# ABC LONDON ATLAS

# How to find a street

The index, page 113, is the key to this atlas, locating every street and road. The system is simple, as this example shows:

| * | Ordnance Mews | NW8 | ....46 | 26 83 | D |
|---|---|---|---|---|---|
| ① | ② | ③ | ④ | ⑤ | ⑥ |

① The asterisk indicates that only the first two letters of the name are shown on the map (e.g. OR).

② The full street name, which may be abbreviated on the map.

③ The postal code or town in which the street falls. Standard postal codes have been used for street names in the London Postal Districts.

   For all other street names Post Town abbreviations have been used as a guide to the location of the street name.

④ The map number on which the street name appears.

⑤ The four figures are the reference system for locating the position of the name on the map.

   The four figures show in which square the centre of the street falls.

   The first two figures can be found along the bottom edge of each map in blue – these apply to the vertical columns.

   The second two figures can be found along the left or right hand side of each map in red – these apply to the horizontal rows.

⑥ The letter provides a more precise location within the square:

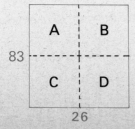

Street names are normally positioned centrally to the length of the street. The abbreviations used on the maps are listed on page 113.

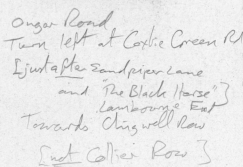

Ongar Road
Turn left at Coxtie Green Rd
[just after Sandpiper Lane
and "The Black Horse"]
Lambourne End
Towards Chigwell Row
[not Collier Row]

First published 1984 by

Ordnance Survey          and      Newnes Books
Romsey Road                        84-88 The Centre
Maybush                            Feltham
Southampton SO9 4DH                Middlesex TW13 4BH

To the best of the Publishers' knowledge, the information
in this atlas was correct at the time of going to press.
No responsibility can be accepted for any errors or their
consequences.

The representation in this atlas of a road, track or path
is no evidence of the existence of a right of way.

Newnes Books is a division of
The Hamlyn Publishing Group Limited

ISBN: 0 600 35134 3 (casebound)
      0 600 35769 4 (paperback)

Printed in Great Britain

# ABC
# LONDON ATLAS

**Key to Maps** — Inside front cover

Key and Legend for Central London Maps — iv-v
*Légende des Plans du Centre de Londres*
*Zeichenerklärungsdiagram und Legende für Innenstadtkarten*

Legend for London Maps — v
*Légende des Cartes de Londres et de ses environs*
*Legende für Aussenbezirkskarten*

Places of Entertainment — vi

Major Hotels — vii

Selected Bus Routes in Central London — vii

Central London Maps at 6 inches to 1 mile — 1-10

London Maps at 3½ inches to 1 mile — 11-112

Index and Reference System explanations and abbreviations — 113

Index to Streets — 114

London Underground Map — Inside back cover

Routes into London — Back cover

 Newnes Books • Ordnance Survey

# Key and Legend : Central London Maps 1-10

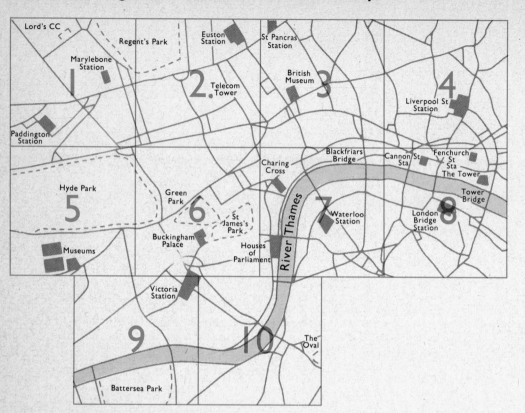

The following symbols appear on Maps 1-10 only.

Other symbols used on these maps will be found on the main legend opposite.

British Rail Station

Play Street *

OXFORD STREET open to buses and taxis only between 7am-7pm, Monday to Saturday

* Restrictions may not apply at all times and to all vehicles

8m — Surface height in metres above sea level

PO — Post Office

Liby — Library

Ch — Church

---

Les symboles suivants ne figurent que sur les Cartes 1 à 10.

Les autres symboles utilisés sur ces cartes sont inclus dans la liste principale des légendes ci-contre.

Die folgenden Zeichen erscheinen nur auf den Karten 1-10.

Andere auf diesen Karten benutzte Zeichen sind in der gegenüberstehenden Hauptlegende enthalten.

Rue réservée aux jeux des enfants *

OXFORD STREET - Circulation interdite (sauf autotus et taxis) du lundi au samedi, de 7 heures à 19 heures

* Les restrictions ne s'appliqueront pas tout le temps et à tous les véhicules

8m — Altitude en mètres au-dessus du niveau de la mer

Gare ferroviaire (British Rail)

Ch — Eglise

Liby — Bibliothèque

PO — Bureau de poste

Als Kinderspielplatz benutzte Strasse *

OXFORD STREET - Nur für Autobusse und Taxis frei 07.00-19.00 Uhr Montag bis Samstag

* Streckenverbote:z.T.nicht ganzzeitig bzw. für alle Fahrzeuge in Kraft

8m — Oberflächenhöhe in Metern über NN

British Rail-Bahnhof

Ch — Kirche

Liby — Bibliothek

PO — Postamt

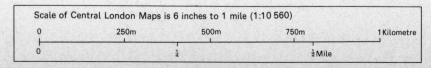

Scale of Central London Maps is 6 inches to 1 mile (1:10 560)

0    250m    500m    750m    1 Kilometre

0    ¼    ½Mile

# Legend : Maps 11-112

For Key to Maps see inside front cover

| | |
|---|---|
| ⇌ British Rail Station | Dual Carriageway |
| ⊖ Underground Station | Main or through road |
| Bus or Coach Station | A 213 / B 266 Road numbers (Dept of Transport) |
| 𝒊 Information Centre | Gate and obstruction to traffic * |
| ◆ Police Station (may not be open 24 hrs) | One way traffic route * |
| ✚ Hospital with Casualty Department | No access in direction of arrow * |
| ✛ Church | Play Street * |
| Important Building | * Restrictions may not apply at all times and to all vehicles |
| ★ Major Hotel | |
| ▲ Youth Hostel | 20 / 21 House numbers (on long roads only) |
| Ⓛ Library | Poly Polytechnic |
| Ⓔ Place of Entertainment | Coll College |
| ☐ Post Office | Sch School |
| P Parking | Mkt Market |
| 12 Adjoining page indicator | CH Club House |
| TH Town Hall | LC Level Crossing |
| Mus Museum | FB Foot Bridge |

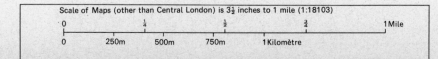

Scale of Maps (other than Central London) is 3½ inches to 1 mile (1:18103)

0    ¼    ½    ¾    1 Mile

0    250m    500m    750m    1 Kilomètre

## LEGENDE

Pour les légendes des schémas, voir à l'intérieur de la couverture avant

| | |
|---|---|
| ⇌ Gare ferroviaire (British Rail) | |
| ⊖ Station de métro | |
| Gare d'autobus ou d'autocar | |
| 𝒊 Bureau de renseignements | |
| ◆ Poste de police (une permanence de 24 heures ne sera pas toujours assurée) | |
| ✚ Centre hospitalier pour accidentés | |
| ✛ Eglise | |
| Edifice important | |
| ★ Grand Hôtel (Cf. page vii) | |
| ▲ Auberge de jeunesse | |
| Ⓛ Bibliothèque | |
| Ⓔ Lieu de distraction (Cf. page vi) | |
| ☐ Bureau de poste | |
| P Parking | |
| 12 Index de la page suivante | |
| Double chaussée | |
| Route principale ou route prioritaire | |
| A 213 / B 266 Numérotation des routes (Ministère du Transport) | |
| Grille et obstacle à la circulation * | |
| Voie de circulation en sens unique * | |
| Pas d'accès dans la direction de la flèche * | |
| Rue réservée aux jeux des enfants * | |
| *Les restrictions ne s'appliqueront pas tout le temps et à tous les véhicules | |
| 20 / 21 Numéros de maisons (seulement sur les routes longues) | |
| TH Hôtel de ville | |
| Mus Musée | |
| Poly Institut universitaire de technologie | |
| Coll Collège | |
| Sch Ecole | |
| Mkt Marché | |
| CH Club | |
| LC Passage à niveau | |
| FB Passerelle | |

## LEGENDE

Zeichenerklärung siehe Innenseite des Umschlages vorne

British Rail-Bahnhof

Untergrundbahnstation

Busbahnhof

Informationsbüro

Polizeiwache (u.U. nicht 24-stündig in Betrieb)

Krankenhaus mit Unfallstation

Kirche

Bedeutendes Bauwerk

Grosses Hotel (siehe S. vii)

Jugendherberge

Bibliothek

Vergnügungsstätte (siehe S. vi)

Postamt

Parkplatz

Nummer der angrenzenden Kartenseite

Zweibahnig

Hauptstrasse, Durchfahrtsstrasse

Strassennummern (Verkehrsministerium)

Schranke, Verkehrssperre *

Einbahnstrasse *

In Pfeilrichtung keine Zufahrt *

Als Kinderspielplatz benutzte Strasse *

*Streckenverbote: z.T. nicht ganzzeitig bzw. für alle Fahrzeuge in Kraft

Hausnummern (nur bei langen Strassen)

Rathaus

Museum

Technische Hochschule

Lehranstalt, Hochschule

Schule

Markt

Clubhaus

Niveau-Ubergang

Fussgängerüberführung

# PLACES OF ENTERTAINMENT

The area covered here appears on maps 2, 3, 6 and 7 in the Atlas

## OTHER CINEMAS, THEATRES AND CONCERT HALLS

An explanation of the referencing system, and abbreviations used are on page 113

### CINEMAS

| | | |
|---|---|---|
| ABC, Edgware Rd. W2 ...1 | 26 81 | B |
| ABC, Fulham Rd. SW10 ...62 | 26 78 | C |
| ABC (Bayswater), Bishop's Bridge Rd. W2 ...1 | 25 81 | D |
| ABC (Beckenham), High St. ...98 | 37 69 | C |
| ABC (Bexleyheath), The Broadway ...79 | 48 75 | D |
| ABC (Catford), Bromley Rd. SE6 ...88 | 37 73 | B |
| ABC (Croydon), London Rd. ...105 | 31 66 | B |
| ABC (Ealing), Uxbridge Rd. W5 ...54 | 17 80 | B |
| ABC (Elephant & Castle), New Kent Rd. SE1 ...63 | 32 79 | C |
| ABC (Enfield), Southbury Rd. ...13 | 33 96 | A |
| ABC (Ewell), Kingston Rd. ...109 | 21 63 | B |
| ABC (Golders Green), Golders Green Rd. NW11 ...35 | 24 87 | A |
| ABC (Hammersmith), King St. W6 ...61 | 22 78 | B |
| ABC (Harrow), Station Rd. ...33 | 15 88 | B |
| ABC (Ilford), High Rd. ...40 | 44 86 | A |
| ABC (Mile End), Mile End Rd. E1 ...57 | 35 82 | C |
| ABC (Putney), High St. SW15 ...73 | 24 76 | A |
| ABC (Romford), South St. ...42 | 51 88 | C |
| ABC (Sidcup), High St. ...90 | 46 71 | A |
| ABC (Streatham), Streatham High Rd. SW16 ...86 | 30 72 | A |
| ABC (Turnpike Lane), Turnpike Parade. N15 ...25 | 31 89 | B |
| ABC (Woodford), High Rd. E18 ...27 | 40 90 | C |
| Academy Cinema, Oxford St. W1 ...2 | 29 81 | C |
| Ace, Rayner's Lane. Har. ...32 | 13 87 | C |
| Ace (Peckham), Peckham High St. ...75 | 33 76 | B |
| Ace (Stoke Newington), Stoke Newington Rd. N16 ...48 | 34 86 | A |
| Ace State (Barkingside), Fairlop Rd. ...28 | 44 90 | C |
| Barbican, Barbican Centre Silk St. EC2 ...4 | 32 81 | A |
| Battersea Arts Centre, Lavender Hill. SW11 ...74 | 27 75 | B |
| Bloomsbury Theatre, Gordon St. WC1 ...2 | 29 82 | C |
| Camden Plaza, Camden High St. NW1 ...47 | 28 88 | B |
| Chelsea Cinema, Kings Road. SW3 ...9 | 27 78 | C |
| Classic, Praed St. W2 ...1 | 27 81 | A |
| Classic (Chelsea), Kings Rd. SW3 ...9 | 26 77 | B |
| Classic (Hampstead), Pond St. NW3 ...47 | 27 85 | C |
| Classic (Hendon), Central Circus. NW4 ...34 | 22 88 | B |
| Classic (Kilburn), Kilburn High Rd. ...46 | 24 84 | B |
| Coronet (Elephant & Castle), New Kent Rd. SE1 ...63 | 32 79 | C |
| Coronet (Northfields), Northfield Ave. W5 ...60 | 17 79 | C |
| Coronet (Notting Hill), Westbourne Gr. W11 ...56 | 25 81 | C |
| Coronet (Well Hall), Well Hall Rd. SE9 ...77 | 42 75 | C |
| Coronet (Woolwich), John Wilson St. ...66 | 43 79 | C |
| Curzon, Curzon St. W1 ...6 | 28 80 | D |
| Curzon (Haringey), Frobisher Rd. N8 ...25 | 31 89 | D |
| Everyman Cinema, Holly Bush Vale. NW3 ...46 | 26 85 | A |
| Film Location (Acton), The Railway High St. W3 ...55 | 20 80 | D |
| Gate (Bloomsbury), Brunswick Sq. WC1 ...3 | 30 82 | C |
| Gate (Mayfair), Mayfair Hotel Stratton St. W1 ...6 | 26 82 | D |
| Gate (Notting Hill), Notting Hill Gate. W11 ...56 | 25 80 | C |
| Granada (Kingston), Clarence St. ...93 | 18 69 | C |
| Granada (Harrow), Sheepcote Rd. ...33 | 15 88 | D |
| Granada (Walthamstow), Hoe St. ...26 | 37 89 | C |
| Institute of Cont Arts, Nash.House The Mall. SW1 ...6 | 29 80 | D |
| Ionic (Golders Green), Finchley Rd. NW11 ...35 | 25 87 | C |
| Minema, Knightsbridge. SW1 ...6 | 28 79 | A |
| National Film Theatre, South Bank. SE1 ...7 | 30 80 | D |
| Odeon (Chelsea), Kensington W8 ...62 | 25 79 | C |
| Odeon, Marble Arch. W1 ...1 | 26 82 | D |
| Odeon (Barking), Longbridge Rd. ...51 | 44 84 | D |
| Odeon (Barnet), Western Parade. ...11 | 25 95 | A |
| Odeon (Bromley), Bromley High St. ...99 | 40 69 | C |
| Odeon (Croydon), North End. ...105 | 32 66 | C |
| Odeon (Hammersmith), Queen Caroline St. W6 ...62 | 23 78 | C |
| Odeon (Holloway), Holloway Rd. N7 ...47 | 30 85 | B |
| Odeon (Ilford), Gants Hill. ...40 | 43 88 | C |
| Odeon (Muswell Hill), Fortis Green Rd. N10 ...24 | 28 89 | D |
| Odeon (Richmond), ...71 | 17 74 | B |
| Odeon (Romford), South St. ...42 | 51 88 | A |
| Odeon (Streatham), Streatham High Rd. ...86 | 30 72 | C |
| Odeon (Swiss Cottage), Finchley Rd. ...46 | 26 84 | D |
| Odeon (Wimbledon). The Broadway. ...95 | 25 70 | C |
| Phoenix, High Rd East Finchley. N2 ...24 | 27 89 | C |
| Rio Cinema, Kingsland High St. Hackney N16 ...48 | 33 85 | D |
| Ritzy (Brixton), Brixton Oval Coldharbour La. SW2 ...75 | 29 73 | C |
| Scala, Pentonville Rd. WC1 ...3 | 30 82 | A |
| Screen on the Green, Upper St. N1 ...48 | 31 83 | B |
| Screen on the Hill, Haverstock Hill. NW3 ...47 | 27 85 | C |
| Studios, Oxford St. W1 ...2 | 29 81 | C |
| Studios (Ealing), Northfield Ave. W13 ...54 | 16 80 | D |
| Studios (Lewisham), Lewisham High St. SE13 ...76 | 35 74 | B |
| Studios (Sutton), Cheam Rd. ...110 | 25 64 | D |
| Times Centa Cinema, Marylebone Rd. NW1 ...2 | 28 82 | C |

### THEATRES

| | | |
|---|---|---|
| Albany Empire, Douglas Way. SE8 ...64 | 37 77 | C |
| Aldwych, Aldwych. WC2 ...3 | 30 81 | D |
| Apollo Vic, Wilton Rd. SW1 ...6 | 29 79 | C |
| Ashcroft, Fairfield Halls High St. Croy. ...105 | 32 65 | D |
| Barbican RSC, Barbican Centre Silk St. EC2 ...4 | 32 81 | A |
| Bloomsbury, Gordon St. WC1 ...2 | 29 82 | D |
| Bush, Shepherds Bush Green. W12 ...62 | 23 79 | A |
| Churchill, ♦ High St. Brom. ...99 | 40 69 | C |
| Cockpit, Gateforth St. NW8 ...1 | 27 82 | C |
| Cottesloe, South Bank. SE1 ...7 | 30 80 | D |
| Drill Hall, Chenies St. WC1 ...2 | 29 81 | B |
| Greenwich, Crooms Hill. SE10 ...64 | 38 77 | C |
| Half Moon, Mile End Rd. E1 ...57 | 35 82 | D |
| Hampstead Theatre Club, Swiss Cottage Centre. NW3 ...46 | 26 84 | C |
| Jeannetta Cochrane, Theobalds Rd. WC1 ...3 | 30 81 | B |
| Jacksons Lane, Archway Rd. N6 ...36 | 28 88 | D |
| Kings Head, Upper St. N1 ...48 | 31 83 | B |
| Lyric (Hammersmith), King St. W6 ...62 | 23 78 | A |
| Lyttleton, South Bank. SE1 ...7 | 30 80 | D |
| Mayfair, Stratton St. W1 ...6 | 28 80 | D |
| Mermaid, Puddle Dock. EC4 ...7 | 31 80 | B |
| National Theatre, South Bank. SE1 ...7 | 30 80 | D |
| New End, New End. NE3 ...35 | 26 86 | C |
| Old Vic, The Cut. SE1 ...63 | 31 79 | A |
| Olivier, South Bank. SE1 ...7 | 30 80 | D |
| Oval House, Kennington Oval. SE11 ...63 | 31 77 | A |
| Palladium, Argyle St. W1 ...2 | 28 80 | D |
| Questors, Mattock Lane. W5 ...54 | 17 80 | A |
| Regents Park (Open Air), Inner Circle. NW1 ...2 | 28 82 | A |
| Riverside Studios, Crisp Rd. W6 ...62 | 23 78 | C |
| Round House, Chalk Farm Rd. NW1 ...47 | 28 84 | C |
| Royal Court, Sloane Sq. SW1 ...9 | 28 78 | A |
| Royalty, Portugal St. WC2 ...3 | 30 81 | D |
| Shaw, Euston Rd. NW1 ...2 | 29 82 | B |
| St Georges, Tufnell Park Rd. N7 ...47 | 30 85 | A |
| Theatre Royal, Gerry Raffles Sq. E15 ...49 | 38 84 | B |
| The Green, Richmond Green. Rich ...71 | 17 75 | D |
| Tower, Cannonbury Tower Cannonbury Pl. N1 ...48 | 31 84 | B |
| Vanbrugh Theatre Club, Malet St. WC1 ...2 | 29 81 | D |
| Victoria Palace, Victoria St. SW1 ...6 | 29 79 | C |
| Westminster, Palace St. SW1 ...6 | 29 79 | C |
| Wimbledon, The Broadway SW19 ...95 | 25 70 | A |
| Young Vic, The Cut. SE1 ...7 | 31 79 | A |

### CONCERT HALLS

| | | |
|---|---|---|
| Barbican, Barbican Centre Silk St. EC2 ...4 | 32 81 | A |
| Central Hall, Storeys Gate. SW1 ...6 | 29 79 | B |
| Conway Hall, Red Lion Sq. WC1 ...3 | 30 81 | B |
| Fairfield Halls, Park La. Croy ...105 | 32 65 | D |
| Hammersmith Palais, Shepherds Bush Rd. W6 ...62 | 23 78 | A |
| Institute of Cont Arts, Nash House The Mall. SW1 ...6 | 29 80 | D |
| The Place, Dukes Rd. WC1 ...2 | 29 82 | B |
| Purcell Room, Q E Hall South Bank. SE1 ...7 | 30 80 | D |
| Queen Elizabeth Hall, South Bank. SE1 ...7 | 30 80 | D |
| Royal Albert Hall, Kensington Gore. SW7 ...5 | 26 79 | B |
| Royal College of Music, Prince Consort Rd. SW7 ...5 | 26 79 | D |
| Royal Festival Hall, South Bank. SE1 ...7 | 30 80 | D |
| Royal Military Sch of Music, Kneller Rd. Twick. ...70 | 14 74 | D |
| Sadlers Wells, Rosebery Ave. EC1 ...3 | 31 82 | A |
| St Johns, Smith Sq. SW1 ...7 | 30 79 | C |
| Wigmore Hall, Wigmore St. W1 ...2 | 28 81 | A |

## INDEX TO WEST END MAP

### ① THEATRES

1 Adelphi
2 Albery
3 Ambassadors
4 Apollo
5 Arts Theatre
6 Astoria
7 Cambridge
8 Coliseum
9 Comedy
10 Criterion
11 Donmar W'House
12 Drury Lane Theatre Royal
13 Duchess
14 Duke of Yorks
15 Fortune
16 Garrick
17 Globe
18 Haymarket Theatre Royal
19 Her Majesty's
20 Lyceum
21 Lyric
22 New London
23 Palace
24 Phoenix
25 Piccadilly
26 Players
27 Prince Edward
28 Prince of Wales
29 Queens
30 Royal Opera House
31 Savoy
32 Shaftesbury
33 St Martins
34 Strand
35 Vaudeville
36 Whitehall
37 Wyndhams

### ㊳ CINEMAS

38 ABC
39 Cinecenta
40 Cinecenta
41 Classic
42 Classic
43 Classic
44 Classic
45 Classic Royal
46 Dominion
47 Empire
48 Eros Cinema
49 Film Centa Cinema
50 Leicester Square Theatre
51 London Pavilion
52 Lumiere Cinema
53 Moulin
54 Odeon
55 Odeon
56 Plaza
57 Prince Charles
58 Roxy
59 Scenes
60 Warner

# MAJOR HOTELS

An explanation of the referencing system, and abbreviations used are on page 113.

| Hotel | Ref | | |
|---|---|---|---|
| Antoinette of Kingston Hotel, 26 Beaufort Rd. King | 93 | 18 68 | C |
| Ariel Hotel, Bath Rd. Hay | 69 | 08 76 | B |
| Athenaeum Hotel, 116 Piccadilly. W1 | 6 | 28 80 | D |
| Baileys Hotel, 140 Gloucester Rd. SW7 | 62 | 26 78 | A |
| Barbican City Hotel, Central St. EC1 | 4 | 32 82 | A |
| Bayswater Fairway Inn, 8-16 Princes Sq. W2 | 5 | 25 80 | B |
| Belgravia Sheraton Hotel, 20 Chesham Pl. SW1 | 6 | 28 79 | C |
| Berkeley, Wilton Pl. SW1 | 6 | 28 79 | A |
| Bloomsbury Crest Hotel, Coram St. WC1 | 3 | 30 82 | C |
| Britannia Hotel, 42 Grosvenor Sq. W1 | 6 | 28 80 | A |
| Bromley Court Hotel, Bromley Hill. Brom | 99 | 39 70 | A |
| Brown's Hotel, Albemarle St. W1 | 6 | 29 80 | A |
| Cavendish Hotel, Jermyn St. W1 | 6 | 29 80 | C |
| Central Park Hotel, 49 Queensborough Terr. W2 | 5 | 26 80 | A |
| Charing Cross, Strand. WC2 | 7 | 30 80 | C |
| Charles Dickens, 66 Lancaster Gate. W2 | 5 | 26 80 | A |
| The Churchill, Portman Sq. W1 | 2 | 27 81 | D |
| Clarendon Hotel, 8-16 Montpelier Row. SE3 | 77 | 39 76 | D |
| Clarendon Court Hotel, Maida Vale. W9 | 1 | 26 82 | C |
| Claridge's, Brook St. W1 | 6 | 28 80 | B |
| Crest Hotel, Empire Way. Wem | 44 | 18 85 | D |
| Cumberland Hotel, Marble Arch. W1 | 1 | 27 81 | D |
| Dorchester, Park La. W1 | 6 | 28 80 | C |
| Eden Park Hotel, 35 Inverness Terr. W2 | 5 | 25 80 | B |
| Europa, Grosvenor Sq. W1 | 6 | 28 80 | A |
| Flemings Hotel, 7-12 Half Moon St. W1 | 6 | 28 80 | D |
| The Gloucester, Harrington Gdns. SW7 | 62 | 26 78 | A |
| Goring Hotel, 15 Beeston Pl. SW1 | 6 | 28 79 | D |
| Great Eastern Hotel, Liverpool St. EC2 | 4 | 33 81 | A |
| Great Western Royal Hotel, Praed St. W2 | 1 | 26 81 | D |
| Grosvenor Hotel, Buckingham Palace Rd. SW1 | 6 | 28 79 | D |
| Grosvenor House, Park La. W1 | 6 | 28 80 | A |
| Heathrow Penta, Bath Rd. Houn | 69 | 08 76 | A |
| Henry VIII Hotel, 19 Leinster Gdns. W2 | 6 | 25 80 | A |
| London Hilton, 22 Park La. W1 | 6 | 28 80 | C |
| Hilton International (Kensington), 179-199 Holland Park Ave, W11 | 62 | 24 79 | A |
| Holiday Inn (Chelsea), 17-25 Sloane St. SW1 | 5 | 27 79 | D |
| Holiday Inn (Marble Arch), 134 George St. W1 | 1 | 27 81 | D |
| Holiday Inn (Swiss Cottage), King Henry's Rd. NW2 | 47 | 27 84 | C |
| Hotel Bristol, Berkeley St. W1 | 6 | 29 80 | C |
| Hotel George, Templeton Pl. SW5 | 62 | 25 78 | A |
| Hotel Russell, Russell Sq. WC1 | 3 | 30 82 | C |
| Howard Hotel, Temple Pl. WC2 | 7 | 30 80 | B |
| The Hyatt Carlton Tower Hotel, Cadogan Pl. SW1 | 5 | 27 79 | D |
| Hyde Park Hotel, Knightsbridge. SW1 | 5 | 27 79 | B |
| Imperial Hotel, Russell Sq. WC1 | 3 | 30 81 | C |
| Inn on the Park, Hamilton Pl Park La. W1 | 6 | 28 80 | A |
| Inter-Continental, 1 Hamilton Pl Hyde Park Cnr. | 6 | 28 79 | A |
| Kenilworth Hotel, Great Russell St. WC1 | 2 | 29 81 | B |
| Kensington Close Hotel, Wrights La. W8 | 62 | 25 79 | B |
| Kensington Palace Hotel, De Vere Gdns. W8 | 5 | 25 79 | B |
| Kingsley Hotel, Bloomsbury Way. WC1 | 3 | 30 81 | A |
| Ladbroke Westmoreland Hotel, 18 Lodge Rd. NW8 | 1 | 27 82 | A |
| Leinster Towers Hotel, 25 Leinster Gdns. W2 | 5 | 26 80 | A |
| London Embassy Hotel, Bayswater Rd. W2 | 56 | 25 80 | B |
| London Forum Hotel, 97 Cromwell Rd. SW5 | 62 | 26 78 | A |
| London International Swallow, Cromwell Rd. SW5 | 62 | 25 78 | B |
| London Metropole Hotel, Edgware Rd. W2 | 1 | 27 81 | A |
| London Penta Hotel, Cromwell Rd. SW5 | 62 | 26 78 | A |
| London Ryan Hotel, Gwynne Pl Kings Cross. WC1 | 3 | 30 82 | B |
| London Tara Hotel, Scarsdale Pl Wrights La. W8 | 62 | 25 79 | D |
| Londoner Hotel, Welbeck St. W1 | 2 | 28 81 | B |
| Mayfair, Stratton St. W1 | 6 | 28 80 | D |
| Mostyn Hotel, Bryanston St. W1 | 1 | 27 81 | D |
| Mount Royal Hotel, Bryanston St. W1 | 1 | 27 81 | D |
| Novotel London, Shortlands, W6 | 62 | 23 78 | B |
| Onslow Court Hotel, 109-113 Queens Gate. SW7 | 62 | 26 78 | B |
| Park Lane, 111 Piccadilly. W1 | 6 | 28 80 | D |
| Park Court Hotel, 75 Lancaster Gate. W2 | 5 | 26 80 | A |
| Park Plaza Hotel, 5 Lancaster Gate. W2 | 5 | 26 80 | A |
| Phoenix Hotel, 1-8 Kensington Gdns Sq. W2 | 56 | 25 80 | B |
| Piccadilly Hotel, 24 Piccadilly. W1 | 6 | 29 80 | A |
| The Portman Intercontinental, Portman Sq. W1 | 2 | 27 81 | D |
| Post House Hotel, 104 Bayswater Rd. W2 | 5 | 25 80 | A |
| Post House Hotel, Haverstock Hill. NW3 | 47 | 27 85 | C |
| Regency Hotel, 100-105 Queens Gate. SW7 | 62 | 26 78 | B |
| Regent Crest Hotel, Carburton St. W1 | 2 | 28 82 | D |
| Rembrandt Hotel, 11 Thurloe Pl. SW7 | 5 | 27 79 | C |
| Richmond Hill Hotel, 146-150 Richmond Hill. Rich | 83 | 18 73 | A |
| The Ritz, Piccadilly. W1 | 6 | 28 80 | D |
| Royal Court Hotel, Sloane Sq. SW1 | 9 | 28 78 | A |
| Royal Garden Hotel, Kensington High St. W8 | 62 | 25 79 | B |
| Royal Horseguards Hotel, Whitehall Ct. SW1 | 7 | 30 80 | C |
| Royal Kensington Hotel, 380 Kensington High St. W14 | 62 | 24 79 | D |
| Royal Lancaster Hotel, Lancaster Terr. W2 | 5 | 26 80 | A |
| Royal Scot Hotel, Kings Cross Rd. WC1 | 3 | 30 82 | B |
| Royal Trafalgar Hotel, Whitcomb St. WC2 | 6 | 29 80 | B |
| Royal National, Bedford Way. WC1 | 3 | 30 82 | C |
| Royal Westminster Hotel, Buckingham Palace Rd. SW1 | 6 | 28 79 | D |
| Rubens Hotel, 39-41 Buckingham Palace Rd. SW1 | 6 | 28 79 | D |
| The Savoy, Savoy Pl. WC2 | 7 | 30 80 | B |
| Savoy Court Hotel, Granville Pl. W1 | 2 | 28 81 | C |
| The Selfridge Hotel, Orchard St. W1 | 2 | 28 81 | C |
| Sheraton Park Hotel, 101 Knightsbridge. SW1 | 5 | 27 79 | B |
| Sherlock Holmes Hotel, Baker St. W1 | 1 | 27 81 | B |
| Skyway Hotel, Bath Rd. Hay | 69 | 08 76 | A |
| St Ermins, Caxton St. W1 | 6 | 29 79 | D |
| St James, Buckingham Gate. SW1 | 6 | 29 79 | C |
| Strand Palace Hotel, Strand. WC2 | 7 | 30 80 | A |
| Tower Hotel, St Katherine's Way. E1 | 4 | 33 80 | D |
| Vanderbilt Hotel, 76-86 Cromwell Rd. SW7 | 62 | 26 78 | A |
| Waldorf Hotel, Aldwych. WC2 | 3 | 30 80 | B |
| Washington Hotel, Curzon St. W1 | 6 | 28 80 | D |
| Westbury Hotel, New Bond St. W1 | 6 | 28 80 | B |
| West Centre Hotel, Lillie Rd. SW6 | 62 | 25 77 | A |
| The White House, Osnaburgh Terr. NW1 | 2 | 28 82 | D |

## SELECTED BUS ROUTES IN CENTRAL LONDON

**INSTRUCTIONS:**
Find your start point along the top or the side of the chart. Trace down the column or along the row until opposite your destination and you will find a list of routes suitable for your journey. If a change of bus is needed the route numbers required will be shown joined by a line; the number nearest the start point will indicate the first bus needed, ask the conductor where to change.

**NOTES:**
Nearest bus route to Buckingham Palace is Hyde Park Corner-Victoria Station. Nearest bus route to the British Museum is Trafalgar Square-Euston Station. A night bus connects all stations on the chart (except Liverpool Street) every Saturday and Sunday during the Summer months.

**KEY:**
30 Regular daily service.
4 Certain days of the week only.
9/3 Change of bus needed.
Night services not shown.

| | Euston | Houses of Parl. | Hyde Pk Cnr | King's X | Liverpool St | London Zoo | Marble Arch | Oxford Circus | Paddington | Piccadilly | Science/V&A | St Paul's | Tower | Trafalgar Sq | Victoria | Waterloo | W/Minster Abbey |
|---|---|---|---|---|---|---|---|---|---|---|---|---|---|---|---|---|---|
| **Albert Hall** | 73 | 9/3 | 9 | 73 | 9/77A | 74/68 | 30 | 73 | 27/30 | 14 | 14,30 | 9 | 9/74 | 9 | 52,52A | 9/4 | 9/3 |
| **Euston Station** | — | 77A | 30 | 73,77A,188 | 9/77A | 74/68 | 30 | 73 | 27/30 | 14 | 14,30 | 18 | 23/77A | 77A | 11/77A | 68,188 | 77A |
| **Houses of Parliament** | 77A | — | 3/9 | 77A/11 | 3/6 | 3,53 | 12,88 | 12,88 | 7/3 | 14 | 7/3 | 6,9,11,15,23 | 23/77A | 23 | 11 | 70,76 | 3 |
| **Hyde Park Corner** | 30 | 3/9 | — | 14,30,73 | 9/18 | 74 | 2,2B,16,30,73,74,137 | 73,137 | 36,36B | 9,14,19,22,38,55 | 14,30,74 | 9 | 9 | 9 | 2,2B,16,36,36B,500 | 4/9 | 9/3 |
| **King's X Station** | 73,77A,188 | 77A/11 | 14,30,73 | — | 18 | 18/3,53 | 30,73 | 73 | 18 | 14 | 14,30,73 | 18 | 18 | 77A | 11,149 | 188 | 77A |
| **Liverpool St Station** | 9/77A | 3/6 | 9/18 | 18 | — | 6 | 6,8,12,15,23,88 | 6,12,15,23,88,159 | 7,15,23 | 6,8,15,23 | 9,14 | 6,9,11,15,23 | 42/78 | 6,9,11,15,23 | 11,149 | 502 | 11 |
| **London Zoo** | 74/68 | 3,53 | 74 | 18/3,53 | 6 | — | 74 | 3,53 | 27/74 | 3,53 | 74 | 3/53 | 23/74 | 3,53 | 3/11 | 53/1 | 53 |
| **Marble Arch** | 30 | 12,88 | 2,2B,16,30,73,74,137 | 30,73 | 6,8,12,15,23,88 | 74 | — | 6,8,12,13,15,23,500 | 7,15,23 | 6,12,15,23,88 | 74 | 6,15,23 | 6 | 3,6,12,13,15,23,53 | 2,2B,16,36,36B,500 | 1/12 | 12 |
| **Oxford Circus** | 73 | 12,88 | 73,137 | 73 | 6,12,15,23,88,159 | 3,53 | 6,8,12,13,15,23,500 | — | 7,15,23 | 3,6,12,13,15,23,53,88 | 7,15,23 | 6,12,15,23,53,88,159 | 8,12,15,23 | 3,6,9,12,13,15,23,88,159 | 3,6,12,13,15,23,53 | 1 | 3,12,53,88,159 |
| **Paddington Station** | 27/30 | 7/3 | 36,36B | 18 | 7,15,23 | 27/74 | 7,15,23 | 7,15,23 | — | 15,23 | 15,23 | 15,23 | 15,23 | 15,23 | 36,36B | 36B/507 | 53,88,159,312 |
| **Piccadilly Circus** | 14 | 14 | 9,14,19,22,38,55 | 14 | 6,8,15,23 | 3,53 | 6,12,15,23,88 | 3,6,12,13,15,23,53,88 | 15,23 | — | 14 | 6,9,15,23 | 15,23 | 3,6,9,11,15,23 | 38,55 | 1,176 | 14/3 |
| **Science, V&A Museums** | 14,30 | 7/3 | 14,30,74 | 14,30,73 | 9,14 | 74 | 74 | 7,15,23 | 15,23 | 14 | — | 14 | 74 | 14 | 52,52A | 52,52A | 11 |
| **St Paul's Cathedral** | 18 | 6,9,11,15,23 | 9 | 18 | 6,9,11,15,23 | 3/53 | 6,15,23 | 6,12,15,23,53,88,159 | 15,23 | 6,9,15,23 | 14 | — | 42 | 6,9,11,15,23 | 11 | 4,513 | 23/11 |
| **Tower of London** | 23/77A | 23/77A | 9 | 18 | 42/78 | 23/74 | 6 | 8,12,15,23 | 15,23 | 15,23 | 74 | 42 | — | 23 | 74 | 513 | 23 |
| **Trafalgar Square** | 77A | 23 | 9 | 77A | 6,9,11,15,23 | 3,53 | 3,6,12,13,15,23,53 | 3,6,9,12,13,15,23,88,159 | 15,23 | 3,6,9,11,15,23 | 23 | 6,9,11,15,23 | 23 | — | 11,24,29 | 1,176 | 23/11 |
| **Victoria Station** | 11/77A | 11 | 2,2B,16,36,36B,500 | 11,149 | 11,149 | 3/11 | 2,2B,16,36,36B,500 | 25,500 | 36,36B | 38,55 | 52,52A | 11 | 74 | 11,24,29 | — | 70,76,149,507 | 23/11 |
| **Waterloo Station** | 68,188 | 70,76 | 4/9 | 188 | 502 | 53/1 | 1/12 | 1 | 36B/507 | 1,176 | 70,76,149,507 | 4,513 | 513 | 1,176 | 70,76,149,507 | — | 70,76 |

(vii)

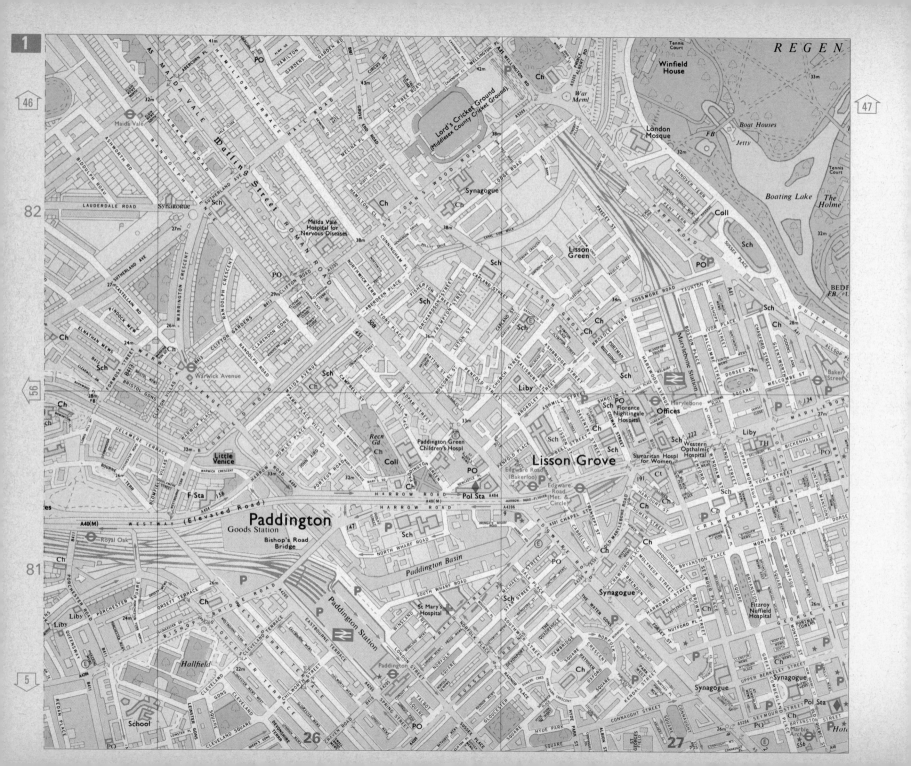

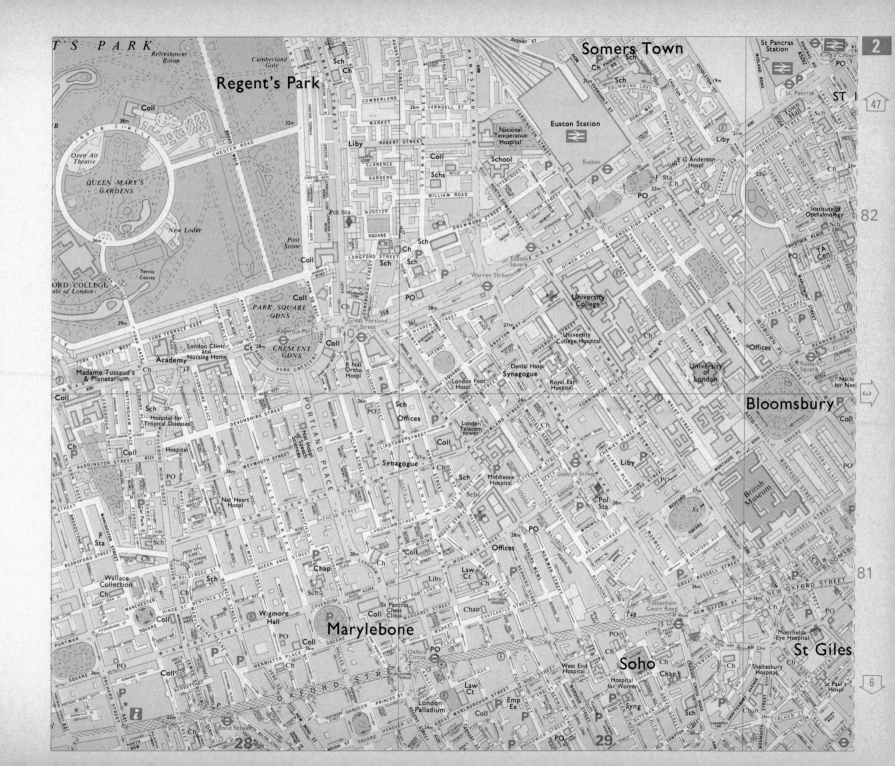

Shoreditch

St Luke's

SPITALFIELDS

Whitechapel

Moorfields Eye Hospital

St Matthew's Hospital

Mildmay Mission Hospital

John Wesley's House

Burial Ground

Barracks

Playing Field

Liverpool Street Station

Broad Street Station

Spitalfields Market

Barbican Centre

Arts Centre

Museum of London

Guild Hall

Law Court Coll

Bank of England

Royal Exchange

Mansion Ho

Nat West Tower

Stock Exchange

St Paul's Cathedral

Old Street

Finsbury Circus

Finsbury Square

Moorgate

Liverpool Street

Shoreditch

CITY ROAD
GREAT EASTERN STREET
OLD STREET
SHOREDITCH HIGH STREET
COMMERCIAL STREET
LONDON WALL
CHEAPSIDE
THREADNEEDLE STREET
CORNHILL
LEADENHALL STREET
ALDGATE
BISHOPSGATE
CANNON STREET
POULTRY
FORE STREET
GRESHAM STREET
CALVERT AVE
COLUMBIA ROAD
BETHNAL GREEN ROAD
HANBURY STREET
FASHION STREET
WENTWORTH STREET
BRUSHFIELD STREET
WORSHIP STREET
FINSBURY PAVEMENT
CHISWELL STREET
BUNHILL ROW
FEATHERSTONE STREET
GOLDEN LANE

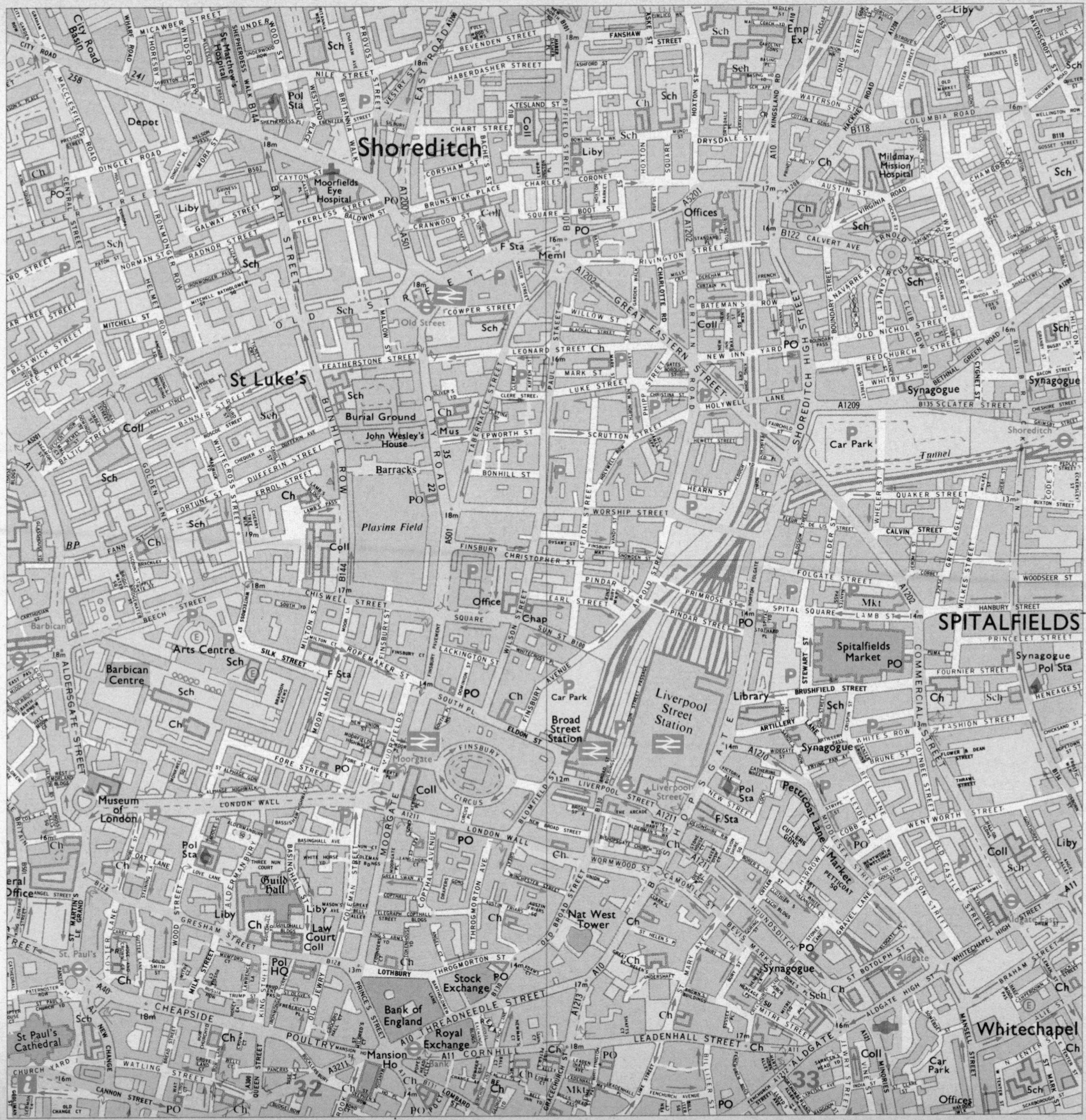

48
82
57
81
8
32
33

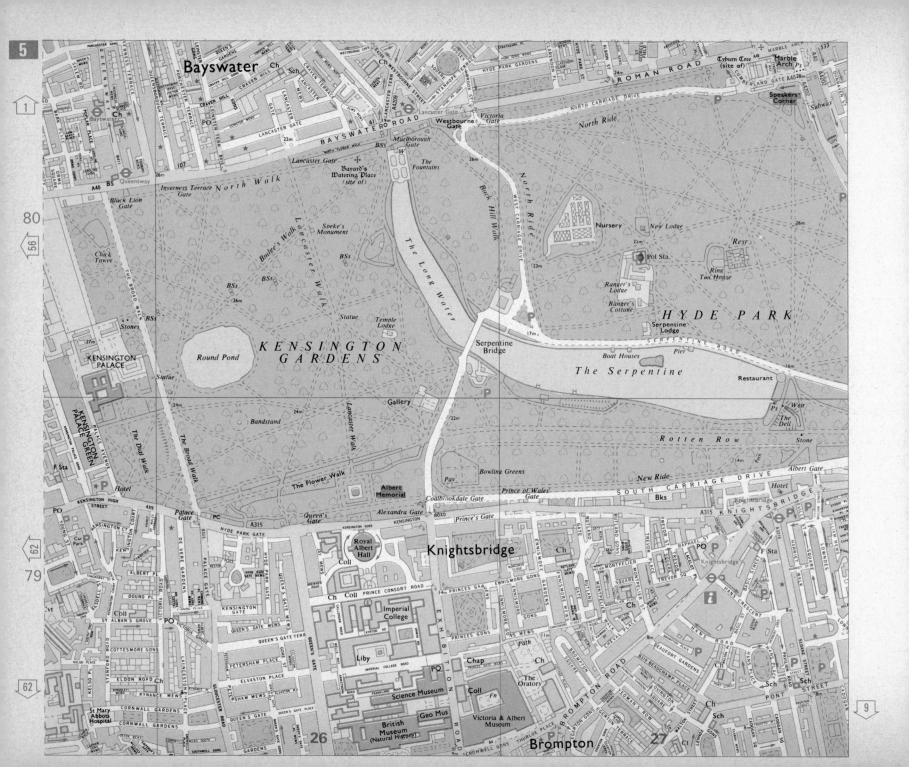

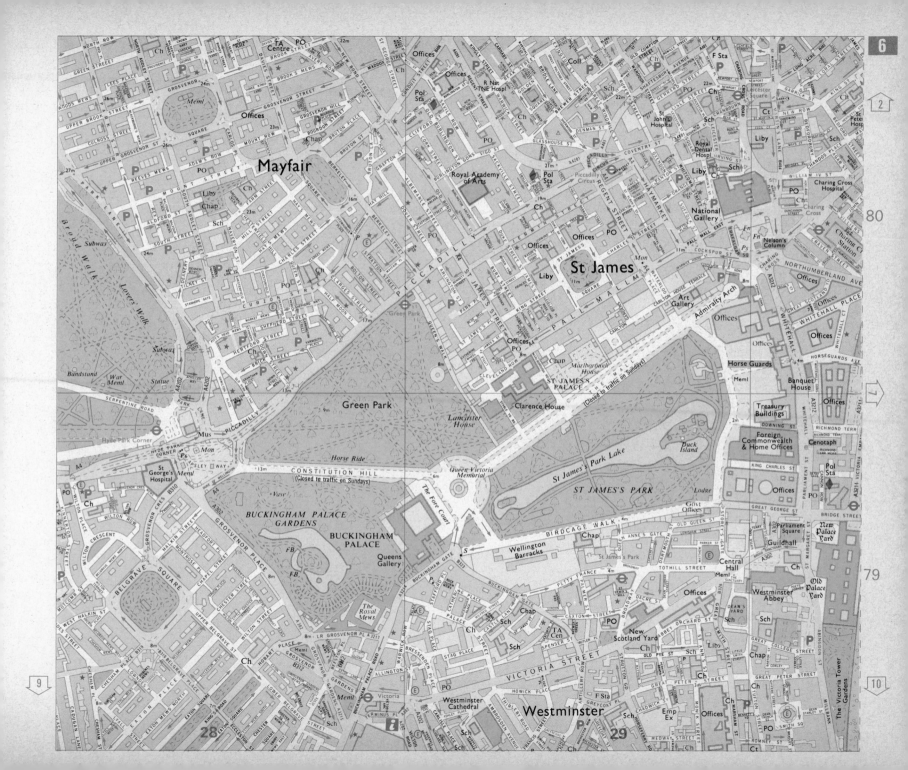

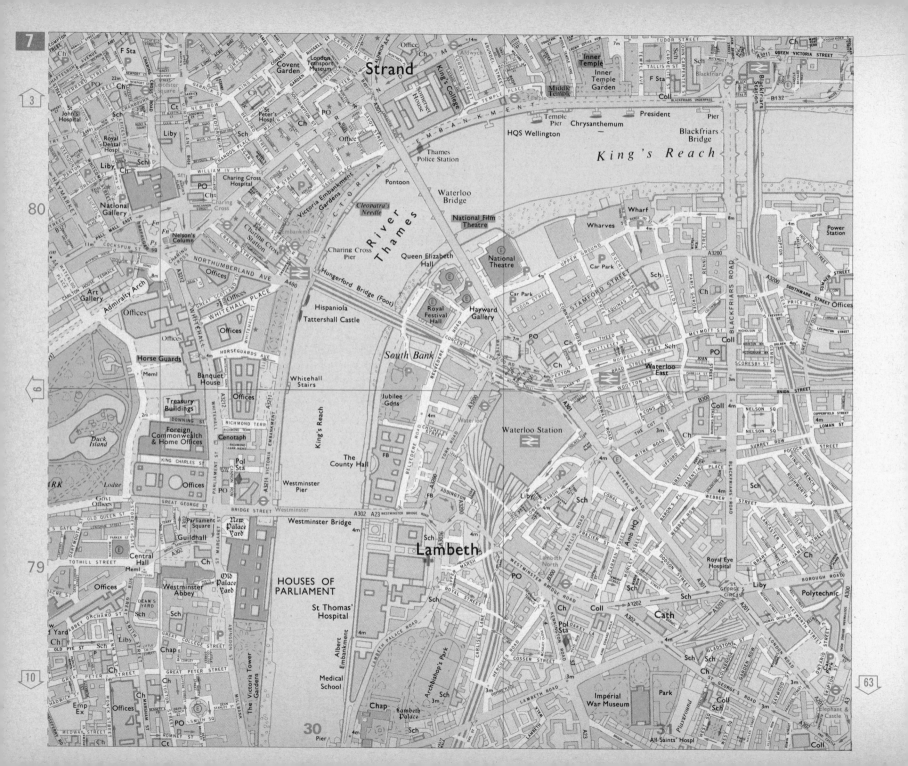

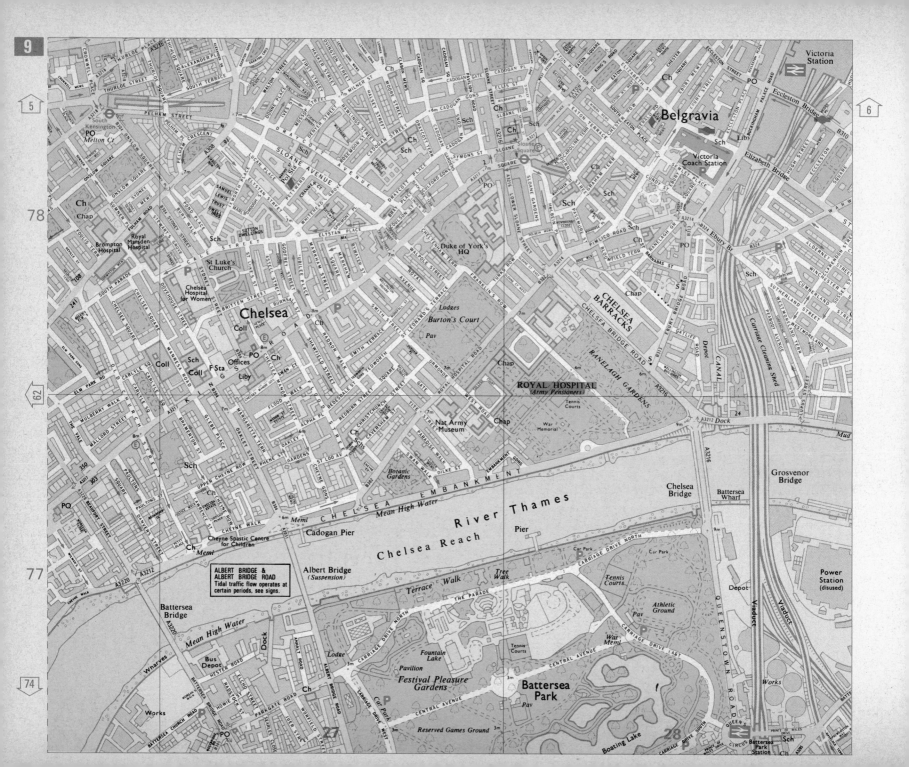

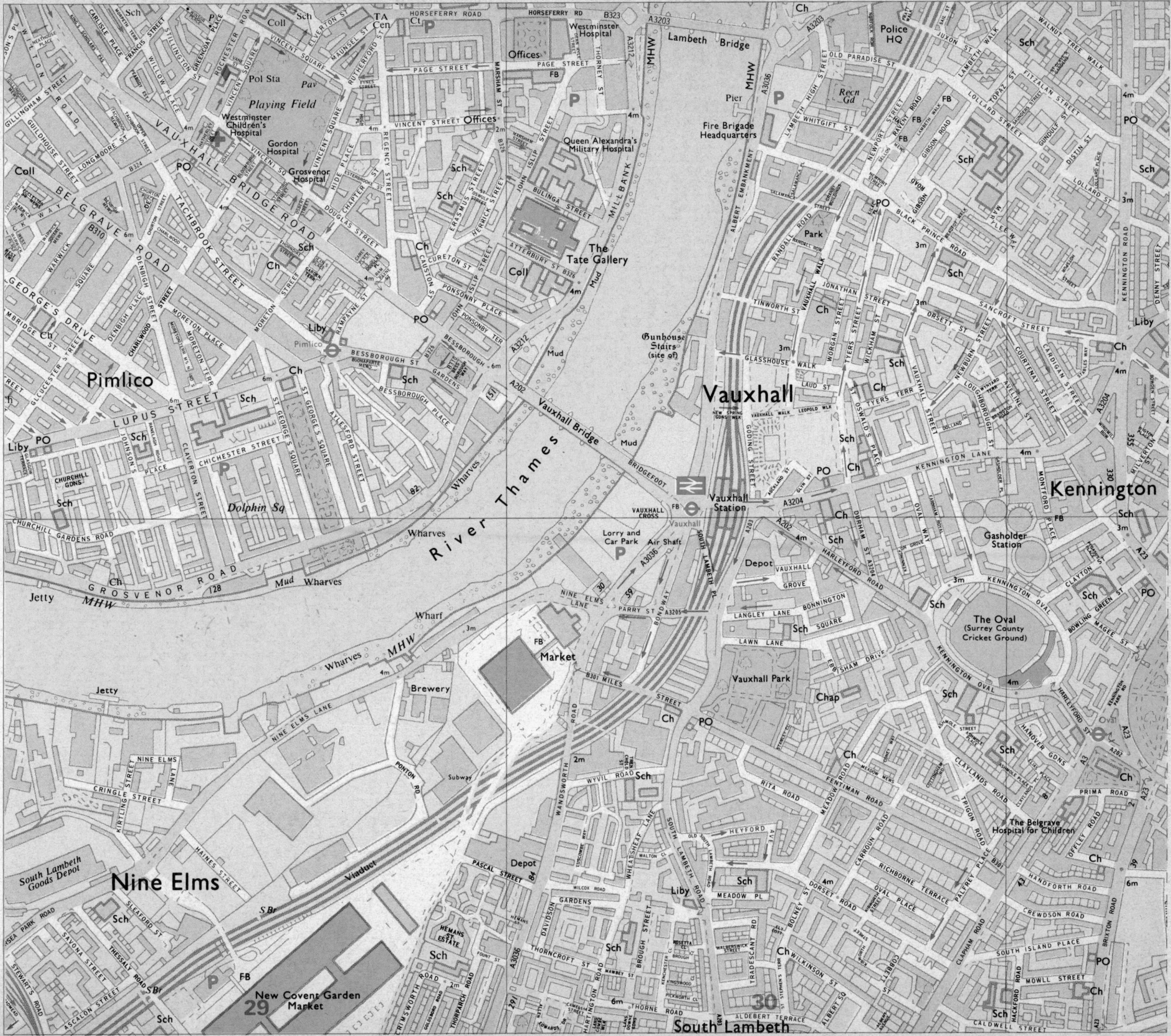

6    7

78

63

77

74

**Pimlico**

**Vauxhall**

**Kennington**

**Nine Elms**

**South Lambeth**

*River Thames*

Sch   Coll   Sch   TA Cen   Ct   P

HORSEFERRY ROAD   HORSEFERRY RD   B323   A3203   Ch

Westminster Hospital   Lambeth Bridge   Police HQ   Sch

Pol Sta   Pav   PAGE STREET   PAGE STREET   FB   MHW   Pier

Offices   A3036

*Playing Field*   VINCENT STREET   Offices   P   Recn Gd   PO

Westminster Children's Hospital   Queen Alexandra's Military Hospital   Fire Brigade Headquarters   LAMBETH WHITGIFT ST   Sch

Gordon Hospital   Grosvenor Hospital   ALBERT EMBANKMENT   LPO   BLACK PRINCE ROAD

Coll   BELGRAVE ROAD   VAUXHALL BRIDGE ROAD   Sch   Park   Sch

Ch   Sch   The Tate Gallery

GEORGES DRIVE   TACHBROOK STREET   Coll   Sch

Liby   Pimlico   Ch   Gunhouse Stairs (site of)   GLASSHOUSE WALK

Sch   BESSBOROUGH ST   Sch   Mud   TINWORTH ST

LUPUS STREET   ST GEORGE'S SQUARE   A202   Vauxhall Bridge   Mud   KENNINGTON LANE

CHICHESTER STREET   Sch   Wharves   BRIDGEFOOT   PO   Ch

Dolphin Sq   P   Wharves   VAUXHALL CROSS   Vauxhall Station   A3204   Gasholder Station

CHURCHILL GARDENS ROAD   Wharves   Lorry and Car Park   Air Shaft   DURHAM ST

GROSVENOR ROAD   Mud   Wharves   P   A3036   Depot   VAUXHALL GROVE   HARLEYFORD ROAD

Jetty   MHW   NINE ELMS LANE   PARRY ST   LANGLEY LANE   The Oval (Surrey County Cricket Ground)

Wharf   BONDWAY   A3205   LAWN LANE   KENNINGTON OVAL

Jetty   Wharves   MHW   FB   Market   Vauxhall Park   Chap   Sch

Brewery   B301   MILES STREET   Ch   PO

NINE ELMS LANE   PONTON RD   Subway   WANDSWORTH ROAD   WYVIL ROAD   RITA ROAD   FENTIMAN ROAD

CRINGLE STREET   Viaduct   PASCAL STREET   HEYFORD   CLAYLANDS ROAD

South Lambeth Goods Depot   Depot   WILCOX ROAD   Liby   MEADOW PL   The Belgrave Hospital for Children

S Br   HEMANS ESTATE   DAVIDSON GARDENS   DORSET ROAD   OVAL PLACE   HANDFORTH ROAD

Sch   THORNCROFT STREET   Ch   RICHBORNE TERRACE   CREWDSON ROAD

P   FB   New Covent Garden Market   Sch   WILKINSON ST   SOUTH ISLAND PLACE   PO

29    30    ALDEBERT TERRACE   CALDWELL STREET   Ch

CH

Monken Mead Brook

A111
A415

Golf Course

Fernyhill Wood

Camlet Hill

Enfield Chase

Leeging Beech Gutter

HADLEY RD
OAK LANE

Vicarage Farm

RIDGE CREST

Rough Lot

Salmon's Brook

97

Trent Park Country Park

Seedfield Spinney

Icehouse Wood

Williams Wood

Hog Hill

Poly

COOMBEHURST CL

Resr

Oak Wood

P

Shaws Wood

FAIRGREEN

BOURNWELL CL
FAIRGRN

FAIRGREEN

COCKFOSTERS RD

Church Wood

Merryhills Brook

TRICTWOOD SIDE
GRAFTON RD
ELMER CL
A110

CASTLEWOOD
RUNDEL RD
NORTHFIELD RD
LINTHORPE RD
GROVE RD

GAMES RD

Golf Course

ENFIELD RD

COTSWOLD WAY

Sch

BINCOTE RD
LINKSIDE

FORDHAM CL
FORDHAM RD

THE PADDOCKS
CHALK LA

Cemy

Boxer's Lake

Sch

GLENBROOK
COTSWOLD CL
CHILTERN
GLENBROOK S

96

MARGARET RD
HAMILTON RD
Mus
HERONS
ROLFE CL

LANGFORD RD
WILTON RD
BEVAN RD
CHURCH WAY
CRES
LANGFORD

COCKFOSTERS PAR
BELMONT CL

NORFOLK
WEST CL
EAST CL

Cockfosters

SILVERCLIFF GDNS
PARK AVE
HIGH TREES

MOUNT PLEASANT
CAMSON RD
EVELYN RD
NORRYS RD
NORRYS

MOUNT AVE

BRAEMAR
HEDDON COURT AVE
STATION APPROACH
GLOUCESTER GDNS

KENT DRI

WESTPOLE AVE

SOUTH C
LODGE
LAKESIDE
LAKESIDE
5TH
LODGE

LOWTHER DRI
NETHERBY RD
MERRYHILLS DRI

GRESTONE GDNS
CULGAITH GDNS
BEWCASTLE GDNS
CORBY
LONSDALE DRIVE N

SILVERDALE
RUSHEY HILL

WORLD'S END LA

Sch

13

WARWICK
HYMUS
BROOK

MOUNT RD
CADDINGTON CL

CRESCENT RISE
A110 BROOKHILL RD

EDGWORTH

ST WILFRID'S
PILGRIM'S RI
CRESCENT RD

BISLEY WAY
ECCLESTON RD

HEDDON COURT PAR

BELMONT AVE
ASHURST RD

PRESTON GDNS
LEYS GDNS

A111

Playing Field

SUSSEX WAY

CLIFTON GDNS

BRANDON GDNS
CURTHWAITE GDNS
BRAMYWOOD GDNS
WOODEND GDNS

BELGRAVE GDNS

GROSVENOR GDNS
SOUTH LODGE DRI
CARLTON AVE

LONSDALE DRI

LINDAL CRES

ROUNDHILL DRI

TARNBANK RD

South Lodge Hospl

Highlands Hospl

JACKSON RD
A110 BARNET RD
E BARNET RD
B193
WELBECK
MIDDLE
OAKLEIGH RD
CHURCHMEAD
CRANSCAPEL RD
CAPEL RD

CAT HILL

DOGGETTS CL
BARONS GATE

THE HOOBE
CHESTNUT GR
THE CLOSE
LAKESIDE CRES

MANSFIELD RD
VERNON

TRENT GDNS

SPEYSIDE
LINDEN WAY

MERRYHILLS CT
STAFFORD RD
TREGENNA CT
CATHERINE CT
CASHBRIDGE

PRIORY CL
POLL INS
BRAMLEY CL

Sports Ground

Poly

GREEN RD

MASEFIELD GR

RESERVOIR RD

ADDISON AVE
AVENUE CL

GWALIOR HOUSE

MERRIVALE

PRINCE GEORGE AVE

OVERTON RD

CHASEVILLE PARK RD

Sch

OAKWOOD CRES

EVERSLEY PK RD
THE BIRCHES
HOLLY HILL

GREEN DRAGON

EVE
EVE

Sch

College

CHASE SIDE

MOHAN CL
FARM LA

DE BOHUN AVE
MONKFRITH AVE

A111

TRENT GDNS

WOOD AVE

BUSH FAIR CT
COWPER GDNS

BEARDOW

LINDEN WAY
ORCHARD

COVERACK CL
CHARTER WAY

OAKWOOD RD
OAKWOOD
FAIRLAWN CL

Oakwood

Oakwood Park

OAKWOOD PARK RD

THE VALE

GLADE
SPRINGBANK
SEYMOUR
MEADOWBANK
BROOKSIDE
HOUNDSDEN RD

95

27
16
28
29
16
30

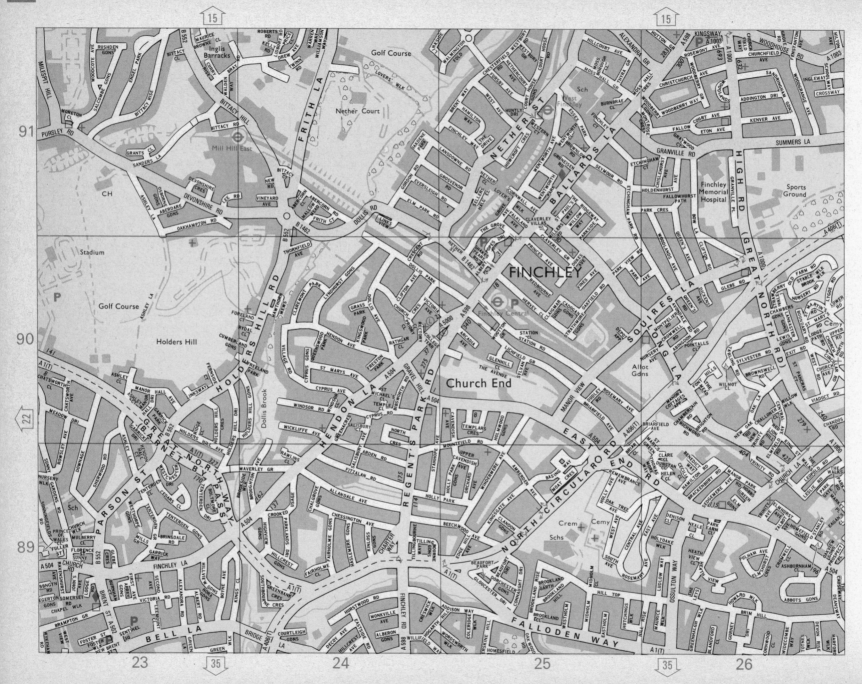

**91**

**90**

**89**

43　　44　　45　　46

Grange Hill

HAINAULT

Claybury Hospital

Hospital Hill Wood

Hospital Hill

Hospital Farm

Fullwell Cross

Fairlop

Fairlop Plain

Hainault Farm

CLAYHALL AVE

Barkingside

Aldborough Hatch

Aldborough Hall Farm

Hargreaves

Willow Fm

FOREST RD

NEW NORTH RD

HAINAULT RD

EASTERN AVE

Playing Fields

Recreation Ground

Sports Ground

Playing Field

Works

Cemy

Recn Gd

Painters Rd

Seven Kings Water

Works
FOREST RD
Hog Hill
A1112
CH P
Five Oaks La
Works

ROMFORD RD
Forest Farm
Cold Blow Farm
ROMFORD RD B 174

PENNINGTON CL
ABRIDGE
STAPLEFORD GDNS
Sch
FRY RD GRIMSTONE
BISCALE LAYBEE
CHARLOTTE
UDALL GDNS GSDEFOE
QUARLES
TUDFIN AVE
BACON
CARTER
JUDITH AVE
LYNWOOD
CARTER CL
SHEILA RD
LYNWOOD DR
Collier Row
DOWNHAM
HAMPDEN
RAMSDEN DR
EATON DR
SILVERMERE AVE
VICTORIA AVE
LARCHWOOD AVE
DOMINION DR
LARCHWOOD
HILLRISE RD
HIGHFIELD
HIGHFIELD GDNS
CLOCKHOUSE LA
BURLAND RD
FELSTEAD RD
ASCENSION RD
HAWKHURST
KINGSHILL
MOUNT PLEASANT RD
PHILAN WAY
BELLE VUE RD
FAIRCROSS DRIVE
GABRIEL RD
HIGHFIELD RD
MERLIN RD
MERLIN GDNS
Sch
B 1459
CHASE CROSS RD
IRBON
GOBIONS AVE
GALLEY
CHELAS WOOD
TWEED WAY
MORAY WAY

FRINTON RD
WILTON RD
HAMLET CL
HAMLET
TAYLOR
PENN GDNS
LODGE LA
RIVERS DALE DR
GELSTHORPE
B 1459
B 174
BIRCH...
BERKELEY AVE
WILTON DR
LAWNS WAY
THE
BOWER CL
312
BARTLOW GDNS

HOG HILL RD
COLLIER ROW RD
HAZELL CRES
BIRDS...
BURCHWALL CL
FULLERS CRES
FULLERS CL
BROCKLEY CRES
EDITH GDNS
SELSDON
MOORLAND
B 174

COLLIER ROW LA
REPULSE
RENOWN CL
RAIDER CL
LOWSHOE LA
WOOD WLK
HULSE AVE
GORING
HILLFOOT
PLAYFIELD AVE
Recn Gd
HORNDON GREEN
HORNDON CL
HILLFOOT RD

ELIZABETH GDNS
LYNTON AVE
CLOVELLY GDNS
ELM CL
ASHDOWN WLK
ELM RD
CHERRYDOWN
LONGMEAD
NEWELL
WILLIAM CL
MOWBLAYS
MOWBRAYS RD
TAPLEY RD
HEATHER WAY
HEATHER GLEN

HOWE
RODNEY
NELSON
ALTANY
VICTORY WAY
ORCHARD RD
NORMAN
KENWAY
FERNDALE
SAFFRON RD
HEATHER DRI

WHITE HART LA
PEARTREE GDNS
ANSON CL
Wks
MAWNEY RD
MAIDSTONE AVE
PROSPECT AVE
PORTNOY

Furze House Farm
Whites Farm
River Rom
REDRIFF RD
WINFLEET AVE
THAMESHILL AVE
MAWSHILL AVE
ASHMOUR GDNS
PRIESTS AVE

Marks Gate
WHALEBONE LANE NO
KINGSHILL AVE
KINGSTON HILL AVE
BEANSLAND
KINGSTON CL
BARHAM CL
VANGUARD
WALMER CL
DUNSTER CL
DOVER
B 175
HAMILTON

BILLET RD
MEAD GR
PERCY RD
LINLEY CRES
CROSS RD
ABBOTTS CL
HAINAULT RD
ROSEDALE RD

Red House Farm
Hainault House
NEWHOUSE AVE
ROSE HATCH AVE
BARDFIELD AVE
PADNALL CT
ANTONY CT
LAWN FARM GR
BIRCH RD
BIRCH CL
KING GEORGE CL
KING GEORGE
RD
PARKSIDE AVE
FIR TREE
Wks
A 125

ROWAN WAY
REYNOLDS GDNS
UPLANDS
DANBURY
CORAL CL
ARNEWAYS AVE
THATCHES
BAGLEYS
SPRING
FOREST RD
SILVER WAY
EPPING CL
Playing Fields
SUSAN CL
BURNHAM

NASH RD
GREGORY RD
LONGGATES
CRABTREE
AVE
FOLES GR
RAMS GR
Cemy
Marks Hall (site of)
ESSEX RD
ESSEX CL
BEAUFORT CL
AMBERLEY WAY
BLENHEIM
BROOKLANDS RD
CHESHAM CL
MEDORA RD
NORTH ST
PARK DR
THE AVENUE
DORSET RD

CAVALIER CL
WOODRUSH WAY
RADNALL RD
SHEEPCOTES RD
LAKE RD
HUTCHINSON
HATCH GR
Warren Farm
PITCAIRN CL
MARLBOROUGH RD
BLANDFORD RD
CROWNMEAD WAY
WINSTON CL
MAWNEY RD
POPLAR ST
CEDAR RD
WILLOW ST
MARLE
BEECH ST
VINE ST
PRETORIA RD
OAK RD
LIME ST
DRUMMOND RD
MARSHALLS
CONO RD

A 12(T)
EASTERN AVE
A1112
EASTERN AVENUE W

FRESHWELL AVE
ROCHFORD
BRON CL
SOMERVILLE GDNS
INVERCLYDE GDNS
SHEPHERDS
CLOSE
WARREN TERR
EAST

91
90
28
89

47
41
48
49
41
50

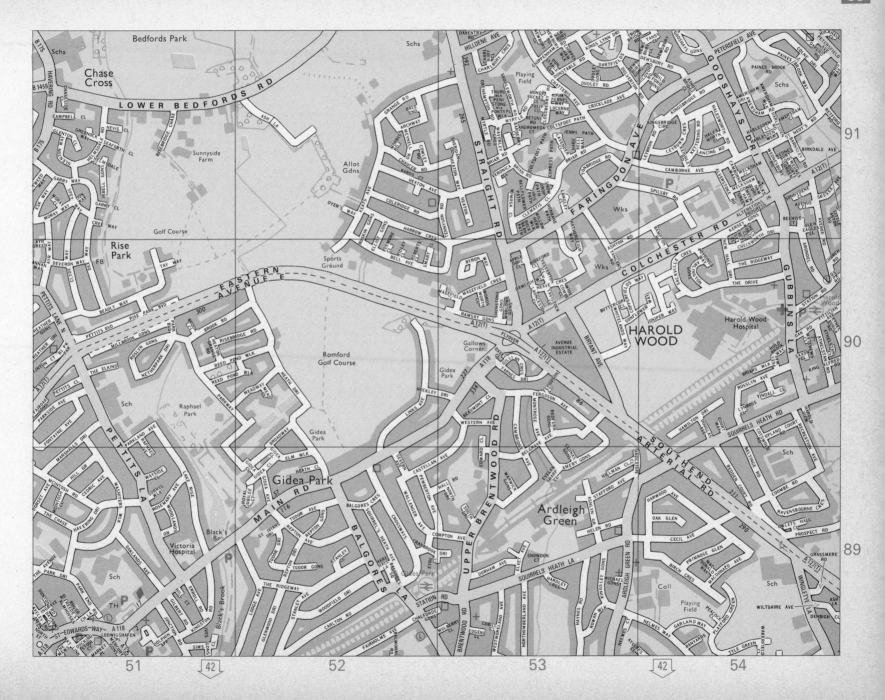

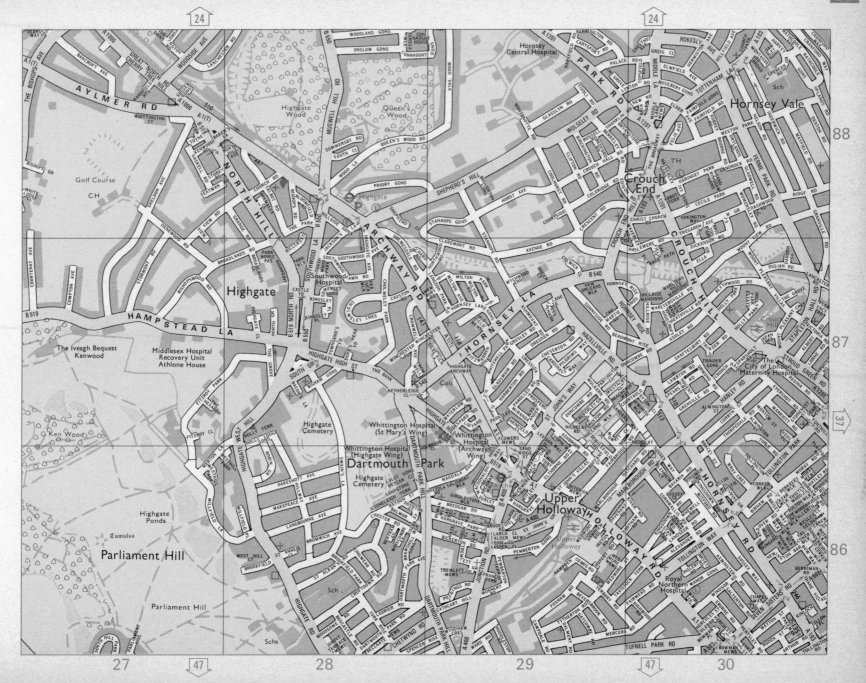

CHADWELL HEATH LA Tech Coll

Goodmayes Hospital

Chadwell Heath Hospital

88

Seven Kings Water

Playing Field

King George Hospital

Newbury Park

King George Hospital West Wing

EASTERN AVE

Gantshill

CRANBROOK RD A123

BARLEY LA

87

Valentines Park

Cranbrook

The Lake

Seven Kings

Goodmayes

THE DRIVE

LEYST

HIGH RD

Seven Kings

A 118

41

Goodmayes

GREEN LA

GOODMAYES LA

River Roding

Ilford

ILFORD HILL

Gordon Fields

The Lake

South Park

WATER LA

Goodmayes Park

Allot Gdns

Schs

86

Playing Field

ROMFORD RD
A 118

43

51

44

45

51

46

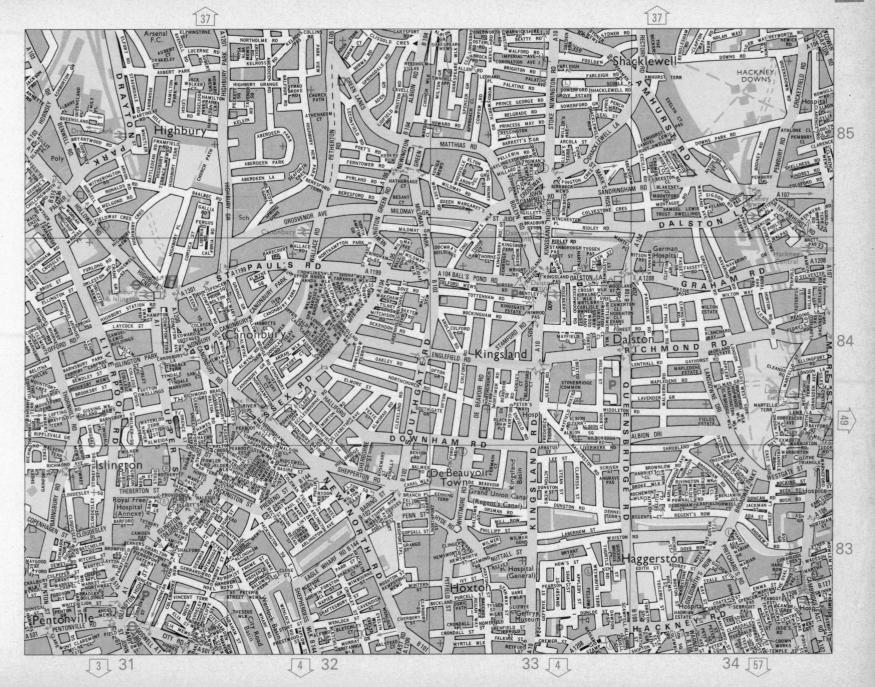

85

84

DAGENHAM

83

Becontree

Parsloes Park

Parsloes Ave

PORTERS AVE

WOOD LA

A 124

A 1150

HEATHWAY

OXLOW LA

REEDE RD

RAINHAM ROAD

Dagenham East

Dagenham Heathway

Becontree

GALE ST

HEDGEMANS RD

DAGENHAM AVE

BROAD ST

BALLARDS RD

Dagenham Old Park

Dagenham Hospital

Beam River

Castle Green

Goresbrook Sports Centre

GORESBROOK RD

Gores Bridge

The Gores

RIPPLE RD

A 13(T)

A 13(T)

NEW RD

Dagenham Dock

Works

Works

Playing Field

Sports Ground

Works

47          48          49          50

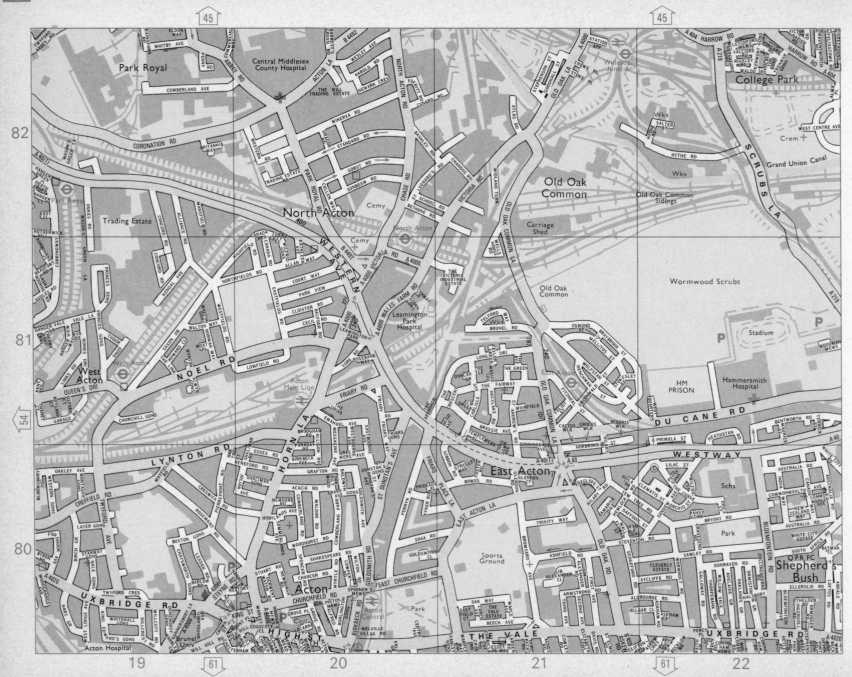

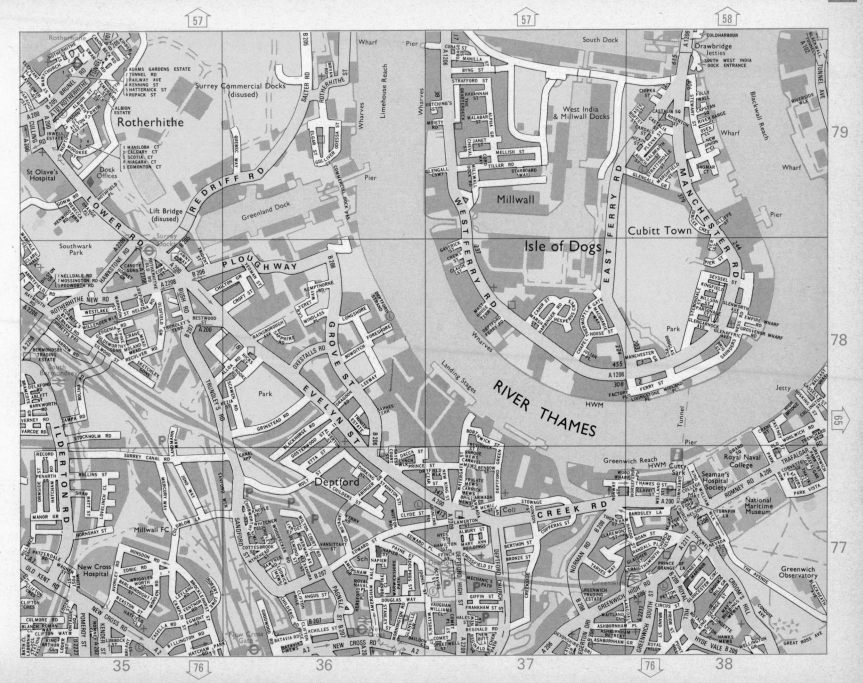

RIVER THAMES

*Gallions Reach*

WESTERN WAY

NATHAN WAY

Dismantled Railway

Abbey Wood

PLUMSTEAD RD

WOOLWICH HIGH ST

PLUMSTEAD HIGH ST

BURRAGE RD

R A Barracks

Plumstead

St Nicholas Hospital

Plumstead Common

Bostall Woods

WOOLWICH

PLUMSTEAD COMMON RD

WOOLWICH COMMON

Park

Turpin's Cave

Cemy

Cemy

79

78

67

77

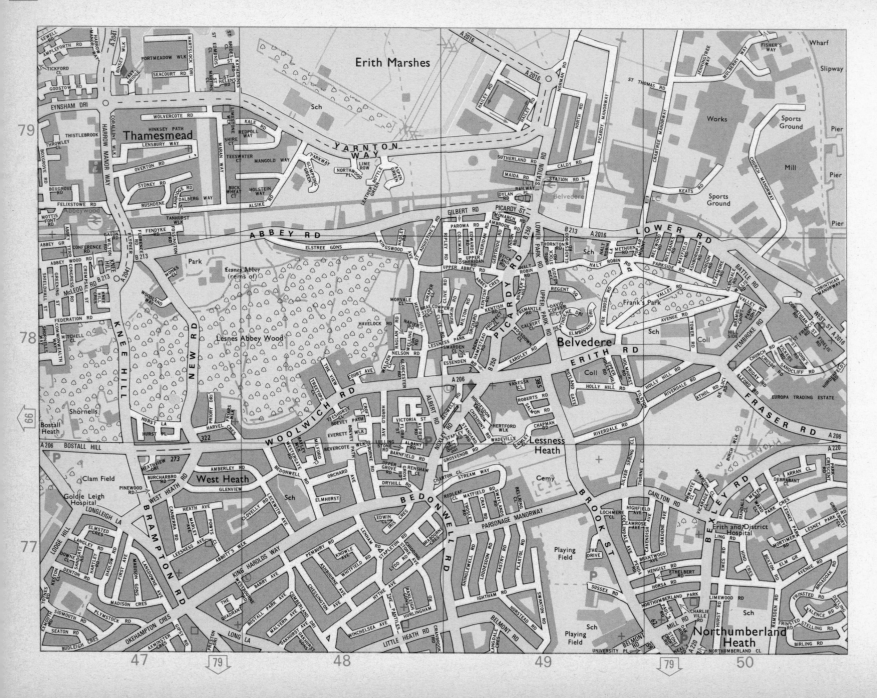

Erith Marshes

Thamesmead

YARNTON WAY

Belvedere

ABBEY RD

Park

Lesnes Abbey
(rems of)

Lesnes Abbey Wood

NEW RD

KNEE HILL

Shornells

Bostall
Heath

A 206 BOSTALL HILL

West Heath

Goldie Leigh
Hospital

WOOLWICH RD

BRAMPTON RD

BEDONWELL RD

Lessness
Heath

BROOK ST

PICARDY RD

Belvedere

ERITH RD

Frank's Park

LOWER RD

FRASER RD

Europa Trading Estate

Erith and District
Hospital

BEXLEY RD

Northumberland
Heath

Works

Sports
Ground

Mill

Sports
Ground

Wharf

Slipway

Pier

Pier

Pier

79

78

77

66

47

48

49

50

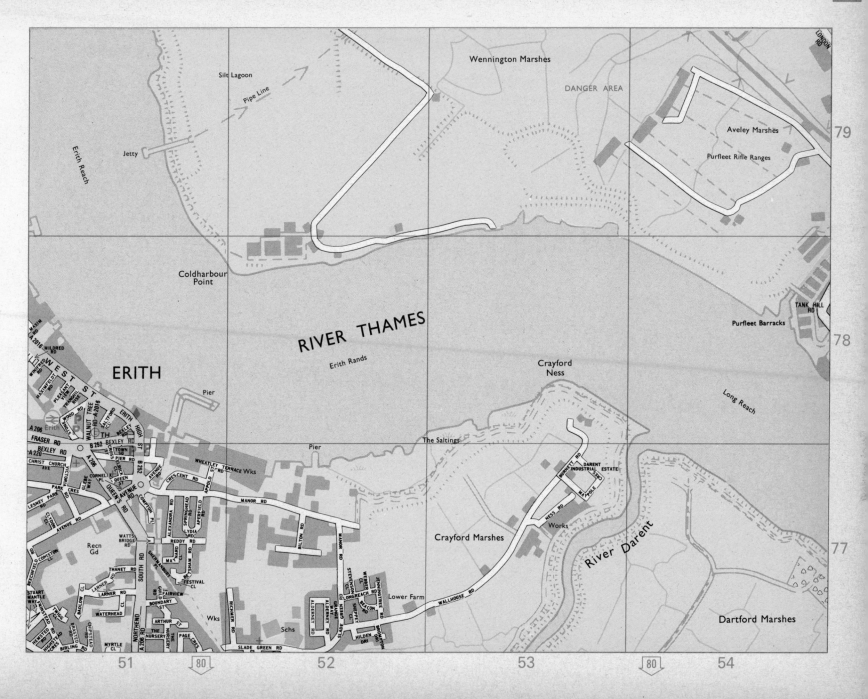

Silt Lagoon

Pipe Line

Wennington Marshes

DANGER AREA

LONDON RD

Aveley Marshes

Purfleet Rifle Ranges

79

Jetty

Erith Reach

Coldharbour
Point

TANK HILL
RD

Purfleet Barracks

RIVER THAMES

Erith Rands

Crayford
Ness

Long Reach

78

ERITH

WEST ST

MAXIM RD
A 2018 MILDRED RD
WINIFRED RD
PLEASANT VIEW RD
TRANQUIL RISE
WALNUT TREE RD · A 2016
SALTFORD CL
BEXLEY RD
ERITH HIGH ST
FRASER RD
A 206 Erith
BEXLEY RD
B 252
A 206
A 220
CHRIST CHURCH
AVE
CORNELL
QUEEN
VICTORIA
PARK CRES
GLEBE WAY
QUEEN'S RD
LESNEY PARK RD
CLYDON
AVENUE RD
Recn
Gd
WATTS
BRIDGE RD
Beechfield CONISTON CL
STUART
MANTLE
WAY
FRINSTEAD RD
HEMSTED RD
HIGHSTEAD CRES
BIRLING
TWIG
OVERDALE RD
BADLOW CL
THANET RD
LARNER RD
LARNER CL
WATERHEAD
MYRTLE
CL
SOUTH RD
NORTHEND
A 206 RD
SHERWANBURY
FAIRVIEW
BOUNDARY ST
THE NURSERY
ARTHUR ST
PAGE CRES

Pier

PIER RD
TOWN
PIER RD
CROSS ST
AVENUE
ALEXANDRA RD
CRESCENT RD
APPOLD ST
SPRINGHEAD
APERFIELD
COMPTON PL
LYDIA RD
REDDY RD
WARD
PELSHAM RD
FESTIVAL
CL
RICHMER RD

Pier

WHEATLEY TERRACE Wks

MANOR RD

BILTON RD

MANOR RD

The Saltings

BURNETT RD
CREALY WAY
DARENT INDUSTRIAL ESTATE
NESS RD

Works

Crayford Marshes

Wks

Schs

ALDERNEY RD
GRANGE RD
SHEPPEY
BEACON
HILDEN DRI
SLADE GREEN RD
STEVENSON RD
LONGREACH RD
WEBBER CL
JENNINGTREE RD
BROMPTON DRI

Lower Farm

WALLHOUSE RD

River Darent

77

Dartford Marshes

51

80

52

53

80

54

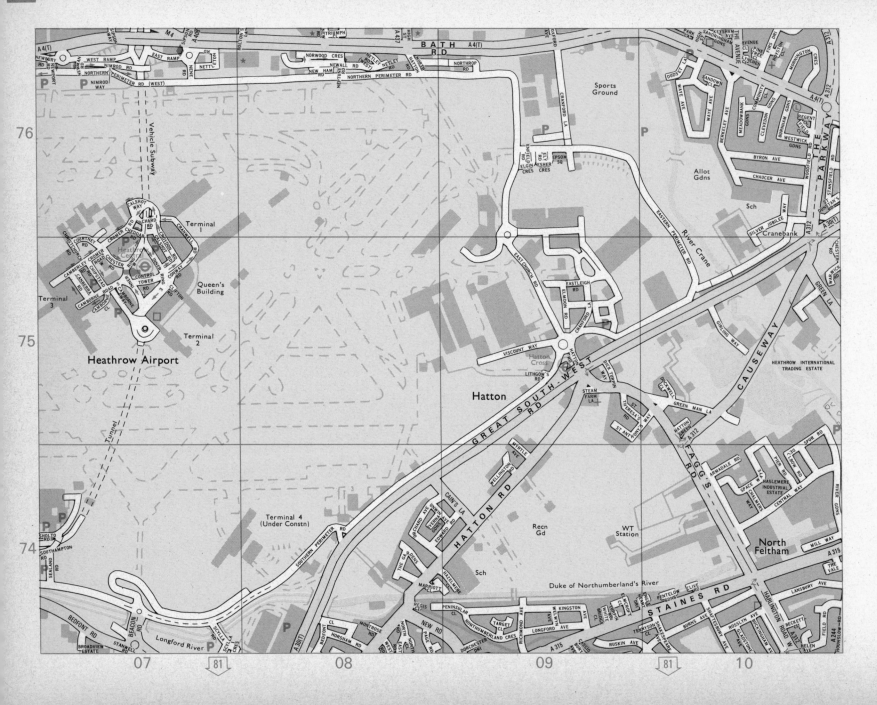

Heathrow Airport

Terminal 1

Terminal 2

Terminal 3

Queen's Building

CONTROL TOWER

Terminal 4
(Under Constn)

Hatton

Hatton Cross

North Feltham

Sports Ground

Allot Gdns

Cranebank

Heathrow International Trading Estate

Haslemere Industrial Estate

Recn Gd

WT Station

BATH RD

A4(T)

GREAT SOUTH-WEST RD

HATTON RD

STAINES RD

THE PARKWAY

CAUSEWAY

FAGG'S RD

Longford River

Duke of Northumberland's River

River Crane

76

75

74

07

08

09

10

81

81

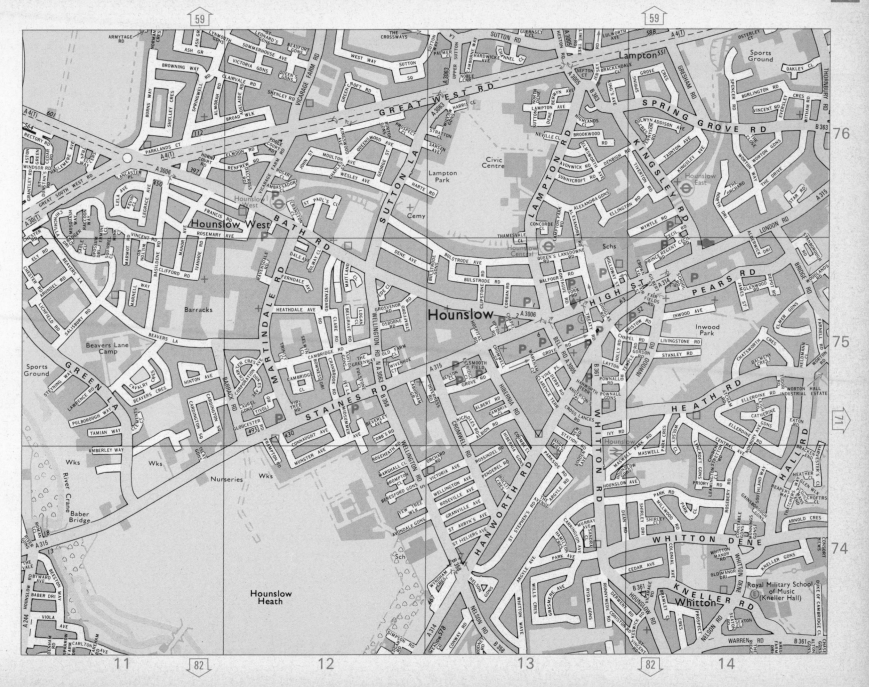

Sports Ground

THE CROSSWAYS

Lampton 551

SPRING GROVE RD

GREAT WEST RD

Civic Centre

Lampton Park

Hounslow East

Hounslow West

Hounslow West

Cemy

KINGSLEY RD

LONDON RD

BATH RD

PEARS RD

Barracks

Hounslow

Hounslow Central

Inwood Park

HIGH ST

Beavers Lane Camp

Sports Ground

GREEN LA

STAINES RD

MARTINDALE RD

WELLINGTON RD

HEATH RD

HALL RD

WHITTON RD

Worton Hall Industrial Estate

River Crane

Baber Bridge

Wks

Wks

Nurseries

Wks

Sch

HANWORTH RD

WHITTON DENE

Hounslow Heath

Sch

KNELLER RD

Royal Military School of Music (Kneller Hall)

Whitton

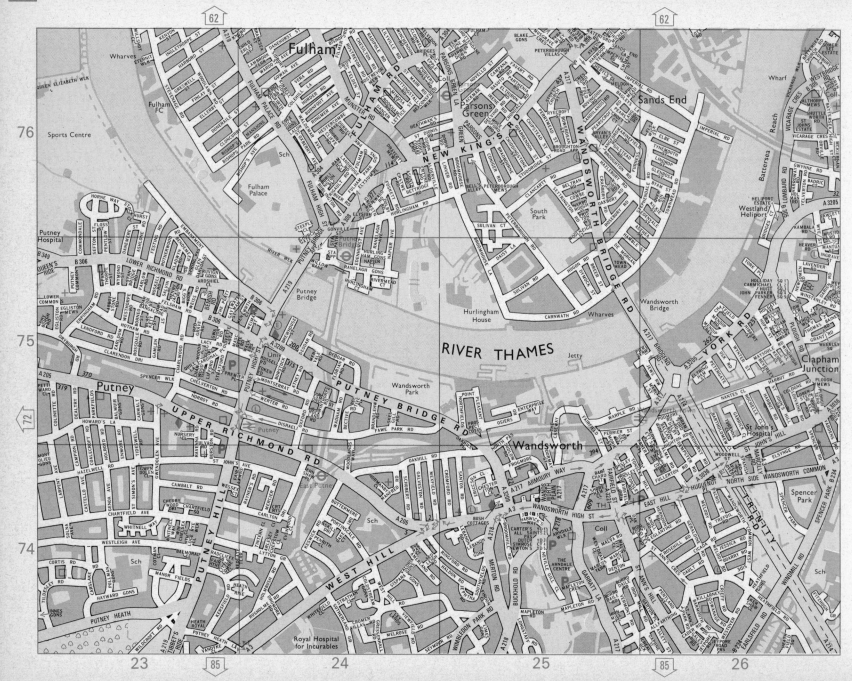

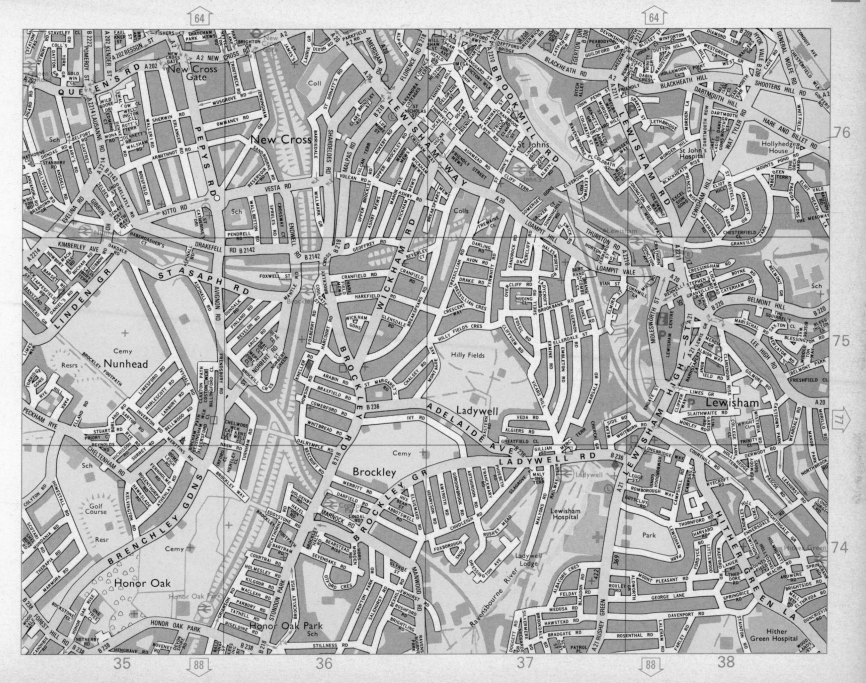

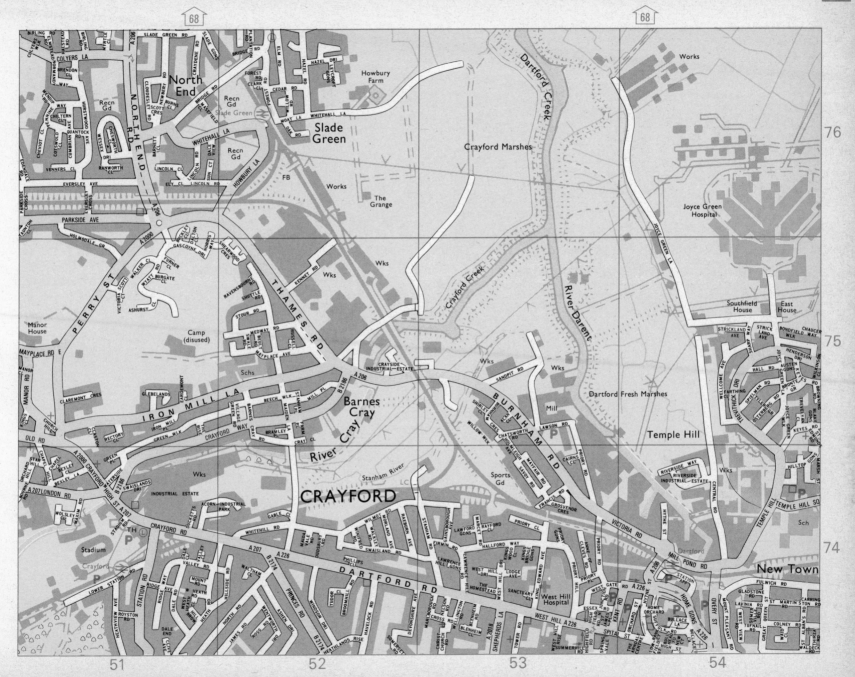

76

75

74

51

52

53

54

COLYERS LA
BIRLING RD
HALSTEAD RD
BRENDON
MYRTLE RD
SLADE GREEN RD
North End
Recn Gd
CRAYDENE RD
SLADE GDNS
BRIDGE RD
FOREST RD
ELM RD
HAZEL DRI
PLANTATION RD
CLARK
CEDAR RD
Works
Howbury Farm
Dartford Creek

CLOUDESLEY RD
Recn Gd
Slade Green
MOAT LA
WHITEHALL LA
Slade Green
Crayford Marshes
Joyce Green Hospital

NORTH END
A 206
WHITEHALL LA
Recn Gd
FB
Works
The Grange

EVERSLEY AVE
LINCOLN RD
HOWBURY LA

PARKSIDE AVE
A 2000
PERRY ST

Manor House
Camp (disused)
THAMES RD
Wks
Crayford Creek
River Darent
Southfield House
East House

IRON MILL LA
Schs
CRAYSIDE INDUSTRIAL ESTATE
A 206
Barnes Cray
Wks
Wks
Dartford Fresh Marshes
Temple Hill

Old Rd
A 2000 CRAYFORD HIGH ST
B 2186
Wks
INDUSTRIAL ESTATE
ACORN INDUSTRIAL PARK
River Cray
Stanham River
Sports Gd
BURNHAM RD
RIVERSIDE INDUSTRIAL ESTATE
Wks

Stadium
CRAYFORD RD
WHITEHILL RD
CRAYFORD
Stanham River
West Hill Hospital
VICTORIA RD
New Town

Crayford
STATION RD
A 207 A 226
DARTFORD RD
Mill Pond Rd
Temple Hill Sq

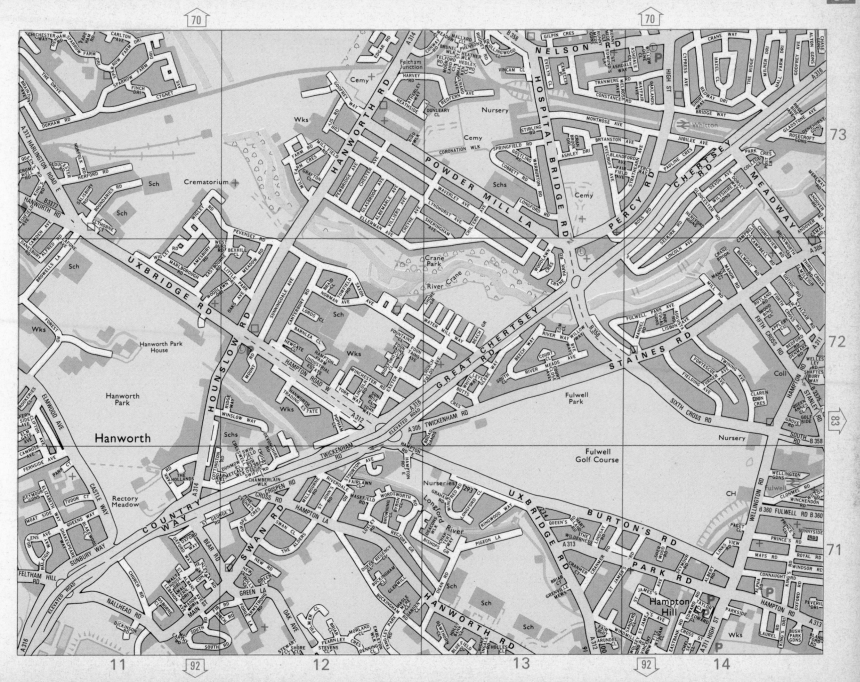

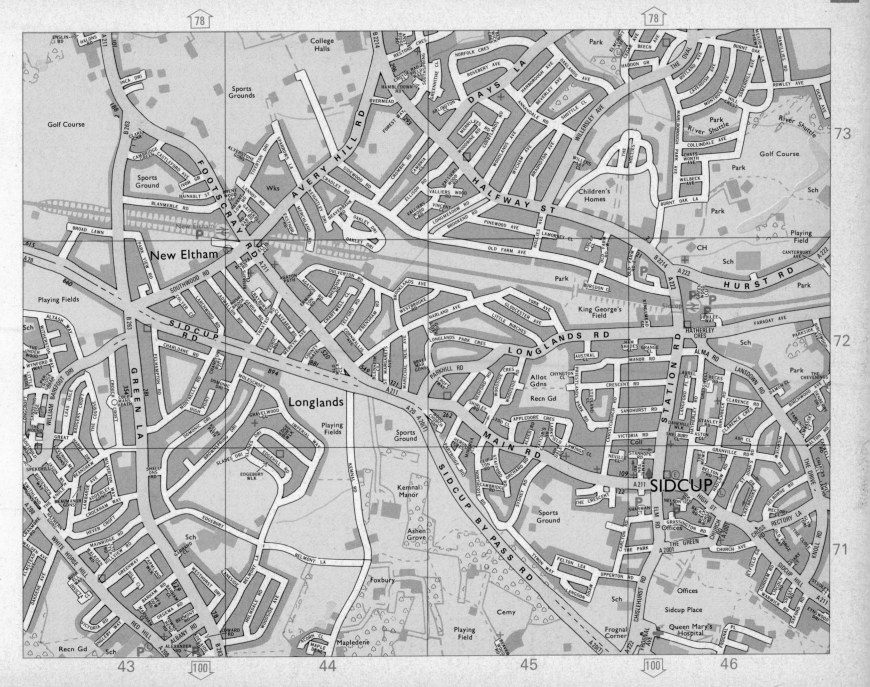

70

69

68

92

83

83

101

101

15　　　　　16　　　　　17　　　　　18

Hospital

BROAD ST
THE CAUSEWAY

National Physical
Laboratory

The Cottage

Bushy
House

Broom
Clumps

COBBLER'S WLK

Lodge

Deer Park

Bushy Park

Heron
Pond

Oval
Plantation

Warren
Plantation

Diana Fountain

Hampton Court
House

Royal
Mews

Hampton Court

Hampton Court Palace

River
Thames

Weirs

The Royal
Paddocks

HAMPTON COURT RD

Stud
House

Hampton Court Park

Kingston Upon
Thames

QUEENS RD

PARK RD

CHESTNUT AVE

SANDY LA

Athletic
Ground

Normansfield
Hospital

School

Recn
Gd

Hampton
Wick

Hampton
Wick

River Thames

BROOM RD

KINGSTON RD

RICHMOND RD

KINGS RD

ACRE RD

LONDON RD

County
Hall

Poly

Fairfield

PORTSMOUTH RD

Kingston

Cromwell Rd

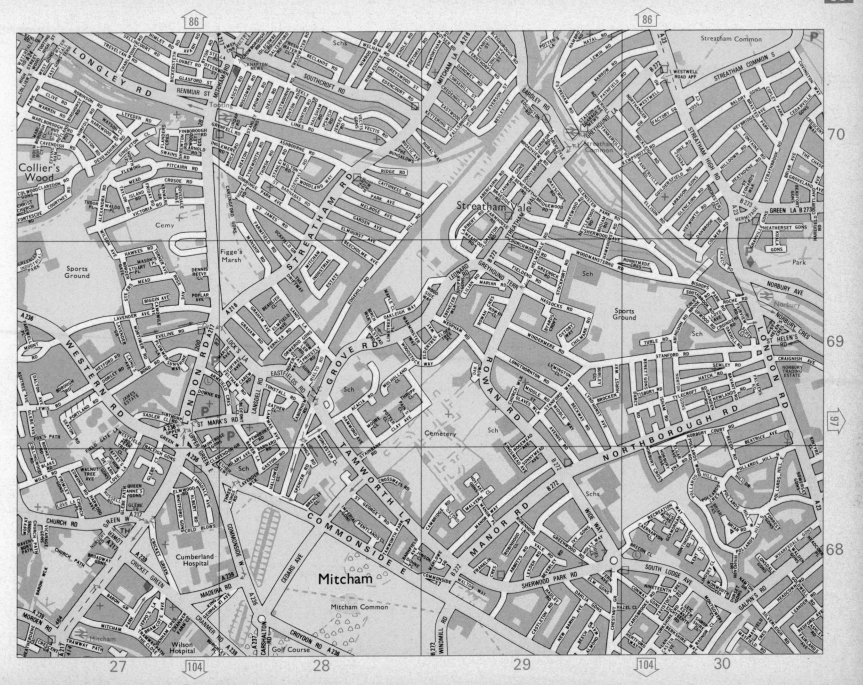

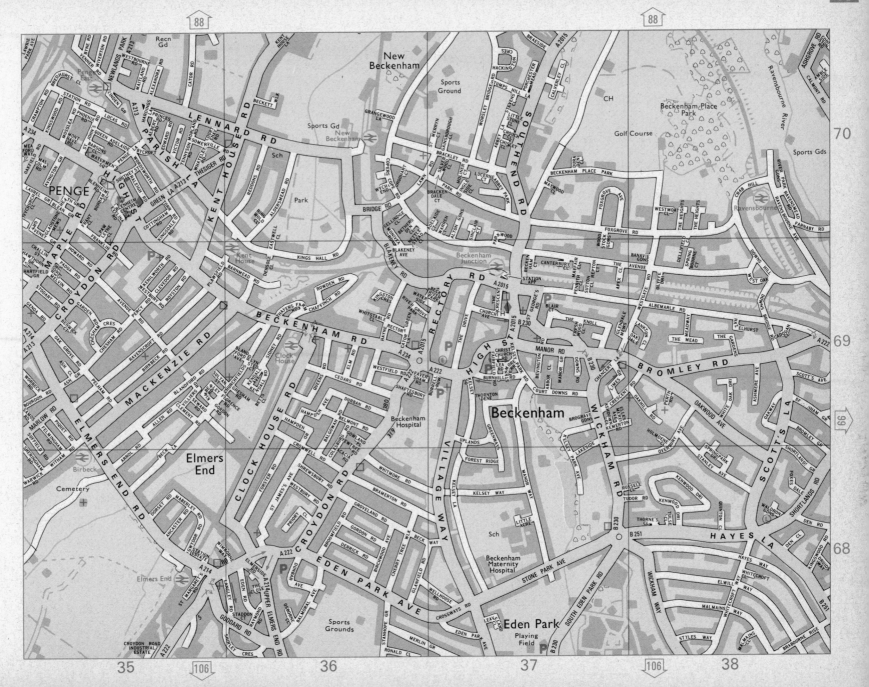

Chislehurst
West

Queen Mary's
Hospital
Frognal
House

SIDCUP BY PASS RD

Sch

Athletic
Ground

Foxbury

PERRY ST

Little Wood

70

Chislehurst

Campden Park
(Golf Course)

Common

Perry Street
Shaw

Bushy
Clump

Scadbury
Park

Icehouse
Wood

Moat

BROMLEY RD

OLD HILL

WATT'S LA

ST PAUL'S CRAY RD

Park Wood

The Drive

MIDFIELD WAY

ST PAUL'S WOOD HILL

CHIPPERFIELD RD

69

Caves

Hawkwood
House

Sch

The
Gorse

Walsingham
Park

St Paul's
Cray

Pond
Wood

Hawkwood
Estate

Tongs Farm

Petts Wood

LEESONS HILL

68

Kyd Brook

Willett Meml.
Wood

BLACKBROOK LA

Aquila

Petts
Wood

St Mary Cray

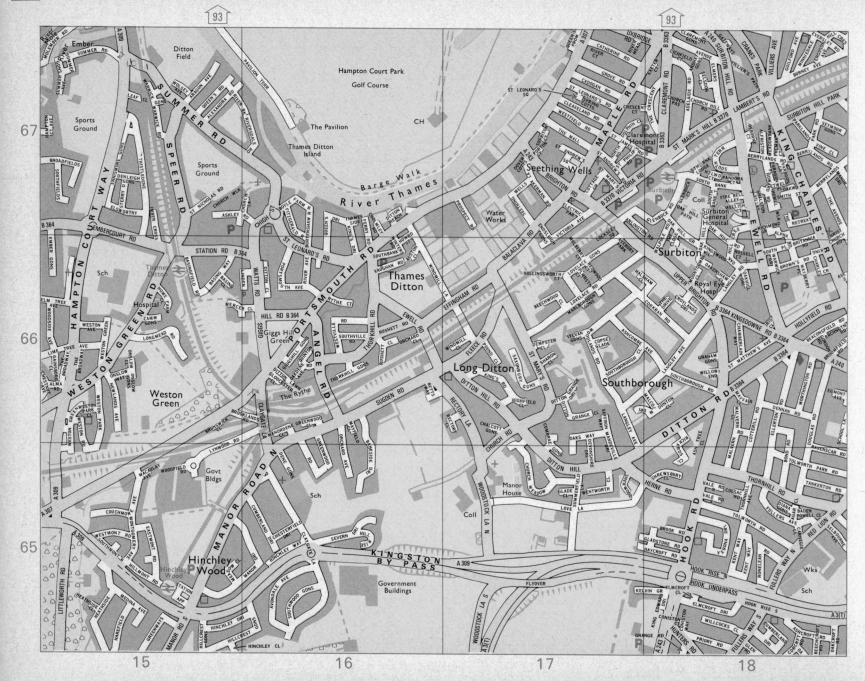

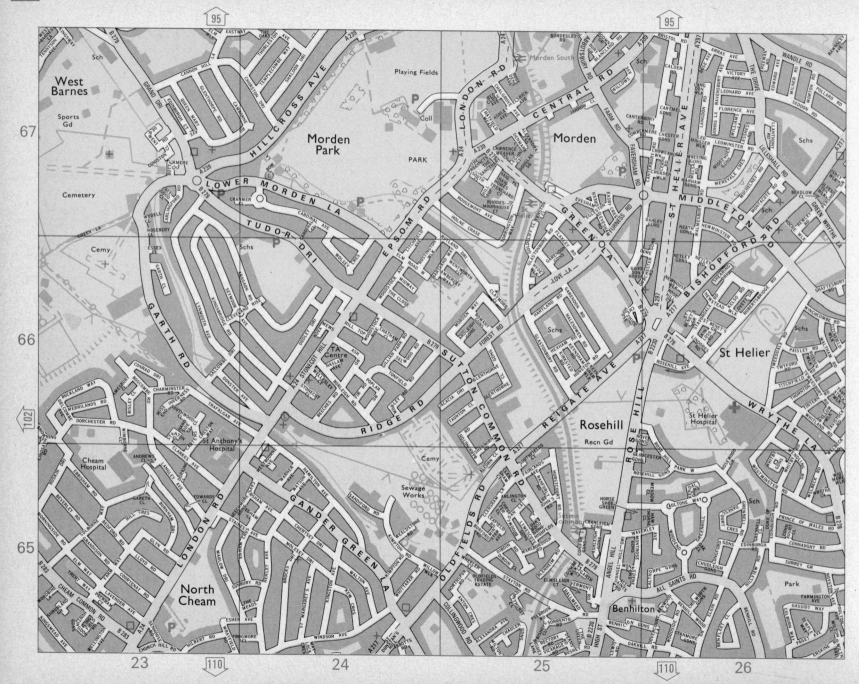

105
105
Recn Gd
Sch
Coombe Park
Coombe Farm
Lloyd Park
South Croydon
Purley Way Playing Fields
Croham Hurst
Breakneck Hill
Golf Course
Allot Gdns
Recn Gd
Resr
CH
FB
Waddon
Coombe Road
Selsdon
Sanderstead
Purley Oaks
STATION APP
SELSDON RD INDUSTRIAL ESTATE
DUPPAS HILL RD
COOMBE RD
OAKS RD
COOMBE LA
DENNING AVE
WARHAM RD
CROHAM RD
WADDON WAY
HALING PARK RD
SELSDON RD
BRIGHTON RD
PURLEY WAY
PAMPISFORD RD
SANDERSTEAD RD
UPPER SELSDON RD
FARLEY RD
CROHAM VALLEY RD
BALLARDS WAY
MANOR WAY
HURST WAY
CARLTON RD
MAYFIELD RD
EDGEHILL RD
HIGHFIELD RD
PURLEY DOWNS RD
BRITON HILL RD
ARKWRIGHT RD
CHURCH WAY
WEST HILL
EAST HILL
OLD FOX FOOTPATH
SOUTH PARK HILL RD
PARK HILL RD
CONDUIT LANE
BALLARDS FARM RD
HOLLINGSWORTH RD
A23
A232
A235
A212
A243
A2022
B275
B274
B243
B269
B271
31
32
33
34
64
63
62

# EXPLANATION OF STREET INDEX AND REFERENCE SYSTEM

## ABBREVIATIONS USED IN THE INDEX

Example:—  * Ordnance Mews. NW8 ............ 46    26 83 D
① ② ③ ④ ⑤⑥

① The asterisk indicates that only the first two letters of the name have been shown on the map e.g. OR.

② This is the full street name, which may have been abbreviated on the map.

③ This is the postal code or town in which the street falls, Standard postal codes have been used for street names in the London Postal Districts.
For all other street names Post Town abbreviations have been used as a guide to the location of the street name.

④ This is the map number on which the street name appears

⑤ The four figures and the letter are the reference system for locating the position of the name on the map.
The four figures show in which square the centre of the street falls.
The first two figures can be found along the bottom edge of each map in blue and these apply to the vertical columns.
The second two figures can be found along the left or right hand side of each map in red and these apply to the horizontal rows.

⑥ The letter provides a more precise location within the square.
The parts of the square to which each letter refers are indicated below.

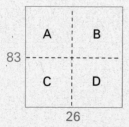

The numerical part of the referencing is based on the National Grid

### Road Names

| | |
|---|---|
| App | Approach |
| Arc | Arcade |
| Ave | Avenue |
| Bvd | Boulevard |
| Bwy | Broadway |
| Bldg/s | Building/s |
| By Ps | By Pass |
| Cswy | Causeway |
| Circ | Circle |
| Circ | Circus |
| Cl | Close |
| Cnr | Corner |
| Ct | Court |
| Cres | Crescent |
| Dri | Drive |
| Dro | Drove |
| E | East |
| Emb | Embankment |
| Espl | Esplanade |
| Fly | Flyover |
| Gdns | Gardens |
| Gr | Grove |
| Hts | Heights |
| Junc | Junction |
| La | Lane |
| N | North |
| Par | Parade |
| Pas | Passage |
| Pl | Place |
| Prec | Precinct |
| Prom | Promenade |
| Rd | Road |
| S | South |
| Sq | Square |
| Strs | Stairs |
| Stps | Steps |
| St | Street |
| Terr | Terrace |
| Wlk | Walk |
| W | West |
| Yd | Yard |

### Postal Districts and Towns

| | |
|---|---|
| Ashf | Ashford |
| Bark | Barking |
| Barn | Barnet |
| Beck | Beckenham |
| Belv | Belvedere |
| Bex | Bexley |
| Bexh | Bexleyheath |
| Brent | Brentford |
| Brom | Bromley |
| Buck H | Buckhurst Hill |
| Cars | Carshalton |
| Chess | Chessington |
| Chig | Chigwell |
| Chis | Chislehurst |
| Croy | Croydon |
| Dag | Dagenham |
| Dart | Dartford |
| E Mol | East Molesey |
| Edg | Edgware |
| Enf | Enfield |
| Eps | Epsom |
| Eri | Erith |
| Esh | Esher |
| Felt | Feltham |
| Grnf | Greenford |
| Hamp | Hampton |
| Har | Harrow |
| Hay | Hayes |
| Horn | Hornchurch |
| Houn | Hounslow |
| Ilf | Ilford |
| Islw | Isleworth |
| King | Kingston on Thames |
| Loug | Loughton |
| Mit | Mitcham |
| Mord | Morden |
| N Mal | New Malden |
| Nthlt | Northolt |
| Orp | Orpington |
| Pnr | Pinner |
| Pur | Purley |
| Rain | Rainham |
| Rich | Richmond |
| Rom | Romford |
| Ruis | Ruislip |
| Shep | Shepperton |
| Sid | Sidcup |
| Sthl | Southall |
| S Croy | South Croydon |
| Stan | Stanmore |
| Sun | Sunbury-on-Thames |
| Surb | Surbiton |
| Sutt | Sutton |
| Stai | Staines |
| Tedd | Teddington |
| Th Hth | Thornton Heath |
| Twick | Twickenham |
| Uxb | Uxbridge |
| Wall | Wallington |
| Walt | Walton on Thames |
| Well | Welling |
| Wem | Wembley |
| W Dray | West Drayton |
| Wdf Gr | Woodford Green |
| W Wick | West Wickham |
| Wor Pk | Worcester Park |

Abbess Cl. SW2 87 31 73 D
Abbeville Rd. N8 24 29 89 D
Abbeville Rd. SW4 74 29 74 A
Abbey Ave. Wem 44 18 83 C
Abbey Cl. Nthlt 53 12 82 B
Abbey Cl. Pnr 20 11 89 A
Abbey Cres. Belv 67 49 78 A
Abbeydale Rd. Wem 45 19 83 A
Abbeyfield Rd. SE16 64 35 78 A
Abbey Gdns. NW8 46 26 83 C
Abbey Gr. SE2 67 47 78 A
Abbey La. Beck 98 37 70 C
Abbey La. E15 49 38 83 D
Abbey Orchard St. SW1 6 29 79 D
Abbey Park. Beck 98 37 70 C
Abbey Rd. Bark 51 44 83 A
Abbey Rd. Belv 67 48 78 A
Abbey Rd. Bexh 79 48 75 C
Abbey Rd. Croy 105 31 65 D
Abbey Rd. E15 50 39 83 A
Abbey Rd. Enf 13 33 95 A
Abbey Rd. Ilf 40 44 88 B
Abbey Rd. NW6 46 25 83 B
Abbey Rd. NW6 46 25 84 D
Abbey Rd. NW8 46 26 83 C
Abbey Rd. SE2 67 47 78 A
Abbey Rd. SW19 95 26 69 A
Abbey St. E13 58 40 82 C
Abbey St. SE1 8 33 79 D
Abbey Terr. SE2 67 47 78 A
Abbey Wlk. E Mol 92 13 68 B
Abbey Wood Rd. SE2 67 47 78 A
Abbor Cl. Beck 98 37 69 D
Abbot Cl. Ruis 32 11 86 D
Abbotsbury Cl. E15 49 38 83 C
Abbotsbury Cl. W14 62 24 79 B
Abbotsbury Gdns. Pnr 32 11 88 C
Abbotsbury Rd. Brom 107 39 65 B
Abbotsbury Rd. Mord 95 25 68 D
Abbotsbury Rd. W14 62 24 79 B
Abbots Cl. N1 48 32 84 A
Abbots Cl. Orp 108 44 66 C
Abbotsford Ave. N15 25 32 89 C
Abbotsford Gdns. Wdf Gn 27 40 91 C
Abbotsford Rd. Ilf 40 46 86 B
Abbots Gdns. N2 23 26 89 D
Abbotshall Ave. N14 16 29 93 C
Abbotshall Rd. SE6 88 38 72 B
Abbots La. SE1 8 33 80 C
Abbotsleigh Cl. Sutt 110 25 63 D
Abbotsleigh Rd. SW16 86 29 71 C
Abbots Park. SW2 87 31 73 C
Abbot's Pl. NW6 46 25 83 B
Abbots Rd. E6 50 41 83 D
Abbots Rd. Edg 22 20 91 D
Abbot St. E8 48 33 84 B
Abbots Terr. N8 36 30 88 C
Abbotstone Rd. SW15 73 23 75 A
Abbots Way. Beck 106 36 67 A
Abbotswell Rd. SE4 76 36 74 B
Abbotswood Gdns. Ilf 27 42 89 B
Abbotswood Gdns. Ilf 28 43 89 C
Abbotswood Rd. SW16 86 29 72 D
Abbott Ave. SW20 95 23 69 B
Abbott Cl. Hamp 92 12 70 A
Abbott Cl. Nthlt 43 12 84 B
Abbott Rd. E14 58 38 81 D
Abbotts Cl. Rom 29 49 89 B
Abbotts Cres. E4 18 38 92 B
Abbotts Cres. Enf 13 31 97 D
Abbotts Dri. Wem 33 16 86 B
Abbottsmede Cl. Twick 83 15 72 B
Abbotts Park Rd. E10 38 38 87 A
Abbotts Rd. Barn 11 25 96 D
Abbotts Rd. Mit 96 29 68 B
Abbotts Rd. Sthl 53 12 80 C
Abbotts Rd. Sutt 110 24 64 A
Abbotts Rd. Sutt 103 24 65 D
Abbott's Wlk. Bexh 67 47 77 D
Abbs Cross Gdns. Horn 42 53 87 D
Abbs Cross. Horn 42 53 87 B
Abbs Cross La. Horn 42 53 86 C
Abchurch La. EC4 8 32 80 B
Abchurch Yd. EC4 8 32 80 B
Abdale Rd. W12 55 22 80 D
Aberavon Rd. E3 57 36 82 A
Abercairn Rd. SW16 96 29 70 C
Aberconway Rd. Mord 95 25 68 D
Abercorn Cl. NW7 23 24 91 C
Abercorn Cl. NW8 7 26 82 A
Abercorn Cres. Har 32 13 87 D
Abercorn Gdns. Har 33 17 87 B
Abercorn Gdns. Rom 40 46 88 D
Abercorn Pl. NW8 46 26 83 C
Abercorn Rd. NW7 23 24 91 C
Abercorn Rd. Stan 21 17 91 C
Abercrombie St. SW11 74 27 76 C
Aberdare Cl. W Wick 106 38 65 A
Aberdare Gdns. NW6 46 26 84 A
Aberdare Gdns. NW7 23 23 91 D
Aberdare Rd. Enf 14 35 96 C
Aberdeen La. N5 48 32 85 C
Aberdeen Park. N5 48 32 85 C
Aberdeen Pl. NW8 1 26 82 D
Aberdeen Rd. Croy 112 32 64 B
Aberdeen Rd. Har 21 15 90 D
Aberdeen Rd. N18 17 34 92 D
Aberdeen Rd. N5 48 32 85 A
Aberdeen Rd. NW10 45 21 85 D
Aberdeen Terr. SE3 76 38 76 D
Aberdour Rd. Ilf 40 46 86 B
Aberdour St. SE1 8 33 79 C
Aberfeldy St. E14 58 38 81 C
Aberford Gdns. SE18 77 42 76 A
Aberfoyle Rd. SW16 96 29 70 D
Abergeldie Rd. SE12 77 40 74 D
Abernethy Rd. SE13 77 39 75 C
Abersham Rd. E8 48 33 85 D
Abery St. SE18 66 45 78 A
Abingdon Cl. NW1 47 29 84 B
Abingdon Cl. SW19 95 26 70 A
Abingdon Rd. N3 23 26 90 C
Abingdon Rd. SW16 96 30 69 A
Abingdon Rd. W8 62 25 79 C
Abingdon St. SE1 7 30 79 C
Abingdon Villas. W8 62 25 79 C
Abinger Ave. Sutt 110 23 62 D
Abinger Cl. Bark 51 46 85 A
Abinger Cl. Brom 99 42 68 A
Abinger Cl. Wall 111 30 64 C
Abinger Ct. W5 54 17 80 A
Abinger Gdns. Islw 71 15 75 A
Abinger Gr. SE8 64 36 77 B
Abinger Mews. W9 56 25 82 C
Abinger Rd. W4 61 21 79 C
Ablett St. SE16 64 35 78 C
Abney Gdns. N16 37 33 86 B
Aboyne Dri. SW20 94 22 69 C
Aboyne Rd. NW10 34 21 86 C
Aboyne Rd. SW17 85 26 72 D
Abridge Gdns. Rom 29 49 91 A
Abridge Way. Bark 51 46 83 D
Abyssinia Cl. SW11 74 27 75 C
Abyssinia Rd. SW11 74 27 75 C
Acacia Ave. Brent 60 16 77 D
Acacia Ave. Horn 42 51 86 B
Acacia Ave. N17 25 32 91 D
Acacia Ave. Ruis 31 10 87 B
Acacia Ave. Wem 44 18 85 C
Acacia Cl. Orp 108 44 67 B
Acacia Cl. Stan 21 15 91 A
Acacia Dri. Sutt 103 25 66 C
Acacia Gdns. NW8 46 26 83 D
Acacia Gdns. W Wick 106 38 65 A
Acacia Gr. N Mal 94 21 68 A
Acacia Gr. SE21 87 32 72 B
Acacia Pl. NW8 46 26 83 D
Acacia Rd. Beck 98 36 68 B
Acacia Rd. E11 39 39 86 B
Acacia Rd. E17 38 36 88 C
Acacia Rd. Enf 13 32 97 B
Acacia Rd. Hamp 92 13 70 A
Acacia Rd. Mit 96 28 69 D
Acacia Rd. N22 25 31 90 A
Acacia Rd. NW8 46 26 83 D
Acacia Rd. W3 55 20 80 A
*Acacia Wlk. SW10 62 26 77 C
Academy Gdns. Croy 105 33 66 D
Academy Gdns. Nthlt 43 11 83 D
Academy Pl. SE18 77 42 76 B
Academy Rd. SE18 65 42 77 D
Acanthus Rd. SW11 74 28 75 A
Accommodation Rd. NW11 35 24 87 D
Acfold Rd. SW6 73 25 76 B
Achilles Rd. NW6 46 25 85 C
Achilles St. SE14 64 36 77 D
Achilles Way. W1 6 28 80 C
Acklam Rd. W10 56 24 81 B
Acklington Dri. NW9 22 21 90 A
Ackmar Rd. SW6 73 25 76 A
Ackroyd Dri. E3 57 36 81 B
Ackroyd Rd. SE23 88 36 73 A
Acland Cres. SE5 75 32 75 B
Acland Rd. NW2 45 22 84 B
Acol Rd. NW6 46 26 84 A
Aconbury Rd. Dag 51 46 83 B
Acorn Cl. Chis 90 44 71 C
Acorn Cl. E4 18 37 92 D
Acorn Cl. Enf 13 31 97 B
Acorn Ct. Ilf 40 45 88 A
Acorn Gdns. SE19 97 33 69 B
Acorn Gdns. W3 55 20 81 B
Acorn Wlk. SE16 57 36 80 C
Acre La. Cars 111 28 64 A
Acre La. SW2 74 30 75 C
Acre La. Wall 111 28 64 B
Acre Rd. Dag 52 49 84 D
Acre Rd. King 93 18 69 B
Acre Rd. SW19 95 26 70 B
Acre Way. Nthwd 19 09 90 B
Acris St. SW18 73 26 74 A
Acton La. NW10 45 20 83 D
Acton La. W3 61 20 79 A
Acton La. W4 61 20 79 D
Acton Mews. E8 48 33 83 B
Acton St. WC1 3 30 82 B
Acuba Rd. SW18 85 25 72 B
Ada Gdns. E14 58 38 81 D
Ada Gdns. E15 50 39 83 B
Adair Rd. W10 56 24 82 C
Adam and Eve Ct. W1 2 29 81 C
Adam and Eve Mews. W8 62 25 79 C
Adam Pl. N16 37 33 86 B
Adams Cl. NW9 34 19 86 B
Adams Ct. EC2 4 32 81 D
Adams Gardens Estate. SE16 64 35 79 A
Adamson Rd. E16 58 40 81 C
Adamson Rd. NW3 46 26 84 D
Adams Rd. Beck 106 36 67 A
Adams Rd. N17 25 33 90 C
Adamsrill Cl. Enf 13 32 95 D
Adamsrill Rd. SE26 88 36 71 A
Adam's Row. W1 6 28 80 A
Adams Sq. Bexh 79 48 75 A
Adam St. WC2 7 30 80 A
Ada Pl. E2 48 34 83 A
Ada Rd. SE5 63 33 77 C
Ada Rd. Wem 33 17 86 D
Adare Wlk. SW16 86 30 72 B
Ada St. E8 48 34 83 B
Adderley Gdns. SE9 90 43 71 A
Adderley Gr. SW11 74 28 74 A
Adderley Rd. Har 21 15 90 B
Adderley St. E14 58 38 81 C
Addington Dri. N12 23 26 91 B
Addington Gr. SE26 88 36 71 A
Addington Rd. Croy 105 31 66 C
Addington Rd. E16 58 39 82 C
Addington Rd. E3 57 37 82 A
Addington Rd. N4 37 31 88 C
Addington Rd. S Croy 112 34 62 D
Addington Rd. W.Wick 107 39 65 C
Addington Sq. SE5 63 32 77 C
Addington St. SE1 7 30 79 B
Addis Cl. Enf 14 35 97 B
Addiscombe Ave. Croy 105 34 66 A
Addiscombe Cl. Har 33 17 88 A
Addiscombe Court Rd. Croy 105 33 65 A
Addiscombe Gr. Croy 105 33 65 A
Addiscombe Rd. Croy 105 34 65 A
Addison Ave. Houn 70 14 76 A
Addison Ave. N14 12 28 95 D
Addison Ave. W11 56 24 80 C
Addison Bridge Pl. W14 62 24 78 B
Addison Cl. Nthwd 19 10 90 A
Addison Cl. Orp 108 44 67 C
Addison Cres. W14 62 24 79 C
Addison Gdns. Surb 93 18 68 D
Addison Gdns. W14 62 23 79 B
Addison Gr. W4 61 21 79 C
Addison Pl. W11 56 24 80 C
Addison Rd. Brom 107 41 67 B
Addison Rd. E11 39 40 88 C
Addison Rd. E17 38 38 88 A
Addison Rd. Enf 14 35 97 B
Addison Rd. Ilf 28 44 90 A
Addison Rd. SE25 97 34 68 C
Addison Rd. W14 62 24 79 A
Addison's Cl. Croy 106 36 65 B
Addison Way. Nthwd 19 09 90 B
Addison Way. NW11 23 25 89 C
Addle Hill. EC4 3 31 81 D
Addle St. EC2 4 32 81 A
Adecroft Way. E Mol 92 14 68 A
Adela Ave. N Mal 94 22 68 D
Adelaide Ave. SE4 76 37 75 C
Adelaide Ct. Beck 98 37 70 C
Adelaide Gdns. Rom 41 48 88 A
Adelaide Gr. W12 55 22 80 C
Adelaide Rd. Chis 90 43 71 D
Adelaide Rd. E10 38 38 86 C
Adelaide Rd. Houn 70 12 76 A
Adelaide Rd. Ilf 40 43 86 B
Adelaide Rd. NW3 47 27 84 C
Adelaide Rd. Rich 71 18 75 D
Adelaide Rd. Sthl 59 12 78 A
Adelaide Rd. Surb 101 18 67 A
Adelaide Rd. Tedd 93 15 70 B
Adelaide Rd. W13 60 16 79 A
Adelaide St. WC2 7 30 80 A
Adelaide Wlk. SW9 75 31 75 C
Adela St. W10 56 24 82 C
Adelina Gr. E1 57 35 81 A
Adeline Pl. WC1 2 29 81 B
Adelphi Cres. Horn 42 52 86 A
Adelphi Terr. WC2 7 30 80 A
Adeney Cl. W6 62 23 77 B
Aden Gr. N16 48 32 85 B
Adenmore Rd. SE6 88 37 73 A
Aden Rd. Enf 14 36 96 C
Aden Rd. Ilf 40 44 87 A
Aden Terr. N16 48 32 85 B
Adie Rd. W6 62 23 79 C
Adine Rd. E13 58 40 82 D
Adler St. E1 57 34 81 C
Adley St. E5 49 36 85 C
Admaston Rd. SE18 66 44 77 A
Admiral Mews. W10 56 23 82 D
Admiral Seymour Rd. SE9 77 42 75 D
Admiral St. SE8 76 37 76 A
Admiral's Wlk. NW3 35 26 86 C
Admiralty Rd. Tedd 93 15 70 B
Adolf St. SE6 88 37 71 B
Adolphus Rd. N4 37 31 87 D
Adolphus St. SE8 64 36 77 D
Adomar Rd. Dag 41 48 86 C
Adpar St. W2 1 26 81 B
Adrian Ave. NW2 34 22 87 D
Adrian Mews. SW10 62 25 77 B
Adrienne Ave. Sthl 53 12 82 B
Adys Rd. SE15 75 34 75 A
Aerodrome Rd. NW4 22 22 89 A
Aerodrome Rd. NW9 22 21 89 B
Aerodrome Way. Houn 59 11 77 A
Aeroville. NW9 22 21 90 C
Affleck St. N1 47 30 83 D
Afghan Rd. SW11 74 27 76 C
Agamemnon Rd. NW6 46 24 85 D
Agar Cl. Surb 101 18 65 B
Agar Gr. NW1 47 29 84 D
Agar Pl. NW1 47 29 84 C
Agar St. WC2 7 30 80 A
Agate Rd. W6 62 23 79 C
Agatha Cl. E1 57 34 80 D
Agaton Path. SE9 90 44 72 A
Agaton Rd. SE9 90 44 72 A
Agave Rd. NW2 46 23 85 A
Agdon St. EC1 3 31 82 D
Agincourt Rd. NW3 47 27 85 B
Agnes Ave. Ilf 51 43 85 B
Agnes Gdns. Dag 52 47 85 B
Agnes Rd. W3 61 21 79 B
Agnes St. E14 57 36 81 D
Agnew Rd. SE23 88 35 73 B
Agricola Pl. Enf 13 33 95 B
Aidan Cl. Dag 52 48 85 A
Aileen Wlk. E15 50 39 84 D
Ailsa Ave. Twick 71 16 74 B
Ailsa Rd. Twick 71 16 74 B
Ailsa St. E14 58 38 81 A
Ainger Mews. NW3 47 27 84 D
Ainger Rd. NW3 47 27 84 D
Ainsdale Cl. Orp 108 44 66 D
Ainsdale Cres. Pnr 20 13 89 A
Ainsdale Rd. W5 54 17 82 D
Ainsley Ave. Rom 41 50 88 C
Ainsley St. E2 57 34 82 B
Ainslie Wlk. SW12 86 28 73 B
Ainslie Wood Cres. E4 18 37 92 D
Ainslie Wood Gdns. E4 18 37 92 D
Ainslie Wood Rd. E4 18 37 92 D
Ainsworth Cl. NW2 34 22 86 C
Ainsworth Estate. NW8 46 26 83 A
Ainsworth Rd. Croy 105 31 65 B
Ainsworth Rd. E9 49 35 84 C
Ainsworth Way. NW8 46 26 83 A
Aintree Ave. E6 50 42 83 A
Aintree Cres. Ilf 28 44 90 C
Aintree Gr. Horn 42 54 86 D
Aintree Rd. Grnf 44 16 83 B
Aintree St. SW6 62 24 77 C
Airdrie Cl. N1 47 30 84 D
Airedale Avenue S. W4 61 21 78 D
Airedale Ave. W4 61 21 78 D
Airedale Rd. SW12 86 27 73 B
Airedale Rd. W5 60 17 79 D
Airlie Gdns. Ilf 40 43 87 D
Airlie Gdns. W8 56 25 80 C
Air St. W1 6 29 80 A
Airthrie Rd. Ilf 40 46 86 B
Aisgill Ave. SW5 62 24 78 D
Aislibie Rd. SE12 77 39 75 C
Aitken Cl. E8 48 34 83 A
Aitken Rd. Barn 11 23 95 A
Aitken Rd. SE6 88 37 72 B
Ajax Ave. NW9 22 21 89 A
Ajax Rd. NW6 46 25 85 C
Akehurst St. SW15 84 22 73 A
Akenside Rd. NW3 46 26 85 D
Akerman Rd. Surb 101 17 67 C
Akerman Rd. SW9 75 31 76 B
Alabama St. SE18 66 45 77 C
Alacross Rd. W5 60 17 79 B
Alan Cl. Dart 80 53 75 C
Alandale Dri. Pnr 19 10 90 B
Alan Dri. Barn 11 24 95 C
Alan Gdns. Rom 41 49 87 A
Alan Rd. SW19 85 24 71 C
Alanthus Cl. SE12 77 39 74 D
Alaska St. SE1 7 31 80 C
Albacore Cres. SE13 76 37 74 D
Alba Gdns. NW11 35 24 88 C
Albany Cl. N15 25 32 89 C
Albany Cl. SW14 72 19 75 D
Albany Courtyard. W1 6 29 80 A
Albany Cres. Edg 22 19 91 C
Albany Mews. SE5 63 32 77 A
Albany Park Ave. Enf 14 35 97 B
Albany Park Rd. King 93 18 70 A
Albany Pas. Rich 71 18 74 B
Albany Pl. Brent 60 18 77 A
Albany Pl. N7 48 31 85 A
Albany Rd. Belv 67 48 77 B
Albany Rd. Brent 60 17 77 B
Albany Rd. Chis 90 43 71 D
Albany Rd. E10 38 37 87 A
Albany Rd. E12 50 41 85 B
Albany Rd. E17 38 36 88 C
Albany Rd. Horn 42 52 87 C
Albany Rd. N18 18 35 92 C
Albany Rd. N4 37 31 88 C
Albany Rd. N Mal 94 20 68 D
Albany Rd. Rich 71 18 74 A
Albany Rd. Rom 41 48 88 D
Albany Rd. SE5 63 33 77 A
Albany Rd. SW19 85 25 71 D
Albany Rd. W13 54 16 80 B
Albany St. NW1 2 28 82 B
Albany The. Tedd 93 17 70 B
Alba Pl. W11 56 24 81 D
Albatross St. SE18 66 45 77 C
Albemarle App. Ilf 40 43 88 D
Albemarle Ave. Twick 82 12 73 D
Albemarle Gdns. Ilf 40 43 88 D
Albemarle Gdns. N Mal 94 20 68 D
Albemarle Rd. Barn 16 27 94 A
Albemarle Rd. Beck 98 38 69 A
Albemarle St. W1 6 29 80 A
Albemarle. SW19 85 23 72 B
Albemarle Way. EC1 3 31 82 D
Alberon Gdns. NW11 23 24 89 D
Alberta Ave. Sutt 110 24 64 D
Alberta Rd. Enf 13 34 95 C
Alberta Rd. Eri 79 50 76 A
Alberta St. SE17 63 31 78 D
Albert Ave. E4 18 37 92 A
Albert Ave. SW8 10 30 77 D
Albert Bridge Rd. SW11 74 27 76 B
Albert Bridge Rd. SW11 9 27 77 D
Albert Bridge. SW3 9 27 77 A
Albert Carr Gdns. SW16 86 30 71 C
Albert Cl. N22 24 29 90 B
Albert Cres. E4 18 37 92 A
Albert Ct. SW19 85 24 73 C
Albert Dri. SW19 85 24 73 C
Albert Emb. SE1 10 30 78 A
Albert Gdns. E1 57 35 81 D
Albert Gr. SW20 95 23 69 B
Albert Mews. W8 5 26 79 C
Albert Palace Mansions. SW11 74 28 76 A
Albert Pl. N3 23 25 90 A
Albert Pl. W8 62 25 79 B
Albert Rd. Barn 11 26 96 C
Albert Rd. Belv 67 48 78 D
Albert Rd. Bex 79 49 74 C
Albert Rd. Brom 107 42 67 A
Albert Rd. Dag 41 49 87 C
Albert Rd. E10 38 38 87 C
Albert Rd. E16 66 43 79 A
Albert Rd. E17 38 37 88 A
Albert Rd. E18 27 40 89 B
Albert Rd. Hamp 82 14 71 C
Albert Rd. Har 20 14 89 A
Albert Rd. Houn 70 13 75 C
Albert Rd. Ilf 40 44 86 C
Albert Rd. King 93 18 69 D
Albert Rd. Mit 96 27 68 B
Albert Rd. N15 37 33 88 C
Albert Rd. N22 24 29 90 A
Albert Rd. N4 36 30 87 B
Albert Rd. N.Mal 102 21 67 B
Albert Rd. NW6 46 24 83 D
Albert Rd. Orp 108 46 67 D
Albert Rd. Rich 71 18 74 B
Albert Rd. Rom 42 51 88 D
Albert Rd. SE20 98 35 70 B
Albert Rd. SE25 105 34 67 B
Albert Rd. SE25 97 34 68 C
Albert Rd. SE9 89 42 72 C
Albert Rd. Sthl 59 11 79 D
Albert Rd. Sutt 110 26 64 D
Albert Rd. Tedd 93 15 70 B
Albert Rd. Twick 83 15 73 D
Albert Rd. W5 54 16 82 D
Albert Sq. E15 50 39 85 C
Albert Sq. SW8 74 30 76 B
Albert Sq. SW8 10 30 77 D
Albert St. N12 15 26 92 C
Albert St. NW1 47 28 83 B
Albert Terrace Mews. NW1 47 28 83 A
Albert Terr. NW1 47 28 83 A
Albert Wlk. E16 66 43 79 A
Albion Ave. N10 24 28 90 A
Albion Ave. SW8 74 29 76 D
Albion Bldgs. EC1 4 32 81 A
Albion Cl. Rom 41 50 88 D
Albion Cl. W2 5 27 80 A
Albion Dri. E8 48 34 84 C
Albion Estate. SE16 64 35 79 A
Albion Gdns. Dag 52 49 85 C
Albion Gdns. W6 61 22 78 B
Albion Gr. N16 48 33 85 A
Albion Mews. N1 48 31 84 C
Albion Mews. W2 5 27 80 A
Albion Pl. EC1 3 31 81 B
Albion Pl. EC2 4 32 81 B
Albion Pl. SE25 97 34 68 A
Albion Rd. Bexh 79 49 75 C
Albion Rd. Dag 52 49 85 C
Albion Rd. E17 26 38 89 A
Albion Rd. Houn 70 13 75 C
Albion Rd. N16 48 33 85 B
Albion Rd. N17 25 34 90 C
Albion Rd. N Mal 94 20 69 A
Albion Rd. Sutt 110 26 63 D
Albion Rd. Twick 83 15 73 C
Albion Sq. E8 48 33 84 D
Albion St. Croy 105 31 66 D
Albion St. SE16 64 35 79 A
Albion St. W2 5 27 80 A
Albion Terr. E8 48 33 84 D
Albion Villas Rd. SE26 88 35 72 C
Albion Way. SE13 76 38 75 C
Albion Way. Wem 34 19 86 D
Albrighton Rd. SE22 75 33 75 A
Albuhera Cl. Enf 13 31 97 A
Albury Ave. Bexh 79 48 76 C
Albury Ave. Islw 60 15 77 D
Albury Ave. Sutt 110 23 62 C
Albury Cl. Hamp 92 13 70 B
Albury Ct. S Croy 112 32 64 A
Albury Ct. Sutt 110 26 64 A
Albury Dri. Pnr 20 11 91 D
Albury St. SE8 64 37 77 A
Albyfield. Brom 99 42 68 B
Albyn Rd. SE8 76 37 76 A
Albyn Rd. SE8 76 37 76 B
Alcester Cres. E5 37 34 86 B
Alcester Rd. Wall 111 28 64 B
Alcock Cl. Wall 111 29 63 D
Alcock Rd. Houn 59 11 77 D
Alconbury Rd. E5 37 34 86 A
Alcorn Cl. Sutt 103 25 65 A
Aldborough Rd. Dag 52 50 84 A
Aldborough Rd. Horn 42 54 86 B
Aldborough Road N. Ilf 28 45 89 D
Aldborough Road S. Ilf 40 45 87 A
Aldbourne Rd. W12 55 22 80 C
Aldbridge St. SE17 63 33 78 C
Aldbury Ave. Wem 45 19 84 D
Aldbury Mews. N9 17 32 94 B
Aldebert Terr. SW8 10 30 77 C
Aldeburgh St. SE10 65 40 78 C
Alden Ave. E15 58 39 82 B
Aldenham St. NW1 47 29 83 D
Aldensley Rd. W6 61 22 79 D
Alderbrook Rd. SW12 86 28 73 B
Alderbury Rd. SW13 61 22 77 A
Alder Gr. NW2 34 22 86 B

Alderholt Way (off Lydney Cl).
SE15 ... 63 33 77C
Aldermanbury. EC2 ... 4 32 81C
Aldermanbury Sq. EC2 ... 4 32 81A
Alderman's Hill. N13 ... 16 30 92B
Alderman's Wlk. EC2 ... 4 33 81A
Aldermary Rd. Brom ... 99 40 69A
Aldermaston St. W10 ... 56 23 81D
Alder Mews. N19 ... 36 29 86A
Alderminster Rd. SE1 ... 63 34 78C
Aldermoor Rd. SE6 ... 88 36 72D
Alderney Ave. Houn ... 59 13 77D
Alderney Gdns. Nthlt ... 43 12 84D
Alderney Rd. E1 ... 57 35 82D
Alderney Rd. Eri ... 68 52 77C
Alderney St. SW1 ... 9 28 78D
Alder Rd. Sid ... 90 45 72D
Alder Rd. SW14 ... 72 20 75B
Alders Ave. Wdf Gn ... 27 39 91A
Aldersbrook Ave. Enf ... 13 33 97C
Aldersbrook Dr. King ... 93 18 70B
Aldersbrook La. E12 ... 39 42 86D
Aldersbrook Rd. E11 ... 39 40 86B
Aldersbrook Rd. E12 ... 39 41 86A
Aldersey Gdns. Bark ... 51 44 84B
Aldersford Cl. SE4 ... 76 35 75D
Aldersgate St. EC1 ... 4 32 81A
Aldersgrove Ave. SE9 ... 89 41 72D
Aldershot Rd. NW6 ... 46 24 83B
Aldersmead Ave. Croy ... 106 35 67D
Aldersmead Rd. Beck ... 98 36 70C
Alderson St. W10 ... 56 24 82C
Alders The. Felt ... 82 12 71A
Alders The. Houn ... 59 12 77B
Alders The. N21 ... 13 31 95C
Alders The. SW16 ... 86 29 71A
Alders The. W Wick ... 106 37 65B
Alderton Cres. NW4 ... 34 22 88B
Alderton Rd. Croy ... 105 34 66A
Alderton Rd. SE24 ... 75 32 75A
Alderville Rd. SW6 ... 73 24 76D
Alderwick Dri. Houn ... 70 14 75B
Alderwood Rd. SE9 ... 78 44 74D
Aldford St. W1 ... 6 28 80C
Aldgate Ave. EC3 ... 4 33 81D
Aldgate. EC3 ... 4 33 81C
Aldgate High St. EC3 ... 4 33 81D
Aldine St. W12 ... 62 23 79A
Aldington Rd. SE18 ... 65 41 79D
Aldis Mews. SW17 ... 86 27 71C
Aldis St. SW17 ... 86 27 71C
Aldred Rd. NW6 ... 46 25 85C
Aldren Rd. SW17 ... 85 26 72C
Aldriche Way. E4 ... 26 38 91A
Aldrich Terr. SW18 ... 85 26 72A
Aldridge Ave. Ruis ... 32 11 86B
Aldridge Ave. Stan ... 21 18 90A
Aldridge Rd Villas. W11 ... 56 24 81B
Aldridge Rise. N.Mal ... 102 21 67C
Aldridge Wlk. N14 ... 16 29 94A
Aldrington Rd. SW16 ... 86 29 71A
Aldsworth Cl. W9 ... 56 25 82D
Aldwick Cl. SE9 ... 90 44 72D
Aldwick Rd. Croy ... 111 30 64B
Aldworth Gr. SE13 ... 76 38 74C
Aldworth Rd. E15 ... 50 39 84C
Aldwych Ave. Ilf ... 28 44 89C
Aldwych Cl. Horn ... 42 52 86A
Aldwych. WC2 ... 3 30 81D
Alers Rd. Bexh ... 79 47 74B
Alexander Ave. NW10 ... 45 22 84D
Alexander Cl. Brom ... 107 40 66C
Alexander Cl. Sid ... 78 45 74C
Alexander Cl. Twick ... 83 15 72B
Alexander Ct. SE3 ... 77 40 76D
Alexander Mews. W2 ... 56 25 81D
Alexander Pl. SW7 ... 9 27 78A
Alexander Rd. Bexh ... 79 47 76D
Alexander Rd. Chis ... 90 43 71D
Alexander Rd. N19 ... 36 30 86A
Alexander Sq. SW3 ... 9 27 78A
Alexander St. W2 ... 56 25 81D
Alexandra Ave. Har ... 32 13 86A
Alexandra Ave. N22 ... 24 29 90B
Alexandra Ave. Sthl ... 53 12 80B
Alexandra Ave. Sutt ... 103 25 65C
Alexandra Ave. SW11 ... 74 28 76A
Alexandra Cl. Ashf ... 91 08 70D
Alexandra Cl. Har ... 32 13 86D
Alexandra Cottages. SE14 ... 76 36 76B
Alexandra Cres. Brom ... 99 39 70B
Alexandra Ct. Wem ... 44 18 85B
Alexandra Dri. SE19 ... 97 33 70A
Alexandra Dri. SE19 ... 87 33 71C
Alexandra Dri. Surb ... 102 19 66A
Alexandra Gdns. Cars ... 111 28 62A
Alexandra Gdns. Houn ... 70 13 76D
Alexandra Gdns. N10 ... 24 28 89D
Alexandra Gdns. W4 ... 61 21 77C
Alexandra Gr. N12 ... 23 25 91B
Alexandra Gr. N4 ... 37 31 87D
Alexandra Park Rd. N10 ... 24 28 90D
Alexandra Park Rd. N22 ... 24 29 90B
Alexandra Pl. Croy ... 105 33 66C
Alexandra Pl. NW8 ... 46 26 83A
Alexandra Pl. SE25 ... 105 32 67B
Alexandra Rd. Ashf ... 91 09 70A
Alexandra Rd. Brent ... 60 17 77B
Alexandra Rd. Croy ... 105 33 66A
Alexandra Rd. E10 ... 38 38 86C
Alexandra Rd. E17 ... 38 36 87B
Alexandra Rd. E18 ... 27 40 89B
Alexandra Rd. Enf ... 14 35 96D
Alexandra Rd. Eri ... 68 51 77B
Alexandra Rd. Houn ... 70 13 76D
Alexandra Rd. King ... 94 19 70C
Alexandra Rd. Mit ... 96 27 70C
Alexandra Rd. N10 ... 24 28 91D
Alexandra Rd. N15 ... 37 32 88B
Alexandra Rd. N8 ... 25 31 89A
Alexandra Rd. N9 ... 17 34 94B
Alexandra Rd. NW4 ... 23 23 89D
Alexandra Rd. NW8 ... 46 26 84C
Alexandra Rd. Rich ... 71 18 76D
Alexandra Rd. Rom ... 41 48 88C
Alexandra Rd. Rom ... 42 51 88D
Alexandra Rd. SE26 ... 98 35 70B
Alexandra Rd. Surb ... 101 15 67B
Alexandra Rd. SW14 ... 72 20 75B
Alexandra Rd. SW19 ... 95 24 70B
Alexandra Rd. Twick ... 71 17 74C
Alexandra Rd. W4 ... 61 20 79B
Alexandra Sq. Mord ... 103 25 67A
Alexandra St. E16 ... 58 40 81A
Alexandra St. SE14 ... 64 36 77C
Alexandra Wlk. SE19 ... 87 33 71C
Alexandra Yd. E9 ... 49 35 83B
Alexandria Rd. W13 ... 54 16 80B
Alexis St. SE16 ... 63 34 78A
Alfearn Rd. E5 ... 49 35 85A
Alford Pl. N1 ... 48 32 83C
Alford Rd. Eri ... 67 50 78C
Alfoxton Ave. N15 ... 25 31 89D
Alfreda St. SW11 ... 74 28 76B
Alfred Gdns. Sthl ... 53 12 80A
Alfred Mews. W1 ... 2 29 81B
Alfred Pl. WC1 ... 2 29 81B
Alfred Rd. Belv ... 67 48 78D
Alfred Rd. E15 ... 50 39 85D
Alfred Rd. Felt ... 82 11 72A
Alfred Rd. King ... 93 18 68B
Alfred Rd. SE25 ... 105 34 67A
Alfred Rd. Sutt ... 110 26 64C
Alfred Rd. W2 ... 56 25 81A
Alfred Rd. W3 ... 55 20 80C
Alfred Salter Hse. SE1 ... 63 33 78B
Alfred's Gdns. Bark ... 51 45 83C
Alfred St. E16 ... 58 39 80B
Alfred St. E3 ... 57 37 82A
Alfred's Way. Bark ... 51 45 83C
Alfreton Cl. SW19 ... 85 23 72D
Alfriston Ave. Croy ... 104 30 66A
Alfriston Ave. Har ... 32 13 87A
Alfriston Rd. SW11 ... 74 27 74B
Alfriston. Surb ... 101 18 67D
Algar Cl. Islw ... 71 16 75A
Algar Rd. Islw ... 71 16 75A
Algarve Rd. SW18 ... 85 25 73D
Algernon Rd. NW4 ... 34 22 88C
Algernon Rd. NW6 ... 46 25 83A
Algernon Rd. SE13 ... 76 37 75D
Algiers Rd. SE13 ... 76 37 75C
Alguin Ct. Stan ... 21 17 91C
Alice Gilliatt Ct. W14 ... 62 24 77B
Alice St. SE1 ... 8 33 79C
Alicia Ave. Har ... 21 17 89C
Alicia Cl. Har ... 21 17 89C
Alicia Gdns. Har ... 21 17 89C
Alie St. E1 ... 4 33 81D
Alington Cres. NW9 ... 34 20 87C
Alington Gr. Wall ... 111 29 62B
Aliwal Rd. SW11 ... 74 27 75C
Alkerden Rd. W4 ... 61 21 78C
Alkham Rd. N16 ... 37 33 86B
Allan Cl. N.Mal ... 102 20 67B
Allandale Ave. N3 ... 23 24 89B
Allandale Rd. Horn ... 42 51 87B
Allan Way. W3 ... 55 20 81A
Allardyce St. SW4 ... 74 30 75D
Allbrook Cl. Tedd ... 83 15 71C
Allcroft Rd. NW5 ... 47 28 84A
Allenby Ave. S Croy ... 112 32 62A
Allenby Cl. Grnf ... 53 13 82A
Allenby Dri. Horn ... 42 54 87D
Allenby Rd. SE23 ... 88 36 72C
Allenby Rd. Sthl ... 53 13 81B
Allen Cl. Sun ... 91 10 69B
Allendale Ave. Sthl ... 53 13 81C
Allendale Cl. SE26 ... 88 35 71D
Allendale Cl. SE5 ... 75 32 76B
Allendale Rd. Grnf ... 44 16 84B
Allen Edwards Dri. SW8 ... 74 30 76A
Allen Rd. Beck ... 98 35 69D
Allen Rd. Croy ... 105 31 66C
Allen Rd. E3 ... 49 36 83D
Allen Rd. N16 ... 48 33 85A
Allen Rd. Sun ... 91 10 69D
Allensbury Pl. N7 ... 47 29 84D
Allens Rd. Enf ... 14 35 95A
Allen St. W8 ... 62 25 79C
Allenswood Rd. SE9 ... 77 42 76D
Allerford Ct. Har ... 32 14 88A
Allerford Rd. SE6 ... 88 37 71B
Allerton Rd. N16 ... 37 32 86A
Allerton Wlk. N7 ... 36 30 86B
Allestree Rd. SW6 ... 62 24 77C
Alleyn Cres. SE21 ... 87 32 72B
Alleyndale Rd. Dag ... 40 47 86A
Alleyn Park. SE21 ... 87 32 72B
Alleyn Park. Sthl ... 59 13 78C
Alleyn Rd. SE21 ... 87 32 72D
Allfarthing La. SW18 ... 73 26 74C
Allgood Cl. Mord ... 103 23 67D
Allgood St. E2 ... 48 33 83D
Allhallows La. EC4 ... 8 32 80B
All Hallows Rd. N17 ... 25 33 90A
Alliance Ct. Ashf ... 81 08 71A
Alliance Rd. E13 ... 58 41 81A
Alliance Rd. SE18 ... 66 46 77C
Alliance Rd. W3 ... 55 19 82D
Allingham Cl. W7 ... 54 15 80B
Allingham Ct. NW3 ... 47 27 85C
Allingham Ct. NW3 ... 47 27 85C
Allingham St. N1 ... 48 32 83C
Allington Ave. N17 ... 25 33 91A
Allington Cl. SW19 ... 85 23 71D
Allington Rd. Har ... 32 14 88A
Allington Rd. NW4 ... 34 22 88D
Allington Rd. Orp ... 108 45 66C
Allington Rd. W10 ... 46 24 83C
Allington St. SW1 ... 6 28 79D
Allison Cl. SE10 ... 76 38 76A
Allison Gr. SE21 ... 87 33 73C
Allison Rd. N8 ... 37 31 88B
Allison Rd. W3 ... 55 20 80A
Allitsen Rd. NW8 ... 47 27 83C
Allnutt Way. SW4 ... 74 29 74B
Alloa Rd. Ilf ... 40 46 86A
Alloa Rd. SE8 ... 64 36 78C
Allonby Gdns. Wem ... 33 17 87C
Alloway Rd. E3 ... 57 36 82A
All Saints' Cl. N9 ... 17 34 93A
All Saints Dri. SE3 ... 77 39 76C
All Saints Pas. SW18 ... 73 25 74A
All Saints Rd. Sutt ... 103 26 65C
All Saints Rd. SW19 ... 95 26 70C
All Saints Rd. W11 ... 56 24 81D
All Saints' Rd. W3 ... 61 20 79C
All Saints St. N1 ... 47 30 83D
Allsop Pl. NW1 ... 1 27 82D
All Souls' Ave. NW10 ... 45 22 83B
All Souls Pl. W1 ... 2 28 81B
Allum Way. N20 ... 15 26 94C
Allwood Cl. SE26 ... 88 35 71B
Alma Ave. E4 ... 26 38 91C
Alma Ave. Horn ... 42 54 86C
Almack Rd. E5 ... 49 35 85A
Alma Cottages. SW9 ... 74 30 75A
Alma Cres. Sutt ... 110 24 64C
Alma Gr. SE1 ... 63 33 78B
Alma Pl. NW10 ... 55 22 82B
Alma Pl. SE19 ... 97 33 70D
Alma Pl. Th Hth ... 105 31 67A
Alma Rd. Cars ... 111 27 64C
Alma Rd. Enf ... 14 36 96C
Alma Rd. Esh ... 101 15 66C
Alma Rd. N10 ... 24 28 91D
Alma Rd. Sid ... 90 46 72C
Alma Rd. Sthl ... 53 12 80A
Alma Rd. SW18 ... 73 26 74A
Alma Rd. SW18 ... 73 26 75C
Alma Row. Har ... 20 14 90B
Alma Sq. NW8 ... 1 26 82A
Alma Sq. NW8 ... 46 26 83C
Alma St. E15 ... 49 38 84B
Alma St. NW5 ... 47 28 84B
Alma Terr. SW18 ... 85 26 73B
Almeida St. N1 ... 48 31 84D
Almeric Rd. SW11 ... 74 27 75D
Almer Rd. SW20 ... 94 22 70C
Almington St. N4 ... 36 30 87D
Almond Ave. Cars ... 104 27 65B
Almond Ave. Uxb ... 31 07 86D
Almond Ave. W5 ... 60 18 79C
Almond Cl. Brom ... 108 43 66A
Almond Cl. Ruis ... 31 09 86D
Almond Cl. SE15 ... 75 34 76C
Almond Cl. Shep ... 91 08 69C
Almond Gr. Brent ... 60 16 77D
Almond Rd. N17 ... 25 34 91C
Almond Rd. SE16 ... 63 34 78B
Almond Way. Brom ... 108 43 66A
Almond Way. Har ... 20 14 90C
Almond Way. Mit ... 96 29 68D
Almorah Rd. Houn ... 70 11 76B
Almorah Rd. N1 ... 48 32 84D
Alnwick Gr. Mord ... 95 25 68D
Alnwick Rd. E16 ... 58 41 81C
Alnwick Rd. SE12 ... 89 40 73B
Alperton La. Wem ... 44 17 83D
Alperton St. W10 ... 56 24 82D
Alpha Cl. NW1 ... 1 27 82C
Alpha Ct. SE25 ... 105 33 67A
Alpha Gr. E14 ... 64 37 79A
Alpha Pl. NW6 ... 46 25 83C
Alpha Pl. SW3 ... 9 27 77A
Alpha Rd. E4 ... 18 37 93D
Alpha Rd. Enf ... 14 36 96C
Alpha Rd. N18 ... 17 34 92C
Alpha Rd. SE14 ... 76 36 76B
Alpha Rd. Surb ... 101 18 67D
Alpha Rd. Tedd ... 82 14 71D
Alpha St. SE15 ... 75 34 76C
Alpine Ave. Surb ... 102 20 65A
Alpine Cl. Croy ... 105 33 65C
Alpine Copse. Brom ... 100 43 69C
Alpine Rd. SE16 ... 64 35 78D
Alpna Rd. Croy ... 105 33 66C
Alric Ave. N Mal ... 94 21 68A
Alric Ave. NW10 ... 45 20 84D
Alroy Rd. N4 ... 37 31 87A
Alsace Rd. SE17 ... 63 33 78C
Alscot Rd. SE1 ... 8 33 79D
Alscot Way. SE1 ... 63 33 78B
Alsike Rd. Belv ... 67 48 79C
Alsom Ave. Wor Pk ... 109 22 64A
Alston Cl. Surb ... 101 16 66B
Alston Rd. Barn ... 11 24 96A
Alston Rd. N18 ... 17 34 92D
Alston Rd. SW17 ... 85 26 71B
Altair Cl. N17 ... 25 33 91B
Altash Way. SE9 ... 89 42 72B
Altash Way. SE9 ... 90 43 72A
Altenburg Ave. W13 ... 60 16 79D
Altenburg Gdns. SW11 ... 74 27 75D
Alt Gr. SW19 ... 95 24 70D
Altham Rd. Pnr ... 20 12 91C
Althea St. SW6 ... 73 25 76D
Althorne Gdns. E18 ... 27 39 89D
Althorne Way. Dag ... 41 49 86A
Althorpe Mews. SW11 ... 73 26 76B
Althorpe Rd. Har ... 32 14 88A
Althorp Rd. SW17 ... 86 27 73D
Altmore Ave. E6 ... 50 42 84D
Alton Ave. Stan ... 21 15 91D
Alton Cl. Islw ... 71 15 76D
Alton Gdns. Beck ... 98 37 70C
Alton Gdns. Twick ... 82 14 73B
Alton Rd. Croy ... 105 31 65C
Alton Rd. N17 ... 25 32 89B
Alton Rd. Rich ... 71 18 75C
Alton Rd. SW15 ... 84 22 73C
Alton St. E14 ... 57 37 81B
Altyre Cl. Beck ... 106 36 67B
Altyre Rd. Croy ... 105 32 65B
Altyre Way. Beck ... 106 36 67B
Alvanley Gdns. NW6 ... 46 25 85D
Alverstoke Rd. Rom ... 30 54 91C
Alverstone Ave. Barn ... 16 27 94A
Alverstone Ave. SW19 ... 85 25 72A
Alverstone Gdns. SE9 ... 90 44 73C
Alverstone Rd. E12 ... 51 43 85A
Alverstone Rd. N Mal ... 94 21 68D
Alverstone Rd. NW2 ... 46 23 84C
Alverstone Rd. Wem ... 33 18 87D
Alverston Gdns. SE25 ... 105 33 67A
Alverton St. SE8 ... 64 36 78D
Alveston Ave. Har ... 21 16 89B
Alvey St. SE17 ... 63 33 78C
Alvington Cres. E8 ... 48 33 85D
Alway Ave. Eps ... 109 20 64D
Alwold Cres. SE12 ... 77 40 74D
Alwyn Ave. W4 ... 61 20 78D
Alwyne La. N1 ... 48 31 84D
Alwyne Pl. N1 ... 48 32 84C
Alwyne Rd. N1 ... 48 32 84C
Alwyne Rd. SW19 ... 95 24 70B
Alwyne Rd. W7 ... 54 15 80A
Alwyne Sq. N1 ... 48 32 84A
Alwyne Villas. N1 ... 48 31 84D
Alwyn Gdns. W3 ... 55 19 81D
Alyth Gdns. NW11 ... 35 25 88C
Amalgamated Dri. Brent ... 60 16 77B
Amazon St. E1 ... 57 34 81D
Ambassador Cl. Houn ... 70 12 76C
Amber Ave. E17 ... 26 36 90A
Amberden Ave. N3 ... 23 25 89A
Ambergate St. SE17 ... 63 31 78D
Amberley Cl. Pnr ... 20 12 89B
Amberley Gdns. Enf ... 17 33 94A
Amberley Gdns. Eps ... 109 21 64B
Amberley Gr. Croy ... 105 33 66B
Amberley Gr. SE26 ... 87 34 71D
Amberley Rd. E10 ... 38 37 87B
Amberley Rd. Enf ... 17 33 94B
Amberley Rd. N13 ... 16 30 93B
Amberley Rd. SE2 ... 67 47 77B
Amberley Rd. W9 ... 56 25 82D
Amberley Way. Houn ... 70 11 74A
Amberley Way. Mord ... 103 25 66A
Amberley Way. Rom ... 29 49 89D
Amber St. E15 ... 49 38 84B
Amberwood Rise. N. Mal ... 102 21 67C
Amblecote Cl. SE12 ... 89 40 72D
Amblecote Rd. SE12 ... 89 40 72D
Ambler Rd. N4 ... 37 31 86D
Ambleside Ave. Beck ... 106 36 67A
Ambleside Ave. SW16 ... 86 29 71B
Ambleside. Brom ... 98 38 70B
Ambleside Cl. E9 ... 49 35 85C
Ambleside Cres. Enf ... 14 35 96B
Ambleside Gdns. Ilf ... 39 42 88A
Ambleside Gdns. Sutt ... 110 26 63A
Ambleside Gdns. Wem ... 33 17 87D
Ambleside Rd. Bexh ... 79 49 76C
Ambleside Rd. NW10 ... 45 21 84D
Ambrey Way. Wall ... 111 29 62B
Ambrook Rd. Belv ... 67 49 79C
Ambrosden Ave. SW1 ... 6 29 79C
Ambrose Ave. NW11 ... 35 24 88D
Ambrose Cl. Orp ... 108 45 65D
Ambrose St. SE16 ... 63 34 78B
Ambrose Wlk. E3 ... 49 37 83C
Amelia St. SE17 ... 63 32 78C
Amen Cnr. EC4 ... 3 31 81D
Amen Cnr. SW17 ... 96 28 70A
Amen Ct. EC4 ... 3 31 81D
America Sq. EC3 ... 8 33 80B
America St. SE1 ... 8 32 80C
Amerland Rd. SW18 ... 73 24 74D
Amersham Ave. N18 ... 25 33 91A
Amersham Ave. N18 ... 17 33 92C
Amersham Cl. Rom ... 30 54 91B
Amersham Dri. Rom ... 30 54 91B
Amersham Gr. SE14 ... 64 36 77D
Amersham Rd. Croy ... 105 32 67D
Amersham Rd. Har ... 33 15 88C
Amersham Rd. Rom ... 30 54 91B
Amersham Rd. SE14 ... 76 35 76B
Amersham Vale. SE14 ... 64 36 77D
Amersham Wlk. Rom ... 30 54 91B
Amery Gdns. NW10 ... 46 23 83A
Amery Gdns. Rom ... 30 53 89B
Amery Rd. Har ... 33 16 86A
Amesbury Ave. SW2 ... 86 30 72B
Amesbury Cl. Wor Pk ... 103 23 66C
Amesbury Dri. E4 ... 14 37 95D
Amesbury Rd. Brom ... 99 41 68B
Amesbury Rd. Dag ... 52 47 84D
Amesbury Rd. Felt ... 82 11 72B
Amethyst Rd. E15 ... 49 38 85B
Amherst Ave. W13 ... 54 17 81C
Amherst Cl. Orp ... 100 46 68D
Amherst Dri. Orp ... 100 46 68C
Amherst Rd. W13 ... 54 17 81C
Amhurst Gdns. Islw ... 71 16 76C
Amhurst Park. N16 ... 37 33 87A
Amhurst Par. N15 ... 37 33 87B
Amhurst Pas. E8 ... 48 34 85C
Amhurst Rd. E8 ... 48 34 85C
Amhurst Rd. N16 ... 48 33 85B
Amhurst Terr. E8 ... 48 34 85A
Amidas Gdns. Dag ... 51 46 85B
Amiel St. E1 ... 57 35 82C
Amies St. SW11 ... 74 27 75B
Amina Way. SE16 ... 63 34 79C
Amis Ave. Eps ... 109 19 64D
Amity Gr. SW20 ... 95 23 69C
Amity Rd. E15 ... 50 39 84D
Amner Rd. SW11 ... 74 28 74C
Amor Rd. W6 ... 62 23 79C
Amos Estate. SE16 ... 57 35 80D
Amott Rd. SE15 ... 75 34 75A
Amour Cl. N7 ... 47 30 84B
Amoy Pl. E14 ... 57 37 80A
Ampleforth Rd. SE2 ... 67 47 79A
Ampthill Rd. N8 ... 24 30 89B
Ampton Pl. WC1 ... 3 30 82B
Ampton St. WC1 ... 3 30 82B
Amroth Cl. SE23 ... 87 34 73D
Amwell Cl. Enf ... 13 32 95B
Amwell St. EC1 ... 3 31 82A
Amyand Cottages. Twick ... 71 16 74D
Amyand La. Twick ... 83 16 73B
Amyand Park Gdns. Twick ... 83 16 73B
Amyand Park Rd. Twick ... 83 16 73A
Amyruth Rd. SE4 ... 76 37 74A
Anatola Rd. N19 ... 36 28 86B
Ancaster Cres. N Mal ... 102 22 67C
Ancaster Rd. Beck ... 98 35 68B
Ancaster St. SE18 ... 66 45 77C
Anchorage Cl. SW19 ... 85 25 71C
Anchor and Hope La. SE7 ... 65 41 78A
Anchor St. SE16 ... 63 34 78B
Anchor Yd. EC1 ... 4 32 82C
Ancill Cl. W6 ... 62 24 77A
Ancona Rd. NW10 ... 45 22 83C
Ancona Rd. SE18 ... 66 44 78D
Andalus Rd. SW9 ... 74 30 75A
Ander Cl. Wem ... 44 17 85B
Anderson Dri. Ashf ... 81 08 71A
Anderson Rd. E9 ... 49 35 84B
Anderson Rd. Ilf ... 27 41 89B
Anderson's Pl. Houn ... 70 13 75D
Anderson St. SW3 ... 9 27 78D
Anderton Cl. SE5 ... 75 32 75B
Anderton Ct. N22 ... 24 29 90D
Andover Cl. Eps ... 109 20 62D
Andover Pl. NW6 ... 46 25 83D
Andover Rd. N7 ... 36 30 86B
Andover Rd. Orp ... 108 45 66C
Andover Rd. Twick ... 82 14 73D
Andre St. E8 ... 48 34 85C
Andrew Borde St. WC2 ... 2 29 81D
Andrew Cl. Dart ... 79 50 74A
Andrew Cl. Ilf ... 28 44 91B
Andrew Pl. SW8 ... 74 29 76B
Andrews Cl. Wor Pk ... 103 23 65B
Andrews Crosse. WC2 ... 3 31 81C
Andrew's Rd. E8 ... 48 34 83B
Andrew St. E14 ... 58 38 81C
Andrews Wlk. SE17 ... 63 31 77B
Andromeda Ct. Rom ... 30 53 91A
Andwell Cl. SE2 ... 66 46 79B
Anerley Gr. SE19 ... 97 33 70D
Anerley Hill. SE19 ... 97 33 70B
Anerley Park Rd. SE20 ... 97 34 70D
Anerley Park SE20 ... 97 34 70D
Anerley Rd. SE19 ... 97 34 70C
Anerley Rd. SE20 ... 97 34 69B
Anerley Station Rd. SE20 ... 97 34 69B
Anerley St. SW11 ... 74 27 76D
Anerley Vale SE19 ... 97 34 70C
Aneurin Bevan Ct. NW2 ... 34 22 86B
Anfield Cl. SW12 ... 86 29 73A
Angel Alley. E1 ... 4 33 81D
Angel Cl. N18 ... 17 34 92A
Angel Ct. EC2 ... 4 32 81D
Angel Ct. SW1 ... 6 29 80C
Angelfield. Houn ... 70 13 74B
Angel Hill Dri. Sutt ... 103 25 65D
Angel Hill. Sutt ... 103 25 65B
Angel La. E15 ... 49 38 84B
Angell Park Gdns. SW9 ... 75 31 75A
Angell Rd. SW9 ... 75 31 75B
Angel Mews. N1 ... 48 31 83C
Angel Pas. EC4 ... 8 32 80B
Angel Pl. N18 ... 17 34 92C
Angel Pl. SE1 ... 8 32 79B
Angel Rd. Har ... 33 15 88C
Angel Rd. Surb ... 101 16 66C
Angel St. EC1 ... 4 32 81C
Angel Way. Rom ... 42 51 88A
Angel Wlk. W6 ... 62 23 78C
Angerstein La. SE3 ... 77 39 76B
Angle Green. Dag ... 41 47 87C
Anglers Cl. Rich ... 83 17 71A
Anglers La. NW5 ... 47 28 84B
Anglesea Ave. SE18 ... 66 43 78B
Anglesea Rd. King ... 93 17 68D

Anglesea Rd. Orp 108 46 67 D
Anglesea Rd. SE18 66 43 78 B
Anglesea St. E1 57 34 82 C
Anglesey Cl. Ashf 81 07 72 C
Anglesey Ct Rd. Cars 111 28 63 A
Anglesey Gdns. Cars 111 28 63 A
Anglesey Rd. Enf 13 34 96 D
Anglesmede Cres. Pnr 20 13 89 A
Anglesmede Way. Pnr 20 13 89 A
Angles Rd. SW16 86 30 71 A
Anglia Wlk. E6 51 43 83 A
Anglo Rd. E3 49 36 83 D
Angns St. SE14 64 36 77 C
Angrave Pas. E8 48 33 83 B
Angus Cl. Chess 109 19 64 C
Angus Dri. Ruis 43 11 85 A
Angus Gdns. NW9 22 20 90 B
Angus Rd. E13 58 41 82 A
Anhalt Rd. SW11 9 27 77 C
Ankerdine Cres. SE18 78 43 76 B
Anlaby Rd. Tedd 83 15 71 C
Anley Rd. W14 62 23 79 B
Anmersh Gr. Stan 21 17 90 B
Annabel Cl. E14 57 37 81 D
Annandale Gr. Ruis 31 08 86 C
Annandale Rd. Croy 105 34 65 A
Annandale Rd. E10 65 39 78 D
Annandale Rd. Sid 90 45 73 B
Annandale Rd. W4 61 21 78 C
Annan Way. Rom 30 51 90 A
Anne Boleyn's Wlk. King 83 18 71 C
Anne Boleyn's Wlk. Sutt 110 24 63 C
Anne of Cleves Rd. Dart 80 53 74 D
Annesley Ave. NW9 22 20 89 B
Annesley Cl. NW10 34 21 86 C
Annesley Dri. Croy 106 36 65 D
Annesley Rd. SE3 77 40 76 B
Anne St. E13 58 40 82 C
Annett Cl. Shep 91 09 68 C
Annette Cl. Har 21 15 90 C
Annette Rd. N7 47 30 85 B
Anne Way. E Mol 92 13 68 D
Anne Way. Ilf 28 44 91 A
Annie Besant Cl. E3 49 36 83 B
Anning St. EC2 4 33 82 C
Annington Rd. N2 24 27 89 B
Annis Rd. E9 49 36 84 A
Ann La. SW10 62 26 77 B
Ann's Cl. SW1 6 28 79 A
Ann St. SE18 66 44 78 B
Annsworthy Ave. Th Hth 97 32 68 B
Ansdell Rd. SE15 76 35 76 C
Ansdell St. W8 62 25 79 D
Ansdell Terr. W8 62 25 79 D
Ansell Gr. Cars 104 28 65 A
Ansell Rd. SW17 86 27 72 D
Anselm Cl. Croy 105 33 65 D
Anselm Rd. Pnr 20 12 91 D
Anselm Rd. SW6 62 25 77 A
Ansford Rd. Brom 88 38 71 B
Ansleigh Pl. W11 56 23 80 B
Anson Cl. Rom 29 49 90 D
Anson Rd. N7 47 29 85 B
Anson Rd. NW2 46 23 85 C
Anstey Rd. E16 58 40 81 B
Anstey Rd. SE15 75 34 75 A
Anstey Wlk. N15 25 32 89 C
Anstice Cl. W4 61 21 77 C
Anstridge Path. SE9 78 44 74 D
Anstridge Rd. SE9 78 44 74 D
Antelope Rd. SE18 65 42 79 D
Anthony Rd. Grnf 44 15 83 C
Anthony Rd. SE25 105 34 67 C
Anthony Rd. Well 78 46 76 A
Anthony St. E1 57 34 81 D
Antill Rd. E3 57 36 82 A
Antill Rd. E3 49 36 83 D
Antill Rd. N15 25 34 89 C
Antill Terr. E1 57 35 81 D
Antlers Hill. E4 14 37 95 B
Anton Cres. Sutt 103 25 65 C
Antoneys Cl. Pnr 20 11 90 D
Anton St. E8 48 34 85 C
Antrim Gr. NW3 47 27 84 B
Antrim Rd. NW3 47 27 84 B
Antrobus Cl. Sutt 110 24 64 D
Antrobus Rd. W4 61 20 79 C
Anvil Rd. Sun 91 10 68 A
Anworth Cl. Wdf Gn 27 40 91 B
Apeldoorn Dri. Wall 111 30 62 A
Aperfield Rd. Eri 68 51 77 B
Apex Cl. Beck 98 37 69 B
Aplin Way. Islw 71 15 76 A
Apollo Ave. Brom 99 40 69 B
Apollo Cl. Horn 42 52 86 A
Apollo Pl. SW10 62 26 77 D
Apothecary St. EC4 3 31 81 D
Appach Rd. SW2 75 31 74 C
Appleby Cl. E4 26 38 91 A
Appleby Cl. N15 37 32 88 B
Appleby Cl. Twick 82 14 72 B
Appleby Rd. E16 58 40 81 C
Appleby Rd. E8 48 34 84 C
Appleby St. E2 48 33 83 D
Appledore Ave. Bexh 79 50 76 D
Appledore Ave. Ruis 32 11 86 C
Appledore Cl. Brom 107 40 67 A
Appledore Cl. Edg 22 19 90 A
Appledore Cl. Rom 30 53 90 A
Appledore Cl. SW17 86 27 72 B
Appledore Cres. Sid 90 45 72 D
Appleford Rd. W10 56 24 82 C
Apple Garth. Brent 60 17 78 B
Applegarth Dri. Ilf 28 45 89 D
Applegarth Rd. W14 62 23 79 D
Apple Gr. Enf 13 33 96 A
Apple Market. King 93 17 69 D
Appleton Gdns. N.Mal 102 22 67 C
Appleton Rd. SE9 77 42 75 A
Appleton Way. Horn 42 53 87 D
Apple Tree Yd. SW1 6 29 80 C
Applewood Cl. NW2 34 22 86 D
Appold St. EC2 4 33 81 A
Appold St. Eri 68 51 77 B
Approach Cl. N16 48 33 85 A
Approach Rd. Ashf 91 08 70 A
Approach Rd. Barn 11 26 96 D
Approach Rd. E2 49 35 83 C
Approach Rd. Edg 22 19 91 A
Approach Rd. SW20 95 23 69 C
Approach The. Enf 13 34 97 D
Approach The. NW4 35 23 88 B
Approach The. Orp 108 45 65 B
Approach The. W3 55 20 81 D
Aprey Gdns. NW4 23 23 89 C
April Cl. Felt 81 10 72 C
April Cl. W7 54 15 80 A
April Glen. SE23 88 35 72 D
April St. E8 48 33 85 B
Apsley Cl. Har 32 14 88 A
Apsley Rd. N Mal 94 20 68 A
Apsley Rd. SE25 97 34 68 D
Apsley Rd. SW18 73 25 74 B
Apsley Way. W1 6 28 79 A
Aquinas St. SE1 7 31 80 C
Arabella Dri. SW15 72 21 75 C
Arabia Cl. E4 18 38 94 B
Arabin Rd. SE4 76 36 75 D
Aragon Ave. Eps 109 22 62 B
Aragon Ave. Surb 101 15 67 B
Aragon Ct. Ilf 28 44 91 C
Aragon Dri. Ilf 28 44 91 C
Aragon Dri. Ruis 32 11 87 D
Aragon Rd. King 83 18 71 C
Aragon Rd. Mord 103 24 66 A
Arandora Cres. Rom 40 46 88 D
Arbery Rd. E3 49 36 83 C
Arbor Ct. N16 37 32 86 B
Arbor Rd. E4 18 38 93 D
Arbour Rd. Enf 14 35 96 B
Arbour Sq. E1 57 35 81 D
Arbroath Rd. SE9 77 42 75 A
Arbury Terr. SE26 87 34 72 D
Arbuthnot La. Bex 79 48 74 C
Arbuthnot Rd. SE14 76 35 76 D
Arbutus St. E8 48 33 83 B
Arcade Pl. Rom 42 51 88 A
Arcade The. Bark 51 44 84 C
Arcade The. E17 26 37 89 C
Arcade. The EC2 4 33 81 A
Arcadia Ave. N3 23 25 90 C
Arcadian Ave. Bex 79 48 74 C
Arcadian Cl. Bex 79 48 74 C
Arcadian Gdns. N22 25 31 91 C
Arcadian Rd. Bex 79 48 74 C
Arcadia St. E14 57 37 81 C
Archbishop's Pl. SW2 86 30 73 B
Archdale Rd. SE22 75 33 75 D
Archel Rd. W14 62 24 77 B
Archer Rd. Orp 108 46 67 A
Archer Rd. SE25 97 34 68 D
Archers Dri. Enf 14 35 97 C
Archer St. W1 6 29 80 B
Archers Wlk. SE15 75 33 76 B
Archery Cl. Har 21 15 89 B
Archery Cl. W2 1 27 81 C
Archery Rd. SE9 77 42 74 B
Arches The. Har 32 13 86 B
Arches. The WC2 7 30 80 C
Archibald Mews. W1 6 28 80 B
Archibald Rd. N7 47 29 85 B
Archibald St. E3 57 37 82 A
Arch St. SE1 8 32 79 C
Archway Cl. SW19 85 25 71 B
Archway Mall. N19 36 29 86 A
Archway Rd. N19 36 29 87 C
Archway Rd. N6 36 28 87 B
Archway. Rom 30 52 91 B
Archway St. SW13 72 21 75 A
Arcola St. E8 48 33 85 D
Arctic St. NW5 47 28 85 D
Arcus Rd. Brom 99 39 70 A
Ardbeg Rd. SE24 75 32 74 B
Arden Cl. Har 32 14 86 D
Arden Cres. Dag 52 47 84 D
Arden Mhor. Pnr 19 10 89 D
Arden Rd. N3 23 24 89 B
Arden Rd. W13 54 17 80 A
Ardfern Ave. SW16 97 31 68 A
Ardfillan Rd. SE6 88 38 72 B
Ardgowan Rd. SE6 89 39 73 C
Ardhay Gdns. Surb 101 18 67 A
Ardilaun Rd. N5 48 32 85 A
Ardleigh Cl. Horn 30 53 89 B
Ardleigh Gdns. Sutt 103 25 66 A
Ardleigh Green Rd. Horn 30 53 89 D
Ardleigh Mews. Ilf 40 43 86 D
Ardleigh Rd. E17 26 36 90 B
Ardleigh Rd. N1 48 33 84 A
Ardleigh Terr. E17 26 36 90 B
Ardley Cl. NW10 34 21 86 C
Ardley Cl. Ruis 31 08 87 A
Ardley Cl. SE6 88 36 72 C
Ardlui Rd. SE27 87 32 72 A
Ardmere Rd. SE13 76 38 74 D
Ardoch Rd. SE6 88 38 72 B
Ardrossan Gdns. Wor Pk 102 22 65 C
Ardshiel Cl. SW15 73 23 75 B
Ardwell Ave. Ilf 40 44 88 A
Ardwell Rd. SW2 86 30 72 A
Ardwick Rd. NW2 46 25 85 A
Argall Ave. E10 38 35 87 D
Argon Mews. SW6 62 25 77 C
Argus Cl. Rom 29 49 90 B
Argus Way. Nthlt 53 12 82 A
Argyle Ave. Houn 70 13 74 C
Argyle Cl. W3 54 16 82 C
Argyle Pass. N17 25 33 90 B
Argyle Pl. W6 61 22 78 B
Argyle Rd. Barn 11 23 96 C
Argyle Rd. E15 50 39 85 A
Argyle Rd. E16 58 41 81 C
Argyle Rd. E1 57 35 82 D
Argyle Rd. Har 32 13 88 D
Argyle Rd. Houn 70 13 74 B
Argyle Rd. Ilf 40 43 86 A
Argyle Rd. N12 15 25 92 D
Argyle Rd. N17 25 34 90 A
Argyle Rd. N18 17 34 92 A
Argyle Rd. W13 54 16 81 A
Argyle Sq. WC1 3 30 82 A
Argyle St. WC1 3 30 82 A
Argyle Wlk. WC1 3 30 82 A
Argyll Ave. Sthl 53 13 80 D
Argyll Cl. SW9 74 30 75 B
Argyll Gdns. Edg 22 19 90 B
Argyll Rd. W8 62 25 79 A
Argyll St. W1 2 29 81 C
Arica Rd. SE4 76 36 75 A
Ariel Rd. NW6 46 25 84 A
Ariel Way. W12 56 23 80 C
Aristotle Rd. SW4 74 29 75 D
Arkell Gr. SE19 97 31 70 D
Arkindale Rd. SE6 88 38 72 C
Arkley Cres. E17 38 36 88 B
Arkley Rd. E17 38 36 88 B
Arklow Rd. SE14 64 36 77 B
Arkwright Rd. NW3 46 26 85 C
Arkwright Rd. S Croy 112 33 62 B
Arlesey Cl. SW15 73 24 74 A
Arlesford Rd. SW9 74 30 75 A
Arlingford Rd. SW2 75 31 74 C
Arlington Ave. N1 48 32 83 A
Arlington Cl. Sid 90 45 73 A
Arlington Cl. Sutt 103 25 65 A
Arlington Cl. Twick 71 17 74 A
Arlington Dri. Cars 104 27 65 B
Arlington Dri. Ruis 31 08 88 D
Arlington Gdns. Ilf 40 43 87 C
Arlington Gdns. Rom 30 54 90 A
Arlington Gdns. W4 61 20 78 B
Arlington. N12 15 25 93 C
Arlington Rd. N14 16 29 94 C
Arlington Rd. NW1 47 28 83 B
Arlington Rd. Rich 83 17 72 B
Arlington Rd. Surb 101 17 67 D
Arlington Rd. Tedd 83 15 71 B
Arlington Rd. Twick 71 17 74 C
Arlington Rd. W13 54 16 81 D
Arlington Rd. Wdf Gn 27 40 91 D
Arlington Sq. N1 48 32 83 A
Arlington St. SW1 6 29 80 C
Arlington Way. EC1 3 31 82 A
Arliss Way. Nthlt 43 11 83 A
Arlow Rd. N21 17 31 94 C
Armada Ct. SE8 64 37 77 A
Armadale Cl. N15 25 34 89 D
Armadale Rd. Felt 69 10 74 A
Armadale Rd. SW6 62 25 77 A
Armada St. SE8 64 37 77 A
Armagh Rd. E3 49 36 83 D
Armfield Cres. Mit 96 27 69 D
Armfield Rd. Enf 13 32 97 B
Arminger Rd. W12 55 22 80 D
Armitage Rd. E10 65 39 78 D
Armitage Rd. NW11 35 24 87 D
Armoury Way. SW18 73 25 74 A
Armstage Rd. Houn 59 11 77 D
Armstead Wlk. Dag 52 49 84 C
Armstrong Ave. Wdf Gn 27 39 91 A
Armstrong Cl. Pnr 31 10 88 C
Armstrong Cres. Barn 11 26 96 B
Armstrong Rd. Felt 82 12 71 C
Armstrong Rd. SW7 5 26 79 D
Armstrong Rd. W3 55 21 80 D
Armstrong Way. Sthl 59 13 79 B
Arnal Cres. SW18 85 24 73 A
Arndale Centre The. Dart 80 54 74 C
Arndale Centre The. SW18 73 25 74 D
Arndale Wlk. SW18 73 25 74 B
Arne Gr. Orp 108 45 65 D
Arne St. WC2 3 30 81 C
Arneways Ave. Rom 29 47 89 B
Arneway St. SW1 6 29 79 D
Arne Wlk. SE3 77 39 75 D
Arnewood Cl. SW15 84 22 73 C
Arney's La. Mit 104 28 67 C
Arngask Rd. SE6 88 38 73 B
Arnhem Way. SE22 75 33 74 A
Arnison Rd. E Mol 92 14 68 D
Arnold Circ. E2 4 33 82 B
Arnold Cl. Har 33 18 87 B
Arnold Cres. Islw 70 14 74 B
Arnold Gdns. N13 17 31 92 D
Arnold Rd. Dag 52 48 84 D
Arnold Rd. E3 57 37 82 A
Arnold Rd. N15 25 33 89 B
Arnold Rd. Nthlt 43 12 84 A
Arnold Rd. SW17 96 27 70 D
Arnos Gr. N14 16 29 93 D
Arnos Rd. N11 16 29 92 A
Arnott Cl. W4 61 20 78 B
Arnould Ave. SE5 75 32 75 D
Arnside Gdns. Wem 33 17 87 D
Arnside Rd. Bexh 79 49 76 A
Arnside St. SE17 63 32 77 B
Arnulf St. SE6 88 37 71 B
Arnull's Rd. SW16 97 31 70 B
Arodene Rd. SW2 74 30 74 D
Arragon Gdns. SW16 96 30 70 C
Arragon Gdns. W Wick 106 37 65 D
Arragon Rd. E6 50 41 83 B
Arragon Rd. Twick 83 16 73 A
Arran Cl. Eri 67 50 77 B
Arran Cl. Wall 111 29 64 A
Arran Dri. E12 39 41 86 B
Arran Rd. SE6 88 38 72 A
Arran Wlk. N1 48 32 84 C
Arras Ave. Mord 103 26 67 A
Arrol Rd. Beck 98 35 68 B
Arrow Rd. E3 57 37 82 B
Arrowscout Wlk (off Wayfarer Rd). Nthlt 53 12 82 A
Arsenal Rd. SE9 77 42 75 B
Arterberry Rd. SW20 95 23 69 B
Artesian Cl. Horn 42 51 87 B
Artesian Rd. W2 56 25 81 C
Arthingworth St. E15 50 39 83 A
Arthurdon Rd. SE4 76 37 74 A
Arthur Gr. SE18 66 44 78 A
Arthur Rd. E6 50 42 83 D
Arthur Rd. King 94 19 70 C
Arthur Rd. N7 36 30 86 D
Arthur Rd. N9 17 33 93 B
Arthur Rd. N.Mal 102 22 67 B
Arthur Rd. Rom 41 47 88 D
Arthur Rd. SW19 85 25 71 A
Arthur St. EC4 8 32 80 B
Arthur St. Eri 68 51 77 D
Artichoke Hill. E1 57 34 80 B
Artichoke Pl. SE5 75 32 76 B
Artillery Cl. Ilf 40 44 88 C
Artillery La. E1 4 33 81 A
Artillery Pas. E1 4 33 81 B
Artillery Pl. SE18 66 43 78 A
Artillery Row. SW1 6 29 79 D
Artizan St. E1 4 33 81 C
Arundel Ave. 109 22 62 D
Arundel Ave. Mord 95 24 68 D
Arundel Ave. S Croy 112 34 62 C
Arundel Cl. Bex 79 48 74 D
Arundel Cl. Croy 105 31 65 D
Arundel Cl. E15 50 39 85 A
Arundel Cl. Hamp 82 13 71 D
Arundel Ct. N17 25 34 90 A
Arundel Dri. Har 43 13 85 A
Arundel Dri. Wdf Gn 27 40 91 C
Arundel Gdns. Edg 22 20 91 D
Arundel Gdns. Ilf 40 46 86 A
Arundel Gdns. N21 17 31 94 C
Arundel Gdns. W11 56 24 80 B
Arundel Gr. N16 48 33 85 C
Arundel Pl. N1 48 31 84 A
Arundel Rd. Barn 12 27 96 A
Arundel Rd. Croy 105 32 67 D
Arundel Rd. Houn 70 11 75 A
Arundel Rd. King 94 20 69 C
Arundel Rd. Rom 30 54 90 B
Arundel Rd. Sutt 110 24 63 D
Arundel Sq. N1 48 31 84 A
Arundel Sq. N7 48 31 84 A
Arundel St. WC2 7 30 80 B
Arundel Terr. SW13 61 22 77 B
Arvon Rd. N5 48 31 85 C
Ascalon St. SW8 10 29 77 C
Ascension Rd. Rom 29 50 91 A
Ascham Dri. E4 26 37 91 C
Ascham End. E17 26 36 90 A
Ascham St. NW5 47 29 85 C
Aschurch Rd. Croy 105 33 66 B
Ascot Cl. Ilf 28 45 91 A
Ascot Cl. Nthlt 43 13 85 C
Ascot Gdns. Sthl 53 13 81 A
Ascot Park. NW10 45 20 85 D
Ascot Rd. Felt 81 07 72 B
Ascot Rd. N15 37 32 88 B
Ascot Rd. N18 17 34 92 A
Ascot Rd. Orp 100 45 68 D
Ascot Rd. SW17 96 28 70 A
Ascott Ave. W5 60 18 79 A
Ashbourne Ave. Bexh 67 48 77 C
Ashbourne Ave. E18 27 40 89 D
Ashbourne Ave. Har 32 14 86 B
Ashbourne Ave. N20 16 27 93 B
Ashbourne Ave. NW11 35 24 88 B
Ashbourne Cl. N12 15 25 92 B
Ashbourne Cl. W5 55 19 81 A
Ashbourne Gr. SE22 75 33 75 D
Ashbourne Gr. W4 61 21 78 C
Ashbourne Rd. Mit 96 28 70 C
Ashbourne Rd. W5 54 18 82 D
Ashbourne Sq. Nthwd 19 09 91 A
Ashbourne Terr. SW19 95 25 70 C
Ashbourne Way. NW11 35 24 88 B
Ashbridge Rd. E11 39 39 87 B
Ashbridge St. NW8 1 27 82 C
Ashbrook Rd. Dag 41 49 86 D
Ashbrook Rd. N19 36 29 86 B
Ashburnam Rd. Rich 83 16 72 D
Ashburn Gdns. SW7 62 26 78 A
Ashburnham Ave. Har 33 15 88 D
Ashburnham Cl. N2 23 26 89 D
Ashburnham Gdns. Har 33 15 88 D
Ashburnham Gr. SE10 64 37 77 D
Ashburnham Pl. SE10 64 37 77 D
Ashburnham Rd. Belv 67 50 78 A
Ashburnham Rd. NW10 46 23 83 C
Ashburnham Rd. SW10 62 26 77 C
Ashburnham Retreat. SE10 64 37 77 D
Ashburn Mews. SW7 62 26 78 A
Ashburn Pl. SW7 62 26 78 A
Ashburton Ave. Croy 105 34 66 D
Ashburton Ave. Ilf 51 45 85 B
Ashburton Cl. Croy 105 34 66 C
Ashburton Gdns. Croy 105 34 65 A
Ashburton Gr. N7 48 31 85 A
Ashburton Rd. Croy 105 34 66 C
Ashburton Rd. E16 58 40 81 C
Ashburton Rd. Ruis 31 10 86 A
Ashburton Terr. E13 50 40 83 C
Ashbury Dri. Uxb 31 07 86 D
Ashbury Gdns. Rom 41 47 88 B
Ashbury Rd. SW11 74 28 76 C
Ashby Ave. Chess 109 19 63 A
Ashby Gr. N1 48 32 84 C
Ashby Mews. SE4 76 36 76 D
Ashby Rd. N15 37 34 88 A
Ashby Rd. SE4 76 36 76 D
Ashby St. EC1 3 31 82 B
Ashby Wlk. Croy 105 32 67 C
Ashchurch Gr. W12 61 22 79 C
Ashchurch Park Villas. W12 61 22 79 C
Ashchurch Terr. W12 61 22 79 A
Ash Cl. Cars 104 27 65 B
Ash Cl. N Mal 94 20 69 D
Ash Cl. Orp 108 44 67 B
Ash Cl. Rom 29 49 91 D
Ash Cl. SE20 98 35 69 C
Ash Cl. Sid 90 46 72 D
Ash Cl. Stan 21 16 91 A
Ashcombe Ave. Surb 101 17 66 B
Ashcombe Park. NW2 34 21 86 C
Ashcombe Rd. Cars 111 28 63 A
Ashcombe Rd. SW19 85 25 71 C
Ashcombe Sq. N Mal 94 20 68 A
Ashcombe St. SW6 73 25 76 D
Ashcroft Ave. Sid 78 46 74 C
Ashcroft Cres. Sid 78 46 74 C
Ashcroft. Pnr 20 13 91 A
Ashcroft Rd. Chess 101 18 65 D
Ashcroft Rd. E3 57 36 82 A
Ashcroft Sq. W6 62 23 78 A
Ash Ct. Eps 109 20 64 A
Ashdale Cl. Twick 82 14 73 A
Ashdale Gr. Stan 21 15 91 B
Ashdale Rd. SE12 89 40 73 D
Ashdale Way. Twick 82 13 73 B
Ashdene Cl. Ashf 91 08 70 C
Ashdene. Pnr 20 11 89 A
Ashdon Cl. Wdf Gn 27 40 91 B
Ashdon Rd. NW10 45 21 83 B
Ashdown Cl. Beck 98 37 69 D
Ashdown Cres. NW5 47 28 85 C
Ashdown Rd. Enf 14 35 97 C
Ashdown Rd. King 93 18 69 C
Ashdown Wlk. Rom 29 49 90 B
Ashenden Rd. E5 49 36 85 C
Ashen Dri. Dart 80 52 74 C
Ashen Gr. SW19 85 25 72 A
Ashentree Ct. EC4 3 31 81 C
Ashfield Ave. Felt 81 10 73 D
Ashfield Cl. Rich 83 18 73 C
Ashfield La. Chis 100 44 70 C
Ashfield Par. N14 16 29 94 D
Ashfield Rd. N14 16 29 93 C
Ashfield Rd. N4 37 32 88 C
Ashfield Rd. W3 55 21 80 D
Ashfield St. E1 57 34 81 B
Ashford Ave. Ashf 91 07 70 B
Ashford Ave. Hay 53 11 81 D
Ashford Ave. N8 24 30 89 C
Ashford Cl. E17 38 36 88 D
Ashford Cres. Enf 14 35 97 C
Ashford Rd. Ashf 91 08 70 C
Ashford Rd. E18 27 40 90 D
Ashford Rd. E6 51 43 84 C
Ashford Rd. Felt 81 09 71 A
Ashford Rd. NW2 46 23 85 B
Ashford St. N1 4 33 82 A
Ash Gr(off Andrew's Rd). E8 48 34 83 B
Ash Gr(off Mare St). E8 48 34 83 B
Ash Gr. Enf 17 33 94 A
Ash Gr. Felt 81 09 73 C
Ash Gr. Houn 70 11 76 B
Ash Gr. N13 17 32 93 C
Ash Gr. NW2 46 24 85 A
Ashgrove Rd. Ashf 81 08 71 D
Ashgrove Rd. Brom 98 38 70 B
Ashgrove Rd. Ilf 40 46 87 C
Ash Gr. SE 20 98 35 69 C
Ash Gr. Sthl 53 13 81 A
Ash Gr. W5 60 18 79 C
Ash Gr. Wem 44 16 85 A
Ash Gr. W Wick 106 38 66 C
Ash Hill Dri. Pnr 20 11 89 A
Ash Hse. SE1 63 33 78 B
Ashington Rd. SW6 73 24 76 D
Ash La. Horn 30 54 89 D
Ashlake Rd. SW16 86 30 71 A
Ashland Pl. W1 2 28 81 A
Ash La. Rom 30 52 91 A
Ashlar Pl. SE18 66 43 78 B
Ashleigh Gdns. Sutt 103 25 65 B
Ashleigh Rd. SE20 97 34 68 B
Ashleigh Rd. SW14 72 21 75 A
Ashley Ave. Ilf 28 43 90 D
Ashley Ave. Mord 103 25 67 A
Ashley Cl. NW4 23 23 90 C
Ashley Cl. Pnr 19 10 90 D
Ashley Cres. N22 25 31 90 C

Ashley Cres. SW11 74 28 75 A
Ashley Ct. NW4 23 23 90 C
Ashley Dri. Twick 82 13 73 D
Ashley Gdns. N13 17 32 92 A
Ashley Gdns. Rich 83 17 72 B
Ashley Gdns. Wem 33 18 86 A
Ashley La. Croy 112 31 64 B
Ashley La. NW4 23 23 89 A
Ashley La. NW7 23 23 91 D
Ashley Pl. SW1 6 29 79 C
Ashley Rd. E4 26 37 91 A
Ashley Rd. E7 50 41 84 C
Ashley Rd. Enf 14 35 97 C
Ashley Rd. Hamp 92 13 69 A
Ashley Rd. N17 25 34 89 A
Ashley Rd. N19 36 30 87 A
*Ashley Rd. Rich 71 18 75 A
Ashley Rd. Surb 101 15 67 D
Ashley Rd. SW19 95 25 70 B
Ashley Rd. Th Hth 96 30 68 D
Ashling Rd. Croy 105 34 66 C
Ashlin Rd. E15 49 38 85 B
Ashlone Rd. SW15 73 23 75 B
Ashlyn Gr. Horn 30 53 89 B
Ashmead. N14 12 29 95 A
Ashmead Rd. Felt 81 10 73 C
Ashmead Rd. SE8 76 37 76 C
Ashmere Ave. Beck 98 38 69 D
Ashmere Cl. Sutt 110 23 64 D
Ashmere Gr. SW2 74 30 75 C
Ashmill St. NW1 1 27 81 A
Ashmole Pl. SW8 10 30 77 B
Ashmole St. SW8 10 30 77 B
Ashmore Ct. Houn 59 13 77 A
Ashmore Gr. Well 78 45 75 A
Ashmore Rd. W9 56 24 82 B
Ashmount Rd. N15 37 33 88 B
Ashmount Rd. N19 36 29 87 B
Ashmour Gdns. Rom 29 50 90 D
Ashness Gdns. Grnf 44 16 84 B
Ashness Rd. SW11 74 27 74 B
Ash Rd. Croy 106 37 65 A
Ash Rd. E15 50 39 85 D
Ash Rd. Shep 91 07 68 C
Ash Rd. Sutt 103 24 66 D
Ashridge Cl. Har 33 17 88 C
Ashridge Cres. SE18 66 44 77 C
Ashridge Ct. N14 12 29 95 A
Ashridge Gdns. N13 16 30 92 C
Ashridge Gdns. Pnr 20 12 89 C
Ashridge Way. Mord 95 24 68 D
Ashridge Way. Sun 91 10 70 A
Ash Row. Brom 108 43 67 C
Ashtead Rd. E5 37 34 87 A
Ashton Cl. Sutt 110 25 64 A
Ashton Gdns. Houn 70 12 75 D
Ashton Gdns. Rom 41 48 88 C
Ashton Rd. E15 49 38 85 D
Ashton Rd. Rom 30 53 90 B
Ashton St. E14 58 38 80 A
Ashtree Ave. Mit 96 27 69 C
Ash Tree Cl. Croy 106 36 67 C
Ash Tree Cl. Surb 101 18 66 C
Ash Tree Dell. NW9 34 20 88 B
Ash Tree Way. Croy 106 36 67 A
Ashurst Cl. Dart 80 51 75 B
Ashurst Cl. Nthwd 19 09 91 C
Ashurst Cl. SE20 97 34 69 B
Ashurst Dri. Ilf 40 43 88 B
Ashurst Rd. Barn 12 27 95 B
Ashurst Rd. N12 16 27 92 C
Ashurst Wlk. Croy 105 34 65 B
Ashvale Rd. SW17 86 27 71 D
Ashville Rd. E11 38 38 86 B
Ashwater Rd. SE12 89 40 73 C
Ashwin St. E8 48 33 84 B
Ashwood Rd. E4 18 38 93 D
Ashworth Rd. W9 56 25 82 B
Aske St. N1 4 33 82 A
Askew Bldgs. W12 61 22 79 A
Askew Cres. W12 61 21 79 B
Askew Rd. W12 61 22 79 A
Askham Ct. W12 55 22 80 C
Askham Rd. W12 55 22 80 C
Askill Dri. SW15 73 24 74 A
Askwith Rd. Rain 52 50 83 D
Asland Rd. E15 50 39 83 A
Aslett St. SW18 85 26 73 A
Aslett St. SW18 73 26 74 C
Asmara Rd. NW2 46 24 85 C
Asmuns Hill. NW11 35 25 88 A
Asmuns Pl. NW11 35 24 88 B
Aspen Cl. N19 36 29 86 A
Aspen Cl. W5 60 18 79 B
Aspen Copse. Brom 99 42 69 D
Aspen Dri. Wem 33 16 86 C
Aspen Gdns. Mit 104 28 67 A
Aspen Gdns. W6 61 22 78 D
Aspen Green. Belv 67 48 79 D
Aspen La. Nthlt 53 12 82 A
Aspenlea Rd. W6 62 23 77 B
Aspinall Rd. SE4 76 35 75 B
Aspinden Rd. SE16 63 34 78 B
Aspley Rd. SW18 73 26 74 C
Asplins Rd. N17 25 34 90 B
Assam St. E1 57 34 81 C
Assembly Pas. E1 57 35 81 A
Assembly Wlk. Cars 104 27 66 A
Astall Cl. Har 21 15 90 A
Astbury Rd. SE15 76 35 76 A
Astell St. SW3 9 27 78 C
Astern Cl. Bexh 79 47 75 D
Aste St. E14 64 38 79 A
Astey's Row. N1 48 32 84 C
Asthall Gdns. Ilf 28 44 89 C
Astle St. SW11 74 28 76 C
Astley Ave. NW2 46 23 85 C
Aston Ave. Har 33 17 87 A
Aston Cl. Sid 90 46 72 C
Aston Green. Houn 70 11 76 C
Aston Rd. SW20 95 23 69 C
Aston Rd. W5 54 17 81 D
Aston St. E14 57 36 81 A
Astonville St. SW18 85 25 73 C
Astor Ave. Rom 41 50 88 C
Astor Cl. King 94 19 70 B
Astoria Wlk. SW9 75 31 75 A
Astrop Mews. W6 62 23 79 C
Astrop Terr. W12 62 23 79 A
Astwood Mews. SW7 62 26 78 A
Asylum Rd. SE15 63 34 77 D
Atalanta St. SW6 62 23 77 D
Atbara Rd. Tedd 93 16 70 B
Atcham Rd. Houn 70 14 75 C
Atheldene Rd. SW18 85 26 73 C
Athelney St. SE6 88 37 72 C
Athelstan Cl. Rom 30 54 90 D
Athelstane Gr. E3 49 36 83 D
*Athelstane Mews. N4 37 31 87 C
Athelstan Rd. King 93 18 68 D
Athelstan Rd. Rom 30 54 90 D
Athelstone Rd. Har 20 14 90 D
Athenaeum Ct. N5 48 32 85 A
Athenaeum Pl. N10 24 28 89 B
Athenaeum Rd. N20 15 26 94 D
Athena Pl. Nthwd 19 09 90 B
Athenlay Rd. SE15 76 35 74 B
Atherden Rd. E5 49 35 85 A
Atherfold Rd. SW9 74 30 75 A
Atherley Way. Houn 82 12 73 B
Atherstone Mews. SW7 62 26 78 A
Atherton Dri. SW19 85 23 71 B
Atherton Hts. Wem 44 17 84 A
Atherton Mews. E7 50 39 84 B
Atherton Pl. Har 20 14 89 B
Atherton Pl. Sthl 53 13 80 A
Atherton Rd. E7 50 39 84 B
Atherton Rd. Ilf 27 42 90 D
Atherton Rd. SW13 61 22 77 C
Atherton St. SW11 74 27 76 C
Athlone Cl. E5 48 34 85 D
Athlone Rd. SW2 87 31 73 A
Athlone St. NW5 47 28 84 A
Athlon Rd. Wem 44 17 83 D
Athol Cl. Pnr 19 10 90 B
Athole Gdns. Enf 13 33 95 A
Athol Gdns. Pnr 19 10 90 B
Athol Rd. Eri 67 50 78 C
Athol Rd. Ilf 40 46 87 A
Athol St. E14 58 38 81 C
Atkinson Rd. E16 58 41 81 A
Atkins Rd. E10 38 37 88 D
Atkins Rd. SW12 86 29 73 B
Atlanta Ct. Th Hth 97 32 68 A
Atlas Gdns. SE7 65 41 78 A
Atlas Mews. N7 47 30 84 B
Atlas Rd. E13 50 40 83 C
Atlas Rd. NW10 55 21 82 A
Atlas Rd. Wem 45 20 85 A
Atley Rd. E3 49 37 83 A
Atney Rd. SW15 73 24 75 C
Atterbury Rd. N4 37 31 88 D
Atterbury St. SW1 10 30 78 A
Attewood Ave. NW10 34 21 86 C
Attewood Rd. Nthlt 43 12 84 A
Attleborough Ct. SE23 87 34 72 B
Attlee Terr. E17 26 37 89 D
Attneave St. WC1 3 31 82 A
Atwater Cl. SW2 87 31 73 C
Atwell Rd. SE15 75 34 76 C
Atwood Ave. Rich 72 19 76 C
Atwood Ho. SE21 87 34 72 C
Atwood Rd. W6 61 22 78 B
Aubert Ct. N5 48 31 85 B
Aubert Park. N5 48 31 85 B
Aubert Rd. N5 48 31 85 B
Aubrey Pl. NW8 46 26 83 C
Aubrey Rd. E17 26 37 89 A
Aubrey Rd. N8 36 30 88 A
Aubrey Rd. W14 56 24 80 D
Aubrey Wlk. W14 56 24 80 D
Aubyn Hill. SE27 87 32 71 A
Aubyn Sq. SW15 72 22 74 A
Auckland Cl. SE19 97 33 69 B
Auckland Gdns. SE19 97 33 69 B
Auckland Hill. SE27 87 32 71 A
Auckland Rd. E10 38 37 86 D
Auckland Rd. Ilf 40 44 87 A
Auckland Rd. King 93 18 68 D
Auckland Rd. SE19 97 33 69 B
Auckland Rd. SW11 74 27 75 C
Auckland Rise. SE19 97 33 69 A
Auckland St. SE11 10 30 78 D
Auden Pl. NW1 47 28 83 A
Audleigh Pl. Chig 28 43 91 A
Audley Ct. E18 27 39 89 D
Audley Ct. Pnr 20 11 90 C
Audley Gdns. Ilf 40 45 86 B
Audley Pl. Sutt 110 25 63 D
Audley Rd. Enf 13 31 97 D
Audley Rd. NW4 34 22 88 D
Audley Rd. Rich 71 18 74 B
Audley Rd. W5 54 18 81 B
Audley Sq. W1 6 28 80 C
Audrey Gdns. Wem 33 16 86 B
Audrey Rd. Ilf 40 43 86 D
Audrey St. E2 48 34 83 C
Augurs La. E13 58 40 82 B
Augusta Rd. Twick 82 14 72 A
Augusta St. E14 57 37 81 D
Augustine Rd. Har 20 14 90 A
Augustine Rd. W14 62 23 79 D
Augustus Cl. Brent 60 17 77 D
Augustus Ct. SE19 97 33 70 C
Augustus Rd. SW19 85 24 73 C
Augustus St. NW1 2 28 82 B
Auila St. NW8 46 26 83 D
Aultone Way. Cars 104 27 65 D
Aultone Way. Sutt 103 26 65 A
Aulton Pl. SE11 63 31 78 C
Aurelia Gdns. Croy 104 30 67 D
Aurelia Rd. Croy 104 30 67 D
Auriel Ave. Dag 52 50 84 B
Auriga Mews. N16 48 33 85 C
Auriol Cl. Wor Pk 102 21 65 C
Auriol Dri. Grnf 43 14 84 D
Auriol Park Rd. Wor Pk 102 21 65 C
Auriol Rd. W14 62 24 78 A
Austen Gdns. Dart 80 54 75 D
Austen Rd. Har 32 13 86 B
Austin Ave. Brom 107 42 67 A
Austin Cl. SE6 88 36 73 B
Austin Ct. E6 50 41 83 A
Austin Friars. EC2 4 32 81 D
Austin Friars Sq. EC2 4 32 81 D
Austin Rd. Orp 108 46 67 A
Austin Rd. SW11 74 28 76 A
Austin's La. Uxb 31 08 86 C
Austin St. E2 4 33 82 B
Austral Cl. Sid 90 45 72 D
Austral Dr. Horn 42 53 87 B
Australia Rd. W12 55 22 80 B
Austral St. SE11 63 31 78 B
Austyn Gdns. Surb 102 19 66 D
Autumn Cl. Enf 13 34 97 A
Autumn St. E3 49 37 83 A
Avalon Cl. Enf 13 31 97 C
Avalon Cl. W13 54 16 81 A
Avalon Rd. Orp 108 46 65 B
Avalon Rd. SW6 73 25 76 B
Avalon Rd. W3 54 16 82 C
Avarn Rd. SW17 96 27 70 B
Avebury Park. Surb 101 17 66 B
Avebury Rd. E11 38 38 87 D
Avebury Rd. Orp 108 44 65 D
Avebury Rd. SW19 95 24 69 B
Avebury St. N1 48 32 83 B
Aveley Rd. Rom 30 51 89 C
Aveline St. SE11 63 31 78 C
Aveling Park Rd. E17 26 37 90 C
Avelon Rd. Rom 29 50 91 B
Ave Maria La. EC4 3 31 81 D
Avenell Rd. N5 48 31 85 B
Avenell Rd. N5 37 31 86 D
Avening Terr. SW18 85 25 73 A
Avening Terr. SW18 85 25 73 A
Avenons Rd. E13 58 40 82 C
Avenue Cl. Houn 69 10 76 B
Avenue Cl. N14 12 29 95 C
Avenue Cl. NW8 47 27 83 A
Avenue Cl. Rom 30 54 91 D
Avenue Cres. W3 61 19 79 B
Avenue Elmers. Surb 101 18 67 A
Avenue Gdns. SE25 97 34 69 C
Avenue Gdns. SW14 72 21 75 A
Avenue Gdns. Tedd 93 15 70 B
Avenue Gdns. W3 61 19 79 B
Avenue Mews. N10 24 28 89 B
Avenue Park Rd. SE27 87 31 72 B
Avenue Par. N21 17 32 94 B
Avenue Rd. Beck 98 35 69 B
Avenue Rd. Belv 67 50 78 A
Avenue Rd. Bexh 79 48 75 A
Avenue Rd. Brent 60 17 78 C
Avenue Rd. E7 50 40 85 B
Avenue Rd. Eri 68 51 77 A
Avenue Rd. Eri 68 51 77 B
Avenue Rd. Felt 81 09 72 D
Avenue Rd. Hamp 92 13 69 B
Avenue Rd. Islw 71 15 76 B
Avenue Rd. King 93 18 68 A
Avenue Rd. N12 15 26 92 A
Avenue Rd. N14 16 29 94 A
Avenue Rd. N15 37 32 88 B
Avenue Rd. N6 36 29 87 B
Avenue Rd. N Mal 94 21 68 C
Avenue Rd. NW10 45 21 83 D
Avenue Rd. NW3 46 26 84 D
Avenue Rd. NW8 47 27 83 A
Avenue Rd. Pnr 20 12 89 A
Avenue Rd. Rom 41 47 87 A
Avenue Rd. Rom 30 54 90 B
Avenue Rd. SE20 98 35 69 A
Avenue Rd. SE25 97 34 69 C
Avenue Rd. Sthl 53 12 80 D
Avenue Rd. Sutt 110 25 62 C
Avenue Rd. SW16 96 29 69 D
Avenue Rd. SW20 94 22 69 D
Avenue Rd. Tedd 93 16 70 A
Avenue Rd. W3 61 19 79 B
Avenue Rd. Wall 111 29 63 C
Avenue Rd. Wdf Gn 27 41 91 A
Avenue S. Surb 102 19 66 A
Avenue Terr. N Mal 94 20 68 A
Avenue The. Barn 11 24 96 A
Avenue The. Beck 98 38 69 A
Avenue The. Bex 79 47 74 D
Avenue The. Brom 107 41 65 D
Avenue The. Brom 99 41 68 B
Avenue The. Croy 105 33 65 C
Avenue The. E11 39 40 88 B
Avenue The. E4 18 38 92 D
Avenue The. Eps 109 22 63 D
Avenue The. Hamp 92 12 70 B
Avenue The. Har 21 15 90 B
Avenue The. Horn 42 53 86 B
Avenue The. Houn 69 10 76 A
Avenue The. Houn 70 13 74 B
Avenue The. N10 24 29 90 C
Avenue The. N11 16 28 92 D
Avenue The. N17 25 33 90 C
Avenue. The. N3 23 25 90 C
Avenue The. N8 25 31 89 A
Avenue The. Nthwd 19 08 91 A
Avenue The. NW6 46 24 83 A
Avenue The. Orp 108 45 65 B
Avenue The. Orp 100 46 70 D
Avenue The. Pnr 32 12 88 D
Avenue The. Pnr 20 12 91 B
Avenue The. Rich 71 18 76 D
Avenue The. Rom 29 50 89 D
Avenue The. SE10 64 38 77 D
Avenue The. Sun 91 10 69 D
Avenue The. Surb 101 18 67 D
Avenue The. Sutt 110 23 63 D
Avenue The. Sutt 110 24 62 B
Avenue The. SW4 74 28 74 A
Avenue The. Twick 71 16 74 B
Avenue The. Uxb 31 07 86 D
Avenue The. W13 54 16 81 D
Avenue The. W4 61 21 79 C
Avenue The. Wem 33 18 87 D
Avenue The. Wor Pk 102 21 65 B
Avenue The. W.Wick 107 39 66 A
Averil Gr. SW16 97 31 70 B
Averill St. W6 62 23 77 B
Avern Cl. E Mol 92 13 68 D
Avern Rd. E Mol 92 13 68 D
Avery Farm Row. SW1 9 28 78 B
Avery Gdns. Ilf 39 42 88 B
Avery Hill Rd. SE9 90 44 73 D
Avery Hill Rd. SE9 78 44 74 D
Avery Row. W1 6 28 80 B
Aviary Cl. E16 58 39 81 B
Aviemore Cl. Beck 106 36 67 D
Aviemore Way. Beck 106 36 67 A
Avignon Rd. SE4 76 35 75 B
Avington Gr. SE20 98 35 70 C
Avington Way (off Daniel Gdns).
SE15 63 33 77 D
Avis Sq. E1 57 35 81 D
Avoca Rd. SW17 86 28 71 A
Avon Cl. Hay 53 11 82 C
Avon Cl. Sutt 110 26 64 A
Avon Cl. Wor Pk 102 22 65 A
Avon Ct. Grnf 53 13 82 D
Avondale Ave. Barn 16 27 94 D
Avondale Ave. Esh 101 16 65 C
Avondale Ave. N12 15 25 92 D
Avondale Ave. NW2 34 21 86 C
Avondale Ave. Wor Pk 102 21 66 D
Avondale Cres. Enf 14 36 96 A
Avondale Cres. Ilf 39 41 88 B
Avondale Ct. E16 58 39 81 A
Avondale Ct. E18 27 40 90 B
Avondale Gdns. Houn 70 12 74 B
Avondale Park Gdns. W11 56 24 80 A
Avondale Park Rd. W11 56 24 80 A
Avondale Rd. Brom 99 39 70 B
Avondale Rd. E16 58 39 81 A
Avondale Rd. E17 38 37 87 A
Avondale Rd. Har 21 15 89 B
Avondale Rd. N13 17 31 93 A
Avondale Rd. N15 37 31 88 B
Avondale Rd. N3 23 26 90 A
Avondale Rd. S Croy 112 32 63 A
Avondale Rd. SE9 89 42 72 A
Avondale Rd. SW14 72 20 75 B
Avondale Rd. SW19 85 25 71 D
Avondale Rd. Well 79 47 76 C
Avondale Rise. SE15 75 33 75 B
Avondale Sq. SE1 63 34 78 C
Avonley Rd. SE14 64 35 77 C
Avon Mews. Pnr 20 12 90 B
Avonmore Pl. W14 62 24 78 B
Avonmore Rd. W14 62 24 78 A
Avonmouth St. SE1 8 32 79 C
Avon Path. S Croy 112 32 63 A
Avon Pl. SE1 8 32 79 A
Avon Rd. E17 26 38 89 B
Avon Rd. Grnf 53 13 82 D
Avon Rd. SE4 76 37 75 A
Avon Rd. Sun 91 09 70 D
Avon Way. E18 27 40 89 A
Avonwick Rd. Houn 70 13 76 D
Avril Way. E4 18 38 92 C
Avro Way. Wall 111 30 63 C
Awlfield Ave. N17 25 32 90 B
Awliscombe Rd. Well 78 45 76 D
Axe St. Bark 51 44 83 A
Axholme Ave. Edg 22 19 90 B
Axminster Cres. Well 79 47 76 A
Axminster Rd. N7 36 30 86 D
Aybrook St. W1 2 28 81 A
Aycliffe Cl. Brom 99 42 68 D
Aycliffe Rd. W12 55 22 80 C
Aylesbury Cl. E7 50 39 84 B
Aylesbury Rd. Brom 99 40 68 A
Aylesbury Rd. SE17 63 32 78 D
Aylesbury St. EC1 3 31 82 D
Aylesbury St. NW10 34 20 86 D
Aylesford Ave. Beck 106 36 67 A
Aylesford St. SW1 10 29 78 D
Aylesham Rd. Orp 108 45 66 B
Aylestone Ave. NW6 46 23 84 D
Aylett Rd. Islw 71 15 76 C
Aylett Rd. SE25 97 34 68 D
Ayley Croft. Enf 13 34 95 A
Aylmer Rd. Dag 41 48 86 C
Aylmer Rd. N2 36 27 88 A
Aylmer Rd. W12 61 21 79 B
Ayloffe Rd. Dag 52 48 84 B
Ayloffs Cl. Horn 30 54 89 C
Ayloff's Wlk. Horn 42 54 88 B
Aylton Estate. SE16 64 35 79 A
Aylward Rd. SE23 88 35 72 B
Aylward Rd. SW20 95 24 68 B
Aylward St. E1 57 35 81 C
Aylward St. E1 57 35 81 D
Aynescombe Path. SW14 72 20 76 C
Aynhoe Rd. W14 62 23 79 D
Aynscombe Angle. Orp 108 46 66 A
Ayr Ct. W3 55 19 81 A
Ayres Cl. E13 58 40 82 A
Ayres Cres. NW10 45 20 84 D
Ayres St. SE1 8 32 79 A
Ayr Green. Rom 30 51 90 A
Ayrsome Rd. N16 37 33 86 C
Ayrton Rd. SW7 5 26 79 D
Ayr Way. Rom 30 51 90 A
Aysgarth Ct. Sutt 103 25 65 D
Aysgarth Rd. SE21 87 33 73 A
Aytoun Pl. SW9 74 30 76 D
Aytoun Rd. SW9 74 30 76 D
Azalea Cl. W7 54 15 80 D
Azalea Wlk. Pnr 31 10 88 D
Azof St. E10 65 39 78 A

Baalbec Rd. N5 48 31 85 D
Babbacombe Gdns. Ilf 27 42 89 C
Babbacombe Rd. Brom 99 40 69 A
Baber Dri. Felt 70 11 74 C
Babington Rd. Dag 52 47 85 A
Babington Rd. Horn 42 52 87 D
Babington Rd. NW4 22 22 89 D
Babington Rd. SW16 86 29 71 D
Babington Rise. Wem 45 19 84 A
Babmaes St. SW1 6 29 80 B
Bacchus Wlk. N1 48 33 83 C
Bache's St. N1 4 32 82 B
Back Alley. EC3 4 33 81 C
Back Church La. E1 57 34 81 C
Back Hill. EC1 3 31 82 C
Backhouse Pl. SE17 63 33 78 A
Back La. Bark 51 44 83 A
Back La. Brent 60 17 77 B
Back La. Edg 22 20 90 A
Back La. N8 36 30 88 A
Back La. NW3 46 26 85 A
Back La. Rich 83 17 72 C
Back La. Rom 41 47 87 B
Back Rd. Sid 90 46 71 A
Bacon Gr. SE1 8 33 79 D
Bacon La. Edg 22 19 90 A
Bacon La. NW9 22 19 89 D
Bacon La. NW9 34 20 88 A
Bacon Link. Rom 29 49 91 B
Bacon's La. N6 36 28 87 C
Bacon St. E2 4 33 82 D
Bacon St. E2 57 34 82 C
Bacton. NW5 47 28 85 C
Bacton St. E2 57 35 82 A
Baddow Cl. Dag 52 49 83 A
Baddows Cl. Wdf Gn 27 41 91 B
Baddow Wlk (off Popham Rd). N1
48 32 83 A
Baden Pl. SE1 8 32 79 B
Baden Powell Cl. Surb 101 18 65 B
Baden Rd. Ilf 51 43 85 D
Baden Rd. N8 24 29 89 D
Badger Cl. Houn 70 11 75 A
Badgers Cl. Enf 13 31 96 B
Badgers Cl. Har 32 14 88 D
Badgers Copse. Orp 108 45 65 B
Badgers Copse. Wor Pk 102 21 65 B
Badgers Croft. N20 15 24 94 C
Badgers Croft. SE9 90 43 72 C
Badgers Wlk. N Mal 94 21 69 C
Badlis Rd. E17 26 37 89 A
Badlow Cl. Eri 68 51 77 C
Badminton Cl. Har 21 15 89 C
Badminton Cl. Nthlt 43 13 84 A
Badminton King 94 19 69 B
Badminton Rd. SW12 74 28 74 C
Badric Ct. SW11 73 26 76 D
Badsworth Rd. SE5 63 32 77 C
Bagleys La. SW6 73 25 76 B
Bagleys Spring. Rom 29 48 89 C
Bagshot Rd. Enf 13 33 95 D
Bagshot St. SE17 63 33 78 C
Bahram Rd. Eps 109 20 62 D
Baildon St. SE8 64 37 77 C
Baillie's Wlk. W5 60 17 79 B
Bainbridge Rd. Dag 52 48 85 B
Bainbridge St. WC1 2 29 81 D
Baird Ave. Sthl 53 14 80 A
Baird Cl. NW9 34 20 88 C
Baird Gdns. SE19 87 33 71 A
Baird Rd. Enf 13 34 96 D
Baird St. EC1 4 32 82 C
Baizdon Rd. SE3 77 39 76 C
Baker La. Mit 96 28 68 A
Baker Pas. NW10 45 21 83 C
Baker Rd. NW10 45 21 83 A
Baker Rd. SE18 77 42 76 A
Bakers' Almshouses. E10 38 37 88 D
Bakers Ave. E17 38 37 88 D
Bakers Ct. SE25 97 33 68 A
Bakers End. SW20 95 24 69 C
Bakers Field. N7 47 30 85 A

Bakers Hall Ct. EC3 8 33 80 A
Bakers Hill. Barn 11 25 97 D
Bakers Hill. E5 38 35 87 C
Baker's La. N6 36 27 88 D
Baker's Mews. W1 2 28 81 C
Bakers Row. E15 50 39 83 C
Baker's Row. EC1 3 31 82 C
Baker St. Enf 13 32 97 B
Baker St. W1 1 27 81 B
Bakewell Way. N Mal 94 21 69 C
Balaams La. N14 16 29 93 B
Balaam St. E13 58 40 82 A
Balaclava Rd. SE1 63 33 78 B
Balaclava Rd. Surb 101 17 67 C
Balben Path. E9 49 35 84 C
Balcaskie Rd. SE9 77 42 74 B
Balchen Rd. SE3 77 41 76 D
Balchier Rd. SE22 75 34 74 D
Balcombe St. NW1 1 27 82 D
Balcorne St. E9 49 35 84 C
Balder Rise. SE12 89 40 72 B
Balderton St. W1 2 28 81 C
Baldewyne Ct. N17 25 34 90 A
Baldock St. E3 49 37 83 D
Baldry Gdns. SW16 96 30 70 B
Baldwin Cres. SE5 75 32 76 A
Baldwin's Gdns. EC1 3 31 81 A
Baldwin St. EC1 4 32 82 B
Baldwin Terr. N1 48 32 83 C
Baldwyn Gdns. W3 55 20 80 B
Balfern Gr. W4 61 21 78 C
Balfern St. SW11 74 27 76 C
Balfe St. N1 47 30 83 C
Balfour App. Ilf 40 43 86 B
Balfour Ave. W7 54 15 80 D
Balfour Gr. N20 16 27 93 C
Balfour Mews. N9 17 34 93 C
Balfour Mews. W1 6 28 80 C
Balfour Pl. W1 6 28 80 A
Balfour Rd. Brom 107 41 67 B
Balfour Rd. Cars 111 27 63 D
Balfour Rd. Har 32 14 88 B
Balfour Rd. Houn 70 13 75 B
Balfour Rd. Ilf 40 44 87 C
Balfour Rd. N5 48 32 85 A
Balfour Rd. SE25 97 34 68 C
Balfour Rd. Sthl 59 11 79 D
Balfour Rd. SW19 95 25 70 D
Balfour Rd. W13 60 16 79 B
Balfour Rd. W3 55 20 81 A
Balfour St. SE17 63 32 78 B
Balgonie Rd. E4 18 38 94 D
Balgores Cres. Rom 30 52 89 B
Balgores La. Rom 30 52 89 D
Balgores Sq. rom 30 52 89 D
Balgowan Cl. N Mal 94 21 68 C
Balgowan Rd. Beck 98 36 69 D
Balgowan St. SE18 66 45 78 B
Balham Gr. SW12 86 28 73 A
Balham High Rd. SW12 86 28 73 D
Balham High Rd. SW17 86 28 72 A
Balham Hill. SW12 86 28 73 B
Balham New Rd. SW12 86 28 73 B
Balham Park Rd. SW12 86 28 73 C
Balham Rd. N9 17 34 93 A
Balham Station Rd. SW12 86 28 73 D
Ballamore Rd. Brom 89 40 72 C
Ballance Rd. E9 49 36 84 A
Ballantine St. SW18 73 26 75 C
Ballard Cl. King 94 20 70 D
Ballards Cl. Dag 52 49 83 B
Ballards Farm Rd. S Croy 112 34 63 A
Ballard's La. N12 23 26 91 A
Ballards La. N3 23 25 91 D
Ballards Rd. Dag 52 49 83 B
Ballards Rd. NW2 34 22 86 A
Ballards Rise. S Croy 112 34 63 A
Ballards Way. Croy 112 34 63 B
Ballards Way. S Croy 112 34 63 B
Ballast Quay. SE10 64 38 78 D
Ballater Rd. S Croy 112 33 64 D
Ballater Rd. SW2 74 30 75 C
Ball Ct. EC3 4 32 81 D
Ballina St. SE23 88 35 73 B
Ballingdon Rd. SW11 74 28 74 C
Balliol Ave. E4 18 38 92 B
Balliol Rd. N17 25 33 90 A
Balliol Rd. W10 56 23 81 D
Balliol Rd. Well 78 46 76 D
Balloch Rd. SE6 88 38 72 B
Ballogie Ave. NW10 45 21 85 A
Ballow Cl. SE5 63 33 77 C
Ball's Pond Pl. N1 48 32 84 B
Ball's Pond Rd. N1 48 33 84 A
Balmain Cl. W5 54 17 80 D
Balmer Rd. E3 49 36 83 D
Balmes Rd. N1 48 32 83 B
Balmoral Ave. Beck 98 36 68 C
Balmoral Cl. SW15 73 23 74 D
Balmoral Cres. E Mol 92 13 68 A
Balmoral Ct. SE27 87 32 71 A
Balmoral Dri. Sthl 53 12 82 D
Balmoral Gdns. Ilf 40 45 87 D
Balmoral Gdns. W13 60 16 79 A
Balmoral Gr. N7 47 30 84 B
Balmoral Mews. W12 61 21 79 D
Balmoral Rd. E10 38 37 86 B
Balmoral Rd. E7 50 41 85 C
Balmoral Rd. Har 43 13 85 A
Balmoral Rd. Horn 42 53 86 D
Balmoral Rd. King 93 18 68 D
Balmoral Rd. NW2 45 22 84 B
Balmoral Rd. Rom 42 52 88 B
Balmoral Rd. Wor Pk 102 22 65 B
Balmoral Way. Sutt 110 25 62 C
Balmore Cres. Barn 12 28 95 A
Balmore St. N19 36 28 86 B
Balmuir Gdns. SW15 73 23 75 C
Balnacraig Ave. NW10 45 21 85 A
Baltic Cl. SW19 95 26 70 D
Baltic St. EC1 4 32 82 C
Baltimore Pl. Well 78 45 76 D
Balvernie Gr. SW18 85 25 73 A
Bamborough Gdns. W12 62 23 79 A
Bamford Ave. Wem 44 18 83 D
Bamford Rd. Bark 51 44 84 A
Bamford Rd. Brom 88 38 71 D
Bamford Way. Rom 29 49 91 B
Bampfylde Cl. Wall 104 29 65 C
Bampton Rd. Rom 30 54 90 A
Bampton Rd. SE23 88 35 72 D
Banavie Gdns. Beck 98 38 69 A
Banbury Ct. Sutt 110 25 63 C
Banbury Ct. WC2 7 30 80 A
Banbury Rd. E9 49 35 84 D
Banbury St. SW11 74 27 76 C
Banchory Rd. SE3 65 40 77 D
Bancroft Ave. N2 36 27 88 A
Bancroft Cl. Ashf 81 07 71 C
Bancroft Ct. Nthlt 43 11 83 A
Bancroft Gdns. Har 20 14 90 A
Bancroft Gdns. Orp 108 45 66 D
Bancroft Rd. E1 57 35 82 B
Bancroft Rd. Har 20 14 90 C
Bandon Rise. Wall 111 29 64 D
Bangalore St. SW15 73 23 75 B
Bangor Cl. Nthlt 43 13 85 D
Bangor Rd. Brent 60 18 77 B
Banim St. W6 61 22 78 B
Banister House. E9 49 35 85 D
Banister Rd. W10 56 23 82 B
Bank Ave. Mit 95 26 69 D
Bank Ct. Dart 80 54 74 C
Bank End. SE1 8 32 80 C
Bankfoot Rd. Brom 89 39 71 A
Bankhurst Rd. SE6 88 36 73 B
Bank La. King 93 18 70 C
Bank La. SW15 72 21 74 A
Bank Mews. Sutt 110 26 63 A
Bank Side Cl. Cars 111 27 63 A
Bankside Dri. Surb 101 16 65 B
Bankside. Enf 13 31 97 B
Bankside. S Croy 112 33 63 B
Bankside. SE1 8 32 80 A
Bankside. Sthl 53 11 80 D
Bankside Way. SE19 97 33 70 A
Banks La. Bexh 79 48 75 D
Bank The. N6 36 28 87 D
Bankton Rd. SW2 75 31 75 C
Bankwell Rd. SE13 77 39 75 C
Banner St. EC1 4 32 82 C
Banning St. E10 65 39 78 C
Bannister Cl. Grnf 43 14 85 D
Bannister Cl. SW2 87 31 73 C
Bannockburn Rd. SE18 66 45 78 B
Banstead Ct. N4 37 32 87 C
Banstead Gdns. N9 17 33 93 C
Banstead Rd. Cars 111 27 63 C
Banstead Rd. Eps 109 22 62 D
Banstead Rd S. Sutt 110 26 62 D
Banstead St. SE15 76 35 75 A
Banstead Way. Wall 111 30 64 C
Banstock Rd. Edg 22 19 91 B
Banton Cl. Enf 13 34 97 D
Bantry St. SE5 63 32 77 D
Banwell Rd. Bex 79 47 74 D
Banyard Rd. SE16 63 34 79 D
Banyards. Horn 30 54 89 C
Baptist Gdns. NW5 47 28 84 A
Barandon Wlk. W11 56 23 80 B
Barbauld Rd. N16 37 33 86 C
Barbel St. SE1 7 31 79 C
Barber Cl. N21 17 31 94 A
Barberry Cl. Rom 30 53 91 C
Barbers Alley. E13 58 40 82 B
Barbers Rd. E15 49 37 83 D
Barbican Rd. Grnf 53 13 81 D
Barb Mews. W6 62 23 79 C
Barbot Cl. N9 17 34 93 C
Barchard St. SW18 73 25 74 B
Barchester Rd. Har 20 14 90 D
Barchester St. E14 57 37 81 B
Barclay Cl. SW6 62 25 77 C
Barclay Rd.Croy 105 32 65 D
Barclay Rd. E11 39 39 87 D
Barclay Rd. E13 58 41 82 C
Barclay Rd. E17 38 38 88 A
Barclay Rd. N18 25 33 91 A
Barclay Rd. SW6 62 25 77 C
Barcombe Ave. SW2 86 30 72 B
Barden St. SE18 66 45 77 C
Bardfield Ave. Rom 29 47 89 B
Bardney Rd. Mord 95 25 68 D
Bardolph Rd. N7 47 30 85 A
Bardolph Rd. Rich 71 18 75 B
Bard Rd. W10 56 23 80 B
Bards Ct. Rom 30 52 91 D
Bardsey Pl. E1 57 35 82 C
Bardsey Wlk. N1 48 32 84 A
Bardsley Cl. Croy 105 33 65 D
Bardsley La. SE10 64 38 77 A
Barfett St. W10 56 24 82 D
Barfield Ave. N20 16 27 93 B
Barfield Rd. Brom 100 43 68 A
Barfield Rd. E11 39 39 87 D
Barford Cl. NW4 22 22 90 A
Barford St. N1 48 31 83 A
Barforth Rd. SE15 75 34 75 B
Barfreston Way. SE20 97 34 69 B
Bargate Cl. N.Mal 102 22 66 A
Bargate Cl. SE18 66 45 78 D
Barge House Rd. E16 66 43 79 B
Barge House St. SE1 7 31 80 C
Bargery Rd. SE6 88 38 73 C
Barge Wlk. E M01 93 15 68 A
Barge Wlk. E Mol 92 14 68 B
Barge Wlk. E Mol 93 15 68 D
Barge Wlk. King 93 17 68 B
Barge Wlk. King 93 17 69 B
Bargrove Cl. SE20 97 34 70 C
Bargrove Cres. SE6 88 36 72 B
Barham Cl. Brom 107 42 66 C
Barham Cl. Chis 90 43 71 D
Barham Cl. Grnf 44 17 84 A
Barham Cl. Rom 29 49 90 D
Barham Rd. Chis 90 43 71 D
Barham Rd. S Croy 112 32 64 C
Barham Rd. SW20 94 22 70 C
Baring Cl. SE12 89 40 72 A
Baring Rd. Barn 11 26 96 B
Baring Rd. Croy 105 34 66 C
Baring Rd. SE12 89 40 72 A
Baring St. N1 48 32 83 B
Barker Ho. SE21 87 34 72 C
Barker Wlk. SW16 86 29 72 D
Barkham Rd. N17 25 33 91 C
Bark Hart Rd. Orp 108 46 66 D
Barking Rd. E16 58 39 81 B
Barking Rd. E6 50 42 83 C
Barkis Way. SE16 63 34 78 D
Bark Pl. W2 56 25 80 B
Barkston Gdns. SW5 62 25 78 B
Barkworth Rd. SE16 64 35 78 C
Barlborough St. SE14 64 35 77 D
Barlby Gdns. W10 56 23 82 D
Barlby Rd. W10 56 23 81 B
Barleycorn Way. E14 57 36 80 B
Barleycorn Way. Horn 42 54 88 D
Barley La. Ilf 40 46 88 C
Barley La. Rom 28 46 89 D
Barley Mow Pas. EC1 3 31 81 B
Barley Mow Pas. W4 61 20 78 D
Barley Mow Way. Shep 91 07 68 C
Barlow Cl. Wall 111 30 63 C
Barlow Pl. W1 6 28 80 B
Barlow Rd. Hamp 92 13 70 C
Barlow Rd. NW6 46 24 84 B
Barlow Rd. W3 55 19 80 D
Barlow St. SE17 63 32 78 B
Barmeston Rd. SE6 88 37 72 B
Barmor Cl. Har 20 13 90 D
Barmouth Ave. Grnf 44 15 83 D
Barmouth Rd. Croy 106 35 65 B
Barmouth Rd. SW18 73 26 74 C
Barnabas Rd. E9 49 35 84 B
Barnard Cl. Chis 100 44 69 B
Barnard Cl. Sun 91 10 70 D
Barnard Cl. Wall 111 29 63 D
Barnard Gdns. N Mal 94 22 68 C
Barnard Gr. E15 50 39 84 D
Barnard Hill. N10 24 28 90 B
Barnard Mews. SW11 74 27 75 C
Barnardo Dri. Ilf 28 44 89 C
Barnardo St. E1 57 35 81 D
Barnard Rd. Enf 13 34 97 D
Barnard Rd. Mit 96 28 69 C
Barnard Rd. SW11 74 27 75 C
Barnard's Inn. EC4 3 31 81 A
Barnards Pl. S Croy 112 31 62 B
Barnby Sq. E15 50 39 83 A
Barnby St. E15 50 39 83 A
Barnby St. NW1 2 29 82 A
Barn Cl. Ashf 81 07 71 D
Barn Cl. Nthlt 43 11 83 C
Barn Cres. Stan 21 17 91 A
Barnehurst Ave. Bexh 79 50 76 C
Barnehurst Ave. Eri 79 50 76 A
Barnehurst Cl. Eri 79 50 76 A
Barnehurst Rd. Bexh 79 50 76 C
Barnes Alley. Hamp 92 14 69 C
Barnes Ave. SW13 61 22 77 C
Barnes Cl. E12 50 41 85 B
Barnes Cray Rd. Dart 80 52 75 C
Barnesdale Cres. Orp 108 46 67 A
Barnes End. N.Mal 102 22 67 A
Barnes High St. SW13 72 21 76 D
Barnes Pikle. W5 54 17 80 B
Barnes Rd. Ilf 51 44 85 C
Barnes Rd. N18 18 35 92 A
Barnes St. E14 57 36 81 C
Barnes Terr. SE8 64 36 78 D
Barnes Wallis Ct. Wem 34 20 86 C
Barnet By Pass. NW7 22 21 91 D
Barnet Dri. Brom 107 42 65 A
Barnet Gr. E2 57 34 82 A
Barnet Hill. Barn 11 25 96 C
Barnet La. Barn 11 25 95 C
Barnet La. N20 15 24 94 B
Barnet Rd. Barn 11 23 96 C
Barnett Cl. Eri 80 51 76 D
Barnett St. E1 57 34 81 D
Barnet Wood Rd. Brom 107 41 65 A
Barney Cl. SE7 65 41 78 C
Barnfield Ave. Croy 106 35 65 A
Barnfield Ave. King 83 18 71 C
Barnfield Ave. Mit 96 28 68 B
Barnfield Gdns. King 83 18 71 C
Barnfield Gdns. SE18 66 43 77 B
Barnfield. N.Mal 102 21 67 C
Barnfield Rd. Belv 67 48 77 B
Barnfield Rd. Edg 22 20 90 A
Barnfield Rd. S Croy 112 33 62 A
Barnfield Rd. SE18 66 43 77 B
Barnfield Rd. W5 54 17 82 C
Barnfield Wood Cl. Beck 106 38 67 D
Barnfield Wood Rd. Beck 106 38 67 B
Barnham Rd. Grnf 53 14 82 A
Barnham St. SE1 8 33 79 A
Barnhill Ave. Brom 107 39 67 B
Barnhill. Pnr 32 11 88 A
Barnhill Rd. Hay 53 11 82 C
Barnhill Rd. Wem 34 20 86 C
Barn Hill. Wem 34 19 87 D
Barnlea Cl. Felt 82 12 72 A
Barnmead Gdns. Dag 52 48 85 D
Barnmead Rd. Beck 98 36 69 A
Barnmead Rd. Dag 52 48 85 D
Barn Rise. Wem 34 19 86 A
Barnsbury Cl. N Mal 94 20 68 C
Barnsbury Cres. Surb 102 20 66 C
Barnsbury Gr. N1 48 31 84 C
Barnsbury La. Surb 102 19 66 D
Barnsbury Park. N1 48 31 84 C
Barnsbury Rd. N1 48 31 83 A
Barnsbury Sq. N1 48 31 84 C
Barnsbury St. N1 48 31 84 C
Barnsbury Terr. N1 48 31 84 C
Barnscroft. SW20 94 22 68 B
Barnsdale Rd. W9 56 24 82 D
Barnsley Rd. Rom 30 54 91 D
Barnsley St. E1 57 34 82 D
Barnstaple La. SE13 76 38 75 C
Barnstaple Rd. Ruis 32 11 86 C
Barn St. N16 37 33 86 A
Barnston Wlk. N1 48 32 83 A
Barn Way. Wem 34 19 87 C
Barnwell Rd. SW2 75 31 74 A
Barnwood Cl. Ruis 31 08 86 B
Barnwood Cl. W9 56 25 82 D
Barnwood Ct. E16 58 40 80 D
Baroness Rd. E2 4 33 82 B
Baronet Gr. N17 25 34 90 A
Baronet Rd. N17 25 34 90 A
Baron Gdns. Ilf 28 44 89 B
Baron Gr. Mit 96 27 68 C
Baron Rd. Dag 41 47 87 D
Baron's Court Rd. W14 62 24 78 C
Barons Ct. NW9 34 20 88 D
Baronsfield Rd. Twick 71 16 74 D
Barons Gate. Barn 12 27 95 C
Barons Keep. W14 62 24 78 C
Barons Mead. Har 21 15 89 C
Baronsmead Rd. SW13 72 22 76 A
Baronsmede. W5 60 18 79 B
Baronsmere Rd. N2 24 27 89 C
Baron's Pl. SE1 7 31 79 A
Barons The. Twick 71 16 74 D
Baron St. N1 48 31 83 C
Baron's Wlk. Croy 106 36 67 C
Baron Wlk. E16 58 39 81 B
Baron Wlk. Mit 96 27 68 C
Barque Mews. SE8 64 37 77 A
Barrack Rd. Houn 70 12 75 C
Barrack Row. Sthl 59 11 78 A
Barracks La. Barn 11 24 96 A
Barratt Ave. N22 24 30 90 D
Barrat Way. Har 20 14 89 B
Barrenger Rd. N10 24 27 90 D
Barrett Rd. E17 26 38 89 C
Barrett's Green Rd. NW10 45 20 83 D
Barrett's Gr. N16 48 33 85 C
Barrett St. W1 2 28 81 C
Barrhill Rd. SW2 86 30 72 A
Barriedale. SE14 76 36 76 C
Barringer Sq. SW17 86 28 71 A
Barrington Cl. NW5 47 28 85 C
Barrington Ct. NW5 47 28 85 C
Barrington Rd. Bexh 79 47 76 D
Barrington Rd. E12 51 43 84 A
Barrington Rd. N8 36 29 88 B
Barrington Rd. Sutt 103 25 66 C
Barrington Rd. SW9 75 31 75 B
Barrington Villas. SE18 78 43 76 A
Barrow Ave. Cars 111 27 62 B
Barrow Cl. N21 17 31 93 B
Barrowdene Cl. Pnr 20 12 90 C
Barrowell Green. N21 17 32 93 A
Barrowfield Cl. N9 18 35 93 C
Barrowgate Rd. W4 61 20 78 D
Barrow Hedges Cl. Cars 111 27 63 C
Barrow Hedges Way. Cars 111 27 63 C
Barrow Hill Cl. Wor Pk 102 21 65 A
Barrow Hill Estate. NW8 47 27 83 C
Barrow Hill Rd. NW8 47 27 83 C
Barrow Hill. Wor Pk 102 21 65 A
Barrow Point Ave. Pnr 20 12 90 C
Barrow Point La. Pnr 20 12 90 C
Barrow Rd. Croy 112 31 64 C
Barrow Rd. SW16 96 29 70 B
Barrs Rd. NW10 45 20 84 D
Barry Ave. Bex h 67 48 77 C
Barry Ave. N15 37 33 88 D
Barry Cl. Orp 108 45 65 C
Barry Rd. NW10 45 20 84 C
Barry Rd. SE22 75 34 74 A
Barset Rd. SE15 76 35 75 A
Barsons Cl. SE20 98 35 70 C
Barston Rd. SE27 87 32 72 C
Barstow Cres. SW2 86 30 73 D
Barter St. WC1 3 30 81 A
Bartholomew Cl. EC1 4 32 81 A
Bartholomew Cl. SW18 73 26 75 C
Bartholomew La. EC2 4 32 81 D
Bartholomew Pl. EC1 4 32 81 A
Bartholomew Rd. NW5 47 29 84 A
Bartholomew St. SE1 8 32 79 D
Bartholomew Villas. NW5 47 29 84 C
Barth Rd. SE18 66 45 78 A
Bartle Ave. E6 50 42 83 C
Bartle Rd. W11 56 24 81 C
Bartlett Ct. EC4 3 31 81 C
Bartlett St. E14 57 37 81 B
Bartlett St. S Croy 112 32 64 D
Bartlow Gdns. Rom 29 50 90 B
Bartolomew Sq. EC1 4 32 82 C
Barton Ave. Rom 41 49 87 D
Barton Cl. Bexh 79 48 74 A
Barton Cl. E9 49 35 85 C
Barton Cl. SE15 75 34 75 B
Barton Green. N Mal 94 20 69 D
Barton Meadows. Ilf 28 44 89 C
Barton Rd. Horn 42 52 87 C
Barton Rd. W14 62 24 78 C
Barton St. SE1 7 30 79 C
Bartram Rd. SE4 76 36 74 C
Bartrip St. E9 49 36 84 B
Barwick Rd. E7 50 40 85 B
Barwood Ave. W Wick 106 37 66 D
Basedale Rd. Dag 51 46 84 D
Bashley Rd. NW10 55 20 82 D
Basildene Rd. Houn 70 11 75 B
Basildon Ave. Ilf 28 43 90 A
Basildon Cl. Sutt 110 25 62 B
Basildon Rd. Bexh 79 48 76 C
Basildon Rd. SE2 66 46 78 A
Basil St. SW3 5 27 79 B
Basil St. SW3 5 27 79 D
Basing Cl. Surb 101 15 66 B
Basing Ct. SE15 75 33 76 B
Basingdon Way. SE5 75 32 75 D
Basing Dri. Bex 79 48 74 D
Basingfield Rd. Surb 101 15 66 B
Basinghall Ave. EC2 4 32 81 D
Basinghall Gdns. Sutt 110 25 62 B
Basinghall St. EC2 4 32 81 D
Basing Hill. NW11 35 24 87 D
Basing Hill. Wem 34 19 87 C
Basing House Yd. E2 4 33 82 A
Basing Pl. E2 4 33 82 A
Basing St. W11 56 24 81 D
Basing Way. N3 23 25 89 B
Basing Way. Surb 101 15 66 B
Basire St. N1 48 32 83 A
Baskerville Rd. SW18 86 27 73 A
Basket Gdns. SE9 77 42 74 A
Baslow Cl. Har 20 14 90 B
Baslow Wlk. E5 49 35 85 B
Basnett Rd. SW11 74 28 75 A
Bassano St. SE22 75 33 74 B
Bassant Rd. SE18 66 45 77 B
Bassein Park Rd. W12 61 21 79 B
Bassett Cl. Sutt 110 25 62 B
Bassett Gdns. Islw 59 14 77 C
Bassett Rd. W10 56 23 81 D
Bassett St. NW5 47 28 84 A
Bassett Way. Grnf 53 13 81 D
Bassingham Rd. SW18 85 26 73 A
Bassingham Rd. Wem 44 17 84 B
Bassishaw Highwalk. EC2 4 32 81 B
Basswood Cl. SE15 75 34 75 B
Bastable Ave. Bark 51 45 83 D
Bastion Rd. SE2 66 46 78 C
Baston Manor Rd. Brom 107 40 65 D
Baston Rd. Brom 107 40 65 B
Bastwick St. EC1 4 32 82 C
Basuto Rd. SW6 73 25 76 A
Batavia Cl. Sun 92 11 69 A
Batavia Mews. SE14 64 36 77 C
Batavia Rd. SE14 64 36 77 C
Batavia Rd. Sun 91 10 69 B
Batchelor St. N1 48 31 83 A
Batchwood Green. Orp 100 46 68 B
Bateman Cl. Bark 51 44 84 A
Bateman Rd. E4 26 37 91 A
Bateman's Bldgs. W1 2 29 81 D
Bateman's Row. EC2 4 33 82 C
Bateman St. W1 2 29 81 D
Bates Cres. Croy 112 31 64 C
Bateson St. SE18 66 45 78 A
Bate St. E14 57 36 80 B
Bath Cl. SE15 64 35 77 C
Bath Ct. EC1 3 31 82 C
Bathgate Rd. SW19 85 23 72 D
Bath Gr. E2 48 34 83 C
Bath House Rd. Croy 104 30 66 C
Bath Pas. King 93 17 69 D
Bath Pas. SE5 63 31 77 D
Bath Pl. Barn 11 24 96 B
Bath Pl. EC2 4 33 82 A
Bath Rd. E7 50 41 84 B
Bath Rd. Hay 69 08 76 A
Bath Rd. Houn 70 12 76 C
Bath Rd. Mit 95 26 68 B
Bath Rd. N9 18 35 93 A
Bath Rd. Rom 41 48 88 C
Bath Rd. W4 61 21 78 A
Baths App. SW6 62 24 77 D
Baths Rd. Brom 99 41 68 D
Bath St. EC1 4 32 82 B
Bath Terr. SE1 8 32 79 C
Bathurst Ave. SW19 95 25 69 B
Bathurst Gdns. NW10 45 22 83 D
Bathurst Mews. W2 5 26 80 B
Bathurst Rd. Ilf 40 43 87 D
Bathurst St. W2 5 26 80 B
Bathway. SE18 66 43 78 A
Batley Pl. N16 37 33 86 D
Batley Rd. Enf 13 32 97 B
Batley Rd. N16 37 33 86 D
Batman Cl. W12 55 22 80 D

Batoum Gdns. W6 62 23 79 C
Batson St. W12 61 22 79 A
Battenberg Wlk. SE19 87 33 71 C
Batten St. SW11 74 27 75 A
Battersby Rd. SE6 88 38 72 D
Battersea Bridge Rd. SW11 74 27 76 A
Battersea Bridge Rd. SW11 9 27 77 C
Battersea Church Rd. SW11 73 26 76 B
Battersea High St. SW11 73 26 76 D
Battersea High St. SW11 74 27 76 C
Battersea Park Rd. SW11 74 27 76 A
Battersea Park Rd. SW8 10 29 77 C
Battersea Rise. SW11 74 27 75 C
Battishill St. N1 48 31 84 D
Battle Bridge La. SE1 8 33 80 C
Battle Bridge Rd. NW1 47 30 83 C
Battle Cl. SW19 95 26 70 A
Battledean Rd. N5 48 31 85 D
Battle Rd. Belv 67 50 78 A
Battle Rd. Eri 67 50 78 B
Batty St. E1 57 34 81 C
Baudwin Rd. SE6 89 39 72 A
Baulk The. SW18 85 25 73 A
Bavant Rd. SW16 96 30 69 D
Bavaria Rd. N19 36 30 86 A
Bavent Rd. SE5 75 32 76 C
Bawdale Rd. SE22 75 33 74 B
Bawdsey Ave. Ilf 28 45 89 D
Bawtree Cl. Sutt 110 26 62 C
Bawtree Rd. SE14 64 36 77 C
Bawtry Rd. N20 16 27 93 D
Baxendale. N20 15 26 93 A
Baxendale St. E2 57 34 82 A
Baxter Rd. E16 58 41 81 C
Baxter Rd. Ilf 51 43 85 D
Baxter Rd. N17 25 34 89 A
Baxter Rd. N18 17 34 92 B
Baxter Rd. N1 48 32 84 B
Bayfield Rd. SE9 77 41 75 D
Bayford Rd. NW10 56 23 82 B
Bayford St. E8 48 34 84 D
Bayham Pl. NW1 47 29 83 C
Bayham Rd. Mord 95 26 68 C
Bayham Rd. W13 54 16 80 D
Bayham Rd. W4 61 20 79 D
Bayham St. NW1 47 29 83 A
Bayhurst Dri. Nthwd 19 09 91 B
Bayley St. WC1 2 29 81 B
Bayley Wlk. SE2 67 48 78 C
Baylis Rd. SE1 7 31 79 A
Baynes Cl. Enf 13 34 97 A
Baynes Mews. NW3 46 26 84 B
Baynes St. NW1 47 29 84 C
Bayonne Rd. W6 62 24 77 A
Bayston Rd. N16 37 33 86 D
Bayswater Rd. W2 5 26 80 B
Baythorne St. E3 57 36 81 B
Baytree Rd. SW2 74 30 75 D
Bazalgette Cl. N.Mal 102 20 67 B
Bazalgette Gdns. N.Mal 102 20 67 B
Bazely St. E14 58 38 80 A
Bazile Rd. N21 13 31 95 C
Beacham Cl. SE7 65 41 77 B
Beachborough Rd. Brom 88 38 71 A
Beachcroft Rd. E11 39 39 86 C
Beachcroft Way. N19 36 29 87 D
Beach Gr. Felt 82 13 72 A
Beachy Rd. E3 49 37 84 C
Beaconfield Terrace Rd. W14 62 24 79 C
Beacon Gr. Cars 111 28 64 A
Beacon Hill. N7 47 30 85 C
Beacon Rd. Eri 68 52 77 D
Beacon Rd. Houn 69 07 74 C
Beacon Rd. SE13 76 38 74 D
Beaconsfield Cl. N11 16 28 92 C
Beaconsfield Cl. SE3 65 40 77 A
Beaconsfield Cl. W4 61 20 78 C
Beaconsfield Rd. Brom 99 41 68 B
Beaconsfield Rd. Croy 105 32 67 D
Beaconsfield Rd. E10 38 38 86 C
Beaconsfield Rd. E16 58 39 82 D
Beaconsfield Rd. E17 38 36 88 D
Beaconsfield Rd. Hay 53 11 80 C
Beaconsfield Rd. N11 16 28 92 A
Beaconsfield Rd. N15 25 33 89 C
Beaconsfield Rd. N9 17 34 93 C
Beaconsfield Rd. N Mal 94 20 69 D
Beaconsfield Rd. NW10 45 21 84 B
Beaconsfield Rd. SE17 63 33 78 C
Beaconsfield Rd. SE3 65 40 77 A
Beaconsfield Rd. SE9 89 42 71 A
Beaconsfield Rd. Sthl 53 12 80 C
Beaconsfield Rd. Surb 101 18 66 B
Beaconsfield Rd. Twick 71 16 74 D
Beaconsfield Rd. W4 61 20 79 D
Beaconsfield Rd. W5 60 17 79 B
Beaconsfield Terr. Rom 41 47 88 D
Beaconsfield Wlk. SW6 73 24 76 B
Beacontree Ave. E17 26 38 90 D
Beacontree Rd. E11 39 39 87 D
Beadlow Cl. Cars 103 26 67 D
Beadman Pl. SE27 87 31 71 B
Beadman St. SE27 87 31 71 B
Beadnell Rd. SE23 88 35 73 D
Beadon Rd. Brom 107 40 67 A
Beadon Rd. Brom 99 40 68 C
Beadon Rd. W6 62 23 78 A
Beaford Gr. SW20 95 24 68 B
Beagle Cl. Felt 81 10 71 B
Beak St. W1 6 29 80 A
Beal Cl. Well 78 46 76 A
Beale Cl. N13 17 31 92 D
Beale Pl. E3 49 36 83 D
Beale Rd. E3 49 36 83 B
Beale Rd. E3 49 36 83 D
Beal Rd. Ilf 40 43 86 A
Beam Ave. Dag 52 49 83 B
Beaminster Gdns. Ilf 28 43 89 B
Beamish Rd. N9 17 34 94 C
Beamway. Dag 52 50 84 D
Beanacre Cl. E9 49 36 84 B
Bean Rd. Bexh 79 47 75 D
Beanshaw. SE9 90 43 71 A
Beansland Gr. Rom 29 48 89 A
Bear Alley. EC4 3 31 81 D
Beardell St. SE19 97 33 70 B
Beardow Gr. N14 12 29 95 C
Beard Rd. King 83 18 71 D
Beardsfield. E13 50 40 83 C
Beard's Hill Cl. Hamp 92 13 69 A
Beard's Hill. Hamp 92 13 69 A
Beardsley Way. W3 61 20 79 B
Beard's Rd. Ashf 91 09 70 A
Bearfield Rd. King 93 18 70 C
Bear Gdns. SE1 8 32 80 C
Bear La. SE1 7 31 80 D
Bear Rd. Felt 82 11 71 B
Bearstead Rise. SE4 76 36 74 B
Bear St. WC2 6 29 80 B
Beatrice Ave. SW16 96 30 69 D
Beatrice Ave. Wem 44 18 85 C
Beatrice Cl. E13 58 40 82 C
Beatrice Cl. Pnr 19 10 89 C
Beatrice Rd. E17 38 37 88 A
Beatrice Rd. Enf 14 35 95 C
Beatrice Rd. N4 37 31 87 A
Beatrice Rd. Rich 71 18 74 B
Beatrice Rd. SE1 63 34 78 A
Beatrice Rd. Sthl 53 12 80 D
Beatson Wlk. SE16 57 36 80 C
Beattock Rise. N10 24 28 89 D
Beatty Rd. N16 48 33 85 A
Beatty Rd. Stan 21 17 91 A
Beatty St. NW1 47 29 83 C
Beattyville Gdns. Ilf 28 43 89 D
Beauchamp Pl. SW3 5 27 79 C
Beauchamp Rd. E7 50 40 84 D
Beauchamp Rd. SE19 97 32 69 B
Beauchamp Rd. Sutt 110 25 64 A
Beauchamp Rd. SW11 74 27 75 D
Beauchamp Rd. Twick 83 16 73 A
Beauchamp St. EC1 3 31 81 A
Beauchamp Terr. SW15 72 22 75 B
Beauclerc Rd. W6 62 23 79 C
Beaufort Ave. Har 21 16 89 B
Beaufort Cl. Rom 29 50 89 C
Beaufort Cl. W5 54 18 81 B
Beaufort Ct. Rich 83 17 71 A
Beaufort Dri. NW11 23 25 89 C
Beaufort Gdns. Houn 70 12 76 A
Beaufort Gdns. Ilf 40 43 87 C
Beaufort Gdns. NW4 35 23 88 C
Beaufort Gdns. SW16 96 30 70 D
Beaufort Gdns. SW3 5 27 79 D
Beaufort Mansions. SW3 62 26 77 B
Beaufort Mews. SW6 62 24 77 B
Beaufort Park. NW11 23 25 89 C
Beaufort Rd. King 93 18 68 C
Beaufort Rd. Rich 83 17 71 A
Beaufort Rd. Ruis 31 08 86 B
Beaufort Rd. Twick 83 17 73 A
Beaufort Rd. W5 54 18 81 B
Beaufort St. SW3 62 26 77 B
Beaufort Way. Eps 109 22 63 C
Beaufoy Rd. N17 25 33 91 C
Beaufoy Wlk. SE11 10 30 78 B
Beaulieu Ave. SE26 87 34 71 B
Beaulieu Cl. Mit 96 28 69 A
Beaulieu Cl. NW9 22 21 89 C
Beaulieu Cl. SE5 75 32 75 B
Beaulieu Cl. Twick 71 17 74 D
Beaulieu Dri. Pnr 32 11 87 B
Beaulieu Gdns. N21 17 32 94 A
Beauly Way. Rom 30 51 90 A
Beaumanor Gdns. SE9 90 43 71 A
Beaumaris Dri. Wdf Gn 27 41 91 D
Beaumont Ave. Har 32 13 88 D
Beaumont Ave. Rich 71 18 75 B
Beaumont Ave. W14 62 24 78 D
Beaumont Ave. Wem 44 17 85 A
Beaumont Cl. Rom 30 53 90 C
Beaumont Cres. W14 62 24 78 D
Beaumont Dri. Ashf 81 08 71 D
Beaumont Gr. E1 57 35 82 D
Beaumont Mews. W1 2 28 81 A
Beaumont Pl. Barn 11 24 97 B
Beaumont Pl. W1 2 29 82 C
Beaumont Rd. E10 38 37 87 B
Beaumont Rd. E10 38 38 87 A
Beaumont Rd. E13 58 40 82 B
Beaumont Rd. Orp 108 44 67 D
Beaumont Rd. SE19 97 32 70 A
Beaumont Rd. SW19 85 24 73 A
Beaumont Rd. W4 61 20 79 C
Beaumont Rise. N19 36 30 87 C
Beaumont Sq. E1 57 35 81 B
Beaumont St. W1 2 28 81 A
Beaumont Wlk. NW3 47 27 84 D
Beauvais Terr. Nthlt 53 11 82 B
Beauval Rd. SE22 75 33 74 D
Beaverbank Rd. SE9 90 44 73 D
Beaver Cl. Hamp 92 13 69 B
Beaver Cl. SE20 97 34 70 C
Beaver Gr (off Jetstar Way). Nthlt 53 12 82 A
Beavers Cres. Houn 70 11 75 D
Beavers La. Houn 70 11 75 A
Beaverwood Rd. Chis 100 45 70 A
Beavor La. W6 61 22 78 A
Bebbington Rd. SE18 66 45 78 A
Beccles Dri. Bark 51 45 84 B
Beccles St. E14 57 36 80 B
Bec Cl. Ruis 32 11 86 D
Beckenham Ct. Beck 98 37 69 A
Beckenham Gdns. N9 17 33 93 C
Beckenham Gr. Brom 98 38 69 D
Beckenham Hill Rd. Beck 88 37 71 D
Beckenham Hill Rd. SE6 88 38 71 C
Beckenham La. Brom 99 39 69 D
Beckenham Place Park. Beck 98 37 70 D
Beckenham Rd. Beck 98 36 69 A
Beckenham Rd. W Wick 106 38 66 A
Beckers The. N16 48 34 85 A
Becket Cl. SE25 105 34 67 C
Becket Fold. Har 33 15 88 B
Becket Rd. N18 18 35 92 A
Becket St. SE1 8 32 79 D
Beckett Cl. Felt 69 10 74 D
Beckett Cl. SW16 86 29 72 B
Becketts Cl. Orp 108 45 65 D
Beckett Wlk. Beck 98 36 70 A
*Beckford Pl. SE17 63 32 78 C
Beckford Rd. Croy 105 33 67 D
Beck La. Beck 98 35 68 B
Becklow Gdns. W12 61 22 79 A
Becklow Gdns. W12 55 22 80 C
Becklow Rd. W12 61 21 79 B
Becklow Rd. W12 61 22 79 A
Beck Rd. E8 48 34 83 B
Beck River Park. Beck 98 37 69 A
Becks Rd. Sid 90 46 72 C
Beckton Rd. E16 58 39 81 B
Beck Way. Beck 98 37 68 A
Beckway Rd. SW16 96 29 69 D
Beckway St. SE17 63 33 78 A
Beckwith Rd. SE24 75 32 74 B
Beclands Rd. SW17 96 28 70 A
Becmead Ave. Har 33 16 88 B
Becmead Ave. SW16 86 29 71 B
Becondale Rd. SE19 87 33 71 C
Becontree Ave. Dag 41 47 86 B
Bective Pl. SW15 73 24 75 D
Bective Rd. E7 50 40 85 A
Bective Rd. SW15 73 24 75 D
Becton Pl. Eri 79 50 76 A
Bedale St. SE1 8 32 80 D
Beddington Farm Rd. Croy 104 30 66 C
Beddington Gdns. Cars 111 28 63 A
Beddington Gdns. Wall 111 28 63 B
Beddington Green. Orp 100 45 69 B
Beddington Gr. Wall 111 29 64 D
Beddington La. Croy 104 29 66 D
Beddington Rd. Ilf 40 45 87 B
Beddington Rd. Orp 100 45 69 B
Bede Cl. Pnr 20 11 90 B
Bedenham Way (off Daniel Gdns). SE15 63 33 77 D
Bede Rd. Rom 41 47 88 C
Bedfont Cl. Felt 69 08 74 C
Bedfont Cl. Mit 96 28 69 C
Bedfont La. Felt 81 09 73 B
Bedfont Rd. Felt 81 08 72 B
Bedfont Rd. Stai 69 07 74 C
Bedford Ave. Barn 11 24 95 B
Bedford Ave. WC1 2 29 81 B
Bedfordbury. WC2 7 30 80 A
Bedford Cl. N10 24 28 91 C
Bedford Ct. WC2 7 30 80 A
Bedford Gdns. Horn 42 53 86 A
Bedford Gdns. W8 56 25 80 C
Bedford Hill. SW12 86 28 72 B
Bedford Hill. SW16 86 29 72 C
Bedford Park. Croy 105 32 66 C
Bedford Pas. SW6 62 24 77 C
Bedford Pl. Croy 105 32 66 D
Bedford Pl. WC1 3 30 81 A
Bedford Rd. E17 26 37 89 A
Bedford Rd. E18 27 40 90 C
Bedford Rd. E6 51 43 83 A
Bedford Rd. Har 32 14 88 C
Bedford Rd. Ilf 40 43 86 D
Bedford Rd. N15 25 33 89 C
Bedford Rd. N22 24 30 90 C
Bedford Rd. N2 24 27 89 A
Bedford Rd. N8 36 29 88 D
Bedford Rd. N9 17 34 94 B
Bedford Rd. Orp 108 46 66 D
Bedford Rd. Sid 90 45 72 C
Bedford Rd. SW4 74 30 75 C
Bedford Rd. Twick 82 14 72 D
Bedford Rd. W13 54 16 80 B
Bedford Rd. W4 61 21 79 C
Bedford Rd. Wor Pk 103 23 65 A
Bedford Row. WC1 3 30 81 B
Bedford Sq. WC1 2 29 81 B
Bedford St. WC2 7 30 80 A
Bedford Way. WC1 2 29 82 D
Bedgebury Gdns. SW19 85 24 72 A
Bedgebury Rd. SE9 77 41 75 D
Bedivere Rd. Brom 89 40 72 C
Bedlow Way. Croy 111 30 64 B
Bedonwell Rd. Bexh 67 48 77 B
Bedonwell Rd. SE2 67 48 77 A
Bedser Dri. Grnf 43 14 85 D
Bedster Gdns. E Mol 92 13 69 D
Bedwardine Rd. SE19 97 33 70 C
Bedwell Rd. Belv 67 49 78 C
Bedwell Rd. N17 25 33 90 A
Bedwin Way. SE16 63 34 78 D
Beeby Rd. E13 58 40 81 B
Beech Ave. Brent 60 16 77 D
Beech Ave. N20 16 27 94 C
Beech Ave. Ruis 31 10 86 D
Beech Ave. S Croy 112 32 62 D
Beech Ave. Sid 90 46 73 A
Beech Ave. W3 55 21 80 C
Beech Cl. Ashf 81 08 71 D
Beech Cl. Cars 104 27 65 B
Beech Cl. Horn 42 52 86 D
Beech Cl. N9 13 34 95 D
Beech Cl. SW15 84 22 73 A
Beech Cl. SW19 95 23 70 A
Beech Copse. Brom 99 42 69 D
Beech Copse. S Croy 112 33 64 C
Beechcroft Ave. Bexh 79 50 76 D
Beechcroft Ave. Har 32 13 87 A
Beechcroft Ave. N Mal 94 20 69 C
Beechcroft Ave. NW11 35 24 87 B
Beechcroft Ave. Sthl 53 12 80 D
Beechcroft. Chis 100 43 70 C
Beechcroft Cl. Houn 59 12 77 C
Beechcroft Gdns. Wem 33 18 86 D
Beechcroft. King 94 19 69 B
Beechcroft Rd. Chess 101 18 65 D
Beechcroft Rd. E18 27 40 90 D
Beechcroft Rd. SW14 72 20 75 A
Beechcroft Rd. SW17 86 27 72 A
Beechdale. N21 16 30 93 B
Beechdale Rd. SW2 74 30 74 D
Beech Dri. N2 24 27 89 B
Beechengrove. Pnr 20 12 89 B
Beechen Pl. SE23 88 35 72 A
Beeches Ave The. Cars 111 27 63 C
Beeches Ct. Brom 99 40 70 A
Beeches Rd. Sutt 103 24 66 C
Beeches Rd. SW17 86 27 72 D
Beeches Wlk. Cars 111 27 62 A
Beechfield Ct. S Croy 112 32 64 A
Beechfield Gdns. Rom 41 50 87 A
Beechfield Rd. Brom 99 41 69 C
Beechfield Rd. Eri 68 51 77 C
Beechfield Rd. N4 37 32 88 C
Beechfield Rd. SE6 88 36 73 D
Beech Gdns. Dag 52 50 84 C
Beech Gdns. W5 60 18 79 C
Beech Gr. Ilf 28 45 91 A
Beech Gr. Mit 96 29 68 D
Beech Gr. N Mal 94 20 68 B
Beech Hall Cres. E4 26 38 91 D
Beech Hall Rd. E4 26 38 91 D
Beech Hill Ave. Barn 11 26 97 B
Beechhill Rd. SE9 78 43 74 A
Beech House Rd. Croy 105 32 65 D
Beech Lawns. N12 15 26 92 D
Beechmont Cl. Brom 89 39 71 C
Beechmore Gdns. Sutt 103 23 65 B
Beechmore Rd. SW11 74 27 76 B
Beechmount Ave. W7 54 15 81 A
Beecholme Ave. Mit 96 28 69 B
Beech Rd. Felt 81 09 73 A
Beech Rd. N11 24 30 91 A
Beech Rd. SW16 96 30 68 B
Beechrow. King 83 18 71 A
Beech St. EC2 4 32 81 A
Beech St. Rom 29 50 89 C
Beech Tree Pl. Sutt 110 25 64 D
Beechvale Cl. N12 16 27 92 C
Beechway. Bex 79 47 74 D
Beech Way. NW10 45 20 84 D
Beech Way. Twick 82 13 72 C
Beech Wlk. Dart 80 52 75 C
Beech Wlk. NW7 22 21 91 A
Beechwood Ave. Grnf 53 13 82 B
Beechwood Ave. Har 32 14 86 C
Beechwood Ave. N3 23 25 89 A
Beechwood Ave. Rich 72 19 76 A
Beechwood Ave. Ruis 31 09 86 B
Beechwood Ave. Sun 91 10 70 A
Beechwood Ave. Th Hth 97 31 68 D
Beechwood Circ. Har 32 13 86 D
Beechwood Cl. Surb 101 17 66 B
Beechwood Cres. Bexh 79 48 75 A
Beechwood Ct. Cars 111 27 64 B
Beechwood Dri. Wdf Gn 27 39 91 B
Beechwood Gdns. Har 32 14 86 C
Beechwood Gdns. Ilf 39 42 88 B
Beechwood Gdns. Ilf 28 43 89 C
Beechwood Park. E18 27 40 89 A
Beechwood Rd. E8 48 33 84 B
Beechwood Rd. N8 24 30 89 C
Beechwood Rd. S Croy 112 33 62 A
Beecroft Rd. SE4 76 36 74 A
Beehive Cl. Ilf 39 42 88 D
Beehive Ct. Rom 30 54 91 D
Beehive La. Ilf 39 42 88 D
Beeleigh Rd. Mord 95 25 68 D
Beer La. King 93 17 69 C
Beer La. King 93 17 69 D
Beeston Cl. E8 48 34 85 C
Beeston Pl. SW1 6 28 79 D
Beeston Rd. Barn 11 26 95 D
Beeston Way. Felt 70 11 74 C
Beethoven St. W10 56 24 82 A
Beeton Cl. Pnr 20 13 91 C
Begbie Rd. SE3 77 41 76 B
Begonia Pl. Hamp 92 13 70 A
Begonia Wlk. W12 55 21 81 D
Beira St. SW12 86 28 73 B
Bekesbourne St. E14 57 36 81 C
Belcroft Cl. Brom 99 39 70 D
Beldham Gdns. E Mol 92 13 68 B
Belfairs Dri. Rom 41 47 87 A
Belfast Rd. N16 37 33 86 B
Belfast Rd. SE25 97 34 68 D
Belfield Rd. Eps 109 21 63 C
Belfont Wlk. N7 47 30 85 A
Belford Gr. SE18 66 43 78 A
Belfort Rd. SE15 76 35 76 C
Belgrade Rd. Hamp 92 13 69 B
Belgrade Rd. N16 48 33 85 A
Belgrave Ave. Rom 30 53 89 A
Belgrave Cl. N14 12 29 95 A
Belgrave Cl. W3 61 20 79 A
Belgrave Cres. Sun 91 10 69 B
Belgrave Ct. E13 58 41 82 C
Belgrave Gdns. N14 12 29 96 D
Belgrave Gdns. NW8 46 25 83 B
Belgrave Mews N. SW1 6 28 79 A
Belgrave Mews S. SW1 6 28 79 C
Belgrave Mews W. SW1 6 28 79 C
Belgrave Pl. SW1 6 28 79 C
Belgrave Rd. E10 38 38 87 C
Belgrave Rd. E11 39 40 86 A
Belgrave Rd. E13 58 41 82 C
Belgrave Rd. E17 38 37 88 C
Belgrave Rd. Houn 70 12 75 B
Belgrave Rd. Ilf 39 42 87 D
Belgrave Rd. Ilf 40 43 86 A
Belgrave Rd. Mit 95 26 68 B
Belgrave Rd. SE25 97 33 68 D
Belgrave Rd. Sun 91 10 69 B
Belgrave Rd. SW13 61 21 77 D
Belgrave Rd. SW1 10 29 78 A
Belgrave Sq. SW1 6 28 79 C
Belgrave St. E1 57 35 81 D
Belgrave Wlk. Mit 95 26 68 B
Belgrave Yd. SW1 6 28 79 D
Belgravia Gdns. Brom 99 39 70 A
Belgravia Mews. King 93 17 68 D
Belgrove St. WC1 3 30 82 A
Belham Wlk. SE5 75 32 76 B
Belhaven St. E3 57 36 82 A
Belinda Rd. SW9 75 31 75 B
Belitha Villas. N1 48 31 84 C
Bellamy Cl. SW5 62 24 78 D
Bellamy Cl. Uxb 31 07 86 C
Bellamy Rd. E4 26 37 91 B
Bellamy St. SW12 86 28 73 B
Bellany Dri. Stan 21 16 90 B
Bellasis Ave. SW2 86 30 72 A
Bell Ave. Rom 30 52 90 B
Bell Cl. Pnr 20 11 89 A
Bell Cl. Ruis 31 09 86 D
Bell Ct. Surb 102 19 65 B
Bell Dri. SW18 85 24 73 A
Bellefield Rd. Orp 108 46 67 B
Bellefields Rd. SW9 74 30 75 B
Bellegrove Cl. Well 78 45 76 D
Bellegrove Rd. Well 78 45 76 C
Bellenden Rd. SE15 75 33 76 D
Belle Staines Pleasaunce. E4 18 37 93 A
Belleville Rd. SW11 74 27 74 B
Belle Vue. Grnf 43 14 83 B
Bellevue Park. Th Hth 97 32 68 C
Bellevue Pl. E1 57 35 82 C
Bellevue Rd. Bexh 79 48 74 B
Bellevue Rd. Horn 42 54 87 D
Bellevue Rd. King 93 18 68 C
Bellevue Rd. N11 16 28 92 B
Belle Vue Rd. Rom 29 50 91 B
Bellevue Rd. SW13 72 22 76 C
Bellevue Rd. SW17 86 27 73 D
Bellevue Rd. W13 54 16 82 D
Bellew St. SW17 85 26 72 C
Bell Farm Ave. Dag 41 50 86 C
Bellfield Ave. Har 20 14 91 B
Bellflower Path. Rom 30 53 91 C
Bellgate Mews. NW5 36 28 86 D
Bell Green La. SE26 88 36 71 B
Bell Green. SE26 88 36 71 B
Bell Hill. Croy 105 32 65 A
Bell House Rd. Rom 41 50 87 C
Bellingham Green. SE6 88 37 72 C
Bellingham Rd. SE6 88 38 72 A
Bell Inn Yd. EC3 4 32 81 D
Bell La. E16 58 40 80 C
Bell La. E1 4 33 81 B
Bell La. NW4 23 23 89 D
Bell La. Twick 83 16 73 C
Bell Meadow. SE19 87 33 71 A
Bellot St. E10 65 39 78 C
Bell Rd. Enf 13 32 97 B
Bell Rd. Houn 70 13 75 D
Bellring Cl. Belv 67 49 77 A
Bell's Alley. SW6 73 25 76 C
Bells Hill. Barn 11 23 96 D
Bell St. NW1 1 27 81 A
Belltrees Gr. SW16 87 31 71 C
Bell Vue Rd. E17 26 38 90 D
Bell Water Gate. SE18 66 43 79 C
Bell Wharf La. EC4 8 32 80 A
Bellwood Rd. SE15 76 35 75 D
Bell Yd. WC2 3 31 81 C
Belmont Ave. Barn 12 27 95 B
Belmont Ave. Horn 42 54 86 B
Belmont Ave. N13 16 30 92 D
Belmont Ave. N17 25 32 89 A
Belmont Ave. N9 17 34 94 C
Belmont Ave. N Mal 94 22 68 C
Belmont Ave. Sthl 59 12 79 C
Belmont Ave. Well 78 45 75 A
Belmont Ave. Wem 44 18 83 B
Belmont Circ. Har 21 16 90 D
Belmont Circ. Stan 21 16 90 B
Belmont Cl. Barn 12 27 96 D
Belmont Cl. N20 15 25 94 D
Belmont Cl. SW4 74 29 75 A
Belmont Gr. SE13 76 38 75 B
Belmont Hill. SE13 76 38 75 B
Belmont La. Chis 90 44 71 C

| | | |
|---|---|---|
| Belmont La. Chis | 90 | 44 71 C |
| Belmont La. Stan | 21 | 17 91 C |
| Belmont Park Cl. SE13 | 77 | 39 75 C |
| Belmont Park Rd. E10 | 38 | 38 88 C |
| Belmont Park. SE13 | 77 | 39 75 C |
| Belmont Rd. Beck | 98 | 36 69 D |
| Belmont Rd. Eri | 79 | 49 76 B |
| Belmont Rd. Har | 21 | 16 89 A |
| Belmont Rd. Horn | 42 | 53 86 D |
| Belmont Rd. Ilf | 40 | 44 86 C |
| Belmont Rd. N15 | 25 | 32 89 C |
| Belmont Rd. N17 | 25 | 32 89 A |
| Belmont Rd. SE25 | 105 | 34 67 B |
| Belmont Rd. Sutt | 110 | 25 62 C |
| Belmont Rd. SW4 | 74 | 29 75 A |
| Belmont Rd. Twick | 82 | 14 72 B |
| Belmont Rd. W4 | 61 | 20 78 B |
| Belmont Rd. Wall | 111 | 29 64 C |
| Belmont Rise. Sutt | 110 | 24 62 B |
| Belmont St. NW1 | 47 | 28 84 C |
| Belmont Terr. W4 | 61 | 20 78 B |
| Belmore St. SW8 | 74 | 29 76 B |
| Belsham St. E9 | 49 | 35 84 A |
| Belsize Ave. N13 | 24 | 30 91 B |
| Belsize Ave. NW3 | 47 | 27 85 C |
| Belsize Ave. W13 | 60 | 16 79 D |
| Belsize Cres. NW3 | 46 | 26 84 B |
| Belsize Ct Garages. NW3 | 46 | 26 85 D |
| Belsize Ct. NW3 | 46 | 26 85 D |
| Belsize Gdns. Sutt | 110 | 25 64 B |
| Belsize Gr. NW3 | 47 | 27 84 A |
| Belsize La. NW3 | 47 | 27 85 C |
| Belsize Mews. NW3 | 46 | 26 84 B |
| Belsize Park Gdns. NW3 | 47 | 27 84 A |
| *Belsize Park Mews. NW3 | 46 | 26 84 B |
| Belsize Park. NW3 | 46 | 26 84 A |
| Belsize Pl. NW3 | 46 | 26 85 D |
| Belsize Rd. Har | 20 | 14 91 D |
| Belsize Rd. NW6 | 46 | 26 84 C |
| Belsize Sq. NW3 | 46 | 26 84 B |
| Belsize Terr. NW3 | 46 | 26 84 B |
| Belson Rd. SE18 | 65 | 42 78 B |
| Beltane Dri. SW19 | 85 | 23 72 D |
| Belthorn Cres. SW12 | 86 | 29 73 A |
| Beltinge Rd. Rom | 30 | 54 89 B |
| Belton Rd. E11 | 50 | 39 85 A |
| Belton Rd. E7 | 50 | 40 84 D |
| Belton Rd. N17 | 25 | 33 89 A |
| Belton Rd. NW2 | 45 | 22 84 A |
| Belton Rd. Sid | 90 | 46 71 A |
| Belton Way. E3 | 57 | 37 81 A |
| Beltran Rd. SW6 | 73 | 25 76 D |
| Beltwood Rd. Belv | 67 | 50 78 A |
| Belvedere Ave. Ilf | 28 | 43 90 D |
| Belvedere Ave. SW19 | 85 | 24 71 C |
| Belvedere Bldgs. SE1 | 7 | 31 79 B |
| Belvedere Cl. Tedd | 83 | 15 71 C |
| Belvedere Ct. N2 | 35 | 26 88 B |
| Belvedere Dri. SW19 | 85 | 24 71 C |
| Belvedere Gr. SW19 | 85 | 24 71 C |
| Belvedere Pl. SE1 | 7 | 31 79 B |
| Belvedere Rd. Bexh | 79 | 48 76 D |
| Belvedere Rd. E10 | 38 | 36 87 C |
| Belvedere Rd. SE19 | 97 | 33 70 D |
| Belvedere Rd. SE1 | 7 | 30 79 B |
| Belvedere Sq. SW19 | 85 | 24 71 C |
| Belvedere Strand. NW9 | 22 | 21 90 D |
| Belvedere Way. Har | 33 | 18 88 C |
| Belvill Allen Cl. SW17 | 86 | 27 71 D |
| Belvior Cl. SE9 | 89 | 42 72 C |
| Belvoir Rd. SE22 | 87 | 34 73 A |
| Belvue Cl. Nthlt | 43 | 13 84 C |
| Belvue Rd. Nthlt | 43 | 13 84 C |
| Bembridge Cl. NW6 | 46 | 24 84 C |
| Bembridge Gdns. Ruis | 31 | 08 86 B |
| Bemerton St. N1 | 47 | 30 83 B |
| Bemish Rd. SW15 | 73 | 23 75 B |
| Bempton Dri. Ruis | 31 | 10 86 D |
| Bemsted Rd. E17 | 26 | 36 89 B |
| Benares Rd. SE18 | 66 | 45 78 B |
| Benbow Rd. W6 | 61 | 22 79 D |
| Benbow St. SE8 | 64 | 37 77 A |
| Benbury Cl. Brom | 88 | 38 71 C |
| Bench Field. S Croy | 112 | 33 64 D |
| Bench The. Rich | 83 | 17 72 C |
| Bencroft Rd. SW16 | 96 | 29 70 C |
| Bencurtis Park. W Wick | 106 | 38 65 D |
| Bendall Mews. NW1 | 1 | 27 81 A |
| Bendemeer Rd. SW15 | 73 | 23 75 B |
| Bendish Rd. E6 | 50 | 42 84 C |
| Bendmore Ave. SE2 | 66 | 46 78 A |
| Bendon Valley. SW18 | 85 | 25 73 A |
| Benedict Cl. Orp | 108 | 45 65 C |
| Benedict Dri. Felt | 81 | 08 73 B |
| Benedict Rd. Mit | 96 | 26 68 B |
| Benedict Rd. SW9 | 74 | 30 75 B |
| Benedict Way. N2 | 23 | 26 89 A |
| Benenden Green. Brom | 107 | 40 67 A |
| Benett Gdns. SW16 | 96 | 30 69 C |
| Benfleet Cl. Sutt | 103 | 26 65 C |
| Bengal Ct. EC3 | 4 | 32 81 D |
| Bengal Rd. Ilf | 40 | 43 86 D |
| Bengarth Dri. Har | 20 | 14 90 D |
| Bengarth Rd. Nthlt | 43 | 12 83 A |
| Bengeworth Rd. Har | 33 | 16 86 C |
| Bengeworth Rd. SE5 | 75 | 32 75 A |
| Benham Cl. SW11 | 73 | 26 75 B |
| Benham Rd. W7 | 54 | 15 81 A |
| Benhill Ave. Sutt | 110 | 25 64 B |
| Benhill Ave. Sutt | 110 | 26 64 A |
| Benhill Rd. SE5 | 75 | 32 76 B |
| Benhill Rd. Sutt | 110 | 26 64 B |
| Benhill Wood Rd. Sutt | 110 | 26 64 A |
| Benhilton Gdns. Sutt | 103 | 25 65 D |
| Benhurst Ave. Horn | 42 | 52 86 D |
| Benhurst Ct. SW16 | 87 | 31 71 C |
| Benhurst La. SW16 | 87 | 31 71 C |
| Benin St. SE13 | 88 | 38 73 B |
| Benjamin Cl. E8 | 48 | 34 83 A |
| Benjamin Cl. Rom | 42 | 52 88 C |
| Benjamin St. EC1 | 3 | 31 81 B |
| Ben Jonson Rd. E1 | 57 | 36 81 A |
| Benledi St. E14 | 58 | 38 81 D |
| Bennerley Rd. SW11 | 74 | 27 74 B |
| Bennet Cl. King | 93 | 17 69 A |
| Bennett Cl. Nthwd | 19 | 09 91 D |
| Bennett Cl. Well | 78 | 46 76 C |
| Bennett Gr. SE13 | 76 | 37 76 B |
| Bennett Park. SE3 | 77 | 39 75 B |
| Bennett Rd. E13 | 58 | 41 82 C |
| Bennett Rd. Rom | 41 | 48 87 A |
| Bennetts Ave. Croy | 106 | 36 65 A |
| Bennetts Ave. Grnf | 44 | 15 83 A |
| Bennett's Castle La. Dag | 52 | 47 85 A |
| Bennett's Castle La. Dag | 41 | 47 86 D |
| Bennetts Cl. N17 | 25 | 33 91 B |
| Bennetts Copse. Chis | 99 | 42 70 A |
| Bennett's Hill. EC4 | 8 | 32 80 A |
| Bennett St. SW1 | 6 | 29 80 C |
| Bennett St. W4 | 61 | 21 77 A |
| Bennetts Way. Croy | 106 | 36 65 B |
| Bennett's Yd. SW1 | 6 | 29 79 D |
| Benningholme Rd. Edg | 22 | 21 91 A |
| Bennington Rd. N17 | 25 | 33 90 A |
| Bennington Rd. Wdf Gn | 27 | 39 91 C |
| Benn's Alley. Hamp | 92 | 13 69 D |
| Benn St. E9 | 49 | 36 84 A |
| Benrek Cl. Ilf | 28 | 44 90 A |
| Bensbury Cl. SW15 | 85 | 23 73 A |
| Bensham Cl. Th Hth | 97 | 32 68 C |
| Bensham Gr. Th Hth | 97 | 32 69 C |
| Bensham La. Croy | 105 | 31 67 D |
| Bensham La. Th Hth | 105 | 31 67 D |
| Bensham Manor Rd. Th Hth | 97 | 32 68 C |
| Ben Smith Way. SE16 | 63 | 34 79 C |
| Benson Ave. E6 | 50 | 41 83 D |
| Benson Cl. Houn | 70 | 13 75 C |
| Benson Rd. Croy | 105 | 31 65 C |
| Benson Rd. SE23 | 88 | 35 73 C |
| Bentfield Gdns. SE9 | 89 | 41 72 D |
| Benthal Rd. N16 | 37 | 34 86 C |
| Bentham Ct. N1 | 48 | 32 84 C |
| Bentham Rd. E9 | 49 | 35 84 B |
| Bentham Wlk. N10 | 45 | 20 85 D |
| Ben Tillet Cl. Bark | 51 | 46 84 C |
| Bentinck Mews. W1 | 2 | 28 81 C |
| Bentinck St. W1 | 2 | 28 81 C |
| Bentley Cl. SW19 | 85 | 25 72 C |
| Bentley Dri. Ilf | 40 | 44 88 C |
| Bentley Rd. N1 | 48 | 33 84 A |
| Benton Gdns. Ilf | 40 | 44 87 D |
| Benton Rd. Ilf | 40 | 44 87 D |
| Benton's La. SE27 | 87 | 32 71 A |
| Benton's Rise. SE27 | 87 | 32 71 D |
| Bentry Cl. Dag | 41 | 48 86 A |
| Bentry Rd. Dag | 41 | 48 86 A |
| Bentworth Rd. W12 | 55 | 22 81 D |
| Benwell Rd. N5 | 48 | 31 85 C |
| Benwick Ct. SE20 | 98 | 35 69 A |
| Benwood Ct. Sutt | 103 | 26 65 C |
| Benworth St. E3 | 57 | 36 82 B |
| Benyon Rd. N1 | 48 | 32 83 B |
| Berber Rd. SW11 | 74 | 27 74 B |
| Bercta Rd. SE9 | 90 | 44 72 A |
| Berenger Wlk. SW10 | 62 | 26 77 D |
| Berenger Wlk. SW10 | 62 | 26 77 D |
| Berens Rd. NW10 | 56 | 23 82 B |
| Berens Way. Chis | 100 | 45 68 B |
| Beresford Ave. N20 | 16 | 27 93 B |
| Beresford Ave. NW10 | 45 | 19 83 A |
| Beresford Ave. Surb | 102 | 20 66 A |
| Beresford Ave. Twick | 71 | 17 74 C |
| Beresford Ave. W7 | 54 | 15 81 A |
| Beresford Dri. Brom | 99 | 42 68 A |
| Beresford Gdns. Enf | 13 | 33 96 C |
| Beresford Gdns. Houn | 70 | 12 74 B |
| Beresford Gdns. Rom | 41 | 48 88 A |
| Beresford Ho. SE21 | 87 | 34 72 C |
| Beresford Rd. E17 | 26 | 37 90 B |
| Beresford Rd. Har | 32 | 14 88 B |
| Beresford Rd. King | 93 | 18 69 B |
| Beresford Rd. N2 | 24 | 27 89 A |
| Beresford Rd. N5 | 48 | 32 85 D |
| Beresford Rd. N8 | 37 | 31 88 B |
| Beresford Rd. N Mal | 94 | 20 68 C |
| Beresford Rd. Sthl | 53 | 11 80 D |
| Beresford Rd. Sutt | 110 | 24 63 D |
| Beresford Sq. SE18 | 66 | 43 78 B |
| Beresford St. SE18 | 66 | 43 79 D |
| Beresford Terr. N5 | 48 | 32 85 C |
| Bere St. E1 | 57 | 35 80 B |
| Berestede Rd. W6 | 61 | 21 78 D |
| Berger Cl. Orp | 108 | 45 67 C |
| Berger Rd. E9 | 49 | 35 84 B |
| Berghem Mews. W14 | 62 | 23 79 D |
| Bergholt Ave. Ilf | 39 | 42 88 A |
| Bergholt Cres. N16 | 37 | 33 87 A |
| Bering Wlk. E16 | 58 | 41 81 D |
| Berkeley Ave. Bexh | 79 | 47 76 B |
| Berkeley Ave. Grnf | 44 | 15 84 A |
| Berkeley Ave. Houn | 69 | 10 76 A |
| Berkeley Ave. Ilf | 28 | 43 90 D |
| Berkeley Ave. Rom | 29 | 50 91 C |
| Berkeley Cl. Brent | 60 | 16 77 A |
| Berkeley Cl. Ruis | 31 | 10 86 C |
| Berkeley Cres. Barn | 11 | 26 95 D |
| Berkeley Ct. N14 | 16 | 29 94 A |
| Berkeley Dri. E Mol | 92 | 13 68 A |
| Berkeley Gdns. N21 | 17 | 32 94 B |
| Berkeley Gdns. W8 | 56 | 25 80 C |
| Berkeley Mews. W1 | 1 | 27 81 D |
| Berkeley Pl. SW19 | 95 | 23 70 B |
| Berkeley Rd. E12 | 50 | 42 85 C |
| Berkeley Rd. N15 | 37 | 32 88 D |
| Berkeley Rd. N8 | 36 | 29 88 D |
| Berkeley Rd. NW9 | 34 | 19 88 A |
| Berkeley Rd. SW13 | 72 | 22 76 A |
| Berkeley Sq. W1 | 6 | 28 80 B |
| Berkeley St. W1 | 6 | 28 80 D |
| Berkeley Waye. Houn | 59 | 12 77 C |
| Berkeley Wlk. N7 | 36 | 30 86 B |
| Berkely Cl. Orp | 108 | 45 66 A |
| Berkhampstead Rd. Belv | 67 | 49 78 C |
| Berkhamsted Ave. Wem | 45 | 19 84 A |
| Berkley Gr. NW1 | 47 | 28 84 C |
| *Berkley Rd. NW1 | 47 | 27 84 D |
| Berkshire Gdns. N13 | 25 | 31 91 A |
| Berkshire Gdns. N18 | 17 | 34 92 D |
| Berkshire Rd. E9 | 49 | 36 84 B |
| Berkshire Way. Mit | 104 | 30 67 A |
| Berkshire Way. Mit | 96 | 30 68 C |
| Bermans Way. NW10 | 45 | 21 85 B |
| Bermondsey St. SE1 | 8 | 33 79 A |
| Bermondsey Trading Estate. SE16 | 64 | 35 78 C |
| Bermondsey Wall E. SE16 | 63 | 34 79 B |
| Bermondsey Wall W. SE16 | 63 | 34 79 A |
| Bermonsey Sq. SE1 | 8 | 33 79 C |
| Bernard Ave. W13 | 60 | 16 79 D |
| Bernard Cassidy St. E16 | 58 | 39 81 B |
| Bernard Gdns. SW19 | 85 | 25 71 C |
| Bernard Rd. N15 | 37 | 33 88 B |
| Bernard Rd. Rom | 41 | 50 87 A |
| Bernard Rd. Wall | 111 | 28 64 B |
| Bernard St. WC1 | 3 | 30 82 C |
| Bernays Cl. Stan | 21 | 17 91 A |
| Bernay's Gr. SW9 | 74 | 30 75 B |
| Bernel Dri. Croy | 106 | 36 65 D |
| Berne Rd. Th Hth | 105 | 32 67 A |
| Berners Mews. W1 | 2 | 29 81 A |
| Berners Pl. W1 | 2 | 29 81 C |
| Berners Rd. N1 | 48 | 31 83 B |
| Berners Rd. N22 | 25 | 31 90 C |
| Berners St. W1 | 2 | 29 81 C |
| Berney Rd. Croy | 105 | 32 66 B |
| Berridge Green. Edg | 22 | 19 91 C |
| Berridge Rd. SE19 | 87 | 33 71 C |
| Berriman Rd. N7 | 36 | 30 86 D |
| Berriton Rd. Har | 32 | 12 87 D |
| Berry Cl. N21 | 17 | 31 94 D |
| Berry Cl. NW10 | 45 | 21 84 C |
| Berryfield Rd. SE17 | 63 | 31 78 D |
| Berryhill Gdns. SE9 | 78 | 43 75 D |
| Berryhill. SE9 | 78 | 43 75 D |
| Berrylands Rd. Surb | 101 | 18 67 D |
| Berrylands. Surb | 102 | 19 67 A |
| Berrylands. SW20 | 95 | 23 68 C |
| Berryman Cl. Dag | 41 | 47 86 C |
| Berryman's La. SE26 | 88 | 35 71 B |
| Berrymead Gdns. W3 | 61 | 20 79 A |
| Berrymede Rd. W4 | 61 | 20 79 D |
| Berry Pl. EC1 | 3 | 31 82 B |
| Berry St. EC1 | 3 | 31 82 D |
| Berry Way. W5 | 60 | 18 79 C |
| Bertal Rd. SW17 | 85 | 26 71 B |
| Berther Rd. Horn | 42 | 54 87 A |
| Berthon St. SE8 | 64 | 37 77 B |
| Bertie Rd. NW10 | 45 | 22 84 A |
| Bertram Cottages. SW19 | 95 | 25 70 C |
| Bertram Rd. Enf | 13 | 34 96 C |
| Bertram Rd. King | 94 | 19 70 C |
| Bertram Rd. NW4 | 34 | 22 88 C |
| Bertram St. N19 | 36 | 28 86 B |
| Bertrand St. SE13 | 76 | 37 75 B |
| Bert Rd. Th Hth | 105 | 32 67 A |
| Bert Way. Enf | 13 | 33 96 D |
| Berwick Ave. Hay | 53 | 11 80 B |
| Berwick Cres. Sid | 78 | 45 74 C |
| Berwick Rd. E16 | 58 | 41 81 C |
| Berwick Rd. E17 | 26 | 36 89 D |
| Berwick Rd. N22 | 25 | 31 90 B |
| Berwick Rd. Well | 78 | 46 76 B |
| Berwick St. W1 | 2 | 29 81 C |
| Berwyn Ave. Houn | 70 | 13 76 B |
| Berwyn Rd. Rich | 72 | 19 75 D |
| Berwyn Rd. SE24 | 87 | 31 73 D |
| Beryl Rd. W6 | 62 | 23 78 D |
| Berystede. King | 94 | 19 70 D |
| Besant Ct. N1 | 48 | 32 85 B |
| Besant Rd. NW2 | 46 | 24 85 A |
| Besant Way. NW10 | 45 | 20 85 C |
| Besant Wlk. N7 | 36 | 30 86 B |
| Besley St. SW16 | 96 | 29 70 A |
| Bessborough Gdns. SW1 | 10 | 29 78 D |
| Bessborough Mews. SW1 | 10 | 29 78 D |
| Bessborough Pl. SW1 | 10 | 29 78 D |
| Bessborough Rd. Har | 32 | 14 87 B |
| Bessborough Rd. SW15 | 84 | 22 73 C |
| Bessborough St. SW1 | 10 | 29 78 D |
| Bessborough Way. SW1 | 10 | 29 78 D |
| Bessemer Rd. SE5 | 75 | 32 76 D |
| Bessingby Rd. Ruis | 31 | 10 86 B |
| Bessingham Wlk. SE4 | 76 | 35 75 D |
| Besson St. SE14 | 76 | 35 76 B |
| Bessy St. E2 | 57 | 35 82 A |
| Bestwood St. SE8 | 64 | 35 78 B |
| Beswick Mews. NW3 | 46 | 25 84 B |
| Betchworth Cl. Sutt | 110 | 26 64 D |
| Betchworth Rd. Ilf | 40 | 45 86 C |
| Betham Rd. Grnf | 53 | 14 82 B |
| Bethany Waye. Felt | 81 | 09 73 A |
| Bethecar Rd. Har | 33 | 15 88 A |
| Bethell Ave. E16 | 58 | 39 82 D |
| Bethell Ave. Ilf | 40 | 43 87 A |
| Bethel Rd. Well | 79 | 47 75 A |
| Bethersden Cl. Beck | 98 | 36 70 D |
| Bethnal Green Rd. E1 | 4 | 33 82 D |
| Bethnal Green Rd. E2 | 57 | 34 82 A |
| Bethune Ave. N11 | 16 | 27 92 B |
| Bethune Rd. N16 | 37 | 33 87 A |
| Bethune Rd. NW10 | 55 | 20 82 D |
| Bethwin Rd. SE5 | 63 | 32 77 C |
| Betony Rd. Rom | 30 | 53 91 B |
| Betsham Rd. Eri | 68 | 51 77 D |
| Betstyle Rd. N11 | 16 | 28 92 B |
| Betterton St. WC2 | 3 | 30 81 C |
| Bettons Park. E15 | 50 | 39 83 A |
| Bettridge Rd. SW6 | 73 | 24 76 D |
| Betts Cl. Beck | 98 | 36 69 C |
| Betts Rd. E16 | 58 | 40 80 B |
| Betts St. E1 | 57 | 34 80 B |
| Betts Way. Surb | 101 | 16 66 C |
| Beulah Ave. Th Hth | 97 | 32 69 C |
| Beulah Cres. Th Hth | 97 | 32 69 C |
| Beulah Gr. Croy | 105 | 32 67 C |
| Beulah Hill. SE19 | 97 | 32 70 D |
| Beulah Path. E17 | 38 | 37 88 B |
| Beulah Rd. E17 | 38 | 37 88 B |
| Beulah Rd. Horn | 42 | 54 86 D |
| Beulah Rd. Sutt | 110 | 25 64 A |
| Beulah Rd. SW19 | 95 | 24 70 D |
| Beulah Rd. Th Hth | 97 | 32 68 A |
| Beult Rd. Dart | 80 | 52 75 C |
| Bevan Ave. Bark | 51 | 46 84 C |
| Bevan Ct. Croy | 112 | 31 64 C |
| Bevan Rd. Barn | 12 | 27 96 D |
| Bevan Rd. SE2 | 66 | 46 78 D |
| Bevan St. N1 | 48 | 32 83 A |
| Bevan Way. Horn | 42 | 54 86 D |
| Bevenden St. N1 | 4 | 32 82 B |
| Bevercote Wlk. Belv | 67 | 48 77 B |
| Beverley Ave. Houn | 70 | 12 75 D |
| Beverley Ave. Sid | 90 | 45 73 B |
| Beverley Ave. SW20 | 94 | 21 69 B |
| Beverley Cl. Enf | 13 | 33 96 C |
| Beverley Cl. Horn | 42 | 54 87 B |
| Beverley Cl. N21 | 17 | 32 94 C |
| Beverley Cl. SW11 | 73 | 26 75 D |
| Beverley Cl. SW13 | 72 | 22 76 C |
| Beverley Cres. Wdf Gn | 27 | 40 91 D |
| Beverley Ct. SE4 | 76 | 36 75 B |
| Beverley Dri. Edg | 22 | 19 89 A |
| Beverley Gdns. Horn | 42 | 54 87 B |
| Beverley Gdns. NW11 | 35 | 24 87 A |
| Beverley Gdns. Stan | 21 | 16 90 A |
| Beverley Gdns. SW13 | 72 | 21 75 B |
| Beverley Gdns. Wem | 34 | 19 87 C |
| Beverley Gdns. Wor Pk | 102 | 22 66 C |
| Beverley Hyrst. Croy | 105 | 33 65 B |
| Beverley La. King | 94 | 21 70 C |
| Beverley La. SW19 | 84 | 21 71 B |
| Beverley Path. SW13 | 72 | 21 76 D |
| Beverley Rd. Bexh | 79 | 50 76 C |
| Beverley Rd. Brom | 107 | 42 65 A |
| Beverley Rd. Dag | 52 | 48 85 A |
| Beverley Rd. E4 | 26 | 38 91 B |
| Beverley Rd. E6 | 58 | 41 82 B |
| Beverley Rd. King | 93 | 17 69 A |
| Beverley Rd. Mit | 96 | 29 68 D |
| Beverley Rd. N Mal | 94 | 22 68 C |
| Beverley Rd. Ruis | 31 | 10 86 B |
| Beverley Rd. SE20 | 97 | 34 69 D |
| Beverley Rd. Sthl | 59 | 12 79 C |
| Beverley Rd. Sun | 91 | 09 69 B |
| Beverley Rd. SW13 | 72 | 21 75 B |
| Beverley Rd. W4 | 61 | 21 78 D |
| Beverley Rd. Wor Pk | 103 | 23 65 A |
| Beverley Way. N Mal | 94 | 22 68 C |
| Beverley Way. SW20 | 94 | 22 69 C |
| Beverly Ct. N14 | 16 | 29 94 A |
| Beversbrook Rd. N19 | 36 | 29 86 D |
| Beverstone Rd. SW2 | 74 | 30 74 B |
| Beverstone Rd. Th Hth | 97 | 31 68 D |
| Bevington Rd. Beck | 98 | 37 69 D |
| Bevington Rd. W10 | 56 | 24 81 A |
| Bevington St. SE16 | 63 | 34 79 A |
| Bevin Way. WC1 | 3 | 31 82 A |
| Bevis Marks. EC3 | 4 | 33 81 C |
| Bewcastle Gdns. Enf | 12 | 30 96 C |
| Bewdley St. N1 | 48 | 31 84 C |
| Bewick St. SW8 | 74 | 28 76 D |
| Bewley St. E1 | 57 | 35 80 A |
| Bewlys Rd. SE27 | 87 | 31 71 D |
| Bexhill Cl. Felt | 82 | 12 72 A |
| Bexhill Rd. N11 | 16 | 29 92 D |
| Bexhill Rd. SE4 | 76 | 36 74 D |
| Bexhill Rd. SW14 | 72 | 20 75 A |
| Bexley Cl. Dart | 80 | 51 74 A |
| Bexley Gdns. N9 | 17 | 32 92 D |
| Bexley La. Dart | 80 | 51 74 A |
| Bexley Rd. Eri | 67 | 50 77 A |
| Bexley Rd. SE9 | 78 | 44 74 A |
| Beynon Rd. Cars | 111 | 27 64 D |
| Bianca Rd. SE15 | 63 | 34 77 A |
| Bibsworth Rd. N3 | 23 | 24 90 D |
| Bibury Cl. SE15 | 63 | 33 77 A |
| Bicester Rd. Rich | 72 | 19 75 B |
| Bickenhall St. W1 | 1 | 27 81 B |
| Bickersteth Rd. SW17 | 96 | 27 70 B |
| Bickersteth Rd. SW17 | 86 | 27 71 D |
| Bickerton Rd. N19 | 36 | 29 86 A |
| Bickley Cres. Brom | 99 | 42 68 C |
| Bickley Park Rd. Brom | 99 | 42 68 B |
| Bickley Rd. Brom | 99 | 42 69 C |
| Bickley Rd. E10 | 38 | 37 87 B |
| Bickley St. SW17 | 86 | 27 71 D |
| Bicknell Rd. SE5 | 75 | 32 75 A |
| Bicknoller Cl. Sutt | 110 | 25 62 D |
| Bicknoller Rd. Enf | 13 | 33 97 B |
| Bicknor Rd. Orp | 108 | 45 66 B |
| Bidborough Cl. Brom | 107 | 39 67 B |
| Bidborough St. WC1 | 3 | 30 82 A |
| Biddenden Way. SE9 | 90 | 43 71 A |
| Bidder St. E16 | 58 | 39 81 A |
| Bidder St. E16 | 58 | 39 82 C |
| Biddestone Rd. N7 | 47 | 30 85 B |
| Biddulph Rd. S Croy | 112 | 32 62 A |
| Biddulph Rd. W9 | 56 | 25 82 B |
| Bideford Ave. Grnf | 44 | 16 83 D |
| Bideford Cl. Edg | 22 | 19 90 A |
| Bideford Cl. Felt | 82 | 12 72 D |
| Bideford Cl. Rom | 30 | 53 90 A |
| Bideford Gdns. Enf | 17 | 33 94 A |
| Bideford Rd. Brom | 89 | 39 72 D |
| Bideford Rd. Ruis | 32 | 11 86 C |
| Bideford Rd. SE2 | 66 | 46 77 D |
| Bidwell Gdns. N11 | 24 | 29 91 C |
| Bidwell St. SE15 | 75 | 34 76 B |
| Bigbury Cl. N17 | 25 | 33 91 C |
| Biggerstaff Rd. E15 | 49 | 38 83 A |
| Biggerstaff St. N4 | 37 | 31 86 A |
| Biggin Ave. Mit | 96 | 27 69 B |
| Biggin Hill. SE19 | 97 | 31 70 D |
| Biggin Way. SE19 | 97 | 32 70 C |
| Bigginwood Rd. SW16 | 97 | 31 70 D |
| Bigg's Row. SW15 | 73 | 23 75 B |
| Big Hill. E5 | 37 | 34 87 D |
| Bigland St. E1 | 57 | 34 81 D |
| Bignold Rd. E7 | 50 | 40 85 A |
| Bigwood Rd. NW11 | 35 | 25 88 D |
| Billet La. Horn | 42 | 53 87 D |
| Billet Rd. E17 | 26 | 36 90 B |
| Billet Rd. Rom | 29 | 47 89 B |
| Billingford Cl. SE4 | 76 | 35 75 D |
| Billing Pl. SW10 | 62 | 25 77 D |
| Billing Rd. SW10 | 62 | 25 77 D |
| Billing St. SW10 | 62 | 25 77 D |
| Billington Rd. SE14 | 64 | 35 77 D |
| Billiter Sq. EC3 | 4 | 33 81 C |
| Billiter St. EC3 | 4 | 33 81 C |
| Billson St. E14 | 64 | 38 78 A |
| Bilsby Gr. SE9 | 89 | 41 71 B |
| Bilton Rd. Eri | 68 | 52 77 A |
| Bilton Rd. Grnf | 44 | 16 83 B |
| Bilton Way. Enf | 14 | 36 97 A |
| Bina Gdns. SW5 | 62 | 26 78 A |
| Bincote Rd. Enf | 12 | 30 96 B |
| Binden Rd. W12 | 61 | 21 79 D |
| Bindon Green. Mord | 95 | 25 68 D |
| Binfield Rd. S Croy | 112 | 33 64 D |
| Binfield Rd. SW4 | 74 | 30 76 A |
| Bingfield St. N1 | 47 | 30 83 B |
| Bingham Pl. W1 | 2 | 28 81 A |
| Bingham Rd. Croy | 105 | 34 66 D |
| Bingham St. N1 | 48 | 32 84 B |
| Bingley Rd. E16 | 58 | 41 81 C |
| Bingley Rd. Grnf | 53 | 14 81 A |
| Bingley Rd. Sun | 91 | 10 70 C |
| Binney St. W1 | 2 | 28 81 C |
| Binns Rd. W4 | 61 | 21 78 C |
| Binsey Wlk. SE2 | 67 | 47 79 A |
| Binton Rd. SW19 | 95 | 26 70 B |
| Binyon Cres. Stan | 21 | 15 91 B |
| Birbeck Gr. W3 | 61 | 20 79 B |
| Birbeck Hill. SE21 | 87 | 31 73 D |
| Birbeck Pl. SE21 | 87 | 32 72 A |
| Birbeck Rd. N12 | 15 | 26 92 C |
| Birbetts Rd. SE9 | 89 | 42 72 B |
| Bircham Path. SE4 | 76 | 35 75 D |
| Birchanger Rd. SE25 | 105 | 34 67 A |
| Birch Ave. N13 | 17 | 32 93 C |
| Birchbeck Rd. Sid | 90 | 46 72 C |
| Birch Cl. Brent | 60 | 16 77 D |
| Birch Cl. E16 | 58 | 39 81 A |
| Birch Cl. N19 | 36 | 29 86 A |
| Birch Cl. Rom | 29 | 49 89 B |
| Birch Cl. SE15 | 75 | 34 76 C |
| Birch Cres. Horn | 30 | 54 89 C |
| Birchdale Gdns. Rom | 41 | 47 87 B |
| Birchdale Rd. E7 | 50 | 41 85 C |
| Birchen Cl. NW9 | 34 | 20 86 B |
| Birchen Gr. NW9 | 34 | 20 86 B |
| Birches Cl. Pnr | 32 | 12 88 A |
| Birches The. N21 | 12 | 30 95 D |
| Birches The. SE7 | 65 | 40 77 B |
| Birchfield Gr. Eps | 110 | 23 62 C |
| Birchfield St. E14 | 57 | 37 80 A |
| Birch Gdns. Dag | 41 | 50 86 C |
| Birch Green. NW9 | 22 | 21 91 C |
| Birch Gr. SE12 | 89 | 39 73 B |
| Birch Gr. Shep | 91 | 09 69 C |
| Birch Gr. W3 | 55 | 19 80 A |
| Birch Gr. Well | 78 | 46 75 C |
| Birchington Cl. Bexh | 79 | 49 76 B |
| Birchington Rd. N8 | 36 | 29 88 D |
| Birchington Rd. NW6 | 46 | 25 83 A |
| Birchington Rd. Surb | 101 | 18 66 B |
| Birchin La. EC3 | 4 | 32 81 D |
| Birchlands Ave. SW12 | 86 | 27 73 B |
| Birchmead Ave. Pnr | 20 | 11 89 C |
| Birch Mead. Orp | 108 | 43 65 A |
| Birchmere Row. SE3 | 77 | 39 76 D |
| Birchmore Wlk. N5 | 37 | 32 86 C |
| Birch Park. Har | 20 | 14 91 C |
| Birch Rd. Felt | 82 | 11 71 C |
| Birch Rd. Rom | 29 | 49 89 B |
| Birch Row. Brom | 108 | 43 66 A |
| Birch Tree Way. Croy | 105 | 34 65 B |
| Birch Wlk. Eri | 67 | 50 77 A |
| Birch Wlk. Mit | 96 | 28 69 B |

Birchwood Ave. Beck 98 36 68 D
Birchwood Ave. N10 24 28 89 C
Birchwood Ave. Sid 90 46 72 B
Birchwood Ave. Sid 90 46 72 D
Birchwood Ave. Wall 104 28 65 C
Birchwood Ct. Edg 22 20 90 C
Birchwood Gr. Hamp 92 13 70 B
Birchwood Rd. Orp 100 45 68 C
Birchwood Rd. SW17 86 28 71 D
Birdbrook Cl. Dag 52 50 84 C
Birdbrook Rd. SE3 77 41 75 A
Birdcage Wlk. SW1 6 29 79 B
Birdham Cl. Brom 107 42 67 A
Birdhurst Ave. S Croy 112 32 64 B
Birdhurst Ct. Wall 111 29 63 C
Birdhurst Gdns. S Croy 112 32 64 B
Birdhurst Rd. S Croy 112 33 64 C
Birdhurst Rd. SW18 73 26 74 A
Birdhurst Rd. SW19 96 27 70 A
Birdhurst Rise. S Croy 112 33 64 C
Bird-in-Bush Rd. SE15 63 34 77 C
Bird-in-hand La. Brom 99 41 69 D
Bird-in-hand Pas. SE23 88 35 72 A
Bird in Hand Path. Croy 105 32 66 B
*Bird In Hand Yd. NW3 46 26 85 A
Birdlip Cl. SE15 63 33 77 A
Birds Farm Ave. Rom 29 49 90 B
Bird St. W1 2 28 81 C
Bird Wlk. Twick 82 12 73 D
Birdwood Cl. Tedd 83 15 71 A
Birkbeck Ave. Grnf 43 14 83 B
Birkbeck Ave. W3 55 20 80 A
Birkbeck Mews. E8 48 33 85 D
Birkbeck Rd. Beck 98 35 69 D
Birkbeck Rd. E8 48 33 85 D
Birkbeck Rd. Enf 13 32 97 B
Birkbeck Rd. Ilf 40 44 88 B
Birkbeck Rd. N17 25 33 90 B
Birkbeck Rd. N8 24 30 89 C
Birkbeck Rd. Rom 41 50 87 D
Birkbeck Rd. SW19 95 25 70 B
Birkbeck Rd. W3 55 20 80 D
Birkbeck Rd. W5 60 17 78 A
Birkbeck St. E2 57 34 82 B
Birkbeck Way. Grnf 43 14 83 B
Birkdale Ave. Pnr 20 13 89 A
Birkdale Ave. Rom 30 54 91 D
Birkdale Cl. Orp 108 44 66 B
Birkdale Rd. SE2 66 46 78 A
Birkdale Rd. W5 54 18 82 C
Birkenhead Ave. King 93 18 69 B
Birkenhead St. WC1 3 30 82 A
Birkhall Rd. SE6 88 38 72 B
Birkwood Cl. SW12 86 29 73 B
Birley Rd. N20 15 26 93 A
Birley St. SW11 74 28 76 C
Birling Rd. Eri 80 51 76 A
Birnam Rd. N4 36 30 86 B
Biscay Rd. W6 62 23 78 D
Biscoe Cl. Houn 59 13 77 A
Biscoe Way. SE13 76 38 75 B
Bisenden Rd. Croy 105 33 65 A
Bisham Cl. Cars 104 27 66 D
Bisham Gdns. N6 36 28 87 D
Bishop Butt Cl. Orp 108 45 65 D
Bishop Craven Cl. Enf 13 31 97 B
Bishopford Rd. Mord 103 26 67 D
Bishop Gr. N2 36 27 88 C
Bishop Ken Rd. Har 21 15 90 B
Bishop King's Rd. W14 62 24 78 A
Bishop Rd. N14 16 28 94 B
Bishops Ave. Brom 99 41 68 A
Bishops Ave. E13 50 40 83 B
Bishops Ave. Rom 41 47 88 C
Bishop's Ave. SW6 73 24 76 C
Bishops Ave The. N2 35 26 88 D
Bishop's Bridge Rd. W2 1 26 81 C
Bishops Cl. Barn 11 23 95 D
Bishop's Cl. E17 26 37 89 D
Bishop's Cl. Enf 13 34 97 D
Bishops Close. Sutt 103 25 65 C
Bishops Cl. Rich 83 17 72 D
Bishops Cl. SE9 90 44 72 A
Bishopscourt. Croy 105 33 65 B
Bishop's Ct. EC4 3 31 81 D
Bishop's Ct. WC2 3 31 81 C
Bishopsgate Church Yd. EC2 4 33 81 C
Bishopsgate. EC2 4 33 81 A
Bishops Gr. Hamp 82 12 71 B
Bishops Gr. N2 36 27 88 C
Bishop's Hall. King 93 17 69 D
Bishop's Mansions. SW6 73 23 76 D
Bishops Park Rd. SW16 96 30 69 A
Bishops Park Rd. SW6 73 24 76 C
Bishop's Pl. Sutt 110 26 64 C
Bishop's Rd. Croy 105 31 66 B
Bishops Rd. N6 36 28 88 C
Bishop's Rd. SW6 62 24 77 B
Bishop's Rd. SW6 62 24 77 D
Bishop's Rd. W7 60 15 79 A
Bishop's Terr. SE11 63 31 78 A
Bishopsthorpe Rd. SE26 88 35 71 B
Bishop St. N1 48 32 83 A
Bishop's Way. E2 49 35 83 C
Bishops Wlk. Chis 100 44 69 A
Bishop's Wlk. Pnr 20 12 89 A
Bishopswood Rd. N6 36 27 87 B
Bishop Way. NW10 45 21 84 C
Bisley Cl. Wor Pk 103 23 66 C
Bispham Rd. NW10 54 18 82 B
Bisson Rd. E15 49 38 83 C
Bisterne Ave. E17 26 38 89 B
Bittacy Cl. NW7 23 23 91 B
Bittacy Ct. NW7 23 24 91 C
Bittacy Hill. NW7 23 23 91 B
Bittacy Park Ave. NW7 15 23 92 D
Bittacy Rd. NW7 23 23 91 B
Bittacy Rise. NW7 23 23 91 B
Bittern Pl. N22 24 30 90 D
Bittern St. SE1 8 32 79 A
Bittoms The. King 93 17 68 B
Bixley Cl. Sthl 59 12 78 B
Blackall St. EC2 4 33 82 C
Blackberry Cl. Shep 91 09 68 C
Blackberry Farm Cl. Houn 59 12 77 C
Blackbird Hill. NW9 34 20 86 A
Blackborne Rd. Dag 52 49 84 B
Black Boy La. N15 37 32 88 A
Blackbrook La. Brom 100 43 68 C
Blackburn Rd. NW6 46 25 84 B
Blackbush Ave. Rom 41 47 88 B
Blackbush Cl. Sutt 110 25 63 D
Blackett St. SW15 73 23 75 B
Blackfen Rd. Sid 78 46 74 C
Blackford Cl. S Croy 112 31 62 B
Blackford's Path. SW15 84 22 73 A
Blackfriars Bridge. EC4 7 31 80 B
Blackfriars Ct. EC4 7 31 80 B
Black Friars La. EC4 3 31 81 D
Blackfriars Pas. EC4 7 31 80 B
Blackfriars Rd. SE1 7 31 80 D
Blackfriars Underpass. EC4 7 31 80 B
Black Gates. Pnr 20 12 89 B
Blackheath Ave. SE10 65 39 77 C
Blackheath Gr. SE3 77 39 76 D
Blackheath Hill. SE10 76 38 76 A
Blackheath Park. SE3 77 40 75 A
Blackheath Rd. SE10 76 37 76 B
Blackheath Rise. SE13 76 38 76 C
Blackheath Vale. SE3 77 39 76 C
Blackheath Village. SE3 77 39 76 D
Black Horse Ct. SE1 8 32 79 D
Blackhorse La. Croy 105 34 66 A
Blackhorse La. E17 26 35 89 B
Blackhorse Rd. E17 26 36 89 C
Blackhorse Rd. SE8 64 36 78 C
Black Horse Rd. Sid 90 46 71 A
Blacklands Rd. SE6 88 38 71 A
Blacklands Terr. SW3 9 27 78 B
Black Lion La. W6 61 22 78 A
Blackmore Ave. Sthl 59 14 80 D
Blackmore's Gr. Tedd 93 16 70 A
Blackpool Rd. SE15 75 34 76 D
Black Prince Rd. SE11 10 30 78 B
Black Prince Rd. SE1 10 30 78 B
Blackshaw Pl. N1 48 33 84 C
Blackshaw Rd. SW17 85 26 71 D
Blackshaw Rd. SW17 96 27 70 A
Black's Rd. W6 62 23 78 A
Blackstock Rd. N4 37 31 86 B
Blackstock Rd. N5 37 31 86 D
Blackstone Ho. SE21 87 34 72 C
Blackstone Rd. NW2 45 23 85 A
Black Swan Yd. SE1 8 33 79 A
Blackthorn Ct. Houn 59 12 77 C
Blackthorne Ave. Croy 106 35 66 C
Blackthorne Dri. E4 18 38 92 B
Blackthorn Gr. Bexh 79 48 75 A
Blackthorn St. E3 57 37 82 C
Blacktree Mews. SW9 75 31 75 A
Blackwall La. E10 65 39 78 B
Blackwall Tunnel App. E14 58 38 81 C
Blackwall Tunnel App. SE10 65 39 79 A
Blackwall Tunnel Northern App.
E14 58 38 81 A
Blackwall Tunnel Northern App.
E3 58 38 82 C
Blackwall Tunnels. SE10 58 39 80 A
Blackwall Way. E14 58 38 80 A
Blackwater Rd. Sutt 110 25 64 D
Blackwater St. SE22 75 33 74 B
Blackwell Cl. E5 49 36 85 A
Blackwell Cl. Har 20 14 91 D
Blackwood St. SE17 63 32 78 D
Blagden's Cl. N14 16 29 93 B
Blagden's La. N14 16 29 93 B
Blagdon Rd. N Mal 94 21 68 D
Blagdon Rd. SE13 76 37 74 D
Blagdon Wlk. Tedd 93 17 70 A
Blagrove Rd. W10 56 24 81 B
Blair Ave. NW9 34 21 87 A
Blair Cl. Sid 78 45 74 A
Blair Ct. Beck 98 37 69 B
Blairderry Rd. SW2 86 30 72 A
Blair St. E14 58 38 81 D
Blake Ave. Bark 51 45 83 B
Blake Cl. Well 78 45 76 A
Blake Gdns. Dart 80 54 75 D
Blake Gdns. SW6 73 25 76 B
Blake Hall Cres. E11 39 40 87 C
Blakehall Rd. Cars 111 27 63 B
Blake Hall Rd. E11 39 40 87 A
Blakemore Rd. SW16 86 30 72 C
Blakemore Rd. Th Hth 104 30 67 B
Blakeney Ave. Beck 98 36 69 B
Blakeney Cl. E8 48 34 85 C
Blakeney Cl. N20 15 26 94 C
Blakeney Rd. Beck 98 36 69 B
Blakenham Rd. SW17 86 27 71 B
Blaker Ct. SE7 65 41 77 C
Blake Rd. Croy 105 33 65 A
Blake Rd. E16 58 39 82 D
Blake Rd. Mit 96 27 68 A
Blake Rd. N11 24 29 91 C
Blaker Rd. E15 49 38 83 C
Blakes Ave. N.Mal 102 21 67 D
Blake's Green. W Wick 106 38 66 C
Blakes La. N.Mal 102 21 67 B
Blakesley Ave. W5 54 17 81 C
Blakesley Wlk. SW20 95 24 69 D
Blake's Rd. SE15 63 33 77 C
Blakes Terr. N.Mal 102 22 67 A
Blakesware Gdns. N9 17 32 94 B
Blakewood Cl. Felt 82 11 71 A
Blanchard Cl. SE9 89 42 72 C
Blanchard Way. E8 48 34 84 A
Blanch Cl. SE15 64 35 77 C
Blanchedowne. SE5 75 32 75 B
Blanche St. E16 58 39 82 D
Blanchland Rd. Mord 103 25 67 B
Blandfield Rd. SW12 86 28 73 A
Blandford Ave. Beck 98 36 69 C
Blandford Ave. Twick 82 13 73 D
Blandford Cl. Croy 104 30 65 C
Blandford Cl. N2 23 26 89 C
Blandford Cl. Rom 29 49 89 D
Blandford Cres. E4 18 38 94 A
Blandford Ct. N1 48 33 84 C
Blandford Rd. Beck 98 35 69 D
Blandford Rd. Sthl 59 13 78 A
Blandford Rd. Tedd 83 15 71 C
Blandford Rd. W4 61 21 79 C
Blandford Rd. W5 60 17 79 B
Blandford Sq. NW1 1 27 82 D
Blandford St. W1 2 28 81 A
Blandford Waye. Hay 53 11 81 C
Bland St. SE9 77 41 75 D
Blanmerle Rd. SE9 90 43 73 D
Blantyre St. SW10 62 26 77 D
Blantyre Wlk. SW10 62 26 77 D
Blashford St. SE13 88 38 73 B
Blawith Rd. Har 21 15 89 D
Blaydon Cl. Ruis 31 09 87 A
Blaydon Wlk. N17 25 34 91 D
Bleak Hill La. SE18 66 45 77 B
Blean Gr. SE20 98 35 70 C
Bleasdale Ave. Grnf 44 16 83 C
Blechynden St. W10 56 23 81 D
Bleddyn Cl. Sid 79 47 74 C
Bledlow Rise. Grnf 43 14 83 C
Bleeding Heart Yd. EC1 3 31 81 A
Blegborough Rd. SW16 96 29 70 A
Blendon Dri. Bex 79 47 74 D
Blendon Path. Brom 99 39 70 D
Blendon Rd. Bex 79 47 74 B
*Blendon Row. SE17 63 32 78 D
Blendon Terr. SE18 66 44 77 A
Blendworth Way (off Lydney Cl).
SE15 63 33 77 C
Blenheim Ave. Ilf 40 43 88 C
Blenheim Centre. SE20 98 35 70 D
Blenheim Cl. Dart 80 53 74 C
Blenheim Cl. Grnf 43 14 83 D
Blenheim Cl. N21 17 32 94 C
Blenheim Cl. Rom 29 50 89 C
Blenheim Cl. SW20 95 23 68 A
Blenheim Cl. Wall 111 29 63 C
Blenheim Cres. Ruis 31 08 86 B
Blenheim Cres. S Croy 112 32 63 C
Blenheim Cres. W11 56 24 81 C
Blenheim Ct. N19 36 30 86 A
Blenheim Ct. Sid 90 44 72 D
Blenheim Ct. Wdf Gn 27 40 91 D
Blenheim Dri. Well 78 45 76 B
Blenheim Gdns. King 94 19 70 D
Blenheim Gdns. NW2 46 23 85 C
Blenheim Gdns. SW2 74 30 74 D
Blenheim Gdns. Wall 111 29 63 C
Blenheim Gdns. Wem 33 18 86 C
Blenheim Gr. SE15 75 34 76 C
Blenheim Park Rd. S Croy 112 32 63 C
Blenheim Pas. NW8 46 26 83 C
Blenheim Rd. Barn 11 23 96 D
Blenheim Rd. Brom 99 42 68 C
Blenheim Rd. Dart 80 53 74 C
Blenheim Rd. E15 50 39 85 A
Blenheim Rd. E17 26 36 89 A
Blenheim Rd. E6 58 41 82 B
Blenheim Rd. Eps 109 21 62 C
Blenheim Rd. Har 32 13 88 D
Blenheim Rd. Nthlt 43 13 84 B
Blenheim Rd. NW8 46 26 83 C
Blenheim Rd. SE20 98 35 70 C
Blenheim Rd. Sutt 103 25 65 D
Blenheim Rd. SW20 95 23 68 A
Blenheim Rd. W4 61 21 79 C
Blenheim St. W1 2 28 81 D
Blenheim Terr. NW8 46 26 83 C
Blenkarne Rd. SW11 74 27 74 D
Bleriot Rd. Houn 59 11 77 C
Blessbury Rd. Edg 22 20 90 A
Blessington Cl. SE13 76 38 75 B
Blessington Rd. SE13 76 38 75 D
Bletchley Ct. N1 48 32 83 D
Bletchley St. N1 48 32 83 C
Bletsoe Wlk. N1 48 32 83 C
Blincoe Cl. SW19 85 23 72 B
Blind Cnr. SE25 97 34 68 D
Blisset St. SE10 76 38 76 A
Blithbury Rd. Dag 51 46 84 B
Blithdale Rd. SE2 66 46 78 A
Blithfield St. W8 62 25 79 D
Blockley Rd. Wem 33 16 86 B
Bloemfontein Ave. W12 55 22 80 D
Bloemfontein Rd. W12 55 22 80 B
Blomfield Rd. W9 1 26 81 A
Blomfield St. EC2 4 32 81 B
Blomfield Villas. W2 1 26 81 A
Blomvill Rd. Dag 41 48 86 C
Blondel St. SW11 74 28 76 C
Blondin Ave. W5 60 17 78 A
Blondin St. E3 49 37 83 C
Bloomburg St. SW1 10 29 78 A
Bloomfield Cres. Ilf 40 43 88 D
Bloomfield Pl. W1 6 28 80 B
Bloomfield Rd. Brom 107 41 67 B
Bloomfield Rd. King 93 18 68 A
Bloomfield Rd. N6 36 28 88 C
Bloomfield Rd. SE18 66 43 78 D
Bloomfield Terr. SW1 9 28 78 C
Bloom Gr. SE27 87 31 72 D
Bloomhall Rd. SE19 87 32 71 D
Bloom Park Rd. SW6 62 24 77 D
Bloomsbury Cl. Eps 109 20 62 D
Bloomsbury Cl. W5 54 18 80 B
Bloomsbury Ct. Pnr 20 12 89 B
Bloomsbury Ct. WC1 3 30 81 A
Bloomsbury Pl. WC1 3 30 81 A
Bloomsbury Sq. WC1 3 30 81 A
Bloomsbury St. WC1 2 29 81 B
Bloomsbury Way. WC1 3 30 81 A
Blore Cl. SW8 74 29 76 B
Blore Ct. W1 6 29 80 B
Blossom Cl. S Croy 112 33 64 D
Blossom Cl. W5 60 18 79 A
Blossom La. Enf 13 32 97 A
Blossom St. E1 4 33 82 C
Blossom Waye. Houn 59 12 77 C
Blount St. E14 57 36 81 C
Bloxam Gdns. SE9 77 42 74 A
Bloxhall Rd. E10 38 36 87 D
Bloxham Cres. Hamp 92 12 69 B
Bloxworth Cl. Wall 104 29 65 C
Blucher Rd. SE5 63 32 77 C
Blue Anchor Alley. Rich 71 18 75 C
Blue Anchor La. SE16 63 34 78 B
Blue Anchor Yd. E1 57 34 80 A
Blue Ball Yd. SW1 6 29 80 C
Bluebell Cl. Orp 108 44 65 A
Bluebell Cl. SE26 87 33 71 A
Bluebell Cl. SE26 87 33 71 B
Bluebell Cl. SE26 87 33 71 B
Bluebird Wlk. Wem 34 19 86 D
Bluefield Cl. Hamp 82 13 71 C
Blundell Rd. Edg 22 21 91 C
Blundell St. N7 47 30 84 A
Blunt Rd. S Croy 112 32 64 D
Blunts Rd. SE9 78 43 74 A
Blurton Rd. E5 49 35 85 B
Blythe Cl. SE6 88 36 73 B
Blythe Hill La. SE6 88 36 73 D
Blythe Hill. Orp 100 46 69 A
Blythe Hill. SE6 88 36 73 B
Blythe Rd. Brom 99 39 69 B
Blythe Rd. W14 62 23 79 D
Blythe Rd. W14 62 24 78 A
Blythe St. E2 57 34 82 B
Blythe Vale. SE6 88 36 73 D
Blyth Rd. E17 38 36 87 B
Blythswood Rd. Ilf 40 46 87 A
Blythwood Rd. N4 36 30 87 B
Blythwood Rd. Pnr 20 11 90 B
Boadicea St. N1 47 30 83 B
Boardman Ave. E4 14 37 95 B
Boar's Head Yd. Brent 60 17 77 D
Boathouse Wlk. Rich 71 18 76 A
Boathouse Wlk. SE15 63 33 77 A
Bobbin Cl. SW4 74 29 75 D
Bockhampton Rd. King 93 18 70 D
Bocking St. E8 49 34 83 B
Boddicott Cl. SW19 85 24 72 A
Bodiam Cl. Enf 13 33 97 C
Bodiam Rd. SW16 96 29 70 D
Bodley Cl. N.Mal 102 21 67 A
Bodley Manor Way. SE24 87 31 73 A
Bodley Rd. N.Mal 102 21 67 A
Bodmin Gr. Mord 103 25 67 B
Bodmin St. SW18 85 25 73 C
Bodnant Gdns. SW20 94 22 68 B
Bodney Rd. E8 48 34 85 D
Boeing Way. Sthl 59 11 79 C
Boevey Path. Belv 67 48 78 D
Bognor Rd. Well 79 47 76 B
Bohemia Pl. E8 49 35 84 A
Bohun Gr. Barn 12 27 95 D
Boileau Rd. SW13 61 22 77 B
Boileau Rd. W5 54 18 81 D
Bolden St. SE8 76 37 76 D
Bolderwood Way. W Wick 106 37 65 B
Boldmere Rd. Pnr 32 11 87 A
Boleyn Ave. Eps 109 22 62 D
Boleyn Ave. Enf 13 34 97 B
Boleyn Dri. E Mol 92 12 68 B
Boleyn Dri. Ruis 32 11 86 B
Boleyn Gdns. Dag 52 50 84 C
Boleyn Gdns. W Wick 106 37 65 B
Boleyn Rd. E6 50 41 83 D
Boleyn Rd. E7 50 40 84 D
Boleyn Rd. N16 48 33 85 C
Boleyn Way. Ilf 28 44 91 A
Bolina Rd. SE16 64 35 78 C
Bolingbroke Gr. SW11 86 27 73 B
Bolingbroke Gr. SW11 74 27 74 A
Bolingbroke Rd. W14 62 23 79 D
Bolingbroke Wlk. SW11 74 27 76 A
Bollo Bridge Rd. W3 61 20 79 C
Bollo Ct. W3 61 20 79 C
Bollo La. W3 61 19 79 D
Bollo La. W4 61 20 78 A
Bolney St. SW8 10 30 77 D
Bolsover St. W1 2 28 82 D
Bolstead Rd. Mit 96 28 69 B
Bolt Ct. EC4 3 31 81 C
Boltmore Cl. NW4 23 23 89 B
Bolton Cres. SE5 63 31 77 D
Bolton Gdns. Brom 99 39 70 B
Bolton Gdns. NW10 46 23 83 D
Bolton Gdns. SW5 62 25 78 D
Bolton Gdns. SW5 62 26 78 C
Bolton Gdns. Tedd 93 16 70 A
Bolton Rd. E15 50 39 84 B
Bolton Rd. Har 20 14 89 D
Bolton Rd. N18 17 33 92 D
Bolton Rd. NW10 45 20 83 A
Bolton Rd. NW8 46 25 83 B
Bolton Rd. W4 61 20 77 C
Bolton's La. Hay 69 08 76 A
Boltons The. Wem 44 15 85 B
Bolton St. W1 6 28 80 D
Bolton The. SW10 62 26 78 C
Bolton Wlk. N7 36 30 86 B
Bombay St. SE16 63 34 78 B
Bomore Rd. W11 56 24 80 A
Bonar Pl. Chis 99 42 70 C
Bonar Rd. SE15 63 34 77 C
Bonchester Cl. Chis 100 43 70 C
Bonchurch Rd. W10 56 24 81 A
Bonchurch Rd. W13 54 16 80 D
Bond Ct. EC4 4 32 81 D
Bondfield Wlk. Dart 80 54 75 B
Bond Gdns. Wall 111 29 64 A
Bond Rd. Mit 96 27 69 D
Bond Rd. Surb 101 18 65 B
Bond St. E15 50 39 85 C
Bond St. W5 54 17 80 B
Bondway. SW8 10 30 77 A
Boneta Rd. SE18 65 42 79 D
Bonfield Rd. SE13 76 38 75 C
Bonham Gdns. Dag 41 47 86 B
Bonham Rd. Dag 41 47 86 D
Bonham Rd. SW2 74 30 74 B
Bonheur Rd. W4 61 20 79 B
Bonhill St. EC2 4 32 82 D
Boniface Gdns. Har 20 13 91 C
Boniface Rd. Uxb 31 07 86 D
Boniface Wlk. Har 20 13 91 C
Bon Marché Terrace Mews. SE27
87 33 71 A
Bonner Hill Rd. King 94 19 68 A
Bonner Rd. E2 49 35 83 C
Bonnersfield Cl. Har 33 16 88 C
Bonnersfield La. Har 33 16 88 C
Bonner St. E2 49 35 83 C
Bonneville Gdns. SW4 74 29 74 C
Bonnington Sq. SW8 10 30 77 B
Bonny St. NW1 47 29 84 C
Bonser Rd. Twick 83 15 72 B
Bonsor St. SE5 63 33 77 C
Bonville Rd. Brom 89 39 71 D
Bookbinders Cott Homes. N20 16 27 93 D
Booker Cl. E14 57 36 81 B
Booker Rd. N18 17 34 92 C
Boones Rd. SE13 77 39 75 C
Boone St. SE13 77 39 75 C
Boord St. SE10 65 39 79 C
Boothby Rd. N19 36 29 86 B
Booth Rd. Croy 105 31 65 B
Booth Rd. NW9 22 21 90 C
Booth's Pl. W1 2 29 81 A
Boot St. N1 4 33 82 A
Bordars Rd. W7 54 15 81 B
Bordars Wlk. W7 54 15 81 A
Borden Ave. Enf 13 32 95 D
Border Cres. SE26 87 34 71 D
Border Gate. Mit 96 27 69 B
Border Rd. SE26 87 34 71 D
Bordesley Rd. Mord 103 25 67 B
Bordesley Rd. Mord 95 25 68 D
Bordon Wlk. SW15 84 22 73 A
Boreas Wlk. N1 48 31 83 D
Boreham Ave. E16 58 40 81 C
Boreham Cl. E10 38 38 87 C
Boreham Rd. N22 25 32 90 C
Borer's Pas. E1 4 33 81 C
Borgard Rd. SE18 65 42 78 B
Borland Rd. SE15 76 35 75 C
Borland Rd. Tedd 93 16 70 D
Borneo St. SW15 73 23 75 A
Borough High St. SE1 8 32 79 A
Borough Hill Croy 105 31 65 D
Borough Rd. Islw 71 15 76 B
Borough Rd. King 94 19 69 A
Borough Rd. Mit 96 27 69 C
Borough Rd. SE1 7 31 79 D
Borough Sq. SE1 8 32 79 A
Borrett Cl. SE17 63 32 78 C
Borrodaile Rd. SW18 73 25 74 D
Borrodale Rd. SW18 73 25 74 D
Borrowdale Ave. Har 21 16 90 C
Borrowdale Cl. Ilf 27 42 89 C
Borthwick Mews. E15 50 39 85 A
Borthwick Rd. E15 50 39 85 A
Borthwick Rd. NW9 34 21 88 D
Borthwick St. SE8 64 37 78 C
Borwick Ave. E17 26 36 89 B
Bosbury Rd. SE6 88 38 72 C
Boscastle Rd. NW5 36 28 86 D
Boscobel Pl. SW1 9 28 78 A
Boscobel St. NW8 1 26 82 D
Boscombe Ave. E10 38 38 87 B
Boscombe Ave. Horn 42 53 87 B
Boscombe Cl. E5 49 36 85 C
Boscombe Rd. SW17 96 28 70 A
Boscombe Rd. SW19 95 25 69 B
Boscombe Rd. W12 61 22 79 A
Boscombe Rd. Wor Pk 103 23 66 D
Bosgrove. E4 18 38 94 C
Boss St. SE1 8 33 79 B
Bostall Hill. SE2 66 46 78 D
Bostall La. SE2 66 46 78 D

Bostall Manorway. SE2 66 46 78 B
Bostall Park Ave. Bexh 67 48 77 C
Bostall Rd. Orp 100 46 70 D
Bostal Row. Bexh 79 48 75 B
Boston Gdns. Brent 60 16 78 B
Boston Gdns. W4 61 21 77 A
Boston Gr. Ruis 31 08 88 C
Boston Manor Rd. Brent 60 16 78 D
Boston Park Rd. Brent 60 17 78 C
Boston Pl. NW1 1 27 82 D
Boston Rd. Croy 105 31 67 C
Boston Rd. Edg 22 20 91 C
Boston Rd. W7 60 15 79 D
Boston St. E2 48 34 83 C
Bostonthorpe Rd. W7 60 15 79 A
Boston Vale. W7 60 16 78 A
Boswell Ct. WC1 3 30 81 A
Boswell Rd. Th Hth 97 32 68 C
Boswell St. WC1 3 30 81 A
Bosworth Cl. E17 26 36 90 B
Bosworth Rd. Barn 11 25 96 B
Bosworth Rd. Dag 41 49 86 C
Bosworth Rd. N11 16 29 92 D
Bosworth Rd. W10 56 24 82 C
Botany Bay La. Chis 100 44 69 C
Boteley Cl. E4 18 38 93 B
Botha Rd. E13 58 41 81 A
Bothwell Cl. E16 58 39 81 B
Bothwell St. W6 62 23 77 B
Botolph Alley. EC3 8 33 80 A
Botolph La. EC3 8 33 80 A
Botsford Rd. SW20 95 24 69 C
Botton Gdns Mews 62 26 78 C
Bott's Mews. W2 56 25 81 C
Boucher Cl. Tedd 83 15 71 D
Boughton Ave. Brom 107 39 66 B
Boughton Rd. SE28 66 45 79 C
Boulcott St. E1 57 35 81 D
Boulogne Rd. Croy 105 32 67 C
Boulton Rd. Dag 41 48 86 D
Bounces La. N9 17 34 93 B
Bounces Rd. N9 18 35 93 A
Boundaries Rd. Felt 82 11 73 C
Boundaries Rd. SW12 86 28 73 C
Boundary Ave. E17 38 36 87 B
Boundary Cl. Ilf 51 45 85 A
Boundary Cl. King 94 19 68 B
Boundary Cl. Sthl 59 13 78 C
Boundary La. E13 58 41 82 D
Boundary La. SE17 63 32 77 A
Boundary Mews. NW8 46 26 83 A
Boundary Pas. E2 4 33 82 D
Boundary Rd. Bark 51 44 83 B
Boundary Rd. Bark 51 44 83 C
Boundary Rd. Cars 111 28 63 C
Boundary Rd. E17 38 37 88 C
Boundary Rd. E6 58 41 82 B
Boundary Rd. Enf 14 35 95 C
Boundary Rd Estate. NW8 46 26 83 A
Boundary Rd. N22 25 32 90 C
Boundary Rd. N2 23 26 90 B
Boundary Rd. NW8 46 26 83 A
Boundary Rd. Pnr 32 11 87 B
Boundary Rd. Rom 42 52 88 C
Boundary Rd. Sid 78 45 74 A
Boundary Rd. SW19 95 26 70 B
Boundary Rd. Wall 111 28 63 C
Boundary Row. SE1 7 31 79 B
Boundary St. E2 4 33 82 D
Boundary St. Eri 68 51 77 D
Boundfield Rd. SE6 89 39 72 A
Bounds Green Rd. N11 24 29 91 B
Bounds Green Rd. N22 24 30 90 A
Bourchier St. W1 6 29 80 B
Bourdon Pl. W1 6 28 80 B
Bourdon Rd. SE20 98 35 69 C
Bourdon St. W1 6 28 80 B
Bourke Cl. NW10 45 21 84 A
Bourke Cl. SW4 74 30 74 C
Bourlet Cl. W1 2 29 81 A
Bourn Ave. Barn 11 26 95 B
Bourn Ave. N15 25 32 89 D
Bournbrook Rd. SE3 77 41 75 B
Bourne Ave. N14 16 30 93 A
Bourne Ave. Ruis 43 11 85 C
Bourne Gdns. E4 18 37 92 B
Bourne Hill. N13 16 30 93 B
Bourne Mead. Bex 79 50 74 B
Bournemouth Rd. SE15 75 34 76 C
Bournemouth Rd. SW19 95 25 69 A
Bourne Pl. W4 61 20 78 D
Bourne Rd. Bex 79 49 74 D
Bourne Rd. Bex 79 50 74 C
Bourne Rd. Brom 99 41 68 D
Bourne Rd. Dart 79 50 74 B
Bourne Rd. E7 39 39 86 D
Bourne Rd. N8 36 30 88 C
Bourne St. Croy 105 31 65 B
Bourne St. SW1 9 28 78 A
Bourne Terr. W2 56 25 81 B
Bourne Terr. W2 56 25 81 B
Bourne The. N14 16 30 94 C
Bourne Vale. Brom 107 40 66 A
Bournevale Rd. SW16 86 30 71 A
Bourne View. Grnf 44 15 85 D
Bourne Way. Brom 107 39 65 B
Bourne Way. Eps 109 20 64 A
Bourne Way. Sutt 110 24 64 D
Bournewood Rd. Orp 108 46 66 B
Bournewood Rd. SE18 66 46 77 C
Bournville Rd. SE6 88 37 73 A
Bournwell Cl. Barn 12 27 97 D
Bousfield Rd. SE14 76 35 76 D
Boutflower Rd. SW11 74 27 75 C
Bouverie Gdns. Har 33 17 88 D
Bouverie Mews. N16 37 33 86 A
Bouverie Pl. W2 1 26 81 D
Bouverie Rd. Har 32 14 88 C
Bouverie Rd. N16 37 33 86 A
Bouverie St. EC4 3 31 81 C
Bovay Pl. N7 47 30 85 B
Bovay St. N7 47 30 85 B
Boveney Rd. SE23 88 35 73 B
Bovill Rd. SE23 88 35 73 B
Bovingdon Ave. Wem 45 19 84 A
Bovingdon Cl. N19 36 29 86 A
Bovingdon La. NW9 22 21 90 A
Bovingdon Rd. SW6 73 25 76 B
Bowater Cl. NW9 34 20 88 B
Bowater Cl. SW4 74 30 74 C
Bowater Pl. SE3 65 40 77 D
Bowater Rd. SE18 65 41 79 D
Bow Churchyard. EC4 4 32 81 C
Bow Common La. E3 57 36 82 D
Bowden Dri. Horn 42 54 87 C
Bowden St. SE11 63 31 78 C
Bowditch. SE8 64 36 78 D
Bowdon Rd. E17 38 37 87 A
Bowen Dri. SE21 87 33 72 C
Bowen Rd. Har 32 14 87 A
Bowen St. E14 57 37 81 D
Bower Ave. SE10 65 39 77 C
Bower Cl. Nthlt 43 11 83 C
Bower Cl. Rom 29 50 91 D
Bowerdean St. SW6 73 25 76 D
Bowerman Ave. SE14 64 36 77 A
Bower St. E1 57 35 81 D
Bowes Cl. Sid 78 46 74 D
Bowes Rd. Dag 52 47 85 A
Bowes Rd. N11 16 29 92 D
Bowes Rd. W3 55 21 80 A
Bowfell Rd. W6 62 23 77 A
Bowford Ave. Bexh 79 48 76 A
Bowie Cl. SW4 86 29 73 B
Bow La. EC4 4 32 81 C
Bow La. Mord 103 24 67 C
Bow La. N12 23 26 91 C
Bowland Rd. SW4 74 29 75 D
Bowland Rd. Wdf Gn 27 41 91 A
Bowl Ct. EC2 4 33 82 C
Bowles Rd. SE1 63 34 77 A
Bowley St. E14 57 36 80 B
Bowling Green Cl. SW15 84 22 73 B
Bowling Green La. EC1 3 31 82 C
Bowling Green Pl. SE1 8 32 79 B
Bowling Green Row. SE18 65 42 78 B
Bowling Green St. SE11 63 31 77 A
Bowling Green Wlk. N1 4 33 82 A
Bowman Ave. E16 58 39 80 B
Bowmans Cl. W13 54 16 80 D
Bowmans Lea. SE23 88 35 73 A
Bowman's Meadow. Wall 104 28 65 D
Bowman's Mews. N7 36 30 86 C
Bowman's Pl. N7 36 30 86 C
Bowmead. SE9 89 42 72 B
Bowmore Wlk. N7 47 29 84 D
Bowness Cl. E8 48 33 84 B
Bowness Cres. SW15 84 21 71 C
Bowness Dri. Houn 70 12 75 C
Bowness Rd. Bexh 79 49 76 D
Bowness Rd. SE6 88 37 73 B
Bowood Rd. Enf 14 35 97 D
Bowood Rd. SW11 74 28 74 A
Bow Rd. E3 57 37 82 D
Bowrons Ave. Wem 44 18 84 C
Bow St. E15 50 39 85 C
Bow St. WC2 3 30 81 C
Bowyer Pl. SE5 63 32 77 C
Bowyer St. SE5 63 32 77 C
Boxall Rd. SE21 87 33 73 A
Boxall Rd. SE21 75 33 74 C
Boxgrove Rd. SE2 67 47 79 C
Boxley Rd. Mord 95 26 68 C
Boxley St. E16 58 40 80 D
Boxmoor Rd. Har 21 16 89 D
Boxmoor Rd. Rom 29 50 91 A
Boxoll Rd. Dag 41 48 86 D
Boxtree La. Har 20 14 91 D
Boxtree Rd. Har 20 14 91 D
Boxworth Gr. N1 47 30 83 B
Boyard Rd. SE18 66 43 78 D
Boyce St. SE1 7 31 80 C
Boyce Way. E13 58 40 82 C
Boycroft Ave. NW9 34 20 88 C
Boyd Ave. Sthl 53 12 80 D
Boyd Cl. King 94 19 70 C
Boydell Ct. NW8 46 26 84 D
Boyd Rd. SW19 95 26 70 B
Boyd St. E1 57 34 81 D
Boyfield St. SE1 7 31 79 B
Boyland Rd. Brom 89 39 71 D
Boyle Ave. Stan 21 16 91 A
Boyle Farm Rd. Surb 101 16 67 C
Boyle St. W1 6 29 80 A
Boyne Ave. NW4 23 23 89 D
Boyne Rd. Dag 41 49 86 C
Boyne Rd. SE13 76 38 75 B
Boyne Terr Mews. W11 56 24 80 D
Boyson Rd. SE17 63 32 77 A
Boyson Wlk. SE17 63 32 77 B
Boythorn Way. SE16 63 34 78 D
Boyton Cl. E1 57 35 82 D
Boyton Cl. N8 24 30 89 A
Boyton Rd. N8 24 30 89 A
Brabant Rd. N22 24 30 90 D
Brabazon Ave. Wall 111 30 63 C
Brabazon Rd. Houn 59 11 77 C
Brabazon Rd. Nthlt 43 13 83 C
Brabazon St. E14 57 37 81 B
Brabourne Cl. SE19 87 33 71 C
Brabourne Cres. Bexh 67 48 77 B
Brabourne Rise. Beck 106 38 67 B
Brabourn Gr. SE15 76 35 76 C
Bracewell Ave. Grnf 44 16 84 A
Bracewell Rd. W10 56 23 81 A
Bracewood Gdns. Croy 105 33 65 D
Bracey St. N4 36 30 86 A
Bracken Ave. Croy 106 37 65 C
Bracken Ave. SW12 86 28 73 A
Brackenbridge Dri. Ruis 32 11 86 D
Brackenbury Gdns. W6 61 22 79 D
Brackenbury Rd. N2 23 26 89 A
Brackenbury Rd. W6 61 22 79 D
Bracken Cl. Houn 82 13 73 A
Brackendale Cl. Houn 70 13 76 B
Brackendale Ct. Beck 98 37 70 C
Brackendale. N21 16 30 93 B
Bracken Dri. Chig 28 43 91 B
Bracken End. Islw 70 14 74 B
Brackenfield Cl. E5 48 34 85 B
Brackenfield Cl. E5 37 34 86 D
Bracken Gdns. SW13 72 22 76 C
Bracken Hill Cl. Brom 99 39 69 B
Bracken Hill La. Brom 99 39 69 B
Brackenhill. Ruis 43 12 85 A
Brackens The. Enf 17 33 94 A
Bracken The. E4 18 38 93 A
Brackenwood. Sun 91 10 69 A
Brackley Cl. Wall 111 30 63 C
Brackley Rd. Beck 98 37 70 C
Brackley Rd. W4 61 21 78 C
Brackley Sq. Wdf Gn 27 41 91 D
Brackley St. EC1 4 32 81 A
Brackley Terr. W4 61 21 78 C
Bracklyn Ct. N1 48 32 83 D
Bracklyn St. N1 48 32 83 D
Bracknell Cl. N22 25 31 90 A
Bracknell Gdns. NW3 46 25 85 B
Bracknell Way. NW3 46 25 85 B
Bracondale Rd. SE2 66 46 78 A
Bradbourne St. SW6 73 25 76 C
Bradbury Cl. Sthl 59 12 78 B
Bradbury St. N16 48 33 85 C
Braddon Rd. Rich 71 18 75 B
Braddyll St. E10 65 39 78 C
Bradenham Ave. Well 78 46 75 C
Bradenham Rd. Har 21 16 89 D
Braden St. W9 56 25 82 D
Bradfield Dri. Bark 51 46 85 C
Bradfield Rd. E16 65 40 79 A
Bradfield Rd. Ruis 43 12 85 C
Bradford Cl. Brom 107 42 66 D
Bradford Cl. SE26 87 34 71 B
Bradford Dri. Eps 109 21 63 B
Bradford Rd. Ilf 40 44 87 D
Bradford Rd. W3 61 21 79 A
Bradgate Rd. SE6 76 37 74 D
Brading Cres. E11 39 40 86 B
Brading Rd. Croy 104 30 67 D
Brading Rd. SW2 86 30 73 B
Bradiston Rd. W9 56 24 82 B
Bradley Cl. N7 47 30 84 B
Bradley Gdns. W13 54 16 81 D
Bradley Rd. N22 24 30 90 D
Bradley Rd. SE19 97 32 70 A
Bradley's Bldgs. N1 48 31 83 C
Bradlord Ho. SE21 87 34 72 C
Bradmead. SW8 10 29 77 C
Bradmore Park Rd. W6 61 22 78 B
Bradstock Rd. E9 49 35 84 B
Bradstock Rd. Eps 109 22 64 D
Brad St. SE1 7 31 80 C
Bradwell Ave. Dag 41 49 86 A
Bradwell Cl. E18 27 39 89 D
Bradwell Mews. N18 17 34 92 A
Brady St. E1 57 34 82 D
Braemar Ave. Bexh 79 50 75 C
Braemar Ave. N22 24 30 90 A
Braemar Ave. NW10 34 20 86 B
Braemar Ave. S Croy 112 32 62 A
Braemar Ave. SW19 85 25 72 A
Braemar Ave. Th Hth 97 31 68 B
Braemar Ave. Wem 44 18 84 C
Braemar Gdns. NW9 22 20 90 B
Braemar Gdns. Sid 90 44 72 D
Braemar Gdns. W Wick 106 38 66 C
Braemar Rd. Brent 60 17 77 B
Braemar Rd. E13 58 39 82 D
Braemar Rd. N15 37 33 88 A
Braemar Rd. Wor Pk 102 22 65 D
Braemore Ct. Barn 12 28 96 C
Braeside Ave. SW19 95 24 69 A
Braeside. Beck 88 37 71 D
Braeside Cl. Pnr 20 13 91 C
Braeside Cres. Bexh 79 50 75 C
Braeside Rd. SW16 96 29 70 C
Braes St. N1 48 31 84 D
Braesyde Cl. Belv 67 48 78 B
Brafferton Rd. Croy 112 32 64 A
Braganza St. SE17 63 31 78 D
Braham St. E1 4 33 81 D
Braid Ave. W3 55 21 81 C
Braid Cl. Felt 82 12 72 B
Braidwood Rd. SE6 88 38 73 D
Braidwood St. SE1 8 33 80 C
Brailsford Rd. SW2 75 31 74 C
Brainton Ave. Felt 82 11 73 A
Braintree Ave. Ilf 27 42 89 C
Braintree Rd. Dag 41 49 86 C
Braintree St. E2 57 35 82 A
Braithwaite Ave. Rom 41 49 87 A
Braithwaite Gdns. Stan 21 17 90 A
Bramalea Cl. N6 36 28 88 C
Bramall Cl. E15 50 39 85 D
Bramber Rd. N12 16 27 92 C
Bramber Rd. W14 62 24 77 B
Bramble Banks. Cars 111 28 62 A
Bramblebury Rd. SE18 66 44 78 C
Bramble Cl. Shep 91 08 68 B
Bramble Cl. Stan 21 17 91 D
Bramble Croft. Eri 67 50 78 A
Brambledown Cl. W.Wick 107 39 67 A
Brambledown Rd. Cars 111 28 63 C
Brambledown Rd. S Croy 112 33 63 C
Brambledown Rd. Wall 111 28 63 D
Bramble Gdns. W12 55 21 80 B
Brambles Cl. Brent 60 16 77 D
Brambles The. Chig 28 44 91 A
Bramblewood Cl. Cars 104 27 66 C
Bramblings The. E4 18 38 92 B
Bramcote Ave. Mit 96 27 68 D
Bramcote Gr. SE16 64 35 78 C
Bramcote Rd. SW15 72 22 75 D
Bramdean Cres. SE12 89 40 73 C
Bramdean Gdns SE12 89 40 73 C
Bramerton Rd. Beck 98 36 68 B
Bramerton St. SW3 9 27 77 A
Bramfield Rd. SW11 74 27 74 B
Bramford Rd. SW18 73 26 75 C
Bramham Gdns. SW5 62 25 78 D
Bramhope La. SE7 65 40 77 B
Bramlands Cl. SW11 74 27 75 A
Bramley Cl. E17 26 36 90 C
Bramley Cl. N14 12 28 95 B
Bramley Cl. Orp 108 43 66 D
Bramley Cl. S Croy 112 32 64 C
Bramley Cl. Twick 70 14 74 C
Bramley Cres. Ilf 40 43 88 C
Bramley Hill. S Croy 112 32 64 A
Bramley Pl. Dart 80 52 75 C
Bramley Rd. Barn 12 29 95 A
Bramley Rd. Sutt 110 23 62 B
Bramley Rd. Sutt 110 26 64 D
Bramley Rd. W11 56 23 80 B
Bramley Rd. W5 60 17 79 C
Bramley St. W10 56 23 81 D
Bramley Way. W Wick 106 37 65 B
Brampton Cl. E5 37 34 86 B
Brampton Gr. Har 21 16 89 D
Brampton Gr. NW4 23 23 89 C
Brampton Gr. Wem 34 19 87 C
Brampton Park Rd. N8 25 31 89 A
Brampton Rd. Bexh 79 48 76 A
Brampton Rd. Croy 105 33 67 D
Brampton Rd. E6 58 41 82 B
Brampton Rd. N15 37 32 88 A
Brampton Rd. NW9 22 19 89 C
Brampton Rd. SE2 67 47 77 A
Bramshaw Rd. E9 49 35 84 B
Bramshaw Rise. N.Mal 102 21 67 C
Bramshill Gdns. NW5 36 28 86 D
Bramshill Rd. NW10 45 21 83 D
Bramshot Ave. SE7 65 40 77 B
Bramston Rd. NW10 45 22 83 C
Bramwell Cl. Sun 92 11 69 D
Brancaster La. Pur 112 32 62 C
Brancaster Rd. E12 50 42 85 B
Brancaster Rd. Ilf 40 45 88 C
Brancaster Rd. SW16 86 30 72 C
Branch Hill. NW3 35 26 86 C
Branch Pl. N1 48 32 83 B
Branch Rd. E14 57 36 81 C
Brancker Cl. Wall 111 30 63 C
Brancker Rd. Har 21 17 89 B
Brandlehow Rd. SW15 73 24 75 D
Brandon Mews. EC2 4 32 81 B
Brandon Rd. E17 26 38 89 A
Brandon Rd. N7 47 30 84 C
Brandon Rd. Sthl 59 12 78 D
Brandon Rd. Sutt 110 25 64 B
Brandon St. SE17 63 32 78 A
Brandram Rd. SE13 77 39 75 C
Brandreth Rd. SW17 86 28 72 B
Brandries The. Wall 104 29 65 D
Brand St. SE10 64 38 77 C
Brandville Gdns. Ilf 28 43 89 B
Brandy Way. Sutt 110 25 63 C
Brangbourne Rd. Brom 88 38 71 D
Brangton Rd. SE11 10 30 78 D
Brangwyn Cres. SW19 95 26 69 D
Branksea St. SW6 73 24 76 A
Branksome Ave. N18 17 33 92 D
Branksome Rd. SW19 95 25 69 A
Branksome Rd. SW2 74 30 74 A
Branksome Way. Har 33 18 88 D
Branksome Way. N Mal 94 20 69 B
Branscombe Gdns. N21 17 31 94 A
Branscombe St. SE13 76 37 75 B
Bransdale Cl. NW6 46 25 83 A
Bransgrove Rd. Edg 21 18 91 D
Branston Cres. Orp 108 44 66 D
Branstone Rd. Rich 71 18 76 B
Brants Wlk. W7 54 15 82 C
Brantwood Ave. Eri 67 50 77 C
Brantwood Ave. Islw 71 16 75 C
Brantwood Cl. E17 26 37 89 B
Brantwood Gdns. Enf 12 30 96 C
Brantwood Gdns. Ilf 27 42 89 C
Brantwood Rd. Bexh 79 49 75 B
Brantwood Rd. N17 25 34 91 A
Brantwood Rd. S Croy 112 32 62 A
Brantwood Rd. SE24 75 32 74 A
Brassey Rd. NW6 46 24 84 B
Brassey Sq. SW11 74 28 75 A
Brassie Ave. W3 55 21 81 C
Brasted Cl. Bexh 79 47 74 B
Brasted Cl. Orp 108 46 65 A
Brasted Cl. SE26 88 35 71 A
Brasted Rd. Eri 68 51 77 C
Brathway Rd. SW18 85 25 73 A
Bratley St. E1 57 34 82 C
Braund Ave. Grnf 53 13 82 D
Braundton Ave. Sid 90 45 73 D
Bravington Pl. W10 56 24 82 D
Bravington Rd. W9 56 24 82 B
Braxfield Rd. SE4 76 36 75 D
Braxted Park. SW16 96 30 70 B
Brayard's Rd. SE15 75 34 76 D
Brayard's. SE15 75 34 76 D
Braybrooke Gdns. SE19 97 33 70 D
Braybrook St. W12 55 21 81 B
Brayburne Ave. SW4 74 29 76 C
Braydon Rd. N16 37 34 87 C
Bray Dr. E16 58 39 80 B
Brayfield Terr. N1 48 31 84 C
Brayford Sq. E1 57 35 81 C
Bray Pl. SW3 9 27 78 B
Bray Rd. NW7 23 23 91 B
Brayton Gdns. Enf 12 29 96 D
Braywood Rd. SE9 78 44 75 D
Bread St. EC4 4 32 81 C
Breakspeare. SE21 87 33 72 D
Breakspear Rd N. Uxb 31 07 88 B
Breakspear Rd. Ruis 31 07 88 D
Breakspear Rd S. Uxb 31 07 87 B
Breakspears Dri. Orp 100 46 69 A
Breakspears Mews. SE4 76 37 76 C
Breakspears Rd. SE4 76 36 75 B
Breamore Cl. SW15 84 22 73 C
Breamore Ct. Ilf 40 46 86 A
Breamore Rd. Ilf 40 45 86 B
Bream's Bldgs. EC4 3 31 81 C
Bream St. E3 49 37 84 C
Breamwater Gdns. Rich 83 16 72 D
Breasley Cl. SW15 72 22 75 D
Brechin Pl. SW7 62 26 78 A
Brecknock Rd. N19 47 29 85 A
Brecknock Rd. N7 47 29 85 D
Brecknock Road Estate. N7 47 29 85 D
Brecon Cl. Mit 96 30 68 A
Brecon Rd. Enf 14 35 96 C
Brecon Rd. W6 62 24 77 A
Bredgar Rd. N19 36 29 86 A
Bredhurst Cl. SE20 98 35 70 A
Bredon Rd. Croy 105 33 66 B
Bredon Rd. SE5 75 32 75 A
Breer St. SW6 73 25 75 B
Breezer's Hill. E1 57 34 80 A
Brember Rd. Har 32 14 86 A
Bremner Rd. SW7 5 26 79 C
Brenchley Cl. Brom 107 39 67 D
Brenchley Cl. Chis 100 43 69 A
Brenchley Gdns. SE23 76 35 74 D
Brenchley Rd. Orp 100 45 69 D
Brendans Cl. Horn 42 54 87 C
Brenda Rd. SW17 86 27 72 B
Brende Gdns. E Mol 92 13 68 D
Brendon Ave. NW10 45 21 85 A
Brendon Cl. Eri 80 51 76 A
Brendon Gdns. Har 43 13 85 B
Brendon Gdns. Ilf 40 45 88 A
Brendon Rd. Dag 41 49 87 C
Brendon Rd. SE9 90 44 72 B
Brendon St. W1 1 27 81 C
Brendon Way. Enf 17 33 94 A
Brenley Cl. Mit 96 28 68 A
Brenley Gdns. SE9 77 41 75 D
Brentcot Cl. W13 54 16 82 D
Brent Cres. NW10 44 18 83 D
Brent Cross Fly. NW2 35 23 87 B
Brent Cross Fly. NW4 35 23 88 C
Brent Ct. NW11 35 23 87 B
Brentfield Cl. NW10 45 20 84 B
Brentfield Gdns. NW11 35 23 87 B
Brentfield. NW10 45 20 84 C
Brentfield Rd. NW10 45 20 84 D
Brentford High St. Brent 60 17 77 D
Brent Green. NW4 35 23 88 B
Brent Green Wlk. Wem 34 20 86 C
Brentham Way. W5 54 17 82 D
Brenthouse Rd. E9 49 35 84 A
Brenthurst Rd. NW10 45 21 84 B
Brent Lea. Brent 60 17 77 C
Brentmead Cl. W7 54 15 80 A
Brentmead Gdns. NW10 44 18 83 D
Brentmead Pl. NW11 35 23 88 D
Brenton St. E14 57 36 81 C
Brent Park Rd. NW4 34 22 87 B
Brent Pl. Barn 11 25 95 A
Brent Rd. Brent 60 17 77 A
Brent Rd. E16 58 40 81 A
Brent Rd. S Croy 112 34 62 B
Brent Rd. SE18 66 43 77 D
Brent Rd. Sthl 59 11 79 C
Brentside. Brent 60 17 77 A
Brentside Cl. W3 54 16 82 C
Brent St. NW4 35 23 88 B
Brent Terr. NW2 35 23 86 A
Brentvale Ave. Sthl 53 14 80 D
Brentvale Ave. Wem 44 18 83 B
Brent View Rd. NW9 34 22 87 A
Brent Way. Brent 60 17 77 D
Brent Way. N3 23 25 91 A
Brent Way. Wem 45 19 84 B
Brentwick Gdns. Brent 60 18 78 A
Brentwood Cl. SE9 90 44 73 C
Brentwood Rd. Rom 42 52 88 D
Brereton Rd. N17 25 33 91 D
Bressenden Pl. SW1 6 29 79 C
Bressey Gr. E18 27 39 90 D

Brett Cl. N16 37 33 86 A
Brett Cl. Nthlt 53 11 82 B
Brett Cres. NW10 45 20 84 D
Brettell St. SE17 63 32 78 D
Brettenham Ave. E17 26 37 90 A
Brettenham Rd. E17 26 37 90 A
Brettenham Rd. N18 17 34 92 B
Brett Gdns. Dag 52 48 84 C
Brettgrave. Eps 109 20 62 C
Brett House Cl. SW15 85 23 73 B
Brett House Cl. SW15 73 23 74 D
Brett Pas. E8 48 34 85 D
Brett Rd. Barn 11 23 95 A
Brett Rd. E8 48 34 85 D
Brewer's Green. SW1 6 29 79 C
Brewers La. Rich 71 17 74 B
Brewer St. W1 6 29 80 A
Brewery Rd. Brom 107 42 66 C
Brewery Rd. N7 47 30 84 A
Brewery Rd. SE18 66 44 78 D
Brewhouse La. E1 57 34 80 D
Brewhouse St. SW15 73 24 75 A
Brewhouse Wlk. SE16 57 36 80 C
Brewhouse Yd. EC1 3 31 82 D
Brewood Rd. Dag 51 46 84 B
Brewster Gdns. W10 56 23 81 A
Brewster Rd. E10 38 37 87 D
Briane Rd. Eps 109 20 62 D
Brian Rd. Rom 41 47 88 A
Briants Cl. Pnr 20 12 90 D
Briant St. SE14 76 35 76 B
Briar Ave. SW16 96 30 70 D
Briarbank Rd. W13 54 16 81 C
Briar Banks. Cars 111 28 62 A
Briar Cl. Hamp 82 12 71 D
Briar Cl. Islw 71 15 74 B
Briar Cl. N13 17 32 93 C
Briar Cl. N2 23 25 89 B
Briar Cres. Nthlt 43 13 84 B
Briar Ct. Hamp 82 13 71 D
Briar Ct. Sutt 110 23 64 A
Briardale Gdns. NW3 35 25 86 C
Briarfield Ave. N2 23 25 89 B
Briarfield Ave. N3 23 25 90 D
Briar Gdns. Brom 107 39 66 D
Briaris Cl. N17 25 34 91 D
Briar La. Cars 111 28 62 A
Briar Pas. SW16 96 30 68 A
Briar Rd. Har 33 17 88 A
Briar Rd. Rom 30 53 91 C
Briar Rd. SW16 96 30 68 B
Briar Rd. Twick 83 15 73 C
Briars Wlk. Rom 30 54 90 D
Briar Wlk. Edg 22 20 91 C
Briar Wlk. SW15 72 22 75 D
Briar Wlk. W10 56 24 82 C
Briarwood Cl. NW9 34 20 88 C
Briarwood Dri. Nthwd 19 10 90 C
Briarwood Rd. Eps 109 22 63 A
Briarwood Rd. SW4 74 29 74 B
Briary Cl. NW3 47 27 84 C
Briary Ct. Sid 90 46 71 D
Briary Gdns. Brom 89 40 71 D
Briary La. N9 17 33 93 D
Brick Ct. EC4 3 31 81 C
Brickett Cl. Ruis 31 08 88 A
Brick Farm Cl. Rich 72 19 76 B
Brickfield Cl. Brent 60 17 77 C
Brickfield Cottages. SE18 66 45 77 B
Brickfield Rd. E3 57 37 82 D
Brickfield Rd. SW19 85 25 71 B
Brickfield Rd. Th Hth 97 31 69 B
Brickfields. Har 33 15 86 A
Brick La. E1 4 33 82 D
Brick La. Enf 13 34 97 D
Brick St. W1 6 28 80 D
Brickwall La. Ruis 31 09 87 D
Brickwood Cl. SE26 87 34 72 D
Brickwood Rd. Croy 105 33 65 A
Bride Ct. EC4 3 31 81 D
Bride La. EC4 3 31 81 D
Bride St. N7 48 31 84 A
Bridewell Pl. EC4 3 31 81 D
Bridford Mews. W1 2 28 81 B
Bridge App. NW1 47 28 84 C
Bridge Ave. W6 62 23 78 C
Bridge Ave. W7 53 14 81 B
Bridge Cl. Enf 13 34 97 D
Bridge Cl. Rom 42 51 88 C
Bridge Cl. Tedd 83 15 71 B
Bridge End. E17 26 38 90 A
Bridgefield. Sutt 110 25 63 A
Bridgefoot. SE1 10 30 78 C
Bridge Foot. Sun 91 10 69 A
Bridge Gate. N21 17 32 94 A
Bridge Gdns. Ashf 91 08 70 C
Bridge Gdns. E Mol 92 14 68 D
Bridgeland Rd. E16 58 40 81 C
Bridge La. NW11 35 24 88 B
Bridge La. SW11 74 27 76 A
Bridgeman Rd. N1 47 30 84 D
Bridgeman Rd. Tedd 93 16 70 A
Bridgeman St. NW8 47 27 83 C
Bridgend Rd. SW18 73 26 75 C
Bridgenhall Rd. Enf 13 33 97 B
Bridgen Rd. Bex 79 48 74 C
Bridge Pl. Croy 105 32 66 D
Bridge Pl. SW1 9 28 78 B
Bridge Rd. Beck 98 36 70 D
Bridge Rd. Bexh 79 48 76 C
Bridge Rd. E15 49 38 83 B
Bridge Rd. E17 38 36 87 B
Bridge Rd. E6 50 42 84 D
Bridge Rd. E Mol 92 14 68 D
Bridge Rd. E Mol 93 15 68 C
Bridge Rd. Eri 80 51 76 B
Bridge Rd. Houn 70 14 75 B
Bridge Rd. Islw 70 14 75 B
Bridge Rd. N22 24 30 90 A
Bridge Rd. N9 17 34 93 C
Bridge Rd. NW10 45 21 84 A
Bridge Rd. Orp 108 46 67 D
Bridge Rd. Sthl 59 13 79 A
Bridge Rd. Sutt 110 25 63 B
Bridge Rd. Twick 71 16 74 D
Bridge Rd. Wall 111 29 64 C
Bridge Rd. Wem 34 19 86 C
Bridge Row. Croy 105 32 66 D
Bridges Ct. SW11 73 26 75 B
Bridges Ct. SW11 73 26 76 D
Bridges La. Croy 111 30 64 A
Bridges Pl. SW6 73 24 76 B
Bridges Rd. SW19 95 25 70 B
Bridges Road Mews. SW19 95 25 70 B
Bridge St. Pnr 20 12 89 A
Bridge St. Rich 71 17 74 B
Bridge St. SW1 7 30 79 A
Bridge St. W4 61 20 78 B
Bridge Terr. E15 49 38 84 D
Bridge The. Har 21 15 89 D
Bridge View. W6 62 23 78 C
Bridgewater Cl. Chis 100 45 68 A
Bridgewater Ct. Wem 44 17 84 A
Bridgewater Gdns. Edg 21 18 90 D
Bridgewater Rd. E15 49 38 83 A
Bridgewater Rd. Wem 44 17 84 C
Bridgewater Sq. EC2 4 32 81 A
Bridgewater St. EC2 4 32 81 A
Bridgeway. Bark 51 45 84 D
Bridge Way. N11 16 29 93 C
Bridge Way. NW11 35 24 88 B
Bridgeway St. NW1 47 29 83 C
Bridge Way. Twick 82 14 73 A
Bridgeway. Wem 44 18 84 D
Bridgewood Cl. SE20 97 34 70 D
Bridgewood Rd. SW16 96 29 70 D
Bridgewood Rd. Wor Pk. 102 22 65 C
Bridgford St. SW18 85 26 72 C
Bridgman Rd. W4 61 20 79 C
Bridgwater Rd. Ruis 31 10 86 D
Bridle Cl. Eps 109 20 64 D
Bridle Cl. Sun 91 10 68 A
Bridle La. W1 6 29 80 A
Bridle Path. Croy 104 30 65 C
Bridle Path The. Wdf Gn 27 39 91 C
Bridlepath Way. Felt 81 09 73 A
Bridle Rd. Croy 106 37 65 A
Bridle Rd. Pnr 32 11 88 A
Bridle Rd The. Pur 111 30 62 C
Bridle Way The. Wall 111 29 64 C
Bridlington Rd. N9 17 34 94 B
Bridport Ave. Rom 41 49 88 D
Bridport Pl. N1 48 32 83 B
Bridport Rd. Grnf 43 13 83 B
Bridport Rd. N18 17 33 92 D
Bridport Rd. Th Hth 97 31 68 A
Bridstow Pl. W2 56 25 81 C
Brief St. SE5 75 31 76 B
Brierley Ave. N9 18 35 94 C
Brierley Cl. Horn 42 53 88 C
Brierley Cl. SE25 97 34 68 C
Brierley Ct. W7 54 15 80 A
Brierley Rd. E11 49 38 85 B
Brierley Rd. SW12 86 29 72 A
Brierly Gdns. E2 49 35 83 C
Brigade Cl. Har 32 14 86 B
Brigade St. SE3 77 39 76 D
Brigadier Ave. Enf 13 32 97 A
Brigadier Hill. Enf 13 32 97 A
Briggeford Cl. E5 37 34 86 A
Brightfield Rd. SE12 77 39 74 B
Brightling Rd. SE4 76 36 74 D
Brightlingsea Pl. E14 57 36 80 B
Brightman Rd. SW18 85 26 73 D
Brighton Ave. E17 38 36 88 B
Brighton Dri. Nthlt 43 13 84 A
Brighton Gr.SE14 76 36 76 A
Brighton Rd. N16 48 33 85 A
Brighton Rd. N2 23 26 90 C
Brighton Rd. Pur 112 31 62 D
Brighton Rd. S Croy 112 32 63 D
Brighton Rd. Surb 101 17 67 D
Brighton Rd. Sutt 110 25 62 B
Brighton Terr. SW9 74 30 75 D
Brightside Rd. SE13 76 38 74 D
Brightside The. Enf 14 36 97 A
Bright St. E14 57 37 81 D
Brightwell Cres. SW17 86 27 71 D
Brig Mews. SE8 64 37 77 A
Brig St. E14 64 38 78 D
Brigstock Rd. Belv 67 49 78 B
Brigstock Rd. Th Hth 97 32 68 C
Brim Hill. N2 23 26 89 D
Brimpsfield Cl. SE2 66 46 79 D
Brimsdown Ave. Enf 14 36 97 A
Brindley St. SE14 76 36 76 B
Brindley Way. Sthl 53 13 80 B
Brindwood Rd. E4 18 37 93 C
Brinkburn Cl. Edg 22 19 89 B
Brinkburn Cl. SE2 66 46 78 A
Brinkburn Gdns. Edg 22 19 89 A
Brinkley Rd. Wor Pk 102 22 66 D
Brinklow Cres. SE18 66 43 77 D
Brinkworth Rd. Ilf 27 42 89 A
Brinkworth Way. E9 49 36 84 B
Brinsdale Rd. NW4 23 23 89 D
Brinsley Rd. Har 20 14 90 D
Brinsley St. E1 57 35 81 C
Brinsworth Cl. Twick 82 14 72 B
Brinton Wlk. SE1 7 31 80 D
Brion Pl. E14 58 38 81 A
Brisane St. SE5 63 32 77 D
Brisbane Ave. SW19 95 25 69 B
Brisbane Rd. E10 38 37 86 B
Brisbane Rd. Ilf 40 44 87 C
Briscoe Rd. SW19 95 26 70 B
Briset Rd. SE9 77 41 75 D
Briset St. EC1 3 31 82 D
Briset Way. N7 36 30 86 B
Bristol Gdns. W9 56 25 82 D
Bristol Mews. W9 56 25 82 D
Bristol Park Rd. E17 26 36 89 C
Bristol Rd. E7 50 41 84 B
Bristol Rd. Grnf 43 13 83 B
Bristol Rd. Mord 103 26 67 A
Briston Gr. N8 36 30 88 C
Bristow Rd. Bexh 79 48 76 A
Bristow Rd. Croy 111 30 64 A
Bristow Rd. Houn 70 14 75 A
Bristow Rd. SE19 87 33 71 C
Britannia Cl. SW4 74 29 75 D
Britannia Rd. Ilf 40 43 86 D
Britannia Rd. N12 15 26 93 C
Britannia Rd. Surb 101 18 66 B
Britannia Rd. SW6 73 25 76 B
Britannia Rd. SW6 62 25 77 D
Britannia Row. N1 48 32 83 A
Britannia St. WC1 3 30 82 B
Britannia Way. NW10 55 19 82 D
Britannia Way. SW6 62 25 77 D
Britannia Wlk. N1 4 32 82 B
Britannia Wlk. N1 4 32 82 B
Britannia Wlk. N1 48 32 83 D
British Grove Pas. W4 61 21 78 D
British Grove Pas. W6 61 21 78 D
British Grove S. W6 61 21 78 D
British Gr. W4 61 21 78 D
British St. E3 57 36 82 B
Briton Hill Rd. S Croy 112 33 62 D
Brittain Rd. Dag 41 48 86 D
Britten Cl. NW11 35 25 87 D
Britten's Ct. E1 57 34 80 D
Britten St. SW3 9 27 78 C
Britton's Ct. EC4 3 31 81 C
Britton St. EC1 3 31 82 B
Brixham Cres. Ruis 31 10 87 C
Brixham Gdns. Ilf 51 45 85 C
Brixham Rd. Well 79 47 76 B
Brixton Hill Ct. SW2 74 30 74 B
Brixton Hill Pl. SW2 86 30 73 A
Brixton Hill. SW2 74 30 74 D
Brixton Oval. SW2 75 31 75 C
Brixton Rd. SW9 75 31 76 C
Brixton Station Rd. SW9 75 31 75 C
Brixton Water La. SW2 75 31 74 A
Broadacre Cl. Uxb 31 07 86 D
Broadbent St. W1 6 28 80 B
Broadberry Ct. N18 17 34 92 D
Broadbridge Cl. SE3 65 40 77 C
Broadcroft Ave. Stan 21 17 90 D
Broadcroft Rd. Orp 108 44 66 B
Broad Ct. WC2 3 30 81 C
Broadfield Cl. NW2 35 23 86 C
Broadfield Cl. Rom 42 51 88 B
Broadfield La. N7 47 30 84 C
Broadfield Rd. SE6 89 39 73 C
Broadfields Ave. N21 17 31 94 A
Broadfields. E Mol 101 15 67 C
Broadfields. Har 20 13 90 D
Broadfield Sq. Enf 13 34 96 B
Broadgates Ave. Barn 11 25 97 B
Broadgates Rd. SW18 85 26 73 D
Broad Green Ave. Croy 105 31 66 B
Broadhead Strand. NW9 22 21 90 B
Broadheath Dri. Chis 89 42 71 D
Broadhinton Rd. SW4 74 28 75 B
Broadhurst Ave. Ilf 51 45 85 B
Broadhurst Cl. NW6 46 26 84 A
Broadhurst Gdns. NW6 46 25 84 B
Broadhurst Gdns. Ruis 32 11 86 A
Broad La. Hamp 92 13 70 A
Broad La. N15 25 34 89 C
Broad La. N8 36 30 88 B
Broadlands Ave. Enf 13 34 96 B
Broadlands Ave. SW16 86 30 72 A
Broadlands Cl. Enf 14 35 96 A
Broadlands Cl. N6 36 28 87 A
Broadlands Cl. SW16 86 30 72 A
Broadlands. E17 26 36 89 A
Broadlands. Felt 82 13 72 C
Broadlands Rd. Brom 89 40 71 B
Broadlands Rd. N6 36 28 87 A
Broadlands Way. N.Mal 102 21 67 D
Broadlawns Ct. Har 21 15 90 B
Broad Lawn. SE9 90 43 73 C
Broadley St. NW8 1 27 81 A
Broadley Terr. NW1 1 27 82 C
Broadmead Ave. Wor Pk 102 22 66 A
Broadmead Cl. Hamp 92 13 70 A
Broadmead Cl. Pnr 20 12 91 C
Broadmead Rd. Hay 53 12 82 C
Broadmead Rd. Wdf Gn 27 40 91 D
Broadmead. SE6 88 37 72 C
Broadoak Rd. Eri 67 50 77 D
Broad Oaks. Surb 102 19 65 B
Broad Oaks Way. Brom 107 39 67 B
Broad Sanctuary. SW1 7 30 79 A
Broad St. Ave. EC2 4 33 81 A
Broad St Bldgs. EC2 4 33 81 A
Broad St. Dag 52 49 84 C
Broadstone Pl. W1 2 28 81 A
Broadstone Rd. Horn 42 52 86 A
Broad Street Market. Dag 52 49 84 C
Broad St. Tedd 93 15 70 B
Broadview. NW9 34 19 88 C
Broadview Rd. SW16 96 29 70 D
Broadwalk. E18 27 39 89 B
Broadwalk La. NW11 35 24 87 B
Broad Walk. N21 16 30 94 D
Broad Walk The. W8 56 25 80 D
Broadwater Rd. N17 25 33 90 C
Broadwater Rd. SW17 86 27 71 A
*Broadway Arc. W6 62 23 78 A
Broadway Ave. Croy 105 32 67 B
Broadway Ave. Twick 71 16 74 D
Broadway. Bexh 79 48 75 D
Broadway Cl. Wdf Gn 27 40 91 B
Broadway Ct. SW19 95 25 70 A
Broadway. E15 49 38 84 D
Broadway. Eps 109 22 64 C
Broadway Gdns. Mit 96 27 68 C
Broadway Market. E8 48 34 83 B
Broadway Mews. N16 37 33 87 B
Broadway Mews. N21 17 31 94 D
Broadway Pl. SW19 95 24 70 B
Broadway. Rom 30 52 90 C
Broadway. Surb 102 19 66 D
Broadway. SW1 6 29 79 B
Broadway The. Dag 41 49 86 A
Broadway The. E13 50 40 83 D
Broadway The. E4 26 38 91 B
Broadway The. Grnf 53 14 82 C
Broad Way The. Har 21 15 90 D
Broadway The. N8 36 30 88 C
Broadway The. N9 17 34 93 C
Broadway The. Pnr 20 12 91 D
Broadway The. Sthl 53 12 80 C
Broadway The. Surb 101 15 66 C
Broadway The. Sutt 110 24 63 A
Broadway The. Sutt 110 26 64 A
Broadway The. SW19 95 25 70 C
Broadway The. W5 54 17 80 B
Broadway The. Wdf Gn 27 40 91 B
Broadway. W13 54 16 80 C
Broadway. W7 54 15 80 C
Broadwick St. W1 2 29 81 C
Broad Wlk. Houn 70 12 76 A
Broad Wlk. Rich 60 18 77 D
Broad Wlk. SE3 77 42 76 C
Broad Wlk The. E Mol 93 15 68 D
Broad Wlk The. Nthwd 19 08 90 C
Broadwood Ave. Ruis 31 09 88 C
Broad Yd. EC1 3 31 82 D
Brocas Cl. NW3 47 27 84 C
Brockdish Ave. Bark 51 45 85 D
Brockenhurst Ave. Wor Pk 102 21 66 C
Brockenhurst Gdns. Ilf 51 44 85 C
Brockenhurst Gdns. NW7 22 21 91 A
Brockenhurst Rd. Croy 105 34 66 B
Brockenhurst Way. SW16 96 29 69 D
Brockham Cl. SW19 85 24 71 D
Brockham Dri. Ilf 40 44 88 A
Brockham Dri. SW2 86 30 73 B
Brockham St. SE1 8 32 79 C
Brockhurst Cl. Stan 21 15 91 B
Brockill Cres. SE4 76 36 75 C
Brocklebank Rd. SW18 85 26 73 A
Brocklehurst St. SE14 64 35 77 D
Brocklesby Rd. SE25 97 34 68 D
Brockley Cres. Rom 29 50 91 C
Brockley Cross. SE4 76 36 75 A
Brockley Footpath. SE15 76 35 75 C
Brockley Footpath. SE4 76 36 74 A
Brockley Gr. SE4 76 36 74 B
Brockley Hall Rd. SE4 76 36 74 A
Brockley Park. SE23 88 36 73 A
Brockley Rd. SE4 76 35 75 D
Brockley Rise. SE23 88 36 73 A
Brockley View. SE23 88 36 73 A
Brockley Way. SE4 76 36 74 A
Brockman Rise. Brom 88 38 71 B
Brock Pl. E3 57 37 82 D
Brock Rd. E13 58 40 81 B
Brocks Dri. Sutt 103 24 65 C
Brockshot Cl. Brent 60 17 77 B
Brock St. SE15 76 35 75 A
Brockwell Cl. Orp 108 45 67 B
Brockwell Park Gdns. SE24 87 31 73 B
Brockworth Cl. SE15 63 33 77 A
Broderick Ho. SE21 87 34 72 C
Brodia Rd. N16 37 33 86 C
Brodie Rd. E4 18 38 93 A
Brodie St. SE1 63 33 78 D
Brodlove La. E1 57 35 80 B
Brodrick Gr. SE2 66 46 78 B
Brodrick Rd. SW17 86 27 72 A
Brograve Gdns. Beck 98 37 69 D
Brograve Rd. N17 25 34 89 A
Broken Wharf. EC4 8 32 80 A
Brokesley St. E3 57 36 82 B
Broke Wlk. E8 48 34 83 A
Bromar Rd. SE5 75 33 75 A
Bromefield. Stan 21 17 90 A
Bromehead Rd. E1 57 35 81 C
Bromehead St. E1 57 35 81 C
Brome Rd. SE9 77 42 75 B
Bromfelde Rd. SW4 74 29 76 D
Bromfelde Wlk. SW4 74 30 76 C
Bromfield St. N1 48 31 83 C
Bromhall Rd. Dag 51 46 84 B
Bromhedge. SE9 89 42 72 D
Bromleigh Ct. SE23 87 34 72 B
Bromley Ave. Brom 99 39 70 C
Bromley Common. Brom 107 41 67 D
Bromley Cres. Brom 99 39 68 B
Bromley Ct. Brom 99 39 70 D
Bromley Gdns. Brom 99 39 68 B
Bromley Gr. Brom 98 38 69 D
Bromley Hall Rd. E14 58 38 81 A
Bromley High St. E3 57 37 82 B
Bromley Hill. Brom 99 39 70 A
Bromley La. Chis 100 44 70 D
Bromley Rd. Beck 98 38 69 C
Bromley Rd. Brom 99 39 69 C
Bromley Rd. Chis 100 44 70 C
Bromley Rd. E10 38 37 88 D
Bromley Rd. E17 26 37 89 A
Bromley Rd. N17 25 34 90 A
Bromley Rd. N18 17 32 92 D
Bromley Rd. SE6 88 37 72 D
Bromley St. E1 57 35 81 D
Brompton Arcade. SW3 5 27 79 B
Brompton Cl. Houn 70 12 74 B
Brompton Dri. Eri 68 52 77 D
Brompton Gr. N2 24 27 89 C
Brompton Pl. SW3 5 27 79 C
Brompton Rd. SW3 5 27 79 C
Brompton Sq. SW3 5 27 79 C
Bromwell's Rd. SW4 74 29 75 C
Bromwich Ave. N6 36 28 86 A
Bromyard Ave. W3 55 21 80 C
Brondesbury Mews. NW6 46 25 84 C
Brondesbury Park. NW2 46 23 84 C
Brondesbury Park. NW6 46 24 84 C
Brondesbury Rd. NW6 46 24 83 D
Brondesbury Villas. NW6 46 25 83 C
Bronholm Rd. SE2 66 46 79 D
Bronsart Rd. SW6 62 24 77 C
Bronson Rd. SW20 95 24 69 C
Bronte Gr. Dart 80 54 75 D
Bronti Cl. SE17 63 32 78 C
Bronze St. SE8 64 37 77 C
Brook Ave. Dag 52 49 84 D
Brook Ave. Edg 22 19 91 B
Brook Ave. Wem 34 19 86 C
Brookbank Ave. W7 53 14 81 B
Brookbank Rd. SE13 76 37 75 B
Brook Cl. Rom 30 51 90 B
Brook Cl. Ruis 31 09 87 A
Brook Cl. SW20 94 22 68 B
Brook Cres. E4 18 37 92 B
Brook Cres. N9 17 34 92 B
Brookdale. N11 16 29 92 A
Brookdale Rd. Bex 79 48 74 C
Brookdale Rd. E17 26 37 89 A
Brookdale Rd. SE6 88 37 73 B
Brookdale Rd. SE6 76 37 74 D
Brookdene Dri. Nthwd 19 09 91 B
Brookdene Rd. SE18 66 45 78 B
Brook Dri. Har 20 14 89 C
Brook Dri. Ruis 31 09 87 A
Brook Dri. SE11 63 31 78 B
Brook Dri. SE11 7 31 79 C
Brook Dri. Sun 91 09 70 A
Brooke Ave. Har 32 14 86 C
Brookehowse Rd. SE6 88 37 72 D
Brookend Rd. Sid 90 45 73 C
Brooke Rd. E17 26 38 89 C
Brooke Rd. E5 37 34 86 D
Brooke Rd. N16 37 34 86 C
Brookes Ct. EC1 3 31 81 A
Brooke's Market. EC1 3 31 81 A
Brooke St. EC1 3 31 81 A
Brookfield Ave. E17 26 38 89 C
Brookfield Ave. NW7 22 22 91 B
Brookfield Ave. NW7 22 22 91 B
Brookfield Ave. Sutt 104 27 65 C
Brookfield Ave. W5 54 17 82 D
Brookfield Cl. Har 33 18 88 A
Brookfield Cl. NW7 22 22 91 B
Brookfield Cres. Har 33 18 88 A
Brookfield Cres. NW7 22 22 91 B
Brookfield Ct. Grnf 53 14 82 A
Brookfield. N6 36 28 86 C
Brookfield Park. NW5 36 28 86 D
Brookfield Path. Wdf Gn 27 39 91 A
Brookfield Rd. E9 49 36 84 A
Brookfield Rd. N9 17 34 93 D
Brookfield Rd. W4 61 20 79 B
Brookfields Ave. Mit 104 27 67 A
Brookfields. Enf 14 35 96 D
Brook Gate. Belv 67 49 78 D
Brook Gate. W1 5 27 80 B
Brook Gdns. E4 18 37 92 B
Brook Gdns. King 94 20 69 A
Brook Gdns. SW13 72 21 75 B
Brook Green. W6 62 23 78 B
Brookhill Cl. Barn 12 27 95 A
Brook Hill Cl. SE18 66 43 78 D
Brookhill Rd. Barn 12 27 95 A
Brooking Rd. E7 50 40 85 A
Brook La. Bex 79 47 74 D
Brook La. Bexh 79 47 74 B
Brook La. Brom 99 40 70 A
Brookland Cl. NW11 23 25 89 C
Brookland Garth. NW11 23 25 89 C
Brookland Hill. NW11 23 25 89 D
Brookland Rise. NW11 23 25 89 C
Brooklands App. Rom 29 50 89 D
Brooklands Ave. SE9 90 44 72 B
Brooklands Ave. SW19 85 25 72 B
Brooklands Cl. Rom 29 50 89 D
Brooklands Cl. Sun 91 09 69 A
Brooklands Dri. Grnf 44 17 83 B
Brooklands Gdns. Horn 42 53 88 C
Brooklands La. Rom 29 50 89 D
Brooklands Park. SE3 77 40 75 A
Brooklands Pas. SW8 74 29 76 B
Brooklands Rd. Rom 29 50 89 D
Brooklands Rd. Surb 101 16 66 C

Brook Lane N. Brent 60 17 78 D
Brook La. SE3 77 40 76 D
Brooklea Cl. NW9 22 21 90 A
Brooklyn Ave. SE25 97 34 68 D
Brooklyn Gr. SE25 97 34 68 D
Brooklyn Rd. Brom 107 41 67 B
Brooklyn Rd. Brom 107 42 67 A
Brooklyn Rd. SE25 97 34 68 D
Brookmead Ave. Brom 107 42 67 B
Brookmead Cl. Orp 108 46 67 D
Brookmead. Croy 104 29 67 C
Brook Mead. Eps 109 21 63 A
Brook Meadow. N12 15 25 93 D
Brookmead Rd. Croy 104 29 67 C
Brookmead Way. Orp 108 46 67 D
Brook Mews N. W2 5 26 80 B
Brookmill Rd. SE8 76 37 76 A
Brook Pl. Barn 11 25 95 A
Brook Rd. Ilf 40 45 88 C
Brook Rd. N22 24 30 90 D
Brook Rd. N2 24 27 91 C
Brook Rd. N8 24 30 89 C
Brook Rd. NW2 34 22 86 C
Brook Rd. Rom 30 51 90 B
Brook Rd. Surb 101 18 65 A
Brook Rd. Th Hth 97 32 68 C
Brook Rd. Twick 71 16 74 C
Brook Road S. Brent 60 17 77 B
Brooksbank St. E9 49 35 84 A
Brooksby Mews. N1 48 31 84 C
Brooksby St. N1 48 31 84 C
Brooksby's Wlk. E9 49 35 85 D
Brookscroft Rd. E17 26 37 90 B
Brookshill. Har 21 15 91 A
Brookside. Barn 12 27 95 C
Brookside. Cars 111 28 64 C
Brookside Cl. Barn 11 24 95 C
Brookside Cl. Har 43 12 85 A
Brookside Cl. Har 33 17 88 B
Brookside Cres. Wor Pk 102 22 66 C
Brookside. Horn 42 54 88 A
Brookside. Ilf 28 44 91 A
Brookside. N21 12 30 95 D
Brookside. Orp 108 45 66 B
Brookside Rd. Hay 53 11 80 A
Brookside Rd. N19 36 29 86 A
Brookside Rd. N9 17 34 92 B
Brookside Rd. NW11 35 24 88 C
Brookside S. Barn 16 28 94 A
Brookside Way. Croy 106 35 67 D
Brookside Wlk.N3 23 24 89 A
Brooks La. W4 61 19 77 A
Brook's Rd. E13 50 40 83 A
Brooks Rd. W4 61 19 78 C
Brook St. Eri 67 49 77 D
Brook St. King 93 17 68 A
Brook St. N17 25 33 90 D
Brook St. W1 6 28 80 B
Brook St. W2 5 26 80 B
Brooksville Ave. NW6 46 24 83 A
Brook Vale. Eri 79 49 76 B
Brookview Rd. SW16 86 29 71 C
Brookville Rd. SW6 62 24 77 D
Brookway. SE3 77 40 75 A
Brook Wlk. Edg 22 20 91 B
Brook Wlk. N2 23 26 90 B
Brookwood Ave. SW13 72 21 76 D
Brookwood Rd. Houn 70 13 76 B
Brookwood Rd. SW18 85 25 73 C
Broom Ave. Orp 100 46 69 D
Broom Cl. Brom 107 42 67 C
Broom Cl. Tedd 93 17 70 D
Broomcroft Ave. Nthlt 53 11 82 A
Broome Rd. Hamp 92 12 69 B
Broome Way. SE5 63 32 77 D
Broomfield Ave. N13 16 30 92 B
Broomfield. E17 38 36 87 B
Broomfield La. N13 16 30 92 B
Broomfield Pl. W13 54 16 80 D
Broomfield Rd. Beck 98 36 68 B
Broomfield Rd. Bexh 79 49 74 A
Broomfield Rd. N13 16 30 92 C
Broomfield Rd. Rich 71 18 76 B
Broomfield Rd. Rom 41 47 87 B
Broomfield Rd. Surb 101 18 66 D
Broomfield Rd. Tedd 93 17 70 A
Broomfield Rd. W13 54 16 80 D
Broomfield St. E14 57 37 81 B
Broomfield. Sun 91 10 69 A
Broom Gdns. Croy 106 37 65 C
Broomgrove Gdns. Edg 22 19 90 A
Broomgrove Rd. SW9 74 30 76 D
Broomhall Rd. S Croy 112 32 62 B
Broomhill Ct. Wdf Gn 27 40 91 A
Broomhill Rd. Dart 80 52 74 D
Broomhill Rd. Ilf 40 46 86 A
Broomhill Rd. Orp 108 46 66 A
Broomhill Rd. SW18 73 25 74 A
Broomhill Rd. Wdf Gn 27 40 91 A
Broomhill Rise. Bexh 79 49 74 A
Broomhill Wlk. Wdf Gn 27 39 91 D
Broomhouse La. SW6 73 25 75 A
Broomhouse Rd. SW6 73 25 76 C
Broomloan La. Sutt 103 25 65 A
Broom Lock. Tedd 93 17 70 A
Broom Mead. Bexh 79 49 74 A
Broom Park. Tedd 93 17 70 D
Broom Rd. Croy 106 37 65 C
Broom Rd. Tedd 93 17 70 A
Broomsleigh St. NW6 46 24 85 D
Broom Water. Tedd 83 17 71 C
Broom Water W. Tedd 83 17 71 C
Broomwood Rd. Orp 100 46 69 D
Broomwood Rd. SW11 74 27 74 D
Broseley Gr. SE26 88 36 71 C
Brougham Rd. E8 48 34 83 A
Brougham Rd. W3 55 20 81 C
Brougham St. SW11 74 27 76 D
Brough Cl. SW8 10 30 77 C
Brough St. SW8 10 30 77 C
Broughton Ave. N3 23 24 89 A
Broughton Ave. Rich 83 17 71 A
Broughton Ct. W13 54 16 80 B
Broughton Dri. SW9 75 31 75 C
Broughton Gdns. N6 36 29 88 C
Broughton Rd. Orp 108 44 65 B
Broughton Rd. SW6 73 25 76 D
Broughton Rd. Th Hth 105 31 67 C
Broughton Rd. W13 54 16 80 B
Broughton Road App. SW6 73 25 76 D
Broughton St. SW8 74 28 76 D
Brouncker Rd. W3 61 20 79 A
Browell's La. Felt 81 10 72 B
Brown Cl. Wall 111 30 63 C
Brownfield St. E14 58 38 81 C
Brown Hart Gdns. W1 6 28 80 A
Brownhill Rd. SE6 88 38 73 B
Browning Ave. Sutt 111 27 64 A
Browning Ave. W7 54 15 81 D
Browning Ave. Wor Pk 102 22 66 D
Browning Cl. Hamp 82 12 71 B
Browning Cl. W9 1 26 82 C
Browning Cl. Well 78 45 76 A
Browning Mews. W1 2 28 81 A
Browning Rd. Dart 80 54 75 D
Browning Rd. E11 39 39 87 B
Browning Rd. E12 50 42 84 B
Browning Rd. Enf 13 32 97 B
Browning St. SE17 63 32 78 A
Browning Way. Houn 70 11 76 B
Brownlea Gdns. Ilf 40 46 86 A
Brownlow Mews. WC1 3 30 82 D
Brownlow Rd. Croy 112 33 64 A
Brownlow Rd. E7 50 40 85 A
Brownlow Rd. E8 48 34 83 A
Brownlow Rd. N11 24 30 91 A
Brownlow Rd. N3 23 25 91 D
Brownlow Rd. NW10 45 21 84 C
Brownlow Rd. W13 54 16 80 C
Brownlow St. WC1 3 30 81 B
Brownrigg Rd. Ashf 81 07 71 A
Brown's Bldgs. EC3 4 33 81 C
Brownspring Dri. SE9 90 44 72 C
Brown's Rd. E17 26 37 89 A
Brown's Rd. Surb 101 18 66 B
Brown St. W1 1 27 81 D
Brownswell Rd. N2 23 26 90 D
Brownswood Rd. N4 37 32 86 A
Broxash Rd. SW11 74 28 74 C
Broxbourne Ave. E18 27 40 89 D
Broxbourne Rd. E7 39 40 86 C
Broxbourne Rd. Orp 108 45 66 B
Broxholm Rd. SE27 87 31 72 C
Broxted Rd. SE6 88 36 72 B
Bruce Ave. Horn 42 53 86 B
Bruce Castle Rd. N17 25 33 90 B
Bruce Cl. Well 78 46 76 B
Bruce Gr. N17 25 33 90 D
Bruce Gr. Orp 108 46 66 C
Bruce Rd. Barn 11 24 96 A
Bruce Rd. E3 57 37 82 B
Bruce Rd. Har 21 15 90 C
Bruce Rd. Mit 96 28 70 C
Bruce Rd. NW10 45 20 84 D
Bruce Rd. SE25 97 32 68 D
Brudenell Rd. SW17 86 28 71 A
Bruffs Meadow. Nthlt 43 12 84 A
Brumfield Rd. Eps 109 20 64 C
Brummel Cl. Bexh 79 50 75 A
Brumwill Rd. W5 44 18 83 C
Brunel Cl. Nthlt 53 12 82 B
Brunel Cl. SE19 97 33 70 B
Brunel Estate. W2 56 25 81 A
Brunel Pl. Sthl 53 13 81 D
Brunel Rd. SE16 64 35 79 A
Brunel Rd. W3 55 21 81 A
Brunel St. E16 58 39 81 D
Brunel Wlk. Houn 82 13 73 A
Brunel Wlk. N15 25 33 89 C
Brune St. E1 4 33 81 B
Brunner Cl. NW11 35 26 88 A
Brunner Rd. E17 38 36 88 B
Brunner Rd. W5 54 17 82 D
Brunswick Ave. N11 16 28 93 C
Brunswick Cl. Bexh 79 47 75 D
Brunswick Cl. Pnr 32 12 88 D
Brunswick Cl. Surb 101 15 66 D
Brunswick Cres. N11 16 28 93 C
Brunswick Ct. SE1 8 33 79 A
Brunswick Gdns. Ilf 28 44 91 C
Brunswick Gdns. W5 54 18 82 C
Brunswick Gdns. W8 56 25 80 C
Brunswick Gr. N11 16 28 93 C
Brunswick Mews. W1 1 27 81 D
Brunswick Park Gdns. N11 16 28 93 A
Brunswick Park Rd. N11 16 28 93 C
Brunswick Park. SE5 75 33 76 A
Brunswick Pl. N1 4 32 82 B
Brunswick Pl. SE19 97 34 70 C
Brunswick Rd. Bexh 79 48 75 C
Brunswick Rd. E10 38 38 87 C
Brunswick Rd. E14 58 38 81 C
Brunswick Rd. King 94 19 69 A
Brunswick Rd. N15 25 33 89 C
Brunswick Rd. Sutt 110 25 64 B
Brunswick Rd. W5 54 18 82 A
Brunswick Sq. WC1 3 30 82 C
Brunswick St. E17 38 38 88 A
Brunswick Villas. SE5 75 33 76 A
Brunswick Way. N11 16 28 92 B
Brunton Pl. E14 57 36 81 C
Brushfield St. E1 4 33 81 B
Brussels Rd. SW11 73 26 75 D
Bruton Cl. Chis 99 42 70 D
Bruton La. W1 6 28 80 B
Bruton Pl. W1 6 28 80 B
Bruton Rd. Mord 95 26 68 C
Bruton St. W1 6 28 80 B
Bruton Way. W13 54 16 81 A
Bryan Ave. NW10 45 22 84 D
Bryan Cl. Sun 91 10 70 C
Bryan Rd. SE16 64 36 79 B
Bryan's Alley. SW6 73 25 76 D
Bryanston Ave. Twick 82 13 73 D
Bryanston Cl. Sthl 59 12 78 B
Bryanstone Rd. N8 36 29 88 D
Bryanston Mews E. W1 1 27 81 B
Bryanston Mews W. W1 1 27 81 D
Bryanston Pl. W1 1 27 81 B
Bryanston Sq. W1 1 27 81 D
Bryanston St. W1 1 27 81 D
Bryant Ave. Rom 30 53 90 D
Bryant Cl. Barn 11 24 95 B
Bryant Ct. E2 48 33 83 D
Bryant Rd. Nthlt 53 11 82 A
Bryant St. E15 50 39 84 C
Bryantwood Rd. N7 48 31 85 C
Brycedale Cres. N14 16 29 93 D
Bryce Rd. Dag 52 47 85 A
Bryden Cl. SE26 88 36 71 C
Brydges Pl. WC2 7 30 80 A
Brydges Rd. E15 49 38 85 D
Brydon Wlk. N1 47 30 83 A
Bryett Rd. N7 36 30 86 C
Brynmaer Rd. SW11 74 27 76 B
Bryn-y-mawr Rd. Enf 13 33 96 D
Bryony Rd. W12 55 22 80 A
Buccleuch House. E5 37 34 87 A
Buchanan Gdns. NW10 45 22 83 D
Buchanan Ho. SE21 87 34 72 C
Buchan Rd. SE15 76 35 75 A
Bucharest Rd. SW18 85 26 73 A
Buckbean Path. Rom 30 53 91 C
Buckden Cl. SE12 77 39 74 D
Buckfast Rd. Mord 95 25 68 D
Buckfast St. E2 57 34 82 A
Buckhold Rd. SW18 73 25 74 C
Buckhurst Ave. Cars 104 27 66 D
Buckhurst St. E1 57 34 82 D
Buckingham Arc. WC2 7 30 80 A
Buckingham Ave. E Mol 92 13 69 D
Buckingham Ave. Felt 69 10 74 D
Buckingham Ave. Grnf 44 16 83 A
Buckingham Ave. N20 15 26 94 B
Buckingham Ave. Th Hth 97 31 69 A
Buckingham Ave. Well 78 45 75 C
Buckingham Cl. Enf 13 33 97 C
Buckingham Cl. Hamp 82 12 71 D
Buckingham Cl. Horn 42 53 88 B
Buckingham Cl. Orp 108 45 66 A
Buckingham Cl. W5 54 17 81 A
Buckingham Ct. NW4 22 22 89 A
Buckingham Ct. Sutt 110 25 62 A
Buckingham Gate. SW1 6 29 79 C
Buckingham Gdns. Edg 21 18 91 C
Buckingham Gdns. E Mol 92 13 69 D
Buckingham Gdns. Th Hth 97 31 69 C
Buckingham La. SE23 88 36 73 A
Buckingham Mews. NW10 45 21 83 D
Buckingham Mews. SW1 6 29 79 C
Buckingham Palace Rd. SW1 9 28 78 B
Buckingham Pl. SW1 6 29 79 C
Buckingham Rd. E10 38 37 86 D
Buckingham Rd. E11 39 41 88 A
Buckingham Rd. E15 50 39 85 D
Buckingham Rd. E18 27 39 90 B
Buckingham Rd. Edg 21 18 91 D
Buckingham Rd. Hamp 82 12 71 D
Buckingham Rd. Har 32 14 88 B
Buckingham Rd. Ilf 40 44 86 B
Buckingham Rd. King 93 18 68 D
Buckingham Rd. Mit 104 30 67 A
Buckingham Rd. N1 48 33 84 A
Buckingham Rd. N22 24 30 90 A
Buckingham Rd. NW10 45 21 83 D
Buckingham Rd. Rich 83 17 72 B
Buckingham St. WC2 7 30 80 C
Buckingham Way. Wall 111 29 62 A
Buckland Cres. NW3 46 26 84 A
Buckland Rd. E10 38 38 86 A
Buckland Rd. Sutt 110 23 62 B
Buckland Rise. Pnr 20 11 90 B
Bucklands Rd. Tedd 93 17 70 A
Buckland St. N1 48 33 83 C
Buckland Way. Wor Pk 103 23 66 C
Buckland Wlk. Mord 95 26 68 C
Buckland Wlk. W3 61 20 79 A
Buck La. NW9 34 20 88 B
Buck La. NW9 22 20 89 D
Buckleigh Ave. SW20 95 24 68 B
Buckleigh Rd. SW16 96 30 70 C
Buckleigh Way. SE19 97 33 70 D
Bucklers Alley. SW6 62 24 77 D
Bucklersbury. EC4 4 32 81 D
Bucklers' Way. Cars 104 27 65 D
Buckle St. E1 4 33 81 D
Buckley Cl. Dart 80 51 76 D
Buckley Rd. NW6 46 24 84 D
Buckley St. SE1 7 31 80 C
Buckmaster Rd. SW11 74 27 75 C
Bucknall St. WC2 3 30 81 C
Buckner Rd. SW2 74 30 75 D
Buckrell Rd. E4 18 38 93 B
Buck St. NW1 47 28 84 D
Buckstone Cl. SE23 76 35 74 C
Buckstone Rd. N18 17 34 92 C
Buckters Rents. SE16 57 36 80 C
Buckthorne Rd. SE4 76 36 74 A
Buckwheat Ct. Belv 67 47 79 D
Buck Wlk. E17 26 38 89 D
Buddings Circ. Wem 34 20 86 C
Budds Alley. Twick 71 17 74 A
Budge Row. EC4 4 32 81 D
Budieigh Cres. Well 79 47 76 A
Budleigh Cres. Well 67 47 77 C
Budoch Ct. Ilf 40 46 86 A
Budoch Dri. Ilf 40 46 86 A
Buer Rd. SW6 73 24 76 C
Bugsby's Way. E10 65 39 78 B
Bugsby's Way. SE7 65 40 78 B
Bulganak Rd. Th Hth 97 32 68 C
Bulinga St. SW1 10 30 78 A
Bullace La. Dart 80 54 74 C
Bullace La. Dart 80 54 74 C
Bullace Row. SE5 75 32 76 B
Bull Alley. Well 78 46 75 B
Bullards Pl. E2 57 35 82 B
Bullbanks Rd. Belv 67 50 78 A
Bullen St. SW11 74 27 76 C
Buller Cl. SE15 63 34 77 C
Buller Rd. Bark 51 45 84 C
Buller Rd. N17 25 34 90 C
Buller Rd. N22 25 31 90 C
Buller Rd. NW10 56 23 82 B
Buller Rd. Th Hth 97 32 68 B
Bullers Wood Dri. Chis 99 42 70 D
Bull Inn Ct. WC2 7 30 80 A
Bullivant St. E14 58 38 80 A
Bull La. Chis 100 44 70 D
Bull La. Dag 41 49 86 D
Bull La. N18 17 33 92 C
Bull Rd. E15 50 39 83 D
Bulls Alley. SW14 72 20 75 B
Bulls Bridge Rd. Sthl 59 11 78 A
Bullsbrook Rd. Hay 53 11 80 C
Bull's Gdn. SW3 9 27 78 A
Bulls Head Pas. EC3 4 33 81 C
Bulls Head Yd. Dart 80 54 74 C
Bull Wharf La. EC4 8 32 80 A
Bull Yd. SE15 75 34 76 A
Bulmer Gdns. Har 33 17 87 B
Bulmer Mews. W11 56 25 80 C
Bulstrode Ave. Houn 70 13 75 A
Bulstrode Gdns. Houn 70 13 75 A
Bulstrode Pl. W1 2 28 81 A
Bulstrode Rd. Houn 70 13 75 A
Bulstrode St. W1 2 28 81 C
Bulwer Court Rd. E11 38 38 87 D
Bulwer Gdns. Barn 11 26 96 C
Bulwer Rd. Barn 11 25 96 D
Bulwer Rd. E11 38 38 87 D
Bulwer Rd. N18 17 33 92 A
Bulwer St. W12 56 23 80 C
Bunces La. Wdf Gn 27 39 91 D
Bungalow Rd. SE25 97 33 68 C
Bungalows The. SW16 96 28 70 D
Bungalow The. Ilf 28 45 90 A
Bunhill Row. EC1 4 32 82 D
Bunhouse Pl. SW1 9 28 78 C
Bunker's Hill. Belv 67 49.78 A
Bunkers Hill. NW11 35 26 87 A
Bunn's La. NW7 22 21 91 D
Bunsen St. E3 49 36 83 C
Buntingbridge Rd. Ilf 40 44 88 B
Bunting Cl. Mit 104 27 67 B
Bunton St. SE18 66 43 79 C
Bunyan Rd. E17 26 36 89 A
Buonaparte Mews. SW1 10 29 78 D
Burbage Cl. SE1 8 32 79 D
Burbage Rd. SE21 87 32 73 B
Burberry Cl. N Mal 94 21 69 C
Burbidge Rd. Shep 91 07 68 C
Burbridge Way. N17 25 33 90 D
Burcham St. E14 58 38 81 C
Burcharbro Rd. SE2 67 47 77 B
Burchell Rd. E10 38 37 87 D
Burchell Rd. SE15 75 34 76 B
Burchett Way. Rom 41 48 88 D
Burchwall Cl. Rom 29 50 91 C
Burcote Rd. SW18 85 26 73 B
Burden Cl. Brent 60 17 78 C
Burdenshott Ave. Rich 72 19 75 D
Burden Way. E11 39 40 86 B
Burder Cl. N1 48 33 84 A
Burder Rd. N1 48 33 84 A
Burdett Ave. SW20 94 21 69 C
Burdett Mews. NW3 46 26 84 B
Burdett Mews. NW3 46 26 84 B
Burdett Mews. W2 56 25 81 D
Burdett Rd. Croy 105 32 67 D
Burdett Rd. E14 57 36 81 D
Burdett Rd. E3 57 36 82 D
Burdett Rd. Rich 71 18 75 B
Burdon La. Sutt 110 24 62 B
Burdon Park. Sutt 110 24 62 B
Burfield Cl. SW17 85 26 71 B
Burford Cl. Dag 41 47 86 C
Burford Cl. Ilf 28 44 89 C
Burford Gdns. N13 16 30 93 D
Burford Rd. Brent 60 18 78 C
Burford Rd. Brom 99 42 68 C
Burford Rd. E15 49 38 83 B
Burford Rd. SE6 88 36 72 B
Burford Rd. Sutt 103 25 65 A
Burford Rd. Wor Pk 102 22 66 A
Burgate Cl. Dart 80 51 75 B
Burges Cl. Horn 42 54 88 D
Burges Rd. E6 50 42 84 D
Burges Rd. E6 51 43 84 C
Burgess Ave. NW9 34 20 88 D
Burgess Cl. Felt 82 12 71 A
Burgess Hill. NW2 46 25 85 A
Burgess Rd. E15 50 39 85 A
Burgess Rd. Sutt 110 25 64 B
Burgess St. E14 57 37 81 A
Burge St. SE1 8 32 79 D
Burghill Rd. SE26 88 36 71 A
Burghley Ave. N Mal 94 20 69 B
Burghley Pl. Mit 96 27 68 D
Burghley Rd. E11 39 39 87 C
Burghley Rd. N8 25 31 89 A
Burghley Rd. NW5 47 28 85 B
Burghley Rd. SW19 85 24 71 A
Burgh St. N1 48 31 83 D
Burgon St. EC4 3 31 81 D
Burgos Gr. SE10 76 37 76 B
Burgoyne Rd. Ashf 91 09 70 B
Burgoyne Rd. N4 37 31 88 D
Burgoyne Rd. SE25 97 33 68 D
Burgoyne Rd. SW9 74 30'75 B
Burgundy St. SE1 63 33 78 D
Burham Cl. SE20 98 35 70 C
Burhill Gr. Pnr 20 12 90 C
Burke Cl. SW15 72 21 75 C
Burke St. E16 58 39 81 B
Burland Rd. Rom 29 50 91 A
Burland Rd. SW11 74 27 74 B
Burleigh Ave. Sid 78 45 74 B
Burleigh Ave. Wall 104 28 65 D
Burleigh Gdns. Ashf 81 08 71 C
Burleigh Gdns. N14 16 29 94 C
Burleigh Rd. Enf 13 33 96 C
Burleigh Rd. Sutt 103 24 66 D
Burleigh St. WC2 7 30 80 B
Burleigh Way. Enf 13 32 96 B
Burley Cl. E4 18 37 92 C
Burley Cl. SW16 96 29 69 D
Burley Rd. E16 58 41 81 A
Burlington Arc. W1 6 29 80 A
Burlington Ave. Rich 72 19 76 A
Burlington Ave. Rom 41 49 88 D
Burlington Cl. Felt 81 08 73 B
Burlington Cl. Orp 108 43 65 B
Burlington Cl. W9 56 25 82 C
Burlington Gdns. Rom 41 48 87 A
Burlington Gdns. W1 6 29 80 A
Burlington Gdns. W3 55 20 80 C
Burlington Gdns. W4 61 20 78 C
Burlington La. W4 61 20 77 D
Burlington La. W4 61 21 77 A
Burlington Mews. W3 55 20 80 C
Burlington Pl. SW6 73 24 76 C
Burlington Rd. Enf 13 32 97 B
Burlington Rd. Islw 70 14 76 B
Burlington Rd. N10 24 28 89 A
Burlington Rd. N17 25 34 90 A
Burlington Rd. N Mal 94 22 68 C
Burlington Rd. SW6 73 24 76 C
Burlington Rd. Th Hth 97 32 69 D
Burlington Rd. W4 61 20 78 B
Burlington Rise. Barn 16 27 94 B
Burma Ct. N16 48 32 85 B
Burma Rd. N16 48 32 85 B
Burmester Rd. SW17 85 26 72 C
Burnaby Cres. W4 61 20 77 A
Burnaby Gdns. W4 61 19 77 B
Burnaby St. SW10 62 26 77 C
Burnbrae Cl. N3 23 25 91 B
Burnbury Rd. SW12 86 29 73 C
Burncroft Ave. Enf 14 35 97 D
Burnell Ave. Rich 83 17 71 C
Burnell Ave. Well 78 46 76 C
Burnell Gdns. Stan 21 17 90 D
Burnell Rd. Sutt 110 25 64 B
Burness Cl. N7 47 30 84 B
Burne St. NW1 1 27 81 A
Burnett Cl. E9 49 35 85 C
Burnett Rd. Eri 68 53 77 B
Burney Ave. Surb 101 18 67 B
Burney St. SE10 64 38 77 C
Burnfoot Ave. SW6 73 24 76 A
Burnham Cres. Dart 80 53 75 C
Burnham Cres. E11 27 41 89 C
Burnham Ct. NW4 23 23 89 C
Burnham Dri. Wor Pk 103 23 65 B
Burnham Estate. E2 57 35 82 A
Burnham Gdns. Houn 69 10 76 B
Burnham Rd. Dag 51 46 83 B
Burnham Rd. Dart 80 53 75 D
Burnham Rd. E4 18 36 92 D
Burnham Rd. Mord 95 25 68 D
Burnham Rd. Rom 29 50 89 B
Burnham St. E2 57 35 82 A
Burnham St. King 94 19 69 A
Burnham Way. W13 60 16 79 D
Burnhill Rd. Beck 98 37 69 C
Burnley Rd. NW10 45 22 85 C
Burnley Rd. SW9 74 30 76 D
Burnsall St. SW3 9 27 78 C
Burns Ave. Felt 69 10 74 C
Burns Ave. Sid 78 46 74 D
Burns Ave. Sthl 53 13 80 A
Burns Cl. Eri 80 51 76 B
Burns Cl. Well 78 45 76 B
Burns Ct. Wall 111 28 63 D
Burnside Cl. Barn 11 25 96 A
Burnside Cl. Twick 71 16 74 C
Burnside Cres. Wem 44 17 83 B
Burn Side. N9 18 35 93 C
Burnside Rd. Dag 41 47 87 C

| Street | Page | Grid |
|---|---|---|
| Burnside St. E3 | 57 | 36 82 A |
| Burn's Rd. NW10 | 45 | 21 83 B |
| Burns Rd. SW11 | 74 | 27 76 D |
| Burns Rd. W13 | 60 | 16 79 B |
| Burns Way. Houn | 70 | 18 83 C |
| Burnt Ash Hill SE12 | 89 | 11 76 B |
| Burnt Ash La. Brom | 89 | 40 73 C |
| Burnt Ash La. SE12 | 77 | 40 71 D |
| Burnthwaite Rd. SW6 | 62 | 39 74 B |
| Burnt Oak Bwy. Edg | 22 | 25 77 C |
| Burnt Oak La. Sid | 90 | 19 90 B |
| Burntwood Ave. Horn | 42 | 20 90 A |
| Burntwood SE18 | 86 | 46 73 B |
| Burntwood Grange Rd. SW18 | 5 | 54 88 C |
| Burntwood La. SW18 | 85 | 27 73 C |
| Burnway. Horn | 42 | 27 79 C |
| Buross St. E1 | 57 | 26 72 B |
| Burrage Gr. SE18 | 66 | 54 87 A |
| Burrage Pl. SE18 | 66 | 34 81 D |
| Burrage Rd. SE18 | 66 | 44 78 A |
| Burrard Rd. E16 | 58 | 43 78 D |
| Burrard Rd. NW6 | 46 | 44 78 C |
| Burr Cl. Bexh | 79 | 40 81 D |
| Burr Cl. E1 | 57 | 25 85 A |
| Burrell Cl. Croy | 106 | 48 75 B |
| Burrell Row. Beck | 98 | 34 80 C |
| Burrell St. SE1 | 7 | 36 67 C |
| Burritt Rd. King | 94 | 37 69 C |
| Burroughs Gdns. NW4 | 22 | 31 80 D |
| Burroughs The. NW4 | 22 | 19 69 C |
| Burrows Mews. SE1 | 7 | 22 89 D |
| Burrows Rd. NW10 | 56 | 22 89 D |
| Burrow Wlk. SE21 | 87 | 31 79 B |
| Burr Rd. SW18 | 85 | 23 82 A |
| Bursar St. SE1 | 8 | 32 73 A |
| Bursdon Cl. Sid | 90 | 25 73 A |
| Bursland Rd. Enf | 14 | 33 80 C |
| Burslem Ave. Ilf | 28 | 45 72 B |
| Burslem St. E1 | 57 | 35 96 D |
| Burstall Rd. N15 | 37 | 46 91 A |
| Burstock Rd. SW15 | 73 | 34 81 D |
| Burston Rd. SW15 | 73 | 33 88 A |
| Burstow Rd. SW20 | 95 | 24 75 C |
| Burtenshaw Rd. Surb | 101 | 23 75 D |
| Burtley Cl. N4 | 37 | 24 69 A |
| Burton Gdns. Houn | 70 | 16 67 C |
| *Burton Gr. SE17 | 63 | 32 87 C |
| Burtonhole Cl. NW7 | 15 | 12 76 B |
| Burtonhole La. NW7 | 15 | 32 78 D |
| Burton La. SW9 | 75 | 23 92 B |
| Burton Mews. SW1 | 9 | 23 92 B |
| Burton Pl. WC1 | 2 | 31 78 C |
| Burton Rd. E18 | 27 | 28 82 B |
| Burton Rd. King | 93 | 29 82 B |
| Burton Rd. NW6 | 46 | 40 89 B |
| Burton Rd. SW9 | 75 | 18 70 C |
| Burton Rd. SW9 | 75 | 24 84 D |
| Burtons Ct. E15 | 49 | 31 76 C |
| Burton's Rd. Hamp | 82 | 31 76 D |
| Burton St. WC1 | 2 | 38 84 D |
| Burts Rd. E16 | 58 | 13 71 B |
| Burwash Rd. SE18 | 66 | 29 82 D |
| Burwell Ave. Grnf | 44 | 41 80 C |
| Burwell Cl. E1 | 57 | 44 78 D |
| Burwell Rd. E10 | 38 | 15 84 A |
| Burwell Wlk. E3 | 57 | 34 81 D |
| Burwood Ave. Brom | 107 | 36 87 C |
| Burwood Ave. Pnr | 32 | 37 82 C |
| Burwood Pl. W2 | 1 | 40 65 B |
| Bury Ave. Ruis | 31 | 11 88 A |
| Bury Cl. EC3 | 4 | 27 81 C |
| Bury Gr. Mord | 103 | 08 88 C |
| Bury Pl. WC1 | 2 | 33 81 C |
| Bury Rd. Dag | 52 | 25 67 B |
| Bury Rd. Enf | 14 | 30 81 A |
| Bury Rd. N22 | 25 | 50 85 C |
| Bury St. EC3 | 4 | 38 96 B |
| Bury St. N9 | 17 | 33 81 C |
| Bury Street W. N9 | 17 | 33 81 C |
| Bury St. Ruis | 31 | 33 94 A |
| Bury St. SW1 | 6 | 08 88 D |
| Bury Wlk. SW3 | 9 | 29 80 C |
| Busby Pl. NW5 | 47 | 27 78 C |
| Busby St. E2 | 57 | 29 84 B |
| Busch Cnr. Islw | 71 | 33 82 D |
| Bushberry Rd. E9 | 49 | 16 76 B |
| Bush Cl. Ilf | 40 | 36 84 A |
| Bush Cottages SW18 | 73 | 44 88 B |
| Bushell Cl. SW2 | 86 | 25 74 A |
| Bushell St. E1 | 57 | 30 72 B |
| Bushell Way. Chis | 90 | 34 80 C |
| Bush Elms Rd. Horn | 42 | 43 71 C |
| Bushey Ave. E18 | 27 | 52 87 A |
| | | 39 89 B |

| Street | Page | Grid |
|---|---|---|
| Bushey Ave. Orp | 108 | 44 66 B |
| Bushey Cl. Uxb | 31 | 07 86 A |
| Bushey Ct. SW20 | 94 | 22 68 B |
| Bushey Ct. SW20 | 95 | 23 69 C |
| Bushey Down. SW12 | 86 | 28 72 B |
| Bushey Hill Rd. SE5 | 75 | 33 76 B |
| Bushey La. Sutt | 110 | 25 64 A |
| Bushey Rd. Croy | 106 | 37 65 A |
| Bushey Rd. E13 | 50 | 41 83 C |
| Bushey Rd. N15 | 37 | 33 88 C |
| Bushey Rd. Sutt | 110 | 25 64 B |
| Bushey Rd. SW20 | 94 | 22 68 B |
| Bushey Rd. Uxb | 31 | 07 86 A |
| Bushey Way. Beck | 106 | 38 67 B |
| Bush Fair Ct. N14 | 12 | 28 95 D |
| Bush Gr. NW9 | 34 | 20 87 A |
| Bushgrove Rd. Dag | 52 | 47 85 B |
| Bush Gr. Stan | 21 | 17 90 B |
| Bush Hill. N21 | 17 | 34 81 D |
| Bush Hill. N21 | 13 | 32 94 A |
| Bush Hill Par. Enf | 12 | 32 95 C |
| Bush Hill Rd. Har | 33 | 32 94 B |
| Bush Hill Rd. N21 | 17 | 18 88 D |
| Bush La. EC4 | 8 | 32 95 D |
| Bushmoor Cres. SE18 | 66 | 43 77 D |
| Bushnell Rd. SW17 | 86 | 23 96 B |
| Bush Rd. E11 | 39 | 40 87 A |
| Bush Rd. E8 | 48 | 34 83 B |
| Bush Rd. Rich | 60 | 18 77 B |
| Bush Rd. SE8 | 64 | 35 78 B |
| Bushway. Dag | 52 | 47 85 A |
| Bushwood. E11 | 39 | 40 87 C |
| Bushwood Rd. Rich | 61 | 19 77 A |
| Bushy Park Gdns. Tedd | 82 | 14 71 D |
| Bushy Park Rd. Tedd | 93 | 16 70 D |
| Bushy Rd. Tedd | 93 | 15 70 D |
| Butcher Row. E14 | 57 | 35 80 B |
| Butcher Row. E1 | 57 | 35 81 D |
| Butchers Rd. E16 | 58 | 40 81 C |
| Bute Ave. Rich | 83 | 18 73 C |
| Bute Ct. Wall | 111 | 29 64 C |
| Bute Gdns. W6 | 62 | 23 78 B |
| Bute Gdns. Wall | 111 | 29 64 C |
| Bute Gdns W. Wall | 111 | 29 64 C |
| Bute Rd. Croy | 105 | 31 66 C |
| Bute Rd. Ilf | 40 | 44 88 A |
| Bute St. Wall | 111 | 29 64 A |
| Bute St. SW7 | 9 | 26 78 B |
| Bute Wlk. N1 | 48 | 28 78 B |
| Butler Ave. Har | 32 | 14 87 B |
| Butler Pl. SW1 | 6 | 29 79 D |
| Butler Rd. Dag | 51 | 46 85 B |
| Butler Rd. Har | 32 | 14 87 A |
| Butler St. E2 | 57 | 35 82 A |
| Butley Ct. 3 | 49 | 36 83 C |
| Buttercup Cl. Rom | 30 | 53 90 B |
| Butterfields. E17 | 38 | 43 74 D |
| Butterfly La. SE9 | 78 | 28 65 C |
| Butter Hill. Wall | 104 | 43 74 D |
| Buttermere Cl. N.Mal | 103 | 23 67 D |
| Buttermere Dri. SW15 | 73 | 24 74 B |
| Buttermere Wlk. E8 | 48 | 33 84 B |
| Butterwick. W6 | 62 | 23 78 B |
| Buttesland St. N1 | 4 | 32 82 B |
| Buttfield Cl. Dag | 52 | 49 84 B |
| Buttmarsh Cl. SE18 | 66 | 43 78 D |
| Buttsbury Rd. Ilf | 51 | 44 85 D |
| Butts Cres. Felt | 82 | 13 72 C |
| Butts Green Rd. Horn | 42 | 53 88 D |
| Buttsmead. Nthwd | 19 | 09 91 C |
| Butts Rd. Brom | 89 | 39 71 C |
| Butts The. Brent | 60 | 17 77 B |
| Butts The. Sun | 92 | 11 68 A |
| Buxted Cl (off Middleton Rd). E8 | | 30 81 A |
| Buxted Cl (off Richmond Rd). E8 | 48 | |
| Buxted Rd. N12 | 16 | 33 84 D |
| Buxton Cl. Wdf Gn | 27 | 27 92 C |
| Buxton Cres. Sutt | 110 | 41 91 B |
| Buxton Dri. E11 | 27 | 24 64 A |
| Buxton Dri. N.Mal | 94 | 32 82 A |
| Buxton Gdns. W3 | 55 | 20 69 D |
| Buxton Rd. E15 | 50 | 19 80 B |
| Buxton Rd. E17 | 26 | 39 85 C |
| Buxton Rd. E4 | 18 | 36 89 C |
| Buxton Rd. Eri | 67 | 38 94 B |
| Buxton Rd. Ilf | 40 | 50 77 D |
| Buxton Rd. N19 | 36 | 45 88 C |
| Buxton Rd. NW2 | 45 | 29 87 D |
| Buxton Rd. SW14 | 72 | 22 84 B |
| Buxton Rd. Th Hth | 105 | 21 75 A |
| Buxton St. E1 | 57 | 31 67 B |
| Buxton St. E1 | 4 | 33 82 D |
| Buxton St. E1 | 57 | 34 82 C |

| Street | Page | Grid |
|---|---|---|
| Byam St. SW6 | 73 | 26 76 C |
| Byards Croft. SW16 | 96 | 29 69 B |
| Byatt Wlk. Hamp | 92 | 12 70 A |
| Bychurch End. Tedd | 83 | 15 71 D |
| Bycroft Rd. Sthl | 53 | 13 82 C |
| Bycroft St. SE20 | 98 | 35 70 D |
| Bycullah Ave. N15 | 37 | 31 97 D |
| Bycullah Rd. Enf | 13 | 31 97 B |
| Byefield Rd. Islw | 71 | 16 75 A |
| Byegrove Rd. N7 | 47 | 30 85 B |
| Bye The. W3 | 55 | 30 68 A |
| Byeways The. Surb | 101 | 19 67 B |
| Bye Ways. Twick | 82 | 13 72 D |
| Bye Way The. Har | 21 | 15 90 B |
| Byeway The. SW14 | 72 | 20 75 A |
| Byfield Gdns. SW13 | 72 | 22 76 A |
| Byford Cl. E15 | 50 | 39 84 C |
| Bygrove Rd. SW19 | 95 | 26 70 B |
| Bygrove St. E14 | 57 | 37 81 D |
| Byland Cl. N21 | 17 | 32 94 A |
| Byland Cl. SE2 | 66 | 30 94 B |
| Byne Rd. Cars | 104 | 46 79 D |
| Byne Rd. SE26 | 88 | 27 65 A |
| Bynes Rd. S Croy | 112 | 35 71 C |
| Byng Pl. WC1 | 2 | 32 63 D |
| Byng St. E14 | 57 | 29 82 D |
| Byng St. E14 | 64 | 23 96 B |
| Bynon Ave. Bexh | 79 | 35 77 A |
| Byrne Rd. SW12 | 86 | 48 75 B |
| Byron Ave. E12 | 50 | 28 72 B |
| Byron Ave. Sutt | 110 | 42 84 B |
| Byron Ave E. Sutt | 110 | 28 90 D |
| Byron Ave. Houn | 69 | 26 64 B |
| Byron Ave. N.Mal | 102 | 10 76 D |
| Byron Ave. NW9 | 22 | 22 67 A |
| Byron Ave. Sutt | 110 | 19 89 B |
| Byron Cl. E8 | 48 | 26 64 B |
| Byron Cl. Hamp | 82 | 34 83 A |
| Byron Cl. N2 | 23 | 12 71 B |
| Byron Ct. Enf | 13 | 26 88 D |
| Byron Gdns. Sutt | 110 | 31 97 D |
| Byron Hill Rd. Har | 33 | 26 64 B |
| Byron Rd. E10 | 38 | 15 86 A |
| Byron Rd. E17 | 26 | 37 87 D |
| Byron Rd. Har | 15 | 37 89 A |
| Byron Rd. NW2 | 34 | 15 88 C |
| Byron Rd. S Croy | 112 | 15 89 B |
| Byron Rd. W5 | 55 | 22 86 B |
| Byron Rd. Wem | 33 | 19 80 C |
| Byron St. E14 | 58 | 17 86 C |
| Byron Way. Nthlt | 53 | 38 81 C |
| Byron Way. Rom | 30 | 12 82 A |
| Bysouth Cl. Ilf | 28 | 53 90 A |
| Bythorn St. SW9 | 74 | 43 90 B |
| Byton Rd. SW17 | 77 | 30 75 D |
| Byward Ave. Felt | 70 | 27 70 B |
| Byward St. EC3 | 8 | 11 74 C |
| Bywater Rd. SW3 | 9 | 33 80 A |
| Byways The. Eps | 109 | 27 78 D |
| Byward St. Sutt | 110 | 21 64 B |
| Bywell Pl. W1 | 2 | 26 62 B |
| Byworth Wlk. N19 | 36 | 29 81 A |
| | | 35 67 D |
| | | 30 87 C |

| Street | Page | Grid |
|---|---|---|
| Cabbell St. NW1 | 1 | 27 81 A |
| Cabinet Way. E4 | 26 | 36 91 B |
| Cable St. E1 | 57 | 35 80 A |
| Cabul Rd. SW11 | 74 | 27 76 C |
| Cactus Wlk. W12 | 55 | 21 81 D |
| Cadbury Cl. Islw | 71 | 16 76 A |
| Cadbury Cl. Sun | 91 | 09 70 C |
| Cadbury Rd. Sun | 91 | 09 70 A |
| Cadbury Way. SE16 | 63 | 34 79 C |
| Caddington Cl. Barn | 12 | 27 95 A |
| Caddington Rd. NW2 | 35 | 24 86 C |
| Cadell Cl. E2 | 57 | 33 83 D |
| Cade Rd. SE10 | 76 | 38 76 B |
| Cader Rd. SW18 | 73 | 26 74 C |
| Cadet Pl. E10 | 65 | 39 78 C |
| Cadiz Rd. Dag | 52 | 50 84 A |
| Cadiz St. SE17 | 63 | 32 78 C |
| Cadley Terr. SE23 | 88 | 35 72 A |
| Cadman Cl. N Mal | 94 | 21 68 C |
| Cadmus Cl. SW4 | 74 | 29 75 B |
| Cadogan Cl. Beck | 98 | 38 69 B |
| Cadogan Cl. E9 | 49 | 36 84 D |
| Cadogan Cl. Har | 32 | 13 85 B |
| Cadogan Cl. Tedd | 83 | 15 71 C |
| Cadogan Cl. Sutt | 110 | 25 63 B |
| Cadogan Gate. SW1 | 9 | 27 78 B |
| Cadogan Gdns. E18 | 27 | 40 89 B |
| Cadogan Gdns. N21 | 17 | 31 95 A |
| Cadogan Gdns. N3 | 23 | 25 90 B |
| Cadogan Gdns. SW3 | 9 | 27 78 B |
| Cadogan La. SW1 | 6 | 28 79 C |

| Street | Page | Grid |
|---|---|---|
| Cadogan Pl. SW1 | 5 | 27 79 D |
| Cadogan Pl. SW1 | 9 | 28 78 A |
| Cadogan Rd. Surb | 101 | 17 67 B |
| Cadogan Sq. SW1 | 9 | 27 78 B |
| Cadogan St. SW3 | 9 | 27 78 B |
| Cadogan Terr. E9 | 49 | 36 84 D |
| Cadoxton Ave. N15 | 37 | 33 88 D |
| Cadwallon Rd. SE9 | 90 | 44 72 A |
| Caedmon Rd. N7 | 47 | 37 85 B |
| Caernarvon Cl. Mit | 96 | 30 68 A |
| Caernarvon Dri. Ilf | 27 | 43 90 A |
| Caesar St. E2 | 4 | 33 82 B |
| Caesars Wlk. Mit | 104 | 27 67 B |
| Cahill St. EC1 | 4 | 32 82 C |
| Cahir St. E14 | 64 | 37 78 B |
| Cain's La. Felt | 69 | 09 74 A |
| Caird St. W10 | 56 | 24 82 B |
| Cairn Ave. W5 | 54 | 17 80 D |
| Cairndale Cl. Brom | 99 | 39 70 D |
| Cairnfield Ave. NW2 | 21 | 21 86 D |
| Cairns Ave. Wdf Gn | 27 | 42 91 B |
| Cairns Cl. Dart | 53 | 74 B |
| Cairns Rd. SW11 | 74 | 27 74 A |
| Cairn Way. Stan | 21 | 15 91 B |
| Cairo New Rd. Croy | 105 | 31 65 B |
| Cairo Rd. E17 | 26 | 37 89 C |
| Caistor Mews. SW12 | 86 | 28 73 B |
| Caistor Park Rd. E15 | 50 | 39 83 B |
| Caistor Rd. SW12 | 86 | 28 73 B |
| Caithness Gdns. Sid | 78 | 28 73 A |
| Caithness Rd. Mit | 96 | 28 70 D |
| Caithness Rd. W14 | 62 | 23 79 D |
| Calabria Rd. N5 | 47 | 31 84 B |
| Calais St. SE5 | 75 | 31 76 B |
| Calbourne Rd. SW12 | 86 | 28 73 A |
| Calcott Wlk. SE9 | 89 | 41 71 B |
| Caldbeck Ave. Wor Pk | 102 | 22 66 D |
| Caldecot Rd. SE5 | 75 | 32 76 C |
| Caldecott Way. E5 | 38 | 35 86 D |
| Calder Ave. Grnf | 54 | 15 83 D |
| Calder Cl. Enf | 13 | 33 96 A |
| Calder Gdns. Edg | 22 | 19 89 A |
| Calderon Pl. W10 | 56 | 23 81 A |
| Calder Rd. Mord | 103 | 26 67 A |
| Caldervale Rd. SW4 | 74 | 29 74 B |
| Calderwood St. SE18 | 66 | 43 78 A |
| Caldwell St. SW9 | 63 | 32 77 D |
| Caldy Rd. Belv | 67 | 31 77 C |
| Caldy Wlk. N1 | 48 | 46 79 D |
| Cale St. SE1 | 8 | 32 84 A |
| Caledonian Rd. N7 | 47 | 32 79 A |
| Caledonia St. N1 | 3 | 30 84 B |
| Caledon Rd. E6 | 50 | 42 83 B |
| Caledon Rd. Wall | 111 | 28 64 A |
| Cale St. SW3 | 9 | 27 78 C |
| Caletock Way. E10 | 65 | 39 78 D |
| Calgary Ct. SE16 | 64 | 35 79 A |
| Calgate Cl. SW9 | 75 | 24 73 C |
| California Rd. N Mal | 94 | 20 68 A |
| Callander Rd. SE6 | 88 | 38 72 A |
| Callard Ave. N13 | 17 | 31 92 B |
| Callcott Rd. NW6 | 46 | 24 84 D |
| Callcott St. W8 | 56 | 25 80 C |
| Callendar Rd. SW7 | 5 | 26 79 D |
| Callis Rd. E17 | 38 | 26 79 D |
| Callow St. SW3 | 62 | 36 88 D |
| Calmington Rd. SE5 | 63 | 26 77 B |
| Calmont Rd. Brom | 99 | 33 77 A |
| Calne Ave. Ilf | 28 | 39 70 A |
| Calonne Rd. SW19 | 85 | 43 90 B |
| Calshot Rd. Houn | 69 | 23 71 B |
| Calshot St. N1 | 47 | 07 75 B |
| Calshot Way. Enf | 13 | 30 83 D |
| Calthorpe Gdns. Sutt | 110 | 31 96 B |
| Calthorpe St. WC1 | 3 | 26 65 C |
| Calva St. Barn | 12 | 30 82 D |
| Calverley Cres. Dag | 41 | 28 96 C |
| Calverley Cl. Beck | 98 | 49 86 A |
| Calverley Gr. N19 | 36 | 37 70 B |
| Calverley Rd. Eps | 109 | 29 87 D |
| Calvert Ave. E2 | 4 | 22 63 A |
| Calvert Cl. Belv | 67 | 33 82 B |
| Calverton Rd. E6 | 51 | 49 78 A |
| Calvert Rd. Barn | 11 | 43 83 A |
| Calvert Rd. E10 | 65 | 23 97 D |
| Calvert's Bldgs. SE1 | 8 | 39 78 D |
| Calvin St. E1 | 4 | 32 80 D |
| Calydon Rd. SE7 | 65 | 40 78 D |
| Camac Rd. Twick | 82 | 14 73 D |
| Cambalt Rd. SW15 | 73 | 28 96 C |
| Camberley Ave. Enf | 13 | 23 74 B |
| Camberley Ave SW20 | 94 | 33 96 C |
| Camberley Rd. Houn | 69 | 22 69 D |
| | | 07 75 A |

| Street | Page | Grid |
|---|---|---|
| Cambert Way. SE3 | 77 | 40 75 D |
| Camberwell Church St. SE5 | 75 | 32 76 B |
| Camberwell Glebe. SE5 | 75 | 33 76 A |
| Camberwell Green. SE5 | 75 | 32 76 B |
| Camberwell Gr. SE5 | 75 | 32 76 B |
| Camberwell New Rd. SE5 | 63 | 31 77 D |
| Camberwell Pas. SE5 | 75 | 32 77 C |
| Camberwell Rd. SE5 | 63 | 32 77 C |
| Camberwell Station Rd. SE5 | 75 | 32 76 B |
| Cambeys Rd. Dag | 52 | 50 85 C |
| Camborne Ave. Rom | 30 | 54 91 C |
| Camborne Ave. W13 | 60 | 17 79 A |
| Camborne Cl. Houn | 70 | 07 75 A |
| Camborne Rd. Croy | 105 | 24 67 A |
| Camborne Rd. Mord | 103 | 24 67 A |
| Camborne Rd. Sutt | 110 | 25 63 D |
| Camborne Rd. SW18 | 85 | 25 73 A |
| Camborne Rd. Well | 78 | 45 76 D |
| Camborne Road S. Houn | 69 | 07 75 A |
| Camborne Way. Houn | 69 | 07 75 A |
| Camborne Way. Houn | 70 | 13 76 A |
| Camborne Way. Rom | 30 | 54 91 C |
| Cambourne Ave. N9 | 17 | 35 94 B |
| Cambourne Mews. W11 | 56 | 24 81 C |
| Cambray Rd. Orp | 108 | 45 66 B |
| Cambray Rd. SW12 | 86 | 29 73 C |
| Cambria Cl. Houn | 70 | 13 75 C |
| Cambria Cl. Sid | 90 | 44 73 D |
| Cambria Ct. Felt | 81 | 10 73 B |
| Cambrian Ave. Ilf | 40 | 45 89 A |
| Cambrian Cl. SE27 | 87 | 31 72 D |
| Cambrian Rd. E10 | 38 | 37 87 A |
| Cambrian Rd. Rich | 71 | 18 74 D |
| Cambria Rd. SE5 | 75 | 32 75 A |
| Cambria St. SW6 | 62 | 25 77 D |
| Cambridge Ave. N Grnf | 44 | 15 85 D |
| Cambridge Ave. N Mal | 94 | 21 69 C |
| Cambridge Ave. NW6 | 46 | 25 83 C |
| Cambridge Ave. Rom | 30 | 53 89 A |
| Cambridge Ave. Well | 78 | 45 75 D |
| Cambridge Circ. WC2 | 2 | 28 81 D |
| Cambridge Cl. Houn | 70 | 12 75 C |
| Cambridge Cl. SW20 | 94 | 23 68 B |
| Cambridge Cottages. Rich | 61 | 19 77 A |
| Cambridge Cres. E2 | 48 | 34 83 D |
| Cambridge Cres. Tedd | 83 | 16 71 C |
| Cambridge Dri. Ruis | 32 | 11 86 B |
| Cambridge Dri. SE12 | 77 | 40 74 A |
| Cambridge Gate Mews. NW1 | 2 | 28 82 D |
| Cambridge Gate. NW1 | 2 | 28 82 D |
| Cambridge Gdns. Enf | 13 | 32 94 C |
| Cambridge Gdns. King | 94 | 19 69 C |
| Cambridge Gdns. N17 | 25 | 32 91 D |
| Cambridge Gdns. N21 | 17 | 32 94 B |
| Cambridge Gdns. NW6 | 46 | 25 83 C |
| Cambridge Gdns. W10 | 56 | 24 81 C |
| Cambridge Green. SE9 | 90 | 43 73 D |
| Cambridge Grove Rd. King | 94 | 19 68 A |
| Cambridge Grove Rd. King | 94 | 19 69 C |
| Cambridge Rd. SE20 | 97 | 34 70 D |
| Cambridge Rd. G. W6 | 61 | 22 78 B |
| Cambridge Heath Rd. E1 | 57 | 35 82 C |
| Cambridge Park. E11 | 39 | 17 73 B |
| Cambridge Park. Twick | 83 | 17 73 B |
| Cambridge Park Rd. E11 | 39 | 17 73 B |
| Cambridge Park. Twick | 83 | 17 74 C |
| Cambridge Pl. E9 | 49 | 35 84 C |
| Cambridge Pl. W8 | 1 | 25 79 B |
| Cambridge Rd. Ashf | 91 | 08 70 C |
| Cambridge Rd. Bark | 51 | 44 84 C |
| Cambridge Rd. Brom | 89 | 40 70 C |
| Cambridge Rd. Cars | 111 | 27 64 C |
| Cambridge Rd. E11 | 39 | 40 88 C |
| Cambridge Rd. E4 | 18 | 38 94 D |
| Cambridge Rd. Hamp | 92 | 12 72 D |
| Cambridge Rd. Har | 32 | 13 88 A |
| Cambridge Rd. Houn | 70 | 12 75 C |
| Cambridge Rd. Ilf | 40 | 45 87 C |
| Cambridge Rd. King | 94 | 19 69 C |
| Cambridge Rd. Mit | 96 | 29 68 A |
| Cambridge Rd. N Mal | 94 | 21 68 A |
| Cambridge Rd. NW6 | 56 | 25 82 A |
| Cambridge Rd. Rich | 61 | 25 83 C |
| Cambridge Rd. SE20 | 97 | 34 68 B |
| Cambridge Rd. Sid | 78 | 32 80 D |
| Cambridge Rd. Sthl | 53 | 12 80 D |
| Cambridge Rd. SW11 | 74 | 27 76 B |
| Cambridge Rd. SW13 | 72 | 21 76 B |
| Cambridge Rd. Tedd | 83 | 16 71 C |
| Cambridge Rd. Twick | 83 | 17 74 D |
| Cambridge Rd. W7 | 60 | 15 79 B |
| Cambridge Road N. W4 | 61 | 19 78 D |

| Street | Page | Grid |
|---|---|---|
| Cambridge Road S. W4 | 61 | 19 78 D |
| Cambridge Row. SE18 | 66 | 43 78 D |
| Cambridge Sq. W2 | 1 | 27 81 C |
| Cambridge St. SW1 | 10 | 29 78 C |
| Cambridge Terr Mews. NW1 | 2 | 28 82 B |
| Cambridge Terr. NW1 | 2 | 28 82 B |
| Cambridge Yd. W7 | 60 | 15 79 B |
| Cambus Rd. E16 | 58 | 40 81 A |
| Camdale Rd. SE18 | 66 | 45 77 D |
| Camden Ave. Felt | 82 | 11 73 C |
| Camden Ave. Hay | 53 | 11 80 B |
| Camden Cl. Chis | 100 | 44 70 C |
| Camden Cnr. Chis | 100 | 43 69 B |
| Camden Gdns. NW1 | 47 | 29 84 C |
| Camden Gdns. Sutt | 110 | 25 64 D |
| Camden Gdns. Th Hth | 97 | 31 68 B |
| Camden Gr. Chis | 100 | 43 70 B |
| Camden High St. NW1 | 47 | 28 83 B |
| Camdenhurst St. E14 | 57 | 36 81 C |
| Camden La. N7 | 47 | 29 84 B |
| Camden Mews. NW1 | 47 | 29 84 B |
| Camden Park Rd. Chis | 100 | 43 70 C |
| Camden Park Rd. NW1 | 47 | 29 84 B |
| Camden Pas. N1 | 48 | 31 83 B |
| Camden Rd. Cars | 111 | 27 64 B |
| Camden Rd. E11 | 39 | 40 88 D |
| Camden Rd. E17 | 38 | 36 88 D |
| Camden Rd. N7 | 47 | 30 85 C |
| Camden Rd. NW1 | 47 | 29 84 C |
| Camden Rd. Sutt | 110 | 25 64 D |
| Camden Row. SE3 | 77 | 39 76 C |
| Camden Sq. NW1 | 47 | 29 84 B |
| Camden Sq. SE15 | 75 | 33 76 B |
| Camden St. NW1 | 47 | 29 83 A |
| Camden Terr. NW1 | 47 | 29 84 B |
| Camden Way. Chis | 100 | 43 70 C |
| Camden Way. Th Hth | 97 | 31 68 A |
| Camel Rd. E16 | 58 | 41 80 D |
| Camelford Wlk. W11 | 56 | 24 81 C |
| Camellia Pl. Twick | 82 | 13 73 B |
| Camellia St. SW8 | 10 | 30 77 C |
| Camelot Cl. SW19 | 85 | 25 74 C |
| Camel Rd. E16 | 58 | 41 80 D |
| Camera Pl. SW10 | 9 | 26 77 B |
| Cameron Cl. N18 | 17 | 34 92 D |
| Cameron Cl. N20 | 16 | 26 93 B |
| Cameron Pl. E1 | 57 | 34 81 D |
| Cameron Rd. Brom | 99 | 40 68 C |
| Cameron Rd. Croy | 105 | 31 67 D |
| Cameron Rd. Ilf | 40 | 45 87 C |
| Cameron Rd. SE6 | 88 | 36 72 B |
| Camerton Cl. E8 | 48 | 33 84 B |
| Camilla Rd. SE16 | 63 | 34 78 B |
| Camlan Rd. Brom | 89 | 39 71 B |
| Camlet St. E2 | 4 | 33 82 D |
| Camlet Way. Barn | 11 | 25 97 B |
| Camley St. N1 | 47 | 29 83 B |
| Camm Gdns. Surb | 101 | 15 66 B |
| Camomile Ave. Mit | 96 | 27 69 B |
| Camomile St. EC3 | 4 | 33 81 C |
| Campana Rd. SW6 | 73 | 25 76 A |
| Campbell Ave. Ilf | 28 | 44 89 C |
| Campbell Cl. Rom | 30 | 51 91 A |
| Campbell Cl. Ruis | 31 | 10 88 C |
| Campbell Cl. SE18 | 66 | 43 76 A |
| Campbell Cl. Twick | 83 | 14 73 B |
| Campbell Ct. NW9 | 34 | 20 88 C |
| Campbell Rd. Croy | 105 | 31 67 D |
| Campbell Rd. E15 | 50 | 39 85 B |
| Campbell Rd. E17 | 26 | 36 89 D |
| Campbell Rd. E3 | 57 | 37 82 A |
| Campbell Rd. E6 | 50 | 42 83 A |
| Campbell Rd. N17 | 25 | 34 90 A |
| Campbell Rd. Twick | 83 | 14 72 B |
| Campbell Rd. W7 | 54 | 15 80 A |
| Campbell St. W2 | 1 | 26 82 D |
| Campdale Rd. N7 | 36 | 29 85 A |
| Campden Cres. Dag | 52 | 47 85 A |
| Campden Cres. Wem | 33 | 16 86 D |
| Campden Gr. W8 | 56 | 25 79 A |
| Campden Hill Gdns. W8 | 56 | 25 80 C |
| Campden Hill Pl. W14 | 56 | 24 80 D |
| Campden Hill Rd. W8 | 62 | 25 79 A |
| Campden Hill Sq. W14 | 56 | 24 80 D |
| Campden Hill. W8 | 62 | 25 79 A |
| Campden House Cl. W8 | 62 | 25 79 A |
| Campden Rd. S Croy | 112 | 33 64 C |
| Campden Rd. Uxb | 31 | 07 86 C |
| Campden St. W8 | 62 | 25 79 A |
| Campen Cl. SW19 | 85 | 24 72 C |
| Camperdown St. E1 | 4 | 33 81 D |
| Campfield Rd. SE9 | 89 | 41 73 B |
| Campian Cl. S Croy | 112 | 33 64 A |
| Campion Rd. Islw | 71 | 15 76 B |

Campion Rd. SW15 73 23 74 A
Campion Terr. NW2 35 23 86 D
Camplin Rd. Har 33 18 88 A
Camplin St. SE14 64 35 77 D
Camp Rd. SW19 84 22 71 D
Camp Rd. SW19 85 23 71 C
Campsbourne Rd. N8 24 30 89 C
Campsbourne The. N8 24 30 89 C
Campsey Gdns. Dag 51 46 84 D
Campsey Rd. Dag 51 46 84 D
Campsfield Rd. N8 24 30 89 A
Campshill Pl. SE13 76 38 74 A
Campshill Rd. SE13 76 38 74 A
Campus Rd. E17 38 36 88 D
Camrose Ave. Edg 21 18 90 B
Camrose Ave. Edg 22 19 91 C
Camrose Ave. Eri 67 49 77 B
Camrose Ave. Felt 82 11 71 A
Camrose Cl. Mord 95 25 68 C
Camrose St. SE2 66 46 78 A
Canada Ave. N18 25 32 91 A
Canada Cres. W3 55 20 82 C
Canada Rd. W3 55 20 81 A
Canada Way. W12 55 22 80 B
Canadian Ave. SE6 88 37 73 D
Canal App. SE8 64 36 77 A
Canal Cl. E2 57 36 82 C
Canal Gr. SE15 63 34 77 A
Canal Head. SE15 75 34 76 A
Canal Rd. E3 57 36 82 C
Canal St. SE5 63 32 77 B
Canal Wlk. N1 48 32 83 B
Canal Wlk. SE26 88 35 71 C
Canberra Cl. Dag 52 50 84 D
Canberra Cres. Dag 52 50 84 D
Canberra Dri. Nthlt 53 11 82 A
Canberra Rd. Bexh 67 47 77 B
Canberra Rd. E6 50 42 83 B
Canberra Rd. Houn 69 07 75 A
Canberra Rd. SE7 65 41 77 B
Canbury Ave. King 93 18 69 B
Canbury Ct. King 93 18 70 C
Canbury Mews. SE26 87 34 72 C
Canbury Park Rd. King 93 18 69 B
Canbury Pas. King 93 18 69 A
Canbury Path. Orp 100 46 68 C
Canbury Pl. King 93 18 69 A
Cancell Rd. SW9 75 31 76 A
Candahar Rd. SW11 74 27 76 C
Candler St. N15 37 33 88 C
Candover Rd. Horn 42 52 87 D
Candover St. W1 2 29 81 A
Candy St. E3 49 36 83 B
Cane Cl Wall 111 30 63 C
Canfield Gdns. NW6 46 26 84 C
Canfield Pl. NW6 46 26 84 A
Canfield Rd. Wdf Gn 27 42 91 C
Canford Ave. Nthlt 43 12 83 B
Canford Cl. Enf 13 31 97 D
Canford Gdns. N.Mal 102 21 67 C
Canford Rd. SW11 74 28 74 A
Canham Rd. SE25 97 33 68 A
Canham Rd. W3 61 21 79 A
Canmore Gdns. SW16 96 29 70 C
Cann Hall Rd. E11 39 39 86 D
Canning Cres. N22 24 30 90 B
Canning Cross. SE5 75 33 76 C
Canning Pas. W8 5 26 79 C
Canning Pl Mews. W8 5 26 79 C
Canning Pl. W8 5 26 79 C
Canning Rd. Croy 105 33 65 B
Canning Rd. E15 50 39 83 C
Canning Rd. E17 26 36 89 A
Canning Rd. Har 21 15 89 B
Canning Rd. N5 37 31 86 D
Cannington Rd. Dag 52 47 84 A
Cannizaro Rd. SW19 85 23 71 D
Cannonbury Ave. Pnr 32 11 88 D
Cannon Cl. Hamp 92 13 70 B
Cannon Cl. SW20 95 23 68 A
Cannon Dri. E14 57 37 80 C
Cannon Hill La. SW20 103 23 67 B
Cannon Hill La. SW20 95 24 68 A
Cannon Hill. N14 16 30 93 C
Cannon Hill. NW6 46 25 85 C
Cannon La. NW3 35 26 86 D
Cannon La. Pnr 32 12 88 C
Cannon Pl. NW3 35 26 86 D
Cannon Pl. SE7 65 42 78 C
Cannon Rd. Bexh 79 48 76 B
Cannon Rd. N14 16 30 93 C
Cannon Row. SW1 7 30 79 A
Cannon St. EC4 8 32 80 A
Cannon Street Rd. E1 57 34 81 D
Cannon Way. E Mol 92 13 68 D
Canon Ave. Rom 41 47 88 A
Canon Beck Rd. SE16 64 35 79 A
Canonbie Rd. SE23 88 35 73 A
Canonbury Gr. N1 48 32 84 C
Canonbury La. N1 48 31 84 D
Canonbury Park N. N1 48 32 84 A
Canonbury Park S. N1 48 32 84 A
Canonbury Pl. N1 48 31 84 B
Canonbury Rd. Enf 13 33 97 A
Canonbury Rd. N1 48 31 84 D
Canonbury Sq. N1 48 31 84 D
Canonbury St. N1 48 32 84 C
Canonbury Villas. N1 48 31 84 D
Canon Murnane Rd. SE1 8 33 79 C
Canon Rd. Brom 99 41 68 B
Canons Cl. Edg 21 18 91 B
Canons Cl. N2 35 26 87 B
Canons Ct. Edg 21 18 91 B
Canons Dri. Edg 21 18 91 B
Canonsleigh Rd. Dag 51 46 84 D
Canons Park Cl. Edg 21 18 91 C
Canon St. N1 48 32 83 A
Canon's Wlk. Croy 106 35 65 D
Canrobert St. E2 57 34 82 B
Canrobert St. E2 48 34 83 D
Cantelowes Rd. NW1 47 29 84 B
Canterbury Ave. Ilf 39 42 87 A
Canterbury Ave. Sid 90 46 72 B
Canterbury Cl. Beck 98 37 69 B
Canterbury Cl. Grnf 53 13 81 B
Canterbury Cres. SW9 75 31 75 A
Canterbury Gr. SE27 87 31 72 D
Canterbury Pl. SE17 63 31 78 B
Canterbury Rd. Croy 105 31 66 A
Canterbury Rd. E10 38 38 88 C
Canterbury Rd. Felt 82 12 72 A
Canterbury Rd. Har 32 13 88 B
Canterbury Rd. Har 32 14 88 A
Canterbury Rd. Mord 103 26 67 C
Canterbury Rd. NW6 46 25 83 C
Canterbury Terr. NW6 46 25 83 C
Cantley Gdns. Ilf 40 44 88 C
Cantley Gdns. SE19 97 33 69 B
Cantley Rd. W7 60 16 79 C
Canton St. E14 57 37 81 C
Cantrell Rd. E3 57 36 82 D
Cantwell Rd. SE18 66 43 77 D
Canute Gdns. SE16 64 35 78 B
Canvey St. SE1 8 32 80 C
Cape Cl. Bark 51 43 84 D
Capel Ave. Wall 111 30 64 D
Capel Cl. Brom 107 42 66 C
Capel Cl. N20 15 26 93 C
Capel Gdns. Ilf 51 45 85 B
Capel Gdns. Pnr 20 12 89 D
Capel Rd. Barn 12 27 95 C
Capel Rd. E12 50 41 85 B
Capel Rd. E7 50 41 85 A
Capener's Cl. SW1 6 28 79 A
Cape Rd. N17 25 34 89 A
Capern Rd. SW18 85 26 73 C
Capitol Way. NW9 22 20 89 A
Capland St. NW8 1 26 82 D
Caple Rd. NW10 45 21 83 D
Capper St. WC1 2 29 82 C
Caprea Cl. Hay 53 11 81 B
Capri Rd. Croy 105 33 66 B
Capstan Ride. Enf 13 31 97 C
Capstan Sq. E14 64 38 79 A
Capstone Rd. Brom 89 39 71 B
Capthorne Ave. Har 32 12 87 D
Capworth St. E10 38 37 87 B
Caradoc Cl. W2 56 25 81 C
Caradoc St. E10 65 39 78 C
Caradon Way. N15 25 32 89 D
Caravelle Gdns (off Javelin Way). Nthlt 53 11 82 B
Caravel Mews. SE8 64 37 77 A
Carberry Rd. SE19 97 33 70 A
Carbery Ave. W3 61 19 79 A
Carbis Rd. E14 57 36 81 D
Carbuncle Pass. N17 25 34 90 C
Carburton St. W1 2 28 82 D
Cardale St. E14 64 38 79 C
Carden Rd. SE15 75 34 75 B
Cardiff Rd. Enf 13 34 96 D
Cardiff Rd. W7 60 16 79 C
Cardiff St. SE18 66 45 77 C
Cardigan Gdns. Ilf 40 46 86 A
Cardigan Rd. E3 49 36 83 D
Cardigan Rd. Rich 71 18 74 C
Cardigan Rd. SW13 72 22 76 C
Cardigan Rd. SW19 95 26 70 A
Cardigan St. SE11 63 31 78 C
Cardigan Wlk. N1 48 32 84 C
Cardinal Ave. King 83 18 71 C
Cardinal Ave. Mord 103 24 67 C
Cardinal Bourne St. SE1 8 32 79 D
Cardinal Cap Alley. SE1 8 32 80 C
Cardinal Cl. Chis 100 45 69 A
Cardinal Cl. Mord 103 24 67 C
Cardinal Cres. N Mal 94 20 69 C
Cardinal Dri. Ilf 28 44 91 A
Cardinal Pl. SW15 73 23 75 D
Cardinal Rd. Felt 81 10 73 D
Cardinal Rd. Ruis 32 11 87 D
Cardinals Way. N19 36 29 87 D
Cardinal's Wlk. Hamp 92 14 70 C
Cardinal's Wlk. Sun 91 09 70 A
Cardine Mews. SE15 63 34 77 D
Cardington Sq. Houn 70 11 75 D
Cardington St. NW1 2 29 82 A
Cardozo Rd. N7 47 30 85 C
Cardrew Ave. N12 15 26 92 D
Cardrew Cl. N12 15 26 92 D
Cardross St. W6 61 22 79 D
Cardwell Rd. N7 47 30 85 A
Cardwell Rd. SE18 66 43 78 A
Carew Cl. N7 36 30 86 B
Carew Rd. Ashf 91 08 70 A
Carew Rd. Mit 96 28 69 C
Carew Rd. N17 25 34 90 C
Carew Rd. Nthwd 19 09 91 B
Carew Rd. Th Hth 97 31 68 D
Carew Rd. W13 60 17 79 A
Carew Rd. Wall 111 29 63 A
Carew St. SE5 75 32 76 C
Carey Ct. Bexh 79 49 74 B
Carey Gdns. SW8 74 29 76 B
Carey La. EC2 4 32 81 C
Carey Pl. SW1 10 29 78 B
Carey Rd. Dag 52 48 85 A
Carey St. WC2 3 30 81 D
Carfax Pl. SW4 74 29 75 D
Carfree Cl. N1 48 31 84 C
Cargill Rd. SW18 85 26 73 C
Cargreen Pl. SE25 97 33 68 D
Cargreen Rd. SE25 97 33 68 D
Carholme Rd. SE23 88 36 73 D
Carisbrook Cl. Enf 13 33 97 B
Carisbrooke Cl. Stan 21 17 90 D
Carisbrooke Rd. Brom 99 41 68 C
Carisbrooke Rd. Mit 96 30 68 C
Carisbrook Rd. E17 38 36 88 A
Carker's La. NW5 47 28 85 D
Carleton Ave. Wall 111 29 62 B
Carleton Rd. N7 47 29 85 B
Carlile Cl. E3 49 36 83 D
Carlinge Rd. NW2 46 24 84 B
Carlingford Gdns. Mit 96 28 70 C
Carlingford Rd. Mord 103 23 67 D
Carlingford Rd. N15 25 31 89 B
Carlingford Rd. NW3 46 26 85 B
Carlisle Ave. EC3 4 33 81 D
Carlisle Ave. W3 55 21 81 C
Carlisle Cl. King 94 19 69 A
Carlisle Gdns. Har 33 17 87 B
Carlisle Gdns. Ilf 39 42 88 C
Carlisle La. SE1 7 30 79 D
Carlisle Mews. King 94 19 69 A
Carlisle Pl. N11 16 28 92 B
Carlisle Pl. SW1 6 29 79 C
Carlisle Rd. E10 38 37 87 C
Carlisle Rd. Hamp 92 13 70 D
Carlisle Rd. N4 37 31 87 A
Carlisle Rd. NW6 46 24 83 A
Carlisle Rd. NW9 22 20 89 A
Carlisle Rd. Rom 42 52 88 A
Carlisle Rd. Sutt 110 24 63 B
Carlisle St. W1 2 29 81 D
Carlisle Wlk. E8 48 33 84 B
Carlos Pl. W1 6 28 80 B
Carlow St. NW1 47 29 83 C
Carlton Ave. Felt 82 11 73 A
Carlton Ave. Felt 70 11 74 C
Carlton Ave. Har 33 16 88 B
Carlton Ave. N14 12 29 95 B
Carlton Avenue E. Wem 33 18 87 C
Carlton Avenue W. Wem 33 16 86 B
Carlton Ave. S Croy 112 33 63 C
Carlton Ave. SE21 75 33 74 C
Carlton Cl. NW3 35 25 86 A
Carlton Cres. Sutt 110 24 64 A
Carlton Ct. Ilf 28 44 89 B
Carlton Ct. SW9 75 31 76 B
Carlton Dri. Ilf 28 44 89 B
Carlton Gdns. SW1 6 29 80 D
Carlton Gdns. W5 54 17 80 A
Carlton Gr. SE15 75 34 76 B
Carlton Hill. NW8 46 26 83 C
Carlton House Terr. SW1 6 29 80 D
Carlton Park Ave. SW20 95 23 69 D
Carlton Par. Orp 108 46 66 B
Carlton Rd. Barn 11 26 95 D
Carlton Rd. E11 39 39 87 D
Carlton Rd. E12 50 41 85 B
Carlton Rd. E17 26 36 90 A
Carlton Rd. Eri 67 50 77 A
Carlton Rd. N11 16 28 92 B
Carlton Rd. N15 25 33 89 D
Carlton Rd. N4 37 31 87 A
Carlton Rd. N Mal 94 21 69 C
Carlton Rd. Rom 30 52 89 C
Carlton Rd. S Croy 112 32 63 D
Carlton Rd. Sid 90 45 71 B
Carlton Rd. Sun 91 09 70 D
Carlton Rd. SW15 73 24 74 A
Carlton Rd. W4 61 20 79 B
Carlton Rd. W5 54 17 81 C
Carlton Rd. Well 78 46 75 B
Carlton Sq. E1 57 35 82 D
Carlton St. SW1 6 29 80 B
Carlton Terr. E11 39 40 88 B
Carlton Terr. N18 17 32 92 D
Carlton Terr. N18 17 32 92 B
Carlton Terr. SE26 88 35 72 C
Carlton Vale. NW6 46 25 83 C
Carluke Cl. SE7 65 41 78 D
Carlwell St. SW17 86 27 71 C
Carlyle Ave. Brom 99 41 68 B
Carlyle Ave. Sthl 53 12 80 B
Carlyle Cl. E Mol 92 13 69 D
Carlyle Cl. N2 35 26 88 C
Carlyle Cl. NW10 45 20 83 B
Carlyle Gdns. Sthl 53 12 80 B
Carlyle Rd. Croy 105 34 65 A
Carlyle Rd. E12 50 42 85 A
Carlyle Rd. W5 60 17 78 A
Carlyle Sq. SW3 62 26 77 B
Carlyon Ave. Har 43 13 85 A
Carlyon Cl. Wem 44 18 83 A
Carlyon Rd. Hay 53 11 81 C
Carlyon Rd. Wem 44 18 83 A
Carmalt Gdns. SW15 73 23 75 C
Carmarthen Pl. SE1 8 33 79 A
*Carmel Ct. W8 62 25 79 B
Carmelite Cl. Har 20 14 90 A
Carmelite Rd. Har 20 14 90 C
Carmelite St. EC4 7 31 80 A
Carmelite Way. Har 20 14 90 C
Carmelite Wlk. Har 20 14 90 A
Carmen St. E14 57 37 81 D
Carmichael Cl. SW11 73 26 75 B
Carmichael Rd. SE25 97 34 68 C
Carminia Rd. SW17 86 28 72 B
Carnaby St. W1 6 29 80 A
Carnac St. SE27 87 32 72 D
Carnanton Rd. E17 26 38 90 B
Carnarvon Ave. Enf 13 33 97 D
Carnarvon Rd. Barn 11 24 96 A
Carnarvon Rd. E10 38 38 88 A
Carnarvon Rd. E15 50 39 84 B
Carnarvon Rd. E18 27 39 90 B
Carnation St. SE2 66 46 78 D
Carnbrook Rd. SE3 77 41 75 B
Carnecke Gdns. SE9 77 42 74 A
Carnegie Cl. Surb 101 18 65 B
Carnegie Pl. SW19 85 23 72 D
Carnegie St. N1 47 30 83 B
Carnforth Cl. Eps 109 19 63 B
Carnforth Rd. SW16 96 29 70 D
Carnoustie Dri. N1 47 30 84 D
Carnwath Rd. SW6 73 25 75 B
Carolina Rd. Th Hth 97 32 69 A
Caroline Cl. Croy 112 33 64 A
Caroline Cl. W2 56 25 80 B
Caroline Ct. Ashf 91 07 70 B
Caroline Gdns. E2 4 33 82 A
Caroline Gdns. SE15 63 34 77 D
Caroline Pl Mews. W2 56 25 80 B
Caroline Pl. SW11 74 28 76 C
Caroline Pl. W2 56 25 80 B
Caroline Rd. SW19 95 24 70 D
Caroline St. E1 57 35 81 D
Caroline Terr. SW1 9 28 78 A
Carol St. NW1 47 29 83 A
Carolyn Dri. Orp 108 46 65 C
Carpenter Gdns. N21 17 31 93 B
Carpenter's Pl. SW4 74 29 75 D
Carpenter's Rd. E15 49 37 84 D
Carpenter St. W1 6 28 80 B
Carrara Wlk. SW9 75 31 75 D
Carriage Dri E. SW11 9 28 77 C
Carriage Dri N. SW11 9 27 77 D
Carriage Drive S. SW11 74 27 76 B
Carriage Dri W. SW11 9 27 77 D
Carrick Gdns. N17 25 33 91 C
Carrick Mews. SE8 64 37 77 A
Carrington Ave. Houn 70 13 74 B
Carrington Rd. Dart 80 54 74 D
Carrington Rd. Rich 72 19 75 C
Carrington St. W1 6 28 80 D
Carrol Cl. E15 50 39 85 D
Carrol Cl. NW5 47 28 85 B
Carron Cl. E14 57 37 81 D
Carroun Rd. SW8 10 30 77 D
Carroway La. Grnf 53 14 82 B
Carrow Rd. Dag 51 46 84 D
Carr Rd. E17 26 37 90 C
Carr Rd. Nthlt 43 14 84 C
Carrs La. N21 13 32 95 A
Carr St. E14 57 36 81 A
Carr St. E14 57 36 81 C
Carshalton Gr. Sutt 110 26 64 D
Carshalton Park Rd. Cars 111 27 64 D
Carshalton Pl. Cars 111 28 64 C
Carshalton Rd. Cars 111 27 64 C
Carshalton Rd. Mit 104 28 67 A
Carshalton Rd. Sutt 110 26 64 D
Carslake Rd. SW15 73 23 74 C
Carson Rd. Barn 12 27 96 D
Carson Rd. E16 58 40 81 A
Carson Rd. SE21 87 32 72 B
Carstairs Rd. SE6 88 38 72 C
Carston Cl. SE12 77 39 74 B
Carswell Cl. Ilf 27 41 89 D
Carswell Rd. SE6 88 38 73 A
Carter Cl. Rom 29 49 91 D
Carter Cl. Wall 111 29 63 D
Carter Dr. Rom 29 49 91 B
Carteret St. SW1 6 29 79 B
Carteret Way. SE8 64 36 78 A
Carterhatch Rd. Enf 14 35 97 D
Carter La. EC4 3 31 81 D
Carter Pl. SE17 63 32 78 C
Carter Rd. E13 50 40 83 B
Carter Rd. SW19 95 26 70 B
Carters Cl. Wor Pk 103 23 66 D
Carters Hill Cl. SE9 89 41 73 C
Carters Rd. N2 24 27 91 C
Carter St. SE17 63 32 78 C
Carter's Yd. SW18 73 25 74 A
Carthew Rd. W6 61 22 79 D
Carthew Villas. W6 61 22 79 D
Carthusian St. EC1 4 32 81 A
Cartins La. WC2 7 30 80 A
Cart La. E4 18 38 94 D
Cartmel Cl. N17 25 34 91 D
Cartmel Gdns. Mord 103 26 67 A
Cartmel Rd. Bexh 79 49 76 A
Cartwright Gdns. WC1 3 30 82 A
Cartwright Rd. Dag 52 48 84 D
Cartwright St. E1 8 33 80 B
Carver Rd. SE24 75 32 74 C
Carville Cres. Brent 60 18 78 A
Carville Pas. Brent 60 18 77 B
Cary Rd. E11 50 39 85 A
Carysfort Rd. N16 48 32 85 B
Carysfort Rd. N8 36 29 88 B
Cascade Ave. N10 24 29 89 C
Casella Rd. SE14 64 35 77 D
Casewick Rd. SE27 87 31 71 B
Casimir Rd. E5 38 35 86 C
Casino Ave. SE24 75 32 74 B
*Caslon Pl. E1 57 34 82 D
Caspian St. SE5 63 32 77 D
Caspian Wlk. E16 58 41 81 D
Cassidy Rd. SW6 62 25 77 C
Cassilda Rd. SE2 66 46 78 A
Cassilis Rd. Twick 71 16 74 D
Cassiobury Ave. Felt 81 09 73 B
Cassiobury Rd. E17 38 36 88 A
Cassland Rd. E9 49 35 84 B
Cassland Rd. Th Hth 97 32 68 D
Cassleden Rd. NW10 45 20 84 D
Casslee Rd. SE6 88 36 73 B
Casson St. E1 57 34 81 A
Castalia Sq. E14 64 38 79 A
Castalia St. E14 64 38 79 A
Castellain Rd. W9 56 25 82 D
Castellan Ave. Rom 30 53 89 A
Castello Ave. SW15 73 23 74 C
Castelnau Gdns. SW13 61 22 77 B
Castelnau Row. SW13 61 22 77 B
Castelnau. SW13 61 22 77 B
Casterbridge Rd. SE3 77 40 75 A
Casterton St. E8 48 34 84 B
Castile Rd. SE18 66 43 78 A
Castillon Rd. SE6 89 39 72 A
Castlands Rd. SE6 88 36 72 B
Castle Ave. E4 18 38 92 D
Castle Ave. Eps 109 22 62 B
Castlebar Hill. W13 54 17 81 A
Castlebar Mews. W5 54 17 81 A
Castlebar Park. W5 54 17 81 A
Castlebar Rd. W5 54 17 81 C
Castle Baynard St. EC4 7 31 80 B
Castle Baynard St. EC4 8 32 80 A
Castle Cl. E9 49 36 85 C
Castle Cl. Sun 91 09 70 C
Castle Cl. SW19 85 23 72 D
Castlecombe Dri. SW19 85 23 73 B
Castlecombe Rd. SE9 89 42 71 A
Castle Ct. EC3 4 32 81 D
Castledine Rd. SE20 97 34 70 D
Castle Dri. Ilf 39 42 88 C
Castleford Ave. SE9 90 43 73 D
Castlegate. Rich 71 18 75 B
Castle Gdns. Dag 51 46 83 B
Castlehaven Rd. NW1 47 28 84 D
Castle La. SW1 6 29 79 C
Castleleigh Ct. Enf 13 32 95 B
Castlemaine Ave. Eps 109 22 62 B
Castlemaine Ave. S Croy 112 33 64 D
Castle Mews. N12 15 26 92 C
Castle Mews. NW1 47 28 84 B
Castle Pl. NW1 47 28 84 B
Castle Pl. W4 61 21 78 A
Castle Rd. Dag 51 46 83 B
Castle Rd. Enf 14 36 97 A
Castle Rd. Islw 71 15 76 D
Castle Rd. N12 15 26 92 C
Castle Rd. Nthlt 43 13 84 D
Castle Rd. NW1 47 28 84 B
Castle Rd. Sthl 59 12 79 D
Castlereagh St. W1 1 27 81 D
Castle St. E6 50 41 83 D
Castle St. King 93 18 69 C
Castleton Ave. Bexh 79 50 76 D
Castleton Ave. Eri 79 50 76 B
Castleton Ave. Wem 44 18 85 A
Castleton Rd. E17 26 38 90 D
Castleton Rd. Ilf 40 46 87 D
Castleton Rd. Mit 96 29 68 D
Castleton Rd. Ruis 32 11 87 D
Castleton Rd. SE9 89 41 71 B
Castletown Rd. W14 62 24 78 C
Castle View Gdns. Ilf 39 42 88 D
Castle Way. Eps 109 22 62 A
Castle Way. Felt 82 11 71 A
Castle Way. SW19 85 23 72 D
Castle Wlk. Sun 92 11 68 A
Castlewood Dri. SE9 77 42 76 D
Castlewood Rd. N15 37 34 88 C
Castlewood Rd. N16 37 34 88 C
Castle Yd. N6 36 28 87 A
Castle Yd. Rich 71 17 74 B
Castle Yd. SE1 7 31 80 D
Caterham Ave. Ilf 28 43 90 C
Caterham Rd. SE13 76 38 75 B
Catesby St. SE17 63 32 78 B
Catford Bwy. SE6 88 37 73 B
Catford Hill. SE6 88 37 73 C
Catford Rd. SE6 88 37 73 A
Cathall Rd. E11 38 38 86 B
Cathay St. SE16 63 34 79 B
Cathcart Dri. Orp 108 45 66 C
Cathcart Hill. N19 36 29 86 C
Cathcart Rd. SW10 62 26 77 A
Cathcart St. NW5 47 28 84 B
Cathedral Pl. EC4 4 32 81 C
Cathedral St. SE1 8 32 80 D
Catherall Rd. N5 37 32 86 C
Catherine Ct. N14 12 29 95 A
Catherine Cl. SW19 85 24 71 D
Catherine Dri. Ashf 91 09 70 B
Catherine Gdns. Houn 70 14 75 D
Catherine Gr. SE10 76 37 76 B
Catherine Pl. SW1 6 29 79 C
Catherine Rd. Rom 42 52 88 B
Catherine Rd. Surb 101 17 67 B
Catherine St. WC2 7 30 80 B
Catherine Wheel Alley. E1 4 33 81 A
Catherine Wheel Rd. Brent 60 17 77 D
Catherine Wheel Yd. SW1 6 29 80 C
Cat Hill. Barn 12 27 95 B
Cathles Rd. SW12 74 28 74 D
Cathnor Rd. W12 61 22 79 B
Catling Cl. SE23 88 35 72 D
Catlin's La. Pnr 19 10 89 D
Catlin St. SE16 63 34 78 D
Caton Pas. SW16 86 30 72 C
Cato Rd. SW4 74 29 75 D
Cator La. Beck 98 36 69 D
Cator Rd.Cars 111 27 64 D

| | | |
|---|---|---|
| Cator Rd. SE26 | 98 | 35 70 B |
| Cator St. SE15 | 63 | 33 77 B |
| Cator St. SE15 | 63 | 33 77 D |
| Cato St. W1 | 1 | 27 81 C |
| Cattistock Rd. SE9 | 89 | 42 71 D |
| Catton St.WC1 | 3 | 30 81 B |
| Caulfield Rd. E6 | 50 | 42 84 D |
| Caulfield Rd. SE15 | 75 | 34 76 D |
| Causeway. Felt | 69 | 10 75 C |
| Causeway. Houn | 69 | 10 75 B |
| Causeway The. Cars | 104 | 28 65 A |
| Causeway The. N2 | 24 | 27 89 C |
| Causeway The. Sutt | 110 | 26 62 A |
| Causeway The. SW18 | 73 | 25 75 D |
| Causeway The. SW19 | 85 | 23 71 C |
| Causeway The. Tedd | 93 | 15 70 B |
| Causeyware Rd. N9 | 18 | 35 94 A |
| Causton Rd. N6 | 36 | 28 87 B |
| Causton St. SW1 | 70 | 29 78 D |
| Cautley Ave. SW4 | 74 | 29 74 A |
| Cavalier Cl. Rom | 29 | 47 89 D |
| Cavalry Cres. Houn | 70 | 11 75 D |
| Cavaye Pl. SW10 | 62 | 26 78 C |
| Cavedish Gdns. Rom | 41 | 48 88 A |
| Cavell Dri. Enf | 13 | 31 97 C |
| Cavell Rd. N17 | 25 | 32 91 D |
| Cavell St. E1 | 57 | 34 81 B |
| Cavendish Ave. Eri | 67 | 50 77 A |
| Cavendish Ave. Har | 44 | 15 85 A |
| Cavendish Ave. N3 | 23 | 25 90 C |
| Cavendish Ave. N Mal | 94 | 22 68 D |
| Cavendish Ave. NW8 | 1 | 26 82 B |
| Cavendish Ave. NW8 | 46 | 26 83 D |
| Cavendish Ave. Sid | 90 | 46 73 A |
| Cavendish Ave. W13 | 54 | 16 81 C |
| Cavendish Ave. Wdf Gn | 27 | 40 91 D |
| Cavendish Ave. Well | 78 | 45 75 B |
| Cavendish Cl. Ashf | 91 | 09 70 B |
| Cavendish Cl. N18 | 17 | 34 92 D |
| Cavendish Cl. NW6 | 46 | 24 84 B |
| Cavendish Cl. NW8 | 1 | 26 82 B |
| Cavendish Ct. EC2 | 4 | 33 81 C |
| Cavendish Dri. E11 | 38 | 38 87 D |
| Cavendish Dri. Edg | 21 | 18 91 B |
| Cavendish Gdns. Bark | 51 | 45 85 D |
| Cavendish Gdns. Ilf | 40 | 43 87 C |
| Cavendish Mews N. W1 | 2 | 28 81 B |
| Cavendish Mews S. W1 | 2 | 28 81 B |
| Cavendish Pl. W1 | 2 | 28 81 D |
| Cavendish Rd. Ashf | 91 | 09 70 B |
| Cavendish Rd. Barn | 11 | 23 96 A |
| Cavendish Rd. Croy | 105 | 31 66 D |
| Cavendish Rd. E4 | 26 | 38 91 A |
| Cavendish Rd. N18 | 17 | 34 92 D |
| Cavendish Rd. N4 | 37 | 31 88 D |
| Cavendish Rd. N Mal | 94 | 21 68 D |
| Cavendish Rd. NW6 | 46 | 24 84 D |
| Cavendish Rd. Sutt | 110 | 26 63 A |
| Cavendish Rd. SW12 | 86 | 28 73 D |
| Cavendish Rd. SW19 | 96 | 27 70 C |
| Cavendish Rd. W4 | 72 | 20 76 A |
| Cavendish Sq. W1 | 2 | 28 81 D |
| Cavendish St. N1 | 48 | 32 83 D |
| Cavendish Terr. Felt | 81 | 10 72 A |
| Cavendish Way. W Wick | 106 | 37 66 D |
| Cavenham Gdns. Horn | 42 | 53 88 A |
| Cavenham Gdns. Ilf | 40 | 44 86 D |
| Cave Rd. E13 | 58 | 40 82 B |
| Cave Rd. Rich | 83 | 17 71 A |
| Caverleigh Way. Wor Pk | 102 | 22 66 A |
| Caverley Gdns. Har | 33 | 17 87 B |
| Caversham Ave. N13 | 17 | 31 93 C |
| Caversham Ave. Sutt | 103 | 24 65 A |
| Caversham Rd. King | 93 | 18 69 D |
| Caversham Rd. N15 | 25 | 32 89 C |
| Caversham Rd. NW5 | 47 | 29 84 A |
| Caversham St. SW3 | 9 | 27 77 B |
| Caverswall St. W12 | 56 | 23 81 C |
| Cavert St. NW1 | 47 | 28 83 A |
| Caveside Cl. Chis | 100 | 43 69 A |
| Cawdor Cres. W7 | 60 | 16 78 A |
| Cawnpore St. SE19 | 87 | 33 71 C |
| Caxton Gr. E3 | 57 | 37 82 A |
| Caxton Rd. N22 | 24 | 30 90 D |
| Caxton Rd. Sthl | 59 | 11 79 D |
| Caxton Rd. SW17 | 85 | 26 71 C |
| Caxton Rd. W12 | 56 | 23 80 D |
| Caxton St. E16 | 58 | 39 80 B |
| Caxton Street N. E16 | 58 | 39 80 B |
| Caxton Street S. E16 | 58 | 39 80 B |
| Caxton St. SW1 | 6 | 29 79 D |
| Caygill Cl. Brom | 99 | 39 68 D |
| Cayley Cl. SE4 | 76 | 36 75 C |
| Cayley Cl. Wall | 111 | 30 63 C |
| Cayton Pl. EC1 | 4 | 32 82 B |
| Cayton Rd. Grnf | 44 | 15 83 C |
| Cayton St. EC1 | 4 | 32 82 B |
| Cazenove Rd. E17 | 26 | 37 90 A |
| Cazenove Rd. N16 | 37 | 34 86 A |
| Cecil Ave. Bark | 51 | 44 84 D |
| Cecil Ave. Enf | 13 | 33 96 D |
| Cecil Ave. Horn | 30 | 54 89 A |
| Cecil Ave. Wem | 44 | 18 85 D |
| Cecil Cl. Ashf | 91 | 08 70 C |
| Cecil Cl. W5 | 54 | 17 81 B |
| Cecil Ct. Barn | 11 | 23 96 B |
| Cecil Ct. Croy | 105 | 33 65 B |
| Cecil Ct. WC2 | 7 | 30 80 A |
| Cecile Park. N8 | 36 | 30 88 C |
| Cecilia Cl. N2 | 23 | 26 89 A |
| Cecilia Rd. E8 | 48 | 34 85 C |
| Cecil Park. Pnr | 20 | 12 89 C |
| Cecil Pl. Mit | 104 | 27 67 B |
| Cecil Rd. Ashf | 91 | 08 70 A |
| Cecil Rd. Croy | 104 | 30 67 D |
| Cecil Rd. E11 | 39 | 39 86 C |
| Cecil Rd. E13 | 50 | 40 83 A |
| Cecil Rd. E17 | 26 | 37 90 A |
| Cecil Rd. Enf | 13 | 32 96 D |
| Cecil Rd. Har | 21 | 15 89 A |
| Cecil Rd. Houn | 70 | 14 76 C |
| Cecil Rd. Ilf | 51 | 43 85 B |
| Cecil Rd. N10 | 24 | 28 90 D |
| Cecil Rd. N14 | 16 | 29 94 C |
| Cecil Rd. NW10 | 45 | 21 83 A |
| Cecil Rd. NW9 | 22 | 20 89 A |
| Cecil Rd. Rom | 41 | 48 87 A |
| Cecil Rd. Sutt | 110 | 24 63 B |
| Cecil Rd. SW19 | 95 | 25 70 D |
| Cecil Rd. W3 | 55 | 20 81 A |
| Cecil Way. Brom | 107 | 40 66 C |
| Cedar Ave. Barn | 16 | 27 94 A |
| Cedar Ave. Enf | 14 | 35 97 C |
| Cedar Ave. Rom | 41 | 48 88 A |
| Cedar Ave. Ruis | 43 | 11 85 C |
| Cedar Ave. Sid | 90 | 46 73 A |
| Cedar Ave. Twick | 70 | 14 74 C |
| Cedar Cl. Brom | 107 | 42 65 C |
| Cedar Cl. E Mol | 93 | 15 68 C |
| Cedar Cl. Rom | 29 | 50 89 C |
| Cedar Cl. SW15 | 84 | 20 71 B |
| Cedar Copse. Brom | 99 | 42 69 D |
| Cedar Cres. Brom | 107 | 42 65 C |
| Cedarcroft Rd. Chess | 101 | 18 65 D |
| Cedar Ct. N10 | 24 | 28 90 C |
| Cedar Ct. SW19 | 85 | 23 72 D |
| Cedar Dri. N2 | 24 | 27 89 C |
| Cedar Dri. Pnr | 20 | 13 91 A |
| Cedar Gdns. Sutt | 110 | 26 63 A |
| Cedar Gr. Bex | 79 | 47 74 D |
| Cedar Gr. Sthl | 53 | 13 81 A |
| Cedar Gr. W5 | 60 | 17 79 B |
| Cedar Hts. Rich | 83 | 18 73 C |
| Cedarhurst Dri. SE9 | 77 | 41 74 A |
| Cedar Lawn Ave. Barn | 11 | 24 95 A |
| Cedar Mount. SE9 | 89 | 41 73 D |
| Cedarne Rd. SW6 | 62 | 25 77 D |
| Cedar Park Gdns. Rom | 41 | 47 87 B |
| Cedar Pl. Nthwd | 19 | 08 91 A |
| Cedar Pl. SE7 | 65 | 41 78 C |
| Cedar Rd. Brom | 99 | 41 69 C |
| Cedar Rd. Croy | 105 | 33 65 A |
| Cedar Rd. E Mol | 93 | 15 68 C |
| Cedar Rd. Eri | 80 | 52 76 A |
| Cedar Rd. Felt | 81 | 08 73 D |
| Cedar Rd. Horn | 42 | 53 86 C |
| Cedar Rd. Houn | 70 | 11 76 C |
| Cedar Rd. N17 | 25 | 33 90 B |
| Cedar Rd. NW2 | 46 | 23 85 A |
| Cedar Rd. Rom | 29 | 50 89 C |
| Cedar Rd. Sutt | 110 | 26 63 A |
| Cedar Rd. Tedd | 83 | 16 71 C |
| Cedar Rise. N14 | 16 | 28 94 B |
| Cedars Ave. E17 | 38 | 37 88 A |
| Cedars Ave. Mit | 96 | 28 68 A |
| Cedars Cl. NW4 | 23 | 23 89 B |
| Cedars Ct. N9 | 17 | 33 93 A |
| Cedars Mews. SW4 | 74 | 28 75 D |
| Cedars Rd. Beck | 98 | 36 69 D |
| Cedars Rd. Croy | 111 | 30 64 A |
| Cedars Rd. E15 | 50 | 39 84 A |
| Cedars Rd. King | 93 | 17 69 A |
| Cedars Rd. Mord | 95 | 25 68 C |
| Cedars Rd. N21 | 17 | 31 93 B |
| Cedars Rd. SW13 | 72 | 22 76 C |
| Cedars Rd. SW4 | 74 | 28 75 B |
| Cedars Rd. W4 | 61 | 20 77 A |
| Cedars The. E9 | 49 | 35 84 D |
| Cedars The. Tedd | 93 | 15 70 B |
| Cedar Terr. Rich | 71 | 18 75 C |
| Cedar Tree Gr. SE27 | 87 | 31 71 D |
| Cedarville Gdns. SW16 | 96 | 30 70 B |
| Cedar Vista. Rich | 60 | 18 77 D |
| Cedar Way. Sun | 91 | 09 70 C |
| Cedric Ave. Rom | 30 | 51 89 A |
| Cedric Rd. SE9 | 90 | 44 72 C |
| Celandie Way. E15 | 58 | 39 82 A |
| Celandine Cl. E14 | 57 | 37 81 A |
| Celbridge Mews. W2 | 56 | 25 81 D |
| Celia Rd. N19 | 47 | 29 85 B |
| Celtic Ave. Brom | 99 | 39 68 A |
| Celtic St. E14 | 57 | 37 81 B |
| Cemetery La. SE7 | 65 | 42 77 A |
| Cemetery Rd. E7 | 50 | 39 85 B |
| Cemetery Rd. N17 | 25 | 33 91 C |
| Cenacle Cl. NW3 | 35 | 25 86 C |
| Centaur St. SE1 | 7 | 30 79 D |
| Centenary Rd. Enf | 14 | 36 96 D |
| Central Ave. E11 | 38 | 38 86 B |
| Central Ave. E Mol | 92 | 12 68 D |
| Central Ave. Enf | 13 | 34 97 D |
| Central Ave. Houn | 70 | 14 75 C |
| Central Ave. N2 | 23 | 25 89 B |
| Central Ave. N2 | 23 | 26 90 D |
| Central Ave. N9 | 17 | 33 93 D |
| Central Ave. Pnr | 32 | 12 87 B |
| Central Ave. SW11 | 9 | 27 77 D |
| Central Ave. Wall | 111 | 30 64 C |
| Central Ave. Well | 78 | 46 76 C |
| Central Circ. NW4 | 34 | 22 88 B |
| Central Dri. Horn | 42 | 54 86 C |
| Central Hill. SE19 | 97 | 33 70 A |
| Central Park Ave. Dag | 41 | 50 86 C |
| Central Park Rd. E6 | 50 | 42 83 C |
| Central Pl. SE25 | 97 | 34 68 C |
| Central Rd. Dart | 80 | 54 74 A |
| Central Rd. Mord | 103 | 25 67 B |
| Central Rd. Wem | 44 | 16 85 D |
| Central Rd. Wor Pk | 102 | 22 65 A |
| Central Sq. E Mol | 92 | 12 68 D |
| Central Sq. NW11 | 35 | 25 88 D |
| Central Sq. Wem | 44 | 18 85 C |
| Central St. EC1 | 4 | 32 82 A |
| Central Way. Cars | 111 | 27 63 C |
| Central Way. Felt | 69 | 10 74 B |
| Central Way. Nthwd | 19 | 09 91 C |
| Centre Ave. N2 | 24 | 27 90 C |
| Centre Ave. W3 | 55 | 20 80 D |
| Centre Common Rd. Chis | 100 | 44 70 C |
| Centre Dri. E7 | 50 | 41 85 B |
| Centre Rd. Dag | 52 | 49 83 D |
| Centre Rd. E11 | 39 | 40 86 A |
| Centre Rd. E7 | 39 | 40 86 C |
| Centre St. E2 | 48 | 34 83 D |
| Centre The. Felt | 81 | 10 73 D |
| Centre Way. N9 | 18 | 35 93 A |
| Centric Cl. NW1 | 47 | 28 83 A |
| Centurion Cl. N7 | 47 | 30 84 D |
| Century Ct. Rich | 83 | 16 71 A |
| Century Rd. E17 | 26 | 36 89 A |
| Cephas Ave. E1 | 57 | 35 82 C |
| Cephas St. E1 | 57 | 35 82 C |
| Ceres Rd. SE18 | 66 | 45 78 B |
| Cerise Rd. SE15 | 75 | 34 76 A |
| Cerne Cl. Hay | 53 | 11 80 A |
| Cerne Rd. Mord | 103 | 26 67 C |
| Cerney Mew. W2 | 5 | 26 80 B |
| Cervantes Ct. Nthwd | 19 | 09 91 D |
| Ceylon Rd. W14 | 62 | 24 79 C |
| Chadacre Ave. Ilf | 27 | 42 89 B |
| Chadacre Rd. Eps | 109 | 22 64 D |
| Chadbourne St. E14 | 57 | 37 81 B |
| Chadbury Ct. NW7 | 22 | 22 90 A |
| Chadd Dri. Brom | 99 | 42 68 A |
| Chadd Green. E13 | 50 | 40 83 A |
| Chadville Gdns. Rom | 41 | 47 88 B |
| Chadway. Dag | 41 | 47 87 C |
| Chadwell Ave. Rom | 40 | 46 87 B |
| Chadwell Heath La. Rom | 28 | 46 89 D |
| Chadwell Heath La. Rom | 41 | 47 88 C |
| Chadwell St. EC1 | 3 | 31 82 A |
| Chadwick Ave. E4 | 18 | 38 92 B |
| Chadwick Cl. Tedd | 93 | 16 70 A |
| Chadwick Rd. E11 | 39 | 39 88 D |
| Chadwick Rd. NW10 | 45 | 21 83 B |
| Chadwick Rd. SE15 | 75 | 33 76 D |
| Chadwick St. SW1 | 6 | 29 79 D |
| Chadwin Rd. E13 | 58 | 40 81 B |
| Chaffinch Ave. Croy | 106 | 35 67 D |
| Chaffinch Cl. Croy | 106 | 35 67 D |
| Chaffinch Rd. Beck | 98 | 36 69 B |
| Chafford Way. Rom | 29 | 47 89 C |
| Chagford St. NW1 | 1 | 27 82 D |
| Chailey Ave. Enf | 13 | 33 97 D |
| Chailey St. E5 | 38 | 35 86 C |
| Chalbury Wlk. N1 | 48 | 31 83 C |
| Chalcombe Rd. SE2 | 66 | 46 79 D |
| Chalcot Cl. Sutt | 110 | 25 63 C |
| Chalcot Cres. NW1 | 47 | 27 83 B |
| Chalcot Gdns. NW3 | 47 | 27 84 B |
| Chalcot Rd. NW1 | 47 | 28 83 A |
| Chalcot Sq. NW1 | 47 | 27 84 D |
| Chalcott Gdns. Surb | 101 | 17 66 C |
| Chalcroft Rd. SE13 | 77 | 39 74 A |
| Chaldon Path. Th Hth | 97 | 31 68 D |
| Chaldon Rd. SW6 | 62 | 24 77 C |
| Chale Rd. SW2 | 74 | 30 74 C |
| Chale Wlk. Sutt | 110 | 25 62 B |
| Chalfont Ave. Wem | 45 | 19 84 B |
| Chalfont Ct. NW9 | 22 | 21 89 B |
| Chalfont Green. N9 | 17 | 33 93 C |
| Chalfont Rd. N9 | 17 | 33 93 D |
| Chalfont Rd. SE25 | 97 | 33 68 B |
| Chalfont Way. W13 | 60 | 16 79 D |
| Chalfont Wlk. Pnr | 20 | 11 90 C |
| Chalford Cl. E Mol | 92 | 13 68 C |
| Chalford Ct. Ilf | 40 | 43 88 B |
| Chalforde Gdns. Rom | 30 | 52 89 D |
| Chalford Rd. SE21 | 87 | 32 71 B |
| Chalford Wlk. Wdf Gn | 27 | 41 91 D |
| Chalgrove Ave. Mord | 103 | 25 67 A |
| Chalgrove Cres. Ilf | 27 | 42 90 C |
| Chalgrove Gdns. N3 | 23 | 24 89 A |
| Chalgrove Rd. E9 | 49 | 35 84 A |
| Chalgrove Rd. N17 | 25 | 34 90 B |
| Chalgrove Rd. Sutt | 110 | 26 63 D |
| Chalice Cl. Wall | 111 | 29 63 B |
| Chalkenden Cl. SE20 | 97 | 34 70 D |
| Chalk Farm Rd. NW1 | 47 | 28 84 C |
| Chalkhill Rd. Wem | 34 | 19 86 D |
| Chalk Hill Rd. WL | 62 | 23 78 B |
| Chalk La. Barn | 12 | 27 96 D |
| Chalklands. Wem | 34 | 20 86 C |
| Chalk Rd. E13 | 58 | 41 81 A |
| Chalkwell Park Ave. Enf | 13 | 33 96 C |
| Challenge Rd. Ashf | 81 | 08 71 B |
| Challice Way. SW2 | 86 | 30 73 D |
| Challin St. SE20 | 98 | 35 69 A |
| Challis Rd. Brent | 60 | 17 78 D |
| Challoner Cl. N2 | 23 | 26 90 D |
| Challoner Cres. W14 | 62 | 24 78 D |
| Challoners Cl. E Mol | 92 | 14 68 D |
| Challoner St. W14 | 62 | 24 78 D |
| Chalmers Rd. Ashf | 81 | 07 71 D |
| Chalmers Road E. Ashf | 81 | 08 71 C |
| Chalmer's Terr. N16 | 37 | 33 86 D |
| Chalmers Way. Felt | 69 | 10 74 B |
| Chalmer's Wlk. SE17 | 63 | 31 77 B |
| Chalsey Rd. SE4 | 76 | 36 75 D |
| Chalthorpe St. WC1 | 3 | 30 82 D |
| Chalton Dri. N2 | 35 | 26 88 D |
| Chalton St. NW1 | 47 | 29 83 D |
| Chamberlain Cottages. SE5 | 75 | 32 76 B |
| Chamberlain Cres. W Wick | 106 | 37 66 D |
| Chamberlain La. Pnr | 19 | 10 89 C |
| Chamberlain Rd. N2 | 23 | 26 90 C |
| Chamberlain Rd. N9 | 17 | 34 93 A |
| Chamberlain Rd. W13 | 60 | 16 79 A |
| Chamberlain St. NW1 | 47 | 27 84 D |
| Chamberlain Way. Pnr | 19 | 10 89 B |
| Chamberlain Way. Surb | 101 | 18 66 A |
| Chamberlain Wlk. Felt | 82 | 12 71 A |
| Chamberlayne Rd. NW10 | 46 | 23 83 D |
| Chambers Gdns. N2 | 23 | 26 90 B |
| Chambers La. NW10 | 46 | 23 84 C |
| Chambers Rd. N7 | 47 | 30 85 A |
| Chambers St. SE16 | 63 | 34 79 A |
| Chamber St. E1 | 8 | 33 80 B |
| Chamber St. E1 | 57 | 34 80 A |
| Chambord St. E2 | 4 | 33 82 B |
| Champion Cres. SE26 | 88 | 36 71 A |
| Champion Gr. SE5 | 75 | 32 75 B |
| Champion Hill. SE5 | 75 | 33 75 A |
| Champion Park. SE5 | 75 | 32 75 B |
| Champion Rd. SE26 | 88 | 36 71 A |
| Champneys Cl. Sutt | 110 | 24 63 D |
| Chancellor Gr. SE21 | 87 | 32 72 C |
| Chancellors Rd. W6 | 62 | 23 78 C |
| Chancellors St. W6 | 62 | 23 78 C |
| Chancelot Rd. SE2 | 66 | 46 78 B |
| Chancel St. SE1 | 7 | 31 80 D |
| Chancery La. Beck | 98 | 37 69 D |
| Chance St. E1 | 4 | 33 82 D |
| Chanctonbury Cl. SE9 | 90 | 43 72 D |
| Chanctonbury Gdns. Sutt | 110 | 25 63 D |
| Chanctonbury Way. N12 | 15 | 25 92 A |
| Chandler Ave. E16 | 58 | 40 81 A |
| Chandler Cl. Hamp | 92 | 13 69 A |
| Chandler St. E1 | 57 | 34 80 D |
| Chandlers Way. SE24 | 87 | 31 73 A |
| Chandos Ave. E17 | 26 | 37 90 C |
| Chandos Ave. N14 | 16 | 29 93 C |
| Chandos Ave. N20 | 15 | 26 94 D |
| Chandos Ave. W5 | 60 | 17 78 B |
| Chandos Cres. Edg | 22 | 19 91 C |
| Chandos Ct. N14 | 16 | 29 93 B |
| Chandos Pl. WC2 | 7 | 30 80 A |
| Chandos Rd. E15 | 49 | 38 85 D |
| Chandos Rd. Har | 32 | 14 88 A |
| Chandos Rd. N17 | 25 | 33 90 D |
| Chandos Rd. N2 | 24 | 27 90 C |
| Chandos Rd. NW10 | 55 | 21 82 C |
| Chandos Rd. NW2 | 46 | 23 85 C |
| Chandos Rd. Pnr | 32 | 11 87 B |
| Chandos St. W1 | 2 | 28 81 B |
| Chandos Way. NW11 | 35 | 25 87 D |
| Change Alley. EC3 | 4 | 32 81 D |
| Channel Cl. Houn | 70 | 13 76 A |
| Channelsea Rd. E15 | 49 | 38 83 B |
| Channing Cl, Horn | 42 | 54 87 B |
| Chanton Dri. Sutt | 110 | 23 62 C |
| Chantrey Rd. SW9 | 74 | 30 75 B |
| Chantry Cl. Har | 33 | 18 88 B |
| Chantry La. Brom | 107 | 41 67 B |
| Chantry Pl. Har | 20 | 13 90 B |
| Chantry Rd. Chess | 109 | 19 64 C |
| Chantry Rd. Har | 20 | 13 90 B |
| Chantry St. N1 | 48 | 31 83 B |
| Chantry Way. Rain | 52 | 50 83 D |
| Chant St. E15 | 49 | 38 84 D |
| Chapel Cl. Dart | 80 | 51 74 A |
| Chapel Ct. N2 | 24 | 27 89 A |
| Chapel Ct. SE1 | 8 | 32 79 B |
| Chapel Farm Rd. SE9 | 89 | 42 72 B |
| Chapel Hill. Dart | 80 | 51 74 A |
| Chapel Hill. N2 | 24 | 27 90 C |
| Chapel House St. E14 | 64 | 37 78 B |
| Chapel La. Houn | 70 | 13 75 A |
| Chapel La. Pnr | 20 | 11 89 B |
| Chapel La. Rom | 41 | 47 87 B |
| Chapel Market. N1 | 48 | 31 83 C |
| Chapel Pl. N17 | 25 | 33 91 C |
| Chapel Pl. N1 | 48 | 31 83 C |
| Chapel Pl. W1 | 2 | 28 81 D |
| Chapel Rd. Bexh | 79 | 49 75 C |
| Chapel Rd. Houn | 70 | 13 75 B |
| Chapel Rd. SE27 | 87 | 32 71 A |
| Chapel Rd. Twick | 83 | 16 73 B |
| Chapel Rd. W13 | 54 | 16 80 D |
| Chapel Side. W2 | 56 | 25 80 B |
| Chapel St. E15 | 49 | 38 84 D |
| Chapel St. Enf | 13 | 32 96 B |
| Chapel St. NW1 | 1 | 27 81 A |
| Chapel Stones. N17 | 25 | 33 90 B |
| Chapel St. SW1 | 6 | 28 79 A |
| Chapel St. W1 | 2 | 29 81 D |
| Chapel Way. Brom | 99 | 40 69 C |
| Chapel Way. N7 | 36 | 30 86 D |
| Chapel Wlk | 23 | 23 89 C |
| Chapel Wlk. Croy | 105 | 32 65 A |
| Chapel Wlk. NW4 | 22 | 22 89 D |
| Chaplaincy Gdns. Horn | 42 | 54 87 C |
| Chaplin Cres. Sun | 91 | 09 70 A |
| Chaplin Rd. Dag | 52 | 48 84 C |
| Chaplin Rd. E15 | 50 | 39 83 B |
| Chaplin Rd. N17 | 25 | 33 89 B |
| Chaplin Rd. NW2 | 45 | 22 84 A |
| Chaplin Rd. Wem | 44 | 17 84 B |
| Chapman Cres. Har | 33 | 18 88 B |
| Chapman Rd. Belv | 67 | 49 78 D |
| Chapman Rd. Croy | 105 | 31 66 C |
| Chapman Rd. E9 | 49 | 36 84 B |
| Chapman St. E1 | 57 | 34 81 D |
| Chapone Pl. W1 | 2 | 29 81 D |
| Chapter House Ct. EC4 | 4 | 32 81 C |
| Chapter Rd. NW2 | 45 | 22 85 D |
| Chapter Rd. SE17 | 63 | 31 78 D |
| Chapter St. SW1 | 10 | 29 78 B |
| Chapter Way. Hamp | 82 | 13 71 A |
| Chara Pl. W4 | 61 | 20 77 B |
| Charcroft Ct. W14 | 62 | 23 79 B |
| Charcroft Gdns. Enf | 14 | 35 96 D |
| Chardin Rd. W4 | 61 | 21 78 A |
| Chardmore Rd. N16 | 37 | 34 87 C |
| Chard Rd. Houn | 69 | 07 76 D |
| Charecroft Way. W12 | 62 | 23 79 B |
| Charford Rd. E16 | 58 | 40 81 A |
| Chargeable La. E13 | 58 | 40 82 C |
| Chargeable St. E16 | 58 | 39 82 D |
| Charing Cross Rd. WC2 | 6 | 29 80 B |
| Charing Cross. SW1 | 7 | 30 80 C |
| Charlbert St. NW8 | 47 | 27 83 C |
| Charlbury Cl. Rom | 30 | 53 91 A |
| Charlbury Cres. Rom | 30 | 53 91 A |
| Charlbury Gdns. Ilf | 40 | 45 86 B |
| Charlbury Gr. W5 | 54 | 17 81 C |
| Charldane Rd. SE9 | 90 | 43 72 D |
| Charlecote Gr. SE26 | 87 | 34 72 D |
| Charlecote Rd. Dag | 41 | 48 86 C |
| Charles Cl. Sid | 90 | 46 71 B |
| Charles Cres. Har | 32 | 14 87 B |
| Charles Ct. Tedd | 83 | 15 71 C |
| Charlesfield. SE9 | 89 | 41 72 C |
| Charles Gringling Wlk. SE18 | 66 | 43 78 A |
| Charles II St. SW1 | 6 | 29 80 D |
| Charles La. NW8 | 47 | 27 83 C |
| Charles Pl. NW1 | 2 | 29 82 A |
| Charles Rd. Dag | 52 | 50 84 B |
| Charles Rd. E7 | 50 | 41 84 C |
| Charles Rd. Rom | 41 | 47 88 D |
| Charles Rd. SW19 | 95 | 25 69 A |
| Charles Rd. W13 | 54 | 16 81 C |
| Charles Sevright Dri. NW7 | 15 | 23 92 D |
| Charles Sq. N1 | 4 | 32 82 B |
| Charles St. E16 | 58 | 41 80 C |
| Charles St. Enf | 13 | 33 95 B |
| Charles St. Houn | 70 | 12 76 D |
| Charles St. SW13 | 72 | 21 76 C |
| Charles St. W1 | 6 | 28 80 D |
| Charleston St. SE17 | 63 | 32 78 A |
| Charleville Circ. SE26 | 87 | 34 71 D |
| Charleville Rd. W14 | 62 | 24 78 D |
| Charlieville Rd. Eri | 67 | 50 77 C |
| Charlmont Rd. SW17 | 86 | 27 71 D |
| Charlmount Rd. SW17 | 96 | 27 70 B |
| Charlotte Despard Ave. SW11 | 74 | 28 76 A |
| Charlotte Gdns. Rom | 29 | 49 91 B |
| Charlotte Mews. W1 | 2 | 29 81 A |
| Charlotte Pl. W1 | 2 | 29 81 A |
| Charlotte Rd. Dag | 52 | 49 84 B |
| Charlotte Rd. EC2 | 4 | 33 82 A |
| Charlotte Rd. SW13 | 72 | 21 76 B |
| Charlotte Rd. Wall | 111 | 29 63 A |
| Charlotte Row. SW4 | 74 | 29 75 A |
| Charlotte St. W1 | 2 | 29 81 A |
| Charlotte Terr. N1 | 47 | 30 83 B |
| Charlton Church La. SE7 | 65 | 41 78 C |
| Charlton Cl. Uxb | 31 | 07 86 B |
| Charlton Cres. Bark | 51 | 45 83 D |
| Charlton Dene. SE7 | 65 | 41 77 C |
| Charlton King's Rd. NW5 | 47 | 29 85 D |
| Charlton La. SE7 | 65 | 41 78 D |
| Charlton La. Shep | 91 | 08 68 D |
| Charlton Park La. SE7 | 65 | 41 77 D |
| Charlton Park Rd. SE7 | 65 | 41 77 B |
| Charlton Pl. N1 | 48 | 31 83 C |
| Charlton Rd. Har | 21 | 18 89 C |
| Charlton Rd. N9 | 18 | 35 94 B |
| Charlton Rd. NW10 | 45 | 20 83 A |
| Charlton Rd. SE3 | 65 | 40 77 D |
| Charlton Rd. SE7 | 65 | 41 77 A |
| Charlton Rd. Shep | 91 | 08 69 C |
| Charlton Rd. Wem | 33 | 18 87 D |
| Charlton Way. SE10 | 77 | 39 76 A |
| Charlton Way. SE3 | 65 | 39 77 D |
| Charlwood Cl. Har | 21 | 15 91 A |
| Charlwood Pl. SW1 | 10 | 29 78 A |
| Charlwood Rd. SW15 | 73 | 23 75 D |
| Charlwood St. SW1 | 10 | 29 78 C |
| Charlwood Terr. SW15 | 73 | 23 75 D |
| Charmian Ave. Stan | 21 | 17 90 D |
| Charminster Ave. SW19 | 95 | 25 69 D |
| Charminster Rd. SE9 | 89 | 41 71 B |
| Charminster Rd. Wor Pk | 103 | 23 66 D |
| Charmouth Ct. Rich | 71 | 18 74 B |
| Charmouth Rd. Well | 79 | 47 76 A |
| Charnock Rd. E5 | 37 | 34 86 D |
| Charnwood Ave. SW19 | 95 | 25 69 D |
| Charnwood Cl. N Mal | 94 | 21 68 C |
| Charnwood Dri. E18 | 27 | 40 89 D |
| Charnwood Pl. N20 | 15 | 26 93 C |
| Charnwood Rd. SE25 | 97 | 32 68 D |
| Charnwood St. E5 | 37 | 34 86 B |
| Charrington Rd. Croy | 105 | 32 65 A |
| Charrington St. NW1 | 47 | 29 83 D |
| Charsley Rd. SE6 | 88 | 37 72 B |
| Chart Cl. Brom | 99 | 39 69 A |
| Chart Cl. Croy | 106 | 35 67 C |
| Charter Ave. Ilf | 40 | 44 87 B |
| Charter Cres. Houn | 70 | 12 75 C |
| Charter Ct. N4 | 37 | 31 87 C |
| Charter Ct. N Mal | 94 | 21 68 A |
| Charterhouse Ave. Wem | 44 | 17 85 C |
| Charterhouse Bldgs. EC1 | 4 | 32 82 C |
| Charterhouse Mews. EC1 | 3 | 31 81 B |
| Charterhouse Rd. Orp | 108 | 46 65 C |
| Charterhouse Sq. EC1 | 3 | 31 81 B |
| Charterhouse St. EC1 | 3 | 31 81 B |
| Charterhouse St. EC1 | 3 | 31 81 B |
| Charteris Rd. NW6 | 46 | 24 83 B |

Charteris Rd. Wdf Gn 27 40 91 B
Charter Rd. King 94 19 68 B
Charter Rd The. Wdf Gn 27 39 91 B
Charters Cl. SE19 87 33 71 C
Charter Sq. King 94 19 69 D
Charter Way. N14 12 29 95 C
Charter Way. N3 23 24 89 D
Chartfield Ave. SW15 73 23 74 A
Chartfield Ave. SW15 73 23 74 A
Chartfield Sq. SW15 73 23 74 B
Chartham Gr. SE27 87 31 72 D
Chartham Rd. SE25 97 34 68 B
Chartley Ave. NW2 34 21 86 C
Chartley Ave. Stan 21 15 91 B
Charton Cl. Belv 67 48 77 B
Chart St. N1 4 32 82 B
Chartwell Cl. SE9 90 44 72 B
Chartwell Pl. Sutt 110 24 64 B
Chartwell Rd. Nthwd 19 09 91 B
Chartwell Way. SE20 97 34 70 B
Charwood. SE27 87 31 71 A
Chase Court Gdns. Enf 13 32 96 A
Chase Cross Rd. Rom 29 50 91 C
Chasefield Rd. SW17 86 27 71 B
Chase Gdns. E4 18 37 92 A
Chase Gdns. Twick 82 14 73 B
Chase Green Ave. Enf 13 32 97 C
Chase Green. Enf 13 32 96 C
Chase Hill. Enf 13 32 96 A
Chase House Gdns. Horn 42 54 88 B
Chase La (Path). Ilf 40 44 88 B
Chase La. Ilf 40 44 88 B
Chaseley St. E14 57 36 81 C
Chasemore Gdns. Croy 112 31 64 C
Chase Rd. NW10 55 20 82 D
Chase Rd. W3 55 20 81 B
Chase Ridings. Enf 13 31 97 C
Chase Side Ave. Enf 13 32 97 D
Chase Side Ave. SW20 95 24 69 C
Chaseside Cl. Rom 30 51 91 A
Chase Side Cres. Enf 13 32 97 A
Chase Side. Enf 13 32 97 C
Chase Side. N14 12 28 95 D
Chase Side. N14 16 29 94 A
Chase Side Pl. Enf 13 32 97 C
Chase The. Bexh 79 49 75 B
Chase The. Brom 99 40 68 B
Chase The. E12 50 41 85 B
Chase The. Edg 22 19 90 B
Chase The. Horn 42 51 86 D
Chase The. Pnr 32 11 88 C
Chase The. Pnr 20 12 89 D
Chase The. Rom 41 48 88 C
Chase The. Rom 41 50 86 D
Chase The. Rom 42 51 86 C
Chase The. Rom 30 51 89 A
Chase The. Stan 21 16 91 A
Chase THE. Sun 91 10 69 B
Chase The. SW16 97 31 70 C
Chase The. SW20 95 24 69 A
Chase The. SW4 74 28 75 B
Chase The. Wall 111 30 64 D
Chaseville Park Rd. N21 12 30 95 B
Chase Way. N14 16 29 94 C
Chasewood Ave. Enf 13 31 97 D
Chateris Rd. N4 37 31 87 C
Chatfield Rd. Croy 105 31 66 D
Chatfield Rd. SW11 73 26 75 A
Chatham Ave. Brom 107 40 66 A
Chatham Ave. N1 4 32 82 B
Chatham Cl. NW11 35 25 88 A
Chatham Cl. Sutt 103 24 66 B
Chatham Pl. E9 49 35 84 A
Chatham Rd. E17 26 36 89 A
Chatham Rd. King 94 19 69 C
Chatham Rd. SW11 74 27 74 B
Chatham St. SE17 63 32 78 B
Chatsfield. Eps 109 22 62 C
Chatsfield Pl. W5 54 18 81 C
Chatsworth Ave. Brom 89 40 71 B
Chatsworth Ave. NW4 23 23 90 C
Chatsworth Ave. Sid 90 46 73 C
Chatsworth Ave. SW20 95 24 69 C
Chatsworth Ave. Wem 44 18 85 D
Chatsworth Cl. NW4 23 23 90 C
Chatsworth Cres. Houn 70 14 75 D
Chatsworth Dri. Enf 13 34 95 C
Chatsworth Estate. E5 49 35 85 B
Chatsworth Gdns. Har 32 13 87 D
Chatsworth Gdns. N.Mal 102 21 67 B
Chatsworth Gdns. W3 55 19 80 D
Chatsworth Pl. Rich 83 16 71 A
Chatsworth Rd. Croy 105 32 65 D
Chatsworth Rd. Dart 80 53 75 C
Chatsworth Rd. E15 50 39 85 D
Chatsworth Rd. E5 49 35 85 B
Chatsworth Rd. E9 49 35 85 D
Chatsworth Rd. NW2 46 23 84 B
Chatsworth Rd. Sutt 110 23 64 B
Chatsworth Rd. W4 61 20 77 A
Chatsworth Rd. W5 54 18 82 D
Chatsworth Rise. W5 54 18 82 D
Chatsworth Way. SE27 87 32 72 C
Chatteris Ave. Rom 30 53 91 B
Chattern Hill. Ashf 81 07 71 B
Chattern Rd. Ashf 81 08 71 A
Chatterton Rd. Brom 107 41 67 B
Chatterton Rd. N4 37 31 86 D
Chatto Rd. SW11 74 27 74 B
Chaucer Ave. Houn 69 10 76 D
Chaucer Ave. Rich 72 19 76 C
Chaucer Cl. N11 16 29 92 D
Chaucer Gdns. Sutt 103 25 65 C
Chaucer Green. Croy 106 35 66 A
Chaucer Rd. E11 39 40 88 C
Chaucer Rd. E17 26 38 90 C
Chaucer Rd. E7 50 40 84 A
Chaucer Rd. Rom 30 52 91 D
Chaucer Rd. SE24 75 31 74 B
Chaucer Rd. Sutt 110 25 64 A
Chaucer Rd. W3 55 20 80 C
Chaucer Rd. Well 78 45 76 B
Chaucer Way. Dart 80 54 75 D
Chauncey Cl. N9 17 34 93 C
Chaundrye Cl. SE9 77 42 74 D
Chauntler Rd. E16 58 40 80 B
Cheam Common Rd. Wor Pk 103 23 65 C
Cheam Mansions. Sutt 110 24 63 C
Cheam Park Way. Sutt 110 24 63 A
Cheam Rd. Eps 109 22 62 C
Cheam Rd. Sutt 110 25 63 A
Cheam St. SE15 75 34 75 B
Cheapside. EC2 4 32 81 C
Cheapside. N13 17 32 92 B
Cheddar Rd. Houn 69 07 76 D
Cheddington Rd. N18 17 33 93 C
Chedworth Cl. E16 58 39 81 C
Cheeseman Cl. Hamp 92 12 70 A
Cheesemans Terr. W14 62 24 78 D
Chelford Rd. Brom 88 38 71 D
Chelmer Cres. Bark 51 46 83 D
Chelmer Rd. E9 49 35 85 D
Chelmsford Ave. Rom 29 50 91 B
Chelmsford Cl. W6 62 23 77 B
Chelmsford Dri. Horn 42 54 86 D
Chelmsford Gdns. Ilf 39 42 87 B
Chelmsford Rd. E11 39 39 87 C
Chelmsford Rd. E17 38 37 88 C
Chelmsford Rd. E18 27 39 90 B
Chelmsford Rd. N14 16 29 94 A
Chelmsford Sq. NW10 46 23 83 A
Chelsea Bridge Rd. SW1 9 28 78 C
Chelsea Bridge. SW8 9 28 77 B
Chelsea Cl. Edg 22 19 90 C
Chelsea Cl. Hamp 82 14 71 C
Chelsea Cl. NW10 45 21 83 A
Chelsea Emb. SW3 9 27 77 B
Chelsea Estate. SW3 9 27 77 A
Chelsea Manor Gdns. SW3 9 27 78 C
Chelsea Manor St. SW3 9 27 78 C
Chelsea Park Gdns. SW3 62 26 77 B
Chelsea Sq. SW3 62 26 78 D
Chelsfield Ave. N9 18 35 94 B
Chelsfield Gdns. SE26 88 35 72 C
Chelsfield Green. N9 18 35 94 B
Chelsham Rd. S Croy 112 32 63 B
Chelsham Rd. SW4 74 29 75 B
Chelston App. Ruis 31 10 86 A
Chelston Rd. Ruis 31 10 87 C
Chelsworth Cl. Rom 30 54 90 B
Chelsworth Dri. Rom 30 54 90 B
Chelsworth Dri. SE18 66 44 77 B
Cheltenham Ave. Twick 83 16 73 A
Cheltenham Cl. Nthlt 43 13 84 B
Cheltenham Gdns. E6 50 42 83 C
Cheltenham Pl. Har 21 18 89 C
Cheltenham Pl. W3 55 19 80 D
Cheltenham Rd. E10 38 38 88 C
Cheltenham Rd. Orp 108 46 65 C
Cheltenham Rd. SE13 76 35 74 A
Cheltenham Terr. SW3 6 27 78 D
Chelverton Rd. SW15 73 23 75 D
Chelwood Cl. Nthwd 19 08 91 C
Chelwood Gdns. Rich 72 19 76 C
Chelwood N20 15 26 93 B
Chelwood Wlk. SE4 76 36 75 C
Chenappa Cl. E13 58 40 82 A
Chenduit Way. Stan 21 15 91 B
Cheney Rd. NW1 47 30 83 C
Cheney Row. E17 26 36 90 B
Cheneys Rd. E11 39 39 86 C
Cheney St. Pnr 32 11 88 A
Chenies Mews. WC1 2 29 82 D
Chenies Pl. NW1 47 29 83 D
Chenies St. WC1 2 29 81 B
Chenies The. Orp 108 45 67 C
Cheniston Gdns. W8 62 25 79 D
Chepstow Ave. Horn 42 54 86 C
Chepstow Cl. SW15 73 24 74 A
Chepstow Cres. Ilf 40 45 88 C
Chepstow Cres. W11 56 25 80 A
Chepstow Gdns. Sthl 53 12 81 D
Chepstow Pl. W2 56 25 80 A
Chepstow Rd. Croy 105 33 65 B
Chepstow Rd. W2 56 25 81 C
Chepstow Rd. W7 60 16 79 C
Chepstow Rise. Croy 105 33 65 C
Chepstow Villas. W11 56 25 80 A
Chepstow Way. SE15 75 33 76 B
Chepstow Way. SE15 63 33 77 D
Chequers Cl. Orp 100 45 68 D
Chequers La. Dag 52 49 83 C
Chequer St. EC1 4 32 82 C
Chequers Way. N13 17 31 92 D
Cherbury St. N1 48 32 83 D
Cherimeya Gdns. E Mol 92 13 68 B
Cherington Rd. W7 54 15 80 D
Cheriton Ave. Brom 107 40 67 A
Cheriton Ave. Ilf 28 43 90 A
Cheriton Cl. W5 54 17 81 A
Cheriton Ct. SE25 105 33 67 A
Cheriton Dri. SE18 66 44 77 B
Cheriton Sq. SW17 86 28 72 B
Cherry Ave. Sthl 53 11 80 D
Cherry Cl. Cars 104 27 65 B
Cherry Cl. Mord 95 24 68 C
Cherry Cl. Ruis 31 09 86 D
Cherry Cl. SW2 87 31 73 A
Cherry Cl. W5 60 17 79 D
Cherry Cres. Brent 60 16 77 D
Cherry Croft. Pnr 20 12 91 D
Cherry Ct. Ilf 28 43 89 B
Cherrydown Ave. E4 18 37 93 C
Cherrydown Cl. E4 18 37 93 C
Cherrydown Wlk. Rom 29 49 90 D
Cherry Garth. Brent 60 17 78 D
Cherry Gdns. Dag 52 48 85 D
Cherry Gdn St. SE16 63 34 79 B
Cherry Hill. Barn 11 25 95 D
Cherry Hill Gdns. Croy 111 30 64 B
Cherry Laurel Wlk. SW2 74 30 74 D
Cherry Orchard Gdns. E Mol 92 12 68 B
Cherry Orchard Rd. Brom 107 42 65 A
Cherry Orchard Rd. Croy 105 32 66 D
Cherry Orchard Rd. E Mol 92 13 68 A
Cherry Orchard. SE7 65 41 77 A
Cherry St. Rom 41 50 88 B
Cherry Tree Hill. N2 36 27 88 B
Cherry Tree Rd. N2 24 27 89 D
Cherry Tree Way. Stan 21 16 91 B
Cherry Tree Wlk. Beck 98 36 68 D
Cherry Tree Wlk. EC1 4 32 82 C
Cherry Way. Eps 109 20 63 B
Cherry Way. Shep 91 09 68 C
Cherry Wlk. Brom 107 40 66 C
Cherrywood Cl. King 94 19 70 C
Cherrywood Ct. Tedd 83 16 71 C
Cherrywood Dri. SW15 73 23 74 B
Cherrywood La. Mord 95 24 68 C
Cherry Wood Way. W5 55 19 81 A
Chertsey Ct. SW14 72 19 75 B
Chertsey Dri. Sutt 103 24 65 A
Chertsey Rd. Ashf 91 08 70 B
Chertsey Rd. E11 38 38 86 B
Chertsey Rd. Felt 81 09 71 A
Chertsey Rd. Ilf 51 44 85 B
Chertsey Rd. Sun 81 09 71 C
Chertsey Rd. Twick 82 14 73 C
Chertsey St. SW17 86 28 71 C
Cherwell Ct. Eps 109 20 64 A
Cheryls Cl. SW6 73 25 76 B
Cheseman St. SE26 87 34 72 D
Chesfield Rd. King 93 18 70 C
Chesham Ave. Orp 108 43 67 D
Chesham Cl. Rom 29 50 89 D
Chesham Cl. Sutt 110 24 62 C
Chesham Cl. SW1 6 28 79 C
Chesham Cres. SE20 98 35 69 A
Chesham Mews. SW1 6 28 79 C
Chesham Pl. SW1 6 28 79 C
Chesham Rd. King 94 19 69 C
Chesham Rd. SE20 98 35 69 A
Chesham Rd. SW19 95 26 70 B
Chesham St. NW10 34 20 86 D
Chesham St. SW1 6 28 79 C
Chesham Terr. W13 60 16 79 B
Cheshire Cl. Mit 96 30 68 A
Cheshire House. Mord 103 25 66 B
Cheshire Rd. N22 24 30 91 B
Cheshire St. E2 4 33 82 D
Cheshire St. E2 57 34 82 C
Chesholm Rd. N16 37 33 86 C
Cheshunt Rd. Belv 67 49 78 C
Cheshunt Rd. E7 50 40 84 B
Chesilton Rd. SW6 73 24 76 B
Chesney St. SW11 74 28 76 A
Chesnut Gr. N17 25 33 89 B
Chessholme Rd. Ashf 91 08 70 A
Chessington Ave. Bexh 67 48 77 C
Chessington Ave. N3 23 24 89 B
Chessington Cl. Eps 109 20 63 A
Chessington Ct. Pnr 20 12 89 D
Chessington Hill Park. Chess 109 19 64 C
Chessington Rd. Eps 109 20 63 D
Chessington Way. W Wick 106 37 65 B
Chesson Rd. W14 62 24 77 B
Chesswood Way. Pnr 20 11 90 D
Chester Ave. Rich 71 18 74 D
Chester Ave. Twick 82 12 73 D
Chester Cl. Ashf 81 08 71 D
Chester Cl N. NW1 2 28 82 B
Chester Cl S. NW1 2 28 82 B
Chester Cl. Sutt 103 25 65 A
Chester Cl. SW15 72 22 75 B
Chester Cl. SW1 6 28 79 D
Chester Ct. Har 33 15 88 D
Chester Dri. Har 32 13 88 C
Chesterfield Cl. SE13 76 38 75 A
Chesterfield Dri. Esh 101 16 65 A
Chesterfield Gdns. N4 37 31 88 B
Chesterfield Gdns. W1 6 28 80 D
Chesterfield Gr. SE22 75 33 74 B
Chesterfield Hill. W1 6 28 80 D
Chesterfield Rd. Barn 11 23 95 B
Chesterfield Rd. E10 38 38 88 C
Chesterfield Rd. Eps 109 20 63 D
Chesterfield Rd. N3 23 25 91 A
Chesterfield Rd. W4 61 20 77 A
Chesterfield St. W1 6 28 80 D
Chesterfield Wlk. SE10 76 38 76 B
Chesterford Gdns. NW3 46 25 85 B
Chesterford Rd. E12 51 43 85 C
Chester Gate. NW1 2 28 82 B
Chester Gdns. Enf 13 34 95 D
Chester Gdns. Mord 103 26 67 A
Chester Mews. SW1 6 28 79 D
Chester Pl. NW1 2 28 82 B
Chester Rd. E11 39 40 88 D
Chester Rd. E16 58 39 82 C
Chester Rd. E17 38 35 88 B
Chester Rd. E7 50 41 84 D
Chester Rd. Houn 69 07 75 A
Chester Rd. Houn 69 10 75 B
Chester Rd. Ilf 40 45 87 B
Chester Rd. N17 25 33 89 A
Chester Rd. N19 36 28 86 B
Chester Rd. N9 17 34 94 D
Chester Rd. Nthwd 19 09 91 D
Chester Rd. NW1 2 28 82 B
Chester Rd. Sid 78 45 74 A
Chester Rd. SW19 95 23 70 A
Chester Row. SW1 9 28 78 A
Chesters Estate The. N Mal 94 21 69 A
Chester Sq Mews. SW1 6 28 79 D
Chester Sq. SW1 9 28 78 B
Chester St. E2 57 34 82 C
Chester St. SW1 6 28 79 D
Chester Terr. NW1 2 28 82 B
Chesterton Cl. Grnf 43 13 83 D
Chesterton Cl. SW18 73 25 74 A
Chesterton Rd. E13 58 40 82 A
Chesterton Rd. W10 56 24 81 A
Chesterton Terr. E13 58 40 82 A
Chesterton Terr. King 94 19 69 C
Chester Way. SE11 63 31 78 A
Chesthunte Rd. N17 25 32 90 C
Chestnut Alley. SW6 62 24 77 B
Chestnut Ave. Brent 60 17 78 B
Chestnut Ave. E7 50 40 85 B
Chestnut Ave. Edg 21 18 91 B
Chestnut Ave. E Mol 93 15 68 B
Chestnut Ave. Eps 109 21 64 A
Chestnut Ave. Esh 101 15 66 C
Chestnut Ave. Hamp 92 13 70 C
Chestnut Ave. Horn 42 52 86 A
Chestnut Ave. N8 36 30 88 A
Chestnut Ave. Nthwd 19 09 90 B
Chestnut Avenue N. E17 26 38 89 D
Chestnut Ave S. E17 38 38 88 B
Chestnut Ave. SW14 72 20 75 B
Chestnut Ave. Tedd 93 15 69 B
Chestnut Ave. Wem 44 16 85 D
Chestnut Ave. W.Wick 107 39 65 C
Chestnut Cl. Ashf 81 07 71 B
Chestnut Cl. Ashf 91 09 70 B
Chestnut Cl. Cars 104 27 66 D
Chestnut Cl. N14 12 29 95 B
Chestnut Cl. N16 37 32 86 B
Chestnut Ct. SW6 62 24 77 B
Chestnut Dri. Bexh 79 48 75 A
Chestnut Dri. E11 39 40 88 C
Chestnut Dri. Har 21 15 90 B
Chestnut Dri. Pnr 32 11 88 D
Chestnut Glen. Horn 42 52 86 A
Chestnut Gr. Barn 12 27 95 B
Chestnut Gr. Ilf 28 45 91 A
Chestnut Gr. Islw 71 16 75 C
Chestnut Gr. Mit 96 29 68 D
Chestnut Gr. N Mal 94 20 68 B
Chestnut Gr. S Croy 112 34 63 D
Chestnut Gr. SW12 86 28 73 C
Chestnut Gr. W5 60 17 79 D
Chestnut Gr. Wem 44 16 85 D
Chestnut La. N20 15 24 94 C
Chestnut Rd. Ashf 81 07 71 B
Chestnut Rd. King 93 18 70 C
Chestnut Rd. N17 25 34 89 A
Chestnut Rd. SE27 87 32 72 C
Chestnut Rd. SW20 95 23 69 D
Chestnut Rd. Twick 83 15 72 A
Chestnut Rise. SE18 66 45 78 C
Chestnut Way. Felt 81 10 72 D
Chestnut Wlk. Shep 91 09 68 C
Cheston Ave. Croy 106 36 66 C
Chesworth Cl. Eri 80 51 76 C
Chettle Cl. SE1 8 32 79 D
Chettle Ct. N8 37 31 88 C
Chetwode Rd. SW17 86 27 72 D
Chetwynd Ave. Barn 16 27 94 D
Chetwynd Rd. NW5 36 28 86 D
Cheval Pl. SW7 5 27 79 C
Cheval St. E14 64 37 79 C
Cheveley Cl. Rom 30 54 90 B
Cheveney Wlk. Brom 99 40 68 A
Chevening Rd. E10 65 39 78 D
Chevening Rd. NW6 46 23 83 D
Chevening Rd. SE19 97 32 70 B
Cheverton Rd. N19 36 29 87 D
Chevet St. E9 49 36 85 C
Cheviot Cl. Bexh 80 51 76 C
Cheviot Cl. Enf 13 32 97 D
Cheviot Cl. Sutt 110 26 62 B
Cheviot Gate. NW2 35 24 86 A
Cheviot Gdns. NW2 35 24 86 A
Cheviot Gdns. SE27 87 31 71 B
Cheviot Rd. Horn 42 52 87 A
Cheviot Rd. SE27 87 31 71 D
Cheviot Way. Ilf 28 45 89 C
Chewton Rd. E17 26 36 89 C
Cheyham Gdns. Sutt 110 23 62 D
Cheyham Way. Sutt 110 24 62 C
Cheyne Ave. E18 27 39 89 B
Cheyne Ave. Twick 82 12 73 D
Cheyne Cl. Brom 107 42 65 C
Cheyne Ct. SW3 9 27 77 B
Cheyne Gdns. SW3 9 27 77 A
Cheyne Hill. Surb 93 18 68 D
Cheyne Mews. SW3 9 27 77 A
Cheyne Path. W13 54 15 81 D
Cheyne Rd. Ashf 91 08 70 B
Cheyne Row. SW3 9 27 77 A
Cheyne Wlk. NW4 35 23 88 C
Cheyne Wlk. Croy 105 34 65 A
Cheyne Wlk. N21 13 31 95 B
Cheyne Wlk. SW10 62 26 77 D
Cheyne Wlk. SW3 62 26 77 B
Cheyne Wlk. SW3 9 27 77 A
Cheyneys Ave. Edg 21 17 91 B
Chichele Gdns. Croy 112 33 64 A
Chichele Rd. NW2 46 23 85 D
Chicheley Gdns. Har 20 14 91 C
Chicheley Rd. Har 20 14 91 C
Chicheley St. SE1 7 30 79 B
Chichester Ave. Ruis 31 09 86 A
Chichester Cl. SE3 77 41 76 A
Chichester Ct. Eps 109 21 62 B
Chichester Ct. Stan 21 18 89 A
Chichester Gdns. Ilf 39 42 87 B
Chichester Rd. Croy 105 33 65 C
Chichester Rd. E11 39 39 86 C
Chichester Rd. N9 17 34 94 C
Chichester Rd. NW6 46 25 83 C
Chichester Rd. W2 56 25 81 B
Chichester Rents. WC2 3 31 81 C
Chichester St. SW1 10 29 78 C
Chichester Way. Felt 82 11 73 A
Chicksand St. E1 4 33 81 B
Chicksand St. E1 57 34 81 A
Chiddingfold. N12 15 25 93 C
Chiddingstone Ave. Bexh 67 48 77 D
Chiddingstone St. SW6 73 25 76 C
Chieveley Rd. Bexh 79 49 75 D
Chignell Pl. W13 54 16 80 C
Chigwell Hill. E1 57 34 80 B
Chigwell Hurst Ct. Pnr 20 11 89 B
Chigwell Rd. E18 27 41 90 C
Chigwell Rd. Wdf Gn 27 42 91 A
Childebert Rd. SW17 86 28 72 B
Childeric Rd. SE14 64 36 77 C
Childerley St. SW6 73 24 76 A
Childers St. SE8 64 36 77 B
Childs Cl. Horn 42 53 88 C
Childs Hill Wlk. NW2 35 24 86 D
Childs La. SE19 97 33 70 A
Child's Pl. SW5 62 25 78 A
Child's St. SW5 62 25 78 A
Childs Way. NW11 35 24 88 B
*Child's Wlk. SW5 62 25 78 A
Chilham Cl. Grnf 44 16 83 C
Chilham Rd. SE9 89 42 71 A
Chilham Way. Brom 107 40 66 A
Chillerton Rd. SW17 86 28 71 D
Chillingworth Gdns. Twick 83 15 72 D
Chillingworth Rd. N7 48 31 85 C
Chilmark Gdns. N.Mal 102 22 67 C
Chilmark Rd. SW16 96 29 69 B
Chiltern Ave. Twick 82 13 73 C
Chiltern Cl. Bexh 80 51 76 A
Chiltern Cl. Uxb 31 07 86 A
Chiltern Dene. Enf 12 30 96 D
Chiltern Dri. Surb 102 19 67 B
Chiltern Gdns. Brom 99 39 68 D
Chiltern Gdns. Horn 42 53 86 C
Chiltern Gdns. NW2 35 23 86 D
Chiltern Rd. E3 57 37 82 C
Chiltern Rd. Ilf 40 45 88 A
Chiltern Rd. Pnr 32 11 88 A
Chiltern Rd. Sutt 110 26 62 C
Chilterns The. Sutt 110 25 62 B
Chiltern St. W1 2 28 81 A
Chilthorne Cl. SE6 88 36 73 B
Chilton Ave. W5 60 17 78 B
Chilton Gr. SE8 64 36 78 A
Chiltonian Industrial Estate. SE12 77 39 74 D
Chilton Rd. Edg 22 19 91 A
Chilton Rd. Rich 72 19 75 A
Chilton St. E2 4 33 82 D
Chilver St. E10 65 39 78 D
Chilworth Gdns. Sutt 103 26 65 C
Chilworth Mews. W2 1 26 81 D
Chilworth St. W2 1 26 81 C
Chimes Ave. N13 17 31 92 B
Chinbrook Cres. SE12 89 40 72 D
Chinbrook Rd. SE12 89 40 72 D
Chinchilla Dri. Houn 70 11 76 C
Chine The. N10 24 29 89 C
Chine The. N21 13 31 95 B
Chine The. Wem 44 16 85 D
Chingford Ave. E4 18 37 93 D
Chingford La. Wdf Gn 27 39 91 B
Chingford Mount Rd. E4 18 37 92 C
Chingford Rd. E17 26 37 90 D
Chingford Rd. E4 26 37 91 C
Chingley Cl. Brom 99 39 70 A
Chinnor Cres. Grnf 43 14 83 C
Chipka St. E14 64 38 79 A
Chipley St. SE14 64 36 77 A
Chipmunk Gr (off Argus Way). Nthlt 53 12 82 A
Chippendale St. E5 38 35 86 D
Chippenham Ave. Wem 45 19 85 D
Chippenham Cl. Pnr 19 09 89 D
Chippenham Gdns. NW6 56 25 82 A
Chippenham Mews. W9 56 25 82 C
Chippenham Rd. Rom 30 53 91 B
Chippenham Rd. W9 56 25 82 C
Chippenham Wlk. Rom 30 53 91 B
Chipperfield Rd. Orp 100 46 69 C
Chipstead Ave. Th Hth 97 31 68 D
Chipstead Cl. SE19 97 33 70 D
Chipstead Gdns. NW2 34 22 86 B
Chipstead Rd. Eri 68 51 77 C
Chipstead Rd. Houn 69 07 75 A
Chipstead St. SW6 73 25 76 C
Chip St. SW4 74 29 75 D
Chisenhale Rd. E3 49 36 83 C
Chisholm Rd. Croy 105 33 65 A
Chisholm Rd. Rich 71 18 74 D
Chisledon Wlk. E9 49 36 84 B

Chislehurst Ave. N12 23 26 91 C
Chislehurst High St. Chis 100 43 70 B
Chislehurst Rd. Brom 99 42 69 C
Chislehurst Rd. Chis 99 42 69 B
Chislehurst Rd. Orp 108 45 67 A
Chislehurst Rd. Rich 71 18 74 A
Chislehurst Rd. Sid 90 46 71 C
Chislet Cl. Beck 98 37 70 C
Chisley Rd. N15 37 33 88 C
Chiswell Sq. SE3 77 40 76 D
Chiswell St. EC1 4 32 81 B
Chiswick Cl. Croy 104 30 65 D
Chiswick Common Rd. W4 61 21 78 A
Chiswick Ct. Pnr 20 12 89 B
Chiswick High Rd. W4 61 20 78 D
Chiswick Lane S. W4 61 21 77 B
Chiswick La. W4 61 21 78 C
Chiswick Mall. W4 61 21 77 B
Chiswick Mall. W6 61 22 78 C
Chiswick Quay. W4 72 20 76 A
Chiswick Rd. N9 17 34 93 A
Chiswick Rd. W4 61 20 78 A
Chiswick Sq. W4 61 21 77 A
Chiswick Village. W4 61 19 77 B
Chitty's La. Dag 41 47 86 B
Chitty St. W1 2 29 81 A
Chivalry Rd. SW11 74 27 74 A
Chivers Rd. E4 18 37 92 B
Choats Manor Way. Dag 52 48 83 D
Chobham Gdns. SW19 85 23 72 B
Chobham Rd. E15 49 38 85 D
Cholmeley Cres. N6 36 28 87 B
Cholmeley Park. N6 36 28 87 B
Cholmley Gdns. NW6 46 25 85 C
Cholmley Rd. Surb 101 16 67 D
Cholmondeley Ave. NW10 45 22 83 C
Cholmondeley Wlk. Rich 71 17 74 A
Choppin's Ct. E1 57 34 80 D
Chorleywood Cres. Orp 100 46 69 C
Choumert Gr. SE15 75 34 76 C
Choumert Rd. SE15 75 33 76 D
Choumert Sq. SE15 75 34 76 C
Chrisp St. E14 57 37 81 D
Christ Church Ave. Tedd 83 16 71 C
Christ Church Ave. Eri 68 51 77 A
Christchurch Ave. Har 21 16 89 D
Christchurch Ave. N12 23 26 91 A
Christchurch Ave. NW6 46 24 84 C
Christchurch Ave. Wem 44 18 84 A
Christchurch Cl. SW19 95 26 70 D
Christchurch Gdns. Har 21 16 89 C
Christchurch Green. Wem 44 18 84 A
Christchurch Hill. NW3 35 26 86 D
Christ Church La. Barn 11 24 97 C
Christchurch Park. Sutt 110 26 63 C
Christ Church Pas. Barn 11 24 96 A
Christchurch Pas. NW3 35 26 86 C
Christ Church Rd. Beck 98 37 69 C
Christchurch Rd. Dart 80 53 74 C
Christchurch Rd. Houn 69 07 75 A
Christchurch Rd. Ilf 40 44 87 C
Christ Church Rd. N8 36 30 88 C
Christchurch Rd. Pur 112 31 62 C
Christchurch Rd. Sid 90 45 72 D
Christ Church Rd. Surb 101 18 67 D
Christ Church Rd. SW14 72 20 74 A
Christchurch Rd. SW19 95 26 70 D
Christchurch Rd. SW2 86 30 73 D
Christchurch Sq. E9 49 35 83 A
Christchurch St. SW3 9 27 77 B
Christchurch Terr. SW3 9 27 77 B
Christchurch Way. E10 65 39 78 C
Christian Fields. SW16 97 31 70 C
Christian St. E1 57 34 81 C
Christie Ct. N4 36 30 86 A
Christie Gdns. Rom 40 46 87 B
Christie Rd. E9 49 36 84 A
Christina St. EC2 4 33 82 C
Christopher Ave. W7 60 16 79 C
Christopher Cl. Sid 78 45 74 B
Christopher Gdns. Dag 52 47 85 D
Christopher Mews. W11 56 24 80 C
Christopher St. EC2 4 32 82 D
Chryssell Rd. SW9 63 31 77 C
Chubworthy St. SE14 64 36 77 A
Chudleigh Cres. Ilf 51 45 85 A
Chudleigh Gdns. Sutt 103 26 65 C
Chudleigh Rd. NW6 46 23 84 D
Chudleigh Rd. SE4 76 37 74 A
Chudleigh Rd. Twick 83 15 73 B
Chudleigh St. E1 57 35 81 D
Chudleigh Way. Ruis 31 10 87 C
Chulsa Rd. SE26 87 34 71 D
Chumleigh St. SE5 63 33 77 A
Chumleigh Wlk. Surb 93 18 68 D
Church Alley. Croy 105 31 66 B
Church App. SE21 87 32 72 D
Church Ave. Beck 98 37 69 A
Church Ave. E4 26 38 91 B
Church Ave. N2 23 26 90 D
Church Ave. Nthlt 43 12 84 D
Church Ave. NW1 47 28 84 B
Church Ave. Pnr 32 12 88 D
Church Ave. Ruis 31 08 87 D
Church Ave. Sid 90 46 71 D
Church Ave. Sthl 59 12 79 C
Church Ave. SW14 72 20 75 B
Churchbury Cl. Enf 13 33 97 C
Churchbury La. Enf 13 33 97 C
Churchbury Rd. Enf 13 33 97 C
Churchbury Rd. SE9 89 41 73 B
Church Cl. N20 16 27 93 C
Church Cl. Nthwd 19 09 91 D
Church Cres. E9 49 35 84 D
Church Cres. N10 24 28 89 D
Church Cres. N20 16 27 93 C
Church Cres. N3 23 24 90 B
Churchcroft Cl. SW12 86 28 73 A
Church Ct. EC4 3 31 81 C
Church Ct. Rich 71 17 74 B
Churchdown. Brom 89 39 71 A
Church Dri. Har 32 13 88 C
Church Dri. NW9 34 20 87 D
Church Dri. W.Wick 107 39 65 C
Church Elm La. Dag 52 49 84 A
Church End. E17 26 37 89 D
Church End. NW4 22 22 89 D
Church Entry. EC4 3 31 81 D
Church Farm La. Sutt 110 24 63 A
Churchfield Ave. N12 23 26 91 B
Churchfield Cl. Har 20 14 89 C
Churchfield Rd. W13 54 17 80 C
Churchfield Rd. W3 55 20 80 C
Churchfield Rd. W7 60 15 79 A
Churchfield Rd. Well 78 46 75 A
Churchfields Ave. Felt 82 12 72 D
Churchfields. E18 27 40 90 A
Churchfields. E Mol 92 13 68 A
Churchfields Rd. Beck 98 36 69 C
Churchfields. SE10 64 38 77 A
Churchfield Way. N12 23 26 91 A
Church Gate. SW6 73 24 75 A
Church Gdns. W5 60 17 79 B
Church Gdns. Wem 44 16 85 A
Church Gr. King 93 17 69 C
Church Gr. SE13 76 37 74 B
Church Hill. Cars 111 27 64 D
Church Hill. Dart 80 51 75 C
Church Hill. E17 26 37 89 D
Church Hill. Har 33 15 87 C
Church Hill. N21 17 31 94 A
Church Hill. Orp 108 46 66 B
Church Hill. Pur 111 30 62 C
Church Hill Rd. E17 26 37 89 D
Church Hill Rd. N20 16 27 94 B
Church Hill Rd. Surb 101 18 67 A
Church Hill Rd. Sutt 110 23 64 B
Church Hill. SE18 65 42 79 D
Church Hill. SE18 66 43 79 C
Church Hill. SW19 85 24 71 D
Church Hill Wood. Orp 108 45 67 B
Churchill Ave. Har 33 16 88 D
Churchill Gdns Rd. SW1 10 29 77 A
Churchill Gdns. SW1 10 29 78 C
Churchill Gdns. W3 55 19 81 C
Churchill Pl. Har 21 15 89 C
Churchill Rd. E16 58 41 81 C
Churchill Rd. Edg 22 19 91 A
Churchill Rd. NW2 45 22 84 B
Churchill Rd. NW5 47 28 85 B
Churchill Rd. S Croy 112 32 63 C
Churchill Terr. E4 18 37 93 C
Churchill Way. Sun 91 10 70 A
Churchill Wlk. E9 49 35 85 C
Church La. Brom 107 42 66 C
Church La. Chis 100 44 69 A
Church La. Dag 52 50 84 C
Church La. E11 39 39 87 C
Church La. E17 26 37 89 D
Church La. Enf 13 32 96 B
Church La. Har 21 15 90 B
Church La. N17 25 33 90 A
Church La. N2 23 26 89 B
Church La. N8 24 30 89 D
Church La. N9 17 34 93 A
Church La. NW9 34 20 87 A
Church La. Pnr 20 12 89 B
Church La. Rom 30 51 89 C
Church La. Surb 101 16 67 C
Church La. SW17 86 28 71 C
Church La. SW19 95 25 69 A
Church La. Tedd 83 15 71 D
Church La. Twick 83 16 73 C
Church La. W5 60 17 79 B
Church La. Wall 104 29 65 D
Churchley Rd. SE26 87 34 71 B
Church Manorway. Eri 67 50 79 D
Church Manor Way. SE28 66 46 79 C
Church Manor Way. SE2 66 45 78 B
Churchmead Cl. Barn 12 27 95 C
Church Meadow. Surb 101 17 65 A
Churchmead Rd. NW10 45 22 84 A
Churchmore Rd. SW16 96 29 69 B
Church Mount. N2 35 26 88 B
Church Pas. Surb 101 18 67 A
Church Path. Bark 51 44 83 A
Church Path. Croy 105 32 65 A
Church Path. E11 39 40 88 A
Church Path. E17 26 37 89 D
Church Path. Mit 96 27 68 A
Church Path. Mit 96 27 68 C
Church Path. N12 15 26 92 A
Church Path. N12 15 26 93 C
Church Path. N17 25 33 91 C
Church Path. N5 48 31 85 D
Church Path. N5 48 32 85 A
Church Path. N8 36 30 88 B
Church Path. NW10 45 21 84 C
Church Path. Rom 42 51 88 A
Church Path. Sthl 59 12 79 D
Church Path. SW14 72 20 75 B
Church Path. SW14 72 20 75 D
Church Path. SW19 95 24 69 D
Church Path. W3 61 20 79 C
Church Pl. Mit 96 27 68 A
Church Pl. SW1 6 29 80 A
Church Pl. W5 60 17 79 B
Church Rd. Ashf 81 07 71 C
Church Rd. Bark 51 44 84 A
Church Rd. Bexh 79 48 75 B
Church Rd. Brom 99 39 68 A
Church Rd. Brom 99 40 69 C
*Church Rd. Croy 112 32 64 A
Church Rd. Croy 105 32 65 C
Church Rd. E10 38 37 87 C
Church Rd. E12 50 42 85 D
Church Rd. E17 26 36 90 C
Church Rd. E Mol 92 14 68 D
Church Rd. Enf 14 35 95 C
Church Rd. Eps 109 20 63 D
Church Rd. Eri 67 50 78 D
Church Rd. Felt 82 11 71 D
Church Rd. Houn 59 13 77 C
Church Rd. Ilf 40 45 88 C
Church Rd. Islw 60 15 77 C
Church Rd. King 93 18 69 D
Church Rd. Mit 95 26 69 D
Church Rd. N17 25 33 91 D
Church Rd. N6 36 28 88 C
Church Rd N. N2 23 26 90 D
Church Rd. Nthlt 43 12 83 A
Church Rd. Nthwd 19 09 91 D
Church Rd. NW10 45 21 84 C
Church Rd. NW4 23 23 89 C
Church Rd. Pur 111 30 62 C
Church Rd. Rich 83 18 71 A
Church Rd. Rich 71 18 74 A
Church Rd. Rom 30 54 90 B
Church Rd. SE19 97 33 70 C
Church Rd. Sid 90 46 71 A
Church Rd S. N2 24 27 90 C
Church Rd. Sthl 59 12 79 D
Church Rd. Surb 101 17 66 C
Church Rd. Sutt 110 24 63 A
Church Rd. SW13 72 22 76 A
Church Rd. SW19 85 24 71 A
Church Rd. SW19 95 26 69 B
Church Rd. Tedd 83 15 71 D
Church Rd. W3 61 20 79 A
Church Rd. W7 54 15 80 A
Church Rd. Wall 104 29 65 D
Church Rd. Well 78 46 76 D
Church Rd. Wor Pk 102 21 66 C
Church Rise. SE23 88 35 72 B
Church Row. Chis 100 44 69 A
Church Row. NW3 46 26 85 A
Church St. Croy 105 32 65 A
Church St. Dag 52 49 84 B
Church St. E15 50 39 83 B
Church St. Enf 13 32 96 B
Church St. Eps 109 22 62 A
Church St. Hamp 92 14 69 A
Church St. Islw 71 16 76 D
Church St. King 93 17 69 D
Church St. N9 17 33 93 A
Church St N. E15 50 39 83 A
Church St. NW8 1 27 82 C
Church St Pas. E15 50 39 83 A
Church Stretton Rd. Houn 70 14 74 A
Church St. Sun 91 10 68 B
Church St. Sutt 110 25 64 D
Church St. Twick 83 16 73 C
Church St. W4 61 21 77 B
Church Terr. NW4 22 22 89 B
Church Terr. Rich 71 17 74 B
Church Terr. SE13 77 39 75 A
Church Vale. N2 24 27 89 B
Church Vale. SE23 88 35 72 B
Churchview Rd. Twick 82 14 72 B
Church Way. Barn 12 27 96 D
Church Way. Edg 22 19 91 A
Church Way. N20 16 27 93 C
Churchway. NW1 2 29 82 B
Church Way. S Croy 112 33 62 D
Churchwell Path. E9 49 35 85 C
Church Wlk. Brent 60 17 77 A
Church Wlk. Enf 13 32 96 B
Church Wlk. N16 48 32 85 B
Church Wlk. N16 37 32 86 D
Church Wlk. NW2 35 24 86 D
Church Wlk. NW4 23 23 89 A
Church Wlk. NW9 34 20 86 B
Church Wlk. Rich 71 17 74 B
Church Wlk. Surb 101 15 67 D
Church Wlk. SW13 72 22 76 A
Church Wlk. SW15 72 22 74 B
Church Wlk. SW16 96 29 69 C
Church Wlk. SW20 95 23 68 A
Churchyard Pas. SE5 75 32 76 B
Churchyard Row. SE11 63 31 78 B
Churnfield. N4 37 31 86 A
Churston Ave. E13 50 40 83 B
Churston Cl. SW2 87 31 73 C
Churston Dri. Mord 103 24 67 A
Churston Gdns. N11 24 29 91 A
Churton Pl. SW1 10 29 78 A
Churton St. SW1 10 29 78 A
Chusan Pl. E14 57 36 81 D
Chyngton Cl. Sid 90 45 72 D
Cibber Rd. SE23 88 35 72 B
Cicada Rd. SW18 73 26 74 A
Cicely Rd. SE15 75 34 76 A
Cinderford Way. Brom 89 39 71 A
Cinnamon St. E1 57 34 80 D
Cintra Park. SE19 97 33 70 B
Circle Gdns. SW19 95 25 68 A
Circle The. NW2 34 21 86 C
Circle The. NW7 22 20 91 B
Circle The. Rich 60 18 77 D
Circuit Rd. SE28 66 45 79 B
Circuits The. Pnr 20 11 89 C
Circular Rd. N17 25 33 89 B
Circular Rd. N2 23 26 90 D
Circular Way. SE18 66 43 77 A
Circus Mews. W1 1 27 81 B
Circus Pl. EC2 4 32 81 B
Circus Rd. NW8 1 26 82 B
Circus Rd. NW8 46 26 83 D
Circus St. SE10 64 38 77 C
Cirencester St. W2 56 25 81 B
Cirencester St. W2 56 25 81 B
Cissbury Ho. SE26 87 34 72 C
Cissbury Rd. N15 37 32 88 B
Cissbury Ring N. N12 15 25 92 C
Cissbury Ring S. N12 15 24 92 D
City Garden Row. N1 48 31 83 D
City Rd. EC1 3 31 82 B
City Rd. EC1 4 32 82 D
Civic Way. Ilf 28 44 89 C
Clabon Mews. SW1 9 27 78 B
Clack La. Ruis 31 08 87 C
Clack St. SE16 64 35 79 A
Clacton Rd. E17 38 36 88 C
Clacton Rd. E6 58 41 82 B
Clacton Rd. N17 25 33 90 D
Claigmar Gdns. N3 23 25 90 B
Claire Ct. N12 15 26 93 C
Claire Ct. Pnr 20 12 91 D
Clairvale. Horn 42 54 87 A
Clairvale Rd. Houn 70 12 76 A
Clairview Rd. SW16 86 28 71 B
Clairville Gdns. W7 54 15 80 D
Clancarty Rd. SW6 73 25 76 C
Clancarty Rd. SW6 73 25 76 C
Clandon Cl. Eps 109 22 63 A
Clandon Cl. W3 61 19 79 B
Clandon Gdns. N3 23 25 89 A
Clandon Rd. Ilf 40 45 86 A
Clandon St. SE8 76 37 76 C
Clanfield Way (off Pentridge St).
SE15 63 33 77 D
Clanricarde Gdns. W2 56 25 80 A
Clapham Common North Side. SW4
74 28 75 D
Clapham Common South Side. SW4
74 29 74 A
Clapham Common West Side. SW4
74 27 75 D
Clapham Cres. SW4 74 29 75 D
Clapham High St. SW4 74 29 75 D
Clapham Junction Estate. SW11
74 27 75 C
Clapham Manor Ct. SW4 74 29 75 A
Clapham Manor St. SW4 74 29 75 B
Clapham Park Rd. SW4 74 29 75 D
Clapham Rd. SW9 74 30 76 C
Clapham Rd. SW9 10 30 77 D
Clapton Common. E5 37 34 87 A
Clapton Pas. E5 49 35 85 C
Clapton Sq. E5 49 35 85 C
Clapton Terr. N16 37 34 87 C
Clapton Way. E5 37 34 86 C
Clara Pl. SE18 66 43 78 A
Clare Cl. N2 23 26 89 A
Clare Cnr. SE9 90 43 73 B
Claredale St. E2 48 34 83 D
Claredon Dri. SW15 73 23 75 C
Claredon Rd. SW19 96 27 70 C
Claredon Rd. Wall 111 28 63 D
Clare Gdns. Bark 51 46 84 C
Clare Gdns. E7 50 40 85 A
Clare Gdns. W11 56 24 81 C
Clare Hall Pl. SE16 64 35 78 A
Clare La. N1 48 32 84 C
Clare Lawn Ave. SW14 72 20 74 B
Clare Market. WC2 3 30 81 D
Claremont Ave. Har 33 18 88 A
Claremont Ave. N.Mal 102 22 67 B
Claremont Ave. Sun 91 10 69 B
Claremont Cl. N1 48 31 83 C
Claremont Cres. Dart 80 51 75 C
Claremont Gdns. Ilf 40 45 86 A
Claremont Gdns. Surb 101 18 67 A
Claremont Gr. Wdf Gn 27 41 91 A
Claremont Park. N3 23 24 90 A
Claremont Rd. Brom 99 42 68 D
Claremont Rd. Croy 105 34 66 C
Claremont Rd. E11 38 38 86 D
Claremont Rd. E17 26 36 90 C
Claremont Rd. E7 50 41 85 C
Claremont Rd. Har 21 15 90 C
Claremont Rd. Horn 42 52 88 C
Claremont Rd. N6 36 29 87 A
Claremont Rd. NW2 35 23 86 B
Claremont Rd. Surb 101 18 67 A
Claremont Rd. Tedd 83 15 71 B
Claremont Rd. Twick 71 17 74 C
Claremont Rd. W13 54 16 81 A
Claremont Rd. W9 46 24 83 D
Claremont Sq. N1 48 31 83 C
Claremont St. E16 66 43 79 A
Claremont St. N18 25 34 91 A
Claremont St. SE10 64 37 77 B
Claremont Way. NW2 35 23 87 B
Clarence Ave. Brom 99 42 68 C
Clarence Ave. Ilf 39 42 88 D
Clarence Ave. Ilf 40 43 88 C
Clarence Ave. N Mal 94 20 69 D
Clarence Ave. SW4 74 29 74 D
Clarence Cres. Sid 90 46 72 D
Clarence Cres. SW4 74 29 74 D
Clarence Gdns. NW1 2 28 82 B
Clarence La. SW15 72 21 74 D
Clarence Mews. E5 48 34 85 D
Clarence Pas. NW1 47 30 83 C
Clarence Pl. E5 48 34 85 D
Clarence Rd. Bexh 79 48 75 C
Clarence Rd. Brom 99 42 68 A
Clarence Rd. Croy 105 32 66 B
Clarence Rd. E12 50 41 85 D
Clarence Rd. E16 58 39 82 C
Clarence Rd. E17 26 35 90 D
Clarence Rd. E5 48 34 85 B
Clarence Rd. Enf 14 35 95 A
Clarence Rd. N15 37 32 88 B
Clarence Rd. N22 24 30 91 C
Clarence Rd. NW6 46 24 84 D
Clarence Rd. Rich 72 19 76 A
Clarence Rd. SE9 89 42 72 A
Clarence Rd. Sid 90 46 72 D
Clarence Rd. Sutt 110 25 64 D
Clarence Rd. SW19 95 25 70 B
Clarence Rd. Tedd 93 16 70 A
Clarence Rd. W4 61 19 78 C
Clarence Rd. Wall 111 28 64 D
Clarence St. King 93 18 69 C
Clarence St. Rich 71 18 75 C
Clarence St. Sthl 59 11 79 D
Clarence Terr. Houn 70 13 75 D
Clarence Way. NW1 47 28 84 D
Clarence Wlk. SW4 74 30 76 C
Clarence Yd. SE17 63 32 78 C
Clarendon Cl. Orp 100 46 68 A
Clarendon Cl. W2 5 27 80 A
Clarendon Cres. Twick 82 14 72 D
Clarendon Cross. W11 56 24 80 A
Clarendon Gdns. Ilf 39 42 87 B
Clarendon Gdns. NW4 22 22 89 B
Clarendon Gdns. W9 1 26 82 C
Clarendon Gdns. Wem 44 18 85 A
Clarendon Green. Orp 100 46 68 C
Clarendon Gr. Mit 96 27 68 B
Clarendon Gr. NW1 2 29 82 B
Clarendon Gr. Orp 100 46 68 C
Clarendon Mews. W2 5 27 80 A
Clarendon Path. Orp 100 46 68 A
Clarendon Pl. W2 5 27 80 A
Clarendon Rd. Croy 105 31 65 B
Clarendon Rd. E11 38 38 87 D
Clarendon Rd. E17 38 37 88 D
Clarendon Rd. E18 27 40 89 A
Clarendon Rd. Har 33 15 88 C
Clarendon Rd. N15 25 32 89 C
Clarendon Rd. N18 17 34 92 C
Clarendon Rd. N22 24 30 90 D
Clarendon Rd. N8 24 30 89 B
Clarendon Rd. W11 56 24 80 A
Clarendon Rd. W5 54 18 82 C
Clarendon Rise. SE13 76 38 75 D
Clarendon St. SW1 9 28 78 D
Clarendon Terr. W9 1 26 82 C
Clarendon Way. Chis 100 45 68 B
Clarendon Way. N21 17 32 94 A
Clarendon Way. Orp 100 46 68 A
Clarendon Wlk. W11 56 24 81 C
Clarens St. SE6 88 36 72 B
Clare Rd. E11 38 38 88 D
Clare Rd. Grnf 43 14 84 B
Clare Rd. Houn 70 12 75 B
Clare Rd. NW10 45 22 84 C
Clare Rd. SE14 76 36 76 B
Clare St. E2 48 34 83 D
Claret Gdns. SE25 97 33 68 C
*Clareville Grove Mews. SW7 62 26 78 A
Clareville Gr. SW7 62 26 78 A
Clareville Rd. Orp 108 44 65 A
Clareville St. SW7 62 26 78 A
Clare Way. Bexh 79 48 76 A
Clarewood Wlk. SW9 75 31 75 D
Clarges Mews. W1 6 28 80 D
Clarges St. W1 6 28 80 D
Claribel Rd. SW9 75 31 76 D
Clarice Way. Wall 111 30 62 A
Claridge Rd. Dag 41 47 87 D
Clarissa Rd. Rom 41 47 87 B
Clarissa St. E8 48 33 83 B
Clark Cl. Eri 80 52 76 A
Clarke Path. N16 37 34 87 C
Clarkes Ave. Wor Pk 103 23 65 B
Clarkes Mews. W1 2 28 81 A
Clarkson Rd. E16 58 39 81 D
Clarkson St. E2 57 34 82 B
Clarksons The. Bark 51 44 83 C
Clark's Pl. EC3 4 33 81 C
Clark's Rd. Ilf 40 44 86 B
Clark St. E1 57 35 81 A
Clark Way. Houn 59 11 77 D
Claston Cl. Dart 80 51 75 C
Claude Rd. E10 38 38 87 C
Claude Rd. E13 50 40 83 B
Claude Rd. SE15 75 34 76 D
Claude St. E14 64 37 78 A
Claudia Pl. SW19 85 24 73 C
Claughton Rd. E13 50 41 83 C
Clauson Ave. Nthlt 43 14 85 C
Clavell St. SE10 64 38 77 A
Claverdale Rd. SW2 87 31 73 A
Clavering Ave. SW13 61 22 77 B
Clavering Cl. Twick 83 16 71 A
Clavering Rd. E12 39 41 86 B
Claverley Gr. N3 23 25 90 B
Claverley Villas. N3 23 25 91 D
Claverton St. SW1 10 29 78 C
Clave St. E1 57 35 80 C
Claxton Gr. W6 62 23 78 D
Claxton Path. SE4 76 35 75 D
Clay Ave. Mit 96 28 69 D
Claybridge Rd. SE12 89 41 71 A
Claybrook Rd. W6 62 23 77 B

Claybury Bwy. Ilf 27 42 89 A
Claybury Rd. Wdf Gn 27 42 91 C
Clayfarm Rd. SE9 90 44 72 A
Claygate La. Esh 101 16 65 A
Claygate La. Surb 101 16 66 C
Claygate Rd. W13 60 16 79 D
Clayhall Ave. Ilf 27 42 90 C
Clayhill Cres. SE9 89 41 71 B
Claylands Pl. SW8 63 31 77 C
Claylands Rd. SW8 10 30 77 B
Claymore Cl. Mord 103 25 66 A
Claypole Rd. E15 49 38 83 C
Clayponds Ave. Brent 60 18 78 C
Clayponds Ave. W5 60 18 78 A
Clayponds Gdns. W5 60 17 78 B
Clayponds La. Brent 60 18 78 C
Clays La. E15 49 37 85 D
Clays Lane Cl. E15 49 37 85 D
Clay St. W1 1 27 81 B
Clayton Ave. Wem 44 18 84 C
Clayton Cres. Brent 60 17 78 D
Clayton Field. NW9 22 21 90 A
Clayton Rd. Islw 71 15 75 A
Clayton Rd. Rom 41 50 87 C
Clayton Rd. SE15 75 34 76 A
Clayton St. SE11 63 31 77 A
Clayton Terr. Hay 53 11 81 B
Clay Wood Cl. Orp 108 45 66 A
Cleanthus Cl. SE18 78 43 76 B
Cleanthus Rd. SE18 78 43 76 B
Clearbrook Way. E1 57 35 81 C
Clearwell Dri. W9 56 25 82 D
Cleaveland Rd. Surb 101 17 67 B
Cleaverholme Cl. SE25 105 34 67 D
Cleaver Sq. SE11 63 31 78 C
Cleaver St. SE11 63 31 78 C
Cleeve Hill. SE23 87 34 73 D
Clegg St. E13 50 40 83 C
Clegg St. E1 57 34 80 D
Clematis Cl. Rom 30 53 91 C
Clematis St. W12 55 22 80 A
Clem Attlee Ct. SW6 62 24 77 B
Clemence St. E14 57 36 81 B
Clement Ave. SW4 74 29 75 D
Clement Cl. NW6 46 23 84 C
Clement Cl. W4 61 20 78 B
Clementhorpe Rd. Dag 52 47 84 A
Clementina Rd. E10 38 36 87 D
Clementine Cl. W13 60 16 79 B
Clement Rd. Beck 98 35 69 D
Clement Rd. SW19 85 24 71 C
Clements Ave. E16 58 40 80 A
Clements Ct. Houn 70 11 75 D
Clements Inn Pas. WC2 3 30 81 D
Clements Inn. WC2 3 30 81 D
Clement's La. EC4 8 32 80 B
Clements La. Ilf 40 43 86 D
Clements Pl. Brent 60 17 78 D
Clements Rd. E6 50 42 84 D
Clements Rd. Ilf 40 43 86 D
Clement's Rd. SE16 63 34 79 D
Clement Way. Horn 42 54 86 D
Clendon Way. SE18 66 44 78 B
Clenham St. SE1 8 32 79 A
Clensham Ct. Sutt 103 25 65 A
Clensham La. Sutt 103 25 65 A
Clenston Mews. W1 1 27 81 D
Clephane Rd. N1 48 32 84 A
Clere Pl. EC2 4 32 82 D
Clere St. EC2 4 32 82 D
Clerkenwell Cl. EC1 3 31 82 C
Clerkenwell Green. EC1 3 31 82 D
Clerkenwell Rd. EC1 3 31 82 D
Clermont Rd. E9 49 35 83 A
Clevedon Cl. N16 37 33 86 C
Clevedon Gdns. Houn 69 10 76 B
Clevedon Pas. N16 37 33 86 B
Clevedon Rd. King 94 19 69 C
Clevedon Rd. SE20 98 35 69 B
Clevedon Rd. Twick 71 17 74 D
Cleveland Ave. Hamp 92 12 70 D
Cleveland Ave. SW20 95 24 69 D
Cleveland Ave. W4 61 21 78 B
Cleveland Gdns. N4 37 32 88 A
Cleveland Gdns. NW2 35 23 86 B
Cleveland Gdns. SW13 72 21 76 D
Cleveland Gdns. W2 1 26 81 C
Cleveland Gdns. Wor Pk 102 21 65 B
Cleveland Gr. E1 57 35 82 C
Cleveland Mews. W1 2 29 81 A
Cleveland Park Ave. E17 26 37 89 C
Cleveland Park Cres. E17 26 37 89 C
Cleveland Pl. SW1 6 29 80 C
Cleveland Rd. E18 27 40 89 A
Cleveland Rd. Ilf 40 43 86 D
Cleveland Rd. Ilf 51 44 85 A
Cleveland Rd. Islw 71 16 75 C
Cleveland Rd. N1 48 32 84 D
Cleveland Rd. N9 17 34 94 B
Cleveland Rd. N Mal 94 21 68 C
Cleveland Rd. SW13 72 21 76 D
Cleveland Rd. W13 54 16 81 B
Cleveland Rd. W4 61 20 79 C
Cleveland Rd. Well 78 45 76 D
Cleveland Rd. Wor Pk 102 21 65 A
Cleveland Rise. Mord 103 23 66 B
Cleveland Row. SW1 6 29 80 C
Cleveland Sq. W2 1 26 81 C
Cleveland St. W1 2 29 81 A
Cleveland Terr. W2 1 26 81 C
Cleveland Way. E1 57 35 82 C
Cleveley Cres. W5 54 18 82 B
Cleveley Cres. W5 44 18 83 C
Cleveleys Rd. E5 37 34 86 D
Clevely Cl. SE7 65 41 78 B
Cleve Rd. NW6 46 25 84 D
Cleverly Estate. W12 55 22 80 C
Cleves Ave. Eps 109 22 62 B
Cleves Rd. E6 50 41 83 D
Cleves Rd. Rich 83 17 72 C
Cleves Way. Hamp 92 12 70 D
Cleves Way. Ruis 32 11 87 D
Cleves Wlk. Ilf 28 44 91 C
Clewer Cres. Har 20 14 90 B
Clifden Rd. Brent 60 17 77 B
Clifden Rd. E9 49 35 85 D
Clifden Rd. Twick 83 15 73 D
Cliffe Rd. S Croy 112 32 64 D
Clifford Ave. Chis 99 42 70 B
Clifford Ave. Ilf 28 43 90 D
Clifford Ave. SW14 72 20 76 C
Clifford Ave. Wall 111 29 64 A
Clifford Cl. Nthlt 43 12 83 A
Clifford Dri. SW9 75 31 75 D
Clifford Gdns. NW10 46 23 83 C
Clifford Gr. Ashf 81 07 71 A
Clifford Rd. Barn 11 25 96 B
Clifford Rd. E16 58 39 82 D
Clifford Rd. E17 26 38 90 C
Clifford Rd. Enf 14 35 95 C
Clifford Rd. Houn 70 11 75 B
Clifford Rd. Rich 83 17 72 B
Clifford Rd. SE25 97 34 68 C
Clifford Rd. Wem 44 17 83 B
Clifford's Inn Pas. EC4 3 31 81 C
Clifford St. W1 6 29 80 A
Clifford Way. NW10 45 21 85 B
Cliff Rd. NW1 47 29 84 B
Cliff Terr. SE8 76 37 76 C
Cliffview Rd. SE13 76 37 75 C
Cliff Villas. NW1 47 29 84 B
Cliff Wlk. E16 58 39 81 B
Cliftan Rd. Grnf 53 14 82 D
Clifton Ave. E17 26 35 89 B
Clifton Ave. Felt 82 11 72 C
Clifton Ave. N3 23 24 90 B
Clifton Ave. Stan 21 16 90 D
Clifton Ave. Sutt 110 25 62 D
Clifton Ave. W12 55 21 80 D
Clifton Ave. Wem 44 18 84 B
Clifton Cres. SE15 64 35 77 C
Clifton Ct. SE25 105 33 67 A
Clifton Gdns. Enf 12 30 96 C
Clifton Gdns. N15 37 33 88 D
Clifton Gdns. NW11 35 24 88 D
Clifton Gdns. W4 61 20 78 B
Clifton Gdns. W9 1 26 82 C
Clifton Gr. E8 48 34 84 A
Clifton Hill. NW6 46 25 83 D
Clifton Hill. NW8 46 26 83 A
Clifton Park Ave. SW20 95 23 69 C
Clifton Pl. W2 1 26 81 D
Clifton Rd. E16 58 39 81 A
Clifton Rd. E7 50 41 84 B
Clifton Rd. Har 21 18 89 D
Clifton Rd. Horn 42 52 88 C
Clifton Rd. Houn 69 07 75 B
Clifton Rd. Ilf 40 44 88 D
Clifton Rd. Islw 70 14 76 D
Clifton Rd. Islw 71 15 76 C
Clifton Rd. King 93 18 70 D
Clifton Rd. King 94 19 69 A
Clifton Rd. N22 24 29 90 A
Clifton Rd. N3 23 26 90 A
Clifton Rd. N8 36 29 88 D
Clifton Rd. NW10 45 22 83 C
Clifton Rd. SE25 97 33 68 C
Clifton Rd. Sid 90 45 71 A
Clifton Rd. Sthl 59 12 78 A
Clifton Rd. SW19 95 23 70 B
Clifton Rd. Tedd 83 15 71 A
Clifton Rd. W9 1 26 82 C
Clifton Rd. Wall 111 28 64 D
Clifton Rd. Well 79 47 75 A
Clifton Rise. SE14 64 36 77 C
Clifton St. EC2 4 33 82 C
Clifton Terr. N4 37 31 86 A
Clifton Villas. W9 1 26 81 A
Clifton Way. SE15 64 35 77 C
Clifton Way. Wem 44 18 83 A
Cline Rd. N11 24 29 91 A
Clinger Ct. N1 48 33 83 A
Clink St. SE1 8 32 80 D
Clinton Ave. E Mol 92 14 68 C
Clinton Ave. Well 78 46 75 C
Clinton Cres. Ilf 28 45 91 A
Clinton Rd. E3 57 36 82 A
Clinton Rd. E7 50 40 85 A
Clinton Rd. N15 25 32 89 D
Clipper Way. SE13 76 38 75 C
Clipstone Rd. Houn 70 13 75 A
Clipstone St. W1 2 29 81 A
Clissold Cl. N2 24 27 89 B
Clissold Cres. N16 48 32 85 B
Clissold Rd. N16 37 32 86 D
Clitheroe Ave. Har 32 13 87 C
Clitheroe Rd. Rom 29 50 91 A
Clitheroe Rd. SW9 74 30 76 C
Clitherow Ave. W7 60 16 79 C
Clitherow Pas. Brent 60 17 78 C
Clitherow Rd. Brent 60 17 78 C
Clitterhouse Cres. NW2 35 23 87 B
Clitterhouse Rd. NW2 35 23 86 A
Clive Ave. Dart 80 51 74 D
Clive Ave. N18 25 34 91 A
Cliveden Cl. N12 15 26 92 A
Cliveden Pl. SW1 9 28 78 A
Cliveden Rd. SW19 95 24 69 B
Clivedon Ct. W13 54 16 81 B
Clive Pas. SE21 87 32 72 D
Clive Rd. Belv 67 49 78 A
Clive Rd. Enf 13 34 96 C
Clive Rd. Felt 69 10 74 C
Clive Rd. Rom 42 52 88 B
Clive Rd. SE21 87 32 72 D
Clive Rd. SW19 96 27 70 A
Clive Rd. Twick 83 16 71 A
Clive Way. Enf 13 34 96 C
Cloak La. EC4 8 32 80 B
Clock House Ave. Bark 51 44 84 C
Clockhouse La. Ashf 81 07 71 A
Clockhouse La. Felt 81 07 72 B
Clockhouse La. Rom 29 50 91 A
Clock House Rd. Beck 98 36 68 A
Clock Pl. SE17 63 31 78 B
Clock Tower Mews. N1 48 32 83 A
Clock Tower Pl. N7 47 30 84 A
Clock Tower Rd. Islw 71 15 75 B
Cloister Gdns. SE25 105 34 67 D
Cloister Rd. NW2 35 24 86 B
Cloister Rd. W3 55 20 81 A
Cloisters Ave. Brom 107 42 67 B
Clonard Way. Pnr 20 13 91 A
Clonbrock Rd. N16 48 33 85 A
Cloncurry St. SW6 73 23 76 D
Clonmel Cl. Har 32 14 87 D
Clonmell Rd. N17 25 32 89 B
Clonmel Rd. SW6 73 24 76 B
Clonmel Rd. Tedd 82 14 71 B
Clonmore St. SW18 85 25 72 A
Closemead Cl. Nthwd 19 08 91 A
Close The. Barn 12 27 95 B
Close The. Beck 98 36 68 C
Close The. Bex 79 49 74 C
Close The. Cars 111 27 62 A
Close The. E4 26 38 91 C
Close The. Ilf 40 45 88 C
Close The. Islw 70 14 76 D
Close The. Mit 96 27 68 D
Close The. N14 16 29 93 B
Close The. N20 15 24 93 B
Close The. N Mal 94 20 69 C
Close The. Orp 108 45 67 C
Close The. Pnr 32 11 87 A
Close The. Pnr 32 12 87 B
Close The. Pur 111 30 62 D
Close The. Pur 112 31 62 D
Close The. Rich 72 19 75 B
Close The. Rom 41 48 88 C
Close The. Surb 101 18 67 C
Close The. Sutt 103 24 66 B
Close The. Wem 44 18 84 A
Close The. Wem 34 20 86 C
Cloth Ct. EC1 3 31 81 B
Cloth Fair. EC1 3 31 81 B
Clothier St. E1 4 33 81 C
Cloth St. EC1 4 32 81 A
Cloudberry Rd. Rom 30 53 91 B
Cloudesdale Rd. SW17 86 28 72 B
Cloudesley Pl. N1 48 31 83 A
Cloudesley Rd. Bexh 79 48 76 B
Cloudesley Rd. Eri 80 51 76 B
Cloudesley Rd. N1 48 31 83 A
Cloudesley Sq. N1 48 31 83 A
Cloudesley St. N1 48 31 83 A
Clouston Cl. Wall 111 30 64 C
Clova Rd. E7 50 40 85 C
Clovelly Ave. NW9 22 21 89 D
Clovelly Ct. Horn 42 54 86 B
Clovelly Gdns. Enf 17 33 94 A
Clovelly Gdns. Rom 29 49 90 B
Clovelly Rd. Bexh 67 48 77 A
Clovelly Rd. N8 24 29 89 D
Clovelly Rd. W4 61 20 79 B
Clovelly Rd. W5 60 17 79 A
Clovelly Way. E1 57 35 81 C
Clovelly Way. Har 32 12 86 B
Clovelly Way. Orp 108 45 67 D
Clover Cl. E11 38 38 86 B
Cloverdale Gdns. Sid 78 45 75 D
Clover Mews. SW3 9 27 77 B
Clove St. E13 58 40 82 C
Clowders Rd. SE6 88 36 72 D
Cloysters Green. E1 57 34 80 C
Cloyster Wood. Edg 21 17 91 B
Club Gardens Rd. Brom 107 40 66 A
Club Row. E2 4 33 82 D
Clumps The. Felt 81 08 71 B
Clunas Gdns. Rom 30 53 89 B
Clunbury Ave. Sthl 59 12 78 D
Clunbury St. N1 48 32 83 B
Cluny Mews. SW5 62 25 78 A
Cluny Pl. SE1 8 33 79 C
Cluse Ct. N1 48 32 83 C
Clutton St. E14 57 37 81 B
Clydach Rd. Enf 13 33 96 D
Clyde Circ. N15 25 33 89 C
Clyde Ct. NW1 47 29 83 D
Clyde Pl. E10 38 37 87 B
Clyde Rd. Croy 105 33 65 B
Clyde Rd. N15 25 33 89 C
Clyde Rd. N22 24 29 90 B
Clyde Rd. Sutt 110 25 64 C
Clyde Rd. Wall 111 29 63 A
Clydesdale Ave. Stan 21 17 89 B
Clydesdale. Enf 14 35 96 D
Clydesdale Gdns. Rich 72 19 75 D
Clydesdale Rd. Horn 42 51 87 B
Clydesdale Rd. W11 56 24 81 D
Clyde St. SE8 64 36 77 B
Clyde Terr. SE23 88 35 72 A
Clyde Vale. SE23 88 35 72 A
Clyde Way. Rom 30 51 90 A
Clydon Cl. Eri 68 51 77 A
Clymping Dene. Felt 81 10 73 B
Clyston St. SW8 74 29 76 C
Coach and Horses Yd. W1 6 29 80 A
Coach House La. SW19 85 23 71 B
Coaldale Wlk. SE21 87 32 73 A
Coalecroft Rd. SW15 73 23 74 A
Coal Wharf Rd. W12 62 23 79 B
Coates Hill Rd. Brom 100 43 69 C
Coate St. E2 48 34 83 C
Coates Wlk (off Burford Rd). Brent 60 18 78 C
Cobar Cl. Barn 11 26 97 B
Cobbett Rd. SE9 77 42 75 A
Cobbett Rd. Twick 82 13 73 C
Cobbetts Ave. Ilf 39 41 88 B
Cobbett St. SW8 10 30 77 D
Cobbler's Wlk. E mol 93 16 69 B
Cobbler's Wlk. Hamp 92 14 69 A
Cobbler's Wlk. Tedd 92 14 70 D
Cobbler's Wlk. Tedd 93 15 70 C
Cobbold Rd. E11 39 39 86 D
Cobbold Rd. NW10 45 21 84 B
Cobbold Rd. W12 61 21 79 B
Cobb's Ct. EC4 3 31 81 D
Cobb's Rd. Houn 70 12 75 D
Cobb St. E1 4 33 81 B
Cobden Path. SE25 105 34 67 B
Cobden Rd. E11 39 39 86 A
Cobden Rd. SE25 105 34 67 A
Cobham Ave. N.Mal 102 22 67 A
Cobham Cl. Brom 107 42 66 A
Cobham Cl. SW11 74 27 74 C
Cobham Cl. Wall 111 30 63 A
Cobham Rd. E17 26 38 90 A
Cobham Rd. Houn 59 11 77 C
Cobham Rd. Ilf 40 45 86 C
Cobham Rd. King 94 19 69 C
Cobham Rd. N22 25 31 89 B
Cobill Cl. Horn 30 53 89 C
Cobland Rd. SE12 89 41 71 A
Coborn Rd. E3 57 36 82 B
Coborn Rd. E3 49 36 83 D
Coborn St. E3 57 36 82 B
Cobourg Rd. SE5 63 33 78 D
Cobourg St. NW1 2 29 82 A
Coburg Cres. SW2 86 30 73 D
Coburg Cres. SW2 87 31 73 C
Coburg Rd. N22 24 30 90 D
Cochrane Mews. NW8 46 26 83 D
Cochrane Rd. SW19 95 24 70 D
Cochrane St. NW8 46 26 83 D
Cockfosters Par. Barn 12 28 96 C
Cockfosters Rd. Barn 12 27 96 B
Cock Hill. EC2 4 33 81 A
Cock La. EC1 3 31 81 B
Cockpit Yd. WC1 3 30 81 B
Cocks Cres. N Mal 94 21 68 D
Cockspur Ct. SW1 6 29 80 D
Code St. E1 4 33 82 D
Codling Way. Wem 44 17 85 B
Codrington Hill. SE23 88 36 73 A
Codrington Mews. W11 56 24 81 D
Cody Cl. Har 21 17 89 B
Cody Cl. Wall 111 29 63 D
Cody Rd. E16 58 39 82 C
Coe's Alley. Barn 11 24 96 C
Cofers Circ. Wem 34 19 86 D
Cogan Ave. E17 26 36 90 A
Coin St. SE1 7 31 80 C
Coity Rd. NW5 47 28 84 A
Cokers La. SE21 87 32 73 D
Coke St. E1 57 34 81 C
Colas Mews. NW6 46 25 83 A
Colbeck Mews. N1 48 31 84 B
Colbeck Mews. SW7 62 26 78 A
Colbeck Rd. Har 32 14 87 A
Colberg Pl. N16 37 33 87 B
Colborne Way. Wor Pk 103 23 65 A
Colburn Ave. Pnr 20 12 91 A
Colburn Way. Sutt 103 26 65 D
Colby Rd. SE19 87 33 71 C
Colchester Ave. E12 39 42 86 D
Colchester Dri. Pnr 32 11 88 B
Colchester Rd. E10 38 38 87 A
Colchester Rd. E17 38 37 88 C
Colchester Rd. Edg 22 20 91 C
Colchester Rd. Nthwd 19 10 90 C
Colchester Rd. Rom 30 54 90 A
Coldbath Sq. EC1 3 31 82 C
Coldbath St. SE13 76 37 76 B
Coldblow La. SE14 64 35 77 B
Cold Blows. Mit 96 27 68 B
Coldershaw Rd. W13 60 16 79 A
Coldershaw Rd. W13 54 16 80 C
Coldfall Ave. N10 24 28 90 C
Coldharbour. E14 64 38 79 A
Coldharbour. E14 58 38 80 C
Coldharbour La. Pur 112 31 62 C
Coldharbour La. SE5 75 32 76 C
Coldharbour La. SW9 75 31 75 D
Coldharbour Pl. SE5 75 32 76 D
Coldharbour Rd. Croy 112 31 64 C
Coldharbour Way. Croy 112 31 64 C
Coldstream Gdns. SW18 73 24 74 D
Colebert Ave. E1 57 35 82 C
Colebrook Cl. SW15 85 23 73 B
Colebrooke Ave. W13 54 16 81 D
Colebrooke Dri. E11 39 41 87 A
Colebrooke Pl. N1 48 31 83 B
Colebrooke Rise. Brom 99 39 69 C
Colebrooke Row. N1 48 31 83 D
Colebrook Rd. E17 26 37 89 C
Colebrook Rd. SW16 96 30 69 A
Colebrook Way. N11 16 28 92 D
Coleby Path. SE5 63 32 77 D
Coledale Dri. Stan 21 17 90 A
Coleford Rd. SW18 73 26 74 A
Colegrave Rd. E15 49 38 85 B
Colegrove Rd. SE15 63 33 77 B
Coleherne Ct. SW5 62 25 78 D
Coleherne Mews. SW10 62 25 78 D
Coleherne Rd. SW10 62 25 78 D
Colehill Gdns. SW6 73 24 76 A
Colehill La. SW6 73 24 76 A
Coleman Fields. N1 48 32 83 A
Coleman Rd. Belv 67 49 78 A
Coleman Rd. Dag 52 48 84 B
Coleman Rd. SE5 63 33 77 C
Colemans Heath. SE9 90 43 72 D
Coleman St Bldgs. EC2 4 32 81 D
Coleman St. EC2 4 32 81 D
Colenso Rd. E5 49 35 85 A
Colenso Rd. Ilf 40 45 87 A
Cole Park Gdns. Twick 71 16 74 C
Cole Park Rd. Twick 71 16 74 C
Colepits Wood Rd. SE9 78 44 74 B
Coleraine Rd. N8 25 31 89 A
Coleraine Rd. SE3 65 39 77 B
Cole Rd. Twick 71 16 74 C
Coleridge Ave. E12 50 42 84 A
Coleridge Ave. Sutt 111 27 64 A
Coleridge Cl. SW8 74 29 76 C
Coleridge Gdns. NW6 46 26 84 C
Coleridge Rd. Croy 106 35 66 A
Coleridge Rd. E17 26 36 89 B
Coleridge Rd. N12 15 26 92 C
Coleridge Rd. N4 37 31 86 A
Coleridge Rd. N8 36 29 88 D
Coleridge Rd. Rom 30 52 91 D
Coleridge Way. Orp 108 46 67 C
Coleridge Wlk. NW11 23 25 89 C
Colesburg Rd. Beck 98 36 69 D
Coles Cres. Har 32 13 86 B
Coles Green Rd. NW2 34 22 86 B
Coleshill Rd. Tedd 93 15 70 A
Colestown St. SW11 74 27 76 C
Cole St. SE1 8 32 79 A
Colet Gdns. W14 62 23 78 B
Coley St. WC1 3 30 82 D
Colfe Rd. SE23 88 36 73 C
Colina Mews. N15 25 31 89 D
Colina Rd. N15 37 31 88 B
Colin Cl. Croy 106 36 65 D
Colin Cl. NW9 22 21 89 C
Colin Cl. W.Wick 107 39 65 D
Colin Cres. NW9 22 21 89 D
Colindale Ave. NW9 22 21 89 A
Colindeep Gdns. NW4 22 22 89 C
Colindeep La. NW4 22 22 89 D
Colindeep La. NW9 22 21 89 D
Colin Dri. NW9 34 21 88 B
Colinette Rd. SW15 73 23 75 C
Colin Gdns. NW9 22 21 89 D
Colin Park Rd. NW9 22 21 89 C
Colin Rd. NW10 45 22 84 A
Coliston Pas. SW18 85 25 73 B
Coliston Rd. SW18 85 25 73 A
Collamore Ave. SW18 86 27 73 C
Collapit Cl. Har 32 13 88 D
College App. SE10 64 38 77 A
College Ave. Har 21 15 90 A
College Cl. E9 49 35 85 C
College Cl. Har 21 15 91 C
College Cl. N18 17 33 92 D
College Cl. Twick 82 14 73 D
College Cres. NW3 46 26 84 A
College Cross. N1 48 31 84 C
College Ct. SW3 9 27 78 D
College Ct. W5 54 18 80 A
College Dri. Ruis 31 10 87 A
College Gdns. E4 18 37 94 D
College Gdns. Enf 13 32 97 B
College Gdns. Ilf 39 42 88 A
College Gdns. N18 17 33 92 D
College Gdns. N.Mal 102 21 67 B
College Gdns. SE21 87 33 73 C
College Gdns. SW17 86 27 72 A
College Green. SE19 97 33 70 C
College Gr. NW1 47 29 83 B
College Hill. EC4 8 32 80 A
College Hill Rd. Har 21 15 90 A
College La. NW5 47 28 85 B
College Park Cl. SE13 76 38 75 D
College Park Rd. N17 25 33 91 B
College Pl. E17 27 39 89 C
College Pl. NW1 47 29 83 A
College Rd. Brom 99 40 69 A
College Rd. Croy 105 32 65 B
College Rd. E17 38 38 88 C
College Rd. Enf 13 32 97 D
College Rd. Har 33 15 88 C
College Rd. Har 21 15 90 A
College Rd. Islw 71 15 76 B
College Rd. N17 25 33 91 B
College Rd. N21 17 31 93 A
College Rd. NW10 46 23 83 C
College Rd. SE19 87 33 71 B
College Rd. SE21 87 33 72 A
College Rd. SW19 95 26 70 B
College Rd. W13 54 16 81 D
College Rd. Wem 33 17 87 D
College Slip. Brom 99 40 69 A
College St. EC4 8 32 80 A
College Terr. E3 57 36 82 B
College Terr. N3 23 24 90 D
College View. SE9 89 41 73 D

College Yd. NW5 47 28 85B
Collent St. E9 49 35 84A
Collerston Rd. E10 65 39 78D
Colless Rd. N15 37 33 88B
Collett Rd. SE16 63 34 79C
Collett Way. Sthl 59 13 79B
Collier Cl. Eps 109 19 63B
Collier Dri. Edg 22 19 90C
Collier Row La. Rom 29 50 90A
Collier Row Rd. Rom 29 49 90A
Collier St. N1 47 30 83D
Colliers Water La. Th Hth 105 31 67A
Collindale Ave. Eri 67 49 77B
Collindale Ave. Sid 90 46 73C
Collingbourne Rd. W12 55 22 80D
Collingham Gdns. SW5 62 25 78B
Collingham Pl. SW5 62 25 78B
Collington St. SE10 64 38 78D
Collingtree Rd. SE23 88 35 71A
Collingwood Ave. N10 24 28 89C
Collingwood Ave. Surb 102 20 66C
Collingwood Cl. SE20 97 34 69B
Collingwood Cl. Twick 82 13 73A
Collingwood Rd. Mit 96 27 68A
Collingwood Rd. N15 25 33 89C
Collingwood Rd. Sutt 110 25 64A
Collingwood St. E1 57 34 82D
Collins Ave. Stan 21 18 90C
Collins Dri. Ruis 32 11 86A
Collinson Wlk. SE1 8 32 79A
Collins Rd. N5 48 32 85A
Collins Sq. SE3 77 39 76D
Collins St. SE3 77 39 76C
Collins Yd. N1 48 31 83B
Collinton Rd. Ilf 40 46 86B
Collinwood Ave. Enf 14 35 96A
Collinwood Gdns. Ilf 28 43 89C
Collis Alley. Twick 83 15 73C
Coll's Rd. SE15 76 35 76A
Collyer Ave. Croy 111 30 64A
Collyer Rd. Croy 111 30 64A
Colman Rd. E16 58 41 81A
Colmar Cl. E1 57 35 82D
Colmer Pl. Har 20 14 91D
Colmer Rd. SW16 96 30 70C
Colmore Rd. Enf 14 35 96C
Colnbrook St. SE1 7 31 79D
Colne Ct. Eps 109 20 64A
Colne Dri. Rom 30 54 91B
Colne Rd. E5 49 36 85A
Colne Rd. N21 17 32 94B
Colne Rd. Twick 83 15 73C
Colne St. E13 58 40 82A
Colney Hatch La. N10 24 28 90A
Colney Hatch La. N11 24 27 91B
Colney Rd. Dart 80 54 74D
Cologne Rd. SW11 73 26 75D
Cologne Rd. SW11 73 26 75D
Colombo Rd. Ilf 40 44 87A
Colombo St. SE1 7 31 80D
Colomb St. E10 65 39 78C
Colonade. WC1 3 30 82C
Colonels Wlk. Enf 13 31 96B
Colonial Ave. Twick 70 14 74C
Colonial Rd. Felt 81 09 73A
Colonnades The. W2 56 25 81D
Colson Rd. Croy 105 33 65A
Colson Way. SW16 86 29 71A
Colsterworth Rd. N15 25 33 89D
Colston Ave. Cars 111 27 64A
Colston Ct. Cars 111 27 64B
Colston Rd. E7 50 41 84B
Colston Rd. SW14 72 20 75C
Coltness Cres. SE2 66 46 78D
Colton Gdns. N17 25 32 89A
Colton Rd. Har 33 15 88A
Coltsfoot Path. Rom 30 53 91C
Columbia Ave. Edg 22 19 90B
Columbia Ave. Wor Pk 102 21 66B
Columbia Rd. E13 58 39 82D
Columbia Rd. E2 4 33 82B
Columbia Rd. E2 48 34 83C
Columbine Ave. S Croy 112 31 63D
Columbine Way. SE13 76 38 76C
Colva Wlk. N19 36 28 86B
Colvestone Cres. E8 48 33 85D
Colview Ct. SE9 89 41 73D
Colville Gdns. W11 56 24 81D
Colville Houses. W11 56 24 81D
Colville Mews. W11 56 24 81D
Colville Pl. W1 2 29 81B
Colville Rd. E11 38 38 86D
Colville Rd. E17 26 36 90C
Colville Rd. N9 17 34 94D
Colville Rd. W11 56 24 81D
Colville Rd. W3 61 19 79D
Colville Sq Mews. W11 56 24 81D
Colville Sq. W11 56 24 81D
Colville Terr. W11 56 24 81D
Colvin Gdns. E11 27 40 89D
Colvin Gdns. E4 18 38 93C
Colvin Gdns. Ilf 28 44 91C
Colvin Rd. E6 50 42 83A
Colvin Rd. Th Hth 105 31 67A
Colwell Rd. SE22 75 33 74B
Colwick Cl. N6 36 29 87B
Colwith Rd. W6 62 23 77A
Colwood Gdns. SW19 95 26 70D
Colworth Gr. SE17 63 32 78A
Colworth Rd. Croy 105 34 66C
Colworth Rd. E11 39 39 87A
Colwyn Ave. Grnf 44 15 83D
Colwyn Cres. Houn 70 14 76A
Colwyn Rd. NW2 34 22 86D
Colyer Cl. SE9 90 43 72B
Colyers Cl. Eri 79 50 76B
Colyers La. Eri 79 50 76B
Colyers Wlk. Eri 80 51 76A
Colyton Cl. Grnf 44 17 84A
Colyton Cl. Well 79 47 76B
Colyton Rd. SE22 75 34 74B
Colyton Way. N18 17 34 92C
Combe Ave. SE3 65 39 77D
Combedale Rd. SE10 65 40 78C
Combemartin Rd. SW18 85 24 73C
Comber Cl. NW2 34 22 86B
Comber Gr. SE5 63 32 77C
Combermere Rd. Mord 103 25 67B
Combermere Rd. SW9 74 30 75B
Comberton Rd. E5 37 34 86B
Combeside. SE18 66 45 77D
Combwell Cres. SE2 66 46 79C
Comely Bank Rd. E17 38 38 88A
Comeragh Rd. W14 62 24 78C
Comerford Rd. SE4 76 36 75D
Comet Pl. SE8 64 37 77C
Comet St. SE8 64 37 77C
Commerce Rd. Brent 60 17 77C
Commerce Rd. N22 24 30 90B
Commerce Way. Croy 104 30 65B
Commercial Dock Pas. SE16 64 36 79D
Commercial Pl. NW1 47 28 84D
Commercial Rd. E14 57 36 81D
Commercial Rd. E1 57 34 81D
Commercial Rd. N18 17 33 92C
Commercial St. E1 4 33 81B
Commercial Way. NW10 45 19 83D
Commercial Way. SE15 63 34 77C
Commerell Pl. E10 65 39 78D
Commerell St. E10 65 39 78C
Commodore St. E2 57 36 82C
Commondale. SW15 73 23 75A
Common Field La. SW17 86 27 71C
Common Rd. SW13 72 22 75A
Commonside. Brom 107 41 65C
Commonside. Brom 107 41 65C
Commonside E. Mit 96 28 68D
Commonside W. Mit 96 28 68A
Common The. Sthl 59 11 78B
Common The. W5 54 18 80C
Commonwealth Ave. W12 55 22 80B
Commonwealth Rd. N17 25 34 91C
Commonwealth Way. SE2 67 47 78C
Community Cl. Houn 69 10 76B
Community Cl. Uxb 31 08 86C
Community Rd. E15 49 38 85D
Community Rd. Grnf 43 14 83A
Como Rd. SE23 88 36 72A
Como St. Rom 29 50 89D
Compass Hill. Rich 71 17 74D
Compayne Gdns. NW6 46 26 84A
Compton Ave. E6 50 41 83D
Compton Ave. N1 48 31 84B
Compton Ave. N6 36 27 87A
Compton Ave. Rom 30 53 89A
Compton Cl. NW1 2 28 82B
Compton Cl. W13 54 16 81C
Compton Cres. N17 25 32 91C
Compton Cres. Nthlt 43 11 83B
Compton Cres. W4 61 20 77A
Compton Pas. EC1 3 31 82D
Compton Pl. Eri 68 51 77B
Compton Pl. WC1 3 30 82C
Compton Rd. Croy 105 34 66D
Compton Rd. N1 48 31 84B
Compton Rd. N21 17 31 94D
Compton Rd. NW10 56 23 82B
Compton Rd. SW19 95 24 70B
Compton Rise. Pnr 32 12 88B
Compton St. EC1 3 31 82D
Compton Terr. N1 48 31 84B
Comreddy Cl. Enf 13 31 97B
Comus Pl. SE17 63 33 78A
Comus Rd. N19 36 29 86D
Comyn Rd. SW11 74 27 75C
Comyns Cl. E16 58 39 81B
Comyns Rd. Dag 52 49 84C
Conaways Cl. Eps 109 22 62C
Concanon Rd. SW2 74 30 75D
Concert Hall App. SE1 7 30 80D
Conchurch Cl. Sutt 110 25 63D
Concorde Cl. Houn 70 13 76D
Concord Rd. Enf 14 35 95A
Concord Rd. W3 55 19 82D
Condell Rd. SW8 74 29 76A
Conder St. E14 57 36 81C
Conderton Rd. SE5 75 32 75A
Condover Cres. SE18 66 43 77D
Conduit Ave. SE10 76 38 76B
Conduit Ave. SE10 64 38 77D
Conduit Ct. WC2 7 30 80A
Conduit La. N18 17 32 92B
Conduit Lane. S Croy 112 34 64C
Conduit Mews. W2 1 26 81D
Conduit Pas. W2 1 26 81D
Conduit Pl. W2 1 26 81D
Conduit Rd. SE18 66 43 78D
Conduit St. W1 6 29 80A
Conduit Way. NW10 45 20 84C
Condult La. Enf 14 35 95D
Conewood St. N5 37 31 86D
Coney Acre. SE21 87 32 73C
Coney Hill Rd. W.Wick 107 39 65B
Coney Way. SW8 10 30 77B
Conference Rd. SE2 67 47 78A
Congleton Gr. SE18 66 44 78C
Congo Rd. SE18 66 44 78D
Congress Rd. SE2 67 47 78A
Congreve Rd. SE9 77 42 75B
Congreve St. SE17 63 33 78A
Conical Cnr. Enf 13 32 97C
Conifer Gdns. Enf 13 33 95C
Conifer Gdns. Sutt 103 25 65B
Conifer Gdns. SW16 86 30 72D
Conifers Cl. Tedd 93 17 70C
Coniger Rd. SW6 73 25 76C
Coningham Mews. W12 55 22 80C
Coningham Rd. W12 61 22 79B
Coningsby Cottages. W5 60 17 79B
Coningsby Gdns. E4 26 37 91B
Coningsby Rd. S Croy 112 32 62A
Coningsby Rd. W5 60 17 79B
Conington Rd. SE13 76 38 76C
Conisbee Ct. N14 12 29 95A
Conisborough Cres. SE6 88 38 72C
Coniscliffe Rd. N13 17 32 93C
Coniston Ave. Bark 51 45 84C
Coniston Ave. Grnf 54 16 82B
Coniston Ave. Well 78 45 75A
Coniston Cl. Bark 51 45 84C
Coniston Cl. Bexh 79 50 76A
Coniston Cl. Eri 68 51 77C
Coniston Cl. N20 15 26 93C
Coniston Cl. N.Mal 103 23 67D
Coniston Cl. W4 61 20 77C
Coniston Ct. SE26 97 34 70B
Conistone Way. N7 47 30 84C
Coniston Gdns. Ilf 27 42 89C
Coniston Gdns. N9 18 35 94C
Coniston Gdns. NW9 34 20 88B
Coniston Gdns. Pnr 19 10 89C
Coniston Gdns. Sutt 110 26 63B
Coniston Gdns. Wem 33 17 87C
Coniston Rd. Bexh 79 50 76A
Coniston Rd. Brom 98 38 70B
Coniston Rd. Brom 99 39 70A
Coniston Rd. Croy 105 34 66A
Coniston Rd. N10 24 28 90D
Coniston Rd. N17 25 34 91A
Coniston Rd. Twick 70 13 74D
Coniston Way. Chess 101 18 65C
Coniston Wlk. E9 49 35 85C
Conlan St. W10 56 24 82C
Conley Rd. NW10 45 21 84A
Conley St. E10 65 39 78C
Connaught Ave. Barn 16 27 94D
Connaught Ave. E4 18 38 94B
Connaught Ave. Enf 13 33 97C
Connaught Ave. Houn 70 12 75C
Connaught Cl. E10 38 36 86A
Connaught Cl. Enf 13 33 97C
Connaught Cl. Sutt 103 26 65B
Connaught Cl. W2 1 27 81C
Connaught Dri. NW11 23 25 89C
Connaught Gdns. N10 36 28 88B
Connaught Gdns. N13 17 31 92B
Connaught House. N10 36 28 88B
Connaught La. Ilf 40 44 86B
Connaught Mews. W2 1 27 81D
Connaught Pl. W2 1 27 81D
Connaught Rd. Barn 11 23 95D
Connaught Rd. E11 39 39 87C
Connaught Rd. E16 58 41 80B
Connaught Rd. E17 38 37 88A
Connaught Rd. Har 21 15 90B
Connaught Rd. Horn 42 53 86D
Connaught Rd. Ilf 40 44 86B
Connaught Rd. N4 37 31 87A
Connaught Rd. N Mal 94 21 68C
Connaught Rd. NW10 45 21 83C
Connaught Rd. Rich 71 18 74B
Connaught Rd. SE18 66 43 78D
Connaught Rd. Sutt 103 26 65B
Connaught Rd. Tedd 82 14 71D
Connaught Rd. W13 54 16 80B
Connaught Sq. W2 1 27 81D
Connaught St. W2 1 27 81C
Connaught Way. N13 17 31 92B
Connell Cres. W5 54 18 82D
Conningsby Rd. N4 37 31 88D
Connington Cres. E4 18 38 93D
Connor Rd. Dag 52 48 85B
Connor St. E9 49 35 83B
Conolly Rd. W7 54 15 80C
Conrad Dri. Wor Pk 103 23 66D
Consfield Ave. N.Mal 102 22 67A
Consort Cl. N11 16 28 92C
Consort Mews. Islw 70 14 74B
Consort Rd. SE15 75 34 76D
Cons St. SE1 7 31 79A
Constable Cl. NW11 35 25 88D
Constable Cres. N15 37 34 88A
Constable Gdns. Edg 22 19 90C
Constable Gdns. Islw 70 14 74B
Constable Wlk. SE21 87 33 72D
Constance Cres. Brom 107 39 66D
Constance Rd. Croy 105 31 66B
Constance Rd. Enf 13 33 95C
Constance Rd. Sutt 110 26 64A
Constance Rd. Twick 82 13 73B
Constantine Rd. NW3 47 27 85A
Constitution Hill. SW1 6 28 79B
Constitution Rise. SE18 78 43 76A
Content St. SE17 63 32 78B
Control Tower Rd. Houn 69 07 75B
Convair Wlk. Nthlt 53 11 82B
Convent Gdns. W11 56 24 81D
Convent Gdns. W5 60 17 78A
Convent Hill. SE19 97 32 70A
Convent Rd. Ashf 81 07 71D
Convent Way. Sthl 59 11 78B
Conway Cl. Stan 21 16 91A
Conway Cres. Grnf 44 15 83C
Conway Cres. Rom 41 47 88C
Conway Dri. Ashf 91 08 70A
Conway Dri. Sutt 110 25 63B
Conway Gdns. Mit 96 30 68C
Conway Gdns. Wem 33 17 87A
Conway Gr. W3 55 20 81B
Conway Rd. Felt 82 11 71D
Conway Rd. Houn 69 07 75B
Conway Rd. Houn 82 13 73A
Conway Rd. Houn 70 13 74C
Conway Rd. N14 16 30 93C
Conway Rd. N15 37 32 88A
Conway Rd. NW2 35 23 86A
Conway Rd. SE18 66 45 78A
Conway Rd. SW20 95 23 69A
Conway St. W1 2 29 82C
Conway Wlk. Hamp 92 12 70B
*Conybeare. NW3 47 27 84C
Conyers Cl. Wdf Gn 27 39 91A
Conyer's Rd. SW16 96 29 70B
Conyer's Rd. SW16 86 29 71D
Conyer St. E3 49 36 83C
Cooden Cl. Brom 99 40 70D
Cookes Cl. E11 39 39 86B
Cookes La. Sutt 110 24 63A
Cookhill Rd. SE2 66 46 79D
Cook's Rd. E15 49 37 83D
Cook's Rd. SE17 63 31 77B
Coolfin Rd. E16 58 40 81D
Coolgardie Ave. E4 18 38 92D
Coolgardie Rd. Ashf 81 08 71C
Coolhurst Rd. N8 36 29 88D
Cool Oak La. NW9 34 21 87B
Coomassie Rd. W9 56 24 82D
Coombe Ave Croy 112 33 64A
Coombe Bank. King 94 21 69A
Coombe Cl. Edg 21 18 90D
Coombe Cl. Houn 70 13 75C
Coombe Cnr. N21 17 31 94D
Coombe Cres. Hamp 92 12 70D
Coombe Dri. Ruis 31 10 86D
Coombe End. King 94 20 70D
Coombefield Cl. N.Mal 102 21 67A
Coombe Gdns. N Mal 94 21 68D
Coombe Gdns. SW20 94 22 69A
Coombe Hill Glade. King 94 21 70C
Coombe Hill Rd. King 94 21 70C
Coombe House Chase. N Mal 94 20 69B
Coombehurst Cl. Barn 12 27 97D
Coombe Lane Flyover. SW20 94 21 69B
Coombe Lane W. King 94 19 69B
Coombe Lea. Brom 99 42 68A
Coombe Lodge. SE7 65 41 77A
Coombe Neville. King 94 20 70D
Coombe Park. King 84 20 71D
Coombe Rd. Croy 112 33 64B
Coombe Rd. Hamp 92 12 70B
Coombe Rd. N22 25 31 90C
Coombe Rd. N Mal 94 21 68A
Coombe Rd. NW10 34 20 86D
Coombe Rd. Rom 30 54 89B
Coombe Rd. SE26 87 34 71B
Coombe Rd. SW20 94 19 69A
Coombe Rd. W13 60 16 79D
Coombe Rd. W4 61 21 78C
Coombe Ridings. King 84 20 71C
Coombe Rise. King 94 20 69A
Coomber Way. Croy 104 29 66B
Coombes Rd. Dag 52 48 83B
Coombe Wlk. Sutt 103 25 65D
Coombe-Wood Dri. Rom 41 48 88D
Coombe Wood Rd. King 84 20 71C
Coombs St. N1 48 31 83D
Coomer Mews. SW6 62 24 77B
Coomer Pl. SW6 62 24 77B
Cooms Wlk. Edg 22 20 90A
Cooperage Cl. N17 25 33 91B
Cooper Ave. E17 26 36 90A
Cooper Cres. Cars 104 27 65D
Cooper Rd. Croy 112 31 64B
Cooper Rd. NW10 45 22 85C
Cooper Rd. NW4 35 23 88D
Coopersale Cl. Wdf Gn 27 41 91C
Coopersale Rd. E9 49 35 85D
Cooper's La. E10 38 37 87D
Coopers La. NW1 47 29 83D
Coopers La. SE12 89 40 72B
Cooper's Rd. SE1 63 33 78D
Cooper's Row. EC3 8 33 80B
Cooper St. E16 58 39 81B
Cooper's Yd. SE19 97 33 70A
Coote Gdns. Dag 41 48 86D
Coote Rd. Bexh 79 48 76B
Coote Rd. Dag 41 48 86D
Copeland Rd. E17 38 37 88D
Copeland Rd. SE15 75 34 76D
Copenhagen Pl. E14 57 36 81D
Copenhagen St. N1 47 30 83B
Cope Pl. W8 62 25 79C
Copers Cope Rd. Beck 98 36 70D
Cope St. SE16 64 35 78B
Copford Cl. Wdf Gn 27 42 91A
Copford Wlk. N1 48 32 83A
Copinger Wlk. Edg 22 19 90B
Copland Ave. Wem 44 17 85D
Copland Cl. Wem 44 17 85C
Copland Rd. Wem 44 18 84A
Copleston Pas. SE5 75 33 75B
Copleston Rd. SE15 75 33 75B
Copley Cl. SE17 63 32 77A
Copley Cl. W7 54 15 81B
Copley Dene. Brom 99 41 69B
Copley Park. SW16 96 30 70B
Copley St. E1 57 35 81B
Copnor Way (off Pentridge St).
SE15 63 33 77D
Coppelia Rd. SE3 77 39 75D
Copperas St. SE8 64 37 77B
Copper Beech Cl. Ilf 28 43 90A
Copperbeech Cl. NW3 46 26 85D
Copperfield App. Chig 28 44 91B
Copperfield. Chig 28 44 91B
Copperfield Mews. N18 17 33 92C
Copperfield Rd. E3 57 36 81A
Copperfield St. SE1 8 32 79A
Copperfields Way. Rom 30 53 90B
Copperfield Way. Chis 100 44 70A
Coppermead Cl. NW2 35 23 86C
Coppermill La. E17 38 35 88B
Copper Mill La. SW17 85 26 71A
Coppets Cl. N12 24 27 91C
Coppetts Rd. N10 24 28 90A
Coppice Cl. Ruis 31 08 88D
Coppice Cl. SW20 95 23 68A
Coppice Dri. SW15 72 22 74D
Coppice The. Enf 13 31 96D
Coppice Way. E18 27 39 89B
Coppice Wlk. N20 15 25 93C
Coppies Gr. N11 16 28 92B
Copping Cl. Croy 112 33 64A
Coppins The. Har 21 15 91A
Coppi The. Ashf 91 07 70B
Coppock Cl. SW11 74 27 76C
Coppsfield. E Mol 92 13 68A
Copse Ave. W Wick 106 37 65D
Copse Cl. Nthwd 19 08 90C
Copse Glade. Surb 101 17 66D
Copse Hill. Sutt 110 25 63D
Copse Hill. SW20 94 22 70C
Copse Wood Way. Nthwd 19 08 90A
Copthall Ave. EC2 4 32 81D
Copthall Bldgs. EC2 4 32 81D
Copthall Cl. EC2 4 32 81D
Copthall Dri. NW7 22 22 91A
Copthall Gdns. NW7 22 22 91C
Copthall Gdns. Twick 83 15 73D
Copthall Rd E. Uxb 31 07 86C
Copthall Rd W. Uxb 31 07 86A
Copthorne Ave. Brom 107 42 65B
Copthorne Ave. Ilf 28 43 91B
Copthorne Ave. SW12 86 29 73B
Coptic St. WC1 3 30 81A
Coral Cl. Rom 29 47 89A
Coralline Wlk. SE2 67 47 79A
Coral St. SE1 7 31 79A
Coram St. WC1 3 30 82C
Coran Cl. N9 18 35 94B
Corban Rd. Houn 70 13 75A
Corbet Cl. Wall 104 28 65A
Corbet Ct. EC3 4 32 81D
Corbet Pl. E1 4 33 81B
Corbet Rd. Eps 109 21 62C
Corbett Gr. N22 24 30 91C
Corbett Rd. E11 39 41 88C
Corbett Rd. E17 26 38 89A
Corbett's La. SE16 64 35 78A
Corbetts Pas. SE16 64 35 78A
Corbicum. E11 39 39 87A
Corbiere Ct. SW19 95 23 70B
Corbins La. Har 32 13 86D
Corbridge Cres. E2 48 34 83D
Corby Cres. Enf 12 30 96C
Corbylands Rd. Sid 90 45 73A
Corbyn St. N4 36 30 87C
Corby Rd. NW10 45 20 83D
Corby Way. E3 57 37 82C
Cordelia St. E14 57 37 81D
Cordingley Rd. Ruis 31 08 86B
Cording St. E14 57 37 81B
Cordova Rd. E3 57 36 82A
Cordwainers Wlk. E13 50 40 83C
Cord Way. E14 64 37 79C
Cordwell Rd. SE13 77 39 74A
Corelli Rd. SE3 77 42 76A
Corfe Ave. Har 43 13 85A
Corfield St. E2 57 34 82B
Corfton Rd. W5 54 18 81A
Corinium Cl. Wem 44 18 85B
Corinne Rd. N19 47 29 85A
Corinthian Manorway. Eri 67 50 78B
Corinthian Rd. Eri 67 50 78B
Corker Wlk. N7 36 30 86B
Corkran Rd. Surb 101 18 66A
Corkscrew Hill. W Wick 106 38 65D
Cork St Mews. W1 6 29 80A
Cork St. W1 6 29 80A
Corlett St. NW1 1 27 81A
Cormont Rd. SE5 75 31 76B
Cornbury Rd. Edg 21 17 91D
Cornelia Pl. Eri 68 51 77A
Cornelia St. N7 47 30 84B
Cornelia St. N7 48 31 84A
Corner Green. SE3 77 40 76C
Corner Mead. NW9 22 21 90B
Corner Par. N18 17 34 92C
Cornerside. Ashf 91 08 70C
Corney Rd. W4 61 21 77A
Cornflower Terr. SE22 75 34 74D
Cornford Cl. Brom 107 40 67A
Cornford Gr. SW12 86 28 72B
Cornhill. EC3 4 32 81D
Cornish Gr. SE20 97 34 69B
Corn Mill Dri. Orp 108 46 66A
Cornmill La. SE13 76 38 75A
Cornshaw Rd. Dag 41 47 87D
Cornthwaite Rd. E5 38 35 86C
Cornwall Ave. E2 57 35 82A

Cornwall Ave. N22 24 30 90 A
Cornwall Ave. N3 23 25 91 C
Cornwall Ave. Sthl 53 13 81 A
Cornwall Ave. Well 78 45 75 B
Cornwall Cl. Bark 51 45 84 B
Cornwall Cres. W11 56 24 81 C
Cornwall Ct. Pnr 20 12 91 D
Cornwall Gdns. NW10 45 22 84 B
Cornwall Gdns. SW7 62 25 79 D
Cornwall Gdns Wlk. SW7 62 25 79 D
Cornwall Gr. W4 61 21 78 C
Cornwallis Ave. N9 18 35 93 A
Cornwallis Ave. SE9 90 44 72 D
Cornwallis Gr. N9 18 35 93 A
Cornwallis Rd. Dag 52 48 85 A
Cornwallis Rd. E17 26 35 89 D
Cornwallis Rd. N19 36 30 86 A
Cornwallis Rd. N9 17 34 93 B
Cornwallis Wlk. SE9 77 42 75 B
Cornwall Mews S. SW7 5 26 79 C
Cornwall Mews W. SW7 62 25 79 D
Cornwall Rd. Croy 105 31 65 B
Cornwall Rd. Har 32 14 88 A
Cornwall Rd. N15 37 32 88 B
Cornwall Rd. N18 17 34 92 C
Cornwall Rd. N4 37 31 87 A
Cornwall Rd. Pnr 20 12 91 D
Cornwall Rd. Ruis 31 09 86 B
Cornwall Rd. SE1 7 31 80 C
Cornwall Rd. Sutt 110 25 62 A
Cornwall Rd. Twick 83 16 73 C
Cornwall St. E1 57 34 80 B
Cornwood Cl. N2 23 26 89 D
Cornwood Dri. E1 57 35 81 C
Cornworthy Rd. Dag 52 47 85 C
Corona Rd. SE12 89 40 73 A
Coronation Ave. N16 48 33 85 B
Coronation Cl. Bex 79 47 74 D
Coronation Cl. Ilf 28 44 89 C
Coronation Rd. E13 58 41 82 A
Coronation Rd. NW10 55 19 82 D
Coronation Wlk. Twick 82 13 73 C
Coronet St. N1 4 33 82 A
Corporation Ave. Houn 70 12 75 C
Corporation Row. EC1 3 31 82 D
Corporation St. E15 50 39 83 D
Corporation St. N7 47 30 85 C
Corrance Rd. SW2 74 30 75 C
Corri Ave. N14 16 29 92 B
Corringham Ct. NW11 35 25 87 A
Corringham Rd. NW11 35 25 87 A
Corringham Rd. NW11 35 25 87 B
Corringham Rd. Wem 34 19 86 A
Corringway. NW11 35 25 87 B
Corringway. W5 55 19 81 A
Corscombe Cl. King 84 20 71 C
Corsehill St. SW16 96 29 70 A
Corseley Way. E9 49 36 84 B
Corsham St. N1 4 32 82 B
Corsica St. N5 48 31 84 B
Cortayne Rd. SW6 73 24 76 D
Cortis Rd. SW15 72 22 74 D
Cortis Terr. SW15 72 22 74 D
Corunna Rd. SW8 74 29 76 A
Corunna Terr. SW8 74 29 76 A
Corvette Sq. SE10 64 38 77 B
Coryton Path. W9 56 24 82 D
Cosbycote Ave. SE24 75 32 74 A
Cosdach Ave. Wall 111 29 63 D
Cosedge Cres. Croy 112 31 64 D
Cosmo Pl. WC1 3 30 81 A
Cossall Wlk. SE15 75 34 76 B
Cosser St. SE1 7 31 79 C
Costa St. SE15 75 34 76 C
Costons Ave. Grnf 53 14 82 B
Costons La. Grnf 53 14 82 B
Coston Wlk. SE4 76 35 75 D
Cosway St. NW1 1 27 81 A
Cotall St. E14 57 37 81 A
Coteford Cl. Pnr 31 10 88 A
Coteford St. SW17 86 28 71 A
Cotelands. Croy 105 33 65 C
Cotesbach Rd. E5 38 35 86 C
Cotesmore Gdns. Dag 52 47 85 A
Cotford Rd. Th Hth 97 32 68 C
Cotham St. SE17 63 32 78 A
Cotherstone. Eps 109 20 62 B
Cotherstone Rd. SW2 86 30 73 D
Cotleigh Rd. NW6 46 25 84 C
Cotleigh Rd. Rom 41 50 88 D
Cotman Cl. NW11 35 26 88 C
Cotman Cl. SW15 73 23 74 D
Cotmandene Cres. Orp 100 46 69 C
Cotman Gdns. Edg 22 19 90 C
Coton Rd. Well 78 46 75 A
Cotsford Ave. N.Mal 102 20 67 B
Cotswold Cl. Bexh 80 51 76 C
Cotswold Cl. King 94 20 70 A
Cotswold Gate. NW2 35 24 87 C
Cotswold Gdns. E6 50 41 83 D
Cotswold Gdns. Ilf 40 44 87 B
Cotswold Gdns. NW2 35 23 86 B
Cotswold Green. Enf 12 30 96 D
Cotswold Rd. Hamp 92 13 70 A
Cotswold Rd. Rom 30 54 90 D
Cotswold Rd. Sutt 110 25 62 D
Cotswold Rise. Orp 108 45 67 D
Cotswold St. SE27 87 31 71 B
Cotswold Way. Enf 12 30 96 D
Cottage Ave. Brom 107 42 66 C
Cottage Cl. Ruis 31 08 87 D
Cottage Green. SE5 63 33 77 C
Cottage Gr. Surb 101 17 67 D
Cottage Gr. SW9 74 30 75 A
Cottage Pl. SW3 5 27 79 C
Cottage Rd. Eps 109 20 63 D
Cottage St. E14 57 37 80 B
Cottage Wlk. N16 37 33 86 D
Cottage Wlk. SE15 75 33 76 B
Cottenham Dr. SW20 94 22 70 D
Cottenham Park Rd. SW20 94 22 69 B
Cottenham Pl. SW20 94 22 70 D
Cottenham Rd. E17 26 36 89 D
Cotterill Rd. Surb 101 18 66 D
Cottesbrook St. SE14 64 36 77 C
Cottesmore Ave. Ilf 28 43 90 C
Cottesmore Gdns. W8 62 25 79 D
Cottingham Chase. Ruis 31 10 86 C
Cottingham Rd. SE20 98 35 70 D
Cottingham Rd. SW8 10 30 77 D
Cottington Rd. Felt 82 11 71 B
Cottington St. SE11 63 31 78 C
Cotton Hill. Brom 88 38 71 B
Cottons App. Rom 41 50 88 B
Cotton's Gdns. E2 4 33 82 A
Cotton's La (Path). E11 39 39 87 B
Cotton St. E14 58 38 80 A
Couchmore Ave. Esh 101 15 65 A
Couchmore Ave. Ilf 27 42 90 D
Coulgate St. SE4 76 36 75 A
Coulson St. SW3 9 27 78 B
Coulter Rd. W6 61 22 79 D
Councillor St. SE5 63 32 77 C
Counter Ct. SE1 8 32 80 D
Counter St. SE1 8 33 80 C
Countess Rd. NW5 47 29 85 C
Countisbury Ave. Enf 17 33 94 B
Country Way. Felt 82 11 71 B
County Gate. Barn 11 25 95 D
County Gate. SE9 90 44 72 C
County Gr. SE5 75 32 76 A
County Rd. Th Hth 97 31 69 D
County St. SE1 8 32 79 C
Coupland Pl. SE18 66 44 78 C
Courage Cl. Horn 42 53 88 C
Courcy Rd. N8 25 31 89 A
Courland Gr. SW8 74 29 76 D
Course The. SE9 90 43 72 C
Courtauld Rd. N19 36 30 87 C
Court Ave. Belv 67 48 78 D
Court Cl. Har 21 18 89 A
Court Close Ave. Twick 82 13 72 D
Court Cl. Twick 82 13 72 D
Court Cl. Wall 111 29 63 D
Court Downs Rd. Beck 98 37 69 D
Court Dri. Croy 111 30 64 B
Court Dri. Sutt 111 27 64 A
Courtenay Ave. Har 20 14 90 A
Courtenay Ave. N6 36 27 87 A
Courtenay Gdns. Har 20 14 90 C
Courtenay Mews. E17 38 36 88 A
Courtenay Pl. E17 38 36 88 A
Courtenay Rd. E11 39 39 86 D
Courtenay Rd. E17 26 35 89 D
Courtenay Rd. SE2 98 35 70 B
Courtenay Rd. Wor Pk 103 23 65 C
Courtenay Sq. SE11 63 31 78 C
Courtenay St. SE11 63 31 78 C
Court Farm Ave. Eps 109 20 64 D
Court Farm Rd. Nthlt 43 13 84 C
Court Farm Rd. SE9 89 42 72 B
Courtfield Ave. Har 33 15 88 B
Courtfield Cres. Har 33 15 88 B
Courtfield Gdns. Ruis 31 09 86 B
Courtfield Gdns. SW5 62 25 78 B
Courtfield Gdns. W13 54 16 81 C
Courtfield Mews. SW7 62 26 78 A
Courtfield Rd. Ashf 91 07 70 B
Courtfield Rd. SW7 62 26 78 A
Courtfield Rise. W Wick 106 38 65 D
Courthill Rd. SE13 76 38 74 A
Courthope Rd. Grnf 43 14 83 D
Courthope Rd. NW3 47 27 85 B
Courthope Rd. SW19 85 24 71 C
Courthope Villas. SW19 95 24 70 C
Court House Gdns. N3 23 25 91 A
Court House Rd. N12 23 25 91 B
Courtland Ave. Ilf 39 42 86 B
Courtland Ave. SW16 96 30 70 D
Courtlands Ave. Brom 107 39 66 D
Courtlands Ave. Hamp 92 12 70 B
Courtlands Ave. Rich 72 19 76 D
Courtlands Ave. SE12 77 40 74 B
Courtlands Cl. Ruis 31 09 87 B
Courtlands Cl. S Croy 112 34 62 C
Courtlands Dri. Eps 109 21 63 B
Courtlands Rd. Surb 102 19 66 A
Courtlands. Rich 72 19 74 A
Courtlands. W5 54 17 81 A
Court Lane Gdns. SE21 87 33 73 A
Court La. SE21 87 33 73 B
Courtleet Dri. Eri 79 49 76 B
Courtleigh Gdns. NW11 23 24 89 C
Courtman Rd. N17 25 32 91 C
Courtmead Cl. SE24 75 32 74 C
Court Mead. Nthlt 53 12 82 B
Courtnell St. W2 56 25 81 C
Courtney Cl. SE19 97 33 70 A
Courtney Cres. Cars 111 27 63 D
Courtney Path. Croy 105 31 65 C
Courtney Rd. Croy 105 31 65 C
Courtney Rd. Houn 69 07 75 A
Courtney Rd. N7 48 31 85 C
Courtney Rd. SW19 96 27 70 C
Courtrai Rd. SE23 76 36 74 C
Court Rd (Orpington By Pass). Orp 108 46 66 D
Court Rd. SE25 97 33 68 B
Court Rd. SE9 89 42 73 D
Court Rd. Sthl 59 12 78 D
Court Royal. SW15 73 24 74 A
Courtside. SE26 88 35 72 C
Courtside. N8 36 29 88 D
Court St. Brom 99 40 69 C
Court St. E1 57 34 81 B
Court The. Ruis 43 12 85 A
Court Way. NW9 22 21 89 C
Court Way. Rom 30 54 90 C
Court Way. Twick 83 15 73 B
Court Way. W3 55 20 81 A
Courtyard The. N1 48 31 84 C
Court Yd. SE9 77 42 74 D
Cousin La. EC4 8 32 80 B
Couthurst Rd. SE3 65 40 77 D
Coval Gdns. SW14 72 19 75 D
Coval La. SW14 72 19 75 D
Coval Rd. SW14 72 20 75 C
Covent Gdn. WC2 7 30 80 A
Coventry Cl. NW6 46 25 83 A
Coventry Cross. E3 58 38 82 C
Coventry Rd. E1 57 34 82 D
Coventry Rd. Ilf 40 43 87 D
Coventry Rd. SE25 97 34 68 C
Coventry St. W1 6 29 80 B
Coverack Cl. Croy 106 36 66 A
Coverack Cl. N14 12 29 95 C
Coverdale Gdns. Croy 105 33 65 D
Coverdale Rd. NW2 46 24 84 C
Coverdale Rd. W12 61 22 79 B
Coverdales The. Bark 51 44 83 D
Coverley Cl. E1 57 34 81 A
Coverton Rd. SW17 86 27 71 C
Covert Rd. Chig 28 45 91 B
Covert The. Nthwd 19 08 90 A
Covert The. Orp 108 45 67 C
Covert Way. Barn 11 26 97 D
Covington Gdns. SW16 97 31 70 D
Covington Way. SW16 97 31 70 C
Cowan St. SE5 63 33 77 A
Cowbridge La. Bark 51 43 84 D
Cowbridge Rd. Har 21 18 89 D
Cowcross St. EC1 3 31 81 B
Cowdenbeath Path. N1 47 30 83 B
Cowden Rd. Orp 108 45 66 B
Cowden St. SE6 88 37 71 A
Cowdrey Cl. Enf 13 33 97 C
Cowdrey Rd. SW17 85 26 71 C
Cowdry Rd. E9 49 36 84 B
Cowen Ave. Har 32 14 86 B
Cowgate Rd. Grnf 53 14 82 B
Cowick Rd. SW17 86 27 71 B
Cowings Mead. Nthlt 43 12 84 A
Cow La. Grnf 43 14 83 D
Cowland Ave. Enf 14 35 96 C
Cowleaze Rd. King 93 18 69 A
Cowley La. E11 39 39 86 C
Cowley Rd. E11 39 40 88 B
Cowley Rd. Ilf 39 42 87 B
Cowley Rd. Rom 30 52 91 D
Cowley Rd. SW14 72 21 75 A
Cowley Rd. SW9 75 31 76 A
Cowley Rd. SW9 63 31 77 C
Cowley Rd. W3 55 21 80 D
Cowley St. SW1 7 30 79 C
Cowling Cl. W11 56 24 80 C
Cowper Ave. E6 50 42 84 C
Cowper Ave. Sutt 110 26 64 B
Cowper Cl. Brom 99 41 68 D
Cowper Cl. Well 78 46 75 A
Cowper Gdns. N14 12 29 95 C
Cowper Gdns. Wall 111 29 63 A
Cowper Rd. Belv 67 49 78 A
Cowper Rd. Brom 99 41 68 D
Cowper Rd. King 83 18 71 D
Cowper Rd. N14 16 28 94 D
Cowper Rd. N16 48 33 85 A
Cowper Rd. N18 17 34 92 C
Cowper Rd. SW19 95 26 70 A
Cowper Rd. W3 55 20 80 D
Cowper Rd. W7 54 15 80 B
Cowper's Ct. EC3 4 32 81 D
Cowper St. EC2 4 32 82 D
Cowper Terr. W10 56 23 81 B
Cowslip Rd. E18 27 40 90 D
Cowthorpe Rd. SW8 74 29 76 B
Cox La. Chess 109 19 64 A
Cox La. Eps 109 19 64 D
Cox La. Eps 109 20 64 C
Coxmount Rd. SE7 65 41 78 D
Cox's Ct. EC1 4 32 81 A
Coxson Pl. SE1 8 33 79 B
Coxs Wlk. SE21 87 34 72 A
Coxwell Rd. SE18 66 44 78 D
Crab Hill. Beck 98 38 70 D
Crabtree Ave. Rom 29 47 89 D
Crabtree Ave. Wem 44 18 83 D
Crabtree La. SW6 62 23 77 D
Crabtree Manorway. Belv 67 50 79 A
Crabtree Wlk. SE15 75 33 76 B
Craddock Rd. Enf 13 33 96 B
Craddock St. NW5 47 28 84 A
Cradley Rd. SE9 90 44 73 D
Cragmuir Park. Wem 44 18 83 B
Craigdale Rd. Horn 42 51 87 B
Craigen Ave. Croy 105 34 66 D
Craigerne Rd. SE3 65 40 77 D
Craig Gdns. E18 27 39 90 D
Craigholm. SE18 78 43 76 A
Craignair Rd. SW2 87 31 73 A
Craignish Ave. SW16 96 30 69 D
Craig Park Rd. N18 17 34 92 B
Craig Rd. Rich 83 17 71 A
Craig's Ct. SW1 7 30 80 C
Craigton Rd. SE9 77 42 75 D
Craigwell Ave. Felt 81 10 72 C
Crail Row. SE17 63 32 78 B
Cramer Ct. SW3 9 27 78 A
Cramer St. W1 2 28 81 A
Crampton Rd. SE20 98 35 70 A
Crampton St. SE17 63 32 78 C
Cranberry Cl. Nthlt 43 11 83 D
Cranberry St. E1 57 34 82 C
Cranborne Ave. Sthl 59 13 78 A
Cranborne Ave. Surb 102 19 65 C
Cranborne Rd. Bark 51 44 83 B
Cranborne Waye. Hay 53 11 80 A
Cranbourn Alley. WC2 6 29 80 B
Cranbourne Ave. E11 27 40 89 D
Cranbourne Dri. Pnr 32 11 88 B
Cranbourne Gdns. Ilf 28 44 89 A
Cranbourne Gdns. NW11 35 24 88 B
Cranbourne Rd. E12 50 42 85 C
Cranbourne Rd. E15 49 38 85 A
Cranbourne Rd. N10 24 28 90 D
Cranbourne Rd. Nthwd 19 09 89 B
*Cranbourn Pas. SE16 63 34 79 B
Cranbourn St. WC2 6 29 80 B
Cranbrook Cl. Brom 107 40 67 C
Cranbrook Dri. Rom 30 53 89 C
Cranbrook Dri. Twick 82 13 73 D
Cranbrook Mews. E17 38 36 88 B
Cranbrook Park. N22 25 31 90 A
Cranbrook Rd. Barn 11 26 95 D
Cranbrook Rd. Bexh 79 48 76 B
Cranbrook Rd. Houn 70 12 75 D
Cranbrook Rd. Ilf 40 43 87 C
Cranbrook Rd. SE8 76 37 76 A
Cranbrook Rd. SW19 95 24 70 C
Cranbrook Rd. Th Hth 97 32 69 C
Cranbrook Rd. W4 61 21 78 C
Cranbrook Rise. Ilf 39 42 87 B
Cranbrook Terr. E2 49 35 83 D
Cranbury Rd. SW6 73 25 76 D
Crane Ave. Islw 71 16 74 A
Crane Ave. W3 55 20 80 A
Cranebrook. Twick 82 14 72 A
Crane Cl. Dag 52 49 84 A
Crane Ct. EC4 3 31 81 C
Crane Ct. Eps 109 20 64 A
Craneford Cl. Twick 83 15 73 B
Craneford Way. Twick 83 15 73 B
Crane Gr. N7 48 31 84 A
Crane Mead Ct. Twick 83 15 73 B
Crane Mead. SE16 64 35 78 B
Crane Park Rd. Twick 82 13 72 B
Crane Rd. Twick 83 15 73 C
Cranes Dr. Surb 93 18 68 D
Cranes Park Ave. Surb 93 18 68 D
Cranes Park Cres. Surb 93 18 68 D
Cranes Park. Surb 101 18 67 B
Crane St. SE10 64 38 78 D
Craneswater Park. Sthl 59 12 78 D
Crane Way. Twick 82 14 73 A
Cranfield Dri. NW7 22 21 91 C
Cranfield Rd E. Cars 111 28 62 A
Cranfield Rd. SE4 76 36 75 B
Cranfield Rd W. Cars 111 28 62 A
Cranford Ave. N13 16 30 92 C
Cranford Cl. SW20 94 22 69 B
Cranford La. Houn 69 09 75 B
Cranford La. Houn 69 09 76 B
Cranford La. Houn 59 11 77 D
Cranford St. E1 57 35 80 B
Cranford Way. N8 36 30 88 B
Cranham Rd. Horn 42 52 88 D
Cranhurst Rd. NW2 46 23 85 C
Cranleigh Cl. Bex 79 49 74 D
Cranleigh Cl. Orp 108 46 65 C
Cranleigh Cl. SE20 97 34 69 D
Cranleigh Gdns. Bark 51 44 84 B
Cranleigh Gdns. Har 33 18 88 A
Cranleigh Gdns. King 93 18 70 B
Cranleigh Gdns. N21 13 31 95 A
Cranleigh Gdns. SE25 97 33 68 A
Cranleigh Gdns. Sthl 53 12 81 D
Cranleigh Gdns. Sutt 103 25 65 B
Cranleigh Rd. Felt 81 09 71 B
Cranleigh Rd. N15 37 32 88 A
Cranleigh Rd. SW19 95 25 68 A
Cranleigh St. NW1 47 29 83 C
Cranley Dri. Ilf 40 44 87 B
Cranley Dri. Ruis 31 09 86 B
Cranley Gdns. N10 24 28 89 D
Cranley Gdns. N13 16 30 93 D
Cranley Gdns. SW7 62 26 78 D
Cranley Gdns. Wall 111 29 63 C
Cranley Mews. SW7 62 26 78 C
Cranley Pl. SW7 62 26 78 B
Cranley Rd. E13 58 40 81 B
Cranley Rd. Ilf 40 44 87 A
Cranmer Ave. W13 60 16 79 D
Cranmer Cl. Mord 103 24 67 C
Cranmer Cl. Ruis 32 11 87 D
Cranmer Cl. Stan 21 17 91 C
Cranmer Ct. Hamp 82 13 71 D
Cranmer Ct. SW4 74 30 75 A
Cranmer Farm Cl. Mit 96 27 68 D
Cranmer Gdns. Dag 52 50 85 A
Cranmer Rd. Croy 105 31 65 D
Cranmer Rd. E7 50 40 85 B
Cranmer Rd. Hamp 82 13 71 D
Cranmer Rd. King 83 18 71 C
Cranmer Rd. SW9 63 31 77 C
Cranmer Terr. SW17 85 26 71 D
Cranmore Ave. Islw 59 14 77 C
Cranmore Rd. Brom 89 39 72 D
Cranmore Rd. Chis 89 42 71 D
Cranmore Way. N10 24 29 89 C
Cranston Cl. Houn 70 12 76 C
Cranston Cl. Ruis 31 08 86 B
Cranston Gdns. E4 18 37 92 D
Cranston Rd. SE23 88 36 72 A
Cranswick Rd. SE16 63 34 78 D
Crantock Rd. SE6 88 38 72 A
Cranwell Rd. Houn 69 07 75 B
Cranwich Ave. N21 17 32 94 B
Cranwich Rd. N16 37 33 87 A
Cranwood St. EC1 4 32 82 B
Cranworth Cres. E4 18 38 94 D
Cranworth Gdns. SW9 75 31 76 A
Craster Rd. SW2 86 30 73 B
Crathie Rd. SE12 77 40 74 D
Crathorn St. SE13 76 38 75 A
Cravan Ave. Felt 81 10 72 A
Craven Ave. Sthl 53 12 81 B
Craven Ave. W5 54 17 80 A
Craven Cl. N16 37 34 87 A
Craven Gdns. Bark 51 45 83 C
Craven Gdns. Ilf 28 44 89 B
Craven Gdns. SW19 85 25 71 D
Craven Hill Gdns. W2 5 26 80 A
Craven Hill Mews. W2 5 26 80 A
Craven Hill. W2 5 26 80 A
Craven Mews. SW11 74 28 75 A
Craven Park Mews. NW10 45 20 83 A
Craven Park. NW10 45 21 83 A
Craven Park Rd. N15 37 34 88 C
Craven Park Rd. NW10 45 21 83 A
Craven Pas. WC2 7 30 80 C
Craven Rd. Croy 105 34 66 D
Craven Rd. King 93 18 69 B
Craven Rd. NW10 45 20 83 B
Craven Rd. W2 1 26 81 D
Craven Rd. W5 54 17 80 A
Craven St. WC2 7 30 80 C
Craven Terr. W2 5 26 80 A
Craven Wlk. N16 37 34 87 A
Crawford Ave. Wem 44 17 85 D
Crawford Cl. Islw 71 15 76 C
Crawford Gdns. Grnf 53 12 82 B
Crawford Gdns. N13 13 31 95 D
Crawford Mews. W1 1 27 81 B
Crawford Pas. EC1 3 31 82 C
Crawford Pl. W1 1 27 81 A
Crawford Rd. SE5 75 32 76 C
Crawford St. W1 1 27 81 B
Crawley Rd. E10 38 37 87 D
Crawley Rd. Enf 17 33 94 A
Crawley Rd. N22 25 32 90 C
Crawshaw Ct. SW9 75 31 76 A
Crawthew Gr. SE22 75 33 75 D
Cray Ave. Orp 108 46 67 B
Craybrooke Rd. Sid 90 46 71 B
Craybury End. SE9 90 44 72 A
Cray Cl. Dart 80 52 75 C
Craydene Rd. Eri 80 51 76 B
Crayford High St. Dart 80 51 74 A
Crayford Rd. Dart 80 51 74 B
Crayford Rd. N7 47 30 85 A
Crayford Way. Dart 80 51 75 C
Crayonne Cl. Sun 91 09 69 A
Cray Rd. Belv 67 49 77 A
Cray Valley Rd. Orp 100 46 68 D
Crealock Gr. Wdf Gn 27 39 91 B
Crealock St. SW18 85 26 73 A
Creasy St. SE1 8 33 79 C
Crebor St. SE22 75 34 74 C
Credenhall Dri. Brom 107 42 66 D
Credenhill St. SW16 96 29 70 A
Crediton Hill. NW6 46 25 85 D
Crediton Rd. E16 58 40 81 C
Crediton Rd. NW10 46 23 83 B
Credon Rd. E13 50 41 83 C
Credon Rd. SE16 63 34 78 D
Creechurch La. EC3 4 33 81 C
Creechurch Pl. EC3 4 33 81 C
Creed La. EC4 3 31 81 D
Creek Rd. E Mol 93 15 68 C
Creek Rd. SE8 64 37 77 A
Creekside SE8 64 37 77 D
Creeland Gr. SE6 88 36 73 D
Cree Way. Rom 30 51 91 C
Crefeld Cl. W6 62 24 77 A
Creffield Rd. W3 55 19 80 A
Creffield Rd. W5 54 18 80 B
Creighton Ave. E6 50 41 83 D
Creighton Ave. N10 24 28 90 C
Creighton Ave. N2 24 27 90 C
Creighton Rd. N17 25 33 91 C
Creighton Rd. NW6 46 23 83 D
Creighton Rd. W5 60 17 79 D
Cremer St. E2 48 33 83 D
Cremorne Gdns. Eps 109 20 62 B
Cremorne Rd. SW10 62 26 77 D
Crescent Ave. Horn 42 51 86 B
Crescent Ct. Surb 101 17 67 B
Crescent Ct. SW4 74 29 74 B
Crescent Dri. Orp 108 44 67 C
Crescent. EC3 8 33 80 B
Crescent Gdns. Ruis 31 10 87 B
Crescent Gdns. SW19 85 25 72 C
Crescent Gr. Mit 96 27 68 C
Crescent Gr. SW4 74 29 75 C
Crescent La. SW4 74 29 74 B
Crescent La. SW4 74 29 74 B
Crescent Pl. SW3 9 27 78 A
Crescent Rd. Barn 12 27 95 A
Crescent Rd. Beck 98 37 69 D
Crescent Rd. Brom 99 40 70 C
Crescent Rd. Dag 41 49 86 D

| | | |
|---|---|---|
| Crescent Rd. E10 | 38 | 37 86 B |
| Crescent Rd. E13 | 50 | 40 83 A |
| Crescent Rd. E18 | 27 | 41 90 A |
| Crescent Rd. E6 | 50 | 41 83 A |
| Crescent Rd. Enf | 13 | 31 96 D |
| Crescent Rd. Eri | 68 | 51 77 B |
| Crescent Rd. King | 94 | 19 70 C |
| Crescent Rd. N11 | 16 | 27 92 B |
| Crescent Rd. N15 | 25 | 31 89 B |
| Crescent Rd. N22 | 24 | 29 90 B |
| Crescent Rd. N3 | 23 | 24 90 B |
| Crescent Rd. N8 | 36 | 29 88 D |
| Crescent Rd. N9 | 17 | 34 94 C |
| Crescent Rd. SE18 | 66 | 43 78 B |
| Crescent Rd. Sid | 90 | 45 72 D |
| Crescent Rd SW20 | 95 | 23 69 B |
| Crescent Rise. Barn | 12 | 27 95 A |
| Crescent Rise. N22 | 24 | 29 90 B |
| Crescent Row. EC1 | 4 | 32 82 C |
| *Crescent St. N1 | 47 | 30 84 D |
| Crescent The. Barn | 11 | 25 97 D |
| Crescent The. Beck | 98 | 37 69 A |
| Crescent The. Croy | 105 | 32 67 D |
| Crescent The. E17 | 38 | 36 88 A |
| Crescent The. E Mol | 92 | 13 68 C |
| Crescent The. Har | 32 | 14 87 C |
| Crescent The. Ilf | 40 | 43 88 C |
| Crescent The. N11 | 16 | 28 92 A |
| Crescent The. N Mal | 94 | 20 69 C |
| Crescent The. NW2 | 34 | 22 86 D |
| Crescent The. Sid | 90 | 45 71 B |
| Crescent The. Sthl | 59 | 12 79 B |
| Crescent The. Surb | 101 | 18 67 A |
| Crescent The. Sutt | 110 | 25 62 C |
| Crescent The. Sutt | 110 | 26 64 D |
| Crescent The. SW13 | 72 | 22 76 C |
| Crescent The. SW19 | 85 | 25 72 C |
| Crescent The. W3 | 55 | 21 81 C |
| Crescent The. Wem | 33 | 16 86 B |
| Crescent The. W.Wick | 107 | 39 67 C |
| Crescentway. N12 | 24 | 27 91 A |
| Crescent Way. SE4 | 76 | 37 75 A |
| Crescent Way. SW16 | 97 | 31 70 C |
| Crescent W. Barn | 11 | 26 97 A |
| Crescent Wood Rd. SE26 | 87 | 34 72 C |
| Cresford Rd. SW6 | 73 | 25 76 B |
| Crespigny Rd. NW4 | 34 | 22 88 D |
| Cressage Cl. Sthl | 53 | 13 82 C |
| Cressent St. SW4 | 74 | 29 75 B |
| Cresset Rd. E9 | 49 | 35 84 A |
| Cressfield Cl. NW5 | 47 | 28 85 C |
| Cressida Rd. N19 | 36 | 29 87 C |
| Cressingham Gr. Sutt | 110 | 26 64 A |
| Cressingham Rd. Edg | 22 | 20 91 D |
| Cressingham Rd. SE13 | 76 | 38 75 A |
| Cressington Cl. N16 | 48 | 33 85 C |
| Cresswell Gdns. SW10 | 62 | 26 78 C |
| Cresswell Park. SE3 | 77 | 39 75 B |
| Cresswell Pl. SW10 | 62 | 26 78 C |
| Cresswell Rd. Felt | 82 | 12 71 A |
| Cresswell Rd. SE25 | 97 | 34 68 C |
| Cresswell Rd. Twick | 71 | 17 74 D |
| Cresswell Way. N21 | 17 | 31 94 A |
| Cressy Ct. E1 | 57 | 35 81 A |
| Cressy Ct. W6 | 61 | 22 79 D |
| Cressy Pl. E1 | 57 | 35 81 A |
| Cressy Rd. NW3 | 47 | 27 85 B |
| Cresta Ct. W5 | 54 | 18 82 D |
| Crestbrook Ave. N13 | 17 | 31 93 D |
| Crestfield St. WC1 | 3 | 30 82 A |
| Crest Gdns. Ruis | 32 | 11 86 C |
| Creston Way. Sutt | 103 | 23 66 D |
| Crest Rd. Brom | 107 | 39 66 B |
| Crest Rd. NW2 | 34 | 22 86 A |
| Crest Rd. S Croy | 112 | 34 63 D |
| Crest The. N13 | 17 | 31 92 A |
| Crest The. NW4 | 35 | 23 88 A |
| Crest The. Surb | 102 | 19 67 A |
| Crest View Dri. Orp | 108 | 44 67 A |
| Crest View. Pnr | 20 | 11 89 D |
| Crestway. SW15 | 72 | 22 74 D |
| Creswick Rd. W3 | 55 | 19 80 B |
| Creswick Wlk. E3 | 57 | 37 82 A |
| Creswick Wlk. NW11 | 23 | 24 89 D |
| Creton St. SE18 | 66 | 43 79 C |
| Crewdson Rd. SW9 | 63 | 31 77 C |
| Crewe Pl. NW10 | 55 | 21 82 B |
| Crews St. E14 | 64 | 37 78 A |
| Crewys Rd. NW2 | 35 | 24 86 B |
| Crewys Rd. SE15 | 75 | 34 76 D |
| Crichton Ave. Wall | 111 | 29 64 D |
| Cricketers Arms Rd. Enf | 13 | 32 97 C |
| Cricketers Ct. SE11 | 63 | 31 78 B |
| Cricketfield Rd. E5 | 48 | 34 85 B |
| Cricket Green. Mit | 96 | 27 68 D |
| Cricket Ground Rd. Chis | 100 | 43 69 B |
| Cricklade Ave. Rom | 30 | 53 91 B |
| Cricklade Ave. SW2 | 86 | 30 72 B |
| Cricklade Ave. SW2 | 87 | 31 72 A |
| Cricklewood Bwy. NW2 | 46 | 23 85 B |
| Cricklewood La. NW2 | 35 | 24 86 D |
| Cridland St. E15 | 50 | 39 83 B |
| Crieff Ct. Tedd | 93 | 17 70 C |
| Crieff Rd. SW18 | 73 | 26 74 C |
| Criffel Ave. SW2 | 86 | 29 72 B |
| Crimscott. SE1 | 8 | 33 79 C |
| Crimsworth Rd. SW8 | 10 | 29 77 D |
| Crinan St. N1 | 47 | 30 83 C |
| Cringle St. SW8 | 10 | 29 77 C |
| Cripplegate St. EC2 | 4 | 32 81 A |
| Crispen Rd. Felt | 82 | 12 71 A |
| Crispin Cl. Croy | 104 | 30 65 A |
| Crispin Cres. Croy | 104 | 29 65 B |
| Crispin Rd. Edg | 22 | 20 91 A |
| Crispin St. E1 | 4 | 33 81 B |
| Crisp Rd. W6 | 62 | 23 78 C |
| Cristowe Rd. SW6 | 73 | 24 76 D |
| Criterion Mews. N19 | 36 | 29 86 B |
| Crockerton Rd. SW17 | 86 | 27 72 B |
| Crockham Way. SE9 | 90 | 43 71 A |
| Crocus Field. Barn | 11 | 24 95 D |
| Crocus Wlk. W12 | 55 | 21 81 D |
| Croft Ave. W Wick | 106 | 38 66 C |
| Croft Cl. Belv | 67 | 48 78 D |
| Croft Cl. Chis | 89 | 42 71 D |
| Croftdown Rd. NW5 | 36 | 28 86 D |
| Crofters Cl. Islw | 70 | 14 74 B |
| Croft Gdns. Ruis | 31 | 09 87 D |
| Croft Gdns. W7 | 60 | 16 79 A |
| Croft Lodge Cl. Wdf Gn | 27 | 40 91 B |
| Crofton Ave. Orp | 108 | 44 65 A |
| Crofton La. Orp | 108 | 44 66 B |
| Crofton Park Rd. SE4 | 76 | 36 74 D |
| Crofton Rd. E13 | 58 | 40 82 D |
| Crofton Rd. Orp | 108 | 44 65 A |
| Crofton Rd. SE5 | 75 | 33 76 C |
| Crofton Terr. Rich | 71 | 18 75 D |
| Crofton Way. Barn | 11 | 25 95 D |
| Crofton Way. Enf | 13 | 31 97 C |
| Croft Rd. Brom | 99 | 40 70 A |
| Croft Rd. Enf | 14 | 36 97 A |
| Croft Rd. Sutt | 111 | 27 64 C |
| Croft Rd. SW16 | 97 | 31 70 C |
| Croft Rd. SW19 | 95 | 26 70 C |
| Crofts Rd. Har | 33 | 16 88 A |
| Crofts St. E1 | 57 | 34 80 A |
| Crofts The. Shep | 91 | 09 68 C |
| Croft St. SE8 | 64 | 36 78 A |
| Croft The. Barn | 11 | 24 96 C |
| Croft The. Edg | 22 | 19 90 B |
| Croft The. Houn | 59 | 12 77 C |
| Croft The. NW10 | 45 | 21 83 D |
| Croft The. Pnr | 32 | 12 87 B |
| Croft The. Ruis | 43 | 11 85 A |
| Croft The. W5 | 54 | 18 81 A |
| Croft The. Wem | 44 | 17 85 C |
| Croftway. NW3 | 46 | 25 85 A |
| Croft Way. Sid | 90 | 45 72 C |
| Crogsland Rd. NW1 | 47 | 28 84 C |
| Croham Cl. S Croy | 112 | 33 63 A |
| Croham Manor Rd. S Croy | 112 | 33 63 A |
| Croham Mount. S Croy | 112 | 33 63 C |
| Croham Park Ave. S Croy | 112 | 33 64 D |
| Croham Rd. S Croy | 112 | 33 64 C |
| Croham Valley Rd. S Croy | 112 | 34 63 C |
| Croindene Rd. SW16 | 96 | 30 69 A |
| Cromartie Rd. N19 | 36 | 29 87 B |
| Crombie Cl. Ilf | 39 | 42 88 B |
| Crombie Mews. SW11 | 74 | 27 76 C |
| Crombie Rd. Sid | 90 | 44 73 D |
| *Cromer Pl (off Andover Rd). Orp | 108 | 45 66 A |
| Cromer Rd. Barn | 11 | 26 96 A |
| Cromer Rd. E10 | 38 | 38 87 B |
| Cromer Rd. Horn | 42 | 53 87 B |
| Cromer Rd. Houn | 69 | 07 76 C |
| Cromer Rd. N17 | 25 | 34 90 C |
| Cromer Rd. Rom | 41 | 48 88 C |
| Cromer Rd. Rom | 41 | 50 88 C |
| Cromer Rd. SE25 | 97 | 34 68 B |
| Cromer Rd. SW17 | 96 | 28 70 A |
| Cromer Road W. Houn | 69 | 07 75 A |
| Cromer St. WC1 | 3 | 30 82 A |
| Cromer Terr. E8 | 48 | 34 85 C |
| Cromer Villas Rd. SW18 | 73 | 24 74 D |
| Cromford Cl. Orp | 108 | 45 65 C |
| Cromford Path. E5 | 49 | 35 85 B |
| Cromford Rd. SW18 | 73 | 25 74 A |
| Cromford Way. N Mal | 94 | 20 69 B |
| Cromlix Cl. Chis | 100 | 43 69 D |
| Crompton St. W2 | 1 | 26 82 D |
| Cromwell Ave. Brom | 99 | 40 68 D |
| Cromwell Ave. N6 | 36 | 28 87 D |
| Cromwell Ave. N.Mal | 102 | 21 67 B |
| Cromwell Ave. W6 | 61 | 22 78 B |
| Cromwell Cl. Brom | 99 | 40 68 D |
| Cromwell Cl. N2 | 23 | 26 89 D |
| Cromwell Cres. SW5 | 62 | 25 78 A |
| Cromwell Ct. Wem | 44 | 18 83 C |
| Cromwell Gdns. SW7 | 5 | 26 79 D |
| Cromwell Gr. W6 | 62 | 23 79 C |
| Cromwell Mews. SW7 | 62 | 26 78 B |
| Cromwell Pl. N6 | 36 | 28 87 D |
| Cromwell Pl. SW14 | 72 | 20 75 A |
| Cromwell Pl. SW7 | 62 | 26 78 D |
| Cromwell Rd. Beck | 98 | 36 68 A |
| Cromwell Rd. Croy | 105 | 32 66 B |
| Cromwell Rd. E17 | 38 | 38 88 A |
| Cromwell Rd. E7 | 50 | 41 84 C |
| Cromwell Rd. Felt | 81 | 10 73 D |
| Cromwell Rd. Houn | 70 | 13 75 C |
| Cromwell Rd. King | 93 | 17 69 D |
| Cromwell Rd. N10 | 24 | 28 91 C |
| Cromwell Rd. N3 | 23 | 26 90 A |
| Cromwell Rd. SW19 | 85 | 25 71 D |
| Cromwell Rd. SW5 | 62 | 25 78 B |
| Cromwell Rd. SW7 | 62 | 26 78 A |
| Cromwell Rd. SW9 | 75 | 31 76 B |
| Cromwell Rd. Tedd | 93 | 16 70 A |
| Cromwell Rd. Wem | 44 | 18 83 C |
| Cromwell Rd. Wor Pk | 102 | 21 65 C |
| Cromwell St. Houn | 70 | 13 75 C |
| Crondace Rd. SW6 | 73 | 25 76 A |
| Crondall Pl. N1 | 48 | 33 83 C |
| Crondall St. N1 | 48 | 33 83 C |
| Crooked Billet Yd. E2 | 4 | 33 82 A |
| Crooked Usage. N3 | 23 | 24 89 A |
| Crooke Rd. SE8 | 64 | 36 78 C |
| Crookham Rd. SW6 | 73 | 24 76 B |
| Crook Log. Bexh | 79 | 47 75 B |
| Crookston Rd. SE9 | 78 | 43 75 A |
| Croombs Rd. E16 | 58 | 41 81 A |
| Croom's Hill Gr. SE10 | 64 | 38 77 C |
| Croom's Hill. SE10 | 64 | 38 77 C |
| Cropley St. N1 | 48 | 32 83 D |
| Croppath Rd. Dag | 52 | 49 85 A |
| Crosby Cl. Felt | 82 | 12 71 A |
| Crosby Ct. SE1 | 8 | 32 79 B |
| Crosby Rd. Dag | 52 | 49 83 B |
| Crosby Rd. E7 | 50 | 40 84 A |
| Crosby Row. SE1 | 8 | 32 79 B |
| Crosby Wlk. E8 | 48 | 33 84 B |
| Crosby Wlk. SE24 | 87 | 31 73 A |
| Crosier Way. Ruis | 31 | 09 86 A |
| Crossbrook Rd. SE3 | 77 | 42 75 A |
| Cross Deep Gdns. Twick | 83 | 15 72 B |
| Cross Deep. Twick | 83 | 16 72 A |
| Crossfield Rd. N17 | 25 | 32 89 A |
| Crossfield Rd. NW3 | 46 | 26 84 B |
| Crossfield St. SE8 | 64 | 37 77 C |
| Crossford St. SW9 | 74 | 30 76 D |
| Crossgate. Grnf | 44 | 16 84 B |
| Cross Key Ct. EC2 | 4 | 32 81 D |
| Cross Keys Cl. W1 | 2 | 28 81 A |
| Cross Keys Sq. EC1 | 4 | 32 81 A |
| Cross La. EC3 | 8 | 33 80 A |
| Cross La. N8 | 24 | 30 89 D |
| Cross Lances Rd. Houn | 70 | 13 75 D |
| Crossland Rd. Th Hth | 105 | 31 67 D |
| Crosslands Ave. Sthl | 59 | 12 78 D |
| Crosslands Ave. W5 | 54 | 18 80 D |
| Crosslands Rd. Eps | 109 | 20 63 B |
| *Crosslet St. SE17 | 63 | 32 78 B |
| Crossley St. N7 | 48 | 31 84 A |
| Crossmead Ave. Grnf | 53 | 13 82 B |
| Crossmead. SE9 | 89 | 42 73 D |
| Cross Rd. Brom | 107 | 42 65 A |
| Cross Rd. Croy | 105 | 32 66 D |
| Cross Rd. Dart | 80 | 53 74 C |
| Cross Rd. Enf | 13 | 33 96 C |
| Cross Rd. Har | 32 | 13 86 D |
| Cross Rd. Har | 32 | 14 88 B |
| Cross Rd. Har | 21 | 16 90 C |
| Cross Rd. King | 93 | 18 70 D |
| Cross Rd. N11 | 16 | 28 92 D |
| Cross Rd. N22 | 25 | 31 91 C |
| Cross Rd. N2 | 24 | 27 90 C |
| Cross Rd. Orp | 108 | 46 67 B |
| Cross Rd. Rom | 41 | 47 87 A |
| Cross Rd. Rom | 41 | 49 89 B |
| Cross Rd. SE5 | 75 | 33 76 C |
| Cross Rd. Sid | 90 | 46 71 B |
| Cross Rd. Sutt | 110 | 25 62 C |
| Cross Rd. Sutt | 110 | 26 64 D |
| Cross Rd. SW19 | 95 | 25 70 C |
| Cross Rd. Wdf Gn | 27 | 42 91 B |
| Cross St. Eri | 68 | 51 77 A |
| Cross St. Hamp | 82 | 14 71 C |
| Cross St. N18 | 17 | 34 92 C |
| Cross St. N1 | 48 | 31 83 B |
| Cross St. SW13 | 72 | 21 75 B |
| Crossthwaite Ave. SE5 | 75 | 32 75 D |
| Crosswall. EC3 | 8 | 33 80 B |
| Crossway Ct. SE4 | 76 | 36 76 C |
| Crossway. Dag | 41 | 47 86 C |
| Crossway. Enf | 17 | 33 94 A |
| Crossway. N12 | 23 | 26 91 B |
| Crossway. N16 | 48 | 33 85 C |
| Crossway. NW9 | 22 | 21 89 D |
| Crossway. NW9 | 22 | 21 89 D |
| Crossway. Orp | 100 | 44 68 D |
| Crossway. Pnr | 19 | 10 90 D |
| Crossway. Ruis | 43 | 11 85 A |
| Crossways Rd. Beck | 98 | 37 68 C |
| Crossways Rd. Mit | 96 | 28 68 B |
| Crossways. Rom | 30 | 52 89 B |
| Crossways. Sutt | 110 | 26 62 B |
| Crossways The. Houn | 59 | 12 77 D |
| Crossways The. Wem | 34 | 19 86 A |
| Crossway. SW20 | 95 | 23 68 C |
| Cross Way The. Har | 21 | 15 90 D |
| Crossway The. N22 | 25 | 31 91 D |
| Crossway The. SE9 | 89 | 41 72 B |
| Crossway. W3 | 54 | 16 82 C |
| Crosswell Cl. Shep | 91 | 08 69 C |
| Croston St. E8 | 48 | 34 83 A |
| Crouch Ave. Bark | 51 | 46 83 D |
| Crouch Cl. Beck | 98 | 37 70 A |
| Crouch Croft. SE9 | 90 | 43 72 C |
| Crouch End Hill. N8 | 36 | 29 88 D |
| Crouch Hall Ct. N19 | 36 | 30 87 C |
| Crouch Hall Rd. N8 | 36 | 29 88 D |
| Crouch Hill. N4 | 36 | 30 87 A |
| Crouch Hill. N8 | 36 | 30 88 C |
| Crouchmans Cl. SE26 | 87 | 34 72 C |
| Crouch Rd. NW10 | 45 | 20 84 D |
| Crowborough Rd. SW17 | 86 | 28 71 C |
| Crowder St. E1 | 57 | 34 80 B |
| Crowhurst Cl. SW9 | 75 | 31 76 C |
| Crowland Gdns. N14 | 16 | 29 94 A |
| Crowland Rd. N15 | 37 | 33 88 B |
| Crowland Rd. Th Hth | 97 | 32 68 D |
| Crowlands Ave. Rom | 41 | 49 88 D |
| Crowland Terr. N1 | 48 | 32 84 D |
| Crowland Wk. Mord | 103 | 26 67 C |
| Crow La. Rom | 41 | 49 87 B |
| Crowley Cres. Croy | 112 | 31 64 C |
| Crowline Wlk. N1 | 48 | 32 84 A |
| Crowmarsh Gdns. SE23 | 88 | 35 73 A |
| Crown Cl. E3 | 49 | 37 83 A |
| Crown Cl. NW3 | 46 | 25 84 B |
| Crown Ct. EC4 | 4 | 32 81 C |
| Crown Ct. SE12 | 77 | 40 74 D |
| Crown Ct. WC2 | 3 | 30 81 C |
| Crowndale Rd. NW1 | 47 | 29 83 C |
| Crown Dale. SE19 | 97 | 32 70 A |
| Crown Dale. SE19 | 87 | 32 71 C |
| Crownfield Ave. Ilf | 40 | 45 88 A |
| Crownfield Rd. E15 | 49 | 38 85 B |
| Crown Hill. Croy | 105 | 32 65 A |
| Crownhill Rd. NW10 | 45 | 21 83 B |
| Crownhill Rd. Wdf Gn | 27 | 42 91 C |
| Crown La. SW16 | 87 | 31 71 C |
| Crown La. Brom | 107 | 42 67 A |
| Crown La. Chis | 100 | 44 69 A |
| Crown La. Mord | 95 | 25 68 B |
| Crown La. N14 | 16 | 29 94 C |
| Crown Lane Gdns. SW16 | 87 | 31 71 C |
| Crown Lane Spur. Brom | 107 | 41 67 D |
| Crownmead Way. Rom | 29 | 49 89 D |
| Crown Office Row. EC4 | 7 | 31 80 A |
| Crown Pas. King | 93 | 17 69 D |
| Crown Pas. SW1 | 6 | 29 80 C |
| Crown Pl. NW5 | 47 | 28 84 B |
| Crown Rd. Enf | 13 | 34 96 D |
| Crown Rd. Ilf | 28 | 44 89 D |
| Crown Rd. Mord | 95 | 25 68 D |
| Crown Rd. N10 | 24 | 28 91 C |
| Crown Rd. N Mal | 94 | 20 69 A |
| Crown Rd. Sutt | 110 | 25 64 B |
| Crown Rd. Twick | 71 | 16 74 D |
| Crown St. Dag | 52 | 50 84 A |
| Crown St. Har | 33 | 15 87 C |
| Crownstone Rd. SW2 | 75 | 31 74 A |
| Crown St. SE5 | 63 | 32 77 C |
| Crown St. W3 | 55 | 19 80 D |
| Crown Terr. Rich | 71 | 18 75 D |
| Crown Wlk. Wem | 33 | 18 86 D |
| Crown Woods Way. SE9 | 78 | 44 74 B |
| Crown Works. E2 | 48 | 34 83 D |
| Crown Yd. Houn | 70 | 14 75 A |
| Crowshott Ave. Stan | 21 | 17 90 B |
| Crows Rd. E15 | 58 | 38 82 B |
| Crowther Ave. Brent | 60 | 18 78 A |
| Crowther Rd. SE25 | 97 | 34 68 C |
| Crowthorne Cl. SW18 | 85 | 24 73 D |
| Crowthorne Rd. W10 | 56 | 23 81 D |
| Croxden Cl. Edg | 22 | 19 89 A |
| Croxden Wlk. Mord | 103 | 26 67 C |
| Croxford Gdns. N22 | 25 | 32 91 C |
| Croxford Way. Rom | 41 | 50 87 D |
| Croxley Cl. Orp | 100 | 46 69 D |
| Croxley Green. Orp | 100 | 46 69 B |
| Croxley Rd. W9 | 56 | 24 82 B |
| Croxted Cl. SE21 | 87 | 32 73 A |
| Croxted Rd. SE21 | 87 | 32 73 D |
| Croyde Ave. Grnf | 53 | 14 82 A |
| Croyde Cl. Sid | 90 | 44 73 B |
| Croydon Fly The. Croy | 105 | 32 65 C |
| Croydon Gr. Croy | 105 | 31 66 D |
| Croydon Rd. Beck | 98 | 36 68 B |
| Croydon Rd. Brom | 107 | 41 65 D |
| Croydon Rd. E13 | 58 | 39 82 D |
| Croydon Rd. Houn | 69 | 07 75 B |
| Croydon Rd. Mit | 104 | 28 67 B |
| Croydon Rd. SE20 | 98 | 35 69 A |
| Croydon Rd. Wall | 104 | 29 65 D |
| Croydon Rd. W.Wick | 107 | 39 65 D |
| Croyland Rd. N9 | 17 | 34 94 C |
| Croylands Dri. Surb | 101 | 18 66 A |
| Croysdale Ave. Sun | 91 | 10 68 A |
| Crozier Dri. S Croy | 112 | 34 62 D |
| Crozier Terr. E9 | 49 | 35 85 D |
| Crucifix La. SE1 | 8 | 33 79 A |
| Cruden St. N1 | 48 | 31 83 B |
| Cruichton Rd. Cars | 111 | 27 63 D |
| Cruickshank St. WC1 | 3 | 31 82 A |
| Cruikshank Rd. E15 | 50 | 39 85 D |
| Crummock Gdns. NW9 | 34 | 21 88 A |
| Crumpsall St. SE2 | 67 | 47 78 A |
| Crundale Ave. NW9 | 34 | 19 88 A |
| Crunden Rd. S Croy | 112 | 32 63 D |
| Crusader Gdns. Croy | 105 | 33 65 C |
| Crusoe Rd. Eri | 67 | 50 78 D |
| Crusoe Rd. Mit | 96 | 27 70 D |
| Crutched Friars. EC3 | 8 | 33 80 A |
| Cruthchley Rd. SE6 | 89 | 39 72 A |
| Crystal Ave. Horn | 42 | 54 86 C |
| Crystal Palace Park Rd. SE26 | 97 | 34 70 B |
| Crystal Palace Park Rd. SE26 | 87 | 34 71 D |
| Crystal Palace Par. SE19 | 87 | 33 71 D |
| Crystal Palace Rd. SE22 | 75 | 34 74 A |
| Crystal Palace Station Rd. SE19 | 97 | 34 70 A |
| Crystal Terr. SE19 | 97 | 32 70 B |
| Cuba Dri. Enf | 14 | 35 97 C |
| Cuba St. E14 | 64 | 37 79 A |
| Cubbit St. WC1 | 3 | 30 82 B |
| Cubitt St. Croy | 111 | 30 64 D |
| Cubitt Terr. SW4 | 74 | 29 75 A |
| Cuckoo Ave. W7 | 54 | 15 81 A |
| Cuckoo Dene. W7 | 54 | 15 81 A |
| Cuckoo Hall La. N9 | 18 | 35 94 A |
| Cuckoo Hill Dri. Pnr | 20 | 11 89 A |
| Cuckoo Hill. Pnr | 20 | 11 89 A |
| Cuckoo Hill Rd. Pnr | 20 | 11 89 D |
| Cuckoo La. W7 | 54 | 15 80 A |
| Cuda's Cl. Eps | 109 | 21 64 B |
| Cuddington Ave. Wor Pk | 102 | 21 65 D |
| Cuddington Way. Sutt | 110 | 24 62 C |
| Cudham St. SE6 | 88 | 38 73 A |
| Cudworth St. E1 | 57 | 34 82 D |
| Cuff Cres. SE9 | 77 | 41 74 D |
| Culford Gdns. SW3 | 9 | 27 78 B |
| Culford Gr. N1 | 48 | 33 84 A |
| Culford Mews. N1 | 48 | 33 84 A |
| Culford Rd. N1 | 48 | 33 84 C |
| Culgaith Gdns. Enf | 12 | 30 96 C |
| Cullen Way. NW10 | 55 | 20 82 C |
| Culling Rd. SE16 | 64 | 35 79 C |
| Cullington Cl. Har | 21 | 16 89 C |
| Cullingworth Rd. NW10 | 45 | 22 85 D |
| Culloden Rd. Enf | 13 | 31 97 D |
| Culloden St. E14 | 58 | 38 81 C |
| Cullum St. EC3 | 8 | 33 80 A |
| Culmington Rd. S Croy | 112 | 32 62 A |
| Culmington Rd. W13 | 54 | 17 80 C |
| Culmore Cross. SW12 | 86 | 28 73 D |
| Culmore Rd. SE15 | 64 | 35 77 C |
| Culmstock Rd. SW11 | 74 | 28 74 A |
| Culpeper Cl. Ilf | 28 | 43 91 B |
| Culpeper St. N1 | 48 | 31 83 C |
| Culross Cl. N15 | 25 | 32 89 C |
| Culross St. W1 | 6 | 28 80 A |
| Culsac Rd. Surb | 101 | 18 65 A |
| Culverden Gdns. SW12 | 86 | 29 72 A |
| Culver Gr. Stan | 21 | 17 90 D |
| Culverhouse Gdns. SW16 | 86 | 30 72 D |
| Culverley Rd. SE6 | 88 | 38 73 C |
| Culvers Ave. Cars | 104 | 27 65 B |
| Culvers Retreat. Cars | 104 | 27 65 B |
| Culverstone Cl. Brom | 107 | 39 67 D |
| Culvers Way. Cars | 104 | 27 65 B |
| Culvert Pl. SW11 | 74 | 28 76 C |
| Culvert Rd. N15 | 37 | 33 88 A |
| Culvert Rd. SW11 | 74 | 27 76 D |
| Culworth St. NW8 | 47 | 27 83 C |
| Cumberland Ave. Horn | 42 | 54 86 C |
| Cumberland Ave. NW10 | 55 | 19 82 B |
| Cumberland Ave. Well | 78 | 45 75 D |
| Cumberland Cl. Eps | 109 | 21 62 C |
| Cumberland Cl. Horn | 42 | 54 86 C |
| Cumberland Cl. SW20 | 95 | 23 70 D |
| Cumberland Cl. Twick | 71 | 16 74 D |
| Cumberland Cres. W14 | 62 | 24 78 A |
| Cumberland Dri. Bexh | 67 | 48 77 C |
| Cumberland Dri. Chess | 101 | 18 65 D |
| Cumberland Dri. Esh | 101 | 16 65 A |
| Cumberland Gate. W1 | 5 | 27 80 B |
| Cumberland Gdns. NW4 | 23 | 24 90 C |
| Cumberland Gdns. WC1 | 3 | 31 82 A |
| Cumberland Market. NW1 | 2 | 28 82 B |
| Cumberland Park. W3 | 55 | 20 80 A |
| Cumberland Pl. NW1 | 2 | 28 82 B |
| Cumberland Pl. Sun | 91 | 10 68 C |
| Cumberland Rd. Brom | 99 | 39 68 B |
| Cumberland Rd. E12 | 50 | 41 85 B |
| Cumberland Rd. E13 | 58 | 40 82 D |
| Cumberland Rd. E17 | 26 | 36 90 C |
| Cumberland Rd. Har | 32 | 13 88 B |
| Cumberland Rd. N22 | 24 | 30 90 D |
| Cumberland Rd. N9 | 18 | 35 94 C |
| Cumberland Rd. Rich | 61 | 19 77 C |
| Cumberland Rd. SE25 | 105 | 34 67 D |
| Cumberland Rd. Stan | 21 | 18 89 B |
| Cumberland Rd. SW13 | 72 | 22 76 A |
| Cumberland Rd. W3 | 55 | 20 80 A |
| Cumberland Rd. W7 | 60 | 15 79 B |
| Cumberland St. SW1 | 9 | 28 78 D |
| Cumberland Terrace Mews. NW1 | 47 | 28 83 D |
| Cumberland Terr. NW1 | 47 | 28 83 D |
| Cumberlow Ave. SE25 | 97 | 34 68 A |
| Cumbernauld Gdns. Sun | 81 | 09 71 D |
| Cumberton Rd. N17 | 25 | 32 90 B |
| Cumbrae Gdns. Surb | 101 | 17 65 B |
| Cumbrian Ave. Bexh | 80 | 51 76 C |
| Cumbrian Gdns. NW2 | 35 | 24 86 A |
| Cumming St. N1 | 47 | 30 83 D |
| Cumnor Gdns. Eps | 109 | 22 63 A |
| Cumnor Rd. Sutt | 110 | 26 63 A |
| Cunard Rd. NW10 | 55 | 20 82 B |
| Cunard St. SE5 | 63 | 33 77 A |
| Cundy Rd. E16 | 58 | 41 81 C |
| Cundy St. SW1 | 9 | 28 78 A |
| Cunliffe Rd. Wor Pk | 109 | 21 64 B |
| Cunliffe St. SW16 | 96 | 29 70 A |
| Cunningham Cl. W Wick | 106 | 37 65 B |
| Cunningham Park. Har | 32 | 14 88 B |
| Cunningham Pl. NW8 | 1 | 26 82 D |
| Cunningham Rd. N15 | 25 | 34 89 C |
| Cunnington St. W4 | 61 | 20 78 A |
| Cupar Rd. SW11 | 74 | 28 76 A |
| Cupola Cl. Brom | 89 | 40 71 D |
| Cureton St. SW1 | 10 | 29 78 B |
| Curlew St. SE1 | 8 | 33 79 B |
| Curnick's La. SE27 | 87 | 32 71 A |
| Curran Ave. Sid | 78 | 45 74 B |
| Curran Ave. Wall | 104 | 28 65 C |
| Currey Rd. Grnf | 43 | 14 84 B |
| Curricle St. W3 | 55 | 21 80 C |
| Currie Hill Cl. SW19 | 85 | 24 71 B |
| Curry Rise. NW7 | 23 | 23 91 B |
| Cursitor St. EC4 | 3 | 31 81 C |
| Curtain Pl. EC2 | 4 | 33 82 C |
| Curtain Rd. EC2 | 4 | 33 82 C |
| Curthwaite Gdns. Enf | 12 | 29 95 B |
| Curtis Field Rd. SW16 | 87 | 31 71 A |
| Curtismill Cl. Orp | 100 | 46 68 B |
| Curtismill Way. Orp | 100 | 46 68 B |
| Curtis Rd. Eps | 109 | 20 64 A |
| Curtis Rd. Horn | 42 | 54 87 B |
| Curtis Rd. Houn | 82 | 12 73 B |
| Curtis St. SE1 | 63 | 33 78 B |
| Curtis Way. SE1 | 63 | 33 78 B |
| Curvan Cl. Eps | 109 | 21 62 D |
| Curve The. W12 | 55 | 22 80 A |
| Curwen Ave. E7 | 50 | 40 85 B |
| Curwen Rd. W12 | 61 | 22 79 A |
| Curzon Ave. Enf | 14 | 35 95 B |

| | | |
|---|---|---|
| Curzon Ave. Stan | 21 | 16 90 A |
| Curzon Cres. Bark | 51 | 45 83 D |
| Curzon Cres. NW10 | 45 | 21 84 C |
| Curzon Gate. W1 | 6 | 28 80 C |
| Curzon Pl. Pnr | 32 | 11 88 A |
| Curzon Pl. W1 | 6 | 28 80 C |
| Curzon Rd. N10 | 24 | 28 90 D |
| Curzon Rd. Th Hth | 105 | 31 67 C |
| Curzon Rd. W5 | 54 | 16 82 D |
| Curzon St. W1 | 6 | 28 80 D |
| Cusack Cl. Twick | 83 | 15 71 B |
| Cutcombe Rd. SE5 | 76 | 37 76 C |
| Cuthbert Rd. Croy | 105 | 31 65 B |
| Cuthbert Rd. E17 | 26 | 38 89 A |
| Cuthbert Rd. N18 | 17 | 34 92 C |
| Cuthbert St. W2 | 1 | 26 82 D |
| Cutlers Gdns. EC2 | 4 | 33 81 C |
| Cutler St. E1 | 4 | 33 81 C |
| Cut. The SE1 | 7 | 31 79 A |
| Cuxton Cl. Bexh | 79 | 48 74 A |
| Cyclamen Way. Eps | 109 | 20 64 C |
| Cygnet Ave. Felt | 82 | 11 73 B |
| Cygnet Cl. Nthwd | 19 | 08 91 A |
| Cygnet St. E1 | 4 | 33 82 D |
| Cygnets The. Felt | 82 | 12 71 A |
| Cynthia St. N1 | 47 | 30 83 D |
| Cyntra Pl. E8 | 48 | 34 84 D |
| Cypress Ave. Twick | 82 | 14 73 A |
| Cypress Gr. Ilf | 28 | 45 91 A |
| Cypress Path. Rom | 30 | 53 91 D |
| Cypress Pl. W1 | 2 | 29 82 C |
| Cypress Rd. Har | 20 | 14 90 D |
| Cypress Rd. SE25 | 97 | 33 69 C |
| Cypress Rd. Sun | 91 | 09 69 A |
| Cyprus Ave. N3 | 23 | 24 90 C |
| Cyprus Gdns. N3 | 23 | 24 90 C |
| Cyprus Pl. E2 | 49 | 35 83 C |
| Cyprus Rd. N3 | 23 | 24 90 D |
| Cyprus Rd. N9 | 17 | 33 93 B |
| Cyprus St (off Bonner St). E2 | 49 | 35 83 C |
| Cyprus St (off Globe Rd). E2 | 49 | 35 83 C |
| Cyrena Rd. SE22 | 75 | 33 74 B |
| Cyril Rd. Bexh | 79 | 48 76 C |
| Cyril Rd. Orp | 108 | 46 66 A |
| Cyrus St. EC1 | 3 | 31 82 D |
| Czar St. SE8 | 64 | 37 77 A |
| Dabbs Hill La. Nthlt | 43 | 12 85 D |
| Dabin Cres. SE10 | 76 | 38 76 A |
| Dacca St. SE8 | 64 | 36 77 B |
| Dace Rd. E3 | 49 | 37 83 A |
| Dacre Ave. Ilf | 28 | 43 90 C |
| Dacre Cl. Grnf | 43 | 13 83 D |
| Dacre Gdns. SE13 | 77 | 39 75 C |
| Dacre Park. SE13 | 77 | 39 75 A |
| Dacre Pl. SE13 | 77 | 39 75 A |
| Dacre Rd. Croy | 104 | 30 66 A |
| Dacre Rd. E11 | 39 | 39 87 D |
| Dacre Rd. E13 | 50 | 40 83 B |
| Dacres Rd. SE23 | 88 | 35 72 D |
| Dacre St. SW1 | 6 | 29 79 D |
| Daerwood Cl. Brom | 107 | 42 66 D |
| Daffodil St. W12 | 55 | 21 80 B |
| Dafforne Rd. SW17 | 86 | 28 72 C |
| Dagenham Ave. Dag | 52 | 48 84 D |
| Dagenham Rd. E10 | 38 | 36 87 D |
| Dagenham Rd. Rain | 52 | 50 84 D |
| Dagenham Rd. Rom | 41 | 50 87 D |
| Dagmar Ave. Wem | 44 | 18 85 B |
| Dagmar Ct. E14 | 64 | 38 79 C |
| Dagmar Gdns. NW10 | 46 | 23 83 D |
| Dagmar Mews. Sthl | 59 | 12 79 C |
| Dagmar Pas. N1 | 48 | 31 83 B |
| Dagmar Rd. Dag | 52 | 50 84 C |
| Dagmar Rd. King | 93 | 18 69 B |
| Dagmar Rd. N4 | 37 | 31 87 A |
| Dagmar Rd. SE25 | 105 | 33 67 A |
| Dagmar Rd. SE5 | 75 | 33 76 A |
| Dagmar Rd. Sthl | 59 | 12 79 C |
| Dagmar Terr. N1 | 48 | 31 83 B |
| Dagnall Park. SE25 | 105 | 33 67 A |
| Dagnall Rd. SE25 | 105 | 33 67 A |
| Dagnall St. SW11 | 74 | 28 76 A |
| Dagnan Rd. SW12 | 86 | 29 73 A |
| Dagonet Gdns. Brom | 89 | 40 72 C |
| Dagonet Rd. Brom | 89 | 40 72 C |
| Dahlia Gdns. Mit | 96 | 29 68 D |
| Dahlia Rd. SE2 | 66 | 46 78 B |
| Dahomey Rd. SW16 | 96 | 29 70 A |
| Daimler Way. Wall | 111 | 30 63 C |
| Daines Cl. E12 | 39 | 42 86 D |
| Dainford Cl. Brom | 88 | 38 71 D |
| Dainton Cl. Brom | 99 | 40 69 B |
| Daintry Way. E9 | 49 | 36 84 B |
| Dairsie Rd. SE9 | 78 | 43 75 A |
| Dairy Wlk. SW19 | 85 | 24 71 A |
| Daisy La. SW6 | 73 | 25 75 A |
| Daisy Rd. E18 | 27 | 40 90 D |
| Dakota Gdns (off Argus Way). Nthlt | 53 | 12 82 A |
| Dalberg Rd. SW2 | 75 | 31 74 A |
| Dalberg Way. Belv | 67 | 47 79 D |
| Dalby Rd. SW18 | 73 | 26 75 C |
| Dalby St. NW5 | 47 | 28 84 B |
| Dalcross Rd. Houn | 70 | 12 76 C |
| Dale Ave. Edg | 21 | 18 90 D |
| Dale Ave. Houn | 70 | 12 75 A |
| Dalebury Rd. SW17 | 86 | 27 72 B |
| Dale Cl. Barn | 11 | 25 95 D |
| Dale Cl. Dart | 80 | 51 74 D |
| Dale Cl. Pnr | 19 | 10 90 B |
| Dale Cl. SE3 | 77 | 40 75 A |
| Dale Ct. King | 93 | 18 70 D |
| Dale End. Dart | 80 | 51 74 D |
| Dale Green Rd. N11 | 16 | 28 93 D |
| Dale Gr. N12 | 15 | 26 92 C |
| Daleham Gdns. NW3 | 46 | 26 84 B |
| Daleham Mews. NW3 | 46 | 26 84 B |
| Dale Park Ave. Cars | 104 | 27 65 B |
| Dale Park Rd. SE19 | 97 | 32 69 B |
| Dale Rd. Dart | 80 | 51 74 D |
| Dale Rd. E16 | 58 | 39 81 A |
| Dale Rd. Grnf | 53 | 13 81 B |
| Dale Rd. NW5 | 47 | 28 85 C |
| Dale Rd. SE17 | 63 | 31 77 B |
| Dale Rd. Sun | 91 | 09 70 D |
| Dale Rd. Sutt | 110 | 24 64 B |
| Daleside Rd. Eps | 109 | 20 63 B |
| Daleside Rd. SW16 | 86 | 28 71 D |
| Dale St. W4 | 61 | 21 78 C |
| Dale The. Brom | 107 | 41 65 D |
| Dale View Ave. E4 | 18 | 38 93 A |
| Dale View Cres. E4 | 18 | 38 93 C |
| Dale View. Eri | 80 | 51 76 D |
| Dale View Gdns. E4 | 18 | 38 93 D |
| Daleview Rd. N15 | 37 | 33 88 C |
| Dalewood Cl. Horn | 42 | 54 87 A |
| Dalewood Gdns. Wor Pk | 102 | 22 65 B |
| Dale Wood Rd. Orp | 108 | 45 66 C |
| Daley St. E9 | 49 | 35 84 B |
| Dalgarno Gdns. W10 | 56 | 23 81 A |
| Dalgarno Way. W10 | 56 | 23 82 C |
| Dalgleish St. E14 | 57 | 36 81 C |
| Daling Way. E3 | 49 | 36 83 C |
| Dalkeith Rd. Ilf | 40 | 44 86 C |
| Dalkeith Rd. SE21 | 87 | 32 73 A |
| Dallas Rd. NW4 | 34 | 22 87 A |
| Dallas Rd. SE26 | 87 | 34 72 D |
| Dallas Rd. Sutt | 110 | 24 63 A |
| Dallas Rd. W5 | 54 | 18 81 B |
| Dallinger Rd. SE12 | 77 | 39 74 D |
| Dalling Rd. W6 | 61 | 22 79 D |
| Dallington St. EC1 | 3 | 31 82 D |
| Dallin Rd. Bexh | 79 | 47 75 D |
| Dallin Rd. SE18 | 66 | 43 77 D |
| Dalmain Rd. SE23 | 88 | 35 73 D |
| Dalmally Pas. Croy | 105 | 33 66 B |
| Dalmally Rd. Croy | 105 | 34 66 A |
| Dalmeny Ave. N7 | 47 | 29 85 D |
| Dalmeny Ave. SW16 | 97 | 31 69 C |
| Dalmeny Cl. Wem | 44 | 17 84 A |
| Dalmeny Cres. Houn | 70 | 14 75 D |
| Dalmeny Rd. Barn | 11 | 26 95 D |
| Dalmeny Rd. Bexh | 79 | 49 76 B |
| Dalmeny Rd. Cars | 111 | 28 63 C |
| Dalmeny Rd. N7 | 47 | 29 85 B |
| Dalmeny Rd. Wor Pk | 102 | 22 65 D |
| Dalmore Rd. SE21 | 87 | 32 72 A |
| Dalrymple Rd. SE4 | 76 | 36 75 C |
| Dalston Gdns. Stan | 21 | 18 90 A |
| Dalston La. E8 | 48 | 34 85 C |
| Dalton Ave. Mit | 96 | 27 69 C |
| Dalton Cl. Dart | 80 | 51 75 B |
| Dalton Cl. Orp | 108 | 45 65 C |
| Dalton St. SE27 | 87 | 31 72 D |
| Dalwood St. SE5 | 75 | 33 76 A |
| Dalyell Rd. SW9 | 74 | 30 75 B |
| Damer Terr. SW10 | 62 | 26 77 C |
| Dames Rd. E7 | 50 | 40 85 A |
| Dame St. N1 | 48 | 32 83 C |
| Damien St. E1 | 57 | 34 81 D |
| Damon Cl. Sid | 90 | 46 72 D |
| Damsonwood Cl. Sthl | 59 | 13 79 C |
| Danbrook Rd. SW16 | 96 | 30 70 C |
| Danbury Cl. Rom | 29 | 47 89 B |
| Danbury Mews. Wall | 111 | 28 64 B |
| Danbury St. N1 | 48 | 31 83 D |
| Danbury Way. Wdf Gn | 27 | 41 91 A |
| Danby St. SE15 | 75 | 33 75 B |
| Dancer Rd. Rich | 72 | 19 75 A |
| Dancer Rd. SW6 | 73 | 24 76 B |
| Dando Cres. SE3 | 77 | 40 75 B |
| Danebury Ave. SW15 | 84 | 22 73 A |
| Daneby Rd. SE6 | 88 | 38 72 A |
| Danecourt Gdns. Croy | 105 | 33 65 D |
| Danecroft Rd. SE24 | 75 | 32 74 B |
| Danehill Wlk. Sid | 90 | 46 72 C |
| Danehurst Gdns. Ilf | 39 | 42 88 B |
| Danehurst St. SW6 | 73 | 24 76 A |
| Daneland. Barn | 12 | 27 95 D |
| Danemead Gr. Nthlt | 43 | 13 85 D |
| Danemere St. SW15 | 73 | 23 75 A |
| Dane Pl. E3 | 49 | 36 83 D |
| Dane Rd. Ashf | 91 | 08 70 B |
| Dane Rd. Ilf | 51 | 44 85 C |
| Dane Rd. N18 | 18 | 35 93 C |
| Dane Rd. Sthl | 53 | 12 80 A |
| Dane Rd. SW19 | 95 | 26 69 A |
| Dane Rd. W13 | 54 | 17 80 C |
| Danesbury Rd. Felt | 81 | 10 73 D |
| Danescourt Cres. Sutt | 103 | 26 65 A |
| Danescroft Ave. NW4 | 35 | 23 88 B |
| Danescroft Gdns. NW4 | 35 | 23 88 B |
| Danescroft. NW4 | 35 | 23 88 B |
| Danes Ct. Wem | 34 | 19 86 D |
| Danesdale Rd. E9 | 49 | 36 84 A |
| Danes Gate. Har | 21 | 15 89 A |
| Danes Rd. Rom | 41 | 50 87 A |
| Dane St. WC1 | 3 | 30 81 B |
| Daneswood Ave. SE6 | 88 | 38 72 C |
| Danethorpe Rd. Wem | 44 | 17 84 B |
| Danetree Rd. Eps | 109 | 20 63 D |
| Danette Gdns. Dag | 41 | 48 86 B |
| Daneville Rd. SE5 | 75 | 32 76 B |
| Dangan Rd. E11 | 39 | 40 88 C |
| Daniel Bolt Cl. E14 | 57 | 37 81 B |
| Daniel Pl. NW4 | 34 | 22 87 B |
| Daniel Rd. W5 | 54 | 18 80 B |
| Daniel's Rd. SE15 | 76 | 35 75 A |
| Dan Leno Wlk. SW6 | 62 | 25 77 D |
| Dansey Pl. W1 | 6 | 29 80 B |
| Dansington Rd. Well | 78 | 46 75 C |
| Danson Cres. Well | 78 | 46 75 B |
| Danson La. Well | 78 | 46 75 D |
| Danson Mead. Well | 79 | 47 75 A |
| Danson Rd. Bex | 79 | 47 74 B |
| Danson Rd. Bex | 79 | 47 74 B |
| Danson Rd. Bexh | 79 | 47 75 D |
| Danson Underpass. Sid | 79 | 47 74 C |
| Dante Rd. SE11 | 63 | 31 78 B |
| Danube St. SW3 | 9 | 27 78 C |
| Danvers Rd. N8 | 24 | 29 89 D |
| Danvers St. SW3 | 62 | 26 77 B |
| Daphne Gdns. E4 | 18 | 38 93 C |
| Daphne St. SW18 | 85 | 26 73 A |
| Daphne St. SW18 | 73 | 26 74 C |
| Daplyn St. E1 | 57 | 34 81 A |
| D'arblay St. W1 | 2 | 29 81 C |
| Darby Cres. Sun | 92 | 11 69 C |
| Darby Gdns. Sun | 92 | 11 69 C |
| Darcy Ave. Wall | 111 | 29 64 A |
| D'arcy Dri. Har | 21 | 17 89 D |
| D'Arcy Gdns. Dag | 52 | 48 83 B |
| D'arcy Gdns. Har | 21 | 18 89 C |
| D'Arcy Rd. Sutt | 110 | 23 64 B |
| Darcy Rd. SW16 | 96 | 30 69 C |
| Dare Gdns. Dag | 41 | 48 86 C |
| Darell Rd. Rich | 72 | 19 75 A |
| Darenth Rd. N16 | 37 | 33 87 D |
| Darenth Rd. Well | 78 | 46 76 A |
| Darfield Rd. SE4 | 76 | 36 74 B |
| Darfield Way. W10 | 56 | 23 81 D |
| Darfur St. SW15 | 73 | 23 75 B |
| Dargate Cl. SE19 | 97 | 33 70 D |
| Darien Rd. SW11 | 73 | 26 75 B |
| Darke St. WC1 | 3 | 30 81 B |
| Darlan Rd. SW6 | 62 | 24 77 D |
| Darlaston Rd. SW19 | 95 | 23 70 D |
| Darley Cl. Croy | 106 | 36 67 C |
| Darley Dri. N Mal | 94 | 20 69 D |
| Darley Rd. N9 | 17 | 33 94 D |
| Darley Rd. SW11 | 74 | 27 74 D |
| Darling Rd. SE4 | 76 | 37 75 A |
| Darling Row. E1 | 57 | 34 82 D |
| Darlington Rd. SE27 | 87 | 31 71 D |
| Darnley Rd. E9 | 49 | 35 84 A |
| Darnley Rd. Wdf Gn | 27 | 40 90 B |
| Darnley Terr. W11 | 56 | 23 80 D |
| Darrell Rd. SE22 | 75 | 34 74 A |
| Darren Cl. N4 | 36 | 30 87 B |
| Darrick Wood Rd. Orp | 108 | 44 65 B |
| Darsley Dri. SW8 | 74 | 30 76 A |
| Dartfields. Rom | 30 | 53 91 B |
| Dartford Ave. Enf | 14 | 35 95 D |
| Dartford Hse. SE1 | 63 | 33 78 B |
| Dartford Rd. Dart | 80 | 52 74 D |
| Dartford St. SE17 | 63 | 32 77 A |
| Dartmouth Cl. W11 | 56 | 24 81 D |
| Dartmouth Ct. SE10 | 76 | 38 76 B |
| Dartmouth Gr. SE10 | 76 | 38 76 B |
| Dartmouth Hill. SE10 | 76 | 38 76 A |
| Dartmouth Park Ave. NW5 | 36 | 28 86 D |
| Dartmouth Park Hill. N19 | 36 | 28 86 B |
| Dartmouth Park Hill. NW5 | 36 | 28 86 D |
| Dartmouth Park Rd. NW5 | 36 | 28 86 D |
| Dartmouth Pl. SE23 | 88 | 35 72 A |
| Dartmouth Pl. W4 | 61 | 21 77 A |
| Dartmouth Rd. Brom | 107 | 40 66 A |
| Dartmouth Rd. E16 | 58 | 40 81 C |
| Dartmouth Rd. NW2 | 46 | 23 84 B |
| Dartmouth Rd. NW4 | 34 | 22 88 C |
| Dartmouth Rd. Ruis | 31 | 10 86 C |
| Dartmouth Rd. SE23 | 88 | 35 72 A |
| Dartmouth Rd. SE26 | 88 | 35 72 C |
| Dartmouth Row. SE10 | 76 | 38 76 A |
| Dartmouth St. SW1 | 6 | 29 79 B |
| Dartmouth Terr. SE10 | 76 | 38 76 B |
| Dartnell Rd. Croy | 105 | 33 66 B |
| Dartrey Wlk. SW10 | 62 | 26 77 C |
| Dart St. W10 | 56 | 24 82 B |
| Darville Rd. N16 | 37 | 33 86 D |
| Darwell Cl. E6 | 51 | 43 83 C |
| Darwin Ct. E13 | 58 | 40 82 B |
| Darwin Ct. NW1 | 47 | 28 83 A |
| Darwin Dri. Sthl | 53 | 13 81 D |
| Darwin Rd. N22 | 25 | 31 90 D |
| Darwin Rd. W5 | 6 | 17 78 A |
| Darwin Rd. Well | 78 | 45 75 B |
| Darwin St. SE17 | 63 | 32 78 B |
| Daryngton Dri. Grnf | 44 | 15 83 C |
| Dashwood Cl. Bexh | 79 | 49 74 A |
| Dashwood Rd. N8 | 36 | 30 88 D |
| Dassett Rd. SE27 | 87 | 31 71 D |
| Datchelor Pl. SE5 | 75 | 32 76 B |
| Datchet Rd. SE6 | 88 | 36 72 B |
| Date St. SE17 | 63 | 32 78 D |
| Daubeney Rd. E5 | 49 | 36 85 A |
| Daubeney Rd. N17 | 25 | 32 91 C |
| Dault Rd. SW18 | 73 | 26 74 C |
| Davenant Rd. N19 | 36 | 29 86 B |
| Davenant St. E1 | 57 | 34 81 A |
| Davenport Rd. SE6 | 76 | 38 74 C |
| Daventry Ave. E17 | 38 | 37 88 C |
| Daventry Rd. Rom | 30 | 52 91 A |
| Daventry St. NW1 | 1 | 27 81 A |
| Davern Cl. E10 | 65 | 39 78 B |
| Davey Cl. N7 | 47 | 30 84 B |
| Davey Rd. E9 | 49 | 37 84 C |
| Davey St. SE15 | 63 | 33 77 B |
| David Ave. Grnf | 54 | 15 82 A |
| David Coffer Ct. Belv | 67 | 49 78 B |
| Davidge St. SE1 | 7 | 31 79 C |
| David Mews. W1 | 2 | 28 81 A |
| David Rd. Dag | 41 | 48 86 A |
| Davidson Gdns. SW8 | 10 | 30 77 C |
| Davidson Rd. Croy | 105 | 33 67 D |
| David's Rd. SE23 | 88 | 35 73 C |
| David St. E15 | 49 | 38 84 B |
| Davids Way. Ilf | 28 | 45 91 C |
| Davies La. E11 | 39 | 39 86 B |
| Davies Mews. W1 | 6 | 28 80 B |
| Davies St. W1 | 6 | 28 80 B |
| Davington Gdns. Dag | 51 | 46 85 D |
| Davington Rd. Dag | 51 | 46 85 D |
| Davinia Cl. Wdf Gn | 27 | 42 91 B |
| Davis Rd. Chess | 109 | 19 64 A |
| Davis Rd. W3 | 61 | 21 79 B |
| Davis St. E13 | 50 | 41 83 C |
| Davisville Rd. W12 | 61 | 22 79 A |
| Dawes Ave. Horn | 42 | 54 86 C |
| Dawes Ave. Islw | 71 | 16 75 C |
| Dawes Rd. SW6 | 62 | 24 77 D |
| Dawes St. SE17 | 63 | 32 78 D |
| Dawlish Ave. Grnf | 44 | 16 83 C |
| Dawlish Ave. N13 | 16 | 30 92 A |
| Dawlish Ave. SW18 | 85 | 25 72 B |
| Dawlish Dri. Ilf | 51 | 45 85 B |
| Dawlish Dri. Pnr | 32 | 12 88 C |
| Dawlish Dri. Ruis | 31 | 10 86 B |
| Dawlish Rd. E10 | 38 | 38 86 B |
| Dawlish Rd. N17 | 25 | 34 89 A |
| Dawlish Rd. NW2 | 46 | 23 84 B |
| Dawlish Wlk. Rom | 30 | 53 90 A |
| Dawnay Gdns. SW18 | 85 | 26 72 B |
| Dawnay Rd. SW18 | 85 | 26 72 B |
| Dawpool Rd. NW2 | 34 | 21 86 B |
| Daws Hill. Enf | 14 | 38 96 A |
| Dawson Ave. Bark | 51 | 45 84 D |
| Dawson Ave. Orp | 100 | 46 69 D |
| Dawson Cl. SE18 | 66 | 44 78 A |
| Dawson Gdns. Bark | 51 | 45 84 D |
| Dawson Pl. W2 | 56 | 25 80 A |
| Dawson Rd. King | 93 | 18 68 B |
| Dawson Rd. NW2 | 46 | 23 85 A |
| Dawson St. E2 | 48 | 33 83 D |
| Dawson Terr. N9 | 18 | 35 94 A |
| Daybrook Rd. SW19 | 95 | 25 68 B |
| Daylesford Ave. SW15 | 72 | 22 75 C |
| Daymar Rd. N22 | 24 | 29 90 B |
| Daymer Gdns. Pnr | 20 | 11 89 C |
| Day's Acre. S Croy | 112 | 33 62 D |
| Daysbrook Rd. SW2 | 86 | 30 73 D |
| Days La. Sid | 90 | 45 73 A |
| Dayton Gr. SE15 | 76 | 35 76 A |
| Deacon Rd. King | 93 | 18 69 B |
| Deacon Rd. NW2 | 45 | 22 84 A |
| Deacons Cl. Pnr | 19 | 10 90 D |
| Deacons Ct. Twick | 83 | 15 72 B |
| Deacons Wlk. Hamp | 82 | 13 71 A |
| Deacon Way. SE17 | 63 | 32 78 A |
| Deacon Way. Wdf Gn | 27 | 42 91 B |
| Deal Rd. SW17 | 96 | 28 70 A |
| Deal St. E1 | 57 | 34 81 A |
| Dealtry Rd. SW15 | 73 | 23 75 C |
| Dean Bradley St. SW1 | 7 | 30 79 C |
| Dean Cl. E9 | 49 | 35 85 C |
| Deancross St. E1 | 57 | 34 81 D |
| Deancross St. E1 | 57 | 35 81 C |
| Dean Ct. Wem | 33 | 17 86 C |
| Dean Dri. Stan | 21 | 18 90 C |
| Deane Ave. Ruis | 43 | 11 85 C |
| Deane Croft Rd. Pnr | 32 | 11 88 C |
| Deane Ct. Nthwd | 19 | 09 90 A |
| Deanery Mews. W1 | 6 | 28 80 C |
| Deanery Rd. E15 | 50 | 39 84 A |
| Deanery St. W1 | 6 | 28 80 C |
| Deane Way. Ruis | 31 | 10 88 D |
| Dean Farrar St. SW1 | 6 | 29 79 D |
| Deanfield Gdns. Croy | 112 | 32 64 B |
| Dean Gdns. E17 | 26 | 38 89 D |
| Deanhill Ct. SW14 | 72 | 19 75 D |
| Deanhill Rd. SW14 | 72 | 19 75 D |
| Dean La. Edg | 22 | 20 91 A |
| Dean Rd. Croy | 112 | 32 64 B |
| Dean Rd. Hamp | 82 | 13 71 C |
| Dean Rd. Houn | 70 | 13 74 B |
| Dean Rd. NW2 | 46 | 23 84 A |
| Dean Ryle St. SW1 | 10 | 30 78 A |
| Dean's Bldgs. SE17 | 63 | 32 78 B |
| Deansbrook Cl. Edg | 22 | 20 91 C |
| Deansbrook Rd. Edg | 22 | 20 91 A |
| Deans Cl. Croy | 105 | 33 65 D |
| Deans Cl. Edg | 22 | 20 91 A |
| Deans Cl. W4 | 61 | 19 77 B |
| Deanscroft Ave. NW9 | 34 | 20 87 C |
| Dean's Ct. EC4 | 3 | 31 81 D |
| Deans La. (Path). W4 | 61 | 19 77 B |
| Dean's Mews. W1 | 2 | 28 81 D |
| Dean's Pl. SW1 | 10 | 29 78 B |
| Deans Rd. Sutt | 103 | 25 65 D |
| Dean's Rd. W7 | 60 | 15 79 B |
| Dean Stanley St. SW1 | 7 | 30 79 C |
| Dean St. E7 | 50 | 40 85 C |
| Dean St. W1 | 2 | 29 81 D |
| Deansway. N2 | 23 | 26 89 D |
| Deansway. N9 | 17 | 33 93 C |
| Dean's Yd. SW1 | 6 | 29 79 D |
| Dean Trench St. SW1 | 7 | 30 79 C |
| Dean Wlk. Edg | 22 | 20 91 A |
| De Arn Gdns. Mit | 96 | 27 68 A |
| Deason St. E15 | 49 | 38 83 A |
| Debden Cl. Wdf Gn | 27 | 41 91 D |
| De Beauvoir Cres. N1 | 48 | 33 83 A |
| De Beauvoir Sq. N1 | 48 | 33 84 C |
| De Beavoir Rd. N1 | 48 | 33 84 C |
| Debenham Ct. E8 | 48 | 34 83 A |
| Debnams Rd. SE16 | 64 | 35 78 A |
| De Bohun Ave. N14 | 12 | 28 95 D |
| Deborah Cl. Islw | 71 | 15 76 A |
| Debrabant Cl. Eri | 67 | 50 77 B |
| Deburgh Rd. SW19 | 95 | 26 70 C |
| Decima St. SE1 | 8 | 33 79 C |
| Decoy Ave. NW11 | 23 | 24 89 C |
| De Crespigny Park. SE5 | 75 | 32 76 D |
| Deeley Rd. SW8 | 74 | 29 76 B |
| Deena Cl. W3 | 54 | 18 81 D |
| Deepdale Ave. Brom | 99 | 39 68 D |
| Deepdale. SW19 | 85 | 23 71 B |
| Deepdene Ave. Croy | 105 | 33 65 D |
| Deepdene Cl. E11 | 27 | 40 89 C |
| Deepdene Ct. Brom | 99 | 39 68 A |
| Deepdene Ct. N21 | 13 | 31 95 D |
| Deepdene Gdns. SW2 | 86 | 30 73 B |
| Deepdene Rd. SE5 | 75 | 32 75 D |
| Deepdene Rd. Well | 78 | 46 75 A |
| Deepwell Cl. Islw | 71 | 16 76 A |
| Deepwood La. Grnf | 53 | 14 82 B |
| Deerbrook Rd. SE24 | 87 | 31 73 D |
| Deerdale Rd. SE24 | 75 | 32 75 C |
| Dee Rd. Rich | 71 | 18 75 D |
| Deerhurst Rd. NW2 | 46 | 23 84 B |
| Deerhurst Rd. SW16 | 86 | 30 71 D |
| Deerleap Gr. E4 | 14 | 37 95 B |
| Deer Park Cl. King | 94 | 19 70 D |
| Deer Park Gdns. Mit | 95 | 26 68 D |
| Deer Park Rd. SW19 | 95 | 26 69 C |
| Deeside Rd. SW17 | 85 | 26 72 D |
| Dee St. E14 | 58 | 38 81 C |
| Dee Way. Eps | 109 | 21 62 C |
| Dee Way. Rom | 30 | 51 90 A |
| Defiance Wlk. SE18 | 65 | 42 79 D |
| Defiant Way. Wall | 111 | 30 63 C |
| Defoe Ave. Rich | 61 | 19 77 C |
| Defoe Rd. N16 | 37 | 33 86 C |
| Defoe Way. Rom | 29 | 49 91 B |
| De Frene Rd. SE26 | 88 | 36 72 C |
| Degema Rd. Chis | 90 | 43 71 D |
| Dehar Cres. NW9 | 34 | 22 87 A |
| De Havilland Rd. Edg | 22 | 19 90 D |
| De Havilland Rd. Houn | 59 | 11 77 C |
| De Havilland Rd. Wall | 111 | 30 63 C |
| Dekker Rd. SE21 | 75 | 33 74 C |
| Delacourt Rd. SE3 | 65 | 40 77 D |
| Delafield Rd. SE7 | 65 | 41 78 C |
| Delaford Rd. SE16 | 64 | 35 78 C |
| Delaford St. SW6 | 62 | 24 77 B |
| Delamare Cres. Croy | 106 | 35 67 C |
| Delamere Gdns. NW7 | 22 | 20 91 B |
| Delamere Rd. Hay | 53 | 11 80 B |
| Delamere Rd. SW20 | 95 | 23 69 B |
| Delamere Rd. W5 | 60 | 18 79 A |
| Delamere St. W2 | 1 | 27 81 A |
| Delamere Terr. W2 | 56 | 25 81 B |
| *Delancey Pas. NW1 | 47 | 29 83 A |
| Delancey St. NW1 | 47 | 28 83 B |
| De Laune St. SE17 | 63 | 31 78 D |
| Delaware Rd. W9 | 56 | 25 82 D |
| Delawyk Cres. SE24 | 75 | 32 74 D |
| Delcombe Ave. Wor Pk | 103 | 23 66 C |
| Delft Way. SE22 | 75 | 33 74 A |
| Delhi Rd. Enf | 17 | 33 94 B |
| Delhi St. N1 | 47 | 30 83 A |
| Delia St. SW18 | 85 | 25 73 B |
| Della Path. E5 | 37 | 34 86 D |
| Dellbow Rd. Felt | 69 | 10 74 B |
| Dell Cl. E15 | 49 | 38 83 B |
| Dell Cl. Wall | 111 | 29 64 B |
| Dell Ct. Horn | 42 | 54 86 A |
| Dell Farm Rd. Ruis | 31 | 08 88 B |
| Dellifield Cl. Beck | 98 | 38 69 A |
| Dell La. Eps | 109 | 22 64 C |
| Dellors Cl. Barn | 11 | 23 95 B |
| Dellow Cl. Ilf | 40 | 44 87 B |
| Dellow St. E1 | 57 | 34 80 B |
| Dell Rd. Eps | 109 | 22 63 A |
| Dell's Mews. SW1 | 10 | 29 78 A |
| Dell The. Brent | 60 | 17 77 A |
| Dell The. Felt | 81 | 10 73 B |
| Dell The. Pnr | 20 | 11 90 D |
| Dell The. SE19 | 97 | 33 70 D |
| Dell The. SE2 | 66 | 46 78 C |
| Dell The. Wem | 44 | 16 85 D |
| Dell Walk. N Mal | 94 | 21 69 C |
| Dell Way. W13 | 54 | 17 81 C |
| Dellwood Gdns. Ilf | 28 | 43 89 A |
| Delme Cres. SE3 | 77 | 40 76 D |
| Delmey Cl. Croy | 105 | 33 65 D |
| Deloraine St. SE8 | 76 | 37 76 A |
| Delorme St. W6 | 62 | 23 77 B |
| Delta Cl. Wor Pk | 102 | 21 65 C |
| Delta Gr. Nthlt | 53 | 11 82 B |
| Delta Rd. Wor Pk | 102 | 21 65 D |
| Delta St. E2 | 57 | 34 82 A |
| De Luci Rd. Eri | 67 | 50 78 C |
| De Lucy St. SE2 | 66 | 46 78 B |
| Delvan Cl. SE18 | 66 | 43 77 C |
| Delvers Mead. Dag | 52 | 50 85 A |
| Delverton Rd. SE17 | 63 | 31 78 D |
| Delvino Rd. SW6 | 73 | 25 76 A |
| Demesne Rd. Wall | 111 | 29 64 D |
| Demeta Cl. Wem | 34 | 20 86 C |
| De Montfort Rd. SW16 | 86 | 30 72 A |
| De Morgan Rd. SW6 | 73 | 25 75 B |
| Dempster Cl. Surb | 101 | 17 66 C |
| Dempster Rd. SW18 | 73 | 26 74 A |
| Denberry Dri. Sid | 90 | 46 72 D |
| Denbigh Cl. Chis | 99 | 42 70 B |
| Denbigh Cl. Horn | 30 | 54 89 D |
| Denbigh Cl. NW10 | 45 | 21 84 C |
| Denbigh Cl. Ruis | 31 | 09 86 B |

Dentigh Cl. Sutt 110 24 64 D
Denbigh Cl. W11 56 24 80 B
Denbigh Gdns. Rich 71 18 74 B
Denbigh Mews. SW1 10 29 78 A
Denbigh Pl. SW1 10 29 78 C
Denbigh Rd. E6 58 41 82 B
Denbigh Rd. Houn 70 13 76 D
Denbigh Rd. Sthl 53 12 81 D
Denbigh Rd. W11 56 24 80 B
Denbigh Rd. W13 54 16 81 D
Denbigh St. SW1 10 29 78 C
Denbigh Terr. W11 56 24 80 B
Denbridge Rd. Brom 99 42 69 D
Den Cl. Beck 98 38 68 C
Dendy St. SW12 86 28 73 C
Dene Ave. Houn 70 12 75 B
Dene Ave. Sid 90 46 73 B
Dene Cl. Brom 107 39 66 D
Dene Cl SE4 76 36 75 A
Dene Cl. Wor Pk 102 21 65 B
Dene Dri. Orp 108 46 65 D
Dene Gdns. Surb 101 16 65 A
Denehurst Gdns. NW4 35 23 88 C
Denehurst Gdns. Rich 72 19 75 C
Denehurst Gdns. Twick 82 14 73 B
Denehurst Gdns. W3 55 19 80 D
Dene Rd. N11 16 27 93 B
Dene Rd. Nthwd 19 08 91 B
Dene The. W13 54 16 81 B
Dene The. Wem 44 18 85 A
Denewood Cl. Barn 11 26 95 A
Denewood Rd. N6 36 27 87 B
Denford St. E10 65 39 78 D
Dengie Wlk (off Maldon Cl). N1 48 32 83 A
Denham Cl. Well 79 47 75 A
Denham Cres. Mit 96 27 68 D
Denham Dri. Ilf 40 44 88 C
Denham Rd. Felt 82 11 73 A
Denham Rd. N20 16 27 93 D
Denham St. SE10 65 40 78 C
Denham Way. Bark 51 45 83 B
Denholme Rd. W9 56 24 82 B
Denison Cl. N2 23 26 89 A
Denison Rd. Felt 81 09 71 B
Denison Rd. SW19 95 26 70 B
Denison Rd. W5 54 17 82 C
Denis Way. SW4 74 29 75 B
Denleigh Gdns. E Mol 101 15 67 C
Denleigh Gdns. N21 17 31 94 A
Denman Dri. Ashf 91 07 70 B
Denman Dri N. NW11 35 25 88 A
Denman Dri. NW11 35 25 88 A
Denman Dri S. NW11 35 25 88 A
Denman Rd. SE15 75 33 76 D
Denman St. W1 6 29 80 B
Denmark Ave. SW19 95 24 70 C
Denmark Ct. Mord 103 25 67 A
Denmark Gdns. Cars 104 27 65 D
Denmark Gr. N1 48 31 83 C
Denmark Hill Dri. NW9 22 22 89 A
Denmark Hill. SE5 75 32 75 B
Denmark Path. SE25 105 34 67 B
Denmark Pl. WC2 2 29 81 D
Denmark Rd. Brom 99 40 69 B
Denmark Rd. Cars 104 27 65 D
Denmark Rd. King 93 18 68 A
Denmark Rd. N8 25 31 89 C
Denmark Rd. NW6 46 24 83 D
Denmark Rd. SE25 105 34 67 B
Denmark Rd. SE5 75 32 76 C
Denmark Rd. SW19 95 23 70 B
Denmark Rd. Twick 82 14 72 D
Denmark Rd. W13 54 16 80 B
Denmark St. E11 39 39 86 C
Denmark St. E13 58 40 81 B
Denmark St. E13 58 40 81 B
Denmark St. N17 25 34 91 D
Denmark St. WC2 2 29 81 D
Denmead Rd. Croy 105 31 66 D
Denmead Way (off Pentridge St). SE15 63 33 77 D
Dennan Rd. Surb 101 18 66 D
Denner Rd. E4 18 37 93 A
Denne Terr. E8 48 33 83 B
Dennett Rd. Croy 105 31 66 A
Dennett's Gr. SE14 76 35 76 D
Dennett's Rd. SE14 76 35 76 A
Denning Ave. Croy 112 31 64 C
Denning Cl. Hamp 82 12 71 D
Denning Cl. NW8 1 26 82 A
Denning Rd. NW3 46 26 85 B
Dennington Park Rd. NW6 46 25 84 A
Dennis Ave. Wem 44 18 85 D
Dennis Cl. Ashf 91 08 70 D
Dennis Park Cres. SW20 95 24 69 A
Dennis Rd. E Mol 101 14 68 C
Dennis Reeve Cl. Mit 96 27 69 B
*Denny Cres. SE11 63 31 78 C
Denny Gdns. Dag 51 46 84 D
Denny Rd. N9 17 34 94 D
Denny St. SE11 63 31 78 C
Den Rd. Brom 98 38 68 C
Densham Rd. E15 50 39 83 A
Densole Cl. Beck 98 36 69 A
Densworth Gr. N9 18 35 93 A
Denton Cl. Barn 11 23 95 A
Denton. NW5 47 28 84 A
Denton Rd. N18 17 33 92 A
Denton Rd. N8 36 30 88 D
Denton Rd. Twick 71 17 74 D
Denton Rd. Well 67 47 77 C
Denton St. SW18 73 25 74 D
Denton Way. E5 38 35 86 D
Dents Rd. SW11 74 27 74 D
Denver Cl. Orp 108 45 67 C
Denver Rd. N16 37 33 87 A
Denyer St. SW3 9 27 78 A
Denzil Rd. NW10 45 21 85 D
Deodar Rd. SW15 73 24 75 C
Deodar Rd. SW15 73 24 75 C
Depot App. N3 23 25 90 B
Depot App. NW2 46 23 85 B
Depot Rd. Houn 70 14 75 B
Depot St SE5 63 32 77 B
Deptford Bridge. SE8 76 37 76 A
Deptford Bwy. SE8 76 37 76 A
Deptford Church St. SE8 64 37 77 C
Deptford Ferry Rd. E14 64 37 78 A
Deptford Green. SE8 64 37 77 A
Deptford High St. SE8 64 37 77 C
Deptford Strand. SE8 64 36 78 B
De Quincey Rd. N17 25 32 90 B
Derby Ave. Har 20 14 90 B
Derby Ave. N12 15 26 92 C
Derby Ave. Rom 41 50 88 C
Derby Gate. SW1 7 30 79 A
Derby Hill Cres. SE23 88 35 72 A
Derby Hill. SE23 88 35 72 A
Derby Rd. Croy 105 31 66 D
Derby Rd. E18 27 39 90 B
Derby Rd. E7 50 41 84 D
Derby Rd. E9 49 35 83 B
Derby Rd. Enf 14 35 95 A
Derby Rd. Grnf 43 13 83 B
Derby Rd. Houn 70 13 75 D
Derby Rd. N18 18 35 92 C
Derby Rd. Surb 102 19 66 C
Derby Rd. Sutt 110 24 63 B
Derby Rd. SW14 72 19 75 D
Derby Rd. SW19 95 25 70 C
Derbyshire St. E2 57 34 82 A
Derby St. W1 6 28 80 C
Dereham Pl. EC2 4 33 82 A
Dereham Rd. Bark 51 45 85 D
Derek Ave. Eps 109 19 64 C
Derek Ave. Wall 111 28 64 B
Derek Ave. Wem 45 19 84 D
Derey Ave. Horn 42 54 86 D
Dericote St. E8 48 34 83 B
Dering Pl. Croy 112 32 64 A
Dering Rd. Croy 112 32 64 A
Dering St. W1 2 28 81 D
Derinton Rd. SW17 86 28 71 A
Derley Rd. Sthl 59 11 79 C
Dermody Gdns. SE13 76 38 74 B
Dermody Rd. SE13 76 38 74 B
Deronda Rd. SE24 87 31 73 D
Deroy Cl. Cars 111 27 63 B
Derrick Ave. S Croy 112 32 62 C
Derrick Gdns. SE7 65 41 78 A
Derrick Rd. Beck 98 36 68 D
Derry Rd. Croy 104 30 65 C
Derry St. W8 62 25 79 B
Dersingham Ave. E12 51 43 85 C
Dersingham Rd. NW2 35 24 86 C
Derwent Ave. Barn 16 27 94 D
Derwent Ave. N18 17 32 92 D
Derwent Ave. NW7 22 20 91 B
Derwent Ave. NW9 34 21 88 A
Derwent Ave. Pnr 20 12 91 A
Derwent Ave. SW15 84 21 71 A
Derwent Ave. Uxb 31 07 86 C
Derwent Cres. Bexh 79 49 76 C
Derwent Cres. N20 15 26 93 C
Derwent Cres. Stan 21 17 90 C
Derwent Dri. Orp 108 44 66 B
Derwent Gdns. Ilf 27 42 89 C
Derwent Gdns. Wem 33 17 87 A
Derwent Gr. SE22 75 33 75 D
Derwent Rd. N13 16 30 93 D
Derwent Rd. N.Mal 103 23 67 D
Derwent Rd. SE20 97 34 69 D
Derwent Rd. Sthl 53 13 81 C
Derwent Rd. Twick 70 13 74 D
Derwent Rd. W5 60 17 79 C
Derwent Rise. NW9 34 21 88 C
Derwent St. E10 65 39 78 C
Derwentwater Rd. W3 55 20 80 C
Derwent Wlk. Wall 111 28 63 D
Desborough Cl. W2 56 25 81 B
Desenfans Rd. SE21 75 33 74 C
Desford Rd. E16 58 39 82 C
Desmond St. SE14 64 36 77 A
Despard Rd. N19 36 29 87 C
Dethick Ct. E3 49 36 83 A
Detling Rd. Brom 89 40 71 C
Detling Rd. Eri 67 50 77 D
Detmond Rd. E5 38 35 86 A
Devana End. Cars 104 27 65 D
Devas Rd. SW20 95 23 69 A
Devas St. E3 57 37 82 D
Devenay Rd. E15 50 39 84 D
Devenish Rd. SE2 66 46 79 A
Deventer Cres. SE22 75 33 74 A
De Vere Cotts. W8 5 26 79 C
De Vere Gdns. Ilf 39 42 87 D
De Vere Gdns. W8 5 26 79 A
Deverell St. SE1 8 32 79 D
De Vere Mews. W8 5 26 79 C
Devereux Ct. WC2 3 31 81 C
Devereux Rd. SW11 74 27 74 D
Deveron Way. Rom 30 51 90 A
Devizes St. N1 48 32 83 B
Devon Ave. Twick 82 14 73 C
Devon Cl. Grnf 44 17 83 A
Devoncroft Gdns. Twick 83 16 73 A
Devon Gdns. N4 37 31 88 D
Devonia Gdns. N18 25 32 91 A
Devonia Rd. N1 48 31 83 D
Devonport Gdns. Ilf 39 42 88 D
Devonport Rd. W12 61 22 79 B
Devonport St. E1 57 35 81 D
Devonport. W2 1 27 81 C
Devon Rd. Bark 51 45 83 A
Devon Rd. Sutt 110 24 62 A
Devon Rise. N2 23 26 89 D
Devonshire Ave. Dart 80 52 74 D
Devonshire Ave. Sutt 110 26 63 C
Devonshire Cl. E15 50 39 85 A
Devonshire Cl. W1 2 28 81 B
Devonshire Cres. NW7 23 23 91 D
Devonshire Dri. SE10 76 37 76 B
Devonshire Dri. Surb 101 17 65 B
Devonshire Gdns. N17 25 32 91 A
Devonshire Gdns. N21 17 32 94 A
Devonshire Gdns. W4 61 20 77 C
Devonshire Gr. SE15 63 34 77 B
Devonshire Hill La. N17 25 32 91 A
Devonshire House. Sutt 110 26 63 C
Devonshire Mews N. W1 2 28 81 B
Devonshire Mews S. W1 2 28 81 B
Devonshire Mews. W4 61 21 78 C
Devonshire Mews W. W1 2 28 81 B
Devonshire Pas. W4 61 21 77 A
Devonshire Pl Mews. W1 2 28 81 A
Devonshire Pl. NW2 35 25 86 C
Devonshire Pl. W1 2 28 82 C
Devonshire Rd. Bexh 79 48 75 C
Devonshire Rd. Croy 105 32 66 B
Devonshire Rd. E16 58 40 81 D
Devonshire Rd. E17 38 37 88 C
Devonshire Rd. Felt 82 12 71 A
Devonshire Rd. Har 32 14 88 D
Devonshire Rd. Horn 42 53 86 B
Devonshire Rd. Ilf 40 45 87 A
Devonshire Rd. N13 17 31 92 A
Devonshire Rd. N17 25 32 91 A
Devonshire Rd. N9 18 35 94 C
Devonshire Rd. NW7 23 23 91 D
Devonshire Rd. Orp 108 46 66 A
Devonshire Rd. Pnr 32 11 88 C
Devonshire Rd. Pnr 20 12 90 B
Devonshire Rd. SE23 88 35 73 C
Devonshire Rd. SE9 89 42 72 A
Devonshire Rd. Sthl 53 13 81 A
Devonshire Rd. Sutt 110 26 63 C
Devonshire Rd. SW19 96 27 70 C
Devonshire Rd. W4 61 21 78 C
Devonshire Rd. W5 60 17 79 C
Devonshire Rd. Wall 111 28 64 A
Devonshire Row. EC2 4 33 81 A
Devonshire Row Mews. W1 2 28 82 D
Devonshire Sq. Brom 99 40 68 D
Devonshire Sq. EC2 4 33 81 C
Devonshire St. W1 2 28 81 B
Devonshire St. W4 61 21 78 C
Devonshire Terr. W2 1 26 81 C
Devonshire Way. Croy 106 36 65 B
Devons Rd. E3 57 37 82 D
Devon St. SE15 63 34 77 B
Devon Waye. Houn 59 12 77 D
Devon Way. Eps 109 19 64 D
De Walden St. W1 2 28 81 A
Dewar St. SE15 75 34 75 A
Dewberry St. E14 58 38 81 A
Dewey Rd. Dag 52 50 84 A
Dewey Rd. N1 48 31 83 C
Dewey St. SW17 86 27 71 D
Dewhurst Rd. W14 62 23 79 D
Dewsbury Cl. Pnr 32 12 88 C
Dewsbury Cl. Rom 30 54 91 A
Dewsbury Gdns. Rom 30 53 91 B
Dewsbury Gdns. Wor Pk 102 22 65 C
Dewsbury Rd. NW10 45 22 85 C
Dewsbury Rd. Rom 30 54 91 A
Dewsbury Terr. NW1 47 28 83 B
Dexter Rd. Barn 11 23 95 D
Dexter Rd. SE24 75 31 75 C
Deyncourt Rd. N17 25 32 90 B
Deynecourt Gdns. E11 27 41 89 C
D'Eynsford Rd. SE5 75 32 76 B
Dhonau Hse. SE1 63 33 78 B
Diadem Ct. W1 2 29 81 D
Dial Walk The. W8 62 25 79 B
Diameter Rd. Orp 108 44 67 C
Diamond Rd. Ruis 43 12 85 A
Diamond St. SE15 63 33 77 C
Diamond Terr. SE10 76 38 76 A
Diana Cl. E18 27 40 90 B
Diana Gdns. Surb 101 18 65 B
Diana Rd. E17 26 36 89 B
Dianthus Cl. SE2 66 46 78 D
Diban Ave. Horn 42 52 86 D
Dibden St. N1 48 32 83 A
Dibdin Cl. Sutt 103 25 65 C
Dibdin Rd. Sutt 103 25 65 A
Dicey Ave. NW2 46 23 85 A
Dickens Ave. N3 23 26 90 A
Dickens Cl. Rich 83 18 72 A
Dickens Dri. Chis 100 44 70 A
Dickens La. N18 17 33 92 C
Dickenson Rd. N8 36 30 87 A
Dickenson's La. SE25 105 34 67 C
Dickenson's Pl. SE25 105 34 67 C
Dickens Rd. E6 50 41 83 D
Dickens Sq. SE1 8 32 79 C
Dickens St. SW8 74 28 76 D
Dickerage La. N Mal 94 20 68 A
Dickinson Rd. Felt 82 11 71 C
Dickson Fold. Pnr 20 11 89 D
Dickson Rd. SE9 77 42 75 A
Dick Turpin Way. Felt 69 09 75 D
Didsbury Cl. E6 50 42 83 B
Digby Cres. N4 37 32 86 A
Digby Estate. E2 57 35 82 A
Digby Gdns. Dag 52 49 83 A
Digby Pl. Croy 105 33 65 D
Digby Rd. Bark 51 45 84 D
Digby Rd. E9 49 35 84 B
Digby St. E2 57 35 82 A
Diggon St. E1 57 35 81 B
Dighton Rd. SW18 73 26 75 C
Dignum St. N1 48 31 83 C
Digswell St. N7 48 31 84 A
Dilhorne Cl. SE12 89 40 72 D
Dilke St. SW3 9 27 77 B
Dillon Pl. N7 36 30 86 D
Dillwyn Cl. SE26 88 36 71 A
Dilston Cl. Nthlt 53 11 82 A
Dilston Gr. SE16 64 35 78 A
Dilton Gdns. SW15 84 22 73 D
Dimes Pl. W6 61 22 78 B
Dimmock Dri. Grnf 43 14 85 D
Dimond Cl. E7 50 40 85 A
Dimsdale Dri. Enf 13 34 95 C
Dimsdale Dri. NW9 34 20 87 C
Dimsdale Wlk. E13 50 40 83 C
Dingle Gdns. E14 57 37 80 A
Dingle Rd. Ashf 81 07 71 D
Dingley La. SW16 86 29 72 B
Dingley Pl. EC1 4 32 82 A
Dingley Rd. EC1 4 32 82 A
Dingwall Ave. Croy 105 32 65 A
Dingwall Gdns. NW11 35 25 88 C
Dingwall Rd. Cars 111 27 62 B
Dingwall Rd. Croy 105 32 65 B
Dingwall Rd. SW18 85 26 73 A
Dinmont St. E2 48 34 83 D
Dinsdale Gdns. Barn 11 25 95 B
Dinsdale Gdns. SE25 105 33 67 A
Dinsdale Rd. SE3 65 39 77 B
Dinsmore Rd. SW12 86 28 73 B
Dinton Rd. King 93 18 70 D
Dirleton Rd. E15 50 39 83 B
Disbrowe Rd. W6 62 24 77 A
Dishforth La. NW9 22 21 90 A
Disney Pl. SE1 8 32 79 A
Disney St. SE1 8 32 79 A
Dison Cl. Enf 14 35 97 B
Disraeli Cl. W4 61 20 78 B
Disraeli Rd. E7 50 40 84 A
Disraeli Rd. NW10 45 20 83 D
Disraeli Rd. SW15 73 24 75 C
Disraeli Rd. W5 54 17 80 D
Diss St. E2 4 33 82 B
Distaff La. EC4 8 32 80 A
Distillery La. W6 62 23 78 C
Distillery Rd. W6 62 23 78 C
Distillery Wlk (off Pottery Rd). Brent 60 18 77 A
Distin St. SE11 63 31 78 A
District Rd. Wem 44 16 85 D
Ditch Alley. SE10 76 37 76 B
Ditchburn St. E14 58 38 80 A
Dittisham Rd. SE9 89 42 71 A
Ditton Cl. Surb 101 16 66 A
Ditton Grange Cl. Surb 101 17 66 D
Ditton Grange Dri. Surb 101 17 66 D
Ditton Hill Rd. Surb 101 17 66 C
Ditton Hill. Surb 101 17 65 B
Ditton Lawn. Surb 101 16 66 C
Ditton Rd. Bexh 79 48 74 A
Ditton Rd. Sthl 59 12 78 D
Ditton Rd. Surb 101 18 66 C
Ditton Reach. Surb 101 16 67 D
Divis Way. SW15 72 22 74 D
Dixon Pl. W Wick 106 37 66 D
Dixon Rd. SE14 76 36 76 A
Dixon Rd. SE25 97 33 68 B
*Dixon's Alley. SE16 63 34 79 B
Dobbin Cl. Har 21 16 90 C
Dobell Rd. SE9 77 42 74 B
Dobree Ave. NW10 45 22 84 D
Dobson Cl. NW6 46 26 84 D
Doby Ct. EC4 8 32 80 A
Dockhead. SE1 8 33 79 B
Dockley Rd. SE16 63 34 79 C
Dock Rd. Brent 60 17 77 D
Dock Rd. E16 58 39 80 B
Dock St. E1 57 34 80 A
Dockwell Cl. Felt 69 10 75 C
Docwra's Blgs. N1 48 33 84 A
Dodbrooke Rd. SE27 87 31 72 D
Doddington Gr. SE17 63 31 78 D
Doddington Pl. SE17 63 31 77 B
Dodsley Pl. N9 18 35 93 C
Dodson St. SE1 7 31 79 A
Dod St. E14 57 37 81 C
Doel Cl. SW19 95 26 70 C
Doggett Rd. SE6 88 37 73 A
Doggett's Cnr. Horn 42 54 86 B
Doggetts Ct. Barn 12 27 95 A
Dog Kennel Hill. SE22 75 33 75 A
Dog La. NW10 45 21 85 A
Doherty Rd. E13 58 40 82 C
Dolben St. SE1 7 31 80 D
Dolby Rd. SW6 73 24 76 D
Dolland St. SE11 10 30 78 D
Dollis Ave. N3 23 24 90 B
Dollis Brook Wlk. Barn 11 24 95 C
Dollis Cres. Ruis 32 11 87 C
Dollis Hill Ave. NW2 34 22 86 D
Dollis Hill La. NW2 34 22 86 C
Dollis Park. N3 23 24 90 B
Dollis Rd. N3 23 24 91 D
Dollis Valley Way. Barn 11 24 95 D
Dolman Rd. W4 61 20 78 B
Dolman St. SW4 74 30 75 D
Dolphin App. Rom 30 51 89 D
Dolphin Cl. Surb 101 17 67 B
Dolphin La. E14 57 37 80 B
Dolphin Rd. Nthlt 43 13 83 C
Dolphin Rd. Sun 91 09 69 A
Dolphin Road N. Sun 91 09 69 A
Dolphin Road S. Sun 91 09 69 A
Dolphin Road W. Sun 91 09 69 A
Dombey St. WC1 3 30 81 B
Dome Hill Park. SE26 87 33 71 A
Domett Cl. SE5 75 32 75 D
Domingo St. EC1 4 32 82 C
Dominion Dr. Rom 29 49 91 B
Dominion Rd. Croy 105 33 66 B
Dominion Rd. Sthl 59 12 79 C
Dominion St. EC2 4 32 81 B
Domonic Dri. SE9 90 43 72 D
Domville Gr. SE5 63 33 78 D
Donald Dri. Rom 41 47 88 A
Donald Rd. Croy 104 30 67 D
Donald Rd. E13 50 40 83 B
Donaldson Rd. NW6 46 24 83 B
Donaldson Rd. SE18 78 43 76 A
Doncaster Dri. Nthlt 43 12 85 D
Doncaster Gdns. N4 37 32 88 C
Doncaster Gdns. Nthlt 43 12 85 D
Doncaster Rd. N9 17 34 94 B
Doncaster Way. Horn 42 54 86 D
Doncel Ct. E4 18 38 94 B
Donegal St. N1 47 30 83 D
Doneraile St. SW6 73 23 76 B
Dongola Rd. E13 58 40 82 B
Dongola Rd. N17 25 33 89 A
Dongola Road W. E13 58 40 82 B
Donington Ave. Ilf 40 44 88 A
Donkey La. Enf 13 34 97 C
Donne Ct. SE24 75 32 74 C
Donnefield Ave. Edg 21 18 91 C
Donne Pl. Mit 96 28 68 D
Donne Pl. SW3 9 27 78 A
Donne Rd. Dag 41 47 86 A
Donnington Rd. Har 33 17 88 D
Donnington Rd. NW10 45 22 83 B
Donnington Rd. Wor Pk 102 22 65 A
Donnybrook Rd. SW16 96 29 70 D
Donovan Ave. N10 24 29 90 C
Donovan Cl. Eps 109 20 62 D
Don Phelan Cl. SE5 75 32 76 B
Don Phelan Cl. SE5 63 32 77 D
Don Way. Rom 30 51 91 C
Doone Cl. Tedd 93 16 70 A
Doon St. SE1 7 31 80 C
Doral Way. Cars 111 27 64 D
Doran Gr. SE18 66 44 77 D
Doran Wlk. E15 49 38 84 C
Dora Rd. SW19 85 25 71 A
Dora St. E14 57 36 81 D
Dorchester Ave. Har 32 14 88 C
Dorchester Ave. N13 17 32 92 A
Dorchester Cl. Nthlt 43 13 85 D
Dorchester Ct. N14 16 28 94 B
Dorchester Ct. SE24 75 32 74 A
Dorchester Dri. Felt 69 09 74 C
Dorchester Dri. SE24 75 32 74 A
Dorchester Gdns. E4 18 37 92 A
Dorchester Gdns. NW11 23 25 89 C
Dorchester Gr. W4 61 21 78 D
Dorchester Mews. N Mal 94 20 68 D
Dorchester Rd. Mord 103 26 66 A
Dorchester Rd. Nthlt 43 13 85 D
Dorchester Rd. Wor Pk 103 23 66 C
Dorchester Way. Har 33 18 88 D
Dorchester Way. Hay 53 11 81 C
Dorcis Ave. Bexh 79 48 76 C
Dordrecht Rd. W3 61 21 79 A
Dore Ave. E12 51 43 85 C
Doreen Ave. NW9 34 20 87 D
Dore Gdns. Mord 103 26 66 A
Dorell Cl. Sthl 53 12 81 B
Dorian Rd. Horn 42 52 87 C
Doria Rd. SW6 73 24 76 D
Doric Way. NW1 2 29 82 B
Dorien Rd. SW20 95 23 69 D
Doris Ave. Eri 79 50 76 A
Doris Rd. Ashf 91 08 70 B
Doris Rd. E7 50 40 84 C
Dorking Cl. SE8 64 36 77 B
Dorking Cl. Wor Pk 103 23 65 B
Dorlcote Rd. SW18 86 27 73 A
Dormans Cl. Nthwd 19 08 91 D
Dorman Way. NW8 46 26 83 B
Dorman Wlk. NW10 45 20 84 B
Dormay St. SW18 73 25 74 B
Dormer Cl. Barn 11 23 95 B
Dormer Cl. E15 50 39 84 B
Dormer's Ave. Sthl 53 13 81 C
Dormers Rise. Sthl 53 13 81 D
Dormer's Wells La. Sthl 53 13 80 B
Dormywood. Ruis 31 09 88 B
Dornberg Cl. SE3 65 40 77 C
Dornberg Rd. SE3 65 40 77 D
Dorncliffe Rd. SW6 73 24 76 C
Dorney Rise. Orp 100 45 68 D
Dornfell St. NW6 46 24 85 D
Dornton Rd. S Croy 112 33 64 C
Dornton Rd. SW12 86 29 72 A
Dorothy Ave. Wem 44 18 84 C
Dorothy Evans Cl. Bexh 79 49 75 D
Dorothy Gdns. Dag 51 46 85 B
Dorothy Rd. SW11 74 27 75 B
Dorrell Pl. SW9 74 30 75 B

| Name | Page | Grid |
|---|---|---|
| Dorrell Pl. SW9 | 75 | 31 75 C |
| Dorrien Wlk. SW16 | 86 | 29 72 B |
| Dorrington Ct. SE25 | 97 | 33 69 C |
| Dorrington Gdns. Horn | 42 | 53 87 D |
| Dorrington St. EC1 | 3 | 31 81 A |
| Dorrit Mews. N18 | 17 | 33 92 C |
| Dorrit St. SE1 | 8 | 32 79 A |
| Dorrit Way. Chis | 100 | 44 70 A |
| Dors Cl. NW9 | 34 | 20 87 D |
| Dorset Ave. Rom | 30 | 50 89 B |
| Dorset Ave. Sthl | 59 | 13 78 A |
| Dorset Ave. Well | 78 | 45 75 D |
| Dorset Cl. NW1 | 1 | 27 81 B |
| Dorset Ct. N1 | 23 | 33 84 C |
| Dorset Dri. Edg | 21 | 18 91 B |
| Dorset Gdns. Mit | 96 | 30 68 D |
| Dorset Mews. SW1 | 6 | 28 79 D |
| Dorset Pl. E15 | 49 | 38 84 B |
| Dorset Pl. SW1 | 10 | 29 78 D |
| Dorset Rd. Beck | 98 | 35 68 B |
| Dorset Rd. E7 | 50 | 41 84 C |
| Dorset Rd. Har | 32 | 14 88 D |
| Dorset Rd. Mit | 96 | 27 69 C |
| Dorset Rd. N15 | 25 | 32 89 D |
| Dorset Rd. N22 | 24 | 30 90 A |
| Dorset Rd. SE9 | 89 | 42 72 A |
| Dorset Rd. Sutt | 110 | 25 62 C |
| Dorset Rd. SW19 | 95 | 25 69 C |
| Dorset Rd. SW8 | 10 | 30 77 D |
| Dorset Rd. W5 | 60 | 17 79 C |
| Dorset Rise. EC4 | 3 | 31 81 D |
| Dorset Sq. Eps | 109 | 20 62 D |
| Dorset Sq. NW1 | 1 | 27 82 D |
| Dorset St. W1 | 2 | 28 81 A |
| Dorset Waye. Houn | 59 | 12 77 D |
| Dorset Way. Twick | 82 | 14 73 D |
| Dorville Cres. W6 | 61 | 22 79 D |
| Dorville Rd. SE12 | 77 | 40 04 A |
| Douai Gr. Hamp | 92 | 14 69 A |
| Doughty Ct. E1 | 57 | 34 80 D |
| Doughty Mews. WC1 | 3 | 30 82 D |
| Doughty St. WC1 | 3 | 30 82 D |
| Douglas Ave. E17 | 26 | 37 90 A |
| Douglas Ave. Rom | 30 | 54 90 C |
| Douglas Ave. Wem | 44 | 18 84 C |
| Douglas Cl. Wall | 111 | 30 63 A |
| Douglas Cres. Hay | 53 | 11 82 D |
| Douglas Dri. Croy | 106 | 37 65 C |
| Douglas Pl. E14 | 58 | 38 78 C |
| Douglas Pl. SW1 | 10 | 29 78 D |
| Douglas Rd. E16 | 58 | 40 81 A |
| Douglas Rd. Horn | 42 | 51 88 D |
| Douglas Rd. Houn | 70 | 13 75 B |
| Douglas Rd. Ilf | 28 | 46 88 C |
| Douglas Rd. King | 94 | 19 69 D |
| Douglas Rd. N1 | 4 | 32 84 C |
| Douglas Rd. N22 | 25 | 31 90 A |
| Douglas Rd. NW6 | 2 | 24 83 B |
| Douglas Rd. Surb | 101 | 18 66 D |
| Douglas Rd. Well | 78 | 46 76 B |
| Douglas Sq. Mord | 103 | 25 67 C |
| Douglas St. SW1 | 10 | 29 78 B |
| Douglas Terr. E17 | 26 | 36 90 A |
| Douglas Way. SE8 | 64 | 36 77 D |
| Doulton Mews. NW3 | 46 | 25 84 B |
| Dounesforth Gdns. SW18 | 85 | 25 73 D |
| Douro Pl. W8 | 62 | 25 79 D |
| Douro St. E3 | 49 | 37 83 C |
| Dove Cl. Nthlt | 53 | 11 82 D |
| Dovecote Ave. N22 | 25 | 31 89 A |
| Dovedale Ave. Har | 33 | 17 88 D |
| Dovedale Ave. Ilf | 28 | 43 90 C |
| Dovedale Cl. Well | 78 | 46 76 C |
| Dovedale Rd. SE22 | 75 | 34 74 D |
| Dovedale Rise. Mit | 96 | 27 70 D |
| Dove House Mead. Bark | 51 | 37 93 A |
| Dovehouse St. SW3 | 9 | 27 78 C |
| Dove Mews. SW5 | 62 | 26 78 C |
| Dove Park. Pnr | 13 | 91 C |
| Dover Cl. Rom | 29 | 50 90 C |
| Dover Cotts. Surb | 101 | 17 67 C |
| Dovercourt Ave. Th Hth | 103 | 31 68 C |
| Dovercourt La. Sutt | 103 | 33 74 D |
| Dovercourt Rd. SE22 | 75 | 30 73 A |
| Dove Rd. N1 | 4 | 33 84 C |
| Doverfield Rd. SW2 | 86 | 30 73 A |
| Dover House Rd. SW15 | 72 | 21 75 C |
| Doridge Gdns. N13 | 17 | 31 92 B |
| Dove Row. E2 | 49 | 34 83 A |
| Dover Park Dri. SW15 | 72 | 22 74 D |
| Dover Rd. E12 | 39 | 41 86 A |
| Dover Rd. N9 | 18 | 35 93 A |
| Dover Rd. Rom | 41 | 48 88 C |
| Dover Rd. SE18 | 78 | 43 76 A |
| Dover Rd. SE19 | 97 | 32 70 B |
| Dover Rd. Well | 78 | 44 76 D |
| Dover St. W1 | 6 | 29 80 C |
| Dover Yd. W1 | 6 | 29 80 C |
| Doves Cl. Brom | 107 | 33 65 A |
| Dovet Cl. SW8 | 74 | 30 76 B |
| Doveton Rd. S Croy | 112 | 32 64 D |
| Doveton St. E1 | 57 | 35 82 C |
| Dove Wlk. SW1 | 9 | 28 79 A |
| Dowanhill Rd. SE6 | 88 | 38 73 D |
| Dowdeswell Cl. SW15 | 72 | 21 75 C |
| Dowding Pl. Stan | 21 | 16 91 A |
| Dower Ave. Wall | 111 | 27 81 B |
| Dowgate Hill. EC4 | 8 | 32 80 B |
| Dowland St. W10 | 56 | 50 89 D |
| Dowlas St. SE5 | 63 | 33 77 C |
| Dowman Cl. SW19 | 95 | 25 70 D |
| Downage. NW4 | 23 | 23 89 A |
| Downbank Ave. Bexh | 79 | 50 76 D |
| Down Barns Rd. Ruis | 32 | 11 86 D |
| Downderry Rd. Brom | 89 | 39 71 A |
| Downe Cl. Well | 78 | 47 77 C |
| Downend. SE18 | 66 | 43 77 D |
| Downe Rd. Mit | 96 | 32 89 D |
| Downes Cl. Twick | 71 | 16 74 D |
| Downes Ct. N21 | 17 | 31 91 D |
| Downfield Cl. W9 | 56 | 25 82 D |
| Downfield. Wor Pk | 102 | 22 66 C |
| Down Hall Rd. King | 93 | 17 69 B |
| Downham Cl. Rom | 29 | 49 91 C |
| Downham Rd. N1 | 4 | 33 84 C |
| Downham Way. Brom | 89 | 40 71 A |
| Downhills Ave. N17 | 25 | 32 89 B |
| Downhills Park Rd. N17 | 25 | 31 89 A |
| Downhills Way. N17 | 25 | 32 89 A |
| Downing Cl. Har | 20 | 14 89 A |
| Downing Dri. Grnf | 44 | 15 83 A |
| Downing Rd. Dag | 52 | 40 04 A |
| Downing St. SW1 | 7 | 30 79 A |
| Downland Cl. N20 | 15 | 24 94 C |
| Downleys Cl. SE9 | 89 | 42 72 A |
| Downman Rd. SE9 | 77 | 42 78 B |
| Down Pl. W6 | 61 | 22 78 D |
| Down Rd. Tedd | 93 | 16 70 B |
| Downs Ave. Chis | 89 | 42 71 D |
| Downs Ave. Pnr | 32 | 12 87 B |
| Downs Bridge Rd. Beck | 98 | 38 69 B |
| Downsell Rd. E15 | 49 | 38 85 B |
| Downsfield Rd. E17 | 26 | 36 88 D |
| Downshall Ave. Ilf | 40 | 45 89 A |
| Downs Hill. Beck | 98 | 38 69 B |
| Downshire Hill. NW3 | 46 | 25 84 C |
| Downside Cl. SW19 | 95 | 26 70 A |
| Downside Cres. NW3 | 47 | 25 84 B |
| Downside Cres. W3 | 54 | 19 69 D |
| Downside Rd. Sutt | 111 | 24 63 A |
| Downside. Twick | 83 | 15 72 D |
| Downside Wlk. Nthlt | 53 | 12 82 C |
| Downs La. E5 | 48 | 34 85 B |
| Downs Park Rd. E5 | 48 | 34 85 B |
| Downs Park Rd. E8 | 48 | 34 85 C |
| Downs Rd. Beck | 98 | 38 69 C |
| Downs Rd. E5 | 48 | 34 85 B |
| Downs Rd. Enf | 13 | 35 96 C |
| Downs Rd. N16 | 48 | 33 85 C |
| Downs Rd. Sutt | 110 | 25 62 D |
| Downs Rd. Th Hth | 97 | 33 69 A |
| Down St. E Mol | 92 | 11 72 D |
| Downs. The. SW20 | 95 | 23 70 D |
| Down St Mews. W1 | 6 | 29 80 A |
| Down St. W1 | 6 | 29 80 D |
| Downsview Gdns. SE19 | 97 | 32 70 C |
| Downs View. Islw | 71 | 16 76 A |
| Downsview Rd. SE19 | 97 | 32 70 C |
| Downsway The. Sutt | 110 | 24 62 A |
| Downton Ave. SW2 | 86 | 30 72 B |
| Downway. N12 | 24 | 27 91 C |
| Dowrey St. N1 | 4 | 31 83 A |
| Dowsett St. N17 | 25 | 33 90 D |
| Doyce St. SE1 | 8 | 32 79 A |
| Doyle Gdns. NW10 | 45 | 22 83 D |
| Doyle Rd. SE25 | 97 | 33 68 C |
| D'Oyley St. SW1 | 9 | 28 78 A |
| Doynton St. N19 | 36 | 28 86 B |
| Draco St. SE17 | 63 | 32 77 A |
| Dragon Yd. WC2 | 3 | 30 81 C |
| Dragoon Rd. SE8 | 64 | 36 78 D |
| Dragor Rd. NW10 | 55 | 19 82 C |
| Drakefell Rd. SE14 | 76 | 35 75 A |
| Drakefell Rd. SE4 | 76 | 36 75 A |
| Drakefield Rd. SW17 | 86 | 28 72 D |
| Drakeley Ct. N5 | 48 | 32 85 B |
| Drake Rd. Chess | 109 | 19 64 C |
| Drake Rd. Croy | 104 | 30 66 B |
| Drake Rd. Har | 32 | 12 86 B |
| Drake Rd. Mit | 104 | 28 67 C |
| Drake Rd. SE4 | 76 | 37 75 A |
| Drake St. Enf | 13 | 32 97 B |
| Drake St. WC1 | 3 | 30 81 C |
| Drakes Dri. Nthwd | 19 | 07 90 B |
| Drakes Wlk. E6 | 50 | 42 83 B |
| Drakewood Rd. SW16 | 96 | 29 70 D |
| Draper Cl. Belv | 67 | 44 78 B |
| Drapers Gdns. EC2 | 4 | 32 81 D |
| Drapers Rd. E15 | 49 | 38 85 B |
| Drapers Rd. Enf | 13 | 31 97 B |
| Drappers Way. SE16 | 63 | 34 78 A |
| Drawell Cl. SE18 | 66 | 45 78 C |
| Drax Ave. SW20 | 94 | 22 70 C |
| Draxmont. SW19 | 95 | 24 70 A |
| Draycot Rd. E11 | 39 | 40 87 B |
| Draycott Ave. Har | 33 | 17 88 C |
| Draycott Ave. SW3 | 9 | 27 78 A |
| Draycott Cl. Har | 33 | 16 88 D |
| Draycott Mews. SW6 | 73 | 24 76 D |
| Draycott Pl. SW3 | 9 | 27 78 B |
| Draycott Terr. SW3 | 9 | 27 78 B |
| Drayford Cl. W9 | 56 | 24 82 D |
| Dray Gdns. SW2 | 74 | 30 74 B |
| Drayson Mews. W8 | 62 | 25 79 A |
| Drayton Ave. Orp | 108 | 43 66 D |
| Drayton Ave. W13 | 54 | 16 80 A |
| Drayton Bridge Rd. W13 | 54 | 16 81 C |
| Drayton Bridge Rd. W7 | 54 | 15 80 B |
| Drayton Gdns. N21 | 17 | 31 91 A |
| Drayton Gdns. SW10 | 62 | 26 78 C |
| Drayton Gdns. W13 | 54 | 16 80 A |
| Drayton Green Rd. W13 | 54 | 16 80 A |
| Drayton Green. W13 | 54 | 16 80 A |
| Drayton Gr. W13 | 54 | 16 80 A |
| Drayton Park. N5 | 48 | 31 85 A |
| Drayton Rd. Croy | 105 | 31 65 B |
| Drayton Rd. E11 | 38 | 38 87 D |
| Drayton Rd. N17 | 25 | 33 90 C |
| Drayton Rd. NW10 | 45 | 21 83 B |
| Drayton Rd. W13 | 54 | 16 80 B |
| Drayton Waye. Har | 33 | 16 88 D |
| Dreadnought St. SE10 | 65 | 37 79 C |
| Dresden Cl. NW3 | 46 | 23 78 C |
| Dresden Rd. N19 | 36 | 16 70 B |
| Dressington Ave. SE13 | 76 | 37 74 C |
| Drew Gdns. Grnf | 44 | 15 84 B |
| Drew Rd. E16 | 58 | 38 85 B |
| Drewstead Rd. SW16 | 86 | 28 72 B |
| Driffield Rd. E3 | 49 | 36 83 C |
| Drift The. Brom | 107 | 41 65 D |
| Driftway The. Mit | 96 | 28 69 A |
| Drinkwater Rd. Har | 32 | 13 86 B |
| Driver's Bldgs. E1 | 57 | 35 82 D |
| Driveway The. Ashf | 91 | 08 70 D |
| Drive The. Bark | 51 | 45 84 D |
| Drive The. Barn | 51 | 24 96 A |
| Drive The. Barn | 51 | 26 95 C |
| Drive The. Beck | 98 | 37 69 A |
| Drive The. Bex | 79 | 47 74 C |
| Drive The. Chis | 100 | 45 68 B |
| Drive The. Chis | 100 | 45 69 A |
| Drive The. E17 | 26 | 37 89 B |
| Drive The. E18 | 27 | 40 89 A |
| Drive The. E4 | 18 | 38 94 B |
| Drive The. Enf | 13 | 32 97 B |
| Drive The. Eps | 109 | 21 63 B |
| Drive The. Eri | 67 | 49 77 D |
| Drive The. Felt | 82 | 11 73 A |
| Drive The. Har | 32 | 13 87 A |
| Drive The. Houn | 70 | 14 76 B |
| Drive The. Ilf | 39 | 42 87 B |
| Drive The. Islw | 70 | 14 76 D |
| Drive The. King | 94 | 20 70 C |
| Drive The. Mord | 103 | 26 67 B |
| Drive The. N11 | 23 | 25 91 B |
| Drive The. N2 | 36 | 27 88 B |
| Drive The. N3 | 23 | 25 91 C |
| Drive The. N7 | 47 | 30 84 B |
| Drive The. Nthwd | 19 | 07 90 A |
| Drive The. NW11 | 35 | 24 87 A |
| Drive The. Orp | 108 | 45 65 B |
| Drive The. Rom | 30 | 50 91 D |
| Drive The. Sid | 101 | 45 73 C |
| Drive The. Surb | 101 | 18 66 A |
| Drive The. SW20 | 95 | 23 70 C |
| Drive The. Th Hth | 97 | 33 68 D |
| Drive The. W3 | 55 | 19 80 D |
| Drive The. Wall | 111 | 29 62 C |
| Drive The. Wem | 34 | 19 85 C |
| Drive The. W Wick | 106 | 39 67 B |
| Dr Johnsons Ave. SW17 | 86 | 28 72 B |
| Droitwich Cl. SE26 | 87 | 36 71 B |
| Dromey Gdns. Har | 21 | 12 86 B |
| Dromore Rd. SW15 | 73 | 28 67 C |
| Dronfield Gdns. Dag | 52 | 47 85 C |
| Droop St. W10 | 56 | 07 90 B |
| Drover La. SE15 | 63 | 32 97 B |
| Drovers' Rd. S Croy | 112 | 32 64 D |
| Druce Rd. SE21 | 75 | 29 70 D |
| Druid St. SE1 | 8 | 33 79 B |
| Druids Way. Brom | 98 | 38 68 D |
| Drumaline Ridge. Wor Pk | 102 | 21 65 A |
| Drummond Ave. Rom | 29 | 50 89 D |
| Drummond Cres. NW1 | 2 | 29 82 B |
| Drummond Dri. Stan | 32 | 65 A |
| Drummond Pl. E11 | 39 | 41 88 C |
| Drummond Rd. Rom | 29 | 50 89 D |
| Drummond Rd. SE16 | 63 | 34 79 D |
| Drummond St. NW1 | 2 | 29 82 C |
| Drum St. E1 | 4 | 33 81 D |
| Drury Lane. WC2 | 3 | 30 81 C |
| Drury Rd. Har | 32 | 14 87 A |
| Dryad St. SW15 | 73 | 23 75 B |
| Dryburgh Gdns. NW9 | 22 | 19 89 A |
| Dryburgh Rd. SW15 | 73 | 23 75 A |
| Dryden Ave. W7 | 54 | 15 81 D |
| Dryden Cl. Ilf | 28 | 45 91 B |
| Dryden Ct. King | 83 | 17 71 B |
| Dryden Ct. SE11 | 63 | 31 78 B |
| Dryden Rd. Enf | 13 | 33 95 D |
| Dryden Rd. Har | 21 | 15 90 B |
| Dryden Rd. SW19 | 95 | 26 70 A |
| Dryden Rd. Well | 78 | 45 76 B |
| Dryden St. WC2 | 3 | 30 81 C |
| Dryden Way. Orp | 108 | 46 66 C |
| Dryfield Cl. NW10 | 45 | 20 84 A |
| Dryfield Rd. Edg | 22 | 20 91 A |
| Dryfield Wlk. SE8 | 64 | 37 77 A |
| Dryhill Rd. Belv | 67 | 48 77 B |
| Drylands Rd. N8 | 36 | 30 88 D |
| Drysdale Ave. E4 | 14 | 37 95 D |
| Drysdale Pl. Nthwd | 19 | 09 91 C |
| Drysdale Pl. N1 | 4 | 33 82 A |
| Drysdale St. N1 | 4 | 33 82 A |
| Du Burstow Terr. W7 | 60 | 15 79 A |
| Ducal St. E2 | 4 | 33 82 B |
| Ducan Cl. Barn | 11 | 26 96 C |
| Du Cane Ct. SW12 | 86 | 28 73 C |
| Du Cane Rd. W12 | 55 | 18 81 C |
| Duchess Mews. W1 | 2 | 29 81 B |
| Duchess of Bedford's Wlk. W8 | 62 | 25 79 A |
| Duchess St. W1 | 2 | 29 81 B |
| Duchy St. SE1 | 7 | 31 80 C |
| Ducie St. SW4 | 74 | 30 75 D |
| Duckett Rd. N4 | 37 | 31 88 D |
| Ducketts Rd. Dart | 80 | 51 74 B |
| Duckett St. E1 | 57 | 36 81 A |
| Ducking Stool Ct. Rom | 30 | 51 89 C |
| Duck La. W1 | 2 | 29 81 D |
| Duck Lees La. E14 | 14 | 36 96 C |
| Duck's Hill Rd. Nthwd | 19 | 07 90 B |
| Ducks Hill Rd. Ruis | 19 | 08 89 C |
| Duck's Wlk. Twick | 71 | 17 74 A |
| Du Cros Dri. Stan | 21 | 17 91 B |
| Du Cros Rd. W3 | 55 | 20 80 C |
| Dudden Hill La. NW10 | 45 | 21 85 D |
| Duddington Cl. SE9 | 89 | 41 71 B |
| Dudley Ave. Har | 21 | 17 89 A |
| Dudley Dri. Mord | 103 | 24 66 A |
| Dudley Gdns. Har | 32 | 14 87 D |
| Dudley Gdns. Rom | | 11 73 A |
| Dudley Gdns. W13 | 60 | 16 79 B |
| Dudley Rd. E17 | 26 | 37 90 C |
| Dudley Rd. Felt | 81 | 08 73 D |
| Dudley Rd. Har | 32 | 14 86 A |
| Dudley Rd. Ilf | 51 | 43 85 B |
| Dudley Rd. King | 93 | 18 68 B |
| Dudley Rd. N3 | 23 | 25 90 D |
| Dudley Rd. NW6 | 2 | 24 83 D |
| Dudley Rd. Rich | 71 | 18 76 D |
| Dudley Rd. Sthl | 59 | 11 79 D |
| Dudley Rd. SW19 | 95 | 25 70 A |
| Dudley St. W2 | 1 | 26 81 B |
| Dudlington Rd. E5 | 48 | 35 86 A |
| Dudmaston Mews. SW3 | 62 | 26 78 D |
| Dudsbury Rd. Dart | 80 | 52 74 B |
| Dudsbury Rd. Sid | 100 | 46 70 B |
| Dudset La. Houn | 68 | 10 76 A |
| Dufferin Ave. EC1 | 4 | 32 82 D |
| Dufferin St. EC1 | 4 | 32 81 D |
| Duffield Cl. Har | 33 | 15 88 B |
| Duff St. E14 | 57 | 37 81 D |
| Dufour's Pl. W1 | 2 | 29 81 C |
| Duke Humphrey Rd. SE3 | 77 | 38 77 B |
| Duke of Cambridge Cl. Twick | 70 | 14 72 D |
| Duke of Edinburgh Rd. Sutt | 103 | 26 65 B |
| Duke of Wellington Pl. SW1 | 6 | 28 79 A |
| Duke of York St. SW1 | 6 | 29 80 C |
| Duke Rd. Ilf | 28 | 44 89 D |
| Duke Rd. W4 | 61 | 20 78 D |
| kes Ave. Edg | 21 | 18 91 B |
| Dukes Ave. Har | 21 | 15 89 C |
| Dukes Ave. Houn | 70 | 12 75 C |
| Dukes Ave. King | 83 | 17 71 B |
| Dukes Ave. N10 | 24 | 28 89 A |
| Dukes Ave. N3 | 23 | 25 90 B |
| Dukes Ave. N Mal | 94 | 21 68 A |
| Dukes Ave. Nthlt | 43 | 12 84 C |
| Dukes Ave. Rich | 83 | 17 71 A |
| Dukes Ave. W4 | 61 | 20 78 D |
| Dukes Cl. Ashf | 81 | 08 71 A |
| Dukes Cl. Hamp | 82 | 12 71 D |
| Dukes Ct. E6 | 51 | 43 83 A |
| Duke's Head Yd. N6 | 36 | 28 87 D |
| Dukes La. W8 | 62 | 25 79 B |
| Dukes Mews. N10 | 24 | 28 89 B |
| Duke's Mews. W1 | 2 | 28 81 C |
| Duke's Pas. E17 | 26 | 38 89 A |
| Dukes Rd. W3 | 55 | 19 82 C |
| Duke's Rd. WC1 | 2 | 29 82 B |
| Duke St Hill. SE1 | 8 | 32 80 D |
| Dukesthorpe Rd. SE26 | 88 | 35 71 B |
| Duke St. Rich | 71 | 17 74 B |
| Duke St St James's. SW1 | 6 | 29 80 C |
| Duke St. Sutt | 110 | 26 64 B |
| Duke St. W1 | 2 | 28 81 C |
| Dukes Way. W.Wick | 107 | 39 65 C |
| Duke's Yd. W1 | 2 | 28 81 C |
| Dulas St. N4 | 37 | 31 87 C |
| Dulford St. W11 | 56 | 24 80 A |
| Dulka Rd. SW11 | 74 | 27 74 B |
| Dulverton Rd. Rom | 30 | 53 91 B |
| Dulverton Rd. Ruis | 31 | 10 86 A |
| Dulverton Rd. SE9 | 90 | 44 72 B |
| Dulwich Common. SE21 | 87 | 33 73 D |
| Dulwich Rd. SE24 | 75 | 31 74 D |
| Dulwich Village. SE21 | 75 | 33 74 C |
| Dulwich Wood Ave. SE19 | 87 | 33 71 C |
| Dulwich Wood Park. SE19 | 87 | 33 71 D |
| Dumbarton Ct. SW2 | 74 | 30 74 D |
| Dumbarton Rd. SW2 | 74 | 30 74 C |
| Dumbleton Cl. King | 94 | 19 69 B |
| Dumbreck Rd. SE9 | 78 | 43 75 A |
| Dumont Rd. N16 | 37 | 33 86 C |
| Dumpton Pl. NW1 | 47 | 28 84 C |
| Dunbar Ave. Beck | 98 | 36 68 C |
| Dunbar Ave. Dag | 52 | 49 86 C |
| Dunbar Ave. SW16 | 97 | 31 69 C |
| Dunbar Ct. Sutt | 110 | 26 64 D |
| Dunbar Gdns. Dag | 52 | 49 85 D |
| Dunbar Rd. E7 | 50 | 40 84 A |
| Dunbar Rd. N22 | 25 | 30 90 A |
| Dunbar Rd. N Mal | 94 | 20 68 C |
| Dunbar St. SE27 | 87 | 31 72 C |
| Dunblane Rd. SE9 | 77 | 42 76 C |
| Dunboyne Rd. NW3 | 47 | 27 85 D |
| Dunbridge St. E2 | 57 | 34 82 D |
| Duncan Ct. N21 | 17 | 31 94 D |
| Duncan Gr. W3 | 55 | 21 81 C |
| Duncannon St. WC2 | 7 | 30 80 A |
| Duncan Rd. E8 | 48 | 34 83 B |
| Duncan Rd. Rich | 71 | 18 75 C |
| Duncan St. N1 | 4 | 31 83 D |
| Duncan Terr. N1 | 4 | 31 83 D |
| Dunch St. E1 | 57 | 34 81 D |
| Duncombe Hill. SE23 | 88 | 36 73 A |
| Duncombe Rd. N19 | 36 | 29 87 D |
| Duncombe Rd. N19 | 36 | 30 87 C |
| Duncrievie Rd. SE13 | 88 | 38 74 D |
| Duncroft. SE18 | 66 | 45 77 C |
| Dundalk Rd. SE4 | 76 | 36 75 A |
| Dundas Gdns. E Mol | 92 | 13 68 B |
| Dundas Rd. SE15 | 76 | 35 76 C |
| Dundee Rd. E13 | 50 | 40 83 D |
| Dundee Rd. SE25 | 105 | 34 67 B |
| Dundee St. E1 | 57 | 34 80 D |
| Dundela Gdns. Eps | 109 | 22 64 B |
| Dundonald Rd. NW10 | 45 | 23 83 B |
| Dundry Ho. SE26 | 87 | 34 72 C |
| Dunedin Rd. E10 | 38 | 38 86 C |
| Dunedin Rd. Ilf | 40 | 44 87 C |
| Dunedin Way. Hay | 53 | 11 82 C |
| Dunelm Gr. SE27 | 87 | 32 72 C |
| Dunelm St. E1 | 57 | 35 81 D |
| Dunfield Rd. SE6 | 88 | 37 71 D |
| Dunford Rd. N7 | 47 | 30 85 B |
| Dunheved Cl. Th Hth | 105 | 31 67 C |
| Dunheved Road N. Th Hth | 105 | 31 67 C |
| Dunheved Rd. S. Th Hth | 105 | 31 67 C |
| Dunheved Road W. Th Hth | 105 | 31 67 C |
| Dunholme Green. N9 | 17 | 33 93 D |
| Dunholme La. N9 | 17 | 33 93 D |
| Dunholme Rd. N9 | 17 | 33 93 D |
| Dunkeld Rd. Dag | 41 | 47 86 A |
| Dunkeld Rd. SE25 | 97 | 32 68 D |
| Dunkery Rd. SE9 | 89 | 42 72 C |
| Dunlace Rd. E5 | 48 | 35 85 B |
| Dunleary Cl. Houn | 82 | 12 73 B |
| Dunloe Ave. N17 | 25 | 32 89 B |
| Dunloe St. E2 | 49 | 33 83 D |
| Dunlop Pl. SE16 | 63 | 34 79 D |
| Dunmore Rd. NW6 | 46 | 24 83 A |
| Dunmore Rd. SW20 | 95 | 23 69 B |
| Dunmow Cl. Felt | 82 | 12 71 A |
| Dunmow Cl. Rom | 41 | 47 88 A |
| Dunmow Rd. E15 | 49 | 38 85 B |
| Dunmow Wlk. N1 | 4 | 32 83 A |
| Dunn Mead. NW9 | 21 | 21 93 D |
| Dunn's Pas. WC1 | 3 | 30 81 C |
| Dunn St. E8 | 48 | 33 85 D |
| Dunollie Pl. NW5 | 47 | 29 85 C |
| Dunollie Rd. NW5 | 47 | 29 85 C |
| Dunoon Rd. SE23 | 88 | 35 73 A |
| Dunraven Dri. Enf | 13 | 31 97 C |
| Dunraven Rd. W12 | 55 | 22 80 C |
| Draven St. W1 | 5 | 27 80 D |
| Dunsany Rd. W14 | 62 | 23 79 D |
| Dunsbury Cl. Sutt | 110 | 25 62 B |
| Dunsford Way. SW15 | 72 | 22 74 D |
| Dunsmore Rd. N16 | 37 | 33 87 C |
| Dunspring La. Ilf | 28 | 43 90 D |
| Dunstable Mews. W1 | 2 | 28 81 A |
| Dunstable Rd. E Mol | 92 | 12 68 D |
| Dunstable Rd. Rich | 71 | 18 75 C |
| Dunstall Rd. SW20 | 95 | 23 70 A |
| Dunstall Way. E Mol | 92 | 13 68 B |
| Dunstan Cl. N2 | 36 | 26 89 A |
| Dunstan Rd. NW11 | 35 | 24 87 D |
| Dunstan's Gr. SE22 | 75 | 34 74 D |
| Dunstan's Rd. SE22 | 75 | 34 74 D |
| Dunster Ave. Mord | 103 | 23 66 D |
| Dunster Cl. Barn | 11 | 23 96 D |
| Dunster Cl. Rom | 29 | 50 90 C |
| Dunster Ct. EC3 | 8 | 33 80 A |
| Dunster Dri. NW9 | 34 | 20 87 C |
| Dunster Way. Har | 32 | 12 86 C |
| Dunsterville Way. SE1 | 8 | 32 79 B |
| Dunston Rd. E8 | 48 | 33 83 B |
| Dunston Rd. SW11 | 74 | 28 75 B |
| Dunston St. E8 | 48 | 33 83 B |
| Dunton Cl. Surb | 101 | 18 66 C |
| Dunton Rd. E10 | 38 | 37 87 B |
| Dunton Rd. Rom | 30 | 51 89 C |
| Dunton Rd. SE1 | 63 | 33 78 B |
| Duntshill Rd. SW18 | 85 | 25 73 D |
| Dunvegan Cl. E Mol | 92 | 13 68 D |
| Dunvegan Rd. SE9 | 89 | 42 75 D |
| Dunwich Rd. Bexh | 79 | 48 76 B |
| Dunworth Mews. W11 | 56 | 24 81 D |
| Duplex Ride. SW1 | 5 | 27 79 B |
| Dupont Rd. SW20 | 95 | 23 69 D |
| Dupont St. E14 | 57 | 36 81 A |
| Duppas Ave. Croy | 112 | 31 64 B |
| Duppas Hill La. Croy | 112 | 31 64 B |
| Duppas Hill Rd. Croy | 112 | 31 64 B |
| Duppas Hill Terr. Croy | 105 | 31 65 D |
| Duppas Rd. Croy | 105 | 31 65 D |
| Dupree Rd. SE7 | 65 | 40 78 D |
| Dura Den Cl. Beck | 98 | 37 70 D |
| Durand Cl. Cars | 104 | 27 66 D |
| Durand Gdns. SW9 | 74 | 30 76 B |
| Durand Way. NW10 | 45 | 20 84 C |
| Durants Park Ave. Enf | 14 | 35 96 D |
| Durants Rd. Enf | 14 | 35 96 D |
| Durant St. E2 | 49 | 34 82 A |
| Durban Gdns. Dag | 52 | 50 84 C |
| Durban Rd. Beck | 98 | 36 69 B |
| Durban Rd. E15 | 49 | 39 82 A |
| Durban Rd. E17 | 26 | 36 90 B |
| Durban Rd. Ilf | 40 | 45 87 C |
| Durban Rd. N17 | 25 | 33 91 B |
| Durban Rd. SE27 | 87 | 32 71 B |
| Durdans Rd. Sthl | 53 | 12 81 D |
| Durell Gdns. Dag | 52 | 47 85 D |
| Durell Rd. Dag | 52 | 47 85 C |
| Durford Cres. SW15 | 84 | 22 73 D |
| Durham Ave. Brom | 99 | 39 68 D |

Durham Ave. Houn 59 12 78 D
Durham Ave. Rom 30 53 89 C
Durham Hill. Brom 89 39 71 B
Durham House St. WC2 7 30 80 A
Durham Pl. SW3 9 27 78 D
Durham Rd. Brom 99 39 68 B
Durham Rd. Dag 52 50 85 C
Durham Rd. E12 50 41 85 B
Durham Rd. E16 58 39 82 C
Durham Rd. Felt 82 11 73 A
Durham Rd. Har 32 13 88 B
Durham Rd. N2 24 27 89 B
Durham Rd. N7 36 30 86 B
Durham Rd. N9 17 34 93 A
Durham Rd. Sid 90 46 71 D
Durham Rd. SW20 94 22 69 B
Durham Rd. W5 60 17 79 D
Durham Rise. SE18 66 44 78 D
Durham Row. E1 57 36 81 A
Durham St. SE11 10 30 77 B
Durham Terr. W2 56 25 81 D
Durley Ave. Pnr 32 12 88 C
Durley Gdns. Mord 103 26 67 C
Durley Rd. N16 37 33 87 A
Durlston Rd. E5 37 34 86 A
Durlston Rd. King 93 18 70 A
Durnford St. N15 37 33 88 A
Durnford St. SE10 64 38 77 A
Durning Rd. SE19 87 32 71 D
Durnsford Ave. SW19 85 25 72 A
Durnsford Rd. N11 24 29 91 D
Durnsford Rd. SW19 85 25 72 D
Durrell Rd. SW6 73 24 76 B
Durrington Ave. SW20 95 23 70 C
Durrington Park Rd. SW20 95 23 69 A
Durrington Rd. E5 49 36 85 A
Dursley Cl. SE3 77 41 76 C
Dursley Gdns. SE3 77 41 76 B
Dursley Rd. SE3 77 41 76 D
Durward St. E1 57 34 81 B
Durweston Mews. W1 1 27 81 B
Durweston St. W1 1 27 81 B
Dury Falls Cl. Horn 42 54 87 D
Dury Rd. Barn 11 24 97 D
Dutch Yd. SW18 73 25 74 A
Duthie St. E14 58 38 80 A
Dutton St. SE10 76 38 76 A
Dye House La. E3 49 37 83 A
Dyers Hall Rd. E11 39 39 87 C
Dyer's La. SW15 72 22 75 D
Dyer's Way. Rom 30 52 91 D
Dykes Way. Brom 99 39 68 B
Dylan Rd. Belv 67 49 79 C
Dylways. SE5 75 32 75 D
Dymchurch Cl. Ilf 28 43 89 A
Dymes Path. SW19 85 23 72 B
Dymock St. SW6 73 25 75 B
Dymoke Rd. Horn 42 51 87 B
Dymond Estate. SW17 86 27 72 C
Dyneley Rd. SE12 89 41 72 C
Dyne Rd. NW6 46 24 84 D
Dynevor Rd. N16 37 33 86 C
Dynevor Rd. Rich 71 18 74 A
Dynham Rd. NW6 46 25 84 C
Dyott St. WC1 2 29 81 D
Dyott St. WC1 3 30 81 C
Dysart Ave. King 83 17 71 A
Dysart St. EC2 4 33 82 C
Dyson Rd. E11 39 39 88 C
Dyson Rd. E15 50 39 84 B
Dyson's Rd. N18 25 34 91 B
Dyson's Rd. N18 17 34 92 D

Eade Rd. N4 37 32 87 A
Eagan's Cl. N2 23 26 89 B
Eagle Ave. Rom 41 48 88 C
Eagle Cl. Enf 14 35 96 C
Eagle Ct. E11 27 40 89 C
Eagle Ct. EC1 3 31 81 B
Eagle Hill. SE19 97 32 70 B
Eagle La. E11 27 40 89 C
Eagle Lodge. NW11 35 24 87 B
Eagle Pl. SW1 6 29 80 A
Eagle Rd. Wem 44 17 84 D
Eaglesfield Rd. SE18 78 43 76 B
Eagle St. WC1 3 30 81 B
Eagle Terr. Wdf.Gn 27 40 91 D
Eaglet Pl. E1 57 35 82 C
Eagle Wharf Rd. N1 48 32 83 C
Eagling Rd. E3 57 37 82 B
Ealdham Sq. SE9 77 41 75 D
Ealing Green. W5 54 17 80 D
Ealing Park Gdns. W5 60 17 78 A
Ealing Rd. Brent 60 17 78 D
Ealing Rd. Nthlt 43 13 84 C
Ealing Rd. Wem 44 18 84 C
Ealing Village. W5 54 18 81 C
Eamont Rd. N Mal 94 21 68 D
Eamont St. NW8 47 27 83 C
Eardemont Cl. Dart 80 51 75 D
Eardley Cres. SW5 62 25 78 C
Eardley Rd. Belv 67 49 78 C
Eardley Rd. SW16 96 29 70 B
Earl Cottages. SE1 63 33 78 D
Earldom Rd. SW15 73 23 75 C
Earle Gdns. King 93 18 70 C
Earlham Gr. E7 50 40 85 C
Earlham Gr. N22 24 30 91 D
Earlham St. WC2 3 30 81 C
Earl Rd. SE1 63 33 78 D
Earl Rd. SW14 72 20 75 C
Earl Rise. SE18 66 44 78 B
Earl's Court Gdns. SW5 62 25 78 B
Earl's Court Rd. SW5 62 25 78 B
Earl's Court Rd. W8 62 25 79 C
Earl's Court Sq. SW5 62 25 78 D
Earls Cres. Har 21 15 89 C
Earlsferry Way. N1 47 30 84 D
Earlsfield Rd. SW18 85 26 73 A
Earlshall Rd. SE9 78 43 75 C
Earlsmead. Har 43 12 85 B
Earlsmead Rd. N15 37 33 88 B
Earlsmead Rd. NW10 56 23 82 A
Earl St. EC2 4 33 81 A
Earls Terr. W8 62 24 79 D
Earlsthorpe Rd. SE26 88 35 71 B
Earlstoke St. EC1 3 31 82 D
Earlston Gr. E9 48 34 83 B
Earls Wlk. Dag 51 46 85 B
Earls Wlk. W8 62 25 79 C
Earlswood Ave. Th Hth 105 31 67 A
Earlswood Cl. E10 65 39 78 C
Earlswood Gdns. Ilf 28 43 89 C
Earlswood St. E10 65 39 78 C
Early Mews. NW1 47 28 83 B
Earnshaw St. WC2 2 29 81 D
Earsby St. W14 62 24 78 A
Easby Cres. Mord 103 25 67 D
Easebourne Rd. Dag 52 47 85 C
Easleys Mews. W1 2 28 81 C
East Acton La. W3 55 21 80 A
East Arbour St. E1 57 35 81 D
East Ave. E12 50 42 84 C
East Ave. E17 38 37 88 B
East Ave. N2 23 26 89 A
East Ave. Sthl 53 12 80 B
East Ave. Wall 111 30 64 D
East Bank. N16 37 33 87 A
Eastbank Rd. Hamp 82 14 71 C
East Barnet Rd. Barn 11 26 95 B
East Boundary Rd. E12 39 42 86 D
Eastbourne Ave. W3 55 20 81 D
Eastbourne Gdns. SW14 72 20 75 A
Eastbourne Mews. W2 1 26 81 C
Eastbourne Rd. Brent 60 17 78 D
Eastbourne Rd. E15 50 39 83 A
Eastbourne Rd. Felt 82 11 72 B
Eastbourne Rd. N15 37 33 88 C
Eastbourne Rd. SW17 96 28 70 A
Eastbourne Rd. W4 61 20 77 A
Eastbourne Terr. W2 1 26 81 C
Eastbournia Ave. N9 17 34 93 D
Eastbrook Ave. Dag 52 50 85 A
Eastbrook Ave. N9 18 35 94 A
Eastbrook Dri. Rom 42 51 86 A
Eastbrook Rd. SE3 77 40 76 B
Eastbury Ave. Bark 51 45 83 A
Eastbury Ave. Enf 13 33 97 B
Eastbury Ave. Nthwd 19 10 91 A
Eastbury Gr. W4 61 21 78 C
Eastbury Rd. King 93 18 70 C
Eastbury Rd. Nthwd 19 09 91 A
Eastbury Rd. Orp 108 44 67 D
Eastbury Rd. Rom 41 50 88 D
Eastbury Sq. Bark 51 45 83 B
Eastbury Terr. E1 57 35 82 D
Eastcastle St. W1 2 29 81 C
Eastcheap. EC3 8 33 80 A
East Churchfield Rd. W3 55 20 80 D
Eastchurch Rd. Houn 69 09 75 A
East Cl. Barn 12 28 96 C
East Cl. Grnf 43 14 83 C
East Cl. W5 55 19 82 C
Eastcombe Ave. SE7 65 40 77 B
Eastcote Ave. Grnf 44 16 85 C
Eastcote Ave. Har 32 14 86 A
Eastcote La. Har 32 13 86 C
Eastcote Lane N. Nthlt 43 13 84 A
Eastcote La. Nthlt 43 12 85 D
Eastcote. Orp 108 45 66 D
Eastcote Rd. Har 32 14 86 C
Eastcote Rd. Pnr 32 11 88 B
Eastcote Rd. Ruis 31 09 87 B
Eastcote Rd. Well 78 44 76 D
Eastcote St. SW9 74 30 76 D
Eastcote View. Pnr 20 11 89 C
East Cres. Enf 13 33 95 B
East Cres. N11 16 28 93 C
Eastcroft Rd. Eps 109 21 63 C
East Cross Route. E3 49 37 83 A
East Cross Route. E9 49 36 84 B
East Ct. Wem 33 17 86 A
Eastdown Park. SE13 76 38 75 D
East Dri. Cars 111 27 62 B
East Dri. Orp 108 46 67 D
East Dulwich Gr. SE22 75 33 74 A
East Dulwich Rd. 75 34 75 C
East End Rd. N2 23 26 89 A
East End Rd. N3 23 25 90 C
East End Way. Pnr 20 12 89 A
East Entrance. Dag 52 49 83 D
Eastern Ave. E11 39 41 88 C
Eastern Ave. Ilf 40 44 88 D
Eastern Avenue E. Rom 30 51 90 B
Eastern Avenue W. Rom 29 49 89 C
Eastern Ave. Pnr 32 12 87 A
Eastern Perimeter Rd. Houn 69 10 76 C
Eastern Rd. E13 50 40 83 D
Eastern Rd. E17 38 38 88 A
Eastern Rd. N22 24 30 90 A
Eastern Rd. N2 24 27 89 D
Eastern Rd. Rom 42 51 88 B
Eastern Rd. SE4 76 37 75 C
Easternville Gdns. Ilf 40 44 88 C
East Ferry Rd. E14 64 37 79 D
Eastfield Ct. W3 55 21 80 C
Eastfield Gdns. Dag 52 49 85 A
Eastfield Rd. Dag 52 49 85 A
Eastfield Rd. E17 26 37 89 C
Eastfield Rd. N8 24 30 89 A
Eastfields. Pnr 32 11 88 A
Eastfields Rd. Mit 96 28 69 C
Eastfields Rd. W3 55 20 81 A
East Gdns. SW17 96 27 70 A
East Gdns. SW17 96 27 70 A
Eastglade. Pnr 20 12 89 B
East Harding St. EC4 3 31 81 C
East Heath Rd. NW3 35 26 86 D
East Hill. S Croy 112 33 62 C
East Hill. SW18 73 26 74 A
East Hill. Wem 34 19 87 C
East Holme. Eri 79 50 76 B
Eastholm. NW11 23 25 89 D
East India Dock Rd. E14 57 37 80 A
East India Dock Rd. E14 58 38 81 D
East India Dock Wall Rd. E14 58 38 80 B
Eastlake Rd. SE5 75 32 76 C
East La. King 93 17 68 B
Eastlands Cres. SE21 87 33 73 B
Eastlands Cres. SE22 75 33 74 D
East La. SE16 63 34 79 A
East La. Wem 33 17 86 C
Eastleigh Ave. Har 32 13 86 B
Eastleigh Cl. NW2 34 21 86 C
Eastleigh Cl. Sutt 110 25 63 D
Eastleigh Rd. Bexh 79 50 75 A
Eastleigh Rd. Houn 69 09 75 B
Eastleigh Wlk. SW15 84 22 73 A
Eastman Rd. W3 61 20 79 B
Eastmead Ave. Grnf 53 13 82 B
Eastmead Cl. Brom 99 42 69 C
East Mead. Ruis 32 11 86 D
Eastmearn Rd. SE21 87 32 72 A
Eastmont Rd. Esh 101 15 65 B
Eastmoor Pl. SE7 65 41 79 D
Eastmoor St. SE7 65 41 78 B
East Mount St. E1 57 34 81 B
Eastney Rd. Croy 105 31 66 D
Eastney St. SE10 64 38 78 D
Eastnor Rd. SE9 90 44 73 C
Easton St. WC1 3 31 82 C
East Park Cl. Rom 41 48 88 A
East Pas. EC1 4 32 81 A
East Pier. E1 57 34 80 D
East Pl. SE27 87 32 71 A
East Poultry Ave. EC1 3 31 81 B
East Ramp. Houn 69 07 76 B
East Rd. Barn 16 28 94 C
East Rd. E15 50 40 83 A
East Rd. Edg 22 20 90 A
East Rd. Felt 81 08 73 B
East Rd. King 93 18 69 A
East Rd. N1 4 32 82 B
East Rd. N2 24 27 90 A
East Rd. Rom 41 48 88 A
East Rd. Rom 41 50 87 B
East Rd. SW19 95 26 70 A
East Rd. Well 78 46 76 D
East Rochester Way. Bex 79 48 74 D
East Rochester Way. Sid 78 46 74 A
East Row. E11 39 40 88 C
East Row. W10 56 24 82 C
Eastry Ave. Brom 107 39 67 D
Eastry Rd. Eri 67 49 77 C
East Sheen Ave. SW14 72 20 75 D
Eastside Rd. NW11 23 24 89 D
East Smithfield. E1 8 33 80 B
East St. Bark 51 44 84 C
East St. Bexh 79 49 75 C
East St. Brent 60 17 77 C
East St. Brom 99 40 69 C
East St. SE17 63 32 78 D
East Surrey Gr. SE15 63 33 77 D
East Tenter St. E1 4 33 81 D
East Towers. Pnr 32 11 88 D
Eastview Ave. SE18 66 45 77 C
East View. Barn 11 24 96 B
East View. E4 18 38 92 C
Eastville Ave. NW11 35 24 88 D
Eastway. Brom 107 40 66 A
East Way. Croy 106 36 65 C
Eastway. E10 49 37 85 A
Eastway. E11 39 40 88 B
Eastway. E9 49 36 85 D
Eastway. Mord 95 24 68 C
Eastway Park. E9 49 36 84 B
East Way. Ruis 31 10 87 C
Eastway. Wall 111 29 64 A
Eastwell Cl. Beck 98 36 69 A
East Wlk. Barn 16 28 94 C
Eastwood Cl. E18 27 40 90 C
Eastwood Rd. E18 27 40 90 D
Eastwood Rd. Ilf 40 46 87 A
Eastwood Rd. N10 24 28 90 C
Eastwood St. SW16 96 29 70 A
Eatington Rd. E10 38 38 88 B
Eaton Cl. SW1 9 28 78 A
Eaton Ct. Chis 100 44 70 A
Eaton Dri. SW9 75 31 75 D
Eaton Dr. King 94 19 70 C
Eaton Dr. Rom 29 49 91 D
Eaton Gate. Nthwd 19 08 91 A
Eaton Gate. SW1 9 28 78 A
Eaton Gdns. Dag 52 48 84 C
Eaton Gr. N19 36 29 86 D
Eaton La. SW1 6 28 79 D
Eaton Mews N. SW1 6 28 79 C
Eaton Mews S. SW1 6 28 79 D
Eaton Mews W. SW1 9 28 78 A
Eaton Park Rd. N13 17 31 93 B
Eaton Pl. SW1 9 28 78 A
Eaton Pl. SW1 6 28 79 C
Eaton Rd. Enf 13 33 96 C
Eaton Rd. Houn 70 14 75 D
Eaton Rd. NW4 35 23 88 A
Eaton Rd. Sutt 110 26 63 B
Eaton Rise. E11 39 41 88 A
Eaton Rise. W5 54 17 81 D
Eaton Row. SW1 6 28 79 D
Eatons Mead. E4 18 37 93 A
Eaton Sq. SW1 6 28 79 C
Eaton Terr Mews. SW1 9 28 78 A
Eaton Terr. SW1 9 28 78 A
Eatonville Rd. SW17 86 27 72 B
Eatonville Villas. SW17 86 27 72 B
Eaton Wlk. SE15 75 33 76 B
Eaton Wlk. SE15 63 33 77 D
Ebbisham Dr. SW8 10 30 77 B
Ebbisham Rd. Wor Pk 103 23 65 A
Ebbsfleet Rd. NW2 46 24 85 A
Ebenezer St. N1 4 32 82 B
Ebenezer Wlk. SW16 96 29 69 A
Ebley Cl. SE15 63 33 77 B
Ebner St. SW18 73 25 74 B
Ebor St. E1 4 33 82 D
Ebrington Rd. Har 33 17 88 D
Ebsworth St. SE23 88 35 73 B
Eburne Rd. N7 36 30 86 C
Ebury Bridge Rd. SW1 9 28 78 C
Ebury Bridge. SW1 9 28 78 D
Ebury Cl. Brom 107 42 65 C
Ebury Mews E. SW1 6 28 79 D
Ebury Mews. SW1 9 28 78 B
Ebury Sq. SW1 9 28 78 B
Ebury St. SW1 9 28 78 B
Ecclesbourne Cl. N13 17 31 92 C
Ecclesbourne Gdns. N13 17 31 92 C
Ecclesbourne Rd. N1 48 32 84 C
Ecclesbourne Rd. Th Hth 105 32 67 A
Eccles Rd. SW11 74 27 75 D
Eccleston Bridge. SW1 9 28 78 B
Eccleston Cl. Barn 12 27 96 D
Eccleston Cl. Orp 108 44 66 D
Eccleston Cres. Rom 40 46 87 B
Ecclestone Ct. Wem 44 18 85 C
Ecclestone Mews. Wem 44 18 85 C
Ecclestone Pl. Wem 44 18 85 D
Eccleston Mews. SW1 6 28 79 C
Eccleston Pl. SW1 9 28 78 B
Eccleston Rd. W13 54 16 80 C
Eccleston Sq Mews. SW1 10 29 78 A
Eccleston Sq Mews. SW1 10 29 78 A
Eccleston Sq. SW1 9 28 78 B
Eccleston St. SW1 9 28 78 B
Echelforde Dri. Ashf 81 07 71 A
Echo Hts. E4 18 37 94 D
Eckersley St. E1 4 33 82 D
Eckford St. N1 48 31 83 C
Eckstein Rd. SW11 74 27 75 C
Eclipse Rd. E13 58 40 81 B
Ector Rd. SE6 89 39 72 A
Edbrooke Rd. W9 56 25 82 C
Eddisbury Ho. SE26 87 34 72 C
Eddiscombe Rd. SW6 73 24 76 D
Eddy Cl. Rom 41 49 88 D
Eddystone Rd. SE4 76 36 74 A
Ede Cl. Houn 70 12 75 B
Edenbridge Rd. E9 49 35 84 D
Edenbridge Rd. Enf 13 33 95 C
Eden Cl. Wem 44 17 83 B
Edencourt Rd. SW16 96 28 70 B
Edendale Rd. Bexh 79 50 76 D
Edenfield Gdns. Wor Pk 102 21 65 B
Eden Gr. E17 38 37 88 B
Eden Gr. N7 47 30 85 D
Edenham Way. W10 56 24 81 B
Edenhurst Ave. SW6 73 24 75 B
Eden Rd. Beck 98 36 68 C
Eden Rd. Croy 112 32 64 B
Eden Rd. E17 38 37 88 B
Eden Rd. SE27 87 31 71 D
Edensor Gdns. W4 61 21 77 C
Edensor Rd. W4 61 21 77 C
Eden St. King 93 18 69 C
Edenvale St. SW6 73 26 76 C
Eden Way. Beck 106 37 67 C
Ederline Ave. SW16 97 31 69 C
Edgarley Terr. SW6 73 24 76 A
Edgar Rd. E3 57 37 82 B
Edgar Rd. Rom 41 47 87 B
Edgar Rd. S Croy 112 32 62 B
Edgeborough Way. Brom 99 41 69 B
Edgebury . Chis 90 43 71 B
Edgebury Wlk. Chis 90 44 71 A
Edgebury Wlk. Chis 90 44 72 C
Edgecombe Cl. King 94 20 70 D
Edgecombe Rd. E11 39 39 87 D
Edgecote Cl. W3 55 19 80 D
Edgecot Gr. N15 37 33 88 A
Edgefield Ave. Bark 51 45 84 D
Edge Hill Ave. N3 23 25 89 C
Edge Hill Ct. SW19 95 23 70 D
Edgehill Gdns. Dag 52 49 85 A
Edgehill Rd. Chis 90 44 71 A
Edgehill Rd. Mit 96 28 69 B
Edgehill Rd. Pur 112 31 62 D
Edgehill Rd. W13 54 17 81 A
Edge Hill. SE18 66 43 77 B
Edge Hill. SW19 95 23 70 D
Edgeley La. SW4 74 29 75 B
Edgeley Rd. SW4 74 29 75 B
Edgel St. SW18 73 25 75 D
Edge Point Cl. SE27 87 31 71 D
Edge St. W8 56 25 80 C
Edgeware Ct. Edg 22 19 91 A
Edgewood Green. Croy 106 35 66 D
Edgeworth Ave. NW4 34 22 88 A
Edgeworth Cl. NW4 34 22 88 A
Edgeworth Cres. NW4 34 22 88 A
Edgeworth Rd. Barn 12 27 96 C
Edgeworth Rd. SE9 77 41 75 C
Edgington Rd. SW16 96 29 70 B
Edgware Rd. Edg 22 19 91 A
Edgware Rd. NW2 34 22 86 B
Edgware Rd. NW9 34 21 88 A
Edgware Rd. W2 1 27 81 A
Edgware Rd. W2 1 27 81 A
Edinburgh Ct. Mord 103 23 67 B
Edinburgh Dri. Uxb 31 07 86 D
Edinburgh Rd. E13 50 40 83 D
Edinburgh Rd. E17 38 37 88 A
Edinburgh Rd. N18 17 34 92 C
Edinburgh Rd. Sutt 103 26 65 B
Edinburgh Rd. W7 60 15 79 B
Edington Rd. Enf 14 35 97 C
Edington Rd. SE2 66 46 79 D
Edison Ave. Horn 42 51 87 D
Edison Cl. Horn 42 51 87 D
Edison Dri. Sthl 53 13 81 D
Edison Gr. SE18 66 45 77 D
Edison Rd. Brom 99 40 69 C
Edison Rd. N8 36 29 88 D
Edison Rd. Well 78 45 76 B
Edis St. NW1 47 28 83 A
Edith Gdns. Surb 102 19 66 B
Edith Gr. SW10 62 26 77 C
Edithna St. SW9 74 30 75 A
Edith Rd. E15 49 38 85 D
Edith Rd. E6 50 41 84 D
Edith Rd. N11 24 29 91 D
Edith Rd. Rom 41 47 88 D
Edith Rd. SE25 105 32 67 B
Edith Rd. SW19 95 25 70 B
Edith Rd. W14 62 24 78 A
Edith Row. SW6 73 25 76 B
Edith St. E2 48 34 83 C
Edith Terr. SW10 62 26 77 C
Edith Villas. W14 62 24 78 D
Edmanson's Cl. N17 25 33 90 B
Edmond Ct. SE15 76 35 76 A
Edmonscote. W13 54 16 81 A
Edmonton Ct. SE16 64 35 79 C
Edmonton Green Shopping Centre. N9 17 34 93 B
Edmund Rd. Mit 96 27 68 A
Edmund Rd. Well 78 46 75 A
Edmunds Cl. Hay 53 11 81 A
Edmund St. SE5 63 32 77 D
Edmunds Wlk. N2 24 27 89 C
Edna Rd. SW20 95 23 69 D
Edna St. SW11 74 27 76 A
Edrick Rd. Edg 22 20 91 A
Edrick Wlk. Edg 22 20 91 A
Edric Rd. SE14 64 35 77 D
Edridge Rd. Croy 105 32 65 D
Edward Ave. E4 26 37 91 B
Edward Ave. Mord 103 26 67 B
Edward Cl. Hamp 82 14 71 C
Edward Cl. N9 17 33 94 B
Edward Cl. Rom 30 53 89 A
Edward Ct. E16 58 40 81 A
Edwardes Sq. W8 62 25 79 C
Edward Gr. Barn 11 26 95 B
Edward Pl. SE8 64 36 77 B
Edward Rd. Barn 11 26 95 B
Edward Rd. Brom 99 41 70 C
Edward Rd. Chis 90 43 71 D
Edward Rd. Croy 105 33 66 A
Edward Rd. E17 38 35 88 B
Edward Rd. Felt 69 09 74 A
Edward Rd. Hamp 82 14 71 C
Edward Rd. Har 20 14 89 A
Edward Rd. Nthlt 43 11 83 C
Edward Rd. Rom 41 48 88 C
Edward Rd. SE20 98 35 70 B
Edward's Ave. Ruis 43 11 85 C
Edwards Cl. Wor Pk 103 23 65 B
Edward's Cottages. N1 48 31 84 B
Edward's La. N16 37 32 86 B
Edwards Mews. W1 2 28 81 C
Edward Sq. N1 47 30 83 B
Edwards Rd. Belv 67 49 78 A
Edward St. E13 58 40 82 C
Edward St. E16 58 40 82 C
Edward St. SE8 64 36 77 B
Edward Temme Ave. E15 50 39 84 D
Edware Ct. Edg 22 19 91 A
Edwina Gdns. Ilf 39 42 88 A
Edwin Ave. E6 51 43 83 C
Edwin Cl. Bexh 67 48 77 B
Edwin Pl. Croy 105 32 66 D
Edwin Rd. Edg 22 20 91 B
Edwin Rd. Twick 83 15 73 C
Edwin's Mead. E9 49 36 85 A
Edwin St. E16 58 40 81 A
Edwin St. E1 57 35 82 C
Edwyn Cl. Barn 11 23 95 D
Effie Pl. SW6 62 25 77 C
Effingham Cl. Sutt 110 25 63 D
Effingham Ct. SW19 96 27 70 C
Effingham Rd. Croy 104 30 66 D
Effingham Rd. N8 25 31 89 D
Effingham Rd. SE12 77 39 74 B
Effingham Rd. Surb 101 17 66 A
Effort St. SW17 86 27 71 C
Effra Par. SW2 75 31 74 A
Effra Rd. SW19 95 25 70 B
Effra Rd. SW2 75 31 74 A
Egan Way. SE16 63 34 78 D
Egbert St. NW1 47 28 83 A

Egdon Way. SE3 77 40 75 B
Egerton Cl. Pnr 19 10 89 C
Egerton Cres. SW3 9 27 78 A
Egerton Dri. SE10 76 37 76 B
Egerton Gdns. Ilf 40 45 86 D
Egerton Gdns Mews. SW3 5 27 79 C
Egerton Gdns. NW10 46 23 83 A
Egerton Gdns. NW4 22 22 89 D
Egerton Gdns. SW3 5 27 79 C
Egerton Gdns. W13 54 16 81 D
Egerton Pl. SW3 5 27 79 C
Egerton Rd. N16 37 33 87 B
Egerton Rd. N Mal 94 21 68 D
Egerton Rd. SE25 97 33 68 A
Egerton Rd. Twick 83 15 73 A
Egerton Rd. Wem 44 18 84 D
Egerton Terr. SW3 5 27 79 C
Egham Cl. Sutt 103 24 65 A
Egham Cres. Sutt 103 24 65 A
Egham Rd. E13 58 40 81 B
Eglantine Rd. SW18 73 26 74 A
Egleston Rd. Mord 103 25 67 D
Eglington Rd. E4 18 38 94 B
Eglington Rd. SE18 66 43 77 B
Eglinton Hill. SE18 66 43 77 D
Egliston Mews. SW15 73 23 75 A
Egliston Rd. SW15 73 23 75 A
Eglon Mews. NW1 47 28 84 C
Egmont Ave. Surb 102 19 66 C
Egmont Rd. N Mal 94 21 68 D
Egmont Rd. Surb 102 19 66 C
Egmont Rd. Sutt 110 26 63 C
Egmont St. SE14 64 35 77 D
Egremont Rd. SE27 87 31 72 C
Eighteenth Rd. Mit 96 30 68 C
Eighth Ave. E12 50 42 85 B
Eileen Rd. SE25 105 32 67 B
Elaine Gr. NW5 47 28 85 C
Elam Cl. SE5 75 31 76 D
Elam St. SE5 75 31 76 D
Eland Pl. Croy 105 31 65 D
Eland Rd. Croy 105 31 65 D
Eland Rd. SW11 74 27 75 B
Elba Pl. SE17 63 32 78 A
Elberon Ave. Croy 104 29 67 C
Elbe St. SW6 73 26 76 C
Elborough Rd. SE25 105 34 67 A
Elborough St. SW18 85 25 73 C
Elbury Dr. E16 58 40 81 C
Elcho St. SW11 9 27 77 C
Elcot Ave. SE15 63 34 77 D
Elder Ave. N8 36 30 88 A
Elderberry Rd. W5 60 18 79 A
Elderfield Rd. E5 49 35 85 A
Elderfield Wlk. E11 39 40 88 B
Elder Oak Cl. SE20 97 34 69 B
Elder Rd. SE27 87 32 71 C
Elderslie Cl. Beck 106 37 67 D
Elderslie Rd. SE9 78 43 74 A
Elder St. E1 4 33 82 D
Elderton Rd. SE26 88 36 71 A
Eldertree Pl. Mit 96 29 69 A
Eldertree Way. Mit 96 29 69 A
Elder Wlk. N1 48 32 83 A
Eldon Ave. Croy 106 35 65 A
Eldon Ave. Houn 59 13 77 C
Eldon Gr. NW3 46 26 85 D
Eldon Park. SE25 97 34 68 D
Eldon Rd. E17 26 36 89 D
Eldon Rd. N22 25 31 90 B
Eldon Rd. N9 18 35 94 C
Eldon Rd. W8 62 25 79 D
Eldon St. EC2 4 32 81 B
Eldon Way. NW10 45 19 83 D
Eldred Rd. Bark 51 45 83 A
Eldridge Cl. Felt 81 10 73 C
Eleanor Ave. Eps 109 20 62 D
Eleanor Cres. NW7 15 23 92 B
Eleanor Gdns. Dag 41 48 86 B
Eleanor Gr. SW13 72 21 75 A
Eleanor Gr. Uxb 31 07 86 D
Eleanor Rd (off Martello St). E8 48 34 84 D
Eleanor Rd (off Richmond Rd). E8 48 34 84 B
Eleanor Rd. E15 50 39 84 B
Eleanor Rd. N11 24 30 91 A
Eleanor St. E3 57 37 82 A
Eleanor Wlk. SE18 65 42 78 B
Electric Ave. SW9 75 31 75 C
Electric La. SW9 75 31 75 C
Electric Par. Surb 101 17 67 D
Elephant and Castle. SE1 7 31 79 D
Elephant La. SE16 64 35 79 A
Elephant Rd. SE17 63 32 78 A
Elers Rd. W13 60 17 79 A
Eley Rd. N18 18 35 92 D
Elfindale Rd. SE24 75 32 74 A
Elfin Gr. Tedd 83 15 71 D
Elford Cl. SE3 77 41 75 C
Elfort Rd. N5 48 31 85 A
Elfrida Cres. SE6 88 37 71 A
Elf Row. E1 57 35 80 B
Elfwine Rd. W7 54 15 81 A
Elgar Ave. Surb 102 19 66 B
Elgar Ave. SW16 96 30 68 A
Elgar Ave. W5 60 18 79 A
Elgar Cl. Uxb 31 07 86 A
Elgar Rd. Houn 82 12 73 B
Elgar St. SE16 64 36 79 C
Elgin Ave. Ashf 91 08 70 A
Elgin Ave. Har 21 16 90 D
Elgin Ave. W9 56 25 82 B
Elgin Cres. Houn 69 09 76 C
Elgin Cres. W11 56 24 80 A
Elgin Dri. Nthwd 19 09 91 C
Elgin Mews N. W9 56 25 82 B
Elgin Mews S. W9 56 25 82 B
Elgin Mews. W11 56 24 81 C
Elgin Rd. Croy 105 33 65 B
Elgin Rd. Ilf 40 45 87 A
Elgin Rd. N22 24 29 90 C
Elgin Rd. Sutt 103 26 65 C
Elgin Rd. Wall 111 29 63 A
Elgood Ave. Nthwd 19 10 91 A
Elham Cl. Brom 99 41 70 D
Elia Mews. N1 48 31 83 D
Elias Pl. SW8 63 31 77 A
Elia St. N1 48 31 83 D
Elibank Rd. SE9 78 43 75 C
Elim St. SE1 8 32 79 D
Eliot Bank. SE23 87 34 72 B
Eliot Cottages. SE3 77 39 76 C
Eliot Dri. Har 32 13 86 B
Eliot Hill. SE13 76 38 76 C
Eliot Park. SE13 76 38 76 C
Eliot Pl. SE3 77 39 76 C
Eliot Rd. Dag 52 47 85 B
Eliot Vale. SE3 76 38 76 D
Elizabeth Ave. Enf 13 31 96 B
Elizabeth Ave. Ilf 40 44 86 B
Elizabeth Ave. N1 48 32 84 D
Elizabeth Bridge. SW1 9 28 78 B
Elizabeth Cl. Barn 11 23 96 B
Elizabeth Cl. Rom 29 49 90 B
Elizabeth Cl. W9 1 26 82 C
Elizabeth Clyde Cl. N15 25 33 89 C
Elizabeth Cottages. Rich 72 19 76 A
Elizabeth Ct. SW1 6 29 79 D
Elizabeth Ct. Tedd 83 15 71 C
Elizabeth Gdns. Stan 21 17 91 A
Elizabeth Gdns. Sun 92 11 68 A
Elizabeth Gdns. W3 55 21 80 D
Elizabeth Mews. NW3 47 27 84 B
Elizabeth Pl. N15 25 33 89 C
Elizabeth Rd. E6 50 41 84 D
Elizabeth Rd. N15 37 33 88 A
Elizabeth Ride. N9 17 34 94 B
Elizabeth Ride. N9 18 35 94 A
Elizabeth St. SW1 9 28 78 A
Elizabeth Terr. SE9 77 42 74 D
Elizabeth Way. Felt 82 11 71 A
Elizabeth Way. SE19 97 32 70 D
Elkington Rd. E13 58 40 82 D
Elkins The. Rom 30 51 90 C
Elkstone Rd. W10 56 24 81 B
Ellaline Rd. W6 62 23 77 B
Ellanby Cres. N18 17 34 92 D
Elland Rd. SE15 76 35 75 C
Ella Rd. N8 36 30 87 A
Ellement Cl. Pnr 32 11 88 B
Ellenborough Pl. SW15 72 22 75 C
Ellenborough Rd. N22 25 32 90 C
Ellenbridge Way. S Croy 112 33 62 B
Ellen Cl. Brom 99 41 68 B
Ellen Ct. N9 18 35 93 A
Ellen St. E1 57 34 81 C
Elleray Rd. Tedd 93 15 70 B
Ellerby St. SW6 73 23 76 B
Ellerdale Cl. NW3 46 26 85 A
Ellerdale Rd. NW3 46 26 85 C
Ellerdale St. SE13 76 37 75 B
Ellerdine Rd. Houn 70 14 75 D
Ellerker Gdns. Rich 71 18 74 C
Ellerman Ave. Twick 82 12 73 D
Ellerslie Gdns. NW10 45 22 83 A
Ellerslie Rd. W12 55 22 80 D
Ellerton Gdns. Dag 52 47 84 C
Ellerton Rd. Dag 52 47 84 C
Ellerton Rd. Surb 101 18 66 D
Ellerton Rd. SW13 72 22 76 A
Ellerton Rd. SW18 85 26 73 D
Ellerton Rd. SW20 94 22 70 C
Ellery Rd. S9 97 32 70 D
Ellery St. SE15 75 34 76 D
Ellesmere Ave. Beck 98 37 69 D
Ellesmere Cl. E11 39 39 88 B
Ellesmere Cl. Ruis 31 08 87 A
Ellesmere Gdns. Ilf 39 42 88 C
Ellesmere Gr. Barn 11 24 95 B
Ellesmere Rd. E3 49 36 83 C
Ellesmere Rd. Grnf 53 14 82 C
Ellesmere Rd. NW10 45 22 85 C
Ellesmere Rd. Twick 71 17 74 C
Ellesmere Rd. W4 61 20 77 B
Ellesmere St. E14 57 37 81 D
Ellingfort Rd. E8 48 34 84 D
Ellingham Rd. E15 49 38 85 B
Ellingham Rd. W12 61 22 79 A
Ellington Ct. N14 16 29 93 B
Ellington Rd. Felt 81 09 71 B
Ellington Rd. Houn 70 13 76 D
Ellington Rd. N10 24 28 89 D
Ellington St. N7 48 31 84 A
Elliot Cl. E15 50 39 84 C
Elliot Gdns. Rom 30 52 91 D
Elliot Gdns. Shep 91 07 68 C
Elliot Rd. NW4 34 22 88 D
Elliot Rd. Stan 21 16 91 A
Elliot Rd. SW9 63 31 77 D
Elliot Rd. W4 61 21 78 A
Elliots Ct. EC4 3 31 81 D
Elliot's Row. SE11 7 31 79 D
Elliott Cl. Wem 34 19 86 C
Elliott Rd. Brom 99 41 68 D
Elliott Rd. Th Hth 97 31 68 D
Elliott's Pl. N1 48 31 83 B
Elliott's Row. SE11 63 31 78 B
Ellis Cl. SE9 90 44 72 A
Elliscombe Rd. SE7 65 41 77 A
Ellis Ct. W7 54 15 81 B
Ellisfield Dri. SW15 84 22 73 A
Ellison Gdns. Sthl 59 12 78 B
Ellison Rd. Sid 90 44 73 D
Ellison Rd. SW16 96 30 70 C
Elliso Rd. SW13 72 21 76 D
Ellis Rd. Mit 104 27 67 D
Ellis St. SW1 9 28 78 A
Ellmore Cl. Rom 30 52 90 B
Ellora Rd. SW16 86 29 71 D
Ellsworth St. E2 57 34 82 B
Elmar Rd. N15 25 32 89 D
Elm Ave. Ruis 31 10 87 B
Elm Ave. W5 54 18 80 D
Elmbank Ave. Barn 11 23 96 C
Elm Bank Gdns. SW13 72 21 76 C
Elmbank. N14 16 29 94 A
Elmbank Way. W7 54 15 81 A
Elmbourne Dri. Belv 67 49 78 B
Elmbourne Rd. SW17 86 28 72 D
Elmbridge Ave. Surb 102 20 67 C
Elmbridge Cl. Ruis 31 10 88 C
Elmbridge Dri. Ruis 31 10 88 C
Elmbridge Rd. Ilf 28 46 91 A
Elmbridge Wlk. E8 48 34 84 C
Elmbrook Gdns. SE9 77 42 75 C
Elmbrook Rd. Sutt 110 24 64 B
Elm Cl. Cars 104 27 66 D
Elm Cl. E11 39 40 88 D
Elm Cl. Har 32 13 88 D
Elm Cl. N19 36 29 86 A
Elm Cl. NW4 35 23 88 B
Elm Cl. Rom 29 49 90 B
Elm Cl. S Croy 112 33 63 A
Elm Cl. Surb 102 20 66 A
Elm Cl. SW20 95 23 68 C
Elm Cl. Twick 82 13 72 B
Elmcourt Rd. SE27 87 31 72 B
Elm Cres. King 93 18 69 A
Elm Cres. W5 54 18 80 C
Elmcroft Ave. E11 27 40 89 D
Elmcroft Ave. N9 13 34 95 D
Elmcroft Ave. NW11 35 24 87 B
Elmcroft Ave. Sid 78 46 74 C
Elmcroft Cl. Chess 101 18 65 C
Elmcroft Cl. E11 27 40 89 D
Elmcroft Cl. Felt 69 09 74 D
Elmcroft Cl. W5 54 17 81 D
Elmcroft Cres. Har 20 13 89 A
Elmcroft Cres. NW11 35 24 87 A
Elmcroft Dri. Ashf 81 07 71 C
Elmcroft Dri. Chess 101 18 65 C
Elmcroft Gdns. NW9 22 19 89 C
Elmcroft Rd. Orp 108 46 66 A
Elmcroft St. E5 49 35 85 A
Elm Ct. EC4 7 31 80 A
Elmdale Rd. N13 16 30 92 D
Elmdene Ave. Horn 42 54 88 B
Elmdene Cl. Beck 106 36 67 B
Elmdene Rd. SE18 66 43 78 D
Elmdene. Surb 102 20 66 C
Elmdon Rd. Houn 69 09 75 B
Elmdon Rd. Houn 70 12 76 C
Elm Dri. Har 32 13 88 D
Elm Dri. Sun 92 11 69 C
Elmer Cl. Enf 12 30 96 B
Elmer Gdns. Edg 22 19 91 D
Elmer Gdns. Islw 70 14 75 B
Elmer Rd. SE6 88 38 73 A
Elmer's Dr. Tedd 93 16 70 B
Elmers End Rd. Beck 98 35 68 A
Elmers End Rd. SE20 98 35 69 C
Elmerside Rd. Beck 98 36 68 C
Elmers Rd. SE25 105 34 66 A
Elmfield Ave. Mit 96 28 69 A
Elmfield Ave. N8 36 30 88 A
Elmfield Ave. Tedd 83 15 71 D
Elmfield Park. Brom 99 40 68 A
Elmfield Rd. Brom 99 40 68 A
Elmfield Rd. E17 38 35 88 D
Elmfield Rd. E4 18 38 93 B
Elmfield Rd. N2 23 26 89 B
Elmfield Rd. Sthl 59 12 79 C
Elmfield Rd. SW17 86 28 72 B
Elmfield Way. S Croy 112 33 62 B
Elm Friars Wlk. N7 47 29 84 D
Elmgate Ave. Felt 82 11 72 C
Elm Gdns. Mit 96 29 68 D
Elm Gdns. N2 23 26 89 A
Elm Green. W3 55 21 81 C
Elm Gr. Eri 67 50 77 D
Elm Gr. Har 32 13 87 A
Elm Gr. Horn 42 54 88 C
Elm Gr. King 93 18 69 A
Elm Gr. N8 36 30 88 C
Elm Gr. NW2 46 23 85 B
Elm Gr. Orp 108 45 66 D
Elmgrove Cres. Har 33 16 88 A
Elmgrove Gdns. Har 33 16 88 A
Elm Grove Par. Wall 104 28 65 C
Elmgrove Rd. Croy 105 34 66 B
Elmgrove Rd. Har 33 15 88 B
Elm Grove Rd. SW13 72 22 76 C
Elm Grove Rd. W5 60 18 79 A
Elm Gr. SE15 75 34 76 C
Elm Gr. Sutt 110 25 64 B
Elm Gr. SW19 95 24 70 C
Elm Hall Gdns. E11 39 40 88 D
Elmhurst Ave. Mit 96 28 70 D
Elmhurst Ave. N2 23 26 89 B
Elmhurst. Belv 67 48 77 A
Elmhurst Dri. E18 27 40 90 C
Elmhurst Dri. Horn 42 53 87 A
Elmhurst Lodge. Sutt 110 26 63 C
Elmhurst Rd. E7 50 40 84 D
Elmhurst Rd. N17 25 33 90 D
Elmhurst Rd. SE9 89 42 72 B
Elmhurst St. SW4 74 29 75 B
Elmington Cl. Bex 79 49 74 D
Elmington Rd. SE5 63 32 77 D
Elmira St. SE13 76 37 75 B
Elm La. SE6 88 36 72 B
Elmlee Cl. Chis 99 42 70 B
Elmley St. SE18 66 44 78 B
Elmore Rd. E11 38 38 86 D
Elmore Rd. Enf 14 35 97 B
Elmore St. N1 48 32 84 D
Elm Park Ave. Horn 42 52 86 D
Elm Park Ave. N15 37 34 88 C
Elm Park Ct. Pnr 20 11 89 A
Elm Park Gdns. NW4 35 23 88 B
Elm Park Gdns. SW10 62 26 78 D
Elm Park La. SW3 62 26 78 D
Elm Park Rd. E10 38 36 87 C
Elm Park Rd. N21 17 32 94 A
Elm Park Rd. N3 23 24 91 D
Elm Park Rd. Pnr 20 11 89 B
Elm Park Rd. SE25 97 33 68 B
Elm Park Rd. SW3 62 26 77 B
Elm Park. Stan 21 17 91 A
Elm Park. SW2 86 30 73 B
Elm Pl. SW7 62 26 78 D
Elm Rd. Barn 11 24 96 D
Elm Rd. Beck 98 36 69 D
Elm Rd. E11 38 38 86 B
Elm Rd. E17 38 38 88 A
Elm Rd. E7 50 39 84 B
Elm Rd. Eps 109 21 63 B
Elm Rd. Eri 80 52 76 A
Elm Rd. Felt 81 08 73 D
Elm Rd. King 93 18 69 B
Elm Rd. N22 25 31 90 B
Elm Rd. N Mal 94 20 68 B
Elm Rd. Rom 29 49 90 D
Elm Rd. Sid 90 46 71 A
Elm Rd. SW14 72 20 75 C
Elm Rd. Th Hth 97 32 68 D
Elm Rd. Wall 104 28 66 C
Elm Rd. Wem 44 18 85 C
Elm Road W. Sutt 103 24 66 B
Elm Row. NW3 35 26 86 C
Elms Ave. N10 24 28 89 B
Elms Ave. NW4 35 23 88 B
Elmscott Gdns. N21 13 32 95 C
Elmscott Rd. Brom 89 39 71 D
Elms Cres. SW4 74 29 74 D
Elms Ct. Wem 44 16 85 A
Elmsdale Rd. E17 26 36 89 D
Elms Gdns. Dag 52 48 85 B
Elms Gdns. Wem 44 16 85 A
Elmshaw Rd. SW15 72 22 74 A
Elmshurst Cres. N2 23 26 89 D
Elmside Rd. Wem 34 19 86 C
Elms La. Wem 44 16 85 A
Elmsleigh Ave. Har 21 17 89 C
Elmsleigh Ct. Sutt 103 25 65 D
Elmsleigh Rd. Twick 82 14 72 B
Elmslie Cl. Wdf Gn 27 42 91 B
Elms Mews. W2 5 26 80 B
Elms Park Ave. Wem 44 16 85 A
Elms Rd. Har 21 15 91 C
Elms Rd. SW4 74 29 74 A
Elmstead Ave. Chis 89 42 71 D
Elmstead Ave. Wem 33 18 86 B
Elmstead Cl. Eps 109 21 64 C
Elmstead Cl. N20 15 25 93 A
Elmstead Gdns. Wor Pk 102 22 65 C
Elmstead Glade. Chis 99 42 70 B
Elmstead La. Chis 89 42 71 D
Elmstead Rd. Eri 80 51 76 A
Elmstead Rd. Ilf 40 45 86 B
Elmsted Cres. Well 67 47 77 A
Elms The. SW13 72 21 75 B
Elmstone Rd. SW6 73 25 76 A
Elm St. WC1 3 30 82 D
Elmsway. Ashf 81 07 71 C
Elmsworth Ave. Houn 70 13 76 D
Elm Terr. Har 20 14 90 B
Elm Terr. NW2 35 25 86 C
Elm Terr. SE9 78 43 74 C
Elmton Way. E5 37 34 86 C
Elm Tree Ave. Esh 101 15 66 A
Elm Tree Cl. Ashf 81 07 71 D
Elm Tree Cl. Nthlt 43 12 83 D
Elm Tree Cl. NW8 1 26 82 B
Elm Tree Rd. NW8 1 26 82 B
Elmtree Rd. Tedd 83 15 71 A
Elm Way. E16 58 39 82 B
Elm Way. Eps 109 20 64 D
Elm Way. NW10 45 21 85 A
Elm Way. NW10 34 21 86 C
Elm Way. Wor Pk 103 23 65 C
Elm Wlk. Brom 107 42 65 D
Elm Wlk. NW3 35 25 86 A
Elm Wlk. Rom 30 52 89 A
Elm Wlk. SW20 95 23 68 D
Elmwood Ave. Felt 81 10 72 D
Elmwood Ave. Har 33 16 88 D
Elmwood Ave. N13 16 30 92 C
Elmwood Cl. Eps 109 22 63 C
Elmwood Cl. Wall 104 28 65 B
Elmwood Cres. NW9 22 20 89 C
Elmwood Ct. Wem 33 16 86 C
Elmwood Dri. Bex 79 48 74 C
Elmwood Dri. Eps 109 22 63 C
Elmwood Gdns. W7 54 15 81 C
Elmwood Rd. Croy 105 31 66 B
Elmwood Rd. Mit 96 27 68 B
Elmwood Rd. SE24 75 32 74 B
Elmwood Rd. W4 61 20 77 A
Elmworth Gr. SE21 87 32 72 B
Elnathan Mews. W9 56 25 82 D
Elphinstone Rd. E17 26 36 90 D
Elphinstone St. N5 48 31 85 B
Elrick Cl. Eri 68 51 77 A
Elrington Rd E8 48 34 84 A
Elsa Rd. Well 79 47 76 C
Elsa St. E14 57 36 81 A
Elsdale St. E9 49 35 84 C
Elsden Mews. E2 49 35 83 C
Elsden Rd. N17 25 33 90 B
Elsenham Rd. E12 51 43 85 C
Elsenham St. SW18 85 24 72 B
Elsham Rd. E11 50 39 85 A
Elsham Rd. W14 62 24 79 A
Elsiedene Rd. N21 17 32 94 A
Elsiemaud Rd. SE4 76 36 74 B
Elsie Rd. SE22 75 33 75 D
Elsinore Rd. SE23 88 36 73 C
Elsley Rd. SW11 74 27 75 B
Elspeth Rd. SW11 74 27 75 D
Elspeth Rd. Wem 44 18 85 C
Elsrick Ave. Mord 103 25 67 A
Elstan Way. Croy 106 36 66 A
Elsted St. SE17 63 32 78 B
Elstow Cl. Ruis 32 11 87 B
Elstow Cl. SE9 78 43 74 A
Elstow Gdns. Dag 52 48 83 A
Elstow Rd. Dag 52 48 83 A
Elstree Gdns. Belv 67 48 78 A
Elstree Gdns. Ilf 51 44 85 C
Elstree Gdns. N9 17 34 94 D
Elstree Hill. Brom 99 39 70 C
Elswick Rd. SE13 76 37 76 D
Elswick St. SW6 73 26 76 C
Elsworthy. E Mol 101 15 67 C
Elsworthy Rd. NW3 47 27 84 C
Elsworthy Rise. NW3 47 27 84 C
Elsworthy Terr. NW3 47 27 84 C
Elsynge Rd. SW18 73 26 74 B
Eltham Green Rd. SE9 77 41 75 C
Eltham High St. SE9 78 43 74 C
Eltham Hill. SE9 77 41 74 B
Eltham Palace Rd. SE9 77 41 74 D
Eltham Park Gdns. SE9 78 43 75 C
Eltham Rd. SE12 77 40 74 A
Eltham Rd. SE9 77 41 74 A
Elthiron Rd. SW6 73 25 76 A
Elthorne Ave. W7 60 16 79 A
Elthorne Ct. Felt 82 11 73 C
Elthorne Park Rd. W7 60 16 79 A
Elthorne Rd. N19 36 29 86 B
Elthorne Rd. NW9 34 20 87 B
Elthorne Way. NW9 34 20 88 D
Elthruda Rd. SE13 76 38 74 D
Eltisley Rd. Ilf 51 43 85 B
Elton Ave. Barn 11 24 95 B
Elton Ave. Grnf 44 15 84 B
Elton Ave. Wem 44 16 85 D
Elton Cl. Tedd 93 17 70 C
Elton Pl. N16 48 33 85 C
Elton Rd. King 94 19 69 A
Eltringham St. SW18 73 26 75 C
Elvaston Mews. SW7 5 26 79 C
Elvaston Pl. SW7 5 26 79 C
Elveden Pl. NW10 45 19 83 C
Elveden Rd. NW10 45 19 83 C
Elvendon Rd. N13 24 30 91 A
Elver Gdns. E2 57 34 82 A
Elverson Rd. SE8 76 37 76 D
Elverton St. SW1 10 29 78 B
Elvet Ave. Rom 30 53 89 C
Elvin Ct. NW9 34 20 87 A
Elvington Green. Brom 107 39 67 B
Elvington La. NW9 22 21 90 A
Elvino Rd. SE26 88 36 71 C
Elwill Way. Beck 98 38 68 D
Elwin St. E2 57 34 82 A
Elwood St. N5 37 31 86 D
Elwyn Gdns. SE12 89 40 73 A
Ely Cl. Eri 80 51 76 D
Ely Cl. N Mal 94 21 69 C
Ely Cottages. SW8 10 30 77 D
Ely Gdns. Dag 41 50 86 C
Ely Gdns. Ilf 39 42 87 A
Elyne Rd. N4 37 31 88 C
Ely Pl. EC1 3 31 81 A
Ely Pl. Wdf Gn 28 43 91 A
Ely Rd. E10 38 38 87 A
Ely Rd. Houn 69 09 76 D
Ely Rd. Houn 70 11 75 A
Ely Rd. Th Hth 105 32 67 B
Elysian Ave. Orp 108 45 67 D
Elysium Pl. SW6 73 24 76 D
Elysium St. SW6 73 24 76 D
Elystan Cl. Wall 111 28 62 A
Elystan Pl. SW3 9 27 78 D
Elystan St. SW3 9 27 78 A
Emanuel Ave. W3 55 20 81 C
Embankment Gdns. SW3 9 27 77 B
Embankment Pl. WC2 7 30 80 C
Embankment. SW15 73 23 75 B
Embankment The. Twick 83 16 73 C
Embassey Ct. Sid 90 46 72 D
Embassy Ct. Well 78 46 75 B
Emba St. SE16 63 34 79 A
Ember Cl. Orp 108 44 66 A
Embercourt Rd. Surb 101 15 67 C
Ember Gdns. Surb 101 15 66 A
Embleton Rd. SE13 76 37 75 D
Embleton Wlk. Hamp 82 12 71 D

Embry Dri. Stan 21 16 91 A
Emden St. SW6 73 25 76 B
Emerald Gdns. Dag 41 49 87 C
Emerald St. WC1 3 30 81 B
Emerson Dri. Horn 42 53 87 B
Emerson Gdns. Har 33 18 88 D
Emerson Rd. Ilf 40 43 87 A
Emerson St. SE1 8 32 80 C
Emery Hill St. SW1 6 29 79 C
Emery St. SE1 7 31 79 C
Emes Rd. Eri 67 50 77 C
Emily Pl. N7 48 31 85 A
Emily St. E16 58 39 81 D
Emlyn Gdns. W12 61 21 79 A
Emlyn Rd. W12 61 21 79 D
Emmanuel Rd. Nthwd 19 09 91 D
Emmanuel Rd. SW12 86 29 73 D
Emma Rd. E13 58 39 82 B
Emma St. E2 48 34 83 D
Emmett St. E14 57 36 80 B
Emmott Ave. Ilf 40 44 88 A
Emmott Cl. E2 57 36 82 C
Emmott Cl. NW11 35 26 88 C
Empire Ave. N18 25 32 91 A
Empire Ct. Wem 34 19 86 D
Empire Rd. Grnf 44 17 84 C
Empire Way. Wem 45 19 85 A
Empire Wharf Rd. E14 64 38 78 B
Empire Yd. N7 36 30 86 C
Empress Ave. E12 39 41 86 B
Empress Ave. E4 26 37 91 D
Empress Ave. Ilf 40 43 86 A
Empress Ave. Wdf Gn 27 39 91 D
Empress Dri. Chis 100 43 70 B
Empress Pl. SW6 62 25 78 C
Empress St. SE17 63 32 77 A
Empson St. E3 57 37 82 D
Emsworth Cl. N9 18 35 94 C
Emsworth Rd. Ilf 28 43 90 D
Emsworth St. SW2 86 30 72 B
Emu Rd. SW8 74 28 76 D
Ena Rd. SW16 96 30 68 A
Enbrook St. W10 56 24 82 A
Endale Cl. Cars 104 27 65 B
Endeavor Way. Bark 51 46 83 C
Endeavour Way. SW19 85 25 71 B
Endell St. WC2 3 30 81 C
Enderby St. E10 65 39 78 C
Enderley Cl. Har 21 15 90 A
Enderley Rd. Har 21 15 90 A
Endersby Rd. Barn 11 23 95 A
Endersleigh Gdns. NW4 22 22 89 C
Endlebury Rd. E4 18 38 93 A
Endlesham Rd. SW12 86 28 73 A
Endsleigh Gdns. Ilf 39 42 87 D
Endsleigh Gdns. Surb 101 17 67 C
Endsleigh Gdns. WC1 2 29 82 D
Endsleigh Pl. WC1 2 29 82 D
Endsleigh Rd. Sthl 59 12 78 A
Endsleigh Rd. W13 54 16 80 A
Endsleigh St. WC1 2 29 82 D
Endway. Surb 102 19 66 B
Endwell Rd. SE4 76 36 75 A
Endymion Rd. N4 37 31 87 B
Endymion Rd. SW2 74 30 74 D
Enfield Rd. Brent 60 17 78 D
Enfield Rd. Enf 12 30 96 A
Enfield Rd. Houn 69 09 76 C
Enfield Rd. N1 48 33 84 C
Enfield Rd. W3 61 19 79 B
Enfield Road E. Brent 60 17 78 D
Enford St. W1 1 27 81 B
Engadine Cl. Croy 105 33 65 D
Engadine St. SW18 85 25 72 A
Engate St. SE13 76 38 75 C
Engel Park. NW7 23 23 91 A
Engineer Cl. SE18 66 43 77 A
Engineers Way. Wem 45 19 85 A
England's La. NW3 47 27 84 B
Englefield Cl. Croy 105 32 67 C
Englefield Cl. Enf 13 31 97 C
Englefield Cl. Orp 100 45 68 D
Englefield Cres. Orp 100 46 68 C
Englefield Path. Orp 100 46 68 C
Englefield Rd. N1 48 33 84 C
Engleheart Dri. Felt 69 09 74 D
Engleheart Rd. SE6 88 38 73 A
Englewood Rd. SW12 74 29 74 C
English Grounds. SE1 8 33 80 C
English St. E3 57 36 82 D
Enid St. SE16 8 33 79 D
Enkel St. N7 36 30 86 D
Enmore Ave. SE25 105 34 67 A
Enmore Gdns. SW14 72 20 74 B
Enmore Rd. SE25 105 34 67 A
Enmore Rd. Sthl 53 13 82 C
Enmore Rd. SW15 73 23 74 A
Ennerdale Ave. Stan 21 17 89 A
Ennerdale Dri. NW9 34 21 88 A
Ennerdale Gdns. Wem 33 17 87 C
Ennerdale Rd. Bexh 79 49 76 A
Ennerdale Rd. Rich 71 18 76 D
Ennersdale Rd. SE13 76 38 74 B
Ennismore Ave. Grnf 44 15 85 C
Ennismore Ave. W4 61 21 78 B
Ennismore Gdns. E Mol 101 15 67 C
Ennismore Gdns Mews. SW7 5 27 79 C
Ennismore Gdns. SW7 5 27 79 A
Ennismore Mews. SW7 5 27 79 C
Ennismore St. SW7 5 27 79 C
Ennis Rd. N4 37 31 87 C
Ennis Rd. SE18 66 44 77 B
Ensign Dri. N13 17 32 93 C
Ensign St. E1 57 34 80 A
Enslin Rd. SE9 90 43 73 A
Ensor Mews. SW7 62 26 78 D
Enstone Rd. Enf 14 36 96 A
Enterprise Way. SW18 73 25 75 C
Epirus Mews. SW6 62 25 77 C
Epirus Rd. SW6 62 25 77 D
Epping Cl. Rom 29 49 89 B
Epping Glade. E4 14 38 95 D
Epping Pl. N1 48 31 84 A
Epping Way. E4 14 37 95 D
Epple Rd. SW6 73 24 76 B
Epsom Cl. Bexh 79 49 75 B
Epsom Cl. Nthlt 43 12 85 D
Epsom Rd. Croy 105 31 65 C
Epsom Rd. E10 38 38 88 C
Epsom Rd. Eps 109 21 62 D
Epsom Rd. Ilf 40 45 88 D
Epsom Rd. Mord 103 24 67 D
Epsom Sq. Houn 69 09 76 D
Epsom Way. Horn 42 54 86 D
Epworth Rd. Islw 60 16 77 D
Epworth St. EC2 4 32 82 D
Erasmus St. SW1 10 29 78 B
Erconwald St. W12 55 21 81 D
Eresby Dri. W Wick 106 37 66 C
Eresby Pl. NW6 46 25 84 C
Erica Gdns. Croy 106 37 65 D
Erica St. W12 55 22 80 A
Eric Cl. E7 50 40 85 A
Ericcson Cl. SW18 73 25 74 A
Eric Rd. E7 50 40 85 A
Eric Rd. NW10 45 21 84 B
Eric Rd. Rom 41 48 87 A
Eric St. E3 57 36 82 D
Eridge Rd. W4 61 20 79 D
Erin Cl. Brom 99 39 70 C
Erindale. SE18 66 44 77 B
Erindale Terr. SE18 66 44 77 B
Erith Cres. Rom 29 50 91 C
Erith High St. Eri 68 51 78 D
Erith Rd. Belv 67 49 78 D
Erith Rd. Bexh 79 49 75 B
Erith Rd. Eri 79 50 76 A
Erlanger Rd. SE14 76 35 76 D
Erlesmere Gdns. W13 60 16 79 C
Ermine Cl. Houn 70 11 76 C
Ermine Rd. N15 37 33 88 D
Ermine Rd. SE13 76 37 75 D
Ermine Side. Enf 13 34 95 A
Ermington Rd. SE9 90 44 72 A
Ernald Ave. E6 58 42 83 C
Erncroft Way. Twick 71 15 74 D
Ernest Ave. SE27 87 31 71 B
Ernest Cl. Beck 106 37 67 A
Ernest Gdns. W4 61 19 77 B
Ernest Gr. Beck 106 36 67 B
Ernest Rd. Horn 42 54 88 D
Ernest Rd. King 94 19 69 D
Ernest Sq. King 94 19 69 D
Ernest St. E1 57 35 82 D
Ernle Rd. SW20 95 23 70 C
Ernshaw Pl. SW15 73 24 74 A
Erpingham Rd. SW15 73 23 75 A
Erridge Rd. SW19 95 25 69 C
Errington Rd. W9 56 24 82 D
Errol Gdns. Hay 53 11 82 C
Errol Gdns. N Mal 94 22 68 C
Erroll Rd. Rom 30 51 89 D
Errol St. EC1 4 32 82 D
Erskine Cl. Sutt 104 27 65 C
Erskine Cres. N15 25 34 89 D
Erskine Hill. NW11 35 25 88 A
Erskine Mews. NW3 47 27 84 D
Erskine Rd. E17 26 36 89 D
Erskine Rd. NW3 47 27 84 D
Erskine Rd. Sutt 103 26 65 D
Erwood Rd. SE7 65 42 78 C
Esam Way. SW16 87 31 71 C
Escott Gdns. SE9 89 42 71 A
Escot Way. Barn 11 23 95 A
Escreet Gr. SE18 66 43 78 A
Esher Ave. Rom 41 50 88 C
Esher Ave. Sutt 103 23 65 D
Esher Cres. Houn 69 09 76 D
Esher Gdns. SW19 85 23 72 B
Esher Rd. Ilf 40 45 86 C
Eskdale Ave. Nthlt 43 12 83 B
Eskdale Cl. Wem 33 17 86 B
Eskdale Rd. Bexh 79 49 76 A
Eskmont Ridge. SE19 97 33 70 C
Esk Rd. E13 58 40 82 D
Esk Way. Rom 30 51 91 C
Esmar Cres. NW9 34 22 87 A
Esmeralda Rd. SE1 63 34 78 A
Esmond Rd. NW6 46 24 83 B
Esmond Rd. W4 61 20 79 D
Esmond St. SW15 73 24 75 C
Esparto St. SW18 85 25 73 A
Essenden Rd. Belv 67 49 78 C
Essenden Rd. S Croy 112 33 63 C
Essendine Rd. W9 56 25 82 A
Essex Ave. Islw 71 15 75 A
Essex Cl. E17 26 36 89 C
Essex Cl. Mord 103 23 66 B
Essex Cl. Rom 29 49 89 D
Essex Cl. Ruis 32 11 87 D
Essex Ct. EC4 3 31 81 C
Essex Ct. SW13 72 21 76 D
Essex Gdns. Horn 42 54 88 B
Essex Gdns. N4 37 31 88 D
Essex Gr. SE19 97 32 70 B
Essex Park Mews. W3 55 21 80 C
Essex Park. N3 23 25 91 B
Essex Place Sq. W4 61 20 78 B
Essex Pl. W4 61 20 78 B
Essex Rd. Bark 51 44 83 B
Essex Rd. Dag 52 50 85 C
Essex Rd. Dart 80 53 74 D
Essex Rd. E10 38 38 88 C
Essex Rd. E12 50 42 84 A
Essex Rd. E17 38 36 88 C
Essex Rd. E18 27 40 90 D
Essex Rd. Enf 13 32 96 D
Essex Rd. N1 48 32 84 C
Essex Rd. NW10 45 21 84 C
Essex Rd. Rom 41 47 87 A
Essex Rd. Rom 29 49 89 D
Essex Rd S. E11 38 38 87 B
Essex Rd. W3 55 20 80 A
Essex Rd. W4 61 20 78 B
Essex St. E7 50 40 85 C
Essex St. WC2 7 31 80 A
Essex Villas. W8 62 25 79 A
Essian St. E1 57 36 81 A
Essoldo Way. Edg 21 18 89 B
Estate Way. E10 38 37 87 C
Estcourt Rd. SE25 105 34 67 D
Estcourt Rd. SW6 62 24 77 D
Estella Ave. N Mal 94 22 68 D
Estelle Rd. NW3 47 28 85 A
Esterbrooke St. SW1 10 29 78 B
Este Rd. SW11 74 27 75 A
Esther Cl. N21 17 31 94 A
Esther Rd. E11 39 39 87 A
Estreham Rd. SW16 96 29 70 B
Estridge Cl. Houn 70 13 75 C
Eswyn Rd. SW17 86 27 71 D
Etchingham Ct. N12 23 26 91 C
Etchingham Park Rd. N3 23 25 91 D
Etchingham Rd. E15 49 38 85 A
Eternit Wlk. SW6 73 23 76 B
Eternity Wlk. SW6 73 23 76 B
Etfield Gr. Sid 90 46 71 D
Ethelbert Cl. Brom 99 40 68 A
Ethelbert Gdns. Ilf 40 43 88 A
Ethelbert Rd. Brom 99 40 68 A
Ethelbert Rd. Eri 67 50 77 C
Ethelbert Rd. SW20 95 23 69 B
Ethelbert St. SW12 86 28 73 D
Ethelburga Rd. Rom 30 54 90 B
Ethelburga St. SW11 74 27 76 A
Etheldene Ave. N10 24 29 89 C
Ethelden Rd. W12 55 22 80 D
Ethel Rd. E16 58 40 81 D
Ethel St. SE17 63 32 78 A
Etheridge Rd. NW4 35 23 87 A
Etherley Rd. N15 37 32 88 A
Etherow St. SE22 87 34 73 A
Etherstone Green. SW16 87 31 71 A
Etherstone Rd. SW16 87 31 71 A
Ethnard Rd. SE15 63 34 77 B
Ethronvi Rd. Bexh 79 48 75 A
Etloe Rd. E10 38 37 86 A
Eton Ave. Barn 12 27 95 C
Eton Ave. Houn 59 12 77 B
Eton Ave. N12 23 26 91 C
Eton Ave. N Mal 94 20 68 D
Eton Ave. NW3 47 27 84 C
Eton Ave. Wem 44 17 85 A
Eton College Rd. NW3 47 27 84 D
Eton Ct. Wem 44 17 85 A
Eton Garages. NW3 47 27 84 A
Eton Gr. NW9 22 19 89 C
Eton Gr. SE13 77 39 75 A
Eton Rd. Ilf 51 44 85 B
Eton Rd. NW3 47 27 84 D
Eton St. Rich 71 18 74 A
Eton Villas. NW3 47 27 84 B
Etta St. SE8 64 36 77 A
Ettrick St. E14 58 38 81 C
Etwell Pl. Surb 101 18 67 D
Eugene Cl. Rom 30 53 89 C
Eugenia Rd. SE16 64 35 78 A
Eureka Rd. King 94 19 69 C
Europa Pl. EC1 4 32 82 A
Eustace Pl. SE18 65 42 78 B
Eustace Rd. Rom 41 47 87 B
Eustace Rd. SW6 62 25 77 C
Euston Rd. Croy 105 31 66 C
Euston Rd. NW1 2 29 82 C
Euston Sq. NW1 2 29 82 B
Euston St. NW1 2 29 82 A
Evandale Rd. SW9 75 31 76 C
Evangelist Rd. NW5 47 28 85 B
Evans Cl. E8 48 33 84 B
Evans Rd. SE6 89 39 72 A
Evanston Ave. E4 26 38 91 C
Evanston Gdns. Ilf 39 42 88 C
Eva Rd. Rom 41 47 87 B
Evelina Mansions. SE5 63 32 77 D
Evelina Rd. SE15 75 34 75 B
Evelina Rd. SE15 76 35 76 C
Evelina Rd. SE20 98 35 70 D
Eveline Rd. Mit 96 27 69 B
Evelyn Ave. NW9 22 20 89 D
Evelyn Ave. Ruis 31 09 88 D
Evelyn Cl. Twick 82 13 73 B
Evelyn Cres. Sun 91 09 69 B
Evelyn Ct. E8 48 34 85 A
Evelyn Ct. N1 48 32 83 D
Evelyn Dri. Pnr 20 11 91 D
Evelyn Gdns. Rich 71 18 75 C
Evelyn Gdns. SW7 62 26 78 D
Evelyn Gr. Sthl 53 12 81 D
Evelyn Gr. W5 54 18 80 D
Evelyn Rd. Barn 12 27 96 D
Evelyn Rd. E16 58 40 80 D
Evelyn Rd. E17 26 38 89 C
Evelyn Rd. Rich 83 17 72 C
Evelyn Rd. Rich 71 18 75 A
Evelyn Rd. SW19 95 25 70 B
Evelyn Rd. W4 61 20 79 D
Evelyn Sharp Cl. Rom 30 53 89 B
Evelyn St. SE8 64 36 78 D
Evelyn Terr. Rich 71 18 75 A
Evelyn Way. Sun 91 09 69 B
Evelyn Way. Wall 111 29 64 B
Evelyn Wlk. N1 48 32 83 D
Evelyn Yd. W1 2 29 81 D
Evenwood Cl. SW15 73 24 74 A
Everard Ave. Brom 107 40 66 C
Everard Way. Wem 33 18 86 C
Everatt Cl. SW18 73 24 74 B
Eve Rd. E11 50 39 85 A
Eve Rd. E15 50 39 83 C
Eve Rd. Islw 71 16 75 C
Eve Rd. N17 25 33 89 A
Everdon Rd. SW13 61 22 77 A
Everest Pl. E14 58 38 81 A
Everest Rd. SE9 77 42 74 B
Everett Cl. Pnr 19 09 89 B
Everett Wlk. Belv 67 48 78 D
Everglade Strand. NW9 22 21 90 B
Everilda St. N1 48 30 83 B
Evering Rd. E5 37 34 86 B
Evering Rd. N16 37 33 86 D
Everington Rd. N10 24 27 90 D
Everington St. W6 62 23 77 B
Everitt Rd. NW10 55 20 82 B
Everleigh St. N4 37 31 87 C
Eversfield Gdns. NW7 22 21 91 C
Eversfield Rd. Rich 71 18 76 D
Eversholt St. NW1 47 29 83 C
Evershot Rd. N4 36 30 87 D
Eversleigh Rd. Barn 11 26 95 A
Eversleigh Rd. E6 50 41 83 B
Eversleigh Rd. N3 23 24 91 D
Eversleigh Rd. SW11 74 28 76 C
Eversley Ave. Bexh 80 51 76 C
Eversley Ave. Wem 34 19 86 A
Eversley Cl. N21 12 30 95 D
Eversley Cres. Islw 70 14 76 B
Eversley Cres. N21 13 31 95 C
Eversley Cres. Ruis 31 09 86 B
Eversley Cross. Bexh 80 51 76 C
Eversley Mount. N21 12 30 95 D
Eversley Park. SW19 84 22 71 D
Eversley Rd. SE19 97 32 70 D
Eversley Rd. SE7 65 40 77 B
Eversley Rd. Surb 101 18 67 B
Eversley Way. Croy 106 37 65 C
Everthorpe Rd. SE15 75 33 75 B
Everton Dri. Stan 21 18 89 B
Everton Rd. Croy 105 34 66 C
Evesham Ave. E17 26 37 90 C
Evesham Cl. Grnf 43 13 83 D
Evesham Cl. Sutt 110 25 63 C
Evesham Green. Mord 103 25 67 D
Evesham Rd. E15 50 39 84 D
Evesham Rd. Mord 103 25 67 D
Evesham Rd. N11 16 29 92 D
Evesham St. W10 56 23 80 B
Evesham Way. Ilf 28 43 89 A
Evesham Way. SW11 74 28 75 A
Evesham Wlk. SE5 75 32 76 D
Evesham Wlk. SW9 75 31 76 A
Ewald Rd. SW6 73 24 76 D
Ewanrigg Terr. Wdf Gn 27 41 91 A
Ewart Gr. N22 25 31 90 A
Ewart Rd. SE23 88 35 73 B
Ewe Cl. N7 47 30 84 A
Ewell By-pass. Eps 109 22 62 A
Ewell Court Ave. Eps 109 21 64 C
Ewell House Gr. Eps 109 21 62 D
Ewellhurst Rd. Ilf 27 42 90 C
Ewell Park Way. Eps 109 22 63 C
Ewell Rd. Surb 101 16 66 B
Ewell Rd. Surb 101 18 66 B
Ewell Rd. Surb 102 19 66 D
Ewell Rd. Sutt 110 23 63 B
Ewelme Rd. SE23 88 35 73 C
Ewen Cres. SW12 87 31 73 A
Ewer St. SE1 8 32 80 C
Ewhurst Ave. S Croy 112 33 62 B
Ewhurst Cl. Sutt 110 23 62 A
Ewhurst Rd. SE4 76 36 74 D
Exbury Rd. SE6 88 37 72 A
Excel Ct. SW1 6 29 80 B
Excelsior Cl. King 94 19 69 C
Excelsior Gdns. SE13 76 38 76 C
Exchange Bldgs. E1 4 33 81 C
Exchange Ct. WC2 7 30 80 A
Exchange St. Rom 42 51 88 A
Exeforde Ave. Ashf 81 07 71 A
Exeter Ct. Surb 101 18 67 A
Exeter Gdns. Ilf 39 42 87 D
Exeter Mews. NW6 46 25 84 B
Exeter Rd. Croy 105 33 66 B
Exeter Rd. Dag 52 49 84 B
Exeter Rd. E16 58 40 81 A
Exeter Rd. E17 38 37 88 A
Exeter Rd. Enf 14 35 96 B
Exeter Rd. Felt 82 12 72 D
Exeter Rd. Har 32 12 86 A
Exeter Rd. N14 16 28 94 B
Exeter Rd. N9 18 35 93 A
Exeter Rd. NW2 46 24 84 A
Exeter Rd. SE15 75 33 76 B
Exeter Rd. SE15 63 33 77 D
Exeter Rd. Well 78 45 76 D
Exeter St. WC2 7 30 80 B
Exford Gdns. SE12 89 40 73 D
Exford Rd. SE12 89 40 73 D
Exhibition Cl. W12 56 23 80 A
Exhibition Rd. SW7 5 26 79 D
Exit Rd. N2 23 26 90 D
Exmoor St. W10 56 23 81 B
Exmouth Market. EC1 3 31 82 C
Exmth Pl. E8 48 34 84 D
Exmouth Rd. Brom 99 40 68 B
Exmouth Rd. E17 38 36 88 B
Exmouth Rd. Ruis 32 11 86 C
Exmouth Rd. Well 79 47 76 A
Exmouth Rd. Well 67 47 77 C
Exmouth St. E1 57 35 81 C
Exning Rd. E16 58 39 82 D
Exon St. SE17 63 33 78 A
Exton Cres. NW10 45 20 84 C
Exton Gdns. Dag 52 47 85 C
Exton St. SE1 7 31 80 C
Eyhurst Ave. Horn 42 52 86 D
Eyhurst Cl. NW2 34 22 86 B
Eylewood Rd. SE27 87 32 71 C
Eynella Rd. SE22 87 33 73 B
Eynham Rd. W12 56 23 81 C
Eynsford Cl. Orp 108 44 66 A
Eynsford Rd. Ilf 40 45 86 A
Eynsham Dri. SE2 66 46 79 D
Eynswood Dri. Sid 90 46 71 D
Eyot Gdns. W6 61 21 78 D
Eyot Green. W4 61 21 78 D
Eyre Cl. Rom 30 52 89 D
Eyre St Hill. EC1 3 31 82 C
Eythorne Rd. SW9 75 31 76 A
Ezra St. E2 4 33 82 B
Ezra St. E2 57 34 82 A

Faber Gdns. NW4 34 22 88 A
Fabian Rd. SW6 62 24 77 D
Factory La. N17 25 33 90 D
Factory Lane. Croy 105 31 65 A
Factory Pl. E14 64 38 78 C
Factory Rd. E16 65 42 79 B
Factory Rd. E16 66 43 79 A
Factory Sq. SW16 96 30 70 A
Factory Yd. W7 54 15 80 C
Fagg's Rd. Felt 69 10 74 A
Fairacre. N Mal 94 21 68 A
Fair Acres. Brom 107 40 67 A
Faacres. Ruis 31 09 87 B
Fairacres. SW15 72 22 75 C
Fairbank Ave. Orp 108 43 65 B
Fairbanks Rd. N17 25 34 89 A
Fairbourne Rd. N17 25 33 89 A
Fairbridge Rd. N19 36 29 87 D
Fairbrook Cl. N13 17 31 92 C
Fairbrook Rd. N13 25 31 91 A
Fairby Hse. SE1 63 33 78 B
Fairby Rd. SE12 77 40 74 B
Fairchild Pl. EC2 4 33 82 C
Fairchild St. EC2 4 33 82 C
Fairclough St. E1 57 34 81 C
Faircross Ave. Bark 51 44 84 A
Faircross Ave. Rom 29 50 91 D
Fair Cross. Bark 51 45 85 C
Fairdale Gdns. SW15 72 22 75 D
Fairfax Av. Eps 109 22 62 B
Fairfax Gdns. SE3 77 41 76 A
Fairfax Pl. NW6 46 26 84 C
Fairfax Rd. N8 25 31 89 C
Fairfax Rd. NW6 46 26 84 C
Fairfax Rd. Tedd 93 16 70 D
Fairfax Rd. W4 61 21 79 C
Fairfield Ave. Edg 22 19 91 D
Fairfield Ave. NW4 35 23 88 C
Fairfield Ave. Ruis 31 08 87 A
Fairfield Ave. Twick 82 13 73 D
Fairfield Cl. Enf 14 36 96 C
Fairfield Cl. Horn 42 52 87 C
Fairfield Cl. N12 15 26 92 A
Fairfield Cl. Sid 78 45 74 D
Fairfield Cres. Edg 22 19 91 B
Fairfield Ct. NW10 45 22 83 A
Fairfield Ct. Ruis 31 08 87 D
Fairfield Dri. Grnf 44 17 83 A
Fairfield Dri. Har 20 14 89 A
Fairfield Dri. SW18 73 25 74 B
Fairfield E. King 93 18 69 C
Fairfield Gdns. N8 36 30 88 A
Fairfield Gr. SE7 65 41 78 D
Fairfield N. King 93 18 69 C
Fairfield Path. Croy 112 33 64 A
Fairfield Path. Croy 105 33 65 C
Fairfield Pl. King 93 18 68 A
Fairfield Rd. Beck 98 37 69 C
Fairfield Rd. Bexh 79 48 76 D
Fairfield Rd. Brom 99 40 70 C
Fairfield Rd. Croy 105 33 65 C
Fairfield Rd. E17 26 36 90 C
Fairfield Rd. E3 49 37 83 C
Fairfield Rd. Enf 14 36 95 A
Fairfield Rd. Ilf 51 43 84 B
Fairfield Rd. King 93 18 69 C
Fairfield Rd. N18 17 34 92 C
Fairfield Rd. N8 36 30 88 A
Fairfield Rd. Orp 108 45 66 A
Fairfield Rd. Sthl 53 12 81 D
Fairfield Rd. Wdf Gn 27 40 91 A
Fairfields Cl. NW9 34 20 88 A
Fairfields Cres. NW9 34 20 88 A
Fairfield S. King 93 18 69 D
Fairfields Rd. Houn 70 14 75 A
Fairfield St. SW18 73 25 74 B
Fairfield St. SW18 73 25 75 D
Fairfield Way. Barn 11 25 95 A
Fairfield Way. Eps 109 21 64 C

Fairfield W. King 93 18 69 C
Fairfoot Rd. E3 57 37 82 C
Fairford Ave. Bexh 79 50 76 B
Fairford Ave. Croy 106 35 67 B
Fairford Cl. Croy 106 36 67 A
Fairford Gdns. Wor Pk 102 21 65 D
Fairgreen. Barn 12 27 96 B
Fairgreen Ct. Barn 12 27 96 B
Fairgreen E. Barn 12 27 96 B
Fairgreen Rd. Th Hth 105 31 67 B
Fairhaven Ave. Croy 106 35 67 D
Fairhazel Gdns. NW6 46 25 84 C
Fairheathe. SW15 73 23 74 D
Fairholme Ave. Rom 30 52 89 D
Fairholme Cl. N3 23 24 89 C
Fairholme. Felt 81 09 73 A
Fairholme Gdns. N3 23 24 89 C
Fairholme Rd. Croy 105 31 66 A
Fairholme Rd. Har 33 15 88 B
Fairholme Rd. Ilf 40 43 88 C
Fairholme Rd. Sutt 110 24 63 B
Fairholme Rd. W14 62 24 78 D
Fairholt Cl. N16 37 33 87 C
Fairholt Rd. N16 37 32 87 D
Fairholt St. SW7 5 27 79 C
Fairkytes Ave. Horn 42 53 87 D
Fairland Rd. E15 50 39 84 D
Fairlands Ave. Sutt 103 25 65 A
Fairlands Ave. Th Hth 105 31 67 A
Fairlands Ct. SE9 78 43 74 C
Fairlawn Ave. Bexh 79 47 76 D
Fairlawn Ave. N2 24 27 89 C
Fairlawn Ave. W4 61 20 78 A
Fairlawn Cl. Felt 82 12 71 B
Fairlawn Cl. King 94 20 70 A
Fairlawn Cl. N14 12 29 95 D
Fairlawn Ct. SE7 65 41 77 C
Fairlawn Dri. Wdf Gn 27 40 91 C
Fairlawnes. Wall 111 28 64 D
Fairlawn Gdns. Sthl 53 12 80 B
Fairlawn Gr. W4 61 20 78 A
Fairlawn Park. SE26 88 36 71 C
Fairlawn Rd. SW19 95 24 70 D
Fairlawns Cl. Horn 42 54 87 B
Fairlawn. SE7 65 41 77 A
Fairlawns. Pnr 20 11 90 D
Fairlawns. Sun 91 10 68 A
Fairlawns. SW15 73 23 74 B
Fairlawns. Twick 71 17 74 C
Fairlea Pl. W5 54 17 81 B
Fairlie Gdns. SE23 88 35 73 A
Fairlight Ave. E4 18 38 93 B
Fairlight Ave. NW10 45 21 83 C
Fairlight Ave. Wdf Gn 27 40 91 A
Fairlight Cl. E4 18 38 93 B
Fairlight Cl. Wor Pk 110 23 64 A
Fairlight Ct. Grnf 43 14 83 D
Fairlight. Hamp 82 13 71 D
Fairlight Rd. SW17 85 26 71 B
Fairlop Gdns. Ilf 28 44 91 C
Fairlop Rd. E11 39 39 87 A
Fairlop Rd. Ilf 28 44 90 C
Fairmead. Brom 99 42 68 D
Fairmead Cl. Brom 99 42 68 D
Fairmead Cl. Houn 59 11 77 D
Fairmead Cl. N Mal 94 20 68 B
Fairmead Gdns. Ilf 39 42 88 A
Fairmead Rd. Croy 105 31 66 A
Fairmead Rd. N19 36 30 86 C
Fairmead. Surb 102 19 66 D
Fairmile Ave. SW16 86 29 71 D
Fairmount Rd. SW2 74 30 74 D
Fairoak Cl. Orp 108 43 66 B
Fairoak Dri. SE9 78 44 74 B
Fairoak Gdns. Rom 30 51 90 C
Fairstead Wlk. N1 48 32 83 A
Fair St. Houn 70 14 75 A
Fair St. SE1 8 33 79 B
Fairthorn Rd. SE10 65 40 78 C
Fairview Ave. Wem 44 17 84 B
Fairview Cl. E17 26 36 90 A
Fairview Cres. Har 32 13 87 C
Fairview Ct. Ashf 81 07 71 C
Fairview. Eri 68 51 77 D
Fairview Gdns. Wdf Gn 27 40 90 B
Fairview Pl. SW2 86 30 73 B
Fairview Rd. Enf 13 31 97 A
Fairview Rd. N15 37 33 88 D
Fairview Rd. Sutt 111 27 64 C
Fairview Rd. SW16 96 30 69 B
Fairwater Ave. Well 78 46 75 C
Fairway Ave. NW9 22 19 89 B
Fairway. Bexh 79 48 74 A
Fairway Cl. Croy 106 36 67 A
Fairway Cl. Eps 109 20 64 A
Fairway Cl. NW11 35 26 87 A
Fairway Dri. Grnf 43 13 84 D
Fairway Gdns. Ilf 51 44 85 C
Fairway. Orp 108 44 67 B
Fairways. Ashf 91 07 70 B
Fairways. Islw 71 15 76 A
Fairways. Stan 21 18 90 C
Fairways. Tedd 93 17 70 D
Fairway. SW20 95 23 68 A
Fairway The. Barn 11 25 95 D
Fairway The. Brom 107 42 67 B
Fairway The. E Mol 92 13 68 B
Fairway The. N13 17 32 93 D
Fairway The. N14 12 28 95 D
Fairway The. N Mal 94 20 69 B
Fairway The. Nthlt 43 14 84 A
Fairway The. Ruis 32 11 86 D
Fairway The. W3 55 21 81 C
Fairway The. Wem 33 16 86 B
Fairweather Cl. N15 25 33 89 C
Fairweather Rd. N16 37 34 88 C
Fairwyn Rd. SE26 88 36 71 A
Falaize Ave. Ilf 51 43 85 B
Falcon Ave. Brom 99 42 68 C
Falconberg Ct. W1 2 29 81 D
Falconberg Mews. W1 2 29 81 D
Falcon Cl. Nthwd 19 09 91 C
Falcon Cl. SE1 7 31 80 D
Falcon Cres. Enf 14 35 95 B
Falcon Ct. E18 27 40 89 B
Falcon Ct. EC4 3 31 81 C
Falconer Wlk. N7 36 30 86 B
Falcon Gr. SW11 74 27 75 A
Falcon Rd. Enf 14 35 95 B
Falcon Rd. Hamp 92 12 70 D
Falcon Rd. SW11 74 27 75 A
Falconry Ct. King 93 18 68 A
Falcon St. E13 58 40 82 C
Falcon Terr. SW11 74 27 75 A
Falcon Way. Har 33 18 88 C
Falcon Way. Sun 91 09 69 C
Falconwood Ave. Well 78 45 76 C
Falconwood Par. Well 78 45 75 D
Falcourt Cl. Sutt 110 25 64 D
Falkirk St. N1 48 33 83 C
Falkland Ave. N11 16 28 92 B
Falkland Ave. N3 23 25 91 C
Falkland Park Ave. SE25 97 33 69 C
Falkland Pl. NW5 47 29 85 C
Falkland Rd. Barn 11 24 97 C
Falkland Rd. N8 25 31 89 C
Falkland Rd. NW5 47 29 85 C
Falloden Way. NW11 23 25 89 D
Fallow Court Ave. N12 23 26 91 A
Fallowhurst Path. N3 23 26 91 C
Fallsbrook Rd. SW16 96 29 70 A
Falmer Rd. E17 26 37 89 B
Falmer Rd. Enf 13 33 96 C
Falmer Rd. N15 37 32 88 B
Falmouth Ave. E4 18 38 92 D
Falmouth Ave. E4 27 39 91 A
Falmouth Cl. N22 24 30 91 D
Falmouth Cl. SE12 77 39 74 B
Falmouth Gdns. Ilf 27 41 89 D
Falmouth Gdns. Ilf 39 42 88 A
Falmouth Rd. SE1 8 32 79 C
Falmouth St. E15 49 38 85 D
Fambridge Cl. SE26 88 36 71 B
Fambridge Rd. Dag 41 49 87 C
Fambridge Rd. SE26 88 36 71 B
Fane St. W14 62 24 78 D
Fann St. EC1 4 32 82 C
Fanshawe Ave. Bark 51 44 84 A
Fanshawe Cres. Dag 52 48 85 D
Fanshawe Cres. Horn 42 53 88 D
Fanshawe Rd. Rich 83 17 71 A
Fanshaw St. N1 4 33 82 A
Fanthorpe St. SW15 73 23 75 A
Faraday Ave. Sid 90 46 72 B
Faraday Cl. N7 47 30 84 B
Faraday Rd. E15 50 39 84 B
Faraday Rd. E Mol 92 13 68 C
Faraday Rd. Sthl 53 13 80 B
Faraday Rd. W10 56 24 81 A
Faraday Rd. W3 55 20 80 A
Faraday Rd. Well 78 46 75 A
Faraday Way. Orp 100 46 68 D
Faraday Way. SE18 65 41 79 D
Fareham Rd. Felt 82 11 73 A
Fareham St. W1 2 29 81 D
Farewell Pl. Mit 96 27 69 A
Faringdon Ave. Brom 108 43 66 A
Faringdon Ave. Rom 30 53 91 D
Faringford Rd. E15 50 39 84 C
Farjeon Rd. SE3 77 41 76 B
Farleigh Ave. Brom 107 40 66 A
Farleigh Pl. N16 48 33 85 B
Farleigh Rd. N16 48 33 85 B
Farley Dri. Ilf 40 45 87 C
Farley Ho. SE26 87 34 72 D
Farley Pl. SE25 97 34 68 C
Farley Rd. S Croy 112 34 62 B
Farley Rd. SE6 88 38 73 A
Farlington Pl. SW15 84 22 73 B
Farlow Rd. SW15 73 23 75 B
Farlton Rd. SW18 85 25 73 B
Farman Gr (off Wayfarer Rd). Nthlt 53 11 82 B
Farm Ave. Har 32 13 88 C
Farm Ave. NW2 35 24 86 D
Farm Ave. SW16 86 30 71 A
Farm Ave. Wem 44 17 84 A
Farm Cl. Barn 11 23 95 A
Farm Cl. Dag 52 50 84 C
Farm Cl. Sthl 3 13 80 B
Farm Cl. Sutt 110 26 63 D
Farm Cl. Uxb 31 07 86 B
Farm Cl. Wall 111 29 62 C
Farm Cl. W.Wick 107 39 65 D
Farmcote Rd. SE12 89 40 73 C
Farm Ct. NW4 22 22 89 A
Farmdale Rd. Cars 111 27 63 C
Farmdale Rd. SE10 65 40 78 C
Farm Dri. Croy 106 36 65 B
Farmer Rd. E10 38 37 87 D
Farmer's Rd. SE5 63 31 77 D
Farmer St. W8 56 25 80 C
Farmfield Cl. N12 15 25 93 C
Farmfield Rd. Brom 89 39 71 C
Farmfield Rd. Mit 96 28 69 A
Farmhouse Rd. SW16 96 29 70 C
Farmilo Rd. E17 38 37 87 A
Farmington Ave. Sutt 103 26 65 D
Farm La. Croy 106 36 65 B
Farm La. N14 12 28 95 D
Farmlands. Enf 13 31 97 A
Farmlands. Pnr 19 10 89 C
Farmlands The. Nthlt 43 13 84 A
Farmland Wlk. Chis 90 43 71 D
Farm La. Pur 111 29 62 C
Farm La. SW6 62 25 77 C
Farmleigh. N14 16 29 94 A
Farm Pl. Dart 80 52 75 C
Farm Pl. W8 56 25 80 C
Farm Rd. Edg 22 19 91 B
Farm Rd. Houn 82 12 73 C
Farm Rd. Mord 103 25 67 B
Farm Rd. N21 17 32 94 B
Farm Rd. Sutt 110 26 63 D
Farmstead Rd. Har 20 14 90 B
Farmstead Rd. SE6 88 37 71 B
Farm St. W1 6 28 80 B
Farm The. SW19 85 23 73 B
Farm Vale. Bex 79 49 74 D
Farmway. Dag 41 47 86 C
Farm Way. Wor Pk 103 23 65 C
Farm Wlk. NW11 35 25 88 A
Farnaby Rd. Brom 99 39 69 A
Farnaby Rd. SE9 77 41 75 C
Farnan Ave. E17 26 37 89 B
Farnan Rd. SW16 86 30 71 C
Farnborough Ave. E17 26 36 89 A
Farnborough Cl. Wem 34 19 86 B
Farnborough Common. Brom 107 42 65 D
Farnborough Way (off Blake's Rd). SE15 63 33 77 D
Farncombe St. SE16 63 34 79 A
Farndale Ave. N13 17 32 93 C
Farndale Cres. Grnf 53 14 82 A
Farnell Mews. SW5 62 25 78 D
Farnell Rd. Islw 70 14 75 B
Farnes Dri. Rom 30 53 90 C
Farnham Cl. N20 15 26 94 A
Farnham Ct. Sutt 110 24 63 A
Farnham Gdns. SW20 94 22 69 D
Farnham Pl. SE1 7 31 80 D
Farnham Rd. Ilf 40 45 87 B
Farnham Rd. Well 79 47 76 C
Farnham Royal. SE11 10 30 78 D
Farningham Rd. N17 25 34 91 C
Farnley Rd. SE25 97 32 68 D
Faro Cl. Brom 100 43 69 C
Faroe Rd. W14 62 23 79 D
Farorna Wlk. Enf 13 31 97 A
Farquhar Rd. SE19 87 33 71 D
Farquhar Rd. SW19 85 25 72 C
Farquharson Rd. Croy 105 32 66 C
Farrance Rd. Rom 41 48 87 A
Farrance St. E14 57 37 81 C
Farrant Ave. N22 25 31 90 D
Farr Ave. Bark 51 46 83 C
Farren Rd. SE23 88 36 72 A
Farrer Rd. Har 21 18 89 C
Farrer Rd. N8 24 29 89 D
Farrier Cl. Sun 91 10 68 C
Farrier Rd. Nthlt 43 13 83 C
Farrier St. NW1 47 28 84 D
Farringdon Rd. EC1 3 31 82 C
Farringdon St. EC4 3 31 81 D
Farrington Ave. Orp 100 46 68 B
Farrins Rents. SE16 57 36 80 C
Farr Rd. Enf 13 32 97 B
Farthing Alley. SE1 63 34 79 A
Farthing Cl. Dart 80 54 75 D
Farthing Fields. E1 57 34 80 D
Farthings Cl. Pnr 31 10 88 D
Farwell Rd. Sid 90 46 71 B
Farwig La. Brom 99 40 69 A
Fashion St. E1 4 33 81 B
Fashoda Rd. Brom 99 41 68 D
Fassett Rd. E8 48 34 84 A
Fassett Rd. King 93 18 68 C
Fassett Sq. E8 48 34 84 A
Fauconberg Rd. W4 61 20 77 A
Faulkner's Alley. EC1 3 31 81 B
Faulkner St. SE14 76 35 76 A
Fauna Cl. Rom 41 47 88 C
Faunce St. SE17 63 31 78 D
Favart Rd. SW6 73 25 76 A
Faversham Ave. Enf 13 32 95 D
Faversham Rd. Beck 98 36 69 D
Faversham Rd. Mord 103 25 67 D
Faversham Rd. SE6 88 36 73 D
Fawcett Cl. SW11 73 26 76 D
Fawcett Estate. E5 37 34 87 C
Fawcett Rd. Croy 105 32 65 C
Fawcett Rd. NW10 45 21 84 D
Fawcett St. SW10 62 26 77 A
Fawe Park Rd. SW15 73 24 75 D
Fawe St. E14 57 37 81 B
Fawkham House. SE1 63 33 78 B
Fawley Rd. N17 25 34 89 C
Fawley Rd. NW6 46 25 85 D
Fawnbrake Ave. SE24 75 32 74 A
Fawn Rd. E13 50 41 83 C
Fawns Manor Rd. Felt 81 08 73 D
Fawood Ave. NW10 45 20 84 D
Faygate Cres. Bexh 79 49 74 A
Faygate Rd. SW2 86 30 72 B
Fayland Ave. SW16 86 29 71 C
Fearnley Cres. Hamp 92 12 70 B
Fearon St. SE10 65 40 78 C
Feathers Pl. SE10 64 38 77 B
Featherstone Ave. SE23 88 35 72 A
Featherstone Rd. NW7 22 22 91 B
Featherstone Rd. Sthl 59 12 79 C
Featherstone St. EC1 4 32 82 D
Featherstone Terr. Sthl 59 12 79 C
Featley Rd. SW9 75 31 75 B
Federal Rd. Grnf 44 17 83 C
Federation Rd. SE2 67 47 78 A
Feildview. SW18 85 26 73 D
Felbridge Ave. Stan 21 16 90 B
Felbridge Cl. Sutt 110 25 62 B
Felbridge Cl. SW16 87 31 71 A
Felbrigge Rd. Ilf 40 45 87 D
Felday Rd. SE13 76 37 74 D
Felden St. SW6 73 24 76 B
Feldman Cl. N16 37 34 87 C
Feldon Cl. Pnr 20 12 91 C
Felgate Mews. W6 61 22 78 B
Felhampton Rd. SE9 90 43 72 D
Felhurst Cres. Dag 52 50 85 A
Felix Ave. N8 36 30 88 C
Felix Rd. W13 54 16 80 A
Felix St. E2 48 34 83 D
Felixstowe Rd. N17 25 33 89 B
Felixstowe Rd. N9 17 34 93 C
Felixstowe Rd. NW10 55 22 82 B
Felixstowe Rd. SE2 66 46 79 D
Fellbrigg Rd. SE22 75 33 74 B
Fellbrigg St. E1 57 34 82 D
Fellbrook. Rich 83 16 72 D
Fellowes Rd. Cars 104 27 65 A
Fellows Ct. E2 48 33 83 D
Fellows Rd. NW3 47 27 84 C
Fell Rd. Croy 105 32 65 C
Felltram Way. SE7 65 40 78 C
Fell Wlk. Edg 22 19 90 B
Felmersham Cl. SW4 74 30 75 C
Felmingham Rd. SE20 98 35 69 C
Felsberg Rd. SW2 86 30 73 A
Fels Cl. Dag 41 49 86 D
Fels Farm Ave. Dag 41 50 86 C
Felsham Rd. SW15 73 23 75 A
Felsham Rd. SW15 73 23 75 B
Felspar Cl. SE18 66 45 78 D
Felstead Ave. Ilf 28 43 90 A
Felstead Rd. E11 39 40 87 B
Felstead Rd. Orp 108 46 65 B
Felstead Rd. Rom 29 50 91 C
Felstead St. E9 49 36 84 B
Felsted Rd. E16 58 41 81 D
Feltham Ave. E Mol 93 15 68 C
Felthambrook Way. Felt 81 10 71 B
Feltham Hill Rd. Ashf 81 07 71 D
Felthamhill Rd. Felt 81 10 71 B
Feltham Rd. Ashf 81 07 71 B
Feltham Rd. Mit 96 28 69 C
Felton Cl. Orp 108 43 67 D
Felton Gdns. Bark 51 45 83 C
Felton Lea. Sid 90 45 71 D
Felton Rd. Bark 51 45 83 C
Felton Rd. W13 60 17 79 A
Felton St. N1 48 32 83 B
Fencepiece Rd. Ilf 28 44 91 C
Fenchurch Ave. EC3 4 33 81 C
Fenchurch Bldgs. EC3 4 33 81 C
Fenchurch St. EC3 8 33 80 A
Fen Ct. EC3 4 33 81 C
Fendall Rd. Eps 109 20 64 C
Fendall St. SE1 8 33 79 C
Fendt Cl. E16 58 39 81 D
Fendyke Rd. Belv 67 47 78 B
Fenelon Pl. W14 62 24 78 B
Fen Gr. Sid 78 45 75 D
Fenham Rd. SE15 63 34 77 D
Fenman Ct. N17 25 34 90 B
Fenn Cl. Brom 99 40 70 A
Fennells Mead. Eps 109 21 62 B
Fennell St. SE18 66 43 77 A
Fenner Cl. SE16 63 34 78 B
Fenner Sq. SW11 73 26 75 B
Fenning St. SE1 8 33 79 A
Fenn St. E9 49 35 85 C
Fenstanton Ave. N12 23 26 91 B
Fen St. E16 58 39 80 B
Fentiman Rd. SW8 10 30 77 D
Fentiman Way. Horn 42 54 87 C
Fenton Cl. Chis 89 42 71 D
Fenton Cl. SW9 74 30 76 D
Fenton Rd. N17 25 32 91 C
Fenton's Ave. E13 50 40 83 D
Fenton St. E1 57 34 81 D
Fenwick Cl. SE18 66 43 77 A
Fenwick Gr. SE15 75 34 75 A
Fenwick Pl. SW9 74 30 75 A
Fenwick Rd. SE15 75 34 75 A
Ferdinand Pl. NW1 47 28 84 C
Ferdinand St. NW1 47 28 84 C
Ferguson Ave. Rom 30 53 90 D
Ferguson Ave. Surb 101 18 67 B
Ferguson Ct. Rom 30 53 90 D
Fergus Rd. N5 48 31 85 D
Fermain Ct. N1 48 33 83 A
Ferme Park Rd. N4 36 30 87 B
Fermor Rd. SE23 88 36 73 C
Fermoy Rd. Grnf 64 13 82 D
Fermoy Rd. W9 56 24 82 D
Fern Ave. Mit 96 29 68 D
Fernbank Ave. Wem 44 15 85 B
Fernbrook Ave. Sid 78 45 74 A
Fernbrook Dri. Har 32 13 87 B
Fernbrook Rd. SE13 77 39 74 C
Ferncliff Rd. E8 48 34 85 C
Ferncroft Ave. N12 24 27 91 B
Ferncroft Ave. NW3 46 25 85 A
Ferncroft Ave. Ruis 32 11 86 A
Ferndale Ave. E17 38 38 88 B
Ferndale Ave. Houn 70 12 75 A
Ferndale. Brom 99 41 69 C
Ferndale Ct. SW9 74 30 75 D
Ferndale Rd. E11 39 39 86 B
Ferndale Rd. E7 50 40 84 D
Ferndale Rd. N15 37 33 88 B
Ferndale Rd. Rom 29 50 90 C
Ferndale Rd. SE25 105 34 67 B
Ferndale Rd. SW4 74 30 75 C
Ferndale Terr. Har 21 15 89 D
Ferndene Rd. SE24 75 32 75 C
Fern Dene. W13 54 16 81 B
Ferndown Way. Rom 41 49 88 D
Ferndown Ave. Orp 108 44 66 D
Ferndown Cl. Pnr 20 12 91 C
Ferndown Cl. Sutt 110 26 63 B
Ferndown. Horn 42 54 88 D
Ferndown. Nthwd 19 10 90 C
Ferndown Rd. SE9 89 41 73 B
Ferne Park Rd. N8 36 30 88 D
Ferney Rd. Barn 16 28 94 C
Fern Gr. Felt 81 10 73 B
Fernhall Dri. Ilf 39 41 88 B
Fernham Rd. Th Hth 97 32 68 A
Fernhead Rd. W9 56 24 82 B
Fernhill Ct. E17 26 38 90 D
Fernhill Ct. King 83 17 71 D
Fernhill Gdns. King 83 18 71 C
Fernholme Rd. SE15 76 35 74 B
Fernhurst Gdns. Edg 22 19 91 A
Fernhurst Rd. Ashf 81 08 71 A
Fernhurst Rd. Croy 105 34 66 D
Fernhurst Rd. SW6 62 24 77 D
Fern La. Houn 59 12 78 D
Fernlea Rd. Mit 96 28 69 A
Fernlea Rd. SW12 86 28 73 D
Fernleigh Cl. Croy 112 31 64 A
Fernleigh Ct. Har 20 13 90 D
Fernleigh Ct. Wem 33 18 87 C
Fernleigh Rd. N21 17 31 93 B
Fernsbury St. WC1 3 31 82 A
Ferns Cl. S Croy 112 34 62 D
Fernshaw Rd. SW10 62 26 77 A
Fernside Ave. Felt 81 10 71 B
Fernside Ct. NW4 23 23 90 D
Fernside Rd. SW12 86 28 73 A
Ferns Rd. E15 50 39 84 B
Fern St. E3 57 37 82 C
Fernthorpe Rd. SW16 96 29 70 A
Ferntower Rd. N5 48 32 85 D
Fernways. Ilf 51 43 85 B
Fernwood Ave. Grnf 44 17 84 A
Fernwood Ave. SW16 86 29 71 B
Fernwood Cl. Brom 99 41 69 C
Fernwood Cres. N20 16 27 93 D
Ferranti Cl. SE18 65 41 79 D
Ferraro Cl. Houn 59 13 77 A
Ferrers Ave. Wall 111 29 64 B
Ferrers Rd. SW16 86 29 71 D
Ferrestone Rd. N8 24 30 89 D
Ferriby Cl. N1 48 31 84 C
Ferrier St. SW18 73 25 75 D
Ferring Cl. Har 32 14 87 C
Ferrings. SE21 87 33 72 C
Ferris Ave. Croy 106 36 65 D
Ferris Rd. SE22 75 34 75 C
Ferron Rd. E5 37 34 86 D
Ferry App. SE18 66 43 79 C
Ferry La. Brent 60 18 77 A
Ferry La. N17 25 34 89 D
Ferry La. Rich 60 18 77 B
Ferry La. SW13 61 21 77 B
Ferrymead Ave. Grnf 43 13 83 D
Ferrymead Dri. Grnf 43 13 83 C
Ferrymead Gdns. Grnf 43 14 83 C
Ferrymoor. Rich 83 16 72 D
Ferry Pl. SE18 66 43 79 C
Ferry Rd. E Mol 92 13 68 A
Ferry Rd. Surb 101 16 67 D
Ferry Rd. SW13 72 22 76 A
Ferry Rd. Tedd 83 16 71 D
Ferry Rd. Twick 83 16 73 D
Ferry Sq. Brent 60 18 77 A
Ferry St. E14 64 38 78 C
Festing Rd. SW15 73 23 75 B
Festival Cl. Eri 68 51 77 D
Festival Wlk. Cars 111 27 64 B
Fetter La. EC4 3 31 81 C
Ffinch St. SE8 64 37 77 C
Field Cl. Brom 99 41 69 C
Field Cl. E4 26 37 91 B
Field Cl. Houn 69 10 76 B
Field Cl. Ruis 31 08 87 C
Field Cl. Uxb 31 07 86 B
Field Ct. WC1 3 30 81 B
Field End. Nthlt 43 11 84 B
Field End Rd. Ruis 32 11 87 D
Fieldend Rd. SW16 96 29 69 A
Field End. Ruis 43 11 84 A
Field End. Twick 83 15 71 B
Field Gate La. Mit 96 27 69 C
Fieldgate St. E1 57 34 81 A
Fieldhouse Rd. SW12 86 29 73 C
Fielding Ave. Twick 82 14 72 C
Fielding Rd. W14 62 23 79 D
Fielding Rd. W4 61 21 79 C
Fieldings The. SE23 88 35 73 C
Fielding St. SE17 63 32 77 A
Field La. Brent 60 17 77 C
Field Lane. Tedd 93 16 70 A
Field La. Tedd 83 16 71 C
Field Mead. NW9 22 21 91 D
Field Pl. EC1 48 31 83 C
Field Pl. N.Mal 102 21 67 D
Field Rd. E7 50 40 85 A
Field Rd. Felt 69 10 74 D

Field Rd. N17 25 33 89 A
Field Rd. W6 62 24 77 D
Fieldsend Rd. Sutt 110 24 64 C
Fields Estate. E8 48 34 84 C
Fieldside Rd. Brom 88 38 71 D
Fields Park Cres. Rom 41 47 88 B
Field St. WC1 3 30 82 B
Field View. Felt 81 08 71 B
Fieldway Cres. N5 48 31 85 C
Fieldway. Dag 52 47 85 A
Field Way. Grnf 43 13 83 B
Field Way. NW10 45 20 84 C
Fieldway. Orp 108 44 67 D
Field Way. Ruis 31 08 87 C
Fife Rd. E16 58 40 81 A
Fife Rd. King 93 18 69 C
Fife Rd. N22 25 31 91 D
Fife Rd. SW14 72 20 74 A
Fife Terr. N1 47 30 83 D
Fifield Path. SE23 88 35 72 D
Fifth Ave. E12 50 42 85 B
Fifth Ave. W10 56 24 82 A
Fifth Cross Rd. Twick 82 14 72 B
Filey Ave. N16 37 34 87 C
Filey Cl. Sutt 110 26 63 C
Filey Waye. Ruis 31 10 86 B
Fillebrook Ave. Enf 13 33 97 D
Fillebrook Rd. E11 39 39 87 A
Filmer Rd. SW6 62 24 77 D
Filston Rd. Eri 67 50 78 C
Finborough Rd. SW10 62 25 77 B
Finborough Rd. SW17 96 27 70 B
Finchale Rd. SE2 66 46 79 C
Finch Ave. SE27 87 32 71 B
Finch Cl. NW10 45 20 84 B
Finchdean Way (off Blake's Rd)
SE15 63 33 77 C
Finch Dri. Felt 82 11 73 B
Finchingfield Ave. Wdf Gn 27 41 91 C
Finch La. EC3 4 32 81 D
Finchley Ct. N3 23 25 91 B
Finchley La. NW4 23 23 89 D
Finchley Park. N12 15 26 92 B
Finchley Pl. NW8 46 26 83 D
Finchley Rd. NW11 35 25 87 A
Finchley Rd. NW3 46 26 85 C
Finchley Rd. NW8 46 26 83 B
Finchley Way. N3 23 25 91 C
Finch's Ct. E14 57 37 80 B
Finck St. SE1 7 30 79 B
Finden Rd. E7 50 41 85 C
Findhorn St. E14 58 38 81 C
Findon Cl. Har 32 13 86 D
Findon Cl. SW18 73 25 74 C
Findon Rd. N9 17 34 94 D
Findon Rd. W12 61 22 79 A
Fine Bush La. Uxb 31 07 88 D
Fingal St. E10 65 39 78 D
Finland Rd. SE4 76 36 75 A
Finlays Cl. Chess 109 19 64 C
Finlay St. SW6 73 23 76 B
Finnis St. E2 57 34 82 D
Finnymore Rd. Dag 52 48 84 C
Finsbury Ave. EC2 4 32 81 B
Finsbury Circ. EC2 4 32 81 B
Finsbury Cottages. N22 24 30 91 C
Finsbury Ct. EC2 4 32 81 B
Finsbury Market. EC2 4 33 81 A
Finsbury Market. EC2 4 33 82 C
Finsbury Park Ave. N4 37 32 87 A
Finsbury Park Rd. N4 37 31 86 B
Finsbury Pavement. EC2 4 32 81 B
Finsbury Rd. N22 24 30 90 B
Finsbury Rd. N22 24 30 91 D
Finsbury Sq. EC2 4 32 81 B
Finsbury St. EC2 4 32 81 B
Finsen Rd. SE5 75 32 75 A
Finstock Rd. W10 56 23 81 D
Finucane Ct. Rich 71 18 75 B
Firbank Cl. E16 58 41 81 B
Firbank Rd. SE15 75 34 76 D
Fircroft Gdns. Har 33 15 86 C
Fircroft Rd. SW17 86 27 72 D
Fir Dene. Orp 108 43 65 C
Firdene. Surb 102 20 66 C
Fire Bell Alley. Surb 101 18 67 C
Firefly Cl. Wall 111 30 63 C
Fire Station Alley. Barn 11 24 96 A
Fir Gr. N.Mal 102 21 67 D
Firhill Rd. SE6 88 37 72 C
Firmin Rd. Dart 80 53 74 A
Fir Rd. Felt 82 11 71 C
Fir Rd. Sutt 103 24 66 D
Firs Ave. N10 24 28 89 C
Firs Ave. SW14 72 20 75 C
Firsby Ave. Croy 106 36 66 C
Firsby Rd. N16 37 34 87 C
Firs Cl. N10 24 28 89 A
Firs Cl. SE23 88 36 73 A
Firscroft. N13 17 32 93 C
Firs Dri. Houn 69 10 76 B
Firs La. N13 17 32 93 C
Firs La. N21 17 32 94 C
Firs Park Ave. N21 17 32 94 D
Firs Park Gdns. N21 17 32 94 D
First Ave. Bexh 67 47 77 C
First Ave. Dag 52 49 83 D
First Ave. E12 50 42 85 C
First Ave. E13 58 40 82 A
First Ave. E17 38 37 88 B
First Ave. E Mol 92 13 68 C
First Ave. Enf 13 33 95 B
First Ave. Eps 109 21 62 A
First Ave. N18 18 35 92 A
First Ave. NW4 23 23 89 C
First Ave. Rom 41 47 88 A
First Ave. SW14 72 21 75 A
First Ave. W10 56 24 82 D
First Ave. W3 55 21 80 D
First Ave. Wem 33 17 86 B
First Cl. E Mol 92 14 68 A
First Cross Rd. Twick 83 15 72 A
Firs The. N20 15 26 94 D
Firs The. SW20 94 22 70 C
Firs The. W5 54 17 81 B
First St. SW3 9 27 78 A
Firstway. SW20 95 23 69 C
First Way. Wem 45 19 85 B
Firs Wlk. Nthwd 19 08 91 B
Firswood Ave. Eps 109 21 64 D
Firth Gdns. SW6 73 24 76 A
Firtree Ave. Mit 96 28 69 C
Fir Tree Cl. Eps 109 21 64 B
Fir Tree Cl. Rom 29 50 89 B
Fir Tree Gr. Cars 111 27 63 D
Fir Tree Rd. Houn 70 12 75 C
Fir Trees Cl. SE16 57 36 80 C
Fir Tree Wlk. Dag 41 50 86 C
Fir Tree Wlk. Enf 13 32 96 B
Fir Wlk. Sutt 110 23 63 B
Fisher Cl. Croy 105 33 66 D
Fisher Cl. Grnf 53 13 82 A
Fisherman Cl. Rich 83 17 71 A
Fisher Rd. Har 21 15 90 D
Fishers Ct. SE14 76 35 76 B
Fisher's La. W4 61 20 78 B
Fisher St. E16 58 40 81 A
Fisher St. WC1 3 30 81 B
Fisher's Way. Belv 67 50 79 B
Fisherton St. NW8 1 26 82 D
Fishponds Rd. SW17 86 27 71 A
Fish St Hill. EC3 8 32 80 B
Fiske Ct. Bark 51 44 83 D
Fiske Ct. N17 25 34 90 A
Fisons Rd. E16 58 40 80 C
Fitzalan Rd. N3 23 24 89 B
Fitzalan St. SE11 63 31 78 A
Fitzgeorge Ave. N Mal 94 20 69 A
Fitz-George Ave. W14 62 24 78 A
Fitzgerald Ave. SW14 72 21 75 A
Fitzgerald Rd. E11 39 40 88 A
Fitzgerald Rd. Surb 101 16 67 C
Fitzgerald Rd. SW14 72 20 75 B
Fitzhardinge St. W1 2 28 81 C
Fitzhugh Gr. SW18 73 26 74 D
Fitzilian Ave. Rom 30 54 90 B
Fitzjames Ave. Croy 105 34 65 A
Fitzjames Ave. W14 62 24 78 A
Fitzjohn Ave. Barn 11 24 96 D
Fitzjohn's Ave. NW3 46 26 85 D
Fitzmaurice Pl. W1 6 28 80 D
Fitzneal St. W12 55 21 81 D
Fitzroy Cl. N6 36 27 87 D
Fitzroy Ct. W1 2 29 82 C
Fitzroy Gdns. SE19 97 33 70 C
Fitzroy Mews. W1 2 29 82 C
Fitzroy Park. N6 36 27 87 D
Fitzroy Rd. NW1 47 28 83 A
Fitzroy Sq. W1 2 29 82 C
Fitzroy St. W1 2 29 82 C
Fitzstephen Rd. Dag 52 47 85 C
Fitzwarren Gdns. N19 36 29 87 C
Fitzwilliam Ave. Rich 71 18 76 D
Fitzwilliam House. Rich 71 17 75 D
Fitzwilliam Rd. SW4 74 29 75 A
Fitz Wygram Cl. Hamp 82 14 71 C
Five Acre. NW9 22 21 90 B
Five Bell Alley. E14 57 36 80 B
Five Elms Rd. Brom 107 41 65 C
Five Elms Rd. Dag 41 48 86 D
Five Oaks La. Chig 29 48 91 A
Fives Ct. SE11 7 31 79 D
Fiveways Rd. W9 75 31 76 C
Fladbury Rd. N15 37 32 88 D
Fladgate Rd. E11 39 39 88 C
Flag Wlk. Pnr 31 10 88 C
Flambard Rd. Har 33 16 88 C
Flamborough Rd. Ruis 31 10 86 C
Flamborough St. E14 57 36 81 C
Flamborough Wlk. E14 57 36 81 C
Flamingo Gdns (off Jetstar Way).
Nthlt 53 12 82 A
Flamstead Gdns. Dag 52 47 84 C
Flamstead Rd. Dag 52 47 84 C
Flamsted Ave. Wem 45 19 84 A
Flamsteed Rd. SE7 65 42 78 C
Flanchford Rd. W12 61 21 79 D
Flanders Cres. SW17 96 27 70 D
Flanders Rd. E6 51 43 83 C
Flanders Rd. W4 61 21 78 A
Flanders Way. E9 49 35 84 C
Flank St. E1 57 34 80 A
Flask Wlk. NW3 46 26 85 B
Flaxley Rd. Mord 103 25 66 B
Flaxman Ct. W1 2 29 81 D
Flaxman Rd. SE5 75 32 76 C
Flaxman Terr. WC1 2 29 82 B
Flaxton Rd. SE18 78 44 76 B
Flaxton Rd. SE18 66 45 77 C
Fleece Rd. Surb 101 17 66 C
Fleece Wlk. N7 47 30 84 A
Fleet La. EC4 3 31 81 D
Fleet Rd. NW3 47 27 85 C
Fleet Sq. WC1 3 30 82 B
Fleet St. EC4 3 31 81 C
Fleet Street Hill. E1 57 34 82 C
Fleetwood Cl. E16 58 41 81 B
Fleetwood Rd. King 94 19 68 B
Fleetwood Rd. NW10 45 22 85 C
Fleetwood Sq. King 94 19 68 B
Fleetwood St. N16 37 33 86 A
Fleming Cl. E17 26 36 90 D
Fleming Ct. Croy 112 31 64 C
Fleming Me. Mit 96 27 70 D
Fleming Rd. E17 26 36 90 D
Fleming Rd. SE17 63 31 77 B
Fleming Rd. Sthl 53 14 81 C
Fleming Way. Islw 71 15 75 D
Flempton Rd. E10 38 36 87 C
Fletcher La. E10 38 38 87 A
Fletcher Path. SE8 64 37 77 C
Fletcher Rd. W4 61 20 79 C
Fletchers Cl. Brom 99 40 68 D
Fletcher St. E1 57 34 80 A
Fletching Rd. E5 38 35 86 C
Fletching Rd. SE7 65 42 77 B
Fletton Rd. N11 24 30 91 C
Fleur Gates. SW19 85 23 73 B
Flexmere Rd. N17 25 33 90 A
Flight App. NW9 22 21 90 D
Flimwell Cl. Brom 89 39 71 C
Flintmill Cres. SE3 77 42 76 C
Flinton St. SE17 63 33 78 C
Flint St. SE17 63 32 78 B
Flitcroft St. WC2 2 29 81 D
*Flockton St. SE16 63 34 79 A
*Flockton St. SE16 63 34 79 A
Flodden Rd. SE5 75 32 76 A
Flood St. SW3 9 27 77 A
Flood Wlk. SW3 9 27 77 A
Flora Cl. E14 57 37 81 D
Flora Gdns. Rom 41 47 88 C
Flora Gdns. W6 61 22 78 B
Floral St. WC2 7 30 80 A
Flora St. Belv 67 48 78 D
Florence Ave. Enf 13 32 96 A
Florence Ave. Mord 103 26 67 A
Florence Cl. Horn 42 54 86 A
Florence Dri. Enf 13 32 96 A
Florence Gdns. W4 61 20 77 A
Florence Rd. Beck 98 36 69 C
Florence Rd. Brom 99 40 69 A
Florence Rd. E13 50 39 83 D
Florence Rd. E6 50 41 83 A
Florence Rd. Felt 81 10 73 D
Florence Rd. King 93 18 70 B
Florence Rd. N4 37 31 87 C
Florence Rd. S Croy 112 32 62 B
Florence Rd. SE14 76 35 76 B
Florence Rd. SE2 67 47 78 A
Florence Rd. Sthl 59 11 79 D
Florence Rd. SW19 95 25 70 B
Florence Rd. W4 61 20 79 D
Florence Rd. W5 54 18 80 A
Florence St. E16 58 39 82 D
Florence St. N1 48 31 84 D
Florence St. NW4 23 23 89 C
Florence Terr. SE14 76 36 76 B
Florfield Pas. E8 48 34 84 B
Florfield Rd. E8 48 34 84 B
Florian Ave. Sutt 110 26 64 B
Florian Rd. SW15 73 24 75 C
Florida Ct. Brom 99 39 68 D
Florida Rd. Th Hth 97 31 69 B
Florida St. E2 57 34 82 A
Floriston Cl. Stan 21 16 90 B
Floriston Gdns. Stan 21 16 90 B
Floriston Rd. Nthlt 43 13 85 D
Floss St. SW6 73 23 76 C
Flower and Dean St. E1 4 33 81 B
Flower House Cl. Brom 88 38 71 C
Flower La. NW7 22 21 91 B
Flowersmead. SW17 86 28 72 A
Flowers Mews. N19 36 29 86 A
Floyd Rd. SE7 65 41 78 C
Fludyer St. SE13 77 39 75 C
Fluer De Lis St. E1 4 33 82 D
Folair Way. SE16 63 34 78 D
Foley St. W1 2 29 81 A
Folgate St. E1 4 33 81 B
Foliot St. W12 55 21 81 D
Folkestone Rd. E17 26 37 89 D
Folkestone Rd. E6 51 43 83 C
Folkestone Rd. N18 17 34 92 A
Folkingham La. NW9 22 21 90 A
Folkington Cnr. N12 15 24 92 D
Follett St. E14 58 38 81 C
Folly La. E17 26 36 91 D
Folly La. E4 26 36 91 A
Folly Wall. E14 64 38 79 A
Fontaine Rd. SW16 96 30 70 D
Fontarabia Rd. SW11 74 28 75 C
Fontayne Ave. Rom 30 51 90 C
Fontenoy Rd. SW12 86 29 72 A
Fonteyne Gdns. Wdf Gn 27 41 90 D
Fonthill Ct. SE23 88 35 73 A
Fonthill Mews. N4 37 31 86 A
Fonthill Rd. N4 37 31 86 A
Font Hills. N2 23 26 90 C
Fontley Way. SW15 84 22 73 A
Fontmell Cl. Ashf 81 07 71 C
Fontmell Park. Ashf 81 07 71 C
Fontwell Cl. Har 21 15 91 C
Fontwell Cl. Nthlt 43 13 84 A
Fontwell Dri. Brom 108 43 67 A
Football La. Har 33 15 87 D
Footbury Hill Rd. Orp 108 46 66 A
Footpath The. SW15 72 22 74 A
Footscray Rd. SE9 78 43 74 C
Footscray Rd. SE9 90 44 73 C
Forbes St. E1 57 34 81 C
Forburg Rd. N16 37 34 87 C
Fordbridge Rd. Sun 90 10 68 C
Ford Cl. Har 32 14 87 B
Ford Cl. Shep 91 07 68 C
Ford Cl. Th Hth 105 31 67 B
Fordcroft Rd. Orp 108 46 67 B
Forde Ave. Brom 99 41 68 A
Fordel Rd. SE6 88 38 73 D
Ford End. Wdf Gn 27 40 91 B
Fordham Cl. Barn 12 27 96 A
Fordham Rd. Barn 12 27 96 A
Fordham St. E1 57 34 81 C
Fordhook Ave. W5 55 19 80 A
Fordingley Rd. W9 56 24 82 B
Fordington Ho. SE26 87 34 72 D
Fordington Rd. N6 24 27 89 D
Fordmill Rd. SE6 88 37 72 A
Ford Rd. Dag 52 49 84 C
Ford Rd. E3 49 36 83 D
Ford's Gr. N21 17 32 94 B
Fords Park Rd. E16 58 40 81 C
Ford Sq. E1 57 34 81 B
Ford St (off Old Ford Rd). E3 49 36 83 C
Ford St (off Roman Rd). E3 49 36 83 C
Ford St. E16 58 39 81 D
Fordwich Cl. Orp 108 45 66 B
Fordwych Rd. NW2 46 24 85 C
Fordyce Rd. SE13 76 38 74 C
Fordyke Rd. Dag 41 48 86 B
Foreign St. SE5 75 31 76 D
Foreland Ct. NW4 23 24 90 A
Foreland St. SE18 66 44 78 B
Foreman Ct. W6 62 23 78 A
Foremark Cl. Chig 28 45 91 B
Foreshore. SE8 64 36 78 B
Forest App. Wdf Gn 27 40 91 C
Fore St Ave. EC2 4 32 81 B
Forest Cl. E11 39 40 88 A
Forest Ct. E11 27 39 89 C
Forestdale. N11 16 29 92 B
Forest Dri. Brom 107 42 65 C
Forest Dri. E12 39 41 86 D
Forest Dri. E17 26 38 89 D
Forest Dri E. E11 38 38 87 B
Forest Dri. Sun 91 09 70 D
Forest Dri. Wdf Gn 27 39 91 C
Forest Dri W. E11 38 38 87 B
Fore St. EC2 4 32 81 B
Forester Rd. SE15 75 34 75 B
Foresters Cl. Wall 111 29 63 D
Foresters Cres. Bexh 79 49 75 D
Foresters Dri. Wall 111 29 62 B
Forest Gate. E7 50 40 85 C
Forest Gate. NW9 34 21 88 A
Forest Gdns. N17 25 33 90 D
Forest Glade. E11 39 39 88 C
Forest Gr. E8 48 33 84 D
Forest Hill Rd. SE23 76 35 74 C
Forestholme Cl. SE23 88 35 72 A
Forest La. E15 50 39 85 C
Forest Mount Rd. Wdf Gr 26 38 91 D
Fore St. N18 17 34 92 A
Fore St. N9 17 34 93 C
Fore St. Pnr 31 10 88 A
Forest Rd. E11 38 38 87 B
Forest Rd. E17 26 37 89 A
Forest Rd. E7 50 40 85 A
Forest Rd. E8 48 33 84 B
Forest Rd. Eri 80 52 76 A
Forest Rd. Felt 82 11 72 A
Forest Rd. Ilf 28 45 91 D
Forest Rd. N17 25 34 89 D
Forest Rd. N9 17 34 94 D
Forest Rd. Rich 61 19 77 C
Forest Rd. Rom 29 49 89 B
Forest Rd. Sutt 103 25 66 A
Forest Ridge. Beck 98 37 68 A
Forest Ridge. Brom 107 42 65 C
Forest Rise. E17 38 38 88 B
Forest Rise. E17 26 38 89 D
Forest Side. E7 50 40 85 B
Forest Side. Wor Pk 102 21 66 D
Forest St. E7 50 40 85 C
Forest The. E11 27 39 89 C
Forest View Ave. E10 38 38 88 B
Forest View. E11 39 39 87 B
Forest View. E4 18 38 94 B
Forest View Rd. E12 50 42 85 A
Forest View Rd. E17 26 38 90 A
Forest Way. N19 36 29 86 A
Forest Way. Orp 108 46 67 A
Forest Way. Sid 90 44 73 B
Forfar Rd. N22 25 31 90 B
Forfar Rd. SW11 74 28 76 A
Forge Cl. Brom 107 40 66 C
Forge La. Felt 82 12 71 C
Forge La. Nthwd 19 09 91 C
Forge La. Sun 91 10 68 A
Forge La. Sutt 110 24 63 C
Forge Pl. NW1 47 28 84 A
Forman Pl. N16 48 33 85 B
Formby Ave. Stan 21 17 89 A
Formosa St. W9 56 25 82 D
Formunt Cl. E16 58 39 81 B
Forres Gdns. NW11 35 25 88 C
Forrester Path. SE26 88 35 71 A
Forrest Gdns. SW16 96 30 68 B
Forset St. W1 1 27 81 C
Forstal Cl. Brom 99 40 68 A
Forster Rd. Beck 98 36 68 A
Forster Rd. Croy 105 32 66 A
Forster Rd. E17 38 36 88 C
Forster Rd. N17 25 33 89 B
Forster Rd. SW2 86 30 73 A
Forsters Cl. Rom 41 48 88 D
Forston St. N1 48 32 83 C
Forsyte Cres. SE19 97 33 69 A
Forsyte Ct. King 94 19 69 B
Forsyth Gdns. SE17 63 31 77 B
Forsyth Pl. Enf 13 33 95 A
Forterie Gdns. Ilf 51 46 85 A
Fortescue Ave. E8 48 34 84 D
Fortescue Ave. Twick 82 14 72 C
Fortescue Rd. Edg 22 20 91 D
Fortescue Rd. SW19 95 26 70 D
Fortess Gr. NW5 47 29 85 C
Fortess Rd. NW5 47 29 85 A
Forthbridge Rd. SW11 74 28 75 C
Forth Cross Rd. Twick 82 14 72 B
Fortis Green Ave. N2 24 27 89 D
Fortis Green. N10 24 28 89 A
Fortis Green. N2 24 27 89 B
Fortis Green Rd. N10 24 28 89 A
Fortismere Ave. N10 24 28 89 C
Fortnam Rd. N19 36 29 86 B
Fortnums Acre. Stan 21 15 91 B
Fort Rd. Nthlt 43 13 84 C
Fort Rd. SE1 63 33 78 B
Fortress Wlk. NW5 47 28 85 D
Fort St. E16 58 40 80 D
Fort St. E1 4 33 81 A
Fortuna Cl. N7 47 30 84 B
Fortunegate Rd. NW10 45 21 84 C
Fortune Green Rd. NW6 46 25 85 A
Fortunes Mead. Nthlt 43 12 84 A
Fortune St. EC1 4 32 82 C
Forty Acre La. E16 58 40 81 A
Forty Ave. Wem 33 18 86 B
Forty Cl. Wem 33 18 86 D
Forty Footpath. SW14 72 20 75 A
Forty La. Wem 34 19 86 B
Forumside. Edg 22 19 91 A
Forum The. E Mol 92 13 68 D
Forum Way. Edg 22 19 91 A
Forval Cl. Mit 104 27 67 B
Fosbury Mews. W2 56 25 80 B
Foscote Mews. W9 56 25 81 A
Foscote Rd. NW4 34 22 88 D
Foskett Rd. SW6 73 24 76 D
Foss Ave. Croy 112 31 64 C
Fossdene Rd. SE7 65 40 78 D
Fosse Way. W13 54 16 81 A
Fossil Rd. SE13 76 37 75 A
Fossington Rd. Belv 67 47 78 B
Foss Rd. SW17 85 26 71 B
Fossway. Dag 41 47 86 A
Foster La. EC2 4 32 81 C
Foster Rd. E13 58 40 82 C
Foster Rd. W3 55 21 80 A
Foster Rd. W4 61 20 78 D
Fosters Cl. Chis 89 42 71 D
Fosters Cl. E18 27 40 90 B
Foster St. NW4 23 23 89 C
Foster Wlk. NW4 23 23 89 C
Fothergill Cl. E13 50 40 83 C
Fotheringham Rd. Enf 13 33 96 D
Foubert's Pl. W1 2 29 81 C
Foulden Rd. N16 48 33 85 B
Foulden Terr. N16 48 33 85 B
Foulis Terr. SW7 62 26 78 D
Foulser Rd. SW17 86 28 72 C
Foulsham Rd. Th Hth 97 32 68 B
Founders Ct. EC2 4 32 81 D
Founders Gdns. SE19 97 32 70 C
Fountain Ct. EC4 7 31 80 A
Fountain Dri. SE19 87 33 71 B
Fountain Pl. SW9 75 31 76 A
Fountain Rd. SW17 85 26 71 B
Fountain Rd. Th Hth 97 32 69 C
Fountains Ave. Felt 82 12 72 D
Fountains Cl. Felt 82 12 72 B
Fountains Cres. N14 16 29 94 A
Fountayne Rd. N15 25 34 89 C
Fountayne Rd. N16 37 34 86 A
Fount St. SW8 10 29 77 D
Fouracres. Enf 14 36 97 A
Four Acres. N12 15 25 93 D
Fourland Wlk. Edg 22 20 91 A
Fournier St. E1 4 33 81 B
Fourth Ave. E12 50 42 85 A
Fourth Ave. Rom 41 50 87 D
Fourth Ave. W10 56 24 82 A
Fourth Way. Wem 45 20 85 A
Four Wents The. E4 18 38 93 B
Fowey Ave. Ilf 39 41 88 B
Fowler Cl. SW11 73 26 75 B
Fowler House. SW8 74 29 76 B
Fowler Rd. E7 50 40 85 A
Fowler Rd. Ilf 28 46 91 B
Fowler Rd. Mit 96 28 69 C
Fowler Rd. N1 48 31 83 B
Fowler's Wlk. W5 54 17 82 D
Fownes St. SW11 74 27 75 A
Foxberry Rd. SE4 76 36 75 A
Foxborough Gdns. SE4 76 37 74 A
Foxbourne Rd. SW17 86 28 72 A
Foxbury Ave. Chis 100 44 70 B
Foxbury Cl. Brom 99 40 70 B
Foxbury Rd. Brom 99 40 70 B
Fox Cl. E16 58 40 81 A
Fox Cl. E1 57 35 82 C
Foxcombe Cl. E6 50 41 83 D
Foxcombe Rd. SW15 84 22 73 C
Foxcroft Rd. SE18 78 43 76 B
Foxdell. Nthwd 19 08 91 B
Foxearth Rd. S Croy 112 34 62 D
Foxes Dale. Brom 98 38 68 B
Foxes Dale. SE3 77 40 75 A
Foxfield Cl. Nthwd 19 09 91 B

| | | | |
|---|---|---|---|
| Foxfield Rd. Orp | 108 | 44 65 | B |
| Foxglove St. W12 | 55 | 21 80 | B |
| Foxgrove Ave. Beck | 98 | 37 70 | D |
| Foxgrove. N14 | 16 | 30 93 | C |
| Foxgrove Rd. Beck | 98 | 38 70 | C |
| Foxham Rd. N19 | 36 | 29 86 | D |
| Fox Hill Gdns. SE19 | 97 | 33 70 | D |
| Fox Hill. SE19 | 97 | 33 70 | D |
| Foxhole Rd. SE9 | 77 | 42 74 | A |
| Foxholt Gdns. NW10 | 45 | 20 84 | C |
| Fox House Rd. Belv | 67 | 49 78 | B |
| Fox & Knot St. EC1 | 3 | 31 81 | B |
| Fox La. N13 | 16 | 30 93 | D |
| Foxlands Cres. Dag | 52 | 50 85 | C |
| Foxlands Rd. Dag | 52 | 50 85 | C |
| Fox La. W5 | 54 | 18 82 | C |
| Foxley Cl. E8 | 48 | 34 85 | C |
| Foxley Ct. Sutt | 110 | 26 63 | C |
| Foxley La. Pur | 111 | 30 62 | C |
| Foxley Rd. SW9 | 63 | 31 77 | D |
| Foxley Rd. Th Hth | 97 | 31 68 | D |
| Foxmore St. SW11 | 74 | 27 76 | B |
| Fox Rd. E16 | 58 | 39 81 | B |
| Fox's Path. Mit | 96 | 27 69 | C |
| Fox's Yd. E2 | 4 | 33 82 | D |
| Foxwell St. SE4 | 76 | 36 75 | A |
| Foxwood Cl. Felt | 87 | 10 72 | D |
| Foxwood Rd. SE3 | 77 | 39 75 | D |
| Foyle Rd. N17 | 25 | 34 90 | B |
| Foyle Rd. SE3 | 65 | 39 77 | B |
| Framfield Rd. N5 | 48 | 31 85 | D |
| Framfield Rd. W7 | 54 | 15 81 | D |
| Framlingham Cl. E5 | 38 | 35 86 | A |
| Framlingham Cres. SE9 | 89 | 42 71 | B |
| Frampton Cl. Sutt | 110 | 25 63 | C |
| Frampton Park Estate. E9 | 49 | 35 84 | C |
| Frampton Park Rd. E9 | 49 | 35 84 | C |
| Frampton Rd. Houn | 70 | 12 74 | A |
| Frampton St. NW8 | 1 | 26 82 | D |
| Francemary Rd. SE4 | 76 | 37 74 | A |
| Frances Rd. E4 | 26 | 37 91 | A |
| Frances St. SE18 | 65 | 42 78 | B |
| Franche Court Rd. SW17 | 85 | 26 72 | C |
| Francis Ave. Bexh | 79 | 49 76 | C |
| Francis Ave. Felt | 87 | 10 72 | C |
| Francis Ave. Ilf | 40 | 44 86 | B |
| Franciscan Rd. SW17 | 86 | 28 71 | A |
| Francis Chichester Way. SW11 | 74 | 28 76 | A |
| Francis Cl. Eps | 109 | 20 64 | B |
| Francis Cl. Shep | 91 | 07 68 | C |
| Francis Gr. SW19 | 95 | 24 70 | B |
| Francis Rd. Croy | 105 | 31 66 | B |
| Francis Rd. Dart | 80 | 53 74 | B |
| Francis Rd. E10 | 38 | 38 86 | A |
| Francis Rd. Grnf | 44 | 17 83 | A |
| Francis Rd. Har | 33 | 16 88 | A |
| Francis Rd. Houn | 70 | 11 76 | D |
| Francis Rd. Ilf | 40 | 44 86 | B |
| Francis Rd. N2 | 24 | 27 89 | D |
| Francis Rd. Pnr | 32 | 11 88 | A |
| Francis Rd. Wall | 111 | 29 63 | A |
| Francis St. E15 | 50 | 39 85 | C |
| Francis St. Ilf | 40 | 44 86 | B |
| Francis St. SW1 | 6 | 29 79 | C |
| Francis Terr. N19 | 36 | 29 86 | C |
| Francombe Gdns. Rom | 42 | 52 88 | C |
| Franconia Rd. SW4 | 74 | 29 74 | B |
| Frank Bailey Wlk. E12 | 51 | 43 84 | A |
| Frank Dixon Cl. SE21 | 87 | 33 73 | C |
| Frank Dixon Way. SE21 | 87 | 33 73 | C |
| Frankfurt Rd. SE24 | 75 | 32 74 | A |
| Frankham St. SE8 | 64 | 37 77 | C |
| Frankland Rd. E4 | 18 | 37 92 | C |
| Frankland Rd. SW7 | 5 | 26 79 | D |
| *Franklin Cl. King | 94 | 19 68 | A |
| Franklin Cl. N20 | 15 | 26 94 | A |
| Franklin Cl. SE27 | 87 | 31 72 | D |
| Franklin Cres. Mit | 96 | 29 68 | C |
| Franklin Pas. SE9 | 77 | 42 75 | A |
| Franklin Rd. Bexh | 79 | 48 76 | A |
| Franklin Rd. SE20 | 98 | 35 69 | A |
| Franklin Sq. SW5 | 62 | 24 78 | D |
| Franklin's Row. SW3 | 9 | 27 78 | D |
| Franklin St. E3 | 57 | 37 82 | B |
| Franklin St. N15 | 37 | 33 88 | C |
| Franklyn Gdns. Ilf | 28 | 44 91 | B |
| Franks Ave. N Mal | 94 | 20 68 | C |
| Frank St. E13 | 58 | 40 82 | C |
| Franks Wood Ave. Orp | 108 | 44 67 | A |
| Franlaw Cres. N13 | 17 | 32 92 | A |
| Franmil Rd. Horn | 42 | 52 87 | C |
| Fransfield Gr. SE26 | 87 | 34 72 | D |
| Frant Cl. SE20 | 98 | 35 70 | C |
| Franthorne Way. SE6 | 88 | 37 72 | D |
| Frantlyn Rd. NW10 | 45 | 21 84 | B |
| Frant Rd. Th Hth | 105 | 31 67 | B |
| Fraser Rd. E17 | 38 | 37 88 | D |
| Fraser Rd. Eri | 67 | 50 78 | D |
| Fraser Rd. Grnf | 44 | 17 83 | A |
| Fraser Rd. N9 | 17 | 34 93 | D |
| Fraser St. W4 | 61 | 21 78 | C |
| Frating Cres. Wdf Gn | 27 | 40 91 | B |
| Frazer Ave. Ruis | 43 | 11 85 | C |
| Frazier St. SE1 | 7 | 31 79 | A |
| Frean St. SE16 | 63 | 34 79 | C |
| Frederica Rd. E4 | 18 | 38 94 | B |
| Frederica St. N7 | 47 | 30 84 | D |
| Frederick Cl. Sutt | 110 | 24 64 | D |
| Frederick Cl. W2 | 5 | 27 80 | B |
| Frederick Cres. Enf | 14 | 35 97 | C |
| Frederick Cres. SW9 | 63 | 31 77 | D |
| Frederick Gdns Sutt | 110 | 24 64 | D |
| Frederick Pl. SE18 | 66 | 43 78 | D |
| Frederick Rd. Rain | 52 | 50 83 | D |
| Frederick Rd. Sutt | 110 | 24 64 | D |
| Frederick Row. EC1 | 3 | 31 82 | B |
| Frederick's Pl. EC2 | 4 | 32 81 | D |
| Frederick's Pl. N12 | 15 | 26 92 | A |
| Frederick St. WC1 | 3 | 30 82 | B |
| Frederick Terr. E8 | 48 | 33 84 | D |
| Frederic Mews. SW1 | 6 | 28 79 | A |
| Frederic St. E17 | 38 | 36 88 | A |
| Freedom St. SW11 | 74 | 27 76 | D |
| Freegrove Rd. N7 | 47 | 30 85 | C |
| Freeland Park. NW4 | 23 | 24 90 | C |
| Freeland Rd. W5 | 54 | 18 80 | B |
| Freelands Gr. Brom | 99 | 40 69 | B |
| Freelands Rd. Brom | 99 | 40 69 | B |
| Freeling St. N1 | 47 | 30 84 | D |
| Freeman Cl. Nthlt | 43 | 12 84 | C |
| Freeman Rd. Mord | 103 | 26 67 | B |
| Freemantle Ave. Enf | 15 | 35 95 | B |
| Freemantle St. SE17 | 63 | 33 78 | C |
| Freeman Way. Horn | 42 | 54 88 | D |
| Freemason's Rd. Croy | 105 | 33 66 | C |
| Freemasons Rd. E16 | 58 | 40 81 | D |
| Freethorpe Cl. SE19 | 97 | 33 69 | A |
| Freke Rd. SW11 | 74 | 28 75 | A |
| Fremantle Rd. Belv | 67 | 49 78 | A |
| Fremantle Rd. Ilf | 28 | 44 90 | C |
| Fremont St. E9 | 49 | 35 83 | A |
| French Ordinary Ct. EC3 | 8 | 33 80 | A |
| French Pl. EC2 | 4 | 33 82 | A |
| French St. Sun | 92 | 11 69 | C |
| Frendsbury Rd. SE4 | 76 | 36 75 | C |
| Frensham Dri. SW15 | 84 | 22 72 | C |
| Frensham Rd. SE9 | 90 | 44 72 | B |
| Frensham St. SE15 | 63 | 34 77 | A |
| Frere St. SW11 | 74 | 27 76 | C |
| Freshfield Cl. SE13 | 76 | 38 75 | D |
| Freshfield Dri. N14 | 16 | 28 94 | B |
| Freshfields. Croy | 106 | 36 66 | D |
| Freshford St. SW18 | 85 | 26 72 | C |
| Freshwater Cl. SW17 | 96 | 28 70 | A |
| Freshwater Ct. Sthl | 53 | 13 82 | A |
| Freshwater Rd. Dag | 41 | 48 87 | C |
| Freshwater Rd. SW17 | 96 | 28 70 | A |
| Freshwell Ave. Rom | 29 | 47 89 | C |
| Fresh Wharf Rd. Bark | 51 | 43 83 | B |
| Freshwood Cl. Beck | 98 | 37 69 | B |
| Freshwood Way. Wall | 111 | 29 62 | A |
| Freston Gdns. Barn | 12 | 28 95 | A |
| Freston Park. N3 | 23 | 24 90 | D |
| Freston Rd. W10 | 56 | 23 80 | B |
| Freta Rd. Bexh | 79 | 48 74 | B |
| Frewin Rd. SW18 | 85 | 26 73 | D |
| Friar Mews. SE27 | 87 | 31 72 | D |
| Friar Rd. Hay | 53 | 11 82 | D |
| Friar Rd. Orp | 108 | 46 67 | A |
| Friars Ave. N20 | 16 | 27 92 | A |
| Friars Cl. Nthlt | 53 | 11 82 | B |
| Friars Gdns. W3 | 55 | 20 81 | D |
| Friars La. Rich | 71 | 17 74 | B |
| Friars Place La. W3 | 55 | 20 80 | B |
| Friars Rd. E6 | 50 | 41 83 | D |
| Friars Stile Pl. Rich | 71 | 18 74 | C |
| Friars Stile Rd. Rich | 71 | 18 74 | C |
| Friar St. EC4 | 3 | 31 81 | D |
| Friars Way. W3 | 55 | 20 81 | D |
| Friars Wlk. N14 | 16 | 28 94 | B |
| Friars Wlk. SE2 | 67 | 47 78 | D |
| Friary Cl. N12 | 16 | 27 92 | C |
| Friary Rd. N12 | 16 | 27 92 | A |
| Friary Rd. SE15 | 63 | 34 77 | C |
| Friary Rd. W3 | 55 | 20 81 | D |
| Friary Way. N12 | 16 | 27 92 | A |
| Friday Rd. Eri | 67 | 50 78 | D |
| Friday Rd. Mit | 96 | 27 70 | D |
| Friday St. EC4 | 8 | 32 80 | A |
| Frideswide Pl. NW5 | 47 | 29 85 | C |
| Friendly Pl. SE10 | 76 | 37 76 | B |
| Friendly Street Mews. SE8 | 76 | 37 76 | C |
| Friendly St. SE8 | 76 | 37 76 | A |
| Friendship Wlk (off Wayfarer Rd). Nthlt | 53 | 11 82 | B |
| Friends' Rd. Croy | 105 | 32 65 | D |
| Friend St. EC1 | 3 | 31 82 | B |
| Friern Barnet La. N11 | 16 | 27 92 | D |
| Friern Barnet La. N20 | 16 | 27 92 | A |
| Friern Barnet Rd. N11 | 16 | 28 92 | C |
| Friern Ct. N20 | 15 | 26 93 | D |
| Friern Mount Dri. N20 | 15 | 26 94 | A |
| Friern Park. N12 | 15 | 26 92 | D |
| Friern Rd. SE22 | 87 | 34 73 | A |
| Friern Rd. SE22 | 75 | 34 74 | C |
| Friern Watch Ave. N12 | 15 | 26 92 | B |
| Frigate Mews. SE8 | 64 | 37 77 | A |
| Frimley Ave. Wall | 111 | 30 64 | D |
| Frimley Gdns. Mit | 96 | 27 68 | A |
| Frimley Rd. Ilf | 40 | 45 86 | C |
| Frimley St. E1 | 57 | 35 82 | D |
| Frimley Way. E1 | 57 | 35 82 | D |
| Fringewood Cl. Nthwd | 19 | 07 90 | B |
| Frinstead Rd. Eri | 68 | 51 77 | C |
| Frinton Dri. Wdf Gr | 26 | 38 91 | D |
| Frinton Mews. Ilf | 40 | 43 88 | C |
| Frinton Rd. E6 | 58 | 41 82 | B |
| Frinton Rd. N15 | 37 | 33 88 | C |
| Frinton Rd. Rom | 29 | 49 91 | C |
| Frinton Rd. SW17 | 96 | 28 70 | A |
| Friston St. SW6 | 73 | 25 76 | D |
| Fritham Cl. N.Mal | 102 | 21 67 | C |
| Frith Ct. NW7 | 23 | 24 91 | C |
| Frith La. NW7 | 23 | 24 91 | A |
| Frith Rd. Croy | 105 | 32 65 | A |
| Frith Rd. E11 | 49 | 38 85 | B |
| Frith St. W1 | 2 | 29 81 | D |
| Frithville Gdns. W12 | 56 | 23 80 | C |
| Frithwood Ave. Nthwd | 19 | 09 91 | B |
| Frizlands La. Dag | 41 | 49 86 | D |
| Frobisher Cl. Pnr | 32 | 11 87 | B |
| Frobisher Rd. N8 | 25 | 31 89 | C |
| Frobisher St. SE10 | 65 | 39 77 | A |
| Frogley Rd. SE22 | 75 | 33 75 | D |
| Frogmore Cl. Sutt | 103 | 24 65 | C |
| Frogmore Ct. Sthl | 59 | 13 78 | A |
| Frogmore Gdns. Sutt | 110 | 24 64 | A |
| Frogmore. SW18 | 73 | 25 74 | A |
| Frognal Ave. Har | 21 | 15 89 | D |
| Frognal Ave. Sid | 100 | 46 70 | A |
| Frognal Cl. NW3 | 46 | 26 85 | C |
| Frognal Cnr. Sid | 100 | 45 70 | B |
| Frognal Gdns. NW3 | 46 | 26 85 | A |
| Frognal La. NW3 | 46 | 25 85 | D |
| Frognal. NW3 | 46 | 26 85 | C |
| Frognal Pl. Sid | 90 | 46 71 | C |
| Frognal Rise. NW3 | 46 | 26 85 | A |
| Frognal Way. NW3 | 46 | 26 85 | A |
| Froissart Rd. SE9 | 77 | 42 74 | A |
| Frome Rd. N22 | 25 | 31 89 | B |
| Frome St. N1 | 48 | 32 83 | C |
| Fromondes Rd. Sutt | 110 | 24 64 | C |
| Frostie Wlk. E1 | 4 | 33 81 | B |
| Froude St. SW8 | 74 | 28 76 | D |
| Fruen Rd. Felt | 81 | 09 73 | B |
| Fryatt Rd. N17 | 25 | 32 91 | D |
| Fryatt St. E14 | 58 | 39 81 | C |
| Fry Cl. Rom | 29 | 49 91 | A |
| Fryent Cl. NW9 | 34 | 19 88 | C |
| Fryent Cres. NW9 | 34 | 21 88 | C |
| Fryent Gr. NW9 | 34 | 21 88 | C |
| Fryent Way. NW9 | 34 | 19 88 | C |
| Frying Pan Alley. E1 | 4 | 33 81 | B |
| Fry Rd. E6 | 50 | 41 84 | D |
| Fry Rd. NW10 | 45 | 21 83 | B |
| Fryston Ave. Croy | 105 | 34 65 | A |
| Fuchsia St. SE2 | 66 | 46 78 | D |
| Fulbeck Dri. NW9 | 22 | 21 90 | A |
| Fulbeck Way. Har | 20 | 14 90 | C |
| Fulbourne Rd. E17 | 26 | 38 90 | C |
| Fulbourne St. E1 | 57 | 34 81 | B |
| Fulbrook Mews. N19 | 47 | 29 85 | A |
| *Fulbrook Rd. N19 | 47 | 29 85 | A |
| Fulford Rd. Eps | 109 | 20 63 | D |
| Fulford St. SE16 | 63 | 34 79 | B |
| Fulham Bwy. SW6 | 62 | 25 77 | C |
| Fulham Ct. SW6 | 73 | 25 76 | A |
| Fulham High St. SW6 | 73 | 24 75 | A |
| Fulham High St. SW6 | 73 | 24 76 | C |
| Fulham Palace Rd. SW6 | 73 | 24 76 | A |
| Fulham Palace Rd. W6 | 62 | 23 77 | B |
| Fulham Park Gdns. SW6 | 73 | 24 76 | D |
| Fulham Park Rd. SW6 | 73 | 24 76 | D |
| Fulham Rd. SW10 | 62 | 26 77 | A |
| Fulham Rd. SW6 | 73 | 24 76 | B |
| Fullbrooks Ave. Wor Pk | 102 | 21 66 | D |
| Fuller Rd. Dag | 52 | 47 85 | A |
| Fuller's Ave. E18 | 27 | 39 91 | D |
| Fullers Ave. Surb | 101 | 18 65 | B |
| Fullers Cl. Rom | 29 | 50 91 | C |
| Fuller's La. Rom | 29 | 50 91 | C |
| Fuller's Rd. E18 | 27 | 39 91 | D |
| Fuller St. E2 | 57 | 34 82 | C |
| Fuller St. NW4 | 23 | 23 89 | C |
| Fullers Way N. Surb | 101 | 18 65 | D |
| Fullers Way S. Chess | 101 | 18 65 | C |
| Fullerton Rd. Cars | 111 | 27 62 | A |
| Fullerton Rd. Croy | 105 | 33 66 | B |
| Fullerton Rd. SW18 | 73 | 26 74 | A |
| Fullwood's Mews. N1 | 4 | 32 82 | B |
| Fulmar Ct. Surb | 101 | 18 67 | D |
| Fulmead St. SW6 | 73 | 25 76 | B |
| Fulmer Cl. Hamp | 82 | 12 71 | C |
| Fulmer Way. W13 | 60 | 16 79 | D |
| Fulready Rd. E10 | 38 | 38 88 | B |
| Fulstone Cl. Houn | 70 | 12 75 | D |
| Fulthorp Rd. SE3 | 77 | 40 76 | C |
| Fulton Mews. W2 | 5 | 26 80 | A |
| Fulton Rd. Wem | 34 | 19 86 | C |
| Fulwell Ave. Ilf | 28 | 43 90 | B |
| Fulwell Ct. Ilf | 28 | 43 90 | A |
| Fulwell Park Ave. Twick | 82 | 14 72 | A |
| Fulwell Rd. Tedd | 82 | 14 71 | B |
| Fulwich Rd. Dart | 80 | 54 74 | D |
| Fulwood Ave. Wem | 44 | 18 83 | D |
| Fulwood Gdns. Twick | 71 | 16 74 | C |
| Fulwood Pl. WC1 | 3 | 30 81 | B |
| Fulwood Wlk. SW19 | 85 | 24 73 | C |
| Furber St. W6 | 61 | 22 79 | D |
| Furham Feild. Pnr | 20 | 13 91 | C |
| Furley Rd. SE15 | 63 | 34 77 | C |
| Furlong Cl. Wall | 104 | 28 66 | C |
| Furlong Rd. N7 | 48 | 31 84 | A |
| Furmage St. SW18 | 85 | 25 73 | A |
| Furneaux Ave. SE27 | 87 | 31 71 | D |
| Furner Cl. Dart | 80 | 51 75 | B |
| Furness Rd. Har | 32 | 13 87 | D |
| Furness Rd. Mord | 103 | 25 67 | D |
| Furness Rd. NW10 | 45 | 22 83 | C |
| Furness Rd. SW6 | 73 | 25 76 | D |
| Furnival St. EC4 | 3 | 31 81 | A |
| Furrow La. E9 | 49 | 35 85 | C |
| Fursby Ave. N3 | 23 | 25 91 | A |
| Further Acre. NW9 | 22 | 21 90 | D |
| Further Green Rd. SE6 | 89 | 39 73 | C |
| Furzedown Dri. SW17 | 86 | 28 71 | D |
| Furzedown Rd. Sutt | 110 | 26 62 | C |
| Furzedown Rd. SW17 | 86 | 28 71 | D |
| Furzefield Cl. Chis | 100 | 43 70 | B |
| Furzefield Rd. SE3 | 65 | 40 77 | D |
| Furze Fm Cl. Rom | 29 | 48 90 | C |
| Furze La. Pur | 111 | 30 62 | C |
| Furze Rd. Th Hth | 97 | 32 68 | A |
| Furze St. E3 | 57 | 37 81 | A |
| Furzewood. Sun | 91 | 10 69 | A |
| Fyfe Way. Brom | 99 | 40 69 | C |
| Fyfield Rd. E17 | 26 | 38 89 | B |
| Fyfield Rd. Enf | 13 | 33 96 | A |
| Fyfield Rd. SW9 | 75 | 31 75 | A |
| Fyfield Rd. Wdf Gn | 27 | 41 91 | C |
| Fynes St. SW1 | 10 | 29 78 | B |
| Gable Cl. Dart | 80 | 52 74 | A |
| Gable Cl. Pnr | 20 | 13 91 | C |
| Gabriel Cl. Felt | 82 | 11 71 | B |
| Gabriel Cl. Rom | 29 | 50 91 | C |
| Gabriel St. SE23 | 88 | 35 73 | D |
| Gaddesden Ave. Wem | 44 | 18 84 | B |
| Gadesden Rd. Eps | 109 | 20 63 | A |
| Gage Rd. E16 | 58 | 39 81 | A |
| Gage St. WC1 | 3 | 30 81 | A |
| Gainford St. N1 | 48 | 31 83 | A |
| Gainsboro Gdns. Grnf | 44 | 15 85 | C |
| Gainsborough Ave. Dart | 80 | 53 74 | A |
| Gainsborough Ave. E12 | 51 | 43 85 | C |
| Gainsborough Cl. Beck | 98 | 37 70 | C |
| Gainsborough Cl. Esh | 101 | 15 66 | C |
| Gainsborough Ct. N12 | 15 | 25 92 | D |
| Gainsborough Gdns. Edg | 22 | 19 90 | C |
| Gainsborough Gdns. Islw | 70 | 14 74 | B |
| Gainsborough Gdns. NW11 | 35 | 24 87 | B |
| Gainsborough Gdns. NW3 | 35 | 26 86 | D |
| Gainsborough Mews. SE26 | 87 | 34 72 | D |
| Gainsborough Rd. Dag | 40 | 46 86 | D |
| Gainsborough Rd. E11 | 39 | 39 87 | B |
| Gainsborough Rd. E15 | 58 | 39 82 | A |
| Gainsborough Rd. Eps | 109 | 20 62 | C |
| Gainsborough Rd. N12 | 15 | 25 92 | D |
| Gainsborough Rd. N.Mal | 102 | 20 66 | B |
| Gainsborough Rd. Rich | 71 | 18 75 | B |
| Gainsborough Rd. W4 | 61 | 21 78 | B |
| Gainsborough Rd. Wdf Gn | 27 | 42 91 | A |
| Gainsborough Sq. Bexh | 79 | 47 75 | B |
| Gainsford Rd. E17 | 26 | 36 89 | D |
| Gainsford St. SE1 | 8 | 33 79 | B |
| Gairloch Rd. SE5 | 75 | 33 76 | C |
| Gaisford St. NW5 | 47 | 29 84 | A |
| Gaitskell Rd. SE9 | 90 | 44 73 | C |
| Galahad Rd. Brom | 89 | 40 71 | A |
| Galata Rd. SW13 | 61 | 22 77 | C |
| Galatea Sq. SE15 | 75 | 34 75 | B |
| Galbraith St. E14 | 64 | 38 79 | C |
| Galeborough Ave. Wdf Gr | 26 | 38 91 | D |
| Gale Cl. Hamp | 92 | 12 70 | A |
| Gale Cl. Mit | 95 | 26 68 | B |
| Galena Rd. W6 | 61 | 22 78 | B |
| Galen Pl. WC1 | 3 | 30 81 | A |
| Galesbury Rd. SW18 | 73 | 26 74 | C |
| Gales Gdns. E2 | 57 | 34 82 | B |
| Gale St. Dag | 52 | 47 84 | D |
| Gale St. E3 | 57 | 37 81 | A |
| Gales Way. Wdf Gn | 27 | 42 91 | C |
| Gallants Farm Rd. Barn | 16 | 27 94 | C |
| Gallery Gdns. Nthlt | 43 | 11 83 | D |
| Gallery Rd. SE21 | 87 | 32 73 | A |
| Galley La. Barn | 11 | 23 96 | C |
| Galleywall Rd. SE16 | 63 | 34 78 | B |
| Galleywood Cres. Rom | 29 | 50 91 | B |
| Galliard Cl. Enf | 14 | 35 95 | C |
| Gallia Rd. N5 | 48 | 31 85 | D |
| Galliard Rd. N9 | 13 | 34 95 | C |
| Gallions Rd. SE7 | 65 | 40 78 | B |
| Gallon Cl. SE7 | 65 | 41 78 | A |
| Gallop The. S Croy | 112 | 34 63 | D |
| Gallop The. Sutt | 110 | 26 62 | B |
| Gallosson Rd. SE18 | 66 | 45 78 | A |
| Galloway Rd. W12 | 55 | 22 80 | C |
| Gallows Cnr. Rom | 30 | 53 90 | A |
| Gallus Cl. N21 | 12 | 30 95 | D |
| Gallus Sq. SE3 | 77 | 40 75 | B |
| Galpin's Rd. Th Hth | 96 | 30 68 | D |
| Galsworthy Ave. Rom | 40 | 46 88 | D |
| Galsworthy Cres. SE3 | 77 | 41 76 | A |
| Galsworthy Rd. King | 94 | 19 69 | B |
| Galsworthy Rd. NW2 | 46 | 24 85 | A |
| Galton St. W10 | 56 | 24 82 | A |
| Galveston Rd. SW15 | 73 | 24 74 | B |
| Galway St. EC1 | 4 | 32 82 | A |
| Gambetta St. SW8 | 74 | 28 76 | D |
| Gambia St. SE1 | 7 | 31 80 | D |
| Gambole Rd. SW17 | 86 | 27 71 | A |
| Games Rd. Barn | 12 | 27 96 | B |
| Gamlen Rd. SW15 | 73 | 23 75 | D |
| Gander Green La. Sutt | 110 | 24 64 | B |
| Gander Green La. Sutt | 103 | 24 65 | B |
| Ganley Ct. SW11 | 73 | 26 75 | B |
| Ganton St. W1 | 2 | 29 81 | C |
| Gantshill Cres. Ilf | 40 | 43 88 | A |
| Gap Rd. SW19 | 85 | 25 71 | D |
| Garage Rd. W3 | 55 | 19 81 | C |
| Garbrand Wlk. Eps | 109 | 21 62 | B |
| Garbutt Pl. W1 | 2 | 28 81 | A |
| Garden Ave. Bexh | 79 | 49 75 | A |
| Garden Ave. Mit | 96 | 28 70 | D |
| Garden City. Edg | 22 | 19 91 | A |
| Garden Cl. Ashf | 91 | 08 70 | A |
| Garden Cl. E4 | 18 | 37 92 | C |
| Garden Cl. Hamp | 82 | 12 71 | D |
| Garden Cl. Nthlt | 43 | 12 83 | A |
| Garden Cl. Ruis | 31 | 09 86 | A |
| Garden Cl. SE12 | 89 | 40 72 | D |
| Garden Cl. SW15 | 84 | 22 73 | B |
| Garden Cl. SW9 | 74 | 30 75 | B |
| Garden Cl. Wall | 111 | 30 64 | C |
| Garden Ct. EC4 | 7 | 31 80 | A |
| Garden Ct. N12 | 15 | 25 92 | A |
| Garden Ct. Rich | 71 | 18 76 | B |
| Garden Ct. SE15 | 75 | 33 76 | B |
| Garden Ct. Wem | 33 | 17 86 | C |
| Gardeners La. EC4 | 8 | 32 80 | A |
| Gardeners Rd. Croy | 105 | 31 66 | D |
| Gardener's Rd. E3 | 49 | 35 83 | D |
| Gardenia Rd. Enf | 13 | 33 95 | C |
| Garden La. Brom | 99 | 40 70 | B |
| Garden La. SW2 | 86 | 30 73 | D |
| Garden Mews. W2 | 56 | 25 80 | A |
| Garden Rd. Brom | 99 | 40 70 | B |
| Garden Rd. NW8 | 1 | 26 82 | A |
| Garden Rd. Rich | 72 | 19 75 | A |
| Garden Rd. SE20 | 98 | 35 69 | A |
| Garden Row. SE1 | 7 | 31 79 | D |
| Garden St. E1 | 57 | 35 81 | B |
| Gardens The. Beck | 98 | 38 69 | D |
| Gardens The. Felt | 69 | 08 74 | D |
| Gardens The. Har | 32 | 14 88 | C |
| Gardens The. N16 | 37 | 33 87 | B |
| Gardens The. N8 | 24 | 30 89 | C |
| Gardens The. Pnr | 32 | 12 88 | D |
| Gardens The. SE22 | 75 | 34 75 | C |
| Gardens Way. E12 | 39 | 42 86 | D |
| Garden Terr. SW1 | 10 | 29 78 | D |
| Garden Way. NW10 | 45 | 20 84 | A |
| Garden Wlk. EC2 | 4 | 33 82 | C |
| Gardiner Ave. NW2 | 46 | 23 85 | C |
| Gardner Cl. E11 | 39 | 40 88 | D |
| Gardner Rd. E13 | 58 | 40 82 | D |
| Gardnor Rd. NW3 | 46 | 26 85 | B |
| Garendon Gdns. Mord | 103 | 25 66 | B |
| Garendon Rd. Mord | 103 | 25 66 | B |
| Gareth Cl. Wor Pk | 103 | 23 65 | B |
| Gareth Gr. Brom | 89 | 40 71 | A |
| Garfield Rd. E13 | 58 | 39 82 | D |
| Garfield Rd. E4 | 18 | 38 94 | D |
| Garfield Rd. Enf | 14 | 35 96 | C |
| Garfield Rd. SW11 | 74 | 28 75 | A |
| Garfield Rd. Twick | 83 | 16 73 | C |
| Garford St. E14 | 57 | 37 80 | A |
| Garibaldi St. SE18 | 66 | 45 78 | A |
| Garland Rd. SE18 | 66 | 44 77 | D |
| Garland Rd. Stan | 21 | 18 90 | A |
| Garland Way. Horn | 30 | 54 89 | C |
| Garlick Hill. EC4 | 8 | 32 80 | A |
| Garlies Rd. SE23 | 88 | 36 72 | C |
| Garman Rd. N17 | 26 | 35 91 | C |
| Garnault Mews. EC1 | 3 | 31 82 | A |
| Garnault Pl. EC1 | 3 | 31 82 | A |
| Garner Rd. E17 | 26 | 38 90 | A |
| Garner St. E2 | 48 | 34 83 | C |
| Garnet Rd. NW10 | 45 | 21 84 | A |
| Garnet Rd. Th Hth | 97 | 32 68 | C |
| Garnet St. E1 | 57 | 35 80 | A |
| Garnett Cl. SE9 | 77 | 42 75 | B |
| Garnett Rd. NW3 | 47 | 27 85 | C |
| Garnham Cl. N16 | 37 | 33 86 | B |
| Garnham St. N16 | 37 | 33 86 | B |
| Garnies Cl. SE15 | 63 | 33 77 | D |
| Garrad's Rd. SW16 | 86 | 29 71 | B |
| Garrard Cl. Bexh | 79 | 49 75 | A |
| Garrard Cl. Chis | 90 | 43 71 | D |
| Garrard Wlk. NW10 | 45 | 21 84 | A |
| Garratt Cl. Croy | 111 | 30 64 | A |
| Garratt La. SW17 | 85 | 26 71 | B |
| Garratt La. SW18 | 85 | 25 73 | D |
| Garratt Rd. Edg | 22 | 19 91 | C |
| Garratt Terr. SW17 | 86 | 27 71 | A |
| Garrett St. EC1 | 4 | 32 82 | C |
| Garrick Ave. NW11 | 35 | 24 88 | C |
| Garrick Cl. Rich | 71 | 17 74 | B |
| Garrick Cl. SW18 | 73 | 26 74 | A |
| Garrick Cl. SW18 | 73 | 26 75 | C |
| Garrick Cl. W5 | 54 | 18 82 | C |
| Garrick Cres. Croy | 105 | 33 65 | A |
| Garrick Dri. NW4 | 23 | 23 90 | D |
| Garrick Gdns. E Mol | 92 | 13 68 | A |
| Garrick Park. NW4 | 23 | 23 90 | D |
| Garrick Rd. Grnf | 53 | 13 82 | D |
| Garrick Rd. NW9 | 34 | 21 88 | D |
| Garrick Rd. Rich | 72 | 19 76 | C |
| Garrick St. WC2 | 7 | 30 80 | A |
| Garrick Way. NW4 | 23 | 23 89 | D |
| Garrick Yd. WC2 | 7 | 30 80 | A |
| Garrowsfield. Barn | 11 | 24 95 | B |
| Garry Cl. Rom | 30 | 51 91 | C |
| Garry Way. Rom | 30 | 51 91 | C |
| Garside Cl. Hamp | 92 | 13 70 | B |
| Garth Cl. King | 83 | 18 71 | D |
| Garth Cl. Mord | 103 | 23 66 | B |
| Garth Cl. Ruis | 32 | 11 87 | D |
| Garth Ct. W4 | 61 | 20 77 | B |
| Garthland Dri. Barn | 11 | 23 95 | A |
| Garthorne Rd. SE23 | 88 | 35 73 | B |
| Garth Rd. King | 83 | 18 71 | D |
| Garth Rd. Mord | 103 | 23 66 | B |
| Garth Rd. NW2 | 35 | 24 86 | B |
| Garth Rd. W4 | 61 | 20 78 | D |
| Garthside. Rich | 83 | 18 71 | C |
| Garth The. Hamp | 92 | 13 70 | B |
| Garth The. Har | 33 | 18 88 | D |
| Garthway. N12 | 24 | 27 91 | A |
| Gartmoor Gdns. SW 19 | 85 | 24 73 | D |
| Gartmore Rd. Ilf | 40 | 45 86 | B |
| Garton Pl. SW18 | 73 | 26 74 | C |
| Garvary Rd. E16 | 58 | 40 81 | D |
| Garway Rd. W2 | 56 | 25 81 | D |
| Gascoigne Gdns. Wdf Gn | 27 | 39 91 | C |
| Gascoigne Pl. E2 | 4 | 33 82 | B |
| Gascoigne Rd. Bark | 51 | 44 83 | A |
| Gascony Ave. NW6 | 46 | 25 84 | C |
| Gascoyne Dri. Dart | 80 | 51 75 | B |
| Gascoyne Rd. E9 | 49 | 35 84 | D |

Gaselee St. E14 58 38 80 A
Gasholder Pl. SE11 10 30 78 D
Gaskarth Rd. Edg 22 20 90 C
Gaskarth Rd. SW12 74 28 74 D
Gaskell Rd. N6 36 27 88 D
Gaskell St. SW4 74 30 76 C
Gaskin St. N1 48 31 83 B
Gaspar Cl. SW7 62 25 78 B
Gaspar Mews. SW5 62 25 78 B
Gassiot Rd. SW17 86 27 71 D
Gassiot Way. Sutt 103 26 65 D
Gastein Rd. W6 62 23 77 B
Gaston Bell Cl. Rich 71 18 75 B
Gaston Rd. Mit 96 28 68 A
Gatcombe Rd. N19 36 29 86 D
Gate End. Nthwd 19 10 91 C
Gateforth St. NW8 1 27 82 C
Gatehill Rd. Nthwd 19 10 91 C
Gatehouse Cl. King 94 20 70 C
Gateley Rd. SW9 74 30 75 B
Gate Mews. SW7 5 27 79 A
Gatesborough St. EC2 4 33 82 C
Gates Green Rd. W.Wick 107 39 65 C
Gateside Rd. SW17 86 27 72 D
Gatestone Ct. SE19 97 33 70 A
Gatestone Rd. SE19 97 33 70 A
Gate St. WC2 3 30 81 D
Gateway Arc. N1 48 31 83 D
Gateway Cl. Nthwd 19 08 91 A
Gateway. SE17 63 32 77 A
Gateways. Surb 101 18 67 A
Gateways. The SW3 9 27 78 A
Gathorne Rd. N22 25 31 90 A
Gathorne St. E2 49 35 83 D
Gatley Ave. Eps 109 19 64 D
Gatliff Rd. SW1 9 28 78 D
Gatling Rd. SE2 66 46 78 C
Gaton Rd. SE2 67 47 79 C
Gatton Cl. Sutt 110 25 62 B
Gatton Rd. SW17 86 27 71 A
Gatward Cl. N21 13 31 95 D
Gatward Green. N9 17 33 93 B
Gatwick Rd. SW18 85 24 73 B
Gatwick Way. Horn 42 54 86 D
Gauden Cl. SW4 74 29 75 B
Gauden Rd. SW4 74 29 75 B
Gauntlet Cl. Nthlt 43 12 84 C
Gauntlett Ct. Wem 44 16 85 D
Gauntlett Rd. Sutt 110 26 64 D
Gaunt St. SE1 7 31 79 D
Gaunt St. SE1 8 32 79 C
Gautrey Rd. SE15 76 35 76 C
*Gavel St. SE17 63 32 78 B
Gaverick St. E14 64 37 78 A
Gavestone Cres. SE12 89 40 73 B
Gavestone Rd. SE12 89 40 73 B
Gavina Cl. Mord 104 27 67 A
Gawber St. E2 57 35 82 A
Gawsworth Cl. E15 50 39 85 D
Gawthorne Ave. NW7 15 24 92 C
Gay Cl. NW12 45 22 85 D
Gaydon La. NW9 22 21 90 A
Gayfere Rd. Eps 109 22 64 C
Gayfere Rd. Ilf 27 42 89 B
Gayfere St. SW1 7 30 79 C
Gayford Rd. W12 61 21 79 B
Gay Gdns. Dag 52 50 85 C
Gayhurst Rd. E8 48 34 84 C
Gaylor Rd. Nthlt 43 12 85 D
Gaynesford Rd. Cars 111 27 63 D
Gaynesford Rd. SE23 88 35 72 B
Gaynes Hill Rd. Wdf Gn 27 42 91 C
Gay Rd. E15 49 38 83 C
Gaysham Ave. Ilf 40 43 88 B
Gaysham Hall. Ilf 28 43 89 B
Gay St. SW15 73 23 75 B
Gayton Cres. NW3 46 26 85 B
Gayton Ct. Har 33 15 88 D
Gayton Rd. Har 33 15 88 D
Gayton Rd. NW3 46 26 85 B
Gayville Rd. SW11 74 27 74 D
Gaywood Cl. SW2 86 30 73 D
Gaywood Cl. SW2 87 31 73 C
Gaywood Rd. E17 26 37 89 A
Gaywood St. SE1 7 31 79 D
Gaza St. SE17 63 31 78 D
Geariesville Gdns. 28 43 89 D
Geary Rd. NW10 45 22 85 C
Geary St. N7 47 30 85 D
Gedeney Rd. N17 25 32 90 C
Gedling Pl. SE1 8 33 79 D
Geere Rd. E15 50 39 83 B
Gees Ct. W1 2 28 81 C
Gee St. EC1 4 32 82 C
Geffrye Ct. N1 48 33 83 C
Geffrye St. E2 48 33 83 D
Geldart Rd. SE15 63 34 77 D
Geldeston Rd. E5 37 34 86 A
Gelsthorpe Rd. Rom 29 49 91 D
Gemini Gr (off Javelin Way). Nthlt 53 11 82 B
General Gordons Pl. SE18 66 43 78 B
General Wolfe Rd. SE10 76 38 76 B
Genesta Rd. SE18 66 44 77 A
Geneva Cl. Shep 91 09 69 C
Geneva Dri. SW9 75 31 75 C
Geneva Gdns. Rom 41 48 88 A
Geneva Rd. King 93 18 68 C
Geneva Rd. Th Hth 105 32 67 A
Genever Cl. E4 18 37 92 C
Genista Rd. N18 17 34 92 D
Genoa Ave. SW15 73 23 74 A
Genoa Rd. SE20 98 35 69 A
Genotin Rd. Enf 13 32 96 B
*Genotin Terr. Enf 13 32 96 D
Gentleman's Row. Enf 13 32 96 A
Gentry Gdns. E13 58 40 82 A
Geoffrey Cl. SE5 75 32 76 C
Geoffrey Gdns. E6 50 42 83 C
Geoffrey Rd. SE4 76 36 75 B
George Comberton Wlk. E12 51 43 85 C
George Cres. N10 24 28 91 C
George Ct. WC2 7 30 80 A
George Downing Estate. N16 37 33 86 B
George Inn Yd. SE1 8 32 80 D
George La. Brom 107 40 66 D
George La. E18 27 40 90 C
George La. SE13 76 38 74 C
George Pl. N17 25 33 89 A
George Rd. E4 26 37 91 A
George Rd. King 94 20 70 C
George Rd. N.Mal 102 21 67 B
George Row. SE16 63 34 79 A
George's Rd. N7 47 30 85 D
George's Sq. SW6 62 24 77 B
George St. Bark 51 44 84 C
George St. Croy 105 32 65 B
George St. E16 58 39 81 D
George St. Houn 70 12 76 D
George St. Rich 71 17 74 B
George St. Rom 42 51 88 D
George St. Sthl 59 12 78 A
George St. Sutt 110 25 64 D
George St. W1 1 27 81 D
George St. W7 54 15 80 C
Georgette Pl. SE10 64 38 77 C
George V Ave. Pnr 20 13 89 A
Georgeville Gdns. Ilf 28 43 89 D
George V Way. Grnf 44 16 83 B
George Wyver Cl. SW18 85 24 73 A
George Yd. EC3 4 32 81 D
George Yd. W1 6 28 80 A
Georgiana St. NW1 47 29 83 A
Georgian Cl. Brom 107 40 66 D
Georgian Cl. Stan 21 16 91 C
Georgian Ct. Wem 45 19 84 B
Georgian Way. Har 32 14 86 B
Georgia Rd. Th Hth 97 31 69 B
Georgina Gdns. E2 4 33 82 B
Geraint Rd. Brom 89 40 71 A
Geraldine Rd. SW18 73 26 74 A
Geraldine Rd. W4 61 19 77 A
Geraldine St. SE11 7 31 79 D
Gerald Mews. SW1 9 28 78 A
Gerald Rd. Dag 41 48 87 D
Gerald Rd. E16 58 39 82 D
Gerald Rd. SW1 9 28 78 A
Gerard Ave. Houn 82 13 73 A
Gerard Rd. Har 33 16 88 C
Gerard Rd. SW13 72 21 76 B
Gerda Rd. SE9 90 44 72 A
Germander Way. E15 58 39 82 A
Gernon Rd. E3 49 36 83 C
Geron Way. NW2 34 22 87 D
Geron Way. NW2 35 23 86 A
Gerrard Gdns. Pnr 31 10 88 A
Gerrard Pl. W1 6 29 80 B
Gerrard Rd. N1 48 31 83 D
Gerrards Cl. N14 12 29 95 A
Gerrard's Ct. W5 60 17 79 D
Gerrard St. W1 6 29 80 B
Gerridge St. SE1 7 31 79 C
Gerry Raffles Sq. E15 49 38 84 B
Gertrude Rd. Belv 67 49 78 A
Gertrude St. SW10 62 26 77 A
Gervase Cl. Wem 34 20 86 C
Gervase Rd. Edg 22 20 90 B
Gervase St. SE15 63 34 77 D
Ghent St. SE6 88 37 72 A
Gibbins Rd. E15 49 38 84 C
Gibbon Rd. King 93 18 70 C
Gibbon Rd. SE15 76 35 76 C
Gibbon Rd. W3 55 21 80 A
Gibbons Rd. NW10 45 21 84 A
Gibbon's Rents. SE1 8 33 80 C
Gibbon Wlk. SW15 72 22 75 C
Gibbs Ave. SE19 87 32 71 D
Gibbs Cl. SE19 87 32 71 D
Gibbs Green. W14 62 24 78 D
Gibbs Rd. N18 18 35 92 A
Gibbs Sq. SE19 87 32 71 D
Gibraltar Cres. Eps 109 21 62 C
Gibraltar Wlk. E2 4 33 82 B
Gibson Cl. E1 57 35 82 C
Gibson Gdns. N16 37 33 86 B
Gibson Rd. SE11 10 30 78 B
Gibson Rd. Sutt 110 25 64 D
Gibson's Hill. SW16 97 31 70 C
Gibson Sq. N1 48 31 83 A
Gibson St. E10 65 39 78 C
Gidea Ave. Rom 30 52 89 A
Gidea Cl. Rom 30 52 89 A
Gideon Cl. Belv 67 49 78 B
Gideon Rd. SW11 74 28 75 A
Giesbach Rd. N19 36 29 86 B
Giffard Rd. N18 17 33 92 C
Giffin St. SE8 64 37 77 C
Gifford Gdns. W7 54 15 81 A
Gifford St. N1 47 30 84 C
Gift La. E15 50 39 83 B
Giggshill Gdns. Surb 101 16 66 C
Giggs Hill. Orp 100 46 69 A
Giggs Hill Rd. Surb 101 16 66 C
Gilbert Gr. Edg 22 20 90 B
Gilbert Pl. WC1 3 30 81 A
Gilbert Rd. Belv 67 49 79 C
Gilbert Rd. Brom 99 40 70 C
Gilbert Rd. Pnr 20 11 89 D
Gilbert Rd. Rom 30 51 89 D
Gilbert Rd. SE11 63 31 78 A
Gilbert Rd. SW19 95 26 70 C
Gilbert St. E15 50 39 85 A
Gilbert St. Houn 70 14 75 A
Gilbert St. W1 2 28 81 C
Gilbey Rd. SW17 86 27 71 C
Gilbourne Rd. SE18 66 45 77 B
Gilda Ave. Enf 14 36 95 A
Gilda Cres. N16 37 34 87 C
Gilda Ct. NW7 22 22 90 A
Gildea St. W1 2 28 81 B
Gilden Cres. NW5 47 28 85 C
Gildersome St. SE18 66 43 77 A
Gilders Rd. Chess 109 19 63 A
Giles Coppice SE19 87 33 71 B
Gilkes Cres. SE21 75 33 74 C
Gilkes Pl. SE21 75 33 74 C
Gill Ave. E16 58 40 81 C
Gillender St. E3 58 38 82 C
Gillespie Rd. N5 37 31 86 D
Gillet Ave. E6 50 42 83 C
Gillett Pl. N16 48 33 85 D
Gillett Rd. Th Hth 97 32 68 D
Gillett St. N16 48 33 85 C
Gillham Terr. N17 25 34 91 C
Gilliam Gr. Pur 112 31 62 C
Gillian Cres. Rom 30 53 90 C
Gillian Park Rd. Sutt 103 24 66 D
Gillian St. SE13 76 37 74 B
Gillies St. NW5 47 28 85 C
Gillingham Mews. SW1 10 29 78 A
Gillingham Rd. NW2 35 24 86 C
Gillingham St. SW1 10 29 78 A
Gillman Dri. E15 50 39 83 B
Gillmans Rd. Orp 108 46 66 D
Gill St. E14 57 36 80 B
Gillum Cl. Barn 16 27 94 D
Gilmore Cl. Uxb 31 07 86 C
Gilmore Cres. Ashf 91 07 70 A
Gilmore Rd. SE13 76 38 75 D
Gilpin Ave. SW14 72 20 75 D
Gilpin Cres. N18 17 33 92 D
Gilpin Cres. Twick 82 13 73 B
Gilpin Rd. E5 49 36 85 A
Gilroy Way. Orp 108 46 66 B
Gilsland Rd. Th Hth 97 32 68 D
Gilstead Rd. SW6 73 25 76 D
Gilston Rd. SW10 62 26 78 C
Gilton Rd. SE6 89 39 72 C
Giltspur St. EC1 3 31 81 B
Gilwell Cl. Enf 14 37 96 D
Gilwell La. Enf 14 38 96 D
Gipsy Hill. SE19 87 33 71 C
Gipsy La. SW15 72 22 75 B
Gipsy Rd. SE27 87 32 71 B
Gipsy Rd. Well 79 47 76 D
Gipsy Road Gdns. SE27 87 32 71 A
Giraud St. E14 57 37 81 D
Girdlers Rd. W4 62 23 78 B
Girdlestone Wlk. N19 36 29 86 A
Girdwood Rd. SW18 85 24 73 A
Girling Way. Felt 69 10 75 A
Gironde Rd. SW6 62 24 77 D
Girton Ave. NW9 22 19 89 A
Girton Cl. Nthlt 43 14 84 A
Girton Gdns. Croy 106 37 65 C
Girton Rd. Nthlt 43 14 84 A
Girton Rd. SE26 88 35 71 D
Gisburn Rd. N8 24 30 89 D
Gissing Wlk (Off Morland Mews). N1 48 31 84 C
Given-Wilson Wlk. E13 50 39 83 D
Gladding Rd. E12 50 41 85 B
Glade Cl. Surb 101 17 65 B
Glade Gdns. Croy 106 36 66 A
Glade La. Sthl 59 13 79 B
Glade Rd. E12 39 42 86 D
Gladeside. Croy 106 35 66 B
Gladeside. N21 16 30 94 B
Gladesmore Rd. N15 37 33 88 D
Gladeswood Rd. Belv 67 49 78 B
Glade The. Brom 99 41 69 D
Glade The. Croy 106 35 67 D
Glade The. Enf 13 31 96 A
Glade The. Eps 109 22 63 A
Glade The. Ilf 27 42 90 B
Glade The. N21 16 30 94 B
Glade The. SE7 65 41 77 C
Glade The. Sutt 110 24 62 A
Glade The. W Wick 106 37 65 D
Gladiator St. SE23 88 36 73 A
Glading Terr. N16 37 33 86 D
Gladsdale Dri. Pnr 19 10 89 D
Gladsmuir Rd. Barn 11 24 97 C
Gladsmuir Rd. N19 36 29 87 C
Gladstone Ave. E12 50 42 84 C
Gladstone Ave. Felt 81 10 73 B
Gladstone Ave. N22 25 31 90 D
Gladstone Ave. Twick 82 14 73 B
Gladstone Mews. N22 25 31 90 C
Gladstone Mews. SE20 98 35 70 C
Gladstone Park Gdns. NW2 34 22 86 D
Gladstone Rd. Croy 105 32 66 B
Gladstone Rd. Dart 80 54 74 D
Gladstone Rd. King 94 19 68 A
Gladstone Rd. Sthl 59 12 79 A
Gladstone Rd. Surb 101 18 65 A
Gladstone Rd. SW19 95 25 70 C
Gladstone Rd. W4 61 20 79 D
Gladstone St. SE1 7 31 79 D
Gladstone Terr. SW11 74 28 76 B
Gladstone Way. Har 21 15 89 A
Gladwell Rd. Brom 99 40 70 A
Gladwell Rd. N8 36 30 88 D
Gladwyn Rd. SW15 73 23 75 B
Gladys Rd. NW6 46 25 84 C
Glaisher St. SE10 64 38 77 C
Glamis Dri. Horn 42 54 87 C
Glamis Pl. E1 57 35 80 A
Glamis Rd. E1 57 35 80 A
Glamis Way. Nthlt 43 14 84 A
Glamorgan Cl. Mit 96 30 68 A
Glamorgan Rd. King 93 17 69 A
Glanfield Rd. Beck 98 36 68 D
Glanville Dri. Horn 42 54 87 D
Glanville Rd. Brom 99 40 68 B
Glanville Rd. SW2 74 30 74 A
Glasbrook Ave. Twick 82 12 73 D
Glasbrook Rd. SE9 89 41 73 B
Glaserton Rd. N16 37 33 87 A
Glasford St. SW17 96 27 70 B
Glasgow Rd. E13 50 40 83 D
Glasgow Rd. N18 17 34 92 D
Glasgow Terr. SW1 10 29 78 C
Glasshill St. SE1 7 31 79 B
Glasshouse Fields. E1 57 35 80 B
Glasshouse St. W1 6 29 80 A
Glasshouse Wlk. SE11 10 30 78 D
Glasshouse Yd. EC1 4 32 82 C
Glasslyn Rd. N8 36 29 88 B
Glassmill La. Brom 99 39 69 D
Glass St. E2 57 34 82 D
Glass Yd. SE18 66 43 79 C
Glastonbury Ave. Wdf Gn 27 41 91 B
Glastonbury Rd. Mord 103 25 66 A
Glastonbury Rd. N9 17 34 94 C
Glastonbury St. NW6 46 24 85 D
Glaucus St. E3 57 37 81 B
Glazbury Rd. W14 62 24 78 C
Glazebro Cl. SE21 87 32 72 B
Glazebrook Rd. Tedd 93 15 70 D
Glebe Ave. Enf 13 31 96 B
Glebe Ave. Har 21 18 89 A
Glebe Ave. Mit 96 27 69 C
Glebe Ave. Uxb 31 07 86 D
Glebe Ave. Wdf Gn 27 40 91 A
Glebe Cres. Har 21 18 89 A
Glebe Cres. NW4 23 23 89 C
Glebe Ct. Mit 96 27 68 B
Glebe Ct. SE3 77 39 75 A
Glebe Gdns. N.Mal 102 21 66 A
Glebe House Dri. Brom 107 40 66 D
Glebe Hyrst. SE19 87 33 71 B
Glebe La. Har 21 18 89 C
Glebelands Ave. E18 27 40 90 C
Glebelands Ave. Ilf 40 44 88 D
Glebelands Cl. SE5 75 33 75 A
Glebelands. Dart 80 51 75 D
Glebelands Rd. Felt 81 10 73 C
Glebe Path. Mit 96 27 68 B
Glebe Pl. SW3 9 27 77 A
Glebe Rd. Brom 99 40 69 A
Glebe Rd. Cars 111 27 63 B
Glebe Rd. Dag 52 49 84 B
Glebe Rd. E8 48 33 84 D
Glebe Rd. N3 23 26 90 A
Glebe Rd. N8 24 30 89 D
Glebe Rd. NW10 45 22 84 A
Glebe Rd. Sutt 110 24 62 A
Glebe Rd. SW13 72 22 76 C
Glebe Side. Twick 71 15 74 D
Glebe Sq. Mit 96 27 68 B
Glebe St. W4 61 21 78 C
Glebe Terr. E3 57 37 82 B
Glebe The. Chis 100 44 69 A
Glebe The. SE3 77 39 75 A
Glebe The. Wor Pk 102 21 66 D
Glebe Way. Eri 68 51 77 A
Glebe Way. Felt 82 13 72 C
Glebe Way. Horn 42 54 87 C
Glebe Way. W Wick 106 38 65 B
Gledhow Gdns. SW5 62 26 78 A
Gledstanes Rd. W14 62 24 78 C
Glegg Pl. SW15 73 23 75 D
Glenaffric Ave. E14 64 38 78 B
Glen Albyn Rd. SW19 85 23 72 B
Glenalla Rd. Ruis 31 09 87 B
Glenalmond Rd. Har 21 18 89 C
Glenalvon Way. SE18 65 42 78 A
Glena Mount. Sutt 110 26 64 A
Glenarm Rd. E5 49 35 85 B
Glen Ave. Ashf 81 07 71 A
Glenavon Rd. E15 50 39 84 C
Glenbarr Cl. SE9 78 43 75 B
Glenbow Rd. Brom 99 39 70 A
Glenbow Rd. Brom 89 39 71 C
Glenbrook N. Enf 12 30 96 D
Glenbrook Rd. NW6 46 25 85 C
Glenbrook S. Enf 12 30 96 D
Glenbuck Ct. Surb 101 18 67 C
Glenbuck Rd. Surb 101 18 67 C
Glenburnie Rd. SW17 86 27 72 D
Glencairn Dri. W5 54 17 82 C
Glencairne Cl. E16 58 41 81 B
Glencairn Rd. SW16 96 30 70 C
Glen Cl. Shep 91 07 68 C
Glencoe Ave. Ilf 40 45 87 A
Glencoe Dri. Dag 52 49 85 A
Glencoe Rd. Hay 53 11 82 D
Glen Cres. Wdf Gn 27 40 91 B
Glendale Ave. N22 25 31 91 C
Glendale Ave. Rom 41 47 87 A
Glendale Cl. SE9 78 43 75 A
Glendale Dri. SW19 85 24 71 D
Glendale Gdns. Wem 33 18 87 C
Glendale Mews. Beck 98 37 69 B
Glendale Rd. Eri 67 50 78 A
Glendall St. SW9 74 30 75 D
Glendarvon St. SW15 73 23 75 B
Glendish Rd. N17 25 34 90 B
Glendower Cres. Orp 108 46 67 C
Glendower Gdns. SW14 72 20 75 B
Glendower Pl. SW7 62 26 78 B
Glendower Rd. E4 18 38 94 D
Glendower Rd. SW14 72 20 75 B
Glendown Rd. SE2 66 46 78 C
Glendun Ct. W3 55 21 80 A
Glendun Rd. W3 55 21 80 A
Gleneagle Mews. SW16 86 29 71 D
Gleneagle Rd. SW16 96 29 70 B
Gleneagle Rd. SW16 86 29 71 D
Gleneagles Cl. Orp 108 44 66 D
Gleneagles Cl. Rom 30 54 91 D
Gleneagles Green. Orp 108 44 66 D
Gleneagles. Stan 21 16 91 B
Gleneldon Mews. SW16 86 30 71 A
Gleneldon Rd. SW16 86 30 71 A
Glenelg Rd. SW2 74 30 74 A
Glenesk Rd. SE9 78 43 75 D
Glenfarg Rd. SE6 88 38 73 D
Glenfield Cres. Ruis 31 08 87 B
Glenfield Rd. Ashf 91 08 70 A
Glenfield Rd. SW12 86 29 73 C
Glenfield Rd. W13 60 16 79 B
Glenfield Terr. W13 54 16 80 D
Glenfinlas Way. SE5 63 31 77 D
Glenforth St. E10 65 39 78 D
Glengall Cswy. E14 64 37 79 C
Glengall Gr. E14 64 38 79 C
Glengall Pas. NW6 46 25 83 A
Glengall Rd. Bexh 79 48 75 A
Glengall Rd. NW6 46 24 83 B
Glengall Rd. SE15 63 33 77 B
Glengall Rd. Wdf Gn 27 40 91 B
Glengall Terr. SE15 63 33 77 B
Glengarnock Ave. E14 64 38 78 A
Glengarry Rd. SE 22 75 33 74 B
Glen Gdns. Croy 112 31 64 A
Glenham Dri. Ilf 40 43 88 B
Glenhead Cl. SE9 78 43 75 B
Glenhill Cl. N3 23 25 90 C
Glenhouse Rd. SE9 78 43 74 A
Glenhurst Ave. NW5 47 28 85 A
Glenhurst Ave. Ruis 31 08 87 A
Glenhurst Rd. Brent 60 17 78 C
Glenhurst Rd. N12 15 26 92 D
Glenhurst Rise. SE19 97 32 70 C
Glenilla Rd. NW3 47 27 84 A
Glenister Park Rd. SW16 96 29 70 D
Glenister Rd. E10 65 39 78 D
Glenister St. E16 66 43 79 A
Glenlea Rd. SE9 78 43 75 C
Glenloch Rd. Enf 14 35 97 C
Glenloch Rd. NW3 47 27 84 A
Glenluce Rd. SE3 65 40 77 A
Glenlyon Rd. SE9 78 43 74 A
Glenmere Ave. NW7 22 22 91 A
Glenmore Rd. NW3 47 27 84 A
Glenmore Rd. Well 78 45 76 B
Glenmore Way. Bark 51 46 83 C
Glenmount Path. SE18 66 44 78 C
Glennie Rd. SE27 87 31 72 C
Glenny Rd. Bark 51 44 84 A
Glenparke Rd. E7 50 40 84 B
Glen Rd. Chess 101 18 65 C
Glen Rd. E13 58 41 82 C
Glen Rd. E17 38 36 88 B
Glen Rise. Wdf Gn 27 40 91 B
Glen Road End. Wall 111 28 62 B
Glenrosa St. SW6 73 26 76 C
Glenroy St. W12 56 23 81 C
Glensdale Rd. SE4 76 36 75 B
Glenshiel Rd. SE9 78 43 74 A
Glenside. Chig 28 43 91 B
Glentanner Way. SW17 85 26 72 D
Glentham Gdns. SW13 61 22 77 B
Glentham Rd. SW13 61 22 77 B
Glen The. Brom 99 39 69 C
Glen The. Croy 106 35 65 D
Glen The. Enf 13 31 96 D
Glen The. Nthwd 19 08 91 D
Glen The. Orp 108 43 65 C
Glen The. Pnr 31 10 88 B
Glen The. Pnr 32 12 87 A
Glen The. Sthl 59 12 78 D
Glen The. Wem 44 17 85 B
Glenthorne Ave. Croy 106 35 66 C
Glenthorne Cl. Sutt 103 25 66 C
Glenthorne Gdns. Ilf 28 43 89 B
Glenthorne Gdns. Sutt 103 25 66 C
Glenthorne Rd. E17 38 36 88 A
Glenthorne Rd. King 93 18 68 D
Glenthorne Rd. N11 16 28 92 B
Glenthorne Rd. W6 61 22 78 B
Glenthorpe Rd. Mord 103 23 67 B
Glenton Cl. Rom 30 51 91 C
Glenton Rd. SE13 77 39 75 C
Glenton Way. Rom 30 51 91 C
Glentworth St. NW1 1 27 82 D
Glenure Rd. SE9 78 43 74 A
Glen View Rd. Brom 99 41 69 D
Glenview. SE2 67 47 77 B
Glenville Gr. SE8 64 36 77 D
Glenville Rd. King 94 19 69 A
Glen Wlk. Islw 70 14 74 B
Glenwood Ave. NW9 34 21 87 C
Glenwood Cl. Har 33 15 88 B
Glenwood Dri. Rom 30 52 89 C
Glenwood Gdns. Ilf 40 43 88 A
Glenwood Gr. NW9 34 20 87 C
Glenwood Rd. Eps 109 22 63 A

Glenwood Rd. Houn 70 14 75 B
Glenwood Rd. N15 37 31 88 B
Glenwood Rd. SE6 88 37 73 C
Glenwood Way. Croy 106 35 67 D
Glenworth Ave. E14 64 38 78 B
Gliddon Rd. W14 62 24 78 C
Glimpsing Green. Belv 67 48 79 C
Globe Pond Rd. SE16 57 36 80 C
Globe Rd. E15 50 39 85 D
Globe Rd. E1 57 35 82 D
Globe Rd. E2 57 35 82 A
Globe Rd. Horn 42 52 88 C
Globe Rd. Wdf Gn 27 41 91 A
Globe Strs. SE16 57 35 80 B
Globe St. SE1 8 32 79 B
Globe Terr. E2 57 35 82 A
Globe Yd. W1 2 28 81 D
Glossop Rd. S Croy 112 32 62 B
Gloster Rd. N Mal 94 21 68 C
Gloucester Ave. NW1 47 28 83 A
Gloucester Ave. Sid 90 45 72 A
Gloucester Ave. Well 78 45 75 D
Gloucester Circ. SE10 64 38 77 C
Gloucester Cl. NW10 45 20 84 C
Gloucester Cl. Surb 101 16 66 C
Gloucester Cres. NW1 47 28 83 B
Gloucester Ct. EC3 8 33 80 A
Gloucester Ct. Rich 61 19 77 C
Gloucester Dri. N4 37 31 86 B
Gloucester Dri. NW11 23 25 89 C
Gloucester Gate Mews. NW1 47 28 83 D
Gloucester Gate. NW1 47 28 83 D
Gloucester Gdns. Barn 12 28 95 A
Gloucester Gdns. Ilf 39 42 87 A
Gloucester Gdns. NW11 35 24 87 B
Gloucester Gdns. Sutt 103 25 65 B
Gloucester Gdns. W2 1 26 81 C
Gloucester Gr. Edg 22 20 90 B
Gloucester Mews. W2 1 26 81 C
Gloucester Mews W. W2 1 26 81 C
Gloucester Pl Mews. W1 1 27 81 B
Gloucester Pl. W1 1 27 81 B
Gloucester Rd. Barn 11 26 95 A
Gloucester Rd. Belv 67 48 78 D
Gloucester Rd. Croy 105 33 66 A
Gloucester Rd. E10 38 37 87 A
Gloucester Rd. E11 39 41 88 A
Gloucester Rd. E12 50 42 85 B
Gloucester Rd. E17 26 35 90 D
Gloucester Rd. Felt 82 11 73 C
Gloucester Rd. Hamp 92 13 70 D
Gloucester Rd. Har 32 13 88 B
Gloucester Rd. Houn 70 12 75 C
Gloucester Rd. King 94 19 69 D
Gloucester Rd. N17 25 32 89 B
Gloucester Rd. N18 17 33 92 D
Gloucester Rd. Rich 61 19 77 C
Gloucester Rd. Rom 42 51 88 C
Gloucester Rd. SE25 105 33 67 C
Gloucester Rd. SW7 62 26 78 A
Gloucester Rd. Tedd 83 15 71 C
Gloucester Rd. Twick 82 14 73 C
Gloucester Rd. W3 61 20 79 A
Gloucester Rd. W5 60 17 79 A
Gloucester Sq. W2 1 27 81 C
Gloucester St. SW1 10 29 78 C
Gloucester Terr. W2 1 26 81 C
Gloucester Way. EC1 3 31 82 A
Gloucester Wlk. W8 62 25 79 A
Glover Rd. Pnr 32 11 88 D
Gloxinia Wlk. Hamp 92 13 70 A
Glycena Rd. SW11 74 27 75 B
Glyde Mews SW3 5 27 79 C
Glyn Ave. Barn 11 26 96 D
Glyn Cl. Eps 109 22 62 A
Glyn Cl. SE25 97 33 69 A
Glyn Ct. SE27 87 31 72 C
Glyndebourne Park. Orp 108 43 65 B
Glynde Rd. Bexh 79 48 75 A
Glynde St. SE4 76 36 74 D
Glyndon Rd. SE18 66 44 78 B
Glyn Dri. Sid 90 46 71 B
Glynfield Rd. NW10 45 21 84 C
Glyn Rd. E5 49 35 85 B
Glyn Rd. Enf 14 35 96 C
Glyn Rd. Wor Pk 103 23 65 D
Glyn St. SE11 10 30 78 D
Glynwood Ct. SE23 88 35 72 A
Goater's Alley. SW6 62 24 77 D
Goat Rd. Mit 104 28 67 C
Goat St. SE1 8 33 79 B
Gobions Ave. Rom 29 50 91 D
Godalming Ave. Wall 111 30 64 D
Godalming Rd. E14 57 37 81 B
Godbold Rd. E15 58 39 82 A
Goddard Cl. Shep 91 07 68 A
Goddard Rd. Beck 98 36 68 C
Goddington Chase. Orp 108 46 65 D
Goddington La. Orp 108 46 65 C
Godfrey Ave. Nthlt 43 12 83 A
Godfrey Ave. Twick 82 14 73 B
Godfrey Hill. SE18 65 42 78 A
Godfrey Rd. SE18 65 42 78 B
Godfrey St. E15 49 38 83 A
Godfrey St. SW3 9 27 78 C
Godfrey Way. Houn 82 12 73 B
Goding St. SE11 10 30 78 C
Godley Rd. SW18 85 26 73 D
Godliman St. EC4 4 32 81 C
Godman Rd. SE15 75 34 76 D
Godolphin Rd. W12 61 22 79 B
Godson Rd. Croy 105 31 65 C
Godson St. N1 48 31 83 C
Godstone Rd. Sutt 110 26 64 A
Godstone Rd. Twick 71 16 74 D
Godstow Rd. SE2 67 47 79 A
Godwin Cl. N1 48 32 83 C
Godwin Rd. Brom 99 41 68 A
Godwin Rd. E7 50 40 85 B
Goffers Rd. SE3 77 39 76 C
Goffs Rd. Ashf 81 08 71 D
Goidel Cl. Wall 111 29 64 B
Golborne Gdns. W10 56 24 82 D
Golborne Mews. W10 56 24 81 A
Golborne Rd. W10 56 24 81 A
Golda Cl. Barn 11 23 95 D
Goldbeaters Gr. Edg 22 21 91 C
Goldbeaters Wlk. Wem 34 19 86 D
Goldcliff Cl. Mord 103 25 66 A
Goldcrest Cl. E16 58 41 81 B
Gold Crest Way. Pur 111 29 62 D
Golden Ct. Rich 71 17 74 B
Golden La. EC1 4 32 82 C
Golden Manor. W7 54 15 80 A
Golden Sq. W1 6 29 80 A
Golden Yd. NW3 46 26 85 A
Golders Gdns. NW11 35 24 87 B
Golders Green Cres. NW11 35 25 87 A
Golders Green Rd. NW11 35 24 87 B
Golders Manor Dri. NW11 35 24 88 C
Golders Park Cl. NW11 35 25 87 C
Golders Rise. NW4 35 23 88 B
Golders Way. NW11 35 24 87 B
Goldhawk Estate. W6 61 22 79 D
Goldhawk Mews. W12 61 22 79 B
Goldhawk Rd. W12 61 22 79 D
Goldhawk Rd. W6 61 21 78 B
Gold Hill. Edg 22 20 91 B
Goldhurst Terr. NW6 46 26 84 C
Golding St. E1 57 34 81 C
Golding Terr. E1 57 34 81 C
Goldington Cres. NW1 47 29 83 D
Goldington St. NW1 47 29 83 D
Goldman Cl. E2 57 34 82 C
Goldsboro Rd. SW8 70 29 77 D
Goldsborough Cres. E4 18 38 93 A
Goldsdown Cl. Enf 14 36 97 C
Goldsdown Rd. Enf 14 36 97 C
Goldsmid St. SE18 66 45 78 C
Goldsmith Ave. E12 50 42 84 A
Goldsmith Ave. NW9 34 21 88 C
Goldsmith Ave. Rom 41 49 87 A
Goldsmith Ave. W3 55 20 80 B
Goldsmith Cl. Har 32 13 87 D
Goldsmith La. NW9 22 20 89 C
Goldsmith Rd. E10 38 37 87 D
Goldsmith Rd. E17 26 35 90 D
Goldsmith Rd. N11 16 27 92 D
Goldsmith Rd. SE15 75 34 76 A
Goldsmith Rd. W3 55 20 80 D
Goldsmiths Cl. W3 55 20 80 D
Goldsmith's Row. E2 48 34 83 C
Goldsmith's Sq. E2 48 34 83 C
Goldsmith St. EC2 4 32 81 C
Goldsworthy Gdns. SE16 64 35 78 C
Goldwell Rd. Th Hth 96 30 68 D
Goldwin Cl. SE15 76 35 76 A
Golf Cl. Stan 21 17 91 C
Golf Club Dri. King 94 20 70 D
Golfe Rd. Ilf 40 44 86 D
Golf Rd. Brom 100 43 68 A
Golf Rd. W5 54 18 81 D
Golf Side Cl. N Mal 94 21 69 C
Golf Side. Twick 82 14 72 D
Goliath Cl. Wall 111 30 63 C
Gollogly Terr. SE7 65 41 78 C
Gomer Gdns. Tedd 93 16 70 A
Gomer Pl. Tedd 93 16 70 A
Gomerset Rd. Sthl 53 13 81 A
Gomm Rd. SE16 64 35 79 C
Gomshall Ave. Wall 111 30 64 C
Gomshall Rd. Sutt 110 23 62 C
Gondar Gdns. NW6 46 24 85 D
Gonson St. SE8 64 37 77 B
Gonston Cl. SW19 85 24 72 A
Gonville Cres. Nthlt 43 13 84 B
Gonville Rd. Th Hth 104 30 67 B
Gonville St. SW6 73 24 75 A
Goodall Rd. E11 38 38 86 C
Gooden Ct. Har 33 15 86 C
Goodenough Rd. SW19 95 24 70 D
Goodge Pl. W1 2 29 81 A
Goodge St. W1 2 29 81 B
Goodhall St. NW10 55 21 82 B
Goodhart Way. W.Wick 107 39 67 C
Goodinge Cl. N7 47 30 84 A
Goodinge Rd. N7 47 30 84 A
Goodman Cres. SW2 86 29 72 B
Goodman Rd. E10 38 38 87 A
Goodman's Stile. E1 57 34 81 C
Goodman's Yd. E1 8 33 80 B
Goodmayes Ave. Ilf 40 46 87 C
Goodmayes La. Ilf 40 45 86 C
Goodmayes Rd. Ilf 40 45 87 C
Goodmead Rd. Orp 108 46 66 A
Goodrich Rd. SE22 75 34 74 C
Goodson House. Mord 103 26 66 A
Goodson Rd. NW10 45 21 84 C
Goods Way. NW1 47 30 83 C
Goodway Gdns. E14 58 38 81 D
Goodwin Gdns. Croy 112 31 63 B
Goodwin Rd. Croy 112 31 64 D
Goodwin Rd. N9 18 35 94 D
Goodwin Rd. W12 61 22 79 B
Goodwins Ct. WC2 7 30 80 A
Goodwin St. N4 37 31 86 A
Goodwood Ave. Horn 42 54 86 C
Goodwood Cl. Mord 95 25 68 C
Goodwood Dri. Nthlt 43 13 84 A
Goodwood Rd. SE14 64 36 77 C
Goodwyn's Vale. N10 24 28 90 B
Goodyers Gdns. NW4 35 23 88 B
Gooseacre La. Har 33 17 88 B
Gooshays Dri. Rom 30 54 91 A
Gooshays Gdns. Rom 30 54 91 A
Gophir La. EC4 8 32 80 B
Gopsall St. N1 48 32 83 B
Gordon Ave. E4 27 39 91 A
Gordon Ave. Horn 42 51 86 B
Gordon Ave. S Croy 112 32 62 C
Gordon Ave. Stan 21 16 91 A
Gordon Ave. SW14 72 21 75 C
Gordon Ave. Twick 71 16 74 B
Gordonbrock Rd. SE4 76 37 74 A
Gordon Cl. E17 38 37 88 C
Gordon Cl. N19 36 29 87 C
Gordon Cres. Croy 105 33 66 D
Gordondale Rd. SW19 85 25 72 A
Gordon Gdns. Edg 22 19 90 D
Gordon Gr. SE5 75 31 76 D
Gordon Hill. Enf 13 32 97 D
Gordon House Rd. NW3 47 28 85 A
Gordon Pl. W8 62 25 79 A
Gordon Rd. Bark 51 45 83 A
Gordon Rd. Beck 98 35 69 D
Gordon Rd. Beck 98 36 68 B
Gordon Rd. Belv 67 50 78 A
Gordon Rd. Cars 111 27 63 B
Gordon Rd. E11 39 40 88 C
Gordon Rd. E12 40 43 86 C
Gordon Rd. E15 49 38 85 A
Gordon Rd. E18 27 40 90 B
Gordon Rd. Enf 13 32 97 D
Gordon Rd. Har 21 15 89 A
Gordon Rd. Houn 70 14 75 C
Gordon Rd. Ilf 51 44 85 B
Gordon Rd. Ilf 40 44 86 D
Gordon Rd. King 93 18 69 B
Gordon Rd. N11 24 29 91 D
Gordon Rd. N3 23 24 91 D
Gordon Rd. N9 17 34 93 B
Gordon Rd. Rich 71 18 76 D
Gordon Rd. Rom 41 48 88 D
Gordon Rd. SE15 75 34 76 D
Gordon Rd. Sid 78 45 74 A
Gordon Rd. Sthl 59 12 78 A
Gordon Rd. Surb 101 18 66 B
Gordon Rd. W4 61 19 77 B
Gordon Rd. W5 54 17 80 A
Gordon Sq. WC1 2 29 82 D
Gordon St. E13 58 40 82 A
Gordon St. WC1 2 29 82 D
Gordon Way. Barn 11 24 96 D
Gore Ct. NW9 34 19 88 A
Gorefield Pl. NW6 46 25 83 C
Gore Rd. E9 49 35 83 B
Gore Rd. SW20 95 23 69 C
Goresbrook Rd. Dag 52 47 83 B
Gore St. SW7 5 26 79 C
Gorham Pl. W11 56 24 80 A
Goring Cl. Rom 29 50 90 A
Goring Gdns. Dag 52 47 85 A
Goring Rd. Dag 52 50 84 B
Goring Rd. N11 24 30 91 A
Goring St. EC3 4 33 81 C
Goring Way. Grnf 43 14 83 C
Gorleston Rd. N15 37 32 89 B
Gorleston St. W14 62 24 78 A
Gorman Rd. SE18 65 42 78 B
Gorringe Park Ave. Mit 96 28 70 C
Gorse Rd. Croy 106 37 65 C
Gorse Rise. SW17 86 28 71 C
Gorseway. Rom 42 51 87 C
Gorst Rd. NW10 55 20 82 D
Gorst Rd. SW11 74 27 74 D
Gorsuch Pl. E2 4 33 82 B
Gosberton Rd. SW12 86 28 73 C
Gosfield Rd. Dag 41 49 86 A
Gosfield St. W1 2 29 81 A
Gosford Gdns. Ilf 39 42 88 B
Goslett Yd. WC2 2 29 81 D
Gosling Cl. Grnf 53 13 82 A
Gosling Way. SW9 75 31 76 A
Gospatrick Rd. N17 25 32 90 C
Gosport Rd. E17 38 36 88 B
Gosport Way (off pentridge St).
SE15 63 33 77 D
Gosport Wlk. N15 25 34 89 D
Gossage Rd. SE18 66 44 78 D
Gosset St. E2 4 33 82 B
Gosset St. E2 57 34 82 A
Gosshill Rd. Chis 100 43 69 C
Gosterwood St. SE8 64 36 78 C
Gostling Rd. Twick 82 13 73 C
Goston Gdns. Th Hth 97 31 68 A
Goswell Pl. EC1 3 31 82 B
Goswell Rd. EC1 3 31 82 B
Gothic Rd. Twick 82 14 72 B
Gottfried Mews. NW5 47 29 85 A
Goudhurst Rd. Brom 89 39 71 D
Gough Rd. E15 50 39 85 B
Gough Rd. Enf 13 34 97 D
Gough Sq. EC4 3 31 81 C
Gough St. WC1 3 30 82 D
Gough Wlk. E14 57 37 81 C
Goulden House. SW11 74 27 76 C
Gould Rd. Felt 81 09 73 A
Gould Rd. Twick 83 15 73 C
Gould Terr. E8 48 34 85 D
Goulston St. E1 4 33 81 D
Goulton Rd. E5 48 34 85 B
Gourley Pl. N15 37 33 88 A
Gourley St. N15 37 33 88 A
Gourock Rd. SE9 78 43 74 A
Govan St. E2 48 34 83 A
Govier Cl. E15 50 39 84 C
Gowan Ave. SW6 73 24 76 A
Gowan Rd. NW10 45 22 84 B
Gower Mews. WC1 2 29 81 B
Gower Pl. WC1 2 29 82 D
Gower Rd. E7 50 40 84 A
Gower Rd. Islw 60 15 77 B
Gower St. WC1 2 29 82 D
Gower's Wlk. E1 57 34 81 C
Gowland Pl. Beck 98 36 69 D
Gowlett Rd. SE15 75 34 75 A
Gowrie Rd. SW11 74 28 75 A
Graburn Way. E Mol 92 14 68 B
Grace Ave. Bexh 79 48 76 D
Gracechurch St. EC3 8 32 80 B
Grace Cl. SE9 89 41 72 D
Gracedale Rd. SW16 86 28 71 D
Gracefield Gdns. SW16 86 30 72 C
Grace Path. SE26 88 35 71 A
Grace Pl. E3 57 37 82 B
Grace Rd. Croy 105 32 67 C
Graces Alley. E1 57 34 80 A
Grace's Mews. SE5 75 33 76 C
Grace's Rd. SE5 75 33 76 C
Grace St. E3 57 37 82 B
Gradient The. SE26 87 34 71 A
Graeme Rd. Enf 13 33 97 C
Graemesdyke Ave. SW14 72 19 75 D
Grafton Cl. Houn 82 12 73 C
Grafton Cl. W13 54 16 81 C
Grafton Cl. Wor Pk 102 21 65 C
Grafton Cres. NW1 47 28 84 B
Grafton Gdns. Dag 41 48 86 A
Grafton Gdns. N4 37 32 88 C
Grafton Mews. W1 2 29 82 C
Grafton Park Rd. Wor Pk 102 21 65 A
Grafton Pl. NW1 2 29 82 B
Grafton Rd. Croy 105 31 66 C
Grafton Rd. Dag 41 48 86 A
Grafton Rd. Enf 12 30 96 B
Grafton Rd. Har 32 14 88 A
Grafton Rd. N Mal 94 21 68 A
Grafton Rd. NW5 47 28 85 C
Grafton Rd. W3 55 20 80 A
Grafton Rd. Wor Pk 102 21 65 C
Grafton Sq. SW4 74 29 75 A
Grafton St. W1 6 28 80 B
Grafton Terr. NW5 47 27 85 D
Grafton Way. W1 2 29 82 C
Grafton Way. W1 2 29 82 C
Grafton Yd. NW5 47 28 84 B
Graham Ave. Mit 96 28 69 A
Graham Ave. W13 60 16 79 B
Graham Cl. Croy 106 37 65 A
Graham Ct. Nthlt 43 12 85 D
Grahame Park Way. NW7 22 21 91 B
Grahame Park Way. NW9 22 22 90 A
Graham Gdns. Surb 101 18 66 C
Graham Rd. Bexh 79 48 75 D
Graham Rd. E13 58 40 82 C
Graham Rd. E8 48 34 84 A
Graham Rd. Hamp 82 13 71 A
Graham Rd. Har 21 15 89 A
Graham Rd. Mit 96 28 69 A
Graham Rd. N15 25 31 89 B
Graham Rd. NW4 34 22 88 D
Graham Rd. SW19 95 24 70 D
Graham Rd. W4 61 20 79 D
Graham St. N1 48 31 83 D
Graham Terr. SW1 9 28 78 A
Grainger Cl. Nthlt 43 14 85 C
Grainger Rd. Islw 71 15 76 D
Grainger Rd. N22 25 32 90 A
Gramer Cl. E11 38 38 86 B
Grampian Cl. Orp 108 45 67 D
Grampian Gdns. NW2 35 24 87 C
Granada St. SW17 86 27 71 D
Granard Ave. SW15 72 22 74 B
Granard Rd. SW12 86 27 73 B
Granby Bldgs. SE11 10 30 78 B
Granby Pl. SE1 7 31 79 A
Granby Rd. SE9 77 42 75 B
Granby St. E2 4 33 82 D
Granby St. E2 57 34 82 A
Granby Terr. NW1 47 29 83 C
Grand Arc. N12 15 26 92 C
Grand Ave. EC1 3 31 81 B
Grand Ave E. Wem 45 19 85 D
Grand Ave. N10 24 28 89 C
Grand Ave. Surb 102 19 67 D
Grand Ave. Wem 45 19 85 C
Grand Depot Rd. SE18 66 43 78 C
Grand Dri. SW20 95 23 68 A
Granden Rd. SW16 96 30 69 C
Grandison Rd. SW11 74 27 74 B
Grandison Rd. Wor Pk 103 23 65 A
Grand Sq. SE10 64 38 77 B
Grand Wlk. E2 57 36 82 C
Granfield St. SW11 73 26 76 B
Grange Ave. Barn 11 27 94 D
Grange Ave. N12 15 26 92 C
Grange Ave. N20 15 24 94 A
Grange Ave. SE25 97 33 69 C
Grange Ave. Stan 21 17 90 C
Grange Ave. Twick 83 15 72 A
Grange Ave. Wdf Gn 27 40 91 C
Grange Cl. E Mol 92 13 68 D
Grange Cl. Houn 59 12 77 B
Grangecliffe Gdns. SE25 97 33 69 C
Grange Cl. Sid 90 46 72 C
Grange Cl. Wdf Gn 27 40 91 C
Grangecourt Rd. N16 37 33 87 C
Grange Ct. Nthlt 43 11 83 C
Grange Ct. Shep 91 07 68 C
Grange Ct. Sutt 110 25 63 D
Grange Ct. Wall 104 28 65 D
Grange Ct. WC2 3 30 81 D
Grangedale Cl. Nthwd 19 09 90 A
Grange Dri. Chis 99 42 70 B
Grange Farm Cl. Har 32 14 86 A
Grange Gdns. N14 16 29 94 D
Grange Gdns. Pnr 20 12 89 C
Grange Gdns. SE25 97 33 69 C
Grange Gr. N1 48 32 84 A
Grangehill Pl. SE9 77 42 75 B
Grangehill Rd. SE9 77 42 75 D
Grange Hill. SE25 97 33 69 C
Grange La. SE21 87 33 72 B
Grange Mansions. Eps 109 21 63 D
Grangemill Rd. SE6 88 37 72 A
Grangemill Way. SE6 88 37 72 A
Grange Park Ave. N21 13 32 95 C
Grange Park Rd. E10 38 37 87 D
Grange Park Rd. Th Hth 97 32 68 B
Grange Park. W5 54 18 80 C
Grange Rd. Chess 101 18 65 C
Grange Rd. E10 38 37 87 C
Grange Rd. E13 58 40 82 B
Grange Rd. E17 38 36 88 A
Grange Rd. Edg 22 20 91 B
Grange Rd. E Mol 92 13 68 D
Grange Rd. Har 32 14 86 B
Grange Rd. Har 33 16 88 A
Grange Rd. Ilf 51 44 85 A
Grange Rd. King 93 18 68 A
Grange Rd. N18 25 34 91 A
Grange Rd. N6 36 28 88 C
Grange Rd. NW10 45 22 84 B
Grange Rd. Orp 108 44 65 A
Grange Rd. Rom 30 52 91 B
Grange Rd. S Croy 112 32 62 A
Grange Rd. SE19 97 32 69 B
Grange Rd. SE1 8 33 79 D
Grange Rd. SE25 97 32 68 B
Grange Rd. Sthl 59 12 79 A
Grange Rd. Sutt 110 25 63 D
Grange Rd. SW13 72 22 76 A
Grange Rd. Th Hth 97 32 68 D
Grange Rd. W4 61 19 78 D
Grange Rd. W5 54 18 80 C
Granger Way. Rom 42 52 88 C
Grange St. N1 48 32 83 B
Grange The. Croy 106 36 65 B
Grange The. E17 38 36 88 A
Grange The. N20 15 26 94 C
Grange The. N.Mal 102 22 67 A
Grange. The SE1 8 33 79 D
Grange The. SW19 95 23 70 B
Grange The. Wem 45 19 84 C
Grange The. Wor Pk 109 20 64 B
Grange Vale. Sutt 110 25 63 D
Grangeview Rd. N20 15 26 94 C
Grange Way. Eri 68 52 77 D
Grangeway Gdns. Ilf 39 42 88 A
Grangeway. N12 15 25 92 B
Grangeway. NW6 46 25 84 C
Grangeway The. N21 13 31 95 C
Grange Wlk. SE1 8 33 79 D
Grangewood Cl. Pnr 31 10 88 A
Grangewood La. Beck 98 36 70 B
Grangewood St. E6 50 41 83 B
Grange Yd. SE1 8 33 79 D
Granham Gdns. N9 17 33 93 B
Granite St. SE18 66 45 78 D
Granleigh Rd. E11 39 39 86 A
Gransden Ave. E8 48 34 84 D
Gransden Rd. W12 61 21 79 B
Grantbridge St. N1 48 31 83 D
Grant Cl. N14 16 29 94 A
Grantham Gdns. Rom 41 48 87 B
Grantham Pl. W1 6 28 80 D
Grantham Rd. E12 51 43 85 A
Grantham Rd. SW9 74 30 76 C
Grantham Rd. W4 61 21 77 C
Grantley Rd. Houn 70 11 76 C
Grantley St. E1 57 35 82 D
Grantock Rd. E17 26 38 90 B
Granton Ave. Horn 42 54 86 B
Granton Rd. Ilf 40 46 87 C
Granton Rd. SW16 96 29 69 A
Grant Pl. Croy 105 33 66 D
Grant Rd. Croy 105 33 66 D
Grant Rd. Har 21 15 89 B
Grant Rd. SW11 74 27 75 A
Grants Cl. NW7 23 23 91 C
Grant St. E13 58 40 82 A
Grant St. N1 48 31 83 C
Grantully Rd. W9 56 25 82 B
Granville Ave. Felt 81 10 72 A
Granville Ave. Houn 70 13 74 A
Granville Ave. N9 18 35 93 C
Granville Cl. Croy 105 33 65 A
Granville Gdns. SW16 96 30 70 D
Granville Gdns. W5 54 18 80 D
Granville Gr. SE13 76 38 75 A
Granville Park. SE13 76 38 75 B
Granville Pl. N12 23 26 91 C
Granville Pl. W1 2 28 81 C
Granville Rd. Barn 11 23 96 B
Granville Rd. E17 38 37 88 D
Granville Rd. E18 27 40 90 D
Granville Rd. Ilf 40 43 86 B
Granville Rd. N12 23 26 91 C
Granville Rd. N13 24 30 91 B
Granville Rd. N22 25 32 90 C

| Name | Pg | Grid |
|---|---|---|
| Granville Rd. N8 | 36 | 30 88 D |
| Granville Rd. NW2 | 35 | 24 86 B |
| Granville Rd. NW6 | 46 | 25 83 C |
| Granville Rd. Sid | 90 | 46 71 B |
| Granville Rd. SW18 | 85 | 24 73 B |
| Granville Rd. SW19 | 95 | 25 70 C |
| Granville Rd. Well | 79 | 47 75 A |
| Granville Sq. WC1 | 3 | 30 82 B |
| Granville St. WC1 | 3 | 30 82 B |
| Grape St. WC2 | 3 | 30 81 C |
| Grasdene Rd. SE18 | 66 | 46 77 C |
| Grasmere Ave. Houn | 70 | 13 74 D |
| Grasmere Ave. Orp | 108 | 43 65 D |
| Grasmere Ave. Ruis | 31 | 08 87 A |
| Grasmere Ave. SW15 | 84 | 21 71 A |
| Grasmere Ave. SW19 | 95 | 25 68 A |
| Grasmere Ave. W3 | 55 | 20 80 B |
| Grasmere Ave. Wem | 33 | 17 87 D |
| Grasmere Ct. N22 | 24 | 30 91 B |
| Grasmere Ct. SE26 | 87 | 34 71 C |
| Grasmere Gdns. Har | 21 | 16 90 C |
| Grasmere Gdns. Ilf | 27 | 42 89 D |
| Grasmere Gdns. Orp | 108 | 43 65 D |
| Grasmere Rd. Bexh | 79 | 50 76 C |
| Grasmere Rd. Brom | 99 | 39 70 D |
| Grasmere Rd. E13 | 50 | 40 83 C |
| Grasmere Rd. N10 | 24 | 28 90 B |
| Grasmere Rd. N18 | 25 | 34 91 A |
| Grasmere Rd. Orp | 108 | 43 65 D |
| Grasmere Rd. SE25 | 105 | 34 67 B |
| Grasmere Rd. SW16 | 86 | 30 71 D |
| Grassington Rd. Sid | 90 | 46 71 A |
| Grassmere Rd. Horn | 30 | 54 89 D |
| Grassmount. Pur | 111 | 29 62 C |
| Grassmount. SE23 | 87 | 34 72 B |
| Grass Park. N3 | 23 | 24 90 B |
| Grassway. Wall | 111 | 29 64 A |
| Grasvenor Ave. Barn | 11 | 25 95 C |
| Grately Way (off Daniel Gdns.). SE15 | 63 | 33 77 D |
| Gratton Rd. W14 | 62 | 24 79 C |
| Gratton Terr. NW2 | 35 | 23 86 D |
| Gravel Hill. Bex | 79 | 49 74 B |
| Gravel Hill Cl. Bex | 79 | 49 74 B |
| Gravel Hill Cl. Bexh | 79 | 49 74 B |
| Gravel Hill. N3 | 23 | 24 90 D |
| Gravel La. E1 | 4 | 33 81 D |
| Gravelly Hill. SW19 | 84 | 22 71 A |
| Gravel Pit La. SE9 | 78 | 44 74 A |
| Gravel Rd. Brom | 107 | 42 65 A |
| Gravel Rd. Twick | 83 | 15 73 C |
| Gravelwood Cl. Chis | 90 | 44 72 C |
| Gravenel Gdns. SW17 | 86 | 27 71 C |
| Graveney Gr. SE20 | 98 | 35 70 C |
| Graveney Rd. SW17 | 86 | 27 71 A |
| Gravesend Rd. W12 | 55 | 22 80 A |
| Graves Estate. Well | 78 | 46 76 D |
| Gray Ave. Dag | 41 | 48 87 D |
| Grayfriars Pas. EC1 | 3 | 31 81 D |
| Graham Cres. N Mal | 94 | 20 68 D |
| Graham Rd. N Mal | 94 | 20 68 D |
| Grayland Cl. Brom | 99 | 41 69 B |
| Grayling Cl. N16 | 37 | 33 86 A |
| *Grayling Sq. E2 | 57 | 34 82 A |
| Grayscroft Rd. SW16 | 96 | 29 70 D |
| Grays Farm Rd. Orp | 100 | 46 69 B |
| Grayshott Rd. SW11 | 74 | 28 75 A |
| Gray's Inn Pl. WC1 | 3 | 30 81 B |
| Gray's Inn Rd. WC1 | 3 | 30 82 D |
| Gray's Inn Sq. WC1 | 3 | 31 81 A |
| Gray St. SE1 | 7 | 31 79 A |
| Grayswood Gdns. SW20 | 94 | 22 69 D |
| Gray's Yd. W1 | 2 | 28 81 C |
| Graywood Ct. N12 | 23 | 26 91 C |
| Grazebrook Rd. N16 | 37 | 32 86 B |
| Grazeley Cl. Bexh | 79 | 50 74 A |
| Great Acre Ct. SW4 | 4 | 29 75 D |
| Great Bell Alley. EC2 | 4 | 32 81 D |
| Great Brownings. SE21 | 87 | 33 72 D |
| Great Bushey Dri. N20 | 15 | 25 94 D |
| Great Cambridge Rd. Enf | 14 | 34 96 C |
| Great Cambridge Rd. N17 | 25 | 32 91 D |
| Great Cambridge Rd. N18 | 17 | 32 92 D |
| Great Cambridge Rd. N9 | 17 | 33 93 A |
| Great Cambridge Rd. N9 | 17 | 33 94 C |
| Great Castle St. W1 | 2 | 28 81 D |
| Great Castle St. W1 | 2 | 29 81 C |
| Great Central Ave. Ruis | 43 | 11 85 C |
| Great Central St. NW1 | 1 | 27 81 B |
| Great Chapel St. W1 | 2 | 29 81 D |
| Great Chertsey Rd. Felt | 82 | 13 72 C |
| Great Chertsey Rd. W4 | 61 | 21 77 A |
| Great Church La. W6 | 62 | 23 78 D |
| Great College St. | | 30 79 C |
| Great Cross Ave. SE10 | 65 | 39 77 C |
| Great Cullings. Rom | 42 | 51 86 A |
| Great Cumberland Mews. W1 | 1 | 27 81 D |
| Great Cumberland Pl. W1 | 1 | 27 81 D |
| Great Dover St. SE1 | 8 | 32 79 D |
| Great Eastern Rd. E15 | 49 | 38 84 B |
| Great Eastern St. EC2 | 4 | 33 82 C |
| Great Elms Rd. Brom | 99 | 41 68 C |
| *Greatfield Cl. N19 | 47 | 29 85 A |
| Greatfield Cl. SE4 | 76 | 37 75 C |
| Great Field. NW9 | 22 | 21 90 A |
| Greatfields Rd. Bark | 51 | 44 83 D |
| Great Gardens Rd. Horn | 42 | 53 88 C |
| Great George St. SW1 | 7 | 30 79 A |
| Great Guildford St. SE1 | 8 | 32 80 C |
| Greatham Wlk. SW15 | 84 | 22 73 C |
| Great Harry Dri. SE9 | 90 | 43 72 C |
| Great James St. WC1 | 3 | 30 81 B |
| Great Marlborough St. W1 | 2 | 29 81 C |
| Great Maze Pond. SE1 | 8 | 32 80 D |
| Great Nelmes Chase. Horn | 54 | 54 88 B |
| Great Newport St. WC2 | 7 | 30 80 A |
| Great New St. EC4 | 3 | 31 81 C |
| Great North Rd. Barn | 11 | 24 96 D |
| Great North Rd. N12 | 23 | 26 91 A |
| Great North Rd. N20 | 15 | 26 94 C |
| Great North Rd. N20 | 15 | 26 94 C |
| Great North Rd. N2 | 24 | 27 89 A |
| Great North Way (Barnet By Pass). NW4 | | 23 90 C |
| Greatorex St. E1 | 57 | 34 81 A |
| Great Ormond St. WC1 | 3 | 30 82 D |
| Great Percy St. WC1 | 3 | 31 82 A |
| Great Peter St. SW1 | 6 | 29 79 D |
| Great Portland St. W1 | 2 | 28 81 B |
| Great Pulteney St. W1 | 2 | 29 80 A |
| Great Queen St. Dart | 80 | 54 74 D |
| Great Queen St. WC2 | 3 | 30 81 C |
| Great Ross Ave. SE10 | 64 | 38 77 D |
| Great Russell St. WC1 | 2 | 29 81 D |
| Great Russell St. WC1 | 3 | 30 81 A |
| Great Scotland Yd. SW1 | 7 | 30 80 C |
| Great Smith St. SW1 | 6 | 29 79 D |
| Great South-West Rd. Felt | 69 | 09 74 A |
| Great South West Rd. Houn | 70 | 11 76 C |
| Great Spilmans. SE22 | 75 | 33 74 A |
| Great St Helen's. EC3 | 4 | 33 81 C |
| Great Strand. NW9 | | 21 90 D |
| Great St Thomas Apostle. EC4 | 4 | 32 80 A |
| Grt Suffolk St. SE1 | 7 | 31 80 D |
| Great Suffolk St. SE1 | 8 | 32 79 A |
| Great Sutton St. EC1 | 3 | 31 82 D |
| Great Swan Alley. EC2 | 4 | 32 81 D |
| Great Thrift. Orp | 100 | 44 68 C |
| Great Titchfield St. W1 | 2 | 29 81 A |
| Great Tower St. EC3 | | 33 80 A |
| Great Trinity La. EC4 | 8 | 32 80 A |
| Great Turnstile. WC2 | 3 | 30 81 B |
| Great Western Rd. W11 | 56 | 25 81 A |
| Great Western Rd. W9 | 56 | 24 82 D |
| Great West Rd. Brent | 60 | 17 78 D |
| Great West Rd. Islw | 60 | 15 77 C |
| Great West Rd. Islw | 60 | 13 76 A |
| Great West Road Chiswick. W4 | 61 | 21 78 D |
| Great Winchester St. EC2 | 4 | 32 81 D |
| Great Windmill St. W1 | 6 | 29 80 B |
| Greatwood. Chis | 100 | 43 70 C |
| Great Woodcote Dri. Pur | 111 | 29 62 D |
| Great Woodcote Park. Pur | 111 | 30 62 C |
| Great Yd. SE1 | 7 | 33 79 A |
| Greaves Pl. SW17 | 86 | 27 71 A |
| Grecian Cres. SE19 | 97 | 31 70 B |
| Greek St. W1 | 2 | 29 81 D |
| Greenacres. Uxb | 31 | 07 86 C |
| Green Acres. Croy | 105 | 33 65 D |
| Greenacres Dri. Stan | 21 | 16 91 D |
| Greenacres. N3 | 23 | 24 90 C |
| Greenacres. SE9 | 78 | 43 74 C |
| Greenacre Wlk. N14 | 16 | 29 93 D |
| Green Arbour Ct. EC4 | 3 | 31 81 D |
| Green Ave. W13 | 60 | 16 79 D |
| Greenaway Gdns. NW3 | 46 | 25 85 B |
| Greenbank Ave. Wem | 44 | 16 85 C |
| Greenbank Cres. NW4 | 23 | 24 89 C |
| Green Bank. E1 | | 34 80 D |
| Green Bank. N12 | 15 | 25 92 B |
| Greenbay Rd. SE7 | 41 | 41 77 D |
| Greenberry St. NW8 | 1 | 27 81 D |
| Greenbrook Ave. Barn | 11 | 26 97 A |
| Green Cl. Brom | 99 | 39 68 A |
| Green Cl. Cars | 104 | 27 65 B |
| Green Cl. Felt | 82 | 12 71 C |
| Green Cl. NW11 | 35 | 26 87 A |
| Green Cl. NW9 | 34 | 20 88 C |
| Greencoat Pl. SW1 | 10 | 29 78 A |
| Greencoat Row. SW1 | 6 | 29 79 C |
| Green Court Ave. Croy | 105 | 34 65 B |
| Greencourt Ave. Edg | 22 | 19 90 B |
| Green Court Gdns. Croy | 105 | 34 65 B |
| Greencourt Rd. Orp | 108 | 45 67 A |
| Greencroft Ave. Ruis | 32 | 11 86 A |
| Greencroft Gdns. Enf | 13 | 33 96 A |
| Greencroft Gdns. NW6 | 46 | 26 84 C |
| Greencroft Rd. Houn | 72 | 12 76 B |
| Green Dale Cl. SE22 | 75 | 33 74 A |
| Green Dale. SE22 | 75 | 33 75 C |
| Green Dragon Ct. SE1 | 8 | 32 80 D |
| Green Dragon La. (Path). Brent | 60 | 18 78 C |
| Green Dragon La. Brent | 60 | 18 78 D |
| Green Dragon La. N21 | 13 | 31 95 C |
| Green Dragon Yd. E1 | 7 | 34 81 A |
| Green Dri. Sthl | 53 | 13 80 C |
| Green End. N21 | 13 | 31 93 B |
| Greenend Rd. W4 | 61 | 21 79 A |
| Greenfield Ave. Surb | 102 | 19 67 D |
| Greenfield Gdns. Dag | 52 | 47 83 B |
| Greenfield Gdns. NW2 | 35 | 24 86 C |
| Greenfield Gdns. Orp | 108 | 44 66 B |
| Greenfield Pas. Barn | 11 | 24 96 A |
| Greenfield Rd. Dag | 52 | 47 83 A |
| Greenfield Rd. E1 | 57 | 34 81 C |
| Greenfield Rd. N15 | 37 | 33 88 A |
| Greenfields. Sthl | 53 | 13 80 A |
| Greenfield Way. Har | 20 | 13 89 B |
| Greenford Ave. Sthl | 53 | 12 80 B |
| Greenford Ave. W7 | 54 | 15 81 C |
| Greenfrd Gdns. Grnf | 53 | 14 82 A |
| Greenford Rd. Grnf | 53 | 14 83 D |
| Greenford Rd. Har | 54 | 15 85 B |
| Greenford Rd. Sutt | 110 | 25 64 B |
| Greengate. Grnf | 54 | 16 84 B |
| Greengate St. E13 | 58 | 40 82 B |
| Greengate St. E13 | 58 | 40 82 B |
| Green Glades. Horn | 42 | 54 88 D |
| Greenhalgh Wlk. N2 | 23 | 26 89 C |
| Greenham Rd. N10 | 24 | 28 90 C |
| Greenheys Cl. Nthwd | 19 | 09 90 A |
| Greenheys Dri. E18 | 27 | 39 90 D |
| Greenhill Cl. Har | | 15 88 C |
| Greenhill Gdns. Nthlt | 43 | 12 83 D |
| Greenhill. E12 | | 42 85 A |
| Greenhill. NW3 | 46 | 26 85 B |
| Greenhill Park. Barn | 11 | 25 95 B |
| Greenhill Park. NW10 | 45 | 21 83 A |
| Greenhill Rd. Har | | 15 88 C |
| Greenhill Rd. NW10 | 45 | 21 83 A |
| Greenhill. NW3 | 46 | 26 85 B |
| Greenhill's Rents. EC1 | 3 | 31 81 B |
| Greenhills Terr. N1 | 48 | 32 84 B |
| Greenhill Ter. Nthlt | 43 | 12 83 D |
| Greenhill Terr. SE18 | 65 | 42 78 D |
| Greenhill Way. Har | 33 | 15 88 C |
| Greenhill Way. Wem | 34 | 19 86 B |
| Greenhithe Cl. Sid | 90 | 45 73 A |
| Greenholm Rd. SE9 | 78 | 43 74 B |
| Green Hundred Rd. SE15 | 63 | 34 77 A |
| Greenhurst Rd. SE27 | 97 | 31 71 C |
| Greening St. SE2 | 67 | 47 78 A |
| Green La. Ashf | | 09 70 B |
| Green La. Chis | 91 | 47 86 B |
| Green La. Edg | 22 | 19 91 A |
| Green La. Enf | 14 | 38 96 B |
| Green La. Felt | 82 | 12 71 C |
| Green La. Houn | 70 | 11 75 C |
| Green La. Ilf | 50 | 45 86 B |
| Green La. Mord | 103 | 23 67 C |
| Green La. Mord | 103 | 25 67 D |
| Green Lane. Th Hth | 97 | 30 69 A |
| Green Lanes. Eps | 109 | 21 62 A |
| Green Lanes. N13 | 17 | 31 93 C |
| Green Lanes. N16 | 48 | 32 85 B |
| Green Lanes. N21 | 17 | 31 94 D |
| Green Lanes. N4 | 37 | 32 87 A |
| Green La. N.Mal | 102 | 20 67 A |
| Green La. Nthwd | 19 | 09 91 C |
| Green La. NW4 | 23 | 23 88 B |
| Green La. Pur | 111 | 29 62 D |
| Green La. SE20 | 98 | 35 70 D |
| Green La. SE9 | 90 | 43 72 A |
| Green La. SE9 | 90 | 43 72 D |
| Green La. SW16 | 96 | 30 70 D |
| Green La. SW16 | 97 | 31 69 A |
| Green La. Th Hth | 97 | 31 69 B |
| Green La. W7 | 60 | 15 79 A |
| Greenlaw Gdns. N.Mal | 102 | 21 66 B |
| Green Lawns. Ruis | 32 | 11 87 C |
| Green La. Wor Pk | | 22 66 C |
| Greenlaw St. SE18 | 66 | 43 79 C |
| Greenleaf Cl. SW2 | 87 | 31 73 A |
| Greenleafe Dri. Ilf | 27 | 43 89 B |
| Greenleaf Rd. E17 | 26 | 36 89 B |
| Greenleaf Rd. E6 | 50 | 41 83 A |
| Green Leas. Ashf | 91 | 09 70 B |
| Greenleaves Ct. Ashf | 91 | 07 70 B |
| Green Man Gdns. W13 | 54 | 16 80 A |
| Green Man La. Felt | 69 | 10 75 C |
| Green Man La. W13 | 54 | 16 80 C |
| Green Man Pas. W13 | 54 | 16 80 D |
| Greenman St. N1 | 48 | 32 83 A |
| Green Moor Link. N21 | 13 | 31 94 B |
| Greenmoor Rd. Enf | 14 | 35 97 C |
| Greenoak Way. SW19 | 85 | 23 71 B |
| Greenock Rd. SW16 | 96 | 29 69 B |
| Greenock Rd. W3 | 61 | 19 79 D |
| Greenock Way. Rom | 30 | 51 91 C |
| Green Pond. Dart | 80 | 51 74 A |
| Green Pond Rd. E17 | 26 | 36 89 A |
| Green Rd. N14 | 12 | 28 95 B |
| Green Rd. N20 | 15 | 26 93 C |
| Greenroof Way. Wem | | 19 86 D |
| Greenshank Cl. W1 | | 29 80 B |
| Greens Ct. Wem | | 17 86 D |
| Green's End. SE18 | 66 | 43 78 B |
| Greenside. Dag | 41 | 47 87 C |
| Greenside Rd. Croy | 105 | 31 66 A |
| Greenside Rd. W12 | 61 | 22 79 A |
| Green St. E13 | | 41 83 A |
| Green St. E7 | 50 | 41 84 A |
| Greenstead Ave. Wdf Gn | 27 | 41 91 A |
| Greenstead Cl. Wdf Gn | 27 | 41 91 A |
| Greenstead Gdns. SW15 | 72 | 22 74 B |
| Greenstead Gdns. Wdf Gn | 27 | 41 91 A |
| Green St. Enf | 14 | 35 97 D |
| Green St. Sun | 91 | 10 69 C |
| Green St. W1 | 2 | 28 80 A |
| Green Terr. EC1 | | 31 82 A |
| Green The. Bexh | 79 | 49 76 A |
| Green The. Brom | 107 | 40 66 A |
| Green The. Brom | 99 | 40 72 C |
| Green The. Cars | 111 | 28 64 A |
| Green The. E11 | 39 | 40 88 D |
| Green The. E15 | 39 | 39 84 B |
| Green The. E4 | 18 | 38 94 D |
| Green The. Houn | | 13 77 A |
| Green The. Mord | 95 | 24 68 C |
| Green The. N14 | | 29 93 D |
| Green The. N21 | 17 | 31 94 A |
| Green The. N9 | 17 | 34 93 A |
| Green The. N Mal | 94 | 20 68 D |
| Green The. Orp | 100 | 46 70 D |
| Green The. Rich | 71 | 17 74 B |
| Green The. Shep | 91 | 09 68 C |
| Green The. Sid | 90 | 46 71 A |
| Green The. Sthl | 59 | 12 79 B |
| Green The. Sutt | 103 | 25 65 D |
| Green The. SW19 | 85 | 23 71 D |
| Green The. Twick | 83 | 15 73 C |
| Green The. W3 | 55 | 21 81 C |
| Green The. Well | 78 | 45 75 C |
| Green The. Wem | 33 | 16 86 A |
| Green Vale. Bexh | 79 | 47 74 B |
| Greenvale Rd. SE9 | 78 | 44 74 B |
| Gen Verges. Stan | 21 | 17 91 D |
| Greenview Ave. Beck | 106 | 36 67 C |
| Greenview Ave. Croy | 106 | 36 67 C |
| Green Walk The. E4 | 18 | 38 94 D |
| Green Way. E17 | 26 | 38 89 D |
| Green Way. Brom | 107 | 42 67 D |
| Greenway. Chis | 90 | 43 71 D |
| Greenway Cl. N20 | 15 | 25 93 A |
| Greenway Cl. N4 | 37 | 32 86 A |
| Greenway Cl. NW9 | 22 | 20 90 D |
| Greenway Ct. Ilf | 40 | 43 87 D |
| Greenway. Dag | 41 | 47 87 C |
| Greenway Gdns. Croy | 106 | 36 65 D |
| Greenway Gdns. Grnf | 53 | 13 82 D |
| Greenway Gdns. Har | 33 | 15 90 C |
| Greenway Gdns. NW9 | 22 | 20 90 D |
| Greenway. Har | 33 | 18 88 A |
| Greenway. N14 | 16 | 30 93 A |
| Greenway. N20 | 15 | 25 93 A |
| Greenways. Pnr | 19 | 12 90 D |
| Greenways. Beck | 98 | 37 69 C |
| Green Way. Esh | 101 | 15 65 D |
| Greenways The. N11 | 24 | 28 91 A |
| Green Way. Sun | 91 | 10 68 C |
| Greenway. SW20 | 95 | 22 69 B |
| Green Way The. Har | 21 | 15 90 A |
| Greenway The. Houn | 70 | 12 75 D |
| Greenway The. NW9 | 22 | 20 90 D |
| Greenway The. Orp | 108 | 46 67 D |
| Greenway The. Pnr | 32 | 12 88 D |
| Greenway The. Uxb | 31 | 09 86 B |
| Greenway. Wall | 111 | 29 64 A |
| Greenwell St. W1 | 2 | 28 81 D |
| Greenwich Church St. SE10 | 64 | 38 77 A |
| Greenwich High Rd. SE10 | 64 | 38 77 C |
| Greenwich Park St. SE10 | 64 | 38 77 B |
| Greenwich South St. SE10 | 76 | 38 76 A |
| Greenwich South St. SE10 | 64 | 38 77 C |
| Green Wlk. Dart | 80 | 51 75 D |
| Green Wlk. Hamp | 92 | 12 70 B |
| Green Wlk. NW4 | 35 | 23 88 B |
| Green Wlk. NW4 | 23 | 23 89 D |
| Green Wlk. Ruis | 31 | 09 87 D |
| Green Wlk. SE1 | 8 | 33 79 C |
| Green Wlk. Sthl | 59 | 13 78 C |
| Green Wlk. Wdf Grn | 27 | 42 91 A |
| Greenwood Ave. Dag | 52 | 50 85 A |
| Greenwood Ave. Enf | 14 | 36 97 A |
| Greenwood Cl. Mord | 95 | 24 68 C |
| Greenwood Cl. Orp | 108 | 46 69 C |
| Greenwood Cl. Sid | 90 | 46 72 A |
| Greenwood Cl. Surb | 101 | 16 66 C |
| Greenwood Dri. E4 | 18 | 38 92 D |
| Greenwood Gdns. Ilf | 28 | 44 91 C |
| Greenwood Gdns. N13 | 17 | 31 93 D |
| Greenwood Park. King | 94 | 21 70 C |
| Greenwood Pl. NW5 | 47 | 28 85 D |
| Greenwood Rd. Croy | 105 | 32 66 A |
| Greenwood Rd. E13 | 50 | 39 83 D |
| Greenwood Rd. E8 | 48 | 34 84 A |
| Greenwood Rd. Islw | 71 | 15 75 B |
| Greenwood Rd. Mit | 96 | 29 68 B |
| Greenwood Rd. Surb | 101 | 16 65 A |
| Green Wrythe Cres. Cars | 104 | 27 66 C |
| Green wrythe La. Cars | 104 | 27 66 C |
| Greer Rd. Har | 20 | 14 90 A |
| Greet St. SE1 | 7 | 31 79 A |
| Gregor Mews. SE3 | 65 | 40 77 C |
| Gregory Cres. SE9 | 89 | 43 73 B |
| Gregory Pl. W8 | 62 | 25 79 B |
| Gregory Rd. Rom | 29 | 47 89 D |
| Gregory Rd. Sthl | 59 | 13 79 C |
| Greig Cl. N8 | 36 | 30 88 A |
| Greig Terr. SE17 | 63 | 31 77 B |
| Grenaby Ave. Croy | 105 | 32 66 B |
| Grenaby Rd. Croy | 105 | 32 66 B |
| Grenada Rd. SE7 | 65 | 41 77 A |
| Grenade St. E14 | 57 | 36 80 B |
| Grena Gdns. Rich | 71 | 18 75 D |
| Grena Rd. Rich | 71 | 18 75 D |
| Grendon Gdns. Wem | 34 | 19 86 A |
| Grendon St. NW8 | 1 | 27 82 C |
| Grenfell Ave. Horn | 42 | 51 87 D |
| Grenfell Gdns. Har | 33 | 18 87 A |
| Grenfell Rd. Mit | 96 | 28 70 A |
| Grenfell Rd. W11 | 56 | 23 80 B |
| Grenfell Wlk. W11 | 56 | 23 80 B |
| Grennell Cl. Sutt | 103 | 26 65 B |
| Grennell Rd. Sutt | 103 | 26 65 A |
| Grenoble Gdns. N13 | 25 | 31 91 A |
| Grenville Cl. Surb | 102 | 20 66 C |
| Grenville Cl. Wor Gn | 27 | 41 91 C |
| Grenville Mews. Hamp | | 13 71 D |
| Grenville Mews. SW7 | 62 | 26 78 A |
| Grenville Pl. SW7 | 62 | 26 78 A |
| Grenville Rd. N19 | 36 | 30 87 C |
| Grenville St. WC1 | 3 | 30 82 C |
| Gresham Ave. N20 | 16 | 27 92 B |
| Gresham Cl. Bex | 79 | 48 74 D |
| Gresham Cl. Enf | 13 | 34 96 A |
| Gresham Dri. Rom | 40 | 46 88 D |
| Gresham Gdns. NW11 | 35 | 24 87 C |
| Gresham Rd. Beck | 98 | 36 69 C |
| Gresham Rd. E16 | 58 | 40 81 D |
| Gresham Rd. E6 | 50 | 42 83 D |
| Gresham Rd. Edg | 21 | 18 91 B |
| Gresham Rd. Hamp | 92 | 13 70 A |
| Gresham Rd. Houn | 70 | 14 76 A |
| Gresham Rd. NW10 | 45 | 20 84 B |
| Gresham Rd. SE25 | 97 | 34 68 C |
| Gresham Rd. SW9 | 75 | 31 75 B |
| Gresham St. EC2 | 4 | 32 81 D |
| Gresham Rd. SW19 | 85 | 25 72 C |
| Gresley Cl. N15 | 25 | 32 89 D |
| Gresley Rd. N19 | 36 | 30 87 C |
| Gressenhall Rd. SW18 | 73 | 24 74 D |
| Gresse St. W1 | 2 | 29 81 D |
| Gresswell Cl. Sid | 90 | 46 72 C |
| Greswell St. SW6 | 73 | 23 76 B |
| Gretton Rd. N17 | 25 | 33 91 C |
| Greville Cl. Twick | 83 | 16 73 B |
| Greville Mews. NW6 | 46 | 25 83 B |
| Greville Pl. NW6 | 46 | 25 83 D |
| Greville Rd. E17 | 26 | 38 89 C |
| Greville Rd. NW6 | 46 | 25 83 D |
| Greville Rd. Rich | 71 | 18 74 D |
| Greville St. EC1 | 3 | 31 81 A |
| Grey Cl. NW11 | 35 | 26 88 C |
| Greycoat Pl. SW1 | 6 | 29 79 D |
| Greycoat St. SW1 | 6 | 29 79 D |
| Greycot Rd. Beck | 88 | 37 71 C |
| Grey Eagle St. E1 | 4 | 33 82 D |
| Greyhound Ct. WC2 | 7 | 31 80 A |
| Greyhound Hill. NW4 | 22 | 22 89 B |
| Greyhound La. SW16 | 96 | 29 70 B |
| Greyhound Rd. N17 | 25 | 33 89 A |
| Greyhound Rd. NW10 | 55 | 22 82 B |
| Greyhound Rd. Sutt | 110 | 26 64 C |
| Greyhound Rd. W14 | 62 | 24 77 A |
| Greyhound Rd. W6 | 62 | 23 77 B |
| Greyhound Terr. SW16 | 96 | 29 69 A |
| Greyladies Gdns. SE10 | 76 | 38 76 C |
| Greys La. Ashf | 81 | 07 71 B |
| Greystead Rd. SE23 | 88 | 35 73 A |
| Greystoke Ave. Pnr | 20 | 13 89 A |
| Greystoke Ct. W5 | 54 | 18 82 D |
| Greystoke Gdns. W5 | 54 | 18 82 D |
| Greystoke Park Terr. W5 | 54 | 18 82 A |
| Greystoke Pl. EC4 | 3 | 31 81 C |
| Greystone Gdns. Har | 33 | 17 88 C |
| Greystone Gdns. Ilf | 28 | 44 90 C |
| Greyswood St. SW16 | 96 | 28 70 B |
| Grey Towers Ave. Horn | 42 | 53 87 D |
| Grey Towers Gdns. Horn | 42 | 53 87 A |
| Grierson Rd. SE23 | 76 | 36 74 C |
| Griffin Manor Way. SE28 | 66 | 44 79 D |
| Griffin Manor Way. SE28 | 66 | 45 79 B |
| Griffin Rd. N17 | 25 | 33 90 C |
| Griffin Rd. SE18 | 66 | 44 78 D |
| Griffin Way. Sun | 91 | 10 69 C |
| Griffiths Cl. Wor Pk | 102 | 22 65 B |
| Griffiths Rd. SW19 | 95 | 25 70 D |
| Grigg's Pl. SE1 | 8 | 33 79 C |
| Griggs Rd. E10 | 38 | 38 88 C |
| Grimsby St. E2 | 4 | 33 82 D |
| Grimsby St. E2 | 57 | 34 82 C |
| Grimsdyke Cres. Barn | 11 | 23 96 A |
| Grimsdyke Rd. Pnr | 20 | 12 91 C |
| Grimsel Path. SE5 | 63 | 31 77 D |
| Grimston Cl. Rom | 29 | 49 91 B |
| Grimston Rd. SW6 | 73 | 24 76 D |
| Grimwade Ave. Croy | 105 | 34 65 C |
| Grimwood Rd. Twick | 83 | 15 73 B |
| Grindal St. SE1 | 7 | 31 79 A |
| Grinling Pl. SE8 | 64 | 37 77 A |
| Grinstead Rd. SE8 | 64 | 36 78 C |
| Grittleton Ave. Wem | 45 | 19 84 B |
| Grittleton Rd. W9 | 56 | 25 82 C |
| Grocers' Hall Ct. EC2 | 4 | 32 81 D |
| Groombridge Cl. Well | 78 | 46 75 A |
| Groombridge Rd. E9 | 35 | 34 84 D |
| Groom Cres. SW18 | 85 | 26 73 B |
| Groomfield Cl. SW17 | 86 | 28 71 A |
| Groom Pl. SW1 | 6 | 28 79 C |
| Grosmont Rd. SE18 | 66 | 45 78 D |
| Grossall Ct. Th hth | 105 | 31 67 C |
| Grosse Way. SW15 | 72 | 22 74 D |
| Grosvenor Ave. Cars | 111 | 28 63 A |
| Grosvenor Ave. Har | 32 | 13 88 D |
| Grosvenor Ave. N5 | 48 | 32 85 C |
| Grosvenor Ave. Rich | 71 | 18 74 A |
| Grosvenor Ave. SW14 | 72 | 21 75 A |
| Grosvenor Bridge. SW8 | | 28 77 B |
| Grosvenor Cottages. SW1 | | 28 78 A |
| Grosvenor Cres. Dart | 80 | 53 74 B |
| Grosvenor Cres Mews. SW1 | | 28 79 A |
| Grosvenor Cres. NW9 | 11 | 19 89 C |
| Grosvenor Cres. SW1 | 6 | 28 79 A |
| Grosvenor Ct. N14 | 16 | 29 94 A |
| Grosvenor Ct. Sutt | 110 | 26 63 A |
| Grosvenor Dri. Horn | 41 | 53 87 A |
| Grosvenor Gdns. E6 | 58 | 41 82 B |
| Grosvenor Gdns. King | 93 | 17 70 B |
| Grosvenor Gdns Mews E. SW1 | | 28 79 A |
| Grosvenor Gdns Mews N. SW1 | | 28 79 D |
| Grosvenor Gdns Mews S. SW1 | | 28 79 D |
| Grosvenor Gdns. N10 | 24 | 28 89 A |
| Grosvenor Gdns. N14 | 12 | 29 95 B |
| Grosvenor Gdns. NW11 | 35 | 24 88 B |
| Groenor Gdns. NW11 | 35 | 24 88 D |
| Grosvenor Gdns. SW14 | 72 | 21 75 B |

Grosvenor Gdns. SW1 6 28 79 D
Grosvenor Gdns. Wall 111 29 63 C
Grosvenor Gdns. Wdf Gn 27 40 91 B
Grosvenor Hill. SW19 95 24 70 A
Grosvenor Hill. W1 6 28 80 B
Grosvenor Park Rd. E17 38 37 88 B
Grosvenor Park. SE5 63 32 77 C
Grosvenor Pl. SW1 6 28 79 B
Grosvenor Rd. Belv 67 49 77 A
Grosvenor Rd. Bexh 79 48 74 A
Grosvenor Rd. Brent 60 17 77 B
Grosvenor Rd. Dag 41 48 87 D
Grosvenor Rd. E10 38 38 87 C
Grosvenor Rd. E11 39 40 88 B
Grosvenor Rd. E6 50 41 83 B
Grosvenor Rd. E7 50 40 84 B
Grosvenor Rd. Houn 70 12 75 B
Grosvenor Rd. Ilf 40 44 86 C
Grosvenor Rd. N10 24 28 90 B
Grosvenor Rd. N3 23 25 91 C
Grosvenor Rd. N9 17 34 94 D
Grosvenor Rd. Orp 108 45 67 C
Grosvenor Rd. Rich 71 18 74 A
Grosvenor Rd. Rom 41 50 87 B
Grosvenor Rd. SE25 97 34 68 C
Grosvenor Rd. Sthl 59 12 79 D
Grosvenor Rd. SW1 10 29 77 A
Grosvenor Rd. Twick 83 16 73 C
Grosvenor Rd. W4 61 20 78 C
Grosvenor Rd. W7 54 16 80 C
Grosvenor Rd. Wall 111 28 64 D
Grosvenor Rd. W Wick 106 37 65 B
Grosvenor Rise E. E17 38 37 88 B
Grosvenor Sq. W1 6 28 80 A
Grosvenor St. W1 6 28 80 B
Grosvenor Terr. SE5 63 32 77 A
Grosvenor Vale. Ruis 31 09 86 B
Grosvenor Wharf Rd. E14 64 38 78 B
Grote's Bldgs. SE3 77 39 76 C
Grote's Pl. SE3 77 39 76 C
Groton Rd. SW18 85 25 72 B
Grotto Ct. SE1 8 32 79 A
Grotto Pas. W1 2 28 81 A
Grotto Rd. Twick 83 15 72 B
Grove Ave. N10 24 29 90 C
Grove Ave. N3 23 25 91 C
Grove Ave. Pnr 20 12 89 C
Grove Ave. Sutt 110 25 63 A
Grove Ave. Twick 83 15 73 D
Grove Ave. W7 54 15 81 C
Grovebury Cl. Eri 67 50 77 B
Grovebury Ct. N14 16 29 94 B
Grovebury Rd. SE2 66 46 79 B
Grove Cl. Brom 107 40 65 A
Grove Cl. King 93 18 68 D
Grove Cl. N14 16 28 94 B
Grove Cl. SE23 88 36 73 C
Grove Cottages. E14 57 37 80 B
Grove Crescent Rd. E15 49 38 84 B
Grove Cres. E18 27 39 90 D
Grove Cres. Felt 82 12 71 A
Grove Cres. King 93 18 68 A
Grove Cres. NW9 22 20 89 D
Grovedale Rd. N19 36 29 86 B
Grove End. NW5 47 28 85 B
Grove End Rd. NW8 1 26 82 B
*Grove Footpath. Surb 93 18 68 C
Grove Gdns. Dag 41 50 86 C
Grove Gdns. Enf 14 35 97 B
Grove Gdns. NW4 22 22 89 C
Grove Gdns. NW8 1 27 82 A
Grove Gdns. Rich 83 16 71 A
Grove Green Rd. E11 38 38 86 B
Grovehill Ct. Brom 99 39 70 B
Grove Hill. E18 27 39 90 D
Grove Hill. Har 33 15 87 A
Grove Hill Rd. Har 33 15 87 B
Grove Hill Rd. SE5 75 33 75 A
Grove House Rd. N8 24 30 89 C
Grove La. King 93 18 68 C
Groveland Ave. SW16 96 30 70 D
Groveland Ct. EC4 4 32 81 C
Groveland Rd. Beck 98 36 68 B
Grovelands Ct. N14 16 29 94 B
Grovelands. E Mol 92 13 68 C
Grovelands Rd. N13 16 30 93 D
Grovelands Rd. N15 37 34 88 C
Grovelands Rd. Orp 100 46 70 D
Groveland Way. N.Mal 102 20 67 B
Grove La. SE5 75 32 76 D
Groveley Rd. Sun 81 09 71 D
Grove Market Pl. SE9 77 42 74 D
Grove Mews. W6 62 23 79 C
Grove Park Ave. E4 26 37 91 D
Grove Park Bridge. W4 61 20 77 C
Grove Park. E11 39 40 88 B
Grove Park Gdns. W4 61 20 77 C
Grove Park Mews. W4 61 20 77 C
Grove Park. NW9 22 20 89 C
Grove Park Rd. N15 25 33 89 C
Grove Park Rd. SE9 89 41 72 B
Grove Park Rd. W4 61 19 77 D
Grove Park. SE5 75 33 76 C
Grove Park Terr. W4 61 19 77 B
Grove Pas. E2 48 34 83 D
Grove Pl. Bark 51 44 84 C
Grove Pl. NW3 35 26 86 D
Grove Pl. W3 55 20 80 C
Grover Ct. SE13 76 37 76 D
Grove Rd. Barn 12 27 96 A
Grove Rd. Belv 67 48 77 B
Grove Rd. Bexh 79 50 75 C
Grove Rd. Brent 60 17 78 C
Grove Rd. E11 39 39 87 B
Grove Rd. E17 38 37 88 B
Grove Rd. E18 27 39 90 D
Grove Rd. E3 57 36 82 A
Grove Rd. E4 18 38 93 C
Grove Rd. E9 49 35 83 B
Grove Rd. Edg 22 19 91 A
Grove Rd. E Mol 92 14 68 D
Grove Rd. Houn 70 13 75 C
Grove Rd. Islw 71 15 76 A
Grove Rd. Mit 96 28 69 C
Grove Rd. N11 16 28 92 D
Grove Rd. N12 15 26 92 D
Grove Rd. N15 37 33 88 A
Grove Rd. Nthwd 19 08 91 B
Grove Rd. NW2 46 23 84 A
Grove Rd. Pnr 32 12 88 B
Grove Rd. Rich 71 18 74 D
Grove Rd. Rom 41 47 88 C
Grove Rd. Surb 101 17 67 B
Grove Rd. Sutt 110 25 63 B
Grove Rd. SW13 72 21 76 D
Grove Rd. SW19 95 26 70 C
Grove Rd. Th Hth 97 31 68 C
Grove Rd. Twick 82 14 72 D
Grove Rd. W3 55 20 80 C
Grove Rd. W5 54 17 80 B
Grovestile Waye. Felt 81 08 73 B
Grove St. N18 25 33 91 B
Grove St. SE8 64 36 78 D
Grove Terrace Mews. NW5 36 28 86 D
Grove Terr. NW5 47 28 85 B
Grove Terr. Rich 83 16 71 A
Grove The. Bexh 79 47 75 D
Grove The. E15 50 39 84 A
Grove The. Enf 13 31 97 C
Grove The. Eps 109 21 62 D
Grove The. Grnf 53 14 81 C
Grove The. Islw 71 15 76 A
Grove The. N13 17 31 92 A
Grove The. N3 23 25 91 C
Grove The. N4 36 30 87 B
Grove The. N6 36 28 87 C
Grove The. N8 36 29 88 B
Grove The. NW11 35 24 87 A
Grove The. NW9 34 20 88 B
Grove The. Rich 83 16 71 A
Grove The. W5 54 18 80 A
Grove The. W Wick 106 38 65 C
Grove Vale. Chis 100 43 70 A
Grove Vale. SE22 75 33 75 D
Groveway. Dag 52 47 85 B
Groveway. SW9 75 31 76 A
Grove Way. Wem 45 20 85 C
Grummant Rd. SE15 75 33 76 B
Grundy St. E14 57 37 81 D
Gruneisen Rd. N3 23 25 91 D
Gubbins La. Rom 30 54 90 B
Gubyon Ave. SE24 75 31 74 B
Guerin Sq. E3 57 36 82 B
Guernsey Cl. Houn 59 13 77 C
Guernsey Gr. SE24 87 32 73 A
Guernsey Rd. E11 38 38 87 D
Guibal Rd. SE12 89 40 73 D
Guildersfield Rd. SW16 96 30 70 C
Guildford Ave. Felt 81 10 72 A
Guildford Gdns. Rom 30 54 91 A
Guildford Gr. SE10 76 37 76 B
Guildford Rd. Croy 105 32 67 D
Guildford Rd. E17 26 38 90 A
Guildford Rd. Ilf 40 45 86 A
Guildford Rd. Rom 30 54 91 A
Guildford Rd. SW8 74 30 76 A
Guildford Way. Wall 111 30 64 C
Guildhall Bldgs. EC2 4 32 81 D
Guildhall Yd. EC2 4 32 81 C
Guildhouse St. SW1 10 29 78 A
Guildown Ave. N12 15 25 92 B
Guild Rd. Eri 68 51 77 D
Guild Rd. SE7 65 41 78 D
Guildsway. E17 26 36 90 B
Guilford Ave. Surb 101 18 67 B
Guilford Pl. WC1 3 30 82 D
Guilford St. WC1 3 30 82 D
Guillemot Pl. N22 24 30 90 D
Guilsborough Cl. NW10 45 21 84 C
Guiness Cl. E9 49 36 84 C
Guinness Ct. EC1 4 32 82 A
Guinness Ct. NW8 47 27 83 A
Guinness Sq. SE1 63 33 78 A
Guinness Trust Bldgs. SW3 9 27 78 B
Guinness Trust. N16 37 33 87 D
Guion Rd. SW6 73 24 76 D
Gulland Wlk. N1 48 32 84 A
Gull Cl. Wall 111 30 63 C
Gulliver Cl. Nthlt 43 12 83 B
Gulliver Rd. Sid 90 45 72 A
Gulliver St. SE16 64 36 79 D
Gumleigh Rd. W5 60 17 78 A
Gumley Gdns. Islw 71 16 75 A
Gumping Rd. Orp 108 44 65 A
Gundulf St. SE11 63 31 78 A
Gundulph Rd. Brom 99 41 68 A
Gunmakers La. E3 49 36 83 A
Gunner La. SE18 66 43 78 C
Gunnersbury Ave. W3 61 19 79 C
Gunnersbury Ave. W4 61 19 78 C
Gunnersbury Ave. W5 54 18 80 D
Gunnersbury Cl. W4 61 19 78 D
Gunnersbury Cres. W3 61 19 79 A
Gunnersbury Ct. W3 61 19 79 B
Gunnersbury Dri. W5 60 18 79 B
Gunnersbury Gdns. W3 61 19 79 A
Gunnersbury La. W3 61 19 79 A
Gunnersbury Mews. W4 61 19 78 D
Gunners Gr. E4 18 38 93 C
Gunners Rd. SW18 85 26 72 B
Gunning St. SE18 66 45 78 A
Gun St. E1 4 33 81 B
Gunstor Rd. N16 48 33 85 A
Gunter Gr. Edg 22 20 90 B
Gunter Gr. SW10 62 26 77 C
Gunterstone Rd. W14 62 24 78 C
Gunthorpe St. E1 4 33 81 D
Gunton Rd. E5 37 34 86 B
Gunton Rd. SW17 96 28 70 A
Gurdon Rd. SE7 65 40 78 C
Gurnell Gr. W13 54 15 82 D
Gurney Cl. E15 50 39 85 C
Gurney Cres. Croy 104 30 66 D
Gurney Dri. N2 23 26 89 C
Gurney Rd. Cars 111 28 64 A
Gurney Rd. E15 50 39 85 C
Gurney Rd. Nthlt 53 11 82 A
Guthrie St. SW3 9 27 78 C
Gutter La. EC2 4 32 81 C
Guyatt Gdns. Mit 96 28 69 C
Guy Rd. Wall 104 29 65 D
Guyscliff Rd. SE13 76 38 74 A
Guy St. SE1 8 32 79 B
Gwalior House. N14 12 29 95 C
Gwalior Rd. SW15 73 23 75 B
Gwendolen Ave. SW15 73 23 74 B
Gwendolen Cl. SW15 73 23 74 B
Gwendoline Ave. E13 50 40 83 B
Gwendwr Rd. W14 62 24 78 C
Gwillim Cl. Sid 78 46 75 A
Gwydor Rd. Beck 98 35 68 B
Gwydyr Rd. Brom 99 39 68 B
Gwynne Ave. Croy 106 35 66 B
Gwynne Park Ave. Wdf Gn 27 42 91 B
Gwynne Pl. WC1 3 30 82 B
Gwynne Rd. SW11 73 26 76 D
Gylcote Cl. SE5 75 32 75 D
Gyles Park. Stan 21 17 90 A
Gyllyngdune Gdns. Ilf 40 45 86 D

Haarlem Rd. W14 62 23 79 D
Haberdasher Pl. N1 4 33 62 A
Haberdasher's Ct. SE14 76 35 76 D
Haberdasher St. N1 4 32 82 B
Haccombe Rd. SW19 95 26 70 A
Hackbridge Park Gdns. Cars 104 27 65 A
Hackbridge Rd. Wall 104 28 65 A
Hackford Rd. SW9 75 31 76 A
Hackford Rd. SW9 63 31 77 C
Hackington Cres. Beck 98 37 70 A
Hackney Gr. E8 48 34 84 B
Hackney Rd. E2 48 34 83 C
Hacton La. Horn 42 54 86 D
Hadden Rd. SE28 66 45 79 C
Hadden Way. Grnf 43 14 84 B
Haddington Rd. Brom 88 38 71 B
Haddon Cl. Enf 13 34 95 C
Haddon Cl. N.Mal 102 21 67 B
Haddon Gr. Sid 90 45 73 B
Haddon Rd. Sutt 110 25 64 B
Haddo St. SE10 64 38 77 A
Haden Ct. N4 37 31 86 A
Hadleigh Cl. E1 57 35 82 C
Hadleigh Rd. N9 17 34 94 B
Hadleigh St. E2 57 35 82 A
Hadley Cl. N21 13 31 95 C
Hadley Gdns. Sthl 59 12 78 D
Hadley Gdns. W4 61 20 78 D
Hadley Gr. Barn 11 24 97 C
Hadley Green. Barn 11 24 97 D
Hadley Green Rd. Barn 11 24 97 D
Hadley Green W. Barn 11 24 97 D
Hadley Highstone. Barn 11 24 97 B
Hadley Rd. Barn 11 25 96 B
Hadley Rd. Belv 67 48 78 B
Hadley Rd. Enf 12 30 97 B
Hadley Rd. Mit 96 29 68 D
Hadley Ridge. Barn 11 24 96 B
Hadley St. NW1 47 28 84 B
Hadley Way. N21 13 31 95 C
Hadley Wood Rd. Barn 11 25 97 D
Hadlow Pl. SE19 97 34 70 C
Hadlow Rd. Sid 90 46 71 A
Hadlow Rd. Well 67 47 77 C
Hadrian Cl. Wall 111 30 63 C
Hadrian Estate. E2 48 34 83 C
Hadrian's Ride. Enf 13 33 95 B
Hadrian St. E10 65 39 78 C
Hadyn Park Rd. W12 61 22 79 A
Hafer Rd. SW11 74 27 75 D
Hafton Rd. SE6 89 39 73 C
Haggard Rd. Twick 83 16 73 B
Haggerstond. E8 48 33 83 B
Hague St. E2 57 34 82 A
Ha-Ha Rd. SE18 65 42 77 B
Haig Homes. Mord 103 25 67 C
Haig Pl. Mord 103 25 67 C
Haig Rd. Stan 21 17 91 A
Haig Road E. E13 58 41 82 A
Haig Road W. E13 58 41 82 A
Haigville Gdns. Ilf 28 43 89 D
Hailes Cl. SW19 95 26 70 A
Haileybury Ave. Enf 13 33 95 D
Hailey Rd. Belv 67 49 79 A
Hailsham Ave. SW2 86 30 72 B
Hailsham Rd. SW17 96 28 70 A
Hailsham Terr. N18 17 32 92 D
Haimo Rd. SE9 77 41 74 B
Hainault Gore. Rom 41 48 88 A
Hainault Gore. Rom 41 48 88 A
Hainault Rd. E11 38 38 87 B
Hainault Rd. Rom 28 46 90 D
Hainault Rd. Rom 41 48 88 D
Hainault Rd. Rom 29 50 89 A
Hainault St. Ilf 40 44 36 A
Hainault St. SE9 90 43 73 D
Haines St. SW8 10 29 77 C
Hainthorpe Rd. SE27 87 31 71 B
Hainton Path. E1 57 34 81 D
Halberd Mews. E5 37 34 86 B
Halbutt St. Dag 52 48 85 D
Halbutt St. Dag 41 48 86 D
Halcomb St. N1 48 33 83 A
Halcot Ave. Bexh 79 49 74 B
Halcrow St. E1 57 34 81 B
Halcyon Way. Horn 42 54 87 D
Haldane Cl. N10 24 28 91 D
Haldane Pl. SW18 85 25 73 D
Haldane Rd. E6 58 41 82 B
Haldane Rd. Sthl 53 14 80 A
Haldane Rd. SW6 62 24 77 B
Haldan Rd. E4 26 38 91 C
Haldon Rd. SW18 73 24 74 D
Hale Cl. E4 18 38 93 C
Hale Dri. NW7 22 20 91 B
Hale End Cl. Ruis 31 10 88 C
Hale End Rd. E17 26 38 90 B
Hale End Rd. E4 26 38 91 B
Hale End Rd. Wdf Gr 26 38 91 D
Hale End. Rom 30 52 91 B
Halefield Rd. N17 25 34 90 B
Hale Gdns. N17 25 34 89 A
Hale Gdns. W3 55 19 80 C
Hale La. NW7 22 21 91 A
Hale Rd. N17 25 34 89 A
Halesowen Rd. Mord 103 25 66 B
Hales St. SE8 64 37 77 C
Hale St. E14 57 37 80 B
Halesworth Cl. E5 38 35 86 A
Halesworth Cl. Rom 30 54 91 C
Halesworth Rd. Rom 30 54 91 A
Halesworth Rd. SE13 76 37 75 B
Hale The. E4 26 38 91 D
Hale The. N17 25 34 89 A
Hale Wlk. W7 54 15 81 A
Half Acre. Brent 60 17 77 B
Half Acre Rd. W7 54 15 80 C
Half Moon Cres. N1 47 30 83 B
Half Moon Ct. EC1 4 32 81 A
Halfmoon Pas. E1 4 33 81 D
Half Moon St. W1 6 28 80 D
Halford Rd. E10 38 38 88 B
Halford Rd. Rich 71 18 74 A
Halford Rd. SW6 62 25 77 A
Halfway St. Sid 90 45 73 C
Haliburton Rd. Twick 71 16 75 C
Haliday Wlk. N1 48 32 84 B
Halidon Cl. E9 49 35 85 C
Halifax Rd. Enf 13 32 97 D
Halifax Rd. Grnf 43 13 83 B
Halifax St. SE26 87 34 72 D
Haling Gr. S Croy 112 32 63 C
Haling Park Gdns. S Croy 112 31 63 B
Haling Park Rd. S Croy 112 32 63 A
Haling Rd. S Croy 112 32 63 B
Halkin Arc. SW1 6 28 79 C
Halkin Mews. SW1 6 28 79 C
Halkin Pl. SW1 6 28 79 C
Halkin St. SW1 6 28 79 A
Hallam Cl. Chis 89 42 71 D
Hallam Gdns. Pnr 20 12 91 C
Hallam Mews. W1 2 28 81 B
Hallam Rd. N15 25 31 89 D
Hallam St. W1 2 28 81 B
Hallam St. W1 2 28 82 D
Halland Way. Nthwd 19 08 91 B
Hall Cl. W5 54 18 81 A
Hall Dri. SE26 88 35 71 C
Hall Dri. W7 54 15 81 C
Halley Pl. E14 57 36 81 A
Halley Rd. E12 50 41 85 D
Halley Rd. E7 50 41 84 A
Halley St. E14 57 36 81 A
Hall Farm Dri. Twick 82 14 73 B
Hallford Way. Dart 80 53 74 A
Hall Gate. NW8 1 26 82 B
Hall Gdns. E4 18 36 92 B
Halliford Cl. Shep 91 08 68 B
Halliford Rd. Sun 91 10 68 C
Halliford St. N1 48 32 84 C
Halliwell Rd. SW2 74 30 74 D
Halliwick Rd. N10 24 28 90 A
Hall La. E4 18 36 92 B
Hall La. NW4 22 22 90 C
Hallmead Rd. Sutt 103 25 65 D
Hall Oak Wlk. NW6 46 24 84 B
Hallon Gdns. E1 4 33 81 B
Hallowell Ave. Croy 111 30 64 A
Hallowell Cl. Mit 96 28 68 A
Hallowell Rd. Nthwd 19 09 91 C
Hall Place Cres. Bex 79 50 74 B
Hall Pl. W2 1 26 81 B
Hall Rd. Dart 80 54 75 D
Hall Rd. E11 49 38 85 B
Hall Rd. E15 49 38 85 B
Hall Rd. E6 50 42 83 B
Hall Rd. Islw 70 14 74 B
Hall Rd. NW8 1 26 82 A
Hall Rd. Rom 41 47 88 D
Hall Rd. Rom 30 52 89 B
Hall Rd. Wall 111 28 62 B
Hall St. EC1 3 31 82 B
Hall St. N12 15 26 92 C
Hallsville Rd. E16 58 39 81 D
Hallswelle Rd. NW11 35 24 88 B
Hall The. SE3 77 40 75 A
Hall View. SE9 89 41 72 B
Halons Rd. SE9 90 43 73 A
Halpin Pl. SE17 63 32 78 B
Halsbrook Rd. SE3 77 41 75 B
Halsbury Rd E. Nthlt 43 14 85 A
Halsbury Rd. W12 55 22 80 D
Halsbury Road W. Nthlt 43 14 85 A
Halsey St. SW3 9 27 78 B
Halsham Cl. Sutt 101 17 66 B
Halsham Cres. Bark 51 45 85 D
Halsmere Rd. SE5 75 31 76 B
Halstead Ct. N1 48 32 83 D
Halstead Gdns. N21 17 32 94 D
Halstead Rd. E11 39 40 88 B
Halstead Rd. Enf 13 33 96 C
Halstead Rd. Eri 80 51 76 A
Halstead Rd. N21 17 32 94 D
Halston Cl. SW11 74 27 74 D
Halstow Rd. NW10 56 23 82 B
Halstow Rd. SE10 65 40 78 C
Halton Cross St. N1 48 31 83 B
Halton Pl. N1 48 32 83 A
Halton Rd. N1 48 31 84 D
Halt Robin La. Belv 67 49 78 B
Halt Robin Rd. Belv 67 49 78 B
Hambalt Rd. SW4 74 29 74 A
Hamble Cl. Ruis 31 09 86 A
Hambledon Gdns. SE25 97 33 68 B
Hambledon Rd. SW18 85 24 73 B
Hambledown Rd. Sid 90 45 73 A
Hamble St. SW6 73 25 75 B
Hambridge Way. SE24 87 31 73 A
Hambro Ave. Brom 107 40 66 C
Hambrook Rd. SE25 97 34 68 B
Hambro Rd. SW16 96 29 70 B
Hambro Rd. SW16 86 29 71 D
Hambrough Rd. Sthl 53 12 80 C
Ham Cl. Rich 83 17 72 C
Hamden Cres. Dag 41 49 86 D
Ham Dip. Rich 84 19 71 A
Hamelin St. E14 58 38 81 C
Ham Farm Rd. Rich 83 17 71 B
Hamfrith Rd. E15 50 39 84 B
Ham Gate Ave. Rich 83 18 71 A
Hamilton Ave. Ilf 40 44 88 A
Hamilton Ave. N9 17 34 94 A
Hamilton Ave. Rom 29 50 90 D
Hamilton Ave. Surb 102 19 65 A
Hamilton Ave. Sutt 103 24 65 A
Hamilton Cl. Barn 12 27 96 D
Hamilton Cl. Felt 81 09 71 D
Hamilton Cl. N17 25 33 89 B
Hamilton Cl. NW8 1 26 82 B
Hamilton Cres. Har 32 12 86 D
Hamilton Cres. Houn 70 13 74 B
Hamilton Cres. N13 17 31 92 A
Hamilton Ct. W5 54 18 80 D
Hamilton Dri. Rom 30 54 90 C
Hamilton Gdns. NW8 1 26 82 A
Hamilton La. N5 48 31 85 B
Hamilton Mews. W1 6 28 79 B
Hamilton Park. N5 48 31 85 B
Hamilton Park W. N5 48 31 85 B
Hamilton Pl. Sun 91 10 70 D
Hamilton Pl. W1 6 28 80 C
Hamilton Rd. Barn 12 27 96 C
Hamilton Rd. Bexh 79 48 75 B
Hamilton Rd. Brent 60 17 77 B
Hamilton Rd. E15 58 39 82 A
Hamilton Rd. E17 26 36 90 C
Hamilton Rd. Felt 81 09 71 B
Hamilton Rd. Har 33 15 88 A
Hamilton Rd. Ilf 51 43 85 B
Hamilton Rd. N2 23 26 89 A
Hamilton Rd. N9 17 34 94 A
Hamilton Rd. NW10 45 22 85 C
Hamilton Rd. NW11 35 24 87 A
Hamilton Rd. Rom 42 52 88 B
Hamilton Rd. SE27 87 32 71 B
Hamilton Rd. Sid 90 46 71 A
Hamilton Rd. Sthl 53 12 80 D
Hamilton Rd. SW19 95 25 70 D
Hamilton Rd. Th Hth 97 32 68 B
Hamilton Rd. Twick 83 15 73 C
Hamilton Rd. W4 61 21 79 A
Hamilton Rd. W5 54 18 80 A
Hamilton Sq. SE1 8 32 79 B
Hamilton St. SE8 64 37 77 A
Hamilton Terr. NW8 1 26 82 A
Hamilton Way. N13 17 31 92 B
Hamilton Way. N3 23 25 91 A
Hamilton Way. Wall 111 29 62 B
Hamish St. SE11 10 30 78 B
Hamlea Cl. SE12 77 40 74 A
Hamlet Cl. Rom 29 49 91 C
Hamlet Gdns. W6 61 22 78 C
Hamlet Rd. Rom 29 49 91 C
Hamlet Rd. SE19 97 34 70 C
Hamlets Way. E3 57 36 82 D
Hamlet The. SE5 75 32 75 B
Hamlin Cres. Pnr 32 11 88 A
Hamlyn Gdns. SE19 97 33 70 C
Hammelton Rd. Brom 99 40 69 A
Hammersley Ave. E16 58 39 81 D
Hammersmith Bridge Rd. W6 62 23 78 C
Hammersmith Bwy. W6 62 23 78 A
Hammersmith Fly. W6 62 23 78 C
Hammersmith Gr. W6 62 23 79 C
Hammersmith Rd. W14 62 24 78 A
Hammersmith Rd. W6 62 23 78 B
Hammett St. EC3 8 33 80 B
Hammond Ave. Mit 96 28 69 D
Hammond Cl. Grnf 43 14 85 D
Hammond Cl. Hamp 92 13 69 A

| | | |
|---|---|---|
| Hammond Rd. Enf | *13* | 34 97 D |
| Hammond Rd. Sthl | *59* | 12 79 C |
| Hammond St. NW5 | *47* | 29 84 A |
| Hamond Sq. N1 | *48* | 33 83 C |
| Ham Park Rd. E15 | *50* | 39 84 D |
| Ham Park Rd. E7 | *50* | 40 84 C |
| Hampden Ave. Beck | *98* | 36 69 C |
| Hampden Cl. NW1 | *47* | 29 83 D |
| Hampden Gurney St. W1 | *1* | 27 81 D |
| Hampden La. N17 | *25* | 34 90 A |
| Hampden Rd (off Comus Rd). N19 | *36* | 29 86 D |
| Hampden Rd (off Holloway Rd). N19 | *36* | 29 86 B |
| Hampden Rd. Beck | *98* | 36 69 C |
| Hampden Rd. Har | *20* | 14 90 C |
| Hampden Rd. King | *94* | 19 68 A |
| Hampden Rd. N10 | *24* | 28 91 C |
| Hampden Rd. N17 | *25* | 34 90 A |
| Hampden Rd. N19 | *36* | 29 86 D |
| Hampden Rd. N8 | *25* | 31 89 C |
| Hampden Rd. Rom | *29* | 49 91 D |
| Hampden Way. N14 | *16* | 28 93 B |
| Hampshire Cl. N18 | *17* | 34 92 D |
| Hampshire Hog La. W6 | *61* | 22 78 B |
| Hampshire Rd. N22 | *24* | 30 91 D |
| Hampshire St. NW5 | *47* | 29 84 B |
| Hampson Way. SW8 | *74* | 30 76 B |
| Hampstead Gdns. NW11 | *35* | 25 88 C |
| Hampstead Green. NW3 | *47* | 27 85 C |
| Hampstead Gr. NW3 | *35* | 26 86 C |
| Hampstead High St. NW3 | *46* | 26 85 B |
| Hampstead Hill Gdns. NW3 | *47* | 27 85 A |
| Hampstead La. N6 | *36* | 27 87 B |
| Hampstead La. NW3 | *35* | 26 87 D |
| Hampstead Rd. NW1 | *2* | 29 82 A |
| Hampstead Sq. NW3 | *35* | 26 86 C |
| Hampstead Way. NW11 | *35* | 25 87 B |
| Hampton Cl. NW6 | *56* | 25 82 A |
| Hampton Cl. SW20 | *95* | 23 70 C |
| Hampton Court Ave. E Mol | *101* | 15 67 A |
| Hampton Court Par. E Mol | *93* | 15 68 C |
| Hampton Court Rd. E Mol | *93* | 15 68 B |
| Hampton Court Rd. Hamp | *92* | 14 69 C |
| Hampton Court Rd. King | *93* | 17 69 C |
| Hampton Court Way. E Mol | *101* | 15 67 A |
| Hampton Court Way. Esh | *101* | 15 65 A |
| Hampton Court Way. Surb | *101* | 16 66 B |
| Hampton Ct. N1 | *48* | 31 84 B |
| Hampton La. Felt | *82* | 12 71 A |
| Hampton Rd. Croy | *105* | 32 67 C |
| Hampton Rd. E11 | *38* | 38 87 D |
| Hampton Rd. E4 | *18* | 36 92 D |
| Hampton Rd. E7 | *50* | 41 85 C |
| Hampton Rd E. Felt | *82* | 12 72 D |
| Hampton Rd. Hamp | *82* | 14 70 D |
| Hampton Rd. Ilf | *51* | 44 85 A |
| Hampton Rd. Tedd | *83* | 15 71 C |
| Hampton Rd. Twick | *82* | 14 72 D |
| Hampton Rd. Wor Pk | *102* | 22 65 B |
| Hampton Rise. Har | *33* | 18 88 C |
| Hampton Road W. Felt | *82* | 12 72 C |
| Hampton St. SE17 | *63* | 31 78 B |
| Ham Ridings. Rich | *83* | 18 71 D |
| Ham Shades Cl. Sid | *90* | 46 72 C |
| Ham Sq. Rich | *83* | 17 72 A |
| Ham St. Rich | *83* | 17 72 A |
| Ham The. Brent | *60* | 17 77 C |
| Ham View. Croy | *106* | 36 67 C |
| Ham Yd. W1 | *6* | 29 80 B |
| Hanameel St. E16 | *58* | 40 80 D |
| Hanbury Rd. N17 | *25* | 34 90 D |
| Hanbury Rd. W3 | *61* | 19 79 D |
| Hanbury St. E1 | *4* | 33 81 B |
| Hanbury St. E1 | *57* | 34 81 A |
| Hancock Rd. E3 | *58* | 38 82 A |
| Hancock Rd. SE19 | *97* | 32 70 B |
| Handa Wlk. N1 | *48* | 32 84 A |
| Handcroft Rd. Croy | *105* | 31 66 B |
| Handcroft Rd. Croy | *105* | 31 66 D |
| Hand Ct. WC1 | *3* | 30 81 B |
| Handel Cl. Edg | *21* | 18 91 B |
| Handel St. WC1 | *3* | 30 82 C |
| Handel Way. Edg | *22* | 19 91 C |
| Handen Rd. SE12 | *77* | 39 74 B |
| Handforth Rd. SW9 | *63* | 31 77 C |
| Handley Rd. E9 | *49* | 35 83 A |
| Handside Cl. Wor Pk | *103* | 23 66 D |
| Hands Wlk. E16 | *58* | 40 81 C |
| Handsworth Ave. E4 | *26* | 38 91 B |
| Handsworth Rd. N17 | *25* | 32 89 B |
| Handtrough Way. E6 | *51* | 43 83 D |
| Hanford Cl. SW18 | *85* | 25 73 C |
| Hanger Ct. W5 | *55* | 19 82 C |
| Hanger Green. W5 | *55* | 19 82 C |
| Hanger Hill. W5 | *54* | 18 81 B |
| Hanger La. W5 | *54* | 18 81 B |
| Hanger Vale La. W5 | *54* | 18 81 D |
| Hanger View Way. W3 | *55* | 19 81 C |
| Hankey Pl. SE1 | *8* | 32 79 B |
| Hanley Rd. N4 | *36* | 30 87 C |
| Hanmer Wlk. N7 | *36* | 30 86 B |
| Hannay Wlk. SW16 | *86* | 29 72 B |
| Hannell Rd. SW6 | *62* | 24 77 C |
| Hannen Rd. SE27 | *87* | 31 72 D |
| Hannibal Rd. E1 | *57* | 35 81 A |
| Hannibal Way. Croy | *111* | 30 63 B |
| Hannington Rd. SW4 | *74* | 28 75 B |
| Hannover Rd. N15 | *25* | 33 89 D |
| Hanover Ave. Felt | *81* | 10 72 A |
| Hanover Cl. Rich | *61* | 19 77 C |
| Hanover Cl. Sutt | *110* | 24 64 A |
| Hanover Gdns. Ilf | *28* | 44 91 C |
| Hanover Gdns. SE11 | *63* | 31 77 A |
| Hanover Park. SE15 | *75* | 34 76 A |
| Hanover Pl. WC2 | *3* | 30 81 C |
| Hanover Rd. NW10 | *46* | 23 83 A |
| Hanover Rd. SW19 | *95* | 26 70 C |
| Hanover Sq. W1 | *2* | 28 81 D |
| Hanover St. Croy | *105* | 31 65 D |
| Hanover St. W1 | *2* | 28 81 D |
| Hanover Terr. Islw | *71* | 16 76 A |
| Hanover Terr Mews. NW1 | *1* | 27 82 B |
| Hanover Terr. NW1 | *1* | 27 82 B |
| Hanover Way. Bexh | *79* | 47 75 B |
| Hanover Yd. N1 | *48* | 31 83 D |
| Hansard Mews. W14 | *62* | 23 79 B |
| Hansart Way. Enf | *13* | 31 97 A |
| Hans Cres. SW1 | *5* | 27 79 D |
| Hanshaw Dri. Edg | *22* | 20 90 B |
| Hansler Gr. E Mol | *92* | 14 68 D |
| Hansler Rd. SE22 | *75* | 33 74 B |
| Hansol Rd. Bexh | *79* | 48 74 A |
| Hanson Cl. SW12 | *86* | 28 73 B |
| Hanson Gdns. Sthl | *59* | 12 79 A |
| Hanson St. W1 | *2* | 29 81 A |
| Hans Pl. SW1 | *5* | 27 79 D |
| Hans Rd. SW3 | *5* | 27 79 D |
| Hans St. SW1 | *5* | 27 79 D |
| Hanway Pl. W1 | *2* | 29 81 D |
| Hanway Rd. W7 | *54* | 15 81 C |
| Hanway St. W1 | *2* | 29 81 D |
| Hanworth Rd. Felt | *81* | 10 73 D |
| Hanworth Rd. Hamp | *82* | 13 71 C |
| Hanworth Rd. Houn | *70* | 13 74 C |
| Hanworth Rd. Sun | *91* | 10 70 C |
| Hanworth Terr. Houn | *70* | 13 75 D |
| Hapgood Cl. Grnf | *43* | 14 85 D |
| Harben Rd. NW6 | *46* | 26 84 C |
| Harberson Rd. E15 | *50* | 39 83 B |
| Harberson Rd. SW12 | *86* | 28 73 D |
| Harberton Rd. N19 | *36* | 29 87 C |
| Harbet Rd. E4 | *18* | 35 92 D |
| Harbet Rd. W2 | *1* | 27 81 A |
| Harbinger Rd. E14 | *64* | 37 78 B |
| Harbledown Rd. SW6 | *73* | 25 76 A |
| Harbord St. SW6 | *73* | 23 76 B |
| Harborough Ave. Sid | *90* | 45 73 B |
| Harborough Rd. SW16 | *86* | 30 71 B |
| Harbour Rd. SE5 | *75* | 32 75 A |
| Harbridge Ave. SW15 | *84* | 22 73 A |
| Harbury Rd. Cars | *111* | 27 63 C |
| Harbut Rd. SW11 | *73* | 26 75 D |
| Harbut Rd. SW11 | *73* | 26 75 D |
| Harcombe Rd. N16 | *37* | 33 86 C |
| Harcourt Ave. E12 | *50* | 42 85 D |
| Harcourt Ave. Sid | *79* | 47 74 C |
| Harcourt Ave. Wall | *111* | 28 64 B |
| Harcourt Cl. Islw | *71* | 16 75 A |
| Harcourt Field. Wall | *111* | 28 64 B |
| Harcourt Rd. Bexh | *79* | 48 75 C |
| Harcourt Rd. E15 | *50* | 39 83 D |
| Harcourt Rd. N22 | *24* | 29 90 B |
| Harcourt Rd. SE4 | *76* | 36 75 B |
| Harcourt Rd. SW19 | *95* | 25 70 C |
| Harcourt Rd. Th Hth | *105* | 31 67 C |
| Harcourt Rd. Wall | *111* | 28 64 B |
| Harcourt St. W1 | *1* | 27 81 A |
| Harcourt Terr. SW10 | *62* | 26 78 C |
| Hardcourts Cl. W Wick | *106* | 37 65 D |
| Hardel Rise. SW2 | *87* | 31 73 D |
| Hardel Wlk. SE24 | *87* | 31 73 A |
| Harden Ct. SE18 | *65* | 42 78 A |
| Hardens Manorway. SE7 | *65* | 41 79 D |
| Harders Rd. Mews. SE15 | *75* | 34 76 B |
| Harders Rd. SE15 | *75* | 34 76 D |
| Hardess St. SE24 | *75* | 32 75 A |
| Hardie Cl. NW10 | *45* | 20 85 D |
| Hardie Rd. Dag | *41* | 50 86 C |
| Harding Cl. SE17 | *63* | 32 77 A |
| Hardinge Rd. N18 | *17* | 33 92 C |
| Hardinge Rd. NW10 | *46* | 23 83 A |
| Hardinge St. E1 | *57* | 35 81 C |
| Harding Rd. Bexh | *79* | 48 76 D |
| Hardings La. SE20 | *98* | 35 70 B |
| Hardley Cres. Horn | *30* | 53 89 D |
| Hardman Rd. King | *93* | 18 69 C |
| Hardman Rd. SE7 | *65* | 40 78 D |
| Hardwicke Ave. Houn | *70* | 13 76 A |
| Hardwicke Rd. N13 | *24* | 30 91 A |
| Hardwicke Rd. Rich | *83* | 17 71 A |
| Hardwicke Rd. W4 | *61* | 20 78 B |
| Hardwicke St. Bark | *51* | 44 83 A |
| Hardwick Green. W13 | *54* | 16 81 B |
| Hardwick St. EC1 | *3* | 31 82 A |
| Hardwick's Way. SW18 | *73* | 25 74 A |
| Hardwidge St. SE1 | *8* | 33 79 A |
| Hardy Cl. Pnr | *32* | 11 87 B |
| Hardy Pas. N22 | *25* | 31 90 C |
| Hardy Rd. SE3 | *65* | 39 77 B |
| Hardy Rd. SW19 | *95* | 25 70 D |
| Hardy Way. Enf | *13* | 31 97 A |
| Hare and Billet Rd. SE3 | *76* | 38 76 D |
| Harebell Way. Rom | *30* | 53 91 D |
| Harecourt Rd. N1 | *48* | 32 84 A |
| Hare Ct. EC4 | *3* | 31 81 C |
| Haredale Rd. SE24 | *75* | 32 75 C |
| Haredon Cl. SE23 | *88* | 35 73 B |
| Harefield Ave. Sutt | *110* | 24 62 A |
| Harefield Cl. Enf | *13* | 31 97 A |
| Harefield. Esh | *101* | 15 65 C |
| Harefield Mews. SE4 | *76* | 36 75 B |
| Harefield Rd. N8 | *36* | 29 88 B |
| Harefield Rd. SE4 | *76* | 36 75 B |
| Harefield Rd. SW16 | *96* | 30 70 D |
| Hare Hall La. Rom | *30* | 52 89 D |
| Hare Marsh. E2 | *57* | 34 82 C |
| Hare Row. E2 | *48* | 34 83 D |
| Haresfield Rd. Dag | *52* | 49 84 A |
| Hare St. SE18 | *66* | 43 79 C |
| Hare Wlk. N1 | *48* | 33 83 C |
| Harewood Ave. Nthlt | *43* | 12 84 D |
| Harewood Ave. NW1 | *1* | 27 82 C |
| Harewood Cl. Nthlt | *43* | 12 84 D |
| Harewood Dri. Ilf | *27* | 42 90 D |
| Harewood Pl. W1 | *2* | 28 81 D |
| Harewood Rd. Islw | *71* | 15 76 B |
| Harewood Rd. S Croy | *112* | 33 63 A |
| Harewood Rd. SW19 | *96* | 27 70 A |
| Harewood Row. NW1 | *1* | 27 81 A |
| Harewood Terr. Sthl | *59* | 12 78 B |
| Harfield Gdns. SE5 | *75* | 33 75 A |
| Harfield Rd. Sun | *92* | 11 69 D |
| Harford Cl. E4 | *18* | 37 94 B |
| Harford Rd. E4 | *18* | 37 94 B |
| Harford St. E2 | *57* | 36 82 C |
| Harford Wlk. N2 | *23* | 26 89 D |
| Hargood Rd. SE3 | *77* | 41 76 A |
| Hargrave Park. N19 | *36* | 29 86 A |
| Hargrave Pl. N7 | *47* | 29 85 D |
| Hargrave Rd. N19 | *36* | 29 86 A |
| Hargwyne St. SW9 | *74* | 30 75 B |
| Haringey Park. N8 | *36* | 30 88 C |
| Haringey Pas. N4 | *37* | 31 88 B |
| Haringey Pas. N8 | *25* | 31 89 C |
| Haringey Rd. N8 | *24* | 30 89 C |
| Harington Terr. N18 | *17* | 32 92 D |
| Harington Terr. N9 | *17* | 32 92 D |
| Harkett Cl. Har | *21* | 15 90 D |
| Harland Ave. Croy | *105* | 34 65 B |
| Harland Ave. SE9 | *90* | 45 72 A |
| Harland Rd. SE12 | *89* | 40 73 C |
| Harlech Gdns. Houn | *59* | 11 77 A |
| Harlech Rd. N14 | *16* | 30 93 C |
| Harlequin Ave. Brent | *60* | 16 77 A |
| Harlequin Rd. Tedd | *93* | 16 70 D |
| Harlescott Rd. SE15 | *76* | 35 75 D |
| Harlesden Cl. Rom | *30* | 54 91 B |
| Harlesden Gdns. NW10 | *45* | 21 83 B |
| Harlesden Rd. NW10 | *45* | 22 83 A |
| Harlesden Rd. Rom | *30* | 54 91 B |
| Harlesden Wlk. Rom | *30* | 54 91 D |
| Harleston Cl. E5 | *38* | 35 86 A |
| Harley Cl. Wem | *44* | 17 84 B |
| Harley Cres. Har | *20* | 14 89 D |
| Harley Ct. N12 | *15* | 26 93 C |
| Harleyford. Brom | *99* | 41 69 A |
| Harleyford Rd. SE11 | *70* | 30 77 B |
| Harleyford St. SE11 | *63* | 31 77 A |
| Harley Gdns. SW10 | *62* | 26 78 C |
| Harley Gr. E3 | *57* | 36 82 B |
| Harley Pl. W1 | *2* | 28 81 B |
| Harley Rd. Har | *20* | 14 89 D |
| Harley Rd. NW10 | *45* | 21 83 C |
| Harley Rd. NW3 | *47* | 27 84 C |
| Harley St. W1 | *2* | 28 81 B |
| Harlington Rd. Bexh | *79* | 48 75 A |
| Harlington Road E. Felt | *82* | 11 73 C |
| Harlington Road W. Felt | *69* | 10 74 D |
| Harlow Gdns. Rom | *29* | 50 91 A |
| Harlow Rd. N13 | *17* | 32 93 D |
| Harlyn Dri. Pnr | *19* | 10 89 B |
| Harman Ave. Wdf Gn | *27* | 39 91 B |
| Harman Cl. E4 | *18* | 38 92 B |
| Harman Cl. NW2 | *35* | 24 86 C |
| Harman Dri. NW2 | *46* | 24 85 A |
| Harman Dri. Sid | *78* | 45 75 D |
| Harman Rd. Enf | *13* | 33 95 B |
| Harmony Cl. Wall | *111* | 30 62 A |
| Harmood Gr. NW1 | *47* | 28 84 D |
| Harmood Pl. NW1 | *47* | 28 84 D |
| Harmood St. NW1 | *47* | 28 84 D |
| Harmsworth St. SE17 | *63* | 31 78 D |
| Harmsworth Way. N20 | *15* | 24 94 D |
| Harness Rd. SE28 | *66* | 46 79 A |
| Harold Ave. Belv | *67* | 48 78 D |
| Harold Ct. Tedd | *83* | 15 71 C |
| Harold Gibbons Ct. SE7 | *65* | 41 77 A |
| Harold Pl. SE11 | *63* | 31 78 C |
| Harold Rd. E11 | *39* | 39 87 C |
| Harold Rd. E13 | *50* | 40 83 B |
| Harold Rd. E4 | *18* | 38 93 C |
| Harold Rd. N15 | *37* | 33 88 B |
| Harold Rd. N8 | *24* | 30 89 D |
| Harold Rd. NW10 | *55* | 20 82 B |
| Harold Rd. SE19 | *97* | 33 70 C |
| Harold Rd. Sutt | *110* | 26 64 B |
| Harold Rd. Wdf Gn | *27* | 40 90 A |
| Haroldstone Rd. E17 | *38* | 36 88 A |
| Harold View. Rom | *30* | 54 90 D |
| Harp Alley. EC4 | *3* | 31 81 D |
| Harpenden Rd. E12 | *39* | 41 86 A |
| Harpenden Rd. SE27 | *87* | 31 72 B |
| Harper Rd. SE1 | *8* | 32 79 C |
| Harper's Yd. N17 | *25* | 33 90 B |
| Harp La. EC3 | *8* | 33 80 A |
| Harp La. EC3 | *8* | 33 80 A |
| Harpley Sq. E1 | *57* | 35 82 D |
| Harpour Rd. Bark | *51* | 44 84 A |
| Harp Rd. W7 | *54* | 15 81 B |
| Harpsden St. SW11 | *74* | 28 76 A |
| Harpur St. WC1 | *3* | 30 81 B |
| Harraden Rd. SE3 | *77* | 41 76 A |
| Harrap St. E14 | *58* | 38 80 B |
| Harriers Cl. W5 | *54* | 18 80 A |
| Harries Rd. Hay | *53* | 11 82 C |
| Harriet Cl. E8 | *48* | 34 83 A |
| Harriet Gdns. Croy | *105* | 34 65 A |
| Harriet St. SW1 | *5* | 27 79 B |
| Harriet Wlk. SW1 | *5* | 27 79 B |
| Harringay Gdns. N15 | *25* | 31 89 D |
| Harringay Rd. N15 | *25* | 31 89 D |
| Harrington Cl. Croy | *104* | 30 65 A |
| Harrington Gdns. SW7 | *62* | 26 78 A |
| Harrington Hill. E5 | *37* | 34 87 D |
| Harrington Rd. E11 | *39* | 39 87 C |
| Harrington Rd. SE25 | *97* | 34 68 D |
| Harrington Rd. SW7 | *62* | 26 78 B |
| Harrington Sq. NW1 | *47* | 29 83 C |
| Harrington St. NW1 | *2* | 29 82 A |
| Harrington St. NW1 | *47* | 29 83 C |
| Harrington Way. SE18 | *65* | 41 79 D |
| Harriott Cl. E10 | *65* | 39 78 B |
| Harris Cl. Enf | *13* | 31 97 B |
| Harris Cl. Houn | *70* | 13 76 A |
| Harrison Cl. Nthwd | *19* | 08 91 A |
| Harrison Rd. Dag | *52* | 49 84 B |
| Harrison's Rise. Croy | *105* | 31 65 D |
| Harrison St. WC1 | *3* | 30 82 A |
| Harris Rd. Bexh | *79* | 48 76 B |
| Harris Rd. Dag | *52* | 48 85 D |
| Harris St. E17 | *38* | 36 87 B |
| Harris St. SE5 | *63* | 32 77 D |
| Harris Way. Sun | *91* | 09 69 A |
| Harrold Rd. Dag | *51* | 46 85 D |
| Harrow Ave. Enf | *13* | 33 95 D |
| Harroway Rd. SW11 | *73* | 26 76 D |
| Harrowby St. W1 | *1* | 27 81 C |
| Harrow Cres. Rom | *30* | 52 91 D |
| Harrowdene Cl. Wem | *44* | 17 85 B |
| Harrowdene Gdns. Tedd | *93* | 16 70 C |
| Harrowdene Rd. Wem | *44* | 17 85 B |
| Harrow Dri. Horn | *42* | 53 87 A |
| Harrow Dri. N9 | *17* | 33 94 D |
| Harrowgate Rd. E9 | *49* | 36 84 C |
| Harrow Green. E11 | *39* | 39 86 C |
| Harrow La. E14 | *57* | 37 80 B |
| Harrow Manor Way. SE2 | *67* | 47 79 C |
| Harrow Park. Har | *33* | 15 86 A |
| Harrow Pl. E1 | *4* | 33 81 D |
| Harrow Rd. Ashf | *81* | 07 72 A |
| Harrow Rd. Bark | *51* | 45 83 A |
| Harrow Rd. Cars | *111* | 27 63 A |
| Harrow Rd. E11 | *39* | 39 86 D |
| Harrow Rd. E6 | *50* | 42 83 A |
| Harrow Rd Fly. NW1 | *1* | 27 81 A |
| Harrow Rd. Ilf | *51* | 44 85 A |
| Harrow Rd. NW10 | *56* | 23 82 A |
| Harrow Rd. W10 | *56* | 24 82 C |
| Harrow Rd. W2 | *1* | 26 81 A |
| Harrow Rd. W9 | *56* | 25 82 C |
| Harrow Rd. Wem | *44* | 16 85 D |
| Harrow Rd. Wem | *45* | 19 84 A |
| Harrow View. Har | *59* | 14 79 D |
| Harrow View Rd. W5 | *54* | 16 82 D |
| Harrow Way. Shep | *91* | 08 69 C |
| Harrow Weald Park. Har | *20* | 14 91 B |
| Harte Rd. Houn | *70* | 12 76 D |
| Hartfield Cres. SW19 | *95* | 24 70 D |
| Hartfield Cres. W.Wick | *107* | 40 65 C |
| Hartfield Gr. SE20 | *98* | 35 69 A |
| Hartfield Rd. SW19 | *95* | 24 70 D |
| Hartfield Terr. E3 | *49* | 37 83 C |
| Hartford Ave. Har | *21* | 16 89 B |
| Hartford Rd. Bex | *79* | 49 74 C |
| Hartford Rd. Eps | *109* | 19 63 B |
| Hart Gr. Sthl | *53* | 13 81 A |
| Hart Gr. W5 | *55* | 19 80 C |
| Hartham Cl. Islw | *71* | 16 76 A |
| Hartham Cl. N7 | *47* | 30 85 C |
| Hartham Rd. Islw | *71* | 16 76 A |
| Hartham Rd. N17 | *25* | 33 90 D |
| Hartham Rd. N7 | *47* | 30 85 C |
| Harting Rd. SE9 | *89* | 42 72 C |
| Hartington Cl. Har | *44* | 15 85 A |
| Hartington Ct. W4 | *61* | 19 77 D |
| Hartington Rd. E16 | *58* | 40 81 D |
| Hartington Rd. E17 | *38* | 36 88 C |
| Hartington Rd. Sthl | *59* | 12 79 C |
| Hartington Rd. SW8 | *10* | 30 77 C |
| Hartington Rd. Twick | *71* | 16 74 D |
| Hartington Rd. W13 | *54* | 16 80 B |
| Hartington Rd. W4 | *72* | 20 76 A |
| Hartismere Rd. SW6 | *62* | 24 77 D |
| Hartlake Rd. E9 | *49* | 36 84 A |
| Hartland Dri. Ruis | *31* | 10 86 D |
| Hartland Dri. Ruis | *43* | 11 85 A |
| Hartland Rd. E15 | *50* | 39 84 D |
| Hartland Rd. Hamp | *82* | 13 71 B |
| Hartland Rd. Horn | *42* | 52 86 A |
| Hartland Rd. Islw | *71* | 16 75 A |
| Hartland Rd. Mord | *103* | 25 66 A |
| Hartland Rd. N11 | *16* | 27 92 D |
| Hartland Rd. NW1 | *47* | 28 84 D |
| Hartland Rd. NW6 | *46* | 24 83 D |
| Hartland Way. Croy | *106* | 36 65 A |
| Hartland Way. Mord | *103* | 24 66 B |
| Hartley Ave. E6 | *50* | 42 83 A |
| Hartley Cl. Brom | *99* | 42 69 D |
| Hartley Hse.SE1 | *63* | 33 78 B |
| Hartley Rd. Croy | *105* | 32 66 A |
| Hartley Rd. E11 | *39* | 39 87 D |
| Hartley Rd. Well | *67* | 47 77 C |
| Hartley St. E2 | *57* | 35 82 A |
| Hartnoll St. N7 | *47* | 30 85 D |
| Harton Cl. Brom | *99* | 41 69 B |
| Harton Rd. N9 | *17* | 34 93 B |
| Harton St. SE8 | *75* | 33 76 A |
| Hartshorn Alley. EC3 | *4* | 33 81 C |
| Harts La. Bark | *51* | 43 84 B |
| Harts La. SE14 | *76* | 36 76 A |
| Hartslock Dri. SE2 | *67* | 47 79 B |
| Hartsmead Rd. SE9 | *89* | 42 72 B |
| Hart St. EC3 | *8* | 33 80 A |
| Hartsway. Enf | *14* | 35 96 C |
| Hartswood Rd. W12 | *61* | 21 79 D |
| Hartsworth Cl. E13 | *50* | 39 83 D |
| Hartville Rd. SE18 | *66* | 45 78 A |
| Hartwell Drive. E4 | *26* | 38 91 A |
| Hartwell St. E8 | *48* | 33 84 B |
| Harvard Hill. W4 | *61* | 19 77 B |
| Harvard La. (Footpath). W4 | *61* | 20 78 C |
| Harvard Rd. Islw | *71* | 15 76 A |
| Harvard Rd. SE13 | *76* | 38 74 A |
| Harvard Rd. W4 | *61* | 19 78 D |
| Harvel Cres. SE2 | *67* | 47 78 D |
| Harvest Bank Rd. W.Wick | *107* | 39 65 D |
| Harvest Ct. Shep | *91* | 07 68 C |
| Harvester Rd. Eps | *109* | 20 62 D |
| Harvester's Cl. Islw | *70* | 14 74 B |
| Harvest Rd. Felt | *81* | 10 72 C |
| Harvey Gdns. E11 | *39* | 39 87 D |
| Harvey Gdns. SE7 | *65* | 41 78 D |
| Harvey Rd. E11 | *39* | 39 87 D |
| Harvey Rd. Houn | *82* | 12 73 B |
| Harvey Rd. Ilf | *51* | 43 85 D |
| Harvey Rd. N8 | *36* | 30 88 B |
| Harvey Rd. Nthlt | *43* | 11 84 C |
| Harvey Rd. SE5 | *75* | 32 76 B |
| Harvey Rd. SE5 | *75* | 32 76 B |
| Harvey's Bldgs. WC2 | *7* | 30 80 A |
| Harvey's La. Rom | *42* | 51 86 A |
| Harvey St. N1 | *48* | 32 83 B |
| Harvington Wlk. E8 | *48* | 34 84 C |
| Harvist Rd. NW6 | *46* | 24 83 C |
| Harwell Cl. Ruis | *31* | 08 87 D |
| Harwell Pas. N2 | *24* | 27 89 D |
| Harwood Ave. Brom | *99* | 40 69 D |
| Harwood Ave. Horn | *30* | 54 89 A |
| Harwood Ave. Mit | *96* | 27 68 A |
| Harwood Rd. SW6 | *62* | 25 77 C |
| Harwoods Yd. N21 | *17* | 31 94 A |
| Harwood Terr. SW6 | *73* | 25 76 B |
| Hascombe Terr. SE5 | *75* | 32 76 D |
| Haselbury Green. N9 | *17* | 33 93 C |
| Haselbury La. N9 | *17* | 33 93 C |
| Haselbury Rd. N18 | *17* | 33 92 A |
| Haselbury Rd. N9 | *17* | 33 93 C |
| Haseley End. SE23 | *88* | 35 73 A |
| Haselrigge Rd. SW4 | *74* | 29 75 D |
| Haseltine Rd. SE26 | *88* | 36 71 B |
| Haselwood Dri. Enf | *13* | 31 96 D |
| Haskard Rd. Dag | *52* | 47 85 B |
| Hasker St. SW3 | *9* | 27 78 A |
| Haslam Ave. Sutt | *103* | 24 66 C |
| Haslam Cl. N1 | *48* | 31 84 C |
| Haslem Cl. Ruis | *31* | 08 86 A |
| Haslemere Ave. Barn | *16* | 27 94 D |
| Haslemere Ave. Houn | *70* | 11 76 C |
| Haslemere Ave. Mit. | *95* | 26 69 D |
| Haslemere Ave. NW4 | *35* | 23 88 D |
| Haslemere Ave. SW18 | *85* | 25 72 B |
| Haslemere Ave. W13 | *60* | 16 79 C |
| Haslemere Ave. W7 | *60* | 16 79 C |
| Haslemere Cl. Hamp | *82* | 12 71 D |
| Haslemere Cl. Wall | *111* | 30 64 C |
| Haslemere Gdns. N3 | *23* | 24 89 D |
| Haslemere Rd. Bexh | *79* | 48 76 D |
| Haslemere Rd. Ilf | *40* | 45 86 B |
| Haslemere Rd. N21 | *17* | 31 94 D |
| Haslemere Rd. N8 | *36* | 30 87 A |
| Haslemere Rd. Th Hth | *105* | 31 67 B |
| Haslett Rd. Shep | *91* | 09 69 C |
| Hasluck Gdns. Barn | *11* | 26 95 C |
| Hassard St. E2 | *48* | 33 83 D |
| Hassendean Rd. SE3 | *65* | 40 77 D |
| Hassett Rd. E9 | *49* | 36 84 A |
| Hassocks Cl. SE26 | *87* | 34 72 D |
| Hassocks Rd. SW16 | *96* | 29 69 B |
| Hassop Rd. NW2 | *46* | 23 85 B |
| Hassop Wlk. SE9 | *89* | 42 71 A |
| Hasted Rd. SE7 | *65* | 41 78 D |
| Hastings Ave. Ilf | *28* | 44 89 C |
| Hastings Cl. Barn | *11* | 26 96 C |
| Hastings Cl. SE15 | *63* | 34 77 C |
| Hastings Pl. Croy | *105* | 33 66 D |
| Hastings Rd. Brom | *107* | 42 65 A |
| Hastings Rd. Croy | *105* | 33 66 D |
| Hastings Rd. N11 | *16* | 29 92 D |
| Hastings Rd. Rom | *42* | 52 88 B |
| Hastings Rd. W13 | *54* | 16 80 B |
| Hastings St. WC1 | *3* | 30 82 A |
| Hatcham Park Mews. SE14 | *76* | 35 76 B |
| Hatcham Park Rd. SE14 | *64* | 35 77 D |
| Hatcham Rd. SE15 | *64* | 35 77 A |
| Hatchard Rd. N19 | *36* | 29 86 B |
| Hatchcroft. NW4 | *22* | 22 89 B |
| Hatchett Rd. Felt | *81* | 08 73 C |
| Hatch Gr. Rom | *29* | 48 89 C |
| Hatch La. E4 | *18* | 38 92 B |
| Hatch Rd. SW16 | *96* | 30 69 C |
| Hatcliffe Cl. SE3 | *77* | 39 75 B |
| Hatcliffe St. E10 | *65* | 39 78 D |
| Hatfield Cl. Ilf | *28* | 43 90 D |
| Hatfield Cl. Mit | *95* | 26 68 D |
| Hatfield Cl. SE14 | *64* | 35 77 D |
| Hatfield Mead. Mord | *103* | 25 67 A |
| Hatfield Rd. Dag | *52* | 48 84 C |
| Hatfield Rd. E15 | *50* | 39 85 C |
| Hatfield Rd. W13 | *54* | 16 80 C |
| Hatfield Rd. W4 | *61* | 20 79 B |
| Hatfields. SE1 | *7* | 31 80 C |
| Hathaway Cl. Stan | *21* | 16 91 A |
| Hathaway Cres. E12 | *50* | 42 84 B |
| Hathaway Gdns. W13 | *54* | 16 81 A |
| Hathaway Rd. Croy | *105* | 31 66 B |
| Hatherleigh Cl. Mord | *95* | 25 68 C |
| Hatherleigh Rd. Ruis | *31* | 10 86 A |
| Hatherleigh Way. Rom | *30* | 53 90 B |
| Hatherley Cres. Sid | *90* | 46 72 A |

| | | |
|---|---|---|
| Hatherley Gdns. E6 | 58 | 41 82 B |
| Hatherley Gdns. N8 | 36 | 30 88 C |
| Hatherley Gr. W2 | 56 | 25 81 D |
| Hatherley Mews. E17 | 26 | 37 89 C |
| Hatherley Rd. E17 | 26 | 37 89 C |
| Hatherley Rd. Rich | 71 | 18 76 B |
| Hatherley Rd. Sid | 90 | 46 72 C |
| Hatherley St. SW1 | 10 | 29 78 A |
| Hathern Gdns. SE9 | 90 | 43 71 A |
| Hatherop Rd. Hamp | 92 | 12 70 D |
| Hathersage Ct. N5 | 48 | 32 85 D |
| Hathorne Cl. SE15 | 76 | 35 76 C |
| Hathway Gdns. Rom | 41 | 47 88 B |
| Hathway St. SE15 | 76 | 35 76 D |
| Hatley Ave. Ilf | 28 | 44 89 C |
| Hatley Cl. N11 | 16 | 27 92 D |
| Hatley Rd. N4 | 36 | 30 86 B |
| Hatteraick St. SE16 | 64 | 35 79 A |
| Hattnn Cl. SE18 | 66 | 44 77 D |
| Hatton Ct. Chis | 99 | 42 70 D |
| Hatton Gdn. EC1 | 3 | 31 81 A |
| Hatton Gdns. Mit | 104 | 27 67 B |
| Hatton Green. Felt | 69 | 10 75 C |
| Hatton Pl. EC1 | 3 | 31 81 A |
| Hatton Rd. Croy | 105 | 31 66 C |
| Hatton Rd. Felt | 69 | 09 74 A |
| Hatton Row. NW8 | 1 | 26 82 D |
| Hatton St. NW8 | 1 | 26 82 D |
| Hatton Wall. EC1 | 3 | 31 81 A |
| Haunch of Venison Yd. W1 | 2 | 28 81 D |
| Havana Cl. Rom | 42 | 51 88 A |
| Havana Rd. SW19 | 85 | 25 72 A |
| Havannah St. E14 | 64 | 37 79 A |
| Havant Rd. E17 | 26 | 38 89 A |
| Havant Way (off Garnies Cl). SE15 | 63 | 33 77 D |
| Havelock Pl. Har | 33 | 15 88 C |
| Havelock Rd. Belv | 67 | 48 78 B |
| Havelock Rd. Brom | 99 | 41 68 C |
| Havelock Rd. Croy | 105 | 33 65 B |
| Havelock Rd. Dart | 80 | 52 74 D |
| Havelock Rd. Har | 21 | 15 89 A |
| Havelock Rd. N17 | 25 | 34 90 C |
| Havelock Rd. Sthl | 59 | 13 79 C |
| Havelock Rd. SW17 | 85 | 26 71 C |
| Havelock St. Ilf | 40 | 46 86 B |
| Havelock St. N1 | 47 | 30 83 A |
| Havelock Terr. SW8 | 74 | 29 76 A |
| Havelock Wlk. SE23 | 88 | 35 72 A |
| Haven Cl. SW19 | 85 | 23 72 D |
| Haven Green Ct. W5 | 54 | 17 81 D |
| Haven Green. W5 | 54 | 17 81 D |
| Havenhurst Rise. Enf | 13 | 31 97 C |
| Haven La. W5 | 54 | 18 81 C |
| Haven Mews. E3 | 57 | 36 81 B |
| Haven Rd. Ashf | 81 | 07 71 B |
| Haven St. NW1 | 47 | 28 84 D |
| Haven The. Rich | 72 | 19 75 A |
| Havenwood. Wem | 34 | 19 86 D |
| Haverfield Gdns. Rich | 61 | 19 77 C |
| Haverfield Rd. E3 | 57 | 36 82 A |
| Haverford Way. Edg | 21 | 18 90 B |
| Haverhill Rd. E4 | 18 | 38 94 C |
| Haverhill Rd. SW12 | 86 | 29 73 C |
| Havering Dri. Rom | 30 | 51 89 A |
| Havering Gdns. Rom | 41 | 47 88 B |
| Havering Rd. Rom | 29 | 50 90 D |
| Havering St. E1 | 57 | 35 81 D |
| Haversham Cl. Twick | 83 | 17 73 B |
| Haverstock Hill. NW3 | 47 | 27 84 B |
| Haverstock Rd. NW5 | 47 | 28 85 C |
| Haverstock St. N1 | 48 | 31 83 D |
| Haverthwaite Rd. Orp | 108 | 44 65 D |
| Havil St. SE5 | 75 | 33 76 A |
| Hawarden Gr. SE24 | 87 | 32 73 A |
| Hawarden Rd. E17 | 26 | 35 89 D |
| Hawbridge Rd. E11 | 38 | 38 87 D |
| Hawes Cl. Nthwd | 19 | 09 91 D |
| Hawes La. W Wick | 106 | 38 66 D |
| Hawes Rd. Brom | 99 | 40 69 B |
| Hawes Rd. N18 | 25 | 34 91 B |
| Hawes St. N1 | 48 | 31 84 D |
| Hawgood St. E3 | 57 | 37 81 A |
| Hawkdene. E4 | 14 | 38 95 D |
| Hawke Park Rd. N22 | 25 | 31 89 B |
| Hawker Cl. Wall | 111 | 30 63 C |
| Hawke Rd. SE19 | 97 | 33 70 A |
| Hawkesbury Rd. SW15 | 72 | 22 74 B |
| Hawkesfield Rd. SE23 | 88 | 36 72 B |
| Hawkesley Cl. Twick | 83 | 16 71 A |
| Hawkes Rd. Mit | 96 | 27 69 B |
| Hawkesworth Cl. Nthwd | 19 | 09 91 C |
| Hawkewood Rd. Sun | 91 | 10 68 B |
| Hawkfield Ct. Islw | 71 | 15 76 C |
| Hawkhurst Gdns. Rom | 29 | 50 91 B |
| Hawkhurst Rd. SW16 | 96 | 29 69 B |
| Hawkhurst Way. N.Mal | 102 | 20 67 B |
| Hawkhurst Wa W Wick | 106 | 37 65 B |
| Hawkinge Wlk. Orp | 100 | 46 68 B |
| Hawkins Cl. Har | 32 | 14 87 B |
| Hawkley Gdns. SE27 | 87 | 31 72 B |
| Hawkridge Cl. Rom | 41 | 47 88 C |
| Hawkshaw Cl. SW2 | 86 | 30 73 A |
| Hawkshead Cl. Brom | 99 | 39 70 C |
| Hawkshead Rd. NW10 | 45 | 21 84 D |
| Hawkshead Rd. W4 | 61 | 21 79 A |
| Hawkslade Rd. SE15 | 76 | 35 74 B |
| Hawksley Rd. N16 | 37 | 33 86 C |
| Hawks Mews. SE10 | 64 | 38 77 C |
| Hawksmoor St. W6 | 62 | 23 77 B |
| Hawksmouth. E4 | 18 | 38 94 A |
| Hawks Pas. King | 93 | 18 69 D |
| Hawks Rd. King | 93 | 18 69 D |
| Hawkstone Rd. SE16 | 64 | 35 78 A |
| Hawkwell Wlk (off Maldon Cl). N1 | 48 | 32 83 A |
| Hawkwood Cres. E4 | 14 | 37 95 D |
| Hawkwood La. Chis | 100 | 44 69 A |
| Hawkwood Mount. E5 | 37 | 34 87 D |
| Hawlands Dri. Pnr | 32 | 12 87 A |
| Hawley Cl. Hamp | 92 | 12 70 B |
| Hawley Cres. NW1 | 47 | 28 84 D |
| Hawley Mews. NW1 | 47 | 28 84 D |
| Hawley Rd. NW1 | 47 | 28 84 D |
| Hawley St. NW1 | 47 | 28 84 D |
| Hawley Way. Ashf | 81 | 07 71 D |
| Hawstead Rd. SE6 | 76 | 37 74 D |
| Hawthorn Ave. N13 | 16 | 30 92 C |
| Hawthorn Ave. Th Hth | 97 | 31 69 B |
| Hawthorn Cl. Hamp | 82 | 13 71 C |
| Hawthorn Cl. Orp | 108 | 44 67 D |
| Hawthorn Ct. Rich | 72 | 19 76 B |
| Hawthorndene Cl. Brom | 107 | 40 65 A |
| Hawthorndene Rd. Brom | 107 | 39 65 B |
| Hawthorn Dri. Har | 32 | 13 88 C |
| Hawthorne Ave. Cars | 111 | 28 63 C |
| Hawthorne Ave. Har | 33 | 16 88 C |
| Hawthorne Ave. Mit | 95 | 26 69 D |
| Hawthorne Ave. Ruis | 31 | 10 87 B |
| Hawthorne Cl. Brom | 99 | 42 68 B |
| Hawthorne Cl. N1 | 48 | 33 84 A |
| Hawthorne Cl. Sutt | 103 | 26 65 A |
| Hawthorne Farm Ave. Nthlt | 43 | 12 83 A |
| Hawthorne Gr. NW9 | 34 | 20 87 A |
| Hawthorne Rd. Brom | 99 | 42 68 B |
| Hawthorne Rd. E17 | 26 | 37 89 A |
| Hawthorne Way. N9 | 17 | 33 93 B |
| Hawthorn Gdns. W5 | 60 | 17 79 D |
| Hawthorn Gr. SE20 | 97 | 34 69 B |
| Hawthorn Hatch. Brent | 60 | 16 77 D |
| Hawthorn Mews. NW7 | 23 | 24 90 A |
| Hawthorn Rd. Bexh | 79 | 48 75 D |
| Hawthorn Rd. Brent | 60 | 16 77 D |
| Hawthorn Rd. N18 | 17 | 33 92 D |
| Hawthorn Rd. N8 | 24 | 30 89 A |
| Hawthorn Rd. NW10 | 45 | 22 84 C |
| Hawthorn Rd. Sutt | 111 | 27 63 A |
| Hawthorn Rd. Wall | 111 | 28 63 D |
| Hawthorn Way. Shep | 91 | 08 68 D |
| Hawthorn Wlk. W10 | 56 | 24 82 C |
| Hawtrey Ave. Nthlt | 43 | 11 83 D |
| Hawtrey Dri. Ruis | 31 | 10 87 A |
| Hawtrey Rd. NW3 | 47 | 27 84 C |
| Haxted Rd. Brom | 99 | 40 69 B |
| Hayant Wlk. SW20 | 95 | 24 68 A |
| Hayburn Way. Horn | 42 | 51 87 D |
| Hay Cl. E15 | 50 | 39 84 C |
| Haycroft Gdns. NW10 | 45 | 22 83 A |
| Haycroft Rd. Surb | 101 | 18 65 C |
| Haycroft Rd. SW2 | 74 | 30 74 A |
| Hay Currie St. E14 | 57 | 37 81 D |
| Hayday Rd. E16 | 58 | 40 81 A |
| Hayden's Pl. W11 | 56 | 24 81 D |
| Hayden Way. Rom | 29 | 50 90 C |
| Haydock Ave. Nthlt | 43 | 13 84 A |
| Haydock Green. Nthlt | 43 | 13 84 A |
| Haydon Cl. NW9 | 22 | 20 89 C |
| Haydon Dri. Pnr | 19 | 10 89 C |
| Haydon Park Rd. SW19 | 85 | 25 71 D |
| Haydon Rd. Dag | 41 | 47 86 A |
| Haydon's Rd. SW19 | 95 | 26 70 A |
| Haydon St. EC3 | 8 | 33 80 B |
| Haydon Wlk. EC3 | 4 | 33 81 D |
| Hayes Chase. W Wick | 106 | 38 67 D |
| Hayes Cl. Brom | 107 | 40 65 A |
| Hayes Cres. NW11 | 35 | 24 88 B |
| Hayes Cres. Sutt | 110 | 23 64 B |
| Hayes Ct. SW2 | 86 | 30 73 C |
| Hayesford Park Dri. Brom | 107 | 39 67 B |
| Hayes Gdn. Brom | 107 | 40 66 C |
| Hayes Hill. Brom | 107 | 39 66 C |
| Hayes Hill Rd. Brom | 107 | 39 66 D |
| Hayes La. Beck | 98 | 38 68 D |
| Hayes La. Brom | 108 | 46 67 C |
| Hayes Mead Rd. Brom | 107 | 39 66 C |
| Hayes Pl. NW1 | 1 | 27 82 C |
| Hayes Rd. Brom | 99 | 40 68 C |
| Hayes Rd. Sthl | 59 | 11 78 A |
| Hayes St. Brom | 107 | 40 66 D |
| Hayes Way. Beck | 98 | 38 68 D |
| Hayes Way. Beck | 99 | 39 68 C |
| Hayes Wood Ave. Brom | 107 | 40 66 D |
| Hayfield Pas. E1 | 57 | 35 82 C |
| Hayfield Rd. Orp | 108 | 46 67 A |
| Hayfield Yd. E1 | 57 | 35 82 C |
| Haygarth Pl. SW19 | 85 | 23 71 D |
| Hay Hill. W1 | 6 | 28 80 B |
| Hayland Cl. NW9 | 22 | 20 89 D |
| Hay La. NW9 | 22 | 20 89 A |
| Hayles St. SE11 | 63 | 31 78 B |
| Hayles St. SE11 | 7 | 31 79 D |
| Haylett Gdns. King | 93 | 17 68 D |
| Hayling Ave. Felt | 81 | 10 72 C |
| Hayling Cl (off Pellerin Rd). N16 | 48 | 33 85 C |
| Hayling Ct. Sutt | 110 | 23 64 A |
| Hayman St. N1 | 48 | 31 84 D |
| Haymarket Arc. SW1 | 6 | 29 80 B |
| Haymarket. SW1 | 6 | 29 80 B |
| Haymer Gdns. Wor Pk | 102 | 22 65 C |
| Haymerle Rd. SE15 | 63 | 34 77 A |
| Hayne Rd. Beck | 98 | 36 69 B |
| Haynes Cl. N17 | 25 | 34 91 D |
| Haynes Cl. SE3 | 77 | 39 75 A |
| Haynes La. SE19 | 97 | 33 70 A |
| Haynes Park Ct. Horn | 42 | 53 88 A |
| Haynes Rd. Horn | 30 | 53 89 D |
| Haynes Rd. Wem | 44 | 18 84 C |
| Hayne St. EC1 | 3 | 31 81 B |
| Hay's La. SE1 | 8 | 33 80 C |
| Haysleigh Gdns. SE20 | 97 | 34 69 C |
| Hay's Mews. W1 | 6 | 28 80 D |
| Haysoms Cl. Rom | 30 | 51 89 C |
| Hay St. E2 | 48 | 34 83 A |
| Hays Wlk. Sutt | 110 | 23 62 D |
| Hayter Rd. SW2 | 74 | 30 74 B |
| Hayton Cl. E8 | 48 | 33 84 B |
| Hayward Cl. Dart | 79 | 50 74 A |
| Hayward Cl. SW19 | 95 | 25 69 B |
| Hayward Gdns. SW15 | 73 | 23 74 C |
| Hayward Rd. N20 | 15 | 26 93 A |
| Hayward's Pl. EC1 | 3 | 31 82 D |
| Haywood Cl. Pnr | 20 | 11 90 D |
| Haywood Rd. Brom | 99 | 41 68 D |
| Hazelbank Rd. SE6 | 88 | 38 72 B |
| Hazelbank Rd. SE6 | 89 | 39 72 A |
| Hazel Bank. Surb | 102 | 20 66 C |
| Hazelbourne Rd. SW12 | 74 | 29 74 C |
| Hazelbrouck Gdns. Ilf | 28 | 44 91 D |
| Hazel Cl. Brent | 60 | 16 77 D |
| Hazel Cl. Horn | 42 | 52 86 D |
| Hazel Cl. Mit | 96 | 29 68 D |
| Hazel Cl. N13 | 17 | 32 92 D |
| Hazel Cl. N19 | 36 | 29 86 A |
| Hazel Cl. SE15 | 75 | 34 76 C |
| Hazel Cl. Twick | 82 | 14 73 A |
| Hazelcroft. Pnr | 20 | 13 91 B |
| Hazel Ct. W5 | 54 | 18 80 A |
| Hazeldene Dri. Pnr | 20 | 11 89 A |
| Hazeldene Rd. Ilf | 40 | 46 86 B |
| Hazeldene Rd. Well | 79 | 47 76 C |
| Hazeldon Rd. SE4 | 76 | 36 74 A |
| Hazel Dri. Eri | 80 | 52 76 B |
| Hazeleigh Gdns. Wdf Gn | 27 | 42 91 A |
| Hazel Gr. Enf | 13 | 34 95 C |
| Hazel Gr. Orp | 108 | 43 65 B |
| Hazel Gr. Rom | 29 | 48 89 A |
| Hazel Gr. SE26 | 88 | 35 71 B |
| Hazel Gr. Wem | 44 | 18 83 A |
| Hazelhurst. Beck | 98 | 38 69 B |
| Hazelhurst Ct. SE6 | 88 | 38 71 C |
| Hazelhurst Rd. SW17 | 85 | 26 71 B |
| Hazel La. Rich | 83 | 18 72 A |
| Hazell Cres. Rom | 29 | 49 90 B |
| Hazellville Rd. N19 | 36 | 29 87 D |
| Hazel Mead. Eps | 109 | 22 62 C |
| Hazelmere Cl. Felt | 69 | 09 74 C |
| Hazelmere Cl. Nthlt | 43 | 12 83 D |
| Hazelmere Gdns. Horn | 42 | 53 88 A |
| Hazelmere Rd. Nthlt | 43 | 12 83 D |
| Hazelmere Rd. NW6 | 46 | 25 83 A |
| Hazelmere Rd. Orp | 100 | 44 68 D |
| Hazelmere Way. Brom | 107 | 40 67 C |
| Hazelmere Wlk. Nthlt | 43 | 12 83 D |
| Hazel Rd. Eri | 80 | 52 76 A |
| Hazel Rd. NW10 | 56 | 23 82 A |
| Hazel Rise. Horn | 42 | 53 88 C |
| Hazeltree La. Nthlt | 53 | 12 82 A |
| Hazel Way. E4 | 26 | 36 91 B |
| Hazel Way. SE1 | 63 | 33 78 B |
| Hazel Wlk. Brom | 108 | 43 67 C |
| Hazelwood Ave. Mord | 95 | 25 68 D |
| Hazelwood Cl. W5 | 60 | 18 79 A |
| Hazelwood Cres. N13 | 17 | 31 92 A |
| Hazelwood Cres. W10 | 56 | 24 82 D |
| Hazelwood Ct. Surb | 101 | 18 67 C |
| Hazelwood Dri. Pnr | 19 | 10 90 D |
| Hazelwood House. N13 | 17 | 31 92 B |
| Hazelwood La. N13 | 17 | 31 92 A |
| Hazelwood Rd. E17 | 38 | 36 88 A |
| Hazelwood Rd. Enf | 13 | 34 95 C |
| Hazlebury Rd. SW6 | 73 | 25 76 D |
| Hazledean Rd. Croy | 105 | 32 65 B |
| Hazledean Rd. NW10 | 45 | 20 84 D |
| Hazledene Rd. W4 | 61 | 20 77 A |
| Hazlemere Gdns. Wor Pk | 102 | 22 66 D |
| Hazlewell Rd. SW15 | 73 | 23 74 A |
| Hazlewood Cres. W10 | 56 | 24 82 C |
| Hazlitt Mews. W14 | 62 | 24 79 C |
| Hazlitt Rd. W14 | 62 | 24 79 C |
| Heacham Ave. Ruis | 31 | 08 86 A |
| Headcorn Pl. Th Hth | 96 | 30 68 B |
| Headcorn Rd. Brom | 89 | 40 71 C |
| Headcorn Rd. N17 | 25 | 33 91 C |
| Headcorn Rd. Th Hth | 96 | 30 68 D |
| Headfort Pl. SW1 | 6 | 28 79 A |
| Headington Rd. SW18 | 85 | 26 72 A |
| Headlam Rd. SW4 | 86 | 29 73 B |
| Headlam St. E1 | 57 | 34 82 D |
| Headley App. Ilf | 40 | 43 88 B |
| Headley Ave. Wall | 111 | 30 64 D |
| Headley Cl. Eps | 109 | 19 63 A |
| Headley Dri. Ilf | 40 | 43 88 D |
| Heads Mews. W11 | 56 | 25 81 C |
| Head St. E1 | 57 | 35 81 D |
| Headstone Dri. Har | 21 | 15 89 A |
| Headstone Gdns. Har | 20 | 14 89 C |
| Headstone La. Har | 20 | 13 90 D |
| Headstone Rd. Har | 33 | 15 88 C |
| Headway Cl. Rich | 83 | 17 71 A |
| Headway The. Eps | 109 | 21 62 B |
| Heald St. SE14 | 76 | 37 76 A |
| Heald St. SE8 | 76 | 37 76 A |
| Healey St. NW1 | 47 | 28 84 B |
| Hearne Rd. W4 | 61 | 19 77 A |
| Hearn Rd. Rom | 42 | 51 88 D |
| Hearn Rise. Nthlt | 43 | 11 83 B |
| Hearn St. EC2 | 4 | 33 82 C |
| Hearnville Rd. SW12 | 86 | 28 73 C |
| Heatham Park. Twick | 83 | 15 73 B |
| Heath Ave. Bexh | 67 | 47 77 B |
| Heath Brow. NW3 | 35 | 26 86 C |
| Heath Cl. NW11 | 35 | 25 87 B |
| Heath Cl. Rom | 30 | 52 89 A |
| Heath Cl. W5 | 54 | 18 82 D |
| Heathcote Ave. Ilf | 27 | 42 90 D |
| Heathcote Ct. Ilf | 27 | 42 90 D |
| Heathcote Gr. E4 | 18 | 38 93 A |
| Heathcote Rd. Twick | 71 | 16 74 B |
| Heathcote St. WC1 | 3 | 30 82 B |
| Heathcroft Ave. Sun | 91 | 09 70 D |
| Heathcroft. NW11 | 35 | 25 87 D |
| Heathcroft. W5 | 54 | 18 82 D |
| Heathdale Ave. Houn | 70 | 12 75 A |
| Heathdene Dri. Belv | 67 | 49 78 B |
| Heathdene Rd. SW16 | 96 | 30 70 D |
| Heathdene Rd. Wall | 111 | 28 63 D |
| Heath Dri. NW3 | 46 | 25 85 B |
| Heath Dri. Rom | 30 | 52 90 C |
| Heath Dri. Sutt | 110 | 26 62 A |
| Heath Dri. SW20 | 95 | 23 68 C |
| Heathedge. SE26 | 87 | 34 72 B |
| Heather Ave. Rom | 29 | 50 90 D |
| Heatherbank. Chis | 100 | 43 69 C |
| Heatherbank. SE9 | 77 | 42 76 D |
| Heather Cl. Hamp | 92 | 12 69 B |
| Heather Cl. Islw | 70 | 14 74 B |
| Heather Cl. Rom | 29 | 50 90 B |
| Heatherdale Cl. King | 94 | 19 70 D |
| Heatherdene Cl. Mit | 96 | 27 68 C |
| Heather Dri. Rom | 30 | 51 90 C |
| Heather Gdns. NW11 | 35 | 24 88 C |
| Heather Gdns. Rom | 29 | 50 90 D |
| Heather Gdns. Sutt | 110 | 25 63 A |
| Heather Glen. Rom | 29 | 50 90 D |
| Heatherlands. Sun | 91 | 10 70 A |
| Heatherley Dri. Ilf | 27 | 42 89 B |
| Heather Park Dri. Wem | 45 | 19 84 C |
| Heather Rd. NW2 | 34 | 21 86 B |
| Heather Rd. SE12 | 89 | 40 73 C |
| Heatherset Gdns. SW16 | 96 | 30 70 D |
| Heatherside Rd. Eps | 109 | 20 63 D |
| Heather Way. Rom | 29 | 50 90 B |
| Heather Way. Stan | 21 | 15 91 B |
| Heather Wlk. Houn | 82 | 13 73 A |
| Heather Wlk. W10 | 56 | 24 82 C |
| Heatherwood Cl. E12 | 39 | 41 86 A |
| Heathfield Ave. SW18 | 85 | 26 73 B |
| Heathfield. Chis | 100 | 44 70 A |
| Heathfield Cl. E16 | 58 | 41 81 B |
| Heathfield Ct. W4 | 61 | 20 78 D |
| Heathfield. E4 | 18 | 38 93 C |
| Heathfield Gdns. NW11 | 35 | 23 88 D |
| Heathfield Gdns. SW18 | 73 | 26 74 D |
| Heathfield Gdns. W4 | 61 | 20 78 C |
| Heathfield La. Chis | 100 | 44 70 A |
| Heathfield N. Twick | 83 | 15 73 B |
| Heathfield Park. NW2 | 46 | 23 84 A |
| Heathfield Rd. Bexh | 79 | 48 75 D |
| Heathfield Rd. Brom | 99 | 39 70 D |
| Heathfield Rd. Croy | 112 | 32 64 B |
| Heathfield Rd. SW18 | 73 | 26 74 D |
| Heathfield Rd. W3 | 61 | 19 79 B |
| Heathfield Rise. Ruis | 31 | 08 87 A |
| Heathfield Sq. SW18 | 85 | 26 73 B |
| Heathfield Sq. SW18 | 73 | 26 74 D |
| Heathfield S. Twick | 83 | 15 73 B |
| Heathfield Terr. SE18 | 66 | 45 77 B |
| Heathfield Terr. W4 | 61 | 20 78 D |
| Heathgate. NW11 | 35 | 25 88 D |
| Heath Gdns. Twick | 83 | 15 72 B |
| Heath Gr. SE20 | 98 | 35 70 C |
| Heath Gr. Sun | 91 | 09 70 D |
| Heath Hurst Rd. NW3 | 47 | 27 85 A |
| Heathhurst Rd. S Croy | 112 | 33 62 A |
| Heathland Rd. N16 | 37 | 33 87 C |
| Heathlands Cl. Sun | 91 | 10 69 C |
| Heathlands Rise. Dart | 80 | 52 74 D |
| Heath La. SE3 | 76 | 38 76 D |
| Heath La. SE3 | 77 | 39 75 A |
| Heathlee Rd. SE3 | 77 | 39 75 D |
| Heathley End. Chis | 100 | 44 70 C |
| Heathman's Rd. SW6 | 73 | 24 76 B |
| Heath Mead. SW19 | 85 | 23 72 D |
| Heath Park Rd. Rom | 42 | 52 88 B |
| Heath Pas. NW3 | 35 | 25 86 B |
| Heath Rd. Dart | 80 | 51 74 D |
| Heath Rd. Har | 32 | 14 87 A |
| Heath Rd. Houn | 70 | 14 75 C |
| Heath Rd. Rom | 41 | 48 87 A |
| Heath Rd. SW8 | 74 | 28 76 D |
| Heath Rd. Th Hth | 97 | 32 68 A |
| Heath Rd. Twick | 83 | 15 73 D |
| Heath Rise. Brom | 107 | 40 67 C |
| Heath Rise. SW15 | 73 | 24 74 C |
| Heath Royal. SW15 | 73 | 23 74 D |
| Heath's Cl. Enf | 13 | 33 97 C |
| Heathside Ave. Bexh | 79 | 48 76 C |
| Heathside Cl. Esh | 101 | 15 65 C |
| Heathside. Esh | 101 | 15 65 C |
| Heathside. Houn | 82 | 12 73 B |
| Heath Side. NW3 | 46 | 26 85 B |
| Heath Side. Orp | 108 | 44 66 A |
| Heathstan Rd. W12 | 55 | 22 81 C |
| Heath St. Bark | 51 | 43 83 B |
| Heath St. NW3 | 46 | 26 85 A |
| Heath The. W7 | 54 | 15 80 C |
| Heathview Ave. Dart | 80 | 51 74 C |
| Heath View Cl. N2 | 23 | 26 89 C |
| Heathview Dri. SE2 | 67 | 47 77 B |
| Heathview Gdns. SW15 | 85 | 23 73 A |
| Heath View. N2 | 23 | 26 89 C |
| Heathview Rd. Th Hth | 97 | 31 68 A |
| Heath Villas. SE18 | 66 | 45 78 D |
| Heathville Rd. N19 | 36 | 30 87 A |
| Heathwall St. SW11 | 74 | 27 75 B |
| Heathway. Croy | 106 | 36 65 D |
| Heathway. Dag | 41 | 48 86 D |
| Heathway. Dag | 52 | 49 85 C |
| Heath Way. Eri | 79 | 50 76 A |
| Heathway. SE3 | 65 | 40 77 C |
| Heathwood Gdns. SE7 | 65 | 42 78 C |
| Heaton Ave. Rom | 30 | 52 91 D |
| Heaton Cl. Rom | 30 | 53 91 C |
| Heaton Grange Rd. Rom | 30 | 51 90 D |
| Heaton Pl. E15 | 49 | 38 85 D |
| Heaton Rd. Mit | 96 | 28 70 C |
| Heaton Rd. SE15 | 75 | 34 76 D |
| Heaton Way. Rom | 30 | 53 91 C |
| Heaver Rd. SW11 | 73 | 26 75 B |
| Heavitree Cl. SE18 | 66 | 44 78 D |
| Heavitree Rd. SE18 | 66 | 44 78 D |
| Hebdon Rd. SW17 | 86 | 27 72 D |
| Heber Rd. NW2 | 46 | 23 85 B |
| Heber Rd. SE22 | 75 | 33 74 D |
| Hebron Rd. W6 | 62 | 23 79 C |
| Hecham Cl. E17 | 26 | 36 90 C |
| Heckfield Pl. SW6 | 62 | 25 77 C |
| Heckford St. E1 | 57 | 35 80 B |
| Hecron St. SE17 | 63 | 31 77 B |
| Hector St. SE18 | 66 | 45 78 A |
| Heddon Cl. Islw | 71 | 16 75 C |
| Heddon Court Ave. Barn | 12 | 27 95 B |
| Heddon Court Par. Barn | 12 | 28 95 A |
| Heddon Rd. Barn | 12 | 27 95 B |
| Heddon St. W1 | 6 | 29 80 A |
| Hedge Hill. Enf | 13 | 31 97 B |
| Hedge La. N13 | 17 | 32 93 C |
| Hedgemans Rd. Dag | 52 | 48 84 C |
| Hedgemans Way. Dag | 52 | 48 84 A |
| Hedgerley Gdns. Grnf | 43 | 14 83 C |
| Hedger's Gr. E9 | 49 | 36 84 A |
| Hedge Wlk. SE6 | 88 | 37 71 D |
| Hedgewood Gdns. Ilf | 40 | 43 88 A |
| Hedgley. Ilf | 27 | 42 89 D |
| Hedgley St. SE12 | 77 | 39 74 B |
| Hedingham Cl. N1 | 48 | 32 84 C |
| Hedingham Rd. Dag | 51 | 46 85 D |
| Hedley Rd. Houn | 82 | 13 73 A |
| Hedley Row. N5 | 48 | 32 85 D |
| Heenan Cl. Bark | 51 | 44 84 A |
| Heene Rd. Enf | 13 | 32 97 B |
| Heigham Rd. E6 | 50 | 42 84 C |
| Heighton Gdns. Croy | 112 | 31 64 D |
| Heights Cl. SW20 | 94 | 22 70 D |
| Heights The. Beck | 98 | 38 70 C |
| Heights The. Nthlt | 43 | 13 85 C |
| Heights The. SE7 | 65 | 41 78 C |
| Helby Rd. SW4 | 74 | 29 74 D |
| Helder Gr SE12 | 89 | 39 73 B |
| Helder St. S Croy | 112 | 32 63 B |
| Heldmann Cl. Houn | 70 | 14 75 D |
| Helena Cl. Wall | 111 | 30 63 C |
| Helena Ct. W5 | 54 | 17 81 B |
| Helena Rd. E13 | 50 | 39 83 D |
| Helena Rd. E17 | 38 | 37 88 A |
| Helena Rd. NW10 | 45 | 22 85 D |
| Helena Rd. W5 | 54 | 17 81 B |
| Helen Ave. Felt | 81 | 10 73 B |
| Helen Cl. E Mol | 92 | 13 68 D |
| Helen Cl. N2 | 23 | 26 89 A |
| Helen Rd. Horn | 30 | 53 89 B |
| Helenslea Ave. NW11 | 35 | 25 87 C |
| Helen's Pl. E2 | 57 | 35 82 A |
| Helen St. SE18 | 66 | 43 78 B |
| Helford Cl. Ruis | 41 | 09 86 A |
| Helgiford Gdns. Sun | 91 | 09 70 C |
| Heliport Estate. SW11 | 73 | 26 76 D |
| Helix Gdns. SW2 | 74 | 30 74 D |
| Helix Rd. SW2 | 75 | 31 74 C |
| Hellings St. E1 | 57 | 34 80 C |
| Helmet Row. EC1 | 4 | 32 82 C |
| Helmsdale Cl. E11 | 39 | 40 88 A |
| Helmsdale Cl. Rom | 30 | 51 91 C |
| Helmsdale Rd. Rom | 30 | 51 91 C |
| Helmsdale Rd. SW16 | 96 | 29 69 B |
| Helmsley Pl. E8 | 48 | 34 84 D |
| Helmsley St. E8 | 48 | 34 84 D |
| Helston Cl. Pnr | 20 | 12 91 D |
| Helvetia St. SE6 | 88 | 36 72 B |
| Hemans St Estate. SW8 | 10 | 29 77 D |
| Hemans St. SW8 | 10 | 30 77 C |
| Hemberton Rd. SW9 | 74 | 30 75 A |
| Hemery Rd. Grnf | 43 | 14 85 D |
| Hemingford Rd. N1 | 47 | 30 84 D |
| Hemingford Rd. Sutt | 110 | 23 64 A |
| Heming Rd. Edg | 22 | 19 91 D |
| Hemington Ave. N11 | 16 | 27 92 D |
| Hemlock Rd. W12 | 55 | 21 80 B |
| Hemming Cl. Hamp | 92 | 13 69 A |
| Hemming St. E1 | 57 | 34 82 C |
| Hempstead Rd. E17 | 26 | 38 90 D |
| Hemp Wlk. SE17 | 63 | 32 78 B |
| Hemp Wlk. SE17 | 63 | 32 78 B |
| Hemstal Rd. NW6 | 46 | 25 84 C |
| Hemsted Rd. Eri | 68 | 51 77 C |
| Hemswell Dri. NW9 | 22 | 21 90 A |
| Hemsworth Ct. N1 | 48 | 33 83 C |
| Hemsworth St. N1 | 48 | 33 83 C |
| Hemus Pl. SW3 | 9 | 27 78 C |
| Henbane Path. Rom | 30 | 53 91 D |
| Henchman St. W12 | 55 | 21 81 D |
| Hendale Ave. NW4 | 22 | 22 89 B |
| Henderson Cl. NW10 | 45 | 20 84 A |
| Henderson Dri. Dart | 80 | 54 75 D |
| Henderson Dri. NW8 | 1 | 26 82 D |
| Henderson Rd. Croy | 105 | 32 67 D |
| Henderson Rd. E7 | 50 | 41 84 A |
| Henderson Rd. N9 | 17 | 34 94 D |
| Henderson Rd. SW18 | 86 | 27 73 A |

Hendham Rd. SW17 86 27 72 B
Hendon Ave. N3 23 24 90 D
Hendon Gdns. Rom 29 50 91 A
Hendon Hall Ct. NW14 23 23 89 B
Hendon La. N3 23 24 90 D
Hendon Park Row. NW11 35 24 88 D
Hendon Rd. N9 17 34 93 A
Hendon Way. NW2 35 24 87 C
Hendren Cl. Grnf 43 14 85 D
Hendre Rd. SE1 63 33 78 A
Hendrick Ave. SW12 86 27 73 B
Heneage La. EC3 4 33 81 C
Heneage Pl. EC3 4 33 81 C
Heneage St. E1 4 33 81 B
Henfield Cl. Bex 79 49 74 C
Henfield Cl. N19 36 29 87 C
Henfield Rd. SW19 95 24 69 B
Hengelo Gdns. Mit 95 26 68 D
Hengist Rd. Eri 67 50 77 C
Hengist Rd. SE12 89 40 73 B
Hengist Way. Brom 99 39 68 C
Hengrave Rd. SE23 88 35 73 B
Henley Ave. Sutt 103 24 65 C
Henley Cl. Grnf 43 14 83 C
Henley Cl. Islw 71 15 76 B
Henley Dr. King 94 21 70 D
Henley Gdns. Pnr 19 10 89 B
Henley Gdns. Rom 41 48 88 A
Henley Rd. E16 65 42 79 B
Henley Rd. Ilf 51 44 85 B
Henley Rd. N18 17 33 92 A
Henley Rd. NW10 46 23 83 A
Henley St. SW11 74 28 76 C
Henley Way. Felt 82 11 71 D
Hennel Cl. SE23 88 35 72 C
Henniker Gdns. E6 58 41 82 B
Henniker Gdns. E6 50 42 83 C
Henniker Mews. SW3 62 26 77 B
Henniker Rd. E15 49 38 85 D
Henningham Rd. N17 25 32 90 B
Henning St. SW11 74 27 76 A
Henrietta Mews. WC1 3 30 82 C
Henrietta Pl. W1 2 28 81 D
Henrietta St. E15 49 38 85 C
Henrietta St. WC2 7 30 80 A
Henriques St. E1 57 34 81 C
Henry Cooper Way. SE9 89 41 72 D
Henry Darlot Dri. NW7 15 23 92 D
Henry Dickens Ct. W11 56 23 80 B
Henry Jackson Rd. SW15 73 23 75 B
Henry Prince Estate. SW18 85 25 73 D
Henry Rd. Barn 11 26 95 B
Henry Rd. E6 50 42 83 C
1Henry Rd. N4 37 32 87 C
Henry's Ave. Wdf Gn 27 39 91 B
Henryson Rd. SE4 76 37 74 A
Henry St. Brom 99 40 69 B
Henry's Wlk. Ilf 28 44 91 D
Hensford Gdns. SE26 87 34 71 B
Henshall St. N1 48 32 84 B
Henshawe Rd. Dag 41 47 86 D
Henshaw St. SE17 63 32 78 B
Henslowe Rd. SE22 75 34 74 A
Henson Ave. NW2 46 23 85 C
Henson Cl. Orp 108 43 65 B
Henson Path. Har 21 17 89 B
Henson Pl. Nthlt 43 11 83 A
Henstridge Pl. NW8 47 27 83 C
*Henty Cl. SW11 74 27 76 A
Henty Wlk. SW15 72 22 74 B
Henville Rd. Brom 99 40 69 B
Henwick Rd. SE9 77 42 75 A
Henwood Rd. SE16 64 35 79 C
Henwood Side. Wdf Gn 27 42 91 B
Hepburn Gdns. Brom 107 39 66 D
Hepple Cl. Islw 71 16 76 D
Hepplestone Cl. SW15 72 22 74 D
Hepscott Rd. E9 49 37 84 C
Hepworth Gdns. Bark 51 46 85 C
Hepworth Rd. SW16 96 30 70 C
Heracles Cl. Wall 111 30 63 C
Herald St. E2 57 34 82 D
Herbal Hill. EC1 3 31 82 C
Herbert Cres. SW1 5 27 79 D
Herbert Gdns. NW10 45 22 83 D
Herbert Gdns. Rom 41 47 87 B
Herbert Gdns. W4 61 19 77 B
Herbert Pl. SE18 66 43 77 B
Herbert Rd. Bexh 79 48 76 C
Herbert Rd. Brom 107 42 67 A
Herbert Rd. E12 50 42 85 A
Herbert Rd. E17 38 36 87 B
Herbert Rd. Horn 42 54 87 B
Herbert Rd. Ilf 40 45 86 A
Herbert Rd. King 93 18 68 B
Herbert Rd. N11 24 30 91 C
Herbert Rd. N15 37 33 88 B
Herbert Rd. NW9 34 22 88 C
Herbert Rd. SE18 66 43 77 B
Herbert Rd. Sthl 53 12 80 D
Herbert Rd. SW19 95 24 70 D
Herbert St. E13 50 40 83 C
Herbert St. NW3 47 28 84 A
Herbrand St. WC1 3 30 82 C
Hercules Pl. N7 36 30 86 C
Hercules Rd. SE1 7 31 79 C
Hercules St. N7 36 30 86 C
Hercules Yd. N7 36 30 86 C
Hereford Ave. Barn 16 27 94 D
Hereford Gdns. Ilf 39 42 87 A
Hereford Gdns. Pnr 32 12 88 A
Hereford Gdns. Twick 82 14 73 C
Hereford Mews. W2 56 25 81 C
Hereford Pl. SE14 64 36 77 D
Hereford Rd. E11 39 40 88 B
Hereford Rd. Felt 82 11 73 C
Hereford Rd. W2 56 25 81 C
Hereford Rd. W3 55 20 80 A
Hereford Rd. W5 60 17 79 C
Hereford Sq. SW7 62 26 78 A
Hereford St. E2 57 34 82 C
Herent Dri. Ilf 27 42 89 B
Hereward Ave. Pur 112 31 62 C
Hereward Gdns. N13 17 31 92 C
Hereward Rd. SW17 86 27 71 B
Herga Ct. Har 33 15 86 A
Herga Rd. Har 21 15 89 D
Heriot Ave. E4 18 37 93 A
Heriot Rd. NW4 35 23 88 A
Herlwyn Ave. Ruis 31 09 86 C
Herlwyn Gdns. SW17 86 27 71 B
Hermes St. N1 48 31 83 C
Hermes Way. Wall 111 29 63 D
Hermiston Ave. N8 36 30 88 A
Hermitage Cl. E18 27 39 89 D
Hermitage Cl. Enf 13 31 97 D
Hermitage Cl. Shep 91 07 68 C
Hermitage Ct. E18 27 40 89 C
Hermitage Ct. NW2 35 25 86 C
Hermitage Gdns. NW2 35 25 86 C
Hermitage Gdns. SE19 97 32 70 C
Hermitage La. Croy 105 34 66 A
Hermitage La. N18 17 32 92 D
Hermitage La. NW2 35 25 86 C
Hermitage La. SW16 96 30 70 D
Hermitage Rd. N15 37 32 88 B
Hermitage Rd. N4 37 32 88 C
Hermitage Rd. SE19 97 32 70 B
Hermitage The. Rich 71 18 74 A
Hermitage The. SE23 88 35 73 C
Hermitage The. SW13 72 21 76 B
Hermitage Wall. E1 57 34 80 C
Hermitage Way. Stan 21 16 90 A
Hermitage Wlk. E18 27 39 89 D
Hermit Pl. NW6 46 25 83 B
Hermit Rd. E16 58 39 82 D
Hermit St. EC1 3 31 82 B
Hermon Hill. E11 27 40 89 C
Hermon Hill. E18 27 40 89 B
Herndon Rd. SW18 73 26 74 A
Herne Cl. NW10 45 20 85 D
Herne Hill Rd. SE24 75 32 75 C
Herne Hill. SE24 75 32 74 A
Herne Mews. N18 17 34 92 A
Herne Pl. SE24 75 31 74 B
Herne Rd. Surb 101 18 65 A
Heron Cl. E17 26 36 90 D
Heron Cl. NW10 45 21 84 A
Heron Cres. Sid 90 45 71 A
Heron Ct. Brom 99 41 68 C
Heron Ct. Rich 71 17 74 B
Herondale Ave. SW18 85 26 73 D
Herongate Rd. E12 39 41 86 A
Heron Hill. Belv 67 48 78 B
Heron Mews. Ilf 40 43 86 B
Heron Rd. Croy 105 33 65 A
Heron Rd. SE24 75 32 75 C
Heron Rd. Twick 71 16 75 C
Heronsforde. W13 54 17 81 C
Herons Rise. Barn 12 27 96 C
Herrick Rd. N5 37 32 86 C
Herrick St. SW1 70 29 78 B
Herries St. W10 46 24 83 C
Herringham Rd. SE7 65 41 79 C
Herring St. SE5 63 33 77 A
Herrongate Cl. Enf 13 33 97 D
Hersant Cl. NW10 45 22 83 A
Herschell Rd. SE23 88 36 73 A
Hersham Cl. SW15 84 22 73 A
Hertford Ave. SW14 72 21 75 C
Hertford Cl. Barn 11 26 96 B
Hertford Ct. N13 17 31 93 C
Hertford Pl. W1 2 29 82 C
Hertford Rd. Bark 51 43 84 D
Hertford Rd. Barn 11 26 96 B
Hertford Rd. Enf 14 35 97 C
Hertford Rd. Ilf 40 45 88 C
Hertford Rd. N1 48 33 84 C
Hertford Rd. N2 24 27 89 A
Hertford Rd. N9 17 34 94 D
Hertford St. W1 6 28 80 D
Hertford Way. Mit 96 30 68 C
Hertford Wlk. Belv 67 49 78 C
Hertley Cl. SE4 76 36 74 A
Hertslet Rd. N7 47 30 85 B
Hertslet Rd. N7 36 30 86 D
Hervey Cl. N3 23 25 90 A
Hervey Park Rd. E17 26 36 89 C
Hervey Rd. SE3 77 40 76 B
Hesketh Pl. W11 56 24 80 A
Hesketh Rd. E7 39 40 86 C
Heslop Rd. SW12 86 27 73 D
Hesper Mews. SW5 62 25 78 B
Hesperus Cres. E14 64 37 78 B
Hessel Rd. W13 60 16 79 B
Hessel St. E1 57 34 81 D
Hestercombe Ave. SW6 73 24 76 A
Hester Rd. N18 17 34 92 C
Hester Rd. SW11 9 27 77 C
Heston Ave. Houn 59 12 77 C
Heston Grange. Houn 59 12 77 B
Heston Grange La. Houn 59 12 77 B
Heston Rd. Houn 59 13 77 A
Heston St. SE8 76 37 76 A
Hetherington Rd. Shep 91 08 69 C
Hetherington Rd. SW4 74 30 75 C
Hetley Rd. W12 61 22 79 B
Hevelius Cl. E10 65 39 78 D
Hever Croft. SE9 90 43 71 A
Hever Gdns. Brom 100 43 69 C
Heverham Rd. SE18 66 45 78 A
Heversham Rd. Bexh 79 49 76 A
Hewer St. W10 56 23 81 B
Hewett Rd. Dag 52 47 85 B
Hewett St. EC2 4 33 82 C
Hewish Rd. N18 17 33 92 A
Hewitt Ave. N22 25 31 90 D
Hewitt Rd. N8 37 31 88 B
Hewlett Rd. E3 49 36 83 C
Hexagon The. N6 36 27 87 D
Hexal Rd. SE6 89 39 72 C
Hexham Gdns. Islw 60 16 77 C
Hexham Rd. Barn 11 25 96 D
Hexham Rd. Mord 103 25 66 D
Hexham Rd. SE27 87 32 72 A
Heybourne Rd. N17 25 34 91 D
Heybridge Ave. SW16 96 30 70 B
Heybridge Dri. Ilf 28 44 89 B
Heybridge Way. E10 38 36 87 D
Heyford Ave. SW20 95 24 68 B
Heyford Ave. SW8 10 30 77 D
Heyford Rd. Mit 96 27 69 C
Heygate St. SE17 63 32 78 A
Heylin Sq. E3 57 36 82 B
Heynes Rd. Dag 52 47 85 A
Heysham Rd. N15 37 32 88 D
Heythorp St. SW18 85 24 72 B
Heywood Ave. NW9 22 21 90 A
Heyworth Rd. E15 50 39 85 B
Heyworth Rd. E5 48 34 85 B
Hibbert Rd. E17 38 36 87 B
Hibbert Rd. Har 21 15 90 D
Hibbert St. SW11 73 26 75 A
Hibernia Gdns. Houn 70 13 74 A
Hibernia Rd. Houn 70 13 75 C
Hichisson Rd. SE15 76 35 74 B
Hickey's Almshouses. Rich 71 18 75 D
Hickin Cl. SE7 65 41 78 B
Hickin St. E14 64 38 79 C
Hickling Rd. Ilf 51 43 85 D
Hickman Ave. E4 26 38 91 A
Hickman Rd. Rom 41 47 87 A
Hickmore Wlk. SW4 74 29 75 A
Hicks Ave. Grnf 54 15 82 A
Hicks Cl. SW11 74 27 75 A
Hicks St. SE8 64 36 78 C
Hidcote Gdns. SW20 94 22 68 B
Hide Pl. SW1 10 29 78 B
Hide Rd. Har 20 14 89 D
Hides St. N7 47 30 84 B
Higgins Wlk. Hamp 92 12 70 A
Higham Hill Rd. E17 26 36 90 C
Higham Path. E17 26 36 89 A
Higham Pl. E17 26 36 89 A
Higham Rd. N17 25 32 89 B
Higham Rd. Wdf Gn 27 40 91 A
Higham Station Ave. E4 26 37 91 B
Higham St. E17 26 36 89 A
Highbanks Cl. SE2 66 46 77 D
Highbanks Rd. Pnr 20 13 91 B
Highbarrow Rd. Croy 105 34 66 C
High Beech. S Croy 112 33 63 C
Highbridge Rd. Bark 51 43 83 B
High Bridge. SE10 64 38 78 D
Highbrook Rd. SE3 77 41 75 B
High Broom Cres. W Wick 106 37 66 B
Highbury Ave. Th Hth 97 31 69 D
Highbury Cl. N.Mal 102 20 67 A
Highbury Cl. W Wick 106 37 65 B
Highbury Cnr. N7 48 31 84 B
Highbury Cres. N5 48 31 85 D
Highbury Gdns. Ilf 40 45 86 A
Highbury Grange. N5 48 32 85 A
Highbury Gr. N5 48 31 85 D
Highbury Hill. N5 48 31 85 B
Highbury Mews. N7 48 31 84 A
Highbury New Park. N5 48 32 85 A
Highbury Park. N5 48 31 85 B
Highbury Pl. N5 48 31 84 B
Highbury Quadrant. N5 37 32 86 C
Highbury Rd. SW19 85 24 71 C
Highbury Station Rd. N1 48 31 84 A
Highbury Terrace Mews. N5 48 31 85 D
Highbury Terr. N5 48 31 85 D
Highclere Rd. N Mal 94 20 68 B
Highclere St. SE26 88 36 71 A
Highcliffe Dri. SW15 72 21 74 D
Highcliffe Gdns. Ilf 39 42 88 A
Highcombe Cl. SE9 89 42 73 C
Highcombe. SE7 65 40 77 B
Highcroft Ave. Wem 45 19 83 A
Highcroft Gdns. NW11 35 24 88 D
Highcroft. NW9 34 21 88 A
Highcroft Rd. N19 36 30 87 A
High Cross Rd. N17 25 34 89 A
Highcross Way. SW15 84 22 73 C
Highdaun Dr. SW16 96 30 68 D
Highdown Rd. SW15 72 22 74 D
Highdown. Wor Pk 102 21 65 B
High Dri. N Mal 94 20 69 C
High Elms Cl. Nthwd 19 08 91 B
Highfield Ave. Eri 67 49 77 B
Highfield Ave. Grnf 44 15 85 C
Highfield Ave. NW11 35 24 87 A
Highfield Ave. NW9 34 20 88 A
High'field Ave. Pnr 32 12 88 B
Highfield Ave. Wem 33 18 86 D
Highfield Cl. Nthwd 19 09 90 A
Highfield Cl. NW9 34 20 88 A
Highfield Cl. Rom 29 50 91 A
Highfield Cl. Surb 101 17 66 C
Highfield Cres. Horn 42 54 86 B
Highfield Cres. Nthwd 19 09 90 A
Highfield Ct. N14 12 29 95 C
Highfield Dri. Brom 99 39 68 D
Highfield Dri. Eps 109 21 63 B
Highfield Dri. W Wick 106 38 65 C
Highfield. Felt 81 10 73 C
Highfield Gdns. NW11 35 24 88 C
Highfield Hill. SE19 97 33 70 C
Highfield Link. Rom 29 50 91 B
Highfield Rd. Bexh 79 48 74 B
Highfield Rd. Brom 99 42 68 D
Highfield Rd. Chis 100 45 68 B
Highfield Rd. Dart 80 53 74 D
Highfield Rd. Felt 81 10 73 C
Highfield Rd. Horn 42 54 86 B
Highfield Rd. Islw 71 15 76 B
Highfield Rd. N21 17 31 94 D
Highfield Rd N. Dart 80 53 74 D
Highfield Rd. Nthwd 19 09 90 A
Highfield Rd. NW11 35 24 88 C
Highfield Rd. Pur 112 31 62 C
Highfield Rd. Rom 29 50 91 A
Highfield Rd. Surb 102 20 66 A
Highfield Rd. Sutt 111 27 64 C
Highfield Rd. W3 55 20 81 A
Highfield Rd. Wdf Gr 27 42 91 C
Highfields. Sutt 103 25 65 A
Highfield Way. Horn 42 54 86 B
Highgate Ave. N6 36 28 87 B
Highgate Cl. N6 36 28 87 A
Highgate High St. N6 36 28 87 D
Highgate Hill. N19 36 29 87 C
Highgate Ho. SE26 87 34 72 C
Highgate Rd. NW5 47 28 85 B
Highgate West Hill. N6 36 28 86 A
Highgrove Rd. Dag 52 47 85 A
Highgrove Way. Ruis 31 10 87 A
High Gr. SE18 78 44 76 B
High Hill Ferry. E5 37 34 87 D
High Hill Ferry. E5 38 35 87 C
High Holborn. WC1 3 30 81 B
Highland Ave. Dag 41 50 86 C
Highland Ave. W7 54 15 81 C
Highland Croft. Beck 88 37 71 D
Highland Park. Felt 81 09 71 B
Highland Rd. Bexh 79 49 75 C
Highland Rd. Brom 99 39 69 B
Highland Rd. Nthwd 19 10 90 C
Highland Rd. SE19 97 33 70 A
Highlands Ave. W3 55 20 80 A
Highlands Cl. Houn 70 13 76 B
Highlands Ct. SE19 97 33 70 A
Highlands Gdns. Ilf 39 42 87 D
Highlands Heath. SW15 85 23 73 A
Highlands Rd. Barn 11 25 95 A
Highlands Rd. Orp 108 46 66 B
Highlands The. Edg 22 19 90 D
High La. W7 53 14 81 D
Highlea Cl. NW9 22 21 90 A
High Level Dri. SE26 87 34 71 A
Highlever Rd. W10 56 23 81 A
Highmead Cres. Wem 44 18 84 D
High Mead. Har 33 15 88 B
High Meadow Cl. Pnr 20 11 89 C
High Meadow Cres. NW9 34 20 88 B
Highmead. SE18 66 45 77 D
High Mead. W.Wick 107 39 65 A
Highmore Rd. SE3 65 39 77 C
High Mount. NW4 34 22 88 C
High Park Ave. Rich 72 19 76 A
High Park Rd. Rich 72 19 76 A
High Path. SW19 95 26 69 A
Highpoint. N6 36 28 87 A
High Point. SE9 90 43 72 D
High Rd. E10 38 37 88 D
High Rd. E18 27 40 90 A
High Rd. Har 21 15 90 A
High Rd. Ilf 40 45 86 A
High Rd. N11 16 28 92 D
High Rd. N12 23 26 91 A
High Rd. N15 37 33 88 B
High Rd. N17 25 33 90 D
High Rd. N22 24 30 90 B
High Rd. N22 25 31 89 A
High Rd. N2 24 27 89 C
High Rd. N8 24 30 89 C
High Rd. NW10 45 22 84 A
High Rd. Rom 41 47 87 B
High Rd. Wem 44 18 85 C
High Road Eastcote. Pnr 31 10 88 B
High Road Ickenham. Uxb 31 08 88 A
High Road Leyton. E10 38 37 87 D
High Road Leyton. E15 49 38 85 A
High Road Leytonstone. E11 39 39 86 A
High Road Woodford Green. Wdf
Wdf Gn 27 39 91 B
Highshore Rd. SE15 75 34 76 C
High St. Barn 11 24 96 A
High St. Beck 98 37 69 C
High St. Brent 60 18 77 A
High St. Brom 99 40 69 C
High St. Cars 111 28 64 A
High St. Croy 105 32 65 C
High St. Dart 80 54 74 C
High St. E11 39 40 88 A
High St. E13 50 40 83 C
High St. E15 49 38 83 A
High St. E17 38 36 88 B
High St. E17 26 37 89 C
Highstead Cres. Eri 68 51 77 C
High St. Edg 22 19 91 A
High St. E Mol 92 13 68 C
High St. Enf 14 35 95 A
High St. Eps 109 22 62 A
High St. Felt 81 10 72 A
High St. Hamp 92 14 70 C
High St. Har 33 15 87 C
High St. Har 21 15 89 A
High St. Hay 69 08 76 B
High St. Horn 42 54 87 C
High St. Houn 69 10 76 A
High St. Houn 70 13 75 B
High St. Ilf 28 44 90 C
High St. King 93 17 68 B
High St. King 93 17 69 B
High St Mews. SW19 85 24 71 C
High St. N14 16 29 93 B
High St. N8 24 30 89 C
High St N. E12 50 42 84 A
High St N. E6 50 42 83 A
High St. N Mal 94 21 68 C
High St. Nthwd 19 09 90 B
Highstone Ave. E11 39 40 88 C



High St. Orp 108 46 66 C
High St. Pnr 20 12 89 A
High Street Colliers Wood. SW19 96 27 70 A
High Street Colliers Wood. SW1 95 26 70 D
High Street Harlesden. NW10 45 21 83 D
High St. Rom 42 51 88 A
High St. Ruis 31 09 87 C
High St. SE20 98 35 70 C
High St. SE25 97 34 68 C
High St. SE25 97 34 68 C
High St S. E6 50 42 83 D
High St. Sid 90 46 71 A
High St. Sthl 53 12 80 D
High St. Surb 101 16 67 C
High St. Sutt 110 24 63 A
High St. Sutt 110 25 64 B
High St. SW19 85 23 71 D
High St. Tedd 83 16 71 C
High St. Th Hth 97 32 68 D
High St. Twick 82 14 73 A
High St. W3 55 20 80 C
High St. W5 54 17 80 B
High St. Wem 44 18 85 B
High St. W Wick 106 37 66 D
High Timber St. EC4 8 32 80 A
High Trees. Barn 12 27 95 A
High Trees. Croy 106 36 66 C
Hightrees Ct. W7 54 15 80 A
High Trees. SW2 87 31 73 C
High View Ave. Wall 111 30 64 D
High View Cl. SE19 97 33 69 D
High View Ct. Har 21 15 91 C
Highview Gdns. N11 16 29 92 C
Highview Gdns. N3 23 24 89 A
High View. Pnr 20 11 89 A
High View Rd. E18 27 39 90 D
High View Rd. N2 24 27 90 B
High View Rd. SE19 97 32 70 B
Highview Rd. Sid 90 46 71 B
Highview Rd. W13 54 16 81 C
Highway The. E14 57 36 80 A
Highway The. E1 57 35 80 A
Highway The. Stan 21 16 91 C
Highway The. Sutt 110 26 62 A
Highwood Ave. N12 15 26 92 A
Highwood Cl. Orp 108 44 65 A
Highwood Dri. Orp 108 44 65 A
Highwood Gdns. Ilf 27 42 89 D
Highwood Rd. N19 36 30 86 C
High Worple. Har 32 12 87 D
Highworth Rd. N11 16 29 92 D
Hilary Ave. Mit 96 28 68 A
Hilary Cl. Eri 79 50 76 A
Hilary Cl. SW6 62 25 77 D
Hilary Rd. Sthl 59 13 79 C
Hilary Rd. Sthl 59 13 79 C
Hilary Rd. W12 55 21 80 B
Hilbert Rd. Sutt 103 23 65 D
Hilborough Cl. SW19 95 26 70 C
Hilborough Rd. E8 48 33 84 D
Hilda Rd. E16 58 39 82 C
Hilda Rd. E16 58 39 82 D
Hilda Rd. E6 50 41 84 D
Hildenborough Gdns. Brom 99 39 70 A
Hilden Dri. Eri 68 52 77 D
Hilden Lea Pl. Brom 99 39 69 C
Hildreth St. SW12 86 28 73 D
Hildyard Rd. SW6 62 25 77 A
Hiley Rd. NW10 56 23 82 A
Hilgrove Rd. NW6 46 26 84 C
Hiliary Gdns. Stan 21 17 90 C
Hillary Rise. Barn 11 25 96 C
Hillbeck Cl. SE15 64 35 77 C
Hillbeck Way. Grnf 43 14 83 B
Hillbrook Rd. SW17 86 28 71 A
Hill Brow. Brom 99 41 69 B
Hill Brow. Dart 80 51 74 D
Hillbrow. N Mal 94 21 68 A
Hillbrow Rd. Brom 99 39 70 A
Hillbury Ave. Har 33 16 88 B
Hillbury Rd. SW17 86 28 72 D
Hill Cl. Barn 11 23 95 A
Hill Cl. Chis 90 43 71 D
Hill Cl. Har 33 15 86 C
Hill Cl. NW11 35 25 88 C
Hill Cl. NW2 34 22 86 D
Hillcote Ave. SW16 97 31 70 C
Hillcourt Ave. N12 23 25 91 B
Hillcourt Rd. SE22 75 34 74 D
Hill Cres. Har 33 16 88 A
Hill Cres. Horn 42 53 88 C
Hill Cres. N20 15 25 93 B
Hill Cres. Surb 101 18 67 B

Hillcrest Ave. NW11 35 24 88 B
Hillcrest Ave. Pnr 20 11 89 D
Hillcrest Cl. Beck 106 36 67 D
Hillcrest Cl. SE26 87 34 71 A
Hillcrest Gdns. Esh 101 15 65 D
Hillcrest Gdns. N3 23 24 89 C
Hill Crest Gdns. NW2 34 22 86 C
Hillcrest. N21 17 31 94 B
Hillcrest. N6 36 28 87 A
Hillcrest Rd. Brom 89 40 71 A
Hillcrest Rd. E17 26 38 90 D
Hillcrest Rd. E18 27 40 90 C
Hillcrest Rd. Horn 42 52 87 A
Hillcrest Rd. Orp 108 46 65 A
Hillcrest Rd. Pur 111 30 62 D
Hillcrest Rd. W3 55 19 80 D
Hillcrest Rd. W5 54 18 81 D
Hill Crest. Sid 90 46 73 B
Hillcrest View. Beck 106 36 67 D
Hill Cres. Wor Pk 103 23 65 A
Hillcroft Ave. Pnr 32 12 88 D
Hillcroft Cres. Ruis 32 11 86 D
Hillcroft Cres. W5 54 18 81 C
Hillcroft Cres. Wem 44 18 85 B
Hillcroome Rd. Sutt 110 26 63 B
Hillcross Ave. Mord 103 24 67 A
Hill Ct. Rom 30 51 89 D
Hill Ct. W5 54 18 82 D
Hilldale Rd. Sutt 110 24 64 B
Hilldene Ave. Rom 30 53 91 A
Hilldown Rd. Brom 107 39 66 D
Hilldown Rd. SW16 96 30 70 D
Hill Dri. NW9 34 20 87 C
Hilldrop Cres. N7 47 29 85 D
Hilldrop Estate. N7 47 29 85 D
Hilldrop La. N7 47 29 85 D
Hilldrop Rd. Brom 99 40 70 B
Hilldrop Rd. N7 47 29 85 D
Hill Dr. SW16 96 30 68 B
Hill End. Orp 108 45 65 B
Hill End. SE18 78 43 76 A
Hillersdon Ave. SW13 72 22 76 C
Hillery Cl. SE17 63 32 78 B
Hill Farm Rd. W10 56 23 81 B
Hillfield Ave. Mord 104 27 67 A
Hillfield Ave. N8 24 30 89 D
Hillfield Ave. NW9 22 21 89 D
Hillfield Ave. Wem 44 18 84 D
Hillfield Cl. Har 20 14 89 C
Hillfield Ct. NW3 47 27 85 C
Hillfield Park Mews. N10 24 28 89 D
Hillfield Park. N10 24 28 89 D
Hillfield Park. N21 17 31 93 A
Hill Field Rd. Hamp 92 12 69 B
Hillfield Rd. NW6 46 24 85 D
Hillfoot Ave. Rom 29 50 90 A
Hillfoot Rd. Rom 29 50 90 A
Hillgate Pl. W8 56 25 80 C
Hillgate St. W8 56 25 80 C
Hill Gr. Rom 30 51 89 A
Hill House Ave. Stan 21 15 91 D
Hill House Cl. N21 17 31 94 A
Hill House Rd. SW16 86 30 71 D
Hilliard Rd. Nthwd 19 09 90 B
Hilliard's Ct. E1 57 35 80 C
Hillier Cl. Barn 11 25 95 D
Hillier Gdns. Croy 112 31 64 C
Hillier Rd. SW11 74 27 74 D
Hillier's La. Croy 104 30 65 C
Hillingdon Rd. Bexh 79 50 75 A
Hillingdon St. SE17 63 31 77 B
Hilngdon St. SE5 63 31 77 D
Hillington Gdns. Wdf Gn 27 41 90 D
Hill La. Ruis 31 08 87 C
Hillman Cl. Horn 30 53 89 B
Hillman St. E8 48 34 84 B
Hillmarton Rd. N7 47 30 85 C
Hillmead Dri. SW9 75 31 75 D
Hillmont Rd. Esh 101 15 65 C
Hillmore Gr. SE26 88 36 71 C
Hill Path. SW16 86 30 71 D
Hill Pl St. E14 57 37 81 C
Hill Rd. Cars 111 27 63 A
Hill Rd. Har 33 16 88 A
Hill Rd. Mit 96 28 70 D
Hill Rd. N10 24 27 90 D
Hill Rd. Nthwd 19 08 91 B
Hill Rd. NW8 46 26 83 C
Hill Rd. Pnr 32 12 88 C
Hill Rd. Sutt 110 25 64 D
Hill Rd. Wem 33 16 86 D
Hillreach. SE18 65 42 78 D
Hill Rise. Esh 101 16 65 B
Hill Rise. Grnf 43 14 83 A
Hillrise Mansions. N19 36 30 87 A
Hill Rise. N9 13 34 95 D
Hill Rise. NW11 23 25 89 D
Hillrise Rd. N19 36 30 87 A
Hillrise Rd. Rom 29 50 91 A
Hill Rise. Rich 71 17 74 B
Hill Rise. Ruis 31 08 87 D
Hill Rise. SE23 87 34 73 D
Hillsboro Rd. SE22 75 33 74 A
Hillside. NW10 45 20 83 A
Hillside Ave. N11 24 27 91 B
Hillside Ave. Wdf Gn 27 41 91 A
Hillside Ave. Wem 44 18 85 B
Hill Side. Barn 11 26 95 A
Hillside Cl. Mord 95 24 68 C
Hillside Cl. NW6 46 25 83 D
Hillside Cres. Har 32 14 87 C
Hillside Cres. Nthwd 19 10 90 A
Hillside Dri. Edg 22 19 91 A
Hillside. Eri 67 50 78 A
Hillside Gdns. Barn 11 24 96 C
Hillside Gdns. E17 26 38 89 B
Hillside Gdns. Har 33 18 87 A
Hillside Gdns. N6 36 28 88 D
Hillside Gdns. Nthwd 19 10 91 C
Hillside Gdns. Wall 111 29 63 C
Hillside Gr. N14 16 29 94 B
Hillside Gr. NW7 22 22 91 C
Hillside La. Brom 107 39 65 B
Hillside La. Brom 107 40 65 A
Hillside Rd. N15 22 20 89 D
Hillside Pas. SW16 86 30 72 B
Hillside Rd. Brom 99 39 68 B
Hillside Rd. Croy 112 31 64 B
Hillside Rd. Dart 80 52 74 C
Hillside Rd. Eps 110 23 62 C
Hilide Rd. N15 37 33 88 C
Hillside Rd. Nthwd 19 10 91 D
Hillside Rd. Pnr 19 10 91 D
Hillside Rd. Sthl 53 13 82 C
Hillside Rd. Sutt 110 24 63 D
Hillside Rd. SW2 87 31 72 A
Hillside Rd. W5 54 18 81 A
Hillside Rise. Nthwd 19 10 91 C
Hillside. SW19 95 23 70 B
Hill's La. Nthwd 19 09 90 A
Hillsleigh Rd. W14 56 24 80 D
Hills Pl. W1 2 29 81 C
Hill St. W1 6 28 80 D
Hillstowe St. E5 38 35 86 C
Hill St. Rich 71 17 74 B
Hilltop Gdns. Dart 80 54 74 B
Hilltop Gdns. Orp 108 45 65 A
Hill Top. Mord 103 25 67 C
Hill Top. NW11 23 25 89 D
Hilltop Rd. NW6 46 25 84 C
Hill Top. Sutt 103 24 66 B
Hill Top View. Wdf Gn 27 42 91 B
Hillview Ave. Har 33 18 88 A
Hillview Ave. Horn 42 53 88 D
Hillview Cl. Pnr 20 12 91 B
Hill View Cres. Ilf 39 42 88 D
Hillview Cres. Orp 108 45 66 D
Hill View Dri. Well 78 45 76 C
Hillview Gdns. Har 20 13 89 C
Hillview Gdns. NW4 23 23 89 D
Hill View Gdns. NW9 34 20 88 B
Hillview Rd. Chis 90 43 71 C
Hillview Rd. NW7 15 23 92 B
Hill View Rd. Orp 108 45 65 B
Hillview Rd. Pnr 20 12 91 D
Hillview Rd. Sutt 103 26 65 D
Hill View Rd. Twick 71 16 74 C
Hillview. SW20 94 22 70 D
Hillway. N6 36 28 86 A
Hillway. NW9 34 21 87 C
Hillworth Rd. SW2 87 31 73 A
Hillyard Rd. W7 54 15 81 A
Hillyard St. SW9 75 31 76 A
Hillyfield. E17 26 36 90 C
Hilly Fields Cres. SE4 76 37 75 A
Hilsea St. E5 49 35 85 A
Hilton Ave. N12 23 26 91 B
Hilversum Cres. SE22 75 33 74 A
Himley Rd. SW17 96 27 70 B
Hinchcliffe Cl. Wall 111 30 63 D
Hinchley Cl. Esh 101 15 65 D
Hinchley Dri. Esh 101 15 65 D
Hinchley Way. Esh 101 16 65 C
Hinckley Rd. SE15 75 34 75 C
Hind Cres. Eri 67 50 77 D
Hind Ct. EC4 3 31 81 C
Hinde Mews. W1 2 28 81 C
Hindes Rd. Har 33 15 88 A
Hinde St. W1 2 28 81 C
Hind Gr. E14 57 37 81 C
Hindhead Gdns. Nthlt 43 12 83 A
Hindhead Way. Wall 111 30 64 C
Hindmans Rd. SE22 75 34 74 A
Hindmarsh Cl. E1 57 34 80 A
Hindrey Rd. E5 48 34 85 D
Hindsley's Pl. SE23 88 35 72 A
Hinkler Cl. Wall 111 30 63 C
Hinkler Rd. Har 21 17 89 B
Hinksey Path. SE2 67 47 79 D
Hinstock Rd. SE18 66 44 77 A
Hinton Ave. Houn 70 11 75 D
Hinton Cl. SE9 89 42 73 C
Hinton Rd. N18 17 33 92 A
Hinton Rd. SE24 75 31 75 B
Hinton Rd. SE24 75 32 75 A
Hinton Rd. Wall 111 29 63 A
Hippodrome Mews. W11 56 24 80 A
Hippodrome Pl. W11 56 24 80 A
Hitcham Rd. E17 38 36 87 B
Hitchin Sq. E3 49 36 83 C
Hitherfield Rd. Dag 41 48 86 A
Hitherfield Rd. SW16 87 31 72 C
Hither Green La. SE13 76 38 74 D
Hitherwell Dri. Har 20 14 90 B
Hitherwood Dri. SE19 87 33 71 B
Hoadly Rd. SW16 86 29 72 B
Hobart Cl. N20 16 27 93 A
Hobart Gdns. Th Hth 97 32 68 B
Hobart Pl. Rich 83 18 73 B
Hobart Pl. SW1 6 28 79 D
Hobart Rd. Dag 52 47 85 B
Hobart Rd. Hay 53 11 82 D
Hobart Rd. Ilf 28 44 90 C
Hobart Rd. Wor Pk 102 22 65 D
Hobbayne Rd. W7 53 14 81 D
Hobbes Wlk. SW15 72 22 74 B
Hobbs Green. N2 23 26 89 A
Hobbs' Pl. N1 48 33 83 A
Hobbs Rd. SE27 87 32 71 A
Hobday St. E14 57 37 81 B
Hobill Wlk. Surb 101 18 67 D
Hoblands End. Chis 100 45 70 A
Hobsons Pl. E1 57 34 81 A
Hobury St. SW10 62 26 77 B
Hocker St. E2 4 33 82 B
Hockley Ave. E6 50 42 83 C
Hockley Dri. Rom 30 53 90 C
Hocroft Ave. NW2 35 24 86 D
Hocroft Rd. NW2 46 24 85 B
Hocroft Wlk. NW2 35 24 86 D
Hodder Dri. Grnf 44 15 83 D
Hoddesdon Rd. Belv 67 49 78 C
Hodford Rd. NW11 35 24 87 D
Hodister Cl. SE5 63 32 77 C
Hodnet Gr. SE16 64 35 78 A
Hodson Cl. Har 32 12 86 D
Hoe St. E17 26 37 89 C
Hofland Rd. W14 62 24 79 C
Hogan Way. E5 37 34 86 A
Hogarth Ave. Ashf 91 08 70 A
Hogarth Cl. E16 58 41 81 B
Hogarth Cl. W5 54 18 81 D
Hogarth Cres. Croy 105 32 66 A
Hogarth Cres. SW19 95 26 69 B
Hogarth Ct. EC3 8 33 80 A
Hogarth Ct. Houn 59 12 77 C
Hogarth Ct. SE19 87 33 71 B
Hogarth Gdns. Houn 59 13 77 C
Hogarth Hill. NW11 23 24 89 D
Hogarth La. W4 61 21 77 A
*Hogarth Pl. SW5 62 25 78 B
Hogarth Rd. Edg 22 19 90 C
Hogarth Rd. SW5 62 25 78 B
Hogarth Roundabout. W4 61 21 77 A
Hogarth Way. Hamp 92 14 69 A
Hog Hill Rd. Rom 29 49 91 C
Hogsmill Way. Eps 109 20 64 A
Holbeach Gdns. Sid 78 45 74 D
Holbeach Rd. SE6 88 37 73 B
Holbeck Row. SE15 63 34 77 C
Holbein Mews. SW1 9 28 78 C
Holbein Pl. SW1 9 28 78 A
Holberton Gdns. NW10 55 22 82 B
Holborn. EC1 3 31 81 A
Holborn Rd. E13 58 40 81 B
Holborn Row. WC2 3 30 81 B
Holbrook Cl. N19 36 28 86 B
Holbrooke Ct. N7 47 30 85 A
Holbrook La. Chis 100 44 70 D
Holbrook Rd. E15 50 39 83 D
Holbrook Way. Brom 107 42 67 B
Holbrook Way. Brom 107 42 67 D
Holburne Cl. SE3 77 41 76 A
Holburne Gdns. SE3 77 41 76 B
Holburne Rd. SE3 77 41 76 B
Holburn Viaduct. EC1 3 31 81 B
Holbutt Gdns. Dag 41 48 86 D
Holcombe Rd. Ilf 40 43 87 A
Holcombe Rd. N17 25 34 89 A
Holcombe St. W6 61 22 78 B
Holcroft Rd. E9 49 35 84 C
Holdbrook Way. Rom 30 54 90 D
Holden Ave. N12 15 25 92 D
Holden Ave. NW9 34 20 87 C
Holdenby Rd. SE4 76 36 74 A
Holdenhurst Ave. N12 23 26 91 C
Holden Rd. N12 15 25 92 B
Holden St. SW11 74 28 76 C
Holdernesse Rd. SW17 86 28 72 A
Holderness Way. SE27 87 31 71 D
Holders Hill Ave. NW4 23 23 89 B
Holders Hill Cres. NW4 23 23 90 D
Holders Hill Dri. NW4 23 23 90 D
Holders Hill Gdns. NW4 23 24 90 C
Holders Hill Rd. NW7 23 24 90 A
Holdsworth Cl. Har 32 14 88 A
Holford Pl. WC1 3 30 82 B
Holford Rd. NW3 35 26 86 C
Holford St. WC1 3 31 82 A
Holgate Ave. SW11 73 26 75 B
Holgate Gdns. Dag 52 49 84 A
Holgate Rd. Dag 52 49 85 C
Holgate St. SE7 65 41 79 D
Holland Ave. Sutt 110 25 62 A
Holland Ave. SW20 94 21 69 B
Holland Cl. Barn 15 26 94 B
Holland Cl. Brom 107 39 65 B
Holland Gdns. W14 62 24 79 C
Holland Gr. SW9 63 31 77 C
Holland Park Ave. Ilf 40 45 88 B
Holland Park Ave. W11 56 24 80 C
Holland Park Gdns. W14 62 24 79 A
Holland Park Mews. W11 56 24 80 D
Holland Park Rd. W14 62 24 79 D
Holland Park. W11 56 24 80 D
Holland Pas (off Basire St). N1 48 32 83 A
Holland Pl. W8 62 25 79 B
Holland Rd. E15 58 39 82 A
Holland Rd. E6 51 43 84 C
Holland Rd. NW10 45 22 83 D
Holland Rd. SE25 105 34 67 A
Holland Rd. W14 62 24 79 C
Holland Rd. Wem 44 17 84 B
Hollands The. Felt 82 11 71 B
Hollands The. Wor Pk 102 21 66 D
Holland St. SE1 7 31 80 D
Holland St. W8 62 25 79 A
Holland Villas Rd. W14 62 24 79 A
Holland Way. Brom 107 39 65 B
Holland Wlk. N19 36 29 87 D
Holland Wlk. W8 62 24 79 B
Hollar Rd. N16 37 33 86 D
Hollen St. W1 2 29 81 D
Holles Cl. Hamp 82 13 71 C
Holles St. W1 2 28 81 D
Hollickwood Ave. N12 24 27 91 B
Holliday Sq. SW11 73 26 75 B
Hollidge Way. Dag 52 49 84 D
Hollies Ave. Sid 90 45 73 D
Hollies Cl. Twick 83 15 72 B
Hollies Rd. W5 60 17 78 A
Hollies The. N20 15 26 94 D
Hollies The. Sid 90 46 73 C
Holligrave Rd. Brom 99 40 69 A
Hollingbourne Ave. Bexh 79 48 76 B
Hollingbourne Gdns. W13 54 16 81 D
Hollingbourne Rd. SE24 75 32 74 A
Hollingsworth Ct. Surb 101 17 66 B
Hollingsworth Rd. Croy 112 34 63 B
Hollington Cres. N Mal 102 22 67 C
Hollington Rd. N17 25 34 90 C
Hollingworth Rd. Orp 108 43 66 B
Hollman Gdns. SW16 97 31 70 B
Holloway Rd. E1 38 38 86 D
Holloway Rd. N19 36 29 86 B
Holloway Rd. N7 47 30 85 B
Holloway St. Houn 70 13 75 B
Hollowfield La. Nthlt 43 11 84 D
Hollowfield Wlk. Nthlt 43 12 84 A
Holly Ave. N2 23 25 89 B
Holly Ave. Stan 21 18 90 C
Hollybank Cl. Hamp 82 13 71 C
Holly Berry La. NW3 46 26 85 A
Hollybrake Cl. Chis 100 44 70 D
Hollybush Cl. E11 39 40 88 A
Hollybush Gdns. E2 57 34 82 B
Hollybush Hill. E11 39 39 88 B
Hollybush Hill. NW3 46 26 85 A
Holly Bush La. Hamp 92 12 70 D
Hollybush Pl. E2 57 34 82 B
Hollybush Rd. King 93 18 70 B
Hollybush St. E13 58 40 82 B
Hollybush St. E13 50 40 83 D
*Hollybush Stps. NW3 46 26 85 A
Holly Bush Vale. NW3 46 26 85 A
Holly Bush Wlk. SW9 75 31 75 D
Holly Cl. Felt 82 12 71 C
Holly Cl. NW10 45 21 84 C
Holly Cres. Beck 106 36 67 B
Holly Cres. Wdf Gr 26 38 91 D
Hollycroft Ave. NW3 35 25 86 C
Hollycroft Ave. Wem 33 18 86 B
Holly Ct. SE26 88 35 71 C
Hollydale Dri. Brom 107 42 65 D
Hollydale Rd. SE15 76 35 76 C
Hollydene. SE13 76 38 74 D
Hollydown Way. E11 38 38 86 D
Hollydown Way. E11 39 39 86 C
Holly Dri. E4 18 37 94 B
Holly Farm Rd. Sthl 59 12 78 C
Hollyfield Ave. N11 16 27 92 D
Hollyfield Rd. Surb 101 18 66 B
Holly Gr. NW9 34 20 87 A
Holly Gr. SE15 75 34 76 C
Holly Hedge Terr. SE13 76 38 74 B
Holly Hill. N21 12 30 95 D
Holly Hill. NW3 46 26 85 A
Holly Hill Rd. Belv 67 49 78 D
Holly Hill Rd. Eri 67 50 78 C
Holly Lodge Gdns. N6 36 28 86 A
Hollymead. Cars 104 27 65 D
Holly Mews. SW10 62 26 78 C
Hollymoor La. Eps 109 20 62 B
Hollymount Cl. SE10 76 38 76 A
Holly Mount. NW3 46 26 85 A
Holly Park Estate. N4 36 30 87 B
Holly Park Gdns. N3 23 25 89 A
Holly Park. N3 23 24 89 B
Holly Park. N4 36 30 87 A
Holly Park Rd. N11 16 28 92 B
Holly Park Rd. W7 54 15 80 D
Holly Rd. E11 39 39 87 B
Holly Rd. Hamp 92 14 70 A
Holly Rd. Houn 70 13 75 D
Holly Rd. Twick 83 16 73 C
Holly Rd. W4 61 20 78 B
Holly St. E8 48 33 84 D
Holly Terr. N6 36 28 87 C
Hollytree Cl. SW19 85 23 73 D
Holly Way. Mit 96 29 68 B
Hollywell Row. EC2 4 33 82 C
Holly Wlk. Enf 13 32 96 B
Holly Wlk. NW3 46 26 85 A
Holly Wlk. Rich 71 18 76 C
Hollywood Mews. SW10 62 26 77 A
Hollywood Rd. E4 18 36 92 C
Hollywood Rd. SW10 62 26 77 A
Hollywood Way. Wdf Gr 26 38 91 D
Holman Rd. Eps 109 20 64 C
Holman Rd. SW11 73 26 76 D
Holmbank Dri. Shep 91 09 68 C
Holmbridge Gdns. Enf 14 35 96 D
Holmbrook Dri. NW4 35 23 88 B
Holmbrook St. E9 49 35 85 D
Holmbury Ct. SW17 86 27 72 D
Holmbury Ct. SW19 96 27 70 C
Holmbury View. E5 37 34 87 D
Holmbush Rd. SW15 73 24 74 C
Holmcote Gdns. N5 48 32 85 C
Holmcroft Way. Brom 107 42 67 B
Holmdale Gdns. NW4 35 23 88 B
Holmdale Rd. Chis 90 44 71 C
Holmdale Rd. NW6 46 25 85 C
Holmdale Terr. N15 37 33 88 C
Holmdene Ave. Har 20 13 89 B
Holmdene Ave. NW7 22 22 91 A
Holmdene Ave. SE24 75 32 74 A
Holmdene Cl. Beck 98 38 69 C
Holmdene Ct. Brom 99 42 68 A
Holmead Rd. SW6 62 25 77 D
Holmefield House. W10 56 24 82 D
Holme Lacey Rd. SE12 77 39 74 D
Holme Rd. E6 50 42 83 A
Holmes Ave. E17 26 36 89 B
Holmes Ave. NW7 15 24 92 C
Holmesdale Ave. SW14 72 19 75 D
Holmesdale Cl. SE25 97 33 68 B
Holmesdale Rd. Bexh 79 47 76 D
Holmesdale Rd. Croy 105 32 67 B
Holmesdale Rd. N6 36 28 87 B
Holmesdale Rd. Rich 71 18 76 B
Holmesdale Rd. SE25 97 33 68 D
Holmesdale Rd. Tedd 93 17 70 A
Holmesley Rd. SE23 76 36 74 C
Holmes Rd. NW5 47 28 85 D
Holmes Rd. SW19 95 26 70 C
Holmes Rd. Twick 83 15 72 B
Holmes Terr. SE1 7 31 79 A
Holme Way. Stan 21 15 91 B
Holmewood Gdns. SW2 86 30 73 B
Holmewood Rd. SE25 97 33 68 A
Holmewood Rd. SW2 86 30 73 B
Holmfield Rd. W4 61 21 78 D
Holmhurst Rd. Belv 67 49 78 D
Holmhurst. SE13 76 38 74 D
Holmleigh Ave. Dart 80 53 74 A
Holmleigh Rd. N16 37 33 87 C
Holmsdale Gr. Bexh 80 51 75 A
Holmshaw Cl. SE26 88 36 71 A
Holmside Ct. SW12 74 28 74 C
Holmside Rd. SW12 74 28 74 C
Holmsley Cl. N.Mal 102 21 66 B
Holms St. E2 48 34 83 C
Holmstall Ave. Edg 22 20 90 C
Holm Wlk. SE3 77 40 76 C
Holmwood Cl. Har 20 14 89 A
Holmwood Cl. Nthlt 43 13 84 B
Holmwood Cl. Sutt 110 23 63 D
Holmwood Gdns. N3 23 25 90 C
Holmwood Gdns. Wall 111 28 63 B
Holmwood Rd. Eps 110 23 62 C
Holmwood Rd. Ilf 40 45 86 A
Holmwood Rd. Sutt 110 23 62 A
Holne Chase. Mord 103 25 67 C
Holne Chase. N2 35 26 88 C
Holness Rd. E15 50 39 84 B
Holroyd Rd. SW15 73 23 74 A
Holstein Way. Belv 67 48 79 C
Holsworthy Sq. WC1 3 30 82 D
Holt Cl. N10 24 28 89 C
Holton St. E1 57 35 82 D
Holt Rd. Wem 33 17 86 C
Holt The. Ilf 28 44 91 A
Holt The. Wall 111 29 64 A
Holtwhite Ave. Enf 13 32 97 C
Holtwhite's Hill. Enf 13 31 97 B
Holwell Pl. Pnr 20 12 89 C
Holwood Park Ave. Brom 107 42 65 D
Holwood Pl. SW4 74 29 75 D
Holwood Rd. Brom 99 40 69 C
Holybourne Ave. SW15 84 22 73 A
Holyhead Cl. E3 57 37 82 A
Holyoake Wlk. N2 23 26 89 A
Holyoake Wlk. W5 54 17 82 C
Holyoak Rd. SE11 63 31 78 B
Holyport Rd. SW6 62 23 77 D
Holyrood Gdns. Edg 22 19 90 D
Holyrood Ave. Har 43 12 85 B
Holyrood Rd. Barn 11 26 95 D
Holyrood St. SE1 8 33 80 C
Holywell La. EC2 4 33 82 C
Home Cl. Cars 104 27 65 B
Home Cl. Nthlt 53 12 82 B
Homecroft Rd. N22 25 32 90 A
Homecroft Rd. SE26 88 35 71 C
Home Farm Cl. Shep 91 09 68 C
Home Farm Cl. Surb 101 15 66 B
Homefarm Rd. W7 54 15 81 D
Homefield Ave. Ilf 40 45 88 A
Home Field. Barn 11 24 95 B
Homefield Cl. NW10 45 20 84 A
Homefield Gdns. Mit 95 26 69 D
Homefield Gdns. N2 23 26 89 B
Homefield Park. Sutt 110 25 63 B
Homefield Rd. Brom 99 41 69 A
Homefield Rd. Edg 22 20 91 B
Homefield Rd. SW19 85 24 71 C
Homefield Rd. Wem 44 16 85 B
Homefield Rise. Orp 108 46 66 C
Homefield St. N1 48 33 83 C
Home Gdns. Dag 41 50 86 C
Home Gdns. Dart 80 54 74 C
Homeland Dri. Sutt 110 25 62 D
Homelands Dri. SE19 97 33 70 C
Homeleigh Rd. SE15 76 35 74 B
Homemead Rd. Brom 107 42 67 B
Homemead Rd. Croy 104 29 67 C
Home Mead. Stan 21 17 90 A
Home Orchard. Dart 80 54 74 C
Home Park Rd. SW19 85 24 72 D
Home Park Wlk. King 93 17 68 D
Homer Ct. Bexh 79 50 76 A
Home Rd. SW11 74 27 76 C
Homer Rd. Croy 106 35 67 D
Homer Rd. E9 49 36 84 A
Homer Row. W1 1 27 81 A
Homersham Rd. King 94 19 69 C
Homer St. W1 1 27 81 A
Homerton Gr. E9 49 35 85 D
Homerton High St. E9 49 35 85 D

Homerton Rd. E9 49 36 85 D
Homerton Row. E9 49 35 85 C
Homerton Terr. E9 49 35 84 A
Homesdale Rd. Brom 99 41 68 A
Homesdale Rd. Orp 108 45 66 A
Homesfield. NW11 35 25 88 A
Homesfield. NW11 23 25 89 C
Homestall Rd. SE22 76 35 74 A
Homestead Paddock. N14 12 28 95 B
Homestead Park. NW2 34 21 86 D
Homestead Rd. Dag 41 48 86 B
Homestead Rd. SW6 62 24 77 D
Homestead The. Dart 80 53 74 C
Homestead The. N11 16 28 92 B
Homewaters Ave. Sun 91 09 69 B
Homewood Cl. Hamp 92 12 70 B
Homewood Cres. Chis 100 45 70 A
Homfield Ave. NW4 35 23 88 B
Homildon Ho. SE26 87 34 72 C
Homington Ct. King 93 18 70 C
Honeybourne Rd. NW6 46 25 85 D
Honeybourne Way. Orp 108 44 66 D
Honeybrook Rd. SW12 86 29 73 A
Honey La. EC2 4 32 81 C
Honeypot Cl. NW9 21 18 89 D
Honeypot La. NW9 21 18 89 D
Honeypot La. Stan 21 18 90 C
Honeysett Rd. N17 25 33 90 D
Honeysuckle Cl. Rom 30 53 91 B
Honeywell Rd. SW11 74 27 74 D
Honeywood Rd. Islw 71 16 75 C
Honeywood Rd. NW10 45 21 83 D
Honeywood Wlk. Cars 111 27 64 B
Honister Cl. Stan 21 16 90 B
Honister Gdns. Stan 21 16 90 B
Honister Pl. Stan 21 16 90 B
Honiton Rd. NW6 46 24 83 D
Honiton Rd. Rom 41 50 88 D
Honiton Rd. Well 78 45 76 D
Honley Rd. SE6 88 38 73 A
Honor Oak Park. SE23 76 35 74 D
Honor Oak Rd. SE23 88 35 73 A
Honor Oak Rise. SE23 76 35 74 C
Hood Ave. N14 12 28 95 D
Hood Ave. Orp 108 46 67 B
Hood Ave. SW14 72 20 74 A
Hood Cl. Croy 105 31 66 D
Hoodcote Gdns. N21 17 31 94 B
Hood Rd. SW20 94 21 70 D
Hood Wlk. Rom 29 49 90 B
Hooke Ct. SE10 76 38 76 A
Hooker's Rd. E17 26 35 89 B
Hook Farm Rd. Brom 107 41 67 B
Hookham Ct. SW8 74 29 76 B
Hook Hill. S Croy 112 33 62 C
Hooking Green. Har 32 13 88 B
Hook La. Well 78 45 75 D
Hook Rd. Chess 101 18 65 C
Hook Rd. Eps 109 20 62 A
Hook Rd. Surb 101 18 65 A
Hook Rise N. Surb 101 18 65 C
Hook Rise N. Surb 102 19 65 C
Hook Rise S. Surb 101 18 65 D
Hook Rise S. Surb 102 19 65 C
Hooks Cl. SE15 75 34 76 B
Hooks Hall Dri. Dag 41 50 86 C
Hook The. Barn 11 26 95 D
Hook Underpass. Surb 101 18 65 C
Hook Wlk. Edg 22 20 91 A
Hooper Rd. E16 58 40 81 C
Hooper's Ct. SW3 5 27 79 B
Hooper's Mews. W3 55 20 80 C
Hooper St. E1 57 34 81 C
Hoop La. NW11 35 25 87 A
Hope Cl. SE12 89 40 72 D
Hope Cl. Wdf Gn 27 41 91 A
Hopedale Rd. SE7 65 40 77 B
Hopefield Ave. NW6 46 24 83 C
Hope Park. Brom 99 39 70 D
Hope St. SW11 73 26 75 B
Hopetown St. E1 4 33 81 B
Hopewell St. SE5 63 32 77 D
Hop Gdns. WC2 7 30 80 A
Hopgood St. W12 56 23 80 C
Hopkins St. W1 2 29 81 D
Hoppers Rd. N21 17 31 94 C
Hopping La. N1 48 31 84 B
Hoppingwood Ave. N Mal 94 21 68 A
Hopton Gdns. N.Mal 102 22 67 C
Hopton Rd. SW16 86 30 71 C
Hopton St. SE1 7 31 80 D
Hopwood Rd. SE17 63 32 77 B
Hopwood Wlk. E8 48 34 84 C
Horace Ave. Rom 41 50 87 D
Horace Rd. E7 50 40 85 B
Horace Rd. Ilf 28 44 89 A
Horace Rd. King 93 18 68 B
Horatio St. E2 48 34 83 C
Horatius Way. Croy 111 30 64 D
Horbury Cres. W11 56 25 80 A
Horbury Mews. W11 56 24 80 B
Horder Rd. SW6 73 24 76 A
Hordle Promenade E (off Garnies Cl). SE15 63 33 77 D
Hordle Promenade N. SE15 63 33 77 D
Hordle Promenade S. SE15 63 33 77 D
Hordle Promenade W (off Blake's Rd). SE15 63 33 77 C
Horle Wlk. SW9 75 31 76 D
Horley Cl. Bexh 79 49 74 A
Horley Rd. SE9 89 42 71 A
Hormead Rd. W9 56 24 82 D
Hornbeam Cres. Brent 60 16 77 D
Hornbeam La. Bexh 79 50 76 C
Hornbeam Rd. Hay 53 11 81 A
Hornbeam Way. Brom 108 43 67 C
Hornbeam Wlk. Rich 83 18 72 D
Hornbuckle Cl. Har 32 14 86 B
Hornby Cl. NW3 46 26 84 D
Horncastle Cl. SE12 89 40 73 A
Horncastle Rd. SE12 89 40 73 A
Hornchurch Rd. Horn 42 52 87 D
Horndean Cl. SW15 84 22 73 C
Horndon Cl. Rom 29 50 90 A
Horndon Green. Rom 29 50 90 A
Horndon Rd. Rom 29 50 90 A
Horne Rd. Shep 91 07 68 C
Horne Way. SW6 73 23 76 C
Hornfair Rd. SE7 65 41 77 D
Hornford Way. Rom 42 51 87 A
Horniman Dri. SE23 88 35 73 A
Horning Cl. SE9 89 42 71 A
Horn La. SE10 65 40 78 A
Horn La. W3 55 20 81 C
Horn La. Wdf Gn 27 40 91 C
Horn Park Cl. SE12 77 40 74 B
Hornpark La. SE12 77 40 74 D
Hornsey La. N6 36 29 87 C
Hornsey Lane Estate. N19 36 29 87 B
Hornsey Lane Gdns. N6 36 29 87 A
Hornsey Park Rd. N8 24 30 89 B
Hornsey Rd. N19 36 30 86 A
Hornsey Rd. N7 36 30 86 D
Hornsey Rise Gdns. N19 36 30 87 A
Hornsey Rise. N19 36 30 87 A
Hornsey St. N7 47 30 85 D
Hornshay St. SE15 64 35 77 A
Horns Rd. Ilf 40 44 88 A
Horn Strs. SE16 57 36 80 D
Hornton Pl. W8 62 25 79 A
Hornton St. W8 62 25 79 A
Horsa Cl. Wall 111 30 63 C
Horsa Rd. Eri 67 50 77 C
Horsa Rd. SE12 89 41 73 A
Horse and Dolphin Yd. W1 6 29 80 B
Horsecroft Cl. Orp 108 46 66 D
Horsecroft Rd. Edg 22 20 91 D
Horse Fair. King 93 17 69 D
Horseferry Pl. SE10 64 38 77 A
Horseferry Rd. SW1 10 29 78 B
Horseguards Ave. SW1 7 30 80 C
Horsell Rd. N5 48 31 85 C
Horsell Rd. Orp 100 46 69 B
Horselydown La. SE1 8 33 80 D
Horsenden Ave. Grnf 44 15 85 D
Horsenden Cres. Grnf 44 15 85 D
Horsenden Lane N. Grnf 44 15 84 D
Horsenden Lane S. Grnf 44 16 83 C
Horse Shoe Alley. SE1 8 32 80 C
Horseshoe Cl. NW2 34 22 86 B
Horse Shoe Cres. Nthlt 43 13 83 C
Horse Shoe Green. Sutt 103 25 65 B
Horseshoe La. Enf 13 32 96 A
Horseshoe La. N20 15 23 94 D
Horse Shoe Yd. W1 6 28 80 B
Horse Yd. N1 48 31 83 B
Horsfeld Gdns. SE9 77 42 74 A
Horsfeld Rd. SE9 77 41 74 B
Horsford Rd. SW2 74 30 74 B
Horsham Ave. N12 16 27 92 C
Horsham Rd. Bexh 79 49 74 B
Horsham Rd. Felt 69 08 74 C
Horsley Rd. Brom 99 40 69 B
Horsley Rd. E4 18 38 93 A
Horsley St. SE17 63 32 77 B
Horsman St. SE5 63 32 77 A
Horsmonden Cl. Orp 108 45 66 B
Horsmonden Rd. SE4 76 36 74 D
Hortensia Rd. SW10 62 26 77 C
Horticultural Pl. W4 61 20 78 D
Horton Ave. NW2 46 24 85 A
Horton La. Eps 09 19 62 B
Horton Rd. E8 48 34 84 B
Horton St. SE13 76 37 75 B
Hortus Rd. E4 18 38 93 A
Hortus Rd. Sthl 59 12 79 B
Hosack Rd. SW17 86 28 72 A
Hoser Ave. SE12 89 40 72 A
Hosier La. EC1 3 31 81 B
Hoskin's Cl. E16 58 41 81 C
Hoskins St. SE10 64 38 78 D
Hospital Bridge Rd. Twick 82 13 73 D
Hospital La. Islw 71 15 74 B
Hospital Rd. Houn 70 13 75 A
Hotham Cl. E Mol 92 13 68 A
Hotham Rd. SW15 73 23 75 A
Hotham St. E15 50 39 83 A
Hothfield Pl. SE16 64 35 79 C
Hotspur Rd. Nthlt 43 13 83 C
Hotspur St. SE11 63 31 78 C
Houblon Rd. Rich 71 18 74 A
Houduras St. EC1 4 32 82 C
Houghton Cl (off Buttermere Wlk). E8 48 33 84 B
Houghton Cl (off Buttermere Wlk). E8 48 33 84 B
Houghton Cl. E8 48 33 84 B
Houghton Cl. Hamp 92 12 70 A
Houghton Rd. N15 25 33 89 D
Houghton St. WC2 3 30 81 D
Houlder Cres. Croy 112 31 64 D
Houndsditch. EC3 4 33 81 C
Houndsfield Rd. N9 17 34 94 B
Hounsden Rd. N21 13 31 95 C
Hounslow Ave. Houn 70 13 74 B
Hounslow Gdns. Houn 70 13 74 B
Hounslow Rd. Felt 81 10 73 B
Hounslow Rd. Felt 82 12 72 A
Hounslow Rd. Twick 70 14 74 C
Housman Way. SE5 63 32 77 D
Houston Rd. SE23 88 36 72 C
Hove Ave. E17 38 36 88 B
Hoveden Rd. NW2 46 24 85 C
Hove Gdns. Sutt 103 25 66 D
Howard Ave. Eps 109 22 62 C
Howard Cl. Ashf 91 09 70 B
Howard Cl. Hamp 92 14 70 C
Howard Cl. N11 16 28 93 A
Howard Cl. NW2 46 24 85 A
Howard Cl. W3 55 19 81 D
Howard Mews. N5 48 31 85 B
Howard Pl. SW1 6 29 79 C
Howard Rd. Bark 51 44 83 B
Howard Rd. Brom 99 40 70 C
Howard Rd. E11 39 39 86 C
Howard Rd. E17 26 37 89 B
Howard Rd. E6 50 42 83 D
Howard Rd. Ilf 51 43 85 B
Howard Rd. Islw 71 15 75 B
Howard Rd. N15 37 33 88 C
Howard Rd. N16 48 33 85 A
Howard Rd. N Mal 94 21 68 D
Howard Rd. NW2 46 23 85 B
Howard Rd. SE20 98 35 69 A
Howard Rd. SE25 105 34 67 C
Howard Rd. Sthl 53 13 81 D
Howard Rd. Surb 101 18 67 D
Howards Cl. Pnr 19 10 90 D
Howard's La. SW15 73 23 75 C
Howard's Rd. E13 58 40 82 A
Howard St. Surb 101 16 66 B
Howard Wlk. N2 23 26 89 D
Howarth Rd. SE2 66 46 78 B
Howberry Cl. Edg 21 17 91 B
Howberry Rd. Edg 21 17 91 B
Howberry Rd. Stan 21 17 91 B
Howberry Rd. Th Hth 97 32 69 D
Howbury La. Eri 80 52 76 C
Howbury Rd. SE15 76 35 75 A
Howcroft Cres. N3 23 25 91 C
Howcroft La. Grnf 53 14 82 B
Howden Ct. SE25 97 33 69 D
Howden Rd. SE25 97 33 69 D
Howden St. SE15 75 34 75 A
Howe Cl. Rom 29 49 90 A
Howell Cl. Rom 41 47 88 B
Howell Hill Gr. Eps 110 23 62 C
Howfield Pl. N17 25 33 89 B
Howgate Rd. SW14 72 20 75 B
Howick Pl. SW1 6 29 79 C
Howie St. SW11 9 27 77 C
Howitt Rd. NW3 47 27 84 A
Howland Mews E. W1 2 29 81 A
Howland St. W1 2 29 81 A
Howletts La. Ruis 31 06 88 C
Howletts Rd. SE24 75 32 74 C
Howley Pl. W2 1 26 81 A
Howley Rd. Croy 105 31 65 D
Howsman Rd. SW13 61 22 77 A
Howson Rd. SE4 76 36 75 C
How's St. E2 48 33 83 D
Hoxton Market. N1 4 33 82 A
Hoxton Sq. N1 4 33 82 A
Hoxton St. N1 48 33 83 C
Hoylake Cres. Uxb 31 07 86 B
Hoylake Gdns. Mit 96 29 68 A
Hoylake Gdns. Ruis 31 10 86 D
Hoylake Rd. W3 55 21 81 C
Hoyle Rd. SW17 86 27 71 C
Hoy St. E16 58 39 81 D
Hubbard Rd. SE27 87 32 71 A
Hubbard St. E15 50 39 83 A
Hubert Gr. SW9 74 30 75 A
Hubert Rd. E6 58 41 82 B
Hucknall Cl. Rom 30 54 91 B
Huddart St. E3 57 36 81 B
Huddlestone Rd. E7 50 39 85 B
Huddlestone Rd. NW2 45 22 84 B
Huddleston Rd. N7 47 29 85 B
Hudson Pl. SE18 66 44 78 C
Hudson Rd. Bexh 79 48 76 D
Hudson Rd. King 93 18 69 A
Hudson's Pl. SW1 10 29 78 A
Huggin Ct. EC4 8 32 80 A
Huggin Hill. EC4 8 32 80 A
Hughan Rd. E15 50 39 85 C
Hughenden Ave. Har 33 16 88 B
Hughenden Gdns. Nthlt 53 11 82 A
Hughenden Rd. Wor Pk 102 22 66 B
Hughes Mansions. E1 57 34 82 C
Hughes Rd. Ashf 91 08 70 A
Hughes Wlk. Croy 105 32 66 A
Hugh Mews. SW1 9 28 78 B
Hugh Pl. SW1 10 29 78 B
Hugh St. SW1 9 28 78 B
Hugon Rd. SW6 73 25 75 B
Hugo Rd. N19 47 29 85 A
Huguenot Pl. SW18 73 26 74 A
Huguenot Sq. SE15 75 34 75 B
Huitt Sq. SW11 73 26 75 B
Hullbridge Mews. N1 48 32 83 A
Hull St. EC1 4 32 82 A
Hulme Pl. SE1 8 32 79 A
Hulse Ave. Bark 51 45 84 A
Hulse Ave. Rom 29 49 90 B
Hulverston Cl. Sutt 110 25 62 B
Humber Rd. NW2 34 22 86 B
Humber Rd. SE3 65 39 77 B
Humberstone Rd. E13 58 41 82 A
Humberton Cl. E9 49 36 85 C
Humbolt Rd. W6 62 24 77 A
Humes Ave. W7 60 15 79 B
Hume Way. Ruis 31 10 88 C
Humphrey St. SE1 63 33 78 D
Humphries Cl. Dag 52 48 85 B
Hundred Acre. NW9 22 21 90 D
Hungerdown. E4 18 38 94 C
Hungerford Bridge (foot). WC2 7 30 80 D
Hungerford La. WC2 7 30 80 C
Hungerford Rd. N7 47 30 85 C
Hungerford St. E1 57 34 81 D
Hunsdon Cl. Dag 52 48 84 A
Hunsdon Rd. SE14 64 35 77 D
Hunslett St. E2 49 35 83 B
Hunston Rd. Mord 103 25 66 D
Hunter Cl. SE1 8 32 79 D
Hunter Rd. Ilf 51 43 85 B
Hunter Rd. SW20 95 23 69 A
Hunter Rd. Th Hth 97 32 69 A
Hunters Cl. SW12 86 28 73 C
Hunters Ct. Rich 71 17 74 B
Hunters Gr. Har 21 17 89 C
Hunters Hall Rd. Dag 52 49 85 D
Hunters Hill. Ruis 32 11 86 D
Hunters Meadow. SE19 87 33 71 A
Hunter Sq. Dag 52 49 85 A
Hunters Rd. Chess 101 18 65 C
Hunter St. WC1 3 30 82 C
Hunters Way. Croy 112 33 64 A
Hunters Way. Enf 13 31 97 A
Hunter Wlk. E13 50 40 83 C
Huntingdon Cl. Mit 96 30 68 A
Huntingdon Gdns. Wor Pk 103 23 65 C
Huntingdon Rd. N2 24 27 89 A
Huntingdon Rd. N9 18 35 94 C
Huntingdon St. E16 58 39 80 B
Huntingdon St. N1 47 30 84 D
Huntingfield Rd. SW15 72 22 74 A
Huntings Rd. Dag 52 49 84 A
Huntley Dri. N3 23 25 91 A
Huntley St. WC1 2 29 82 D
Huntley Way. SW20 94 22 69 C
Huntly Rd. SE25 97 33 68 C
Hunton St. E1 57 34 82 C
Hunt Rd. Sthl 59 13 79 C
Hunts Cl. SE3 77 40 76 C
Hunt's Ct. WC2 6 29 80 B
Hunt's La. E15 49 38 83 C
Huntsman Rd. Ilf 28 46 91 A
Huntsman St. SE17 63 33 78 A
Hunts Mead Cl. Chis 99 42 70 D
Hunts Mead. Enf 14 35 96 B
Huntsmoor Rd. Eps 109 20 64 D
Huntspill St. SW17 85 26 72 C
Hunts Slip Rd. SE21 87 33 72 A
Hunt St. W11 56 23 80 D
Huntsworth Mews. NW1 1 27 82 D
Huntsworth Mews. NW1 1 27 82 D
Hurley Rd. Grnf 53 13 81 B
Hurlingham Ct. SW6 73 24 75 B
Hurlingham Gdns. SW6 73 24 75 B
Hurlingham Rd. Bexh 67 48 77 D
Hurlingham Rd. SW6 73 24 76 D
Hurlock St. N5 37 31 86 D
Hurlstone Rd. SE25 105 33 67 A
Hurn Court Rd. Houn 70 11 76 D
Hurnford Cl. S Croy 112 33 62 C
Huron Rd. SW17 86 28 72 C
Hurren Cl. SE3 77 39 75 A
Hurry Cl. E15 50 39 84 C
Hurst Ave. E4 18 37 93 C
Hurst Ave. N6 36 29 88 C
Hurstbourne Gdns. Bark 51 45 84 A
Hurstbourne Rd. SE23 88 36 73 C
Hurst Cl. Brom 107 39 66 D
Hurst Cl. Chess 109 19 64 C
Hurst Cl. E4 18 37 93 C
Hurst Cl. Nthlt 43 12 85 D
Hurst Cl. NW11 35 25 88 D
Hurstcourt Rd. Sutt 103 25 65 B
Hurstdene Ave. Brom 107 39 66 D
Hurstdene Gdns. N16 37 33 87 A
Hurstfield. Brom 107 40 67 A
Hurstfield Rd. E Mol 92 13 68 A
Hurst La. E Mol 92 14 68 A
Hurstlands Cl. Horn 42 53 88 C
Hurst La. SE2 67 47 78 D
Hurstleigh Gdns. Ilf 28 43 90 A
Hurst Lodge. Wem 44 18 84 D
Hurst ParkE Mol 92 13 69 D
Hurst Pl. SE2 67 47 78 D
Hurst Rd. Croy 112 32 64 D
Hurst Rd. E17 26 37 89 B
Hurst Rd. E Mol 92 13 68 B
Hurst Rd. Eri 67 50 77 C
Hurst Rd. N21 17 31 94 C
Hurst Rd. Sid 90 46 72 B
Hurst Rd. Walt 92 11 68 D
Hurst Rise. Barn 11 25 96 A
Hurst St. SE24 75 31 74 D
Hurstview Grange. S Croy 112 31 63 D
Hurst View Rd. S Croy 112 33 63 C
Hurst Way. S Croy 112 33 63 A
Hurstway Walk. W11 56 23 80 B
Hurstwood Ave. Bexh 80 51 76 C
Hurstwood Ave. E18 27 40 89 D
Hurstwood Ave. Eri 80 51 76 B
Hurstwood Dri. Brom 99 42 68 B
Hurstwood Rd. NW11 23 24 89 D
Huson Cl. NW3 47 27 84 C
Husseywell Cres. Brom 107 40 66 C
Hutching's St. E14 64 37 79 A
Hutchings Wlk. NW11 23 25 89 D
Hutchins Cl. E15 49 38 84 C
Hutchinson Ct. Rom 29 47 89 D
Hutchinson Ct. Rom 29 47 89 D
Hutchinson Terr. Wem 33 17 86 D
Hutton Cl. Grnf 43 14 85 D
Hutton Cl. Wdf Gn 27 40 91 B
Hutton Gdns. Har 20 14 91 C
Hutton Gr. N12 15 25 92 D
Hutton Gr. N12 23 26 91 A
Hutton La. Har 20 14 91 D
Hutton St. EC4 3 31 81 C
Hutton Wlk. Har 20 14 91 C
Huxbear St. SE4 76 36 74 B
Huxley Cl. Nthlt 43 12 83 A
Huxley Dri. Rom 40 46 87 B
Huxley Gdns. NW10 44 18 83 D
Huxley Pl. N13 17 31 93 D
Huxley Rd. E10 38 38 86 A
Huxley Rd. N18 17 33 92 A
Huxley Rd. Well 78 45 75 B
Huxley Sayze. N18 17 32 92 D
Huxley St. W10 56 24 82 A
Hyacinth Cl. Hamp 92 13 70 A
Hyacinth Rd. SW15 84 22 73 C
Hyde Cl. Barn 11 24 96 B
Hyde Cl. E13 50 40 83 C
Hyde Cres. NW9 34 21 88 A
Hyde Estate Rd. NW9 34 21 88 B
Hydefield Cl. N21 17 32 94 D
Hydefield Ct. N9 17 33 93 A
Hyde La. SW11 74 27 76 A
Hyde Park Ave. N21 17 32 94 D
Hyde Park Cnr. SW1 6 28 79 A
Hyde Park Cres. W2 1 27 81 C
Hyde Park Gate Mews. SW7 5 26 79 A
Hyde Park Gate. SW7 5 26 79 A
Hyde Park Gate. W8 5 26 79 A
Hyde Park Gdns Mews. W2 5 27 80 A
Hyde Park Gdns. N21 17 32 94 C
Hyde Park Gdns. W2 5 27 80 A
Hyde Park Sq Mews. W2 1 27 81 C
Hyde Park Sq. W2 1 27 81 C
Hyde Park St. W2 1 27 81 C
Hyde Rd. Bexh 79 48 76 D
Hyde Rd. N1 48 33 83 A
Hyde Rd. Rich 71 18 74 B
Hydeside Gdns. N9 17 33 93 B
*Hyde's Pl. N1 48 31 84 C
Hyde St. SE8 64 37 77 A
Hyde Terr. Ashf 91 09 70 A
Hyde The. NW9 22 21 89 C
Hydethorpe Ave. N9 17 33 93 B
Hydethorpe. SW12 86 29 73 C
Hyde Vale. SE10 76 38 76 B
Hyde Way. N9 17 33 93 B
Hyde Wlk. Mord 103 25 66 A
Hyland Cl. Horn 42 52 87 B
Hylands Rd. E17 26 38 90 D
Hyland Way. Horn 42 52 87 B
Hylton St. SE18 66 45 78 B
Hyndewood. SE23 88 35 72 D
Hyndman St. SE15 63 34 77 B
Hynton Rd. Dag 41 47 86 A
Hyperion House. SW2 74 30 74 D
Hyperion Pl. Eps 109 20 62 B
Hyrstdene. S Croy 112 31 64 B
Hyson Rd. SE16 63 34 78 D
Hythe Ave. Bexh 67 48 77 D
Hythe Cl. N18 17 34 92 A
Hythe Path. Th Hth 97 32 68 B
Hythe Rd. NW10 55 22 82 C
Hythe Rd. Th Hth 97 32 69 D
Hythe St. Dart 80 54 74 C

Ian Ct. SE23 88 35 72 A
Ian Sq. Enf 14 35 97 B
Ibbotson Ave. E16 58 39 81 D
Ibbott St. E1 57 35 82 C
Iberian Ave. Wall 111 30 64 A
Ibis La. W4 72 20 76 A
Ibscott Cl. Dag 52 50 84 A
Ibsley Gdns. SW15 84 22 73 C
Ibsley Way. Barn 12 27 96 C
Iceland Rd. E3 49 37 83 A
Ickburgh Estate. E5 37 34 86 B
Ickburgh Rd. E5 37 34 86 D
Ickenham Cl. Ruis 31 08 86 B
Ickenham Rd. Ruis 31 08 87 D
Ickleton Rd. SE9 89 42 71 A
Icknield Dri. Ilf 40 43 88 B
Ickworth Park Rd. E17 26 36 89 C
Ida Rd. N15 25 32 89 D
Ida St. E14 58 38 81 C
Iden Cl. Brom 99 39 68 A
Idlecombe Rd. SW17 96 28 70 A
Idmiston Rd. E15 50 39 85 D
Idmiston Rd. SE27 87 32 72 A
Idmiston Rd. Wor Pk 102 21 66 B
Idmiston Sq. Wor Pk 102 21 66 B
Idol La. EC3 8 33 80 A
Idonia St. SE8 64 37 77 C
Iffley Rd. W6 61 22 79 D
Ifield Rd. SW10 62 25 77 B
Ightham Rd. Eri 67 49 77 C
Ilbert St. W10 56 24 82 A
Ilchester Gdns. W2 56 25 80 B
Ilchester Pl. W14 62 24 79 D
Ilchester Rd. Dag 52 47 85 C
Ildersly Gr. SE21 87 32 72 B
Ilderton Rd. SE15 64 35 77 A
Ilderton Rd. SE16 64 35 78 C
Ilex Rd. NW10 45 21 84 B
Ilex Way. SW16 87 31 71 C
Ilford Hill. Ilf 40 43 86 C
Ilford La. Ilf 40 43 86 C
Ilford La. Ilf 51 44 85 C
Ilfracombe Gdns. Rom 40 46 87 B
Ilfracombe Rd. Brom 89 39 72 D

| | | | |
|---|---|---|---|
| Iliffe St. SE17 ........63 | 31 78 D | Inner Temple La. EC4 ........3 | 31 81 C |
| Iliffe Yd. SE17 ........63 | 31 78 D | Innes Cl. SW20 ........95 | 24 69 C |
| Ilkley Cl. SE19 ........97 | 32 70 B | Innes Gdns. SW15 ........72 | 22 74 D |
| Ilkley Rd. E16 ........58 | 41 81 A | Innes Yd. Croy ........105 | 32 65 C |
| Illingworth Cl. Mit ........95 | 26 68 B | Inniskilling Rd. E13 ........50 | 41 83 C |
| Illingworth Way. Enf ........13 | 33 95 A | Inskip Cl. E10 ........38 | 37 86 B |
| Ilmington Rd. Har ........33 | 17 88 D | Inskip Dri. Horn ........42 | 54 87 C |
| Ilminster Gdns. SW11 ........74 | 27 75 C | Inskip Rd. Dag ........41 | 47 87 D |
| Imber Cl. N14 ........16 | 29 94 A | Institute Pl. E8 ........48 | 34 85 D |
| Imber Cross. E Mol ........101 | 15 67 D | Instone Cl. Wall ........111 | 30 63 C |
| Imber St. N1 ........48 | 32 83 B | Insurance St. WC1 ........3 | 31 82 A |
| Impact Cl. SE20 ........97 | 34 69 D | Interger Gdns. E11 ........38 | 38 87 B |
| Imperial Ave. N16 ........48 | 33 85 A | International Ave. Houn ........59 | 11 78 C |
| Imperial Cl. Har ........32 | 13 88 C | Inverary Pl. SE18 ........66 | 44 77 B |
| Imperial College Rd. SW7 ........5 | 26 79 D | Inver Cl. E5 ........38 | 35 86 A |
| Imperial Ct. Har ........32 | 13 87 A | Inverclyde Gdns. Rom ........29 | 47 89 D |
| Imperial Dri. Har ........32 | 13 88 C | Inveresk Gdns. Wor Pk ........102 | 22 65 C |
| Imperial Gdns. Mit ........96 | 26 68 B | Inverforth Cl. NW3 ........35 | 26 88 A |
| Imperial Mews. E6 ........50 | 41 83 D | Inverforth Rd. N11 ........16 | 28 92 D |
| Imperial Rd. Felt ........81 | 09 73 A | Inverine Rd. SE7 ........65 | 40 78 D |
| Imperial Rd. N22 ........17 | 30 90 A | Invermead Cl. W6 ........61 | 24 78 A |
| Imperial Rd. SW6 ........73 | 25 76 B | Inverness Ave. Enf ........13 | 33 97 A |
| Imperial Rd. SW6 ........73 | 26 76 C | Inverness Dri. Ilf ........28 | 45 91 A |
| Imperial Sq. SW6 ........73 | 26 76 C | Inverness Mews. W2 ........56 | 25 80 B |
| Imperial St. E3 ........58 | 38 82 A | Inverness Pl. W2 ........56 | 25 80 B |
| Imperial Way. Chis ........90 | 44 72 C | Inverness Rd. Houn ........70 | 13 75 C |
| Imperial Way. Croy ........112 | 31 63 A | Inverness Rd. N18 ........17 | 34 92 D |
| Imperial Way. Har ........33 | 18 88 C | Inverness Rd. Sthl ........59 | 12 78 A |
| Inca Dri. SE9 ........90 | 43 73 B | Inverness St. NW1 ........47 | 28 83 B |
| Inchmerry Rd. SE6 ........88 | 38 73 C | Inverness Terr. W2 ........56 | 25 80 B |
| Independents Rd. SE3 ........77 | 39 75 B | Inverton Rd. SE15 ........76 | 35 75 D |
| Inderwick Rd. N8 ........36 | 30 88 D | Invicta Cl. Chis ........90 | 43 71 C |
| India St. EC3 ........4 | 33 81 D | Invicta Gr. Ntht ........53 | 12 82 B |
| India Way. W12 ........55 | 22 80 B | Invicta Rd. SE3 ........65 | 40 77 A |
| Indus Rd. SE7 ........65 | 41 77 C | Inville Rd. SE17 ........63 | 32 78 D |
| Ingal Rd. E13 ........58 | 40 82 C | Inville Wlk. SE17 ........63 | 32 78 D |
| Ingate Pl. SW8 ........74 | 28 76 B | Inwood Ave. Houn ........70 | 14 75 A |
| Ingatestone Rd. E12 ........39 | 41 87 C | Inwood Cl. Croy ........106 | 36 65 A |
| Ingatestone Rd. SE25 ........105 | 34 67 B | Inwood Rd. Houn ........70 | 14 75 C |
| Ingatestone Rd. Wdf Gn ........27 | 40 91 D | Inworth St. SW11 ........74 | 27 77 C |
| Ingersoll Rd. W12 ........55 | 22 80 D | Inworth Wlk. N1 ........48 | 32 83 A |
| Ingestre Pl. W1 ........6 | 29 80 A | Ipswich Rd. SW17 ........96 | 28 70 A |
| Ingestre Rd. E7 ........50 | 40 85 A | Ireland Yd. EC4 ........3 | 31 81 D |
| Ingestre Rd. NW5 ........47 | 28 85 B | Irene Rd. Orp ........108 | 45 66 B |
| Ingham Rd. NW6 ........46 | 25 85 A | Irene Rd. SW6 ........73 | 25 76 A |
| Inglebert St. EC1 ........3 | 31 82 A | Ireton Rd. N19 ........36 | 29 86 B |
| Ingleborough St. SW9 ........75 | 30 77 C | Irfield Cl. SE4 ........76 | 36 74 A |
| Ingleby Dri. Har ........32 | 14 86 D | Iris Ave. Bex ........79 | 48 74 C |
| Ingleby Rd. Dag ........52 | 49 84 B | Iris Cl. Surb ........101 | 18 66 B |
| Ingleby Rd. Ilf ........40 | 43 87 D | Iris Cres. Bexh ........67 | 50 86 C |
| Ingleby Rd. N7 ........36 | 30 86 C | Iris Path. Rom ........30 | 53 91 C |
| Ingleby Way. Chis ........90 | 43 71 C | Iris Rd. Eps ........109 | 19 64 D |
| Ingleby Way. Wall ........111 | 29 63 D | Iris Way. E4 ........26 | 36 91 B |
| Ingle Cl. Pnr ........20 | 12 89 A | Irkdale Ave. Enf ........13 | 33 97 B |
| Ingledew Rd. SE18 ........66 | 44 78 D | Irongate Wharf Rd. W2 ........1 | 26 81 B |
| Inglefield Sq. E1 ........57 | 34 80 D | Iron Mill La. Dart ........80 | 51 75 D |
| Inglehurst Gdns. Ilf ........39 | 42 88 B | Iron Mill Pl. Dart ........80 | 51 75 D |
| Inglelow Rd. SW8 ........74 | 28 76 D | Iron Mill Rd. SW18 ........73 | 25 74 D |
| Inglemere Rd. Mit ........96 | 27 70 D | Iron Mill Rd. SW18 ........73 | 25 74 D |
| Inglemere Rd. SE23 ........88 | 35 72 D | Irongate Ph. N1 ........48 | 32 81 D |
| Inglesham Wlk. E9 ........49 | 36 84 B | Ironmonger La. EC2 ........4 | 32 81 A |
| Ingleside Cl. Beck ........98 | 37 70 C | Ironmonger Pas. EC1 ........4 | 32 82 A |
| Ingleside Gr. SE3 ........65 | 39 77 B | Ironmonger Row. EC1 ........4 | 32 82 A |
| Inglethorpe St. SW6 ........73 | 23 76 B | Irons Way. Rom ........29 | 50 91 C |
| Ingleton Ave. Well ........78 | 46 75 A | Irvine Ave. Har ........21 | 16 89 B |
| Ingleton Rd. Cars ........111 | 27 62 B | Irvine Cl. N20 ........16 | 27 93 A |
| Ingleton Rd. N18 ........25 | 34 91 A | Irvine Way. Orp ........108 | 45 66 B |
| Ingleton St. SW9 ........75 | 31 76 C | Irving Ave. Ntht ........43 | 11 83 B |
| Ingleway. N12 ........24 | 27 91 A | Irving Gr. SW9 ........74 | 30 76 D |
| Inglewood. Chis ........100 | 44 70 B | Irving Rd. W14 ........62 | 23 79 D |
| Inglewood Cl. Chig ........28 | 45 91 B | Irving St. WC2 ........6 | 29 80 B |
| Inglewood Copse. Brom ........99 | 42 69 D | Irwell Estate. SE16 ........64 | 35 79 A |
| Inglewood Rd. Bexh ........79 | 50 75 D | Irwin Ave. SE18 ........66 | 45 77 C |
| Inglewood Rd. NW6 ........46 | 25 85 C | Irwin Gdns. NW10 ........45 | 22 83 B |
| Inglis Rd. Croy ........105 | 33 66 D | Isabella Rd. E9 ........49 | 35 85 C |
| Inglis Rd. W5 ........54 | 18 80 B | Isabella St. SE1 ........3 | 31 80 D |
| Inglis St. SE5 ........75 | 32 76 A | Isabel St. SW9 ........74 | 30 76 B |
| Ingram Ave. NW11 ........35 | 26 87 A | Isbell Gdns. Rom ........30 | 51 91 C |
| Ingram House. King ........93 | 17 69 A | Isel Way. SE22 ........75 | 33 74 A |
| Ingram Rd. N2 ........24 | 27 89 C | Isham Rd. SW16 ........96 | 28 69 D |
| Ingram Rd. Th Hth ........97 | 32 69 A | Isis Rd. SE18 ........66 | 44 77 A |
| Ingram Way. Grnf ........43 | 14 83 B | Isis St. SW18 ........85 | 26 72 A |
| Ingrave Rd. Rom ........30 | 51 89 C | Island Rd. Mit ........96 | 27 70 D |
| Ingrave St. SW11 ........74 | 27 75 A | Island Row. E14 ........57 | 36 81 D |
| Ingress St. W4 ........61 | 21 78 C | Islay Gdns. Houn ........70 | 11 74 B |
| Inigo Jones Rd. SE7 ........65 | 42 77 C | Islay Wlk. N1 ........48 | 32 84 A |
| Inigo Pl. WC2 ........7 | 30 80 A | Isledon Rd. N7 ........37 | 31 86 C |
| Inkerman Rd. NW5 ........47 | 28 84 B | Islehurst Cl. Chis ........100 | 43 69 A |
| Inks Green. E4 ........18 | 38 92 C | Islington Green ........48 | 31 83 B |
| Inman Rd. NW10 ........45 | 21 84 C | Islington High St. N1 ........48 | 31 83 C |
| Inman Rd. SW18 ........85 | 26 73 A | Islington Park St. N1 ........48 | 31 84 C |
| Inner Circ. NW1 ........2 | 28 82 A | Islip Gdns. Edg ........22 | 20 91 D |
| Inner Park Rd. SW19 ........85 | 23 72 B | Islip Gdns. Ntht ........43 | 12 84 C |
| Inner Ring E. Houn ........69 | 07 75 B | Islip Manor Rd. Ntht ........43 | 12 84 C |
| Inner Ring W. Houn ........69 | 07 75 A | Islip St. NW5 ........47 | 29 85 C |
| Inner Staithe. W4 ........72 | 20 76 A | | |

| | | | |
|---|---|---|---|
| Ismailia Rd. E7 ........50 | 40 84 D | James La. E10 ........38 | 38 87 A |
| Isom Cl. E13 ........58 | 24 69 C | James La. E11 ........39 | 38 88 C |
| Ivanhoe Dri. Har ........21 | 16 90 D | Jameson St. W8 ........56 | 25 80 C |
| Ivanhoe Rd. Houn ........70 | 11 75 B | James Pl. N17 ........25 | 33 90 B |
| Ivanhoe Rd. SE5 ........80 | 33 75 B | James Rd. Dart ........80 | 52 74 C |
| Ivatt Pl. W14 ........62 | 24 78 D | James St. Bark ........51 | 44 84 C |
| Ivatt Way. N15 ........25 | 32 89 A | James St. Enf ........14 | 33 95 B |
| Iveagh Ave. NW10 ........45 | 19 83 C | James St. Houn ........70 | 14 75 B |
| Iveagh Cl. E9 ........35 | 35 83 B | James St. W1 ........2 | 28 81 C |
| Iveagh Cl. Nthwd ........19 | 07 90 B | James St. WC2 ........7 | 30 80 A |
| Iveagh Cl. NW10 ........45 | 19 83 C | Jamestown Rd. NW1 ........47 | 28 83 B |
| Ivedon Rd. Well ........79 | 47 76 C | Jane St. E1 ........57 | 34 81 D |
| Ive Farm Cl. E10 ........38 | 37 86 A | Janet St. E14 ........57 | 37 79 C |
| Ive Farm La. E10 ........38 | 37 86 A | *Janeway Pl. SE16 ........63 | 34 79 B |
| Iveley Rd. SW4 ........74 | 29 76 C | Janeway St. SE16 ........63 | 34 79 A |
| Iver Ct. N1 ........48 | 32 84 A | Janice Mews. Ilf ........40 | 43 86 D |
| Ivere Dri. Barn ........11 | 26 95 D | Jansen Wlk. SW11 ........73 | 26 75 B |
| Iverhurst Cl. Bexh ........78 | 47 74 B | Janson Cl. E15 ........50 | 39 85 C |
| Iver Rd. Rom ........30 | 52 90 A | Janson Rd. E15 ........50 | 39 85 C |
| Iverna Ct. W8 ........62 | 25 79 C | Japan Cres. N4 ........36 | 33 89 A |
| Iverna Gdns. Felt ........69 | 08 74 B | Japan Rd. Rom ........41 | 50 87 B |
| Iverna Gdns. W8 ........62 | 25 79 C | Jardin St. SE5 ........63 | 33 77 A |
| Iverson Rd. NW6 ........46 | 25 84 A | Jarrett Cl. SW2 ........87 | 31 73 D |
| Ives Gdns. Rom ........30 | 51 89 D | Jarrow Cl. Mord ........103 | 25 67 B |
| Ives Rd. E16 ........58 | 39 81 A | Jarrow Rd. N15 ........25 | 34 89 D |
| Ives St. SW3 ........9 | 27 78 A | Jarrow Rd. Rom ........41 | 47 88 C |
| Ivestor Terr. S ........88 | 35 73 A | Jarrow Rd. SE16 ........64 | 35 78 A |
| Ivimey St. E2 ........57 | 34 82 A | Jarrow Way. E9 ........49 | 36 85 B |
| Ivinghoe Cl. Enf ........13 | 33 97 A | Jarvis Cl. Barn ........11 | 23 95 B |
| Ivinghoe Rd. Dag ........51 | 46 85 D | Jarvis Rd. Dag ........41 | 48 86 A |
| Ivor Gr. SE9 ........90 | 43 73 D | Jarvis Rd. S Croy ........112 | 32 63 B |
| Ivor Pl. NW1 ........1 | 27 82 D | Jarvis Rd. SE22 ........75 | 33 75 C |
| Ivor St. NW1 ........47 | 29 84 C | Jasmin Cl. SE1 ........3 | 31 80 D |
| Ivorydown. Brom ........89 | 40 71 A | Jocelyn Rd. Rich ........71 | 18 75 A |
| Ivybridge La. WC2 ........7 | 30 80 A | Jasmine Gdns. Croy ........106 | 37 65 D |
| Ivydale Rd. Cars ........104 | 30 70 C | Jasmine Gdns. Har ........32 | 13 86 A |
| Ivychurch Cl. SE20 ........98 | 35 70 C | Jasmine Gr. SE20 ........97 | 34 69 B |
| Ivy Church La. SE17 ........63 | 33 78 D | Jasmin Rd. Eps ........109 | 20 64 D |
| Ivy Cl. Har ........43 | 12 85 B | Jason Cl. W13 ........53 | 17 80 A |
| Ivy Cl. Pnr ........20 | 11 87 A | Jason Ct. W1 ........2 | 28 81 C |
| Ivy Cl. Sun ........92 | 11 69 C | Jason Wlk. SE9 ........90 | 43 71 A |
| Ivy Cottages. E14 ........57 | 37 80 B | Jasper Pas. SE19 ........97 | 33 70 B |
| Ivy Cres. W4 ........61 | 20 78 A | Jasper Rd. SE19 ........97 | 33 70 B |
| Ivydale Rd. SE15 ........76 | 35 75 D | Javelin Way. Ntht ........53 | 11 82 B |
| Ivydale Rd. SE15 ........76 | 35 75 D | Jaycroft. Enf ........13 | 31 97 A |
| Ivyday Gr. SW16 ........86 | 30 72 D | Jay Mews. SW7 ........5 | 26 79 A |
| Ivydene Cl. Sutt ........110 | 26 64 A | Jebb Ave. SW2 ........74 | 30 74 C |
| Ivydene Rd. E8 ........48 | 34 84 C | Jebb St. E3 ........49 | 37 83 C |
| Ivy Gdns. Mit ........96 | 29 86 B | Jedburgh Rd. E13 ........58 | 41 82 A |
| Ivy Gdns. N8 ........36 | 30 88 C | Jedburgh St. SW11 ........74 | 28 75 C |
| Ivyhouse Rd. Dag ........52 | 48 84 A | Jeddo Rd. W12 ........61 | 21 79 B |
| Ivyhouse Rd. Uxb ........31 | 07 86 D | John Mc Kenna Wlk. SE16 ........63 | 34 79 C |
| Ivy La. Houn ........70 | 12 75 D | John Newton Ct. Well ........78 | 46 75 B |
| Ivymount Rd. SE27 ........87 | 31 72 C | John Parker Cl. Dag ........52 | 49 84 D |
| Ivy Rd. E16 ........58 | 40 81 C | John Parker Sq. SW11 ........73 | 26 75 B |
| Ivy Rd. E17 ........38 | 37 88 C | John Penn St. SE13 ........77 | 37 76 B |
| Ivy Rd. Houn ........70 | 13 75 D | Jeffrey's Pl. NW1 ........47 | 29 84 C |
| Ivy Rd. N14 ........16 | 29 94 B | Jeffrey's Rd. Enf ........14 | 36 96 D |
| Ivy Rd. NW2 ........46 | 23 85 A | Jeffrey's Rd. SW4 ........74 | 30 76 C |
| Ivy Rd. SE4 ........76 | 36 75 D | Jeffrey's St. NW1 ........47 | 29 84 C |
| Ivy St. N1 ........48 | 33 83 C | Jeffs Rd. Sutt ........110 | 24 64 B |
| Ivy Wlk. Dag ........52 | 48 84 A | Jeken Rd. SE9 ........77 | 41 75 C |
| Ivy Wlk. Nthwd ........79 | 48 75 D | Jelf Rd. SW2 ........75 | 31 74 A |
| Izane Rd. Bexh ........79 | | Jellicoe Gdns. Stan ........21 | 15 91 B |
| | | Jellicoe Rd. N17 ........25 | 32 91 D |
| | | Jengar Cl. Sutt ........110 | 25 64 B |
| Jack Barnett Way. N22 ........24 | 30 90 D | Jenkins La. Bark ........51 | 43 85 A |
| Jack Cornwell St. E12 ........51 | 43 86 A | Jenkins Rd. E13 ........58 | 40 82 D |
| Jackets La. Nthwd ........19 | 07 91 D | Jenner Pl. SW13 ........61 | 22 77 B |
| Jackman St. E8 ........48 | 34 83 B | Jenner Rd. N16 ........37 | 34 86 A |
| Jackson Rd. Bark ........51 | 44 83 B | Jennett Rd. Croy ........105 | 31 65 C |
| Jackson Rd. Barn ........12 | 27 95 C | Jennifer Rd. Brom ........89 | 39 72 D |
| Jackson Rd. Brom ........107 | 42 66 D | Jennings Rd. SE22 ........75 | 33 74 D |
| Jackson Rd. N7 ........47 | 30 85 B | Jennings Way. Barn ........11 | 23 96 A |
| Jackson's La. N6 ........36 | 35 79 A | Jenningtree Rd. Eri ........68 | 52 77 D |
| Jackson's Pl. Croy ........105 | 45 77 C | Jenningtree Way. Belv ........67 | 50 79 A |
| Jackson St. SE18 ........66 | 22 83 B | Jenny Path. Rom ........30 | 53 91 D |
| Jack Walker Ct. N5 ........48 | 35 85 C | Jenton Ave. Bexh ........79 | 48 76 C |
| Jacob St. SE1 ........3 | 34 79 A | Jephson Rd. E7 ........50 | 41 84 C |
| Jacob's Well Mews. W1 ........2 | 30 76 B | Jephson St. SE5 ........75 | 32 76 B |
| Jacqueline Cl. Nthlt ........43 | 12 83 A | Jephtha Rd. SW18 ........73 | 26 74 D |
| Jaffray Pl. SE27 ........87 | 31 71 B | Jeppo's La. Mit ........96 | 27 68 D |
| Jaffray Rd. Brom ........99 | 41 68 D | Jerdan Pl. SW6 ........62 | 25 77 C |
| Jaggard Way. SW12 ........86 | 27 73 B | Jeremiah St. E14 ........57 | 37 81 D |
| Jago Cl. SE18 ........66 | 44 77 A | Jeremy's Green. N18 ........18 | 35 92 A |
| Jago Wlk. SE5 ........63 | 32 77 D | Jermyn St. SW1 ........6 | 29 80 C |
| Jamaica Rd. SE16 ........64 | 34 79 C | Jerningham Ave. Ilf ........28 | 43 90 D |
| Jamaica Rd. Th Hth ........105 | 31 67 D | Jerningham Rd. SE14 ........76 | 36 76 A |
| Jamaica St. E1 ........57 | 35 81 A | Jerome Cres. NW8 ........1 | 27 82 C |
| James Ave. Dag ........41 | 48 87 D | Jerome St. E1 ........4 | 33 82 D |
| James Ave. NW2 ........45 | 23 85 C | Jerome St. E1 ........4 | 33 82 D |
| James Bedford Cl. Pnr ........20 | 11 90 C | Jerrard St. SE13 ........76 | 37 75 B |
| James Boswell Cl. SW16 ........87 | 31 71 A | Jerrold St. N1 ........48 | 33 83 C |
| James Cl. E13 ........50 | 40 83 C | Jersey Ave. Stan ........21 | 17 90 C |
| James Cl. Rom ........42 | 52 88 A | Jersey Dri. Orp ........108 | 44 67 D |
| James St. Enf ........14 | 32 83 A | Jersey Rd. E11 ........38 | 38 87 D |
| James Dudson Ct. NW10 ........45 | 20 84 B | Jersey Rd. E16 ........58 | 41 81 D |
| James Gdns. N22 ........25 | 32 91 C | Jersey Rd. Houn ........70 | 13 76 B |

| | | | |
|---|---|---|---|
| Jersey Rd. Houn ........59 | 13 77 D | Jordan Rd. Grnf ........44 | 17 83 A |
| Jersey Rd. Ilf ........51 | 43 85 B | Jordans Cl. Dag ........52 | 49 85 B |
| Jersey Rd. Islw ........59 | 14 77 D | Jordans Cl. Islw ........71 | 15 76 C |
| Jersey Rd. SW17 ........96 | 28 70 B | Joseph Ct. N15 ........37 | 33 87 A |
| Jersey Rd. W7 ........60 | 16 79 A | Josephine Ave. SW2 ........74 | 30 74 D |
| Jersey St. E2 ........57 | 34 82 B | Joseph Powell Cl. SW12 ........74 | 29 74 C |
| Jerusalem Pas. EC1 ........3 | 31 82 D | Joseph St. E3 ........57 | 36 82 D |
| Jervis Ct. W1 ........2 | 28 81 D | Joshua St. E14 ........58 | 38 81 C |
| Jerviston Gdns. SW16 ........97 | 31 70 A | Jossiline Ct. E3 ........49 | 36 83 C |
| Jesmond Ave. Wem ........44 | 18 84 B | Joubert St. SW11 ........74 | 27 76 D |
| Jesmond Rd. Croy ........105 | 33 66 B | Jowett St. SE15 ........63 | 33 77 D |
| Jessam Ave. E5 ........37 | 34 87 D | Joyce Ave. N18 ........17 | 33 92 D |
| Jessamine Rd. W7 ........54 | 15 80 D | Joyce Green La. Dart ........80 | 54 75 A |
| Jesse Rd. E10 ........38 | 38 87 C | Joyce Green Wlk. Dart ........80 | 54 75 D |
| Jessica Rd. SW18 ........73 | 26 74 A | Joyce Wlk. SW2 ........75 | 31 74 C |
| Jessop Rd. SE24 ........75 | 32 75 C | Joydon Dri. Rom ........40 | 46 88 D |
| Jessops Way. Croy ........104 | 29 67 C | Jubilee Ave. E4 ........26 | 38 91 C |
| Jessup Cl. SE18 ........66 | 44 78 A | Jubilee Ave. Rom ........41 | 50 88 A |
| Jetstar Way. Ntht ........53 | 12 82 A | Jubilee Ave. Twick ........82 | 14 73 C |
| Jewel Rd. E17 ........27 | 37 89 A | Jubilee Cl. King ........93 | 17 69 A |
| Jewry St. EC3 ........4 | 33 81 D | Jubilee Cl. NW9 ........34 | 20 88 D |
| Jews Row. SW18 ........73 | 26 75 C | Jubilee Cl. Pnr ........20 | 11 90 C |
| Jews Wlk. SE26 ........87 | 34 71 B | Jubilee Cl. Rom ........41 | 49 88 B |
| Jeymer Ave. NW2 ........46 | 23 85 C | Jubilee Cres. E14 ........64 | 38 79 C |
| Jeymer Dri. Grnf ........43 | 14 83 A | Jubilee Cres. N9 ........17 | 34 94 C |
| Jeypore Rd. SW18 ........73 | 26 74 C | Jubilee Dri. Ruis ........43 | 12 85 A |
| Jeypore Road Pas. SW18 ........73 | 26 74 C | Jubilee Gdns. Sthl ........53 | 13 81 C |
| Jillian Cl. Hamp ........92 | 13 70 C | Jubilee Pl. SW3 ........9 | 27 78 C |
| Joan Cres. SE9 ........89 | 41 73 B | Jubilee Rd. Grnf ........44 | 16 83 B |
| Joan Gdns. Dag ........41 | 48 86 A | Jubilee Rd. Sutt ........110 | 23 63 B |
| Joan Rd. Dag ........41 | 48 86 A | Jubilee St. E1 ........57 | 35 81 A |
| Joan St. SE1 ........3 | 31 80 D | Jubilee Way. Chess ........102 | 19 65 D |
| Jocelyn Rd. Rich ........71 | 18 75 A | Jubilee Way. Sid ........90 | 46 72 A |
| Jockey's Fields. WC1 ........3 | 30 81 B | Jubilee Way. SW19 ........95 | 26 69 B |
| Jodrell Rd. E3 ........49 | 36 84 D | Judd St. WC1 ........3 | 30 82 A |
| Joel St. Nthwd ........19 | 10 90 C | Jude St. E16 ........58 | 39 81 D |
| Joel St. Pnr ........19 | 10 89 C | Judges' Wlk. NW3 ........35 | 26 86 C |
| Johanna St. SE1 ........7 | 31 79 A | Judith Ave. Rom ........29 | 49 91 B |
| John Adam St. WC2 ........7 | 30 80 A | Juer St. SW11 ........9 | 27 77 C |
| John Aird Ct. W2 ........1 | 26 81 A | Juglands Rd. Orp ........108 | 46 66 C |
| John Barnes Wlk. E15 ........50 | 39 84 B | Julia Gdns. Bark ........52 | 45 84 C |
| John Burns Dri. Bark ........51 | 45 84 C | Julian Ave. W3 ........55 | 19 80 B |
| John Campbell Rd. N16 ........48 | 33 85 C | Julian Cl. Barn ........11 | 25 96 B |
| John Carpenter St. EC4 ........7 | 31 80 B | Julian Pl. E14 ........64 | 37 78 D |
| John Felton Rd. SE16 ........63 | 34 79 A | Julia St. NW5 ........47 | 28 85 C |
| John Fisher St. E1 ........57 | 34 80 A | Julien Rd. W5 ........62 | 17 79 C |
| John Glynes Ct. SW15 ........72 | 22 75 D | Junction App. SE13 ........76 | 38 75 A |
| John Islip St. SW1 ........10 | 29 78 C | Junction Ave. W10 ........56 | 23 82 A |
| John Mc Kenna Wlk. SE16 ........63 | 34 79 C | Junction Mews. W2 ........1 | 27 81 C |
| John Newton Ct. Well ........78 | 46 75 B | Junction Pl. W2 ........1 | 26 81 D |
| John Parker Cl. Dag ........52 | 49 84 D | Junction Rd. Ashf ........81 | 08 71 C |
| John Parker Sq. SW11 ........73 | 26 75 B | Junction Rd. Dart ........80 | 53 74 D |
| John Penn St. SE13 ........77 | 37 76 B | Junction Rd. E13 ........50 | 40 83 D |
| John Perrin Pl. Har ........33 | 18 88 A | Junction Rd. Har ........33 | 15 88 C |
| John Prince's St. W1 ........2 | 28 81 D | Junction Rd. N17 ........25 | 34 89 A |
| John Rennie Wlk. E1 ........57 | 34 80 D | Junction Rd. N19 ........36 | 29 86 C |
| John Roll Way. SE16 ........63 | 34 79 C | Junction Rd. Rom ........42 | 54 94 C |
| John Ruskin St. SE5 ........63 | 31 77 B | Junction Rd. S Croy ........112 | 32 64 D |
| John's Ave. NW4 ........22 | 23 89 C | Junction Rd. W5 ........60 | 17 78 B |
| John's Cl. Ashf ........81 | 08 71 A | Juniper Cl. Barn ........11 | 23 95 C |
| Johns La. Mord ........103 | 26 67 A | Juniper Gdns. SW16 ........96 | 29 69 A |
| John's Mews. WC1 ........3 | 30 82 D | Juniper Rd. Ilf ........40 | 43 86 C |
| Johnson Cl. E8 ........48 | 34 83 A | Juniper St. E1 ........57 | 35 80 A |
| Johnson Rd. Brom ........107 | 41 67 B | Juno Way. SE14 ........64 | 35 77 B |
| Johnson Rd. Croy ........105 | 32 66 B | Juniper Way. Rom ........30 | 54 90 A |
| Johnson Rd. Houn ........59 | 11 77 C | Jupiter Way. N7 ........47 | 30 84 B |
| Johnson's Cl. Cars ........104 | 27 65 D | Jupp Rd. E15 ........49 | 38 84 B |
| Johnsons Dri. Hamp ........92 | 14 69 A | Jupp Rd W. E15 ........49 | 38 83 B |
| Johnson St. E1 ........57 | 35 80 A | Justice Wlk. SW3 ........9 | 27 77 A |
| Johnson St. Sthl ........59 | 11 79 D | Justin St. Brent ........60 | 17 77 D |
| John Spencer Sq. N1 ........48 | 31 84 B | Jute La. Enf ........14 | 36 96 A |
| John's Pl. E1 ........57 | 34 81 D | Jutland Rd. E13 ........58 | 40 82 C |
| John's St. E15 ........50 | 39 83 B | Jutland Rd. SE6 ........88 | 38 73 A |
| John's Terr. Croy ........105 | 33 66 C | Jutsums Ave. Rom ........41 | 49 88 D |
| Johnston Rd. Wdf Gn ........27 | 40 91 A | Jutsums La. Rom ........41 | 49 88 B |
| Johnston Terr. NW2 ........35 | 23 87 A | Juxon Cl. Har ........20 | 13 90 B |
| John St. SE25 ........34 | 34 68 C | Juxon St. SE11 ........10 | 30 78 B |
| John St. WC1 ........3 | 30 82 D | Jveington Way. SE12 ........89 | 40 73 D |
| John St. E15 ........50 | 37 81 D | |
| John Wilson St. SE18 ........66 | 43 78 A | Kaduna Cl. Pnr ........31 | 10 88 B |
| John Woolley Cl. SE13 ........77 | 39 75 C | Kale Rd. Belv ........67 | 48 79 A |
| Joiners Arms Yd. SE5 ........75 | 32 76 B | Kambala Rd. SW11 ........73 | 26 75 B |
| Joiner St. SE1 ........3 | 32 80 D | Kangley Bridge Rd. SE26 ........88 | 36 71 D |
| Joint Rd. N2 ........24 | 27 90 A | Karen Cr. Brom ........99 | 39 69 B |
| Jollys La. Har ........44 | 16 85 D | Kashgar Rd. SE18 ........66 | 45 78 B |
| Jollys La. Hay ........53 | 12 81 A | Kashmir Rd. SE7 ........65 | 41 77 D |
| Jonathan St. SE11 ........10 | 30 78 B | Kassala Rd. SW11 ........74 | 27 76 B |
| Jones Rd. E13 ........58 | 40 82 D | Katharine St. Croy ........105 | 32 65 C |
| Jones St. W1 ........2 | 28 80 B | Katherine Gdns. Ilf ........28 | 44 91 C |
| Jonson Cl. Mit ........96 | 28 68 B | Katherine Gdns. SE9 ........77 | 41 75 D |
| Joram Way. SE16 ........63 | 34 78 D | Katherine Rd. E6 ........50 | 42 83 A |
| Jordan Hill. N2 ........24 | 13 76 B | Katherine Rd. E7 ........50 | 41 84 B |

Katherine Sq. W11 56 24 80 C
Kathleen Ave. W3 55 20 81 A
Kathleen Ave. Wem 44 18 84 C
Kathleen Rd. SW11 74 27 75 B
Kayemoor Rd. Sutt 111 27 63 A
Kay Rd. SW9 74 30 76 C
Kay St. E15 49 38 84 D
Kay St. E2 48 34 83 C
Kay St. Well 78 46 76 B
Kean St. WC2 3 30 81 D
Keates Estate. N16 37 33 86 B
Keats Ave. Rom 30 52 91 D
Keats Cl. Chig 28 44 91 A
Keats Gr. NW3 47 27 85 A
Keats Pl. EC2 4 32 81 D
Keats Rd. Belv 67 50 79 C
Keats Rd. Well 78 45 76 B
Keats Way. Croy 106 35 67 C
Keats Way. Grnf 53 13 81 B
Keble Cl. Nthlt 43 14 85 C
Keble Cl. Wor Pk 102 21 66 D
Keble St. SW17 85 26 71 A
Kechill Gdns. Brom 107 40 66 A
Kedleston Dri. Orp 108 45 67 B
Keeble Cl. SE18 66 43 78 B
Keedonwood Rd. Brom 89 39 71 D
Keeley Rd. Croy 105 32 65 A
Keeley St. WC2 3 30 81 D
Keeling Rd. SE9 77 41 74 B
Keemor Cl. SE18 66 43 77 C
Keen's Rd. Croy 112 32 64 A
Keen's Yd. N1 48 31 84 B
Keep The. King 93 18 70 D
Keep The. SE3 77 40 76 C
Keeton's Rd. SE16 63 34 79 D
Keevil Dri. SW19 85 24 73 A
Keighley Cl. N7 47 30 85 A
Keighley Rd. Rom 30 54 91 C
Keightley Dri. SE9 90 44 73 C
Keildon Rd. SW11 74 27 75 D
Keir Hardie Way. Bark 51 46 84 C
Keith Gr. W12 61 22 79 A
Keith Rd. Bark 51 44 83 D
Keith Rd. E17 26 36 90 B
Keith Way. Horn 42 54 87 A
Kelbrook Rd. SE3 77 42 75 A
Kelby Path. SE9 90 43 72 D
Kelceda Cl. NW2 34 22 86 A
Kelday Rd. E3 49 37 84 C
Kelfield Gdns. W10 56 23 81 D
Kelland Rd. E13 58 40 82 C
Kellaway Rd. SE3 77 41 76 D
Kellerton Rd. SE13 77 39 74 A
Kellett Rd. SW2 75 31 75 C
Kelling Gdns. Croy 105 31 66 B
Kellino St. SW17 86 27 71 B
Kellner Rd. SE28 66 45 79 D
Kell St. SE1 7 31 79 D
Kelly Cl. Shep 91 09 69 C
Kelly Rd. NW7 23 24 91 A
Kelly St. NW1 47 28 84 B
Kelly Way. Rom 41 48 88 C
Kelman Cl. SW4 74 29 76 D
Kelmore Gr. SE22 75 34 75 C
Kelmscott Cl. E17 26 36 90 B
Kelmscott Gdns. W12 61 22 79 C
Kelmscott Rd. SW11 74 27 74 B
Kelross Pas. N5 48 32 85 A
Kelross Rd. N5 48 32 85 A
Kelsall Cl. SE3 77 40 76 D
Kelsey La. Beck 98 37 68 A
Kelsey Park Ave. Beck 98 37 69 D
Kelsey Park Rd. Beck 98 37 69 C
Kelsey Rd. Orp 100 46 69 D
Kelsey Sq. Beck 98 37 69 C
Kelsey St. E2 57 34 82 C
Kelsey Way. Beck 98 37 68 A
Kelsie Way. Ilf 28 45 91 A
Kelso Pl. W8 62 25 79 D
Kelso Rd. Cars 103 26 66 A
Kelston Rd. Ilf 28 43 90 D
Kelvedon Cl. King 94 19 70 A
Kelvedon Lodge. Ilf 28 43 90 C
Kelvedon Rd. SW6 73 24 76 B
Kelvedon Way. Wdf Gn 27 42 91 B
Kelvin Ave. N13 24 30 91 B
Kelvin Ave. Tedd 93 15 70 A
Kelvinbrook. E Mol 92 13 68 B
Kelvin Cl. Eps 109 19 63 A
Kelvin Cres. Har 21 15 91 C
Kelvin Dri. Twick 71 16 74 D
Kelvin Gdns. Sthl 53 13 81 C
Kelvin Gr. Chess 101 18 65 C
Kelvin Gr. SE26 87 34 72 D
Kelvington Cl. Croy 106 36 66 A
Kelvington Rd. SE15 76 35 74 B
Kelvin Par. Orp 108 45 66 C
Kelvin Rd. N5 48 32 85 A
Kelvin Rd. Well 78 46 75 A
Kemble Dri. Brom 107 42 65 C
Kemble Rd. Croy 105 31 65 D
Kemble Rd. N17 25 34 90 A
Kemble Rd. SE23 88 35 73 D
Kemble St. WC2 3 30 81 D
Kemerton Rd. Beck 98 37 69 D
Kemerton Rd. Croy 105 33 66 B
Kemerton Rd. SE5 75 32 75 A
Kemey's St. E9 49 36 85 C
Kemnal Rd. Chis 100 44 70 A
Kemnal Rd. Chis 90 44 71 B
Kemnal Warren. Chis 100 44 70 B
Kempe Rd. NW6 46 23 83 D
Kemp Gdns. Croy 105 32 67 C
Kempis Way. SE22 75 33 74 A
Kemplay Rd. NW3 46 26 85 B
Kemp Rd. Dag 41 47 87 D
Kemp's Ct. W1 2 29 81 D
Kemps Dri. E14 57 37 80 A
Kemps Dri. Nthwd 19 09 91 D
Kempsford Gdns. SW5 62 25 78 C
Kempsford Rd. SE11 63 31 78 A
Kempshott Rd. SW16 96 30 70 C
Kempson Rd. SW6 62 25 77 D
Kempthorne Rd. SE8 64 36 78 B
Kempton Ave. Horn 42 54 86 D
Kempton Ave. Nthlt 43 13 85 C
Kempton Ave. Sun 91 10 69 B
Kempton Cl. Eri 67 50 77 A
Kempton Rd. E6 50 42 83 B
Kempton Rd. Hamp 92 12 69 C
Kempton Wlk. Croy 106 36 67 C
Kempt St. SE18 66 43 77 A
Kemsing Cl. Brom 107 39 65 B
Kemsing Cl. Th Hth 97 32 68 C
Kemsing Rd. SE10 65 40 78 C
Kenbury Cl. Uxb 31 07 86 C
Kenbury St. SE5 75 32 76 C
Kenchester Cl. SW8 70 30 77 C
Kendal Ave. Bark 51 45 83 A
Kendal Ave. N18 17 32 92 B
Kendal Ave. W3 55 19 81 B
Kendale Rd. Brom 89 39 71 C
Kendal Gdns. N18 17 32 92 B
Kendal Gdns. Sutt 103 26 65 A
Kendall Ave. Beck 98 36 69 C
Kendall Ave. S Croy 112 32 62 B
Kendall Ave S. S Croy 112 32 62 B
Kendall Pl. W1 2 28 81 A
Kendall Rd. Beck 98 36 69 C
Kendall Rd. Islw 71 16 76 C
Kendal Par. N18 17 32 92 B
Kendal Rd. NW10 45 22 85 A
Kendal St. W2 1 27 81 C
Kender St. SE14 76 35 76 A
Kendoa Rd. SW4 74 29 75 D
Kendon Cl. E11 39 40 88 B
Kendra Hall Rd. S Croy 112 31 63 D
Kendrey Gdns. Twick 83 15 73 A
Kendrick Mews. SW7 62 26 78 B
Kendrick Pl. SW7 62 26 78 B
Kenelm Cl. Har 33 16 86 C
Kenerne Dri. Barn 11 24 95 A
Kenilford Rd. SW12 86 28 73 B
Kenilworth Ave. E17 26 37 89 A
Kenilworth Ave. Har 43 12 85 B
Kenilworth Ave. SW19 85 25 71 A
Kenilworth Cres. Enf 13 33 97 A
Kenilworth Ct. SW15 73 24 75 A
Kenilworth Gdns. Horn 42 53 86 D
Kenilworth Gdns. Ilf 40 45 86 B
Kenilworth Gdns. SE18 78 43 76 D
Kenilworth Gdns. Sthl 53 12 82 B
Kenilworth Rd. E3 49 36 83 C
Kenilworth Rd. Eps 109 22 64 C
Kenilworth Rd. NW6 46 24 83 B
Kenilworth Rd. Orp 108 44 67 C
Kenilworth Rd. SE20 98 35 69 B
Kenilworth Rd. W5 54 18 80 C
Kenley Ave. NW9 22 21 90 C
Kenley Cl. Chis 100 45 68 A
Kenley Gdns. Horn 42 54 86 B
Kenley Gdns. Th Hth 97 31 68 D
Kenley Rd. King 94 19 69 D
Kenley Rd. SW19 95 25 68 B
Kenley Rd. Twick 71 16 74 D
Kenley Wlk. Sutt 110 23 64 B
Kenley Wlk. W11 56 24 80 A
Kenlor Rd. SW17 85 26 71 D
Kenmare Dri. Mit 96 27 70 D
Kenmare Gdns. N13 17 32 92 A
Kenmare Rd. Th Hth 105 31 67 C
Kenmere Gdns. Wem 45 19 83 A
Kenmere Rd. Well 79 47 76 C
Kenmont Gdns. NW10 55 22 82 B
Kenmore Ave. Har 21 16 89 A
Kenmore Cl. Rich 61 19 77 C
Kenmore Gdns. Edg 22 19 90 D
Kenmore Rd. Har 21 17 89 B
Kenmure Rd. E8 48 34 85 D
Kennard Rd. E15 49 38 84 D
Kennard Rd. N11 16 27 92 D
Kennard St. SW11 74 28 76 A
Kennedy Ave. Enf 14 35 95 C
Kennedy Cl. E13 50 40 83 C
Kennedy Cl. Orp 108 44 66 D
Kennedy Cl. Pnr 20 12 91 B
Kennedy Ct. Ashf 81 08 71 C
Kennedy Path. W7 54 15 82 D
Kennedy Rd. Bark 51 45 83 A
Kennedy Rd. W7 54 15 82 C
*Kennedy Wlk. SE17 63 32 78 B
Kennet Cl. SW11 73 26 75 D
Kenneth Ave. Ilf 51 43 85 B
Kenneth Cres. NW12 45 22 85 D
Kenneth Gdns. Stan 21 16 91 A
Kenneth Rd. Rom 41 48 87 A
Kennet Rd. Dart 80 52 75 A
Kennet Rd. Islw 71 15 75 B
Kennet Rd. W9 56 24 82 D
Kennet Wharf La. EC4 8 32 80 A
Kenninghall Rd. E5 37 34 86 D
Kenninghall Rd. N18 18 35 92 C
Kenning St. SE16 64 35 79 A
Kennings Way. SE11 63 31 78 D
Kenning Terr. N1 48 33 83 A
Kennington Gr. SE11 10 30 77 B
Kennington La. SE11 10 30 78 D
Kennington La. SE11 63 31 78 C
Kennington Oval. SE11 10 30 77 B
Kennington Park Gdns. SE11 63 31 77 B
Kennington Park Pl. SE11 63 31 77 A
Kennington Park Rd. SE11 63 31 78 C
Kennington Rd. SE11 63 31 78 A
Kennington Rd. SE1 7 31 79 C
Kennoldes. SE21 87 32 72 B
Kenny Rd. NW7 15 24 92 C
Kenrick Pl. W1 2 28 81 A
Kensal Rd. W10 56 24 82 C
Kensington Ave. E12 50 42 84 B
Kensington Ave. Th Hth 97 31 69 A
Kensington Church Ct. W8 62 25 79 B
Kensington Church St. W8 62 25 79 B
Kensington Church Wlk. W8 62 25 79 B
Kensington Court Mews. W8 62 25 79 D
Kensington Court Pl. W8 62 25 79 D
Kensington Ct. W8 62 25 79 B
Kensington Dri. Wdf Gn 27 41 90 D
Kensington Gate. W8 5 26 79 C
Kensington Gdns. Ilf 39 42 87 D
Kensington Gdns Sq. W2 56 25 81 D
Kensington Gore. SW7 5 26 79 B
Kensington High St. W14 62 24 79 D
Kensington High St. W8 62 25 79 C
Kensington Mall. W8 56 25 80 C
Kensington Mansions. SW5 62 25 78 C
Kensington Palace Gdns. W8 62 25 79 B
Kensington Palace Gdns. W8 56 25 80 D
Kensington Park Gdns. W11 56 24 80 B
Kensington Park Mews. W11 56 24 81 D
Kensington Park Rd. W11 56 24 80 B
Kensington Pl. W8 56 25 80 C
Kensington Rd. Grnf 53 13 82 A
Kensington Rd. Nthlt 43 13 83 C
Kensington Rd. Rom 41 50 88 C
Kensington Rd. SW7 5 26 79 B
Kensington Sq. W8 62 25 79 D
Kensington Terr. S Croy 112 32 63 D
Kent Ave. Dag 52 49 83 C
Kent Ave. W13 54 16 81 B
Kent Ave. Well 78 45 74 B
Kent Cl. Mit 96 30 68 C
Kent Ct. W3 55 19 81 C
Kent Ct. W3 55 19 81 C
Kent Dri. Barn 12 28 95 A
Kent Dri. Tedd 83 15 71 C
Kentford Way. Nthlt 43 12 83 A
Kent Gdns. Ruis 31 10 88 C
Kent Gdns. W13 54 16 81 B
Kent House La. Beck 88 36 71 C
Kent House Rd. Beck 98 36 70 C
Kent House Rd. SE26 88 36 71 C
Kentish Bldgs. SE1 8 32 80 D
Kentish Rd. Belv 67 49 78 A
Kentish Town Rd. NW1 47 28 84 D
Kentish Town Rd. NW5 47 28 85 D
Kentmere Rd. SE18 66 45 78 A
Kenton Ave. Har 33 15 87 B
Kenton Ave. Sthl 53 13 80 A
Kenton Ave. Sun 92 12 69 C
Kenton Ct. Har 33 16 88 D
Kenton Gdns. Har 33 17 88 A
Kenton La. Har 21 16 90 D
Kenton Park Ave. Har 21 17 89 D
Kenton Park Cl. Har 21 17 89 C
Kenton Park Cres. Har 21 17 89 D
Kenton Park Rd. Har 21 17 89 C
Kenton Rd. E9 49 35 84 B
Kenton Rd. Har 33 17 88 A
Kenton St. WC1 3 30 82 C
Kent Pas. NW1 1 27 82 B
Kent Rd. Dag 52 49 85 D
Kent Rd. Dart 80 54 74 C
Kent Rd. E Mol 92 14 68 C
Kent Rd. N21 17 32 94 B
Kent Rd. Orp 108 46 67 D
Kent Rd. Rich 61 19 77 C
Kent Rd. W4 61 20 79 C
Kent Rd. W Wick 106 37 66 D
Kent St. E13 58 40 82 B
Kent St. E2 48 33 83 D
Kent Terr. NW1 1 27 82 A
Kent View Gdns. Ilf 40 45 86 A
Kent Way. SE15 75 33 76 B
Kent Way. Surb 101 18 65 C
Kentwell Cl. SE4 76 36 75 C
Kent Wlk. SW9 75 31 75 D
Kentwode Green. SW13 61 22 77 C
Kent Yd. SW7 5 27 79 A
Kenver Ave. N12 23 26 91 B
Kenward Rd. SE9 77 41 74 B
Kenway Rd. SW5 62 25 78 B
Kenway. Rom 29 50 90 C
Ken Way. Wem 34 20 86 C
Kenwood Ave. N14 12 29 95 B
Kenwood Cl. NW3 35 26 87 D
Kenwood Dri. Beck 98 38 68 A
Kenwood Gdns. E18 27 40 89 B
Kenwood Gdns. Ilf 40 43 88 A
Kenwood Rd. N6 36 27 88 D
Kenwood Rd. N9 17 34 94 C
Kenworthy Rd. E9 49 36 84 A
Kenwyn Dri. NW2 34 21 86 D
Kenwyn Rd. SW20 95 23 69 A
Kenwyn Rd. SW4 74 29 75 D
Kenya Rd. SE7 65 41 77 D
Kenyngton Dri. Sun 81 10 71 C
Kenyngton Pl. Har 33 17 88 A
Kenyon St. SW6 62 23 77 D
Keogh Rd. E15 50 39 84 B
Kepiel Rd. Dag 52 48 85 A
Kepler Rd. SW4 74 30 75 C
Keppel Rd. E6 50 42 83 B
Keppel Row. SE1 8 32 80 C
Keppel St. WC1 2 29 81 B
*Kerbela St. E2 57 34 82 C
Kerbey St. E14 57 37 81 D
Kerfield Pl. SE5 75 32 76 B
Kernow Cl. Horn 42 54 86 A
Kerri Cl. Barn 11 23 96 C
Kerridge Ct. N1 48 33 84 C
Kerrison Pl. W5 54 17 80 D
Kerrison Rd. E15 49 38 83 B
Kerris Rd. SW11 74 27 75 A
Kerrison Rd. W5 54 17 80 D
Kerry Cl. E16 58 40 81 D
Kerry Rd. SE14 64 36 77 B
Kersey Gdns. Rom 30 54 91 D
Kersey Gdns. SE9 89 42 71 A
Kersfield Rd. SW15 73 23 74 D
Kershaw Cl. SW18 73 26 74 D
Kershaw Rd. Dag 41 49 86 C
Kersley Mews. SW11 74 27 76 B
Kersley Rd. N16 37 33 86 C
Kersley St. SW11 74 27 76 D
Kerswell Cl. N15 37 33 88 A
Kerwick Cl. N7 47 30 84 D
Keslake Rd. NW6 46 23 83 D
Kessock Cl. N17 37 34 88 B
Kesteven Cl. Chig 28 45 91 B
Kestlake Rd. Bex 79 47 74 C
Kestlake Rd. Bex 79 47 74 C
Keston Cl. N18 17 32 92 D
Keston Cl. Well 67 47 77 C
Keston Mark. Brom 107 42 65 C
Keston Rd. N17 25 32 89 D
Keston Rd. SE15 75 34 75 A
Keston Rd. Th Hth 105 31 67 C
Kestrel Ave. SE24 75 32 74 A
Keswick Ave. Horn 42 53 87 D
Keswick Ave. SW15 84 21 71 C
Keswick Ave. SW19 95 25 69 C
Keswick Cl. Sutt 110 26 64 A
Keswick Gdns. Ilf 27 42 89 C
Keswick Gdns. Ruis 31 08 88 D
Keswick Gdns. Wem 44 18 85 A
Keswick Mews. W5 54 18 80 C
Keswick Rd. Bexh 79 49 76 A
Keswick Rd. Orp 108 46 66 A
Keswick Rd. SW15 73 24 74 A
Keswick Rd. Twick 70 14 74 C
Keswick Rd. W.Wick 107 39 65 A
Kettering Rd. Rom 30 54 91 C
Kettering St. SW16 96 29 70 A
Kett Gdns. SW2 74 30 74 B
Kettlebaston Rd. E10 38 36 87 D
Kevelioc Rd. N17 25 32 90 A
Kevin Cl. Houn 70 11 76 D
Kevington Cl. Orp 100 45 68 D
Kevington Dri. Chis 100 45 68 D
Kevington Dri. Orp 100 46 68 C
Kew Bridge Ct. W4 61 19 78 C
Kew Bridge Rd. Brent 60 18 77 B
Kew Cres. Sutt 103 24 65 D
Kewferry Dri. Nthwd 19 08 91 A
Kewferry Rd. Nthwd 19 08 91 A
Kew Foot Rd. Rich 71 18 75 A
Kew Gardens Rd. Rich 60 18 77 D
Kew Gardens Rd. Rich 61 19 77 C
Kew Green. Rich 60 18 77 B
Kew Meadow Path. Rich 72 19 76 B
Kew Rd. Brent 60 18 77 B
Kew Rd. N2 24 27 90 A
Kew Rd. Rich 71 18 76 D
Kew Rd. Rich 61 19 77 A
Key Cl. E1 57 35 82 C
Keyes Rd. Dart 80 54 75 D
Keyes Rd. NW2 46 23 85 D
Keymer Rd. SW2 86 30 72 B
Keynes Cl. N2 24 27 89 D
Keynsham Gdns. SE9 77 42 74 A
Keynsham Rd. Mord 103 25 66 D
Keynsham Rd. SE9 77 42 74 A
Keynsham Wlk. Mord 103 25 66 D
Keyse Rd. SE1 8 33 79 D
Keysham Ave. Houn 69 10 76 A
Keystone Cres. N1 47 30 83 C
Keywood Dri. Sun 91 10 70 A
Keyworth Pl. SE1 7 31 79 D
Keyworth St. SE1 7 31 79 D
Kezia St. SE8 64 36 78 C
Khama Rd. SW17 86 27 71 A
Khartoum Rd. E13 58 40 82 B
Khartoum Rd. Ilf 51 43 85 D
Khartoum Rd. SW17 85 26 71 B
Khyber Rd. SW11 74 27 76 C
Kibworth St. SW8 10 30 77 D
Kidbrooke Gdns. SE3 77 40 76 A
Kidbrooke Gr. SE3 77 40 76 B
Kidbrooke La. SE9 77 42 75 C
Kidbrooke Park Cl. SE3 77 40 76 B
Kidbrooke Park Rd. SE3 77 40 75 B
Kidbrooke Way. SE3 77 40 76 D
Kidderminster Pl. Croy 105 31 66 D
Kidderminster Rd. Croy 105 32 66 A
Kidderpore Ave. NW3 46 25 85 A
Kidderpore Gdns. NW3 46 25 85 A
Kidd Pl. SE7 65 42 78 C
Kidlington Way. NW9 22 21 90 A
Kidron Way. E9 49 35 83 A
Kielder Cl. Chig 28 45 91 B
Kiffen St. EC2 4 32 82 D
Kilburn High Rd. NW6 46 25 84 C
Kilburn La. W10 56 23 82 B
Kilburn La. W9 46 24 83 D
Kilburn Park Rd. NW6 56 25 82 A
Kilburn Pl. NW6 46 25 83 A
Kilburn Priory. NW6 46 25 83 B
Kilburn Sq. NW6 46 25 83 A
Kilburn Vale Estate. NW6 46 25 83 A
Kilburn Vale. NW6 46 25 83 B
Kildare Cl. Ruis 32 11 87 C
Kildare Gdns. W2 56 25 81 C
Kildare Rd. E16 58 40 81 A
Kildare Terr. W2 56 25 81 C
Kildare Wlk. E14 57 37 81 C
Kildoran Rd. SW2 74 30 74 A
Kildowan Rd. Ilf 40 46 87 C
Kilgour Rd. SE23 76 36 74 C
Kilkie St. SW6 73 26 76 C
Killarney Rd. SW18 73 26 74 C
Killearn Rd. SE6 88 38 73 D
Killester Gdns. Wor Pk 110 23 64 A
Killick St. N1 47 30 83 D
Killieser Ave. SW2 86 30 72 A
Killip Cl. E16 58 39 81 D
Killowen Ave. Nthlt 43 14 85 C
Killowen Rd. E9 49 35 84 B
Killyon Rd. SW8 74 29 76 C
Kilmaine Rd. SW6 62 24 77 C
Kilmarsh Rd. W6 62 23 78 A
Kilmartin Ave. SW16 97 31 68 A
Kilmartin Rd. Ilf 40 46 86 A
Kilmeston Way (off Daniel Gdns). SE15 63 33 77 D
Kilmington Rd. SW13 61 22 77 A
Kilmorey Gdns. Twick 71 16 75 D
Kilmorey Rd. Twick 71 16 75 D
Kilmorie Rd. SE23 88 36 73 C
Kiln Ct. E14 57 36 80 B
Kilner St. E14 57 37 81 A
Kiln Pl. NW5 47 28 85 C
Kiln Way. Nthwd 19 09 91 A
Kilravock St. W10 56 24 82 A
Kilsby Wlk. Dag 51 46 84 B
Kimbell Gdns. SW6 73 24 76 A
Kimberley Ave. E6 50 42 83 C
Kimberley Ave. Ilf 40 45 87 A
Kimberley Ave. Rom 41 50 88 C
Kimberley Ave. SE15 76 35 75 A
Kimberley Gdns. Enf 13 33 96 B
Kimberley Gdns. N4 37 31 88 B
Kimberley Rd. Beck 98 35 69 D
Kimberley Rd. E11 38 38 86 B
Kimberley Rd. E16 58 39 82 D
Kimberley Rd. E17 26 36 90 B
Kimberley Rd. N17 25 34 90 C
Kimberley Rd. N18 25 34 91 B
Kimberley Rd. NW6 46 24 83 A
Kimberley SW9 74 30 75 A
Kimberley Rd. Th Hth 105 31 67 B
Kimber Rd. SW18 85 25 73 A
Kimble Rd. SW19 95 26 70 B
Kimbolton Cl. SE12 77 39 74 D
Kimbolton Row. SW3 9 27 78 A
Kimmeridge Gdns. SE9 89 42 71 A
Kimmeridge Rd. SE9 89 42 71 A
Kimpton Rd. SE5 75 32 76 B
Kimpton Rd. Sutt 103 24 65 B
Kinburn St. SE16 64 35 79 B
Kincaid Rd. SE15 63 34 77 D
Kinch Gr. Har 33 18 87 B
Kinder St. E1 57 34 81 D
Kinfauns Ave. Horn 42 53 88 C
Kinfauns Rd. Ilf 40 46 87 D
Kinfauns Rd. SW2 87 31 72 A
King Alfred Ave. SE6 88 37 71 A
King Alfred Rd. Rom 30 54 90 D
King and Queen St. SE17 63 32 78 C
King Arthur Cl. SE15 64 35 77 C
King Charles Cres. Surb 101 18 66 B
King Charles' Rd. Surb 101 18 67 D
King Charles St. SW1 7 30 79 A
King Charles Wlk. SW19 85 24 73 C
King David La. E1 57 35 80 A
Kingdon Rd. NW6 46 25 84 A
King Edward Ave. Dart 80 53 74 D
King Edward Dri. Chess 101 18 65 C
King Edward Rd. Barn 11 25 96 D
King Edward Rd. E10 38 38 87 C
King Edward Rd. E17 26 36 89 A
King Edward Rd. Rom 42 51 88 D
King Edward's Gdns. W3 55 19 80 C
King Edward's Gr. Tedd 93 17 70 A
King Edward's Rd. Bark 51 44 83 B
King Edward's Rd. E9 49 35 83 A
King Edward's Rd. Enf 14 35 96 D
King Edward's Rd. N9 17 34 94 B
King Edward's Rd. Ruis 31 08 87 D
King Edward St. EC1 4 32 81 C
King Edward Wlk. SE1 7 31 79 C
Kingfield Rd. W5 54 17 82 D
Kingfield St. E14 64 38 78 A
Kingfisher Ct. E Mol 93 15 68 C
Kingfisher Dri. Rich 83 16 71 B
Kingfisher Pl. N22 24 30 90 D
King Gdns. Croy 112 31 64 D
King George Ave. E16 58 41 81 D
King George Cl. Rom 29 50 89 A
King George St. SE10 64 38 77 C
King George V1 Ave. Mit 96 27 68 D
Kingham Cl. SW18 85 26 73 A
Kingham Cl. W11 62 23 79 B
King Harolds Way. Bexh 67 48 77 C
King Henry's Rd. King 94 19 68 B
King Henry's Rd. NW3 47 27 84 C
King Henry St. N16 48 33 85 C
King Henry's Wlk. N1 48 33 84 A
Kinghorn St. EC1 4 32 81 A
King James St. SE1 7 31 79 B
King John Ct. EC2 4 33 82 C

King John St. E1 57 35 81 B
King John's Wlk. SE9 89 41 73 D
King John's Wlk. SE9 77 42 74 C
Kinglake St. SE17 63 33 78 C
Kingly Ct. W1 6 29 80 A
Kingly St. W1 6 29 80 A
Kingsand Rd. SE12 89 40 72 A
King's Arms Alley (Path). Brent 60 17 77 B
King's Arms Yd. EC2 4 32 81 D
Kings Arms Yd. Rom 42 51 88 A
King's Ave. Ashf 91 09 70 B
Kings Ave. Brom 99 39 70 B
Kings Ave. Cars 111 27 63 D
King's Ave. Grnf 53 13 81 D
King's Ave. Houn 70 13 76 B
Kings Ave. N10 24 28 89 A
King's Ave. N21 17 31 94 D
Kings Ave. N Mal 94 21 68 D
Kings Ave. Rom 41 48 88 D
Kings Ave. SW12 86 29 73 D
Kings Ave. SW4 74 30 74 C
Kings Ave. W5 54 17 81 D
King's Ave. Wdf Gn 27 40 91 B
King's Bench St. SE1 7 31 79 B
King's Bench Wlk. EC4 3 31 81 C
Kingsbridge Ave. W3 60 18 79 B
Kingsbridge Circ. Rom 30 54 91 A
Kingsbridge Cl. Rom 30 54 91 A
Kingsbridge Cres. Sthl 53 12 81 B
Kingsbridge Gdns. Dart 80 53 74 D
Kingsbridge Rd. Bark 51 44 83 D
Kingsbridge Rd. Mord 103 23 66 B
Kingsbridge Rd. Rom 30 54 91 A
Kingsbridge Rd. Sthl 59 12 78 B
Kingsbridge Rd. W10 56 23 81 C
Kingsbury Rd. N1 48 33 84 A
Kingsbury Rd. NW9 34 20 88 A
Kingsbury Terr. N1 48 33 84 A
Kings Cl. Dart 80 51 75 C
King's Cl. E10 38 37 87 B
Kingsclere Cl. SW15 84 22 73 A
Kingscliffe Gdns. SW19 85 24 73 D
Kings Cl. Nthwd 19 09 91 B
Kings Cl. NW4 23 23 89 D
King's College Rd. NW3 47 27 84 C
Kings College Rd. Ruis 37 09 88 D
Kingscote Rd. Croy 105 34 66 B
Kingscote Rd. N Mal 94 20 68 B
Kingscote Rd. W4 61 20 79 D
Kingscote St. EC4 7 31 80 B
Kingscourt Rd. SW16 86 30 72 C
King's Cres. N4 37 32 86 C
Kingscroft Rd. NW2 46 24 84 B
Kingscroft. SW4 74 30 74 C
King's Cross Bridge. WC1 3 30 82 A
King's Cross. N1 3 30 82 A
King's Cross Rd. WC1 3 30 82 B
Kings Ct. E13 50 40 83 B
King's Ct. SE1 8 32 79 A
Kingsdale Gdns. W11 56 23 80 D
Kingsdale Rd. SE18 66 45 77 B
Kingsdale Rd. SE20 98 35 70 D
Kingsdown Ave. S Croy 112 32 62 A
Kingsdown Ave. W13 60 16 79 B
Kingsdown Ave. W3 55 21 80 A
Kingsdown Cl. W10 56 23 81 D
Kingsdowne Rd. Surb 101 18 66 B
Kingsdown Rd. E11 39 39 86 C
Kingsdown Rd. N19 36 30 86 A
Kingsdown Rd. Sutt 110 24 64 C
Kingsdown Way. Brom 107 40 66 A
Kingsdown Way. Brom 107 40 67 C
King's Dri. Surb 101 16 66 B
Kings Dri. Surb 102 19 67 C
King's Dri. Tedd 82 14 71 D
Kings Dri. Wem 34 19 86 B
Kingsend. Ruis 31 09 87 C
Kings Farm Ave. Rich 72 19 75 C
Kingsfield Ave. Har 32 14 88 A
Kingsfield Rd. Har 32 14 87 B
Kingsford Ave. Wall 111 30 63 C
Kingsford St. NW5 47 27 85 D
Kingsgate Ave. N3 23 25 89 A
Kingsgate Cl. Bexh 79 48 76 A
Kingsgate Estate. N1 48 33 84 A
Kingsgate Pl. NW6 46 25 84 C
Kingsgate Rd. NW6 46 25 84 C
Kingsgate. Wem 34 20 86 C
Kings Gdns. Ilf 40 44 87 D
Kingsground. SE9 89 42 73 A
Kingsground. SE9 77 42 74 C
Kings Gr. Rom 42 52 88 A
King's Gr. SE15 75 34 76 B
Kings Hall Rd. Beck 98 36 69 A
Kings Head Hill. E4 18 38 94 A
Kings Head Pas. SW4 74 29 75 D
King's Head Yd. SE1 8 32 80 D
King's Highway. SE18 66 45 77 B
Kingshill Ave. Har 21 16 89 D
Kingshill Ave. Har 33 17 88 A
Kingshill Ave. Nthlt 53 11 82 A
Kingshill Ave. Rom 29 50 91 A
Kingshill Ave. Wor Pk 102 22 66 B
Kingshill Dri. Har 21 16 89 B
Kingshold Rd. E9 49 35 84 C
Kingsholm Gdns. SE9 77 42 75 C
Kingshurst Rd. SE12 89 40 73 A
King's Keep. Surb 93 18 68 C
Kingsland Green. N16 48 33 84 A
Kingsland High St. E8 48 33 85 D
Kingsland Pas. E8 48 33 84 A
KingslandRd. E13 58 41 82 A
Kingsland Rd. E2 48 33 83 B
Kingsland Rd. E8 48 33 84 C
King's La. Sutt 110 26 64 D
King's Lawn Cl. SW15 72 22 74 B
Kingsley Ave. Houn 70 14 76 C
Kingsley Ave. Sthl 53 13 80 A
Kingsley Ave. Sutt 110 26 64 B
Kingsley Ave. W13 54 16 81 C
Kingsley Cl. Dag 52 49 85 B
Kingsley Cl. NW2 35 26 88 A
Kingsley Dri. Wor Pk 102 21 65 B
Kingsley Gdns. E4 18 37 92 C
Kingsley Gdns. Horn 30 53 89 D
Kingsley Mews. W8 62 25 79 D
Kingsley Pl. N6 36 28 87 A
Kingsley Rd. Croy 105 31 66 C
Kingsley Rd. E17 26 38 90 C
Kingsley Rd. E7 50 40 84 C
Kingsley Rd. Har 20 12 89 D
Kingsley Rd. Har 32 14 86 C
Kingsley Rd. Houn 70 14 76 C
Kingsley Rd. Ilf 28 44 90 A
Kingsley Rd. N13 17 31 92 B
Kingsley Rd. NW6 46 24 83 B
Kingsley Rd. SW19 85 25 71 D
Kingsley St. SW11 74 27 75 B
Kingsley Way. N2 35 26 88 A
Kingsley Wood Dri. SE9 89 42 72 D
Kingslyn Cres. SE19 97 33 69 A
Kings Lynn Dri. Rom 30 53 91 B
King's Mall. W6 62 23 78 A
Kingsman Par. SE18 65 42 79 D
Kingsman St. SE18 65 42 78 B
Kingsmead Ave. Mit 96 29 68 A
Kingsmead Ave. N9 17 34 94 D
Kingsmead Ave. NW9 34 20 87 B
Kingsmead Ave. Rom 42 51 88 D
Kingsmead Ave. Sun 92 11 69 C
Kingsmead Ave. Surb 102 19 65 A
Kingsmead Ave. Wor Pk 102 22 65 D
Kingsmead. Barn 11 25 96 C
Kingsmead Cl. Eps 109 20 63 D
Kingsmead Cl. Sid 90 46 72 A
Kingsmead Dri. Nthlt 43 12 84 D
Kingsmead Rd. SW2 87 31 72 A
King's Mead Way. E9 49 36 85 A
Kingsmere Park. NW9 34 20 87 C
Kingsmere Rd. SW19 85 23 72 B
King's Mews. SW4 74 30 74 A
King's Mews. WC1 3 30 82 D
Kingsmill Gdns. Dag 52 48 85 D
Kingsmill Rd. Dag 52 48 85 D
Kingsmill Terr. NW8 46 26 83 D
Kingsnympton Park. King 94 19 70 B
King's Orchard. SE9 77 42 74 C
King's Paddock. Hamp 92 14 69 A
Kingspark Ct. E18 27 40 89 A
King's Pas. King 93 17 69 B
King's Pas. King 93 17 69 B
King's Pas. King 93 17 69 D
King's Pl. SE1 8 32 79 A
Kings Pl. W4 61 20 78 A
King Sq. EC1 4 32 82 A
King's Rd. Bark 51 44 84 C
King's Rd. Barn 11 23 96 A
Kings Rd Bungalows. Har 32 12 86 D
King's Rd. E11 39 39 87 A
King's Rd. E4 18 38 94 D
King's Rd. E6 50 41 83 A
King's Rd. Felt 82 11 73 C
Kings Rd. Har 32 12 86 B
King's Rd. King 93 18 70 C
Kings Rd. Mit 96 28 68 A
King's Rd. N17 25 33 90 B
King's Rd. N18 17 34 92 A
King's Rd. N22 24 30 90 B
King's Rd. NW10 45 22 84 D
Kings Rd. Rich 71 18 74 B
King's Rd. Rom 42 52 88 A
King's Rd. SE25 97 34 68 A
King's Rd. Surb 101 17 66 C
Kings Rd. Sutt 110 25 62 D
King's Rd. SW10 62 26 77 C
King's Rd. SW19 95 25 70 A
King's Rd. SW1 6 28 79 C
Kings Rd. SW3 9 27 78 C
King's Rd. SW6 62 25 77 D
King's Rd. Tedd 82 14 71 D
King's Rd. Twick 71 16 74 D
Kings Rd. W5 54 17 81 B
Kings Ride Gate. Rich 72 19 75 C
King's Scholars' Pas. SW1 10 29 78 A
King St. E13 58 40 82 C
King St. EC2 4 32 81 C
King's Terr. NW1 47 29 83 A
Kingsthorpe Rd. SE26 88 35 71 B
King St. N17 25 33 90 B
King St. N2 23 26 89 C
Kingston Ave. Felt 69 09 74 D
Kingston Ave. Sutt 103 24 65 C
Kingston By Pass. Esh 101 15 65 D
Kingston By Pass. N.Mal 102 21 67 A
Kingston By Pass. Surb 101 18 65 D
Kingston By Pass. Surb 102 19 65 C
Kingston By Ps. N Mal 102 21 67 A
Kingston By Ps. SW15 84 21 71 A
Kingston By Ps. SW20 94 21 69 B
Kingston Cl. Nthlt 43 12 83 B
Kingston Cl. Rom 29 48 89 A
Kingston Cl. Tedd 93 16 70 B
Kingston Cres. Beck 98 36 69 B
Kingston Hall Rd. King 93 17 68 B
Kingston Hill Ave. Rom 29 48 89 A
Kingston Hill. King 94 19 70 B
Kingston La. Tedd 93 16 70 B
Kingston Rd. Ashf 91 07 70 A
Kingston Rd. Barn 11 26 95 B
Kingston Rd. Eps 109 21 64 C
Kingston Rd. Ilf 51 44 85 A
Kingston Rd. King 94 19 68 B
Kingston Rd. N9 17 34 93 A
Kingston Rd. N Mal 94 20 68 D
Kingston Rd. Rom 30 51 89 D
Kingston Rd. Sthl 59 12 79 B
Kingston Rd. Surb 102 19 65 B
Kingston Rd. SW15 84 22 73 D
Kingston Rd. SW19 95 25 69 A
Kingston Rd. SW20 95 24 69 C
Kingston Rd. Tedd 93 16 70 B
Kingston Rd. Wor Pk 102 20 65 C
Kingston Vale. SW15 84 21 72 C
Kingstown St. NW1 47 28 83 A
King St. Rich 71 17 74 B
King St. Sthl 59 12 79 C
King St. SW1 6 29 80 C
King St. Twick 83 16 73 C
King St. W3 55 20 80 C
King St. W6 61 22 78 A
King St. WC2 7 30 80 A
Kingsway Cres. Har 20 14 89 C
Kings Way. Croy 111 30 64 D
Kingsway. Enf 13 34 95 B
Kings Way. Har 21 15 89 C
Kingsway. N12 23 26 91 A
Kingsway. N. Mal 103 23 67 A
Kingsway. Orp 108 44 67 B
Kingsway Rd. Sutt 110 24 63 C
Kingsway. SW14 72 19 75 B
Kingsway The. Eps 109 21 62 D
Kingsway. WC2 3 30 81 D
Kingsway. Wem 44 18 85 A
Kingsway. W.Wick 107 39 65 D
Kingswear Rd. Ruis 31 10 86 A
Kingswood Ave. Belv 67 48 78 B
Kingswood Ave. Brom 99 39 68 C
Kingswood Ave. Hamp 92 13 70 B
Kingswood Ave. Houn 70 12 76 D
Kingswood Ave. NW6 46 24 83 C
Kingswood Ave. Th Hth 105 31 67 A
Kingswood Cl. Dart 80 53 74 C
Kingswood Cl. N20 15 26 94 A
Kingswood Cl. N.Mal 102 21 67 D
Kingswood Cl. Orp 108 44 66 B
Kingswood Cl. Surb 101 18 66 A
Kingswood Cl. SW8 10 30 77 C
Kingswood Dri. Cars 104 27 66 D
Kingswood Dri. SE19 87 33 71 B
Kingswood Park. N3 23 24 90 D
Kingswood Pl. SE13 77 39 75 C
Kingswood Rd. Brom 99 39 68 A
Kingswood Rd. Ilf 40 46 87 A
Kingswood Rd. SE20 98 35 70 A
Kingswood Rd. SW19 95 24 70 D
Kingswood Rd. SW2 86 30 73 A
Kingswood Rd. W4 61 20 79 C
Kingswood Way. Wall 111 30 64 C
Kingsworth Cl. Beck 106 36 67 A
Kingthorpe Rd. NW10 45 20 84 D
Kingwear Rd. NW5 36 28 86 D
King William La. E10 65 39 78 C
King William St. EC4 8 32 80 B
King William Wlk. SE10 64 38 77 A
Kingwood Rd. SW6 62 24 77 C
Kinlet Rd. SE18 78 44 76 A
Kinloch Dri. NW9 34 21 87 A
Kinloch St. N7 36 30 86 D
Kinloss Gdns. N3 23 24 89 D
Kinloss Rd. Cars 103 26 66 A
Kinnaird Ave. Brom 99 39 70 B
Kinnaird Ave. W4 61 20 77 C
Kinnaird Cl. Brom 99 39 70 B
Kinnaird Way. Wdf Gn 27 42 91 B
Kinnear Rd. W12 61 21 79 B
Kinnerton Pl N. SW1 5 27 79 B
Kinnerton Pl S. SW1 5 27 79 B
Kinnerton St. SW1 6 28 79 A
Kinnerton Yd. SW1 6 28 79 A
Kinnoul Rd. W6 62 24 77 A
Kinross Ave. Wor Pk 102 22 65 A
Kinross Cl. Har 33 18 88 B
Kinross Cl. Sun 81 09 71 D
Kinross Dri. Sun 81 09 71 D
Kinsale Rd. SE15 75 34 75 A
Kintore Way. SE1 63 33 78 B
Kintyre Cl. SW16 96 30 68 B
Kinveachy Gdns. SE7 65 42 78 C
Kinver Rd. SE26 88 35 71 A
Kipling Pl. Stan 21 15 91 B
Kipling Rd. Bexh 79 48 76 A
Kipling St. SE1 8 32 79 B
Kipling Terr. N9 17 32 93 B
Kippington Dri. SE9 89 41 73 D
Kirby Cl. Eps 109 21 64 D
Kirby Cl. Ilf 28 45 91 A
Kirby Cl. Nthwd 19 09 91 B
Kirby Estate. SE16 63 34 79 D
Kirby Gr. SE1 8 33 79 A
Kirby St. EC1 3 31 81 A
Kirchen Rd. W13 54 16 80 B
Kirkdale Rd. E11 39 39 87 A
Kirkdale. SE26 88 35 71 A
Kirkey Rd. SW19 95 25 69 A
Kirkham St. SE18 66 45 77 A
Kirkland Ave. Ilf 28 43 90 C
Kirkland Wlk (off Crosby Wlk). E8 48 33 84 B
Kirk La. SE18 66 44 77 A
Kirklees Rd. Dag 52 47 85 C
Kirklees Rd. Th Hth 105 31 67 A
Kirkly Cl. S Croy 112 33 62 A
Kirkman Pl. W1 2 29 81 B
Kirkmichael Rd. E14 58 38 81 C
Kirk Rd. E17 38 36 88 D
Kirkside Rd. SE3 65 40 77 A
Kirk's Pl. E14 57 36 81 B
Kirkstall Ave. N17 25 32 89 D
Kirkstall Gdns. SW2 86 30 73 C
Kirkstall Rd. SW2 86 30 73 C
Kirksted Rd. Mord 103 25 66 D
Kirkstone Way. Brom 99 39 70 C
Kirkton Rd. N15 25 33 89 C
Kirkwall Pl. E2 57 35 82 A
Kirkwood Rd. SE15 75 34 76 D
Kirn Rd. W13 54 16 80 B
Kirtley Rd. SE26 88 36 71 A
Kirtling St. SW8 10 29 77 C
Kirton Cl. W4 61 20 78 B
Kirton Gdns. E2 4 33 82 B
Kirton Rd. E13 50 41 83 C
Kirton Wlk. Edg 22 20 91 C
Kirwyn Way. SE5 63 31 77 D
Kitcat Terr. E3 57 37 82 A
Kitchener Rd. Dag 52 49 84 B
Kitchener Rd. E17 26 37 90 B
Kitchener Rd. E7 50 40 84 B
Kitchener Rd. N17 25 33 89 A
Kitchener Rd. N2 24 27 89 A
Kitchener Rd. Th Hth 97 32 68 B
Kitley Gdns. SE19 97 33 69 B
Kitson Rd. SE5 63 32 77 D
Kitson Rd. SW13 72 22 76 A
Kittiwake Rd. Nthlt 53 11 82 B
Kitto Rd. SE14 76 35 76 D
Kitt's End Rd. Barn 11 24 97 B
Kiver Rd. N19 36 30 86 A
Klea Ave. SW4 74 29 74 C
Knapdale Cl. SE23 87 34 72 B
Knapmill Rd. SE6 88 37 72 B
Knapmill Way. SE6 88 37 72 B
Knapp Cl. NW10 45 21 84 A
Knapp Rd. E3 57 37 82 C
Knaresborough Pl. SW5 62 25 78 B
Knatchbull Rd. NW10 45 20 83 B
Knatchbull Rd. SE5 75 31 76 B
Knebworth Ave. E17 26 37 90 A
Knebworth Rd. N16 48 33 85 A
Knee Hill Cres. SE2 67 47 78 A
Knee Hill. SE2 67 47 78 C
Kneller Gdns. Islw 70 14 74 D
Kneller Rd. N.Mal 102 21 66 A
Kneller Rd. SE4 76 36 75 C
Kneller Rd. Twick 70 14 74 D
Knightland Rd. E5 37 34 86 B
Knighton Cl. Rom 41 50 88 D
Knighton Cl. S Croy 112 31 62 B
Knighton Park Rd. SE26 88 35 71 D
Knighton Rd. E7 39 40 86 C
Knighton Rd. Rom 41 50 88 C
Knightrider St. EC4 7 32 80 C
Knight's Ave. W5 60 18 79 A
Knightsbridge Gdns. Rom 41 50 88 B
Knightsbridge Green. SW1 5 27 79 B
Knightsbridge. SW1 5 27 79 B
Knightsbridge. SW7 5 27 79 A
Knights Cl. E9 49 35 85 C
Knight's Hill. SE21 87 31 73 D
Knight's Hill. SE27 87 31 71 B
Knight's Hill Sq. SE27 87 31 71 B
Knight's La. N9 17 34 93 C
Knight's Park. King 93 18 68 A
Knights Rd. E16 65 40 79 A
Knights Way. Ilf 28 44 91 A
Knight's Wlk. SE11 63 31 78 B
Knightwood Cres. N.Mal 102 21 67 C
Knivett Rd. SW6 62 25 77 A
Knobs Hill Rd. E15 49 37 83 B
Knockholt Rd. SE9 77 41 74 B
Knole Cl. Croy 106 35 67 C
Knole The. SE9 90 43 71 A
Knoll Cres. Nthwd 19 09 90 C
Knoll Dri. N14 16 28 94 A
Knollmead. Surb 102 20 66 C
Knoll Rd. Bex 79 49 74 C
Knoll Rd. Sid 90 46 71 B
Knoll Rd. SW18 73 26 74 A
Knoll Rise. Orp 108 45 66 D
Knolls Cl. Wor Pk 102 22 65 D
Knoll The. Beck 98 37 69 B
Knoll The. Brom 107 40 66 C
Knoll The. W13 54 17 81 A
Knolly's Cl. SW16 87 31 72 C
Knolly's Rd. SW16 87 31 72 C
Knottisford St. E2 57 35 82 B
Knotts Green Rd. E10 38 38 88 C
Knowle Ave. Bexh 67 48 77 D
Knowle Cl. SW9 75 31 75 A
Knowle Rd. Brom 107 42 65 A
Knowle Rd. Twick 83 15 73 C
Knowles Hill Cres. SE13 76 38 74 B
Knowles Wlk. SW4 74 29 75 A
Knowlton Green. Brom 107 39 67 B
Knowsley Ave. Sthl 53 13 80 D
Knowsley Rd. SW11 74 27 76 D
Knox Rd. E7 50 40 84 A
Knox St. W1 1 27 81 B
Knoyle St. SE14 64 36 77 A
Kohat Rd. SW19 85 25 71 D
Kosuth St. E10 65 39 78 C
Kramer Mews. SW5 62 25 78 D
Kreisel Wlk. Rich 60 18 77 B
Kuala Gdns. SW16 96 30 69 B
Kuhn Way. E7 50 40 85 C
Kydbrook Cl. Orp 108 44 66 A
Kylemore Cl. E6 50 41 83 D
Kylemore Rd. NW6 46 25 84 C
Kymberley Rd. Har 33 15 88 C
Kyme Rd. Horn 42 51 88 D
Kynance Gdns. Stan 21 17 90 A
Kynance Mews. SW7 5 26 79 C
Kynance Pl. SW7 5 26 79 C
Kynaston Ave. N16 37 33 86 D
Kynaston Ave. Th Hth 105 32 67 A
Kynaston Cl. Har 20 14 91 D
Kynaston Cres. Th Hth 105 32 67 A
Kynaston Rd. Brom 89 40 71 C
Kynaston Rd. Enf 13 32 97 B
Kynaston Rd. N16 37 33 86 C
Kynaston Rd. Orp 108 46 66 B
Kynaston Rd. Th Hth 105 32 67 A
Kynaston Wood. Har 20 14 91 D
Kynersley Cl. Cars 104 27 65 D
Kynoch Rd. N18 18 35 92 B
Kyrle Rd. SW11 74 28 74 C
Kyverdale Rd. N16 37 33 87 D

Laburnum Ave. Horn 42 52 86 A
Laburnum Ave. N17 25 32 91 D
Laburnum Gr. Houn 70 12 75 D
Laburnum Ave. N9 17 33 93 B
Laburnum Ave. Sutt 104 27 65 C
Laburnum Cl. E4 26 36 91 B
Laburnum Cl. SE15 64 35 77 C
Laburnum Cres. Sun 91 10 69 B
Laburnum Gdns. N21 17 32 93 A
Laburnum Gr. N21 17 32 93 A
Laburnum Gr. N Mal 94 20 69 D
Laburnum Gr. NW9 34 20 87 A
Laburnum Gr. Ruis 31 08 88 D
Laburnum Gr. Sthl 53 12 82 D
Laburnum Rd. Mit 96 28 69 C
Laburnum Rd. SW19 95 26 70 C
Laburnum St. E2 48 33 83 B
Laburnum Way. Brom 108 43 66 B
Lacey Wlk. E3 49 37 83 C
Lackington St. EC2 4 32 81 B
Lacock Cl. SW19 95 26 70 A
Lacon Rd. SE22 75 34 74 A
Lacy Dri. Hamp 92 12 69 B
Lacy Rd. SW15 73 23 75 D
Ladas Rd. SE27 87 32 71 C
Ladbroke Cres. W11 56 24 81 C
Ladbroke Gdns. W11 56 24 80 B
Ladbroke Gr. W10 56 24 81 A
Ladbroke Gr. W11 56 24 80 B
Ladbroke Mews. W11 56 24 80 C
Ladbroke Rd. Enf 13 33 95 D
Ladbroke Rd. W11 56 24 80 D
Ladbroke Sq. W11 56 24 80 B
Ladbroke Terr. W11 56 24 80 D
Ladbroke Wlk. W11 56 24 80 D
Ladbrook Cl. Pnr 32 12 88 B
Ladbrook Rd. SE25 97 32 68 D
Ladderstile Ride. King 84 20 71 C
Ladderswood Way. N11 16 29 92 C
Ladycroft Rd. SE13 76 37 75 B
Ladycroft Wlk. Stan 21 17 90 D
Ladygate La. Ruis 31 08 88 C
Lady Hay. Wor Pk 102 21 65 B
Lady Margaret Rd. N19 47 29 85 A
Lady Margaret Rd. Sthl 53 12 81 B
Ladysmith Ave. E6 50 42 83 C
Ladysmith Ave. Ilf 40 45 87 A
Ladysmith Rd. E16 58 39 82 B
Ladysmith Rd. Enf 13 33 97 D
Ladysmith Rd. Har 21 15 90 C
Ladysmith Rd. N17 25 34 90 C
Ladysmith Rd. N18 17 34 92 D
Ladysmith Rd. SE9 78 43 74 C
Lady Somerset Rd. NW5 47 28 85 B
Ladywell Rd. SE13 76 37 74 B
Ladywell St. E15 50 39 83 B
Ladywood Ave. Orp 108 45 67 A
Ladywood Rd. Surb 102 19 65 A
Lafone Ave. Felt 82 11 72 A
Lafone St. SE1 8 33 79 B
Lagonda Ave. Ilf 28 45 91 B
Laing Cl. Ilf 28 44 91 B
Laing Dean. Nthlt 43 11 83 A
Laing's Ave. Mit 96 27 69 D
Lainson St. SW18 85 25 73 A
Lairdale Cl. SE21 87 32 73 A
Lairs Cl. N7 47 30 84 A
Laitwood Rd. SW12 86 28 73 D
Lake Ave. Brom 99 40 70 A
Lake Cl. SW19 85 24 71 D
Lakedale Rd. SE18 66 45 78 C
Lakefield Rd. N22 25 31 90 D
Lake Gdns. Dag 52 49 85 C
Lake Gdns. Rich 83 16 72 B
Lake Gdns. Wall 104 28 65 D
Lakehall Gdns. Th Hth 105 31 67 B
Lakehall Rd. Th Hth 105 31 67 B
Lake House Rd. E11 39 40 86 A
Lakehurst Rd. Eps 109 21 64 C
Lakeland Cl. Har 20 14 91 B
Lakenheath. N14 12 29 95 B
Lake Rd. Croy 106 36 65 B
Lake Rd. Rom 29 47 89 D
Lake Rd. SW19 85 24 71 D
Lake Rise. Rom 30 51 89 B
Lakeside Ave. Ilf 27 41 89 D
Lakeside. Beck 98 37 68 B
Lakeside Cl. Ruis 19 08 89 D
Lakeside Cl. SE25 97 34 69 C
Lakeside Cl. Sid 79 47 74 C
Lakeside Cres. Barn 12 27 95 B
Lakeside Dri. Brom 107 42 65 C
Lakeside. Enf 12 29 96 D

| Street | Page | Grid |
|---|---|---|
| Lakeside Rd. N13 | 16 | 30 93 D |
| Lakeside Rd. W14 | 62 | 23 79 D |
| Lakeside. W13 | 54 | 17 81 C |
| Lakeside. Wall | 111 | 28 64 B |
| Lakeside Way. Wem | 45 | 19 85 A |
| Lakeswood Rd. Orp | 108 | 44 67 C |
| Lake View. Edg | 21 | 18 91 B |
| Lakeview Rd. SE27 | 87 | 31 71 D |
| Lakeview Rd. Well | 78 | 46 75 D |
| Lakis Cl. NW3 | 46 | 26 85 A |
| Laleham Rd. SE6 | 88 | 38 73 A |
| Laleham Rd. Shep | 91 | 07 68 C |
| Lalor St. SW6 | 73 | 24 76 C |
| Lambarde Ave. SE9 | 90 | 43 71 A |
| Lamberhurst Rd. Dag | 41 | 48 87 D |
| Lamberhurst Rd. SE27 | 87 | 31 71 C |
| Lambert Ave. Rich | 72 | 19 75 B |
| Lambert Rd. E16 | 58 | 40 81 D |
| Lambert Rd. N12 | 15 | 26 92 D |
| Lambert Rd. SW2 | 74 | 30 74 B |
| Lambert's Pl. Croy | 105 | 32 66 D |
| Lambert's Rd. Surb | 101 | 18 67 B |
| Lambert St. N1 | 48 | 31 84 C |
| Lambert Way. N12 | 23 | 26 91 A |
| Lambert Way. N12 | 23 | 26 91 A |
| Lambert Way. N12 | 15 | 26 92 C |
| Lambert Way. N12 | 15 | 26 92 C |
| Lambert Wlk. Wem | 33 | 17 86 D |
| Lambeth Bridge. SW1 | 10 | 30 78 A |
| Lambeth High St. SE1 | 10 | 30 78 B |
| Lambeth Hill. EC4 | 8 | 32 80 A |
| Lambeth Mews. SE11 | 10 | 30 78 B |
| Lambeth Palace Rd. SE1 | 7 | 30 79 D |
| Lambeth Rd. Croy | 105 | 31 66 D |
| Lambeth Rd. SE1 | 7 | 31 79 C |
| Lambeth Wlk. SE11 | 10 | 30 78 B |
| Lamb La. E8 | 48 | 34 84 D |
| Lamble St. NW5 | 47 | 28 85 C |
| Lambley Rd. Dag | 51 | 46 84 B |
| Lamb Mews. N1 | 48 | 31 83 B |
| Lambolle Pl. NW3 | 47 | 27 84 A |
| Lambolle Rd. NW3 | 47 | 27 84 A |
| Lambourn Cl. NW5 | 47 | 29 85 A |
| Lambourn Cl. W7 | 60 | 15 79 B |
| Lambourne Ave. SW19 | 85 | 24 71 B |
| Lambourne Gdns. Bark | 51 | 45 84 D |
| Lambourne Gdns. E4 | 18 | 37 93 A |
| Lambourne Gdns. Enf | 13 | 33 97 D |
| Lambourne Gdns. Horn | 42 | 53 86 B |
| Lambourne Gr. King | 94 | 19 69 D |
| Lambourne Pl. SE3 | 77 | 40 76 B |
| Lambourne Rd. Bark | 51 | 45 84 D |
| Lambourne Rd. E11 | 38 | 38 87 A |
| Lambourne Rd. Ilf | 40 | 45 86 A |
| Lambourn Rd. SW4 | 74 | 28 75 B |
| Lambrook Terr. SW6 | 73 | 24 76 A |
| Lamb's Bldgs. EC1 | 4 | 32 82 D |
| Lamb's Conduit Pas. WC1 | 3 | 30 81 B |
| Lamb's Conduit St. WC1 | 3 | 30 82 D |
| Lambscroft Ave. SE9 | 89 | 41 72 D |
| Lambs Meadow. Wdf Gn | 27 | 41 90 D |
| Lamb's Pas. EC1 | 4 | 32 82 D |
| Lamb St. E1 | 4 | 33 81 B |
| Lamb's Terr. N9 | 17 | 33 93 A |
| Lambs Wlk. Enf | 13 | 32 97 C |
| Lambton Pl. W11 | 56 | 24 81 D |
| Lambton Rd. N19 | 36 | 30 87 C |
| Lambton Rd. SW20 | 95 | 23 69 A |
| Lamb Wlk. SE1 | 8 | 33 79 A |
| Lamerock Rd. Brom | 89 | 39 71 B |
| Lamerton St. SE8 | 64 | 37 77 A |
| Lamerton Way. Ilf | 28 | 43 90 D |
| Lamford Cl. N17 | 25 | 32 91 D |
| Lamington St. W6 | 61 | 22 78 B |
| *Lamlash St. SE11 | 63 | 31 78 B |
| Lammas Ave. Mit | 96 | 28 69 C |
| Lammas Green. SE26 | 87 | 34 72 D |
| Lammas Park Gdns. W5 | 54 | 17 80 C |
| Lammas Park Rd. W5 | 60 | 17 79 B |
| Lammas Rd. E10 | 38 | 36 87 C |
| Lammas Rd. E9 | 49 | 35 84 D |
| Lammas Rd. Rich | 71 | 17 71 A |
| Lammermoor Rd. SW12 | 86 | 28 73 B |
| Lamont Rd Pas. SW10 | 62 | 26 77 B |
| Lamont Rd. SW10 | 62 | 26 77 B |
| Lamorbey Cl. Sid | 90 | 45 73 D |
| Lamorna Cl. Orp | 108 | 46 66 A |
| Lamorna Gr. Stan | 21 | 17 90 D |
| Lampard Gr. N16 | 37 | 33 87 D |
| *Lampern Sq. E2 | 57 | 34 82 A |
| Lampeter Sq. W6 | 62 | 24 77 A |
| Lampmead Rd. SE12 | 77 | 39 75 D |
| Lamport Cl. SE18 | 65 | 42 78 B |
| Lampton Ave. Houn | 70 | 13 76 B |
| Lampton House Cl. SW19 | 85 | 23 71 B |
| Lampton Park Rd. Houn | 70 | 13 76 D |
| Lampton Rd. Houn | 70 | 13 76 D |
| Lanacre Ave. NW9 | 22 | 21 90 A |
| Lanark Cl. W5 | 54 | 17 81 A |
| Lanark Pl. W9 | 1 | 26 82 C |
| Lanark Rd. W9 | 46 | 25 83 D |
| Lanark Rd. W9 | 1 | 26 82 A |
| Lanata Wlk. Hay | 53 | 11 82 D |
| Lanbury Rd. SE15 | 76 | 35 75 D |
| Lancashire Ct. W1 | 6 | 28 80 B |
| Lancaster Ave. Bark | 51 | 45 84 C |
| Lancaster Ave. E18 | 27 | 40 89 D |
| Lancaster Ave. Mit | 104 | 30 67 A |
| Lancaster Ave. SE27 | 87 | 32 72 A |
| Lancaster Ave. SW19 | 85 | 23 71 D |
| Lancaster Cl. Brom | 99 | 39 68 D |
| Lancaster Cl. King | 83 | 17 71 D |
| Lancaster Cottages. Rich | 71 | 18 74 C |
| Lancaster Ct. Sutt | 110 | 25 63 C |
| Lancaster Ct. SW6 | 62 | 25 77 C |
| Lancaster Dri. NW3 | 47 | 27 84 A |
| Lancaster Garages. NW3 | 47 | 27 84 A |
| Lancaster Gate. W2 | 5 | 26 80 A |
| Lancaster Gdns. King | 83 | 17 71 D |
| Lancaster Gdns. SW19 | 85 | 24 71 C |
| Lancaster Gdns. W13 | 60 | 16 79 B |
| Lancaster Gr. NW3 | 47 | 27 84 A |
| Lancaster Mews. Rich | 71 | 18 74 C |
| Lancaster Mews. W2 | 5 | 26 80 A |
| Lancaster Park. Rich | 71 | 18 74 A |
| Lancaster Pl. Houn | 70 | 11 76 C |
| Lancaster Pl. SW19 | 85 | 23 71 D |
| Lancaster Pl. Twick | 83 | 16 73 A |
| Lancaster Pl. WC2 | 7 | 30 80 B |
| Lancaster Rd. Barn | 11 | 26 95 B |
| Lancaster Rd. E11 | 39 | 39 86 A |
| Lancaster Rd. E17 | 26 | 35 90 D |
| Lancaster Rd. E7 | 50 | 40 84 D |
| Lancaster Rd. Enf | 13 | 32 97 B |
| Lancaster Rd. Har | 32 | 13 88 A |
| Lancaster Rd. N11 | 24 | 29 91 B |
| Lancaster Rd. N18 | 17 | 33 92 D |
| Lancaster Rd. N4 | 37 | 31 87 A |
| Lancaster Rd. Nthlt | 43 | 14 84 A |
| Lancaster Rd. NW10 | 45 | 22 85 C |
| Lancaster Rd. SE25 | 97 | 34 68 A |
| Lancaster Rd. Sthl | 53 | 12 80 A |
| Lancaster Rd. SW19 | 85 | 24 71 C |
| Lancaster Rd. W11 | 56 | 24 81 C |
| Lancaster St. SE1 | 7 | 31 79 B |
| Lancaster Terr. W2 | 5 | 26 80 B |
| Lancefield St. W10 | 56 | 24 82 B |
| Lancell St. N16 | 37 | 33 86 A |
| Lancelot Ave. Wem | 44 | 17 85 B |
| Lancelot Cres. Wem | 44 | 17 85 B |
| Lancelot Gdns. Barn | 16 | 28 94 A |
| Lancelot Pl. SW7 | 5 | 27 79 B |
| Lancelot Rd. Ilf | 28 | 45 91 C |
| Lancelot Rd. Well | 78 | 46 75 C |
| Lancelot Rd. Wem | 44 | 17 85 D |
| Lance Rd. Har | 32 | 14 87 A |
| Lancey Cl. SE7 | 65 | 41 78 B |
| Lanchester Rd. N6 | 36 | 27 88 B |
| Lancing Gdns. N9 | 17 | 33 94 D |
| Lancing Rd. Croy | 104 | 30 66 B |
| Lancing Rd. Felt | 81 | 09 72 B |
| Lancing Rd. Ilf | 40 | 44 88 D |
| Lancing Rd. Orp | 108 | 46 65 B |
| Lancing Rd. Rom | 30 | 54 91 C |
| Lancing Rd. W13 | 54 | 16 80 B |
| Lancing St. NW1 | 2 | 29 82 B |
| Landcroft Rd. SE22 | 75 | 33 74 D |
| Landells Rd. SE22 | 75 | 34 74 C |
| Landford Rd. SW15 | 73 | 23 75 A |
| Landgrove Rd. SW19 | 85 | 25 71 C |
| Landmann Way. SE14 | 64 | 35 78 D |
| Landon Pl. SW1 | 5 | 27 79 D |
| Landon Way. Ashf | 91 | 07 70 B |
| Landon Wlk. E14 | 57 | 37 80 B |
| Landor Rd. SW9 | 74 | 30 75 A |
| Landor Wlk. W12 | 61 | 22 79 A |
| Landport Way (off Garnies Cl). SE15 | 63 | 33 77 D |
| Landra Gdns. N21 | 13 | 31 95 D |
| Landridge Rd. SW6 | 73 | 24 76 D |
| Landrock Rd. N8 | 36 | 30 88 D |
| Landscape Rd. Wdf Gn | 27 | 40 91 D |
| Landsdowne Ave. Bexh | 67 | 47 77 D |
| Landseer Ave. E12 | 51 | 43 85 C |
| Landseer Cl. Edg | 22 | 19 90 C |
| Landseer Cl. SW19 | 95 | 26 69 B |
| Landseer Rd. Enf | 13 | 34 95 A |
| Landseer Rd. N19 | 36 | 30 86 A |
| Landseer Rd. N.Mal | 102 | 20 66 B |
| Landseer Rd. Sutt | 110 | 25 63 A |
| Landstead Rd. SE18 | 66 | 44 77 D |
| Lane App. NW7 | 15 | 24 92 C |
| Lane Cl. NW2 | 34 | 22 86 D |
| Lane End. Bexh | 79 | 49 75 B |
| Lanercost Cl. SW2 | 87 | 31 72 A |
| Lanercost Gdns. N14 | 16 | 29 94 A |
| Lanercost Rd. SW2 | 87 | 31 72 A |
| Laneside Ave. Dag | 41 | 48 87 B |
| Laneside. Chis | 90 | 44 71 C |
| Lane The. NW8 | 46 | 26 83 C |
| Lane The. SE3 | 77 | 40 75 A |
| Laneway. SW15 | 72 | 22 74 B |
| Lanfranc Rd. E3 | 49 | 36 83 C |
| Lanfranc St. SE1 | 7 | 31 79 C |
| Lanfrey Pl. W14 | 62 | 24 78 D |
| Langbourne Ave. N6 | 36 | 28 86 A |
| Langbrook Rd. SE3 | 77 | 41 76 D |
| Langcroft Cl. Cars | 104 | 27 65 D |
| Langdale Ave. Mit | 96 | 27 68 B |
| Langdale Ave. Orp | 108 | 43 65 D |
| Langdale Cl. SE17 | 63 | 32 77 A |
| Langdale Cres. Bexh | 79 | 49 76 A |
| Langdale Rd. SE10 | 64 | 38 77 C |
| Langdale Rd. Th Hth | 97 | 31 68 C |
| Langdale St. E1 | 57 | 34 81 D |
| Langdon Cres. E6 | 51 | 43 83 C |
| Langdon Ct. NW10 | 45 | 20 83 A |
| Langdon Dri. NW9 | 34 | 20 87 C |
| Langdon Park Rd. N6 | 36 | 29 87 A |
| Langdon Pl. SW14 | 72 | 20 75 A |
| Langdon Rd. Brom | 99 | 40 68 B |
| Langdon Rd. E6 | 51 | 43 83 A |
| Langdon Rd. Mord | 103 | 26 67 A |
| Langdon Shaw. Sid | 90 | 45 71 D |
| Langdon Wlk. Mord | 103 | 26 67 A |
| Langford Cl. E8 | 48 | 34 85 C |
| Langford Cl. N15 | 37 | 33 88 C |
| Langford Cl. NW8 | 46 | 26 83 C |
| Langford Cres. Barn | 12 | 27 96 D |
| Langford Green. SE5 | 75 | 33 75 A |
| Langford Pl. NW8 | 46 | 26 83 C |
| Langford Pl. Sid | 90 | 46 72 C |
| Langford Rd. Barn | 12 | 27 96 D |
| Langford Rd. SW6 | 73 | 25 76 B |
| Langford Rd. SW6 | 73 | 25 76 D |
| Langford Rd. Wdf Gn | 27 | 41 91 A |
| Langham Cl. N15 | 25 | 31 89 B |
| Langham Ct. Horn | 42 | 53 87 B |
| Langham Dri. Rom | 40 | 46 88 D |
| Langham Gdns. Edg | 22 | 20 91 C |
| Langham Gdns. N21 | 13 | 31 95 B |
| Langham Gdns. Rich | 83 | 17 71 A |
| Langham Gdns. W13 | 54 | 16 80 B |
| Langham Gdns. Wem | 33 | 17 86 A |
| Langham House Cl. Rich | 83 | 17 71 B |
| Langham Pl. N15 | 25 | 31 89 B |
| Langham Pl. W1 | 2 | 28 81 B |
| Langham Rd. Edg | 22 | 20 91 A |
| Langham Rd. N15 | 25 | 32 89 A |
| Langham Rd. SW20 | 95 | 23 69 A |
| Langham Rd. Tedd | 93 | 16 70 B |
| Langham St. W1 | 2 | 28 81 B |
| Langhedge Cl. N18 | 25 | 33 91 B |
| Langhedge La. N18 | 25 | 33 91 B |
| Langholm Cl. SW12 | 86 | 29 73 B |
| Langhorne Rd. Dag | 52 | 49 84 C |
| Langland Cres. Stan | 21 | 17 90 D |
| Langland Ct. Nthwd | 19 | 08 91 C |
| Langland Dri. Pnr | 20 | 12 91 C |
| Langland Gdns. Croy | 106 | 36 65 B |
| Langland Gdns. NW3 | 46 | 25 85 D |
| Langler Rd. NW10 | 46 | 23 83 C |
| Langley Ave. Ruis | 31 | 10 86 B |
| Langley Ave. Surb | 101 | 18 66 C |
| Langley Ave. Wor Pk | 103 | 23 65 B |
| Langley Cl. Rom | 30 | 53 91 D |
| Langley Cres. Dag | 52 | 47 84 D |
| Langley Cres. E11 | 39 | 41 87 A |
| Langley Ct. WC2 | 7 | 30 80 A |
| Langley Dri. E11 | 39 | 40 87 B |
| Langley Dri. W3 | 61 | 19 79 B |
| Langley Gdns. Dag | 52 | 47 84 D |
| Langley Gdns. Orp | 108 | 43 67 D |
| Langley Gr. N Mal | 94 | 21 69 C |
| Langley La. SW8 | 10 | 30 77 B |
| Langley Oaks Ave. S Croy | 112 | 34 62 C |
| Langley Park. NW7 | 22 | 21 91 A |
| Langley Park Rd. Sutt | 110 | 26 63 A |
| Langley Rd. Beck | 98 | 36 68 C |
| Langley Rd. Islw | 71 | 15 76 D |
| Langley Rd. Surb | 101 | 18 66 A |
| Langley Rd. SW19 | 95 | 25 69 A |
| Langley Rd. Well | 67 | 47 77 A |
| Langley St. WC2 | 3 | 30 81 C |
| Langley Way. W.Wick | 107 | 39 66 A |
| Langmore Ct. Bexh | 79 | 47 75 B |
| Langroyd Rd. SW17 | 86 | 27 72 B |
| Langside Ave. SW15 | 72 | 22 75 C |
| Langside Cres. N14 | 16 | 29 93 D |
| Lang St. E1 | 57 | 35 82 C |
| Langthorn Ct. EC2 | 4 | 32 81 D |
| Langthorne Rd. E11 | 49 | 38 85 B |
| Langthorne Rd. E11 | 38 | 38 86 C |
| Langthorne St. SW6 | 62 | 23 77 D |
| Langton Ave. N20 | 15 | 26 94 B |
| Langton Cl. WC1 | 3 | 30 82 D |
| Langton Rd. E Mol | 92 | 14 68 C |
| Langton Rd. Har | 20 | 14 91 C |
| Langton Rd. NW2 | 35 | 23 86 C |
| Langton Rd. SW9 | 63 | 31 77 D |
| Langton Rise. SE23 | 87 | 34 73 B |
| Langton St. SW10 | 62 | 26 77 A |
| Langton Way. Croy | 112 | 33 64 A |
| Langton Way. SE3 | 77 | 40 76 A |
| Langtry Rd. Nthlt | 43 | 11 83 D |
| Langtry Rd. NW8 | 46 | 25 83 B |
| Langtry Wlk. NW8 | 46 | 26 83 A |
| Langwood Chase. Tedd | 93 | 17 70 A |
| Lanhill Rd. W9 | 56 | 25 82 C |
| Lanier Rd. SE13 | 76 | 38 74 D |
| Lankaster Gdns. N2 | 23 | 26 90 B |
| Lankers Dri. Har | 32 | 12 88 D |
| Lankton Cl. Beck | 98 | 38 69 A |
| Lannoy Rd. SE9 | 90 | 44 73 C |
| Lanrick Rd. E14 | 58 | 39 81 C |
| Lanridge Rd. Belv | 67 | 47 79 D |
| Lansbury Ave. Bark | 51 | 46 84 C |
| Lansbury Ave. Felt | 69 | 10 74 D |
| Lansbury Ave. N18 | 17 | 33 92 C |
| Lansbury Ave. Rom | 41 | 48 88 A |
| Lansbury Cl. NW10 | 45 | 20 85 C |
| Lansbury Gdns. E14 | 58 | 38 81 D |
| Lansbury Rd. Enf | 14 | 35 97 B |
| Lansbury Way. N18 | 17 | 33 92 C |
| Lanscombe Wlk. SW8 | 10 | 30 77 C |
| Lansdell Rd. Mit | 96 | 28 69 C |
| Lansdowne Ave. Orp | 108 | 43 66 D |
| Lansdowne Cl. SW20 | 95 | 23 70 D |
| Lansdowne Cl. Twick | 83 | 15 73 D |
| Lansdowne Cres. W11 | 56 | 24 80 A |
| Lansdowne Ct. Pur | 112 | 31 62 D |
| Lansdowne Ct. Wor Pk | 102 | 22 65 A |
| Lansdowne Dri. E8 | 48 | 34 84 C |
| Lansdowne Gdns. SW8 | 74 | 30 76 A |
| Lansdowne Gr. NW10 | 45 | 21 85 A |
| Lansdowne Hill. SE27 | 87 | 31 72 D |
| Lansdowne La. SE7 | 65 | 41 78 D |
| Lansdowne Mews. SE7 | 65 | 41 78 D |
| Lansdowne Mews. W11 | 56 | 24 80 D |
| Lansdowne Pl. SE19 | 97 | 33 70 D |
| Lansdowne Pl. SE1 | 8 | 32 79 D |
| Lansdowne Rd. Brom | 99 | 40 70 D |
| Lansdowne Rd. Croy | 105 | 32 66 D |
| Lansdowne Rd. E11 | 39 | 39 86 B |
| Lansdowne Rd. E17 | 38 | 37 88 C |
| Lansdowne Rd. E18 | 27 | 40 89 A |
| Lansdowne Rd. E4 | 18 | 37 93 A |
| Lansdowne Rd. Eps | 109 | 20 63 D |
| Lansdowne Rd. Har | 33 | 15 87 A |
| Lansdowne Rd. Houn | 70 | 13 75 B |
| Lansdowne Rd. Ilf | 40 | 45 87 B |
| Lansdowne Rd. N10 | 24 | 29 90 C |
| Lansdowne Rd. N3 | 23 | 25 91 C |
| Lansdowne Rd. N7 | 25 | 34 90 A |
| Lansdowne Rd. Stan | 21 | 17 91 A |
| Lansdowne Rd. SW20 | 95 | 23 70 C |
| Lansdowne Rd. W11 | 56 | 24 80 A |
| Lansdowne Rd. W1 | 6 | 28 80 D |
| Lansdowne Rise. W11 | 56 | 24 80 A |
| Lansdowne Terr. WC1 | 3 | 30 82 C |
| Lansdowne Way. SW8 | 74 | 30 76 A |
| Lansdowne Wlk. W11 | 56 | 24 80 D |
| Lansdown Rd. E7 | 50 | 41 84 C |
| Lansdown Rd. Sid | 90 | 46 72 D |
| Lansfield Ave. N18 | 17 | 34 92 A |
| Lantern Cl. SW15 | 72 | 22 75 C |
| Lantern Cl. Wem | 44 | 17 85 D |
| Lant St. SE1 | 8 | 32 79 A |
| Lanvanor Rd. SE15 | 76 | 35 76 C |
| Lapford Cl. W9 | 56 | 24 82 D |
| Lapponum Wlk. Hay | 53 | 11 82 D |
| Lapse Wood Wlk. SE23 | 87 | 34 73 D |
| Lapstone Gdns. Har | 33 | 17 88 C |
| Larbert Rd. SW16 | 96 | 29 70 C |
| Larby Pl. Eps | 9 | 21 62 C |
| Larch Ave. W3 | 55 | 21 80 C |
| Larch Cl. N19 | 36 | 29 86 A |
| Larch Cl. SW12 | 86 | 28 72 B |
| Larch Cres. Eps | 109 | 19 63 B |
| Larch Cres. Hay | 53 | 11 81 B |
| Larch Dene. Orp | 108 | 43 65 A |
| Larches Ave. SW14 | 72 | 20 75 D |
| Larches The. N13 | 17 | 32 93 C |
| Larch Green. NW9 | 22 | 21 90 A |
| Larch Rd. NW2 | 46 | 23 85 A |
| Larch Tree Way. Croy | 106 | 37 65 C |
| Larch Way. Brom | 108 | 43 66 A |
| Larchwood Ave. Rom | 29 | 49 91 B |
| Larchwood Cl. Rom | 29 | 50 91 A |
| Larchwood Rd. SE9 | 90 | 43 72 B |
| Larcom St. SE17 | 63 | 32 78 A |
| Larden Rd. W3 | 61 | 21 79 A |
| Largewood Ave. Surb | 102 | 19 65 A |
| Larissa St. SE17 | 63 | 32 78 D |
| Larkbere Rd. SE26 | 88 | 36 71 A |
| Larkfield Ave. Har | 21 | 16 89 B |
| Larkfield Cl. Brom | 107 | 40 65 A |
| Larkfield Rd. Rich | 71 | 18 75 C |
| Larkfield Rd. Sid | 90 | 45 72 D |
| Larkhall La. SW4 | 74 | 30 76 C |
| Larkhall Rise. SW4 | 74 | 29 76 D |
| Lark Row. E2 | 49 | 35 83 A |
| Larksfield Gr. Enf | 13 | 34 97 B |
| Larkshall Cres. E4 | 18 | 38 92 A |
| Larkshall Rd. E4 | 18 | 38 93 D |
| Larkspur Cl. N17 | 25 | 32 91 D |
| Larkspur Ct. Wall | 111 | 28 63 B |
| Larkspur Way. Eps | 109 | 20 64 C |
| Larkswood Ct. E4 | 18 | 38 92 D |
| Larkswood Rd. E4 | 18 | 37 92 B |
| Larkswood Rise. Pnr | 20 | 11 89 C |
| Larkway Cl. NW9 | 22 | 20 89 D |
| Larnach Rd. W6 | 62 | 23 77 B |
| Larne Rd. Ruis | 31 | 09 87 B |
| Larner Rd. Eri | 68 | 51 77 C |
| Larpent Ave. SW15 | 73 | 23 74 A |
| Larwood Cl. Grnf | 43 | 14 85 D |
| Lascelles Ave. Har | 32 | 14 87 B |
| Lascelles Cl. E11 | 38 | 38 86 B |
| Lascott's Rd. N22 | 24 | 30 91 B |
| Lassa Rd. SE9 | 77 | 42 74 B |
| Lassell St. SE10 | 64 | 38 78 D |
| Latchett Rd. E18 | 27 | 40 90 B |
| Latchingdon Gdns. Wdf Gn | 27 | 42 91 A |
| Latchmere Cl. Rich | 83 | 18 71 C |
| Latchmere La. King | 93 | 18 70 B |
| Latchmere La. King | 83 | 18 71 D |
| Latchmere Pas. SW11 | 74 | 27 76 D |
| Latchmere Rd. King | 93 | 18 70 B |
| Latchmere Rd. SW11 | 74 | 27 76 D |
| Latchmere St. SW11 | 74 | 27 76 D |
| Lateward Rd. Brent | 60 | 17 77 B |
| Latham Cl. Twick | 83 | 16 73 A |
| Latham Rd. Bexh | 79 | 49 74 A |
| Latham Rd. Twick | 83 | 15 73 B |
| Lathkill Cl. Enf | 17 | 34 94 A |
| Lathom Rd. E6 | 50 | 42 84 D |
| Latimer Ave. E6 | 50 | 42 83 B |
| Latimer Cl. Pnr | 20 | 11 90 A |
| Latimer Cl. Wor Pk | 109 | 22 64 B |
| Latimer Gdns. Pnr | 20 | 11 90 A |
| Latimer Pl. W10 | 56 | 23 81 C |
| Latimer Rd. Barn | 11 | 25 96 B |
| Latimer Rd. Croy | 105 | 31 65 D |
| Latimer Rd. E7 | 50 | 40 85 B |
| Latimer Rd. N15 | 37 | 33 88 C |
| Latimer Rd. SW19 | 95 | 25 70 B |
| Latimer Rd. Tedd | 83 | 15 71 D |
| Latimer Rd. W10 | 56 | 23 81 C |
| Latimer. SE17 | 63 | 33 78 C |
| Latimer St. E1 | 57 | 35 81 B |
| Latona Rd. SE15 | 63 | 34 77 A |
| La Tourne Gdns. Orp | 108 | 44 65 C |
| Latymer Ct. W6 | 62 | 23 78 B |
| Latymer Rd. N9 | 17 | 33 94 D |
| Latymer Way. N9 | 17 | 33 93 A |
| Lauder Cl. Nthlt | 43 | 11 83 D |
| Lauderdale Dri. Rich | 83 | 17 72 D |
| Lauderdale Rd. W9 | 56 | 25 82 B |
| Laud St. Croy | 105 | 32 65 C |
| Laud St. SE11 | 10 | 30 78 D |
| Laughton Rd. Nthlt | 43 | 11 83 B |
| Launcelot Rd. Brom | 89 | 40 71 A |
| Launcelot St. SE1 | 7 | 31 79 A |
| Launceston Cl. Rom | 30 | 53 90 A |
| Launceston Ct. Th Hth | 105 | 31 67 C |
| Launceston Gdns. Grnf | 44 | 17 84 C |
| Launceston Pl. W8 | 5 | 26 79 C |
| Launceston Rd. Grnf | 44 | 17 83 A |
| Launch St. E14 | 64 | 38 79 C |
| Laundry Rd. W6 | 62 | 24 77 A |
| Laura Cl. E11 | 39 | 41 88 A |
| Laura Cl. Enf | 13 | 33 95 A |
| Lauradale Rd. N2 | 24 | 27 89 D |
| Laura Pl. E5 | 49 | 35 85 A |
| Laurel Ave. Twick | 83 | 15 73 D |
| Laurel Bank Rd. Enf | 13 | 32 97 B |
| Laurel Cl. Ilf | 28 | 44 91 B |
| Laurel Cl. N19 | 36 | 29 86 A |
| Laurel Cl. Sid | 90 | 46 72 C |
| Laurel Cres. Croy | 106 | 37 65 C |
| Laurel Cres. Rom | 42 | 51 87 C |
| Laurel Ct. SE25 | 105 | 33 67 A |
| Laurel Dri. N21 | 17 | 31 94 A |
| Laurel Gdns. E4 | 18 | 37 94 B |
| Laurel Gdns. Houn | 70 | 12 75 C |
| Laurel Gdns. W7 | 54 | 15 80 C |
| Laurel Gr. SE20 | 98 | 35 70 C |
| Laurel Gr. SE26 | 88 | 36 71 A |
| Laurel Manor. Sutt | 110 | 26 63 C |
| Laurel Park. Har | 21 | 15 91 D |
| Laurel Rd. Hamp | 82 | 14 71 D |
| Laurel Rd. SW13 | 72 | 22 76 C |
| Laurel Rd. SW20 | 94 | 22 69 B |
| Laurel St. E8 | 48 | 33 84 B |
| Laurel View. N12 | 15 | 25 93 D |
| Laurel Way. E18 | 27 | 39 89 D |
| Laurel Way. N20 | 15 | 25 93 C |
| Laurence Pountney Hill. EC4 | 8 | 32 80 B |
| Laurence Pountney La. EC4 | 8 | 32 80 B |
| Laurie Gr. SE14 | 76 | 36 76 A |
| Laurie Rd. W7 | 54 | 15 81 A |
| Laurier Rd. Croy | 105 | 33 66 B |
| Laurier Rd. NW5 | 36 | 28 86 D |
| Laurie Wlk. Rom | 42 | 51 88 A |
| Lauriston Rd. E9 | 49 | 35 84 D |
| Lauriston Rd. SW19 | 95 | 23 70 B |
| Lausanne Rd. N8 | 25 | 31 89 C |
| Lausanne Rd. SE15 | 76 | 35 76 C |
| Lavell St. N16 | 48 | 32 85 B |
| Lavender Ave. Mit | 96 | 27 69 B |
| Lavender Ave. NW9 | 34 | 20 87 C |
| Lavender Ave. Wor Pk | 103 | 23 65 C |
| Lavender Cl. Rom | 30 | 53 91 D |
| Lavender Cl. SW3 | 62 | 26 77 B |
| Lavender Cl. Wall | 111 | 28 64 B |
| Lavender Ct. E Mol | 92 | 13 68 B |
| Lavender Gdns. Enf | 13 | 31 97 B |
| Lavender Gdns. SW11 | 74 | 27 75 D |
| Lavender Gr. E8 | 48 | 34 84 C |
| Lavender Gr. Mit | 96 | 27 69 A |
| Lavender Hill. Enf | 13 | 31 97 B |
| Lavender Hill. SW11 | 74 | 27 75 B |
| Lavender Rd. Croy | 104 | 30 67 D |
| Lavender Rd. Enf | 13 | 32 97 B |
| Lavender Rd. Eps | 109 | 19 64 D |
| Lavender Rd. Sutt | 110 | 26 64 B |
| Lavender Rd. SW11 | 73 | 26 75 B |
| Lavender Rd. Wall | 111 | 28 64 A |
| Lavender St. E15 | 50 | 39 84 A |
| Lavender Sweep. SW11 | 74 | 27 75 D |
| Lavender Terr. SW11 | 74 | 27 75 A |
| Lavender Vale. Wall | 111 | 29 63 B |
| Lavender Way. Croy | 106 | 35 67 D |
| Lavender Wlk. Mit | 96 | 28 68 A |
| Lavender Wlk. SW11 | 74 | 27 75 D |
| Lavengro Rd. SE27 | 87 | 32 72 A |
| Lavenham Rd. SW18 | 85 | 25 73 C |
| Lavernock Rd. Bexh | 79 | 49 76 C |
| Lavers Rd. N16 | 37 | 33 86 C |
| Laverstoke Gdns. SW15 | 84 | 22 73 A |
| Laverton Mews. SW5 | 62 | 25 78 B |
| Laverton Pl. SW5 | 62 | 25 78 B |
| Lavidge Rd. SE9 | 89 | 42 72 B |
| Lavina Gr. N1 | 47 | 30 83 D |
| Lavington Rd. Croy | 111 | 30 64 B |
| Lavington Rd. W13 | 54 | 16 80 D |
| Lavington St. SE1 | 7 | 31 80 D |
| Lavinia Rd. Dart | 80 | 54 74 D |
| Lawdon Gdns. Croy | 112 | 31 64 B |
| Lawford Cl. Wall | 111 | 30 62 A |
| Lawford Gdns. Dart | 80 | 53 74 A |
| Lawford Rd. NW5 | 47 | 29 84 A |
| Lawford Rd. W4 | 61 | 20 77 C |
| Lawless St. E14 | 57 | 37 80 B |
| Lawley Rd. N14 | 16 | 28 94 B |
| Lawley St. E5 | 49 | 35 85 A |
| Lawn Cl. Brom | 99 | 40 70 B |
| Lawn Cl. N9 | 17 | 33 94 B |
| Lawn Cl. N Mal | 94 | 21 69 C |
| Lawn Cl. Ruis | 31 | 09 86 D |
| Lawn Cres. Rich | 72 | 18 76 D |
| Lawn Dri. E7 | 50 | 41 85 B |
| Lawn Farm Gr. Rom | 29 | 48 89 A |
| Lawn Gdns. W7 | 54 | 15 80 C |
| Lawn La. SW8 | 10 | 30 77 B |
| Lawn Park Gr. Rom | 29 | 48 89 C |
| Lawn Pl. SE15 | 75 | 33 76 B |
| Lawn Pl. SE15 | 63 | 33 77 D |
| Lawn Rd. Beck | 98 | 36 70 D |

Lawn Rd. NW3 47 27 85 D
Lawns Ct. Wem 33 18 86 B
Lawns Ct. Wem 34 19 86 A
Lawnside. SE3 77 39 75 D
Lawns The. E4 18 37 92 C
Lawns The. Pnr 20 13 91 C
Lawns The. SE19 97 32 69 B
Lawns The. SE3 77 39 75 B
Lawns The. Sid 90 46 71 B
Lawns The. Sutt 110 24 63 C
Lawns Way. Rom 29 50 91 C
Lawn Terr. SE3 77 39 75 A
Lawn Vale. Pnr 20 12 90 C
Lawrence Ave. E12 51 43 85 A
Lawrence Ave. E17 26 36 90 A
Lawrence Ave. N13 17 31 92 B
Lawrence Ave. N.Mal 102 21 66 A
Lawrence Cl. E3 49 37 83 C
Lawrence Cl. N15 25 33 89 C
Lawrence Cres. Dag 41 49 86 D
Lawrence Cres. Edg 22 19 90 C
Lawrence Hill. E4 18 37 93 A
Lawrence Hill Gdns. Dart 80 53 74 C
Lawrence Hill Rd. Dart 80 53 74 C
Lawrence La. EC2 4 32 81 C
Lawrence Pl. N1 47 30 83 A
Lawrence Rd. E13 50 40 83 B
Lawrence Rd. E6 50 42 83 A
Lawrence Rd. Hamp 92 12 70 D
Lawrence Rd. Houn 70 11 75 C
Lawrence Rd. N15 25 33 89 C
Lawrence Rd. N18 17 34 92 B
Lawrence Rd. Pnr 32 11 88 B
Lawrence Rd. Rich 83 17 71 A
Lawrence Rd. Rom 42 52 88 B
Lawrence Rd. SE25 97 33 68 D
Lawrence Rd. W5 60 17 78 B
Lawrence's Bldgs. N16 37 33 86 D
Lawrence St. E16 58 39 81 B
Lawrence St. SW3 9 27 77 A
Lawrence Weaver Cl. Mord 103 25 67 C
Lawrence Yd. N15 25 33 89 C
Lawrie Park Ave. SE26 87 34 71 D
Lawrie Park Cres. SE26 87 34 71 D
Lawrie Park Gdns. SE26 87 34 71 D
Lawrie Park Rd. SE6 88 35 71 C
Lawson Cl. E16 58 41 81 A
Lawson Cl. SW19 85 23 72 D
Lawson Rd. Dart 80 53 75 D
Lawson Rd. Enf 14 35 97 A
Lawson Rd. Sthl 53 13 82 C
Law St. SE1 8 32 79 D
Lawton Rd. Barn 11 26 96 B
Lawton Rd. E10 38 38 87 C
Lawton Rd. E3 57 36 82 A
Laxfield Ct. E8 48 34 83 A
Laxley Cl. SE5 63 31 77 D
Laxton Pl. NW1 2 28 82 D
Layard Rd. Enf 13 33 97 B
Layard Rd. SE16 63 34 78 B
Layard Rd. Th Hth 97 32 69 D
Layard Sq. SE16 63 34 78 B
Laycock St. N1 48 31 84 A
Layer Gdns. W3 55 19 80 A
Layfield Cl. NW4 34 22 87 B
Layfield Cres. NW4 34 22 87 B
Layfield Rd. NW4 34 22 87 B
Layhams Rd. W Wick 106 38 65 D
Laymead Cl. Nthlt 43 12 84 A
Laystall St. EC1 3 31 82 C
Layton Cres. Croy 112 31 64 D
Layton Ct. Brent 60 17 78 D
Layton Rd. Brent 60 17 78 D
Layton Rd. Houn 70 13 75 D
Layton Rd. N1 48 31 83 C
Layton's La. Sun 91 09 69 D
Lazar Wlk. N7 36 30 86 B
Lazell Wlk. SE9 89 41 73 D
Lazenby Ct. WC2 7 30 80 A
Leabank Cl. Har 33 15 86 C
Leabank View N15 37 34 88 C
Leabourne Rd. N16 37 34 87 A
Lea Bridge Rd. E10 38 36 87 B
Lea Bridge Rd. E5 38 35 86 C
Leacroft Ave. SW12 86 27 73 B
Leadale Ave. E4 18 37 93 A
Leadale Rd. N15 37 34 88 C
Leadale Rd. N16 37 34 88 C
Leadenhall Ave. EC3 4 33 81 C
Leadenhall Market. EC3 4 33 81 C
Leadenhall Pl. EC3 4 33 81 C
Leadenhall St. EC3 4 33 81 C
Leadenham Ct. E3 57 37 82 C
Leader Ave. E12 51 43 85 C
Leadings The. Wem 34 20 86 C
Leaf Cl. E Mol 101 15 67 A
Leaf Cl. Nthwd 19 08 91 D
Leaf Gr. SE27 87 31 71 C
Leafield Cl. SW16 97 31 70 B
Leafield Rd. Sutt 103 25 65 A
Leafield Rd. SW20 95 24 68 B
Leafy Oak Rd. SE12 89 41 72 C
Leafy Way. Croy 105 33 65 B
Lea Gdns. Wem 44 18 85 B
Leagrave St. E5 38 35 86 C
Lea Hall Rd. E10 38 37 87 C
Leaholme Waye. Ruis 31 08 88 C
Leahurst Rd. SE13 76 38 74 B
Leahurst Rd. SE13 77 39 74 C
Leake Ct. SE1 7 30 79 B
Leake St. SE1 7 30 79 B
Lealand Rd. N15 37 33 88 D
Leamington Ave. Brom 89 41 71 C
Leamington Ave. E17 38 37 88 A
Leamington Ave. Mord 95 24 68 D
Leamington Ave. Orp 108 45 65 C
Leamington Cl. Brom 89 41 71 C
Leamington Cl. E12 50 42 85 C
Leamington Cl. Houn 70 14 74 A
Leamington Cres. Har 32 12 86 D
Leamington Gdns. Ilf 40 45 86 B
Leamington Park. W3 55 20 81 B
Leamington Rd. Sthl 59 11 78 B
Leamington Rd Villas. W11 56 24 81 B
Leamouth Rd. E14 58 38 80 B
Leander Rd. Nthlt 43 13 83 C
Leander Rd. SW2 75 31 74 C
Leander Rd. Th Hth 96 30 68 D
Lea Rd. Beck 98 37 69 C
Lea Rd. Enf 13 32 97 B
Lea Rd. Sthl 59 12 78 A
Leas Dale. SE9 90 43 72 C
Leas Green. Chis 100 45 70 B
Leaside Ave. N10 24 28 89 C
Leaside Rd. E5 38 35 87 C
Leasowes Rd. E10 38 37 87 C
Leather Bottle Green. Belv 67 48 79 D
Leather Cl. Mit 96 28 69 C
Leatherdale St. E1 57 35 82 B
*Leatherdale St. E1 57 35 82 C
Leather Gdns. E15 50 39 83 A
Leatherhead Cl. N16 37 33 87 C
Leather La. EC1 3 31 81 A
Leathermarket St. SE1 8 33 79 A
Leathersellers Cl. Barn 11 24 96 A
Leathsale Rd. Har 32 13 86 D
Leathwaite Rd. SW11 74 27 74 B
Leathwell Rd. SE8 76 37 76 D
Lea Vale. Bexh 79 50 75 D
Lea Valley Rd. E4 14 37 95 C
Lea Valley Rd. Enf 14 36 95 A
Leaveland Cl. Beck 98 37 68 C
Leaver Gdns. Grnf 44 15 83 C
Leavesden Rd. Stan 21 16 91 A
Lea View House. E5 37 34 87 D
Lebanon Ave. Felt 82 11 71 C
Lebanon Ct. Twick 83 16 73 B
Lebanon Gds. SW18 73 25 74 C
Lebanon Park. Twick 83 16 73 B
Lebanon Rd. Croy 105 33 65 A
Lebanon Rd. SW18 73 25 74 A
Lebrun Sq. SE3 77 40 75 B
Lechmere App. Wdf Gn 27 41 90 C
Lechmere Ave. Wdf Gn 27 41 90 D
Lechmere Rd. NW2 45 22 84 B
Leckford Rd. SW18 85 26 73 C
Leckwith Ave. Bexh 67 48 77 A
Lecky St. SW7 62 26 78 D
Leconfield Ave. SW13 72 21 75 B
Leconfield Rd. N5 48 32 85 B
Leda e. Enf 14 35 97 B
Leda Rd. SE18 65 42 79 D
Ledbury Mews N. W11 56 25 81 C
Ledbury Mews W. W11 56 25 80 A
Ledbury Pl. Croy 112 32 64 A
Ledbury Rd. Croy 112 32 64 B
Ledbury Rd. W11 56 25 81 C
Ledbury St. SE15 63 34 77 C
Ledrington Rd. SE19 97 34 70 A
Ledway Dri. Wem 33 18 87 B
Lee Ave. Rom 41 48 88 C
Leechcroft Ave. Sid 78 45 74 B
Leechcroft Rd. Wall 104 28 65 C
Lee Church St. SE13 77 39 75 C
Lee Cl. E17 26 35 90 A
Lee Conservancy Rd. E9 49 36 85 D
Leecroft Rd. Barn 11 24 96 C
Leeds Pl. N4 36 30 87 D
Leeds Rd. Ilf 40 44 87 D
Leeds St. N18 17 34 92 C
Leegate. SE12 77 39 74 B
Lee Green. Orp 108 46 67 A
Lee Green. SE12 77 39 74 B
Lee High Rd. SE12 77 39 75 D
Lee High Rd. SE13 76 38 75 D
Leeke St. WC1 3 30 82 B
Leeland Rd. W13 54 16 80 C
Leeland Terr. W13 54 16 80 C
Leeland Way. NW10 45 21 85 B
Leemount Cl. NW4 23 23 89 D
Lee Park. SE3 77 39 75 D
Lee Park Way. N18 18 35 92 B
Lee Park Way. N9 18 36 93 C
Lee Rd. Enf 13 34 95 C
Lee Rd. Grnf 44 17 83 A
Lee Rd. NW7 23 23 91 D
Lee Rd. SE3 77 39 75 D
Lee Rd. SW19 95 25 69 B
Lees Ave. Nthwd 19 09 90 B
Leeside. Barn 11 24 95 C
Leesideres. NW11 35 24 88 D
Leeside Rd. N17 26 35 91 A
Leesness Ave. Bexh 67 47 77 D
Leeson Rd. SE24 75 31 75 C
Leesons Hill. Chis 100 45 68 B
Leesons Hill. Orp 100 46 68 B
Leesons Way. Orp 100 45 69 D
Lees Pl. W1 6 28 80 A
Lee St. E8 48 33 83 B
Lees The. Croy 106 36 65 B
Lee Terr. SE3 77 39 75 A
Lee View. Enf 13 31 97 B
Leeward Gdns. SW19 95 24 70 A
Leeway. SE8 64 36 78 D
Lefevre Wlk. E3 49 37 83 A
Leffern Rd. W12 61 22 79 A
Lefroy Rd. W12 61 21 79 B
Legard Rd. N5 37 31 86 D
Legatt Rd. SE9 77 41 74 B
Leggatt Rd. E15 49 38 83 C
Legge St. SE13 76 38 74 A
Leghorn Rd. NW10 45 22 83 C
Leghorn Rd. SE18 66 44 78 D
Legion Cl. N1 48 31 84 C
Legion Ct. Mord 103 25 67 C
Legion Rd. Grnf 43 14 83 C
Legon Ave. Rom 41 50 87 C
Legrace Ave. Houn 70 11 76 D
Leicester Ave. Mit 96 30 68 C
Leicester Cl. Wor Pk 110 23 64 A
Leicester Ct. WC2 6 29 80 B
Leicester Gdns. Ilf 40 45 87 A
Leicester Pl. WC2 6 29 80 B
Leicester Rd. Barn 11 25 96 D
Leicester Rd. Croy 105 33 66 A
Leicester Rd. E11 39 40 88 B
Leicester Rd. N2 24 27 89 A
Leicester Rd. NW10 45 20 84 D
Leicester Sq. WC2 6 29 80 B
Leicester St. WC2 6 29 80 B
Leigham Ave. SW16 86 30 72 C
Leigham Court Rd. SW16 86 30 72 D
Leigham Dri. Islw 60 15 77 C
Leigham Vale. SW16 87 31 72 A
Leigh Ave. Ilf 27 41 89 D
Leigh Cl. N Mal 94 20 68 D
Leigh Ct. Har 33 15 87 C
Leigh Gdns. NW10 46 23 83 C
Leigh Orchard Cl. SW16 86 30 72 D
Leigh Pl. EC1 3 31 81 A
Leigh Pl. Well 78 46 76 C
Leigh Rd. E10 38 38 87 A
Leigh Rd. E6 51 43 84 C
Leigh Rd. Houn 70 14 75 D
Leigh Rd. N5 48 31 85 B
Leigh St. WC1 3 30 82 A
Leighton Ave. E12 51 43 85 C
Leighton Ave. Pnr 20 12 89 A
Leighton Cl. Edg 22 19 90 C
Leighton Cres. NW5 47 29 85 C
Leighton Gdns. NW10 46 23 83 C
Leighton Gr. NW5 47 29 85 C
Leighton Pl. NW5 47 29 85 C
Leighton Rd. Enf 13 34 95 A
Leighton Rd. Har 20 14 90 D
Leighton Rd. NW5 47 29 85 C
Leighton Rd. W13 60 16 79 A
Leighton St. Croy 105 31 66 D
Leinster Gdns. W2 1 26 81 C
Leinster Mews. W2 5 26 80 A
Leinster Pl. W2 1 26 81 C
Leinster Rd. N10 24 28 89 D
Leinster Rd. NW6 56 25 82 A
Leinster Sq. W2 56 25 81 D
Leinster Terr. W2 5 26 80 A
Leith Cl. NW9 34 20 87 D
Leithcote Gdns. SW16 86 30 71 B
Leithcote Path. SW16 86 30 72 D
Leith Hill Green. Orp 100 46 69 A
Leith Hill. Orp 100 46 69 A
Leith Rd. N22 25 31 90 B
Leith Yd. NW6 46 25 83 A
Lela Ave. Houn 70 11 76 C
Lelitia Cl. E8 48 34 83 A
Leman Pas. E1 57 34 81 C
Leman St. E1 57 34 81 C
Lemark Cl. Stan 21 17 91 A
Le May Ave. SE12 89 40 72 D
Lemna Rd. E11 39 39 87 A
Lemon St. E1 4 33 81 D
Lemonwell Dri. SE9 78 44 74 A
Lemsford Cl. N15 37 34 88 A
Lena Gdns. W6 62 23 79 C
Lenham Rd. Bexh 67 48 77 B
Lenham Rd. SE12 77 39 75 D
Lenham Rd. Sutt 110 26 64 C
Lenham Rd. Th Hth 97 32 69 D
Lennard Ave. W.Wick 107 39 65 C
Lennard Cl. W.Wick 107 39 65 A
Lennard Rd. Beck 98 36 70 C
Lennard Rd. Brom 107 42 66 D
Lennard Rd. Croy 105 32 66 C
Lennard Rd. SE20 98 35 70 B
Lennox Cl. Rom 42 51 88 D
Lennox Gdns. Croy 112 31 64 B
Lennox Gdns. Ilf 39 42 87 D
Lennox Gdns Mews. SW1 9 27 78 B
Lennox Gdns. NW10 45 21 85 B
Lennox Gdns. SW1 5 27 79 D
Lennox Rd. E17 38 37 88 C
Lennox Rd. N4 37 31 86 A
Lenor Cl. Bexh 79 48 75 C
Lensbury Way. SE2 67 47 79 D
Lens Rd. E7 50 41 84 C
Lenthall Rd. E8 48 34 84 C
Lenthal Pl. SW7 62 26 78 A
Lenthorp Rd. E10 65 39 78 B
Lentmead Rd. Brom 89 39 72 D
Lenton Rise. Rich 71 18 75 A
Lenton St. SE18 66 44 78 B
Lenton Terr. N4 37 31 86 A
Lenville Way. SE16 63 34 78 C
Leo Ct. Brent 60 17 77 D
Leof Cres. SE6 88 37 71 D
Leominster Rd. Mord 103 26 67 C
Leominster Wlk. Mord 103 26 67 C
Leonard Ave. Mord 103 26 67 A
Leonard Ave. Rom 41 50 87 D
Leonard Ct. Har 21 15 90 A
Leonard Pl. N16 48 33 85 A
Leonard Rd. E4 26 37 91 A
Leonard Rd. E7 50 40 85 A
Leonard Rd. N9 17 34 93 C
Leonard Rd. Sthl 59 11 79 D
Leonard Rd. SW16 96 29 69 A
Leonard St. EC2 4 33 82 C
Leontine Cl. SE15 63 34 77 C
Leopards Ct. EC1 3 31 81 A
Leopold Ave. SW19 85 24 71 D
Leopold Rd. E17 38 37 88 A
Leopold Rd. N18 18 35 92 C
Leopold Rd. N18 18 35 92 C
Leopold Rd. N2 23 26 89 B
Leopold Rd. NW10 45 21 84 C
Leopold Rd. SW19 85 24 71 D
Leopold Rd. W5 54 18 80 D
Leopold St. E3 57 36 81 B
Leopold Wlk. SE11 10 30 78 D
Leo St. SE15 63 34 77 D
Leppoc Rd. SW4 74 29 74 B
Leroy St. SE1 8 33 79 C
Lescombe Cl. SE23 88 36 72 C
Lescombe Rd. SE23 88 36 72 C
Leslie Gdns. Sutt 110 25 63 C
Leslie Gr. Croy 105 33 66 C
Leslie Grove Pl. Croy 105 33 66 C
Leslie Park Rd. Croy 105 33 66 C
Leslie Prince Ct. SE5 63 32 77 D
Leslie Rd. E11 49 38 85 B
Leslie Rd. E16 58 40 81 D
Leslie Rd. N2 23 26 89 B
Leslie Smith Sq. SE18 66 43 77 A
Lesney Park. Eri 67 50 77 B
Lesney Park Rd. Eri 67 50 77 B
Lessada St. E3 49 35 83 D
Lessar Ave. SW4 74 29 74 C
Lessingham Ave. Ilf 28 43 89 A
Lessingham Ave. SW17 86 28 71 A
Lessing St. SE23 88 35 73 D
Lessington Ave. Rom 41 50 88 C
Lessness Park. Belv 67 49 78 C
Lessness Rd. Belv 67 49 78 C
Lessness Rd. Mord 103 26 67 A
Lester Ave. E15 58 39 82 C
Leswin Pl. N16 37 33 86 D
Leswin Rd. N16 37 33 86 D
Letchford Gdns. NW10 55 22 82 A
Letchford Mews. NW10 55 22 82 A
Letchworth Ave. Felt 81 09 73 B
Letchworth Cl. Brom 107 40 67 A
Letchworth Dri. Brom 107 40 67 A
Letchworth St. SW17 86 27 71 B
Lethbridge Cl. SE10 76 38 76 A
Letterstone Rd. SW6 62 24 77 D
Lettice St. SW6 73 24 76 B
Lett Rd. E15 49 38 84 D
Lettsom St. SE5 75 33 76 C
Lettsom Wlk. E13 50 40 83 C
Leucha Rd. E17 38 36 88 A
Levana Cl. SW 19 85 24 73 C
Levehurst Way. SW4 74 30 76 C
Levendale Rd. SE23 88 36 72 B
Leven Rd. E14 58 38 81 D
Leverett St. SW3 9 27 78 A
Leverholme Gdns. SE9 90 43 71 A
Leverington Pl. N1 4 32 82 B
Leverson St. SW16 96 29 70 A
Lever St. EC1 4 32 82 A
Leverton Pl. NW5 47 29 85 C
Leverton St. NW5 47 29 85 C
Levett Gdns. Ilf 40 46 86 C
Levett Rd. Bark 51 45 84 A
Levine Gdns. Bark 52 47 83 D
Levison Way. N19 36 29 86 B
Lewes Cl. Nthlt 43 13 84 A
Lewesdon Cl. SW19 85 23 73 D
Lewes Rd. Brom 99 41 69 D
Lewes Rd. N12 16 27 92 C
Leweston Pl. N16 37 33 87 B
Lewgars Ave. NW9 34 20 88 C
Lewin Rd. Bexh 79 48 75 C
Lewin Rd. SW16 96 29 70 B
Lewis Ave. E17 26 37 90 A
Lewis Cres. NW10 45 20 85 D
Lewis Gdns. N2 23 26 90 D
Lewis Gr. SE13 76 38 75 A
Lewisham Centre. SE13 76 38 75 A
Lewisham High St. SE13 76 38 75 C
Lewisham Hill. SE13 76 38 76 C
Lewisham Park. SE13 76 38 74 A
Lewisham Rd. SE13 76 38 76 C
Lewisham St. SW1 6 29 79 B
Lewisham Way. SE14 76 36 76 B
Lewisham Way. SE4 76 37 76 C
Lewis Rd. Horn 42 53 88 C
Lewis Rd. Mit 96 27 69 C
Lewis Rd. Rich 71 17 74 B
Lewis Rd. Sthl 59 12 79 A
Lewis Rd. Sutt 110 25 64 B
Lewis Rd. Well 79 47 75 A
Lewis St. NW1 47 28 84 D
Lexden Dri. Rom 40 46 88 D
Lexden Rd. Mit 96 29 68 D
Lexden Rd. W3 55 19 80 D
Lexham Gardens Mews. W8 62 25 79 D
Lexham Gdns. W8 62 25 78 D
Lexham Mews. W8 62 25 79 C
Lexham Wlk. W8 62 25 79 D
Lexington Ct. Pur 112 32 62 C
Lexington St. W1 6 29 80 A
Lexington Way. Barn 11 23 96 D
Lexton Gdns. SW12 86 29 73 D
Leyborne Ave. W13 60 17 79 A
Leyborne Park. Rich 72 19 76 A
Leybourne Cl. Brom 107 40 67 C
Leybourne Rd. E11 39 39 87 D
Leybourne Rd. NW1 47 28 84 D
Leybourne Rd. NW9 34 19 88 A
*Leybourne St. NW1 47 28 84 D
Leybridge Ct. SE12 77 40 74 A
Leyburn Cl. E17 26 37 89 D
Leyburn Cres. Rom 30 54 91 C
Leyburn Gdns. Croy 105 33 65 A
Leyburn Gr. N18 25 34 91 A
Leyburn Rd. N18 25 34 91 B
Leyburn Rd. Rom 30 54 91 C
Leycroft Gdns. Eri 80 52 76 B
Leyden Mansions. N19 36 30 87 A
Leyden St. E1 4 33 81 B
Leyes Rd. E16 58 41 81 D
Leyfield. Wor Pk 102 21 66 D
Leyland Ave. Enf 14 36 97 C
Leyland Rd. SE12 77 40 74 A
Leylands. SW18 73 24 74 D
Leylang Rd. SE14 64 35 77 D
Leys Ave. Dag 52 50 84 C
Leys Cl. Dag 52 50 84 D
Leys Cl. Har 32 14 88 B
Leysdown Ave. Bexh 79 50 75 C
Leysdown Rd. SE9 89 42 72 B
Leysfield Rd. W12 61 22 79 C
Leys Gdns. Barn 12 28 95 A
Leyspring Rd. E11 39 39 87 D
Leys Rd E. Enf 14 36 97 A
Leys Rd W. Enf 14 36 97 A
Leys The. Har 33 18 88 D
Leys The. N2 23 26 89 C
Ley St. Ilf 40 44 87 D
Leyswood Dri. Ilf 40 45 88 A
Leyswood Dri. Ilf 28 45 89 C
Leythe Rd. W3 61 20 79 A
Leyton Grange. E10 38 37 86 A
Leyton Green Rd. E10 38 38 88 C
Leyton Park Rd. E10 38 38 86 C
Leyton Rd. E15 49 38 85 D
Leyton Rd. SW19 95 26 70 C
Leytonstone Rd. E15 50 39 85 C
Leyton Way. E11 39 39 87 B
Leywick St. E15 50 39 83 C
Liardet St. SE14 64 36 77 A
Liberia Rd. N5 48 31 84 B
Liberty Ave. SW19 95 26 69 B
Liberty St. SW9 74 30 76 B
Liberty The. Rom 42 51 88 A
Libra Rd. E13 50 40 83 C
Libra Rd. E3 49 36 83 D
Library Pl. E1 57 34 80 B
Library St. SE1 7 31 79 B
Lichen Ct. Ilf 28 43 89 B
Lichfield Ct. Rich 71 18 74 A
Lichfield Ct. Surb 101 18 67 A
Lichfield Gdns. Rich 71 18 74 A
Lichfield Gr. N3 23 25 90 C
Lichfield Rd. Dag 41 47 86 C
Lichfield Rd. E3 57 36 82 A
Lichfield Rd. E6 58 41 82 B
Lichfield Rd. Houn 70 11 75 A
Lichfield Rd. N9 17 34 93 A
Lichfield Rd. Nthwd 19 10 89 A
Lichfield Rd. NW2 46 24 85 A
Lichfield Rd. Rich 71 18 76 B
Lidbury Rd. NW7 15 24 92 C
Liddell Cl. Har 21 17 89 B
Liddell Gdns. NW10 46 23 83 C
Lidding Rd. Har 33 17 88 B
Liddington Rd. E15 50 39 83 B
Liddon Rd. Brom 99 41 68 B
Liddon Rd. E13 58 40 82 B
Lidfield Rd. N16 48 32 85 B
Lidiard Rd. SW18 85 26 72 B
Lidlington Pl. NW1 47 29 83 C
Lidyard Rd. N19 36 29 87 C
Liffler Rd. SE18 66 45 78 C
Liffords Pl. SW13 72 21 76 D
Lifford St. SW15 73 23 75 D
Lightcliffe Rd. N13 17 31 93 C
Lightfoot Rd. N8 24 30 89 C
Lightley Cl. Wem 44 18 83 B
Ligonier St. E2 4 33 82 D
Lilac Cl. E4 26 36 91 B
Lilac Gdns. Croy 106 37 65 C
Lilac Gdns. Rom 42 51 87 C
Lilac Gdns. W5 60 17 79 D
Lilac Pl. SE11 10 30 78 B
Lilac St. W12 55 22 80 A
Lilburne Gdns. SE9 77 42 74 A
Lilburne Rd. SE9 77 42 74 A
Lilburne Wlk. NW10 45 20 84 A
Lile Cres. W7 54 15 81 A
Lilestone St. NW8 1 27 82 C
Lilford Rd. SE5 75 31 76 D
Lilian Ave. W3 61 19 79 A
Lilian Board Way. Grnf 43 14 85 D
Lilian Gdns. Wdf Gn 27 40 90 B
Lilian Rd. SW13 61 22 77 B
Lilian Rd. SW16 96 29 69 A
Lillechurch Rd. Dag 52 47 85 C
Lilleshall Rd. Mord 103 26 67 D
Lillie Rd. SW6 62 24 77 B
Lillieshall Rd. SW4 74 29 75 A
Lillie Yd. SW6 62 25 77 A
Lilliput Ave. Nthlt 43 12 83 B
Lilliput Rd. Rom 41 50 87 B
Lily Cl. W14 62 24 78 A
Lily Gdns. Wem 44 17 83 C
Lily Pl. EC1 3 31 81 A
Lily Rd. E17 38 37 88 C
Lilyville Rd. SW6 73 24 76 B
Limbourne Ave. Dag 41 48 87 B
Limburg Rd. SW11 74 27 75 C

Lime Cl. Cars 104 27 65 B
Lime Cres. Sun 92 11 69 C
Limecroft Cl. Eps 109 20 63 D
Lime Ct. Horn 42 53 87 A
Limedene Cl. Pnr 20 11 90 B
Lime Gr. Ilf 28 45 91 B
Lime Gr. N20 15 24 94 B
Lime Gr. N Mal 94 20 68 B
Lime Gr. Orp 108 43 65 B
Lime Gr. Ruis 31 10 87 B
Lime Gr. Sid 78 45 74 D
Lime Gr. Twick 71 16 74 C
Lime Gr. W12 62 23 79 A
Limehouse Cswy. E14 57 36 80 B
Limehouse Fields Estate. E14 57 36 81 A
Limerick Cl. SW12 86 29 73 A
Lime Row. Belv 67 48 79 D
Limerston St. SW10 62 26 77 B
Limes Ave. Cars 104 27 66 D
Limes Ave. Chig 28 44 91 B
Limes Ave. Croy 105 31 65 C
Limes Ave. E11 27 40 89 D
Limes Ave. E12 39 42 86 D
Limes Ave. N12 15 26 92 A
Limes Ave. NW11 35 24 87 A
Limes Ave. NW7 22 21 91 A
Limes Ave. SE20 97 34 70 D
Limes Ave. SW13 72 21 76 D
Limes Ave The. N11 16 29 92 C
Limes Cl. Ashf 81 07 71 C
Limesdale Gdns. Edg 22 20 90 C
Limes Field Rd. SW14 72 21 75 A
Limesford Rd. SE15 76 35 75 D
Limes Gdns. SW18 73 25 74 C
Limes Gr. SE13 76 38 75 C
Limes Pl. Croy 105 32 66 B
Limes Rd. Beck 98 37 69 D
Limes Rd. Croy 105 32 66 B
Lime St. E17 26 36 89 C
Lime St. EC3 4 33 81 C
Limes The. Brom 107 42 65 A
Limestone Wlk. Belv 67 47 79 B
Lime St Pas. EC3 4 33 81 C
Lime St. Rom 29 50 89 C
Limes Wlk. SE15 75 34 75 D
Limes Wlk. SE15 76 35 75 C
Limes Wlk. W5 60 17 79 B
Lime Tree Ave. Esh 101 15 66 C
Lime Tree Ave. SE20 97 34 69 B
Lime Tree Ave. Surb 101 15 66 C
Lime Tree Ave. W8 62 24 79 B
Limetree Cl. SW2 86 30 73 D
Lime Tree Gr. Croy 106 36 65 D
Limetree Pl. Mit 96 28 69 B
Lime Tree Rd. Houn 70 13 76 B
Lime Wlk. E Mol 93 15 68 D
Limewood Cl. W13 54 17 81 C
Limewood Rd. Eri 67 50 77 C
Limpsfield Ave. SW19 85 23 72 B
Limpsfield Ave. Th Hth 104 30 67 B
Linacre Rd. NW2 45 22 84 B
Linchmere Rd. SE12 89 39 73 B
Lincoln Ave. N14 16 29 93 A
Lincoln Ave. Rom 42 51 87 C
Lincoln Ave. SW19 85 23 72 D
Lincoln Ave. Twick 82 14 72 A
Lincoln Cl. Eri 80 51 76 D
Lincoln Cl. Grnf 43 14 83 A
Lincoln Cl. Har 32 12 88 B
Lincoln Cres. Enf 13 33 95 A
Lincoln Ct. Enf 13 32 96 D
Lincoln Ct. N16 37 32 87 B
Lincoln Gdns. Ilf 39 42 87 A
Lincoln Green Rd. Orp 108 45 67 B
Lincoln Mews. NW6 46 24 83 B
Lincoln Rd. E13 58 40 82 D
Lincoln Rd. E18 27 40 90 A
Lincoln Rd. E7 50 41 84 B
Lincoln Rd. Enf 13 34 95 A
Lincoln Rd. Eri 80 51 76 D
Lincoln Rd. Felt 82 12 72 D
Lincoln Rd. Har 32 12 88 B
Lincoln Rd. Mit 104 30 67 A
Lincoln Rd. N2 24 27 89 A
Lincoln Rd. N Mal 94 20 68 A
Lincoln Rd. Nthwd 19 09 89 B
Lincoln Rd. SE25 97 34 68 B
Lincoln Rd. Sid 90 46 71 D
Lincoln Rd. Wem 44 17 84 B
Lincoln Rd. Wor Pk 102 22 66 D
Lincoln's Inn Fields. WC2 3 30 81 D
Lincoln St. E11 39 39 86 A
Lincoln St. SW3 9 27 78 B
Lincoln Way. Enf 13 34 95 B
Lincoln Way. Sun 91 09 69 A
Lincoln Wlk. Eps 109 20 62 D
Lincombe Rd. Brom 89 39 72 D
Lindal Cres. Enf 12 30 96 D
Lindales The. N17 25 33 91 B
Lindal Rd. SE4 76 36 74 B
Lindbergh Rd. Wall 111 30 63 C
Linden Ave. Enf 13 34 97 A
Linden Ave. Houn 70 13 74 B
Linden Ave. NW10 46 23 83 D
Linden Ave. Ruis 31 10 86 D
Linden Ave. Th Hth 97 31 68 D
Linden Ave. Wem 44 18 85 D
Linden Cl. N14 12 29 95 C
Linden Cl. Ruis 31 10 87 C
Linden Cl. Surb 101 15 66 B
Linden Cres. Grnf 44 15 84 B
Linden Cres. King 93 18 69 D
Linden Cres. Wdf Gn 27 40 91 B
Lindenfield. Chis 100 43 69 D
Linden Gdns. Enf 13 34 97 A
Linden Gdns. W2 56 25 80 A
Linden Gdns. W4 61 20 78 D
Linden Gr. N Mal 94 21 68 A
Linden Gr. SE15 76 35 75 A
Linden Gr. SE26 98 35 70 A
Linden Gr. Tedd 83 15 71 D
Linden Lawns. Wem 44 18 85 B
Linden Lea. N2 35 26 88 A
Linden Leas. W Wick 106 38 65 B
Linden Mews. W2 56 25 80 A
Linden Pas. W4 61 20 78 D
Linden Rd. Hamp 92 13 69 A
Linden Rd. N10 24 28 89 D
Linden Rd. N11 16 28 93 A
Linden Rd. N15 25 32 89 C
Lindens The. N12 15 26 92 D
Lindens The. W4 72 20 76 A
Linden St. Rom 29 50 89 D
Linden Way. N14 12 29 95 C
Linden Way. Pur 111 29 62 C
Lindeth Cl. Stan 21 16 91 B
Lindfield Gdns. NW3 46 26 85 C
Lindfield Rd. Croy 105 33 67 D
Lindfield Rd. W5 54 17 82 C
Lindfield St. E14 57 37 81 C
Lindisfarne Rd. Dag 41 47 86 C
Lindisfarne Rd. SW20 94 22 70 C
Lindisfarne Way. E9 49 36 85 A
Lindley Ct. King 93 17 70 C
Lindley Rd. E10 38 38 86 A
Lindley St. E1 57 35 81 A
Lindore Rd. SW11 74 27 75 D
Lindores Rd. Cars 103 26 66 A
Lindo St. SE15 76 35 76 C
Lind Rd. Sutt 110 26 64 C
Lindrop St. SW6 73 26 76 C
Lindsay Dri. Har 33 18 88 B
Lindsay Rd. Hamp 82 13 71 B
Lindsay Rd. Wor Pk 102 22 65 B
Lindsell Rd. Bark 51 44 83 A
Lindsell St. SE10 76 38 76 A
Lindsey Cl. Brom 99 42 68 A
Lindsey Cl. Mit 96 30 68 C
Lindsey Ct. N13 17 31 93 C
Lindsey Rd. Dag 41 47 86 C
Lindsey St. EC1 3 31 81 B
Lindsey Way. Horn 42 53 88 A
Lind St. SE8 76 37 76 D
Lindum Rd. Tedd 93 17 70 C
Lindway. SE27 87 31 71 D
Linford Rd. E17 26 38 89 A
Linford St. SW8 74 29 76 A
Lingards Rd. SE13 76 38 75 C
Lingey Cl. Sid 90 45 72 B
Lingfield Ave. Horn 42 54 86 D
Lingfield Ave. King 93 18 68 D
Lingfield Cl. Enf 13 33 95 C
Lingfield Cl. Nthwd 19 09 91 C
Lingfield Cres. SE9 78 44 75 D
Lingfield Gdns. N9 17 34 94 B
Lingfield Rd. SW19 95 23 70 B
Lingfield Rd. Wor Pk 103 23 65 C
Lingham St. SW9 74 30 76 C
Lingholm Way. Barn 11 23 95 B
Ling Rd. E16 58 40 81 A
Ling Rd. Eri 67 50 77 A
Ling's Coppice. SE21 87 32 72 B
Lingwell Rd. SW17 86 27 72 C
Lingwood. Bexh 79 49 76 D
Lingwood Gdns. Islw 60 15 77 C
Lingwood Rd. E5 37 34 87 A
Linhope St. NW1 1 27 82 D
Linkfield. Brom 107 40 67 C
Linkfield. E Mol 92 13 68 B
Linkfield Rd. Islw 71 15 76 D
Link La. Wall 111 30 63 A
Linklea Cl. NW9 22 21 91 C
Link Rd. Dag 52 49 83 D
Link Rd. Felt 81 09 73 B
Link Rd. N11 16 28 92 A
Link Rd. Wall 104 28 66 C
Links Ave. Mord 95 25 68 C
Links Ave. Rom 30 52 90 C
Linkscroft Ave. Ashf 91 07 70 B
Links Dri. N20 15 25 94 D
Links Gdns. SW16 97 31 70 C
Linkside. Enf 13 31 96 A
Linkside Gdns. Enf 12 30 96 B
Linkside. N12 23 24 91 B
Linkside. N Mal 94 21 69 C
Links Rd. NW2 34 21 86 B
Links Rd. SW17 96 28 70 A
Links Rd. W3 55 19 81 C
Links Rd. W Wick 106 38 66 C
Link St. E9 49 35 85 C
Links The. E17 26 36 89 C
Links View Cl. Stan 21 16 91 A
Links View. N3 23 24 91 D
Links View Rd. Croy 106 37 65 C
Links View Rd. Hamp 82 14 71 A
Links Way. Beck 106 37 67 C
Linksway. Nthwd 19 08 90 A
Linksway. NW4 23 23 90 D
Link The. Enf 14 36 97 A
Link The. Nthlt 43 12 85 D
Link The. Pnr 32 11 87 A
Link The. W3 55 19 81 D
Link The. Wem 33 17 87 C
Linkway. Barn 11 25 95 D
Link Way. Brom 107 42 66 A
Linkway. Dag 52 47 85 A
Link Way. Horn 42 54 87 C
Linkway. N4 37 32 87 A
Linkway. Pnr 20 11 90 B
Link Way. Rich 83 16 72 B
Linkway. SW20 94 22 68 B
Linkway The. Sutt 110 26 62 B
Linkwood Wlk. N7 47 29 84 D
Linley Cres. Rom 29 50 89 A
Linley Ct. Sutt 110 26 64 A
Linley Rd. N17 25 33 90 C
Linnell Cl. NW11 35 25 88 D
Linnell Dr. NW11 35 25 88 D
Linnell Rd. N18 17 34 92 C
Linnell Rd. SE5 75 33 76 C
Linnet Mews. SW12 86 28 73 A
Linnett Cl. E4 18 38 92 A
Linom Rd. SW4 74 30 75 C
Linscott Rd. E5 49 35 85 A
Linsey St. SE16 63 34 78 A
Linsey St. SE16 63 34 79 C
Linstead St. NW6 46 25 84 C
Linstead Way. SW18 85 24 73 A
Linsted Ct. SE9 78 45 74 C
Linthorpe Ave. Wem 44 17 84 A
Linthorpe Rd. Barn 12 27 96 A
Linthorpe Rd. N16 37 33 87 A
Linton Cl. Well 78 46 76 B
Linton Ct. Rom 30 51 90 C
Linton Gr. SE27 87 32 71 C
Linton Rd. Bark 51 44 84 C
Lintons The. Bark 51 44 84 C
Linton St. N1 48 32 83 A
Linver Rd. SW6 73 25 76 C
Linwood Way (off Daniel Gdns). SE15 63 33 77 D
Linzee Rd. N8 24 30 89 C
Lion Ave. Twick 83 15 73 D
Lionel Gdns. SE9 77 41 74 B
Lionel Mews. W10 56 24 81 A
Lionel Rd. Brent 60 18 78 A
Lionel Rd. SE9 77 41 74 B
Lion Gate Gdns. Rich 71 18 75 B
Lion Rd. Bexh 79 48 75 D
Lion Rd. Croy 105 32 67 A
Lion Rd. N9 17 34 93 A
Lion Rd. Twick 83 15 73 D
Lions Cl. SE9 89 41 72 D
Lion Way. Brent 60 17 77 D
Liphook Cres. SE23 88 35 73 A
Lipton Rd. E1 57 35 81 D
Lisbon Ave. Twick 82 14 72 A
Lisburne Rd. NW3 47 27 85 B
Lisford St. SE15 75 33 76 B
Lisgar Terr. W14 62 24 78 B
Liskeard Cl. Chis 100 44 70 A
Liskeard Gdns. SE3 77 40 76 A
Lisle Cl. NW2 35 24 86 C
Lisle St. WC2 6 29 80 B
Lismore Cl. Islw 71 16 76 C
Lismore Rd. N17 25 32 89 B
Lismore Rd. S Croy 112 33 63 A
Lismore Wlk. N1 48 32 84 A
Lissenden Gdns. NW5 47 28 85 A
Lisson Gr. NW8 1 27 82 C
Lisson St. NW1 1 27 81 A
Liss Way (off Cator St). SE15 63 33 77 D
Lister Gdns. N18 17 32 92 C
Lister Mews. N7 47 30 85 B
Lister Rd. E11 39 39 87 D
Liston Rd. N17 25 34 90 A
Liston Rd. SW4 74 29 75 A
Liston Way. Wdf Gn 27 41 91 C
Listowel Rd. Dag 41 49 86 C
Listria Park. N16 37 33 86 A
Litchfield Ave. E15 50 39 84 A
Litchfield Ave. Mord 103 24 66 B
Litchfield Gdns. NW10 45 22 84 A
Litchfield Rd. Sutt 110 26 64 A
Litchfield St. WC2 6 29 80 B
Litchfield Way. NW11 35 26 88 A
Lithgow's Rd. Houn 69 09 75 D
Lithos Rd. NW3 46 26 84 A
Litlington St. SE16 63 34 78 B
Little Acre. Beck 98 37 68 A
Little Albany St. NW1 2 28 82 D
Little Argyll St. W1 2 29 81 C
Little Aston Rd. Rom 30 54 91 D
Little Birches. Sid 90 45 72 A
Little Boltons The. SW10 62 26 78 C
Little Bornes. SE21 87 33 71 A
Little Britain. EC1 4 32 81 A
Little Brownings. SE23 87 34 72 B
Littlebury Rd. SW4 74 29 75 B
Little Bury St. N9 17 33 94 A
Little Cedars. N12 15 26 92 A
Little Chester St. SW1 6 28 79 D
Little College La. EC4 8 32 80 B
Little College St. SW1 7 30 79 C
Little Combe Cl. SW15 73 23 74 D
Littlecombe. SE7 65 40 77 B
Littlecote Cl. SW19 85 24 73 A
Littlecroft. SE9 78 43 75 A
Little Ct. W.Wick 107 39 65 A
Littledale. SE2 66 46 77 A
Little Dimocks. SW12 86 28 72 B
Little Dorrit Ct. SE1 8 32 79 A
Little Ealing La. W5 60 17 79 C
Little Edward St. NW1 47 28 83 D
Little Essex St. WC2 7 31 80 A
Little Ferry Rd. Twick 83 16 73 D
*Littlefield Cl. N19 47 29 85 A
Littlefield Rd. Edg 22 20 91 C
Little Gearies. Ilf 28 43 89 D
Little George St. SW1 7 30 79 A
Little Green. Rich 71 17 75 D
Little Green St. NW5 47 28 85 B
Littlegrove. Barn 12 27 95 C
Little Haven. SE19 97 32 70 C
Little Heath Rd. Bexh 67 48 77 D
Littleheath Rd. S Croy 112 34 62 B
Little Heath. Rom 28 46 89 D
Little Heath. SE7 65 42 78 C
Little Ilford La. E12 50 42 85 B
Littlejohn Rd. Orp 108 46 67 B
Littlejohn Rd. W7 54 15 81 D
Little Marlborough St. W1 2 29 81 C
Littlemede. SE9 89 42 72 D
Littlemoor Rd. Ilf 40 44 86 D
Littlemore Rd. SE2 66 46 79 A
Little Moss La. Pnr 20 12 90 C
Little Newport St. WC2 6 29 80 B
Little New St. EC4 3 31 81 C
Little Orchard Cl. Pnr 20 12 90 C
Little Park Dri. Felt 82 12 72 A
Little Park Gdns. Enf 13 32 96 B
Little Portland St. W1 2 29 81 C
Little Queen's Rd. Tedd 93 15 70 B
Little Rd. Croy 105 33 66 C
Little Redlands. Brom 99 42 69 C
Littlers Cl. SW19 95 26 69 B
Little Russell St. WC1 3 30 81 A
Little Sanctuary. SW1 7 30 79 A
Little Smith St. SW1 6 29 79 D
Little Somerset St. E1 4 33 81 D
Little St James's St. SW1 6 29 80 C
Little St Leonards. SW14 72 20 75 A
Littlestone Cl. Beck 98 37 70 A
Little Strand. NW9 22 21 90 A
Little Thrift. Orp 100 44 68 C
Little Titchfield St. W1 2 29 81 A
Littleton Cres. Har 33 15 86 B
Littleton Rd. Ashf 91 08 70 C
Littleton Rd. Har 33 16 86 C
Littleton St. SW18 85 26 72 A
Little Trinity La. EC4 8 32 80 A
Littlewood Cl. W13 60 16 79 D
Littlewood. SE13 76 38 74 C
Littleworth Rd. Esh 101 15 65 C
Livermere Rd. E8 48 33 83 B
Liverpool Gr. SE17 63 32 78 D
Liverpool Rd. E10 38 38 88 C
Liverpool Rd. E16 58 39 81 A
Liverpool Rd. King 94 19 70 C
Liverpool Rd. N1 48 31 84 C
Liverpool Rd. N7 48 31 84 A
Liverpool Rd. Th Hth 97 32 68 A
Liverpool Rd. W5 60 17 79 B
Liverpool St. EC2 4 33 81 A
Livesey Pl. SE15 63 34 77 A
Livingstone Ct. E10 38 38 88 C
Livingstone Pl. E14 64 38 78 C
Livingstone Rd. E15 49 38 83 A
Livingstone Rd. E17 38 37 88 D
Livingstone Rd. Houn 70 14 75 C
Livingstone Rd. N13 24 30 91 A
Livingstone Rd. Sthl 53 11 80 B
Livingstone Rd. SW11 73 26 75 B
Livingstone Rd. Th Hth 97 32 69 D
Livingstone Wlk. SW11 73 26 75 B
Livonia St. W1 2 29 81 C
Lizard St. EC1 4 32 82 A
Lizhan St. SE3 65 40 77 D
Llanelly Rd. NW2 35 24 86 B
Llanover Rd. SE18 66 43 77 C
Llanover Rd. Wem 33 17 86 D
Llanthony Rd. Mord 103 26 67 D
Llanvanor Rd. NW2 35 24 86 B
Llewellyn St. SE16 63 34 79 A
Lloyd Ave. SW16 96 30 69 A
Lloyd Baker St. WC1 3 31 82 A
Lloyd Ct. Pnr 32 11 88 B
Lloyd Park Ave. Croy 112 33 64 B
Lloyd Rd. Dag 52 48 84 D
Lloyd Rd. E17 26 35 89 D
Lloyd Rd. E6 50 42 83 B
Lloyd Rd. Wor Pk 103 23 65 D
Lloyd's Ave. EC3 8 33 80 A
Lloyd's Pl. SE3 77 39 76 C
Lloyd Sq. WC1 3 31 82 A
Lloyd's Row. EC1 3 31 82 B
Lloyd St. WC1 3 31 82 A
Lloyds Way. Beck 106 36 67 B
Loampit Hill. SE13 76 37 76 D
Loampit Vale. SE13 76 37 75 B
Loats Rd. SW4 74 30 74 C
Lobby Rd. SE28 66 45 79 A
Locarno Rd. Grnf 53 14 82 D
Locarno Rd. W3 55 20 80 C
Lochaber Rd. SE13 77 39 75 C
Lochaline St. W6 62 23 77 A
Lochinvar Estate. SW12 86 28 73 B
Lochinvar St. SW12 86 28 73 B
Lochmere Cl. Eri 67 49 77 B
Lochnagar St. E14 58 38 81 A
Lock Chase. SE3 77 39 75 A
Lockesley Dri. Orp 108 46 67 C
Locket Rd. Har 21 15 90 D
Lockfield Ave. Enf 14 36 97 B
Lockhart Cl. N7 47 30 84 B
Lockhart St. E3 57 36 82 D
Lockhurst St. E5 49 35 85 B
Lockier Wlk. Wem 33 17 86 D
Lockington Rd. SW8 74 28 76 B
Lockmead Rd. N15 37 34 88 C
Lockmead Rd. SE13 76 38 75 A
Lock Rd. Rich 83 17 71 A
Lock's La. Mit 96 28 69 C
Locksley Sq. Surb 101 17 67 D
Locksley St. E14 57 36 81 B
Locksmeade Rd. Rich 83 17 71 A
Lockwood Rd. Ilf 40 44 86 A
Lockwood Sq. SE16 63 34 79 D
Lockwood Way. Chess 109 19 64 C
Lockwood Way. E17 26 35 90 D
Lockwood Wlk. Rom 42 51 88 A
Lockyer St. SE1 8 32 79 B
Loddiges Rd. E9 49 35 84 C
Loder St. SE15 64 35 77 C
Lodge Ave. Croy 105 31 65 C
Lodge Ave. Dag 51 46 84 B
Lodge Ave. Dart 80 53 74 C
Lodge Ave. Har 21 18 89 C
Lodge Ave. Rom 30 52 89 C
Lodge Ave. SW14 72 21 75 A
Lodge Cl. Edg 21 18 91 B
Lodge Cl. Islw 71 16 76 B
Lodge Cl. N18 17 32 92 C
Lodge Cl. Orp 108 46 66 D.
Lodge Cl. Wall 104 28 66 C
Lodge Cres. Orp 108 46 66 D
Lodge Ct. Horn 42 54 86 A
Lodge Dri. N13 17 31 92 A
Lodge Gdns. Beck 106 36 67 B
Lodge Hill. Ilf 27 42 89 C
Lodge Hill. Well 67 47 77 A
Lodge La. Bex 79 47 74 D
Lodge La. N12 15 26 92 C
Lodge La. Rom 29 49 91 C
Lodge Path. N2 23 26 90 D
Lodge Pl. Sutt 110 25 64 D
Lodge Rd. Brom 99 41 70 C
Lodge Rd. Croy 105 31 66 B
Lodge Rd. NW4 23 23 89 C
Lodge Rd. NW8 1 27 82 A
Lodge Rd. Sutt 110 25 64 D
Lodge Rd. Wall 111 28 64 D
Lodge The. Tedd 93 15 70 B
1Lodge Villas. Wdf Gn 27 39 91 D
Lodge Way. Shep 91 08 69 C
Lodore Gdns. NW9 34 21 88 A
Lodore St. E14 58 38 81 C
Loftie St. SE16 63 34 79 A
Lofting Rd. N1 48 31 84 C
Loftus Rd. W12 55 22 80 D
Logan Cl. Enf 14 35 97 B
Logan Cl. Houn 70 12 75 B
Logan Mew. W8 62 25 78 A
Logan Pl. W8 62 25 78 A
Logan Rd. N9 17 34 93 B
Logan Rd. Wem 33 18 86 A
Logs Hill. Chis 99 42 69 A
Logs Hill Cl. Chis 99 42 69 A
Lollard Pl. SE11 63 31 78 A
Lollard St. SE11 10 30 78 B
Lollard St. SE11 63 31 78 A
Loman St. SE1 7 31 79 B
Lomas St. E1 57 34 81 A
Lombard Ave. Enf 14 35 97 A
Lombard Ave. Ilf 40 45 87 C
Lombard Ct. EC4 8 32 80 B
Lombard La. EC4 3 31 81 C
Lombard Rd. N11 16 29 92 C
Lombard Rd. SW11 73 26 76 D
Lombard Rd. SW19 95 26 69 C
Lombard St. EC3 4 32 81 D
Lombard Wall. SE7 65 40 78 B
Lombardy Pl. W2 56 25 80 B
Lomond Cl. N15 25 33 89 C
Lomond Cl. Wem 44 18 84 D
Lomond Gr. SE5 63 32 77 D
Lona Cl. SE6 88 37 73 A
Loncroft Rd. SE5 63 33 77 A
Londesborough Rd. N16 48 33 85 A
London Bridge. EC4 8 32 80 B
London Bridge St. SE1 8 32 80 D
London Fields East Side. E8 48 34 84 D
London Fields West Side. E8 48 34 84 C
London La. Brom 99 39 70 D
London La. E8 48 34 84 D
London Mews. W2 1 26 81 D
London Rd. Ashf 81 07 73 C
London Rd. Bark 51 43 84 D
London Rd. Brent 60 17 77 C
London Rd. Brom 99 39 69 B
London Rd. Croy 105 31 66 B
London Rd. Dart 79 50 74 B
London Rd. E13 50 40 83 C
London Rd. Enf 13 32 96 D
London Rd. Eps 109 22 63 D
London Rd. Har 33 15 86 A
London Rd. Houn 70 14 75 B
London Rd. Islw 71 15 76 D
London Rd. King 93 18 69 D
London Rd. Mit 96 27 69 D
London Rd. Mit 104 28 66 A
London Rd. Mord 103 25 67 A
London Rd. Mord 95 25 68 D
London Rd. Rom 41 49 88 D
London Rd. SE1 7 31 79 D
London Rd. SE23 88 35 73 C
London Rd. S Ock 68 54 79 B
London Rd. Sutt 103 23 65 D
London Rd. SW17 96 27 70 B
London Rd. Th Hth 105 31 67 A
London Rd. Twick 83 16 73 A
London Rd. Twick 71 16 74 C
London Rd. Wall 104 28 65 C
London Rd. Wem 44 18 84 A
London St. EC3 8 33 80 A
London St. W2 1 26 81 D
London Wall. EC2 4 32 81 A
Longacre Pl. Cars 111 28 63 A
Longacre Rd. E17 26 38 90 B
Long Acre. WC2 3 30 81 C

| | | |
|---|---|---|
| Longbeach Rd. SW11 | 74 | 28 75 A |
| Longberrys. NW2 | 35 | 24 86 D |
| Longbridge Rd. Bark | 51 | 45 84 A |
| Longbridge Rd. Dag | 51 | 46 85 B |
| Longbridge Way. SE13 | 76 | 38 74 A |
| Longbury Dri. Orp | 100 | 46 69 D |
| Longcrofte Rd. Edg | 21 | 17 91 D |
| Longcroft. SE9 | 90 | 43 72 C |
| Longdon Wood. Brom | 107 | 42 65 C |
| Longdown Rd. SE6 | 88 | 37 71 A |
| Long Dri. Grnf | 43 | 13 83 B |
| Long Dri. Ruis | 43 | 11 85 B |
| Long Dri. W3 | 55 | 21 81 C |
| Long Elmes. Har | 20 | 14 90 A |
| Longfellow Rd. E17 | 38 | 36 88 D |
| Longfellow Rd. Wor Pk | 102 | 22 66 D |
| Longfield Ave. E17 | 26 | 36 89 C |
| Longfield Ave. Horn | 42 | 51 87 B |
| Longfield Ave. NW7 | 22 | 22 91 C |
| Longfield Ave. W5 | 54 | 17 80 A |
| Longfield Ave. Wall | 104 | 28 66 C |
| Longfield Ave. Wem | 33 | 18 87 C |
| Longfield. Brom | 99 | 39 69 B |
| Longfield Cres. SE26 | 88 | 35 72 C |
| Longfield Dri. SW14 | 72 | 19 74 B |
| Long Field. NW9 | 22 | 21 91 D |
| Longfield Rd. W5 | 54 | 17 81 C |
| Longfield St. SW18 | 85 | 25 73 A |
| Longfield Wlk. W5 | 54 | 17 81 C |
| Longford Ave. Felt | 69 | 09 74 D |
| Longford Ave. Sthl | 53 | 13 80 B |
| Longford Cl. Hamp | 82 | 13 71 A |
| Longford Cl. Hay | 53 | 11 80 B |
| Longford Ct. Eps | 109 | 20 64 A |
| Longford Gdns. Hay | 53 | 11 80 B |
| Longford Gdns. Sutt | 103 | 26 65 A |
| Longford Rd. Twick | 82 | 13 73 D |
| Longford St. NW1 | 2 | 28 82 D |
| Longford Wlk. SE24 | 87 | 31 73 A |
| Long Grove Rd. Eps | 109 | 19 62 D |
| Longhayes Ave. Rom | 29 | 47 89 D |
| Longhayes Ct. Rom | 29 | 47 89 D |
| Longhayes Ct. Rom | 29 | 47 89 D |
| Longheath Gdns. Croy | 106 | 35 67 B |
| Longhedge St. SW11 | 74 | 28 76 C |
| 1Longhill Rd. SE6 | 88 | 38 72 D |
| Longhope Cl. SE15 | 63 | 33 77 B |
| Longhurst Rd. Croy | 105 | 34 67 D |
| Longhurst Rd. Croy | 106 | 35 67 C |
| Longhurst Rd. SE13 | 77 | 39 74 A |
| Long La. Bexh | 79 | 48 76 B |
| Long La. Croy | 106 | 35 67 C |
| Long La. EC1 | 3 | 31 81 B |
| Long La. N3 | 23 | 25 90 B |
| Longland Ct. SE1 | 63 | 34 78 C |
| Longland Dri. N20 | 15 | 25 93 B |
| Longlands Park Cres. Sid | 90 | 45 72 A |
| Longlands Rd. Sid | 90 | 45 72 D |
| Long La. SE1 | 8 | 32 79 B |
| Long La. Uxb | 31 | 07 86 D |
| Longleat Rd. Enf | 13 | 33 95 A |
| Longleat Way. Felt | 81 | 08 73 B |
| Longleigh La. Bexh | 67 | 47 77 A |
| Longleigh La. SE2 | 67 | 47 77 A |
| Longley Ave. Wem | 44 | 18 83 B |
| Longley Rd. Croy | 105 | 31 66 B |
| Longley Rd. Har | 20 | 14 89 D |
| Longley Rd. SW17 | 96 | 27 70 A |
| Long Leys. E4 | 26 | 37 91 B |
| Longley St. SE1 | 63 | 34 78 A |
| Longmead. Chis | 100 | 43 69 C |
| Long Mead. NW9 | 22 | 21 90 B |
| Longmeadow Rd. Sid | 90 | 45 73 C |
| Longmead Rd. Eps | 109 | 21 62 C |
| Longmead Rd. Surb | 101 | 15 66 B |
| Longmead Rd. SW17 | 86 | 27 71 B |
| Longmore Ave. Barn | 11 | 26 95 D |
| Longmore St. SW1 | 10 | 29 78 A |
| Longnor Rd. E1 | 57 | 35 82 B |
| Long Pond Rd. SE3 | 77 | 39 76 A |
| Longport Cl. Ilf | 28 | 46 91 A |
| Long Rd. SW4 | 74 | 29 75 C |
| Longreach Ct. Bark | 51 | 44 83 D |
| Longreach Rd. Eri | 68 | 52 77 D |
| Longridge La. Sthl | 53 | 13 81 D |
| Longridge Rd. SW5 | 62 | 25 78 A |
| Long's Ct. WC2 | 6 | 29 80 B |
| Longshaw Rd. E4 | 18 | 38 93 D |
| Longshore. SE8 | 64 | 36 78 B |
| Longstaff Cres. SW18 | 85 | 25 73 A |
| Longstaff Rd. SW18 | 85 | 25 73 A |
| Longstaff Rd. SW18 | 73 | 25 74 C |
| Long St. E2 | 4 | 33 82 B |
| Long St. E2 | 48 | 33 83 D |
| Longstone Ave. NW10 | 45 | 21 83 B |
| Longstone Rd. SW17 | 86 | 28 71 D |
| Longthornton Rd. SW16 | 96 | 29 69 D |
| Longton Ave. SE26 | 87 | 34 71 A |
| Longton Gr. SE26 | 87 | 34 71 B |
| Longview Way. Rom | 29 | 50 90 B |
| Longville Rd. SE11 | 63 | 31 78 B |
| Long Walk. N Mal | 94 | 20 68 A |
| Long Wlk. SE18 | 66 | 43 77 B |
| Long Wlk. SE1 | 8 | 33 79 C |
| Long Wlk. SW13 | 72 | 21 76 D |
| Longwood Dri. SW15 | 72 | 22 74 C |
| Longwood Gdn. Ilf | 28 | 43 89 A |
| Long Yd. WC1 | 3 | 30 82 D |
| Loning The. NW9 | 22 | 21 89 D |
| Lonsdale Ave. E6 | 58 | 41 82 D |
| Lonsdale Ave. Rom | 41 | 50 88 C |
| Lonsdale Ave. Wem | 44 | 18 84 A |
| Lonsdale Cl. Pnr | 20 | 12 91 C |
| Lonsdale Cl. SE9 | 89 | 41 72 D |
| Lonsdale Cres. Ilf | 40 | 43 88 D |
| Lonsdale Dri. Enf | 12 | 30 95 A |
| Lonsdale Drive N. Enf | 12 | 30 96 C |
| Lonsdale Gdns. Th Hth | 96 | 30 68 D |
| Lonsdale Mews. Rich | 72 | 19 76 A |
| Lonsdale Mews. W11 | 56 | 24 81 D |
| Lonsdale Pl. N1 | 48 | 31 84 C |
| Lonsdale Rd. Bexh | 79 | 48 76 D |
| Lonsdale Rd. E11 | 39 | 39 87 B |
| Lonsdale Rd. NW6 | 46 | 24 83 B |
| Lonsdale Rd. SE25 | 97 | 34 68 D |
| Lonsdale Rd. Sthl | 59 | 11 79 D |
| Lonsdale Rd. SW13 | 61 | 22 77 A |
| Lonsdale Rd. W11 | 56 | 24 81 D |
| Lonsdale Rd. W4 | 61 | 21 78 B |
| Lonsdale Sq. N1 | 48 | 31 84 C |
| Lon Sq. E2 | 48 | 34 83 C |
| Loobert Rd. N15 | 25 | 33 89 A |
| Looe Gnds. Ilf | 28 | 43 90 D |
| Loop Rd. Chis | 100 | 44 70 A |
| Lopen Rd. N18 | 17 | 33 92 A |
| Loraine Cl. Enf | 14 | 35 95 A |
| Loraine Rd. N7 | 47 | 30 85 B |
| Loraine Rd. W4 | 61 | 19 77 B |
| Lord Ave. Ilf | 27 | 42 89 B |
| Lord Chancellor Wlk. King | 94 | 20 69 A |
| Lorden Wlk. E2 | 57 | 34 82 A |
| Lord Gdns. Ilf | 27 | 42 89 D |
| Lord Hills Rd. W2 | 56 | 25 81 B |
| Lord Holland La. SW9 | 75 | 31 76 C |
| Lord Napier Pl. W6 | 61 | 22 78 C |
| Lord North St. SW1 | 7 | 30 79 C |
| Lord Roberts Mews. SW6 | 62 | 25 77 D |
| Lord Roberts Terr. SE18 | 66 | 43 78 C |
| Lordsbury Field. Wall | 111 | 29 62 C |
| Lords Cl. Felt | 82 | 12 72 A |
| Lords Cl. SE21 | 87 | 32 72 A |
| Lordship Gr. N16 | 37 | 32 86 B |
| Lordship La. N17 | 25 | 32 90 B |
| Lordship La. N22 | 25 | 31 90 A |
| Lordship La. SE22 | 75 | 33 74 D |
| Lordship Park Mews. N16 | 37 | 32 86 A |
| Lordship Park. N16 | 37 | 32 86 B |
| Lordship Pl. SW3 | 9 | 27 77 A |
| Lordship Rd. N16 | 37 | 32 87 D |
| Lordship Rd. Nthlt | 43 | 12 84 C |
| Lordship Terr. N16 | 37 | 33 86 A |
| Lordsmead Rd. N17 | 25 | 33 90 C |
| Lord Warwick St. SE18 | 65 | 42 79 D |
| Lorenzo St. N1 | 47 | 30 83 D |
| Lorenzo St. WC1 | 3 | 30 82 B |
| Loretto Gdns. Har | 21 | 18 89 C |
| Lorian Cl. N12 | 15 | 25 92 B |
| Loring Rd. Islw | 71 | 15 76 D |
| Loring Rd. N20 | 16 | 27 93 A |
| Loris Rd. W6 | 62 | 23 79 C |
| Lorne Ave. Croy | 106 | 35 66 B |
| Lorne Cl. NW8 | 1 | 27 82 A |
| Lorne Gdns. Croy | 106 | 35 66 B |
| Lorne Gdns. E11 | 27 | 41 89 C |
| Lorne Gdns. W11 | 62 | 23 79 B |
| Lorne Rd. E17 | 38 | 37 88 A |
| Lorne Rd. E7 | 50 | 41 85 A |
| Lorne Rd. Har | 21 | 15 90 D |
| Lorne Rd. N4 | 36 | 30 87 D |
| Lorne Rd. Rich | 71 | 18 74 B |
| Lorn Rd. SW9 | 75 | 31 76 C |
| Lorraine Park. Har | 21 | 15 91 C |
| Lorrimore Rd. SE17 | 63 | 31 77 B |
| Lorrimore Sq. SE17 | 63 | 31 77 B |
| Losberne Way. SE16 | 63 | 34 78 C |
| Lothair Rd. W5 | 60 | 17 79 B |
| Lothair Road. N4 | 37 | 31 88 D |
| Lothair Road S. N4 | 37 | 31 87 B |
| Lothbury. EC2 | 4 | 32 81 D |
| Lothian Mews. SW9 | 63 | 31 77 D |
| Lothian Rd. SW9 | 75 | 31 76 B |
| Lothian Rd. SW9 | 63 | 31 77 D |
| Lothrop St. W10 | 56 | 24 82 A |
| Lots Rd. SW10 | 62 | 26 77 C |
| Loubet Rd. SW17 | 96 | 27 70 B |
| Loudoun Ave. Ilf | 40 | 43 88 B |
| Loudoun Rd. NW8 | 46 | 26 83 A |
| Loudwater Cl. Sun | 91 | 10 68 C |
| Loudwater Rd. Sun | 91 | 10 68 C |
| Loughborough Park. SW9 | 75 | 31 75 D |
| Loughborough Rd. SW9 | 75 | 31 76 C |
| Loughborough St. SE11 | 10 | 30 78 D |
| Lough Rd. N7 | 47 | 30 84 B |
| Louisa Gdns. E1 | 57 | 35 82 D |
| Louisa St. E1 | 57 | 35 82 D |
| Louise Rd. E15 | 50 | 39 84 A |
| Louisville Rd. SW17 | 86 | 28 72 C |
| Louvaine Rd. SW11 | 73 | 26 75 D |
| Lovat Cl. NW2 | 34 | 21 86 D |
| Lovat La. EC3 | 8 | 33 80 A |
| Lovatt Cl. Edg | 22 | 19 91 B |
| Lovatt Dri. Ruis | 31 | 09 88 B |
| Lovat Wlk. Houn | 59 | 12 77 C |
| Loveday Rd. W13 | 54 | 16 80 D |
| Lovegrove St. SE1 | 63 | 34 77 A |
| Lovekyn Cl. King | 93 | 18 69 D |
| Love La. Bex | 79 | 49 74 C |
| Love La. Brom | 99 | 40 69 C |
| Lovelace Ave. Brom | 108 | 43 67 C |
| Lovelace Gdns. Bark | 51 | 46 85 C |
| Lovelace Gdns. Surb | 101 | 17 66 B |
| Lovelace Green. SE9 | 77 | 42 75 B |
| Lovelace Rd. Barn | 16 | 27 94 A |
| Lovelace Rd. SE21 | 87 | 32 73 C |
| Lovelace Rd. Surb | 101 | 17 66 B |
| Love La. EC2 | 4 | 32 81 C |
| Love La. Mit | 96 | 27 68 A |
| Love La. Mord | 103 | 25 66 B |
| Love La. N17 | 25 | 33 91 C |
| Love La. Pnr | 20 | 12 89 A |
| Love La. SE18 | 66 | 43 78 B |
| Love La. SE25 | 97 | 34 68 B |
| Love La. Surb | 101 | 17 65 B |
| Love La. Sutt | 110 | 24 63 B |
| Lovel Ave. Well | 78 | 46 76 C |
| Love La. Wdf Gn | 27 | 42 91 B |
| Lovelinch Cl. SE15 | 64 | 35 77 A |
| Lovell Rd. Rich | 83 | 17 72 C |
| Lovell Rd. Sthl | 53 | 13 81 D |
| Loveridge Mews. NW6 | 46 | 24 84 B |
| Loveridge Rd. NW6 | 46 | 24 84 B |
| Lovers' Wlk. N3 | 23 | 25 91 C |
| Lovers' Wlk. NW7 | 23 | 24 91 B |
| Lovers' Wlk. SE10 | 65 | 39 77 C |
| Lovett Dri. Cars | 103 | 26 66 B |
| Lovett's Pl. SW18 | 73 | 25 75 D |
| Lovett Way. NW10 | 45 | 20 85 C |
| Love Wlk. SE5 | 75 | 32 76 D |
| Lovibonds Ave. Orp | 108 | 44 65 C |
| Lowbrook Rd. Ilf | 51 | 43 85 B |
| Low Cross Wood La. SE21 | 87 | 33 72 D |
| Lowden Rd. N9 | 17 | 34 94 D |
| Lowden Rd. SE24 | 75 | 32 75 C |
| Lowden Rd. Sthl | 53 | 12 80 A |
| Lowe Ave. E16 | 58 | 40 81 A |
| Lowell St. E14 | 57 | 36 81 C |
| Lowen Rd. Rain | 52 | 50 83 D |
| Lower Addiscombe Rd. Croy | 105 | 34 66 C |
| Lower Bedfords Rd. Rom | 30 | 51 91 B |
| Lower Belgrave St. SW1 | 6 | 28 79 D |
| Lower Boston Rd. W7 | 60 | 15 79 A |
| Lower Broad St. Dag | 52 | 49 83 A |
| Lower Camden. Chis | 99 | 42 69 B |
| Lower Church St. Croy | 105 | 31 65 B |
| Lower Clapton Rd. E5 | 48 | 34 85 B |
| Lower Common S. SW15 | 72 | 22 75 B |
| Lower Coombe St. Croy | 112 | 32 64 A |
| Lower Downs Rd. SW20 | 95 | 23 69 B |
| Lower Drayton Pl. Croy | 105 | 31 65 B |
| Lower George St. Rich | 71 | 17 74 B |
| Lower Gravel Rd. Brom | 107 | 42 66 D |
| Lower Green W. Mit | 96 | 27 68 A |
| Lower Grosvenor Pl. SW1 | 6 | 28 79 D |
| Lower Hall La. E4 | 18 | 36 92 C |
| Lower Hampton Rd. Sun | 92 | 11 69 D |
| Lower Ham Rd. King | 93 | 17 70 D |
| Lower Ham Rd. King | 83 | 17 71 D |
| Lower James St. W1 | 6 | 29 80 A |
| Lower John St. W1 | 6 | 29 80 A |
| Lower Kendal Ave. Enf | 12 | 30 95 A |
| Lower Maidstone Rd. N11 | 24 | 29 91 A |
| Lower Mall. W6 | 61 | 22 78 D |
| Lower Mall. W6 | 62 | 23 78 C |
| Lower Mardyke Ave. Rain | 52 | 50 83 C |
| Lower Marsh La. King | 94 | 19 68 B |
| Lower Marsh. SE1 | 7 | 31 79 A |
| Lower Merton Rise. NW3 | 47 | 27 84 C |
| Lower Morden La. Mord | 103 | 24 67 C |
| Lower Mortlake Rd. Rich | 71 | 18 75 D |
| Lower Moss La. Rom | 42 | 51 88 D |
| Lower Park Rd. Belv | 67 | 49 78 A |
| Lower Park Rd. N11 | 16 | 29 92 C |
| Lower Rd. Belv | 67 | 49 79 D |
| Lower Rd. Eri | 67 | 50 78 B |
| Lower Rd. Har | 32 | 14 87 D |
| Lower Rd. N2 | 24 | 27 90 A |
| Lower Rd. Orp | 108 | 46 67 D |
| Lower Rd. SE16 | 64 | 35 79 C |
| Lower Rd. SE8 | 64 | 35 78 B |
| Lowerd. Sutt | 110 | 26 64 A |
| Lower Richmond Rd. Rich | 72 | 19 75 A |
| Lower Richmond Rd. SW14 | 72 | 20 75 A |
| Lower Richmond Rd. SW15 | 73 | 23 75 B |
| Lower Sloane St. SW1 | 9 | 28 78 C |
| Lower Sq. Islw | 71 | 16 75 B |
| Lower Staithe. W4 | 72 | 20 76 A |
| Lower Station Rd. Dart | 80 | 51 74 C |
| Lower Strand. NW9 | 22 | 21 90 D |
| Lower Sunbury Rd. Hamp | 92 | 13 69 C |
| Lower Teddington Rd. King | 93 | 17 69 B |
| Lower Terr. NW3 | 35 | 26 86 C |
| Lower Thames St. EC3 | 8 | 33 80 A |
| Lowestoft Cl. E5 | 38 | 35 86 A |
| Loweswater Cl. Wem | 33 | 17 86 B |
| Lowfield Rd. NW6 | 46 | 25 84 C |
| Lowfield Rd. W3 | 55 | 20 81 C |
| Lowfield St. Dart | 80 | 54 74 C |
| Low Hall Cl. E4 | 18 | 37 94 B |
| Low Hall La. E17 | 38 | 36 88 C |
| Lowick Rd. Har | 33 | 15 88 A |
| Lowland Gdns. Rom | 41 | 49 88 D |
| Lowlands Rd. Har | 33 | 15 87 A |
| Lowlands Rd. Pnr | 32 | 11 88 C |
| Lowman Rd. N7 | 47 | 30 85 B |
| Lowndes Cl. SW1 | 6 | 28 79 C |
| Lowndes Pl. SW1 | 6 | 28 79 C |
| Lowndes Sq. SW1 | 5 | 27 79 B |
| Lowndes St. SW1 | 6 | 28 79 C |
| Lownds Ave. Brom | 99 | 40 69 C |
| Lowood St. E1 | 57 | 35 80 A |
| Lowshoe La. Rom | 29 | 49 90 B |
| Lowswood Cl. Nthwd | 19 | 08 90 A |
| Lowther Dri. Enf | 12 | 30 96 C |
| Lowther Hill. SE23 | 88 | 36 73 A |
| Lowther Rd. E17 | 26 | 36 90 C |
| Lowther Rd. King | 93 | 18 69 B |
| Lowther Rd. N7 | 48 | 31 85 C |
| Lowther Rd. Stan | 21 | 18 89 B |
| Lowther Rd. SW13 | 72 | 21 76 B |
| Lowth Rd. SE5 | 75 | 32 76 C |
| Loxford Ave. E6 | 50 | 41 83 D |
| Loxford La. Ilf | 51 | 44 85 D |
| Loxford Rd. Bark | 51 | 43 84 B |
| Loxham Rd. E4 | 26 | 37 91 D |
| Loxham St. WC1 | 3 | 30 82 A |
| Loxley Cl. SE26 | 88 | 35 71 D |
| Loxley Rd. Hamp | 82 | 12 71 B |
| Loxley Rd. SW18 | 85 | 26 73 D |
| Loxton Rd. SE23 | 88 | 36 73 C |
| Loxwood Rd. N17 | 25 | 33 89 A |
| Lubbock Rd. Chis | 99 | 42 70 D |
| Lubbock St. SE14 | 64 | 35 77 C |
| Lucan Pl. SW3 | 9 | 27 78 A |
| Lucan Rd. Barn | 11 | 24 96 A |
| Lucas Ave. E13 | 50 | 40 83 B |
| Lucas Ave. Har | 32 | 13 86 A |
| Lucas Ct. SE26 | 88 | 36 71 D |
| Lucas Rd. SE20 | 98 | 35 70 A |
| Lucas Sq. NW11 | 35 | 25 88 C |
| Lucas St. SE8 | 76 | 37 76 A |
| Lucerne Cl. N13 | 16 | 30 93 C |
| Lucerne Ct. Beck | 98 | 37 70 C |
| Lucerne Gr. E17 | 26 | 38 89 D |
| Lucerne Mews. W8 | 56 | 25 80 C |
| Lucerne Rd. N5 | 48 | 31 85 B |
| Lucerne Rd. Orp | 108 | 45 66 D |
| Lucerne Rd. Th Hth | 97 | 32 68 C |
| Lucerne Way. Rom | 30 | 53 91 B |
| Lucey Rd. SE16 | 63 | 34 79 C |
| Lucey Way. SE16 | 63 | 34 79 C |
| Lucie Ave. Ashf | 91 | 07 70 B |
| Lucien Rd. SW17 | 86 | 28 71 A |
| Lucien Rd. SW19 | 85 | 25 72 B |
| Lucknow St. SE18 | 66 | 45 77 C |
| Lucorn Cl. SE12 | 77 | 39 74 D |
| Lucy Cres. W3 | 55 | 20 81 A |
| Lucy Gdns. Dag | 41 | 48 86 C |
| Luddesdon Rd. Eri | 67 | 49 77 C |
| Ludford Cl. NW9 | 22 | 21 90 C |
| Ludgate Bwy. EC4 | 3 | 31 81 D |
| Ludgate Circ. EC4 | 3 | 31 81 D |
| Ludgate Ct. EC4 | 3 | 31 81 D |
| Ludgate Hill. EC4 | 3 | 31 81 D |
| Ludgate Sq. EC4 | 3 | 31 81 D |
| Ludham. NW5 | 47 | 27 85 D |
| Ludlow Cl. Har | 43 | 12 85 B |
| Ludlow Rd. Felt | 81 | 10 71 A |
| Ludlow Rd. W5 | 54 | 17 82 C |
| Ludlow St. EC1 | 4 | 32 82 C |
| Ludlow Way. N2 | 23 | 26 89 C |
| Ludovick Wlk. SW15 | 72 | 21 75 D |
| Ludwick Mews. SE14 | 64 | 36 77 C |
| Ludwigshafen Pl. Rom | 30 | 51 89 C |
| Luffield Rd. SE2 | 66 | 46 79 D |
| Luffman Rd. SE12 | 89 | 40 72 D |
| Lugard Rd. SE15 | 75 | 34 76 B |
| Luke St. EC2 | 4 | 33 82 C |
| Lukin Cres. E4 | 18 | 38 93 D |
| Lukin St. E1 | 57 | 35 81 C |
| Lullingstone Cl. Orp | 100 | 46 70 D |
| Lullingstone Cres. Orp | 100 | 46 70 D |
| Lullingstone Rd. Belv | 67 | 48 77 B |
| Lullington Garth. N12 | 15 | 24 92 D |
| Lullington Rd. Dag | 52 | 48 84 C |
| Lullington Rd. SE20 | 97 | 34 70 C |
| Lulot Gdns. N6 | 36 | 28 86 B |
| Lulworth Ave. Houn | 59 | 14 77 C |
| Lulworth Ave. Wem | 33 | 17 87 A |
| Lulworth Cl. Har | 32 | 12 86 D |
| Lulworth Dri. Pnr | 32 | 12 87 A |
| Lulworth Gdns. Har | 32 | 12 86 B |
| Lulworth Rd. SE15 | 75 | 34 76 D |
| Lulworth Rd. SE9 | 89 | 42 72 A |
| Lulworth Rd. Well | 78 | 45 76 D |
| Lulworth Waye. Hay | 53 | 11 81 C |
| Lumley Cl. Belv | 67 | 49 78 C |
| Lumley Ct. WC2 | 7 | 30 80 A |
| Lumley Gdns. Sutt | 110 | 24 64 C |
| Lumley Rd. Sutt | 110 | 24 64 C |
| Lumley St. W1 | 2 | 28 81 C |
| Luna Rd. Th Hth | 97 | 32 68 A |
| Lundy Wlk. N1 | 48 | 32 84 C |
| Lunham Rd. SE19 | 97 | 33 70 A |
| Luntley Pl. E1 | 57 | 34 81 A |
| Lupin Cl. SW2 | 87 | 31 72 B |
| Lupton Cl. SE12 | 89 | 40 71 B |
| Lupton St. NW5 | 47 | 29 85 A |
| Lupus St. SW1 | 10 | 29 78 C |
| Lurgan Ave. W6 | 62 | 23 77 B |
| Lurline Gdns. SW11 | 74 | 28 76 A |
| Luscombe Way. SW8 | 10 | 30 77 C |
| Lushington Rd. NW10 | 45 | 22 83 D |
| Lushington Rd. SE6 | 88 | 37 71 D |
| Luther Rd. Tedd | 83 | 15 71 D |
| Luton Pl. SE10 | 64 | 38 77 C |
| Luton Rd. E13 | 58 | 40 82 C |
| Luton Rd. E17 | 26 | 36 89 B |
| Luton St. NW8 | 1 | 26 82 D |
| Lutton Terr. NW3 | 46 | 26 85 A |
| Luttrell Ave. SW15 | 72 | 22 74 B |
| Lutwyche Rd. SE6 | 88 | 36 72 B |
| Luxborough St. W1 | 2 | 28 81 A |
| Luxemburg Gdns. W6 | 62 | 23 78 B |
| Luxfield Rd. SE9 | 89 | 42 73 C |
| Luxford St. SE16 | 64 | 35 78 B |
| Luxmore St. SE4 | 76 | 36 76 B |
| Luxor St. SE5 | 75 | 32 76 C |
| Lxworth Pl. SW3 | 9 | 27 78 A |
| Lyall Ave. SE21 | 87 | 33 71 B |
| Lyall Mews. SW1 | 6 | 28 79 C |
| Lyall Mews W. SW1 | 6 | 28 79 C |
| Lyall St. SW1 | 6 | 28 79 C |
| Lyal Rd. E3 | 49 | 36 83 C |
| Lycett Pl. W12 | 61 | 22 79 A |
| Lych Gate Rd. Orp | 108 | 46 66 C |
| Lyconby Gdns. Croy | 106 | 36 66 A |
| Lydd Cl. Sid | 90 | 45 72 C |
| Lydden Ct. SE9 | 78 | 45 74 C |
| Lydden Gr. SW18 | 85 | 25 73 A |
| Lydden Rd. SW18 | 85 | 25 73 A |
| Lydd Rd. Bexh | 67 | 48 77 D |
| Lydeard Rd. E6 | 50 | 42 84 D |
| Lydford Cl (off Truman's Rd) N16 | 48 | 33 85 C |
| Lydford Rd. N15 | 37 | 32 88 B |
| Lydford Rd. NW2 | 46 | 23 84 B |
| Lydford Rd. W9 | 56 | 24 82 D |
| Lydhurst Ave. SW2 | 86 | 30 72 B |
| Lydhurst Rd. Grnf | 53 | 13 82 D |
| Lydia Rd. Eri | 68 | 51 77 B |
| Lydney Cl. SE15 | 63 | 33 77 C |
| Lydney Cl. SW19 | 85 | 24 72 A |
| Lydon Rd. SW4 | 74 | 29 75 A |
| Lydstep Rd. Chis | 90 | 43 71 A |
| Lyford Rd. SW18 | 86 | 27 73 C |
| Lyford St. SE18 | 65 | 42 78 A |
| Lygoe Rd. N2 | 23 | 26 90 B |
| Lygon Pl. SW1 | 6 | 28 79 D |
| Lyham Cl. SW2 | 74 | 30 74 C |
| Lyham Rd. SW2 | 74 | 30 74 A |
| Lymbourne Cl. Sutt | 110 | 25 62 C |
| Lyme Farm Rd. SE12 | 77 | 40 75 C |
| Lyme Gr. E9 | 49 | 35 84 C |
| Lymer Ave. SE19 | 87 | 33 71 D |
| Lyme Rd. Well | 78 | 46 76 B |
| Lymescote Gdns. Sutt | 103 | 25 65 A |
| Lyme St. NW1 | 47 | 29 84 C |
| Lyminge Cl. Sid | 90 | 45 71 B |
| Lyminge Gdns. SW18 | 86 | 27 73 C |
| Lymington Ave. N22 | 25 | 31 90 D |
| Lymington Cl. SW16 | 96 | 29 69 D |
| Lymington Dri. Ruis | 31 | 08 86 B |
| Lymington Gdns. Eps | 109 | 21 64 D |
| Lymington Rd. Dag | 41 | 47 87 D |
| Lymington Rd. NW6 | 46 | 25 84 B |
| Lympstone Gdns. SE15 | 63 | 34 77 C |
| Lynbridge Gdns. N13 | 17 | 31 92 B |
| Lynbrook Cl. Rain | 52 | 50 83 D |
| Lynbrook Cl. SE15 | 63 | 33 77 C |
| Lynchen Cl. Houn | 69 | 10 76 B |
| Lynch Wlk. SE8 | 64 | 36 77 B |
| Lyncott Cres. SW4 | 74 | 28 75 D |
| Lyncroft Ave. Pnr | 32 | 12 88 A |
| Lyncroft Gdns. Eps | 109 | 21 62 B |
| Lyncroft Gdns. Houn | 70 | 14 74 A |
| Lyncroft Gdns. NW6 | 46 | 25 85 C |
| Lyncroft Gdns. W13 | 54 | 17 80 C |
| Lyndale Ave. NW2 | 35 | 24 86 D |
| Lyndale Cl. SE3 | 65 | 39 77 B |
| Lyndale. NW2 | 46 | 24 85 B |
| Lynden Hyrst. Croy | 105 | 33 65 B |
| Lyndhurst Ave. N12 | 24 | 27 91 B |
| Lyndhurst Ave. NW7 | 22 | 21 91 A |
| Lyndhurst Ave. Pnr | 19 | 10 90 B |
| Lyndhurst Ave. Sthl | 53 | 13 80 D |
| Lyndhurst Ave. Sun | 91 | 10 68 A |
| Lyndhurst Ave. Surb | 102 | 19 66 D |
| Lyndhurst Ave. SW16 | 96 | 29 69 D |
| Lyndhurst Ave. Twick | 82 | 13 73 C |
| Lyndhurst Cl. Bexh | 79 | 49 75 B |
| Lyndhurst Cl. Croy | 105 | 33 65 D |
| Lyndhurst Cl. NW10 | 34 | 20 86 D |
| Lyndhurst Ct. Sutt | 110 | 25 63 C |
| Lyndhurst Dri. E10 | 38 | 38 87 A |
| Lyndhurst Dri. Horn | 42 | 53 87 A |
| Lyndhurst Dri. N.Mal | 102 | 21 66 B |
| Lyndhurst Gdns. Bark | 51 | 45 84 A |
| Lyndhurst Gdns. Enf | 13 | 33 96 C |
| Lyndhurst Gdns. Ilf | 40 | 44 88 D |
| Lyndhurst Gdns. N3 | 23 | 24 90 A |
| Lyndhurst Gdns. NW3 | 46 | 26 85 D |
| Lyndhurst Gdns. Pnr | 19 | 10 90 B |
| Lyndhurst Gr. SE15 | 75 | 33 76 D |
| Lyndhurst Rd. Bexh | 79 | 49 75 B |
| Lyndhurst Rd. E4 | 26 | 38 91 C |
| Lyndhurst Rd. N18 | 17 | 34 92 A |
| Lyndhurst Rd. N22 | 25 | 31 91 A |
| Lyndhurst Rd. NW3 | 46 | 26 85 D |
| Lyndhurst Rd. Th Hth | 97 | 31 68 C |
| Lyndhurst Sq. SE15 | 75 | 33 76 B |
| Lyndhurst Way. SE15 | 75 | 33 76 D |
| Lyndhurst Way. Sutt | 110 | 25 62 A |
| Lyndon Ave. Pnr | 20 | 12 91 A |
| Lyndon Ave. Sid | 78 | 45 74 B |
| Lyndon Ave. Wall | 104 | 28 65 C |
| Lyndon Rd. Belv | 67 | 49 78 A |
| Lyne Cres. E17 | 26 | 36 90 B |
| Lynegrove Ave. Ashf | 81 | 08 71 C |
| Lyneham Wlk. E5 | 49 | 36 85 C |
| Lyneham Wlk. Pnr | 19 | 09 89 B |
| Lynette Ave. SW4 | 74 | 29 74 C |
| Lynford Gdns. Ilf | 40 | 45 86 B |
| Lynmere Rd. Well | 78 | 46 76 D |
| Lynmouth Ave. Enf | 12 | 33 95 D |
| Lynmouth Ave. Mord | 103 | 23 66 B |
| Lynmouth Dri. Ruis | 31 | 10 86 D |
| Lynmouth Gdns. Grnf | 44 | 17 84 C |
| Lynmouth Gdns. Houn | 70 | 11 76 B |
| Lynmouth Rd. E17 | 38 | 36 88 A |
| Lynmouth Rd. Grnf | 44 | 16 83 B |
| Lynmouth Rd. N16 | 37 | 33 87 D |
| Lynmouth Rd. N2 | 24 | 27 89 D |
| Lynmouth Rise. Orp | 100 | 46 68 D |
| Lynn Cl. Ashf | 81 | 08 71 D |
| Lynn Cl. Har | 20 | 14 90 D |
| Lynnett Rd. Dag | 41 | 47 86 B |
| Lynne Way. Nthlt | 43 | 11 83 D |
| Lynne Way. NW10 | 45 | 21 84 A |
| Lynn Rd. E11 | 39 | 39 86 C |
| Lynn Rd. Ilf | 40 | 44 87 B |
| Lynn Rd. SW12 | 86 | 28 73 B |

Lynn Rd. SW12 74 28 74 D
Lynn St. Enf 13 32 97 B
Lynross Cl. Rom 30 54 90 D
Lynstead Cl. Bexh 79 49 74 B
Lynstead Cl. Brom 99 41 69 C
Lynsted Ct. Beck 98 36 69 C
Lynsted Gdns. SE9 77 41 75 D
Lynton Ave. N12 15 26 92 B
Lynton Ave. NW9 22 21 89 D
Lynton Ave. Orp 100 46 68 D
Lynton Ave. Rom 29 49 90 B
Lynton Ave. W13 54 16 81 C
Lynton Cl. Islw 71 15 75 D
Lynton Cres. Ilf 40 43 88 D
Lynton Gdns. Enf 17 33 94 A
Lynton Gdns. N11 24 29 91 B
Lynton Mead. N20 15 25 93 B
Lynton Rd. Croy 105 31 67 C
Lynton Rd. E4 18 37 92 D
Lynton Rd. Har 32 12 86 A
Lynton Rd. N8 36 30 88 A
Lynton Rd. N.Mal 102 20 67 B
Lynton Rd. NW6 46 24 83 D
Lynton Rd. SE1 63 34 78 A
Lynton Rd. W3 55 19 80 B
Lynwood Cl. E18 27 41 90 A
Lynwood Cl. Har 32 12 86 C
Lynwood Cl. Rom 29 49 91 B
Lynwood Ct. King 94 19 69 D
Lynwood Dri. Nthwd 19 09 90 B
Lynwood Dri. Wor Pk 102 22 65 A
Lynwood Dr. Rom 29 49 91 D
Lynwood Gdns. Croy 111 30 64 B
Lynwood Gdns. Sthl 53 12 81 D
Lynwood Gr. N21 17 31 94 C
Lynwood Gr. Orp 108 45 66 C
Lynwood Rd. Surb 101 15 65 B
Lynwood Rd. SW17 86 27 71 B
Lynwood Rd. W5 54 18 82 C
Lyon Meade. Stan 21 17 90 A
Lyon Park Ave. Wem 44 18 84 B
Lyon Rd. Har 33 15 88 D
Lyon Rd. Rom 42 51 87 B
Lyon Rd. SW19 95 26 69 A
Lyonsdown Ave. Barn 11 26 95 C
Lyonsdown Rd. Barn 11 26 95 A
Lyons Pl. NW8 1 26 82 D
Lyon St. N1 47 30 84 D
Lyon Way. Grnf 44 15 83 A
Lyoth Rd. Orp 108 44 65 A
Lyric Rd. SW13 72 21 76 B
Lysander Gr. N19 36 29 87 D
Lysander Rd. Croy 111 30 63 B
Lysander Rd. Ruis 31 08 86 B
Lysander Way. Orp 108 44 65 C
Lysias Rd. SW12 74 28 74 D
Lysia St. SW6 62 23 77 D
Lysons Wlk. SW15 72 22 74 A
Lytchet Rd. Brom 99 40 70 D
Lytchet Way. Enf 14 35 97 A
Lytchgate Cl. S Croy 112 33 63 C
Lytcott Gr. SE22 75 33 74 B
Lytham Gr. W5 54 18 82 B
Lytham St. SE17 63 32 78 D
Lyttleton Cl. NW3 47 27 84 C
Lyttleton Rd. E10 38 38 86 C
Lyttleton Rd. N8 25 31 89 A
Lyttlton Ct. NW2 35 26 88 A
Lytton Ave. N13 17 31 93 A
Lytton Cl. N2 35 26 88 B
Lytton Cl. Nthlt 43 12 84 D
Lytton Gdns. Wall 111 29 64 B
Lytton Gr. SW15 73 24 74 C
Lytton Rd. Barn 11 26 96 C
Lytton Rd. E11 39 39 87 A
Lytton Rd. Pnr 20 12 91 C
Lytton Rd. Rom 42 52 88 B
Lyveden Rd. SE3 65 40 77 D
Lyveden Rd. SW17 96 27 70 B

Maberley Cres. SE19 97 34 70 C
Maberley Rd. Beck 98 35 68 B
Maberley Rd. SE19 97 34 69 A
Mabledon Pl. WC1 2 29 82 B
Mablethorpe Rd. SW6 62 24 77 C
Mabley St. E9 49 36 84 A
Mabley St. E9 49 36 85 C
Macaret Cl. N20 15 26 94 A
Macaulay Ave. Esh 101 15 65 A
Macaulay Rd. E6 50 41 83 D
Macaulay Rd. SW4 74 28 75 B
Macaulay Sq. SW4 74 28 75 D
Macbean St. SE18 66 43 79 D
Macbeth St. W6 61 22 78 D
Macclesfield Rd. EC1 4 32 82 A
Macclesfield Rd. SE25 106 35 67 A
Macclesfield St. W1 6 29 80 B
Macdonald Ave. Dag 41 49 86 D
Macdonald Ave. Horn 30 54 89 D
Macdonald Rd. E17 26 38 90 C
Macdonald Rd. E7 50 40 85 A
Macdonald Rd. N11 16 27 92 D
Macdonald Rd. N19 36 29 86 A
Macdonald Way. Horn 30 54 89 C
Macduff Rd. SW11 74 28 76 A
Mace St. E2 49 35 83 D
Macfarlane Rd. W12 56 23 80 C
Mac Farren Pl. NW1 2 28 82 C
Macgregor Rd. E16 58 41 81 A
Machell Rd. SE15 76 35 75 A
Mackay Rd. SW4 74 28 75 B
Mackennal St. NW8 47 27 83 C
Mackenzie Rd. Beck 98 35 69 D
Mackenzie Rd. N7 47 30 84 B
Mackeson Rd. NW3 47 27 85 B
Mackie Rd. SW2 87 31 73 A
Mackintosh La. E9 49 35 85 D
Macklin St. WC2 3 30 81 C
Mackrow Wlk. E14 58 38 80 A
Macks Rd. SE16 63 34 78 A
Mackworth St. NW1 2 29 82 A
Maclean Rd. SE23 76 36 74 C
Macleod St. SE17 63 32 78 C
Maclise Rd. W14 62 24 79 C
Macoma Rd. SE18 66 44 77 B
Macoma Terr. SE18 66 44 77 B
Macquarie Way. E14 64 37 78 B
Macready Pl. N7 47 30 85 A
Macroom Rd. W9 56 24 82 B
Mada Rd. Orp 108 43 65 D
Maddams St. E3 57 37 82 D
Maddison Cl. Tedd 93 15 70 B
Maddock Way. SE17 63 31 77 B
Maddox St. W1 6 29 80 A
Madeira Ave. Brom 99 39 70 C
Madeira Gr. Wdf Gn 27 41 91 A
Madeira Rd. E11 39 39 87 C
Madeira Rd. Mit 96 27 68 D
Madeira Rd. N13 13 31 95 D
Madeley Rd. W5 54 18 81 C
Madeline Rd. SE20 97 34 70 C
Maderira Rd. SW16 86 30 71 C
Madison Cres. Bexh 67 47 77 C
Madison Gdns. Bexh 67 47 77 C
Madison Gdns. Brom 99 39 68 B
Madras Pl. N7 48 31 84 A
Madras Rd. Ilf 51 43 85 B
Madrid Rd. SW13 61 22 77 C
Madron St. SE17 63 33 78 C
Mafeking Ave. Brent 60 18 77 A
Mafeking Ave. E6 50 42 83 C
Mafeking Ave. Ilf 40 44 87 B
Mafeking Rd. E16 58 39 82 D
Mafeking Rd. Enf 13 33 96 B
Mafeking Rd. N17 25 34 90 C
Magdala Ave. N19 36 29 86 A
Magdala Rd. Islw 71 16 75 A
Magdala Rd. S Croy 112 32 63 D
Magdalene Cl. SE15 75 34 76 D
Magdalen Pas. E1 8 33 80 B
Magdalen Rd. Shep 91 07 68 A
Magdalen Rd. SW18 85 26 73 D
Magdalen St. SE1 8 33 80 A
Magee St. SE11 63 31 77 A
Magnin Cl. E8 48 34 83 A
Magnolia Cl. King 94 19 70 B
Magnolia Ct. Har 33 18 87 B
Magnolia Ct. Rich 72 19 76 B
Magnolia Ct. Sutt 110 25 63 D
Magnolia Ct. SW4 74 30 75 C
Magnolia Rd. W4 61 19 77 B
Magnolia Way. Eps 109 20 64 C
Magnolia Wharf. W4 61 19 77 B
Magpie Alley. EC4 3 31 81 C
Magpie Hall Cl. Brom 107 42 67 C
Magpie Hall La. Brom 107 42 67 C
Magpie Hall La. Brom 107 42 67 D
Maguire Dri. Rich 83 17 71 A
Maguire St. SE1 8 33 79 B
Mahlon Ave. Ruis 43 11 84 A
Mahogany Cl. SE16 57 36 80 C
Maida Ave. E4 18 37 94 B
Maida Ave. W2 1 26 82 C
Maida Rd. Belv 67 49 79 C
Maida Vale Rd. Dart 80 52 74 A
Maida Vale. W9 1 26 82 A
Maida Way. E4 18 37 94 B
Maiden La. Dart 80 52 75 C
Maiden La. N7 47 29 84 D
Maiden La. WC2 7 30 80 A
Maiden Rd. E15 50 39 84 C
Maidstone Ave. Rom 29 50 90 C
Maidstone Bldgs. SE1 8 32 80 D
Maidstone Hill. SE10 76 38 76 A
Maidstone Rd. N11 24 29 91 B
Maidstone St. E2 48 34 83 C
Mail Coach Yd. E2 4 33 82 A
Main Ave. Enf 13 33 95 B
Main Rd. Rom 30 52 89 A
Main Rd. Sid 90 45 71 B
Mainridge Rd. Chis 90 43 71 A
Main St. Felt 82 11 71 D
Maismore St. SE15 63 34 77 A
Maitland Cl. Houn 70 12 75 B
Maitland Cl. SE10 64 37 77 D
Maitland Park Estate. NW3 47 27 84 B
Maitland Park Rd. NW3 47 27 84 B
Maitland Park Villas. NW3 47 27 84 B
Maitland Rd. E15 50 39 84 B
Maitland Rd. SE26 98 35 70 B
Maize Row. E14 57 36 81 D
Majendie Rd. SE18 66 44 78 D
Major Rd. E15 49 38 85 D
Major Rd. SE16 63 34 79 C
Makepeace Ave. N6 36 28 86 A
Makepeace Rd. Nthlt 43 12 83 A
Makins St. SW3 9 27 78 A
Malabar St. E14 64 37 79 A
Malam Gdns. E14 57 37 80 B
Malbrook Rd. SW15 72 22 75 D
Malcolm Cres. NW4 34 22 88 C
Malcolm Ct. E7 50 39 84 B
Malcolm Dri. Surb 101 18 66 C
Malcolm Pl. E2 57 35 82 C
Malcolm Rd. E1 57 35 82 C
Malcolm Rd. SE20 98 35 70 C
Malcolm Rd. SE25 105 34 67 C
Malcolm Rd. SW19 95 24 70 A
Malcolm Way. E11 27 40 89 C
Malden Ave. Grnf 44 15 84 A
Malden Ave. SE25 97 34 68 B
Malden Cres. NW1 47 28 84 A
Malden Ct. N Mal 94 22 68 B
Malden Ct. N Mal 94 22 68 B
Malden Green Ave. Wor Pk 102 22 66 C
Malden Hill Gdns. N Mal 94 21 68 A
Malden Hill. N Mal 94 21 68 A
Malden Park. N.Mal 102 21 67 D
Malden Pl. NW5 47 28 85 C
Malden Rd. N.Mal 102 21 67 B
Malden Rd. NW3 47 28 84 A
Malden Rd. Sutt 110 23 64 A
Malden Rd. Wor Pk 102 22 66 C
Malden Way. N.Mal 102 21 67 A
Maldon Cl. N1 48 32 83 A
Maldon Cl. SE5 75 33 75 A
Maldon Rd. N9 17 33 93 D
Maldon Rd. Rom 41 50 87 A
Maldon Rd. W3 55 20 80 A
Maldon Rd. Wall 111 28 64 D
Maldon Wlk. Wdf Gn 27 41 91 A
Malet St. WC1 2 29 81 B
Maley Ave. SE27 87 31 72 B
Maley Pl. WC1 2 29 82 D
Malford Ct. E18 27 40 90 C
Malford Gr. E18 27 39 89 B
Malfort Rd. SE5 75 33 75 A
Malham Rd. SE23 88 35 73 D
Mallams Mews. SW9 75 31 75 B
Mallard Cl. Barn 15 26 94 B
Mallard Cl. Barn 11 26 95 D
Mallard Cl. E9 49 36 84 B
Mallard Cl. Houn 82 13 73 A
Mallard Pl. N22 24 30 90 D
Mallard Pl. Twick 83 16 72 C
Mallards Rd. Wdf Gn 27 40 91 D
Mallard Way. Nthwd 19 08 91 C
Mallard Way. NW9 34 20 87 A
Mallet Dri. Nthlt 43 12 85 D
Mallet Rd. SE13 76 38 74 D
Malling Cl. Croy 106 35 67 C
Malling Gdns. Mord 103 26 67 C
Malling Way. Brom 107 39 66 B
Mallinson Rd. Croy 104 29 65 D
Mallinson Rd. SW11 74 27 74 B
Mallord St. SW3 62 26 77 B
Mallory Cl. SE4 76 36 75 C
Mallory Gdns. Barn 16 28 94 A
Mallory St. NW8 1 27 82 C
Mallow Mead. NW7 23 24 91 C
Mallow St. EC1 4 32 82 D
Mallows The. Uxb 31 07 86 D
Mall Rd. W6 61 22 78 D
Mall The. Brent 60 17 77 B
Mall The. Brom 99 40 68 A
Mall The. Croy 105 32 65 A
Mall The. Dag 52 49 84 A
Mall The. E15 49 38 84 D
Mall The. Har 33 18 88 D
Mall The. N14 16 30 93 C
Mall The. Surb 101 17 67 B
Mall The. SW14 72 20 74 A
Mall. The SW1 6 29 80 D
Mall The. W5 54 18 80 A
Malmains Cl. Beck 98 38 68 D
Malmains Way. Beck 98 38 68 D
Malmesbury Cl. Pnr 19 10 89 C
Malmesbury Rd. E16 58 39 81 A
Malmesbury Rd. E18 27 39 90 B
Malmesbury Rd. E3 49 37 83 C
Malmesbury Rd. Mord 103 26 67 C
Malmesbury Terr. E16 58 39 81 B
Malpas Dri. Pnr 32 11 88 B
Malpas Rd. Dag 52 47 84 B
Malpas Rd. E8 48 34 85 D
Malpas Rd. SE4 76 36 76 D
Malta Rd. E10 38 37 87 A
Malta St. EC1 3 31 82 D
Maltby Cl. Orp 108 46 66 C
Maltby Rd. Chess 109 19 63 A
Maltby St. SE1 8 33 79 D
Malthouse Dri. Felt 82 11 71 D
Maltings Cl. SW13 72 21 76 C
Maltings The. Orp 108 45 66 D
Malton Rd. W10 56 24 81 C
Malton St. SE18 66 45 77 A
Maltravers St. WC2 7 31 80 A
Malt St. SE1 63 34 77 A
Malva Cl. SW18 73 25 74 D
Malva Rd. SW18 73 25 74 B
Malvern Ave. Bexh 67 48 77 C
Malvern Ave. E4 26 38 91 D
Malvern Ave. Har 32 12 86 D
Malvern Cl. Mit 96 29 68 A
Malvern Cl. Surb 101 18 66 C
Malvern Cl. Uxb 31 07 86 A
Malvern Cl. W10 56 24 81 B
Malvern Dri. Felt 82 11 71 D
Malvern Dri. Ilf 51 45 85 B
Malvern Gdns. Har 21 18 89 C
Malvern Gdns. NW2 35 24 86 A
Malvern Mews. NW6 56 25 82 A
Malvern Pl. W9 56 24 82 B
Malvern Rd. E11 39 39 86 B
Malvern Rd. E6 50 42 83 A
Malvern Rd. E8 48 34 84 C
Malvern Rd. Hamp 92 13 69 A
Malvern Rd. Horn 42 52 88 C
Malvern Rd. N17 25 34 89 A
Malvern Rd. N8 25 31 89 A
Malvern Rd. NW6 56 25 82 A
Malvern Rd. Surb 101 18 66 C
Malvern Rd. Th Hth 97 31 68 C
Malvern Terr. N1 48 31 83 A
Malvern Terr. N9 17 33 94 D
Malvern Way. W13 54 16 81 B
Malwood Rd. SW12 74 28 74 D
Malyons Rd. SE13 76 37 74 B
Malyons Terr. SE13 76 37 74 B
Managers St. E14 58 38 80 C
Manaton Cl. SE15 75 34 75 B
Manaton Cres. Sthl 53 13 81 C
Manbey Gr. E15 50 39 84 A
Manbey Park Rd. E15 50 39 84 A
Manbey Rd. E15 50 39 84 A
Manbey St. E15 50 39 84 A
Manchester Dri. W10 56 24 82 C
Manchester Gr. E14 64 38 78 C
Manchester Rd. E14 64 38 79 C
Manchester Rd. N15 37 32 88 D
Manchester Rd. Th Hth 97 32 68 A
Manchester Sq. W1 2 28 81 C
Manchester St. W1 2 28 81 A
Manchester Way. Dag 52 49 85 B
Manchuria Rd. SW11 74 28 74 C
Manciple St. SE1 8 32 79 B
Mandalay Rd. SW4 74 29 74 A
Mandarin St. E14 57 37 80 A
Mandela Cl. NW10 45 20 84 C
Mandeville Cl. SE3 65 40 77 C
Mandeville Dri. Surb 101 17 66 D
Mandeville Pl. W1 2 28 81 C
Mandeville Rd. Islw 71 16 76 C
Mandeville Rd. N14 16 29 93 A
Mandeville Rd. Nthlt 43 13 84 A
Mandeville St. E5 49 36 85 A
Mandrake Rd. SW17 86 27 72 D
Mandrell Rd. SW2 74 30 74 A
Manette St. W1 2 29 81 D
Manfred Rd. SW15 73 24 74 B
Manger Rd. N7 47 30 84 A
Mangold Way. Belv 67 48 79 C
Manilla St. E14 64 37 79 A
Maniloba Ct. SE16 64 35 79 A
Manister Rd. SE2 66 46 79 C
Manley Ct. N16 37 33 86 D
Manley St. NW1 47 28 83 A
Manmouth Ave. King 93 17 70 C
Manningford Cl. EC1 3 31 82 B
Manning Gdns. Har 33 17 87 B
Manning Rd. Dag 52 49 84 C
Manning Rd. E17 38 36 88 A
Manningtree Cl. SW18 85 24 73 C
*Manningtree St. E1 57 34 81 C
Mannin Rd. Rom 40 46 88 D
Mannock Rd. N22 25 31 89 B
Mann's Cl. Islw 71 15 74 B
Manns Rd. Edg 22 19 91 A
Manoel Rd. Twick 82 14 72 A
Manor Alley. W4 61 21 78 C
Manor Ave. Horn 42 53 88 A
Manor Ave. Houn 70 11 76 D
Manor Ave. Nthlt 43 12 84 D
Manor Ave. SE4 76 36 76 D
Manorbrook. SE3 77 40 75 C
Manor Cl. Barn 11 24 96 C
Manor Cl. Dag 52 50 84 B
Manor Cl. Dart 80 51 75 C
Manor Cl. E17 26 36 90 C
Manor Cl. NW9 34 19 88 B
Manor Cl. Rom 42 52 88 A
Manor Cl. Ruis 31 09 87 D
Manor Cl. Wor Pk 102 21 66 C
Manor Cottages App. N2 23 26 90 C
Manor Cottages. Nthwd 19 09 90 B
Manor Court Rd. W7 54 15 80 A
Manor Cres. Horn 42 53 88 A
Manor Cres. Surb 102 19 67 C
Manor Ct. N14 16 29 93 B
Manor Ct. SW16 86 30 72 C
Manor Ct. Twick 82 14 72 A
Manordene Cl. Surb 101 16 66 C
Manor Dri. Eps 109 21 63 A
Manor Dri. Esh 101 16 65 C
Manor Dri. Felt 82 11 71 C
Manor Dri. N14 16 28 94 D
Manor Dri. N20 16 27 93 D
Manor Dri. Sun 91 10 69 C
Manor Dri. Surb 102 19 67 C
Manor Drive N. N.Mal 102 20 66 B
Manor Drive N. Wor Pk 102 21 66 C
Manor Drive The. Wor Pk 102 21 66 C
Manor Dri. Wem 44 18 85 B
Manor Farm Rd. Th Hth 97 31 69 C
Manor Farm Rd. Wem 44 17 83 D
*Manorfield Cl. N19 47 29 85 A
Manor Fields. SW15 73 23 74 D
Manor Gate. Nthlt 43 12 84 C
Manorgate Rd. King 94 19 69 A
Manor Gdns. Hamp 92 14 70 C
Manor Gdns. N7 36 30 86 C
Manor Gdns. Rich 71 18 75 D
Manor Gdns. Ruis 43 11 85 C
Manor Gdns. S Croy 112 33 63 B
Manor Gdns. Sun 91 10 69 C
Manor Gdns. SW20 95 24 69 D
Manor Gdns. W3 61 19 78 A
Manor Gr. Beck 98 37 69 D
Manor Gr. Rich 72 19 75 A
Manor Gr. SE15 64 35 77 A
Manor Hall Ave. NW4 23 23 90 D
Manor Hall Dri. NW4 23 23 90 D
Manor Hall Gdns. E10 38 37 87 C
Manor House Dri. NW6 46 23 84 D
Manor House Estate. Stan 21 16 91 B
Manor La. Felt 81 10 72 A
Manor Lane Terr. SE13 77 39 74 A
Manor La. SE12 77 39 74 C
Manor La. SE13 77 39 74 A
Manor La. Sun 91 10 69 D
Manor La. Sutt 110 26 64 C
Manor Mews. NW6 46 25 83 C
Manor Mews. SE4 76 36 76 D
Manor Mount. SE23 88 35 73 C
Manor Park. Chis 100 44 69 B
Manor Park Cl. W Wick 106 37 66 D
Manor Park Cres. Edg 22 19 91 A
Manor Park Dri. Har 20 13 89 B
Manor Park Gdns. Edg 22 19 91 A
Manor Park Rd. Chis 100 44 69 B
Manor Park Rd. E12 50 41 85 B
Manor Park Rd. N2 23 26 89 A
Manor Park Rd. NW10 45 21 83 B
Manor Park Rd. Sutt 110 26 64 C
Manor Park Rd. W Wick 106 37 66 D
Manor Park. Rich 71 18 75 D
Manor Park. SE13 77 39 74 A
Manor Pl. Chis 100 44 69 D
Manor Pl. Felt 81 10 73 C
Manor Pl. Mit 96 29 68 A
Manor Pl. SE17 63 32 78 C
Manor Pl. Sutt 110 25 64 B
Manor Rd. Ashf 81 07 71 C
Manor Rd. Bark 51 45 84 B
Manor Rd. Barn 11 24 96 C
Manor Rd. Beck 98 37 69 D
Manor Rd. Chig 28 43 91 A
Manor Rd. Dag 52 50 84 B
Manor Rd. Dart 80 51 75 C
Manor Rd. E10 38 37 87 A
Manor Rd. E15 58 39 82 A
Manor Rd. E17 26 36 90 C
Manor Rd. E Mol 92 14 68 D
Manor Rd. Enf 13 32 97 D
Manor Rd. Eri 68 52 77 A
Manor Rd. Har 33 16 88 C
Manor Rd. Mit 96 29 68 A
Manor Rd. N16 37 33 87 C
Manor Rd. N17 25 34 90 B
Manor Rd. N22 24 30 91 A
Manor Rd. N. Esh 101 15 65 B
Manor Rd N. Surb 101 16 66 C
Manor Rd N. Wall 111 28 64 B
Manor Rd. Rich 71 18 75 D
Manor Rd. Rom 41 47 88 D
Manor Rd. Rom 42 52 88 A
Manor Rd. Ruis 31 08 87 D
Manor Rd. SE25 9 34 68 A
Manor Rd S. Esh 101 15 65 D
Manor Rd. Sid 90 46 72 C
Manor Rd. Sutt 110 24 63 D
Manor Rd. SW20 95 24 69 D
Manor Rd. Tedd 16 16 71 D
Manor Rd. Twick 82 14 72 B
Manor Rd. W13 54 16 80 A
Manor Rd. Wall 111 28 64 D
Manor Rd. Wdf Gn 27 42 91 B
Manor Rd. W Wick 106 37 65 B
Manorside. Barn 11 24 96 C
Manor Sq. Dag 41 47 86 B
Manor St Estate. SW3 9 27 77 A
Manor Vale. Brent 60 17 78 C
Manor View. N3 23 25 90 D
Manor Way. Beck 98 37 68 B
Manor Way. Bexh 79 50 75 B
Manor Way. Brom 107 42 67 C
Manor Way. E4 18 38 92 B
Manorway. Enf 17 33 94 A
Manor Way. Har 20 13 89 D
Manor Way. Mit 96 29 68 A
Manor Way. NW9 22 21 89 C
Manor Way. Orp 100 44 68 C
Manor Way. Ruis 31 09 87 D
Manor Way. S Croy 112 33 63 B
Manor Way. SE3 77 40 75 C
Manor Way. Sthl 59 11 78 B
Manor Way The. Wall 111 28 64 B
Manor Way. Wor Pk 102 21 66 D
Manresa Rd. SW3 9 27 78 C
Mansard Cl. Pnr 20 11 89 B
Mansel Gr. E17 26 37 90 A
Mansell Rd. Grnf 53 13 81 B
Mansell Rd. W3 61 20 79 B
Mansell St. E1 8 33 80 B
Mansell St. E1 4 33 81 D
Mansel Rd. SW19 95 24 70 A
Manse Rd. N16 37 33 86 D
Mansergh Cl. SE18 65 42 77 C
Mansfield Ave. Barn 12 28 95 C
Mansfield Ave. N15 25 32 89 D
Mansfield Cl. N9 13 34 95 C
Mansfield Gdns. Horn 42 53 86 B
Mansfield Hill. E4 18 37 94 D
Mansfield Hts. N2 36 27 88 B
Mansfield Mews. W1 2 28 81 B
Mansfield Pl. NW3 46 26 85 A
Mansfield Pl. S Croy 112 32 63 B
Mansfield Rd. E11 39 40 88 D
Mansfield Rd. E17 26 36 89 D
Mansfield Rd. Ilf 40 43 86 A
Mansfield Rd. NW3 47 28 85 A
Mansfield Rd. S Croy 112 32 63 B
Mansfield Rd. W3 55 19 82 D
Mansfield St. W1 2 28 81 B
Mansford St. E2 48 34 83 C
Manship Rd. Mit 96 28 69 A
Mansion House Pl. EC4 4 32 81 D
Mansion House St. EC2 4 32 81 D
Manson Mews. SW7 62 26 78 B
Manson Pl. SW7 62 26 78 B

Manstead Gdns. Rom 41 47 87 A
Manston Ave. Sthl 59 13 78 A
Manstone Rd. NW2 46 24 85 C
Mantell St. N1 48 31 83 C
Manthorpe Rd. SE18 66 44 78 C
Mantilla Rd. SW17 86 28 71 A
Mantle Rd. SE4 76 36 75 A
Manton Ave. W7 60 16 79 A
Manton Rd. SE2 66 46 78 A
Mantua St. SW11 73 26 75 B
Mantus Cl. E1 57 35 82 C
Mantus Rd. E1 57 35 82 C
Manus Way. N20 15 26 94 C
Manville Gdns. SW17 86 28 72 D
Manville Rd. SW17 86 28 72 D
Manwood Rd. SE4 76 36 74 D
Many Gates. SW12 86 28 72 B
Mapesbury Rd. NW2 46 24 84 A
Mape St. E2 57 34 82 D
Maple Ave. E4 26 36 91 B
Maple Ave. Har 32 13 86 B
Maple Ave. W3 55 21 80 C
Maple Cl. Horn 42 52 86 D
Maple Cl. Mit 96 28 69 B
Maple Cl. N16 37 34 88 C
Maple Cl. Nthlt 53 11 82 B
Maple Cl. Orp 108 44 67 B
Maple Cl. Ruis 31 10 88 D
Maple Cl. SW4 74 29 74 D
Maple Cres. Sid 78 46 74 C
Maple Ct. N Mal 94 21 68 A
Mapledale Ave. Croy 105 34 65 D
Mapledene Estate. E8 48 34 84 C
Mapledene Rd. E8 48 34 84 C
Maple Gdns. Edg 22 21 91 C
Maple Gr. Brent 60 16 77 D
Maple Gr. NW9 34 20 87 A
Maple Gr. Sthl 53 12 81 B
Maple Gr. W5 60 17 79 D
Mapleleafe Gdns. Ilf 28 43 89 B
Maple Pl. W1 2 29 81 A
Maple Rd. E11 39 39 88 C
Maple Rd. Hay 53 11 82 D
Maple Rd. Nthlt 53 11 82 A
Maple Rd. SE20 98 35 70 C
Maple Rd. Surb 101 17 67 B
Maples Pl. E1 57 34 81 B
Maplestead Rd. Dag 51 46 83 B
Maplestead Rd. SW2 86 30 73 B
Maple St. Rom 29 50 89 C
Maple St. W1 2 29 82 C
Maplethorpe Rd. Th Hth 97 31 68 D
Mapleton Cl. Brom 107 40 67 C
Mapleton Cres. SW18 73 25 74 D
Mapleton Rd. Enf 13 34 97 D
Mapleton Rd. SW18 73 25 74 C
Mapleton Rd. SW18 73 25 74 D
Mapleton Way. Felt 81 10 72 C
Maple Wlk. Sutt 110 25 62 D
Maple Wlk. W10 56 23 82 D
Maplin Cl. N21 12 30 95 D
Maplin Rd. E16 58 40 81 C
Maplin St. E3 57 36 82 B
Mapperley Dri. Wdf Gn 27 39 91 C
Maran Way. Belv 67 47 79 D
Marban Rd. W9 56 24 82 B
Marble Arch. W1 5 27 80 B
Marble Cl. W3 55 19 80 D
Marble Hill Cl. Twick 83 16 73 B
Marble Hill Gdns. Twick 83 16 73 B
Marbrook Ct. SE12 89 41 72 C
Marcellina Way. Orp 108 45 65 D
Marcet Rd. Dart 80 53 74 A
Marchant Rd. E11 38 38 86 B
Marchbank Rd. SW5 62 24 77 B
March Ct. SW15 72 22 75 D
Marchmont Rd. Rich 71 18 74 B
Marchmont Rd. Wall 111 29 63 C
Marchmont St. WC1 3 30 82 C
March Rd. Twick 83 16 73 A
March's Pl. SW15 73 23 75 B
Marchwood Cl. SE5 63 33 77 C
Marchwood Cres. W5 54 17 81 D
Marcia Rd. SE1 63 33 78 A
Marcilly Rd. SW18 73 26 74 B
Marco Way. Sthl 53 13 81 D
Marcon Pl. E8 48 34 85 D
Marco Rd. W6 62 23 79 C
Marcus Ct. E15 50 39 83 A
Marcus St. E15 50 39 83 B
Marcus St. SW18 73 25 74 D
Marcus Terr. SW18 73 25 74 D
Mardale Dri. NW9 34 20 88 B
Mardell Rd. Croy 106 35 67 B
Marden Ave. Brom 107 40 67 C
Marden Cres. Bex 79 50 74 A
Marden Cres. Croy 104 30 67 D
Marden Rd. Croy 104 30 67 D
Marden Rd. N17 25 33 90 C
Marden Rd. Rom 42 51 88 C
Marden Sq. SE16 63 34 79 D
Marder Rd. W13 60 16 79 A
Marechal Neil Ave. Sid 90 44 72 D
Maresfield. Croy 105 33 65 C
Maresfield Gdns. NW3 46 26 84 A
Mare St. E8 48 34 84 D
Margaret Ave. E4 14 37 95 D
Margaret Bondfield Ave. Bark 51 46 84 C
Margaret Cl. Rom 42 52 88 B
Margaret Ct. W1 2 29 81 C
Margaret Dri. Horn 42 54 87 B
Margaret Rd. Barn 11 26 96 D
Margaret Rd. Bex 79 47 74 D
Margaret Rd. N16 37 33 87 D
Margaret Rd. Rom 42 52 88 B
Margaret St. W1 2 29 81 C
Margaretta Terr. SW3 9 27 77 A
Margaretting Rd. E12 39 41 87 C
Margaret Way. Ilf 39 42 88 C
Margate Rd. SW2 74 30 74 A
Margery Park Rd. E7 50 40 84 A
Margery Rd. Dag 41 47 86 D
Margery St. WC1 3 31 82 A
Margin Dri. SW19 85 23 71 B
Margravine Gdns. W6 62 23 78 D
Margravine Rd. W6 62 23 77 B
Marham Gdns. Mord 103 26 67 C
Marham Gdns. SW18 86 27 73 C
Maria Cl. SE1 63 34 78 A
Mariam Gdns. Horn 42 54 86 B
Marian Ct. E9 49 35 85 C
Marian Ct. Sutt 110 25 64 D
Marian Pl. E2 48 34 83 D
Marian Rd. SW16 96 29 69 A
Marian Sq. E2 48 34 83 C
Marian St. E2 48 34 83 D
Marian Way. NW10 45 21 84 D
Maria Terr. E1 57 35 82 D
Maria Theresa Cl. N.Mal 102 20 67 B
Maribor. SE10 64 38 77 C
Maricas Ave. Har 20 14 90 B
Mariette Way. Wall 111 30 62 A
Marigold St. SE16 63 34 79 B
Marigold Way. E4 26 36 91 B
Marina Ave. N.Mal 102 22 67 B
Marina Cl. Brom 99 40 68 A
Marina Dri. Well 78 45 76 C
Marina Gdns. Rom 41 49 88 B
Marina Way. Tedd 93 17 70 D
Marinefield Rd. SW6 73 25 76 D
Mariner Gdns. Rich 83 17 72 C
Mariner Rd. E12 51 43 85 A
Marine St. SE16 63 34 79 C
Marion Cl. Ilf 28 44 91 D
Marion Cres. Orp 108 46 67 A
Marion Rd. Th Hth 105 32 67 B
Marischal Rd. SE13 76 38 75 B
Maritime St. E3 57 36 82 D
Marius Rd. SW17 86 28 72 A
Marjorie Cr. SW11 74 28 75 C
Mark Ave. E4 14 37 95 D
Mark Cl. Bexh 79 48 76 A
Market Ct. W1 2 29 81 C
Market Hill. SE18 66 43 79 C
Market La. Edg 22 20 90 A
Market Link. Rom 30 51 89 C
Market Mews. W1 6 28 80 D
Market Pl. Bexh 79 49 75 C
Market Pl. Brent 60 17 77 D
Market Pl. Enf 13 32 96 B
Market Pl. King 93 17 69 D
Market Pl. N2 23 26 89 B
Market Pl. N2 24 27 89 A
Market Pl. Rom 42 51 88 A
Market Pl. SE16 63 34 78 B
Market Pl. SE18 66 43 78 B
Market Pl. W1 2 29 81 C
Market Pl. W3 55 20 80 C
Market Rd. N7 47 30 84 A
Market Rd. Rich 72 19 75 A
Market Sq. Brom 99 40 69 C
Market Sq. E14 57 37 81 D
Market Sq The. N9 17 34 93 B
Market St. E6 51 43 83 C
Market St. SE18 66 43 78 A
Market Way. E14 57 37 81 D
Market Way. Wem 44 18 85 C
Markfield Gdns. E4 18 37 94 B
Markfield Rd. N15 37 34 88 A
Markham Pl. SW3 9 27 78 D
Markham Sq. SW3 9 27 78 D
Markham St. SW3 9 27 78 C
Markhole Cl. Hamp 92 12 70 D
Markhouse Ave. E17 38 36 88 C
Markhouse Pas. E17 38 36 88 D
Markhouse Rd. E17 38 36 88 D
Mark La. EC3 8 33 80 A
Markmanor Ave. E17 38 36 87 B
Mark Rd. N22 25 31 90 D
Marksbury Ave. Rich 72 19 75 A
Marks Rd. Rom 41 50 88 B
Mark St. E15 50 39 84 C
Mark St. EC2 4 33 82 C
Mark St. EC2 4 33 82 C
Markway. Sun 92 11 69 C
Markway The. Sun 92 11 69 C
Markwell Cl. SE26 87 34 71 B
Markyate Rd. Dag 51 46 85 D
Marlan Cl. Hay 53 11 82 D
Marlands Rd. Ilf 27 42 89 B
Marlborough Ave. E8 48 34 83 A
Marlborough Ave. N14 16 29 93 C
Marlborough Ave. Ruis 31 08 88 D
Marlborough Bldgs. SW3 9 27 78 A
Marlborough Cl. N20 16 27 93 D
Marlborough Cl. Orp 108 45 67 D
Marlborough Cl. SE17 63 32 78 A
Marlborough Cl. SW19 96 27 70 A
Marlborough Cres. W4 61 21 79 C
Marlborough Dri. Ilf 27 42 89 A
Marlborough Gdns. N20 16 27 93 D
Marlborough Gdns. Surb 101 17 66 B
Marlborough Gr. SE1 63 34 78 C
Marlborough Hill. Har 21 15 89 C
Marlborough Hill. NW8 46 26 83 A
Marlborough La. SE7 65 41 77 C
Marlborough Park Ave. Sid 90 46 73 C
Marlborough Pl. NW8 46 26 83 C
Marlborough Rd. Bexh 79 47 75 B
Marlborough Rd. Brom 99 41 68 C
Marlborough Rd. Dag 52 47 85 C
Marlborough Rd. Dart 80 53 74 C
Marlborough Rd. E15 50 39 85 A
Marlborough Rd. E18 27 40 89 A
Marlborough Rd. E4 26 37 91 B
Marlborough Rd. E7 50 41 84 C
Marlborough Rd. Felt 82 11 72 B
Marlborough Rd. Hamp 92 13 70 A
Marlborough Rd. Islw 60 16 77 D
Marlborough Rd. N19 36 30 86 A
Marlborough Rd. N22 24 30 91 B
Marlborough Rd. N9 17 33 94 D
Marlborough Rd. Rich 71 18 74 D
Marlborough Rd. Rom 29 49 89 D
Marlborough Rd. S Croy 112 32 63 C
Marlborough Rd. Sthl 59 11 79 C
Marlborough Rd. Sutt 103 25 65 A
Marlborough Rd. SW19 95 26 70 B
Marlborough Rd. SW19 96 27 70 A
Marlborough Rd. SW1 6 29 80 C
Marlborough Rd. W4 61 20 78 B
Marlborough Rd. W5 60 17 79 B
Marlborough St. SW3 9 27 78 A
Marlborough Yd. N19 36 29 86 B
Marler Rd. SE23 88 36 73 D
Marley Ave. Bexh 67 47 77 B
Marley Cl. Grnf 53 13 82 A
Marley Wlk. NW2 46 23 84 A
Marlingdene Cl. Hamp 92 13 70 A
Marlings Cl. Chis 100 45 68 C
Marlings Park Ave. Chis 100 45 68 A
Marloes Cl. Wem 44 17 85 B
Marloes Rd. W8 62 25 79 D
Marlow Cl. Ilf 28 44 90 A
Marlow Cl. SE20 97 34 68 B
Marlow Cres. Twick 71 15 74 D
Marlow Dri. Sutt 103 23 65 D
Marlowe Cl. Chis 100 44 70 B
Marlowe Gdns. Rom 30 53 90 A
Marlowe Gdns. SE9 78 43 74 C
Marlowe Rd. E17 26 38 89 C
Marlowe Sq. Mit 96 29 68 C
Marlowes The. Bexh 79 50 75 D
Marlowes The. NW8 46 26 83 B
Marlow Rd. SE20 97 34 68 B
Marlow Rd. Sthl 59 12 79 D
Marl St. SW18 73 26 75 C
Marlton St. E10 65 39 78 D
Marmion App. E4 18 37 92 A
Marmion Ave. E4 18 36 92 B
Marmion Cl. E4 18 37 92 A
Marmion Mews. SW11 74 28 75 A
Marmion Rd. SW11 74 28 75 C
Marmont Rd. SE15 75 34 76 A
Marmora Rd. SE22 76 35 74 C
Marmot Rd. Houn 70 11 75 B
Marnadon Rd. SE18 66 45 78 B
Marne Ave. N11 16 28 92 B
Marne Ave. Well 78 46 75 A
Marnell Way. Houn 70 11 75 B
Marne St. W10 56 24 82 A
Marney Rd. SW11 74 28 75 C
Marnham Ave. NW2 46 24 85 A
Marnham Cres. Grnf 43 13 83 D
Marnock Rd. SE4 76 36 74 B
Maroon St. E14 57 36 81 A
Marquess Rd. N1 48 32 84 B
Marquis Cl. Wem 44 18 84 D
Marquis Rd. N22 24 30 91 B
Marquis Rd. N4 36 30 87 D
Marquis Rd. NW1 47 29 84 B
Marrick Cl. SW15 72 22 75 C
Marriott Cl. Felt 69 08 74 D
Marriott Rd. Barn 11 23 96 B
Marriott Rd. E15 50 39 83 A
Marriott Rd. N10 24 27 90 B
Marriott Rd. N4 36 30 87 D
Marriotts Cl. NW9 34 21 88 D
Marryat Pl. SW19 85 24 71 A
Marryat Rd. SW19 85 24 71 A
Marryatt Ct. W5 54 18 81 D
Marsala Rd. SE13 76 37 75 D
Marsden Rd. N9 17 34 93 B
Marsden Rd. SE15 75 33 75 B
Marsden St. NW5 47 28 84 A
Marshall Cl. Har 32 14 87 B
Marshall Cl. Houn 70 12 74 B
Marshall Gdns. SE1 7 31 79 D
Marshall Rd. N17 25 32 90 B
Marshalls Dri. Rom 30 51 89 A
Marshalls Gr. SE18 65 42 78 A
Marshalls Rd. Rom 29 50 89 D
Marshall's Rd. Sutt 110 25 64 B
Marshall St. W1 2 29 81 C
Marshalsea Rd. SE1 8 32 79 A
Marsham Cl. Chis 90 43 71 D
Marsham St. SW1 10 29 78 B
Marsh Ave. Eps 109 21 62 C
Marsh Ave. Mit 96 28 69 C
Marshbrook Cl. SE3 77 41 75 B
Marsh Dri. NW9 34 21 88 D
Marsh Farm Rd. Twick 83 15 73 D
Marshfield St. E14 64 38 79 C
Marshgate La. E15 49 37 83 B
Marshgate Path. SE18 66 44 79 C
Marsh Green Rd. Dag 52 49 83 A
Marsh Hill. E9 49 36 85 C
Marsh La. E10 38 36 86 B
Marsh La. N17 25 34 90 B
Marsh La. Stan 21 17 91 B
Marsh Rd. Pnr 20 12 89 C
Marsh Rd. Wem 44 17 83 D
Marsh St. Dart 80 54 74 B
Marsh St. E14 64 37 78 B
Marsland Cl. SE17 63 31 78 D
Marston Ave. Dag 41 49 86 C
Marston Cl. Dag 41 49 86 C
Marston Cl. NW6 46 26 84 C
Marston Rd. Ilf 27 42 90 C
Marston Rd. Tedd 83 16 71 D
Marston Way. SE19 97 32 70 C
Marsworth Ave. Pnr 20 11 90 B
Martaban Rd. N16 37 33 86 B
Martello St. E8 48 34 84 D
Martello Terr. E8 48 34 84 D
Martell Rd. SE21 87 32 72 D
Martel Pl. E8 48 33 84 B
Marten Rd. E17 26 37 90 C
Martens Ave. Bexh 79 50 75 C
Martens Cl. Bexh 79 50 75 C
Martha Ct. E2 48 34 83 D
Martha Rd. E15 50 39 84 A
Martha St. E1 57 35 81 C
Marthorne Cres. Har 20 14 90 D
Martin Bowes Rd. SE9 77 42 75 B
Martin Cres. Croy 105 31 66 C
Martindale Rd. Houn 70 12 75 A
Martindale Rd. SW12 86 28 73 B
Martindale. SW14 72 20 74 A
Martin Dene. Bexh 79 48 74 B
Martin Dri. Nthlt 43 12 85 D
Martineau Rd. N5 48 31 85 B
Martineau St. E1 57 35 80 A
Martingale Cl. Sun 91 10 68 C
Martingales Cl. Rich 83 17 72 D
Martin Gdns. Dag 52 47 85 B
Martin Gr. Mord 95 25 68 A
Martin La. EC4 8 32 80 B
Martin Rd. Dag 52 47 85 B
Martin Rise. Bexh 79 48 74 B
Martins Cl. W Wick 106 38 66 D
Martins Mount. Barn 11 25 96 D
Martin's Rd. Brom 99 39 69 D
Martins Slip. Brom 99 39 69 D
Martins Wlk. N10 24 28 90 A
Martin Way. Mord 95 24 68 B
Martin Way. SW20 95 24 68 A
Martlet Gr. Nthlt 53 11 82 B
Martlett Ct. WC2 3 30 81 C
Martley Dri. Ilf 40 43 88 B
Marton Cl. SE6 88 37 72 C
Marton Rd. N16 37 33 86 A
Marvels Cl. SE12 89 40 72 B
Marvels La. SE12 89 41 72 C
Marville Rd. SW6 62 24 77 D
Marvin St. E8 48 34 84 B
Marwood Cl. Well 78 46 75 B
Marwood Way. SE16 63 34 78 D
Mary Adelaide Cl. SW15 84 21 72 C
Mary Ann Buildings. SE8 64 37 77 A
Maryatt Ave. Har 32 13 86 B
Marybank. SE18 65 42 78 B
Mary Cl. Har 21 18 89 D
Mary Datchelor Cl. SE5 75 32 76 B
Maryland Park. E15 50 39 85 C
Maryland Point. E15 50 39 84 A
Maryland Rd. E15 49 38 85 D
Maryland Rd. N22 25 31 91 A
Maryland Rd. Th Hth 97 31 69 B
Maryland Sq. E15 50 39 85 C
Marylands Rd. W9 56 25 82 C
Maryland St. E15 50 39 85 C
Maryland Way. Sun 91 10 69 C
Maryland Wlk. N1 48 32 83 A
Marylebone High St. W1 2 28 81 A
Marylebone La. W1 2 28 81 C
Marylebone Mews. W1 2 28 81 B
Marylebone Pas. W1 2 29 81 C
Marylebone Rd. NW1 1 27 81 B
Marylebone St. W1 2 28 81 A
Marylee Way. SE11 10 30 78 B
Maryon Gr. SE7 65 42 78 A
Maryon Mews. NW3 47 27 85 A
Maryon Rd. SE18 65 42 78 A
Maryon Rd. SE7 65 42 78 A
Mary Peters Dri. Grnf 43 14 85 D
Mary Pl. W11 56 24 80 A
Mary Rose Cl. Hamp 92 13 69 A
Mary St. E16 58 39 81 B
Mary's Terr. Twick 83 16 73 A
Mary St. N1 48 32 83 A
Mary Terr. NW1 47 29 83 A
Masbro Rd. W14 62 23 79 D
Mascalls Ct. SE7 65 41 77 A
Mascalls Rd. SE7 65 41 77 A
Mascotte Rd. SW15 73 23 75 D
Mascotts Cl. NW2 34 22 86 D
Masefield Ave. Stan 21 15 91 B
Masefield Ave. Sthl 53 13 80 A
Masefield Cl. Eri 80 51 76 B
Masefield Cl. Rom 30 53 90 A
Masefield Cres. N14 12 29 95 C
Masefield Cres. Rom 30 53 90 A
Masefield La. Hay 53 11 82 C
Masefield Rd. Hamp 82 12 71 B
Masefield View. Orp 108 44 65 C
Mashie Rd. W3 55 21 81 C
Mashiters Hill. Rom 29 50 90 B
Mashiters Wlk. Rom 30 51 89 A
Maskall Cl. SW2 87 31 73 C
Maskell Rd. SW17 85 26 72 C
Maskelyne Cl. SW11 74 27 76 A
Mason Cl. Bexh 79 49 75 B
Mason Cl. E16 58 40 80 A
Mason Cl. Hamp 92 12 69 B
Mason Cl. SW20 95 23 69 B
Mason's Arms Mews. W1 6 28 80 B
Mason's Ave. Croy 105 32 65 C
Mason's Ave. EC2 4 32 81 D
Masons Ave. Har 21 15 89 D
Mason's Green La. W3 55 19 81 A
Mason's Hill. Brom 99 40 68 D
Masons Hill. SE18 66 43 78 B
Mason's Pl. EC1 4 32 82 A
Mason's Pl. Mit 96 27 69 B
Mason St. SE17 63 32 78 B
Mason's Yd. SW19 85 23 71 D
Mason's Yd. SW1 6 29 80 C
Massey Cl. N11 16 28 92 D
Massie Rd. E8 48 34 84 A
Massinger St. SE17 63 33 78 A
Massingham St. E1 57 35 82 D
Masson Ave. Ruis 43 11 84 A
Master Gunners' Pl. SE18 65 42 77 C
Master Gunners' Pl. SE18 77 42 76 A
Master's St. E1 57 35 81 B
Mast House Terr. E14 64 37 78 A
Maswell Park Cres. Houn 70 14 74 A
Maswell Park Rd. Houn 70 13 74 B
Matcham Rd. E11 39 39 86 D
Matfield Cl. Brom 107 40 67 A
Matfield Rd. Belv 67 49 77 A
Matham Gr. SE22 75 33 75 D
Matheson Rd. W14 62 24 78 B
Mathews Ave. E6 51 43 83 C
Mathews Park Ave. E15 50 39 84 B
Matilda St. N1 47 30 83 B
Matlock Cres. Sutt 110 24 64 A
Matlock Gdns. Horn 42 54 86 C
Matlock Gdns. Sutt 110 24 64 A
Matlock Pl. Sutt 110 24 64 A
Matlock Rd. E10 38 38 88 C
Matlock St. E14 57 36 81 C
Matlock Way. N Mal 94 20 69 B
Matlow Ct. NW9 22 21 89 B
Matrimony Pl. SW8 74 29 76 C
Matthew Cl. W10 56 23 82 D
Matthew Parker St. SW1 6 29 79 B
Matthews Cl. Rom 30 54 90 D
Matthews Rd. Grnf 43 14 85 D
Matthews St. SW11 74 27 76 D
Matthias Rd. N16 48 33 85 C
Mattingly Way (off Daniel Gdns). SE15 63 33 77 D
Mattison Rd. N4 37 31 88 D
Mattock La. W13 54 16 80 D
Mattock La. W5 54 17 80 A
Maude Rd. E17 38 36 88 A
Maude Rd. SE5 75 33 76 A
Maudesville Cottages. W7 54 15 80 C
Maude Terr. E17 26 36 89 C
Maud Gdns. Bark 51 45 83 D
Maud Gdns. E13 50 39 83 D
Maudlins Green. E1 57 34 80 C
Maud Rd. E10 38 38 86 C
Maud Rd. E13 50 39 83 B
Maudslay Rd. SE9 77 42 75 B
Maud St. E16 58 39 81 B
Mauleverer Rd. SW2 74 30 74 A
Maundeby Wlk. NW10 45 21 84 A
Maunder Rd. W7 54 15 80 D
Maunsel St. SW1 10 29 78 B
Maurice Ave. N22 25 31 90 D
Maurice Browne Cl. NW7 23 23 91 B
Maurice Ct. Brent 60 17 77 D
Maurice St. W12 55 22 81 D
Maurice Wlk. NW11 23 26 89 C
Maurier Cl. Nthlt 43 11 83 A
Mauritius Rd. E10 65 39 78 A
Maury Rd. N16 37 34 86 C
Mavelstone Cl. Brom 99 42 69 A
Mavelstone Rd. Brom 99 42 69 A
Maverton Rd. E3 49 37 83 A
Mavis Ave. Eps 109 21 64 C
Mavis Cl. Eps 109 21 64 C
Mavis Gr. Horn 42 54 86 A
Mawbey Pl. SE1 63 33 78 D
Mawbey Rd. SE1 63 33 78 D
Mawbey St. SW8 10 30 77 C
Mawney Cl. Rom 29 49 90 D
Mawney Rd. Rom 29 49 89 B
Mawson Cl. SW20 95 24 69 C
Mawson La. W4 61 21 77 B
Maxey Gdns. Dag 52 48 85 A
Maxey Rd. Dag 52 48 85 A
Maxey Rd. SE18 66 44 78 A
Maxilla Gdns. W10 56 23 81 D
Maxilla Wlk. W10 56 23 81 D
Maximfeldt Rd. Eri 68 51 78 C
Maxim Rd. Dart 80 51 74 A
Maxim Rd. Eri 68 51 78 A
Maxim Rd. N21 13 31 95 C
Maxted Park. Har 33 15 87 A
Maxted Rd. SE15 75 34 75 A
Maxwell Gdns. Orp 108 45 65 D
Maxwell Rd. Ashf 91 08 70 A
Maxwell Rd. Nthwd 19 08 91 D
Maxwell Rd. SW6 62 25 77 D
Maxwell Rd. Well 78 46 75 A
Mayall Rd. SE24 75 31 74 B
May Ave. Orp 108 46 67 B
Maybank Ave. E18 27 40 90 D
Maybank Ave. Wem 44 16 85 C
Maybank Gdns. Pnr 31 10 88 A
Maybank Rd. E18 27 41 90 A
Mayberry Pl. Surb 101 18 66 B
Maybourne Cl. SE26 87 34 71 D
Maybrick Rd. Horn 42 53 88 C
Maybury Cl. Orp 108 43 67 B
Maybury Gdns. NW10 45 22 84 B

Maybury Rd. Bark 51 46 83 C
Maybury Rd. E13 58 41 82 C
Maybury St. SW17 86 27 71 C
Maybush Rd. Horn 42 54 87 A
Maychurch Cl. Stan 21 17 91 D
Maycock Gr. Nthwd 19 09 91 B
Maycroft. Pnr 19 10 90 D
Maycross Ave. Mord 95 25 68 C
Mayday Gdns. SE3 77 42 76 C
Mayday Rd. Croy 105 31 67 D
Mayerne Rd. SE9 77 41 74 B
Mayesbrook Rd. Bark 51 45 83 B
Mayesbrook Rd. Dag 40 46 86 D
Mayesford Rd. Rom 41 47 87 A
Mayes Rd. N22 24 30 90 D
Mayeswood Rd. SE12 89 41 71 A
Mayfair Ave. Bexh 79 47 76 B
Mayfair Ave. Ilf 40 43 86 A
Mayfair Ave. Rom 41 47 88 D
Mayfair Ave. Twick 82 14 73 A
Mayfair Ave. Wor Pk 102 22 66 C
Mayfair Cl. Beck 98 37 69 B
Mayfair Cl. Surb 101 18 66 C
Mayfair Gdns. N17 25 32 91 B
Mayfair Gdns. Wdf Gn 27 40 91 C
Mayfair Pl. W1 6 28 80 D
Mayfair Rd. Dart 80 53 74 B
Mayfair Terr. N14 16 29 94 B
Mayfield Ave. Har 33 16 88 B
Mayfield Ave. N12 15 26 92 B
Mayfield Ave. N14 16 29 93 B
Mayfield Ave. Orp 108 45 66 B
Mayfield Ave. W13 60 16 79 B
Mayfield Ave. W4 61 21 78 A
Mayfield Ave. Wdf Gn 27 40 91 A
Mayfield. Bexh 79 48 75 B
Mayfield Cl. Ashf 91 07 70 B
Mayfield Cl. E8 48 33 84 B
Mayfield Cl. SE20 97 34 69 B
Mayfield Cl. Surb 101 16 66 D
Mayfield Cres. N9 13 34 95 D
Mayfield Cres. Th Hth 96 30 68 D
Mayfield Dri. Pnr 20 12 89 D
Mayfield Gdns. NW4 35 23 88 D
Mayfield Gdns. W7 54 15 81 A
Mayfield Rd. Belv 67 50 78 A
Mayfield Rd. Brom 107 42 67 A
Mayfield Rd. Dag 41 47 87 C
Mayfield Rd. E13 58 39 82 D
Mayfield Rd. E17 26 36 90 C
Mayfield Rd. E4 18 38 93 B
Mayfield Rd. E8 48 33 84 D
Mayfield Rd. Enf 14 35 97 D
Mayfield Rd. N8 36 30 88 D
Mayfield Rd. S Croy 112 32 62 B
Mayfield Rd. Sutt 110 26 63 B
Mayfield Rd. SW19 95 24 69 B
Mayfield Rd. Th Hth 104 30 67 B
Mayfield Rd. W3 55 19 80 A
Mayfields Cl. Wem 34 19 86 A
Mayfields. Wem 34 19 86 A
Mayflower Cl. Ruis 31 08 88 C
Mayflower Rd. SW9 74 30 75 A
Mayflower St. SE16 64 35 79 A
Mayfly Gdns (off Seaspite Cl).
Nthlt 53 11 82 B
Mayford Cl. SW12 86 27 73 B
Mayford. NW1 47 29 83 C
Mayford Rd. SW12 86 28 73 A
May Gdns. Wem 54 17 82 A
Maygood St. N1 48 31 83 C
Maygreen Cres. Horn 42 52 87 A
Maygrove Rd. NW6 46 24 84 B
Mayhew Cl. E4 18 37 93 C
Mayhill Rd. Barn 11 24 95 C
Mayhill Rd. SE7 65 40 77 B
Maynard Cl. Eri 68 51 77 D
Maynard Rd. E17 38 38 88 A
Maynards. Horn 42 54 87 A
Mayola Rd. E5 49 35 85 A
Mayo Rd. NW10 45 21 84 A
Mayo Rd. SE25 105 32 67 B
Mayow Rd. SE23 88 35 72 D
Mayow Rd. SE26 88 35 71 B
Mayplace Ave. Dart 80 52 75 C
Mayplace Cl. Bexh 79 49 75 B
Mayplace La. SE18 66 43 77 B
Mayplace Rd E. Bexh 79 50 75 B
Mayplace Rd E. Dart 80 51 75 C
Mayplace Rd W. Bexh 79 49 75 C
Maypole Cres. Eri 68 53 77 B
Maypole Cres. Ilf 28 44 91 D
May Rd. E13 50 40 83 C
May Rd. E4 26 37 91 A
May Rd. Twick 83 15 73 C
Mayroyd Ave. Surb 102 19 65 A
May's Buildings Mews. SE10 64 38 77 D
Mays Ct. WC2 7 30 80 A
May's Hill Rd. Brom 99 39 68 A
Mays La. Barn 11 24 95 A
Maysoule Rd. SW11 73 26 75 D
Mays Rd. Tedd 82 14 71 D
May St. W14 62 24 78 D
Mayswood Gdns. Dag 52 50 84 B
Mayton St. N7 36 30 86 D
Maytree Ct. Nthlt 53 12 82 A
Maytree Wlk. SW2 87 31 72 A
Mayville Rd. E11 39 39 86 A
Mayville Rd. E11 39 39 86 C
Mayville Rd. Ilf 51 43 85 B
Maywin Dri. Horn 42 54 87 D
Maywood Cl. Beck 98 37 70 D
Maze Hill. SE10 65 39 77 A
Maze Hill. SE3 65 39 77 C
Mazenod Ave. NW6 46 25 84 C
Maze Rd. Rich 61 19 77 C
Mcadam Dri. Enf 13 31 97 D
McAuley Cl. SE1 7 31 79 C
McCall Cl. SW4 74 30 76 C
Mc Call Cres. SE7 65 42 78 C
Mc Carthy Rd. Felt 82 11 71 C
Mc Crone Mews. NW3 46 26 84 B
McCullum Rd. E3 49 36 83 D
Mc Dermott Cl. SW11 74 27 75 A
Mc Dermott Rd. SE15 75 34 75 A
McDougall Ct. Rich 72 19 76 C
Mcdowall Cl. E16 58 40 81 A
Mc Dowall Rd. SE5 75 32 76 A
McEntee Ave. E17 26 36 90 A
McEwen Way. E15 49 38 83 B
McGrath Rd. E15 50 39 84 B
McGregor Rd. W11 56 24 81 B
Mcintosh Cl. Rom 30 51 89 A
McIntosh Cl. Wall 111 30 63 C
Mcintosh Rd. Rom 30 51 89 A
McKay Rd. SW20 94 22 70 D
McKerrell Rd. SE15 75 34 76 A
Mckiernan Ct. SW11 73 26 76 D
Mc Leod Rd. SE2 66 46 78 A
McLeod Rd. SE2 67 47 78 A
McLeod's Mews. SW7 62 25 78 B
Mcmillan St. SE8 64 37 77 A
Mc Neil Rd. SE5 75 33 76 C
Meadbrook. SW20 95 23 68 C
Mead Cl. Har 20 14 90 B
Mead Cl. Rom 30 52 90 C
Mead Cres. E4 18 38 92 A
Mead Cres. Sutt 111 27 64 A
Meadcroft Rd. SE11 63 31 77 B
Mead Ct. NW9 34 20 88 B
Meade Cl. W4 61 19 77 A
Mead Field. Har 32 12 86 D
Meadfoot Rd. SW16 96 29 69 A
Mead Gr. Rom 29 48 89 A
Meadlands Dri. Rich 83 17 72 B
Meadow Ave. Croy 106 35 67 D
Meadowbank Cl. SW6 62 23 77 C
Meadowbank Gdns. Houn 69 10 76 B
Meadowbank. N21 12 30 95 D
Meadowbank. NW3 47 27 84 D
Meadowbank Rd. NW9 34 20 87 B
Meadowbank. SE3 77 39 75 B
Meadowbank. Surb 101 18 67 D
Meadow Cl. Barn 11 24 95 D
Meadow Cl. Chis 90 43 71 D
Meadow Cl. E4 18 37 94 D
Meadow Cl. Enf 14 36 97 A
Meadow Cl. Esh 101 15 65 D
Meadow Cl. Houn 82 13 73 A
Meadow Cl. Nthlt 43 13 83 C
Meadow Cl. Rich 83 18 73 C
Meadow Cl. Ruis 31 09 88 D
Meadow Cl. SE6 88 37 71 C
Meadow Cl. Sutt 103 26 65 A
Meadow Cl. SW20 95 23 68 C
Meadowcourt Rd. SE3 77 39 75 D
Meadow Croft. Brom 99 42 68 B
Meadowcroft Rd. N13 17 31 93 A
Meadow Dri. N10 24 28 89 B
Meadow Dri. NW4 23 23 90 C
Meadow Garth. NW10 45 20 84 A
Meadow Hill. N.Mal 102 21 67 C
Meadowlands. Horn 42 54 87 A
Meadow Mews. SW8 10 30 77 B
Meadow Pl. SW8 10 30 77 C
Meadow Rd. Ashf 81 08 71 D
Meadow Rd. Bark 51 46 84 C
Meadow Rd. Brom 99 39 69 C
Meadow Rd. Dag 52 48 84 B
Meadow Rd. Felt 82 12 72 A
Meadow Rd. Pnr 20 12 89 C
Meadow Rd. Rom 41 50 87 C
Meadow Rd. Sthl 53 12 80 B
Meadow Rd. Sutt 111 27 64 C
Meadow Rd. SW19 95 26 70 C
Meadow Rd. SW8 10 30 77 D
Meadow Row. SE1 8 32 79 C
Meadows End. Sun 91 10 69 A
Meadows Gdns. Edg 22 20 91 A
Meadowside Rd. Sutt 110 24 62 A
Meadowside. SE9 77 41 75 C
Meadowside. Twick 83 17 73 B
Meadow Stile. Croy 105 32 65 C
Meadow The. Chis 100 44 70 A
Meadowview Rd. Bex 79 48 74 D
Meadowview Rd. Eps 109 21 62 A
Meadowview Rd. SE6 88 37 71 C
Meadow View Rd. Th Hth 105 31 67 B
Meadow View. Sid 90 46 73 B
Meadow Waye. Houn 59 12 77 C
Meadow Way. NW9 34 20 88 B
Meadow Way. Orp 108 43 65 C
Meadow Way. Ruis 31 10 88 D
Meadow Way The. Har 21 15 90 A
Meadow Way. Wem 44 17 85 B
Meadow Wlk. Dag 52 48 84 B
Meadow Wlk. E18 27 40 89 C
Meadow Wlk. Eps 109 21 63 B
Meadow Wlk. Wall 104 28 65 D
Mead Path. SW17 85 26 71 D
Mead Path. SW19 95 26 70 B
Mead Plat. NW10 45 20 84 B
Mead Pl. Croy 105 32 66 C
Mead Pl. E9 49 35 84 A
Mead Rd. Chis 100 44 70 A
Mead Rd. Edg 22 19 91 A
Mead Rd. Rich 83 17 72 C
Mead Row. SE1 7 31 79 C
Meads La. Ilf 40 45 87 B
Meads Rd. Enf 14 36 97 A
Meads Rd. N22 25 31 90 D
Meads The. Edg 22 20 91 B
Meads The. Sutt 103 24 65 C
Mead The. Beck 98 38 69 A
Mead The. N2 23 26 90 C
Mead The. Uxb 31 07 86 A
Mead The. W13 54 16 81 B
Mead The. Wall 111 29 63 B
Mead The. W Wick 106 38 66 D
Meadvale Rd. Croy 105 33 67 D
Meadvale Rd. W5 54 17 82 C
Meadway. Ashf 81 07 71 A
Meadway. Barn 11 25 96 C
Meadway. Beck 98 38 69 A
Mead Way. Brom 107 39 67 D
Meadway Cl. Barn 11 25 96 C
Meadway Cl. NW11 35 25 88 D
Meadway Cl. Pnr 20 13 91 B
Mead Way. Croy 106 36 65 A
Meadway Ct. NW11 35 25 88 D
Meadway Ct. W5 54 18 82 D
Meadway Gate. NW11 35 25 88 C
Meadway Gdns. Ruis 31 08 88 D
Meadway. Ilf 51 45 85 A
Meadway. N14 16 30 93 A
Meadway. NW11 35 25 88 C
Meadway. Rom 30 52 90 C
Mead Way. Ruis 31 08 88 D
Meadway. Surb 102 20 66 C
Meadway. SW20 95 23 68 C
Meadway The. SE3 76 38 76 D
Meadway. Twick 82 14 73 D
Meaford Way. SE20 97 34 70 D
Meaford Way. SE20 98 35 70 C
Meanley Rd. E12 50 42 85 C
Meard St. W1 2 29 81 D
Meath Cl. Orp 108 46 67 B
Meath Rd. E15 50 39 83 D
Meath Rd. Ilf 40 44 86 C
Meath St. SW11 74 28 76 B
Mechanic's Path. SE8 64 37 77 C
Mecklenburgh Pl. WC1 3 30 82 D
Mecklenburgh Sq. WC1 3 30 82 D
Medburn St. NW1 47 29 83 D
Medcroft Gdns. SW14 72 20 75 C
Medebourne Cl. SE3 77 40 75 A
Medesenge Way. N13 25 31 91 B
Medfield St. SW15 84 22 73 B
Medhurst Rd. E3 49 36 83 C
Median Rd. E5 49 35 85 C
Medina Ave. Esh 101 15 65 C
Medina Gr. N7 37 31 86 C
Medina Rd. N7 37 31 86 C
Medland Cl. Cars 104 28 66 C
Medlar Cl. Nthlt 43 11 83 D
Medlar St. SE5 75 32 76 A
Medley Rd. NW6 46 25 84 A
Medora Rd. Rom 29 50 89 D
Medora Rd. SW2 86 30 73 B
Medusa Rd. SE6 76 37 74 D
Medway Bldgs. S3 49 36 83 C
Medway Cl. Croy 106 35 67 C
Medway Cl. Ilf 51 44 85 C
Medway Dri. Grnf 44 15 83 D
Medway Gdns. Wem 44 16 85 A
Medway Par. Grnf 44 15 83 D
Medway Rd. Dart 80 52 75 A
Medway Rd. E3 49 36 83 C
Medway St. SW1 6 29 79 D
Medwin St. SW4 74 30 75 D
Meerbrook Rd. SE3 77 41 75 A
Meeson Rd. E15 50 39 84 D
Meeson St. E5 49 36 85 A
Meeting Field Path. E9 49 35 84 A
Meetinghouse Alley. E1 57 34 80 D
Meeting House La. SE15 63 34 77 D
Mehetabel Rd. E9 49 35 85 C
Melanda Cl. Chis 89 42 71 D
Melanie Cl. Bexh 79 48 76 A
Melba Way. SE13 76 37 76 B
Melbourne Ave. N13 24 30 91 B
Melbourne Ave. Pnr 20 13 89 B
Melbourne Ave. W13 54 16 80 C
Melbourne Cl. Orp 108 45 66 A
Melbourne Cl. Wall 111 29 64 C
Melbourne Ct. SE20 97 34 70 C
Melbourne Gdns. Rom 41 48 88 A
Melbourne Gr. SE22 75 33 75 D
Melbourne Mews. SW9 75 31 76 A
Melbourne Pl. WC2 3 30 81 D
Melbourne Rd. E10 38 37 87 B
Melbourne Rd. E17 26 36 89 C
Melbourne Rd. E6 50 42 83 D
Melbourne Rd. Ilf 40 43 87 D
Melbourne Rd. SW19 95 25 69 A
Melbourne Rd. Tedd 93 17 70 A
Melbourne Rd. Wall 111 29 64 C
Melbourne Sq. SW9 75 31 76 A
Melbourne Way. Enf 13 33 95 D
Melbury Ave. Sthl 59 13 79 D
Melbury Cl. Chis 99 42 70 B
Melbury Ct. W8 62 25 79 C
Melbury Dri. SE5 63 33 77 C
Melbury Gdns. SW20 94 22 69 B
Melbury Rd. Har 33 18 88 B
Melbury Rd. W14 62 24 79 D
Melbury Terr. NW1 1 27 82 C
Melcombe Gdns. Har 33 18 88 D
Melcombe Pl. NW1 1 27 81 B
Melcombe St. NW1 1 27 82 D
Meldon Cl. SW6 73 25 76 B
Meldrum Rd. Ilf 40 46 86 A
Melfield Gdns. SE6 88 38 71 C
Melford Ave. Bark 51 45 84 B
Melford Ct. SE22 87 34 73 A
Melford Rd. E11 39 39 86 A
Melford Rd. E17 26 36 89 D
Melford Rd. Ilf 40 44 86 B
Melford Rd. SE22 87 34 73 C
Melfort Ave. Th Hth 97 31 68 B
Melfort Rd. Th Hth 97 31 68 B
Melgund Rd. N5 48 31 85 C
Melina Pl. NW8 1 26 82 B
Melina Rd. W12 61 22 79 B
Melior Pl. SE1 8 33 79 A
Melior St. SE1 8 33 79 A
Meliot Rd. SE6 88 38 72 B
Melksham Cl. Rom 30 54 91 D
Melksham Dri. Rom 30 54 91 D
Melksham Gdns. Rom 30 54 91 D
Melksham Green. Rom 30 54 91 D
Meller Cl. Croy 104 30 65 C
Melling St. SE18 66 45 77 A
Mellish Cl. Bark 51 45 83 B
Mellish Ct. Surb 101 18 67 C
Mellish St. E14 64 37 79 C
Mellison Rd. SW17 86 27 71 C
Mellitus St. W12 55 21 81 B
Mellows Rd. Ilf 27 42 89 B
Mellows Rd. Wall 111 29 64 D
Mells Cres. SE9 89 42 71 B
Mell St. E10 65 39 78 C
Melody Rd. SW18 73 26 74 A
Melody Rd. SW18 73 26 74 C
Melon Pl. W8 62 25 79 A
Melon Rd. SE15 75 34 76 A
Melrose Ave. Grnf 43 13 83 D
Melrose Ave. Mit 96 28 70 D
Melrose Ave. N22 25 31 90 B
Melrose Ave. NW2 46 23 85 C
Melrose Ave. SW16 97 31 68 A
Melrose Ave. SW19 85 25 72 C
Melrose Ave. Twick 82 13 73 B
Melrose Cl. Grnf 43 13 83 D
Melrose Dri. Sthl 53 13 80 C
Melrose Gdns. Edg 22 19 90 D
Melrose Gdns. N Mal 94 20 68 B
Melrose Gdns. W6 62 23 79 C
Melrose Rd. Har 20 12 89 D
Melrose Rd. SW13 72 21 76 D
Melrose Rd. SW18 73 24 74 D
Melrose Rd. SW19 95 25 69 A
Melrose Rd. W3 61 20 79 C
Melrose Terr. W6 62 23 79 C
Melsa Rd. Mord 103 26 67 C
Meltham Way. SE16 63 34 78 D
Melthorne Dri. Ruis 32 11 86 C
Melthorpe Gdns. SE3 77 42 76 A
Melton Cl. Ruis 32 11 87 C
Melton Ct. SW7 62 26 78 B
Melton Gdns. Rom 42 51 87 B
Melton Pl. Eps 109 20 62 B
Melton St. NW1 2 29 82 B
Melville Ave. Grnf 44 15 85 D
Melville Ave. S Croy 112 33 64 D
Melville Ave. SW20 94 22 70 C
Melville Ct. W4 61 19 78 C
Melville Gdns. N13 17 31 92 D
Melville Rd. E17 26 36 89 B
Melville Rd. NW10 45 20 84 D
Melville Rd. Rom 29 49 90 B
Melville Rd. SW13 72 22 76 A
Melville St. N1 48 32 84 C
Melville Villas Rd. W3 55 20 80 D
Melvin Rd. SE20 98 35 69 A
Melyn Cl. NW19 47 29 85 A
Memel Ct. EC1 4 32 82 C
Memel St. EC1 4 32 82 C
Memorial Ave. E15 58 39 82 A
Memorial Cl. Houn 59 12 77 B
Mendip Cl. SE26 88 35 71 A
Mendip Cres. SW11 73 26 75 A
Mendip Dri. NW2 35 24 86 A
Mendip Rd. Bexh 80 51 76 A
Mendip Rd. Horn 42 52 87 A
Mendip Rd. Ilf 40 45 88 A
Mendip Rd. SW11 73 26 75 A
Mendora Rd. SW6 62 24 77 D
Mendoza Cl. Horn 42 54 88 A
Menelik Rd. NW2 46 24 85 B
Meness Path. SE18 66 43 77 A
Menlo Gdns. SE19 97 32 70 D
Menotti St. E2 57 34 82 C
Menthone Pl. Horn 42 53 87 B
Mentmore Cl. Har 33 17 88 C
Mentmore Terr. E8 48 34 84 D
Meon Rd. W3 61 20 79 A
Meopham Rd. Mit 96 29 69 A
Mepham Cres. Har 20 14 91 C
Mepham Gdns. Har 20 14 91 C
Mepham St. SE1 7 31 80 C
Mera Dri. Bexh 79 49 75 C
Mercator Rd. SE13 76 38 75 D
Merccia Gr. SE13 76 38 75 C
Mercer Cl. Surb 101 15 66 B
Merceron St. E1 57 34 82 D
Mercer Pl. Pnr 20 11 90 C
Mercers Cl. E10 65 39 78 B
Mercers Rd. N19 36 29 86 D
Mercer St. WC2 3 30 81 C
Merchant St. E3 57 36 82 B
Merchiston Rd. SE6 88 38 72 B
Merchland Rd. SE9 90 44 73 C
Mercier Rd. SW15 73 24 74 A
Mercury Gdns. Rom 42 51 88 B
Mercury Way. SE14 64 35 77 B
Mercy Terr. SE13 76 37 74 B
Merebank La. Croy 111 30 64 D
Mere Cl. Orp 108 43 65 B
Mere Cl. SW15 85 23 73 B
Meredith Ave. NW2 46 23 85 C
Meredith Cl. Pnr 20 11 91 D
Meredith St. E13 58 40 82 A
Meredith St. EC1 3 31 82 B
Meredyth Rd. SW13 72 22 76 C
Mere End. Croy 106 35 66 B
Mereside. Orp 108 43 65 A
Meretone Cl. SE4 76 36 75 C
Meretune Ct. Mord 95 24 68 B
Merevale Cres. Mord 103 26 67 C
Mereway Rd. Twick 83 15 73 C
Merewood Cl. Brom 100 43 69 C
Merewood Rd. Bexh 79 50 76 C
Mereworth Cl. Brom 107 39 67 B
Mereworth Dri. SE18 66 44 77 C
Merhsam Rd. Th Hth 97 32 69 D
Meridan Rd. SE7 65 41 77 D
Meriden Cl. Brom 99 41 70 D
Meriden Cl. Ilf 28 44 90 A
Meridian Wlk. N17 25 33 91 A
Merifield Rd. SE9 77 41 75 C
Merino Pl. Sid 78 46 74 C
Merivale Rd. Har 32 14 87 A
Merivale Rd. SW15 73 24 75 C
Merlewood Dri. Chis 99 42 69 B
Merley Ct. NW9 34 20 87 C
Merlin Cl. Croy 112 33 64 A
Merlin Cl. Nthlt 53 11 82 A
Merlin Cl. Rom 29 50 91 B
Merlin Cres. Edg 21 18 90 B
Merlin Gdns. Brom 89 40 72 C
Merlin Gdns. Rom 29 50 91 B
Merlin Gr. Beck 106 37 67 A
Merlin Gr. Ilf 28 44 91 C
Merlin Rd. E12 39 41 86 B
Merlin Rd. Rom 29 50 91 B
Merlin Rd. Well 78 46 75 C
Merlins Ave. Har 32 12 86 D
Merlin St. WC1 3 31 82 A
Mermaid Ct. SE1 8 32 79 B
Merredene St. SW2 74 30 74 D
Merrick Rd. Sthl 59 12 79 B
Merrick Rd. Sthl 59 12 79 D
Merrick Sq. SE1 8 32 79 D
Merridene. N21 13 31 95 D
Merrielands Cres. Dag 52 48 83 D
Merrilands Rd. Wor Pk 103 23 66 C
Merrilees Rd. Sid 90 45 73 A
Merriman Rd. SE3 77 41 76 A
Merrington Rd. SW6 62 25 77 A
Merritt Rd. SE4 76 36 74 B
Merrivale Ave. Ilf 27 41 89 D
Merrivale. N14 12 29 95 D
Merrow Rd. Sutt 110 23 62 B
Merrows Cl. Nthwd 19 08 91 A
Merrow St. SE17 63 32 78 D
Merrow Wlk. SE17 63 32 78 D
Merrydown Way. Chis 99 42 69 A
Merryfield. SE3 77 39 76 D
Merryhill Cl. E4 18 37 94 B
Merryhills Ct. N14 12 29 95 A
Merryhills Dri. Enf 12 29 96 D
Merryweather Ct. N.Mal 102 21 67 A
Mersey Rd. E17 26 36 89 B
Mersham Dri. NW9 34 19 88 B
Merten Rd. Rom 41 48 87 A
Merthyr Terr. SW13 61 22 77 B
Merton Ave. Nthlt 43 14 85 C
Merton Ave. W4 61 21 78 B
Merton Gdns. Orp 108 43 67 B
Merton Hall Gdns. SW20 95 24 69 A
Merton Hall Rd. SW19 95 24 69 A
Merton High St. SW19 95 26 70 C
Merton La. N6 36 27 86 B
Merton Mansions. SW20 95 23 69 D
Merton Rd. Bark 51 45 84 D
Merton Rd. E17 38 38 88 C
Merton Rd. Har 32 14 87 C
Merton Rd. Ilf 40 45 87 B
Merton Rd. SE25 105 34 67 A
Merton Rd. SW18 85 25 73 C
Merton Rd. SW19 95 25 70 D
Merton Rise. NW3 47 27 84 C
Merton Way. E Mol 92 14 68 A
Merttins Rd. SE15 76 35 74 B
Mervan Rd. SW2 75 31 75 C
Mervyn Ave. SE9 90 44 72 A
Mervyn Rd. W13 60 16 79 C
Messaline Ave. W3 55 20 80 A
Messent Rd. SE9 77 41 74 A
Messeter Pl. SE9 78 43 74 C
Messina Ave. NW6 46 25 84 C
Metcalf Rd. Ashf 81 07 71 D
Metcalf Wlk. Felt 82 12 71 A
Meteor St. SW11 74 28 75 C
Meteor Way. Wall 111 30 63 C
Methering Way. NW9 22 21 90 A
Methley St. SE11 63 31 78 C
Methuen Cl. Edg 22 19 91 C
Methuen Park. N10 24 28 89 B
Methuen Rd. Belv 67 49 78 B
Methuen Rd. Bexh 79 48 75 D
Methuen Rd. Edg 22 19 91 C
Methwold Rd. W10 56 23 81 B
Mews The. Ilf 39 41 88 B
Mews The. N1 48 32 83 A
Mews The. Rom 30 51 89 C
Mews The. Sid 90 46 71 A
Mexfield Rd. SW15 73 24 74 B
Meyer Rd. Eri 67 50 77 B

Meymott St. SE1 7 31 80 D
Meynell Cres. E9 49 35 84 D
Meynell Gdns. E9 49 35 84 D
Meynell Rd. E9 49 35 84 D
Meynell Rd. Rom 30 52 91 D
Meyrick Rd. NW10 45 22 84 A
Meyrick Rd. SW11 74 27 75 A
Miall Wlk. SE26 88 36 71 A
Micawber St. N1 4 32 82 A
Michael Gaynor Cl. W7 54 15 80 D
Michael Gdns. Horn 30 53 89 D
Michael Rd. E11 39 39 87 D
Michael Rd. SE25 97 33 68 A
Michael Rd. SW6 73 25 76 B
Michaels Cl. SE13 77 39 75 A
Micheldever Rd. SE12 77 39 74 D
Michelham Gdns. Twick 83 15 72 D
Michel's Row. Rich 71 18 75 C
Michigan Ave. E12 50 42 85 B
Michleham Down. N12 15 24 92 B
Mickleham Cl. Orp 100 46 69 C
Mickleham Gdns. Sutt 110 24 63 A
Mickleham Rd. Orp 100 46 69 C
Micklethwaite Rd. SW6 62 25 77 A
Midcroft. Ruis 31 09 87 C
Middle Dartrey Wlk. SW10 62 26 77 D
Middlefielde. W13 54 16 81 B
Middlefield Gdns. Ilf 40 43 88 D
Middle Field. NW8 46 26 83 B
Middleham Gdns. N18 25 34 91 A
Middleham Rd. N18 25 34 91 B
Middle La. N8 36 30 88 A
Middle Lane Mews. N8 36 30 88 A
Middle La. Tedd 93 15 70 B
Middle Park Ave. SE9 89 42 73 C
Middle Path. Har 32 14 87 D
Middle Rd. Barn 12 27 95 C
Middle Rd. E13 50 40 83 C
Middle Rd. Har 32 14 87 D
Middle Rd. N2 24 27 90 A
Middle Rd. SW16 96 29 69 D
Middle Row. W10 56 24 82 C
Middlesborough Rd. N18 17 34 92 C
Middlesex Pas. EC1 3 31 81 B
Middlesex Pl. E9 49 35 84 A
Middlesex Rd. Mit 104 30 67 A
Middlesex St. E1 4 33 81 D
Middle St. Croy 105 32 65 C
Middle St. EC1 4 32 81 A
Middle Temple La. EC4 7 31 80 A
Middleton Ave. E4 18 36 93 D
Middleton Ave. Grnf 43 14 83 D
Middleton Ave. Sid 100 46 70 B
Middleton Bldgs. W1 2 29 81 A
Middleton Cl. E4 18 36 93 D
Middleton Dri. Pnr 19 10 89 A
Middleton Gdns. Ilf 40 43 88 D
Middleton Gr. N7 47 30 85 C
Middleton Mews. N7 47 30 85 C
Middleton Rd. Cars 104 27 66 A
Middleton Rd. E8 48 33 84 D
Middleton Rd. Eps 109 20 62 D
Middleton Rd. Mord 103 26 67 C
Middleton Rd. NW11 35 25 87 A
Middleton St. E2 57 34 82 B
Middleton Way. SE13 76 38 75 D
Middle Way. Hay 53 11 82 C
Middleway. NW11 35 25 88 B
Middle Way. SW16 96 29 69 D
Middle Way The. Har 21 15 90 D
Middle Yd. SE1 8 33 80 C
Midfield Ave. Bexh 79 50 75 A
Midfield Par. Bexh 79 50 75 A
Midfield Way. Orp 100 46 69 B
Midford Pl. W1 2 29 82 C
Midholm Cl. NW11 23 25 89 D
Midholm. NW11 23 25 89 D
Midholm Rd. Croy 106 36 65 A
Midholm. Wem 34 19 87 C
Midhope St. WC1 3 30 82 A
Midhurst Ave. Croy 105 31 66 A
Midhurst Ave. N10 24 28 89 A
Midhurst Hill. Bexh 79 49 74 A
Midhurst Rd. W13 60 16 79 C
Midland Pl. E14 64 38 78 C
Midland Rd. E10 38 38 87 A
Midland Rd. NW1 3 30 82 A
Midland Rd. NW1 47 30 83 C
Midland Terr. NW10 55 21 82 C
Midland Terr. NW2 35 23 86 D
Midleton Rd. N Mal 94 20 69 C
Midlothian Rd. E3 57 36 82 D
Midmoor Rd. SW12 86 29 73 C
Midmoor Rd. SW19 95 24 69 A
Midstrath Rd. NW10 45 21 85 A
Midsummer Ave. Houn 70 12 75 D
Midway. Sutt 103 24 66 B
Midwood Cl. NW2 34 22 86 D
Miers Cl. E6 51 43 83 A
Mighell Ave. Ilf 39 41 88 B
Milborne Gr. SW10 62 26 78 C
Milborne St. E9 49 35 84 A
Milborough Cres. SE12 77 39 74 C
Milcote St. SE1 7 31 79 B
Mildenhall Rd. E5 38 35 86 C
Mildmay Ave. N1 48 32 84 B
Mildmay Gr. N1 48 32 85 D
Mildmay Park. N1 48 32 85 D
Mildmay Rd. Ilf 40 43 86 D
Mildmay Rd. N1 48 33 85 C
Mildmay Rd. Rom 41 50 88 A
Mildmay St. N1 48 32 84 B
Mildred Ave. Nthlt 43 13 85 D
Mildred Rd. Eri 68 51 78 C
Mile End Pl. E1 57 35 82 D
Mile End Rd. E1 57 35 82 D
Mile End Rd. E3 57 36 82 B
Mile End The. E17 26 35 90 A
Mile Rd. Croy 104 29 66 D
Mile Rd. Wall 104 29 66 C
Milespit Hill. NW7 23 23 91 A
Miles Pl. NW8 1 26 81 B
Miles Pl. Surb 93 18 68 D
Miles Rd. Mit 96 27 68 A
Miles Rd. N8 24 30 89 A
Miles St. SW8 10 30 77 A
Milestone Cl. Sutt 110 26 63 D
Milestone Rd. SE19 97 33 70 B
Miles Way. N20 16 27 93 A
Milfoil St. W12 55 22 80 A
Milford Cl. SE2 67 48 77 A
Milford Gdns. Edg 22 19 91 C
Milford Gdns. Wem 44 17 85 D
Milford Gr. Sutt 110 26 64 A
Milford La. WC2 7 31 80 A
Milford La. WC2 7 31 80 A
Milford Rd. Sthl 53 13 80 A
Milford Rd. W13 54 16 80 D
Milford St. SW8 74 28 75 B
Milford Way. SE15 75 33 76 B
Milk St. Brom 99 40 70 B
Milk St. EC2 4 32 81 C
Milkwell Gdns. Wdf Gn 27 40 91 D
Milkwood Rd. SE24 75 31 75 D
Milk Yd. E1 57 35 80 A
Millais Ave. E12 51 43 85 C
Millais Gdns. Edg 22 19 90 C
Millais Rd. E11 49 38 85 B
Millais Rd. Enf 13 33 95 B
Millais Rd. N.Mal 102 21 66 A
Millais Way. Eps 109 20 64 A
Millard Cl (off Boleyn Rd). N16 48 33 85 C
Millard Terr. Dag 52 49 84 A
Millbank. SW1 10 30 78 A
Millbank Way. SE12 77 40 74 A
Millbourne Rd. Felt 82 12 71 A
Mill Bridge. Barn 11 24 95 B
Millbrook Ave. Well 78 44 75 D
Millbrook Gdns. Rom 41 48 88 C
Millbrook Gdns. Rom 30 51 90 A
Millbrook Pas. SW9 75 31 75 B
Millbrook Rd. N9 17 34 94 D
Millbrook Rd. SW9 75 31 75 B
Mill Cl. Cars 104 28 65 A
Mill Cnr. Barn 11 24 97 B
Millender Wlk. SE16 64 35 78 A
Miller Cl. Pnr 20 11 90 C
Miller Rd. Croy 105 31 66 C
Miller Rd. SW19 95 26 70 B
Miller's Ave. E8 48 33 85 D
Miller's Ct. W6 61 21 78 D
Miller's Terr. E8 48 33 85 D
Miller St. NW1 47 29 83 C
Millers Yd. N3 23 25 91 D
Millet Rd. Grnf 43 13 83 D
Mill Farm Ave. Sun 91 09 70 C
Mill Farm Cl. Pnr 20 11 90 C
Mill Farm Cres. Houn 82 12 73 C
Millfield Ave. E17 26 36 90 A
Mill Field Cres. Houn 82 12 73 D
Millfield. King 93 18 68 B
Millfield La. N6 36 27 86 B
Millfield Pl. N6 36 28 86 A
Millfield Rd. Edg 22 20 90 C
Millfields Cl. Orp 100 46 68 D
Millfields Rd. E5 38 35 86 D
Millfield. Sun 91 08 69 B
Mill Footpath. Rom 42 51 88 D
Mill Gdns. SE26 87 34 72 D
Mill Green. Mit 104 28 66 A
Mill Green Rd. Mit 104 28 66 A
Millgrove St. SW11 74 28 76 C
Mill Hill Gr. W3 55 19 80 D
Mill Hill Rd. SW13 72 22 76 C
Mill Hill Rd. W3 61 19 79 B
Mill Hill. SW13 72 22 75 A
Mill Hill Terr. W3 55 19 80 D
Millhouse Pl. SE27 87 31 71 C
Millicent Fawcett Ct. N17 25 33 90 B
Millicent Rd. E10 38 36 87 D
Milligan St. E14 57 36 80 B
Milling Rd. Edg 22 20 91 D
Mill La. Cars 111 28 64 A
Mill La. Croy 104 30 65 D
Mill La. Enf 14 37 96 B
Mill La. Eps 109 21 62 B
Mill La. NW6 46 24 85 D
Mill La. Rom 41 48 88 C
Mill La. SE18 66 43 78 C
Millman Mews. WC1 3 30 82 D
Millman St. WC1 3 30 82 D
Millmark Gr. SE14 76 36 76 C
Millmarsh La. Enf 14 36 97 D
Mill Mead Rd. N17 25 34 89 A
Mill Park Ave. Horn 42 54 86 A
Mill Plat Ave. Islw 71 16 76 C
Mill Plat. Islw 71 16 76 C
Mill Pl. Chis 100 43 69 B
Mill Pl. Dart 80 52 75 C
Mill Pl. E14 57 36 81 C
Mill Pl. King 93 18 68 B
Mill Pond Rd. Dart 80 54 74 C
Mill Rd. E16 58 40 80 D
Mill Rd. Eri 67 50 77 C
Mill Rd. Ilf 40 43 86 C
Mill Rd. SE13 76 38 75 A
Mill Rd. SW19 95 26 70 C
Mill Rd. Twick 82 14 72 A
Mill Row. N1 48 33 83 A
Mills Ct. EC2 4 33 82 A
Mills Gr. NW4 23 23 89 B
Millshot Cl. SW6 73 23 76 A
Millside. Cars 104 27 65 B
Mills Row. W4 61 20 78 B
Mill St. King 93 18 68 A
Millstream Rd. SE1 8 33 79 B
Mill St. SE1 8 33 79 B
Mill St. W1 6 29 80 A
Mill Vale. Brom 99 39 69 D
Mill View Gdns. Croy 106 35 65 D
Millwall Dock Rd. E14 64 37 79 C
Millward Wlk. SE18 66 43 77 A
Mill Way. Felt 69 10 74 B
Millway Gdns. Nthlt 43 12 84 B
Millwood Rd. Houn 70 14 74 A
Millwood St. W10 56 24 81 A
Mill Yd. E1 57 34 80 A
Milman Cl. Pnr 20 11 89 B
Milman Rd. NW6 46 24 83 C
Milman's St. SW10 62 26 77 B
Milne Feild. Pnr 20 13 91 C
Milne Gdns. SE9 77 42 74 A
Milner Dri. Twick 82 14 73 B
Milner Pl. Cars 111 28 64 A
Milner Pl. N1 48 31 83 A
Milner Rd. Dag 41 47 86 A
Milner Rd. E15 58 39 82 A
Milner Rd. King 93 17 68 B
Milner Rd. Mord 103 26 67 B
Milner Rd. SW19 95 25 69 B
Milner Rd. Th Hth 97 32 68 B
Milner Sq. N1 48 31 84 C
Milner St. SW3 9 27 78 B
Milnthorpe Rd. W4 61 20 77 B
Milo Rd. SE22 75 33 74 D
Milroy Wlk. SE1 7 31 80 D
Milson Rd. W14 62 24 79 C
Milton Ave. Barn 11 24 95 B
Milton Ave. Croy 105 32 66 B
Milton Ave. E6 50 42 84 C
Milton Ave. Horn 42 51 86 B
Milton Ave. N6 36 29 87 A
Milton Ave. NW10 45 20 83 B
Milton Ave. NW9 22 20 89 A
Milton Ave. Sutt 111 27 64 A
Milton Cl. N2 35 26 88 C
Milton Cl. Sutt 103 26 65 D
Milton Court Rd. SE14 64 36 77 A
Milton Cres. Ilf 40 44 88 C
Milton Ct. EC2 4 32 81 B
Milton Ct. King 83 18 71 A
Milton Ct. Uxb 31 07 86 D
Milton Gr. N11 16 29 92 D
Milton Gr. N16 48 33 85 A
Milton Park. N6 36 29 87 A
Milton Pl. N7 48 31 85 C
Milton Rd. Belv 67 49 78 A
Milton Rd. Croy 105 32 66 B
Milton Rd. E17 26 37 89 C
Milton Rd. Hamp 92 13 70 C
Milton Rd. Har 21 15 89 C
Milton Rd. Mit 96 28 70 C
Milton Rd. N15 25 31 89 D
Milton Rd. N6 36 29 87 A
Milton Rd. NW9 34 22 87 A
Milton Rd. Rom 42 52 88 C
Milton Rd. SE24 75 31 74 B
Milton Rd. Sutt 103 25 65 C
Milton Rd. SW14 72 20 75 B
Milton Rd. SW19 95 26 70 A
Milton Rd. W3 55 20 80 D
Milton Rd. W7 54 15 80 B
Milton Rd. Wall 111 29 63 B
Milton Rd. Well 78 45 76 B
Milton St. EC2 4 32 81 B
Milverton Rd. Ilf 40 45 86 B
Milverton Rd. NW6 46 23 84 C
Milverton St. SE11 63 31 78 C
Milverton Way. SE9 90 43 71 A
Milward St. E1 57 34 81 B
Mimosa Cl. Rom 30 53 91 C
Mimosa Rd. Hay 53 11 81 A
Mimosa St. SW6 73 24 76 B
Minard Rd. SE6 89 39 73 C
Mina Rd. SE17 63 33 78 C
Mina Rd. SW19 95 25 69 A
Minchenden Cres. N14 16 29 93 D
Minchenden Ct. N14 16 29 93 B
Mincing La. EC3 8 33 80 A
Minden Rd. SE20 97 34 69 B
Minehead Rd. Har 32 13 86 C
Minehead Rd. SW16 86 30 71 D
Mineral St. SE18 66 45 78 A
Minera Mews. SW1 9 28 78 A
Minerva Cl. Sid 90 45 71 A
Minerva Rd. E4 26 37 91 D
Minerva Rd. King 93 18 69 D
Minerva Rd. NW10 55 20 82 B
Minerva St. E2 48 34 83 C
Minet Ave. NW10 45 21 83 C
Minet Gdns. NW10 45 21 83 C
Minet Rd. SW9 75 31 76 D
Minford Gdns. W14 62 23 79 B
Mingard Wlk. N7 36 30 86 B
Ming St. E14 57 37 80 A
Mink Ct. Houn 70 11 76 C
Minniedale. Surb 101 18 67 B
Minnow St. SE17 63 33 78 A
Minories. EC3 8 33 80 B
Minshull St. SW8 74 29 76 B
Minson Rd. E9 49 35 83 B
Minstead Gdns. SW15 84 21 73 B
Minstead Way. N.Mal 102 21 67 C
Minster Ave. Sutt 103 25 65 A
Minster Ct. W5 54 18 82 D
Minster Dri. Croy 112 33 64 A
Minster Gdns. E Mol 92 12 68 D
Minsterley Ave. Shep 91 09 68 C
Minster Rd. Brom 99 40 70 D
Minster Rd. NW2 46 24 85 C
Minster Way. Horn 42 54 87 D
Minster Wlk. N8 24 30 89 C
Minstrel Gdns. Surb 93 18 68 D
Mintern Cl. N13 13 31 95 D
Minterne Ave. Sthl 59 13 78 A
Minterne Rd. Har 33 18 88 B
Minterne Waye. Hay 53 11 81 C
Mintern St. N1 48 32 83 D
Minton Mews. NW3 46 25 84 B
Mint Rd. Wall 111 28 64 B
Mint St. SE1 8 32 79 A
Mint Wlk. Croy 105 32 65 C
Mirabel Rd. SW6 62 24 77 D
Miranda Rd. N19 36 29 87 C
Mirfield St. SE7 65 41 79 D
Miriam Rd. SE18 66 45 78 C
Mirro Path. SE9 89 41 72 C
Missenden Gdns. Mord 103 26 67 C
Mission Gr. E17 38 36 88 A
Mission Pl. SE15 75 34 76 A
Mission Sq (off Pottery Rd). Brent 60 18 77 A
Mitcham Garden Village. Mit 104 28 67 A
Mitcham La. SW16 86 29 71 D
Mitcham Park. Mit 96 27 68 C
Mitcham Rd. Croy 104 30 66 B
Mitcham Rd. Ilf 40 45 87 B
Mitcham Rd. SW17 86 27 71 D
Mitcham Rd. SW17 96 28 70 A
Mitchell Cl. SE2 67 47 78 A
Mitchell Rd. N13 17 32 92 C
Mitchell Rd. Orp 108 45 65 D
Mitchell St. EC1 4 32 82 C
Mitchell Way. Brom 99 40 69 A
Mitchell Way. NW10 45 20 84 A
Mitchison Rd. N1 48 32 84 B
Mitchley Rd. N17 25 34 89 A
Mitford Rd. N19 36 30 86 A
Mitre Cl. Sutt 110 26 63 D
Mitre Ct. EC2 4 32 81 C
Mitre Ct. EC4 3 31 81 C
Mitre Rd. SE1 7 31 79 A
Mitre Sq. EC3 4 33 81 C
Mitre St. EC3 4 33 81 C
Mitre The. E14 57 36 80 B
Moat Cres. N3 23 25 89 B
Moat Ct. Har 34 19 88 A
Moat Dri. E13 50 41 83 C
Moat Dri. Har 20 14 89 D
Moat Dri. Ruis 31 09 87 A
Moat Farm Rd. Nthlt 43 12 84 D
Moat La. E Mol 93 15 68 B
Moat La. Eri 80 52 76 A
Moat Pl. SW9 74 30 75 B
Moat Pl. W3 55 19 81 D
Moat Side Enf 14 35 96 D
Moat Side. Felt 82 11 71 A
Moat The. N Mal 94 21 69 A
Moberly Rd. SW4 86 29 73 B
Modbury Gdns. NW5 47 28 84 A
Modder Pl. SW15 73 23 75 D
Model Cottages. SW14 72 20 75 A
Model Farm Cl. SE9 89 42 72 C
Modern Ct. EC4 3 31 81 D
Moffat Ct. SW19 85 25 71 C
Moffat Gdns. Mit 96 27 68 A
Moffat Rd. N13 24 30 91 A
Moffat Rd. SW17 86 27 71 B
Moffat Rd. Th Hth 97 32 69 D
Mogden La. Islw 71 15 74 B
Mohan Cl. N14 12 28 95 D
Moiety Rd. E14 64 37 79 A
Moira Cl. N17 25 33 90 C
Moira Rd. SE9 77 42 75 D
Moir Cl. S Croy 112 34 62 A
Moland Mead. SE16 64 35 78 D
Mole Abbey Gdns. E Mol 92 13 68 B
Mole Ct. Eps 109 20 64 A
Molember Rd. E Mol 101 15 67 A
Molescroft. SE9 90 44 72 C
Molesey Ave. E Mol 92 12 68 D
Molesey Dri. Sutt 103 24 65 C
Molesford Rd. SW6 73 25 76 A
Molesham Cl. E Mol 92 13 68 B
Molesham Way. E Mol 92 13 68 B
Molesworth St. SE13 76 37 75 A
Moliner Ct. Beck 98 37 70 C
Mollison Ave. Enf 14 36 96 A
Mollison Ave. Enf 14 36 97 B
Mollison Dri. Wall 111 30 63 C
Mollison Way. Edg 22 19 90 C
Molyneux St. W1 1 27 81 A
Monarch Cl. Felt 81 09 73 A
Monarch Ct. N2 35 26 88 B
Monarch Rd. Belv 67 49 79 C
Monarch's Way. Ruis 31 09 87 C
Mona Rd. SE15 76 35 76 C
Mona St. E16 58 39 81 B
Monastery Gdns. Enf 13 32 97 D
Monaveen Gdns. E Mol 92 13 68 B
Monck St. SW1 6 29 79 D
Monclar Rd. SE5 75 33 75 C
Moncorvo Pl. SW7 5 27 79 A
Moncrieff St. SE15 75 34 76 C
Monega Rd. E12 50 41 84 B
Monega Rd. E7 50 41 84 A
Mongers La. Eps 109 22 62 C
Monier Rd. E3 49 37 84 C
Monivea Rd. Beck 98 36 70 D
Monk Dri. E16 58 40 80 A
Monkfrith Ave. N14 12 28 95 D
Monkfrith Cl. N14 16 28 94 B
Monkfrith Way. N14 16 28 94 B
Monkham's Ave. Wdf Gn 27 40 91 B
Monkleigh Rd. Mord 95 24 68 C
Monks Ave. Barn 11 26 95 C
Monks Cl. Enf 13 32 97 C
Monks Cl. Ruis 43 11 85 B
Monks Cl. SE2 67 47 78 B
Monksdene Gdns. Sutt 103 25 65 D
Monks Dri. W3 55 19 81 C
Monks Orchard Rd. Beck 106 37 66 A
Monks Park Gdns. Wem 45 19 84 D
Monks Park. Wem 45 20 84 A
Monks Rd. Enf 13 32 97 C
Monk St. SE18 66 43 78 A
Monks Way. Beck 106 37 67 C
Monks Way. Orp 108 44 66 D
Monkswood Gdns. Ilf 28 43 89 A
Monkton Rd. Well 78 45 76 D
Monkton St. SE11 63 31 78 A
Monkville Ave. NW11 23 24 89 D
Monkwell Sq. EC2 4 32 81 A
Monmouth Ave. E18 27 40 89 B
Monmouth Cl. Mit 96 30 68 C
Monmouth Cl. Well 78 46 75 C
Monmouth Pl. W2 56 25 81 D
Monmouth Rd. Dag 52 48 85 D
Monmouth Rd. N9 17 34 93 B
Monmouth Rd. N9 18 35 93 A
Monmouth Rd. W2 56 25 81 C
Monmouth St. WC2 3 30 81 C
Monnery Rd. N19 36 29 86 C
Monnow Rd. SE1 63 34 78 A
Monoux Gr. E17 26 37 90 A
Monroe Cres. Enf 13 34 97 B
Monroe Dri. SW14 72 19 74 B
Monro Gdns. Har 21 15 91 C
Monsell Rd. N4 37 31 86 D
Monson Rd. NW10 45 22 83 D
Monson Rd. SE14 64 35 77 D
Mons Way. Brom 107 42 67 C
Montacute Rd. Mord 103 26 67 D
Montacute Rd. SE6 88 36 73 B
Montagu Cres. N18 17 34 92 B
Montague Ave. SE4 76 37 75 C
Montague Ave. W7 54 15 80 D
Montague Cl. SE1 8 32 80 D
Montague Gdns. W5 55 19 80 A
Montague Pl. E14 58 38 80 A
Montague Pl. WC1 2 29 81 B
Montague Rd. Croy 105 31 66 D
Montague Rd. E11 39 39 86 B
Montague Rd. E8 48 34 85 C
Montague Rd. Houn 70 13 75 B
Montague Rd. N15 25 34 89 C
Montague Rd. N8 36 30 88 B
Montague Rd. Rich 71 18 74 C
Montague Rd. Sthl 59 12 78 A
Montague Rd. SW19 95 25 70 D
Montague Rd. W13 54 16 81 D
Montague Rd. W7 60 15 79 B
Montague Sq. SE14 64 35 77 C
Montague St. WC1 3 30 81 A
Montague Waye. Sthl 59 12 79 C
Montagu Gdns. N18 17 34 92 B
Montagu Gdns. Wall 111 29 64 A
Montagu Mansions. W1 1 27 81 B
Montagu Mews N. W1 1 27 81 B
Montagu Mews S. W1 1 27 81 D
Montagu Mews W. W1 1 27 81 D
Montagu Pl. W1 1 27 81 B
Montagu Rd. N18 18 35 92 A
Montagu Rd. N9 18 35 93 A
Montagu Rd. NW4 34 22 88 C
Montagu Row. W1 1 27 81 B
Montagu Sq. W1 1 27 81 D
Montagu St. W1 1 27 81 D
Montana Cl. S Croy 112 32 62 D
Montana Rd. SW17 86 28 72 C
Montana Rd. SW20 95 23 69 A
Montbelle Rd. SE9 90 43 72 D
Montcalm Cl. Brom 107 40 67 C
Montcalm Rd. SE7 65 41 77 D
Montclare St. E2 4 33 82 D
Monteagle Ave. Bark 51 44 84 A
Monteagle Way. E5 37 34 86 C
Monteagle Way. SE15 75 34 75 B
Montefiore Ct. N16 37 33 87 D
Montefiore St. SW8 74 28 76 D
Monteith Rd. E3 49 36 83 B
Montem Rd. N Mal 94 21 68 C
Montem Rd. SE23 88 36 73 B
Montem St. N4 36 30 87 D
Montenotte Rd. N8 36 29 88 A
Montesole Ct. Pnr 20 11 90 C
Montford Pl. SE11 63 31 78 C
Montford Rd. Sun 91 10 68 C
Montfort Gdns. Ilf 28 44 91 A
Montfort Pl. SW19 85 23 73 D
Montgolfier Wlk (off Argus Way). Nthlt 53 12 82 A
Montgomery Ave. Esh 101 15 65 A
Montgomery Cl. Mit 96 30 68 C
Montgomery Cl. Sid 78 45 74 D
Montgomery Rd. Edg 21 18 91 B
Montgomery Rd. W4 61 20 78 A
Montholme Rd. SW11 74 27 74 D
Monthope Rd. E1 57 34 81 A
Montolieu Gdns. SW15 73 23 74 A

Montpelier Ave. W5 54 17 81 A
Montpelier Ct. W5 54 17 81 B
Montpelier Gdns. E6 58 41 82 B
Montpelier Gdns. E6 50 42 83 C
Montpelier Gdns. Rom 41 47 87 A
Montpelier Gr. NW5 47 29 85 C
Montpelier Mew. SW7 5 27 79 C
Montpelier Pl. SW7 5 27 79 C
Montpelier Rd. N3 23 26 90 A
Montpelier Rd. Pur 112 31 62 D
Montpelier Rd. SE15 75 34 76 B
Montpelier Rd. Sutt 110 26 64 A
Montpelier Rd. W5 54 17 81 B
Montpelier Rise. Wem 33 17 87 D
Montpelier Row. SE3 77 39 76 D
Montpelier Row. Twick 83 17 73 A
Montpelier Sq. SW7 5 27 79 A
Montpelier St. SW7 5 27 79 C
Montpelier Terr. SW7 5 27 79 A
Montpelier Vale. SE3 77 39 76 D
Montpelier Wlk. SW7 5 27 79 C
Montpellier Rise. NW11 35 24 87 A
Montpellier Way. NW11 35 24 87 A
Montrave Rd. SE20 98 35 70 C
Montreal Pl. WC2 7 30 80 B
Montreal Rd. Ilf 40 44 87 A
Montrell Rd. SW2 86 30 73 C
Montrose Ave. Edg 22 20 90 B
Montrose Ave. NW6 46 24 83 C
Montrose Ave. Rom 30 53 90 C
Montrose Ave. Sid 90 46 73 A
Montrose Ave. Twick 82 13 73 B
Montrose Ave. Well 78 45 75 A
Montrose Cl. Ashf 81 08 71 C
Montrose Cl. Well 78 45 75 B
Montrose Cres. N12 23 26 91 A
Montrose Cres. Wem 44 18 84 A
Montrose Gdns. Mit 96 27 69 D
Montrose Gdns. Sutt 103 25 65 B
Montrose Pl. SW1 6 28 79 A
Montrose Rd. Felt 69 08 74 D
Montrose Rd. Har 21 15 90 D
Montrose Way. SE23 88 35 73 D
Montserrat Ave. Wdf Gr 26 38 91 D
Montserrat Rd. SW15 73 24 75 C
Monument St. EC3 8 32 80 B
Monza St. E1 57 35 80 C
Moodkee St. SE16 64 35 79 C
Moody St. E1 57 35 82 B
Moon La. Barn 11 24 96 B
Moon St. N1 48 31 83 B
Moorcroft Rd. SW16 86 30 72 C
Moorcroft Way. Pnr 32 12 88 A
Moordown. SE18 78 43 76 B
Moore Cl. Mit 96 28 69 D
Moore Cl. SW14 72 20 75 A
Moore Cl. Wall 111 30 63 C
Moorefield Rd. N17 25 33 90 D
Moorehead Way. SE3 77 40 75 A
Mooreland Rd. Brom 99 39 70 D
Moore Park Rd. SW6 62 25 77 D
Moore Rd. SE19 97 32 70 A
Moore St. SW3 9 27 78 B
Moore Wlk. E7 50 40 85 A
Moorey Cl. E15 50 39 83 B
Moorfield Ave. W5 54 17 82 D
Moorfield Rd. Enf 14 35 97 A
Moorfield Rd. Orp 108 46 66 A
Moorfields. EC2 4 32 81 B
Moorfields Highwalk. EC2 4 32 81 B
Moorgate. EC2 4 32 81 B
Moorgate Pl. EC2 4 32 81 D
Moorhouse Rd. Har 21 17 89 B
Moorhouse Rd. W2 56 25 81 C
Moorings The. E16 58 41 81 A
Moor La. Chess 109 19 63 A
Moor La. EC2 4 32 81 B
Moor La. EC2 4 32 81 B
Moorland Cl. Houn 82 13 73 A
Moorland Cl. Rom 29 49 90 B
Moorland Rd. SW9 75 31 75 D
Moorlands Ave. NW7 22 22 91 B
Moormead Dri. Eps 109 21 64 C
Moor Mead Rd. Twick 71 16 74 C
Moor Park Rd. Nthwd 19 08 91 B
Moor Pl. EC2 4 32 81 B
Moorside Rd. Brom 89 39 71 B
Moor St. W1 2 29 81 D
Morant St. E14 57 37 80 A
Mora Rd. NW2 46 23 85 A
Mora St. EC1 4 32 82 A
Morat St. SW9 74 30 76 B
Moravian Cl. SW3 62 26 77 B
Moravian Pl. SW10 62 26 77 B
Moravian St. E2 57 35 82 A
Moray Cl. Rom 30 51 91 C
Moray Mews. N4 36 30 86 B
Moray Rd. N4 36 30 86 B
Moray Rd. N4 37 31 87 C
Moray Way. Rom 30 51 91 C
Mordaunt Gdns. Dag 52 48 84 C
Mordaunt Rd. NW10 45 20 83 B
Mordaunt St. SW9 74 30 75 B
Morden Ct. Mord 95 25 68 D
Morden Gdns. Grnf 44 15 85 D
Morden Gdns. Mit 95 26 68 D
Morden Hall Rd. Mord 95 26 68 C
Morden Hill. SE13 76 38 76 C
Morden La. SE13 76 38 76 A
Morden Rd. Mord 95 26 68 D
Morden Rd. SE3 77 40 76 C
Morden Rd. SW19 95 25 69 C
Morden Road Mews. SE3 77 40 76 C
Morden St. SE13 76 37 76 B
Morden Way. Sutt 103 25 66 A
Morden Wharf Rd. SE10 65 39 79 C
Morder Rd. Rom 41 48 87 A
Mordon Rd. Ilf 40 45 87 B
Morecambe St. SE17 63 32 78 C
Morecambe Terr. N18 17 32 92 B
More Cl. E16 58 39 81 D
More Cl. W14 62 24 78 A
Morecoombe Cl. King 94 19 70 D
Moredred Rd. SE6 89 39 72 A
Moree Way. N18 17 34 92 A
Moreland Ct. NW2 35 25 86 C
Moreland St. EC1 3 31 82 B
Moreland Way. E4 18 38 93 C
Morella Rd. SW12 86 27 73 B
Moremead Rd. SE6 88 37 71 A
Morena St. SE6 88 37 73 B
Moresbury Wlk. SW8 74 29 76 C
Moresby Ave. Surb 102 19 66 B
Moresby Rd. E5 37 34 87 D
Moreton Ave. Islw 71 15 76 A
Moreton Cl. E5 38 35 86 A
Moreton Cl. N15 37 32 88 D
Moreton Cl. NW7 23 23 91 A
Moreton Pl. SW1 10 29 78 C
Moreton Rd. N15 37 32 88 D
Moreton Rd. S Croy 112 32 64 D
Moreton Rd. Wor Pk 102 22 65 B
Moreton St. SW1 10 29 78 D
Moreton Terr Mews N. SW1 10 29 78 C
Moreton Terr Mews S. SW1 10 29 78 C
Moreton Terr. SW1 10 29 78 C
Morford Cl. Ruis 31 10 87 B
Morford Way. Ruis 31 10 87 B
Morgan Ave. E17 26 38 89 D
Morgan Cl. Dag 52 49 84 C
Morgan Cl. Nthwd 19 09 91 B
Morgan Ct. Ashf 81 07 71 D
Morgan Rd. Brom 99 40 70 C
Morgan Rd. N7 48 31 85 C
Morgan Rd. W10 56 24 81 B
Morgans La. SE1 8 33 80 C
Morgan St. E16 58 39 81 B
Morgan St. E3 57 36 82 A
Morgan St. E3 57 36 82 B
Morgan's Wlk. SW11 9 27 77 C
Morgan Way. Wdf Gn 27 42 91 B
Morie St. SW18 73 25 74 B
Morieux Rd. E10 38 36 87 D
Moring Rd. SW17 86 28 71 A
Morkyns Wlk. SE21 87 33 72 C
Morland Ave. Croy 105 33 66 C
Morland Ave. Dart 80 52 74 B
Morland Cl. Hamp 82 12 71 D
Morland Cl. NW11 35 25 87 D
Morland Estate. E8 48 34 84 C
Morland Gdns. Sthl 53 13 80 D
Morland Mews. N1 48 31 84 C
Morland Rd. Croy 105 33 66 B
Morland Rd. Dag 52 49 84 C
Morland Rd. E17 38 35 88 B
Morland Rd. Har 21 18 89 C
Morland Rd. Ilf 40 43 86 B
Morland Rd. SE20 98 35 70 B
Morland Rd. Sutt 110 26 64 C
Morley Ave. E4 26 38 91 D
Morley Ave. N18 17 34 92 A
Morley Ave. N22 25 31 90 D
Morley Cl. Orp 108 43 65 B
Morley Crescent E. Stan 21 17 89 B
Morley Crescent W. Stan 21 17 89 A
Morley Cres. Ruis 32 11 86 A
Morley House. E5 37 34 86 A
Morley Rd. Bark 51 44 83 B
Morley Rd. Chis 100 44 69 A
Morley Rd. E10 38 38 87 C
Morley Rd. E15 50 39 83 D
Morley Rd. Rom 41 48 88 A
Morley Rd. S Croy 112 33 62 D
Morley Rd. SE13 76 38 75 C
Morley Rd. Sutt 103 24 66 D
Morley Rd. Twick 71 17 74 D
Morley St. SE1 7 31 79 A
Morna Rd. SE5 75 32 76 C
Morning La. E9 49 35 84 A
Morningside Rd. Wor Pk 103 23 65 A
Mornington Ave. Brom 99 41 68 B
Mornington Ave. Ilf 40 43 87 A
Mornington Ave. W14 62 24 78 B
Mornington Cres. Houn 69 10 76 B
Mornington Cres. NW1 47 29 83 C
Mornington Gr. E3 57 37 82 A
Mornington Mews. SE5 75 32 76 A
Mornington Pl. NW1 47 29 83 C
Mornington Rd. Ashf 81 08 71 C
Mornington Rd. E11 39 39 87 D
Mornington Rd. E4 18 38 94 B
Mornington Rd. SE8 64 36 77 D
Mornington St. NW1 47 28 83 D
Mornington Terr. NW1 47 28 83 D
Mornington Wlk. Rich 83 17 71 A
Mornington Rd. Grnf 53 13 82 D
Morocco St. SE1 8 33 79 A
Morpeth Gr. E9 49 35 83 B
Morpeth Rd. E9 49 35 83 B
Morpeth St. E2 57 35 82 B
Morpeth Terr. SW1 10 29 78 A
Morpeth Wlk. N17 25 34 91 D
Morrab Gdns. Ilf 40 45 86 D
Morris Ave. E12 50 42 85 D
Morris Cl. Orp 108 45 65 C
Morris Gdns. SW18 85 25 73 A
Morrish Rd. SW2 86 30 73 A
Morrison Ave. N17 25 33 89 A
Morrison Rd. Bark 52 48 83 C
Morrison St. SW11 74 28 75 A
Morris Pl. N4 37 31 86 A
Morris Rd. Dag 41 48 86 B
Morris Rd. E14 57 37 81 B
Morris Rd. E15 50 38 85 A
Morris Rd. Islw 71 15 75 B
Morris Rd. Rom 30 52 91 D
Morris St. E1 57 34 81 D
Morse Cl. E13 58 40 82 A
Morshead Rd. W9 56 25 82 B
Morston Gdns. SE9 89 42 71 B
Morten Cl. SW4 74 29 74 D
Morteyne Rd. N17 25 32 90 B
Mortgramit Sq. SE18 66 43 79 C
Mortham St. E15 50 39 83 A
Mortimer Cl. NW2 35 24 86 D
Mortimer Cl. SW16 86 29 72 B
Mortimer Cres. NW6 46 25 83 B
Mortimer Cres. Wor Pk 102 20 65 D
Mortimer Estate. NW6 46 25 83 B
Mortimer Market. WC1 2 29 82 C
Mortimer Pl. NW6 46 25 83 B
Mortimer Rd. Eri 67 50 77 B
Mortimer Rd. Mit 96 27 69 D
Mortimer Rd. N1 48 33 84 C
Mortimer Rd. NW10 56 23 82 A
Mortimer Rd. Orp 108 46 66 C
Mortimer Rd. W13 54 17 81 C
Mortimer Sq. W11 56 23 80 B
Mortimer St. W1 2 29 81 A
Mortimer Terr. NW5 47 28 85 B
Mortlake Cl. Croy 104 30 65 C
Mortlake High St. SW14 72 20 75 B
Mortlake Rd. E16 58 40 81 D
Mortlake Rd. Ilf 51 44 85 B
Mortlake Rd. Rich 72 19 76 D
Mortlock Cl. SE15 75 34 76 B
Mortlock Ct. E12 50 41 85 B
Morton Cres. N14 16 29 92 B
Morton Ct. Nthlt 43 14 85 C
Morton Gdns. Wall 111 29 64 C
Morton Mews. SW5 62 25 78 B
Morton Rd. E15 50 39 84 D
Morton Rd. Mord 103 26 67 B
Morton Rd. N1 48 32 84 C
Morton Way. N14 16 29 92 B
Morvale Cl. Belv 67 48 78 B
Morval Rd. SW2 75 31 74 A
Morven Rd. SW17 86 27 72 D
Morville St. E3 49 37 83 C
Morwell St. WC1 2 29 81 B
Moscow Pl. W2 56 25 80 B
Moscow Rd. W2 56 25 80 B
Moselle Ave. N22 25 31 90 D
Moselle Cl. N8 24 30 89 B
Moselle Pl. N17 25 33 91 C
Moselle St. N17 25 33 91 C
Moslyn Mews. Har 33 16 88 A
Mossborough Cl. N12 23 25 91 B
Mossbury Rd. SW11 74 27 75 A
Moss Cl. Pnr 20 12 90 D
Mossdown Cl. Belv 67 49 78 A
Mossford Ct. Ilf 28 43 90 D
Mossford Green. Ilf 28 44 89 A
Mossford La. Ilf 28 44 90 C
Mossford St. E3 57 36 82 D
Moss Gdns. Felt 81 10 72 A
Moss Hall Cres. N12 23 26 91 A
Moss Hall Gr. N12 23 25 91 B
Mossington Rd. SE16 64 35 78 A
Moss La. Pnr 20 12 90 D
Moss La. Rom 42 51 88 D
Mosslea Rd. Brom 107 41 67 B
Mosslea Rd. Orp 108 44 65 C
Mosslea Rd. SE20 98 35 70 A
Mossop St. SW3 9 27 78 A
Moss Rd. Dag 52 49 84 C
Mossville Gdns. Mord 95 24 68 D
Mostyn Ave. Wem 44 18 85 D
Mostyn Gdns. NW10 46 23 83 D
Mostyn Gr. E3 49 37 83 C
Mostyn Rd. Edg 22 21 91 C
Mostyn Rd. SW19 95 24 69 D
Mostyn Rd. SW9 75 31 76 A
Mosul Way. Brom 107 42 67 C
Motcomb St. SW1 6 28 79 C
Motley St. SW8 74 29 76 C
Motspur Park. N.Mal 102 22 67 C
Mottingham Gdns. SE9 89 41 73 D
Mottingham La. SE12 89 41 73 A
Mottingham La. SE9 89 41 73 D
Mottingham Rd. N9 18 35 94 B
Mottingham Rd. SE9 89 42 72 D
Mottisfont Rd. SE2 66 46 79 D
Moulins Rd. E9 49 35 84 D
Moulton Ave. Houn 70 12 76 C
Moundfield Rd. N16 37 34 88 C
Mound The. SE9 90 43 72 C
Mountacre Cl. SE26 87 34 71 A
Mount Adon Park. SE22 87 34 73 A
Mount Angelus Rd. SW15 84 21 73 B
Mount Ararat Rd. Rich 71 18 74 A
Mount Ash Rd. SE26 87 34 72 D
Mount Ave. E4 18 37 93 D
Mount Ave. Sthl 53 13 81 C
Mount Ave. W5 54 17 81 B
Mountbatten Cl. SE18 66 45 77 A
Mountbatten Cl. SE19 87 33 71 C
Mountbel Rd. Stan 21 16 90 C
Mount Cl. Barn 12 28 96 C
Mount Cl. Brom 99 42 69 A
Mount Cl. Cars 111 28 62 A
Mount Cl. W5 54 17 81 A
Mountcombe Cl. Surb 101 18 66 A
Mount Ct. W.Wick 107 39 65 A
Mount Dri. Bexh 79 48 74 A
Mount Dri. Har 32 12 88 B
Mount Dri. Wem 34 20 86 A
Mountearl Gdns. SW16 86 30 72 D
Mount Echo Ave. E4 18 37 94 B
Mount Echo Dri. E4 18 37 94 D
Mount Ephraim La. SW16 86 29 72 D
Mount Ephraim Rd. SW16 86 29 72 D
Mountfield Rd. E6 51 43 83 C
Mountfield Rd. N3 23 25 89 A
Mountfield Rd. W5 54 18 81 C
Mountford Rd. E8 48 34 85 C
Mountford St. E1 57 34 81 C
Mountford Terr. N1 48 31 84 C
Mountfort Cres. N1 48 31 84 C
Mount Gdns. SE26 87 34 72 D
Mountgrove Rd. N5 37 32 86 C
Mounthurst Rd. Brom 107 39 66 B
Mountjoy Cl. SE2 66 46 79 B
Mount Mills. EC1 3 31 82 B
Mount Nod Rd. SW16 86 30 72 D
Mount Park Ave. Har 33 15 86 A
Mount Park Ave. S Croy 112 31 62 B
Mount Park. Cars 111 28 62 A
Mount Park Cres. W5 54 17 81 D
Mount Park Rd. Har 32 14 86 D
Mount Park Rd. Pnr 31 10 88 A
Mount Park Rd. W5 54 17 81 D
Mount Pleasant. Barn 12 27 96 D
Mount Pleasant Cres. N4 36 30 87 B
Mount Pleasant. Eps 109 21 62 D
Mount Pleasant Hill. E5 38 35 86 A
Mount Pleasant. Ilf 51 44 85 C
Mount Pleasant Rd. Dart 80 54 74 D
Mount Pleasant Rd. E17 26 36 90 C
Mount Pleasant Rd. N17 25 33 90 C
Mount Pleasant Rd. N Mal 94 20 68 A
Mount Pleasant Rd. NW10 46 23 83 A
Mount Pleasant Rd. Rom 29 50 91 B
Mount Pleasant Rd. SE13 76 38 74 C
Mount Pleasant Rd. W5 54 17 82 C
Mount Pleasant. Ruis 32 11 86 B
Mount Pleasant. SE27 87 32 71 A
Mount Pleasant Villas. N4 36 30 87 B
Mount Pleasant. WC1 3 31 82 C
Mount Pleasant. Wem 44 18 83 B
Mount Pleasant Wlk. Bex 79 50 74 A
Mount Pleasant Wlk. Bex 79 50 74 A
Mount Pl. W3 55 19 80 D
Mount Rd. Barn 12 27 95 A
Mount Rd. Bexh 79 48 74 A
Mount Rd. Chess 109 19 64 A
Mount Rd. Dag 41 48 87 D
Mount Rd. Dart 80 51 74 D
Mount Rd. Felt 82 12 72 C
Mount Rd. Ilf 51 43 85 D
Mount Rd. Mit 96 27 69 C
Mount Rd. Mit 96 27 69 C
Mount Rd. N Mal 94 20 68 B
Mount Rd. NW2 35 23 86 C
Mount Rd. NW4 34 22 88 C
Mount.Rd. SE19 97 33 70 A
Mount Rd. SW19 85 25 72 A
Mount Row. W1 6 28 80 B
Mountsfield Ct. SE13 76 38 74 D
Mountside. Stan 21 16 90 A
Mounts Pond Rd. SE13 76 38 76 D
Mounts Pond Rd. SE3 76 38 76 D
Mounts Pond Rd. SE3 77 39 76 C
Mount Sq The. NW3 35 26 86 C
Mount Stewart Ave. Har 33 17 87 B
Mount St. W1 6 28 80 A
Mount Terr. E1 57 34 81 B
Mount The. E5 37 34 86 B
Mount The. Eps 109 21 62 D
Mount The. Eps 109 22 64 B
Mount The. N20 15 26 93 A
Mount The. N Mal 94 21 68 A
Mount The. NW3 35 26 86 C
Mount The. Wem 34 20 86 A
Mount Vernon. NW3 46 26 85 A
Mountview Ct. N15 25 31 89 D
Mountview. Nthwd 19 09 91 B
Mount View Rd. E4 18 38 94 B
Mount View Rd. N4 36 30 87 B
Mount View Rd. NW9 34 20 88 B
Mountview Rd. Orp 108 46 66 A
Mount View. W5 54 17 81 B
Mount Villas. SE27 87 31 72 D
Mount Way. Cars 111 28 62 A
Mountwood Cl. S Croy 112 34 62 D
Mountwood. E Mol 92 13 68 B
Movers La. Bark 51 45 83 A
Mowatt Cl. N19 36 29 87 D
Mowbray Rd. Barn 11 26 95 A
Mowbray Rd. NW6 46 24 84 C
Mowbray Rd. Rich 83 17 72 C
Mowbray Rd. SE19 97 33 69 B
Mowbrays Cl. Rom 29 50 90 A
Mowbrays Rd. Rom 29 50 90 C
Mowlem St. E2 48 34 83 D
Mowll St. SW9 63 31 77 C
Moxon Cl. E13 50 39 83 D
Moxon St. Barn 11 24 96 B
Moxon St. W1 2 28 81 A
Moye Cl. E2 48 34 83 C
Moyers Rd. E10 38 38 87 A
Moylan Rd. W6 62 24 77 A
Moyne Pl. NW10 45 19 83 C
Moyser Rd. SW16 86 28 71 D
Moyser Rd. SW16 96 29 70 A
Mozart St. W10 56 24 82 B
Muchelney Rd. Mord 103 26 67 D
Muggeridge Rd. Dag 52 49 85 B
Muirdown Ave. SW14 72 20 75 D
Muirfield. W3 55 21 81 C
Muirkirk Rd. SE6 88 38 73 C
Muir Rd. E5 37 34 86 C
Mulberry Cl. E4 18 37 93 A
Mulberry Cl. Nthlt 43 12 83 C
Mulberry Cl. NW3 46 26 85 B
Mulberry Cl. NW4 23 23 89 A
Mulberry Cl. Rom 30 53 89 C
Mulberry Cl. SW16 86 29 71 A
Mulberry Cres. Brent 60 17 77 C
Mulberry Ct. Bark 51 45 84 D
Mulberry Ct. Surb 101 17 66 B
Mulberry La. Croy 105 33 66 D
Mulberry Pl. W6 61 22 78 C
Mulberry St. E1 57 34 81 C
Mulberry Way. Belv 67 50 79 A
Mulberry Way. E18 27 40 90 D
Mulberry Way. Ilf 28 44 89 C
Mulberry Wlk. SW3 62 26 77 B
Mulgrave Rd. Croy 105 32 65 D
Mulgrave Rd. Har 33 16 86 A
Mulgrave Rd. NW10 45 21 85 B
Mulgrave Rd. Sutt 110 25 63 A
Mulgrave Rd. SW6 62 24 77 B
Mulgrave Rd. W5 54 17 82 D
Mulholland Cl. Mit 96 28 69 D
Mulkern Rd. N19 36 29 87 D
Mullberry Mews. Wall 111 29 63 A
Muller Rd. SW4 74 29 74 D
*Mullet Gdns. E2 57 34 82 A
Mullins Path. SW14 72 20 75 B
Mullion Cl. Har 20 13 90 B
Mull Wlk. N1 48 32 84 B
Mulready St. NW8 1 27 82 C
Multi Way. W3 61 21 79 A
Multon Rd. SW18 85 26 73 D
Mumford Ct. EC2 4 32 81 C
Mumford Rd. SE24 75 31 74 B
Muncaster Cl. Ashf 81 07 71 A
Muncaster Rd. Ashf 81 07 71 D
Muncaster Rd. SW11 74 28 74 A
Mundania Rd. SE22 76 35 74 A
Munday Rd. E16 58 40 80 A
Munden St. W14 62 24 78 A
Mundford Rd. E5 38 35 86 A
Mund St. W14 62 24 78 D
Mundy St. N1 4 33 82 A
Munnings Gdns. Islw 70 14 74 B
Munro Mews. W10 56 24 81 A
Munster Ave. Houn 70 12 74 A
Munster Ct. Tedd 93 17 70 A
Munster Gdns. N13 17 32 92 A
Munster Rd. SW6 73 24 76 B
Munster Sq. NW1 2 28 82 D
Munton Rd. SE17 63 32 78 A
Murchison Rd. E10 38 38 86 A
Murdock St. SE15 63 34 77 B
Murfett Cl. SW19 85 24 72 A
Muriel St. N1 47 30 83 B
Murillo Rd. SE13 76 38 75 D
Murphy St. SE1 7 31 79 A
Murray Ave. Brom 99 40 69 D
Murray Ave. Houn 70 13 74 B
Murray Cres. Pnr 20 11 90 B
Murray Gr. N1 48 32 83 D
Murray Mews. NW1 47 29 84 D
Murray Rd. Nthwd 19 09 91 C
Murray Rd. Orp 100 46 68 B
Murray Rd. Rich 83 17 72 A
Murray Rd. SW19 95 23 70 B
Murray Rd. W5 60 17 78 A
Murray Sq. E16 58 40 81 D
Murray St. NW1 47 29 84 C
Murrays Yd. SE18 66 43 78 B
Murray Terr. NW3 46 26 85 B
Murtwell Dri. Chig 28 44 91 A
Musard Rd. W6 62 24 77 A
Musbury St. E1 57 35 81 C
Muscatel Pl. SE5 75 33 76 A
Muschamp Rd. Cars 104 27 65 A
Muschamp Rd. SE15 75 33 75 B
Muscovy St. EC3 8 33 80 A
Museum Pas. E2 57 35 82 A
Museum St. WC1 3 30 81 C
Musgrave Cres. SW6 73 25 76 A
Musgrave Ct. SW11 74 27 76 A
Musgrave Rd. Islw 71 15 76 B
Musgrove Cl. Barn 11 26 97 A
Musgrove Rd. SE14 76 36 76 A
Musjid Rd. SW11 73 26 76 D
Musquash Way. Houn 70 11 76 C
Muston Rd. E5 37 34 86 B
Muswell Ave. N10 24 28 90 D
Muswell Hill Bwy. N10 24 28 89 B
Muswell Hill. N10 24 29 89 C
Muswell Hill Pl. N10 24 28 89 D
Muswell Hill Rd. N10 24 28 89 C
Muswell Hill Rd. N6 36 28 88 C
Muswell Mews. N10 24 28 89 B
Muswell Rd. N10 24 28 90 D
Mutrix Rd. NW6 46 25 83 A
Mutton Pl. NW1 47 28 84 A
Muybridge Rd. N Mal 94 20 69 C
Myatt Rd. SW9 75 31 76 B
Mycenae Rd. SE3 65 40 77 A
Myddelton Ave. Enf 13 33 97 B
Myddelton Cl. Enf 13 33 97 B
Myddelton Gdns. N21 17 32 94 A
Myddelton Park. N20 15 26 93 B
Myddelton Pas. EC1 3 31 82 A
Myddelton Sq. EC1 3 31 82 A

Myddelton St. EC1 3 31 82 A
Myddelton Rd. N22 24 30 91 D
Myddelton Rd. N8 24 30 89 C
Mylis Cl. SE26 87 34 71 B
Mylne Cl. W6 61 22 78 C
Mylne St. EC1 3 31 82 A
Mylne St. EC1 48 31 83 C
Mynster Rd. Tedd 93 17 70 A
Myra St. SE2 66 46 78 A
Myrdle St. E1 57 34 81 C
Myron Pl. SE13 76 38 75 A
Myrtle Alley. SE18 66 43 79 C
Myrtle Ave. Felt 69 09 74 A
Myrtle Ave. Ruis 31 10 87 B
Myrtleberry Cl. E8 48 33 84 B
Myrtle Cl. Barn 16 27 94 D
Myrtle Cl. Eri 80 51 76 A
Myrtledene Rd. SE2 66 46 78 C
Myrtle Gdns. W7 54 15 80 C
Myrtle Gr. N Mal 94 20 69 C
Myrtle Rd. Croy 106 37 65 C
Myrtle Rd. E17 38 36 88 C
Myrtle Rd. E6 50 42 83 A
Myrtle Rd. Hamp 92 14 70 A
Myrtle Rd. Houn 70 14 76 C
Myrtle Rd. Ilf 40 43 86 B
Myrtle Rd. N13 17 32 93 C
Myrtle Rd. Rom 30 53 91 A
Myrtle Rd. Sutt 110 26 64 C
Myrtle Rd. W3 55 20 80 C
Myrtleside Cl. Nthwd 19 08 91 D
Myrtle Wlk. N1 48 33 83 C
Mysore Rd. SW11 74 27 75 D
Myton Rd. SE21 87 32 72 D

Nadine St. SE7 65 41 78 C
Nagle Cl. E17 26 38 90 D
Nag's Head La. Well 78 46 75 B
Nags Head Rd. Enf 14 36 96 D
Nairne Gr. SE24 75 32 74 B
Nairn Rd. Ruis 43 11 84 A
Nairn St. E14 58 38 81 A
Naish Ct. N1 47 30 83 A
Nallhead Rd. Felt 82 11 71 C
Namton Dr. Th Hth 96 30 68 D
Nanescombe. SE12 89 40 73 C
Nankin St. E14 57 37 81 C
Nansen Rd. SW11 74 28 75 A
Nansen Village. N12 15 25 92 B
Nantes Cl. SW18 73 26 75 C
Nantes Pas. E1 4 33 81 B
Nant Rd. NW2 35 24 86 B
Nant St. E2 57 34 82 B
Napier Ave. SW6 73 24 75 B
Napier Cl. SE8 64 36 77 D
Napier Cl. W14 62 24 79 D
Napier Ct. SW6 73 24 75 B
Napier Gr. N1 48 32 83 C
Napier Pl. W14 62 24 79 D
Napier Rd. Ashf 91 08 70 D
Napier Rd. Belv 67 48 78 B
Napier Rd. Brom 99 40 68 D
Napier Rd. E11 39 39 86 C
Napier Rd. E15 50 39 83 C
Napier Rd. E6 51 43 83 C
Napier Rd. Enf 14 35 95 B
Napier Rd. Islw 71 16 75 C
Napier Rd. N17 25 33 89 A
Napier Rd. NW10 55 22 82 B
Napier Rd. S Croy 112 32 63 D
Napier Rd. SE25 97 34 68 D
Napier Rd. W14 62 24 79 D
Napier Rd. Wem 44 17 84 B
Napier St. SE8 64 36 77 D
Napier Terr. N1 48 31 84 D
Napoleon Rd. E5 48 34 85 B
Napoleon Rd. E5 37 34 86 D
Napoleon Rd. Twick 83 16 73 B
Narbonne Ave. SW4 74 29 74 A
Narboro Ct. Rom 42 52 88 C
Narborough St. SW6 73 25 76 D
Narcissus Rd. NW6 46 25 85 C
Narford Rd. E5 37 34 86 A
Narrow St. E14 57 36 80 A
Narrow St. W3 55 19 80 D
Narrow Way. Brom 107 42 67 C
Nascot St. W12 56 23 81 C
Naseby Cl. Islw 71 15 76 A
Naseby Cl. NW6 46 26 84 C
Naseby Rd. Dag 41 49 86 C
Naseby Rd. Ilf 27 42 90 B
Naseby Rd. SE19 97 32 70 B
Nash Green. Brom 99 40 70 A
Nash Rd. N9 18 35 93 A
Nash Rd. Rom 29 47 89 D
Nash Rd. SE4 76 36 74 A
Nasmyth St. W6 61 22 79 D
Nassau Rd. SW13 72 21 76 B
Nassau St. W1 2 29 81 A
Nassington Rd. NW3 47 27 85 A
Natalie Cl. Felt 81 08 73 B
Natal Rd. Ilf 51 43 85 B
Natal Rd. N11 24 30 91 A
Natal Rd. SW16 96 29 70 B
Natal Rd. Th Hth 97 32 68 B
Nathans Rd. Wem 33 17 86 A
Nathan Way. SE28 66 45 79 D
Nation Way. E4 18 38 94 C
Naval Row. E14 58 38 80 A
Navarino Gr. E8 48 34 84 A
Navarino Rd. E8 48 34 84 A
Navarre Gdns. Rom 29 49 91 B
Navarre Rd. E6 50 42 83 C
Navarre St. E2 4 33 82 D
Navenby Wlk. E3 57 37 82 C
Navestock Cres. Wdf Gn 27 41 90 A
Navy St. SW4 74 29 75 B
Naylor Cl. Enf 14 35 95 B
Naylor Rd. N20 15 26 93 A
Naylor Rd. SE15 63 34 77 D
Neal Ave. Sthl 53 12 82 D
Neal Cl. Nthwd 19 10 90 A
Nealden St. SW9 74 30 75 B
Neale Cl. N2 23 26 89 A
Neal St. WC2 3 30 81 C
Neal's Yd. Eri 67 50 77 C
Neal's Yd. WC2 3 30 81 C
Near Acre. NW9 22 21 90 B
Neasden Cl. NW10 45 21 85 C
Neasden La. NW10 34 20 86 D
Neasden La. NW10 45 21 85 A
Neasham Rd. Dag 51 46 85 D
Neate St. SE5 63 33 77 A
Neath Gdns. Mord 103 26 67 C
Neathouse Pl. SW1 10 29 78 A
Neats Acre. Ruis 31 08 87 B
Neave Cres. Rom 30 53 90 B
Nebraska St. SE1 8 32 79 B
Neckinger Estate. SE16 8 33 79 D
Neckinger St. SE1 8 33 79 D
Nectarine Way. SE13 76 37 76 D
Needham Rd. W11 56 25 81 C
Needham Terr. NW2 35 23 86 D
Neeld Cres. NW4 34 22 88 B
Neeld Cres. Wem 45 19 85 C
Neil Cl. Ashf 81 08 71 C
Nelgarde Rd. SE6 88 37 73 A
Nella Rd. W6 62 23 77 B
Nelldale Rd. SE16 64 35 78 A
Nelmes Cl. Horn 42 54 88 B
Nelmes Cres. Horn 42 54 88 B
Nelmes Ct. Horn 30 53 89 D
Nelmes Rd. Horn 42 54 88 C
Nelmes Way. Horn 30 54 89 C
Nelson Cl. Croy 105 31 66 D
Nelson Cl. Rom 29 49 90 B
Nelson Gdns. E2 57 34 82 A
Nelson Gdns. Houn 70 13 74 C
Nelson Grove Rd. SW19 95 26 69 A
Nelson Pas. EC1 4 32 82 A
Nelson Pl. N1 48 31 83 D
Nelson Pl. Sid 90 46 71 A
Nelson Pl. W3 55 19 80 D
Nelson Rd. Belv 67 48 78 D
Nelson Rd. Brom 99 41 68 C
Nelson Rd. Dart 80 53 74 C
Nelson Rd. E11 27 40 89 D
Nelson Rd. E4 26 37 91 B
Nelson Rd. Enf 14 35 95 B
Nelson Rd. Har 33 15 87 C
Nelson Rd. Houn 70 13 74 C
Nelson Rd. N15 25 33 89 C
Nelson Rd. N8 36 30 88 D
Nelson Rd. N9 17 34 93 B
Nelson Rd. N.Mal 102 20 67 B
Nelson Rd. SE10 64 38 77 A
Nelson Rd. Sid 90 46 71 A
Nelson Rd. Stan 21 17 91 A
Nelson Rd. SW19 95 26 70 C
Nelson Rd. Twick 82 13 73 B
Nelson Sq. SE1 7 31 79 B
Nelsons Row. SW4 74 29 75 D
Nelson St. E16 58 39 80 B
Nelson St. E1 57 34 81 D
Nelson St. E6 50 42 83 D
Nelson St. E6 51 43 83 A
Nelson Terr. N1 48 31 83 D
Nelson Wlk. SE16 57 36 80 C
Nelwyn Ave. Horn 42 54 88 B
Nemoure Rd. W3 55 20 80 A
Nene Rd. Houn 69 07 76 B
Nepaul Rd. SW11 74 27 76 C
Nepean St. SW15 84 22 73 A
Neptune Rd. Har 32 14 88 D
Neptune Rd. Houn 69 08 76 B
Neptune St. SE16 64 35 79 C
Nero Ct. Brent 60 17 77 D
Nesbit Cl. SE3 77 39 76 C
Nesbit Rd. SE9 77 41 75 D
Nesbitts Alley. Barn 11 24 96 B
Ness Rd. Eri 68 53 77 B
Ness St. SE16 63 34 79 C
*Nesta Rd. Wdf Gn 27 39 91 B
Nestor Ave. N21 13 31 95 D
Netheravon Rd. W4 61 21 78 D
Netheravon Rd. W7 54 15 80 D
Netheravon Road S. W4 61 21 78 D
Netherbury Rd. W5 60 17 79 D
Netherby Gdns. Enf 12 30 96 C
Netherby Rd. SE23 88 35 73 A
Nether Cl. N3 23 25 91 C
Nethercourt Ave. N3 23 25 91 A
Netherfield Gdns. Bark 51 44 84 D
Netherfield Rd. N12 15 25 92 D
Netherfield Rd. SW17 86 28 72 C
Netherford Rd. SW4 74 29 76 C
Netherhall Gdns. NW3 46 26 85 C
Netherhall Way. NW3 46 26 85 C
Netherlands Rd. Barn 11 26 95 D
Netherleight Cl. N6 36 28 87 D
Netherpark Dri. Rom 30 51 90 D
Nether St. N12 15 25 92 D
Nether St. N3 23 25 91 C
Netherton Gr. SW10 62 26 77 A
Netherton Rd. N15 37 32 88 D
Netherton Rd. Twick 71 16 74 B
Netherwood Rd. W14 62 23 79 B
Netherwood St. NW6 46 24 84 B
Netley Cl. Sutt 110 23 64 D
Netley Gdns. Mord 103 26 66 A
Netley Rd (West). Houn 69 08 76 B
Netley Rd. Brent 60 18 77 A
Netley Rd. E17 38 36 88 B
Netley Rd. Houn 69 08 76 B
Netley Rd. Ilf 40 44 88 B
Netley Rd. Mord 103 26 66 A
Netley St. NW1 2 29 82 A
Nettlecombe Cl. Sutt 110 25 62 B
Nettleden Ave. Wem 45 19 84 A
Nettlefold Pl. SE27 87 31 72 D
Nettlestead Cl. Beck 98 36 70 D
Nettleton Rd. Houn 69 07 76 B
Nettleton Rd. SE14 76 35 76 B
Nettlewood Rd. SW16 96 29 70 D
Neuchatel Rd. SE6 88 36 72 B
Nevada St. SE10 64 38 77 A
Nevern Pl. SW5 62 25 78 A
Nevern Rd. SW5 62 25 78 A
Nevern Sq. SW5 62 25 78 A
Neville Ave. N Mal 94 20 69 B
Neville Cl. E11 39 39 86 D
Neville Cl. Houn 70 13 76 D
Neville Cl. NW1 47 29 83 D
Neville Cl. NW6 46 24 83 D
Neville Cl. SE15 75 34 76 A
Neville Cl. Sid 90 45 71 B
Neville Cl. W3 61 20 79 A
Neville Dri. N2 35 26 88 C
Neville Gdns. Dag 41 47 86 B
Neville Gill Cl. SW18 73 25 74 D
Neville Rd. Croy 105 32 66 B
Neville Rd. Dag 41 47 86 B
Neville Rd. E7 50 40 84 D
Neville Rd. Ilf 28 44 90 A
Neville Rd. King 94 19 69 C
Neville Rd. NW6 46 24 83 D
Neville Rd. Rich 83 17 72 A
Neville Rd. W5 54 17 82 D
Neville's Ct. NW2 34 22 86 C
Neville's Ct. NW2 34 22 86 C
Neville St. SW7 62 26 78 D
Neville Terr. SW7 62 26 78 D
Neville Wlk. Cars 104 27 66 A
Nevill Pl. N22 24 30 90 B
Nevill Rd. N16 48 33 85 A
Nevill Rd. N16 37 33 86 C
Nevin Dri. E4 18 37 94 D
Nevis Cl. Rom 30 51 91 A
Nevis Rd. SW17 86 28 72 A
Newall Rd. Houn 69 08 76 A
Newark Cres. NW10 55 20 82 B
Newark Rd. S Croy 112 32 63 B
Newark St. E1 57 34 81 B
Newark Way. NW4 22 22 89 A
New Barns Ave. Mit 96 29 68 D
New Barn St. E13 58 40 82 D
Newbery Rd. Eri 80 51 76 B
Newbolt Ave. Sutt 110 23 64 D
Newbolt Rd. Stan 21 15 91 B
New Bond St. W1 6 28 80 B
Newborough Green. N Mal 94 20 68 D
New Brent St. NW4 35 23 88 A
New Bridge St. EC4 3 31 81 D
New Broad St. EC2 4 33 81 A
New Broadway. W5 54 17 80 B
Newburgh Rd. W3 55 20 80 D
Newburgh St. W1 2 29 81 C
New Burlington Mews. W1 6 29 80 A
New Burlington Pl. W1 6 29 80 A
New Burlington St. W1 6 29 80 A
Newburn St. SE11 10 30 78 D
Newbury Cl. Nthlt 43 12 84 B
Newbury Cl. Rom 30 53 91 B
Newbury Gdns. Eps 109 21 64 B
Newbury Gdns. Horn 42 54 86 D
Newbury Gdns. Rom 30 53 91 B
Newbury Mews. NW5 47 28 84 A
Newbury Rd. Brom 99 40 68 A
Newbury Rd. E4 26 38 91 A
Newbury Rd. Houn 69 07 76 A
Newbury Rd. Ilf 40 45 88 C
Newbury Rd. Rom 30 53 91 B
Newbury St. EC1 4 32 81 A
Newbury Way. Nthlt 43 12 84 B
New Butt La. SE8 64 37 77 C
Newby Cl. Enf 13 33 97 C
Newby Pl. E14 58 38 80 A
Newby St. SW8 74 28 75 B
Newcastle Ave. Ilf 28 46 91 A
Newcastle Cl. EC4 3 31 81 D
Newcastle Ct. EC4 8 32 80 A
Newcastle Pl. W2 1 26 81 B
Newcastle Row. EC1 3 31 82 C
New Cavendish St. W1 2 28 81 B
New Change. EC4 4 32 81 C
New Chapel Sq. Felt 81 10 73 D
New Charles St. EC1 3 31 82 B
New Church Rd. SE5 63 32 77 B
New Church Rd. SE5 63 32 77 C
New City Rd. E13 58 41 82 A
New Cl. Felt 82 12 71 C
New Cl. SW19 95 26 68 A
New Colebrooke Ct. Cars 111 28 63 C
New College Mews. N1 48 31 84 C
Newcombe Park. Wem 44 18 83 B
Newcombe St. W8 56 25 80 C
Newcome Gdns. SW16 86 30 71 A
Newcomen Rd. E11 39 39 86 D
Newcomen Rd. SW11 73 26 75 B
Newcomen St. SE1 8 32 79 B
New Compton St. WC2 3 30 81 C
Newcourt St. NW8 47 27 83 C
New Coventry St. W1 6 29 80 B
New Cross Gate. SE14 76 35 76 B
New Cross Rd. SE14 76 35 76 B
New Ct. Dart 80 54 74 C
New Ct. EC4 7 31 80 A
New Ct. Nthlt 43 13 85 D
Newdales Cl. N9 17 34 93 A
Newdene Ave. Nthlt 43 11 83 D
Newell St. E14 57 36 80 B
New End. NW3 35 26 86 C
New End Sq. NW3 46 26 85 B
Newent Cl. Cars 104 27 66 D
Newent Cl. SE15 63 33 77 C
New Farm Ave. Brom 99 40 68 C
New Farm La. Nthwd 19 09 90 A
New Fetter La. EC4 3 31 81 C
Newfield Cl. Hamp 92 13 69 A
Newfield Rise. NW2 34 22 86 D
New Forest La. Chig 28 43 91 A
Newgale Gdns. Edg 21 18 90 B
Newgate Cl. Felt 82 12 72 C
Newgate. Croy 105 32 66 C
Newgate St. EC1 3 31 81 D
New Goulston St. E1 4 33 81 D
New Hall Dri. Rom 30 54 90 A
New Ham Rd. Houn 69 08 76 A
Newham's Row. SE1 8 33 79 A
Newham Way. E16 58 40 81 B
Newhaven Cres. Ashf 81 08 71 D
Newhaven Gdns. SE9 77 41 75 D
Newhaven Rd. SE25 105 32 67 B
New Heston Rd. Houn 59 12 77 D
Newhouse Ave. Rom 29 47 89 B
Newhouse Cl. N.Mal 102 21 66 A
Newhouse Wlk. Mord 103 26 66 A
Newick Cl. Bex 79 49 74 D
Newick Rd. E5 48 34 85 B
Newick Rd. E5 38 35 86 C
Newing Green. Brom 99 41 70 D
Newington Barrow Way. N7 36 30 86 D
Newington Butts. SE11 63 31 78 B
Newington Cswy. SE1 8 32 79 C
Newington Green. N5 48 32 85 D
Newington Green Rd. N1 48 32 85 D
New Inn Bwy. EC2 4 33 82 C
New Inn Pas. WC2 3 30 81 D
New Inn Sq. EC2 4 33 82 C
New Inn St. EC2 4 33 82 C
New Inn Yd. EC2 4 33 82 C
New Kent Rd. SE1 63 32 78 B
New King's Rd. SW6 73 25 76 C
New King St. SE8 64 37 77 A
Newland Cl. Pnr 20 12 91 B
Newland Ct. Wem 34 19 86 A
Newland Dri. Enf 13 34 97 B
Newland Gdns. W13 60 16 79 A
Newland Rd. N8 24 30 89 A
Newlands Ave. Surb 101 15 66 C
Newlands Cl. Sthl 59 12 78 C
Newlands Cl. Wem 44 17 84 A
Newlands Ct. SE9 78 43 74 C
Newlands Park. SE26 88 35 71 D
Newlands Pl. Barn 11 23 95 B
Newlands Rd. SW16 96 30 69 C
Newlands The. Wall 111 29 63 D
New London St. EC3 8 33 80 A
New Lydenburg St. SE7 65 41 79 C
Newlyn Gdns. Har 32 12 87 B
Newlyn Rd. Barn 11 24 96 D
Newlyn Rd. N17 25 33 90 B
Newlyn Rd. Well 78 45 76 D
Newman Cl. Horn 42 54 88 A
Newman Pas. W1 2 29 81 A
Newman Rd. Brom 99 40 69 A
Newman Rd. Croy 104 30 66 D
Newman Rd. E13 58 40 82 B
Newman Rd. E17 38 35 88 B
Newman Rd. Houn 69 07 76 A
Newman's Ct. EC3 4 32 81 D
Newman's Row. WC2 3 30 81 B
Newman St. W1 2 29 81 A
Newman's Way. Barn 11 26 97 A
Newmarket Ave. Nthlt 43 13 85 D
Newmarket Green. SE9 89 41 73 B
Newminster Rd. Mord 103 26 67 C
New Mount St. E15 49 38 84 D
Newnes Path. SW15 72 22 75 D
Newnham Ave. Ruis 32 11 87 C
Newnham Cl. Nthlt 43 14 84 A
Newnham Gdns. Nthlt 43 14 84 A
Newnham Rd. N22 24 30 90 B
Newnhams Cl. Brom 99 42 68 B
Newnham Terr. SE1 7 31 79 C
Newnham Way. Har 33 18 88 A
New North Pl. EC2 4 33 82 C
New North Rd. Ilf 28 45 91 B
New North Rd. N1 48 32 83 B
New North St. WC1 3 30 81 B
Newnton Cl. N4 37 32 87 B
New Oak Rd. N2 23 26 90 C
New Orleans Wlk. N19 36 29 87 B
New Oxford St. WC1 3 30 81 C
New Park Ave. N13 17 32 92 D
New Park Cl. Nthlt 43 12 84 A
New Park Estate. N18 18 35 92 C
New Park Rd. Ashf 81 08 71 C
New Park Rd. SW2 86 30 73 A
New Place Sq. SE16 63 34 79 D
New Plaistow Rd. E15 50 39 83 A
Newport Ave. E13 58 40 82 D
Newport Ct. WC2 6 29 80 B
Newport Pl. WC2 6 29 80 B
Newport Rd. E10 38 38 86 B
Newport Rd. E17 26 36 89 C
Newport Rd. Houn 69 07 76 A
Newport Rd. SW13 72 22 76 A
Newport St. SE11 10 30 78 B
Newquay Cres. Har 32 12 86 A
Newquay Rd. SE6 88 38 72 A
New Quebec St. W1 1 27 81 D
New Rd. Brent 60 17 77 B
New Rd. Dag 52 49 83 D
New Rd. E1 57 34 81 B
New Rd. E4 18 37 92 B
New Rd. E Mol 92 13 68 A
New Rd. Felt 69 08 74 D
New Rd. Felt 81 10 73 D
New Rd. Felt 82 12 71 C
New Rd. Har 44 15 85 B
New Rd. Hay 69 08 76 A
New Rd. Houn 70 13 75 D
New Rd. Ilf 40 45 86 A
New Rd. King 94 19 70 C
New Rd. Mit 104 28 66 C
New Rd. N17 25 33 90 B
New Rd. N2 24 27 90 A
New Rd. N8 36 30 88 A
New Rd. N9 17 34 93 A
New Rd. NW7 23 24 91 C
New Rd. Orp 108 46 66 A
New Rd. Rain 52 50 83 C
New Rd. Rich 83 17 71 A
New Rd. SE2 67 47 78 D
New Rd. Shep 91 07 68 B
New Rd. Well 78 46 76 D
New River Cres. N13 17 31 92 B
New River Wlk. N1 48 32 84 C
New Row. WC2 7 30 80 A
Newry Rd. Twick 71 16 74 A
Newsam Ave. N15 37 32 88 B
New Spring Gdns Wlk. SE11 10 30 78 C
New Sq. WC2 3 30 81 D
Newstead Ave. Orp 108 45 65 A
Newstead Rd. SE12 89 39 73 B
Newstead Way. SW19 85 24 71 A
Newstead Wlk. Cars 103 26 66 A
New St. EC2 4 33 81 A
New Street Hill. Brom 89 41 71 C
New Street Hill. SE12 89 41 71 D
New Street Sq. EC4 3 31 81 C
Newton Ave. N10 24 28 90 B
Newton Ave. W3 61 20 79 A
Newton Gr. W4 61 21 78 A
Newton Rd. E15 49 38 85 D
Newton Rd. Har 21 15 90 C
Newton Rd. Islw 71 15 76 D
Newton Rd. N15 37 34 88 A
Newton Rd. NW2 35 23 86 C
Newton Rd. SW19 95 24 70 C
Newton Rd. W2 56 25 81 D
Newton Rd. Well 78 46 75 A
Newton Rd. Wem 44 18 84 D
Newton St. WC2 3 30 81 C
Newton's Yd. SW18 73 25 74 A
Newton Way. N18 17 32 92 C
Newton Wlk. Edg 22 19 90 B
Newton Wlk. Edg 22 20 90 A
Newtown St. SW11 74 28 76 B
New Trinity Rd. N2 23 26 90 D
New Turnstile. WC2 3 30 81 B
New Union Cl. E14 64 38 79 C
New Union St. EC2 4 32 81 B
New Wanstead. E11 39 40 88 C
New Way Rd. NW9 22 21 89 C
New Wharf Rd. N1 47 30 83 C
Newyears Green La. Uxb 31 07 88 C
New Zealand Way. W12 55 22 80 B
Niagara Ave. W5 60 17 78 A
Niagara Ct. SE16 64 35 79 C
Nibthwaite Rd. Har 33 15 88 A
Nicholas Cl. Grnf 43 13 83 D
Nicholas Gdns. W5 60 17 79 B
Nicholas La. EC4 8 32 80 B
Nicholas Rd. Croy 111 30 64 A
Nicholas Rd. Dag 41 48 86 D
Nicholas Rd. E1 57 35 82 C
Nicholas Way. Nthwd 19 08 90 A
Nicholay Rd. N19 36 29 86 B
Nicholay Rd. N19 36 29 87 D
Nichol Cl. N14 16 29 94 D
Nicholes Rd. Houn 70 13 75 C
Nichol La. Brom 99 40 70 D
Nicholl St. E2 48 34 83 A
Nicholsfield Wlk. N7 47 30 85 D
Nichols Green. W5 54 18 81 D
Nicholson Rd. Croy 105 33 66 D
Nicholson St. SE1 7 31 80 D
Nicola Cl. Har 20 14 90 D
Nicola Cl. S Croy 112 32 63 A
Nicoll Pl. NW4 34 22 88 D
Nicoll Rd. NW10 45 21 83 A
Nicosia Rd. SW18 86 27 73 A
Niederwald Rd. SE26 88 36 71 A
Nigel Cl. Nthlt 43 12 83 A
Nigel Mews. Ilf 51 43 85 B
Nigel Playfair Ave. W6 61 22 78 D
Nigel Rd. E7 50 41 85 C
Nigel Rd. SE15 75 34 75 A
Nigeria Rd. SE7 65 41 77 D
Nightingale Cl. Car 104 28 65 A
Nightingale Cl. W4 61 20 77 A
Nightingale Dri. Eps 109 19 63 B
Nightingale Gr. SE13 76 38 74 B
Nightingale La. Brom 99 41 69 D
Nightingale La. E11 39 40 88 B
Nightingale La. N8 24 30 89 A
Nightingale La. Rich 83 18 73 A
Nightingale La. SW12 74 28 74 C

Nightingale Pl. SE18 .... 66 43 77 A
Nightingale Rd. Cars .... 104 27 65 D
Nightingale Rd. E5 .... 37 34 86 D
Nightingale Rd. Hamp .... 92 13 70 A
Nightingale Rd. N22 .... 24 30 91 D
Nightingale Rd. N9 .... 18 35 94 D
Nightingale Rd. NW10 .... 45 21 83 D
Nightingale Rd. Orp .... 108 44 67 C
Nightingale Rd. W7 .... 54 15 80 D
Nightingale Sq. SW12 .... 86 28 73 A
Nightingale Vale. SE18 .... 66 43 77 A
Nightingale Wlk. SW4 .... 74 28 74 D
Nile Path. SE18 .... 66 43 77 A
Nile Rd. E13 .... 50 41 83 C
Nile St. N1 .... 4 32 82 B
Nile Terr. SE15 .... 63 33 78 D
Nimbus Rd. Eps .... 109 20 62 D
Nimegen Way. SE22 .... 75 33 74 B
Nimrod Pas. N1 .... 48 33 84 A
Nimrod Rd. Houn .... 69 07 76 A
Nimrod Rd. SW16 .... 86 28 71 D
Nimrod Way. Houn .... 69 07 76 A
Nine Acres Cl. E12 .... 50 42 85 C
Nine Elms La. SW8 .... 10 29 77 B
Nineteenth Rd. Mit .... 96 30 68 C
Nisbet House. E9 .... 49 35 85 D
Nithdale Rd. SE18 .... 66 43 77 D
Nithsdale Gr. Ruis .... 31 08 86 C
Niton Cl. Barn .... 11 23 95 D
Niton Rd. Rich .... 72 19 75 A
Niton St. SW6 .... 62 23 77 D
Nobel Rd. N18 .... 18 35 92 A
Noble Cnr. Houn .... 70 13 76 A
Noble St EC2 .... 4 32 81 C
Noel Park Rd. N22 .... 25 31 90 C
Noel Rd. N1 .... 48 31 83 D
Noel Rd. W3 .... 55 19 81 D
Noel Sq. Dag .... 52 47 85 A
Noel St. W1 .... 2 29 81 C
Nolan Way. E5 .... 48 34 85 A
Nolton Pl. Edg .... 21 18 90 B
Nonsuch Cl. Ilf .... 28 43 91 B
Nonsuch Court Ave. .... 109 22 62 D
Nonsuch Wlk. Sutt .... 110 23 62 D
Nora Gdns. NW4 .... 23 23 89 D
Norbiton Ave. King .... 94 19 69 C
Norbiton Common Rd. King .... 94 19 68 B
Norbiton Hall. King .... 93 18 69 D
Norbiton Rd. E14 .... 57 36 81 D
Norbroke St. W12 .... 55 21 80 B
Norburn St. W10 .... 56 24 81 A
Norbury Ave. Houn .... 70 14 75 D
Norbury Ave. SW16 .... 96 30 69 B
Norbury Ave. Th Hth .... 97 31 69 D
Norbury Brook. Th Hth .... 105 32 67 A
Norbury Cl. SW16 .... 97 31 69 A
Norbury Court Rd. SW16 .... 96 30 69 C
Norbury Cres. SW16 .... 97 31 69 C
Norbury Cross. SW16 .... 96 30 68 A
Norbury Gdns. Rom .... 41 47 88 B
Norbury Hill. SW16 .... 97 31 70 D
Norbury Rd. E4 .... 18 37 92 C
Norbury Rd. Th Hth .... 97 32 69 C
Norbury Rise. SW16 .... 96 30 68 A
Norcombe Gdns. Har .... 33 17 88 A
Norcott Cl. Hay .... 53 11 82 C
Norcott Rd. N16 .... 37 34 86 C
Norcroft Gdns. SE22 .... 87 34 73 A
Norcutt Rd. Twick .... 83 15 73 C
Nordenfeldt Rd. Eri .... 67 50 78 D
Norfolk Ave. N13 .... 25 31 91 B
Norfolk Ave. N15 .... 37 33 88 D
Norfolk Ave. S Croy .... 112 34 62 C
Norfolk Cl. Barn .... 12 28 96 C
Norfolk Cl. N13 .... 25 31 91 B
Norfolk Cl. N2 .... 24 27 89 A
Norfolk Cl. Twick .... 71 16 74 D
Norfolk Cres. Sid .... 90 45 73 A
Norfolk Cres. W2 .... 1 27 81 C
Norfolk Gdns. Bexh .... 79 48 76 B
Norfolk House Rd. SW16 .... 86 30 72 C
Norfolk Pl. W2 .... 1 26 81 D
Norfolk Pl. Well .... 78 46 76 C
Norfolk Rd. Bark .... 51 45 84 C
Norfolk Rd. Barn .... 11 25 96 A
Norfolk Rd. Dag .... 52 49 85 D
Norfolk Rd. E17 .... 26 35 90 D
Norfolk Rd. E6 .... 51 43 83 A
Norfolk Rd. Enf .... 13 34 95 B
Norfolk Rd. Felt .... 82 11 73 C
Norfolk Rd. Har .... 32 13 88 B
Norfolk Rd. Ilf .... 40 45 87 A
Norfolk Rd. NW10 .... 45 21 84 C
Norfolk Rd. NW8 .... 46 26 83 B
Norfolk Rd. Rom .... 41 50 88 C
Norfolk Rd. SW19 .... 96 27 70 A
Norfolk Rd. Th Hth .... 97 32 68 A
Norfolk Row. SE11 .... 10 30 78 B
Norfolk Sq. Mews. W2 .... 1 26 81 D
Norfolk Sq. W2 .... 1 26 81 D
Norfolk St. E7 .... 50 40 85 C
Norgrove St. SW12 .... 86 28 73 A
Norhyrst Ave. SE25 .... 97 33 68 B
Norland Pl. W11 .... 56 24 80 C
Norland Rd. W11 .... 56 23 80 D
Norlands Cres. Chis .... 100 43 69 B
Norland Sq. W11 .... 56 24 80 C
Norley Vale. SW15 .... 84 22 73 C
Norlington Rd. E10 .... 38 38 87 C
Norlington Rd. E11 .... 38 38 87 D
Norman Ave. Felt .... 82 12 78 B
Norman Ave. N22 .... 25 32 90 A
Norman Ave. S Croy .... 112 32 62 C
Norman Ave. Sthl .... 53 12 80 A
Norman Ave. Twick .... 83 17 73 A
Normanby Cl. SW15 .... 73 24 74 B
Norman Cl. Orp .... 108 44 65 C
Norman Cl. Rom .... 29 49 90 D
Norman Cres. Houn .... 59 11 77 D
Norman Cres. Pnr .... 20 11 90 A
Normand Mews. W14 .... 62 24 77 A
Normand Rd. W14 .... 62 24 77 B
Normandy Ave. Barn .... 11 24 96 D
Normanby Rd. NW10 .... 45 21 85 B
Normandy Rd. SW9 .... 75 31 76 A
Normandy Terr. E16 .... 58 40 81 D
Normandy Way. Eri .... 80 51 76 A
Norman Gr. E3 .... 49 36 83 C
Normanhurst. Ashf .... 81 07 71 C
Normanhurst Ave. Bexh .... 79 47 76 B
Normanhurst Ave. Well .... 79 47 76 B
Normanhurst Dri. Twick .... 71 16 74 B
Normanhurst Rd. Orp .... 100 46 69 D
Normanhurst Rd. SW2 .... 86 30 72 B
Norman Rd. Ashf .... 91 08 70 B
Norman Rd. Belv .... 67 49 79 B
Norman Rd. E11 .... 39 39 86 A
Norman Rd. Horn .... 42 52 87 B
Norman Rd. Ilf .... 51 43 85 D
Norman Rd. N15 .... 37 33 88 B
Norman Rd. SE10 .... 64 37 77 D
Norman Rd. Sutt .... 110 25 64 C
Norman Rd. SW19 .... 95 26 70 C
Norman Rd. Th Hth .... 105 31 67 B
Normans Cl. NW10 .... 45 20 84 B
Normansfield Ave. Tedd .... 93 17 70 C
Normanshire Dri. E4 .... 18 37 92 B
Normans Mead. NW10 .... 45 20 84 B
Norman St. EC1 .... 4 32 82 A
Normanton Ave. SW19 .... 85 25 72 A
Normanton Rd. S Croy .... 112 33 63 A
Normanton St. SE23 .... 88 35 72 B
Norman Way. N14 .... 16 30 93 A
Norman Way. W3 .... 55 19 81 B
Normington Cl. SW16 .... 87 31 71 C
Norrice Lea. N2 .... 35 26 88 B
Norris St. SW1 .... 6 29 80 B
Norris Way. Dart .... 80 51 75 B
Norroy Rd. SW15 .... 73 23 75 D
Norrys Cl. Barn .... 12 27 96 D
Norrys Rd. Barn .... 12 27 96 D
Norseman Way. Grnf .... 43 13 83 B
Norstead Pl. SW15 .... 84 22 72 A
North Access Rd. E17 .... 38 35 88 D
North Acre. NW9 .... 22 21 90 A
North Acton Rd. NW .... 45 20 82 B
Northall Rd. Bexh .... 79 50 76 C
Northampton Bldgs. EC1 .... 3 31 82 C
Northampton Gr. N1 .... 48 32 85 D
Northampton Park. N1 .... 48 32 84 B
Northampton Rd. Croy .... 105 34 65 A
Northampton Rd. EC1 .... 3 31 82 C
Northampton Rd. Enf .... 14 36 96 C
Northampton Sq. EC1 .... 3 31 82 B
Northampton St. N1 .... 48 32 84 C
Northanger Rd. SW16 .... 96 30 70 A
North Audley St. W1 .... 6 28 80 A
North Ave. Cars .... 111 28 63 C
North Ave. Har .... 32 13 88 D
North Ave. N18 .... 17 34 92 A
North Ave. Rich .... 72 19 76 A
North Ave. Sthl .... 53 12 80 B
North Ave. W10 .... 56 23 82 A
North Ave. W13 .... 54 16 81 B
North Bank. NW8 .... 1 27 82 A
Northbank Rd. E17 .... 26 38 90 C
North Birkbeck Rd. E11 .... 38 38 86 D
Northborough Rd. SW16 .... 96 30 69 C
Northbourne. Brom .... 107 40 66 A
Northbourne Rd. SW4 .... 74 29 74 B
Northbrook Dri. Nthwd .... 19 09 91 C
Northbrook Rd. Barn .... 11 24 95 C
Northbrook Rd. Croy .... 105 32 67 B
Northbrook Rd. Ilf .... 40 43 86 A
Northbrook Rd. N22 .... 24 30 91 C
Northbrook Rd. SE13 .... 77 39 74 A
Northburgh St. EC1 .... 3 31 82 D
North Carriage Dri. W2 .... 5 27 80 A
Northchurch Rd. N1 .... 48 32 84 D
Northchurch Rd. Wem .... 45 19 84 A
Northchurch Terr. N1 .... 48 33 84 C
North Circular Rd. E17 .... 26 38 90 A
North Circular Rd. E18 .... 27 40 90 A
North Circular Rd. E4 .... 26 36 91 B
North Circular Rd. Ilf .... 27 42 89 D
North Circular Rd. N11 .... 24 29 91 A
North Circular Rd. N12 .... 23 26 90 B
North Circular Rd. N12 .... 24 27 91 C
North Circular Rd. N13 .... 17 31 92 C
North Circular Rd. N18 .... 17 34 92 C
North Circular Rd. N3 .... 23 25 89 B
North Circular Rd. N3 .... 23 25 89 B
North Circular Rd. NW10 .... 45 19 84 D
North Circular Rd. NW11 .... 35 24 88 A
North Circular Rd. NW2 .... 34 22 87 C
North Circular Rd. NW2 .... 34 22 87 C
North Circular Rd. W3 .... 61 19 79 C
North Circular Rd. W4 .... 61 19 78 A
North Circular Rd. W5 .... 54 18 81 D
North Circular Rd. Wdf Gn .... 27 41 90 D
North Cl. Barn .... 11 23 95 A
North Cl. Bexh .... 79 47 75 D
North Cl. Dag .... 52 49 83 A
North Cl. Felt .... 69 08 74 D
Northcliffe Cl. Wor Pk .... 102 21 65 C
Northcliffe Dri. N20 .... 15 24 94 D
North Cl. Mord .... 95 24 68 C
North Common Rd. W5 .... 54 18 80 A
Northcote Ave. Islw .... 71 16 74 A
Northcote Ave. Sthl .... 53 12 80 A
Northcote Ave. Surb .... 102 19 66 B
Northcote Ave. W5 .... 54 18 80 A
Northcote. Pnr .... 20 11 90 C
Northcote Rd. Croy .... 105 32 67 D
Northcote Rd. E17 .... 26 36 89 C
Northcote Rd. N Mal .... 94 20 68 B
Northcote Rd. NW10 .... 45 21 84 C
Northcote Rd. Sid .... 90 45 71 A
Northcote Rd. SW11 .... 74 27 74 B
Northcote Rd. Twick .... 71 16 74 A
Northcott Ave. N22 .... 24 30 90 A
North Countess Rd. E17 .... 26 36 90 B
Northcourt. W1 .... 2 29 81 A
North Cres. N3 .... 23 24 90 D
North Cres. WC1 .... 2 29 81 B
Northcroft Rd. Eps .... 109 21 63 C
Northcroft Rd. W13 .... 60 16 79 D
North Crofts. SE23 .... 87 34 73 D
North Cross Rd. Ilf .... 28 44 89 C
North Cross Rd. SE22 .... 75 33 74 B
Northdene Gdns. N15 .... 37 33 88 D
North Dene. Houn .... 70 13 76 B
Northdown Cl. Ruis .... 31 09 86 D
Northdown Gdns. Ilf .... 40 45 88 A
Northdown Rd. Horn .... 42 52 87 B
Northdown Rd. Sutt .... 110 25 62 C
Northdown Rd. Well .... 79 47 76 C
Northdown St. N1 .... 47 30 83 D
North Dri. Houn .... 70 14 76 C
North Dri. Rom .... 30 53 89 A
North Dri. Ruis .... 31 09 87 A
North Dri. SW16 .... 86 29 71 A
North End Ave. NW3 .... 35 26 86 A
North End Cre. W14 .... 62 24 78 B
North End. Croy .... 105 32 65 A
North End. NW3 .... 35 26 86 A
Northend Rd. Eri .... 80 51 76 B
North End Rd. NW11 .... 35 25 87 D
North End Rd. SW6 .... 62 25 77 A
North End Rd. W14 .... 62 24 78 D
North End Rd. Wem .... 34 19 86 C
North End Way. NW3 .... 35 26 86 A
Northern Ave. N9 .... 17 33 93 B
Northernhay Wlk. Mord .... 95 24 68 C
Northern Perimeter Rd (West). Houn .... 69 07 76 A
Northern Perimeter Rd. Houn .... 69 08 76 B
Northern Rd. E13 .... 50 40 83 D
Northey Ave. Sutt .... 110 24 62 C
North Eyot Gdns. W6 .... 61 21 78 D
Northey St. E14 .... 57 36 80 A
Northfield Ave. Pnr .... 20 11 89 D
Northfield Ave. W13 .... 60 16 79 B
Northfield Ave. W5 .... 60 17 79 C
Northfield Cres. Sutt .... 110 24 64 A
Northfield Gdns. Dag .... 52 48 85 B
Northfield Path. Dag .... 52 48 85 B
Northfield Rd. Barn .... 12 27 96 A
Northfield Rd. Dag .... 52 48 85 B
Northfield Rd. E6 .... 50 42 84 D
Northfield Rd. Enf .... 13 34 95 B
North Field Rd. Houn .... 59 11 77 B
Northfield Rd. N16 .... 37 33 87 A
Northfield Rd. W13 .... 60 16 79 B
Northfields Rd. W3 .... 55 20 81 A
Northfields. SW18 .... 73 25 75 C
North Folgate. E1 .... 4 33 81 A
Northgate. Nthwd .... 19 08 91 C
North Gdns. SW19 .... 95 26 70 D
North Gower St. NW1 .... 2 29 82 A
North Green. NW9 .... 22 21 91 C
North Gr. N15 .... 37 32 88 B
North Gr. N6 .... 36 28 87 A
North Hatton Rd. Houn .... 69 08 76 B
North Hill Ave. N6 .... 36 27 88 D
North Hill. N6 .... 36 28 88 C
North Hyde La. Houn .... 59 12 77 A
North Hyde La. Sthl .... 59 12 78 C
Northiam. N12 .... 15 25 93 C
Northiam St. E2 .... 48 34 83 B
Northiam St. E9 .... 49 35 83 A
Northington St. WC1 .... 3 30 82 D
Northlands St. SE5 .... 75 32 76 C
North La. Tedd .... 93 15 70 B
North Lodge Cl. SW15 .... 73 23 74 B
North Mall. N9 .... 17 34 93 B
North Mews. WC1 .... 3 30 82 D
Northolme Gdns. Edg .... 22 19 90 A
Northolme Rd. N5 .... 48 32 85 A
Northolme Rise. Orp .... 108 45 65 A
Northolt Ave. Ruis .... 43 11 85 C
Northolt Gdns. Grnf .... 44 15 85 D
Northolt Rd. Har .... 32 14 86 C
Northover. Brom .... 89 39 72 D
North Park. SE9 .... 78 43 74 C
North Pas. SW18 .... 73 25 75 C
North Pl. Mit .... 96 27 70 D
North Pl. Tedd .... 93 15 70 B.
North Pole Rd. W10 .... 56 23 81 A
Northport St. N1 .... 48 33 83 A
North Rd. Belv .... 67 49 79 D
North Rd. Brent .... 60 18 77 A
North Rd. Brom .... 99 40 69 B
North Rd. Dart .... 80 52 74 C
North Rd. Edg .... 22 19 90 B
North Rd. Felt .... 69 08 74 D
North Rd. Ilf .... 40 45 86 A
North Rd. N2 .... 24 27 90 A
North Rd. N6 .... 36 28 87 A
North Rd. N7 .... 47 30 84 A
North Rd. N9 .... 17 34 94 D
North Rd. Rich .... 72 19 76 C
North Rd. Rom .... 41 48 88 A
North Rd. SE18 .... 66 45 78 A
North Rd. Sthl .... 53 13 80 A
North Rd. Surb .... 101 17 67 D
North Rd. SW19 .... 95 26 70 A
North Rd. W5 .... 60 17 79 D
North Rd. W Wick .... 106 37 66 D
Northrop Rd. Houn .... 69 09 76 A
North Row. W1 .... 6 28 80 A
Northside Rd. Brom .... 99 40 69 A
North Side Wandsworth Common. SW18 .... 73 26 74 B
Northspur Rd. Sutt .... 103 25 65 C
North Sq. N9 .... 17 34 93 B
North Sq. NW11 .... 35 25 88 A
North St. Bark .... 51 44 84 C
North St. Bexh .... 79 49 75 C
North St. Brom .... 99 40 69 A
North St. Cars .... 111 27 64 B
North St. E13 .... 50 40 83 D
Northstead Rd. SW2 .... 87 31 72 A
North St. Horn .... 42 53 87 D
North St. Islw .... 71 16 75 A
North St. NW4 .... 35 23 88 A
North St Pas. E13 .... 50 40 83 D
North St. Rom .... 29 50 89 D
North St. Rom .... 29 50 89 D
North St. Rom .... 42 51 88 A
North St. SW4 .... 74 29 75 A
North Tenter St. E1 .... 4 33 81 D
North Terr. SW3 .... 5 27 79 C
Northumberland Alley. EC3 .... 4 33 81 C
Northumberland Ave. E12 .... 39 41 87 C
Northumberland Ave. Enf .... 13 34 97 B
Northumberland Ave. Horn .... 42 53 88 A
Northumberland Ave. Islw .... 60 16 77 C
Northumberland Ave. WC2 .... 7 30 80 C
Northumberland Ave. Well .... 78 45 75 A
Northumberland Cl. Eri .... 67 50 77 C
Northumberland Cres. Felt .... 69 09 74 C
Northumberland Gdns. Mit .... 104 29 67 B
Northumberland Gdns. N9 .... 17 33 93 D
Northumberland Gr. N17 .... 25 34 91 D
Northumberland Park. Eri .... 67 50 77 C
Northumberland Park. N17 .... 25 34 91 C
Northumberland Pl. Rich .... 71 17 74 B
Northumberland Pl. W2 .... 56 25 81 C
Northumberland Rd. Barn .... 15 26 94 A
Northumberland Rd. E17 .... 38 37 87 A
Northumberland Rd. Har .... 32 13 88 A
Northumberland St. WC2 .... 7 30 80 C
Northumberland Way. Eri .... 79 50 76 B
Northumbria St. E14 .... 57 37 81 C
North Verbena Gdns. W6 .... 61 22 78 C
Northview Cres. NW10 .... 45 21 85 B
Northview Dri. Wdf Gn .... 27 41 90 D
North View. Pnr .... 32 11 87 A
North View Rd. N8 .... 24 29 89 B
North View. SW19 .... 85 23 71 C
North View. W5 .... 54 17 82 C
North Villas. NW1 .... 47 29 84 B
Northway. Mord .... 95 24 68 C
North Way. N11 .... 24 29 91 A
North Way. N9 .... 18 35 93 B
Northway. NW11 .... 35 25 88 B
North Way. NW9 .... 22 19 89 B
North Way. Pnr .... 20 11 89 D
Northway Rd. Croy .... 105 33 66 B
Northway Rd. SE5 .... 75 32 75 A
Northway. Wall .... 111 29 64 A
North West Pier. E1 .... 57 34 80 D
Northwest Pl. N1 .... 48 31 83 C
North Wharf Rd. W2 .... 1 26 81 B
Northwick Ave. Har .... 33 16 88 D
Northwick Circ. Har .... 33 17 88 C
Northwick Cl. NW8 .... 1 26 82 D
Northwick Park Rd. Har .... 33 15 88 D
Northwick Rd. Wem .... 44 17 83 B
Northwick Terr. NW8 .... 1 26 82 D
Northwick Wlk. Har .... 33 15 87 B
Northwold Dri. Pnr .... 20 11 89 A
Northwold Rd. E5 .... 37 34 86 A
Northwold Rd. N16 .... 37 33 86 B
Northwood Gdns. Grnf .... 44 15 85 D
Northwood Gdns. Ilf .... 28 43 89 C
Northwood Gdns. N12 .... 15 26 92 D
Northwood Hills Circ. Nthwd .... 19 10 90 A
Northwood Pl. Belv .... 67 48 79 D
Northwood Rd. Cars .... 111 28 63 A
Northwood Rd. N6 .... 36 28 87 B
Northwood Rd. SE23 .... 88 36 73 D
Northwood Rd. Th Hth .... 97 32 69 A
Northwood Way. Nthwd .... 19 10 91 C
Northwood Way. SE19 .... 97 33 70 A
North Woolwich Rd. E16 .... 58 40 80 D
North Worple Way. SW14 .... 72 20 75 B
Norton Ave. Surb .... 102 19 66 B
Norton Cl. E4 .... 18 37 92 C
Norton Gdns. SW16 .... 96 30 69 C
Norton Rd. Dag .... 52 50 84 B
Norton Rd. E10 .... 38 36 87 D
Norton Rd. Wem .... 44 17 84 B
Norval Rd. Wem .... 33 16 87 D
Norway Pl. E14 .... 57 36 81 D
Norway St. SE10 .... 64 37 77 B
Norwich Rd. E7 .... 50 40 85 C
Norwich Rd. Grnf .... 43 13 83 B
Norwich Rd. Nthwd .... 19 09 89 B
Norwich Rd. Th Hth .... 97 32 68 A
Norwich St. EC4 .... 3 31 81 C
Norwich Wlk. Edg .... 22 20 91 C
Norwood Ave. Rom .... 42 51 87 A
Norwood Ave. Wem .... 44 18 83 D
Norwood Cl. Sthl .... 59 13 78 A
Norwood Cres. Houn .... 69 08 76 A
Norwood Dri. Har .... 32 13 88 C
Norwood Gdns. Hay .... 53 11 82 C
Norwood Gdns. Sthl .... 59 12 78 B
Norwood Green Rd. Sthl .... 59 13 78 A
Norwood High St. SE27 .... 87 32 71 A
Norwood Park Rd. SE27 .... 87 32 71 C
Norwood Rd. SE24 .... 87 31 73 B
Norwood Rd. SE27 .... 87 31 72 B
Norwood Rd. Sthl .... 59 12 78 B
Notley St. SE5 .... 63 32 77 D
Notson Rd. SE25 .... 97 34 68 D
Notting Barn Rd. W10 .... 56 23 82 D
Nottingdale Sq. W11 .... 56 24 80 C
Nottingham Ave. E16 .... 58 41 81 C
Nottingham Ct. WC2 .... 3 30 81 C
Nottingham Pl. W1 .... 2 28 81 A
Nottingham Rd. E10 .... 38 38 88 C
Nottingham Rd. Islw .... 71 15 76 D
Nottingham Rd. S Croy .... 112 32 64 C
Nottingham Rd. SW17 .... 86 27 73 D
Nottingham St. W1 .... 2 28 81 A
Notting Hill Gate. W11 .... 56 25 80 C
Nova Mews. Mord .... 103 24 66 A
Novar Cl. Orp .... 108 45 66 B
Nova Rd. Croy .... 105 32 66 A
Novar Rd. SE9 .... 90 44 73 C
Novello St. SW6 .... 73 25 76 A
Nowell Rd. SW13 .... 61 22 77 A
Nower Hill. Pnr .... 20 12 89 D
Noyna Rd. SW17 .... 86 27 72 D
Nuding Cl. SE13 .... 76 37 75 A
Nugent Rd. N19 .... 36 30 87 C
Nugent Rd. SE25 .... 97 33 68 B
Nugent's Park. Pnr .... 20 12 90 B
Nugent Terr. NW8 .... 46 26 83 C
Nun Ct. EC2 .... 4 32 81 D
Nuneaton Rd. Dag .... 52 48 84 C
Nunhead Cres. SE15 .... 75 34 75 B
Nunhead Gr. SE15 .... 76 35 75 A
Nunhead La. SE15 .... 75 34 75 B
Nunhead Pas. SE15 .... 75 34 75 B
Nunnington Cl. SE9 .... 89 42 72 C
Nunn's Rd. Enf .... 13 32 97 C
Nupton Dri. Barn .... 11 23 95 C
Nursery Ave. Bexh .... 79 48 75 B
Nursery Ave. Croy .... 106 35 65 B
Nursery Ave. N3 .... 23 26 90 C
Nursery Cl. Croy .... 106 35 65 B
Nursery Cl. Enf .... 14 35 97 B
Nursery Cl. Eps .... 109 21 62 C
Nursery Cl. Felt .... 81 10 73 B
Nursery Cl. Orp .... 108 46 66 A
Nursery Cl. Rom .... 41 47 88 B
Nursery Cl. SW15 .... 73 23 75 D
Nursery Ct. N17 .... 25 33 91 D
Nursery Gdns. Enf .... 14 35 97 B
Nursery Gdns. Sun .... 91 09 69 D
Nursery La. E7 .... 50 40 84 B
Nursery La. W10 .... 56 23 81 A
Nursery Rd. E9 .... 49 35 84 A
Nursery Rd. Mit .... 96 27 68 A
Nursery Rd. N14 .... 16 29 94 A
Nursery Rd. N2 .... 23 26 90 B
Nursery Rd. Pnr .... 20 11 89 A
Nursery Rd. Sun .... 91 09 69 D
Nursery Rd. Sutt .... 110 26 64 A
Nursery Rd. SW19 .... 95 24 70 C
Nursery Rd. SW19 .... 95 25 69 D
Nursery Rd. SW9 .... 74 30 75 D
Nursery Rd. Th Hth .... 97 32 68 D
Nursery Row. Barn .... 11 24 96 A
Nursery St. N17 .... 25 33 91 D
Nursery The. Eri .... 68 51 77 D
Nursery Wlk. NW4 .... 23 23 89 A
Nursery Wlk. Rom .... 41 50 88 D
Nurstead Rd. Eri .... 67 49 77 C
Nutbourne St. W10 .... 56 24 82 A
Nutbrook St. SE15 .... 75 34 75 A
Nutbrowne Rd. Dag .... 52 48 83 B
Nutcroft Rd. SE15 .... 63 34 77 D
Nutfield Cl. N18 .... 25 34 91 A
Nutfield Gdns. Ilf .... 40 46 86 A
Nutfield Gdns. Nthlt .... 43 11 83 C
Nutfield Pas. Th Hth .... 97 31 68 D
Nutfield Pl. Th Hth .... 97 31 68 D
Nutfield Rd. E15 .... 49 38 85 A
Nutfield Rd. NW2 .... 34 22 86 C
Nutfield Rd. SE22 .... 75 33 75 D
Nutfield Rd. Th Hth .... 97 31 68 D
Nutfield Way. Orp .... 108 43 65 B
Nutford Pl. W1 .... 1 27 81 D
Nuthurst Ave. SW2 .... 86 30 72 B
Nutley Terr. NW3 .... 46 26 84 B
Nuttall St. N1 .... 48 33 83 C
Nutter La. E11 .... 39 41 88 A
Nutt St. SE15 .... 63 33 77 D
Nutty La. Shep .... 91 08 68 A
Nutwell St. SW17 .... 86 27 71 C
Nuxley Rd. Belv .... 67 49 78 C
Nyanza St. SE18 .... 66 44 77 B
Nye Bevan Estate. E5 .... 38 35 86 D
Nylands Ave. Rich .... 72 19 76 C
Nymans Gdns. SW20 .... 94 22 68 B
Nynehead St. SE14 .... 64 36 77 C
Nyon Gr. SE6 .... 88 36 72 B
Nyssa Cl. Wdf Gn .... 27 42 91 B
Nyton Cl. N19 .... 36 30 87 C

Oak Ave. Croy .... 106 37 65 B
Oak Ave. Enf .... 12 30 97 B
Oak Ave. Hamp .... 92 12 70 B
Oak Ave. Houn .... 59 12 77 C
Oak Ave. N10 .... 24 28 91 D

Oak Ave. N17 ...25 33 91 C
Oak Ave. N8 ...24 30 89 C
Oak Ave. Uxb ...31 07 86 B
Oakbank Gr. SE24 ...75 32 75 C
Oakbrook Cl. SE12 ...89 40 71 B
Oakbury Rd. SW6 ...73 25 76 D
Oak Cl. N14 ...16 28 94 B
Oak Cl. Sutt ...103 26 65 A
Oakcombe Cl. N Mal ...94 21 69 A
Oak Cottage Cl. SE6 ...89 39 73 D
Oak Cres. E18 ...58 39 81 A
Oakcroft Cl. Pnr ...19 10 90 D
Oakcroft Rd. Chess ...101 18 65 D
Oakcroft Rd. SE13 ...76 38 76 D
*Oakcroft Villas. Chess ...101 18 65 D
Oakdale Av. Har ...33 18 88 A
Oakdale Ave. Nthwd ...19 10 90 C
Oakdale. Beck ...98 38 69 A
Oakdale. N14 ...16 28 94 D
Oakdale Rd. E11 ...38 38 86 B
Oakdale Rd. E18 ...27 40 90 D
Oakdale Rd. E7 ...50 40 84 D
Oakdale Rd. Eps ...109 20 62 B
Oakdale Rd. N4 ...37 32 88 D
Oakdale Rd. SE15 ...76 35 75 A
Oakdale Rd. SW16 ...86 30 71 C
Oakdene Ave. Chis ...90 43 71 A
Oakdene Ave. Chis ...90 43 71 A
Oakdene Ave. Eri ...67 50 77 A
Oakdene Ave. Surb ...101 16 66 C
Oak Dene Cl. Horn ...42 52 88 D
Oakdene Cl. Pnr ...20 12 91 D
Oakdene Dri. Surb ...102 20 66 C
Oakdene Park. N3 ...23 24 91 D
Oakdene Rd. Orp ...108 46 67 C
Oak Dene. W13 ...54 16 81 B
Oakden St. SE11 ...63 31 78 A
Oake Ct. SW15 ...73 24 74 A
Oakenshaw Cl. Surb ...101 18 66 A
Oakeshott Av. N6 ...36 28 86 A
Oakey La. SE1 ...7 31 79 C
Oakfield Av. Har ...21 16 89 B
Oakfield Cl. N8 ...36 30 87 A
Oakfield Cl. N.Mal ...102 21 67 B
Oakfield. E4 ...18 37 92 D
Oakfield Gdns. Beck ...106 37 67 A
Oakfield Gdns. Cars ...104 27 66 D
Oakfield Gdns. Grnf ...53 14 82 B
Oakfield Gdns. N18 ...17 33 92 A
Oakfield Gdns. SE19 ...87 33 74 D
Oakfield Rd. Ashf ...81 07 71 D
Oakfield Rd. Croy ...105 32 66 C
Oakfield Rd. E17 ...26 36 90 C
Oakfield Rd. E6 ...50 42 83 A
Oakfield Rd. Ilf ...40 43 89 B
Oakfield Rd. N14 ...16 30 93 A
Oakfield Rd. N3 ...23 25 90 B
Oakfield Rd. N4 ...37 31 87 A
Oakfield Rd. N8 ...37 31 88 C
Oakfield Rd. Orp ...108 48 66 A
Oakfield Rd. SE20 ...97 34 70 D
Oakfield Rd. SW19 ...85 23 72 D
Oakfields Rd. NW11 ...35 24 88 C
Oakfield St. SW10 ...62 26 77 A
Oakford Rd. NW5 ...47 29 85 A
Oak Gdns. Croy ...106 37 65 A
Oak Gdns. Edg ...22 20 90 C
Oak Glade. Nthwd ...19 07 90 B
Oak Glen. Horn ...30 54 89 A
Oak Gr. NW2 ...46 24 85 A
Oak Grove Rd. SE20 ...98 35 69 C
Oak Gr. Ruis ...31 10 86 D
Oak Gr. Sun ...91 10 70 D
Oak Gr. W Wick ...106 38 66 C
Oakhall Ct. E11 ...39 40 88 D
Oakhall Ct. Sun ...81 09 71 D
Oakhall Dri. Sun ...81 09 71 D
Oak Hall Rd. E11 ...39 40 88 D
Oakham Cl. SE6 ...88 36 72 B
Oakham Dri. Brom ...99 39 68 D
Oakhampton Cl. N12 ...15 26 92 D
Oakhampton Rd. NW7 ...23 23 91 D
Oakhill Ave. NW3 ...46 25 85 B
Oakhill Av. Pnr ...20 12 90 C
Oak Hill Cl. Wdf Gr ...26 38 91 D
Oak Hill Cres. Surb ...101 18 66 A
Oak Hill Cres. Wdf Gn ...27 39 91 C
Oakhill Ct. SW19 ...95 23 70 D
Oakhill Dri. Surb ...101 18 66 A
Oak Hill Gdns. Wdf Gn ...27 39 90 A
Oak Hill Gr. Surb ...101 18 67 C
Oak Hill Park Mews. NW3 ...46 26 85 A
Oak Hill Park. NW3 ...46 25 85 B
Oak Hill Path. Surb ...101 18 67 C
Oakhill Pl. SW15 ...73 25 74 A

Oakhill Rd. Beck ...98 38 69 C
Oakhill Rd. Orp ...108 45 65 B
Oak Hill Rd. Surb ...101 18 67 C
Oakhill Rd. Sutt ...103 32 75 C
Oakhill Rd. SW15 ...73 24 74 B
Oakhill Rd. SW15 ...73 25 74 A
Oakhill Rd. SW16 ...96 30 69 B
Oak Hill. Surb ...101 18 66 A
Oak Hill Way. NW3 ...46 25 85 B
Oak Hill. Wdf Gn ...27 39 91 C
Oakhouse Rd. Bexh ...99 49 74 A
Oakhurst Ave. Barn ...16 27 94 A
Oakhurst Ave. Bexh ...99 48 77 C
Oakhurst Cl. E17 ...27 39 89 C
Oakhurst Gdns. Bexh ...99 48 77 C
Oakhurst Gdns. E17 ...27 39 89 C
Oakhurst Gr. SE22 ...75 34 75 C
Oakhurst Rise. Cars ...111 27 62 B
Oakington Ave. Har ...32 13 87 A
Oakington Ave. Wem ...33 18 86 D
Oakington Dri. Sun ...92 11 69 C
Oakington Manor Dri. Wem ...19 25 C
Oakington Rd. W9 ...56 25 82 C
Oakington Way. N8 ...36 30 87 A
Oak La. E14 ...57 36 80 B
Oak La. Islw ...71 15 75 C
Oak La. N11 ...24 29 91 B
Oak La. N2 ...23 26 90 D
Oaklands Ave. Islw ...60 15 77 B
Oaklands Ave. N9 ...13 34 95 D
Oaklands Ave. Rom ...36 51 89 D
Oaklands Ave. Sid ...90 45 73 B
Oaklands Ave. Th Hth ...68 31 68 C
Oaklands Ave. W Wick ...106 37 65 D
Oaklands Cl. Bexh ...79 48 74 B
Oaklands Cl. Orp ...108 45 67 C
Oaklands Gate. Nthwd ...19 09 91 A
Oaklands Gr. W12 ...55 22 80 C
Oaklands La. Barn ...11 23 96 C
Oaklands Mews. NW2 ...46 23 85 B
Oaklands. N21 ...16 30 93 B
Oaklands Park Ave. Ilf ...40 44 86 A
Oaklands Pas. NW2 ...23 85 B
Oaklands Pl. SW4 ...74 29 75 D
Oaklands Rd. Bexh ...79 48 75 D
Oaklands Rd. Croy ...39 70 C
Oaklands Rd. N20 ...15 24 94 B
Oaklands Rd. NW2 ...33 74 D
Oaklands Rd. SW14 ...72 07 71 D
Oaklands Rd. W7 ...32 66 C
Oaklands. Twick ...82 36 90 C
Oaklands. W13 ...54 42 83 A
Oakland Way. Eps ...109 16 73 A
Oak La. Twick ...83 30 93 A
Oakleafe Gdns. Ilf ...28 43 89 B
Oaklea Pas. King ...93 17 68 B
Oakleigh Ave. Edg ...22 19 90 D
Oakleigh Ave. N20 ...16 27 94 C
Oakleigh Ave. Surb ...102 19 65 A
Oakleigh Cl. N20 ...15 24 94 B
Oakleigh Ct. Barn ...12 27 95 C
Oakleigh Ct. Edg ...22 20 90 C
Oakleigh Gdns. N20 ...15 26 94 C
Oakleigh Park Ave. Chis ...100 43 69 A
Oakleigh Park N. N20 ...16 26 94 D
Oakleigh Park S. N20 ...16 27 94 C
Oakleigh Rd. Pnr ...20 12 91 B
Oakleigh Road N. N20 ...16 27 93 A
Oakleigh Road S. N11 ...16 28 92 A
Oakleigh Way. Mit ...28 69 B
Oakleigh Way. Surb ...102 19 66 D
Oakley Ave. Bark ...51 45 84 D
Oakley Ave. Croy ...111 30 64 B
Oakley Ave. W5 ...54 19 80 A
Oakley Cl. Islw ...70 14 76 B
Oakley Cl. W7 ...36 72 B
Oakley Cres. EC1 ...39 68 D
Oakley Dri. Brom ...107 42 65 C
Oakley Dri. SE9 ...25 85 B
Oakley Gdns. N8 ...36 30 88 B
Oakley Gdns. SW3 ...27 77 A
Oakley Pl. SE1 ...63 33 78 D
Oakley Rd. Brom ...107 42 65 A
Oakleyd. Har ...33 15 88 C
Oakley Rd. N1 ...32 84 D
Oakley Rd. SE25 ...105 34 67 B
Oakley Sq. NW1 ...29 83 A
Oakley St. SW3 ...27 77 A
Oakley Wk. W6 ...26 85 A
Oakley Yd. E2 ...25 85 B
Oak Lodge Dri. W Wick ...106 37 66 B
Oakmead Ave. Brom ...107 40 67 C
Oakmeade. Pnr ...20 13 91 B

Oakmead Rd. Croy ...104 29 67 D
Oakmead Rd. SW12 ...86 28 73 D
Oakmere Rd. SE2 ...66 46 77 A
Oakmont Pl. Orp ...108 44 66 D
Oak Pl. SW18 ...73 25 74 B
Oak Rd. Eri ...67 50 77 C
Oak Rd. Eri ...80 52 76 C
Oak Rd. N Mal ...94 20 69 D
Oak Rd. Rom ...30 54 90 B
Oakridge Rd. Brom ...89 39 71 A
Oaks Ave. Felt ...82 12 72 A
Oaks Ave. Rom ...29 50 90 C
Oaks Ave. SE19 ...87 33 71 C
Oaks Ave. Wor Pk ...109 22 64 B
Oaksford Ave. SE26 ...87 34 72 D
Oakshade Rd. Brom ...88 38 71 B
Oakshaw Rd. SW18 ...85 25 73 B
Oaks La. Croy ...106 35 65 C
Oaks La. Ilf ...40 45 88 A
Oaks La. Ilf ...40 45 89 C
Oaks The. N12 ...15 25 92 B
Oaks The. Ruis ...31 09 87 A
Oaks The. SE18 ...66 44 78 C
Oaks The. Wdf Gn ...27 39 91 C
Oaks Track. Cars ...111 28 60 D
Oaks Track. Wall ...111 28 62 D
Oak St. Rom ...29 50 88 A
Oaks Way. Cars ...111 27 63 D
Oaks Way. Surb ...101 17 66 D
Oakthorpe Rd. N13 ...17 31 93 D
Oaktree Ave. N13 ...17 31 92 C
Oak Tree Ave. N2 ...23 25 89 B
Oak Tree Cl. W5 ...54 17 81 C
Oak Tree Cl. W3 ...55 17 81 C
Oak Tree Dell. NW9 ...34 19 88 B
Oak Tree Dri. N20 ...15 24 94 D
Oak Tree Gdns. Brom ...89 40 71 D
Oakview Gdns. N2 ...23 26 89 D
Oakview Gr. Croy ...106 36 66 C
Oakview Rd. SE6 ...88 37 71 D
Oak Village. NW5 ...47 28 85 A
Oakway. Brom ...98 38 69 D
Oakway Cl. Bex ...80 48 74 C
Oak Way. Croy ...106 35 67 D
Oak Way. Felt ...81 09 73 C
Oak Way. N14 ...16 28 94 B
Oakways. SE9 ...78 45 78 A
Oakway. SW20 ...95 23 68 C
Oak Way. W3 ...55 21 80 C
Oakwood Ave. Beck ...98 38 69 C
Oakwood Ave. Brom ...99 40 68 B
Oakwood Ave. Mit ...95 26 69 D
Oakwood Ave. N14 ...16 29 94 B
Oakwood Ave. Sthl ...53 13 80 A
Oakwood Chase. Horn ...42 54 88 D
Oakwood Cl. Chis ...99 41 70 A
Oakwood Cl. N14 ...16 29 95 C
Oakwood Cl. Wdf Gn ...27 40 90 B
Oakwood Cres. Grnf ...44 16 84 B
Oakwood Cres. N21 ...12 30 95 D
Oakwood Ct. W14 ...61 24 79 D
Oakwood Dri. Bexh ...79 50 75 C
Oakwood Dri. Edg ...22 20 91 A
Oakwood Dri. SE19 ...97 33 70 A
Oakwood Gdns. Ilf ...45 86 B
Oakwood Gdns. Orp ...108 44 65 A
Oakwood Gdns. Sutt ...103 25 65 A
Oakwood La. W14 ...62 24 79 D
Oakwood Pk. Croy ...105 31 67 C
Oakwood Pl. Croy ...105 31 67 C
Oakwood Rd. NW11 ...35 25 88 B
Oakwood Rd. Orp ...108 44 65 A
Oakwood Rd. Pnr ...19 10 90 D
Oakwood Rd. SW20 ...94 21 69 C
Oakwood. Surb ...101 18 67 D
Oakwood View. N14 ...16 29 94 B
Oakwood. Wall ...111 28 62 B
Oakworth Rd. W10 ...56 23 81 B
Oast House Way. Orp ...100 44 73 D
Oatfield Rd. Orp ...108 45 66 D
Oat La. EC2 ...4 32 81 C
Oatland Rise. E17 ...26 36 90 C
Oatlands Rd. Enf ...14 35 97 A
Oban Rd. E13 ...58 41 82 A
Oban Rd. SE25 ...97 32 68 D
Oban St. E14 ...58 38 80 D
Oberstein Rd. SW11 ...73 26 75 D
Oborne Cl. SE24 ...75 32 74 A
Observatory Gdns. W8 ...62 25 79 A
Observatory Rd. SW14 ...72 20 75 C
Occupation La. SE18 ...78 43 76 B

Occupation La. W5 ...60 17 78 B
Occupation La. SE17 ...63 32 78 C
Ocean St. E1 ...57 35 81 B
Ockendon Rd. N1 ...48 32 84 B
Ockham Dri. Orp ...100 46 70 C
Ockley Ct. Sutt ...110 50 77 C
Ockley Rd. Croy ...104 30 66 B
Ockley Rd. SW16 ...86 30 72 C
Octavia Cl. Mit ...104 27 67 A
Octavia Rd. Islw ...71 15 75 B
Octavia St. SW11 ...74 27 76 A
Octavius St. SE8 ...64 39 78 C
Odard Rd. E Mol ...92 13 68 C
Odessa Rd. E7 ...50 40 85 A
Odessa Rd. NW10 ...45 22 83 C
Odessa St. SE16 ...6 36 79 D
Odger St. SW11 ...74 27 76 A
Odhams Wlk. WC2 ...3 30 81 C
Offa's Mead. E9 ...49 36 85 A
Offenham Rd. SE9 ...89 42 71 B
Offerton Rd. SW4 ...74 29 75 A
Offham Slope. N12 ...15 24 92 D
Offley Rd. SW9 ...63 31 77 C
Offord Cl. N17 ...25 34 91 A
Offord Rd. N1 ...48 31 84 C
Ogilby St. SE18 ...65 42 78 B
Oglander Rd. SE15 ...75 33 75 B
Ogle St. W1 ...2 29 81 A
Oglethorpe Rd. Dag ...41 49 86 C
Ohio Rd. E13 ...58 39 82 D
Oil Mill La. W6 ...61 22 78 C
Okeburn Rd. SW17 ...86 28 71 C
Okehampton Cres. Well ...78 46 76 B
Okehampton Rd. NW10 ...46 23 83 B
Okehampton Rd. Rom ...53 91 A
Olaf St. W11 ...56 23 80 B
Old Bailey. EC4 ...3 31 80 C
Old Barge House Alley. SE1 ...7 31 80 C
Old Barn Cl. Sutt ...110 24 63 C
Old Barn Way. Bexh ...79 50 75 B
Old Barrack Yd. SW1 ...6 28 79 A
Old Barrowfield. E15 ...50 39 83 A
Old Bethnal Green Rd. E2 ...57 34 82 B
Old Bldgs. WC2 ...3 31 81 C
Old Bond St. W1 ...6 29 80 A
Oldborough Rd. Wem ...33 17 86 A
Old Brewery Mews. NW3 ...46 26 85 B
Old Bridge Cl. Nthlt ...43 13 82 C
Old Bridge St. King ...93 17 69 D
Old Broad St. EC3 ...4 33 81 C
Old Bromley Rd. Brom ...88 38 71 D
Old Brompton Rd. SW5 ...62 25 78 D
Old Brompton Rd. SW7 ...62 26 78 B
Old Burlington St. W1 ...6 29 80 A
Oldbury Pl. W1 ...2 28 80 D
Oldbury Rd. Enf ...13 34 97 C
Old Castle St. E1 ...33 81 D
Old Cavendish St. W1 ...2 29 80 D
Old Change Ct. EC4 ...4 32 81 D
Old Charlton Rd. Shep ...91 08 68 C
Oldchurch Gdns. Rom ...41 50 87 B
Old Church La. NW9 ...34 20 86 D
Old Church La. Stan ...21 17 91 A
Old Church Rd. E1 ...57 35 81 D
Old Church Rd. E4 ...18 37 93 A
Oldchurch Rd. Rom ...42 51 88 C
Oldchurch Rise. Rom ...42 51 87 A
Old Church St. SW3 ...66 26 78 D
Old Clem Sq. SE18 ...66 43 77 B
Old Compton St. W1 ...2 29 81 D
Old Cote Dri. Houn ...59 13 77 A
Old Court Pl. W8 ...62 25 79 B
Old Deer Park Gdns. Rich ...71 18 75 A
Old Devonshire Rd. SW12 ...86 28 73 B
Old Dock Cl. Rich ...61 19 77 A
Old Dover Rd. SE3 ...65 40 77 D
Old Farm Ave. N14 ...16 29 94 A
Old Farm Ave. Sid ...90 45 72 B
Old Farm Pas. Hamp ...92 14 69 A
Old Farm Rd E. Sid ...90 46 72 A
Old Farm Rd. Hamp ...92 12 70 B
Old Farm Rd. N2 ...23 26 90 B
Old Farm Rd W. Sid ...90 45 72 B
Old Fold Cl. Barn ...11 24 97 B
Old Fold La. Barn ...11 24 97 B
Old Fold View. Barn ...11 23 96 A
Old Ford Rd. E2 ...49 35 83 C
Old Ford Rd. E2 ...49 36 83 A
Old Forge Way. Sid ...90 46 71 B
Old Fox Footpath. S Croy ...112 33 62 A
Old Gloucester St. WC1 ...3 30 81 A
Old Hall Cl. Pnr ...20 12 90 A
Old Hall Dri. Pnr ...20 12 90 A
Old Hatch Manor. Ruis ...31 10 87 A
Old Hill. Chis ...100 43 69 A
Oldhill St. N16 ...37 34 87 C
Old Homesdale Rd. Brom ...99 41 68 C
Old House Cl. Eps ...109 21 62 D
Old House Cl. SW19 ...85 24 71 C
Old Howlett's La. Ruis ...31 08 88 D
Old Jamaica Rd. SE16 ...63 34 79 C
Old James St. SE15 ...75 34 75 B
Old Jewry. EC2 ...4 32 81 D
Old Kenton La. NW9 ...34 19 88 B
Old Kent Rd. SE15 ...63 33 78 D
Old Kent Rd. SE1 ...63 33 78 B
Old Kingston Rd. Wor Pk ...102 20 65 C
Old Malden La. Wor Pk ...102 21 65 A
Old Manor Dri. Islw ...70 14 74 C
Old Manor Way. Bexh ...79 50 76 D
Old Manor Yd. SW5 ...25 78 B
Old Market Sq. E2 ...33 82 B
Old Marylebone Rd. NW1 ...2 27 81 A
Old Mill Ct. E18 ...27 41 89 A
Old Mill Rd. SE18 ...66 44 77 B
Old Montague St. E1 ...57 34 81 A
Old Nichol St. E2 ...4 33 82 D
Old North St. WC1 ...3 30 81 B
Old Oak Common La. NW10 ...55 21 82 C
Old Oak Common La. W3 ...55 21 81 D
Old Oak La. NW10 ...55 21 82 B
Old Oak Rd. W3 ...55 21 80 B
Old Orchard. Sun ...92 11 69 C
Old Palace La. Rich ...71 17 74 A
Old Palace Rd. Croy ...105 32 65 C
Old Palace Yd. Rich ...71 17 74 B
Old Paradise St. SE11 ...10 30 78 B
Old Park Ave. Enf ...13 32 96 C
Old Park Ave. SW12 ...74 28 74 C
Old Park Gr. Enf ...13 32 96 C
Old Park La. W1 ...6 28 80 D
Old Park Mews. Houn ...59 12 77 D
Old Park Rd. N13 ...17 31 93 D
Old Park Rd. SE2 ...66 46 78 C
Old Park Ridings. N21 ...13 32 95 A
Old Park View. Enf ...13 31 96 B
Old Perry St. Chis ...100 45 70 C
Old Pye St. SW1 ...6 29 79 D
Old Quebec St. W1 ...2 28 81 D
Old Queen St. SW1 ...6 29 79 B
Old Rd. Bexh ...79 50 75 D
Old Rd. Enf ...14 35 97 A
Old Rd. SE13 ...77 39 75 C
Old Rectory Gdns. Edg ...22 19 91 A
Oldridge Rd. SW12 ...86 28 73 B
Old Rope Wlk. Sun ...91 10 68 B
Old Rope Wlk. Sun ...9 11 68 A
Old Ruislip Rd. Nthlt ...43 11 83 C
Old Schools La. Eps ...109 21 62 B
Old Seacoal La. EC4 ...3 31 81 D
Old South Lambeth Rd. SW8 ...10 30 77 C
Old Sq. WC2 ...3 31 81 B
Old St. E13 ...50 41 83 C
Old St. EC1 ...4 32 82 D
Oldstead Rd. Brom ...88 38 71 B
Old St. EC1 ...4 32 82 D
Old Swan Yd. Cars ...111 27 64 B
Old Town. Croy ...105 31 65 B
Old Town. SW4 ...74 29 76 A
Old Tranyard. SE18 ...66 45 78 A
Old Woolwich Rd. SE10 ...64 38 78 D
O'Leary Sq. E1 ...57 35 81 A
Oley Pl. E1 ...35 81 B
Olga St. E3 ...49 36 83 C
Olinda Rd. N16 ...37 33 88 D
Oliphant St. W10 ...56 23 82 B
Oliver Ave. SE25 ...97 33 68 B
Oliver Cl. E10 ...38 36 86 B
Oliver Ct. SE18 ...66 44 78 A

Oldfield Rd. Hamp ...92 12 69 B
Oldfield Rd. N16 ...37 33 86 C
Oldfield Rd. NW10 ...45 21 84 D
Oldfield Rd. SW19 ...95 24 70 A
Oldfield Rd. W3 ...61 21 79 B
Oldfields Circ. Nthlt ...43 14 84 A
Oldfields Rd. Sutt ...103 25 65 A
Old Fish St Hill. EC4 ...8 32 80 A
Olive Rd. E13 ...58 41 82 A
Olive Rd. NW2 ...46 23 85 A
Olive Rd. SW19 ...95 26 70 C
Olive Rd. W5 ...60 17 79 D
Oliver Gr. SE25 ...97 33 68 D
Oliver Rd. E10 ...38 37 86 D
Oliver Rd. E17 ...38 38 88 A
Oliver Rd. N Mal ...94 20 69 C
Oliver Rd. Sutt ...110 26 64 B
Oliver's Yd. EC2 ...32 82 D
Olivette St. SW15 ...73 23 75 B
Ollerton Green. E3 ...49 36 83 B
Ollerton Rd. N11 ...16 29 92 D
Olley Cl. Wall ...111 30 63 C
Ollgar Cl. W12 ...55 21 80 D
Olliffe St. E14 ...64 38 79 C
Olmar St. SE1 ...34 77 A
Olney Rd. SE17 ...63 32 77 A
Olorane Gdns. NW3 ...35 25 86 C
Olron Cres. Bexh ...79 48 74 A
Olven Rd. SE18 ...66 44 77 A
Olveston Wlk. Cars ...103 26 67 D
Olyffe Ave. Well ...78 46 76 C
Olyffe Dri. Beck ...98 38 69 A
Olympia Wy. W14 ...62 24 79 C
Olympia Yd. W2 ...56 25 80 B
Olympic Way. Grnf ...43 13 83 B
Olympic Way. Wem ...34 19 85 A
Omeara St. SE1 ...8 32 80 C
Omega Pl. N1 ...47 30 83 C
Omega St. SE14 ...76 37 76 A
Ommaney Rd. SE14 ...76 36 76 A
Ondine Rd. SE15 ...75 33 75 D
O'Neill Path. SE18 ...43 77 A
One Tree Cl. SE23 ...76 35 74 C
Ongar Cl. Rom ...41 48 88 A
Ongar Rd. SW6 ...62 25 77 A
Onra Rd. E17 ...38 37 87 A
Onslow Av. Rich ...71 18 74 A
Onslow Ave. Sutt ...110 24 62 D
Onslow Cl. E4 ...18 38 93 B
Onslow Cl. Surb ...101 15 66 C
Onslow Gdns. E18 ...27 41 89 A
Onslow Gdns. N10 ...36 28 88 B
Onslow Gdns. N21 ...13 31 95 A
Onslow Gdns. Surb ...101 15 66 C
Onslow Gdns. Wall ...111 29 63 C
Onslow Mews E. SW7 ...62 26 78 B
Onslow Mews W. SW7 ...62 26 78 B
Onslow Rd. Croy ...105 31 66 A
Onslow Rd. N Mal ...94 22 68 C
Onslow Rd. Rich ...18 74 C
Onslow Sq. SW7 ...62 26 78 B
Onslow St. EC1 ...3 31 82 C
Onslow Way. Surb ...101 15 66 C
Onslow Gdns. Chis ...26 78 D
Ontario St. SE1 ...31 79 D
Opal Mews. Ilf ...40 43 88 B
Opal St. SE11 ...63 31 78 D
Openshaw Rd. SE2 ...66 46 78 B
Openview. SW18 ...85 26 72 B
Ophir Terr. SE15 ...34 76 A
Oppidans Rd. NW3 ...47 27 84 D
Orange Ct. E1 ...57 34 80 C
Orange Hill Rd. Edg ...22 20 91 C
Orange Pl. SE16 ...64 35 79 C
Orange Row. E1 ...57 34 81 A
Orangery La. SE9 ...77 42 74 B
Orange St. WC2 ...6 29 80 B
Orange Yd. W1 ...29 81 D
Oratory La. SW3 ...9 27 78 C
Orbain Rd. SW6 ...62 24 77 C
Orbel St. SW11 ...74 27 76 A
Orb St. SE17 ...63 32 78 A
Orchard Ave. Ashf ...91 08 70 A
Orchard Ave. Belv ...78 47 77 B
Orchard Ave. Croy ...106 37 66 C
Orchard Ave. Felt ...80 07 74 B
Orchard Ave. Houn ...59 12 77 C
Orchard Ave. Mit ...28 66 C
Orchard Ave. N14 ...16 29 94 A
Orchard Ave. N20 ...15 26 93 B
Orchard Ave. N3 ...23 25 89 A
Orchard Ave. N Mal ...94 21 68 A
Orchard Ave. Sthl ...53 12 80 D
Orchard Cl. Ashf ...91 08 70 A
Orchard Cl. Bexh ...79 48 76 A
Orchard Cl. Edg ...21 18 91 A
Orchard Cl. Surb ...101 16 66 B
Orchard Cl. SW20 ...95 23 68 C

Orchard Cl. Wem 44 18 83 A
Orchard Cres. Enf 13 33 97 B
Orchard Ct. Wor Pk 102 22 66 C
Orchard Dri. SE3 77 39 76 C
Orchard Gate. Grnf 44 16 84 B
Orchard Gate. NW9 22 21 89 C
Orchard Gr. Croy 106 36 66 A
Orchard Gr. Edg 22 19 90 B
Orchard Green. Orp 108 45 65 A
Orchard Gr. Har 33 18 88 B
Orchard Gr. Orp 108 45 66 D
Orchard Hill. Dart 80 51 74 A
Orchard Hill. SE13 76 37 76 B
Orchard La. SW20 94 22 69 B
Orchardleigh Ave. Enf 14 35 97 C
Orchardmede. N21 13 32 95 D
Orchard Pl. E14 58 39 81 C
Orchard Pl. N17 25 33 91 D
Orchard Rd. Barn 11 24 96 D
Orchard Rd. Belv 67 49 78 A
Orchard Rd. Brent 60 17 77 A
Orchard Rd. Brom 99 41 69 A
Orchard Rd. Dag 52 49 83 A
Orchard Rd. Enf 14 35 95 A
Orchard Rd. Hamp 92 13 70 C
Orchard Rd. Houn 70 12 74 B
Orchard Rd. King 93 18 69 C
Orchard Rd. Mit 104 28 66 C
Orchard Rd. N6 36 28 87 B
Orchard Rd. Rich 72 19 75 A
Orchard Rd. Rom 29 49 90 D
Orchard Rd. Sid 90 45 71 A
Orchard Rd. Sun 91 10 70 D
Orchard Rd. Sutt 110 25 64 A
Orchard Rd. Twick 71 16 74 B
Orchard Rd. Well 78 46 75 B
Orchard Rise. Croy 106 36 66 D
Orchard Rise E. Sid 78 45 74 B
Orchard Rise. King 94 20 69 A
Orchard Rise. Rich 72 19 75 D
Orchard Rise W. Sid 78 45 74 A
Orchardson St. NW8 1 26 82 D
Orchard Sq. W14 62 24 78 D
Orchard St. Dart 80 54 74 C
Orchard St. E17 26 36 89 C
Orchard St. W1 2 28 81 C
Orchard The. Eps 109 21 63 D
Orchard The. Houn 70 14 76 C
Orchard The. N21 13 32 95 D
Orchard The. NW11 35 25 88 A
Orchard The. SE3 76 38 76 D
Orchard The. W4 61 20 78 B
Orchard Way. Beck 106 36 67 B
Orchard Way. Croy 106 36 66 A
Orchard Way. Enf 13 33 96 A
Orchard Way. Sutt 110 26 64 B
Orchid Rd. N14 16 29 94 A
Orchid St. W12 55 22 80 A
Orchis Way. Rom 30 54 91 B
Orde Hall St. WC1 3 30 81 B
Ordell Rd. E3 49 36 83 D
Ordnance Cl. Felt 81 10 72 A
Ordnance Cres. SE10 65 39 79 A
Ordnance Hill. NW8 46 26 83 D
*Ordnance Mews. NW8 46 26 83 D
Ordnance Rd. E16 58 39 81 B
Ordnance Rd. SE18 66 43 77 A
Oregon Ave. E12 50 42 85 B
Oregon Sq. Orp 108 44 66 D
Orford Gdns. Twick 83 15 72 B
Orford Rd. E17 38 37 88 B
Orford Rd. E17 26 37 89 D
Orford Rd. E18 27 40 89 B
Organ La. E4 18 38 93 A
Oriel Ct. NW3 46 26 85 A
Oriel Gdns. Ilf 27 42 89 B
Oriel Pl. NW3 46 26 85 A
Oriel Rd. E9 49 36 84 A
Oriel Way. Nthlt 43 13 84 D
Oriental Rd. E16 58 41 80 D
Oriental St. E14 57 37 80 A
Orient St. SE11 63 31 78 B
Orient Way E5 38 35 86 D
Orissa Rd. SE18 66 45 78 C
Orkney St. SW11 74 28 76 C
Orlando Gdns. Eps 109 20 62 D
Orlands Rd. SW4 74 29 75 A
Orleans Ct. Twick 83 16 73 B
Orleans Rd. SE19 97 32 70 B
Orleans Rd. Twick 83 17 73 A
Orleston Mews. N7 48 31 84 A
Orleston Rd. N7 48 31 84 A
Orley Farm Rd. Har 33 15 86 C
Orlop St. E10 65 39 78 C
Ormanton Rd. SE26 87 34 71 A
Orme Ct Mews. W2 56 25 80 B
Orme Ct. W2 56 25 80 B
Orme La. W2 56 25 80 B
Ormeley Rd. SW12 86 28 73 D
Orme Rd. King 94 19 69 D
Ormerod Gdns. Mit 96 28 69 A
Ormesby Way. Har 33 18 88 B
Orme Sq. W2 56 25 80 B
Ormiston Gr. W12 55 22 80 D
Ormiston Rd. SE10 65 40 78 C
Ormond Ave. Hamp 92 13 69 B
*Ormond Ave. Rich 71 17 74 B
Ormond Cl. WC1 3 30 81 A
Ormond Cres. Hamp 92 13 69 B
Ormond Dri. Hamp 92 13 70 D
Ormonde Ave. Eps 109 20 62 D
Ormonde Ave. Orp 108 44 65 A
Ormonde Gate. SW3 9 27 78 D
Ormonde Pl. SW1 9 28 78 A
Ormonde Rd. SW14 72 20 75 A
Ormonde Terr. NW8 47 27 83 B
Ormond Mews. WC1 3 30 82 C
Ormond Rd. N19 36 30 87 C
Ormond Rd. Rich 71 17 74 B
Ormond Yd. SW1 6 29 80 C
Ormsby Gdns. Grnf 43 14 83 C
Ormsby Pl. N16 37 33 86 D
Ormsby St. E2 48 33 83 D
Ormsby. Sutt 110 25 63 D
Ormside St. SE15 64 35 77 A
Ornan Rd. NW3 47 27 85 C
Oronsay Wlk. N1 48 32 84 B
Orpen Wlk. N16 37 33 86 C
Orpheus St. SE5 75 32 76 B
Orpington Gdns. N18 17 33 93 C
Orpington Rd. Chis 100 45 68 A
Orpington Rd. N21 17 31 94 D
Orpwood Cl. Hamp 92 12 70 B
Orsett St. SE11 10 30 78 D
Orsett Terr. W2 1 26 81 C
Orsett Terr. Wdf Gn 27 41 91 C
Orsman Rd. N1 48 33 83 A
Orton St. E1 57 34 80 C
Orville Rd. SW11 73 26 76 D
Orwell Ct. E8 48 34 83 A
Osbaldeston Rd. N16 37 34 87 C
Osberton Rd. SE12 77 40 74 A
Osbert St. SW1 10 29 78 B
Osborn Cl. E8 48 34 83 A
Osborne Cl. Beck 98 36 68 C
Osborne Cl. Felt 82 11 71 C
Osborne Cl. Horn 42 52 88 D
Osborne Ct. Surb 101 18 67 C
Osborne Ct. W5 54 18 81 A
Osborne Gdns. NW7 23 23 91 D
Osborne Gdns. Th Hth 97 32 69 C
Osborne Gr. E17 26 36 89 D
Osborne Pl. Sutt 110 26 64 D
Osborne Rd. Belv 67 48 77 B
Osborne Rd. Dag 52 48 85 D
Osborne Rd. E10 38 37 86 B
Osborne Rd. E7 50 40 85 D
Osborne Rd. E9 49 36 84 B
Osborne Rd. Enf 14 36 97 C
Osborne Rd. Horn 42 53 88 C
Osborne Rd. Houn 70 12 75 B
Osborne Rd. King 93 18 70 C
Osborne Rd. N13 17 31 93 C
Osborne Rd. N4 37 31 87 C
Osborne Rd. NW2 45 22 84 B
Osborne Rd. Sthl 53 14 81 C
Osborne Rd. Th Hth 97 32 69 C
Osborne Rd. W3 61 19 79 B
Osborne Sq. Dag 52 48 85 B
Osborn La. SE23 88 36 73 A
Osborn St. E1 4 33 81 B
Osborn St. E1 57 34 81 C
Osborn Terr. SE3 77 39 75 D
Oscar St. SE8 76 37 76 A
Oscar St. SE8 76 37 76 C
Oseney Cres. NW5 47 29 84 B
O'Shea Gr. E3 49 36 83 B
Osidge La. N14 16 28 94 D
Osiers Rd. SW18 73 25 75 C
Osier St. E1 57 35 82 C
Osier Way. E10 38 37 86 D
Osier Way. Mit 104 27 67 B
Oslac Rd. SE6 88 37 71 D
Osman Cl. N15 37 32 88 D
Osman Rd. N9 17 34 93 C
Osman Rd. W6 62 23 79 C
Osmond Cl. Har 32 14 86 A
Osmond Gdns. Wall 111 29 64 C
Osmund St. W12 55 21 81 B
Osnaburgh St. NW1 2 28 82 D
Osnaburgh Terr. NW1 2 28 82 D
Osney Wlk. Cars 103 26 67 D
Ospringe Ct. SE9 78 44 74 D
Ospringe Rd. NW5 47 29 85 A
Osric Path. N1 48 33 83 C
Ossian Rd. N4 36 30 87 B
Ossington Bldgs. W1 2 28 81 A
Ossington Cl. W2 56 25 80 A
Ossington St. W2 56 25 80 B
Ossory Rd. SE15 63 34 77 A
Ossulston St. NW1 2 29 82 B
Ossulston St. NW1 2 29 82 B
Ossulton Way. N2 23 26 89 C
Ostade Rd. SW2 86 30 73 B
Ostend Pl. SE17 63 32 78 A
Osten Mews. SW7 62 25 79 D
Osterberg Rd. Dart 80 54 75 D
Osterley Ave. Islw 59 14 77 D
Osterley Cres. Islw 71 15 76 B
Osterley Ct. Islw 70 14 76 B
Osterley Ct. Islw 59 14 77 D
Osterley La. Islw 59 14 78 A
Osterley La. Sthl 59 13 78 D
Osterley Park Rd. Sthl 59 12 79 D
Osterley Park View Rd. W7 60 15 79 A
Osterley Rd. Islw 60 15 77 C
Osterley Rd. N16 48 33 85 A
Osterly Gdns. Th Hth 97 32 69 C
Oswald Rd. Sthl 53 12 80 C
Oswald's Mead. E9 49 36 85 A
Oswald St. E5 38 35 86 D
Osward Pl. N9 17 34 93 B
Osward Rd. SW17 86 27 72 B
Oswin St. SE11 63 31 78 B
Oswin St. SE11 7 31 79 D
Oswyth Rd. SE5 75 33 76 C
Otford Cl. Bex 79 49 74 D
Otford Cl. Brom 100 43 68 A
Otford Cres.SE4 76 36 74 D
Othello Cl. SE11 63 31 78 D
Otho Ct. Brent 60 17 77 D
Otis St. E3 58 38 82 A
Otley App. Ilf 40 43 88 D
Otley Dri. Ilf 40 43 88 D
Otley Rd. E16 58 41 81 C
Otley Terr. E5 38 35 86 D
Ottawa Gdns. Dag 52 50 84 D
Ottaway St. E5 37 34 86 C
Otterbourne Rd. Croy 105 32 65 A
Otterbourne Rd. E4 18 38 93 D
Otterburn Gdns. Islw 60 16 77 C
Otterburn St. SW17 96 27 70 B
Otterden St. SE6 88 37 71 A
Otter Rd. Grnf 53 14 82 C
Otto Cl. SE26 87 34 72 D
Otto St. SE17 63 31 77 B
Oulton Cl. E5 38 35 86 A
Oulton Cres. Bark 51 45 85 D
Oulton Rd. N15 37 32 88 B
Ouseley Rd. SW12 86 27 73 D
Outer Circ. NW1 1 27 82 D
Outgate Rd. NW10 45 21 84 D
Outram Pl. N1 47 30 83 A
Outram Rd. Croy 105 33 65 B
Outram Rd. E6 50 42 83 A
Outram Rd. N22 24 29 90 B
Outwich St. EC3 4 33 81 C
Oval Pl. SW8 10 30 77 D
Oval Rd. Croy 105 33 66 C
Oval Rd. NW1 47 28 83 B
Oval Road N. Dag 52 49 83 B
Oval Road S. Dag 52 49 83 D
Oval The. E2 48 34 83 D
Oval The. Sid 90 46 73 A
Oval Way. SE11 10 30 77 B
Overbrae. Beck 88 37 71 C
Overbrook Wlk. Edg 22 19 91 C
Overbury Ave. Beck 98 38 68 A
Overbury Rd. N15 37 32 88 D
Overbury St. E5 49 35 85 B
Overcliff Rd. SE13 76 37 75 A
Overcourt Cl. Sid 78 46 74 D
Ordale Ave. N Mal 94 20 69 D
Overdale Rd. W5 60 17 79 C
Overdown Rd. SE6 88 37 71 B
Overhill Rd. Pur 112 31 62 C
Overhill Rd. SE22 87 34 73 A
Overhill Way. Beck 106 38 67 B
Overlea Rd. E5 37 34 87 A
Overmead. Sid 90 44 73 B
Overstand Cl. Beck 106 37 67 A
Overstone Gdns. Croy 106 36 66 B
Overstone Rd. W6 62 23 78 A
Over Strand. NW9 22 21 90 B
Overton Cl. Islw 71 15 76 B
Overton Cl. NW10 45 20 84 A
Overton Dri. E11 39 40 87 B
Overton Dri. Rom 41 47 87 A
Overton Rd. E10 38 36 87 C
Overton Rd. N14 12 30 95 A
Overton Rd. SE2 67 47 79 D
Overton Rd. Sutt 110 25 63 C
Overton Rd. SW9 75 31 76 C
Overton's Yd. Croy 105 32 65 C
Overy St. Dart 80 54 74 C
Ovesdon Ave. Har 32 12 87 D
Ovett Cl. SE19 97 33 70 A
Ovex Cl. E14 64 38 79 A
Ovington Gdns. SW3 5 27 79 C
Ovington Mews. SW3 5 27 79 C
Ovington Sq. SW3 5 27 79 C
Ovington St. SW3 9 27 78 B
Owen Gdns. Wdf Gn 27 42 91 A
Owenite St. SE2 66 46 78 B
Owen Rd. Hay 53 11 82 A
Owen Rd. N13 17 32 92 C
Owen's Ct. EC1 3 31 82 B
Owen's Row. EC1 3 31 82 B
Owen St. EC1 48 31 83 D
Owens Way. SE23 88 36 73 A
Owen Way. NW10 45 20 84 A
Owgan Cl. SE5 63 32 77 D
Owlets Hall Cl. Horn 30 54 89 B
Oxberry Ave. SW6 73 24 76 C
Oxendon St. SW1 6 29 80 B
Oxenford St. SE15 75 33 75 B
Oxenpark Ave. Wem 33 18 87 A
Oxestalls Rd. SE8 64 36 78 C
Oxford Ave. Hay 69 09 76 B
Oxford Ave. Houn 59 13 78 C
Oxford Ave. SW20 95 24 69 C
Oxford Ave. W10 56 23 82 A
Oxford Circus Ave. W1 2 29 81 C
Oxford Circ. W1 2 29 81 C
Oxford Cl. Ashf 91 08 70 C
Oxford Cl. Mit 96 29 68 A
Oxford Cl. N9 17 34 93 B
Oxford Cres. N.Mal 102 20 67 D
Oxford Ct. EC4 8 32 80 B
Oxford Ct. W3 55 19 81 C
Oxford Dri. Ruis 32 11 86 B
Oxford Gdns. N20 15 26 94 D
Oxford Gdns. N21 17 32 94 A
Oxford Gdns. W10 56 23 81 D
Oxford Gdns. W4 61 19 77 B
Oxford Rd. Cars 111 27 64 C
Oxford Rd. E15 49 38 84 B
Oxford Rd. Enf 13 34 95 B
Oxford Rd. Har 32 14 88 C
Oxford Rd. Har 21 15 89 B
Oxford Rd. Ilf 51 44 85 C
Oxford Rd. N4 37 31 87 C
Oxford Rd. N9 17 34 93 B
Oxford Rd. NW6 46 25 83 C
Oxford Rd. Rom 30 54 91 B
Oxford Rd. SE19 97 32 70 B
Oxford Rd. Sid 90 46 71 D
Oxford Rd. SW15 73 24 75 C
Oxford Rd. Tedd 82 14 71 D
Oxford Rd. W5 54 17 80 B
Oxford Rd. Wall 111 29 64 C
Oxford Road N. W4 61 19 78 D
Oxford Road S. W4 61 19 78 D
Oxford Sq. W2 1 27 81 C
Oxford St. W1 2 28 81 D
Oxford Way. Felt 82 11 71 B
Oxford Wlk. Sthl 53 12 80 D
Oxgate Gdns. NW2 34 22 86 B
Oxgate La. NW2 34 22 86 B
Oxhawth Cres. Brom 108 43 67 D
Oxhey Dri. Nthwd 19 10 91 B
Oxhey La. Pnr 20 13 91 B
Ox La. Eps 109 22 62 A
Oxleas Cl. Well 78 44 76 D
Oxleay Rd. Har 32 13 87 C
Oxleigh Cl. N.Mal 102 21 67 A
Oxley Cl. Rom 30 53 90 C
Oxleys Rd. NW2 34 22 86 D
Oxlow La. Dag 52 49 85 A
Oxonian St. SE22 75 33 75 D
Oxted Cl. Mit 95 26 68 B
Oxtoby Way. SW16 96 29 69 B
Ozins Way. E16 58 40 81 C

Pace Pl. E1 57 34 81 D
Pacific Rd. E16 58 40 81 C
Packham Ct. Wor Pk 103 23 65 C
Packington Sq. N1 48 32 83 A
Packington St. N1 48 32 83 A
Packmores Rd. SE9 78 44 74 B
Padbury Ct. E2 4 33 82 B
Paddenswick Rd. W6 61 22 79 C
Paddington Green. W2 1 26 81 B
Paddington St. W1 2 28 81 A
Paddock Cl. Nthlt 43 13 83 C
Paddock Cl. SE26 88 35 71 B
Paddock Gdns. SE19 97 33 70 A
Paddock Rd. NW2 34 22 86 A
Paddock Rd. Ruis 32 11 86 D
Paddocks Cl. Har 43 13 85 B
Paddocks The. Barn 12 27 96 B
Paddocks The. Wem 34 19 86 B
Paddock Way. Chis 100 44 70 D
Paddook Rd. Bexh 79 48 75 C
Padfield Rd. SE5 75 32 75 A
Padnall Ct. Rom 29 47 89 B
Padnall Ct. Rom 29 47 89 B
Padnall Rd. Rom 29 47 89 D
Padstow Rd. Enf 13 31 97 B
Padua Rd. SE20 98 35 69 A
Pagden St. SW8 74 28 76 B
Pageant Strs. SE16 57 36 80 C
Pageant Wlk. Croy 105 33 65 C
Page Cl. Hamp 92 12 70 A
Page Cl. Har 33 18 88 D
Page Cres. Croy 112 31 64 D
Page Cres. Eri 68 51 77 D
Page Green Rd. N15 37 34 88 A
Page Green Terr. N15 37 33 88 B
Page Heath La. Brom 99 41 68 B
Page Heath Villas 99 41 68 B
Page High. N22 25 31 89 A
Pagehurst Rd. Croy 105 34 66 B
Page Rd. Felt 81 08 73 B
Page's Hill. N10 24 28 90 C
Page's La. N10 24 28 90 C
Pages La. N10 24 28 90 C
Page St. NW7 22 22 91 C
Page St. SW1 10 29 78 B
Page's Wlk. SE1 63 33 78 A
Page's Yd. W4 61 21 77 A
Paget Ave. Sutt 103 26 65 D
Paget Cl. Hamp 82 14 71 B
Paget Gdns. Chis 100 43 69 B
Paget Rd. Ilf 51 43 85 B
Paget Rd. N16 37 32 87 D
Paget Rise. SE18 66 43 77 C
Paget St. EC1 3 31 82 B
Paget Terr. SE18 66 43 77 A
Pagnell St. SE14 64 36 77 D
Pagoda Ave. Rich 71 18 75 B
Pagoda Gdns. SE3 76 38 76 D
Paignton Rd. N15 37 33 88 C
Paignton Rd. Ruis 31 10 86 C
Paine Ct. SE3 65 39 77 B
Paines Brook Rd. Rom 30 54 91 B
Paines Brook Way. Rom 30 54 91 B
Paines Cl. Pnr 20 12 89 A
Paine's La. Pnr 20 12 90 C
Pain's Cl. Mit 96 28 69 D
*Painsthorpe Rd. N16 37 33 86 C
Painters Rd. Ilf 28 46 89 A
Paisley Rd. Cars 103 26 66 D
Paisley Rd. N22 25 31 90 B
Pakeman St. N7 36 30 86 D
Pakenham Cl. SW12 86 28 73 C
Pakenham St. WC1 3 30 82 D
Palace Ave. W8 62 25 79 B
Palace Court Gdns. N10 24 29 89 A
Palace Ct. Har 33 18 88 C
Palace Ct. W2 56 25 80 B
Palace Gates Rd. N22 24 29 90 B
Palace Gate. W8 5 26 79 A
Palace Gdn Mews. W8 56 25 80 C
Palace Gdns. Enf 13 32 96 D
Palace Gdns Terr. W8 56 25 80 D
Palace Gr. Brom 99 40 69 B
Palace Green. W8 56 25 80 D
Palace Gr. SE19 97 33 70 D
Palace Mews. SW1 9 28 78 A
Palace Pl. SW1 6 29 79 C
Palace Rd. Brom 99 40 69 B
Palace Rd. E Mol 92 14 68 B
Palace Rd. King 93 17 68 D
Palace Rd. N11 24 30 91 C
Palace Rd. N8 36 29 88 B
Palace Rd. Ruis 43 12 85 A
Palace Rd. SE19 97 33 70 D
Palace Rd. SW2 87 31 72 A
Palace Sq. SE19 97 33 70 D
Palace St. SW1 6 29 79 C
Palace View. Brom 99 40 68 B
Palace View. Croy 106 36 65 D
Palace View Rd. E4 18 37 92 D
Palace View. SE12 89 40 72 A
Palamos Rd. E10 38 37 87 C
Palatine Ave. N16 48 33 85 B
Palatine Rd. N16 48 33 85 A
Palemo Rd. NW10 45 22 83 C
Palestine Gr. SW19 95 26 69 B
Palewell Cl. Orp 100 46 69 D
Palewell Common Dri. SW14 72 20 74 B
Palewell Park. SW14 72 20 75 D
Palfrey Pl. SW8 10 30 77 D
Palfrey Pl. SW8 63 31 77 C
Palgrave Ave. Sthl 53 13 80 A
Palgrave Rd. W12 61 21 79 D
Palissy St. E2 4 33 82 B
Pallant Way. Orp 108 43 65 C
Pallet Way. SE18 77 42 76 A
Palliser Rd. W14 62 24 78 C
Pall Mall E. SW1 6 29 80 D
Pall Mall Pl. SW1 6 29 80 C
Pall Mall. SW1 6 29 80 D
Palmar Cres. Bexh 79 49 76 C
Palmar Rd. Bexh 79 49 76 C
Palmeira Rd. Bexh 79 47 75 B
Palmer Ave. Sutt 110 23 64 A
Palmer Cl. Houn 70 13 76 A
Palmer Cres. King 93 18 68 A
Palmer Pl. N5 48 31 85 C
Palmer Rd. E13 58 40 82 D
Palmers Gr. E Mol 92 13 68 C
Palmers La. Enf 14 35 97 A
Palmers Pas. SW14 72 20 75 A
Palmer's Rd. E2 49 35 83 D
Palmer's Rd. N11 16 29 92 C
Palmers Rd. SW14 72 20 75 A
Palmerston Cres. N13 16 30 92 D
Palmerston Cres. SE18 66 44 77 A
Palmerston Ct. Surb 101 17 66 B
Palmerston Gr. SW19 95 25 70 C
Palmerston Rd (off Hemstal Rd) NW6 46 25 84 C
Palmerston Rd (off Kilburn High Rd). NW6 46 24 84 D
Palmerston Rd. Cars 111 27 64 B
Palmerston Rd. E17 26 36 89 D
Palmerston Rd. E7 50 40 84 B
Palmerston Rd. Har 21 15 89 B
Palmerston Rd. N22 24 30 91 B
Palmerston Rd. Sutt 110 26 64 C
Palmerston Rd. SW14 72 20 75 C
Palmerston Rd. SW19 95 25 70 C
Palmerston Rd. Th Hth 105 32 67 B
Palmerston Rd. W3 61 20 79 C
Palmerston Way. SW8 9 28 77 D
Palmer St. SW1 6 29 79 D
Palm Gr. W5 60 18 79 C
Palm Rd. Rom 41 50 88 A
Palm St. E3 57 36 82 A
Pamber St. W10 56 23 81 D
Pamela Gdns. Pnr 31 10 88 B
Pampisford Rd. Pur 112 31 62 D
Pampisford Rd. S Croy 112 31 62 B
Pams Way. Eps 109 20 64 D
Pancras La. EC4 4 32 81 D
Pancras Rd. NW1 47 29 83 D
Pandora Ct. Surb 101 18 67 C
Pandora Rd. NW6 46 25 84 A
Panfield Mews. Ilf 40 43 88 C
Panfield Rd. SE2 66 46 79 C
Pangbourne Ave. W10 56 23 81 A
Panhard Pl. Sthl 53 13 80 B
Pank Ave. Barn 11 26 95 A
Panmure Rd. SE26 87 34 72 D
Pansy Gdns. W12 55 22 80 A
Pantiles The. Bexh 67 48 77 D
Pantiles The. Brom 99 42 68 A
Panton St. SW1 6 29 80 B
Panyer Alley. EC4 4 32 81 C
Papillions Wlk. SE3 77 40 76 C
Papworth Way. SE24 87 31 73 A
Parade Mews. SE27 87 31 72 B
Parade The. Sun 91 09 70 D
Parade. The SW11 9 27 77 D
Paradise Pas. N7 48 31 84 A
Paradise Rd. Rich 71 18 74 A
Paradise Rd. SW4 74 30 76 C
Paradise Row. E2 57 34 82 B
Paradise St. SE16 63 34 79 B
Paradise Wlk. SW3 9 27 77 B
Paragon Gdns. SE1 63 32 78 B
Paragon Gr. Surb 101 18 67 D
*Paragon Mews. SE1 63 32 78 B
Paragon Pl. SE3 77 39 76 D
Paragon Pl. Surb 101 18 67 D
Paragon Rd. E9 49 35 84 A
Paragon The. SE3 77 40 76 C
Parbury Rd. SE23 76 36 74 C

Parchmore Rd. Th Hth 97 32 68 A
Parchmore Way. Th Hth 97 32 69 C
Pardoner St. SE1 8 32 79 D
Pardon St. EC1 3 31 82 D
Parfett St. E1 57 34 81 C
Parfrey St. W6 62 23 77 B
Parham Dri. Ilf 40 43 88 B
Paris Gdn. SE1 7 31 80 D
Parish La. SE20 98 35 70 D
Park App. Well 78 46 75 D
Park Ave. E15 50 39 84 A
Park Ave. Bark 51 44 84 A
Park Ave. Brom 99 39 70 B
Park Ave. Cars 111 28 63 A
Park Ave. E6 51 43 83 C
Park Ave. Enf 13 33 95 C
Park Ave. Houn 70 13 74 D
Park Ave. Ilf 40 43 87 C
Park Ave. Mit 96 28 70 D
Park Ave. N13 17 31 93 C
Park Ave. N18 17 34 92 A
Park Ave. N22 24 30 90 B
Park Ave. N3 23 25 90 B
Park Ave N. N8 24 29 89 D
Park Avenue East. Eps 109 22 63 A
Park Avenue Mews. Mit 96 28 70 D
Park Avenue N. NW10 45 22 85 D
Park Avenue Rd. N17 25 34 91 D
Park Avenue West. Eps 109 22 63 A
Park Ave. NW10 54 18 82 B
Park Ave. NW10 44 18 83 D
Park Ave. NW11 35 25 87 D
Park Ave. NW2 45 22 84 B
Park Ave. Orp 108 43 65 A
Park Ave. Orp 108 46 65 C
Park Ave. Ruis 31 09 88 C
Park Ave S. N8 24 29 89 D
Park Ave. Sthl 53 13 80 C
Park Ave. SW14 72 20 75 D
Park Ave. W Wick 106 38 65 A
Park Bvd. Rom 30 51 90 B
Park Chase. Wem 44 18 85 B
Park Cl. Cars 111 27 63 B
Park Cl. E9 49 35 83 A
Park Cl. Hamp 92 14 69 A
Park Cl. Har 21 15 90 A
Park Cl. Houn 70 14 74 A
Park Cl. N20 15 26 92 B
Park Cl. NW10 54 18 82 B
Park Cl. NW2 34 22 86 D
Park Cl. SW1 5 27 79 B
Park Cl. W14 62 24 79 D
Park Cottages. Twick 71 16 74 D
Park Crescent Rd. Eri 67 50 77 B
Park Cres. Enf 13 32 96 D
Park Cres. Eri 67 50 77 B
Park Cres. Har 21 15 90 A
Park Cres. Horn 42 52 87 A
Park Cres Mews E. W1 2 28 82 D
Park Cres Mews W. W1 2 28 82 D
Park Cres. N3 23 26 91 C
Park Cres. Twick 82 14 73 D
Park Cres. W1 2 28 82 D
Park Croft. Edg 22 20 90 A
Parkcroft Rd. SE12 89 39 73 B
Park Ct. E17 38 37 88 B
Park Ct. King 93 17 69 A
Park Ct. N12 15 26 92 D
Park Ct. N Mal 94 20 68 D
Park Ct. Wem 44 18 85 C
Parkdale Cres. Wor Pk 102 20 65 D
Parkdale Rd. SE18 66 45 78 C
Park Dri. Dag 41 50 86 C
Park Dri. Har 32 13 87 A
Park Dri. Har 21 15 91 A
Park Dri. N21 13 32 95 C
Park Dri. NW11 35 25 87 D
Park Dri. SE7 65 42 77 A
Park Dri. SW14 72 20 75 D
Park Dri. W3 61 19 79 C
Park Dr. Rom 29 50 89 D
Park End. Brom 99 39 69 B
Park End. NW3 47 27 85 A
Park End Rd. Rom 30 51 89 C
Parke Rd. Sun 91 10 68 C
Parke Rd. SW13 61 22 77 C
Parker Mews. WC2 3 30 81 C
Parker Rd. Croy 112 32 64 A
Parker's Bldgs. SE16 8 33 79 D
Parkers Rd. N2 24 27 90 A
Parker's Row. SE1 8 33 79 B
Parker St. WC2 3 30 81 C
Park Farm Cl. N2 23 26 89 A
Park Farm Cl. Pnr 31 10 88 B
Park Farm Rd. Brom 99 41 69 B
Park Farm Rd. King 93 18 70 C
Parkfield Ave. Felt 81 10 72 C
Parkfield Ave. Har 20 14 90 C
Parkfield Ave. Nthlt 43 12 83 C
Parkfield Ave. SW14 72 21 75 C
Parkfield Cl. Edg 22 19 91 B
Parkfield Cl. Nthlt 43 12 83 C
Parkfield Cres. Felt 81 10 72 C
Parkfield Cres. Har 20 14 90 C
Parkfield Cres. Ruis 32 12 86 A
Parkfield Dri. Nthlt 43 11 83 D
Parkfield Gdns. Har 20 13 89 B
Parkfield. Islw 71 15 76 A
Parkfield Rd. Felt 81 10 72 C
Parkfield Rd. Har 32 14 86 C
Parkfield Rd. Nthlt 43 12 83 C
Parkfield Rd. NW10 45 22 84 D
Parkfield Rd. SE14 76 36 76 B
Parkfield Rd. Uxb 37 07 86 B
Parkfields Ave. NW9 34 21 87 C
Parkfields Ave. SW20 94 22 69 D
Parkfields. Croy 106 36 66 D
Parkfields Rd. King 83 18 71 D
Parkfields. SW15 73 23 75 C
Parkfield St N1 48 31 83 C
Parkfield Way. Brom 107 42 67 B
Parkgate Ave. Barn 11 26 97 A
Parkgate Cl. King 94 19 70 B
Parkgate Cres. Barn 11 26 97 A
Parkgate Gdns. SW14 72 20 74 B
Park Gate. N21 16 30 94 B
Park Gate. N2 23 26 89 B
Parkgate Rd. SW11 9 27 77 C
Parkgate Rd. Wall 111 28 64 D
Parkgate. SE3 77 39 75 B
Park Gate. W5 54 17 81 B
Park Gdns. Eri 67 50 78 B
Park Gdns. King 83 18 71 D
Park Gdns. NW9 22 19 89 B
Park Gr. Bexh 79 50 75 C
Park Gr. Brom 99 40 69 B
Park Gr. E15 50 40 83 A
Park Gr. N11 24 29 91 D
Park Grove Rd. E11 39 39 86 A
Park Hall Rd. N2 24 27 89 C
Park Hall Rd. SE21 87 32 72 D
Parkham St. SW11 74 27 76 A
Park Hill. Brom 99 42 68 D
Park Hill. Cars 111 27 63 B
Park Hill Cl. Cars 111 27 64 C
Parkhill Cl. Horn 42 53 86 A
Park Hill Ct. SW17 86 27 72 D
Park Hill Rd. Brom 99 39 69 C
Park Hill Rd. Croy 105 33 65 C
Parkhill Rd. E4 18 38 94 A
Parkhill Rd. NW3 47 27 85 D
Parkhill Rd. Sid 90 45 72 C
Park Hill Rd. Wall 111 28 63 D
Park Hill. Rich 71 18 74 D
Park Hill Rise. Croy 105 33 65 D
Park Hill. SE23 87 34 73 D
Park Hill. SW4 74 29 74 B
Park Hill. W5 54 17 81 B
Park Hill Wlk. NW3 47 27 85 D
Parkholme Rd. E8 48 34 84 A
Park House Gdns. Twick 71 17 74 A
Park House Pas. N6 36 28 87 A
Parkhouse St. SE5 63 32 77 D
Parkhurst. Eps 109 20 62 C
Parkhurst Rd. Bex 79 49 74 C
Parkhurst Rd. E12 51 43 85 A
Parkhurst Rd. E17 26 36 89 C
Parkhurst Rd. N11 16 28 92 B
Parkhurst Rd. N17 25 34 90 C
Parkhurst Rd. N22 24 30 91 B
Parkhurst Rd. N7 47 30 85 A
Parkhurst Rd. Sutt 110 26 64 B
Park La. Cars 111 28 64 C
Park La. Croy 105 32 65 D
Park La. E15 49 38 83 B
Park La. Har 32 13 86 D
Park La. Horn 42 52 87 A
Park La. Houn 69 10 76 A
Park La. N17 25 34 91 C
Park La. N18 17 33 93 C
Park La. N9 17 33 93 D
Parkland Ave. Rom 30 51 90 D
Parkland Gr. Ashf 81 07 71 A
Parkland Rd. Ashf 81 07 71 A
Parkland Rd. N22 24 30 90 D
Parkland Rd. Wdf Gn 27 40 91 D
Parklands Ct. Houn 70 11 76 D
Parklands Dri. N3 23 24 89 A
Parklands Rd. SW16 86 28 71 D
Parklands. Surb 101 18 67 B
Parklands Way. Wor Pk 102 21 65 A
Park Lane Cl. N17 25 34 91 C
Park La. Rich 71 17 75 D
Park La. Rom 41 47 88 D
Park La. Sutt 110 24 63 A
Park La. Tedd 93 15 70 B
Park La. W1 6 28 80 A
Park La. Wem 44 18 85 A
Park Lawn. Th Hth 97 32 69 C
Parklea Cl. NW9 22 21 90 A
Parkleigh Rd. SW19 95 25 69 D
Parkleys. King 83 18 71 A
Parkleys. Rich 83 17 71 B
Park Mansions Arc. SW1 5 27 79 B
Parkmead Gdns. NW7 22 21 91 B
Park Mead. Har 32 13 86 D
Park Mead. Sid 78 46 74 B
Park Mead. Sid 79 47 74 C
Parkmead. SW15 72 22 74 D
Park Par. NW10 45 21 83 D
Park Pl. Hamp 92 14 70 A
Park Pl. SW1 6 29 80 C
Park Pl Villas. W2 1 26 81 A
Park Pl. W3 61 19 78 A
Park Pl. W5 54 17 80 D
Park Pl. Wem 44 18 85 B
Park Rd. Ashf 81 07 71 D
Park Rd. Barn 11 24 96 D
Park Rd. Barn 12 27 96 C
Park Rd. Barn 12 26 97 A
Park Rd. Beck 98 37 70 C
Park Rd. Brom 99 40 69 B
Park Rd. Chis 100 43 70 B
Park Rd. E10 38 37 87 C
Park Rd. E12 39 40 87 D
Park Rd. E15 50 40 83 A
Park Rd. E17 38 36 88 B
Park Rd. E6 50 41 83 A
Park Rd. E Mol 92 14 68 C
Park Rd. Felt 82 11 71 B
Park Rd. Hamp 82 14 71 C
Park Rd. Houn 70 14 74 A
Park Rd. Ilf 40 44 86 D
Park Rd. Islw 71 16 76 D
Park Rd. King 83 17 69 A
Park Rd. King 94 19 70 A
Park Rd. N11 24 30 91 C
Park Rd. N14 16 29 94 D
Park Rd. N15 25 31 89 D
Park Rd. N18 17 34 92 A
Park Rd. N2 23 26 89 B
Park Rd. N8 36 29 88 B
Park Rd. N Mal 94 20 68 D
Park Rd. NW10 45 20 83 A
Park Rd. NW4 34 22 87 B
Park Rd. NW9 34 20 87 B
Park Rd. Rich 71 18 74 D
Park Rd. SE25 97 33 68 C
Park Rd. Sun 91 10 70 D
Park Rd. Surb 101 18 67 B
Park Rd. Sutt 110 24 63 A
Park Rd. SW19 95 26 70 B
Park Rd. Tedd 93 15 70 B
Park Rd. Twick 71 17 74 C
Park Rd. W4 61 20 77 B
Park Rd. W7 54 15 80 B
Park Rd. Wall 111 28 64 D
Park Rd. Wall 104 28 65 B
Park Rd. Wem 44 18 84 A
Park Ridings. N8 25 31 89 A
Park Rise. Har 21 15 90 A
Park Rise Rd. SE23 88 36 73 C
Park Rise. SE23 88 36 73 C
Park Road E. W3 61 20 79 A
Park Road. NW1 1 27 82 C
Park Road N. W3 61 19 79 B
Park Road N. W4 61 20 78 D
Park Row. SE10 64 38 77 B
Park Royal Rd. NW10 55 20 82 C
Parkshot. Rich 71 17 75 D
Parkside Ave. Bexh 80 51 76 C
Parkside Ave. Brom 99 42 68 C
Parkside Ave. Rom 29 50 89 B
Parkside Ave. Rom 30 51 90 C
Parkside Ave. SW19 85 23 71 D
Parkside Cres. Surb 102 20 67 C
Parkside Cross. Bexh 80 51 76 C
Parkside Estate. E9 49 35 83 A
Parkside Gdns. Barn 16 28 94 A
Parkside Gdns. SW19 85 23 71 B
Parkside. Hamp 82 14 71 D
Parkside. N3 23 25 91 D
Park Side. NW2 45 22 85 B
Parkside. NW7 22 22 91 A
Parkside Rd. Belv 67 50 78 A
Parkside Rd. Houn 70 13 74 B
Parkside. SE3 65 39 77 D
Parkside. Sid 90 46 72 B
Parkside St. SW11 74 28 76 A
Parkside. Sutt 110 24 63 A
Parkside. SW19 85 23 71 B
Parkside Way. Har 20 14 89 C
Park Sq E. NW1 2 28 82 D
Park Sq Mews. NW1 2 28 82 D
Park Sq W. NW1 2 28 82 D
Park St. Croy 105 32 65 A
Parkstead Rd. SW15 72 22 74 B
Parkstone Ave. Horn 42 54 88 C
Parkstone Ave. N18 17 33 92 D
Parkstone Rd. E17 26 38 89 A
Parkstone Rd. SE15 75 34 76 C
Park St. SE1 8 32 80 C
Park St. Tedd 93 15 70 A
Park St. W1 6 28 80 A
Park Terr. Wor Pk 102 22 66 C
Park The. Cars 111 27 64 D
Park The. N6 36 28 88 C
Park The. NW11 35 25 87 D
Park The. SE19 97 33 70 D
Park The. Sid 90 46 71 A
Park The. W5 54 17 80 D
Parkthorne Cl. Har 32 13 88 D
Parkthorne Dri. Har 32 13 88 D
Parkthorne Rd. SW12 86 29 73 B
Park View Cres. N11 16 28 92 B
Park View Gdns. Ilf 27 42 89 D
Park View Gdns. NW4 35 23 88 A
Park View. N21 16 30 94 B
Park View. N5 48 32 85 A
Park View. N Mal 94 21 68 A
Park View. Pnr 20 12 90 B
Park View Rd. Bexh 79 47 75 B
Parkview Rd. Croy 105 34 66 C
Park View Rd. N17 25 34 90 C
Park View Rd. N3 23 25 90 B
Park View Rd. NW10 45 21 85 B
Park View Rd. Pnr 19 10 91 D
Park View Rd. SE9 90 43 72 B
Park View Rd. Sthl 53 13 80 C
Park View Rd. W5 54 18 81 A
Park View Rd. Well 79 47 75 A
Park View. W3 55 20 81 A
Park View. Wem 45 19 85 D
Park Village E. NW1 47 28 83 D
Park Village W. NW1 47 28 83 D
Park Villas. Rom 41 47 88 D
Parkville Rd. SW6 62 24 77 D
Park Vista. SE10 64 38 77 B
Parkway. Belv 67 48 79 C
Park Way Ct. Ruis 31 09 87 D
Park Way. Edg 22 19 90 B
Park Way. E Mol 92 13 68 B
Park Way. Enf 13 31 97 C
Park Way. Felt 81 10 73 B
Parkway. Ilf 40 45 86 D
Parkway. N14 16 30 93 A
Park Way. N20 16 27 92 B
Park Way. NW11 35 24 88 A
Parkway. NW1 47 28 83 B
Parkway. Rom 30 51 90 D
Park Way. Ruis 31 10 87 C
Parkway. SW20 95 23 68 D
Parkway The. Houn 69 10 76 B
Park West Pl. W2 1 27 81 C
Park West. W2 1 27 81 C
Park Wlk. N6 36 28 87 A
Park Wlk. SW10 62 26 77 B
Parkwood. Beck 98 37 70 C
Parkwood Gr. Sun 91 10 68 A
Parkwood. N11 24 28 91 A
Parkwood. N20 16 27 93 D
Parkwood Rd. Islw 71 16 76 A
Parkwood Rd. SW19 85 24 71 D
Parliament Hill. NW3 47 27 85 A
Parliament St. SW1 7 30 79 A
Parma Cres. SW11 74 27 75 D
Parmiter Pl. E2 49 35 83 C
Parmiter St. E2 48 34 83 D
Parmuir Rd. SW20 94 22 69 B
Parnell Rd. E3 49 36 83 B
Parnham St. E14 57 36 81 C
Parolles Rd. N19 36 29 87 C
Paroma Rd. Belv 67 49 79 C
Parr Ave. Eps 109 22 62 B
Parr Ct. Felt 82 11 71 A
Parr Rd. E6 50 41 83 B
Parr Rd. Stan 21 18 90 A
Parrs Cl. S Croy 112 32 62 B
Parr's Pl. Hamp 92 13 70 C
Parr St. N1 48 32 83 D
Parry Cl. Eps 109 22 63 C
Parry Pl. SE18 66 43 78 B
Parry Rd. SE25 97 33 68 A
Parry St. SW8 10 30 77 A
Parsifal Rd. NW6 46 25 85 C
Parsloes Ave. Dag 52 48 85 D
Parsonage Gdns. Enf 13 32 97 C
Parsonage La. Enf 13 32 97 D
Parsonage Manorway. Belv 67 49 77 A
Parsonage St. E14 64 38 78 A
Parsons Green La. SW6 73 25 76 A
Parsons Green. SW6 73 25 76 A
Parson's Mead. Croy 105 31 66 D
Parsons Mead. E Mol 92 14 68 A
Parsons Rd. E13 50 41 83 C
Parson St. NW4 23 23 89 A
Parthenia Rd. SW6 73 25 76 A
Partingdale La. NW7 15 23 92 D
Partington Cl. N19 36 29 87 D
Partridge Dri. Orp 108 44 65 C
Partridge Green. SE9 90 43 72 C
Partridge Rd. Sid 90 45 71 A
Partridge Way. N22 24 30 90 A
Pascal St. SW8 10 29 77 D
Pascoe Rd. SE13 76 38 74 B
Pasley Cl. SE17 63 32 78 C
Pasquier Rd. E17 26 36 89 A
Passage The. Rich 71 17 74 B
Passey Pl. SE9 77 42 74 D
Passfield Dri. E14 57 37 81 B
Passfields. SE6 88 38 72 C
Passing Alley. EC1 3 31 82 D
Passmore Gdns. N11 24 29 91 B
Passmore St. SW1 9 28 78 C
Pasteur Gdns. N18 17 32 92 C
Paston Cl. E5 38 35 86 D
Paston Cres. SE12 89 40 73 B
Pastor St. SE11 63 31 78 B
Pasture Cl. Wem 33 16 86 D
Pasture Rd. Dag 52 48 85 D
Pasture Rd. SE6 89 39 73 D
Pasture Rd. Wem 33 16 86 D
Pastures The. N20 15 24 94 D
Patcham Terr. SW11 74 28 76 B
Paternoster Row. EC4 4 32 81 C
Paternoster Sq. EC4 3 31 81 D
Pater St. W8 62 25 79 C
Pates Manor Dri. Felt 81 08 73 B
Pathfield Rd. SW16 96 29 70 B
Path The. SW19 95 25 69 B
Patience Rd. SW11 74 27 76 C
Patio Cl. SW4 74 29 74 D
Patmore St. SW8 74 29 76 A
Patmos Rd. SW9 75 31 76 B
Paton Cl. E3 57 37 82 A
Paton St. EC1 4 32 82 C
Patricia Ct. SE2 66 46 77 D
Patricia Dri. Horn 42 54 87 C
Patrick Connolly Gdns. E3 57 37 82 B
Patrick Pas. SW11 74 27 76 C
Patrick Rd. E13 58 41 82 A
Patriot Sq. E2 48 34 83 D
Patrol Pl. SE6 76 37 74 D
Patshull Pl. NW5 47 29 84 A
Patshull Rd. NW5 47 29 84 A
Patten Alley. Rich 71 17 74 B
Pattenden Rd. SE6 88 36 73 D
Patten Rd. SW18 86 27 73 A
Patterdale Cl. Brom 99 39 70 A
Patterdale Rd. SE15 64 35 77 C
Patterson Rd. SE19 97 33 70 B
Pattison Rd. NW2 35 25 86 C
Pattison Wlk. SE18 66 44 78 C
Paul Cl. E15 50 39 84 C
Paulet Rd. SE5 75 31 76 B
Paul Gdns. Croy 105 33 65 B
Paulhan Rd. Har 21 17 89 D
Paulin Dri. N21 17 31 94 B
Pauline Cres. Twick 82 14 73 C
Paul St. E15 50 39 83 A
Paul St. EC2 4 33 82 C
Paultons Sq. SW3 62 26 77 B
Paultons St. SW3 62 26 77 B
Pauntley St. N19 36 29 87 C
Paved Ct. Rich 71 17 74 B
Paveley St. NW8 1 27 82 C
Paveley St. NW8 1 27 82 A
Pavement Mews. Rom 41 47 87 B
Pavement Sq. Croy 105 34 66 C
Pavement The. SW4 74 29 75 C
Pavet Cl. Dag 52 49 84 B
Pavilion Rd. Ilf 39 42 87 B
Pavilion Rd. SW1 5 27 79 D
Pavilion St. SW1 5 27 79 D
Pavilion Terr. 101 16 67 A
Pavilion Way. Ruis 32 11 86 A
Pawleyne Cl. SE20 98 35 70 C
Pawsey Cl. E13 50 40 83 A
Pawson's Rd. Croy 105 32 67 A
Paxford Rd. Wem 33 16 86 B
Paxton Cl. Rich 71 18 76 D
Paxton Pl. SE27 87 33 71 A
Paxton Rd. Brom 99 40 70 C
Paxton Rd. N17 25 34 91 C
Paxton Rd. W4 61 21 77 A
Paynell Ct. SE3 77 39 75 A
Payne Rd. E3 49 37 83 D
Payne St. SE8 64 36 77 D
Peabody Ave. SW1 9 28 78 D
*Peabody Bldgs. SE17 63 32 78 B
Peabody Bldgs. SE5 75 32 76 B
Peabody Cl. SE10 76 37 76 B
Peabody Cottages. N17 25 33 90 A
Peabody Estate. E1 57 34 80 A
Peabody Estate. E1 57 35 80 B
Peabody Estate. E2 48 34 83 D
Peabody Estate. N1 48 32 83 A
Peabody Estate. SE1 8 32 80 C
Peabody Estate. SE24 87 31 73 B
Peabody Estate. SW1 10 29 78 A
Peabody Estate. SW6 62 24 77 B
Peabody Estate. W10 56 23 82 C
Peabody Estate. W6 62 23 78 C
Peabody Hill. SE21 87 31 73 D
Peabody Yd. N1 48 32 83 A
Peace Gr. Wem 34 19 86 B
Peace St. E1 57 34 82 C
Peaches Cl. Sutt 110 24 63 C
Peachum Rd. SE3 65 39 77 B
Peacock Ave. Felt 81 08 73 D
Peacock Cl. Horn 30 54 89 C
Peacock St. SE17 63 31 78 B
Peacock Wlk. N6 36 28 87 B
Peacock Yd. SE17 63 31 78 B
Peakes Pl. SE18 66 43 78 B
Peaketon Ave. Ilf 39 41 88 B
Peak Hill Ave. SE26 88 35 71 A
Peak Hill Gdns. SE26 88 35 71 A
Peak Hill. SE26 88 35 71 A
Peaks Hill. Pur 111 30 62 C
Peaks Hill Rise. Pur 111 30 62 C
Peak The. SE26 88 35 72 C
Peal Gdns. W3 54 16 82 C
Peall Rd. Croy 104 30 67 D
Pearcefield Ave. SE23 88 35 73 C
Pear Cl. NW9 22 20 89 D
Pearcroft Rd. E11 38 38 86 B
Peardon St. SW8 74 28 76 D
Peareswood Gdns. Stan 21 17 90 B
Pearfield Rd. SE23 88 36 72 C
Pearl Rd. E17 26 37 89 A
Pearl St. E1 57 34 80 D
Pearman St. SE1 7 31 79 A
Pear Pl. SE1 7 31 79 A
Pearscroft Ct. SW6 73 25 76 B
Pearscroft Rd. SW6 73 25 76 B
Pearson's Ave. SE14 76 37 76 A
Pearson St. E2 48 33 83 D
Pears Rd. Houn 70 13 75 D
Pear Tree Cl. Eri 79 50 76 B
Pear Tree Cl. Mit 96 27 69 C
Pear Tree Ct. EC1 3 31 82 C
Peartree Gdns. Dag 51 46 85 B
Peartree Gdns. Rom 29 49 90 D
Pear Tree Rd. Ashf 81 08 71 C
Peartree Rd. Enf 13 33 96 A
Pear Tree St. EC1 4 32 82 C
Peary Pl. E2 57 35 82 A
Pebworth Rd. Har 33 16 86 A
Peckarmans Wood. SE26 87 34 72 C
Peckett Sq. N5 48 32 85 A
Peckford Pl. SW9 75 31 76 C
Peckham Gr. SE15 63 33 77 C
Peckham High St. SE15 75 34 76 A
Peckham Hill St. SE15 63 34 77 C
Peckham Park Rd. SE15 63 34 77 A
Peckham Rd. SE15 75 33 76 B
Peckham Rd. SE5 75 33 76 A
Peckham Rye. SE15 75 34 75 D
Peckwater St. NW5 47 29 85 C
Pedlars Wlk. N7 47 30 85 C
Pedley St. E1 4 33 82 D
Pedley St. E1 57 34 82 C
Pedro St. E5 49 35 85 B
Pedworth Rd. SE16 64 35 78 A
Peek Cres. SW19 85 23 71 D
Peel Dri. Ilf 27 42 90 C
Peel Gr. E2 49 35 83 C
Peel Pass. W8 56 25 80 C
Peel Prec. NW6 46 25 83 C
Peel Rd. E18 27 39 90 B

| | | | |
|---|---|---|---|
| Peel Rd. Har | 21 | 15 89 | B |
| Peel Rd. NW6 | 46 | 25 83 | C |
| Peel Rd. Wem | 33 | 17 86 | D |
| Peel St. W8 | 56 | 25 80 | C |
| Peel Way. Rom | 30 | 54 90 | D |
| Peerage Way. Horn | 42 | 54 87 | B |
| Peerless St. EC1 | 4 | 32 82 | B |
| Pegamoid Rd. N18 | 18 | 35 92 | A |
| Pegamoid Rd. N18 | 18 | 35 93 | D |
| Pegasus Pl. SE11 | 63 | 31 77 | A |
| Pegasus Rd. Croy | 112 | 31 63 | A |
| Pegelm Gdns. Horn | 42 | 54 87 | B |
| Pegg Rd. Houn | 59 | 11 77 | D |
| Pegley Gdns. SE12 | 89 | 40 72 | A |
| Pegwell St. SE18 | 66 | 45 77 | C |
| Pekin St. E14 | 57 | 37 81 | C |
| Peldon Ct. Rich | 71 | 18 74 | B |
| Peldon Pas. Rich | 71 | 18 75 | D |
| Peldon Wlk. N1 | 48 | 31 83 | B |
| Pelham Ave. Bark | 51 | 45 83 | B |
| Pelham Cl. SE5 | 75 | 33 75 | A |
| Pelham Cres. SW7 | 9 | 27 78 | A |
| Pelham Pl. SW7 | 9 | 27 78 | A |
| Pelham Rd. Beck | 98 | 35 69 | C |
| Pelham Rd. Bexh | 79 | 49 75 | A |
| Pelham Rd. E18 | 27 | 40 89 | B |
| Pelham Rd. Ilf | 40 | 44 86 | B |
| Pelham Rd. N15 | 25 | 33 89 | D |
| Pelham Rd. N22 | 25 | 31 90 | C |
| Pelham Rd. SW19 | 95 | 25 70 | C |
| Pelham St. SW7 | 9 | 27 78 | A |
| *Pelican Pas. E1 | 57 | 35 82 | C |
| Pelican Wlk. SW9 | 75 | 31 75 | D |
| Pelier St. SE17 | 63 | 32 77 | A |
| Pelinore Rd. SE6 | 89 | 39 72 | A |
| Pellant Rd. SW6 | 62 | 24 77 | C |
| Pellatt Gr. N22 | 25 | 31 90 | A |
| Pellatt Rd. SE22 | 75 | 33 74 | B |
| Pellerin Rd. N16 | 48 | 33 85 | C |
| Pelling St. E14 | 57 | 37 81 | C |
| Pellipar Cl. N13 | 17 | 31 93 | C |
| Pellipar Gdns. SE18 | 65 | 42 78 | D |
| Pelly Rd. E13 | 50 | 40 83 | C |
| Pelton Ave. Sutt | 110 | 25 62 | D |
| Pelton Rd. E10 | 65 | 39 78 | C |
| Pembar Ave. E17 | 26 | 36 89 | A |
| Pember Rd. NW10 | 56 | 23 82 | B |
| Pemberton Ave. Rom | 30 | 52 89 | B |
| Pemberton Gdns. N19 | 36 | 29 86 | C |
| Pemberton Gdns. Rom | 41 | 48 88 | A |
| Pemberton Pl. E8 | 49 | 35 84 | C |
| Pemberton Rd. E Mol | 92 | 14 68 | C |
| Pemberton Rd. N4 | 37 | 31 88 | B |
| Pemberton Row. EC4 | 3 | 31 81 | C |
| Pemberton Terr. N19 | 36 | 29 86 | C |
| Pembridge Ave. Twick | 82 | 12 73 | D |
| Pembridge Cres. W11 | 56 | 25 80 | A |
| Pembridge Gdns. W2 | 56 | 25 80 | A |
| Pembridge Mews. W11 | 56 | 25 80 | A |
| Pembridge Pl. W2 | 56 | 25 80 | A |
| Pembridge Rd. W11 | 56 | 25 80 | A |
| Pembridge Sq. W2 | 56 | 25 80 | A |
| Pembridge Villas. W11 | 56 | 25 80 | A |
| Pembroke Ave. Enf | 13 | 34 97 | B |
| Pembroke Ave. Har | 21 | 16 89 | B |
| Pembroke Ave. Surb | 102 | 19 67 | B |
| Pembroke Cl. SW1 | 6 | 28 79 | A |
| Pembroke Gdns Cl. W8 | 62 | 25 79 | C |
| Pembroke Gdns. Dag | 41 | 49 86 | D |
| Pembroke Gdns. W8 | 62 | 25 78 | A |
| Pembroke Mews. W8 | 62 | 25 79 | C |
| Pembroke Pl. Edg | 22 | 19 91 | C |
| Pembroke Pl. Islw | 71 | 15 76 | C |
| Pembroke Pl. W8 | 62 | 25 79 | C |
| Pembroke Rd. Brom | 99 | 41 69 | C |
| Pembroke Rd. E17 | 38 | 37 88 | B |
| Pembroke Rd. Eri | 67 | 50 78 | B |
| Pembroke Rd. Grnf | 53 | 13 82 | D |
| Pembroke Rd. Ilf | 40 | 45 87 | B |
| Pembroke Rd. Mit | 96 | 28 69 | C |
| Pembroke Rd. N10 | 24 | 28 91 | C |
| Pembroke Rd. N13 | 17 | 32 93 | C |
| Pembroke Rd. N15 | 37 | 33 88 | B |
| Pembroke Rd. N8 | 24 | 30 89 | C |
| Pembroke Rd. Ruis | 31 | 09 87 | D |
| Pembroke Rd. SE25 | 97 | 33 68 | C |
| Pembroke Rd. W8 | 62 | 25 78 | A |
| Pembroke Rd. Wem | 33 | 17 86 | D |
| Pembroke Sq. W8 | 62 | 25 79 | C |
| Pembroke St. N1 | 47 | 30 84 | C |
| Pembroke Studios. W8 | 62 | 24 79 | D |
| Pembroke Villas. Rich | 71 | 17 75 | D |
| Pembroke Villas. W8 | 62 | 25 78 | A |
| Pembroke Wlk. W8 | 62 | 25 78 | A |
| Pembury Ave. Wor Pk | 102 | 22 66 | A |
| Pembury Cl. Brom | 107 | 39 66 | B |
| Pembury Cl. E5 | 48 | 34 85 | D |
| Pembury Pl. E5 | 48 | 34 85 | D |
| Pembury Rd. Bexh | 67 | 48 77 | A |
| Pembury Rd. E5 | 48 | 34 85 | D |
| Pembury Rd. N17 | 25 | 33 90 | B |
| Pembury Rd. SE25 | 97 | 34 68 | C |
| Pemdevon Rd. Croy | 105 | 31 66 | A |
| Pemell Cl. E1 | 57 | 35 82 | C |
| Penally Pl. N1 | 48 | 32 83 | B |
| Penang St. E1 | 57 | 34 80 | D |
| Penarth Cl. Sutt | 110 | 26 63 | C |
| Penarth St. SE15 | 6 | 35 77 | A |
| Penberth Rd. SE6 | 88 | 38 73 | C |
| Penbury Rd. Sthl | 59 | 12 78 | D |
| Pencraig Way SE15 | 63 | 34 77 | B |
| Penda Rd. Eri | 67 | 49 77 | D |
| Pendarves Rd. SW20 | 95 | 23 69 | A |
| Penda's Mead. E9 | 49 | 36 85 | A |
| Pendennis Rd. N17 | 25 | 32 89 | B |
| Pendennis Rd. SW16 | 86 | 30 71 | A |
| Penderel Rd. Houn | 70 | 13 74 | A |
| Penderry Rise. SE6 | 88 | 38 72 | B |
| Penderyn Way. N7 | 47 | 29 85 | B |
| Pendle Ho. SE26 | 87 | 34 72 | C |
| Pendle Rd. SW16 | 86 | 29 71 | C |
| Pendlestone Rd. E17 | 38 | 37 88 | B |
| Pendragon Rd. Brom | 89 | 40 72 | C |
| Pendrell Rd. SE4 | 76 | 36 76 | C |
| Pendrell St. SE18 | 66 | 44 77 | B |
| Pendula Dri. Hay | 53 | 11 81 | B |
| Penerley Rd. SE6 | 88 | 38 73 | C |
| Penfold Pl. NW1 | 1 | 27 81 | A |
| Penfold Rd. N9 | 18 | 35 94 | D |
| Penfold St. NW1 | 1 | 27 81 | A |
| Penfold St. NW8 | 1 | 26 82 | D |
| Penford Gdns. SE9 | 77 | 41 75 | B |
| Penford St. SE5 | 75 | 31 76 | D |
| Pengarth Rd. Bex | 79 | 47 74 | D |
| Penge La. SE20 | 98 | 35 70 | D |
| Penge Rd. SE20 | 97 | 34 68 | A |
| Penge Rd. SE25 | 97 | 34 68 | A |
| Penhall Rd. SE7 | 65 | 41 78 | B |
| Penhill Rd. Bex | 79 | 47 74 | C |
| Penhurst Rd. Ilf | 28 | 44 91 | C |
| Penhurst Wlk. Brom | 107 | 39 67 | B |
| Penifather La. Grnf | 53 | 14 82 | D |
| Peninsular Cl. Felt | 69 | 09 74 | C |
| Penistone Rd. SW16 | 96 | 30 70 | C |
| Penistone Wlk. Rom | 30 | 53 91 | A |
| Penketh Dri. Har | 32 | 14 86 | D |
| Penmon Rd. SE2 | 66 | 46 79 | C |
| Pennack Rd. SE15 | 63 | 33 77 | B |
| Pennant Terr. E17 | 26 | 36 90 | D |
| Pennard Rd. W12 | 62 | 23 79 | A |
| Pennards The. Sun | 92 | 11 68 | A |
| Pennart Mews. W8 | 62 | 25 78 | B |
| Penn Cl. Grnf | 43 | 13 83 | D |
| Penn Cl. Har | 21 | 17 89 | C |
| Penner Cl. SW19 | 85 | 24 72 | A |
| Pennethorne Cl. E9 | 49 | 35 83 | A |
| Pennethorne Rd. SE15 | 63 | 34 77 | D |
| Penn Gdns. Chis | 100 | 43 69 | D |
| Penn Gdns. Rom | 29 | 49 91 | C |
| Pennine Dri. NW2 | 35 | 23 86 | B |
| Pennine La. NW2 | 35 | 24 86 | A |
| Pennine Way. Bexh | 80 | 51 76 | A |
| Pennington Cl. Rom | 29 | 49 91 | A |
| Pennington St. E1 | 57 | 34 80 | B |
| Penn La. Bex | 79 | 48 74 | C |
| Penn Rd. N7 | 47 | 30 85 | C |
| Penn St. N1 | 48 | 32 83 | B |
| Pennyfields. E14 | 57 | 37 80 | A |
| Pennymore Wlk. W9 | 56 | 24 82 | D |
| Penny Rd. NW10 | 55 | 19 82 | B |
| Penpoll Rd. E8 | 48 | 34 84 | B |
| Penpool La. Well | 78 | 46 75 | B |
| Penrhyn Ave. E17 | 26 | 37 90 | A |
| Penrhyn Cres. E17 | 26 | 37 90 | A |
| Penrhyn Cres. SW14 | 72 | 20 75 | C |
| Penrhyn Gdns. King | 93 | 17 68 | D |
| Penrhyn Gr. E17 | 26 | 37 90 | A |
| Penrhyn Rd. King | 93 | 18 68 | A |
| Penrith Cl. Beck | 98 | 37 69 | B |
| Penrith Cl. SW15 | 73 | 24 74 | A |
| Penrith Pl. SE27 | 87 | 31 72 | B |
| Penrith Rd. Ilf | 28 | 45 91 | B |
| Penrith Rd. N15 | 37 | 32 88 | B |
| Penrith Rd. N Mal | 94 | 20 68 | D |
| Penrith Rd. Th Hth | 97 | 32 69 | C |
| Penrith St. SW16 | 96 | 29 70 | A |
| Penrose Gr. SE17 | 63 | 32 78 | C |
| Penrose St. SE17 | 63 | 32 78 | C |
| Penryn St. NW1 | 47 | 29 83 | D |
| Penry St. SE1 | 63 | 33 78 | A |
| Pensbury Pl. SW8 | 74 | 29 76 | C |
| Pensbury St. SW8 | 74 | 29 76 | C |
| Pensford Ave. Rich | 72 | 19 76 | C |
| Penshurst Ave. Sid | 78 | 46 74 | C |
| Penshurst Green. Brom | 107 | 39 67 | B |
| Penshurst Rd. Bexh | 79 | 48 76 | B |
| Penshurst Rd. E9 | 49 | 35 84 | D |
| Penshurst Rd. N17 | 25 | 33 91 | C |
| Penshurst Rd. Th Hth | 105 | 31 67 | B |
| Penshurst Way. Sutt | 110 | 25 63 | C |
| Penstock Path. N22 | 24 | 30 89 | B |
| Pentelow Gdns. Felt | 69 | 10 74 | C |
| Pentire Rd. E17 | 26 | 38 90 | B |
| Pentland Cl. NW11 | 35 | 24 86 | A |
| Pentlands Cl. Mit | 96 | 28 68 | B |
| Pentland St. SW18 | 73 | 26 74 | C |
| Pentland Way. Ruis | 31 | 08 86 | C |
| Pentlow St. SW15 | 73 | 23 75 | A |
| Pentney Rd. E4 | 18 | 38 94 | D |
| Pentney Rd. SW12 | 86 | 29 73 | C |
| Pentney Rd. SW19 | 95 | 24 69 | A |
| Penton Gr. N1 | 48 | 31 83 | C |
| Penton Pl. SE17 | 63 | 31 78 | D |
| Penton Rise. WC1 | 3 | 30 82 | B |
| Penton St. N1 | 48 | 31 83 | C |
| Pentonville Rd. N1 | 47 | 30 83 | D |
| Pentridge St. SE15 | 63 | 33 77 | D |
| Pentyre Ave. N18 | 17 | 32 92 | D |
| Penwerris Ave. Islw | 59 | 14 77 | C |
| Penwith Rd. SW18 | 85 | 25 72 | B |
| Penwortham Rd. S Croy | 112 | 32 62 | D |
| Penwortham Rd. SW16 | 96 | 29 70 | A |
| Penylan Pl. Edg | 22 | 19 91 | C |
| Penywern Rd. SW5 | 62 | 25 78 | C |
| Penzance Pl. W11 | 56 | 24 80 | C |
| Penzance St. W11 | 56 | 24 80 | C |
| Peony Gdns. W12 | 55 | 22 80 | A |
| Peploe Rd. NW6 | 46 | 23 83 | D |
| Pepper St. SE1 | 8 | 32 79 | A |
| Peptha Rd. SW18 | 73 | 25 74 | C |
| Pepys Cres. Barn | 11 | 23 95 | B |
| Pepys Rd. SE14 | 76 | 35 76 | D |
| Pepys Rd. SW20 | 95 | 23 69 | A |
| Pepys Rise. Orp | 108 | 45 66 | D |
| Pepys St. EC3 | 8 | 33 80 | A |
| Perceval Ave. NW3 | 47 | 27 85 | C |
| Perch St. E8 | 48 | 33 85 | B |
| Percival Ct. N17 | 25 | 33 91 | D |
| Percival Gdns. Rom | 41 | 47 88 | D |
| Percival Rd. Enf | 13 | 33 96 | D |
| Percival Rd. Felt | 81 | 09 72 | B |
| Percival Rd. Horn | 42 | 53 88 | C |
| Percival Rd. Orp | 108 | 44 65 | A |
| Percival Rd. SW14 | 72 | 20 75 | C |
| Percival St. EC1 | 3 | 31 82 | B |
| Percival Way. Eps | 109 | 20 64 | B |
| Percy Ave. Ashf | 81 | 07 71 | C |
| Percy Bryant Rd. Sun | 91 | 09 70 | C |
| Percy Circ. WC1 | 3 | 30 82 | B |
| Percy Gdns. Enf | 14 | 35 95 | B |
| Percy Gdns. Islw | 71 | 16 75 | A |
| Percy Gdns. Wor Pk | 102 | 21 66 | C |
| Percy Mews. W1 | 2 | 29 81 | B |
| Percy Pl. W12 | 55 | 22 80 | C |
| Percy Rd. Bexh | 79 | 48 76 | C |
| Percy Rd. E11 | 39 | 39 87 | A |
| Percy Rd. E16 | 58 | 39 81 | A |
| Percy Rd. Hamp | 92 | 13 70 | C |
| Percy Rd. Ilf | 40 | 46 87 | A |
| Percy Rd. Islw | 71 | 16 75 | C |
| Percy Rd. Mit | 104 | 28 66 | A |
| Percy Rd. N12 | 15 | 26 92 | C |
| Percy Rd. N21 | 17 | 32 94 | A |
| Percy Rd. Rom | 29 | 49 89 | B |
| Percy Rd. SE20 | 98 | 35 69 | B |
| Percy Rd. SE25 | 105 | 34 67 | A |
| Percy Rd. Twick | 82 | 13 73 | D |
| Percy Rd. W12 | 61 | 22 79 | A |
| Percy St. W1 | 2 | 29 81 | B |
| Percy Way. Twick | 82 | 14 73 | C |
| Peregrine Rd. Sun | 91 | 09 69 | D |
| Peregrine Way. SW19 | 95 | 23 70 | C |
| Perham Rd. W14 | 62 | 24 78 | D |
| Perifield. SE21 | 87 | 32 73 | C |
| Perimeade Rd. Grnf | 44 | 17 83 | C |
| Periton Rd. SE9 | 77 | 41 75 | D |
| Perivale Gdns. W13 | 54 | 16 82 | D |
| Perivale Grange. Grnf | 54 | 16 82 | A |
| Perivale La. Grnf | 54 | 16 82 | A |
| Perkin Cl. Wem | 44 | 16 85 | D |
| Perkins Rd. Ilf | 40 | 44 88 | B |
| Perkins Rents. SW1 | 6 | 29 79 | D |
| Perks Cl. SE3 | 77 | 39 76 | C |
| Perlock Ave. Har | 32 | 14 87 | C |
| Perpins Rd. SE9 | 78 | 45 74 | C |
| Perran Rd. SW2 | 87 | 31 72 | B |
| Perran Wlk (off Clayponds La). Brent | 60 | 18 78 | C |
| Perren St. NW5 | 47 | 28 84 | B |
| Perrers Rd. W6 | 61 | 22 78 | B |
| Perring Estate. E3 | 57 | 37 81 | A |
| Perrin Rd. Wem | 44 | 16 85 | B |
| Perrin's Ct. NW3 | 46 | 26 85 | A |
| Perrin's La. NW3 | 46 | 26 85 | A |
| Perrins Wlk. NW3 | 46 | 26 85 | A |
| Perrott St. SE18 | 66 | 44 78 | A |
| Perry Cl. Rain | 52 | 50 83 | D |
| Perry Ct. N15 | 37 | 33 88 | C |
| Perryfield Way. NW9 | 34 | 21 87 | B |
| Perryfield Way. Rich | 83 | 16 72 | D |
| Perry Garth. Nthlt | 43 | 11 83 | A |
| Perry Gdns. N9 | 17 | 33 93 | C |
| Perry Hall Cl. Orp | 108 | 46 66 | A |
| Perry Hall Rd. Orp | 108 | 46 66 | A |
| Perry Hill. SE6 | 88 | 35 72 | D |
| Perry How. Wor Pk | 102 | 21 66 | D |
| Perrymans Farm Rd. Ilf | 40 | 44 88 | B |
| Perry Mead. Enf | 13 | 31 97 | D |
| Perrymead St. SW6 | 73 | 25 76 | D |
| Perryn Rd. SE16 | 63 | 34 79 | D |
| Perryn Rd. W3 | 55 | 20 80 | B |
| Perry Rise. SE23 | 88 | 36 72 | C |
| Perry's Pl. W1 | 2 | 29 81 | D |
| Perry St. Chis | 100 | 45 70 | A |
| Perry St. Dart | 80 | 51 75 | A |
| Perry Vale. SE23 | 88 | 35 72 | B |
| Perserverance Pl. Rich | 71 | 18 75 | C |
| Persfield Cl. Eps | 109 | 22 62 | C |
| Persfield Mews. Eps | 109 | 21 62 | D |
| Pershore Cl. Ilf | 40 | 43 88 | B |
| Pershore Gr. Cars | 103 | 26 67 | D |
| Pert Cl. N11 | 24 | 28 91 | B |
| Perth Ave. Hay | 53 | 11 82 | C |
| Perth Ave. NW9 | 34 | 21 87 | A |
| Perth Cl. SW20 | 94 | 22 69 | C |
| Perth Rd. Bark | 51 | 44 83 | B |
| Perth Rd. Beck | 98 | 38 69 | C |
| Perth Rd. E10 | 38 | 36 87 | D |
| Perth Rd. E13 | 50 | 40 83 | D |
| Perth Rd. Ilf | 40 | 43 87 | B |
| Perth Rd. N22 | 25 | 31 90 | B |
| Perth Rd. N4 | 37 | 31 87 | C |
| Perth Terr. Ilf | 40 | 44 87 | A |
| Perwell Ave. Har | 32 | 12 87 | D |
| Peter Ave. NW10 | 45 | 22 84 | D |
| Peterborough Gdns. Ilf | 39 | 42 87 | A |
| Peterborough Mews. SW6 | 73 | 25 76 | C |
| Peterborough Rd. Cars | 104 | 27 66 | B |
| Peterborough Rd. E10 | 38 | 38 88 | D |
| Peterborough Rd. E17 | 38 | 38 88 | A |
| Peterborough Rd. Har | 33 | 15 87 | B |
| Peterborough Rd. SW6 | 73 | 25 75 | A |
| Peterborough Villas. SW6 | 73 | 25 76 | B |
| Petergate. SW11 | 73 | 26 75 | C |
| Peters Cl. Stan | 21 | 17 91 | B |
| Petersfield Ave. Rom | 30 | 54 91 | B |
| Petersfield Cl. N18 | 17 | 32 92 | C |
| Petersfield Rd. W3 | 61 | 20 79 | A |
| Petersfield Rise. SW15 | 84 | 22 73 | D |
| Petersham Cl. Rich | 83 | 17 72 | B |
| Petersham Cl. Sutt | 110 | 25 64 | C |
| Petersham Dri. Orp | 100 | 46 68 | A |
| Petersham Gdns. Orp | 100 | 45 69 | D |
| Petersham La. SW7 | 5 | 26 79 | C |
| Petersham Mews. SW7 | 5 | 26 79 | C |
| Petersham Pl. SW7 | 5 | 26 79 | C |
| Petersham Rd. Rich | 83 | 18 73 | C |
| Peter's Hill. EC4 | 8 | 32 80 | A |
| Peter's La. EC1 | 3 | 31 81 | B |
| Peters Path. SE26 | 87 | 34 71 | B |
| Peter St. E2 | 4 | 33 82 | B |
| Peterstone Rd. SE2 | 66 | 46 79 | B |
| Peterstow Cl. SW19 | 85 | 24 72 | A |
| Peter St. W1 | 6 | 29 80 | B |
| Petherton Ct. Har | 33 | 15 88 | D |
| Petherton Rd. N5 | 48 | 32 85 | D |
| Petley Rd. W6 | 62 | 23 77 | D |
| Peto Pl. NW1 | 2 | 28 82 | D |
| Peto Street N. E16 | 58 | 39 80 | B |
| Peto Street S. E16 | 58 | 39 80 | B |
| Petrie Cl. NW2 | 46 | 24 84 | A |
| Pettits Bvd. Rom | 30 | 51 90 | C |
| Pettits Cl. Rom | 30 | 51 90 | C |
| Pettits Lane N. Rom | 30 | 51 90 | A |
| Pettits La. Rom | 30 | 51 89 | A |
| Pettit's Pl. Dag | 52 | 49 85 | C |
| Pettit's Rd. Dag | 52 | 49 85 | C |
| Pettiward Cl. SW15 | 73 | 23 75 | C |
| Pettley Gdns. Rom | 41 | 50 88 | B |
| Pettman Cres. SE28 | 66 | 44 79 | D |
| Pettsgrove Ave. Wem | 44 | 17 85 | C |
| Pett's Hill. Nthlt | 43 | 13 85 | D |
| Petts La. Shep | 91 | 07 68 | C |
| Pett St. SE18 | 65 | 42 78 | A |
| Petts Wood Rd. Orp | 108 | 44 67 | B |
| Petty France. SW1 | 6 | 29 79 | C |
| Petworth Gdns. SW20 | 94 | 22 68 | B |
| Petworth Rd. Bexh | 79 | 49 74 | A |
| Petworth Rd. N12 | 16 | 27 92 | C |
| Petworth St. SW11 | 74 | 27 76 | A |
| Petyt Pl. SW3 | 9 | 27 77 | A |
| Petyward. SW3 | 9 | 27 78 | A |
| Pevensey Ave. Enf | 13 | 33 97 | C |
| Pevensey Ave. N11 | 16 | 29 92 | D |
| Pevensey Cl. Islw | 59 | 14 77 | C |
| Pevensey Rd. E7 | 50 | 40 85 | A |
| Pevensey Rd. Felt | 82 | 12 73 | C |
| Pevensey Rd. SW17 | 85 | 26 71 | B |
| Peveril Dri. Tedd | 82 | 14 71 | D |
| Pewsey Cl. E4 | 18 | 37 92 | C |
| Peyton Pl. SE10 | 64 | 38 77 | C |
| Phelp St. SE17 | 63 | 32 77 | B |
| Phene St. SW3 | 9 | 27 77 | A |
| Philan Way. Rom | 29 | 50 91 | B |
| Philbeach Gdns. SW5 | 62 | 25 78 | C |
| Philchurch Pl. E1 | 57 | 34 81 | C |
| Philip Ave. Rom | 41 | 50 87 | D |
| Philip Gdns. Croy | 106 | 36 65 | B |
| Philip La. N15 | 25 | 33 89 | A |
| Philipot Path. SE9 | 77 | 42 74 | D |
| Philipot Path. SE9 | 78 | 43 74 | C |
| Philippa Gdns. SE9 | 77 | 41 74 | B |
| Philip Rd. SE15 | 75 | 34 75 | A |
| Philip St. E13 | 58 | 40 82 | C |
| Philip Wlk. SE15 | 75 | 34 75 | B |
| Phillimore Gardens Cl. W8 | 62 | 25 79 | C |
| Phillimore Gdns. NW10 | 46 | 23 83 | A |
| Phillimore Gdns. W8 | 62 | 25 79 | A |
| Phillimore Pl. W8 | 62 | 25 79 | A |
| Phillimore Wlk. W8 | 62 | 25 79 | C |
| Phillipp St. N1 | 48 | 33 83 | A |
| Phillips Cl. Dart | 80 | 52 74 | D |
| Phillips Way. Brom | 99 | 40 69 | C |
| Philpot La. EC3 | 8 | 33 80 | A |
| Philpot St. E1 | 57 | 34 81 | D |
| Phineas Pett Rd. SE9 | 77 | 42 75 | A |
| Phipp's Bridge Rd. Mit | 95 | 26 68 | B |
| Phipp's Bridge Rd. SW19 | 95 | 26 69 | C |
| Phipp St. EC2 | 4 | 33 82 | C |
| Phoebeth Rd. SE4 | 76 | 37 74 | A |
| Phoenix Dri. Brom | 107 | 41 65 | D |
| Phoenix Rd. NW1 | 47 | 29 83 | D |
| Phoenix Rd. SE20 | 98 | 35 70 | A |
| Phoenix St. WC2 | 2 | 29 81 | D |
| Phoenix Way. Houn | 59 | 11 77 | B |
| Phoenix Pl. WC1 | 3 | 30 82 | D |
| Phyllis Ave. N.Mal | 102 | 22 67 | B |
| Picardy Manorway. Belv | 67 | 49 79 | D |
| Picardy Rd. Belv | 67 | 49 78 | A |
| Picardy St. Belv | 67 | 49 79 | C |
| Piccadilly Arc. SW1 | 6 | 29 80 | C |
| Piccadilly Circ. W1 | 6 | 29 80 | B |
| Piccadilly Pl. W1 | 6 | 29 80 | A |
| Piccadilly. W1 | 6 | 29 80 | C |
| Pickard St. EC1 | 3 | 31 82 | B |
| Pickering Ave. E6 | 51 | 43 83 | C |
| Pickering Mews. W2 | 56 | 25 81 | D |
| Pickering Pl. SW1 | 6 | 29 80 | C |
| Pickering St. N1 | 48 | 32 83 | A |
| Pickets St. SW12 | 86 | 28 73 | B |
| Pickett Croft. Stan | 21 | 17 90 | B |
| Pickett's Lock La. N9 | 18 | 35 93 | B |
| Pickford Cl. Bexh | 79 | 48 76 | C |
| Pickford La. Bexh | 79 | 48 76 | C |
| Pickford Rd. Bexh | 79 | 48 75 | A |
| Pickhurst Green. Brom | 107 | 39 66 | B |
| Pickhurst La. Brom | 107 | 39 66 | D |
| Pickhurst La. W.Wick | 107 | 39 67 | C |
| Pickhurst Mead. Brom | 107 | 39 66 | B |
| Pickhurst Park. Brom | 107 | 39 67 | B |
| Pickhurst Rise. W.Wick | 107 | 39 66 | C |
| Pickle Herring St. SE1 | 8 | 33 80 | C |
| Pickwick Ct. SE9 | 89 | 42 73 | C |
| Pickwick Mews. N18 | 17 | 33 92 | C |
| Pickwick Pl. Har | 33 | 15 87 | A |
| Pickwick Rd. SE21 | 63 | 32 78 | A |
| Pickwick St. SE1 | 8 | 32 79 | A |
| Pickwick Way. Chis | 100 | 44 70 | A |
| Pickworth Cl. SW8 | 10 | 30 77 | C |
| Picton Pl. W1 | 2 | 28 81 | C |
| Picton St. SE5 | 63 | 32 77 | D |
| Piedmont Rd. SE18 | 66 | 44 78 | D |
| Piermont Rd. SE22 | 75 | 34 74 | B |
| Pier Rd. E16 | 65 | 42 79 | B |
| Pier Rd. E16 | 66 | 43 79 | A |
| Pier Rd. Eri | 68 | 51 77 | A |
| Pier Rd. Felt | 69 | 10 74 | B |
| Pierrepoint Rd. W3 | 55 | 19 80 | B |
| Pierrepont Arc. N1 | 48 | 31 83 | D |
| Pierrepont Row. N1 | 48 | 31 83 | D |
| Pier St. E14 | 64 | 38 78 | A |
| Pier Terr. SW18 | 73 | 26 75 | C |
| Pigeon La. Hamp | 82 | 13 71 | A |
| Pigott St. E14 | 57 | 37 81 | C |
| Pike Cl. Brom | 89 | 40 71 | D |
| Pike's End. Pnr | 19 | 10 89 | D |
| Pilgrimage St. SE1 | 8 | 32 79 | B |
| Pilgrim Hill. SE27 | 87 | 32 71 | A |
| Pilgrim's La. NW3 | 46 | 26 85 | B |
| Pilgrim's Pl. NW3 | 46 | 26 85 | B |
| Pilgrim's Rise. Barn | 12 | 27 95 | A |
| Pilgrim St. EC4 | 3 | 31 81 | D |
| Pilgrims Way. N19 | 36 | 29 87 | D |
| Pilgrims Way. NW9 | 34 | 19 87 | D |
| Pilgrim's Way. S Croy | 112 | 33 64 | D |
| Pilkington Rd. Orp | 108 | 44 65 | A |
| Pilkington Rd. SE15 | 75 | 34 76 | D |
| Pillmans Cl. Sid | 100 | 46 70 | B |
| Pilsden Cl. SW19 | 85 | 23 73 | D |
| Pilton Estate The. Croy | 105 | 31 65 | B |
| Pilton Pl. SE17 | 63 | 32 78 | C |
| Pimlico Rd. SW1 | 9 | 28 78 | C |
| Pimlico Wlk. N1 | 4 | 33 82 | A |
| Pimpernel Way. Rom | 30 | 53 91 | B |
| Pinchin St. E1 | 57 | 34 80 | A |
| Pincott Rd. Bexh | 79 | 49 75 | C |
| Pincott Rd. SW19 | 95 | 26 69 | A |
| Pindar St. EC2 | 4 | 33 81 | A |
| Pindock Mews. W9 | 56 | 25 82 | D |
| Pine Apple Ct. SW1 | 6 | 29 79 | C |
| Pine Ave. W Wick | 106 | 37 66 | D |
| Pine Cl. N14 | 16 | 29 94 | A |
| Pine Cl. N19 | 36 | 29 86 | A |
| Pine Cl. Nthwd | 19 | 09 91 | A |
| Pinefield Cl. E14 | 57 | 37 80 | A |
| Pine Gdns. Ruis | 31 | 10 86 | D |
| Pine Gdns. Surb | 102 | 19 67 | C |
| Pine Gr. N20 | 15 | 25 94 | C |
| Pine Gr. N4 | 36 | 30 86 | B |
| Pine Gr. SW19 | 85 | 24 71 | D |
| Pinehurst Wlk (off Andover Rd). Orp | 108 | 45 66 | C |
| Pine Rd. N11 | 16 | 28 93 | A |
| Pine Rd. NW2 | 46 | 23 85 | B |
| Pine Ridge. Cars | 111 | 28 62 | A |
| Pines Rd. Brom | 99 | 42 69 | C |
| Pine St. EC1 | 3 | 31 82 | C |
| Pines The. Sun | 91 | 10 68 | A |
| Pine Tree Cl. Houn | 69 | 10 76 | B |
| Pine Wlk. Cars | 110 | 26 62 | D |
| Pine Wlk. Surb | 102 | 19 67 | C |
| Pinewood Ave. Pnr | 20 | 13 91 | B |
| Pinewood Ave. Sid | 90 | 45 73 | C |
| Pinewood Cl. Croy | 106 | 36 65 | C |
| Pinewood Cl. Orp | 108 | 44 66 | D |
| Pinewood Cl. Pnr | 20 | 13 91 | B |
| Pinewood Ct. SW4 | 74 | 29 74 | D |
| Pinewood Gr. W5 | 54 | 17 81 | C |
| Pinewood Pl. Eps | 109 | 20 64 | B |
| Pinewood Rd. Brom | 99 | 40 68 | C |
| Pinewood Rd. Felt | 81 | 10 72 | D |
| Pinewood Rd. SE2 | 67 | 47 77 | B |
| Pine Wood. Sun | 91 | 10 69 | A |
| Pinfold Rd. SW16 | 86 | 30 71 | A |
| Pinkham Way. N11 | 24 | 28 91 | C |
| Pinley Gdns. Dag | 51 | 46 83 | B |
| Pinnacle Hill. Bexh | 79 | 49 75 | D |
| Pinnell Rd. SE9 | 77 | 41 75 | D |
| Pinner Ct. Pnr | 20 | 13 89 | C |
| Pinner Green. Pnr | 20 | 11 90 | C |
| Pinner Gr. Pnr | 32 | 12 88 | A |
| Pinner Hill. Pnr | 19 | 10 91 | D |
| Pinner Hill Rd. Pnr | 20 | 11 90 | C |
| Pinner Park Ave. Har | 20 | 14 90 | C |
| Pinner Park Gdns. Har | 20 | 14 90 | C |
| Pinner Rd. Har | 32 | 14 88 | D |
| Pinner Rd. Nthwd | 19 | 10 90 | A |
| Pinner Rd. Pnr | 19 | 10 90 | D |
| Pinner Rd. Pnr | 20 | 13 89 | C |
| Pinner View. Har | 32 | 14 88 | A |
| Pinn Way. Ruis | 31 | 09 87 | A |
| Pintail Rd. Wdf Gn | 27 | 40 91 | D |
| Pinto Way. SE3 | 77 | 40 75 | D |
| Piper Cl. N7 | 47 | 30 84 | B |
| Piper Rd. King | 94 | 19 68 | A |
| Pipers Green. NW9 | 34 | 20 88 | A |
| Pipewell Rd. Cars | 104 | 27 67 | C |
| Pippin Cl. Croy | 106 | 36 66 | D |
| Pippins Ct. Ashf | 91 | 07 70 | B |
| Piquet Rd. SE20 | 98 | 35 69 | C |

Pirbright Rd. SW18 85 25 73 C
Pirie St. E16 58 40 80 D
Pitcairn Cl. Rom 29 49 89 C
Pitcairn Rd. Mit 96 27 70 D
Pitcairn St. SW8 74 28 75 B
Pitchford St. E15 50 39 84 C
Pitfield St. N1 4 33 82 A
Pitfield St. N1 48 33 83 C
Pitfield Way. Enf 14 35 97 A
Pitfield Way. NW10 45 20 84 A
Pitfold Cl. SE12 77 40 74 D
Pitfold Rd. SE12 77 40 74 C
Pitlake. Croy 105 31 65 B
Pitman St. SE5 63 32 77 C
Pitsea Pl. E1 57 35 81 D
Pitsea St. E1 57 35 81 D
Pitshanger La. W5 54 17 82 C
Pitsmead Ave. Brom 107 40 66 A
Pitt Cres. SW19 85 25 71 B
Pitt Rd. Th Hth 105 32 67 A
Pitt's Ct. SE1 8 33 80 C
Pitt's Head Mews. W1 6 28 80 C
Pitt St. SE15 75 33 76 B
Pitt St. SE15 63 33 77 D
Pitt St. W8 62 25 79 A
Pittville Gdns. SE25 97 34 68 A
Pixfield Ct. Brom 99 39 69 D
Pixley St. E14 57 36 81 D
Place Farm Ave. Orp 108 44 66 D
Plaistow Gr. Brom 99 40 70 D
Plaistow Gr. E15 50 39 83 B
Plaistow La. Brom 99 41 69 A
Plaistow Park Rd. E13 50 40 83 D
Plaistow Rd. E15 50 39 83 D
Plane St. SE26 87 34 72 D
Plane Tree Cres. Felt 81 10 72 D
Plane Tree Wlk. SE19 97 33 70 A
Plantagenet Cl. Wor Pk 109 20 64 B
Plantagenet Gdns. Rom 41 47 87 B
Plantagenet Pl. Rom 41 47 87 B
Plantagenet Rd. Barn 11 26 96 C
Plantain Pl. SE1 8 32 79 B
Plantation Rd. Eri 80 52 76 A
Plantation The. SE3 77 40 76 C
Plashet Gr. E6 50 41 84 D
Plashet Rd. E13 50 40 84 D
Plassy Rd. SE6 88 37 73 B
Platford Green. Horn 30 54 89 C
Platina St. EC2 4 32 82 D
Plato Rd. SW2 74 30 75 C
Platt's La. NW3 35 25 86 C
Platts Rd. Enf 14 35 97 A
Platt St. NW1 47 29 83 D
Platt The. SW15 73 23 75 B
Plawsfield Rd. Beck 98 35 69 B
Plaxtol Cl. Brom 99 41 69 A
Plaxtol Rd. Eri 67 49 77 C
Playfair St. W6 62 23 78 C
Playfield Ave. Rom 29 50 90 A
Playfield Cres. SE22 75 33 74 B
Playfield Rd. Edg 22 20 90 C
Playford Rd. N4 36 30 86 B
Playford Rd. N4 37 31 86 A
Playgreen Way. SE6 88 37 71 A
Playhouse Yd. EC4 3 31 81 D
Pleasance Rd. Orp 100 46 68 B
Pleasance Rd. SW15 72 22 74 B
Pleasance The. SW15 72 22 75 D
Pleasant Gr. Croy 106 36 65 D
Pleasant Pl. N1 48 31 84 D
Pleasant Row. NW1 47 28 83 B
Pleasant View. Eri 68 51 78 C
Pleasant Way. Wem 44 17 83 C
Plender Pl. NW1 47 29 83 A
Plender St. NW1 47 29 83 A
Pleshey Rd. N7 47 29 85 B
Plesman Way. Wall 111 30 62 A
Plevna Cres. N15 37 33 88 C
Plevna Rd. Hamp 92 13 69 B
Plevna Rd. N9 17 34 93 D
Plevna St. E14 64 38 79 C
Pleydell Ave. SE19 97 33 70 D
Pleydell Ave. W6 61 21 78 B
Pleydell St. EC4 3 31 81 C
Plimsoll Cl. E14 57 37 81 D
Plimsoll Rd. N4 37 31 86 D
Plimsoll Rd. N5 37 31 86 D
Plough Alley. E1 57 34 80 C
Plough Ct. EC4 8 32 80 B
Plough La Cl. Wall 111 30 64 C
Plough La. Pur 111 30 62 D
Plough La. SE22 75 33 74 D
Plough La. SW17 85 26 71 A
Plough La. SW19 85 25 71 D
Plough La. Wall 111 30 64 C
Ploughmans End. Islw 70 14 74 B
Plough Mews. SW11 73 26 75 D
Plough Pl. EC4 3 31 81 C
Plough Rd. Eps 109 20 63 D
Plough Rd. SW11 73 26 75 D
Plough St. E1 57 34 81 C
Plough Terr. SW11 73 26 75 D
Ploughway. SE16 64 36 78 A
Plough Yd. EC2 4 33 82 C
Plough Yd. EC2 4 33 82 C
Plumber's Pl. EC1 3 31 82 C
Plumbers Row. E1 57 34 81 C
Plumbridge St. SE10 76 38 76 A
Plum Garth. Brent 60 17 78 B
Plum La. SE18 66 44 77 C
Plummer La. Mit 96 27 69 D
Plummer Rd. SW4 86 29 73 B
Plumpton Ave. Horn 42 54 86 D
Plumpton Cl. Nthlt 43 13 84 A
Plumstead Common Rd. SE18 66 44 77 A
Plumstead High St. SE18 66 45 78 A
Plumstead Rd. SE18 66 44 78 A
Plumtree Ct. EC4 3 31 81 D
Plymouth Rd. Brom 99 40 69 B
Plymouth Rd. E16 58 40 81 A
Plympton Ave. NW6 46 24 84 D
Plympton Pl. NW8 1 27 82 C
Plympton Rd. NW6 46 24 84 D
Plympton St. NW8 1 27 82 C
Plymstock Rd. Well 67 47 77 C
Pocklington Cl. NW9 22 21 90 C
Pocklington Ct. SW15 84 22 73 C
Pocock St. SE1 7 31 79 B
Podmore Rd. SW18 73 26 75 C
Poets Corner. SW1 7 30 79 C
Poet's Rd. N5 48 32 85 D
Pointalls Cl. N3 23 26 90 C
Point Cl. SE10 76 38 76 A
Point Hill. SE10 76 38 76 A
Point Pleasant. SW18 73 25 75 C
Poland St. W1 2 29 81 C
Polebrook Rd. SE3 77 41 75 A
Pole Cat Alley. Brom 107 39 65 B
Polecroft La. SE6 88 36 72 B
Pole Hill Rd. E4 18 38 94 A
Polesden Gdns. SW20 94 22 69 D
Polesworth Rd. Dag 52 47 84 D
Pollard Cl. E16 58 40 80 A
Pollard Cl. N7 47 30 85 B
Pollard Rd. Mord 103 26 67 B
Pollard Rd. N20 16 27 93 A
Pollard Row. E2 57 34 82 A
Pollards Cres. SW16 96 30 68 A
Pollards Hill E. SW16 96 30 68 B
Pollards Hill N. SW16 96 30 68 B
Pollards Hill S. SW16 96 30 68 B
Pollards Hill W. SW16 96 30 68 B
Pollard St. E2 57 34 82 A
Pollards Wood Rd. SW16 96 30 68 A
Pollen St. W1 2 29 81 C
Pollitt Dri. NW8 1 26 82 D
Polperro Cl. Orp 108 45 67 D
Polsted Rd. SE6 88 36 73 B
Polthorne Gr. SE18 66 44 78 B
Polworth Rd. SW16 86 30 71 C
Polygon Rd. NW1 47 29 83 D
Polygon The. SW4 74 29 75 C
Polytechnic St. SE18 66 43 78 A
Pomell Way. E1 4 33 81 D
Pomeroy St. SE14 76 35 76 A
Pomfret Rd. SE5 75 32 75 A
Pond Cl. SE3 77 39 76 D
Pond Cottage La. W Wick 106 37 66 C
Pond Cottages. SE21 87 33 73 C
Ponder St. N7 47 30 84 D
Pondfield Rd. Brom 107 39 66 C
Pondfield Rd. Dag 52 49 85 D
Pondfield Rd. Orp 108 43 65 D
Pond Green. Ruis 31 09 86 A
Pond Hill Gdns. Sutt 110 24 63 A
Pond Mead. SE21 75 32 74 D
Pond Pl. SW3 9 27 78 C
Pond Rd. E15 50 39 83 C
Pond Rd. SE3 77 39 76 D
Pond St. NW3 47 27 85 B
Pond Way. Tedd 93 17 70 A
Ponler St. E1 57 34 81 D
Ponsard Rd. NW10 55 22 82 B
Ponsford St. E9 49 35 84 A
Ponsonby Pl. SW1 10 29 78 D
Ponsonby Rd. SW15 84 22 73 B
Ponsonby Terr. SW1 10 29 78 D
Pontefract Rd. Brom 89 39 71 D
Ponton Rd. SW8 10 29 77 D
Pont St Mews. SW1 5 27 79 D
Pont St. SW1 5 27 79 D
Pontypool Pl. SE1 7 31 79 B
Pontypool Wlk. Rom 30 53 91 A
Pool Cl. Beck 88 37 71 C
Poole Cl. Ruis 31 09 86 A
Poole Court Rd. Houn 70 12 76 C
Poole Rd. E9 49 35 84 B
Poole Rd. Eps 109 20 63 B
Poole Rd. Horn 42 54 87 B
Pooles Bldgs. EC1 3 31 82 C
Pooles La. Dag 52 48 83 C
Pooles La. SW10 62 26 77 C
Pooles Park. N4 37 31 86 A
Poole St. N1 48 32 83 B
Poolsford Rd. NW9 22 21 89 C
Poonah St. E1 57 35 81 B
Pope Rd. Brom 107 41 67 B
Pope's Ave. Twick 83 15 72 A
Popes Dri. N3 23 25 90 A
Popes Gr. Croy 106 36 65 D
Pope's Gr. Twick 83 15 72 B
Pope's Head Alley. EC3 4 32 81 D
Pope's La. W5 60 18 79 C
Pope's La. W5 61 19 79 C
Pope's Rd. SW9 75 31 75 A
Pope St. SE1 8 33 79 A
Popham Cl. Felt 82 12 72 D
Popham Rd (off Brittania Row). N1 48 32 83 A
Popham Rd (off New North Rd). N1 48 32 83 A
Popham St. N1 48 32 83 A
Poplar Ave. Mit 96 27 69 B
Poplar Ave. Orp 108 43 65 B
Poplar Ave. Sthl 59 13 79 D
Poplar Bath St. E14 57 37 80 B
Poplar Cl. Pnr 20 11 90 B
Poplar Cres. Eps 109 20 63 A
Poplar Ct. Nthlt 43 11 83 C
Poplar Ct. SW19 85 25 71 C
Poplar Farm Cl. Eps 109 20 63 A
Poplar Gdns. N Mal 94 20 69 D
Poplar Gr. N Mal 94 20 68 B
Poplar Gr. W6 62 23 79 A
Poplar Gr. Wem 34 20 86 C
Poplar High St. E14 57 37 80 B
Poplar Mews. W12 56 23 80 C
Poplar Pl. W2 56 25 80 B
Poplar Rd. Ashf 81 08 71 C
Poplar Rd. SE24 75 32 75 C
Poplar Rd. Sutt 103 24 66 D
Poplar Rd. SW19 95 25 69 C
Poplar Road S. SW19 95 25 68 A
Poplars Ave. NW2 46 23 84 A
Poplars Cl. Ruis 31 09 87 C
Poplars Rd. E17 38 37 88 D
Poplars The. N14 12 28 95 B
Poplar St. Rom 29 50 89 C
Poplar Way. Felt 81 10 72 D
Poplar Way. Ilf 28 44 89 C
Poplar Wlk. Croy 105 32 66 C
Poplar Wlk. SE24 75 32 75 A
Poplar Wlk. SE24 75 32 75 C
Poppins Ct. EC4 3 31 81 D
Poppleton Rd. E11 39 39 88 C
Popular Mount. Belv 67 50 78 A
Porchester Gdn Mews. W2 56 25 81 D
Porchester Gdns. W2 56 25 80 B
Porchester Mead. Beck 98 37 70 B
Porchester Mews. W2 56 25 81 D
Porchester Pl. W2 1 27 81 C
Porchester Rd. King 94 19 69 D
Porchester Rd. W2 56 25 81 D
Porchester Sq. W2 56 25 81 D
Porchester Terr N. W2 56 25 81 D
Porchester Terr. W2 5 26 80 A
Porchfield Cl. Sutt 110 25 62 D
Porch Way. N20 16 27 93 D
Porcupine Cl. SE9 89 42 72 A
Porden Rd. SW2 74 30 75 D
Porlock Ho. SE26 87 34 72 C
Porlock Rd. Enf 17 33 94 B
Porlock St. SE1 8 32 79 B
Porrington Cl. Chis 100 43 69 A
Portal Cl. SE27 87 31 72 C
Portbury Cl. SE15 75 34 76 A
Portchester Cl. Horn 42 54 88 C
Port Cres. E13 58 40 82 D
Portelet Rd. E1 57 35 82 D
Porten Rd. W14 62 24 79 C
Porters Ave. Dag 52 47 85 C
Porter St. W1 1 27 81 B
Porteus Rd. W2 1 26 81 A
Portgate Cl. W9 56 24 82 D
Porthcawe Rd. SE26 88 36 71 B
Porthkerry Ave. Well 78 46 75 C
Portia Ct. Bark 51 46 84 C
Portia Way. E3 57 36 82 D
Portinscale Rd. SW15 73 24 74 B
Portland Ave. N16 37 33 87 B
Portland Ave. N.Mal 102 21 66 B
Portland Ave. Sid 78 46 74 C
Portland Crescent W. Stan 21 17 89 B
Portland Cres. Felt 81 08 71 B
Portland Cres. Grnf 53 14 81 A
Portland Cres. SE9 89 42 72 A
Portland Cres. Stan 21 18 90 C
Portland Gdns. N4 37 31 88 D
Portland Gdns. Rom 41 47 88 B
Portland Gr. SW8 74 30 76 B
Portland Mews. W1 2 29 81 C
Portland Pl. SE25 97 34 68 C
Portland Pl. W1 2 28 81 B
Portland Rd. Brom 89 41 71 C
Portland Rd. King 93 18 68 B
Portland Rd. Mit 96 27 69 C
Portland Rd. N15 25 33 89 D
Portland Rd. SE25 105 34 67 B
Portland Rd. SE9 89 42 72 A
Portland Rd. Sthl 59 12 79 D
Portland Rd. W11 56 24 80 C
Portland Rise. N4 37 32 87 C
Portland St. SE17 63 32 78 D
Portland Terr. Rich 71 17 75 D
Portland Wlk. SE17 63 32 77 B
Portman Bldgs. NW1 1 27 82 C
Portman Cl. Bexh 79 47 75 B
Portman Cl. W1 2 28 81 C
Portman Dri. Wdf Gn 27 41 90 D
Portman Gdns. NW9 22 20 90 D
Portman Mews S. W1 2 28 81 C
Portman Pl. E2 57 35 82 A
Portman Rd. King 93 18 69 D
Portman Sq. W1 2 28 81 C
Portman St. W1 2 28 81 C
Portman Towers. W1 1 27 81 D
Portmeadow Wlk. SE2 67 47 79 B
Portmeers Cl. E17 38 36 88 D
Portnall Rd. W9 56 24 82 B
Portnoi Cl. Rom 29 50 90 D
Portobello Ct Estate. W11 56 24 81 D
Portobello Mews. W11 56 25 80 A
Portobello Rd. W10 56 24 81 A
Portobello Rd. W11 56 24 81 D
Porton Ct. Surb 101 17 67 C
Portpool La. EC1 3 31 81 A
Portree Cl. N22 24 30 91 D
Portree St. E14 58 38 81 D
Portsdown Mews. NW11 35 24 88 D
Portsea Mews. W2 1 27 81 C
Portsea Pl. W2 1 27 81 C
Portslade Rd. SW8 74 29 76 C
Portsmouth Ave. Surb 101 16 66 A
Portsmouth Rd. Esh 101 15 65 A
Portsmouth Rd. Surb 101 16 66 B
Portsmouth Rd. SW15 85 23 73 A
Portsmouth St. WC2 3 30 81 D
Portsoken St. E1 8 33 80 B
Portswood Pl. SW15 84 21 73 B
Portswood Pl. SW15 72 21 74 D
Portugal Gdns. Twick 82 14 72 A
Portugal St. WC2 3 30 81 D
Portway Cres. Eps 109 22 62 A
Portway. E15 50 39 83 B
Portway. Eps 109 22 62 A
Portway Gdns. SE18 65 41 77 D
Postern Green. Enf 13 31 96 A
Post La. Twick 82 14 73 D
Post Office Alley. W4 61 19 77 B
Post Office App. E7 50 40 85 D
Post Office Ct. EC4 4 32 81 D
Postway Mews. Ilf 40 43 86 D
Potier St. SE1 8 32 79 D
Potter Cl. Mit 96 28 69 D
Potter Heights Cl. Pnr 19 10 91 D
Potterne Cl. SW19 85 23 73 B
Potters Fields. SE1 8 33 80 C
Potters Gr. N Mal 94 20 68 C
Potter's La. Barn 11 25 96 C
Potter's La. SW16 96 29 70 B
Potter's Rd. Barn 11 25 96 D
Potter St. Nthwd 19 10 90 B
Potter St. Pnr 19 10 90 B
Potter Street Hill. Pnr 19 10 91 D
Pottery La. W11 56 24 80 C
Pottery Rd. Brent 60 18 77 A
Pottery St. SE16 63 34 79 B
Pott St. E2 57 34 82 B
Poulett Gdns. Twick 83 16 73 C
Poulett Rd. E6 50 42 83 D
Poulner Way. SE15 63 33 77 D
Poulton Ave. Sutt 103 26 65 D
Poulton Ave. Sutt 104 27 65 C
Poulton Cl. E8 48 34 85 D
Poultry. EC2 4 32 81 D
Pound Cl. Orp 108 44 65 B
Pound Cl. Surb 101 17 66 C
Pound Court Dri. Orp 108 45 66 B
Pound La. NW10 45 22 84 A
Pound Park Rd. SE7 65 41 78 B
Pound Pl. SE9 78 43 74 C
Pound St. Cars 111 27 64 D
Pountney Rd. SW11 74 28 75 A
Poverest Rd. Orp 108 46 67 A
Powder Mill La. Twick 82 13 73 C
Powell Cl. Edg 21 18 91 B
Powell Cl. Wall 111 30 63 C
Powell Gdns. Dag 52 49 85 A
Powell Rd. E5 37 34 86 D
Powell's Wlk. W4 61 21 77 A
Power Rd. W4 61 19 78 B
Powerscroft Rd. E5 49 35 85 A
Powers Ct. Twick 83 17 73 B
Powis Gdns. NW11 35 24 87 B
Powis Gdns. W11 56 24 81 D
Powis Mews. W11 56 24 81 D
Powis Pl. WC1 3 30 82 C
Powis Rd. E3 57 37 82 B
Powis Sq. W11 56 24 81 D
Powis St. SE18 66 43 79 C
Powis Terr. W11 56 24 81 D
Powlett Pl. NW1 47 28 84 D
Pownall Gdns. Houn 70 13 75 D
Pownall Rd. E8 48 34 83 A
Pownall Rd. Houn 70 13 75 D
Powster Rd. Brom 89 40 71 D
Powys Cl. Bexh 67 47 77 B
Powys La. N13 16 30 92 A
Powys La. N14 16 30 92 A
Poynders Ct. SW4 74 29 74 C
Poynders Gdns. SW4 86 29 73 A
Poynders Rd. SW4 86 29 73 B
Poynings Rd. N19 36 29 86 C
Poynings Way. N12 15 25 92 C
Poynings Way. Rom 30 54 90 A
Poyntell Cres. Chis 100 44 69 B
Poynter Rd. Enf 13 34 95 A
Poynter Rd. N17 25 34 90 C
Poyntz Rd. SW11 74 27 76 D
Poyser St. E2 48 34 83 D
Praed Mews. W2 1 26 81 D
Praed St. W2 1 26 81 D
Pragel St. E13 50 41 83 C
Pragnell Rd. SE12 89 40 72 B
Prague Pl. SW2 74 30 74 A
Prah Rd. N4 37 31 86 A
Prairie St. SW8 74 28 76 D
Pratt Mews. NW1 47 29 83 A
Pratt St. NW1 47 29 83 A
Pratt Wlk. SE11 10 30 78 B
Prayle Gr. NW2 35 23 87 B
Prayle Gr. NW2 35 23 87 D
Prebend Gdns. W6 61 21 78 B
Prebend St. N1 48 32 83 A
Precincts The. Mord 103 25 67 C
Premier Pl. SW15 73 23 75 D
Prendergast Rd. SE3 77 39 75 A
Prentice Ct. SW19 85 24 71 D
Prentis Rd. SW16 86 29 71 B
Prentiss Ct. SE7 65 41 78 B
Presburg Rd. N.Mal 102 21 67 A
Prescelly Pl. Edg 21 18 90 B
Prescot St. E1 8 33 80 B
Prescott Ave. Orp 108 43 67 D
Prescott Pl. SW4 74 29 75 D
President. EC1 4 32 82 A
Press Rd. NW10 34 20 86 D
Prestbury Rd. E7 50 41 84 C
Prestbury Sq. SE9 89 42 71 B
Prested Rd. SW11 74 27 75 C
Preston Ave. E4 26 38 91 B
Preston Cl. SE1 63 33 78 A
Preston Cl. Twick 83 15 72 C
Preston Dri. Bexh 79 47 76 B
Preston Dri. E11 39 41 88 A
Preston Dri. Eps 109 21 63 B
Preston Gdns. Ilf 39 42 88 D
Preston Gdns. NW10 45 21 84 A
Preston Hill. Har 33 18 88 D
Preston Pl. NW2 45 22 84 A
Preston Pl. Rich 71 18 74 A
Preston Rd. Brom 107 40 65 A
Preston Rd. E11 39 39 88 C
Preston Rd. Har 33 18 87 A
Preston Rd. SE19 97 31 70 B
Preston Rd. SW20 94 22 70 C
Preston Rd. Wem 33 18 86 A
Preston's Rd. E14 58 38 80 C
Preston Waye. Har 33 18 87 C
Prestwick Cl. Sthl 59 12 78 C
Prestwood Ave. Har 21 16 89 D
Prestwood Cl. Har 21 16 89 D
Prestwood Gdns. Croy 105 32 66 A
Prestwood St. N1 48 32 83 C
Pretoria Ave. E17 26 36 89 C
Pretoria Cres. E4 18 38 94 C
Pretoria Rd. E11 38 38 87 D
Pretoria Rd. E16 58 39 82 D
Pretoria Rd. E4 18 38 94 D
Pretoria Rd. Ilf 51 43 85 D
Pretoria Rd. N17 25 33 91 B
Pretoria Rd. Rom 41 50 88 A
Pretoria Rd. SW16 86 29 71 C
Pretoria Road N. N18 25 33 91 B
Prevost Rd. N11 16 28 93 A
Price Cl. NW7 23 24 91 A
Price's St. SE1 7 31 80 D
Price's Yd. N1 47 30 83 B
Price Way. Hamp 92 12 70 A
Pricklers Hill. Barn 11 25 95 B
Prickley Wood. Brom 107 39 66 D
Priddy's Yd. Croy 105 32 65 A
Prideaux Pl. W3 55 20 80 B
Prideaux Pl. WC1 3 30 82 B
Prideaux Rd. SW9 74 30 75 A
Pridham Rd E. Th Hth 97 32 68 D
Priestfield Rd. SE23 88 36 72 C
Priestlands Park Rd. Sid 90 45 72 D
Priestley Cl. N16 37 33 87 B
Priestley Gdns. Rom 40 46 88 D
Priestley Way. E17 26 35 89 B
Priestley Way. NW2 34 22 87 C
Priestley Way. NW9 34 22 87 C
Priestly Rd. Mit 96 28 69 C
Priests Ave. Rom 29 50 90 D
Priests Bridge. SW14 72 21 75 A
Priests Bridge. SW15 72 21 75 B
Priest's Ct. EC2 4 32 81 C
Prima Rd. SW 9 63 31 77 C
Primrose Ave. Enf 13 33 97 A
Primrose Ave. Rom 40 46 87 B
Primrose Cl. Har 32 12 86 D
Primrose Gdns. NW3 47 27 84 A
Primrose Gdns. Ruis 43 11 85 C
Primrose Glen. Horn 30 54 89 C
Primrose Hill Ct. NW3 47 27 84 D
Primrose Hill. EC4 3 31 81 C
Primrose Hill Rd. NW3 47 27 84 D
Primrose Hill Studios. NW1 47 28 83 A
Primrose Rd. E10 38 37 87 D
Primrose Rd. E18 27 40 90 D
Primrose St. EC2 4 33 81 A
Primrose Way. Wem 44 17 83 D
Primula St. W12 55 22 81 C
Prince Albert Rd. NW1 47 28 83 A
Prince Albert Rd. NW8 47 27 83 C
Prince Arthur Mews. NW3 46 26 85 A
Prince Arthur Rd. NW3 46 26 85 C
Prince Charles Dri. NW4 35 23 87 A
Prince Charles Rd. SE3 77 39 76 B
Prince Charles Way. Wall 104 28 65 D
Prince Cl. SW17 86 27 72 D
Prince Consort Dri. Chis 100 44 69 B
Prince Consort Rd. SW7 5 26 79 D
Princedale Rd. W11 56 24 80 C
Prince Edward Rd. E9 49 36 84 B
Prince George Ave. N14 12 29 95 B
Prince George Rd. N16 48 33 85 A
Prince George's Ave. SW20 95 23 69 C
Prince George's Rd. SW19 95 26 69 B
Prince Henry Rd. SE7 65 41 77 D
Prince Imperial Rd. Chis 100 43 70 D
Prince Imperial Rd. SE18 77 43 76 A
Prince John Rd. SE9 77 42 74 A
Princelet St. E1 4 33 81 B
Prince of Orange La. SE10 64 38 77 C
Prince of Wales Cl. NW4 22 22 89 D
Prince of Wales Cl. NW4 23 23 89 C
Prince of Wales Dri. SW11 74 28 76 A
Prince of Wales Dri. SW11 9 28 77 D
Prince of Wales Rd. E16 58 41 81 C
Prince of Wales Rd. NW5 47 28 84 A
Prince Of Wales Rd. SE3 77 39 76 B
Prince Of Wales Rd. Sutt 103 26 65 B
Prince of Wales Terr. W4 61 21 78 C
Prince of Wales Terr. W8 62 25 79 B
Prince Rd. Croy 112 31 64 D
Prince Rd. SE25 105 33 67 A
Prince Rd. SE25 97 33 68 C
Prince Regent La. E13 58 41 82 C

Prince Regent La. E16 58 4181 C
Prince Regent Rd. Houn 70 1475 A
Prince Rupert Rd. SE9 77 4275 B
Princes Arc. SW1 6 2980 C
Princes Ave. Cars 111 2762 B
Prince's Ave. Grnf 53 1381 D
Princes Ave. N10 24 2889 B
Princes Ave. N13 17 3192 C
Princes Ave. N22 24 2990 B
Princes Ave. N3 23 2590 B
Princes Ave. NW9 22 1989 D
Princes Ave. Orp 108 4567 A
Princes Ave. Surb 102 1965 A
Princes Ave. W3 61 1979 C
Princes Cl. NW9 22 1989 C
Prince's Cl. Tedd 82 1471 B
Princes Ct. Wem 44 1885 C
Princes Dri. Har 21 1589 A
Princes Gate Mews. SW7 5 2679 D
Princes Gdns. SW7 5 2679 D
Princes Gdns. W3 55 1981 C
Princes Gdns. W5 54 1782 C
Princes La. N10 24 2889 B
Prince's Mews. W2 56 2580 B
Princes Park Ave. NW11 35 2488 A
Prince's Plain. Brom 107 4266 D
Princes Pl. W11 56 2480 C
Princes Rd. Dart 80 5274 C
Princes Rd. Felt 81 0972 D
Princes Rd. Ilf 28 4489 D
Princes Rd. King 94 1970 C
Princes Rd. N18 18 3592 A
Princes Rd. Rich 71 1874 B
Princes Rd. Rich 71 1876 B
Princes Rd. Rom 42 5288 A
Princes Rd. SE20 98 3570 B
Prince's Rd. SW14 72 2075 B
Prince's Rd. SW19 95 2570 A
Prince's Rd. Tedd 82 1471 B
Princes Rd. W13 54 1680 D
Princes Rise. SE13 76 3876 C
Princess Ave. Wem 33 1886 A
Princess Cres. N4 37 3186 B
Princess May Rd. N16 48 3385 A
Princess Mews. NW3 46 2684 B
Princess Par. Orp 108 4365 C
Prince's Sq. W2 56 2580 B
Princess Rd. Croy 105 3267 C
Princess Rd. NW1 47 2883 A
Princess Rd. NW6 46 2583 C
Princess St. SE1 7 3179 D
Princess's Wlk. Rich 60 1877 C
Princes St. Bexh 79 4875 B
Prince's St. EC2 4 3281 D
Princes St. N17 25 3391 A
Princes St. Rich 71 1874 A
Princes St. Sutt 110 2664 B
Princes St. W1 2 2881 D
Prince's Terr. E13 50 4083 B
Prince St. SE8 64 3777 A
Princes Way. Croy 111 3064 D
Princes Way. Ruis 43 1285 A
Princes Way. SW19 85 2473 C
Princes Way. W.Wick 107 3965 D
Princes Yd. W11 56 2480 C
Princethorpe Rd. SE26 88 3571 B
Princeton St. WC1 3 3081 B
Pringle Gdns. SW16 86 2971 A
Pring St. W10 56 2380 B
Printer St. EC4 3 3181 C
Printing House Yd. E2 4 3382 A
Priolo Rd. SE7 65 4178 C
Prior Ave. Sutt 111 2763 C
Prior Bolton St. N1 48 3184 B
Prioress St. SE1 8 3379 C
Prioress Wlk. SE27 87 3172 D
Priors Croft. E17 26 3690 D
Priors Field. Nthlt 43 1284 A
Priorsford Ave. Orp 100 4668 D
Priors Gdns. Ruis 43 1185 C
Priors Mead. Enf 13 3397 A
Priors Park. Horn 42 5386 C
Prior St. SE10 64 3877 C
Priory Ave. E17 38 3788 A
Priory Ave. E4 18 3793 C
Priory Ave. N8 24 2989 D
Priory Ave. Orp 108 4467 D
Priory Ave. Sutt 110 2364 B
Priory Ave. W4 61 2179 C
Priory Ave. Wem 44 1585 B
Priory Cl. Beck 98 3668 A
Priory Cl. Chis 99 4269 B
Priory Cl. Dart 80 5374 B
Priory Cl. E18 27 4090 A
Priory Cl. E4 18 3693 D
Priory Cl. Hamp 92 1269 B
Priory Cl. N14 12 2895 B
Priory Cl. N20 15 2494 B
Priory Cl. N3 23 2490 B
Priory Cl. Ruis 31 0987 D
Priory Cl. Sun 91 1070 C
Priory Cl. SW19 95 2569 B
Priory Cl. Wem 44 1585 B
Priory Cres. SE19 97 3270 C
Priory Cres. Sutt 110 2364 B
Priory Cres. Wem 33 1686 C
Priory Ct. E17 26 3690 D
Priory Ct. E6 50 4183 B
Priory Ct. SE15 76 3575 C
Priory Ct. SW8 74 2976 B
Priory Dri. SE2 67 4778 D
Priory Gdns. Dart 80 5374 B
Priory Gdns. Hamp 92 1269 B
Priory Gdns. N6 36 2888 D
Priory Gdns. SW13 72 2175 B
Priory Gdns. W4 61 2178 A
Priory Gdns. Wem 44 1685 A
Priory Gr. SW8 74 3076 A
Priory Hill. Dart 80 5374 D
Priory Hill. Wem 44 1685 A
Priory Lane. E Mol 92 1368 D
Priory La. SW15 72 2174 B
Priory Mews. SW8 74 2976 B
Priory Park Rd. NW6 46 2483 B
Priory Park Rd. Wem 44 1685 A
Priory Park. SE3 77 3975 B
Priory Pl. Dart 80 5374 D
Priory Rd. Bark 51 4484 D
Priory Rd. Chess 101 1865 C
Priory Rd. Croy 105 3166 A
Priory Rd. Dart 80 5374 B
Priory Rd. E6 50 4183 B
Priory Rd. Hamp 92 1370 C
Priory Rd. Houn 70 1474 A
Priory Rd. N8 24 2989 D
Priory Rd. NW6 46 2584 D
Priory Rd. Rich 61 1977 C
Priory Rd. Sutt 110 2364 B
Priory Rd. SW19 95 2670 D
Priory Rd. W4 61 2079 D
Priory St. E3 57 3782 B
Priory Terr. NW6 46 2583 B
Priory The. SE3 77 3975 D
Priory Way. Har 20 1389 D
Priory Way. Sthl 59 1179 D
Priory Wlk. SW10 62 2678 C
Priscilla Rd. E3 57 3782 A
Pritchard's Rd. E2 48 3483 C
Priter Rd. SE16 63 3479 C
Priter Way. SE16 63 3479 C
Private Rd. Enf 13 3395 A
Probert Rd. SW2 75 3174 A
Probyn Rd. SW2 87 3172 B
Procter St. WC1 3 3081 B
Proctors Cl. Felt 81 1073 C
Progress Way. Croy 104 3065 B
Progress Way. Enf 13 3495 A
Progress Way. N22 25 3190 A
Promenade Approach Rd. W4 61 2177 C
Promenade The. W4 72 2176 A
Proof Butts Rd. SE28 66 4579 A
Prospect Cl. Belv 67 4978 A
Prospect Cl. Houn 70 1276 B
Prospect Cl. Ruis 32 1187 B
Prospect Cl. SE26 87 3471 B
Prospect Cottages. SW18 73 2575 C
Prospect Cres. Twick 70 1474 C
Prospect Hill. E17 26 3789 D
Prospect Pl. Brom 99 4068 B
Prospect Pl. N17 25 3391 C
Prospect Pl. N2 23 2689 D
Prospect Pl. NW2 35 2486 D
Prospect Pl. Rom 29 5090 C
Prospect Pl. W4 61 2078 D
Prospect Rd. Barn 11 2596 D
Prospect Rd. Horn 30 5489 B
Prospect Rd. N2 24 2789 A
Prospect Rd. NW2 35 2586 C
Prospect Rd. Surb 101 1767 C
Prospect Rd. Wdf Gn 27 4191 A
Prospect Ring. N2 24 2789 A
Prospect St. SE16 63 3479 B
Prospect Vale. SE18 65 4278 A
Prospect Wlk. E2 57 3582 B
Prospero Rd. N19 36 2987 D
Prothero Gdns. NW4 34 2288 B
Prothero Rd. SW6 62 2477 D
Prout Gr. NW10 45 2185 B
Prout Rd. E5 37 3486 D
Provence St. N1 48 3283 C
Providence Ct. W1 6 2880 A
Providence Pl. N1 48 3183 B
Providence Row. N1 47 3083 D
*Providence Yd. E2 57 3482 A
Provost Rd. NW3 47 2784 D
Provost St. N1 4 3282 B
Prowse Pl. NW1 47 2984 C
Pruden Cl. N14 16 2993 A
Prudent Pas. EC2 4 3281 C
Prusom St. E1 57 3480 D
Pryors The. NW3 35 2686 D
Pudding La. EC3 8 3280 B
Pudding Mill La. E15 49 3783 B
Puddle Dock. EC4 7 3180 B
Pugh's Pl. W1 2 2981 C
Pulborough Rd. SW18 85 2473 B
Pulborough Way. Houn 70 1175 C
Pulford Rd. N15 37 3288 D
Pulham Ave. N2 23 2689 D
Puller Rd. Barn 11 2496 A
Pullman Ct. SW2 86 3073 D
Pullman Gdns. SW15 73 2374 C
Pulross Rd. SW9 74 3075 B
Pulteney Cl. E3 49 3683 B
Pulteney Rd. E18 27 4089 B
Pulteney Terr. N1 47 3083 B
Pulton Pl. SW6 62 2577 C
Puma Ct. E1 4 3381 B
Pump Alley. Brent 60 1777 D
Pump Cl. Nthlt 43 1383 C
Pump Ct. EC4 3 3181 C
Pumping Station Rd. W4 61 2177 C
Pump Pail N. Croy 105 3265 C
Pump Pail S. Croy 105 3265 C
Punderson's Gdns. E2 57 3482 B
Purbeck Ave. N.Mal 102 2167 D
Purbeck Dri. NW2 35 2386 B
Purbeck Dri. NW2 35 2486 A
Purbeck Rd. Horn 42 5287 A
Purberry Gr. Eps 109 2162 D
Purbrook St. SE1 8 3379 C
Purcell Cres. SW6 62 2477 C
Purcell Rd. Grnf 53 1381 B
Purcell St. N1 48 3383 C
Purchese St. NW1 47 2983 D
Purdy St. E3 57 3782 D
Purland Cl. Dag 41 4887 D
Purland Rd. SE28 66 4679 A
Purleigh Ave. Wdf Gn 27 4291 A
Purley Ave. NW2 35 2486 A
Purley Bury Ave. Pur 112 3262 C
Purley Cl. Ilf 28 4390 C
Purley Ct. Pur 112 3162 D
Purley Downs Rd. Pur 112 3162 C
Purley Oaks Rd. S Croy 112 3262 D
Purley Park Rd. Pur 112 3162 D
Purley Pl. N1 48 3184 D
Purley Rd. N9 17 3393 C
Purley Rd. S Croy 112 3263 D
Purley Way. Croy 112 3164 A
Purley Way. Pur 112 3162 C
Purnell Pl. SE16 57 3580 D
Purneys Rd. SE9 77 4175 D
Purrett Rd. SE18 66 4578 D
Pursers Cross Rd. SW6 73 2476 B
Pursley Rd. NW7 22 2291 D
Purves Rd. NW10 55 2282 B
Purves Rd. NW10 46 2383 C
Putney Bridge App. SW6 73 2475 A
Putney Bridge Rd. SW15 73 2475 D
Putney Common. SW15 73 2375 A
Putney Heath La. SW15 73 2374 D
Putney Heath. SW15 73 2374 C
Putney High St. SW15 73 2475 C
Putney Hill. SW15 85 2373 B
Putney Hill. SW15 73 2374 B
Putney Park Ave. SW15 72 2275 C
Putney Park La. SW15 72 2274 B
Pycombe Cnr. N12 15 2492 B
Pylbrook Rd. Sutt 103 2565 D
Pym Cl. Barn 11 2695 B
Pymers Mead. SE21 87 3273 C
Pymmes Cl. N13 16 3092 D
Pymmes gardens N. N9 17 3393 D
Pymmes Gardens S. N9 17 3393 D
Pymmes Green Rd. N11 16 2993 C
Pymmes Rd. N13 24 3091 A
Pymms Brook Dri. Barn 12 2796 C
Pynchester Cl. Uxb 31 0786 A
*Pynfolds. SE16 63 3479 B
Pynham Cl. SE2 66 4679 D
Pyrland Rd. N5 48 3285 D
Pyrland Rd. Rich 71 1874 D
Pyrmont Gr. SE27 87 3172 D
Pyrmont Rd. Ilf 40 4486 A
Pyrmont Rd. W4 61 1977 A
Pytchley Cres. SE19 97 3270 A
Pytchley Rd. SE22 75 3375 A

Quadrangle The. E17 26 3690 D
Quadrangle. The W2 1 2781 C
Quadrant Arc. Rom 42 5188 A
Quadrant Arc. W1 6 2980 A
Quadrant Cl. NW4 34 2288 B
Quadrant Gr. NW5 47 2785 D
Quadrant Rd. N2 24 2790 A
Quadrant Rd. Rich 71 1775 D
Quadrant Rd. Th Hth 97 3168 D
Quadrant The. Bexh 67 4777 D
Quadrant The. Rich 71 1775 D
Quadrant The. Sutt 110 2663 A
Quadrant The. SW20 95 2469 A
Quaggy Wlk. SE3 77 4075 C
Quainton St. NW10 34 2086 D
Quaker La. Sthl 59 1379 C
Quakers Course. NW9 22 2190 B
Quakers La. Islw 71 1676 A
Quaker St. E1 4 3382 D
Quakers Wlk. N21 13 3295 D
Quality Ct. WC2 3 3181 C
Quantock Ct. Grnf 44 1585 C
Quantock Gdns. NW2 35 2386 B
Quantock Rd. Bexh 80 5176 C
Quarles Cl. Rom 29 4991 C
Quarley Way (off Pentridge St). SE15 63 3377 D
Quarrendon St. SW6 73 2576 C
Quarr Rd. Cars 104 2767 C
Quarry Park Rd. Sutt 110 2463 B
Quarry Rd. SW18 73 2674 C
Quarry Rise. Sutt 110 2463 B
Quarterdeck The. E14 64 3779 A
Quartermile La. E10 49 3785 B
Quartermile La. E15 49 3785 B
Quebec Mews. W1 1 2781 D
Quebec Rd. Hay 53 1181 C
Quebec Rd. Ilf 40 4487 A
Quebec Way. SE16 64 3679 C
Queen Adelaide Rd. SE20 98 3570 C
Queen Alexandra's Ct. SW19 85 2471 D
Queen Anne Ave. Brom 99 3968 B
Queen Anne Gate. Bexh 79 4775 B
Queen Anne Mews. W1 2 2881 B
Queen Anne Rd. E9 49 3584 B
Queen Annes Cl. Twick 82 1472 D
Queen Anne's Gate. SW1 6 2979 B
Queen Anne's Gdns. Enf 13 3395 C
Queen Anne's Gdns. Mit 96 2768 B
Queen Anne's Gdns. W4 61 2179 C
Queen Anne's Gdns. W5 60 1879 A
Queen Anne's Gr. Enf 13 3395 C
Queen Anne's Gr. W4 61 2179 C
Queen Anne's Gr. W5 60 1879 A
Queen Anne's Pl. Enf 13 3395 D
Queen Anne St. W1 2 2881 B
Queenborough Gdns. Ilf 28 4389 C
Queen Caroline St. W6 62 2378 C
Queen Elizabeth Gdns. Mord 95 2568 C
Queen Elizabeth Rd. E17 26 3689 A
Queen Elizabeth Rd. King 93 1869 D
Queen Elizabeth's Cl. N16 37 3286 B
Queen Elizabeth's Dri. N14 16 3094 C
Queen Elizabeth St. SE1 8 3379 B
Queen Elizabeth's Wlk. N16 37 3286 B
Queen Elizabeth's Wlk. Wall 111 2964 B
Queen Elizabeth Wlk. SW13 72 2276 B
Queenhill Rd. S Croy 112 3462 D
Queenhithe. EC4 8 3280 A
Queen Margaret's Gr. N1 48 3385 C
Queen Mary Ave. Mord 103 2367 B
Queen Mary Rd. SE19 97 3170 B
Queen Mary Rd. Shep 91 0869 C
Queen Mary's Ave. Cars 111 2763 D
Queens Acre. Sutt 110 2463 C
Queens Ave. Felt 82 1171 A
Queen's Ave. Grnf 53 1481 C
Queens Ave. N10 24 2889 B
Queens Ave. N20 15 2693 B
Queen's Ave. N21 17 3194 D
Queen's Ave. N3 23 2690 A
Queens Ave. Stan 21 1789 A
Queensberry House. Rich 71 1774 B
Queensberry Mews W. SW7 62 2678 B
Queensberry Pl. SW7 62 2678 B
Queensberry Way. SW7 62 2678 B
Queensborough Mews. W2 5 2680 A
Queensborough Pas. W2 5 2680 A
Queensborough Terr. W2 5 2680 A
Queensbridge Ct. E2 48 3383 D
Queensbridge Park. Islw 71 1574 A
Queensbridge Rd. E2 48 3383 B
Queensbridge Rd. E8 48 3384 D
Queensbury Ct. Th Hth 97 3269 C
Queensbury Rd. NW9 34 2087 B
Queensbury Rd. Wem 44 1883 D
Queensbury Station Par. Edg 21 1889 B
Queensbury St. N1 48 3284 C
Queen's Circ. SW11 9 2877 D
Queen's Club Gdns. W14 62 2477 A
Queen's Cl. Wall 111 2864 D
Queenscourt. Wem 44 1885 A
Queen's Cres. NW5 47 2884 A
Queens Cres. Rich 71 1874 B
Queenscroft Rd. SE9 77 4174 D
Queen's Ct. King 94 1970 C
Queen's Ct. Rich 71 1874 D
Queensdale Cres. W11 56 2380 D
Queensdale Pl. W11 56 2480 C
Queensdale Rd. W11 56 2480 C
Queensdale Wlk. W11 56 2480 C
Queensdown Rd. E5 48 3485 B
Queens Dri. E10 38 3787 A
Queen's Dri. N4 37 3186 B
Queen's Dri. Surb 101 1667 C
Queens Dri. Surb 102 1967 C
Queen's Dri. W3 55 1981 C
Queen's Elm Sq. SW3 62 2678 D
Queensferry Wlk. N15 25 3489 D
Queensfield Ct. Sutt 110 2364 A
Queensgate Gdns. Chis 100 4469 B
Queen's Gate Gdns. SW7 5 2679 C
Queen's Gate Mews. SW7 5 2679 C
Queen's Gate Pl Mews. SW7 5 2679 C
Queensgate Pl. NW6 46 2584 C
Queen's Gate Pl. SW7 5 2679 C
Queen's Gate. SW7 5 2679 C
Queen's Gate. SW7 5 2679 C
Queen's Gate Terr. SW7 5 2679 C
Queen's Gdns. Houn 70 1276 A
Queens Gdns. NW4 35 2388 A
Queens Gdns. Rain 52 5083 D
Queen's Gdns. W2 5 2680 A
Queen's Gdns. W5 54 1782 C
Queen's Grove. NW8 46 2683 B
Queen's Grove Rd. E4 18 3894 D
Queen's Head St. N1 48 3183 B
Queen's Head Yd. SE1 8 3280 D
Queens La. N10 24 2889 B
Queensland Ave. N18 25 3291 A
Queensland Ave. SW19 95 2569 B
Queensland Pl. N7 48 3185 A
Queensland Rd. N7 48 3185 A
Queen's Market. E13 50 4183 A
Queensmead Ave. 109 2262 D
Queensmead. NW8 46 2683 B
Queen's Mead Rd. Brom 99 3969 D
Queensmere Cl. SW19 85 2372 B
Queensmere Rd. SW19 85 2372 B
Queen's Mews. W2 56 2580 B
Queensmill Rd. SW6 62 2377 D
Queens Parade Cl. N11 16 2792 D
Queens Park Ct. W10 56 2382 B
Queens Park Gdns. Felt 81 0972 D
Queens Park Rd. Rom 30 5490 B
Queens Pas. Chis 100 4370 B
Queen's Pl. Mord 95 2568 C
Queen's Prom. King 93 1768 D
Queen Sq Pl. WC1 3 3082 C
Queen Sq. WC1 3 3081 A
Queen's Rd. Bark 51 4484 C
Queens Rd. Barn 11 2396 B
Queens Rd. Beck 98 3669 C
Queen's Rd. Brom 99 4069 C
Queen's Rd. Chis 100 4370 B
Queen's Rd. Croy 105 3267 C
Queen's Rd. E11 39 3987 A
Queen's Rd. E17 38 3688 D
Queen's Rd. Enf 13 3396 C
Queen's Rd. Eri 68 5177 A
Queen's Rd. Felt 81 1073 D
Queen's Rd. Hamp 82 1371 B
Queen's Rd. Houn 70 1375 B
Queens Rd. Ilf 40 4486 A
Queen's Rd. Mit 95 2668 B
Queens Rd. Mord 95 2568 C
Queen's Rd. N11 24 3091 A
Queen's Rd. N3 23 2690 A
Queen's Rd. N9 17 3493 B
Queen's Rd. N.Mal 102 2167 B
Queen's Rd. NW4 35 2388 A
Queen's Rd. Rich 71 1874 D
Queen's Rd. SE15 76 3576 A
Queen's Rd. Sthl 59 1279 A
Queen's Rd. Surb 101 1567 B
Queens Rd. Sutt 110 2562 C
Queen's Rd. SW14 72 2075 B
Queen's Rd. SW19 95 2570 A
Queen's Rd. Tedd 93 1570 B
Queen's Rd. Twick 83 1673 C
Queen's Rd. W5 54 1881 C
Queen's Rd. Wall 111 2864 D
Queens Rd W. E13 50 4083 D
Queen's Rd. Well 78 4676 D
Queen's Ride. Rich 60 1877 C
Queen's Ride. Rich 84 2073 C
Queen's Ride. SW13 72 2275 A
Queen's Ride. SW15 72 2275 B
Queen's Rise. Rich 71 1874 D
Queen's Row. SE17 63 3277 B
Queen St. Bexh 79 4875 B
Queen St. Croy 105 3265 C
Queen St. EC4 8 3280 A
Queen St. Eri 68 5177 A
Queens Terr. E13 50 4083 B
Queen's Terr. Islw 71 1675 C
Queens Terr. NW8 46 2683 D
Queensthorpe Rd. SE26 88 3571 B
Queen St. N17 25 3391 A
Queenstown Rd. SW11 74 2776 B
Queenstown Rd. SW8 9 2877 D
Queen St Pl. EC4 8 3280 A
Queen St. Rom 41 5088 D
Queen St. W1 6 2880 D
Queensville Rd. SW12 86 2973 B
Queensway. Croy 112 3164 C
Queensway. Enf 14 3596 C
Queens Way. Felt 82 1171 A
Queens Way. NW4 35 2388 A
Queensway. Orp 108 4467 C
Queensway. Sun 91 1069 D
Queensway. W2 56 2580 B
Queensway. W.Wick 107 3965 C
Queens Well Ave. N20 16 2792 A
Queens Wlk. E4 18 3894 D
Queens Wlk. Har 21 1589 C
Queens Wlk. NW9 34 2086 A
Queens Wlk. Ruis 43 1185 B
Queen's Wlk. SW1 6 2980 C
Queen's Wlk. W5 54 1781 A
Queenswood Ave. E17 26 3890 A
Queenswood Ave. Hamp 92 1370 B
Queenswood Ave. Houn 70 1276 D
Queenswood Ave. Th Hth 105 3167 A
Queenswood Ave. Wall 111 2964 B
Queenswood Ct. SE27 87 3271 A
Queenswood Ct. SW4 74 3074 A
Queenswood Gdns. E11 39 4086 B
Queenswood Park. N3 23 2490 C
Queen's Wood Rd. N10 36 2888 D
Queenswood Rd. SE23 88 3672 C
Queenswood Rd. Sid 78 4574 D
Queen Victoria Ave. Wem 44 1784 D
Queen Victoria St. EC4 8 3280 A
Quemerford Rd. N7 47 3085 D
Quentin Pl. SE13 77 3975 A
Quentin Rd. SE13 77 3975 A
Quernmore Cl. Brom 99 4070 A
Quernmore Rd. Brom 99 4070 A
Quernmore Rd. N4 37 3188 C
Querrin St. SW6 73 2676 C
Quex Mews. NW6 46 2583 A
Quex Rd. NW6 46 2583 A
Quick Pl. N1 48 3183 B
Quick Rd. W4 61 2178 C
Quicksilver Pl. N22 24 3090 D
Quicks Rd. SW19 95 2570 D
Quick St. N1 48 3183 D
Quickswood. NW3 47 2784 C
Quiet Nook. Brom 107 4165 D
Quill La. SW15 73 2375 D
Quilp St. SE1 8 3279 A
Quilter St. E2 57 3482 A
Quinta Dri. Barn 11 2395 A
Quintin Ave. SW20 95 2469 B
Quinton Cl. Beck 98 3868 A
Quinton Cl. Wall 111 2864 B
Quinton Rd. Surb 101 1666 C
Quinton St. SW18 85 2672 A
Quixley St. E14 58 3880 B
Quorn Rd. SE22 75 3375 A

Rabbit Row. W8 56 2580 C
Rabbits Rd. E12 50 4285 A
Raby Rd. N Mal 94 2068 D
Raby St. E14 57 3681 C
Raccoon Way. Houn 70 1176 C
Racton Rd. SW6 62 2577 A
Radbourne Ave. W5 60 1778 A
Radbourne Cl. E5 49 3585 B
Radbourne Cres. E17 26 3889 B

Radbourne Rd. SW12 86 29 73 D
Radcliffe Ave. Enf 13 32 97 A
Radcliffe Ave. NW10 45 22 83 C
Radcliffe Gdns. Cars 111 27 63 C
Radcliffe Path. SW8 74 29 76 C
Radcliffe Rd. Croy 105 33 65 D
Radcliffe Rd. Har 21 16 90 C
Radcliffe Rd. N21 17 31 94 D
Radcliffe Sq. SW15 73 23 74 D
Radcliffe Way. Nthl 53 11 82 B
*Radcot St. SE11 63 31 78 C
Raddington Rd. W10 56 24 81 A
Radfield Way. Sid 90 44 73 B
Radford Rd. SE13 76 38 74 C
Radipole Rd. SW6 73 24 76 B
Radland Rd. E16 58 40 81 C
Radlet Ave. SE26 87 34 72 B
Radlett Cl. E7 50 39 84 B
Radlett Pl. NW8 47 27 83 A
Radley Ave. Ilf 51 46 85 A
Radley Gdns. Har 21 18 89 C
Radley Mews. W8 62 25 79 D
Radley Rd. N17 25 33 90 C
Radley's La. E18 27 40 90 C
Radleys Mead. Dag 52 49 84 B
Radley Sq. E5 38 35 86 A
Radlix Rd. E10 38 37 87 C
Radnor Ave. Har 33 15 88 A
Radnor Ave. Well 78 46 74 B
Radnor Cl. Chis 100 45 70 A
Radnor Cl. Mit 96 30 68 C
Radnor Cres. Ilf 39 42 88 B
Radnor Gdns. Enf 13 33 97 A
Radnor Gdns. Twick 83 15 72 B
Radnor Mews. W2 1 26 81 D
Radnor Pl. W2 1 27 81 C
Radnor Rd. Har 33 15 88 A
Radnor Rd. NW6 46 24 83 A
Radnor Rd. SE15 63 34 77 C
Radnor Rd. Twick 83 15 72 B
Radnor St. EC1 4 32 82 A
Radnor Wlk. Croy 106 36 67 D
Radnor Wlk. SW3 9 27 78 D
Radstock Ave. Har 21 16 89 B
Radstock St. SW11 9 27 77 C
Raeburn Ave. Dart 80 52 74 B
Raeburn Ave. Surb 102 19 67 D
Raeburn Cl. King 93 17 70 D
Raeburn Cl. NW11 35 26 88 C
Raeburn Rd. Edg 22 19 90 A
Raeburn Rd. Sid 78 45 74 C
Raeburn St. SW2 74 30 75 C
Rafford Way. Brom 99 40 68 B
Raggleswood. Chis 100 43 69 A
Raglan Ct. S Croy 112 31 64 D
Raglan Ct. Wem 44 18 85 B
Raglan Rd. Belv 67 48 78 B
Raglan Rd. Brom 99 41 68 C
Raglan Rd. E17 38 38 88 B
Raglan Rd. Enf 17 33 94 B
Raglan Rd. SE18 66 44 78 C
Raglan St. NW5 47 28 84 B
Raglan Way. Nthlt 43 14 84 A
Ragley Cl. W3 61 20 79 A
Raider Cl. Rom 29 49 90 B
Railey Mews. NW5 47 29 85 B
Railshead Rd. Islw 71 16 75 D
Railton Rd. SE24 75 31 74 B
Railway App. Har 21 15 89 D
Railway App. SE1 8 32 80 D
Railway App. Twick 83 16 73 A
Railway Ave. SE16 64 35 79 A
Railway Pas. Tedd 93 16 70 A
Railway Pl. Belv 67 49 79 C
Railway Pl. EC3 8 33 80 A
Railway Pl. SW19 95 24 70 B
Railway Rd. Tedd 83 15 71 B
Railway Rise. SE22 75 33 75 C
Railway Side. SW13 72 21 75 A
Railway St. N1 47 30 83 C
Railway St. Rom 41 47 87 A
Railway Terr. E17 26 38 90 A
Railway Terr. Felt 81 10 73 C
Railway Terr. SE13 76 37 74 B
Rainborough Cl. NW10 45 20 84 A
Rainbow St. SE5 63 33 77 C
Raine St. E1 57 34 80 D
Rainham Cl. SE9 78 45 74 C
Rainham Cl. SW11 74 27 74 C
Rainham Rd. NW10 56 23 82 B
Rainham Road N. Dag 41 49 86 D
Rainham Road S. Dag 52 50 84 A
Rainhill Way. E3 57 37 82 A
Rainsborough Ave. SE8 64 36 78 A
Rainsford Rd. NW10 45 19 83 D
Rainsford St. W2 1 27 81 C
Rainsford Way. Horn 42 52 87 C
Rainton Rd. SE7 65 40 78 C
Rainville Rd. W6 62 23 77 A
Raisins Hill. Pnr 19 10 89 B
Raith Ave. N14 16 29 93 D
Raleana Rd. E14 58 38 80 C
Raleigh Ave. Wall 111 29 64 B
Raleigh Cl. NW4 35 23 88 A
Raleigh Cl. Pnr 32 11 87 B
Raleigh Cl. Ruis 31 09 86 B
Raleigh Ct. Wall 111 28 63 B
Raleigh Dri. N20 16 27 93 C
Raleigh Dri. Surb 102 20 66 C
Raleigh Gdns. Mit 96 27 68 B
Raleigh Gdns. SW2 74 30 74 D
Raleigh Mews. N1 48 31 83 B
Raleigh Rd. Enf 13 32 96 D
Raleigh Rd. Felt 81 09 72 B
Raleigh Rd. N2 24 27 90 C
Raleigh Rd. N8 25 31 89 C
Raleigh Rd. Rich 71 18 75 B
Raleigh Rd. SE20 98 35 70 D
Raleigh Rd. Sthl 59 12 78 C
Raleigh St. N1 48 31 83 B
Raleigh Way. Felt 82 11 71 C
Raleigh Way. N14 16 29 94 D
Ralston St. SW3 9 27 78 D
Rama Ct. Har 33 15 86 A
Rambler Cl. SW16 86 29 71 A
Ramelagh Gdns. E11 39 41 88 A
Ramilles Cl. SW2 74 30 74 C
Ramillies Pl. W1 2 29 81 C
Ramillies Rd. Sid 78 46 74 D
Ramillies Rd. W4 61 20 79 D
Ramillies St. W1 2 29 81 C
Ramily Ct. SW6 73 24 76 D
Rampart St. E1 57 34 81 D
Rampayne St. SW1 10 29 78 D
Ram Pl. E9 49 35 84 A
Rampton Cl. E4 18 37 93 C
Ramsay Gdns. Rom 30 53 90 A
Ramsay Rd. E7 39 39 86 D
Ramsay Rd. W3 61 20 79 A
Ramscroft Cl. N9 17 33 94 A
Ramsdale Rd. SW17 86 28 71 D
Ramsden Dr. Rom 29 49 91 C
Ramsden Rd. Eri 67 50 77 D
Ramsden Rd. N11 16 27 92 D
Ramsden Rd. Orp 108 46 66 D
Ramsden Rd. SW12 86 28 73 A
Ramsey Rd. NW9 34 21 88 D
Ramsey Rd. Th Hth 104 30 67 D
Ramsey St. E2 57 34 82 C
Ramsey Way. N14 16 29 94 A
Ramsey Wlk. N1 48 32 84 B
Ramsgate St. E8 48 33 84 B
Ramsgill App. Ilf 28 45 89 D
Ramsgill Dri. Ilf 28 45 89 D
Rams Gr. Rom 29 48 89 C
Ramulis Dri. Hay 53 11 82 D
Rancliffe Gdns. SE9 77 42 75 C
Rancliffe Rd. E6 50 42 83 C
Randall Ave. NW2 34 21 86 D
Randall Cl. Eri 67 50 77 A
Randall Cl. SW11 74 27 76 A
Randall Ct. NW7 22 22 91 C
Randall Dri. Horn 42 53 86 D
Randall Pl. SE10 64 38 77 C
Randall Rd. Rom 42 51 88 D
Randall Rd. SE11 10 30 78 B
Randall Row. SE11 10 30 78 B
Randell's Rd. N1 47 30 83 A
Randle Rd. Rich 83 17 71 A
Randlesdown Rd. SE6 88 37 72 D
Randolph App. E16 58 41 81 C
Randolph Ave. W9 1 26 82 A
Randolph Cl. Bexh 79 50 75 A
Randolph Cl. King 84 20 71 C
Randolph Cres. W9 1 26 82 C
Randolph Gdns. NW6 46 25 83 D
Randolph Mews. W9 1 26 82 C
Randolph Rd. E17 38 37 88 B
Randolph Rd. Sthl 59 12 79 B
Randolph Rd. W9 1 26 82 C
Randolph St. NW1 47 29 84 C
Randon Cl. Har 20 13 90 D
Ranelagh Ave. SW13 72 22 76 C
Ranelagh Ave. SW6 73 24 75 B
Ranelagh Dri. Twick 71 16 74 B
Ranelagh Gdns. Ilf 40 43 87 A
Ranelagh Gdns. SW6 73 24 75 B
Ranelagh Gdns. W4 61 20 77 C
Ranelagh Gr. SW1 9 28 78 C
Ranelagh Mews. W5 60 17 79 B
Ranelagh Pl. N.Mal 102 21 67 A
Ranelagh Rd. E11 50 39 85 A
Ranelaghd. E15 50 39 83 C
Ranelagh Rd. E6 51 43 83 C
Ranelagh Rd. N17 25 33 89 A
Ranelagh Rd. N22 24 30 90 B
Ranelagh Rd. NW10 45 21 83 D
Ranelagh Rd. SW1 10 29 78 C
Ranelagh Rd. W5 60 17 79 B
Ranelagh Rd. Wem 44 17 84 B
Ranelegh Rd. Sthl 53 11 80 D
Ranfurly Rd. Sutt 103 25 65 A
Rangefield Rd. Brom 89 39 71 D
Rangemoor Rd. 15 37 33 88 B
Rangers Sq. SE10 76 38 76 B
Rangoon St. EC3 4 33 81 D
Rankin Cl. NW9 22 21 89 A
Ranleigh Gdns. Bexh 67 48 77 D
Ranmere St. SW12 86 28 73 D
Ranmoor Cl. Har 20 14 89 D
Ranmoor Gdns. Har 20 14 89 D
Ranmore Ave. Croy 105 33 65 D
Ranmore Ct. SW20 95 23 69 B
Ranmore Path. Orp 100 46 68 C
Ranmore Rd. Sutt 110 23 62 B
Rannoch Rd. W6 62 23 77 B
Rannock Ave. NW9 34 21 87 A
Ransom Rd. SE7 65 41 78 A
Ranston St. NW1 1 27 81 A
Ranulf Rd. NW2 46 24 85 B
Ranwell Cl. E3 49 36 83 B
Ranworth Cl. Eri 80 51 76 C
Ranworth Rd. N9 18 35 93 A
Raphael Ave. Rom 30 51 89 B
Raphael St. SW7 5 27 79 B
Rashleigh St. SW8 74 28 76 D
Rasper Rd. N20 15 26 93 A
Rastell Ave. SW2 86 29 73 D
Ratcliffe Cross St. E1 57 35 81 D
Ratcliffe La. E14 57 36 81 C
Ratcliffe Orchard. E1 57 35 80 B
Ratcliff Rd. E7 50 41 85 C
Rathbone Pl. W1 2 29 81 D
Rathbone St. E16 58 39 81 D
Rathbone St. W1 2 29 81 A
Rathcoole Ave. N8 36 30 88 B
Rathcoole Gdns. N8 36 30 88 B
Rathfern Rd. SE6 88 36 73 B
Rathgar Ave. W13 54 17 80 C
Rathgar Cl. N3 23 24 90 D
Rathgar Rd. SW9 75 31 75 B
Rathlin Wlk. N1 48 32 84 A
Rathmell Dri. SW4 74 29 74 D
Rathmore Rd. SE7 65 40 78 D
Rattray Rd. SW2 75 31 74 A
Raul Rd. SE15 75 34 76 A
Raveley St. NW5 47 29 85 A
Ravendale Rd. Sun 91 09 69 D
Ravenet St. SW11 74 28 76 B
Ravenfield Rd. SW17 86 27 72 D
Ravenhill Rd. E13 50 41 83 C
Ravenna Rd. SW15 73 23 75 D
Ravenor Ct. Grnf 53 13 82 D
Ravenor Park Rd. Grnf 53 13 82 B
Raven Rd. E18 27 41 90 C
Raven Rd. SE11 10 30 78 B
Raven Row. E1 57 34 81 B
Ravensbourne Ave. Brom 98 38 69 B
Ravensbourne Cres. Rom 30 54 89 B
Ravensbourne Gdns. Ilf 28 43 90 B
Ravensbourne Gdns. W13 54 16 81 B
Ravensbourne Park Cres. SE6 88 36 73 B
Ravensbourne Park. SE6 88 37 73 A
Ravensbourne Pl. SE13 76 37 76 D
Ravensbourne Rd. Brom 99 40 68 A
Ravensbourne Rd. Dart 80 52 75 A
Ravensbourne Rd. SE6 88 36 73 D
Ravensbourne Rd. Twick 71 17 74 C
Ravensbury Ave. Mord 103 26 67 A
Ravensbury Gr. Mit 95 26 68 D
Ravensbury La. Mit 95 26 68 D
Ravensbury Path. Mit 95 26 68 D
Ravensbury Path. Mit 96 27 68 A
Ravensbury Rd. Orp 100 46 68 C
Ravensbury Rd. SW18 85 25 72 B
Ravensbury Terr. SW18 85 25 72 B
Ravenscar Rd. Brom 89 39 71 A
Ravenscar Rd. Surb 101 18 65 B
Ravens Cl. Brom 99 39 69 D
Ravens Cl. Enf 13 33 97 C
Ravenscourt Cl. Horn 42 54 86 C
Ravenscourt Cl. Ruis 31 08 87 A
Ravenscourt Dri. Horn 42 54 86 A
Ravenscourt Gdns. W6 61 22 78 A
Ravenscourt Gr. Horn 42 54 86 A
Ravenscourt Park. W6 61 22 78 A
Ravenscourt Pl. W6 61 22 78 B
Ravenscourt Rd. Orp 100 46 69 D
Ravenscourt Rd. W6 61 22 78 B
Ravenscourt Sq. W6 61 22 79 C
Ravenscourt. Sun 91 09 69 B
Ravenscraig Rd. N11 16 29 92 A
Ravenscroft Ave. NW11 35 24 87 B
Ravenscroft Ave. W6 61 22 78 A
Ravenscroft Ave. Wem 33 18 87 B
Ravenscroft Cl. E16 58 40 81 A
Ravenscroft. E2 4 33 82 B
Ravenscroft Park. Barn 11 23 96 B
Ravenscroft Rd. Beck 98 35 69 D
Ravenscroft Rd. E16 58 40 81 A
Ravenscroft Rd. W4 61 20 78 A
Ravensdale Ave. N12 15 26 92 B
Ravensdale Gdns. SE19 97 32 70 D
Ravensdale Rd. Houn 70 12 75 A
Ravensdale Rd. N16 37 33 88 D
Ravensdon St. SE11 63 31 78 C
Ravensfield. Dag 52 47 85 B
Ravensfield Gdns. Eps 109 21 64 A
Ravenshaw St. NW6 46 24 85 D
Ravenshill. Chis 100 43 69 B
Ravenshurst Ave. NW4 23 23 89 C
Ravenslea Rd. SW12 86 27 73 D
Ravensmead Rd. Brom 98 38 70 D
Ravensmede Way. W4 61 21 78 B
Ravens Mews. SE12 77 40 74 A
Ravenstone Rd. N8 25 31 89 A
Ravenstone Rd. NW9 34 21 88 D
Ravenstone St. SW12 86 28 73 C
Ravens Way. SE12 77 40 74 A
Ravenswood Ave. Surb 102 19 65 A
Ravenswood Ave. W Wick 106 38 66 C
Ravenswood Cres. Har 32 12 86 B
Ravenswood Cres. W Wick 106 38 66 C
Ravenswood Ct. King 94 19 70 B
Ravenswood Gdns. Islw 71 15 76 A
Ravenswood Park. Nthwd 19 10 91 A
Ravenswood Rd. Croy 105 31 65 D
Ravenswood Rd. E17 38 38 88 A
Ravenswood Rd. E17 26 38 89 C
Ravenswood Rd. SW12 86 28 73 B
Ravensworth Rd. NW10 55 22 82 B
Ravensworth Rd. SE9 89 42 71 B
Ravent Rd. SE11 10 30 78 B
Ravey St. EC2 4 33 82 C
Ravine Gr. SE18 66 45 77 A
Ravleigh Ave. Tedd 93 15 70 A
Rawlings St. SW3 9 27 78 B
Rawlins Cl. N3 23 24 89 A
Rawnsley Ave. Mit 104 27 67 A
Rawreth Wlk (off Basire St). N1 48 32 83 A
Rawson St. SW11 74 28 76 B
Rawsthorne Pl. EC1 3 31 82 B
Rawstone Wlk. E13 50 40 83 C
Rawstorne St. EC1 3 31 82 B
Raydean Rd. Barn 11 25 95 B
Raydons Gdns. Dag 52 48 85 C
Raydons Rd. Dag 52 48 85 C
Raydon St. N19 36 28 86 B
Rayfield Cl. Brom 107 42 67 C
Rayford Ave. SE12 89 39 73 B
Rayford Cl. Dart 80 53 74 A
Ray Gdns. Bark 51 46 83 C
Rayleas Cl. SE18 78 43 76 B
Rayleigh Cl. N13 17 32 93 D
Rayleigh Ct.King 93 18 69 D
Rayleigh Rd. N13 17 32 93 D
Rayleigh Rd. SW19 95 24 69 B
Rayleigh Rd. Wdf Gn 27 41 91 C
Rayleigh Rise. S Croy 112 33 63 A
Ray Lodge Rd. Wdf Gn 27 41 91 B
Raymead Ave. Th Hth 105 31 67 A
Raymead Pas. Th Hth 105 31 67 A
Raymere Gdns. SE18 66 45 77 C
Raymond Ave. E18 27 39 90 D
Raymond Ave. W13 60 16 79 C
Raymond Cl. SE26 88 35 71 C
Raymond Rd. Beck 98 36 68 C
Raymond Rd. Ilf 40 44 87 B
Raymond Rd. SW19 95 24 70 A
Raymouth Rd. SE16 63 34 78 B
Rayne Ct. E18 27 39 89 D
Rayners Cl. Wem 44 17 85 D
Rayners La. Har 32 13 86 B
Rayners La. Pnr 32 12 88 D
Rayner's Rd. SW15 73 24 74 A
Raynes Ave. E11 39 41 87 A
Raynesfield. SW20 95 23 68 A
Raynham Ave. N18 17 34 92 C
Raynham Rd. N18 17 34 92 C
Raynham Rd. W6 61 22 78 B
Raynham Terr. N18 17 34 92 C
Raynham. W2 1 27 81 C
Raynor Cl. Sthl 53 12 80 D
Raynor Pl. N1 48 32 83 A
Raynton Cl. Har 32 12 87 A
Rays Ave. N18 18 35 92 C
Rays Rd. N18 18 35 92 A
Ray St. EC1 3 31 82 C
Ray Wlk. N7 36 30 86 B
Reade Wlk. NW10 45 21 84 C
Reading La. E8 48 34 84 B
Reading Rd. Nthlt 43 14 85 C
Reading Rd. Sutt 110 26 64 C
Reading Way. NW7 15 24 92 C
Reapers Way. Islw 70 14 74 B
Reardon Path. E1 57 34 80 D
Reardon St. E1 57 34 80 D
Reaston St. SE14 64 35 77 D
Rebecca Terr. SE16 64 35 79 C
Reckitt Rd. W4 61 21 78 C
Record St. SE15 64 35 77 A
Recovery St. SW17 86 27 71 C
Recreation Ave. Rom 41 50 88 A
Recreation Ave. Rom 30 54 90 D
Recreation Rd. Brom 99 39 69 D
Recreation Rd. SE26 88 35 71 B
Recreation Rd. Sthl 59 12 78 A
Recreation Way. Mit 96 30 68 A
Rector St. N1 48 32 83 A
Rectory Cl. Dart 80 51 75 C
Rectory Cl. E4 18 37 93 C
Rectory Cl. N3 23 24 90 B
Rectory Cl. Shep 91 07 68 A
Rectory Cl. Sid 90 46 71 B
Rectory Cl. Surb 101 17 66 C
Rectory Cl. SW20 95 23 68 A
Rectory Cres. E11 39 41 88 C
Rectory Field Cres. SE7 65 41 77 C
Rectory Gdns. N8 24 30 89 C
Rectory Gdns. Nthlt 43 12 83 B
Rectory Gdns. SW4 74 29 75 A
Rectory Gr. Croy 105 31 65 B
Rectory Green. Beck 98 36 69 B
Rectory Gr. Hamp 82 12 71 B
Rectory Gr. SW4 74 29 75 A
Rectory La. Edg 22 19 91 A
Rectory La. Sid 90 46 71 B
Rectory La. Surb 101 17 66 C
Rectory La. SW17 96 28 70 A
Rectory La. SW17 86 28 71 C
Rectory La. Wall 111 29 64 A
Rectory Orchard The. SW19 85 24 71 A
Rectory Park Ave. Nthlt 53 12 82 B
Rectory Pl. SE18 66 43 78 A
Rectory Rd. Beck 98 37 69 A
Rectory Rd. Dag 52 49 84 D
Rectory Rd. E12 50 42 85 D
Rectory Rd. E17 26 37 89 D
Rectory Rd. E8 48 34 85 A
Rectory Rd. Houn 70 11 76 C
Rectory Rd. N16 37 33 86 D
Rectory Rd. Sthl 59 12 79 D
Rectory Rd. Sutt 103 25 65 D
Rectory Rd. SW13 72 22 76 C
Rectory Rd. W3 55 19 80 D
Rectory Sq. E1 57 35 81 B
Rectory Way. Uxb 31 07 86 B
Reculver Mews. N18 17 34 92 A
Reculver Rd. SE16 64 35 78 D
Redanchof Cl. SW3 9 27 77 A
Redan Pl. W2 56 25 81 D
Redan St. W14 62 23 79 D
Redan Terr. SE5 75 32 76 C
Redberry Gr. SE26 88 35 72 C
Redbourne Ave. N3 23 25 90 A
Redbridge Gdns. SE5 63 33 77 C
Redbridge Lane E. Ilf 39 42 88 A
Redbridge Lane W. E11 39 41 88 C
Redburn St. SW3 9 27 77 B
Redcar Cl. Nthlt 43 13 84 B
Redcar St. SE5 63 32 77 C
Redcastle Cl. E1 57 35 80 A
Red Cedars Rd. Orp 108 45 66 A
Redchurch St. E2 4 33 82 D
Redcliffe Gdns. Ilf 40 43 87 C
Redcliffe Gdns. SW10 62 25 77 B
Redcliffe Mews. SW10 62 25 78 B
Redcliffe Pl. SW10 62 26 77 A
Redcliffe Rd. SW10 62 26 77 A
Redcliffe Sq. SW10 62 25 78 D
Redcliffe St. SW10 62 25 77 B
Redcliffe Wlk. Wem 34 19 86 D
Redclose Ave. Mord 103 25 67 A
Redclyffe Rd. E6 50 41 83 A
Redcroft Rd. Sthl 53 14 81 C
Redcross Way. SE1 8 32 80 C
Redden Court Rd. Horn 30 54 89 B
Redden Court Rd. Rom 30 54 89 A
Reddington Cl. S Croy 112 33 62 A
Reddins Rd. SE15 63 34 77 A
Reddons Rd. Beck 98 36 70 C
Reddy Rd. Eri 68 51 77 B
Rede Pl. W2 56 25 80 A
Redesdale Gdns. Islw 60 16 77 C
Redesdale St. SW3 9 27 78 D
Redfern Ave. Houn 82 13 73 A
Redfern Gdns. Rom 30 53 90 D
Redfern Rd. NW10 45 21 84 C
Redfern Rd. SE6 88 38 73 A
Redfield La. SW5 62 25 78 B
Redfield Mews. SW5 62 25 78 A
Redford Ave. Th Hth 96 30 68 D
Redford Ave. Wall 111 30 63 A
Redford Wlk. N1 48 32 83 A
Redgates Dri. Brom 107 40 65 B
Redgate Terr. SW15 73 23 74 D
Redgrave Rd. SW15 73 23 75 B
Red Hill. Chis 90 43 71 D
Redhill Dri. Edg 22 20 90 C
Redhill St. NW1 2 28 82 B
Red House La. Bexh 79 48 75 C
Red House Rd. Croy 104 29 67 D
Redington Gdns. NW3 46 25 85 B
Redington Rd. NW3 46 25 85 B
Redland Gdns. E Mol 92 12 68 D
Redlands. N15 25 32 89 D
Redlands Rd. Enf 14 36 97 A
Redlands Way. SW2 86 30 73 B
Redlaw Way. SE16 63 34 78 C
Redleaf Cl. Belv 67 49 77 A
Redleaves Ave. Ashf 91 07 70 B
Redlees Cl. Islw 71 16 75 C
Red Lion Cl. SE17 63 32 77 B
Red Lion Ct. EC4 3 31 81 C
Red Lion Hill. N2 23 26 90 D
Red Lion La. SE18 78 43 76 A
Red Lion Pl. SE18 78 43 76 A
Red Lion Rd. Surb 102 19 66 C
Red Lion Row. SE17 63 32 77 A
Red Lion Sq. WC1 3 30 81 B
Red Lion St. Rich 71 17 74 B
Red Lion St. WC1 3 30 81 B
Red Lion Yd. W1 6 28 80 C
Red Lodge Rd. W Wick 106 38 66 B
Redman's Rd. E1 57 35 81 A
Redmead La. E1 57 34 80 C
Redmore Rd. W6 61 22 78 B
Red Oak Cl. Orp 108 43 65 B
Red Path. E9 49 36 84 B
Red Pl. W1 6 28 80 A
Redpoll Way. Belv 67 47 79 D
Red Post Hill. SE24 75 32 74 B
Redriffe Rd. E13 50 39 83 B
Redriff Rd. Rom 29 49 90 D
Redriff Rd. SE16 64 35 79 D
Redruth Cl. N22 24 30 91 D
Redruth House. Sutt 110 25 63 D
Redruth Rd. E9 49 35 83 A
Redston Rd. N8 24 29 89 D
Redvers Rd. N22 24 31 90 C
Redvers St. E2 4 33 82 A
Redwald Rd. E5 49 36 85 A
Redway Dri. Twick 82 14 73 A
Redwing Path. SE18 66 44 79 B
Redwood Cl. SE16 57 36 80 C
Redwood Ct. Surb 101 17 66 B
Redwoods. SW15 84 22 73 C
Reece Mews. SW7 62 26 78 B
Reed Ave. Orp 108 45 65 C
Reed Cl. E16 58 40 81 A
Reed Cl. SE12 77 40 74 A
Reede Gdns. Dag 52 49 85 D
Reede Rd. Dag 52 49 84 B
Reede Way. Dag 52 49 84 B
Reedham Cl. N15 25 34 89 D
Reedham St. SE15 75 34 75 A
Reedholm Villas. N16 48 32 85 B
Reed Pond Wlk. Rom 30 51 90 D
Reed Rd. N17 25 33 90 D
Reedsfield Rd. Ashf 81 07 71 B
Reed's Pl. NW1 47 29 84 B
Reedworth St. SE11 63 31 78 A
Rees Gdns. Croy 105 33 67 D
Reesland Cl. E12 51 43 84 A
Rees St. N1 48 32 83 A
Reets Farm Cl. NW9 34 21 88 C
Reeves Ave. NW9 34 20 87 B
Reeves Cnr. Croy 105 31 65 B
Reeves Mews. W1 6 28 80 A

| | | | |
|---|---|---|---|
| Reeves Pl. N1 | 48 | 33 83 | C |
| Reeves Rd. E3 | 57 | 37 82 | D |
| Reform Row. N17 | 25 | 33 90 | D |
| Reform St. SW11 | 74 | 27 76 | D |
| Regal Cl. W5 | 54 | 17 81 | B |
| Regal Cres. Wall | 104 | 28 65 | D |
| Regal Ct. N18 | 17 | 33 92 | D |
| Regal Ct. Wem | 44 | 17 85 | B |
| Regal La. NW1 | 47 | 28 83 | A |
| Regal Way. Har | 33 | 18 88 | C |
| Regan Way. N1 | 48 | 33 83 | C |
| Regarth Ave. Rom | 42 | 51 88 | C |
| Regency Cl. Hamp | 82 | 12 71 | D |
| Regency Cl. W5 | 54 | 18 81 | C |
| Regency Ct. Sutt | 110 | 25 64 | B |
| Regency Ct. Tedd | 93 | 16 70 | B |
| Regency Dri. Ruis | 31 | 09 87 | C |
| Regency Mews. Islw | 71 | 15 74 | A |
| Regency Mews. NW10 | 45 | 22 84 | A |
| Regency St. SW1 | 10 | 29 78 | B |
| Regency Way. Bexh | 79 | 47 75 | B |
| Regency Wlk. Croy | 106 | 36 67 | D |
| Regent Cl. Har | 33 | 18 88 | C |
| Regent Cl. Houn | 69 | 10 76 | B |
| Regent Cl. N12 | 15 | 26 92 | C |
| Regent Pl. Croy | 105 | 33 66 | D |
| Regent Pl. W1 | 6 | 29 80 | A |
| Regent Rd. SE24 | 75 | 31 74 | B |
| Regent Rd. Surb | 102 | 19 67 | A |
| Regents Ave. N13 | 17 | 31 92 | C |
| Regents Cl. S Croy | 112 | 33 63 | A |
| Regents Ct. E8 | 48 | 34 83 | A |
| Regents Mews. NW8 | 46 | 26 83 | C |
| Regent's Park Barracks. NW1 | 47 | 28 83 | D |
| Regent's Park Rd. N3 | 23 | 24 90 | D |
| Regent's Park Rd. NW1 | 47 | 27 83 | B |
| Regent's Park Rd. NW1 | 47 | 28 84 | C |
| Regent's Park Terr. NW1 | 47 | 28 83 | B |
| Regent's Pl. SE3 | 77 | 40 76 | C |
| Regent Sq. Belv | 67 | 49 78 | B |
| Regent Sq. E3 | 57 | 37 82 | B |
| Regent Sq. WC1 | 3 | 30 82 | A |
| Regent's Row. E8 | 48 | 34 83 | A |
| Regent St. NW10 | 56 | 23 82 | B |
| Regent St. SW1 | 6 | 29 80 | B |
| Regent St. W1 | 6 | 29 80 | A |
| Regent St. W4 | 61 | 19 78 | C |
| Regina Cl. Barn | 11 | 23 96 | B |
| Reginald Rd. E7 | 50 | 40 84 | A |
| Reginald Rd. Nthwd | 19 | 09 91 | D |
| Reginald Rd. SE8 | 64 | 37 77 | C |
| Reginald Sq. SE8 | 64 | 37 77 | C |
| Regina Rd. N4 | 36 | 30 87 | D |
| Regina Rd. SE25 | 97 | 34 68 | A |
| Regina Rd. Sthl | 59 | 11 78 | A |
| Regina Rd. W13 | 54 | 16 80 | C |
| Regina Terr. W13 | 54 | 16 80 | D |
| Regis Ct. Felt | 69 | 08 74 | D |
| Regnart Bldgs. NW1 | 2 | 29 82 | C |
| Reid Cl. Pnr | 19 | 10 89 | C |
| Reidhaven Rd. SE18 | 66 | 45 78 | A |
| Reigate Ave. Sutt | 103 | 25 66 | D |
| Reigate Rd. Brom | 89 | 40 72 | C |
| Reigate Rd. Eps | 109 | 22 62 | C |
| Reigate Rd. Ilf | 40 | 45 86 | B |
| Reigate Way. Wall | 111 | 30 64 | C |
| Reighton Rd. E5 | 37 | 34 86 | A |
| Relay Rd. W12 | 56 | 23 80 | C |
| Relf Rd. SE15 | 75 | 34 75 | A |
| Relko Ct. Eps | 109 | 20 62 | D |
| Relko Gdns. Sutt | 110 | 26 64 | D |
| Relton Mews. SW7 | 5 | 27 79 | C |
| Rembrandt Cl. SW1 | 9 | 28 78 | C |
| Rembrandt Rd. Edg | 22 | 19 90 | C |
| Rembrandt Rd. SE13 | 77 | 39 75 | C |
| Remembrance Ave. N2 | 23 | 25 89 | B |
| Remington Rd. N15 | 37 | 32 88 | D |
| Remington St. N1 | 48 | 31 83 | D |
| Remnant St. WC2 | 3 | 30 81 | D |
| Rempstone Mews. N1 | 48 | 32 83 | D |
| Remus Rd. E3 | 49 | 37 84 | C |
| Rendlesham Rd. E5 | 37 | 34 86 | C |
| Rendlesham Rd. Enf | 13 | 31 97 | B |
| Renforth St. SE16 | 64 | 35 79 | A |
| Renfrew Rd. Houn | 70 | 12 76 | C |
| Renfrew Rd. King | 94 | 20 70 | C |
| Renfrew Rd. SE11 | 63 | 31 78 | B |
| Renmuir St. SW17 | 96 | 27 70 | B |
| Rennell St. SE13 | 76 | 38 75 | A |
| Renness Rd. E17 | 26 | 36 89 | A |
| Rennets Cl. Sid | 78 | 45 74 | A |
| Rennets Wood Rd. SE9 | 78 | 44 74 | B |
| Rennie St. SE1 | 7 | 31 80 | D |
| Renown Cl. Croy | 105 | 31 66 | D |
| Renown Cl. Rom | 29 | 49 90 | B |
| Rensburg Rd. E17 | 38 | 35 88 | D |
| Renshaw Cl. Belv | 67 | 48 77 | B |
| Renters Ave. NW4 | 35 | 23 88 | C |
| Renton Cl. SW2 | 74 | 30 74 | D |
| Renwick Rd. Bark | 51 | 46 83 | D |
| Repens Way. Hay | 53 | 11 82 | D |
| Rephidim St. SE1 | 8 | 33 79 | C |
| Replingham Rd. SW18 | 85 | 25 73 | C |
| Reporton Rd. SW6 | 62 | 24 77 | C |
| Repository Rd. SE18 | 65 | 42 78 | D |
| Repton Ave. Rom | 30 | 52 89 | A |
| Repton Ave. Wem | 44 | 17 85 | A |
| Repton Cl. Cars | 111 | 27 64 | C |
| Repton Ct. Beck | 98 | 37 69 | B |
| Repton Dri. Rom | 30 | 52 89 | C |
| Repton Gdns. Rom | 30 | 52 89 | A |
| Repton Gr. Ilf | 27 | 42 90 | B |
| Repton Rd. Har | 21 | 18 89 | D |
| Repton Rd. Orp | 108 | 46 65 | C |
| Repton St. E14 | 57 | 36 81 | C |
| Repulse Cl. Rom | 29 | 49 90 | B |
| Reservoir Rd. N14 | 12 | 29 95 | A |
| Reservoir Rd. Ruis | 19 | 08 89 | D |
| Reservoir Rd. SE4 | 76 | 36 76 | C |
| Resolution Wlk. SE18 | 65 | 42 79 | D |
| Restell Cl. SE3 | 65 | 39 77 | A |
| Restmor Way. Wall | 104 | 28 65 | A |
| Reston Pl. SW7 | 5 | 26 79 | A |
| Restons Cres. SE9 | 78 | 45 74 | C |
| Retcar Cl. N6 | 36 | 28 86 | B |
| Retford Rd. Rom | 30 | 54 91 | B |
| Retford St. N1 | 48 | 33 83 | C |
| Retingham Way. E4 | 18 | 37 93 | B |
| Retreat Cl. Har | 33 | 17 88 | A |
| Retreat Pl. E9 | 49 | 35 84 | A |
| Retreat Rd. Rich | 71 | 17 74 | B |
| Retreat The. Har | 32 | 13 87 | A |
| Retreat The. NW9 | 34 | 20 88 | B |
| Retreat The. Surb | 101 | 18 67 | D |
| Retreat The. SW14 | 72 | 21 75 | A |
| Retreat The. Th Hth | 97 | 32 68 | D |
| Retreat The. Wor Pk | 102 | 22 65 | B |
| Revell Rd. King | 94 | 19 69 | B |
| Revell Rd. Sutt | 110 | 24 63 | B |
| Revelon Rd. SE4 | 76 | 36 75 | A |
| Revelstoke Rd. SW18 | 85 | 25 72 | A |
| Reventlow Rd. SE9 | 90 | 44 73 | C |
| Reverdy Rd. SE1 | 63 | 34 78 | A |
| Revesby Rd. Cars | 104 | 27 67 | C |
| Review Rd. Dag | 52 | 49 83 | B |
| Review Rd. NW2 | 34 | 21 86 | B |
| Rewell St. SW6 | 62 | 26 77 | C |
| Rewley Rd. Cars | 103 | 26 67 | D |
| Rex Ave. Ashf | 81 | 07 71 | C |
| Rex Pl. W1 | 6 | 28 80 | C |
| Reydon Ave. E11 | 39 | 41 88 | C |
| Reynard Cl. Brom | 100 | 43 68 | A |
| Reynard Dri. SE19 | 97 | 33 70 | D |
| Reynardson Rd. N17 | 25 | 32 91 | C |
| Reynolds Ave. E12 | 51 | 43 85 | C |
| Reynolds Ave. Rom | 41 | 47 87 | A |
| Reynolds Cl. Cars | 104 | 27 66 | D |
| Reynolds Cl. NW11 | 35 | 25 87 | B |
| Reynolds Ct. E11 | 39 | 39 86 | D |
| Reynolds Ct. Rom | 29 | 47 89 | B |
| Reynolds Ct. Rom | 29 | 47 89 | B |
| Reynolds Dri. Eng | 22 | 19 89 | A |
| Reynolds Pl. Rich | 71 | 18 74 | D |
| Reynolds Pl. SE3 | 65 | 40 77 | D |
| Reynolds Rd. Hay | 53 | 11 82 | C |
| Reynolds Rd. N.Mal | 102 | 20 66 | B |
| Reynolds Rd. SE15 | 76 | 35 74 | A |
| Reynolds Rd. W4 | 61 | 20 79 | C |
| Reynolds Way. Croy | 112 | 33 64 | A |
| Rheidol Mew. N1 | 48 | 32 83 | C |
| Rheidol Terr. N1 | 48 | 32 83 | A |
| Rheola Cl. N17 | 25 | 33 90 | B |
| Rhoda St. E2 | 4 | 33 82 | D |
| Rhodes Ave. N22 | 24 | 29 90 | A |
| Rhodesia Rd. E11 | 38 | 38 86 | B |
| Rhodesia Rd. SW9 | 74 | 30 76 | C |
| Rhodes-moorhouse Ct. Mord | 103 | 25 67 | C |
| Rhodes St. N7 | 47 | 30 85 | D |
| Rhodeswell Rd. E14 | 57 | 36 81 | B |
| Rhododendron Dell. Rich | 71 | 18 76 | A |
| Rhododendron Dell. Rich | 60 | 18 77 | C |
| Rhondda Gr. E3 | 57 | 36 82 | A |
| Rhyl Rd. Grnf | 44 | 15 83 | D |
| Rhyl St. NW5 | 47 | 28 84 | A |
| Rhys Ave. N11 | 24 | 29 91 | D |
| Ribble Cl. Wdf Gn | 27 | 41 91 | A |
| Ribblesdale Ave. Nthlt | 43 | 13 84 | B |
| Ribblesdale Rd. N8 | 24 | 30 89 | D |
| Ribblesdale Rd. SW16 | 86 | 28 71 | D |
| Ribchester Ave. Grnf | 54 | 15 82 | B |
| Ribston Cl. Brom | 107 | 42 66 | D |
| Ricardo St. E14 | 57 | 37 81 | D |
| Ricards Rd. SW19 | 85 | 24 71 | D |
| Richards Ave. Rom | 41 | 50 88 | C |
| Richards Cl. Har | 33 | 16 88 | A |
| Richardson Rd. E15 | 50 | 39 83 | C |
| Richardson's Mews. W1 | 2 | 29 82 | C |
| Richards Pl. E17 | 26 | 37 89 | A |
| Richard's Pl. SW3 | 9 | 27 78 | A |
| Richard St. E1 | 57 | 34 81 | D |
| Richbell Pl. WC1 | 3 | 30 81 | B |
| Richborne Terr. SW8 | 10 | 30 77 | D |
| Richborough Rd. NW2 | 46 | 24 85 | A |
| Richford Rd. E15 | 50 | 39 83 | B |
| Richford St. W6 | 62 | 23 79 | C |
| Richlands Ave. Eps | 109 | 22 64 | C |
| Rich La. SW5 | 62 | 25 78 | D |
| Richmer Rd. Eri | 68 | 52 77 | C |
| Richmond Ave. E4 | 18 | 38 92 | D |
| Richmond Ave. Felt | 69 | 09 74 | C |
| Richmond Ave. N1 | 48 | 31 83 | A |
| Richmond Ave. NW10 | 46 | 23 84 | A |
| Richmond Ave. SW20 | 95 | 24 69 | A |
| Richmond Bldgs. W1 | 2 | 29 81 | D |
| Richmond Cl. E17 | 38 | 36 88 | D |
| Richmond Cres. E4 | 18 | 38 92 | D |
| Richmond Cres. N1 | 48 | 31 83 | A |
| Richmond Cres. N9 | 17 | 34 94 | C |
| Richmond Ct. Mit | 95 | 26 68 | B |
| Richmond Gdns. Har | 21 | 15 91 | D |
| Richmond Gdns. NW4 | 22 | 22 89 | C |
| Richmond Green. Croy | 104 | 30 65 | C |
| Richmond Green. Rich | 71 | 17 74 | B |
| Richmond Gr. N1 | 48 | 31 84 | D |
| Richmond Gr. Surb | 101 | 18 67 | D |
| Richmond Hill Ct. Rich | 71 | 18 74 | C |
| Richmond Hill. Rich | 71 | 18 74 | C |
| Richmond Ho. SE26 | 87 | 34 72 | C |
| Richmond Mews. W1 | 2 | 29 81 | D |
| Richmond Park Rd. King | 93 | 18 70 | C |
| Richmond Park Rd. SW14 | 72 | 20 75 | D |
| Richmond Pl. SE18 | 66 | 44 78 | A |
| Richmond Rd. Barn | 11 | 26 95 | A |
| Richmond Rd. Croy | 104 | 30 65 | C |
| Richmond Rd. E11 | 38 | 38 86 | B |
| Richmond Rd. E4 | 18 | 38 94 | D |
| Richmond Rd. E7 | 50 | 40 85 | D |
| Richmond Rd. E8 | 48 | 34 84 | C |
| Richmond Rd. Ilf | 40 | 44 86 | C |
| Richmond Rd. Islw | 71 | 16 75 | A |
| Richmond Rd. King | 93 | 18 70 | C |
| Richmond Rd. N11 | 24 | 30 91 | A |
| Richmond Rd. N15 | 37 | 33 88 | C |
| Richmond Rd. N2 | 23 | 26 90 | C |
| Richmond Rd. Rom | 42 | 51 88 | D |
| Richmond Rd. SW20 | 94 | 22 69 | B |
| Richmond Rd. Th Hth | 97 | 31 68 | C |
| Richmond Rd. Twick | 83 | 16 73 | B |
| Richmond Rd. W5 | 60 | 18 79 | A |
| Richmond St. E13 | 50 | 40 83 | C |
| Richmond Terr Mews. SW1 | 7 | 30 79 | A |
| Richmond Terr. SW1 | 7 | 30 79 | A |
| Richmond Way. E11 | 39 | 40 86 | A |
| Richmond Way. W12 | 62 | 23 79 | B |
| Richmond Way. W14 | 62 | 23 79 | B |
| Richmount Gdns. SE3 | 77 | 40 75 | A |
| Rich St. E14 | 57 | 36 80 | B |
| Rickard Cl. SW2 | 87 | 31 73 | C |
| Rickards Cl. Surb | 101 | 18 65 | A |
| Rickards Ct. Sthl | 53 | 14 80 | C |
| Rickett St. SW6 | 62 | 25 77 | A |
| Rickman St. E1 | 57 | 35 82 | C |
| Rickmansworth Rd. Nthwd | 19 | 08 91 | D |
| Rickmansworth Rd. Pnr | 20 | 11 90 | C |
| Rickthorne Rd. N19 | 36 | 30 86 | A |
| Rickyard Path. SE9 | 77 | 42 75 | C |
| Ridding La. Grnf | 44 | 15 85 | D |
| Riddlesdown Rd. Pur | 112 | 32 62 | C |
| Riddons Rd. SE12 | 89 | 41 71 | A |
| Rideout St. SE18 | 65 | 42 78 | B |
| Ride The. Brent | 60 | 17 78 | C |
| Ride The. Enf | 14 | 35 96 | A |
| Ridgdale St. E3 | 49 | 37 83 | D |
| Ridge Ave. Dart | 80 | 51 74 | D |
| Ridge Ave. N21 | 17 | 32 94 | B |
| Ridgebrook Rd. SE3 | 77 | 41 75 | B |
| Ridge Cl. NW4 | 23 | 23 90 | D |
| Ridge Cl. NW9 | 22 | 20 89 | D |
| Ridge Crest. Enf | 12 | 30 97 | B |
| Ridge Hill. NW11 | 35 | 24 87 | C |
| Ridge Langley. S Croy | 112 | 34 62 | A |
| Ridgemount Ave. Croy | 106 | 35 65 | B |
| Ridgemount Cl. SE20 | 97 | 34 70 | D |
| Ridgemount Gdns. Enf | 13 | 31 97 | D |
| Ridge Park. Pur | 111 | 29 62 | D |
| Ridge Rd. Mit | 96 | 28 70 | D |
| Ridge Rd. N21 | 17 | 32 94 | B |
| Ridge Rd. N8 | 36 | 30 88 | D |
| Ridge Rd. NW2 | 35 | 24 86 | D |
| Ridge Rd. Sutt | 103 | 24 66 | D |
| Ridge's Yd. Croy | 105 | 31 65 | D |
| Ridge The. Barn | 11 | 24 95 | B |
| Ridge The. Orp | 108 | 44 65 | B |
| Ridge The. Pur | 111 | 29 62 | D |
| Ridge The. Surb | 102 | 19 67 | A |
| Ridge The. Twick | 82 | 14 73 | B |
| Ridgeview Cl. Barn | 11 | 23 95 | D |
| Ridgeview Rd. N20 | 15 | 26 93 | C |
| Ridgeway Ave. Barn | 12 | 27 95 | D |
| Ridgeway. Brom | 107 | 40 65 | A |
| Ridgeway Cres Gdns. Orp | 108 | 45 65 | C |
| Ridgeway Cres. Orp | 108 | 45 65 | C |
| Ridge Way. Dart | 80 | 51 74 | D |
| Ridgeway Dri. Brom | 89 | 40 71 | B |
| Ridgeway E. Sid | 78 | 45 74 | B |
| Ridge Way. Felt | 82 | 12 72 | C |
| Ridgeway Gdns. Ilf | 39 | 42 88 | A |
| Ridgeway Gdns. SW19 | 95 | 23 70 | D |
| Ridgeway Pl. SW19 | 95 | 24 70 | A |
| Ridgeway Rd. Islw | 71 | 15 76 | A |
| Ridgeway Road N. Islw | 60 | 15 77 | C |
| Ridge Way. SE19 | 97 | 33 70 | A |
| Ridgeway. SW19 | 95 | 23 70 | B |
| Ridgeway The. Croy | 104 | 30 65 | D |
| Ridgeway The. E4 | 18 | 38 94 | C |
| Ridgeway The. Enf | 13 | 31 97 | C |
| Ridgeway The. Har | 32 | 12 88 | B |
| Ridgeway The. Har | 33 | 17 88 | C |
| Ridgeway The. N11 | 16 | 27 92 | B |
| Ridgeway The. N14 | 16 | 30 93 | A |
| Ridgeway The. N3 | 23 | 25 91 | D |
| Ridgeway The. NW11 | 35 | 24 87 | D |
| Ridgeway The. NW7 | 15 | 23 92 | C |
| Ridgeway The. NW9 | 22 | 20 89 | D |
| Ridgeway The. Rom | 30 | 52 89 | C |
| Ridgeway The. Rom | 30 | 54 90 | B |
| Ridgeway The. Ruis | 31 | 10 87 | A |
| Ridge Way The. S Croy | 112 | 33 62 | C |
| Ridgeway The. Stan | 21 | 17 91 | A |
| Ridgeway The. W3 | 61 | 19 79 | C |
| Ridgeway W. Sid | 78 | 45 74 | A |
| Ridgewell Cl. Dag | 52 | 49 83 | B |
| Ridgewell Cl. N1 | 48 | 32 83 | A |
| Ridgewell Rd. E16 | 58 | 41 81 | A |
| Ridgmount Gdns. WC1 | 2 | 29 81 | B |
| Ridgmount Pl. WC1 | 2 | 29 81 | B |
| Ridgmount Rd. SW18 | 73 | 25 74 | B |
| Ridgmount St. WC1 | 2 | 29 81 | B |
| Ridgway Rd. SW9 | 75 | 31 75 | B |
| Ridgway The. Sutt | 110 | 26 63 | D |
| Riding House St. W1 | 2 | 29 81 | A |
| Ridings Ave. N21 | 13 | 32 95 | A |
| Ridings The. Barn | 15 | 26 94 | B |
| Ridings The. Sun | 91 | 10 69 | A |
| Ridings The. Surb | 102 | 19 67 | A |
| Ridings The. W5 | 54 | 18 82 | D |
| Riding The. NW11 | 35 | 24 87 | B |
| Ridley Ave. W13 | 60 | 16 79 | D |
| Ridley Cl. Rom | 30 | 52 90 | B |
| Ridley Rd. Brom | 99 | 39 68 | B |
| Ridley Rd. E7 | 50 | 41 85 | A |
| Ridley Rd. E8 | 48 | 33 85 | D |
| Ridley Rd. NW10 | 45 | 22 83 | C |
| Ridley Rd. SW19 | 95 | 25 70 | D |
| Ridley Rd. Well | 78 | 46 76 | B |
| Ridsdale Rd. SE20 | 97 | 34 69 | B |
| Riefield Rd. SE9 | 78 | 44 75 | C |
| Riffel Rd. NW2 | 46 | 23 85 | C |
| Rifle Ct. SE11 | 63 | 31 77 | A |
| Rifle Pl. W11 | 56 | 23 80 | D |
| Rifle St. E14 | 57 | 37 81 | B |
| Rigault Rd. SW6 | 73 | 24 76 | C |
| Rigby Cl. Croy | 105 | 31 65 | C |
| Rigby Mews. Ilf | 40 | 43 86 | B |
| Rigden St. E14 | 57 | 37 81 | D |
| Rigeley Rd. NW10 | 55 | 22 82 | A |
| Rigg App. E10 | 38 | 36 87 | C |
| Rigge Pl. SW4 | 74 | 29 75 | D |
| Riggindale Rd. SW16 | 86 | 29 71 | B |
| Riley Rd. SE1 | 8 | 33 79 | B |
| Riley St. SW10 | 62 | 26 77 | D |
| Ring Cl. Brom | 99 | 40 70 | D |
| Ringcroft St. N7 | 48 | 31 85 | C |
| Ringer's Rd. Brom | 99 | 40 68 | A |
| Ringford Rd. SW18 | 73 | 25 74 | C |
| Ringles Ct. E6 | 51 | 43 83 | B |
| Ringmer Ave. SW6 | 73 | 24 76 | A |
| Ringmer Gdns. N19 | 36 | 30 86 | A |
| Ringmer Pl. N21 | 13 | 32 95 | B |
| Ringmer Way. Brom | 107 | 42 67 | B |
| Ringmore Rise. SE23 | 87 | 34 73 | B |
| Ringshall Rd. Orp | 100 | 46 68 | A |
| Ringslade Rd. N22 | 24 | 30 90 | D |
| Ringstead Rd. SE6 | 88 | 37 73 | B |
| Ringstead Rd. Sutt | 110 | 26 64 | D |
| Ring Way. N11 | 24 | 29 91 | A |
| Ringway. Sthl | 59 | 12 78 | C |
| Ringwold Cl. Beck | 98 | 36 70 | C |
| Ringwood Ave. Croy | 104 | 30 66 | A |
| Ringwood Ave. Horn | 42 | 53 86 | B |
| Ringwood Ave. N2 | 24 | 27 89 | B |
| Ringwood Cl. Pnr | 20 | 11 89 | A |
| Ringwood Gdns. SW15 | 84 | 22 73 | C |
| Ringwood Rd. E17 | 38 | 36 88 | D |
| Ringwood Way. Hamp | 82 | 13 71 | A |
| Ringwood Way. N21 | 17 | 31 94 | B |
| Ripley Gdns. Sutt | 110 | 26 64 | A |
| Ripley Gdns. SW14 | 72 | 20 75 | B |
| Ripley Rd. Belv | 67 | 49 78 | A |
| Ripley Rd. E16 | 58 | 41 81 | C |
| Ripley Rd. Enf | 13 | 32 97 | A |
| Ripley Rd. Hamp | 92 | 13 70 | C |
| Ripley Rd. Ilf | 40 | 45 86 | B |
| Ripley Villas. W5 | 54 | 17 81 | C |
| Ripon Cl. Nthlt | 43 | 13 84 | B |
| Ripon Gdns. Ilf | 39 | 42 87 | A |
| Ripon Rd. N17 | 25 | 32 89 | B |
| Ripon Rd. N9 | 17 | 34 94 | B |
| Ripon Rd. SE18 | 66 | 43 78 | B |
| Rippersley Rd. Well | 78 | 46 76 | A |
| Ripple Rd. Bark | 51 | 45 83 | A |
| Ripple Rd. Dag | 52 | 48 83 | A |
| Ripplevale Gr. N1 | 48 | 31 84 | C |
| Rippolson Rd. SE18 | 66 | 45 78 | D |
| Ripston Rd. Ashf | 81 | 08 71 | D |
| Risborough Dri. Wor Pk | 102 | 22 66 | B |
| Risborough St. SE1 | 7 | 31 79 | B |
| Risdon St. SE16 | 64 | 35 79 | A |
| Risebridge Chase. Rom | 30 | 51 91 | B |
| Risebridge Rd. Rom | 30 | 52 90 | A |
| Risedale Rd. Bexh | 79 | 50 75 | A |
| Riseholme St. E9 | 49 | 36 84 | B |
| Riseldine Rd. SE23 | 76 | 36 74 | C |
| Rise Park Bvd. Rom | 30 | 51 90 | B |
| Rise Park Par. Rom | 30 | 51 90 | C |
| Rise The. Dart | 80 | 51 75 | D |
| Rise The. E11 | 39 | 40 88 | A |
| Rise The. Eps | 109 | 21 62 | D |
| Rise The. Grnf | 44 | 16 85 | C |
| Rise The. N13 | 17 | 31 92 | A |
| Rise The. NW7 | 22 | 21 91 | B |
| Rise The. Wem | 45 | 21 85 | A |
| Rising Hill Cl. Nthwd | 19 | 08 91 | A |
| Risinghill St. N1 | 48 | 31 83 | C |
| Risingholme Cl. Har | 21 | 15 90 | A |
| Risingholme Rd. Har | 21 | 15 90 | C |
| Risings The. E17 | 26 | 38 89 | D |
| Rising Sun Ct. EC1 | 3 | 31 81 | B |
| Risley Ave. N17 | 25 | 32 90 | B |
| Rita Rd. SW8 | 10 | 30 77 | D |
| Ritches Rd. N15 | 37 | 32 88 | A |
| Ritchie Rd. Croy | 105 | 34 67 | D |
| Ritchie St. N1 | 48 | 31 83 | C |
| Ritchings Ave. E17 | 26 | 36 89 | C |
| Ritherdon Rd. SW17 | 86 | 28 72 | B |
| Ritson Rd. E8 | 48 | 34 84 | A |
| Ritter St. SE18 | 66 | 43 77 | A |
| Rivenhall Gdns. E18 | 27 | 39 89 | D |
| River Ave. N13 | 17 | 31 93 | D |
| River Ave. Surb | 101 | 16 66 | A |
| River Bank. E Mol | 92 | 13 68 | A |
| Riverbank. E Mol | 93 | 15 68 | C |
| River Bank. N21 | 17 | 32 94 | A |
| River Bank. Surb | 101 | 15 67 | B |
| River Barge Cl. E14 | 64 | 38 79 | A |
| River Cl. E11 | 39 | 41 88 | C |
| River Cl. Ruis | 31 | 09 88 | D |
| Rivercourt Rd. W6 | 61 | 22 78 | D |
| River Ct. Surb | 101 | 17 67 | B |
| Riverdale Gdns. Twick | 71 | 17 74 | A |
| Riverdale Rd. Belv | 67 | 49 78 | D |
| Riverdale Rd. Bex | 79 | 48 74 | D |
| Riverdale Rd. Eri | 67 | 50 78 | C |
| Riverdale Rd. Felt | 82 | 12 71 | B |
| Riverdale Rd. SE18 | 66 | 45 78 | D |
| Riverdale Rd. Twick | 71 | 17 74 | C |
| Riverdene Rd. Ilf | 40 | 43 86 | D |
| River Front. Enf | 13 | 33 96 | A |
| River Gdns. Cars | 104 | 28 65 | C |
| River Gdns. Felt | 69 | 10 74 | B |
| River Grove Park. Beck | 98 | 36 69 | B |
| Riverhead Cl. E17 | 26 | 35 90 | D |
| Riverholme Dri. Eps | 109 | 21 62 | A |
| River Ho. SE26 | 87 | 34 72 | D |
| River La. Rich | 83 | 17 73 | D |
| Rivermead Cl. Tedd | 83 | 16 71 | D |
| Rivermead Ct. SW6 | 73 | 24 75 | B |
| River Meads Ave. Twick | 82 | 13 72 | D |
| Rivermead. Surb | 101 | 17 67 | B |
| River Park Gdns. Brom | 98 | 38 70 | D |
| River Park Rd. N22 | 24 | 30 90 | D |
| River Pl. N1 | 48 | 32 84 | C |
| River Rd. Bark | 51 | 45 83 | C |
| River Reach. Tedd | 83 | 17 71 | C |
| Riversdale Rd. N5 | 37 | 32 86 | C |
| Riversdale Rd. Rom | 29 | 49 91 | D |
| Riversdale Rd. Surb | 101 | 16 67 | C |
| Riversfield Rd. Enf | 13 | 33 96 | A |
| River Side Ave. Rich | 71 | 18 76 | A |
| Riverside Cl. King | 93 | 17 68 | D |
| Riverside Cl. W7 | 54 | 15 82 | C |
| Riverside Cl. Wall | 104 | 28 65 | D |
| Riverside Dri. Mit | 104 | 27 67 | A |
| Riverside Dri. Rich | 83 | 17 72 | A |
| Riverside Dri. W4 | 72 | 21 76 | A |
| Riverside Gdns. Enf | 13 | 32 97 | D |
| Riverside Gdns. W6 | 61 | 22 78 | D |
| Riverside Gdns. Wem | 44 | 18 83 | C |
| Riverside Mansions. E1 | 57 | 35 80 | C |
| Riverside. NW4 | 34 | 22 87 | B |
| Riverside Rd. E15 | 49 | 38 83 | C |
| Riverside Rd. N15 | 37 | 34 88 | C |
| Riverside Rd. SW17 | 85 | 26 72 | C |
| Riverside. SE7 | 65 | 41 79 | C |
| Riverside. Twick | 83 | 16 73 | D |
| Riverside Way. Dart | 80 | 54 74 | A |
| Riverside Wlk. E10 | 65 | 39 78 | A |
| Riverside Wlk. Islw | 71 | 15 75 | A |
| River St. EC1 | 3 | 31 82 | A |
| River Terr. W6 | 62 | 23 78 | C |
| Riverton Cl. W9 | 56 | 24 82 | B |
| River View. Enf | 13 | 32 96 | A |
| Riverview Gdns. SW13 | 61 | 22 77 | B |
| River View Gdns. Twick | 83 | 15 72 | B |
| Riverview Gr. W4 | 61 | 19 77 | B |
| Riverview Park. SE6 | 88 | 37 72 | A |
| Riverview Rd. Eps | 109 | 20 64 | B |
| Riverview Rd. W4 | 61 | 19 77 | B |
| River Way. Eps | 109 | 20 64 | D |
| Riverway. N13 | 17 | 31 92 | A |
| River Way. SE10 | 65 | 39 79 | D |
| River Way. Twick | 82 | 13 72 | B |
| River Wlk. SW6 | 62 | 23 77 | C |
| River Wlk. SW6 | 73 | 24 75 | A |
| River Wlk. SW6 | 73 | 24 75 | A |
| River Wlk. W6 | 62 | 23 77 | A |
| Riverwood La. Chis | 100 | 44 69 | D |
| Rivington Ave. Wdf Gn | 27 | 41 90 | D |
| Rivington Cres. NW9 | 22 | 21 91 | D |
| Rivington Ct. NW10 | 45 | 22 83 | A |
| Rivington Pl. EC2 | 4 | 33 82 | A |
| Rivington St. EC2 | 4 | 33 82 | A |
| Rivington Wlk. E8 | 48 | 34 83 | A |
| Rivulet Rd. N17 | 25 | 32 91 | C |
| Rixsen Rd. E12 | 50 | 42 85 | C |
| Roach Rd. E3 | 49 | 37 84 | C |
| Roads Pl. N19 | 36 | 30 86 | A |
| Roan St. SE10 | 64 | 38 77 | A |
| Robb Rd. Stan | 21 | 16 91 | A |
| Robert Adam St. W1 | 2 | 28 81 | C |
| Roberta St. E2 | 57 | 34 82 | A |
| Robert Cl. W9 | 1 | 26 82 | C |
| Robert Keen Cl. SE15 | 75 | 34 76 | A |
| Robert Lowe Cl. SE14 | 64 | 35 77 | D |
| Roberton Dri. Brom | 99 | 41 69 | A |
| Robert's Alley. W5 | 60 | 17 79 | B |
| Robertsbridge Rd. Cars | 103 | 26 66 | B |
| Roberts Cl. Rom | 30 | 52 90 | B |
| Roberts Cl. Sutt | 110 | 23 63 | D |
| Roberts Ct. SE20 | 98 | 35 69 | A |
| Roberts Mews. SW1 | 6 | 28 79 | C |
| Robertson St. SW8 | 74 | 28 76 | D |
| Roberts Rd. Belv | 67 | 49 78 | C |
| Roberts Rd. E17 | 26 | 37 90 | B |
| Roberts Rd. NW7 | 23 | 24 91 | A |
| Robert St. Croy | 105 | 32 65 | C |
| Robert St. E16 | 66 | 43 79 | B |
| Robert St. NW1 | 2 | 29 82 | A |
| Robert St. SE18 | 66 | 44 78 | B |
| Robert St. WC2 | 7 | 30 80 | A |
| Robeson St. E3 | 57 | 36 81 | B |
| Robina Cl. Bexh | 79 | 47 75 | B |
| Robina Cl. Ilf | 28 | 45 91 | A |
| Robin Cl. Rom | 29 | 50 91 | D |
| Robin Ct. Wall | 111 | 29 64 | C |
| Robin Gr. Har | 33 | 18 88 | D |
| Robin Gr. N6 | 36 | 28 86 | A |
| Robin Grove Church Wlk. Brent | 60 | 17 77 | A |
| Robin Hill Dri. Chis | 99 | 42 70 | A |
| Robinhood Cl. Mit | 96 | 29 68 | A |

Robin Hood Dri. Har 21 15 91 D
Robin Hood Gdns. E14 58 38 80 A
Robin Hood Green. Orp 108 46 67 A
Robin Hood La. Bexh 79 48 74 A
Robin Hood La. E14 58 38 80 A
Robinhood La. Mit 96 29 68 A
Robin Hood La. Sutt 110 25 64 C
Robin Hood La. SW15 84 21 71 A
Robin Hood Rd. SW19 84 22 71 C
Robin Hood Way. Grnf 44 15 84 B
Robin Hood Way. SW15 84 21 71 A
Robin Hood Way. SW20 94 21 70 B
Robins Ct. SE12 89 41 72 C
Robins Gr. W.Wick 107 40 65 C
Robinson Rd. Dag 52 49 85 A
Robinson Rd. E2 49 35 83 C
Robinson Rd. SW17 96 27 70 A
Robinson Rd. SW17 96 27 70 B
Robinson's Cl. W13 54 16 81 A
Robinson St. SW3 9 27 77 B
Robin Way. Orp 100 46 68 B
Robinwood Pl. SW15 84 20 71 B
Robsart St. SW9 75 31 76 C
Robson Ave. NW10 45 22 84 C
Robson Cl. Enf 13 31 97 D
Robson Rd. SE27 87 32 72 C
Roch Ave. Edg 21 18 90 D
Rochdale Rd. E17 38 37 87 A
Rochdale Rd. SE2 66 46 78 B
Rochelle Cl. SW11 73 26 75 D
Rochelle St. E2 4 33 82 B
Rochemont Wlk. E8 48 34 83 A
Roche Rd. SW16 96 30 69 B
Rochester Ave. Brom 99 40 69 D
Rochester Ave. Felt 81 09 72 B
Rochester Cl. Enf 13 33 97 A
Rochester Cl. Sid 78 46 74 B
Rochester Cl. SW16 96 30 70 C
Rochester Dri. Bex 79 49 74 C
Rochester Dri. Pnr 32 11 88 B
Rochester Gdns. Croy 105 33 65 C
Rochester Gdns. Ilf 39 42 87 B
Rochester Mews. NW1 47 29 84 C
Rochester Pl. NW1 47 29 84 C
Rochester Rd. Cars 111 27 64 B
Rochester Rd. Nthwd 19 09 89 B
Rochester Rd. NW1 47 29 84 A
Rochester Row. SW1 10 29 78 A
Rochester Sq. NW1 47 29 84 C
Rochester St. SW1 6 29 79 D
Rochester Terr. NW1 47 29 84 A
Rochester Way. SE3 77 41 76 C
Rochester Way. SE9 77 42 75 C
Rochester Wlk. SE1 8 32 80 D
Roche Wlk. Cars 103 26 67 D
Rochford Ave. Rom 41 47 88 A
Rochford Cl. E6 50 41 83 D
Rochford Way. Croy 104 30 67 C
Rochford Wlk. E8 48 34 84 C
Rock Ave. SW14 72 20 75 B
Rockbourne Mews. SE23 88 35 73 D
Rockbourne Rd. SE23 88 35 73 D
Rockchase Gdns. Horn 42 54 88 C
Rockford Ave. Grnf 44 16 83 D
Rock Gdns. Dag 52 49 85 D
Rock Grove Way. SE16 63 34 78 A
Rockhall Rd. NW2 46 23 85 B
Rockhampton Cl. SE27 87 31 71 A
Rockhampton Rd. S Croy 112 33 63 A
Rockhampton Rd. SE27 87 31 71 A
Rock Hill. SE26 87 33 71 B
Rockingham Ave. Horn 42 52 88 D
Rockingham Cl. SW15 72 21 75 D
Rockingham St. SE1 8 32 79 C
Rockland Rd. SW15 73 24 75 C
Rocklands Dri. Stan 21 17 90 C
Rockley Rd. W14 62 23 79 B
Rockmount Rd. SE18 66 45 78 D
Rockmount Rd. SE19 97 32 70 B
Rocks La. SW13 72 22 76 D
Rock St. N4 37 31 86 A
Rockware Ave. Grnf 43 14 83 B
Rockware Ave. Grnf 44 15 83 A
Rockwell Gdns. SE19 87 33 71 A
Rockwell Rd. Dag 52 49 85 D
Rockwood Pl. W12 62 23 79 A
Rocliffe St. N1 48 31 83 D
Rocombe Cres. SE23 88 35 73 A
Rocque La. SE3 77 39 75 B
Rodborough Rd. NW11 35 25 87 C
Roden Ct. N6 36 29 87 B
Roden Gdns. SE25 105 33 67 C
Rodenhurst Rd. SW4 74 29 74 D
Roden St. Ilf 40 43 86 C
Roden St. N7 36 30 86 D
Roden Way. Ilf 40 43 86 C
Roderick Rd. NW3 47 27 85 B
Roding Ave. Bark 51 43 84 D
Roding Ave. Wdf Gn 27 42 91 A
Roding Lane N. Wdf Gn 27 42 90 A
Roding Lane S. Ilf 27 41 89 D
Roding Lodge. Ilf 39 41 88 D
Roding Rd. E5 49 36 85 C
Rodings The. Wdf Gn 27 41 91 A
Rodmarton St. W1 1 27 81 B
Rodmel Slope. N12 15 24 92 D
Rodmere St. E10 65 39 78 C
Rodmill La. SW2 86 30 73 A
Rodney Cl. Croy 105 31 66 D
Rodney Cl. N.Mal 102 21 67 A
Rodney Cl. Pnr 32 12 87 A
Rodney Gdns. Pnr 32 11 88 A
Rodney Pl. E17 26 36 90 D
Rodney Pl. SE17 63 32 78 A
Rodney Pl. SW19 95 26 69 A
Rodney Rd. E11 27 40 89 D
Rodney Rd. Mit 96 27 68 A
Rodney Rd. N.Mal 102 21 67 A
Rodney Rd. SE17 63 32 78 B
Rodney Rd. Twick 82 13 73 A
Rodney St. N1 47 30 83 D
Rodney Way. Rom 29 49 90 B
Rodsley St. SE1 63 34 77 A
Rodway Rd. Brom 99 40 69 B
Rodway Rd. SW15 84 22 73 A
Rodwell Rd. SE22 75 33 74 D
Roebourne Way. E16 66 43 79 A
Roebuck Cl. Felt 81 10 71 B
Roebuck Cl. N17 25 33 91 B
Roebuck Rd. Chess 109 19 64 A
Roebuck Rd. Ilf 28 46 91 B
Roedean Ave. Enf 14 35 97 A
Roedean Cl. Enf 14 35 97 A
Roedean Cres. SW15 72 21 74 C
Roe End. NW9 22 20 89 C
Roe Green. NW9 34 20 88 A
Roehampton Cl. SW15 72 22 75 C
Roehampton Dri. Chis 100 44 70 A
Roehampton Gate. SW15 72 21 74 C
Roehampton High St. SW15 84 22 73 A
Roehampton La. SW15 72 22 74 A
Roehampton Vale. SW15 84 21 72 B
Roe La. NW9 22 20 89 C
Roe Way. Wall 111 30 63 A
Rofant Rd. Nthwd 19 09 91 A
Roffey St. E14 64 38 79 A
Roger Reede's Almhouses. Rom 30 51 89 C
Rogers Estate. E2 57 35 82 A
Rogers Gdns. Dag 52 49 85 C
Rogers Rd. Dag 52 49 85 C
Rogers Rd. E16 58 39 81 D
Rogers Rd. SW17 86 27 71 A
Rogers Ruff. Nthwd 19 08 90 A
Roger St. WC1 3 30 82 D
Rogers Wlk. N12 15 25 93 D
Rojack Rd. SE23 88 35 73 D
Rokeby Gdns. Wdf Gn 27 40 90 A
Rokeby Pl. SW20 94 22 70 D
Rokeby Rd. SE4 76 36 76 D
Rokeby St. E15 50 39 83 A
Rokesby Cl. Well 78 44 76 D
Rokesby Pl. Wem 44 17 85 D
Rokesly Ave. N8 36 30 88 A
Roland Gdns. SW10 62 26 78 C
Roland Gdns. SW7 62 26 78 C
Roland Rd. E17 26 38 89 D
Roland Way. SE17 63 32 78 D
Roland Way. SW7 62 26 78 C
Roland Way. Wor Pk 102 21 65 B
Roles Gr. Rom 29 48 89 C
Rolfe Cl. Barn 12 27 96 C
Rollesby Rd. Chess 109 19 63 A
Rolleston Ave. Orp 108 43 67 D
Rolleston Cl. Orp 108 43 66 B
Rolleston Rd. S Croy 112 32 63 D
Roll Gdns. Ilf 40 43 88 A
Rollins St. SE15 64 35 77 A
Rollit Cres. Houn 70 13 74 A
Rollit St. N7 48 31 85 C
Rolls Bldgs. EC4 3 31 81 C
Rollscourt Ave. SE24 75 32 74 A
Rolls Park Ave. E4 18 37 92 D
Rolls Park Rd. E4 18 37 92 D
Rolls Pas. EC4 3 31 81 C
Rolls Rd. SE1 63 33 78 A
Rolt St. SE14 64 36 77 A
Rolvenden Gdns. Brom 99 41 70 D
Roman Cl. Felt 70 11 74 A
Roman Cl. Rain 52 50 83 D
Romanhurst Ave. Brom 99 39 68 C
Romanhurst Gdns. Brom 99 39 68 C
Roman Rd. E2 57 35 82 A
Roman Rd. E3 49 36 83 C
Roman Rd. Ilf 51 43 84 B
Roman Rd. N10 24 28 91 D
Roman Rd. N2 24 27 90 A
Roman Rd. W4 61 21 78 B
Roman Rise. SE19 97 32 70 B
Roman Way. Croy 105 31 65 B
Roman Way. Enf 13 33 95 B
Roman Way. N7 47 30 84 B
Roman Way. SE15 64 35 77 C
Romany Gdns. E17 26 36 90 A
Romany Gdns. Sutt 103 25 66 A
Romany Rise. Orp 108 44 66 C
Roma Rd. E17 26 36 89 A
Romberg Rd. SW17 86 28 72 C
Romborough Gdns. SE13 76 38 74 A
Romborough Way. SE13 76 38 74 A
Rom Cres. Rom 42 51 87 B
Romero Sq. SE3 77 41 75 C
Romeyn Rd. SW16 86 30 72 D
Romford Rd. Chig 29 48 91 C
Romford Rd. E12 50 42 85 B
Romford Rd. E15 50 39 84 A
Romford Rd. E7 50 40 85 D
Romford Rd. Rom 29 48 91 D
Romford St. E1 57 34 81 B
Romilly Rd. N4 37 31 86 D
Romilly St. W1 2 29 81 D
Rommany Rd. SE27 87 32 71 B
Romney Chase. Horn 42 54 88 D
Romney Cl. Ashf 81 08 71 C
Romney Cl. Har 32 13 87 A
Romney Cl. N17 25 34 90 B
Romney Cl. NW11 35 26 87 C
Romney Cl. SE14 64 35 77 C
Romney Dri. Brom 99 41 70 D
Romney Dri. Har 32 13 87 A
Romney Gdns. Bexh 79 48 76 B
Romney Rd. N.Mal 102 20 67 D
Romney Rd. SE10 64 38 77 B
Romney St. SW1 7 30 79 C
Romola Rd. SE24 87 31 73 D
Romsey Gdns. Dag 52 47 83 B
Romsey Rd. Dag 52 47 83 B
Romsey Rd. W13 54 16 80 B
Ronald Ave. E15 58 39 82 A
Ronald Cl. Beck 106 36 67 B
Ronalds Rd. Brom 99 40 69 A
Ronalds Rd. N5 48 31 85 C
Ronald St. E1 57 35 81 C
Ronaldstone Rd. Sid 78 45 74 C
Rona Rd. NW3 47 28 85 A
Rona Wlk. N1 48 32 84 B
Rondu Rd. NW2 46 24 85 C
Ronelean Rd. Surb 101 18 65 D
Roneo Cnr. Horn 42 51 87 D
Ronver Rd. SE12 89 39 73 D
Rood La. EC3 8 33 80 A
Rookby Ct. N21 17 31 93 B
Rookeries Cl. Felt 82 11 72 C
Rookery Cl. NW9 34 21 88 B
Rookery Cres. Dag 52 49 84 D
Rookery La. Brom 107 41 67 D
Rookery Rd. SW4 74 29 75 C
Rookery Way. NW9 34 21 88 B
Rooke Way. E10 65 39 78 D
Rookfield Ave. N10 24 29 89 C
Rookfield Cl. N10 24 29 89 C
Rookley Cl. Sutt 110 25 62 D
Rooksmead Rd. Sun 91 10 69 C
Rookstone Rd. SW17 86 27 71 D
Rookwood Ave. N Mal 94 22 68 C
Rookwood Ave. Wall 111 29 64 B
Rookwood Rd. N16 37 33 87 B
Roosevelt Way. Dag 52 50 84 B
Ropemakers Fields. E14 57 36 80 B
Ropemaker St. EC2 4 32 81 B
Roper La. SE1 8 33 79 A
Ropers Ave. E4 18 38 92 C
Roper St. SE9 78 43 74 C
Ropers Wlk. SE24 87 31 73 A
Roper Way. Mit 96 28 69 C
Ropery St. E3 57 36 82 D
Rope Walk Gdns. E1 57 34 81 C
Rope Yard Rails. SE18 66 43 79 D
Ropley St. E2 48 34 83 C
Rosa Alba Mews. N5 48 32 85 A
Rosa Ave. Ashf 81 07 71 A
Rosaline Rd. SW6 62 24 77 C
Rosamond St. SE26 87 34 72 D
Rosary Cl. Houn 70 12 76 C
Rosary Gdns. Ashf 81 07 71 B
Rosary Gdns. SW7 62 26 78 A
Rosaville Rd. SW6 62 24 77 D
Roscoe St. EC1 4 32 82 C
Roscoff Cl. Edg 22 20 90 A
Roseacre Cl. Horn 42 54 87 B
Roseacre Cl. W13 54 16 81 B
Roseacre Rd. Well 78 46 75 B
Roseacre Rd. Well 79 47 75 A
Rose Alley. SE1 8 32 80 C
Rose and Crown Ct. EC2 4 32 81 C
Rose and Crown Yd. SW1 6 29 80 C
Rose Ave. E18 27 40 90 D
Rose Ave. Mit 96 27 69 B
Rose Ave. Mord 103 26 67 A
Rosebank Ave. Wem 44 15 85 B
Rose Bank Cl. N12 16 27 92 C
Rosebank Gdns. E3 49 36 83 D
Rosebank Gr. E17 26 36 89 B
Rosebank Rd. E17 38 37 88 D
Rosebank Rd. W7 60 15 79 A
Rosebank. SE20 97 34 70 D
Rosebank. SW6 62 23 77 C
Rosebank Villas. E17 26 37 89 C
Rosebank Way. W3 55 20 81 D
Rosebank Wlk. N7 47 29 84 D
Roseberry Gdns. N4 37 32 88 C
Roseberry Gdns. Orp 108 45 65 C
Roseberry Pl. E8 48 33 84 B
Roseberry Sq. EC1 3 31 82 C
Roseberry St. SE16 63 34 78 B
Rosebery Ave. E12 50 42 84 B
Rosebery Ave. EC1 3 31 82 C
Rosebery Ave. Har 43 12 85 B
Rosebery Ave. N17 25 34 90 C
Rosebery Ave. N Mal 94 21 69 C
Rosebery Ave. Sid 90 45 73 A
Rosebery Ave. Th Hth 97 32 69 C
Rosebery Cl. Mord 103 23 67 D
Rosebery Gdns. N8 36 30 88 A
Rosebery Gdns. Sutt 110 25 64 B
Rosebery Gdns. W13 54 16 81 C
Rosebery Mews. N10 24 29 90 C
Rosebery Rd. Houn 70 14 74 A
Rosebery Rd. King 94 19 69 D
Rosebery Rd. N10 24 29 90 C
Rosebery Rd. N9 17 34 93 A
Rosebery Rd. Sutt 110 24 63 B
Rosebery Rd. SW2 74 30 74 C
Rosebery Sq. King 94 19 69 D
Rosebine Ave. Twick 82 14 73 B
Rosebury Rd. SW6 73 25 76 D
Rosebury Vale. Ruis 31 10 86 A
Rosecourt Rd. Croy 104 30 67 D
Rosecroft Ave. NW3 35 25 86 C
Rose Croft Gdns. NW2 34 22 86 C
Rosecroft Gdns. Twick 82 14 73 D
Rosecroft Rd. Sthl 53 13 82 C
Rosecroft Wlk. Pnr 32 11 88 B
Rosecroft Wlk. Wem 44 17 85 D
Rosedale Cl. SE2 66 46 79 D
Rosedale Cl. Stan 21 16 91 B
Rosedale Cl. W7 60 15 79 B
Rosedale Gdns. Dag 51 46 84 D
Rose Dale. Orp 108 43 65 B
Rosedale Rd. Dag 51 46 84 D
Rosedale Rd. E7 50 41 85 C
Rosedale Rd. Eps 109 22 64 C
Rosedale Rd. Rich 71 18 75 C
Rosedale Rd. Rom 29 50 89 A
Rosene Ave. Croy 104 30 66 B
Rosedene Ave. Grnf 53 13 82 A
Rosedene Ave. Mord 103 25 67 A
Rosedene Ave. SW16 86 30 72 D
Rosedene Gdns. Ilf 28 43 89 C
Rosedene. NW6 46 23 83 B
Rosedene Terr. E10 38 37 86 B
Rosedew Rd. W6 62 23 77 B
Rose End. Wor Pk 103 23 66 D
Rosefield Gdns. E14 57 37 80 A
Rose Garden Cl. Edg 21 18 91 A
Rose Gdns. Felt 81 10 72 A
Rose Gdns. Sthl 53 13 82 C
Rose Gdns. W5 60 17 79 D
Rose Glen. NW9 22 20 89 D
Rose Glen. Rom 42 51 87 C
Rosehart Mews. W11 56 25 81 C
Rosehatch Ave. Rom 29 47 89 B
Roseheath Rd. Houn 70 12 74 B
Rosehill Ave. Sutt 103 26 66 C
Rosehill Ct. Mord 103 26 66 A
Rosehill Gdns. Grnf 44 15 85 D
Rosehill Gdns. Sutt 103 26 65 A
Rosehill. Hamp 92 13 69 A
Rose Hill Park W. Sutt 103 26 65 A
Rosehill Rd. SW18 73 26 74 A
Rose Hill. Sutt 103 25 66 D
Roseland Cl. N17 25 32 91 D
Rose La. Rom 29 48 89 C
Roseleigh Ave. N5 48 31 85 B
Roseleigh Cl. Twick 71 17 74 D
Rosemary Ave. E Mol 92 13 68 C
Rosemary Ave. Enf 13 33 97 A
Rosemary Ave. Houn 70 11 76 D
Rosemary Ave. N2 23 25 89 D
Rosemary Ave. N3 23 25 90 D
Rosemary Ave. N9 17 34 94 D
Rosemary Ave. Rom 30 51 89 B
Rosemary Dri. Ilf 39 41 88 B
Rosemary Gdns. Dag 41 48 87 D
Rosemary La. SW14 72 20 75 A
Rosemary Rd. SE15 63 33 77 D
Rosemary Rd. SE15 63 33 77 D
Rosemary Rd. Well 78 45 76 B
Rosemary St. N1 48 32 83 B
Rosemead Ave. Felt 81 09 72 B
Rosemead Ave. Mit 96 29 68 A
Rosemead Ave. Wem 44 18 85 C
Rosemead. NW9 34 22 87 A
Rosemont Ave. N12 23 26 91 A
Rosemont Rd. NW3 46 26 84 A
Rosemont Rd. Rich 71 18 74 C
Rosemont Rd. W3 55 19 80 B
Rosemont Rd. Wem 44 18 83 A
Rosemoor St. SW3 9 27 78 B
Rosemount Dri. Brom 99 42 68 D
Rosemount Rd. N Mal 94 20 68 A
Rosemount Rd. W13 54 16 81 C
Rosenau Cres. SW11 74 27 76 B
Rosenau Rd. SW11 74 27 76 B
Rosendale Rd. SE21 87 32 72 A
Roseneath Ave. N21 17 31 94 D
Roseneath Rd. SW11 74 28 74 C
Roseneath Wlk. Enf 13 33 96 C
Rosenthal Rd. SE6 76 38 74 C
Rosenthorpe Rd. SE15 76 35 74 B
Roserton St. E14 64 38 79 A
Rosery The. Croy 106 35 67 D
Roses The. Wdf Gn 27 39 91 D
Rose St. WC2 7 30 80 A
Rosetta Cl. SW8 10 30 77 C
Roseveare Rd. SE12 89 41 71 A
Roseville Ave. Houn 70 13 74 A
Rosevine Rd. SW20 95 23 69 A
Rose Way. SE12 77 40 74 A
Roseway. SE21 75 32 74 D
Rose Wlk. Surb 102 19 67 B
Rose Wlk. W Wick 106 38 65 B
Rosewood Ave. Grnf 44 16 84 A
Rosewood Ct. Brom 99 41 69 B
Rosewood Ct. King 94 19 70 C
Rosewood Gr. Sutt 103 26 65 A
Rosher Cl. E15 49 38 84 D
Rosina St. E9 49 35 84 B
Roskeen Ct. SW20 95 23 70 C
Roskell Rd. SW15 73 23 75 B
Roskild Ct. Wem 44 18 85 B
Roslin Rd. W3 61 19 79 D
Roslin Way. Brom 89 40 71 C
Roslyn Cl. Mit 95 26 69 D
Roslyn Gdns. Rom 30 51 90 D
Roslyn Rd. N15 37 33 88 A
Rosmead Rd. W11 56 24 80 A
Rosoman Pl. EC1 3 31 82 C
Rosoman St. EC1 3 31 82 C
Rossall Cl. Horn 42 52 88 C
Rossall Cres. NW10 54 18 82 B
Ross Ave. Dag 41 48 87 D
Ross Ave. NW7 15 24 92 C
Ross Cl. Har 20 14 91 C
Ross Ct. SW15 85 23 73 B
Rossdale Dri. Enf 14 35 95 C
Rossdale Dri. NW9 34 20 87 C
Rossdale Rd. SW15 73 23 75 C
Rossdale. Sutt 111 27 64 C
Rosse Mews. SE3 77 40 76 B
Rossendale St. E5 37 34 86 B
Rossindel Rd. Houn 70 13 74 A
Rossington St. E5 37 34 86 A
Rossiter Rd. SW12 86 28 73 D
Rossland Cl. Bexh 79 49 74 B
Rosslyn Ave. Barn 12 27 95 C
Rosslyn Ave. Dag 41 48 87 B
Rosslyn Ave. Felt 69 10 74 C
Rosslyn Ave. Rom 30 54 90 D
Rosslyn Ave. SW13 72 21 75 B
Rosslyn Cl. W.Wick 107 39 65 D
Rosslyn Cres. Har 21 15 89 D
Rosslyn Cres. Wem 33 18 86 C
Rosslyn Hill. NW3 46 26 85 D
Rosslyn Mews. NW3 46 26 85 B
Rosslyn Park Mews. NW3 46 26 85 D
Rosslyn Rd. Bark 51 44 84 D
Rosslyn Rd. E17 26 38 89 C
Rosslyn Rd. Twick 71 17 74 C
Rossmore Rd. NW1 1 27 82 C
Ross Par. Wall 111 28 63 B
Ross Rd. Dart 80 52 74 C
Ross Rd. SE25 97 33 68 A
Ross Rd. Twick 82 14 73 C
Ross Rd. Wall 111 29 64 C
Ross Way. SE9 77 42 75 A
Rosswood Gdns. Wall 111 29 63 A
Rostella Rd. SW17 85 26 71 B
Rostrevor Ave. N15 37 33 88 D
Rostrevor Gdns. Sthl 59 12 78 C
Rostrevor Rd. SW6 73 24 76 B
Rotary St. SE1 7 31 79 D
Rothbury Gdns. Islw 60 16 77 C
Rothbury Rd. E9 49 36 84 D
Rothbury Wlk. N17 25 34 91 C
Rotherfield Rd. Cars 111 28 64 C
Rotherfield St. N1 48 32 84 C
Rotherham Wlk. SE1 7 31 80 D
Rotherhill Ave. SW16 96 29 70 B
Rotherhithe New Rd. SE16 63 34 78 D
Rotherhithe Old Rd. SE16 64 35 78 B
Rotherhithe St. SE16 64 35 79 A
Rotherhithe St. SE16 57 36 80 C
Rotherhithe Tunnel. E1 57 35 80 B
Rothermere Rd. Croy 111 30 64 D
Rotherwick Hill. W5 55 19 82 C
Rotherwick Rd. NW11 35 25 87 A
Rotherwood Rd. SW15 73 23 75 B
Rothery St. N1 48 31 83 B
Rothesay Ave. Grnf 43 14 84 B
Rothesay Ave. Rich 72 19 75 D
Rothesay Ave. SW20 95 24 69 C
Rothesay Rd. SE25 97 33 68 C
Rothsay Rd. E7 50 41 84 A
Rothsay St. SE1 8 33 79 C
Rothschild Rd. W4 61 20 79 C
Rothschild St. SE27 87 31 71 B
Rothwell Gdns. Dag 52 47 83 A
Rothwell Rd. Dag 52 47 83 A
Rothwell St. NW1 47 27 83 B
Roth Wlk. N7 36 30 86 B
Rouel Rd. SE16 63 34 78 A
Rouel Rd. SE16 63 34 79 C
Rougemont Ave. Mord 103 25 67 C
Roundacre. SW19 85 23 73 B
Round Gr. Croy 106 35 66 B
Roundhay Cl. SE23 88 35 72 B
Roundhill Dri. Enf 12 30 96 D
Round Hill. SE26 88 35 72 C
Roundtable Rd. Brom 89 39 72 D
Roundtree Rd. Wem 44 16 85 D
Roundway Rd. Ilf 27 42 90 D
Roundways. Ruis 31 09 86 D
Roundway The. N17 25 32 91 D
Roundwood. Chis 100 43 69 D
Roundwood Cl. Ruis 31 08 87 B
Roundwood Rd. NW10 45 21 84 D
Rounton Rd. E3 57 37 82 C
Roupell Rd. SW2 86 30 73 D
Roupell St. SE1 7 31 80 C
Rouse Gdns. SE21 87 33 71 A
Routh Rd. SW18 86 27 73 A
Rover Ave. Ilf 28 45 91 B
Rowallan Rd. SW6 62 24 77 C
Rowan Ave. E4 26 36 91 B
Rowan Cl. N Mal 94 21 69 C
Rowan Cl. SW16 96 29 69 A
Rowan Cl. W5 60 18 79 A
Rowan Cl. Wem 33 16 86 C
Rowan Cres. SW16 96 29 69 A
Rowan Dri. NW9 22 22 89 A
Rowan Gdns. Croy 105 33 65 D
Rowan Rd. Bexh 79 48 75 A
Rowan Rd. Brent 60 16 77 D
Rowan Rd. SW16 96 29 69 C
Rowan Rd. W6 62 23 78 B
Rowans The. N13 17 32 93 C
Rowans The. Sun 81 09 71 D
Rowan Terr. W6 62 23 78 B
Rowantree Cl. N21 17 32 94 D
Rowantree Rd. Enf 13 31 97 D
Rowantree Rd. N21 17 32 94 D
Rowan Way. Rom 29 47 89 A
Rowan Wlk. Brom 107 42 65 D
Rowan Wlk. Horn 30 53 89 D
Rowan Wlk. N19 36 29 86 A
Rowan Wlk. N2 35 26 88 A
Rowan Wlk. W10 56 24 82 C
Rowben Cl. N20 15 25 94 D
Rowberry Cl. SW6 62 23 77 D

Rowcross Pl. SE1 63 33 78 D
Rowcross St. SE1 63 33 78 D
Rowdell Rd. Nthlt 43 13 83 A
Rowden Rd. Beck 98 36 69 B
Rowden Rd. E4 26 37 91 B
Rowden Rd. Eps 109 20 64 A
Rowditch La. SW11 74 28 76 C
Rowdon Ave. NW10 45 22 84 D
Rowdowns Rd. Dag 52 48 84 D
Rowe Gdns. Bark 51 46 83 C
Rowe La. E9 49 35 85 C
Rowena Cres. SW11 74 27 76 C
Rowe Wlk. Har 32 13 86 C
Rowfant Rd. SW17 86 28 72 A
Rowhill Rd. E5 48 34 85 B
Rowington Cl. W2 56 25 81 B
Rowland Ave. Har 21 17 89 A
Rowland Ct. E16 58 39 82 D
Rowland Gr. SE26 87 34 72 D
Rowland Hill Ave. N17 25 32 91 B
Rowland Hill St. NW3 47 27 85 C
Rowlands Ave. Pnr 20 13 91 B
Rowlands Cl. NW7 22 22 91 C
Rowlands Rd. Dag 41 48 86 B
Rowland Way. Ashf 91 08 70 D
Rowland Way. SW19 95 25 69 B
Rowley Ave. Sid 90 46 73 B
Rowley Cl. Wem 44 18 84 D
Rowley Gdns. N4 37 32 87 A
Rowley Rd. N15 37 32 88 A
Rowley Way. NW8 46 26 83 A
Rowlls Rd. King 93 18 68 B
Rowney Gdns. Dag 52 47 84 A
Rowney Rd. Dag 51 46 84 B
Rowntree Clifford Cl. E13 58 40 82 B
Rowntree Rd. Twick 83 15 73 C
Rowse Cl. E15 49 38 83 A
Rowsley Ave. NW4 23 23 89 A
Rowstock Gdns. N7 47 29 85 D
Rowton Rd. SE18 66 44 77 C
Roxborough Ave. Har 33 15 87 A
Roxborough Ave. Islw 60 15 77 D
Roxborough Park. Har 33 15 87 A
Roxborough Rd. Har 32 14 88 D
Roxbourne Cl. Nthlt 43 11 84 B
Roxburgh Rd. SE27 87 31 71 D
Roxburn Way. Ruis 31 09 86 D
Roxby Pl. SW6 62 25 77 A
Roxeth Green Ave. Har 32 14 86 A
Roxeth Gr. Har 43 13 85 B
Roxeth Hill. Har 32 14 86 B
Roxley Rd. SE13 76 37 74 D
Roxwell Rd. Bark 51 46 83 C
Roxll Rd. W12 61 22 79 A
Roxwell Way. Wdf Gn 27 41 91 C
Roxy Ave. Rom 41 47 87 A
Royal Arc. W1 6 29 80 A
Royal Ave. SW3 9 27 78 D
Royal Ave. Wor Pk 102 21 65 A
Royal Circ. SE27 87 31 72 C
Royal Cl. Wor Pk 102 21 65 A
Royal College St. NW1 47 29 83 A
Royal Cres Mews. W11 56 23 80 D
Royal Cres. Ruis 32 12 86 C
Royal Cres. W11 56 23 80 C
Royal Exchange Ave. EC3 4 32 81 D
Royal Exchange Bldgs. EC3 4 32 81 D
Royal Hill. SE10 64 38 77 C
Royal Hospital Rd. SW3 9 27 78 D
Royal Jubilee Ct. Rom 30 52 89 A
Royal Mint St. E1 8 33 80 B
Royal Naval Pl. SE14 64 36 77 D
Royal Oak Pl. SE22 75 34 74 D
Royal Oak Rd. Bexh 79 48 75 D
Royal Oak Rd. E8 48 34 84 B
Royal Opera Arc. SW1 6 29 80 D
Royal Par. Chis 100 44 70 C
Royal Par. SE3 77 39 76 D
Royal Pl. SE10 64 38 77 C
Royal Rd. E16 58 41 81 D
Royal Rd. SE17 63 31 77 B
Royal Rd. Tedd 82 14 71 D
Royal St. SE1 7 30 79 D
Royal Victor Pl. E3 49 35 83 D
Royal Wlk. Wall 104 28 65 D
Roycraft Ave. Bark 51 45 83 D
Roycroft Cl. E18 27 40 90 B
Roycroft Cl. SW2 87 31 73 C
Roydene Rd. SE18 66 45 78 C
Roydon Cl. SW11 74 27 76 D
Roy Gdns. Ilf 40 45 88 B
Roy Gr. Hamp 92 13 70 B
Royle Cl. Rom 42 52 88 B
Royle Cres. W3 54 16 82 C
Roy Rd. Nthwd 19 09 91 D
Roysden St. NW1 47 29 84 C
Royston Ave. E4 18 37 92 D
Royston Ave. Sutt 103 26 65 D
Royston Ave. Wall 111 29 64 B
Royston Cl. Houn 69 10 76 B
Royston Gdns. Ilf 39 41 88 D
Royston Gr. Pnr 20 13 91 A
Royston Park Rd. Pnr 20 12 91 B
Royston Rd. Dart 80 51 74 D
Royston Rd. Rich 71 18 74 A
Royston Rd. SE20 98 35 69 B
Royston St. E2 49 35 83 C
Roystons The. Surb 102 19 67 B
Rozel Rd. SW4 74 29 75 A
Rubastic Rd. Sthl 59 11 79 C
Rubens Rd. Nthlt 43 11 83 D
Rubens St. SE6 88 36 72 B
Ruby Rd. E17 26 37 89 A
Ruby St. SE15 63 34 77 B
Ruby Triangle. SE15 63 34 77 B
Ruckholt Cl. E10 38 37 86 D
Ruckholt Rd. E10 38 37 86 D
Rucklidge Ave. NW10 45 22 83 C
Rucklidge Pas. NW10 45 21 83 D
Rudall Cres. NW3 46 26 85 B
Ruddstreet Cl. SE18 66 43 78 B
Rudland Rd. Bexh 79 49 75 B
Rudloe Rd. SW12 86 29 73 A
Rudolph Rd. E13 50 39 83 D
Rudolph Rd. NW6 46 25 83 C
Rudyard Gr. NW7 22 20 91 A
Ruffetts Cl. S Croy 112 34 63 D
Ruffetts The. S Croy 112 34 63 D
Rufford Cl. Har 33 16 88 C
Rufford St. N1 47 30 83 A
Rufus Cl. Ruis 32 12 86 C
Rufus St. N1 4 33 82 A
Rugby Ave. Grnf 43 14 84 B
Rugby Ave. N9 17 33 94 D
Rugby Ave. Wem 44 17 85 A
Rugby Cl. Har 21 15 89 C
Rugby Gdns. Dag 52 47 84 A
Rugby Lane. Sutt 110 23 62 B
Rugby Rd. Dag 52 47 84 A
Rugby Rd. Islw 71 15 74 A
Rugby Rd. NW9 22 19 89 D
Rugby Rd. Twick 71 15 74 C
Rugby Rd. W4 61 21 79 A
Rugby St. WC1 3 30 82 D
Rugg St. E14 57 37 80 A
Ruislip Cl. Grnf 53 13 82 D
Ruislip Ct. Ruis 31 09 86 B
Ruislip Rd. Grnf 53 13 82 A
Ruislip Rd. Nthlt 43 11 83 D
Ruislip Road E. Grnf 53 14 82 C
Ruislip Road E. W13 54 16 82 C
Ruislip Road E. W7 54 15 82 C
Ruislip St. SW17 86 27 71 B
Rumbold Rd. SW6 62 25 77 D
Rum Cl. E1 57 35 80 A
Rumsey Cl. Hamp 92 12 70 B
Rumsey Rd. SW9 74 30 75 B
Runbury Circ. NW9 34 20 86 B
Runcorn Cl. N15 25 34 89 D
Runcorn Pl. W11 56 24 80 A
Rundell Cres. NW4 34 22 88 B
Runham St. SE17 63 32 78 D
Runnelfield. Har 33 15 86 C
Running Horse Yd. Brent 60 18 77 A
Runnymede Cl. Twick 82 13 73 B
Runnymede Cres. SW16 96 30 69 A
Runnymede Gdns. Grnf 44 15 83 C
Runnymede Gdns. Twick 82 13 73 B
Runnymede Rd. Twick 70 13 74 D
Runnymede. SW19 95 26 69 B
Runway The. Ruis 43 11 85 C
Rupack St. SE16 64 35 79 A
Rupert Ave. Wem 44 18 85 C
Rupert Ct. W1 6 29 80 B
Rupert Gdns. SW9 75 31 76 D
Rupert Rd (off Holloway Rd). N19 36 29 86 B
Rupert Rd (off Yerbury Rd). N19 36 29 86 D
Rupert Rd. N19 36 29 86 D
Rupert Rd. NW6 46 24 83 D
Rupert Rd. W4 61 21 79 C
Rupert St. W1 6 29 80 B
Rural Way. SW16 96 29 70 C
Ruscoe Rd. E16 58 39 81 D
Ruscombe Way. Felt 81 09 73 B
Rusham Rd. SW12 86 27 73 B
Rushbrook Cres. E17 26 36 90 B
Rushbrook Rd. SE9 90 44 72 A
Rushcroft Rd. E4 26 37 91 D
Rushcroft Rd. SW2 75 31 75 C
Rushden Cl. SE19 97 32 70 D
Rushdene Ave. Barn 16 27 94 A
Rushdene Cl. Nthlt 43 11 83 C
Rushdene Cres. Nthlt 53 11 82 A
Rushdene Rd. Pnr 32 11 88 D
Rushdene. SE2 67 47 79 D
Rushden Gdns. Ilf 28 43 89 A
Rushden Gdns. NW7 23 23 91 A
Rushen Wlk. Cars 103 26 66 D
Rushet Rd. Orp 100 46 69 C
Rushett Cl. Surb 101 16 66 C
Rushett Rd. Surb 101 16 66 B
Rushey Cl. N Mal 94 20 68 D
Rushey Green. SE6 88 37 73 B
Rushey Hill. Enf 12 30 96 D
Rushey Mead. SE13 76 37 74 A
Rushford Rd. SE4 76 36 74 D
Rush Green Gdns. Rom 41 50 87 C
Rush Green Rd. Rom 41 49 87 D
Rushgrove Ave. NW9 22 21 89 D
Rush Grove St. SE18 65 42 78 B
Rush Hill Mews. SW11 74 28 75 A
Rush Hill Rd. SW11 74 28 75 A
Rushmead Cl. Croy 112 33 64 B
Rushmead. E2 57 34 82 B
Rushmead. Rich 83 16 72 D
Rushmere Ct. Wor Pk 102 22 65 A
Rushmoor Cl. Pnr 19 10 89 D
Rushmore Cl. Brom 99 42 68 A
Rushmore Cres. E5 49 35 85 B
Rushmore Rd. E5 49 35 85 B
Rusholme Ave. Dag 41 49 86 C
Rusholme Gr. SE19 87 33 71 C
Rusholme Rd. SW15 73 24 74 C
Rushout Ave. Har 33 16 88 D
Rush The. SW19 95 24 69 B
Rushton St. N1 48 32 83 D
Rushworth St. SE1 7 31 79 B
Ruskin Ave. E12 50 42 84 A
Ruskin Ave. Felt 69 09 74 D
Ruskin Ave. Rich 61 19 77 C
Ruskin Ave. Well 78 46 76 C
Ruskin Cl. NW11 35 25 88 D
Ruskin Ct. SE9 77 42 74 D
Ruskin Dri. Orp 108 45 65 C
Ruskin Dri. Well 78 46 75 A
Ruskin Dri. Wor Pk 103 23 65 A
Ruskin Gdns. Har 21 18 89 D
Ruskin Gdns. Rom 30 52 91 D
Ruskin Gdns. W5 54 17 82 D
Ruskin Gr. Well 78 46 76 C
Ruskin Rd. Belv 67 49 78 A
Ruskin Rd. Cars 111 28 64 C
Ruskin Rd. Croy 105 31 65 B
Ruskin Rd. Islw 71 15 75 B
Ruskin Rd. N17 25 33 90 B
Ruskin Rd. Sthl 53 12 80 A
Ruskin Way. SW19 95 26 69 B
Ruskin Wlk. Brom 107 42 67 D
Ruskin Wlk. N9 17 34 93 A
Ruskin Wlk. SE24 75 32 74 A
Rusland Ave. Orp 108 44 65 D
Rusland Park Rd. Har 21 15 89 C
Rusper Rd. Dag 52 47 84 A
Rusper Rd. N22 25 32 89 A
Russell Ave. N22 25 31 90 D
Russell Cl. Beck 98 38 68 A
Russell Cl. Bexh 79 49 75 C
Russell Cl. Dart 80 52 75 C
Russell Cl. NW10 45 20 84 C
Russell Cl. Ruis 32 11 86 A
Russell Ct. Brom 99 39 70 D
Russell Ct. Surb 101 18 66 A
Russell Ct. SW1 6 29 80 C
Russell Ct. Wall 111 29 64 C
Russell Gdns Mews. W14 62 24 79 C
Russell Gdns. N20 16 27 93 A
Russell Gdns. NW11 35 24 88 C
Russell Gdns. Rich 83 17 72 A
Russell Gdns. W1 62 24 79 C
Russell Green Cl. Pur 112 31 62 C
Russell Gr. SW9 63 31 77 C
Russell Hill. Pur 111 30 62 D
Russell Hill Rd. Pur 112 31 62 C
Russell La. N20 16 27 93 B
Russell Pl. SW1 10 29 78 D
Russell Rd. E10 38 37 88 D
Russell Rd. E16 58 40 81 D
Russell Rd. E17 26 36 89 B
Russell Rd. E4 18 36 92 B
Russell Rd. Mit 96 27 68 A
Russell Rd. N13 24 30 91 B
Russell Rd. N15 37 33 88 A
Russell Rd. N20 16 27 93 A
Russell Rd. N8 36 29 88 D
Russell Rd. Nthlt 43 14 85 C
Russell Rd. NW9 34 21 88 D
Russell Rd. SW19 95 25 70 C
Russell Rd. Twick 71 15 74 D
Russell Rd. W14 62 24 79 C
Russell's Footpath. SW16 86 30 71 C
Russell Sq. WC1 3 30 81 A
Russell St. WC2 7 30 80 A
Russell Yd. SW15 73 24 75 C
Russel Rd. N 13 24 30 91 B
Russet Cres. N7 47 30 85 D
Russets Cl. E4 18 38 93 D
Russet Way. SE13 76 37 76 D
Russia Ct. EC2 4 32 81 C
Russia Dock Rd. SE16 57 36 80 C
Russia La. E2 49 35 83 C
Russia Row. EC2 4 32 81 C
Rusthall Ave. W4 61 20 79 D
Rusthall Cl. Croy 106 35 67 C
Rustic Ave. SW16 96 28 70 D
Rustic Pl. Wem 44 17 85 B
Rustington Wlk. Mord 103 24 66 B
Ruston Ave. Surb 102 19 66 B
Ruston Mews. W11 56 24 81 C
Ruston St. E3 49 36 83 B
Rust Sq. SE5 63 32 77 D
Rutford Rd. SW16 86 30 71 C
Ruth Cl. Har 21 18 89 D
Rutherford Cl. Sutt 110 26 63 B
Rutherford St. SW1 10 29 78 B
Rutherford Way. Wem 45 19 85 A
Rutherglen Rd. SE2 66 46 77 A
Rutherwyke Cl. Eps 109 22 63 A
Ruthin Rd. SE3 65 40 77 A
Ruthven St. E9 49 35 83 B
Rutland Ave. Sid 90 46 73 A
Rutland Cl. Eps 109 20 62 D
Rutland Cl. SW14 72 20 75 A
Rutland Ct. W3 55 19 81 C
Rutland Dri. Mord 103 25 66 A
Rutland Dri. Rich 83 17 73 D
Rutland Gate. Belv 67 49 78 D
Rutland Gate. Brom 99 39 68 D
Rutland Gate Mews. SW7 5 27 79 A
Rutland Gate. SW7 5 27 79 A
Rutland Gdns. Croy 112 33 64 A
Rutland Gdns. Dag 52 47 85 C
Rutland Gdns Mews. SW7 5 27 79 A
Rutland Gdns. N4 37 32 88 C
Rutland Gdns. SW7 5 27 79 A
Rutland Gdns. W13 54 16 81 A
Rutland Gr. W6 61 22 78 D
Rutland Mews E. SW7 5 27 79 C
Rutland Mews S. SW7 5 27 79 C
Rutland Mews W. SW7 5 27 79 C
Rutland Park. NW2 46 23 84 A
Rutland Park. SE6 88 36 72 B
Rutland Pl. EC1 3 31 81 B
Rutland Rd. E11 39 40 88 B
Rutland Rd. E17 38 37 88 C
Rutland Rd. E7 50 41 84 D
Rutland Rd. E9 49 35 83 B
Rutland Rd. Har 32 14 88 C
Rutland Rd. Ilf 40 43 86 D
Rutland Rd. Sthl 53 13 81 A
Rutland Rd. SW19 96 27 70 C
Rutland Rd. Twick 82 14 72 B
Rutland St. SW7 5 27 79 C
Rutland Wlk. SE6 88 36 72 B
Rutley Cl. SE11 63 31 77 B
Rutlish Rd. SW19 95 25 69 A
Rutter Gdns. Mit 95 26 68 D
Rutt's Terr. SE14 76 35 76 B
Ruvigny Gdns. SW15 73 23 75 B
Ruxley Cl. Eps 109 19 64 D
Ruxley La. Eps 109 20 64 C
Ryan Cl. SE3 77 41 75 C
Rycroft Way. N17 25 33 89 B
Ryculff Sq. SE3 77 39 76 D
Rydal Cl. NW4 23 24 90 A
Rydal Cres. Grnf 54 17 82 A
Rydal Dri. Bexh 79 49 76 A
Rydal Gdns. NW9 34 21 88 A
Rydal Gdns. SW15 84 21 71 C
Rydal Gdns. Twick 70 13 74 D
Rydal Gdns. Wem 33 17 87 C
Rydal Rd. SW16 86 29 71 B
Rydal Way. Enf 14 35 95 C
Rydal Way. Ruis 43 11 85 A
Ryde Pl. Twick 71 17 74 D
Ryder Cl. Brom 89 40 71 D
Ryder Ct. SW1 6 29 80 C
Ryder's Terr. NW8 46 26 83 C
Ryder St. SW1 6 29 80 C
Ryder Yd. SW1 6 29 80 C
Ryde Vale Rd. SW17 86 29 72 A
Rydons Cl. SE9 77 42 75 A
Rydon St. N1 48 32 83 A
Rydston Cl. N7 47 30 84 D
Rye Cl. Bex 79 49 74 D
Ryecotes Mead. SE21 87 33 73 C
Ryecroft Ave. Ilf 28 43 90 D
Ryecroft Ave. Twick 82 13 73 D
Ryecroft Cres. Barn 11 23 95 A
Ryecroft Rd. Orp 108 44 67 D
Ryecroft Rd. SE13 76 38 74 A
Ryecroft Rd. SW16 97 31 70 A
Ryecroft St. SW6 73 25 76 B
Ryedale. SE22 75 34 74 D
Ryefield Cres. Nthwd 19 10 90 C
Ryefield Path. SW15 84 22 73 C
Ryefield Rd. SE19 97 32 70 A
Rye Hill Park. SE15 76 35 75 C
Ryelands Cres. SE9 77 41 74 C
Rye La. SE15 75 34 76 C
Rye Pas. SE15 75 34 75 A
Rye Rd. SE15 76 35 75 D
Rye The. N14 16 29 94 A
Rye Way. Edg 21 18 91 B
Rye Wlk. SW15 73 23 74 B
Ryfold Rd. SW19 85 25 72 C
Ryhope Rd. N11 16 28 92 B
Ryland Cl. Felt 81 09 71 B
Rylandes Rd. NW2 34 22 86 C
Rylandes Rd. S Croy 112 34 62 D
Ryland Rd. NW5 47 28 84 B
Rylett Cres. W12 61 21 79 D
Rylett Rd. W12 61 21 79 D
Rylston Rd. N13 17 32 92 D
Rylston Rd. SW6 62 24 77 D
Rymer Rd. Croy 105 33 66 A
Rymer Rd. SW18 73 26 74 A
Rymer St. SE24 75 31 74 D
Rysbrack St. SW3 5 27 79 D
Rythe Ct. Surb 101 16 66 A

Sabbarton St. E16 58 39 81 D
Sabella Ct. E3 49 36 83 D
Sabine Rd. SW11 74 28 75 A
Sable Cl. Houn 70 11 75 A
Sable St. N1 48 31 84 D
Sach Rd. E5 37 34 86 B
Sackville Ave. Brom 107 40 66 C
Sackville Cl. Har 32 14 86 D
Sackville Cres. Rom 30 54 90 A
Sackville Gdns. Ilf 39 42 87 D
Sackville Rd. Sutt 110 25 63 C
Sackville St. W1 6 29 80 A
Saddlecombe Way. N12 15 25 92 C
Saddlers Cl. Pnr 20 13 91 A
Saddlers Ride. E Mol 92 14 69 C
Saddlescombe Way. N12 15 25 92 C
Saddleworth Rd. Rom 30 53 91 A
Sadler Cl. Mit 96 27 69 D
Saffron Cl. NW11 35 24 88 D
Saffron Hill. EC1 3 31 81 A
Saffron Rd. Rom 29 50 90 D
Saffron St. EC1 3 31 81 A
Saffron Way. Surb 101 17 66 D
Sage Way. WC1 3 30 82 B
Saigasso Cl. E16 58 41 81 D
Sail St. SE11 7 30 79 D
Sainfoin Rd. SW17 86 28 72 A
Sainsbury Rd. SE19 87 33 71 C
St Agatha's Dri. King 93 18 70 B
St Agatha's Gr. Cars 104 27 66 D
St Agnes Cl. E9 49 35 83 A
St. Agnes Pl. SE11 63 31 77 B
St Aidan's Rd. SE22 75 34 74 D
St Aidan's Rd. W13 60 16 79 B
St Albans Ave. Felt 82 11 71 D
St Albans Ave. W4 61 20 79 D
St Albans Cres. N22 25 31 90 A
St Alban's Cres. Wdf Gn 27 40 90 A
St Alban's Gdns. Tedd 83 16 71 C
St Alban's Gr. Cars 104 27 66 A
St Alban's Gr. W8 62 25 79 D
St Alban's Mews. W2 1 26 81 B
St Alban's Pl. N1 48 31 83 B
St Alban's Rd. 45 20 83 A
St Albans Rd. Barn 11 24 97 C
St Alban's Rd. Dart 80 54 74 D
St Albans Rd. Ilf 40 45 87 B
St Albans Rd. King 93 18 70 A
St Alban's Rd. NW5 36 28 86 D
St Albans Rd. Sutt 110 24 64 B
St Alban's Rd. Wdf Gn 27 40 91 C
St Alban's St. SW1 6 29 80 B
St Albans Terr. W6 62 24 77 A
St Albans Terr. W6 62 24 77 A
St Alfege Pas. SE10 64 38 77 A
St Alfege Rd. SE7 65 41 77 B
St Alphage Gdn. EC2 4 32 81 A
St Alphage Highwalk. EC2 4 32 81 A
St Alphage Wlk. Edg 22 20 90 C
St Alphege Rd. N9 18 35 94 A
St Alphonsus Rd. SW4 74 29 75 D
St Amunds Cl. SE6 88 37 71 A
St Andrews Ave. Wem 44 16 85 A
St Andrew's Cl. Islw 71 15 76 A
St Andrew's Cl. N12 15 26 92 A
St Andrew's Cl. NW2 34 22 86 D
St Andrews Cl. Ruis 32 11 86 B
St Andrew's Cl. Shep 91 08 68 D
St Andrews Cl. Stan 21 17 90 C
St Andrew's Ct. SW18 85 26 72 A
St Andrews Dri. Orp 108 46 66 B
St Andrews Dri. Stan 21 17 90 A
St Andrew's Gr. N16 37 32 87 D
St Andrew's Hill. EC4 3 31 81 D
St Andrew's Mews. N16 37 33 87 C
St Andrew's Pl. NW1 2 28 82 D
St Andrew's Rd. Cars 104 27 65 C
St Andrew's Rd. Croy 112 32 64 A
St Andrew's Rd. E11 39 39 88 C
St Andrew's Rd. E13 58 40 82 B
St Andrews Rd. E17 26 36 90 C
St Andrew's Rd. Enf 13 32 96 B
St Andrew's Rd. Ilf 39 42 87 B
St Andrews Rd. N9 18 35 94 A
St Andrew's Rd. NW10 45 22 84 B
St Andrew's Rd. NW1 35 24 88 D
St Andrews Rd. NW9 34 20 87 D
St Andrews Rd. Rom 41 50 88 D
St Andrew's Rd. Surb 101 17 67 D
St Andrew's Rd. W14 62 24 77 A
St Andrew's Rd. W3 55 21 81 C
St Andrew's Rd. W7 60 15 79 A
St Andrew's Sq. Surb 101 17 67 D
St Andrew's Sq. W11 56 24 81 C
St Andrew St. EC4 3 31 81 A
St Anne's Cl. N6 36 28 86 C
St Anne's Ct. W1 2 29 81 D
St Annes Gdns. NW10 54 18 82 B
St Anne's Pas. E14 57 36 81 D
St Annes Rd. E11 38 38 86 B
St Anne's Rd. Wem 44 17 85 D
St Anne's Row. E14 57 36 81 D
St Anne St. E14 57 36 81 D
St Ann's. Bark 51 44 83 A
St Ann's Cres. SW18 73 26 74 C
St Ann's Gdns. NW5 47 28 84 A
St Ann's Hill. SW18 73 26 74 C
St Ann's La. SW1 6 29 79 D
St Ann's Park Rd. SW18 73 26 74 C
St Ann's Pas. SW13 72 21 75 A
St Ann's Rd. Bark 51 44 83 A
St Ann's Rd. Har 33 15 88 C
St Ann's Rd. N15 37 32 88 B
St Ann's Rd. N9 17 33 94 D
St Anns Rd. SW13 72 21 76 D
St Ann's Rd. W11 56 23 80 D
St Ann's St. SW1 6 29 79 D
St Ann's Terr. NW8 46 26 83 D
St Ann's Villas Rd. W11 56 23 80 D
St Ann's Way. S Croy 112 31 63 B
St Anselm's Pl. W1 6 28 80 B
St Anthony's Ave. Wdf Gn 27 41 91 C
St Anthony's Cl. E1 57 34 80 C
St Anthonys Cl. SW17 86 27 72 A
St Anthony's Ct. Orp 108 43 65 B
St Anthony's Way. Felt 69 09 75 D
St Antony's Rd. E7 50 40 84 D
St Arvans Cl. Croy 105 33 65 C
St Asaph Rd. SE4 76 35 75 B
St Aubyn's Ave. Houn 70 13 74 A
St Aubyn's Ave. SW19 85 24 71 D
St Aubyns Cl. Orp 108 45 65 D
St Aubyns Gdns. Orp 108 45 65 D
St Aubyn's Rd. SE19 97 33 70 B
St Audrey Ave. Bexh 79 49 76 C
St Augustine's Ave. Brom 107 42 67 A
St Augustine's Ave. S Croy 112 32 63 C
St Augustine's Ave. W5 44 18 83 C
St Augustine's Ave. Wem 33 18 86 C
1St Augustine's Ct. E11 39 39 87 D
St Augustine's Rd. Belv 67 48 78 B
St Augustine's Rd. NW1 47 29 84 D
St Austell Cl. Edg 21 18 90 D
St Austell Rd. SE13 76 38 76 D
St Awdry's Rd. Bark 51 44 84 D
St Awdry's Wlk. Bark 51 44 84 D
St Barnabas Rd. E17 38 37 88 C
St Barnabas Rd. Mit 96 28 70 C

St Barnabas' Rd. Sutt 110 26 64 D
St Barnabas Rd. Wdf Gn 27 41 91 C
St Barnabas St. SW1 9 28 78 C
St Barnabas Terr. E9 49 35 85 D
St Barnabas Villas. SW8 74 30 76 A
St Bartholemew's Rd. E6 50 42 83 D
St Benedict's Cl. SW17 86 28 71 C
St Benets Cl. SW17 86 27 72 A
St Benet's Gr. Cars 103 26 66 A
St Benet's Pl. EC3 8 32 80 B
St Bernards Cl. SE27 87 32 71 B
St Bernards. Croy 105 33 65 C
St Bernard's Rd. E6 50 42 83 A
St Blaise Ave. Brom 99 40 69 D
St Botolph St. EC3 4 33 81 D
St Bride's Ave. EC4 3 31 81 D
St Bride's Ave. Edg 21 18 90 B
St Brides Cl. Belv 67 47 79 B
St Bride's Pas. EC4 3 31 81 D
St Bride St. EC4 3 31 81 D
St Catherines Cl. SW17 86 27 72 A
St Catherine's Ct. W4 61 21 79 C
St Catherine's Dri. SE14 76 35 76 D
St Catherines Farm Ct. Ruis 31 08 88 C
St Catherines Rd. E4 18 37 93 A
St Catherines Rd. Ruis 31 08 88 D
St Chad's Gdns. Rom 41 48 87 A
St Chad's Pl. WC1 3 30 82 B
St Chad's Rd. Rom 41 48 87 A
St Chad's St. WC1 3 30 82 A
St Charles Pl. W10 56 24 81 A
St Charles Sq. W10 56 24 81 A
St Christopher's Cl. Islw 71 15 76 A
St Christopher's Pl. W1 2 28 81 C
St Clair Cl. Ilf 27 42 90 D
St Clair Dri. Wor Pk 109 22 64 B
St Clair Rd. E13 50 40 83 D
St Clair's Rd. Croy 105 33 65 A
St Clare St. EC3 4 33 81 D
St Clement Danes. SW17 85 26 71 B
St Clement's Ct. EC4 8 32 80 B
St Clement's Hts. SE26 87 34 72 C
St Clement's La. WC2 3 30 81 D
St Clements St. N1 48 31 84 C
St Cloud Rd. SE27 87 32 71 B
St Crispin's Cl. Sthl 53 12 81 D
St Cross St. EC1 3 31 81 A
St Cuthberts Gdns. Pnr 20 12 91 D
St Cuthbert's Rd. NW2 46 24 84 B
St Cyprian's St. SW17 86 27 71 B
St Davids Cl. Wem 34 20 86 C
St David's Cl. W Wick 106 37 66 B
St David's Dri. Edg 21 18 90 B
St David's Pl. NW4 34 22 87 B
St Denis Rd. SE27 87 32 71 B
St Dionis Rd. SW6 73 24 76 D
St Donatt's Rd. SE14 76 36 76 B
St Dunstan's Alley. EC3 8 33 80 A
St Dunstan's Ave. W3 55 20 80 B
St Dunstan's Ct. EC4 3 31 81 C
St Dunstan's Gdns. W3 55 20 80 B
St Dunstan's Hill. EC3 8 33 80 A
St Dunstan's Hill. Sutt 110 24 64 A
St Dunstan's La. Beck 106 38 67 A
St Dunstan's La. EC3 8 33 80 A
St Dunstan's Rd. E7 50 41 84 A
St Dunstan's Rd. Felt 81 09 72 D
St Dunstan's Rd. Houn 70 11 76 C
St Dunstan's Rd. SE25 97 33 68 D
St Dunstan's Rd. W6 62 23 78 D
St Dunstan's Rd. W7 60 15 79 A
St Edmunds Ave. Ruis 31 08 88 D
St Edmunds Cl. Belv 67 47 79 B
St Edmund's Cl. NW8 47 27 83 B
St Edmunds Cl. SW17 86 27 72 A
St Edmunds Dri. Stan 21 16 90 A
St Edmund's La. Twick 82 13 73 B
St Edmunds Rd. Dart 80 54 75 D
St Edmund's Rd. Ilf 39 42 88 D
St Edmunds Rd. N9 17 34 94 A
St Edmund's Terr. NW8 47 27 83 B
St Edward's Cl. NW11 35 25 88 C
St Edwards Way. Rom 30 51 89 C
St Egberts Way. E4 18 38 94 C
St Elmo Rd. W12 61 21 79 B
St Erkenwald Rd. Bark 51 44 83 B
St Ermin's Hill. SW1 6 29 79 D
St Ervan's Rd. W10 56 24 81 A
St Faith's Cl. Enf 13 32 97 A
St Faith's Rd. SE21 87 31 73 D
St Fidelis' Rd. Eri 67 50 78 B
St Fillans Rd. SE6 88 38 73 C
St Francis Cl. Orp 108 45 67 C
St Francis' Rd. Eri 67 50 78 B
St Francis Rd. SE22 75 33 75 C
St Gabriel's Rd. NW2 46 23 85 D
St George's Ave. E7 50 40 84 D
St George's Ave. Horn 42 54 87 B
St George's Ave. N7 47 29 85 B
St George's Ave. NW9 22 20 89 D
St George's Ave. Sthl 53 12 80 B
St George's Ave. W5 60 17 79 B
St George's Circ. SE1 7 31 79 D
St George's Cl. NW11 35 24 88 D
St Georges Cl. Wem 33 16 86 C
St George's Dri. SW1 10 29 78 C
St George's Dri. Uxb 31 07 86 A
St Georges Field. W2 1 27 81 C
St George's Gdns. Surb 102 19 65 B
St George's Gr. SW17 85 26 72 D
St George's La. EC3 8 32 80 B
St George's Mews. NW1 47 27 84 D
St George's Rd. Beck 98 37 69 B
St Georges Rd. Brom 99 42 68 B
St Georges Rd. Dag 52 48 85 A
St George's Rd. E10 38 38 86 C
St George's Rd. E7 50 40 84 B
St George's Rd. Felt 82 11 71 B
St George's Rd. Ilf 39 42 87 B
St George's Rd. King 94 19 70 C
St George's Rd. Mit 96 28 68 B
St George's Rd. N13 16 30 93 B
St George's Rd. N9 17 34 93 C
St George's Rd. NW11 35 24 88 D
St Georges Rd. Orp 108 44 67 D
St George's Rd. Rich 71 18 75 B
St George's Rd. SE1 7 31 79 D
St George's Rd. SW19 95 24 70 B
St George's Rd. Twick 71 16 74 B
St Georges Rd. W4 61 20 79 B
St George's Rd. W7 54 15 80 D
St George's Rd. Wall 111 28 64 D
St Georges Rd W. Brom 99 42 69 C
St George's Sq. E7 50 40 84 D
St George's Sq. N Mal 94 21 68 A
St George's Sq. SW1 10 29 78 D
St George's Terr. NW1 47 27 84 D
St George St. W1 6 28 80 B
St George's Way. SE15 63 33 77 A
St George's Wlk. Croy 105 32 65 C
St Gerards Cl. SW4 74 29 74 A
St German's Pl. SE3 77 40 76 A
St German's Rd. SE23 88 36 73 C
St Giles Ave. Dag 52 49 84 D
St Giles Circ. W1 2 29 81 D
St Giles Cl. Dag 52 49 84 D
St Giles High St. WC2 2 29 81 D
St Giles Pl. WC2 2 29 81 D
St Giles Rd. SE5 75 33 76 A
St Gothard Rd. SE27 87 32 71 B
St Helena Rd. SE16 64 35 78 B
St Helena St. WC1 3 31 82 A
St Helen's Cres. SW16 96 30 69 B
St Helen's Gdns. W10 56 23 81 D
St Helen's Pl. EC3 4 33 81 C
St Helens Rd. Belv 67 47 79 B
St Helen's Rd. Ilf 39 42 88 D
St Helen's Rd. SW16 96 30 69 B
St Helen's Rd. W13 54 17 80 C
St Helier Ave. Mord 103 26 67 A
St Heliers Ave. Houn 70 13 74 A
St Helier's Rd. E10 38 38 88 C
St Hilda's Cl. NW6 46 23 83 B
St Hildas Cl. SW17 86 27 72 A
St Hilda's Rd. SW13 61 22 77 B
St Hughes Cl. SW17 86 27 72 A
St Hugh's Rd. SE20 97 34 69 B
St Ivians Dri. Rom 30 52 89 A
St James Ave. N20 16 27 93 C
St James Ave. Eps 109 22 62 C
St James' Ave. Sutt 110 25 64 C
St James' Ave. W13 54 16 80 C
St James Cl. N20 16 27 93 C
St James' Cl. N.Mal 102 21 67 B
St James Cl. Ruis 32 11 86 A
St James Cottages. Rich 71 17 74 B
St James Ct. Croy 105 31 66 B
St James' Ct. SW1 6 29 79 C
St James' Gdns. Wem 44 18 84 C
St Jame's Gr. SW11 74 27 76 D
St James Pl. Dart 80 53 74 D
St James Rd. Cars 104 27 65 C
St James Rd. E15 50 39 85 D
St James' Rd. Mit 96 28 70 C
St James' Rd. N9 17 34 93 B
St James' Rd. Surb 101 17 67 D
St James' Rd. Sutt 110 25 64 C
St James's App. EC2 4 33 82 C
St James's Ave. Beck 98 36 68 A
St James's Ave. E2 49 35 83 C
St James's Ave. Hamp 82 14 71 C
St James's Cl. SE18 66 44 78 C
St James's Cl. SW17 86 27 72 B
St James's Cres. SW9 75 31 75 A
St James's Dri. SW17 86 27 73 D
St James's Gdns. W11 56 24 80 C
St James's La. N10 24 28 89 D
St James's Market. SW1 6 29 80 B
St James's Park. Croy 105 32 66 A
St James's Pas. EC3 4 33 81 C
St James's Path. E17 38 36 88 B
St James's Pl. SW1 6 29 80 C
St James's Rd. Croy 105 32 66 A
St James's Rd. Hamp 82 13 71 D
St James's Rd. King 93 17 68 A
St James's Rd. SE16 63 34 79 C
St James's Rd. SE1 63 34 78 C
St James's Row. EC1 3 31 82 D
St James's. SE14 76 36 76 A
St James's Sq. SW1 6 29 80 D
St James's St. E17 38 36 88 A
St James's St. SW1 6 29 80 C
St James's Terrace Mews, NW8 47 27 83 B
St James's Terr. NW8 47 27 83 D
St James St. W6 62 23 78 C
St James's Wlk. EC1 3 31 82 D
St James Wlk. SE15 63 33 77 D
St Joan's Rd N9 17 33 94 D
St John's Ave. N11 16 27 92 D
St John's Ave. NW10 45 21 83 B
St John's Ave. SW15 73 23 74 B
St John's Church Rd. E9 49 35 85 C
St John's Cl. Wem 44 18 85 C
St John's Cres. SW9 75 31 75 A
St John's Ct. Islw 71 15 76 D
St John's Ct. N4 37 31 86 B
St Johns Estate. SW11 73 26 76 B
St John's Gdns. W11 56 24 80 B
St John's Gr. N19 36 29 86 A
St John's Gr. Rich 71 18 75 C
St John's Gr. SW13 72 21 76 D
St John's Hill Gr. SW11 73 26 75 D
St John's Hill. SW11 73 26 75 D
St John's Hill. SW18 73 26 74 B
St John's La. EC1 3 31 81 B
St John's Park. SE3 65 40 77 C
St John's Pas. SW19 95 24 70 A
St John's Path. EC1 3 31 82 D
St John's Pl. EC1 3 31 82 D
St John's Rd. Bark 51 45 83 A
St John's Rd. Cars 104 27 65 C
St John's Rd. Croy 105 31 65 D
St John's Rd. E16 58 40 81 C
St John's Rd. E17 26 38 90 C
St John's Rd. E4 18 37 92 B
St John's Rd. E6 50 42 83 A
St John's Rd. E Mol 92 14 68 D
St John's Rd. Eri 67 50 78 D
St John's Rd. Felt 82 12 71 B
St John's Rd. Har 33 15 88 D
St Johns Rd. Ilf 40 45 87 A
St John's Rd. Islw 71 15 76 D
St John's Rd. King 93 17 69 A
St John's Rd. N15 37 33 88 C
St Johns Rd. N Mal 94 20 68 A
St John's Rd. NW11 35 24 88 D
St John's Rd. Orp 108 45 67 C
St John's Rd. Rich 71 18 75 C
St John's Rd. SE20 98 35 70 A
St John's Rd. Sid 90 46 71 B
St John's Rd. Sthl 59 12 79 C
St John's Rd. Sutt 103 25 65 B
St John's Rd. SW11 74 27 75 C
St John's Rd. SW19 95 24 70 A
St John's Rd. Well 78 46 75 B
St John's Rd. Wem 44 18 85 C
St John's Sq. EC1 3 31 82 D
St John St. EC1 3 31 82 D
St John St. EC1 48 31 83 C
St John's Terr. E7 50 40 84 B
St John's Terr. SE18 66 44 77 B
St John's Terr. W10 56 23 82 D
St John's Vale. SE8 76 37 76 C
St John's Villas. N19 36 29 86 B
St John's Way. N19 36 29 87 D
St John's Wood High St. NW8 47 27 83 C
St John's Wood Park. NW8 46 26 83 B
St John's Wood Rd. NW8 1 26 82 B
St John's Wood Terr. NW8 47 27 83 C
St Joseph's Dri. Sthl 53 12 80 C
St Joseph's Rd. N9 18 35 94 A
St Joseph's St. SW8 74 28 76 B
St Judes Ct. Wdf Gn 27 42 91 C
St Jude's Rd. E2 48 34 83 D
St Jude St. N1 48 33 85 C
St Julian's Cl. SW16 87 31 71 A
St Julian's Farm Rd. SE27 87 31 71 B
St Julian's Rd. NW6 46 25 83 A
St Katharine's Way. E1 8 33 80 B
St Katherine's Prec. NW1 47 28 83 D
St Katherines Rd. Belv 67 47 79 B
St Katherine's Row. EC3 8 33 80 A
St Keverne Rd. SE9 89 42 71 A
St Kilda Rd. Orp 108 45 66 D
St Kilda Rd. W13 60 16 79 A
St Kilda's Rd. Har 33 15 88 C
St Kilda's Rd. N16 37 33 87 C
St Laurence's Cl. NW6 46 23 83 B
St Lawrence Cl. Edg 21 18 91 D
St Lawrence Dri. Pnr 31 10 88 B
St Lawrence St. E14 58 38 80 C
St Lawrence Terr. W10 56 24 81 A
St Lawrence Way. SW9 75 31 76 C
St Leonard's Ave. E4 26 38 91 B
St Leonards Ave. Har 33 17 88 A
St Leonards Cl. Well 78 46 75 A
St Leonard's Gdns. Houn 70 12 76 A
St Leonards Gdns. Ilf 51 44 85 C
St Leonard's Rd. Croy 105 31 65 B
St Leonards Rd. E14 58 38 81 A
St Leonard's Rd. E14 58 38 81 C
St Leonard's Rd. NW10 55 20 82 D
St Leonard's Rd. Surb 101 16 66 A
St Leonard's Rd. Surb 101 17 67 B
St Leonards Rd. SW14 72 20 75 A
St Leonard's Rd. W13 54 17 80 A
St Leonard's Sq. NW5 47 28 84 A
St Leonard's Sq. Surb 101 17 67 B
St Leonard's St. E3 57 37 82 B
St Leonard's Terr. SW3 9 27 78 D
St Leonards Wlk. SW16 96 30 70 D
St Loo Ave. SW3 9 27 77 A
St Louis Rd. SE27 87 32 71 B
St Loy's Rd. N17 25 33 89 B
St Luke's Ave. Ilf 51 43 85 D
St Luke's Ave. SW4 74 29 75 D
St Lukes Cl. SE25 105 34 67 D
St Luke's Mews. W11 56 24 81 D
St Luke's Rd. W11 56 24 81 B
St Luke's Sq. E16 58 39 81 D
St Luke's St. SW3 9 27 78 C
St Luke's Yd. W9 46 24 83 D
St Malo Ave. N9 18 35 93 C
St Margarets Ave. Ashf 81 07 71 D
St Margaret's Ave. Har 32 14 86 C
St Margaret's Ave. N15 25 31 89 D
St Margarets Ave. N20 15 26 94 C
St Margarets Ave. Sid 90 44 72 D
St Margaret's Ave. Sutt 103 24 65 C
St Margarets. Bark 51 44 83 B
St Margaret's Cres. SW15 72 22 74 B
St Margaret's Ct. SE1 8 32 80 D
St Margaret's Dri. Twick 71 16 74 B
St Margaret's Gr. E11 39 39 86 D
St Margaret's Gr. SE18 66 44 78 C
St Margaret's Gr. Twick 71 16 74 C
St Margaret's Pas. SE13 77 39 75 A
St Margaret's Path. SE18 66 44 78 C
St Margaret's Rd. Beck 98 35 68 D
St Margaret's Rd. E12 39 41 86 A
St Margaret's Rd. Islw 71 16 75 D
St Margaret's Rd. N17 25 33 89 A
St Margaret's Rd. NW10 56 23 82 A
St Margarets Rd. Ruis 31 08 88 D
St Margaret's Rd. SE4 76 36 75 D
St Margaret's Rd. Twick 71 16 74 D
St Margaret's Rd. W7 60 15 79 A
St Margaret's Terr. SE18 66 44 78 C
St Margaret St. SW1 7 30 79 A
St Mark's Cl. Barn 11 25 96 B
St Mark's Cres. NW1 47 28 83 A
St Marks Gate. E9 49 36 84 D
St Mark's Gr. SW10 62 25 77 D
St Mark's Hill. Surb 101 18 67 A
St Mark's Pl. SW19 95 24 70 B
St Mark's Pl. W11 56 24 81 C
St Mark's Rd. Brom 99 40 68 B
St Mark's Rd. Enf 13 33 95 B
St Mark's Rd. Mit 96 28 69 C
St Mark's Rd. SE25 97 34 68 C
St Mark's Rd. Tedd 93 16 70 D
St Mark's Rd. W10 56 23 81 D
St Mark's Rd. W5 54 18 80 C
St Mark's Rd. W7 60 15 79 A
St Mark's Rise. E8 48 33 85 D
St Mark's Sq. NW1 47 28 83 A
St Mark St. E1 4 33 81 D
St Martin's App. Ruis 31 09 87 A
St Martin's Ave. E6 50 41 83 D
St Martins Cl. Belv 67 47 79 B
St Martin's Cl. Enf 13 34 97 B
St Martin's Cl. NW1 47 29 83 A
St Martin's Ct. WC2 7 30 80 A
St Martin's La. WC2 7 30 80 A
St Martin's Le Grand. EC1 4 32 81 C
St Martin's Pl. WC2 7 30 80 A
St Martin's Rd. Dart 80 54 74 D
St Martin's Rd. N2 23 26 90 B
St Martin's Rd. N9 17 34 93 B
St Martin's Rd. SW9 74 30 76 D
St Martin's St. WC2 6 29 80 B
St Martin's Way. SW17 85 26 72 C
St Mary Abbot's Pl. W8 62 24 79 D
St Mary Abbots Terr. W14 62 24 79 D
St Mary at Hill. EC3 8 33 80 A
St Mary Ave. Wall 104 28 65 D
St Mary Axe. EC3 4 33 81 C
St Marychurch St. SE16 64 35 79 A
St Mary Rd. E17 26 37 89 D
St Mary' Rd. N9 18 35 94 C
St Mary's App. E12 50 42 85 D
St Mary's Ave. Brom 99 39 68 A
St Mary's Ave. E11 39 40 87 B
St Mary's Ave. N3 23 24 90 C
St Marys Ave. Sthl 59 13 78 B
St Mary's Ave. Tedd 93 15 70 B
St Marys. Bark 51 44 83 B
St Mary's Cl. Eps 109 21 62 B
St Mary's Cl. N17 25 34 90 A
St Mary's Cl. Orp 100 46 69 D
St Mary's Cl. Sun 91 10 68 C
St Mary's Cres. Islw 60 15 77 C
St Mary's Cres. NW4 22 22 89 B
St Mary's Dri. Felt 81 08 73 A
St Mary's Gdns. SE11 63 31 78 A
St Mary's Green. N2 23 26 89 A
St Mary's Gr. N1 48 31 84 B
St Mary's Gr. Rich 71 18 75 D
St Mary's Gr. SW13 72 22 75 B
St. Mary's Gr. W4 61 19 77 B
St Mary's Mansions. W2 1 26 81 B
St Mary's Path. N1 48 31 83 B
St Mary's Pl. W5 60 17 79 B
St Mary's Rd. Barn 16 27 94 B
St Mary's Rd. E10 38 38 86 A
St Mary's Rd. E13 50 40 83 D
St Marys Rd. Ilf 40 44 86 B
St.Mary's Rd. N2 23 26 90 B
St Mary's Rd. N8 24 30 89 C
St Mary's Rd. NW10 45 20 83 A
St Mary's Rd. NW11 35 24 87 A
St Mary's Rd. S Croy 112 32 62 B
St Mary's Rd. SE15 76 35 76 C
St Mary's Rd. SE25 97 33 68 A
St Mary's Rd. Surb 101 17 66 C
St Mary's Rd. Surb 101 17 67 D
St Mary's Rd. SW19 85 24 71 C
St Mary's Rd. W5 60 17 79 B
St Mary's Rd. Wor Pk 102 21 65 A
St Mary's Sq. W2 1 26 81 B
St Mary's Sq. W5 60 17 79 B
St Mary's Terr. W2 1 26 81 B
St Mary St. SE18 66 43 79 C
St Mary's Wlk. SE11 63 31 78 A
St Matthew's Ave. Surb 101 18 66 D
St Matthews Dri. Brom 99 42 68 B
St Matthew's Rd. SW2 74 30 74 B
St Matthews Rd. SW2 74 30 75 D
St Matthew's Rd. W5 54 18 80 C
St Matthew's Row. E2 57 34 82 C
St Matthew St. SW1 6 29 79 D
St Matthias Cl. NW9 34 21 88 B
St Maur Rd. SW6 73 24 76 B
St Merryn Cl. SE18 66 44 77 D
St Merryn Ct. Beck 98 37 70 C
St Michael's Alley. EC3 4 32 81 D
St Michaels Ave. N9 18 35 94 A
St Michael's Ave. Wem 45 19 85 C
St Michaels Cl. Brom 99 42 68 A
St Michael's Cl. N12 16 27 92 C
St Michael's Cl. N3 23 24 90 D
St Michael's Cres. Pnr 32 12 88 C
St Michael's Gdns. W10 56 24 81 A
St Michaels Rd. Ashf 81 07 71 C
St Michael's Rd. Croy 105 32 66 C
St Michael's Rd. NW2 46 23 85 A
St Michael's Rd. SW9 74 30 76 D
St Michael's Rd. Wall 111 29 63 A
St Michael's Rd. Well 78 46 75 B
St Michael's St. W2 1 27 81 C
St Michael's Terr. N22 24 30 90 A
St Mildred's Ct. EC2 4 32 81 D
St Mildreds Rd. SE12 89 39 73 B
St Neot's Rd. Rom 30 54 91 D
St Nicholas Ave. Horn 42 52 86 C
St Nicholas Rd. SE18 66 45 78 B
St Nicholas Rd. Surb 101 15 67 D
St Nicholas Rd. Sutt 110 25 64 D
St Nicholas St. SE8 76 36 76 B
St Nicholas Way. Sutt 110 25 64 D
St Nicolas La. Chis 99 42 69 A
St Norbert Green. SE4 76 36 75 C
St Norbert Rd. SE4 76 36 75 C
St Normans Way. Eps 109 22 62 C
St Olaf's Rd. SW6 62 24 77 C
St Olave's Ct. EC2 4 32 81 D
St Olave's Gdns. SE11 63 31 78 A
St Olave's Rd. E6 51 43 83 A
St Olaves Wlk. SW16 96 29 69 D
St Oswald's Pl. SE11 10 30 78 D
St Oswald's Rd. SW16 97 31 69 B
St Oswulf St. SW1 10 29 78 B
St Pancras Ct. N2 23 26 90 D
St Pancras Way. NW1 47 29 83 A
St Paul's Alley. EC4 3 31 81 D
St Paul's Ave. Har 21 18 89 D
St Paul's Ave. NW2 46 23 84 A
St Paul's Ave. SE16 57 35 80 D
St Paul's Church Yd. EC4 4 32 81 C
St Paul's Church Yd. EC4 4 32 81 C
St Paul's Cl. Ashf 81 08 71 C
St Paul's Cl. Houn 70 12 76 C
St Pauls Cl. SE7 65 41 78 D
St Pauls Cl. W5 60 18 79 B
St Paul's Cray Rd. Chis 100 44 69 B
St Paul's Cres. NW1 47 29 84 D
St Paul's Dri. E15 49 38 85 D
St Paul's Pl. N1 48 32 84 B
St Pauls Rd. Bark 51 44 83 A
St Paul's Rd. Brent 60 17 77 B
St Paul's Rd. Eri 67 50 77 C
St Paul's Rd. N11 16 28 92 D
St Paul's Rd. N17 25 34 90 A
St Paul's Rd. N1 48 32 84 A
St Pauls Rd. Rich 71 18 75 B
St Paul's Rd. Th Hth 97 32 68 A
St Paul's Sq. Brom 99 40 69 C
St Paul St. N1 48 32 83 A
St Paul's Way. E3 57 36 81 B
St Paul's Way. N3 23 25 91 D
St Paul's Wood Hill. Orp 100 45 69 D
St Peter's Alley. EC3 4 32 81 D
St Peters Ave. N2 24 27 91 C
St Peter's Ave. E17 27 39 89 C
St Peter's Ave. E2 48 34 83 C
St Peter's Ave. N18 17 34 92 A
St Petersburgh Mews. W2 56 25 80 B
St Petersburgh Pl. W2 56 25 80 B
St Peters Cl. Chis 100 44 70 D
St Peter's Cl. E2 48 34 83 C
St Peters Cl. Ilf 28 45 89 D
St Peters Cl. Ruis 32 11 86 B
St Peters Cl. SW17 86 27 72 A
St Peter's Ct. NW4 35 23 88 A
St Peters Ct. SE3 77 39 74 B
St Peter's Gdns. SE27 87 31 71 A
St Peter's Gr. W6 61 22 78 A
St Peter's Rd. Croy 112 32 64 B
St Peter's Rd. E Mol 92 13 68 C
St Peters Rd. King 94 19 69 C
St Peter's Rd. N9 17 34 94 D
St Peter's Rd. N9 18 35 94 C
St Peter's Rd. Sthl 53 13 81 A
St Peter's Rd. Twick 71 16 74 B
St Peter's Rd. W6 61 22 78 C
St Peter's Sq. E2 48 34 83 C
St Peter's Sq. W6 61 21 78 D
St Peter's St. N1 48 31 83 D
St Peter's Street Mews. N1 48 32 83 C
St Peter's St. S Croy 112 32 64 D
St Peter's Terr. SW6 62 24 77 D
St Peter's Villas. W6 61 22 78 A
St Peter's Way. N1 48 33 84 C
St Peters Way. W5 54 17 81 B
St Philips Ave. N2 24 27 91 C
St Philip's Ave. Wor Pk 102 22 65 B
St Philip Sq. SW8 74 28 76 D
St Philip's Rd. E8 48 34 84 A
St Philip's Rd. Surb 101 17 67 D
St Philip St. SW8 74 28 76 D
St Philip's Way. N1 48 32 83 A
St Quentin Rd. Well 78 45 75 B
St Quintin Ave. W10 56 23 81 B
St Quintin Gdns. W10 56 23 81 A
St Quintin Rd. E13 58 40 82 B
St Raphael's Way. NW10 45 20 85 C
St Regis Cl. N10 24 28 90 B
St Ronans Cres. Wdf Gn 27 40 91 C
St Rule St. SW8 74 29 76 C

St Saviors Cl. E17 38 3788 C
St Saviour's Rd. Croy 105 3267 C
St Saviour's Rd. SW2 74 3074 B
Saints Dri. E7 50 4185 D
St Silas Pl. NW5 47 2884 A
St Simon's Ave. SW15 73 2374 A
St Stephen's Ave. E17 38 3888 A
St Stephen's Ave. W12 61 2279 B
St Stephen's Ave. W13 54 1681 D
St Stephen's Cl. E17 38 3788 B
St Stephen's Cl. NW8 47 2783 A
St Stephen's Cl. Sthl 53 1381 A
St Stephen's Cres. Th Hth 97 3168 A
St Stephen's Cres. W2 56 2581 C
St Stephen's Gdns. Twick 71 1774 C
St Stephen's Gdns. W2 56 2581 C
St Stephen's Gr. SE13 76 3875 A
St Stephen's Mews. W2 56 2581 A
St Stephen's Pas. Twick 71 1774 C
St Stephens Rd. Barn 11 2395 B
St Stephen's Rd. E17 38 3788 B
St Stephen's Rd. E3 49 3683 D
St Stephens Rd. E6 50 4184 C
St Stephen's Rd. Houn 70 1374 B
St Stephen's Rd. W13 54 1681 D
St Stephen's Row. EC4 4 3281 D
St Stephen's Terr. SW8 70 3077 D
St Swithin's La. EC4 8 3280 B
St Swithun's Rd. SE13 76 3874 D
St Theresa's Rd. Felt 69 0975 D
St Thomas' Dri. Orp 108 4466 C
St Thomas Dri. Pnr 20 1290 A
St Thomas Gdns. Ilf 51 4484 A
St Thomas' Gdns. NW5 47 2884 A
St Thomas Rd. Belv 67 5079 A
St Thomas Rd. E16 58 4081 C
St Thomas Rd. N14 16 2994 B
St Thomas' Rd. W4 61 2077 C
St Thomas's Pl. E9 49 3584 C
St Thomas's Rd. N4 37 3186 C
St Thomas's Rd. NW10 45 2083 A
St Thomas's Sq. E9 49 3584 C
St Thomas St. SE1 8 3280 D
St Thomas's Way. SW6 62 2477 D
St Ursula Gr. Pnr 32 1288 A
St Ursula Rd. Sthl 53 1381 C
St Vincent Rd. Twick 70 1474 C
St Vincent St. W1 2 2881 A
St Wilfrid's Cl. Barn 12 2795 A
St Wilfrid's Rd. Barn 12 2795 A
St Winefride's Ave. E12 50 4285 C
St Winifred's Rd. Tedd 93 1670 B
Salamanca Pl. SE1 10 3078 B
Salamanca St. SE11 10 3078 B
Salamanca St. SE1 10 3078 B
Salcombe Dri. Mord 103 2366 D
Salcombe Dri. Rom 41 4888 D
Salcombe Gdns. NW7 23 2391 A
Salcombe Rd. E17 38 3687 B
Salcombe Rd. N16 48 3385 C
Salcombe Way. Ruis 31 1086 A
Salcott Rd. Croy 111 3064 B
Salcott Rd. SW11 74 2774 B
Salehurst Cl. Har 33 1888 A
Salehurst Rd. SE4 76 3674 D
Salem Pl. Croy 105 3265 C
Salem Rd. W2 56 2580 B
Sale Pl. W2 1 2781 C
Sale St. E2 57 3482 C
Salford Rd. SW2 86 2973 D
Salisbury Ave. Bark 51 4584 C
Salisbury Ave. N3 23 2489 B
Salisbury Ave. Sutt 110 2463 B
Salisbury Cl. SE17 63 3278 B
Salisbury Cl. Wor Pk 102 2165 D
Salisbury Ct. EC4 3 3181 D
Salisbury Ct. N3 23 2490 D
Salisbury Gdns. SW19 95 2470 C
Salisbury Mews. SW6 62 2477 D
Salisbury Plain. NW4 35 2388 B
Salisbury Pl. W1 1 2781 B
Salisbury Rd. Barn 11 2496 A
Salisbury Rd. Brom 107 4267 A
Salisbury Rd. Cars 111 2763 B
Salisbury Rd. Dag 52 4984 B
Salisbury Rd. E10 38 3886 A
Salisbury Rd. E12 50 4285 C
Salisbury Rd. E17 38 3888 A
Salisbury Rd. E4 18 3793 C
Salisbury Rd. E7 50 4084 A
Salisbury Rd. Felt 82 1173 C
Salisbury Rd. Har 32 1488 B
Salisbury Rd. Houn 70 1175 A
Salisbury Rd. Ilf 40 4586 A
Salisbury Rd. N22 25 3190 D
Salisbury Rd. N4 37 3188 B
Salisbury Rd. N9 17 3493 C
Salisbury Rd. N Mal 94 2068 B
Salisbury Rd. Pnr 19 1089 C
Salisbury Rd. Rich 71 1875 C
Salisbury Rd. Rom 42 5288 B
Salisbury Rd. SE25 105 3467 C
Salisbury Rd. Sthl 59 1278 A
Salisbury Rd. SW19 95 2470 C
Salisbury Rd. W13 60 1679 B
Salisbury Rd. Wor Pk 102 2165 D
Salisbury Sq. EC4 3 3181 C
Salisbury St. NW8 1 2782 C
Salisbury St. W3 61 2079 A
Salisbury Terr. SE15 76 3575 A
Salisbury Wlk. N19 36 2986 A
Salix Cl. Sun 91 1070 D
Salman Rd. E13 50 3983 D
Salmond Cl. Stan 21 1691 A
Salmon La. E14 57 3681 C
Salmon Rd. Belv 67 4978 C
Salmons Rd. N9 17 3494 C
Salmon St. E14 57 3681 D
Salmon St. NW9 34 2087 A
Salomons Rd. E13 58 4181 A
Salop Rd. E17 38 3588 D
Saltash Cl. Sutt 110 2464 B
Saltash Rd. Ilf 28 4491 D
Saltash Rd. Well 79 4776 A
Saltcoats Rd. W4 61 2179 A
Saltcroft Cl. NW9 34 1987 D
Salterford Rd. SW17 96 2870 A
Salter Rd. SE16 57 3680 C
Salters Hall Ct. EC4 8 3280 B
Salter's Hill. SE19 87 3271 D
Salters Rd. E17 26 3889 D
Salters Rd. W10 56 2382 D
Salter St. E14 57 3780 A
Salter St. NW10 55 2282 A
Salterton Rd. N7 36 3086 D
Saltford Cl. Eri 68 5178 C
Saltoun Rd. SW2 75 3175 C
Saltram Cl. N15 25 3389 D
Saltram Cres. W9 56 2582 A
Saltwell St. E14 57 3780 A
Saltwood Gr. SE17 63 3278 D
Salusbury Rd. NW6 46 2483 A
Salvador. SW17 86 2771 D
Salvia Gdns. Grnf 44 1683 C
Salvin Rd. SW15 73 2375 B
Salway Cl. Wdf Gn 27 4091 C
Salway Pl. E15 49 3884 B
Salway Rd. E15 49 3884 B
Samantha Cl. E17 38 3687 B
Sam Bartram Cl. SE7 65 4178 C
Samels Ct. W6 61 2278 C
Samford St. NW8 1 2782 C
Samos Cl. SE3 65 3977 D
Samos Rd. SE20 97 3469 D
Sampson Ave. Barn 11 2395 B
Sampson St. E1 57 3480 C
Samson St. E13 50 4183 C
Samuel Johnson Cl. SW16 87 3171 A
Samuel Lewis Buildings. N1 48 3184 C
Samuel Lewis Trust Dwellings 9 2778 A
Samuel Lewis Trust Dwellings (off Dalston La). E8 48 3485 C
Samuel Lewis Trust Dwellings (off Downs Park Rd). E8 48 3485 C
Samuel Lewis Trust Dwellings. SW6 62 2577 C
Samuel Lewis Trust Dwellings. W14 62 2478 A
Samuel Lewis Trust Estate. N15 37 3388 C
Samuel St. SE18 65 4278 B
Sancroft Cl. NW2 34 2286 D
Sancroft Rd. Har 21 1690 C
Sancroft St. SE11 63 3178 C
Sanctuary Cl. Dart 80 5374 D
Sanctuary St. SE1 8 3279 A
Sanctuary. The. SW1 6 2979 D
Sanctuary The. Bex 79 4774 D
Sanctuary The. Mord 103 2567 C
Sandall Cl. W5 54 1882 C
Sandall Rd. NW5 47 2984 A
Sandall Rd. W5 54 1882 C
Sandal Rd. N18 17 3492 C
Sandal Rd. N Mal 94 2168 C
Sandal St. E15 50 3983 A
Sandalwood Cl. E2 57 3682 C
Sandalwood Rd. Felt 81 1072 D
Sandbach Pl. SE18 66 4478 C
Sandbourne Ave. SW19 95 2569 D
Sandbourne Rd. SE4 76 3676 C
Sandbrook Cl. NW7 22 2091 B
Sandbrook Rd. N16 37 3386 C
Sandby Green. SE9 77 4275 A
Sandcliff Rd. Eri 67 5078 D
Sanddown Ct. Sutt 110 2563 D
Sandell's Ave. Ashf 81 0871 C
Sandell St. SE1 7 3179 A
Sanders Cl. Hamp 82 1471 C
Sanders La. NW7 23 2391 D
Sanderson Cl. NW5 47 2885 B
Sanderstead Ave. NW2 35 2486 A
Sanderstead Cl. SW4 86 2973 A
Sanderstead Rd. E10 38 3687 C
Sanderstead Rd. Orp 108 4667 D
Sanderstead Rd. S Croy 112 3262 B
Sanders Way. N19 36 2987 D
Sandfield Gdns. Th Hth 97 3168 B
Sandfield Pas. Th Hth 97 3269 C
Sandfield Pl. Th Hth 97 3268 A
Sandfield Rd. Th Hth 97 3168 B
Sandford Ave. N22 25 3290 A
Sandford Ct. N16 37 3387 C
Sandford Rd. Bexh 79 4875 A
Sandford Rd. Brom 99 4068 D
Sandford Row. SE17 63 3278 D
Sandford St. SW6 62 2577 D
Sandgate Rd. Well 67 4777 C
Sandgate St. SE15 63 3477 B
Sandhills. Wall 111 2964 B
Sandhurst Ave. Har 32 1388 D
Sandhurst Ave. Surb 102 1966 B
Sandhurst Cl NW9 22 1989 A
Sandhurst Cl. S Croy 112 3362 A
Sandhurst Dri. Ilf 51 4585 B
Sandhurst Rd. Bexh 79 4774 B
Sandhurst Rd. Enf 14 3595 D
Sandhurst Rd. NW9 22 1989 A
Sandhurst Rd. Orp 108 4665 C
Sandhurst Rd. SE6 88 3873 C
Sandhurst Rd. Sid 90 4672 C
Sandhurst Way. S Croy 112 3363 D
Sandiford Rd. Sutt 103 2465 B
Sandiland Cres. Brom 107 3965 B
Sandilands. Croy 105 3465 B
Sandilands Rd. SW6 73 2576 B
Sandison St. SE15 75 3475 B
Sandland St. WC1 3 3081 B
Sandling Rise. SE9 90 4372 C
Sandlings The. N22 25 3189 B
Sandmere Rd. SW4 74 3075 C
Sandown Ave. Dag 52 5084 A
Sandown Ave. Horn 42 5386 B
Sandown Cl. Houn 69 1076 A
Sandown Dri. Cars 111 2862 A
Sandown Rd. SE25 105 3467 B
Sandown Way. Nthlt 43 1285 C
Sandpit Pl. SE7 65 4278 C
Sandpit Rd. Brom 89 3971 C
Sandpit Rd. Dart 80 5375 C
Sandpits Rd. Rich 83 1772 B
Sandra Cl. Houn 70 1374 B
Sandra Cl. N22 25 3290 C
Sandridge Cl. Har 21 1589 C
Sandridge St. N19 36 2986 A
Sandringham Ave. SW20 95 2469 C
Sandringham Cl. Enf 13 3397 C
Sandringham Cl. Ilf 28 4489 A
Sandringham Cres. Har 32 1386 D
Sandringham Dri. Well 78 4576 C
Sandringham Gdns. Houn 69 1076 A
Sandringham Gdns. Ilf 28 4489 A
Sandringham Gdns. N12 23 2691 B
Sandringham Gdns. N8 36 3088 C
Sandringham Mews. W5 54 1780 B
Sandringham Rd. Th Hth 105 3267 A
Sandringham Rd. Bark 51 4584 B
Sandringham Rd. Brom 89 4071 C
Sandringham Rd. E10 238 3888 D
Sandringham Rd. E7 50 4185 C
Sandringham Rd. E8 48 3385 D
Sandringham Rd. N22 25 3290 C
Sandringham Rd. Nthlt 43 1384 C
Sandringham Rd. NW11 35 2487 A
Sandringham Rd. NW2 45 2284 B
Sandringham Rd. Wor Pk 102 2265 D
Sandrock Rd. SE13 76 3775 A
Sands End La. SW6 73 2576 B
Sandstone Pl. N6 36 2886 B
Sandstone Rd. SE12 89 4072 B
Sands Way. Wdf Gn 27 4291 B
Sandtoft Rd. SE7 65 4077 B
Sandwell Cres. NW6 46 2584 A
Sandwich St. WC1 3 3082 A
Sandy Bury. Orp 108 4465 D
Sandycombe Rd. Felt 81 1073 C
Sandycombe Rd. Rich 72 1976 C
Sandycoombe Rd. Twick 71 1774 C
Sandycroft. SE2 66 4677 A
Sandy Dri. Felt 81 0973 C
Sandy Hill Ave. SE18 66 4378 D
Sandyhill Rd. Ilf 51 4385 B
Sandy Hill Rd. SE18 66 4378 D
Sandy Hill Rd. Wall 111 2962 A
Sandy La. King 93 1769 A
Sandy La. Mit 96 2869 A
Sandy La. Nthwd 19 1091 B
Sandy La N. Wall 111 2964 D
Sandy La. Orp 108 4666 A
Sandy La. Rich 83 1772 B
Sandy La. Sutt 110 2462 A
Sandy La S. Wall 111 2963 C
Sandy La. Tedd 93 1670 D
Sandy Lodge Way. Nthwd 19 0991 A
Sandymount Ave. Stan 21 1791 B
Sandy Rd. NW3 35 2586 B
Sandy Ridge. Chis 100 4370 A
Sandy's Row. E1 4 3381 A
Sandy Way. Croy 106 3665 D
Sanford La. N16 37 3386 B
Sanford St. SE14 64 3677 A
Sanford Terr. N16 37 3386 D
Sanford Wlk. N16 37 3386 B
Sanford Wlk. SE14 64 3677 A
Sangley Rd. SE25 97 3368 C
Sangley Rd. SE6 88 3873 C
Sangora Rd. SW11 73 2675 D
Sansom Rd. E11 39 3986 B
Sansom St. SE5 75 3276 B
Sansom St. SE5 63 3277 D
Sans Wlk. EC1 3 3182 D
Santley St. SW4 74 3075 D
Santos Rd. SW18 73 2574 A
Sapphire Rd. SE8 64 3678 A
Saracen Cl. Croy 105 3267 D
Saracen's Head Yd. EC3 4 3381 D
Saracen St. E14 57 3781 C
Sarah St. N1 4 3382 A
Saratoga Rd. E5 49 3585 A
Sardinia St. WC2 3 3081 D
Sark Cl. Houn 59 1377 C
Sark Wlk. E16 58 4081 D
*Sarnesfield Rd. Enf 13 3296 B
Sarre Rd. NW2 46 2485 D
Sarsen Ave. Houn 70 1276 D
Sarsfeld Rd. SW12 86 2773 D
Sarsfield Rd. Grnf 44 1783 C
Sartor Rd. SE15 76 3575 D
Satchell Mead. NW9 22 2190 B
Satchwell Rd. E2 57 3482 A
Sauls Green. E11 39 3986 C
Saunders Ness Rd. E14 64 3878 B
Saunders Rd. SE18 66 4578 D
Saunders St. SE11 63 3178 A
Saunderton Rd. Wem 44 1685 D
Saunton Rd. Horn 42 5286 A
Savage Gdns. EC3 8 3380 A
Savernake Rd. N9 13 3495 C
Savernake Rd. NW3 47 2785 B
Savile Cl. N.Mal 102 2167 A
Savile Gdns. Croy 105 3365 B
Savile Cres. Ashf 91 0870 B
Saville Rd. Rom 41 4887 B
Saville Rd. Twick 83 1573 D
Saville Rd. W4 61 2079 D
Saville Row. Enf 14 3597 D
Saville Row. W1 6 2980 A
Savill Gdns. SW20 94 2268 A
Savill Row. Wdf Gn 27 3991 B
Savona Cl. SW19 95 2370 D
Savona St. SW8 10 2977 C
Savoy Bldgs. WC2 7 3080 B
Savoy Cl. E15 50 3983 A
Savoy Ct. WC2 7 3080 A
Savoy Hill. WC2 7 3080 B
Savoy Pl. WC2 7 3080 B
Savoy Rd. Dart 80 5374 B
Savoy Row. WC2 7 3080 B
Savoy Steps. WC2 7 3080 B
Savoy St. WC2 7 3080 B
Savoy Way. WC2 7 3080 B
Sawkins Cl. SW19 85 2472 A
Sawley Rd. W12 55 2280 C
Sawtry Cl. Cars 104 2766 A
Sawyer's Hill. Rich 84 1973 A
Sawyers Lawn. W13 54 1681 C
Sawyer St. SE1 8 3279 A
Saxby Rd. SW2 86 3073 A
Saxham Rd. Bark 51 4583 D
Saxlingham Rd. E4 18 3893 D
Saxon Ave. Felt 82 1272 B
Saxonbury Ave. Sun 92 1168 A
Saxonbury Cl. Mit 95 2668 B
Saxonbury Gdns. Surb 101 1766 C
Saxon Cl. Rom 30 5490 D
Saxon Dr. W3 55 1981 B
Saxon Gdns. Sthl 53 1280 A
Saxon Rd. Ashf 91 0870 B
Saxon Rd. Brom 99 3970 D
Saxon Rd. E3 49 3683 D
Saxon Rd. Ilf 51 4385 D
Saxon Rd. N22 25 3190 B
Saxon Rd. SE25 105 3267 B
Saxon Rd. Sthl 53 1280 A
Saxon Rd. Wem 34 2086 C
Saxon Way. N14 12 2995 D
Saxton Cl. SE13 76 3875 B
Saxville Rd. Orp 100 4669 D
Sayer St. SE17 63 3278 A
Sayes Court Rd. Orp 100 4668 D
Sayes Court St. SE8 64 3677 B
Scads Hill Cl. Orp 108 4567 D
Scala St. W1 2 2981 A
Scales Rd. N17 25 3489 A
Scampston Mews. W10 56 2381 D
Scandrett St. E1 57 3480 D
Scarba Wlk. N1 48 3284 B
Scarborough Rd. E11 38 3887 D
Scarborough Rd. N4 37 3187 C
Scarborough Rd. N9 18 3594 A
Scarborough St. E1 4 3381 D
Scarbrook Rd. Croy 105 3265 C
Scarle Rd. Wem 44 1784 B
Scarlet Rd. SE6 89 3972 C
Scarlette Manor Way. SE24 87 3173 A
Scarsbrook Rd. SE3 77 4175 B
Scarsdale Pl. W8 62 2579 D
Scarsdale Rd. Har 32 1486 C
Scarsdale Villas. W8 62 2579 C
Scarth Rd. SW13 72 2275 A
Scawen Rd. SE8 64 3678 C
Scawfell St. E2 48 3383 D
Scaynes Link. N12 15 2592 A
Sceaux Gdns. SE5 75 3376 A
Sceptre Rd. E2 57 3582 A
Schofield Wlk. SE3 65 4077 D
Scholars Rd. E4 18 3894 D
Scholars Rd. SW12 86 2973 C
Scholefield Rd. N19 36 2986 B
Scholefield Rd. N19 36 2987 D
School App. E2 4 3382 A
Schoolhouse La. E1 57 3580 B
School House La. Tedd 93 1770 C
School La. King 93 1769 A
School La. Pnr 20 1289 C
School La. Surb 101 1866 D
School La. Well 78 4675 B
School Pas. King 93 1869 D
School Pas. Sthl 53 1280 B
School Rd. Ashf 91 0770 B
School Rd. Chis 100 4470 C
School Rd. Dag 52 4983 A
School Rd. E12 50 4285 B
School Rd. E Mol 92 1468 D
School Rd. Hamp 92 1470 A
School Rd. Houn 70 1475 A
School Rd. King 93 1769 A
School Rd. NW10 55 2082 D
School Road Ave. Hamp 92 1470 A
School Way. Dag 41 4786 C
Schoolway. N12 23 2691 B
School Wlk. Sun 91 1068 A
Schubert Rd. SW15 73 2474 B
Sclater St. E1 4 3382 D
Scoble Pl. N16 48 3385 B
Scoles Cres. SW2 87 3173 C
Scoresby St. SE1 7 3180 D
Scorton Ave. Grnf 44 1683 C
Scotch Common W13 54 1681 B
Scoter Cl. Wdf Gn 27 4091 D
Scot Gr. Pnr 20 1191 D
Scotia Ct. SE16 64 3579 C
Scotland Green. N17 25 3390 D
Scotland Green Rd. Enf 14 3595 B
Scotland Green Rd N. Enf 14 3696 C
Scotland Pl. SW1 7 3080 C
Scotsdale Cl. Orp 100 4568 C
Scotsdale Cl. Sutt 110 2463 C
Scotsdale Rd. SE12 77 4074 D
Scotswood St. EC1 3 3182 C
Scotswood Wlk. N17 25 3491 C
Scott Cl. Eps 109 2064 C
Scott Cl. SW16 96 3069 B
Scott Cres. Eri 80 5176 B
Scott Cres. Har 32 1387 D
Scott Ellis Gdns. NW8 1 2682 B
Scottes Rd. Dag 41 4787 D
Scott Gdns. Houn 59 1177 D
Scott Lidgett Cres. SE16 63 3479 A
Scott's Ave. Brom 98 3869 D
Scott's Ave. Sun 91 0970 A
Scotts Dri. Hamp 92 1370 D
Scotts Farm Rd. Eps 109 2063 A
Scott's La. Brom 98 3869 D
Scottsas. SE18 66 4378 B
Scotts Rd. Brom 99 4070 C
Scott's Rd. E10 38 3887 C
Scotts Rd. Sthl 59 1179 D
Scott's Rd. W12 61 2279 B
Scott St. E1 57 3482 D
Scott's Way. Sun 91 0970 C
Scott's Yd. EC4 8 3280 B
Scoulding Rd. E16 58 4081 C
Scouler St. E14 58 3880 B
Scout La. SW4 74 2975 A
Scovell Cres. SE1 8 3279 A
Scovell Rd. SE1 8 3279 A
Scrafton Rd. Ilf 40 4386 D
Scrattons Terr. Bark 52 4783 B
Scriven St. E8 48 3383 B
Scrooby St. SE6 76 3774 D
Scrubs La. NW10 55 2282 D
Scrubs La. W10 56 2381 A
Scrutton Cl. SW12 86 2973 B
Scrutton St. EC2 4 3382 C
Scudamore La. NW9 22 2089 C
Scutari Rd. SE22 76 3574 A
Scylla Cres. Felt 81 0773 B
Scylla Rd. Felt 69 0774 D
Scylla Rd. SE15 75 3475 B
Seabright St. E2 57 3482 B
Seabrook Dri. W.Wick 107 3965 A
Seabrook Gdns. Rom 41 4987 A
Seabrook Rd. Dag 41 4786 D
Seacoal La. EC4 3 3181 D
Seacourt Rd. SE2 67 4779 B
Seafield Rd. N11 16 2992 B
Seaford Cl. Ruis 31 0886 B
Seaford Rd. E17 26 3789 B
Seaford Rd. Enf 13 3396 C
Seaford Rd. N15 37 3388 A
Seaford Rd. W13 54 1680 D
Seaford St. WC1 3 3082 A
Seaforth Ave. N Mal 94 2268 D
Seaforth Cl. Rom 30 5191 C
Seaforth Cres. N5 48 3285 C
Seaforth Gdns. Eps 109 2164 D
Seaforth Gdns. N21 17 3194 C
Seaforth Pl. SW1 6 2979 C
Seager Pl. E3 57 3681 B
Seagrave Cl. E1 57 3581 B
Seagrave Rd. SW6 62 2577 A
Seagry Rd. E11 39 4087 B
Sealand Rd. Houn 69 0774 C
Sealand Wlk. Nthlt 53 1282 A
Seal St. E8 48 3385 B
Searle Ct. N4 36 3087 D
Searles Cl. SW11 9 2777 C
Searles Rd. SE1 63 3278 B
Sears St. SE5 63 3277 D
Seasprite Cl. Nthlt 53 1182 B
Seaton Ave. Ilf 51 4585 D
Seaton Cl. E13 58 4082 C
Seaton Cl. SE11 63 3178 D
Seaton Cl. Twick 70 1474 D
Seaton Gdns. Ruis 31 1086 A
Seaton Pl. NW1 2 2982 C
Seaton Rd. Mit 96 2769 C
Seaton Rd. Twick 70 1474 C
Seaton Rd. Well 67 4777 C
Seaton Rd. Wem 44 1883 C
Seaton St. N18 17 3492 C
Sebastian St. EC1 3 3182 B
Sebastopol Rd. N9 17 3493 C
Sebbon St. N1 48 3184 D
Sebert Rd. E7 50 4085 B
Sebright Pas. E2 48 3483 C
Sebright Rd. Barn 11 2396 B
Secker Cres. Har 20 1490 A
Secker St. SE1 7 3180 C
Second Ave. Dag 52 4983 D
Second Ave. E12 50 4285 C
Second Ave. E13 58 4082 A
Second Ave. E17 38 3788 A
Second Ave. Enf 13 3395 B
Second Ave. N18 18 3592 A
Second Ave. NW4 23 2389 D
Second Ave. Rom 41 4788 A
Second Ave. SW14 72 2175 A
Second Ave. W10 56 2482 C
Second Ave. W3 55 2180 D

| | | |
|---|---|---|
| Second Ave. Wem | 33 | 17 86 B |
| Second Cl. E Mol | 92 | 14 68 C |
| Second Cross Rd. Twick | 83 | 15 72 A |
| Second Way. Wem | 45 | 19 85 B |
| Sedan Way. SE17 | 63 | 33 78 C |
| Sedcote Rd. Enf | 14 | 35 95 B |
| Sedding St. SW1 | 9 | 28 78 A |
| Seddon Rd. Mord | 103 | 26 67 B |
| Seddon St. WC1 | 3 | 30 82 B |
| Sedgebrook Rd. SE3 | 77 | 41 75 B |
| Sedgecombe Ave. Har | 33 | 17 88 A |
| Sedgeford Rd. W3 | 55 | 21 80 D |
| Sedgehill Rd. SE6 | 88 | 37 71 D |
| Sedgemere Ave. N2 | 23 | 26 89 A |
| Sedgemoor Dri. Dag | 52 | 49 85 A |
| Sedgeway. SE6 | 89 | 39 73 D |
| Sedgewood Cl. Brom | 107 | 39 66 B |
| Sedgmoor Pl. SE5 | 63 | 33 77 C |
| Sedgwick Rd. E10 | 38 | 38 86 A |
| Sedgwick St. E9 | 49 | 35 85 D |
| Sedleigh Rd. SW18 | 73 | 24 74 D |
| Sedlescombe Rd. SW6 | 62 | 25 77 A |
| Sedley Pl. W1 | 2 | 28 81 D |
| Seeley Dri. SE21 | 87 | 33 71 B |
| Seelig Ave. NW9 | 34 | 22 87 A |
| Seely Rd. SW17 | 96 | 28 70 A |
| Seething La. EC3 | 8 | 33 80 A |
| Seething Wells La. Surb | 101 | 17 67 C |
| Sefton Ave. Har | 20 | 14 90 B |
| Sefton Ave. NW7 | 22 | 20 91 B |
| Sefton Cl. Orp | 100 | 45 68 D |
| Sefton Ct. Houn | 70 | 13 76 B |
| Sefton Rd. Croy | 105 | 34 66 C |
| Sefton Rd. Eps | 109 | 20 62 D |
| Sefton Rd. Orp | 100 | 45 68 D |
| Sefton St. SW15 | 73 | 23 75 A |
| Sekforde St. EC1 | 3 | 31 82 D |
| Selbie Ave. NW10 | 45 | 21 85 D |
| Selborne Ave. E12 | 51 | 43 85 A |
| Selborne Ave. E17 | 38 | 36 88 B |
| Selborne Gdns. Grnf | 44 | 16 83 C |
| Selborne Gdns. NW4 | 22 | 22 89 C |
| Selborne Rd. Croy | 105 | 33 65 D |
| Selborne Rd. E17 | 38 | 37 88 A |
| Selborne Rd. Ilf | 40 | 43 86 A |
| Selborne Rd. N14 | 16 | 30 93 C |
| Selborne Rd. N22 | 24 | 30 90 B |
| Selborne Rd. SE5 | 75 | 32 76 D |
| Selborne Rd. Sid | 90 | 46 71 B |
| Selbourne Ave. Surb | 102 | 19 65 C |
| Selbourne Rd. N Mal | 94 | 21 69 C |
| Selby Chase. Ruis | 31 | 10 86 B |
| Selby Cl. Chis | 100 | 43 70 A |
| Selby Gdns. Sthl | 53 | 13 82 C |
| Selby Green. Cars | 104 | 27 66 A |
| Selby Rd. Ashf | 91 | 08 70 A |
| Selby Rd. Cars | 104 | 27 66 A |
| Selby Rd. E11 | 39 | 39 86 C |
| Selby Rd. E13 | 58 | 40 81 B |
| Selby Rd. N17 | 25 | 33 91 A |
| Selby Rd. SE20 | 97 | 34 69 C |
| Selby Rd. W5 | 54 | 17 82 C |
| Selby St. E1 | 57 | 34 82 C |
| Selcroft Rd. E10 | 65 | 39 78 D |
| Selden Rd. SE15 | 76 | 35 76 C |
| Seldon Wlk. N7 | 36 | 30 86 B |
| Selhurst New Rd. SE25 | 105 | 33 67 C |
| Selhurst Pl. SE25 | 105 | 33 67 C |
| Selhurst Rd. N9 | 17 | 33 93 C |
| Selhurst Rd. SE25 | 105 | 33 67 A |
| Selinas La. Dag | 41 | 48 87 B |
| Selkirk Rd. SW17 | 86 | 27 71 A |
| Selkirk Rd. Twick | 82 | 14 73 C |
| Sellers Hall Cl. N3 | 23 | 25 91 C |
| Sellincourt Rd. SW17 | 96 | 27 70 B |
| Sellindge Cl. Beck | 98 | 36 70 D |
| Sellon Mews. SE11 | 10 | 30 78 B |
| Sellons Ave. NW10 | 45 | 21 83 B |
| Selous St. NW1 | 47 | 29 83 A |
| Selsdon Ave. S Croy | 112 | 32 63 B |
| Selsdon Cl. Rom | 29 | 50 90 A |
| Selsdon Cl. Surb | 101 | 18 67 A |
| Selsdon Rd. E11 | 39 | 40 87 A |
| Selsdon Rd. E13 | 50 | 41 83 C |
| Selsdon Rd. NW2 | 34 | 21 86 B |
| Selsdon Rd. S Croy | 112 | 32 63 B |
| Selsdon Rd. SE27 | 87 | 31 71 B |
| Selsea Pl. N16 | 48 | 33 85 C |
| Selsey Cres. Well | 79 | 47 76 B |
| Selsey St. E14 | 57 | 37 81 A |
| Selway Cl. Pnr | 19 | 10 89 B |
| Selwood Dri. Barn | 11 | 23 95 B |
| Selwood Pl. SW7 | 62 | 26 78 D |
| Selwood Rd. Croy | 105 | 34 66 D |
| Selwood Rd. Sutt | 103 | 24 66 D |
| Selwood Terr. SW7 | 62 | 26 78 D |
| Selworthy Cl. E11 | 39 | 40 88 A |
| Selworthy Rd. SE6 | 88 | 36 72 D |
| Selwyn Ave. E4 | 26 | 38 91 A |
| Selwyn Ave. Ilf | 40 | 45 88 D |
| Selwyn Ave. Rich | 71 | 18 75 B |
| Selwyn Cl. Houn | 70 | 12 75 C |
| Selwyn Cres. Well | 78 | 46 75 D |
| Selwyn Ct. Edg | 22 | 19 91 D |
| Selwyn Pl. Orp | 100 | 46 68 B |
| Selwyn Rd. E13 | 50 | 40 83 B |
| Selwyn Rd. E3 | 49 | 36 83 D |
| Selwyn Rd. N.Mal | 102 | 20 67 B |
| Selwyn Rd. NW10 | 45 | 21 84 C |
| Semley Pl. SW1 | 9 | 28 78 B |
| Semley Rd. SW16 | 96 | 30 69 C |
| Senate St. SE15 | 76 | 35 76 C |
| Seneca Rd. SW4 | 74 | 30 75 C |
| Seneca Rd. Th Hth | 97 | 32 68 C |
| Senga Rd. Wall | 104 | 28 66 C |
| Senhouse Rd. Sutt | 103 | 23 65 D |
| Senior St. W2 | 56 | 25 81 B |
| Senior St. W2 | 56 | 25 81 B |
| Senlac Rd. SE12 | 89 | 40 73 D |
| Sennen Rd. Enf | 17 | 33 94 B |
| Sennen Wlk. SE9 | 89 | 42 72 C |
| Senrab St. E1 | 57 | 35 81 D |
| Sentinel Sq. NW4 | 23 | 23 89 C |
| September Way. Stan | 21 | 16 91 B |
| Sequoia Gdns. Orp | 108 | 45 66 B |
| Sequoia Park. Pnr | 20 | 13 91 B |
| Serbin Cl. E10 | 38 | 38 87 A |
| Serjeants' Inn. EC4 | 3 | 31 81 C |
| Serle St. WC2 | 3 | 30 81 D |
| Sermon La. EC4 | 4 | 32 81 C |
| Serpentine Rd. W2 | 5 | 27 80 D |
| Serviden Dri. Brom | 99 | 41 69 B |
| Servius Ct. Brent | 60 | 17 77 D |
| Setchell Rd. SE1 | 63 | 33 78 B |
| Setchell Way. SE1 | 63 | 33 78 B |
| Seth St. SE16 | 64 | 35 79 A |
| Seton Gdns. Dag | 52 | 47 84 C |
| Settle Rd. E13 | 50 | 40 83 C |
| Settles St. E1 | 57 | 34 81 C |
| Settrington Rd. SW6 | 73 | 25 76 D |
| Seven Kings Rd. Ilf | 40 | 44 86 B |
| Sevenoaks Cl. Bexh | 79 | 49 75 D |
| Sevenoaks Ct. Nthwd | 19 | 08 91 C |
| Sevenoaks Rd. Orp | 108 | 46 65 C |
| Sevenoaks Rd. SE4 | 76 | 36 74 D |
| Seven Sisters Rd. N15 | 37 | 33 88 A |
| Seven Sisters Rd. N4 | 37 | 32 87 A |
| Seventh Ave. E12 | 50 | 42 85 B |
| Severn Ave. Rom | 30 | 52 89 B |
| Severn Dri. Esh | 101 | 16 65 A |
| Severn Way. NW10 | 45 | 21 85 D |
| Severus Rd. SW11 | 74 | 27 75 C |
| Seville St. SW1 | 5 | 27 79 B |
| Sevington Rd. NW4 | 34 | 22 88 D |
| Sevington St. W9 | 56 | 25 82 D |
| Seward Rd. Beck | 98 | 35 69 D |
| Seward Rd. W7 | 60 | 16 79 A |
| Seward St. EC1 | 4 | 32 82 A |
| Sewardstone Gdns. E4 | 14 | 37 95 B |
| Sewardstone Rd. E2 | 49 | 35 83 C |
| Sewardstone Rd. E4 | 18 | 37 94 B |
| Sewardstone Rd. Enf | 14 | 37 96 B |
| Sewdley St. E5 | 49 | 35 85 B |
| Sewell Rd. SE2 | 66 | 46 79 B |
| Sewell St. E13 | 58 | 40 82 A |
| Seymer Dri. Grnf | 43 | 13 83 B |
| Seymer Rd. Rom | 29 | 50 89 B |
| Seymour Ave. Eps | 109 | 22 62 B |
| Seymour Ave. Mord | 103 | 23 66 B |
| Seymour Ave. N17 | 25 | 34 90 C |
| Seymour Cl. Pnr | 20 | 12 90 B |
| Seymour Cl. SW20 | 94 | 22 70 D |
| Seymour Ct. N10 | 24 | 28 90 C |
| Seymour Ct. N21 | 12 | 30 95 D |
| Seymour Gdns. Felt | 82 | 11 71 A |
| Seymour Gdns. Ilf | 39 | 42 87 D |
| Seymour Gdns. Ruis | 32 | 11 87 D |
| Seymour Gdns. Surb | 101 | 18 67 B |
| Seymour Gdns. Twick | 83 | 16 73 B |
| Seymour Mews. W1 | 2 | 28 81 C |
| Seymour Pl. SE25 | 97 | 34 68 D |
| Seymour Pl. W1 | 1 | 27 81 D |
| Seymour Rd. Cars | 111 | 28 64 C |
| Seymour Rd. E10 | 38 | 36 87 D |
| Seymour Rd. E4 | 18 | 37 94 D |
| Seymour Rd. E6 | 50 | 41 83 D |
| Seymour Rd. E Mol | 92 | 14 68 C |
| Seymour Rd. Hamp | 82 | 14 71 C |
| Seymour Rd. King | 93 | 17 69 B |
| Seymour Rd. Mit | 104 | 28 66 A |
| Seymour Rd. N3 | 23 | 25 91 D |
| Seymour Rd. N8 | 37 | 31 88 B |
| Seymour Rd. N9 | 17 | 34 93 B |
| Seymour Rd. SW18 | 73 | 24 74 D |
| Seymour Rd. SW19 | 85 | 23 72 D |
| Seymour Rd. W4 | 61 | 20 78 A |
| Seymour St. W1 | 1 | 27 81 D |
| Seymour Terr. SE20 | 97 | 34 69 B |
| Seymour Villas. SE20 | 97 | 34 69 B |
| Seymour Way. Sun | 91 | 09 70 A |
| Seymour Wlk. SW10 | 62 | 26 77 A |
| Seyssel St. E14 | 64 | 38 78 A |
| Shaa Rd. W3 | 55 | 20 80 B |
| Shacklegate La. Tedd | 83 | 15 71 A |
| Shackleton Cl. SE23 | 87 | 34 72 B |
| Shackleton Cl. SE23 | 88 | 35 72 A |
| Shackleton Ct. W12 | 61 | 22 79 B |
| Shackleton Rd. Sthl | 53 | 12 80 B |
| Shacklewell La. E8 | 48 | 33 85 D |
| Shacklewell Rd. N16 | 48 | 33 85 B |
| Shacklewell Row. E8 | 48 | 33 85 B |
| Shacklewell St. E2 | 4 | 33 82 B |
| Shadbolt Cl. Wor Pk | 102 | 21 65 B |
| Shad Thames. SE1 | 8 | 33 79 B |
| Shadwell Ct. Nthlt | 43 | 12 83 D |
| Shadwell Dri. Nthlt | 53 | 12 82 B |
| Shadwell Gdns. E1 | 57 | 35 80 A |
| Shadwell Pierhead. E1 | 57 | 35 80 A |
| Shadwell Pl. E1 | 57 | 35 80 A |
| Shaef Way. Tedd | 93 | 16 70 C |
| Shafter Rd. Dag | 52 | 50 84 A |
| Shaftesbury Ave. | 32 | 14 87 C |
| Shaftesbury Ave. Barn | 11 | 26 96 C |
| Shaftesbury Ave. Enf | 14 | 35 97 D |
| Shaftesbury Ave. Felt | 81 | 10 73 A |
| Shaftesbury Ave. Har | 33 | 18 88 C |
| Shaftesbury Ave. Sthl | 59 | 13 79 C |
| Shaftesbury Ave. W1 | 6 | 29 80 B |
| Shaftesbury Circ. Har | 32 | 14 87 C |
| Shaftesbury Mews. W8 | 62 | 25 79 C |
| Shaftesbury Rd. Beck | 98 | 36 69 D |
| Shaftesbury Rd. Cars | 104 | 27 66 A |
| Shaftesbury Rd. E10 | 38 | 37 87 C |
| Shaftesbury Rd. E17 | 38 | 37 88 D |
| Shaftesbury Rd. E4 | 18 | 38 94 D |
| Shaftesbury Rd. E7 | 50 | 41 84 C |
| Shaftesbury Rd. N18 | 25 | 33 91 B |
| Shaftesbury Rd. N19 | 36 | 30 87 C |
| Shaftesbury Rd. Rich | 71 | 18 75 A |
| Shaftesbury Rd. Rom | 42 | 51 88 D |
| Shaftesburys The. Bark | 54 | 44 83 A |
| Shaftesbury St. N1 | 48 | 32 83 D |
| Shaftesbury Waye. Hay | 53 | 11 81 C |
| Shaftesbury Way. Twick | 82 | 14 72 D |
| Shafto Mews. SW1 | 5 | 27 79 D |
| Shafton Rd. E9 | 49 | 35 83 B |
| Shafts Ct. EC3 | 4 | 33 81 C |
| Shakespeare Ave. Felt | 69 | 10 74 C |
| Shakespeare Ave. Hay | 53 | 11 82 C |
| Shakespeare Ave. N11 | 16 | 29 92 C |
| Shakespeare Ave. NW10 | 45 | 20 83 B |
| Shakespeare Cres. E12 | 50 | 42 84 B |
| Shakespeare Cres. NW10 | 45 | 20 83 B |
| Shakespeare Dri. Har | 33 | 18 88 D |
| Shakespeare Gdns. N2 | 24 | 27 89 D |
| Shakespeare Mews. N16 | 48 | 33 85 A |
| Shakespeare Rd. Bexh | 79 | 48 76 A |
| Shakespeare Rd. E17 | 26 | 35 90 D |
| Shakespeare Rd. N3 | 23 | 25 90 A |
| Shakespeare Rd. Rom | 42 | 51 88 D |
| Shakespeare Rd. W3 | 55 | 20 80 C |
| Shakespeare Rd. W7 | 54 | 15 80 B |
| Shakespeare Sq. Ilf | 28 | 44 91 A |
| Shakespeare Way. Felt | 82 | 11 71 A |
| Shakspeare Wlk. N16 | 48 | 33 85 A |
| Shalcomb St. SW10 | 62 | 26 77 A |
| Shaldon Dri. Mord | 103 | 24 67 A |
| Shaldon Dri. Ruis | 32 | 11 86 C |
| Shaldon Rd. Edg | 21 | 18 90 D |
| Shalfleet Dri. W10 | 56 | 23 80 B |
| Shalford Ct. N1 | 48 | 31 83 C |
| Shalimar Gdns. W3 | 55 | 20 80 A |
| Shalimar Rd. W3 | 55 | 20 80 A |
| Shallons Rd. SE9 | 90 | 43 71 B |
| Shalstone Rd. SW14 | 72 | 19 75 B |
| Shalston Villas. Surb | 101 | 18 67 D |
| Shamrock Rd. Croy | 104 | 30 67 D |
| Shamrock St. SW4 | 74 | 29 75 B |
| Shamrock Way. N14 | 16 | 28 94 D |
| Shandon Rd. SW4 | 74 | 29 74 C |
| Shand St. SE1 | 8 | 33 79 A |
| Shand St. SE1 | 8 | 33 80 C |
| Shandy St. E2 | 57 | 36 82 C |
| Shanklin Rd. N15 | 25 | 34 89 C |
| Shanklin Rd. N8 | 36 | 29 88 B |
| Shanklin Way. SE15 | 63 | 33 77 D |
| Shannon Cl. Sthl | 59 | 11 78 D |
| Shannon Corner. N Mal | 94 | 22 68 C |
| Shannon Gr. SW9 | 74 | 30 75 D |
| Shannon Pl. NW8 | 47 | 27 83 C |
| Shap Cres. Cars | 104 | 27 66 D |
| Shap St. E2 | 48 | 33 83 D |
| Shardcroft Ave. SE24 | 75 | 31 74 B |
| Shardeloes Rd. SE14 | 76 | 36 76 D |
| Shard's Sq. SE15 | 63 | 34 77 A |
| Sharman Ct. Sid | 90 | 46 71 A |
| Sharnbrooke Cl. Well | 79 | 47 75 A |
| Sharon Cl. Surb | 101 | 17 66 C |
| Sharon Gdns. E9 | 49 | 35 83 A |
| Sharon Rd. Enf | 14 | 36 97 C |
| Sharon Rd. W4 | 61 | 20 78 D |
| Sharples Hall St. NW1 | 47 | 27 83 B |
| Sharps La. Ruis | 31 | 08 87 D |
| Sharp Way. Dart | 80 | 54 75 B |
| Sharratt St. SE15 | 64 | 35 77 A |
| Sharstead St. SE17 | 63 | 31 78 D |
| Sharvel La. Nthlt | 43 | 11 83 A |
| Shaver's Pl. SW1 | 6 | 29 80 B |
| Shaw Ave. Bark | 52 | 48 83 C |
| Shawbrooke Rd. SE9 | 77 | 41 75 D |
| Shawbury Rd. SE22 | 75 | 33 74 B |
| Shawfield Park. Brom | 99 | 41 69 D |
| Shawfield St. SW3 | 9 | 27 78 C |
| Shawford Rd. Eps | 109 | 20 63 B |
| Shaw Gdns. Bark | 52 | 48 83 C |
| Shaw Path. Brom | 89 | 39 72 D |
| Shaw Rd. Brom | 89 | 39 72 D |
| Shaw Rd. Enf | 14 | 35 97 B |
| Shaw Sq. E17 | 26 | 36 90 A |
| Shaw Way. Wall | 111 | 30 63 C |
| Shearing Dri. Cars | 103 | 26 66 A |
| Shearling Way. N7 | 47 | 30 84 A |
| Shearman Rd. SE3 | 77 | 39 75 D |
| Shears Ct. Sun | 91 | 09 70 C |
| Shearwood Cres. Dart | 80 | 52 75 A |
| Sheaveshill Ave. NW9 | 22 | 21 89 C |
| Sheaveshill Ct. NW9 | 22 | 21 89 C |
| Sheba St. E1 | 4 | 33 82 D |
| Sheen Common Dri. Rich | 72 | 19 75 C |
| Sheen Court Rd. Rich | 72 | 19 75 C |
| Sheendale Rd. Rich | 71 | 18 75 D |
| Sheenewood. SE26 | 87 | 34 71 B |
| Sheen Gate Gdns. SW14 | 72 | 20 75 C |
| Sheen Gr. N1 | 48 | 31 83 A |
| Sheen La. SW14 | 72 | 20 75 C |
| Sheen Park. Rich | 71 | 18 75 C |
| Sheen Rd. Orp | 100 | 45 68 D |
| Sheen Rd. Rich | 71 | 18 75 D |
| Sheen Way. Wall | 111 | 30 64 D |
| Sheen Wood. SW14 | 72 | 20 74 A |
| Sheepcote La. SW11 | 74 | 27 76 D |
| Sheepcote Rd. Har | 33 | 15 88 D |
| Sheepcotes Rd. Rom | 29 | 48 89 C |
| Sheephouse Way. N.Mal | 102 | 21 66 A |
| Sheep La. E8 | 48 | 34 83 B |
| Sheerwater Rd. E16 | 58 | 41 81 B |
| Sheffield Sq. E3 | 57 | 36 82 B |
| Sheffield St. WC2 | 3 | 30 81 D |
| Sheffield Terr. W8 | 56 | 25 80 C |
| Shefton Rise. Nthwd | 19 | 10 91 C |
| Sheila Cl. Rom | 29 | 49 91 D |
| Sheila Rd. Rom | 29 | 49 91 D |
| Sheilings The. Horn | 42 | 54 88 B |
| Shelbourne Cl. Pnr | 20 | 12 89 B |
| Shelbourne Rd. N17 | 25 | 34 90 B |
| Shelburne Rd. N7 | 47 | 30 85 B |
| Shelbury Cl. Sid | 90 | 46 72 C |
| Shelbury Rd. SE22 | 75 | 34 74 B |
| Sheldon Ave. Ilf | 28 | 43 90 D |
| Sheldon Ave. N6 | 36 | 27 88 D |
| Sheldon Cl. SE20 | 97 | 34 69 B |
| Sheldon Rd. Bexh | 79 | 48 76 B |
| Sheldon Rd. Dag | 52 | 48 84 C |
| Sheldon Rd. N18 | 17 | 33 92 A |
| Sheldon Rd. NW2 | 46 | 23 85 B |
| Sheldon St. Croy | 105 | 32 65 C |
| Sheldrake Pl. W8 | 62 | 25 79 A |
| Sheldrick Cl. SW19 | 95 | 26 69 D |
| Shelford Pl. N16 | 37 | 32 86 D |
| Shelford Rd. Barn | 11 | 23 95 C |
| Shelford Rise. SE19 | 97 | 33 70 D |
| Shelgate Rd. SW11 | 74 | 27 74 B |
| Shell Cl. Brom | 107 | 42 67 C |
| Shelley Ave. E12 | 50 | 42 84 A |
| Shelley Ave. Grnf | 53 | 14 82 B |
| Shelley Ave. Horn | 42 | 51 87 D |
| Shelley Cl. Grnf | 53 | 14 82 B |
| Shelley Cl. Orp | 108 | 45 65 C |
| Shelley Cres. Houn | 70 | 11 76 B |
| Shelley Cres. Sthl | 53 | 12 81 D |
| Shelley Dri. Well | 78 | 45 76 A |
| Shelley Gdns. Wem | 33 | 17 86 A |
| Shellness Rd. E5 | 48 | 34 85 D |
| Shell Rd. SE13 | 76 | 37 75 B |
| Shellwood Rd. SW11 | 74 | 27 76 D |
| Shelmerdine Cl. E3 | 57 | 37 81 A |
| Shelson Ave. Felt | 81 | 09 71 B |
| Shelton Rd. SW19 | 95 | 25 69 A |
| Shelton St. WC2 | 3 | 30 81 C |
| Shenfield Rd. Wdf Gn | 27 | 40 91 D |
| Shenfield St. N1 | 48 | 33 83 C |
| Shenley Ave. Ruis | 31 | 09 86 B |
| Shenley Rd. Houn | 70 | 12 76 A |
| Shenley Rd. SE5 | 75 | 33 76 A |
| Shenstone Cl. Bexh | 79 | 50 75 D |
| Shenstone Gdns. Ilf | 28 | 46 89 C |
| Shenstone Gdns. Rom | 30 | 53 90 A |
| Shepherd Cl. W1 | 6 | 28 80 A |
| Shepherdess Pl. N1 | 4 | 32 82 B |
| Shepherdess Wlk. N1 | 48 | 32 83 C |
| Shepherd Market. W1 | 6 | 28 80 D |
| Shepherd's Bush Green. W12 | 62 | 23 79 A |
| Shepherd's Bush Market. W12 | 62 | 23 79 A |
| Shepherd's Bush Pl. W12 | 62 | 23 79 B |
| Shepherd's Bush Rd. W6 | 62 | 23 79 C |
| Shepherd's Cl. N6 | 36 | 28 88 D |
| Shepherds Cl. Orp | 108 | 45 65 D |
| Shepherds Cl. Rom | 41 | 47 88 B |
| Shepherd's Hill. N6 | 36 | 29 88 C |
| Shepherds La. Dart | 80 | 53 74 C |
| Shepherd's La. E9 | 49 | 35 84 A |
| Shepherd's Path. NW3 | 46 | 26 85 D |
| Shepherds Pl. W1 | 6 | 28 80 A |
| Shepherd St. W1 | 6 | 28 80 D |
| Shepherd's Wlk. NW3 | 46 | 26 85 D |
| Shepley Cl. Cars | 104 | 28 65 C |
| Sheppard Cl. Surb | 93 | 18 68 C |
| Sheppard's Ct. Har | 33 | 15 87 A |
| Sheppard St. E16 | 58 | 39 82 D |
| Shepperd St. E3 | 57 | 37 82 D |
| Shepperton Rd. N1 | 48 | 32 83 B |
| Shepperton Rd. Orp | 108 | 44 67 C |
| Sheppey Cl. Eri | 68 | 52 77 D |
| Sheppey Gdns. Dag | 52 | 47 84 C |
| Sheppey Rd. Dag | 52 | 47 84 C |
| Sheppey Wlk. N1 | 48 | 32 84 A |
| Sherard Rd. SE9 | 77 | 42 74 A |
| Sheraton St. W1 | 2 | 29 81 D |
| Sherborne Ave. Enf | 14 | 35 97 C |
| Sherborne Ave. Sthl | 59 | 13 78 A |
| Sherborne Cres. Cars | 104 | 27 66 A |
| Sherborne Gdns. NW9 | 22 | 19 89 A |
| Sherborne Gdns. W13 | 54 | 16 81 B |
| Sherborne La. EC4 | 8 | 32 80 B |
| Sherborne Rd. Felt | 81 | 08 73 D |
| Sherborne Rd. Orp | 108 | 45 67 B |
| Sherborne Rd. Sutt | 103 | 25 66 C |
| Sherborne St. N1 | 48 | 32 83 B |
| Sherboro Rd. N15 | 37 | 33 88 D |
| Sherbrooke Cl. Bexh | 79 | 49 75 C |
| Sherbrooke Rd. SW6 | 62 | 24 77 C |
| Sherbrook Gdns. N21 | 17 | 31 94 B |
| Shere Ave. Sutt | 110 | 23 62 C |
| Sheredan Rd. E4 | 18 | 38 92 D |
| Shere Rd. Ilf | 40 | 43 88 A |
| Sherfield Gdns. SW15 | 72 | 21 74 D |
| Sheridan Cl. Rom | 30 | 53 91 C |
| Sheridan Cres. Chis | 100 | 43 69 D |
| Sheridan Gdns. Har | 33 | 17 88 D |
| Sheridan Pl. Har | 33 | 15 87 A |
| Sheridan Rd. Belv | 67 | 49 78 A |
| Sheridan Rd. Bexh | 79 | 48 75 A |
| Sheridan Rd. E12 | 50 | 42 85 D |
| Sheridan Rd. E7 | 39 | 39 86 D |
| Sheridan Rd. Rich | 83 | 17 72 C |
| Sheridan Rd. SW19 | 95 | 24 69 B |
| Sheridan St. E1 | 57 | 35 81 C |
| Sheridan Wlk. Cars | 111 | 27 64 D |
| Sheridan Wlk. NW11 | 35 | 25 88 C |
| Sheringham Ave. E12 | 50 | 42 85 B |
| Sheringham Ave. N14 | 12 | 29 95 D |
| Sheringham Ave. Rom | 41 | 50 88 C |
| Sheringham Ave. Twick | 82 | 13 73 C |
| Sheringham Dri. Bark | 51 | 46 85 C |
| Sheringham Rd. N7 | 48 | 31 84 A |
| Sheringham Rd. SE20 | 98 | 35 68 A |
| Sherington Avenue. Pnr | 20 | 13 91 C |
| Sherington Rd. SE7 | 65 | 40 77 B |
| Sherland Rd. Twick | 83 | 15 73 D |
| Sherlies Ave. Orp | 108 | 45 65 A |
| Sherlock Mews. W1 | 2 | 28 81 A |
| Shermanbury Pl. Eri | 68 | 51 77 D |
| Sherman Rd. Brom | 99 | 40 69 A |
| Shernhall St. E17 | 38 | 38 88 A |
| Shernhall St. E17 | 26 | 38 89 C |
| Sherrard Rd. E12 | 50 | 41 85 D |
| Sherrard Rd. E7 | 50 | 41 84 A |
| Sherrards Way. Barn | 11 | 25 95 D |
| Sherrick Green Rd. NW10 | 45 | 22 85 D |
| Sherriff Rd. NW6 | 46 | 25 84 A |
| Sherringham Ave. Felt | 81 | 10 72 D |
| Sherringham Ave. N17 | 25 | 34 90 C |
| Sherrock Gdns. NW4 | 22 | 22 89 C |
| Shert Path. SE18 | 66 | 43 77 B |
| Sherwin Rd. SE14 | 76 | 35 76 B |
| Sherwood Ave. E18 | 27 | 40 89 D |
| Sherwood Ave. Grnf | 44 | 15 85 C |
| Sherwood Ave. Ruis | 31 | 09 88 C |
| Sherwood Ave. SW16 | 96 | 29 70 D |
| Sherwood Cl. Bex | 79 | 47 74 C |
| Sherwood Cl. SW15 | 72 | 22 75 B |
| Sherwood Cl. W13 | 54 | 16 80 D |
| Sherwood Gdns. Bark | 51 | 44 84 D |
| Sherwood Park Ave. Sid | 78 | 46 74 D |
| Sherwood Park Rd. Mit | 96 | 29 68 D |
| Sherwood Park Rd. Sutt | 110 | 25 64 C |
| Sherwood Rd. Croy | 105 | 34 66 D |
| Sherwood Rd. Hamp | 82 | 14 71 C |
| Sherwood Rd. Har | 32 | 14 86 A |
| Sherwood Rd. Ilf | 28 | 44 89 D |
| Sherwood Rd. NW4 | 23 | 23 89 A |
| Sherwood Rd. SW19 | 95 | 24 70 D |
| Sherwood Rd. Well | 78 | 45 75 A |
| Sherwood St. N20 | 15 | 26 93 D |
| Sherwood St. W1 | 6 | 29 80 A |
| Sherwood. Surb | 101 | 17 65 B |
| Sherwood Terr. N20 | 15 | 26 93 D |
| Sherwood Way. W Wick | 106 | 38 65 A |
| Shetland Rd. E3 | 49 | 36 83 D |
| Shield Dri. Brent | 60 | 16 77 B |
| Shieldhall St. SE2 | 67 | 47 78 A |
| Shield Rd. Ashf | 81 | 08 71 B |
| Shifford Path. SE23 | 88 | 35 72 D |
| Shillibeer Pl. W1 | 1 | 27 81 A |
| Shillingford St. N1 | 48 | 31 84 D |
| Shillington St. SW11 | 74 | 27 76 C |
| Shillitoe Rd. N13 | 17 | 32 92 C |
| Shinfield St. W12 | 56 | 23 81 C |
| Shinglewell Rd. Eri | 67 | 49 77 C |
| Ship Alley. W4 | 61 | 19 77 A |
| Ship and Mermaid Row. SE1 | 8 | 33 79 A |
| Shipka Rd. SW12 | 86 | 28 73 D |
| Ship Lane Pas. SW14 | 72 | 20 76 C |
| Ship La. SW14 | 72 | 20 76 C |
| Shipman Rd. E16 | 58 | 41 81 C |
| Shipman Rd. SE23 | 88 | 35 72 B |
| Ship St. SE8 | 76 | 37 76 A |
| Ship Tavern Pas. EC3 | 8 | 33 80 A |
| Shipton Cl. Dag | 41 | 47 86 D |
| Shipton St. E2 | 4 | 33 82 B |
| Shipwright Yd. SE1 | 8 | 33 80 C |
| Shirburn Cl. SE23 | 88 | 35 73 A |
| Shirbutt St. E14 | 57 | 37 80 B |
| Shirebrook Rd. SE3 | 77 | 41 75 B |
| Shire Ct. Belv | 67 | 47 79 D |
| Shirehall Cl. NW4 | 35 | 23 88 D |
| Shirehall Gdns. NW4 | 35 | 23 88 D |
| Shirehall La. NW4 | 35 | 23 88 D |
| Shirehall Park. NW4 | 35 | 23 88 D |
| Shires The. Rich | 83 | 18 71 A |
| Shirland Mews. W9 | 56 | 24 82 B |
| Shirland Rd. W9 | 56 | 25 82 C |
| Shirley Ave. Croy | 106 | 35 66 C |
| Shirley Ave. Sutt | 110 | 24 62 D |
| Shirley Ave. Sutt | 111 | 27 64 A |
| Shirley Church Rd. Croy | 106 | 36 65 C |
| Shirley Cl. Dart | 80 | 53 75 C |
| Shirley Cl. Houn | 70 | 14 74 A |
| Shirley Cres. Beck | 98 | 36 68 C |
| Shirley Dri. Houn | 70 | 14 74 A |
| Shirley Gdns. Bark | 51 | 45 84 A |
| Shirley Gdns. Horn | 42 | 53 86 A |
| Shirley Gdns. W7 | 54 | 16 80 C |
| Shirley Gr. N9 | 18 | 35 94 B |
| Shirley Gr. SW11 | 74 | 28 75 A |
| Shirley House Dri. SE7 | 65 | 41 77 C |
| Shirley Hts. Wall | 111 | 29 62 A |
| Shirley Oaks. Croy | 106 | 35 66 D |
| Shirley Park Rd. Croy | 106 | 35 66 C |
| Shirley Rd. Croy | 105 | 34 66 D |
| Shirley Rd. E15 | 50 | 39 84 C |
| Shirley Rd. Enf | 13 | 32 96 A |
| Shirley Rd. Sid | 90 | 45 72 C |
| Shirley Rd. W4 | 61 | 20 79 B |
| Shirley Rd. Wall | 111 | 29 62 A |
| Shirley St. E16 | 58 | 39 81 D |
| Shirley St. N1 | 47 | 30 83 B |
| Shirley Way. Croy | 106 | 36 65 D |
| Shirlock Rd. NW3 | 47 | 27 85 B |
| Shobden Rd. N17 | 25 | 32 90 B |

| | | |
|---|---|---|
| Shoebury Rd. E6 | 50 | 42 84 D |
| Shoe La. EC4 | 3 | 31 81 C |
| Sholto Rd. Houn | 69 | 07 74 A |
| Shooters Ave. Har | 21 | 17 89 C |
| Shooters Hill Rd. SE10 | 76 | 38 76 B |
| Shooters Hill Rd. SE18 | 77 | 42 76 A |
| Shooters Hill Rd. SE3 | 77 | 39 76 B |
| Shooters Hill. SE18 | 78 | 43 76 A |
| Shooters Hill. Well | 78 | 44 76 C |
| Shooters Rd. Enf | 13 | 31 97 B |
| Shoot-up Hill. NW2 | 46 | 24 84 A |
| Shore Cl. Felt | 81 | 10 73 A |
| Shore Cl. Hamp | 82 | 12 71 C |
| Shoreditch High St. E1 | 4 | 33 82 C |
| Shore Gr. Felt | 82 | 13 72 A |
| Shoreham Cl. Croy | 106 | 35 67 C |
| Shoreham Cl. SW18 | 73 | 25 74 B |
| Shoreham Rd. Orp | 100 | 46 69 D |
| Shoreham Way. Brom | 107 | 40 67 C |
| Shore Pl. E9 | 49 | 35 84 C |
| Shore Rd. E9 | 49 | 35 84 C |
| Shorncliffe Rd. SE1 | 63 | 33 78 D |
| Shorndean St. SE6 | 88 | 38 73 C |
| Shorne Cl. Sid | 78 | 46 74 D |
| Shornefield Cl. Brom | 100 | 43 68 A |
| Shornells Way. SE2 | 67 | 47 78 C |
| Shorrolds Rd. SW6 | 62 | 25 77 C |
| Shortcroft Rd. Eps | 109 | 21 63 D |
| Shortcrofts Rd. Dag | 52 | 48 84 B |
| Shorter St. E1 | 8 | 33 80 B |
| Shortfield. Wall | 111 | 28 63 B |
| Shortgate. N12 | 15 | 24 92 B |
| Shortlands Cl. N18 | 17 | 32 93 D |
| Shortlands Gdns. Brom | 99 | 39 69 C |
| Shortlands Gr. Brom | 98 | 38 68 B |
| Shortlands Rd. Brom | 99 | 39 69 C |
| Shortlands Rd. E10 | 38 | 37 87 B |
| Shortlands Rd. King | 93 | 18 70 D |
| Shortlands. W6 | 62 | 23 78 B |
| Short Rd. E11 | 39 | 39 86 A |
| Short Rd. E15 | 49 | 38 83 B |
| Short Rd. W4 | 61 | 21 77 A |
| Shorts Croft. NW9 | 22 | 19 89 D |
| Shorts Gdns. WC2 | 3 | 30 81 C |
| Shorts Rd. Cars | 111 | 27 64 C |
| Short St. SE1 | 7 | 31 79 A |
| Short Way. N12 | 24 | 27 91 A |
| Shortway. SE9 | 77 | 42 75 A |
| Short Way. Twick | 82 | 14 73 A |
| Shotfield. Wall | 111 | 28 63 B |
| Shottendane Rd. SW6 | 73 | 25 76 A |
| Shottery Cl. SE9 | 89 | 42 72 C |
| Shottfield Ave. SW14 | 72 | 21 75 C |
| Shoulder of Mutton Alley. E14 | 57 | 36 80 A |
| Shouldham St. W1 | 1 | 27 81 A |
| Shrapnel Cl. SE18 | 65 | 42 77 C |
| Shrapnel Rd. SE9 | 77 | 42 75 B |
| Shrewsbury Ave. Har | 21 | 18 89 C |
| Shrewsbury Ave. SW14 | 72 | 20 75 D |
| Shrewsbury Cl. Surb | 101 | 18 65 A |
| Shrewsbury Cres. NW10 | 45 | 20 83 B |
| Shrewsbury La. SE18 | 78 | 43 76 B |
| Shrewsbury Mews. W2 | 56 | 25 81 A |
| Shrewsbury Rd. Beck | 98 | 36 68 A |
| Shrewsbury Rd. Cars | 104 | 27 66 A |
| Shrewsbury Rd. E7 | 50 | 41 84 B |
| Shrewsbury Rd. N11 | 24 | 29 91 B |
| Shrewsbury Rd. W2 | 56 | 25 81 C |
| Shrewsbury Wlk. Islw | 71 | 16 75 A |
| Shrewton Rd. SW17 | 96 | 27 70 D |
| Shroffold Rd. Brom | 89 | 39 72 D |
| Shropshire Cl. Mit | 96 | 30 68 C |
| Shropshire Pl. WC1 | 2 | 29 82 D |
| Shropshire Rd. N22 | 24 | 30 91 D |
| Shroton St. NW1 | 1 | 27 81 A |
| Shrubberies The. E18 | 27 | 40 90 C |
| Shrubbery Gdns. N21 | 17 | 31 94 B |
| Shrubbery Rd. N9 | 17 | 34 93 C |
| Shrubbery Rd. Sthl | 53 | 13 80 C |
| Shrubbery Rd. SW16 | 86 | 30 71 A |
| Shrubbery The. E11 | 39 | 40 88 B |
| Shrubland Gr. Wor Pk | 103 | 23 65 C |
| Shrubland Rd. E10 | 38 | 37 87 A |
| Shrubland Rd. E17 | 38 | 37 88 A |
| Shrubland Rd. E8 | 48 | 34 83 A |
| Shrublands Ave. Croy | 106 | 37 65 C |
| Shrublands Cl. Chig | 28 | 44 91 A |
| Shrublands Cl. N20 | 15 | 26 93 B |
| Shuna Wlk. N1 | 48 | 32 84 B |
| Shurland Ave. Barn | 11 | 26 95 D |
| Shuttle Cl. Sid | 90 | 45 73 B |
| Shuttlemead. Bex | 79 | 48 74 A |
| Shuttle Rd. Dart | 80 | 52 75 A |
| Shuttle St. E1 | 57 | 34 82 C |
| Shuttleworth Rd. SW11 | 74 | 27 76 C |
| Sibella Rd. SW4 | 74 | 29 76 D |
| Sibley Cl. Bexh | 79 | 48 74 A |
| Sibley Gr. E12 | 50 | 42 84 D |
| Sibthorpe Rd. SE12 | 89 | 41 73 A |
| Sibthorp Rd. Mit | 96 | 27 69 D |
| Sibton Rd. Cars | 104 | 27 66 A |
| Sicilian Ave. WC1 | 3 | 30 81 A |
| Sickert Ct (off Canonbury St). N1 | 48 | 32 84 C |
| Sickert Ct (off Northampton St). N1 | 48 | 32 84 C |
| Sidbury St. SW6 | 73 | 24 76 A |
| Sidcup By Pass Rd. Sid | 100 | 46 70 A |
| Sidcup Hill. Sid | 90 | 46 71 D |
| Sidcup Rd. SE9 | 77 | 41 74 C |
| Sidcup Rd. SE9 | 89 | 42 73 D |
| Siddon La. NW1 | 1 | 27 82 D |
| Siddons Rd. Croy | 105 | 31 65 C |
| Siddons Rd. N17 | 25 | 34 90 A |
| Siddons Rd. SE23 | 88 | 36 72 A |
| Side Rd. E17 | 38 | 36 88 B |
| Sidewood Rd. SE9 | 90 | 44 73 D |
| Sidford Pl. SE1 | 7 | 30 79 D |
| Sidings The. E11 | 38 | 38 87 D |
| Sidmouth Ave. Islw | 71 | 15 76 C |
| Sidmouth Dri. Ruis | 31 | 10 86 B |
| Sidmouth Rd. E10 | 38 | 38 86 C |
| Sidmouth Rd. NW2 | 46 | 23 84 C |
| Sidmouth Rd. Orp | 100 | 46 68 D |
| Sidmouth Rd. SE15 | 75 | 33 76 B |
| Sidmouth Rd. Well | 67 | 47 77 C |
| Sidmouth St. WC1 | 3 | 30 82 B |
| Sidney Ave. N13 | 16 | 30 92 D |
| Sidney Gdns. Brent | 60 | 17 77 B |
| Sidney Gr. EC1 | 3 | 31 82 B |
| Sidney Gr. EC1 | 48 | 31 83 D |
| Sidney Rd. Beck | 98 | 36 69 C |
| Sidney Rd. E7 | 39 | 40 86 C |
| Sidney Rd. Har | 20 | 14 89 A |
| Sidney Rd. N22 | 24 | 30 91 D |
| Sidney Rd. SE25 | 105 | 34 67 A |
| Sidney Rd. SW9 | 74 | 30 76 D |
| Sidney Rd. Twick | 71 | 16 74 D |
| Sidney Sq. E1 | 57 | 35 81 A |
| Sidney St. E1 | 57 | 35 81 A |
| Sidworth St. E8 | 48 | 34 84 D |
| Siebert Rd. SE3 | 65 | 40 77 A |
| Siemens Rd. SE18 | 65 | 41 79 D |
| Sigdon Pas. E8 | 48 | 34 85 C |
| Sigdon Rd. E8 | 48 | 34 85 C |
| Sigs The. Pnr | 31 | 10 88 D |
| Silbury Ho. SE26 | 87 | 34 72 C |
| Silbury St. N1 | 4 | 32 82 B |
| Silchester Rd. W10 | 56 | 23 81 D |
| Silecroft Rd. Bexh | 79 | 49 76 A |
| Silesia Bldgs. E8 | 48 | 34 84 D |
| Silex St. SE1 | 7 | 31 79 B |
| Silk Cl. SE12 | 77 | 40 74 A |
| Silkfield Rd. NW9 | 34 | 21 88 B |
| Silk Mills Pas. SE13 | 76 | 37 76 D |
| Silk Mills Path. SE13 | 76 | 38 76 C |
| Silksteam Rd. Edg | 22 | 20 90 A |
| Silk St. EC2 | 4 | 32 81 A |
| Silsoe Rd. N22 | 24 | 30 89 B |
| Silver Birch Ave. E4 | 26 | 36 91 B |
| Silver Cl. Har | 20 | 14 91 D |
| Silvercliffe.Gdns. Barn | 12 | 27 96 C |
| Silver Cres. W4 | 61 | 19 78 B |
| Silverdale Ave. Ilf | 40 | 45 88 B |
| Silverdale Cl. Nthlt | 43 | 12 85 D |
| Silverdale Cl. Sutt | 110 | 24 64 B |
| Silverdale Cl. W7 | 54 | 15 80 D |
| Silverdale Dri. Sun | 91 | 10 69 D |
| Silverdale. Enf | 12 | 30 96 C |
| Silverdale Rd. Bexh | 79 | 49 76 D |
| Silverdale Rd. E4 | 26 | 38 91 B |
| Silverdale Rd. Orp | 100 | 44 68 C |
| Silverdale Rd. Orp | 100 | 46 68 A |
| Silverdale. SE26 | 88 | 35 71 A |
| Silverhall St. Islw | 71 | 16 75 A |
| Silverholme Cl. Har | 33 | 18 87 A |
| Silver Jubilee Way. Houn | 69 | 10 76 D |
| Silver La. W Wick | 106 | 38 65 B |
| Silverleigh Rd. Th Hth | 105 | 31 67 A |
| Silvermere Ave. Rom | 29 | 49 91 B |
| Silvermere Rd. SE6 | 76 | 37 74 D |
| Silver Pl. W1 | 6 | 29 80 A |
| Silver Rd. W12 | 56 | 23 80 B |
| Silver Spring Cl. Eri | 67 | 49 77 B |
| Silver St. Enf | 13 | 32 96 B |
| Silver St. N18 | 17 | 33 92 A |
| Silverston Way. Stan | 21 | 17 91 A |
| Silverthorne Rd. SW8 | 74 | 28 76 D |
| Silverthorn Gdns. E4 | 18 | 37 93 A |
| Silverton Rd. W6 | 62 | 23 77 B |
| Silvertown By-Pass. E16 | 58 | 41 80 D |
| Silvertown Way. E16 | 58 | 39 80 B |
| Silvertree La. Grnf | 53 | 14 82 B |
| Silver Way. Rom | 29 | 49 89 B |
| Silver Wlk. SE16 | 57 | 36 80 D |
| Silverwood Cl. Beck | 98 | 37 70 C |
| Silverwood Cl. Nthwd | 19 | 08 90 A |
| Silvester Rd. SE22 | 75 | 34 74 A |
| Silvester St. SE1 | 8 | 32 79 B |
| Silwood St. SE16 | 64 | 35 78 C |
| Simla Cl. SE14 | 64 | 36 77 A |
| Simmons Cl. N20 | 16 | 27 93 A |
| Simmons La. E4 | 18 | 38 93 B |
| Simmons Rd. SE18 | 66 | 43 78 D |
| Simmons Way. N20 | 16 | 27 93 A |
| Simms Cl. Cars | 104 | 27 65 A |
| Simms Rd. SE1 | 63 | 34 78 A |
| Simnel Rd. SE12 | 89 | 40 73 B |
| Simon Cl. W11 | 56 | 25 80 A |
| Simonds Rd. E10 | 38 | 37 86 A |
| Simone Cl. Brom | 99 | 41 69 B |
| Simons Wlk. E15 | 49 | 38 85 D |
| Simpson Rd. Houn | 70 | 12 74 D |
| Simpson Rd. Rich | 83 | 17 71 A |
| Simpson's Rd. Brom | 99 | 40 68 A |
| Simpson's Rd. E14 | 57 | 37 80 B |
| Simrose Ct. SW18 | 73 | 25 74 A |
| Sims Cl. Rom | 30 | 51 89 D |
| Sims Wlk. SE3 | 77 | 39 75 D |
| Sinclair Ct. Beck | 98 | 37 70 C |
| Sinclair Gdns. W14 | 62 | 23 79 B |
| Sinclair Gr. NW11 | 35 | 23 88 D |
| Sinclair Rd. E4 | 18 | 36 92 D |
| Sinclair Rd. W14 | 62 | 24 79 C |
| Sinclare Cl. Enf | 13 | 33 97 B |
| Singapore Rd. W13 | 54 | 16 80 C |
| Singer St. EC2 | 4 | 32 82 B |
| Singleton Cl. Croy | 105 | 32 66 A |
| Singleton Cl. SW17 | 96 | 27 70 D |
| Singleton Rd. Dag | 52 | 48 85 D |
| Singleton Scarp. N12 | 15 | 25 92 C |
| Sinnott Rd. E17 | 26 | 35 90 A |
| Sion Ct. Twick | 83 | 16 73 D |
| Sion Rd. Twick | 83 | 16 73 D |
| Sipson Rd. W.Dray | 69 | 07 76 B |
| Sipson Way. W.Dray | 69 | 07 76 A |
| Sir Alexander Cl. W3 | 55 | 21 80 D |
| Sir Alexander Rd. W3 | 55 | 21 80 D |
| Sirdar Rd. Mit | 96 | 28 70 A |
| Sirdar Rd. N22 | 25 | 32 90 C |
| Sirdar Rd. W11 | 56 | 24 80 A |
| Sir Thomas More Estate. SW3 | 62 | 26 77 B |
| Sise La. EC4 | 4 | 32 81 D |
| Sisley Rd. Bark | 51 | 45 83 B |
| Sispara Gdns. SW18 | 73 | 24 74 D |
| Sissinghurst Rd. Croy | 105 | 34 66 A |
| Sisters Ave. SW11 | 74 | 27 75 D |
| Sistova Rd. SW12 | 86 | 28 73 D |
| Sittingbourne Ave. Enf | 13 | 32 95 D |
| Siverst Cl. Nthlt | 43 | 13 84 B |
| Siviter Way. Dag | 52 | 49 84 D |
| Siward Rd. Brom | 99 | 41 68 A |
| Siward Rd. N17 | 25 | 32 90 B |
| Siward Rd. SW17 | 85 | 26 72 C |
| Sixth Ave. E12 | 50 | 42 85 B |
| Sixth Ave. W10 | 56 | 24 82 A |
| Sixth Cross Rd. Twick | 82 | 14 72 C |
| Skardu Rd. NW2 | 46 | 24 85 C |
| Skeena Hill SW18 | 85 | 24 73 A |
| Skeffington Rd. E6 | 50 | 42 83 B |
| Skelbrook St. SW18 | 85 | 26 72 A |
| Skelgill Rd. SW15 | 73 | 24 75 D |
| Skelley Rd. E15 | 50 | 39 84 D |
| Skelton Cl. E8 | 48 | 33 84 B |
| Skelton Rd. E7 | 50 | 40 84 A |
| Skelton's La. E10 | 38 | 37 87 B |
| Skelwith Rd. W6 | 62 | 23 77 A |
| Sketchley Gdns. SE16 | 64 | 35 78 D |
| Sketty Rd. Enf | 13 | 33 96 B |
| Skiers St. E15 | 50 | 39 83 A |
| Skiffington Cl. SW2 | 87 | 31 73 C |
| Skin Market Pl. SE1 | 8 | 32 80 C |
| Skinner Ct. E2 | 48 | 34 83 D |
| Skinner Pl. SW1 | 9 | 28 78 A |
| Skinners La. EC4 | 8 | 32 80 A |
| Skinner St. EC1 | 3 | 31 82 C |
| Skipton St. SE1 | 7 | 31 79 D |
| Skipworth Rd. E9 | 49 | 35 83 A |
| Skomer Wlk. N1 | 48 | 32 84 C |
| Sky Peals Rd. Wdf Gr | 26 | 38 90 D |
| Sladebrook Rd. SE3 | 77 | 41 75 B |
| Sladedale Rd. SE18 | 66 | 45 78 C |
| Slade Gdns. Eri | 80 | 51 76 B |
| Slade Green Rd. Eri | 68 | 52 77 C |
| Sladen Pl. E5 | 48 | 34 85 B |
| Slades Cl. Enf | 13 | 31 96 A |
| Slades Dri. Chis | 90 | 44 72 C |
| Slades Dri. SE9 | 90 | 44 71 A |
| Slades Gdns. Enf | 13 | 31 96 A |
| Slades Hill. Enf | 13 | 31 96 A |
| Slades Rise. Enf | 13 | 31 96 A |
| Slade The. SE18 | 66 | 44 77 A |
| Slade Wlk. SE17 | 63 | 32 77 A |
| Slagrove Pl. SE13 | 76 | 37 74 B |
| Slaidburn St. SW10 | 62 | 26 77 A |
| Slaithwaite Rd. SE13 | 76 | 38 75 C |
| Slaney Pl. N7 | 48 | 31 85 C |
| Sleaford St. SW8 | 10 | 29 77 C |
| Slewins Cl. Horn | 42 | 53 88 A |
| Slewins La. Horn | 42 | 53 88 A |
| Slindon Ct. N16 | 37 | 33 86 D |
| Slingsby Pl. WC2 | 7 | 30 80 A |
| Slippers Pl. SE16 | 63 | 34 79 D |
| Sloane Ave. SW3 | 9 | 27 78 A |
| Sloane Ct E. SW3 | 9 | 28 78 C |
| Sloane Ct W. SW3 | 9 | 28 78 C |
| Sloane Gdns. Orp | 108 | 44 65 C |
| Sloane Gdns. SW1 | 9 | 28 78 A |
| Sloane Sq. SW1 | 9 | 28 78 A |
| Sloane St. SW1 | 5 | 27 79 D |
| Sloane Terr. SW1 | 9 | 28 78 A |
| Sloane Wlk. Croy | 106 | 36 67 D |
| Slough La. NW9 | 34 | 20 88 C |
| Sly St. E1 | 57 | 34 81 D |
| Smallberry Ave. Islw | 71 | 15 76 D |
| Smallbrook Mews. W2 | 1 | 26 81 D |
| Smalley Cl. N16 | 37 | 33 86 D |
| Smallwood Rd. SW17 | 85 | 26 71 B |
| Smardale Rd. SW18 | 73 | 26 74 D |
| Smarden Cl. Belv | 67 | 49 78 C |
| Smarden Gr. SE9 | 89 | 42 71 B |
| Smart Cl. Rom | 30 | 52 90 B |
| Smart's Pl. N18 | 17 | 34 92 C |
| Smart's Pl. WC2 | 3 | 30 81 C |
| Smart St. E2 | 57 | 35 82 B |
| Smeaton Rd. SW18 | 85 | 25 73 A |
| Smedley St. SW8 | 74 | 29 76 D |
| Smeed Rd. E3 | 49 | 37 84 C |
| Smithfield St. EC1 | 3 | 31 81 B |
| Smith Hill. Brent | 60 | 18 77 A |
| Smithies Rd. SE2 | 66 | 46 78 B |
| Smith's Ct. W1 | 6 | 29 80 A |
| Smith's Ct. W1 | 6 | 29 80 B |
| Smithson Rd. N17 | 25 | 32 90 B |
| Smith Sq. SW1 | 7 | 30 79 C |
| Smith St. Surb | 101 | 18 67 D |
| Smith St. SW3 | 9 | 27 78 D |
| Smith's Yd. Croy | 105 | 32 65 C |
| Smith Terr. SW3 | 9 | 27 78 D |
| Smithwood Cl. SW19 | 85 | 24 72 A |
| Smithy St. E1 | 57 | 35 81 A |
| Smock Wlk. Croy | 105 | 32 67 C |
| Smoothfield. Houn | 70 | 13 75 C |
| Smyrk's Rd. SE17 | 63 | 33 78 C |
| Smyrna Rd. NW6 | 46 | 25 84 C |
| Smythe St. E14 | 57 | 37 80 B |
| Snakes La. Barn | 12 | 29 96 A |
| Snakes La. Wdf Gn | 27 | 40 91 B |
| Snaresbrook Rd. E11 | 27 | 39 89 D |
| Snarsgate St. W10 | 56 | 23 81 A |
| Sneath Ave. NW11 | 35 | 24 87 A |
| Snell's Park. N18 | 25 | 33 91 B |
| Sneyd Rd. NW2 | 46 | 23 85 A |
| Snowbury Rd. SW6 | 73 | 25 76 D |
| Snowbury Rd. SW6 | 73 | 25 76 D |
| Snowden St. EC2 | 4 | 33 82 C |
| Snowdon Ct. Rom | 30 | 53 89 C |
| Snowdrop Cl. Hamp | 92 | 13 70 A |
| Snowdrop Path. Rom | 30 | 53 91 D |
| Snowfields. SE1 | 8 | 32 79 B |
| Snow Hill. EC1 | 3 | 31 81 B |
| Snowshill Rd. E12 | 50 | 42 85 C |
| Soames St. SE15 | 75 | 33 75 B |
| Soames Wlk. N Mal | 94 | 21 69 A |
| Socket La. Brom | 107 | 40 67 D |
| Soho Sq. W1 | 2 | 29 81 D |
| Soho St. W1 | 2 | 29 81 D |
| Solebay St. E2 | 57 | 36 82 C |
| Solent Rd. NW6 | 46 | 25 85 C |
| Soley Mews. WC1 | 3 | 31 82 A |
| Solna Ave. SW15 | 73 | 23 74 A |
| Solna Rd. N21 | 17 | 32 94 B |
| Solomon's Pas. SE15 | 75 | 34 75 D |
| Solon New Rd. SW4 | 74 | 30 75 C |
| Solon Rd. SW2 | 74 | 30 75 C |
| Solway Cl. E8 | 48 | 33 84 B |
| Solway Cl. Houn | 70 | 12 75 A |
| Solway Rd. N22 | 25 | 31 90 B |
| Solway Rd. SE22 | 75 | 34 75 C |
| Somaford Gr. Barn | 11 | 26 95 D |
| Somali Rd. NW2 | 46 | 24 85 D |
| Somerby Rd. Bark | 51 | 44 84 D |
| Somerfield Rd. N4 | 37 | 31 86 B |
| Somerford Cl. Pnr | 19 | 10 89 C |
| Somerford Gr. N16 | 48 | 33 85 B |
| Somerford Gr. N17 | 25 | 34 91 C |
| Somerford Grove Estate. N16 | 48 | 33 85 B |
| Somerford St. E1 | 57 | 34 82 D |
| Somerhill Ave. Sid | 90 | 46 73 B |
| Somerhill Rd. Well | 78 | 46 76 D |
| Somerleyton Pas. SW9 | 75 | 31 75 D |
| Somerleyton Rd. SW9 | 75 | 31 75 C |
| Somersby Gdns. Ilf | 39 | 42 88 B |
| Somers Cl. NW1 | 47 | 29 83 D |
| Somers Cres. W2 | 1 | 27 81 C |
| Somerset Ave. SW20 | 94 | 22 69 D |
| Somerset Ave. Well | 78 | 45 75 D |
| Somerset Cl. Eps | 109 | 21 62 A |
| Somerset Cl. N.Mal | 102 | 21 67 C |
| Somerset Cl. Wdf Gn | 27 | 40 90 C |
| Somerset Estate. SW11 | 73 | 26 76 B |
| Somerset Estate. SW11 | 74 | 27 76 A |
| Somerset Gdns. N6 | 36 | 28 87 A |
| Somerset Gdns. SE13 | 76 | 37 76 D |
| Somerset Gdns. SW16 | 96 | 30 68 B |
| Somerset Gdns. Tedd | 83 | 15 71 C |
| Somerset Rd. Barn | 11 | 26 95 A |
| Somerset Rd. Brent | 60 | 17 77 B |
| Somerset Rd. Dart | 80 | 52 74 D |
| Somerset Rd. E17 | 38 | 37 88 C |
| Somerset Rd. Har | 32 | 14 88 A |
| Somerset Rd. King | 93 | 18 69 D |
| Somerset Rd. N17 | 25 | 33 89 B |
| Somerset Rd. N18 | 17 | 33 92 D |
| Somerset Rd. NW4 | 23 | 23 89 C |
| Somerset Rd. Orp | 108 | 46 66 A |
| Somerset Rd. SW19 | 85 | 23 72 D |
| Somerset Rd. Tedd | 83 | 15 71 C |
| Somerset Rd. W13 | 54 | 17 80 C |
| Somerset Rd. W4 | 61 | 20 79 D |
| Somerset Sq. W14 | 62 | 24 79 B |
| Somerset Waye. Houn | 59 | 12 77 C |
| Somersham Rd. Bexh | 79 | 48 76 C |
| Somers Pl. SW2 | 86 | 30 73 B |
| Somers Rd. E17 | 26 | 36 89 D |
| Somers Rd. SW2 | 74 | 30 74 D |
| Somers Town Estate. NW1 | 47 | 29 83 C |
| Somerton Ave. Rich | 72 | 19 75 B |
| Somerton Rd. NW2 | 35 | 24 86 C |
| Somerton Rd. SE15 | 75 | 34 75 D |
| Sometrees Ave. SE12 | 89 | 40 72 B |
| Somervell Rd. Har | 43 | 13 85 C |
| Somerville Rd. Dart | 80 | 54 74 D |
| Somerville Rd. Rom | 41 | 47 88 A |
| Somerville Rd. SE20 | 98 | 35 70 D |
| Sonderburg Rd. N7 | 36 | 30 86 D |
| Sondes St. SE17 | 63 | 32 77 B |
| Sonia Ct. Har | 33 | 15 88 D |
| Sonia Gdns. Houn | 59 | 13 77 C |
| Sonia Gdns. N12 | 15 | 26 92 A |
| Sonia Gdns. NW10 | 45 | 21 85 B |
| Sonning Rd. SE25 | 105 | 34 67 C |
| Sophia Cl. N7 | 47 | 30 84 B |
| Sophia Rd. E10 | 38 | 37 87 D |
| Sophia Rd. E16 | 58 | 40 81 D |
| Sopwith Rd. Houn | 59 | 11 77 C |
| Sorrel Wlk. Rom | 30 | 51 89 B |
| Sorrento Rd. Sutt | 103 | 25 65 D |
| Sotheby Rd. N5 | 37 | 32 86 C |
| Sotheran Cl. E8 | 48 | 34 83 A |
| Sotheron Rd. SW6 | 62 | 25 77 D |
| Soudan Rd. SW11 | 74 | 27 76 B |
| Souldern Rd. W14 | 62 | 23 79 D |
| Sounding's Alley. E3 | 49 | 37 83 A |
| South Access Rd. E17 | 38 | 36 88 C |
| South Acre. NW9 | 22 | 21 90 D |
| South Africa Rd. W12 | 55 | 22 80 B |
| Southall Ct. Sthl | 53 | 12 80 B |
| Southall La. Sthl | 59 | 11 78 A |
| Southall Pl. SE1 | 8 | 32 79 B |
| Southampton Bldgs. WC2 | 3 | 31 81 A |
| Southampton Gdns. Mit | 104 | 30 67 A |
| Southampton Pl. WC1 | 3 | 30 81 A |
| Southampton Rd. Houn | 69 | 07 74 C |
| Southampton Rd. NW5 | 47 | 27 85 D |
| Southampton Row. WC1 | 3 | 30 81 A |
| Southampton St. WC2 | 7 | 30 80 A |
| Southampton Way. SE5 | 75 | 33 76 B |
| Southampton Way. SE5 | 63 | 33 77 C |
| Southam St. W10 | 56 | 24 82 C |
| South Audley Sq. W1 | 6 | 28 80 C |
| South Ave. Cars | 111 | 28 63 C |
| South Ave. E4 | 18 | 37 94 B |
| South Ave. N2 | 23 | 25 89 D |
| South Avenue Gdns. Sthl | 53 | 12 80 B |
| South Ave. Rich | 72 | 19 76 C |
| South Ave. Sthl | 53 | 12 80 B |
| South Ave. W10 | 56 | 23 82 A |
| South Bank Lodge. Surb | 101 | 18 67 C |
| Southbank. Surb | 101 | 16 66 B |
| South Bank. Surb | 101 | 18 67 C |
| South Bank Terr. Surb | 101 | 18 67 C |
| South Birkbeck Rd. E11 | 38 | 38 86 D |
| South Black Lion La. W6 | 61 | 22 78 C |
| South Bolton Gdns. SW10 | 62 | 25 78 D |
| South Border The. Pur | 111 | 30 62 C |
| Southborough Cl. Surb | 101 | 17 66 D |
| Southborough La. Brom | 107 | 42 67 B |
| Southborough Rd. Brom | 99 | 42 68 C |
| Southborough Rd. E9 | 49 | 35 83 B |
| Southborough Rd. Surb | 101 | 18 66 C |
| South Boundary Rd. E12 | 39 | 42 86 D |
| Southbourne Ave. NW9 | 22 | 20 90 D |
| Southbourne. Brom | 107 | 40 66 A |
| Southbourne Cl. Pnr | 32 | 12 87 A |
| Southbourne Cres. NW4 | 23 | 24 89 C |
| Southbourne Gdns. Ilf | 51 | 44 85 C |
| Southbourne Gdns. Ruis | 31 | 10 86 D |
| Southbourne Gdns. Ruis | 32 | 11 87 C |
| Southbourne Gdns. SE12 | 77 | 40 74 B |
| Southbridge Pl. Croy | 112 | 32 64 A |
| Southbridge Rd. Croy | 112 | 32 64 A |
| Southbridge Way. Sthl | 59 | 12 79 A |
| Southbrook Rd. SE12 | 77 | 39 74 D |
| Southbrook Rd. SW16 | 96 | 30 69 A |
| Southbury Ave. Enf | 13 | 34 96 C |
| Southbury Rd. Enf | 13 | 33 96 D |
| South Carriage Dri. SW1 | 5 | 27 79 B |
| South Carriage Dri. SW7 | 5 | 27 79 A |
| Southchurch Rd. E6 | 50 | 42 83 D |
| South Cl. Barn | 11 | 24 96 B |
| South Cl. Bexh | 79 | 47 75 D |
| South Cl. Dag | 52 | 49 83 A |
| South Cl. Mord | 103 | 25 67 C |
| South Cl. N6 | 36 | 28 88 D |
| South Cl. Pnr | 20 | 11 90 B |
| South Cl. Pnr | 32 | 12 87 B |
| South Cl. Twick | 82 | 13 72 C |
| Southcombe St. W14 | 62 | 24 78 A |
| Southcote Ave. Felt | 81 | 10 72 A |
| Southcote Ave. Surb | 102 | 19 66 B |
| Southcote Rd. E17 | 38 | 35 88 B |
| Southcote Rd. N19 | 47 | 29 85 A |
| Southcote Rd. S Croy | 112 | 33 62 D |
| Southcote Rd. SE25 | 105 | 34 67 D |
| Southcote Rise. Ruis | 31 | 08 87 B |
| South Countess Rd. E17 | 26 | 36 89 B |
| South Cres. WC1 | 2 | 29 81 B |
| Southcroft Ave. Well | 78 | 45 75 A |
| Southcroft Ave. W Wick | 106 | 38 65 A |
| Southcroft Rd. Orp | 108 | 45 65 C |
| Southcroft Rd. SW17 | 96 | 28 70 A |
| South Cross Rd. Ilf | 28 | 44 89 C |
| South Croxted Rd. SE21 | 87 | 32 72 D |
| Southdale. Chig | 28 | 44 91 B |
| Southdean Gdns. SW19 | 85 | 24 72 B |
| Southdene Ct. N11 | 16 | 29 93 C |
| Southdown Ave. W7 | 60 | 16 78 A |
| Southdown Cres. Har | 32 | 14 87 C |
| Southdown Cres. Ilf | 40 | 45 88 A |
| Southdown Dri. SW20 | 95 | 23 70 D |
| Southdown Rd. Cars | 111 | 28 62 A |
| Southdown Rd. Horn | 42 | 52 87 B |
| Southdown Rd. SW20 | 95 | 23 69 B |
| South Dri. E12 | 39 | 42 86 D |
| South Dri. Rom | 30 | 53 89 A |
| South Dri. Ruis | 31 | 09 87 C |
| South Dri. Sutt | 110 | 24 62 A |
| South Ealing Rd. W5 | 60 | 17 79 D |
| South Eastern Ave. N9 | 17 | 33 93 D |
| South Eaton Pl. SW1 | 9 | 28 78 A |
| South Eden Park Rd. Beck | 106 | 37 67 B |
| South Edwardes Sq. W8 | 62 | 25 79 C |
| Southend Arterial Rd Horn | 30 | 54 89 B |
| Southend Arterial Rd. Rom | 30 | 53 90 D |
| South End Cl. NW3 | 47 | 27 85 A |
| Southend Cl. SE9 | 78 | 43 74 D |
| Southend Cres. SE9 | 78 | 43 74 D |
| South End. Croy | 112 | 32 64 A |
| South End Green. NW3 | 47 | 27 85 A |
| Southend La. SE26 | 88 | 36 71 B |
| Southend La. SE6 | 88 | 37 71 B |
| Southend Rd. Beck | 98 | 37 70 C |
| Southend Rd. E18 | 27 | 40 90 A |
| Southend Rd. E6 | 50 | 42 84 D |
| South End Rd. NW3 | 47 | 27 85 A |
| South End Row. W8 | 62 | 25 79 D |
| South End. W8 | 62 | 25 79 D |
| Southern Ave. Felt | 81 | 10 73 C |
| Southern Ave. SE25 | 97 | 33 68 B |

Southern Gr. E3 57 36 82 D
Southern Perimeter Rd. Houn 69 08 74 A
Southern Rd. E13 50 40 83 D
Southern Rd. N2 24 27 89 D
Southern Row. W10 56 24 82 C
Southern St. N1 47 30 83 D
Southern Way. Rom 41 49 88 C
Southern Way. Rom 41 49 88 C
Southerton Rd. W6 62 23 78 A
South Esk Rd. E7 50 41 84 A
Southey Rd. N15 37 33 88 A
Southey Rd. SW19 95 25 70 C
Southey Rd. SW9 75 31 76 A
Southey St. SE20 98 35 70 D
Southfield. Barn 11 23 95 D
Southfield Cottages. W7 60 15 79 B
Southfield Gdns. Twick 83 15 71 B
Southfield Park. Har 20 13 89 D
Southfield Rd. Chis 100 46 68 A
Southfield Rd. Enf 14 35 95 C
Southfield Rd. W4 61 20 79 B
Southfield Rd. W4 61 21 79 C
Southfields Ave. Ashf 91 07 70 B
Southfields. E Mol 101 15 67 C
Southfields. NW4 22 22 89 B
Southfields Rd. SW18 73 25 74 C
Southfields. Sutt 103 25 65 A
Southfleet Rd. Orp 108 45 65 C
South Gate Ave. Felt 81 08 71 B
Southgate Gr. N1 48 32 84 D
Southgate Rd. N1 48 32 84 D
Southgate Way. N2 24 27 90 A
South Gdns. SW19 95 26 70 D
South Gr. E17 38 36 88 B
South Gr. N15 37 32 88 B
South Gr. N6 36 28 87 C
South Hill Ave. Har 32 14 86 D
South Hill. Chis 99 42 70 B
South Hill Gr. Har 44 15 85 A
South Hill Park. NW3 47 27 85 A
South Hill Rd. Brom 99 39 68 C
Southill La. Pnr 19 10 89 D
Southill Rd. Chis 99 42 70 D
South Island Pl. SW9 63 31 77 C
South La. King 93 17 68 B
South Lambeth Pl. SW8 10 30 77 A
South Lambeth Rd. SW8 10 30 77 C
Southland Rd. SE18 66 45 77 D
Southlands Gr. Brom 99 42 68 A
Southlands Rd. Brom 99 41 68 D
Southland Way. Houn 70 14 74 B
South Lane W. N Mal 94 20 68 D
South La. N.Mal 102 21 66 A
South Lodge Ave. 96 30 68 C
South Lodge Cres. Enf 12 29 96 D
South Lodge Dri. N14 12 29 95 B
South Mall. N9 17 34 93 C
South Mead. Eps 109 21 63 D
South Mead. NW9 22 21 90 B
Southmead Rd. SW19 85 24 73 C
South Molton La. W1 2 28 81 D
South Molton Rd. E16 58 40 81 C
South Molton St. W1 2 28 81 D
Southmont Rd. Esh 101 15 65 C
Southmoor Way. E9 49 36 85 D
South Norwood Hill. SE25 97 33 68 B
Southold Rise. SE9 90 43 72 C
Southolm St. SW11 74 28 76 B
Southover. Brom 99 40 70 A
Southover. Brom 89 40 71 C
Southover. N12 15 25 92 A
South Parade. SW3 62 26 78 D
South Park Cres. Ilf 40 45 86 C
South Park Cres. SE6 89 39 73 D
South Park Dri. Bark 51 45 85 C
South Park Dri. Ilf 40 45 86 C
South Park Gr. N Mal 94 20 68 C
South Park Hill Rd. S Croy 112 32 64 B
South Park Rd. Ilf 40 44 86 D
South Park Rd. SW19 95 25 70 A
South Park Terr. Ilf 40 45 86 C
South Park Way. Ruis 43 11 85 C
South Par. W4 61 20 78 B
South Pl. EC2 4 32 81 B
South Pl Mews. EC2 4 32 81 B
South Pl. Surb 101 18 66 B
Southport Rd. SE18 66 44 78 B
South Rd. Edg 22 19 90 B
South Rd. Eri 68 51 77 D
South Rd. Felt 82 11 71 C
South Rd. Hamp 92 12 70 B
South Rd. N9 17 34 94 C
South Rd. Rom 41 47 88 A
South Rd. Rom 41 48 88 C
South Rd. SE23 88 35 72 B
South Rd. Sthl 53 12 80 D
South Rd. SW19 95 26 70 A
South Rd. Twick 82 14 72 D
South Rd. W5 60 17 78 B
South Rise. Cars 111 27 62 A
South Row. SE3 77 39 76 D
Southsea Rd. King 93 18 68 C
Southside Common. SW19 95 23 70 B
South Side. W6 61 21 79 D
Southspring. Sid 90 44 73 B
South Sq. NW11 35 25 88 D
South Sq. WC1 3 31 81 A
South St. Brom 99 40 69 C
South St. Enf 14 35 95 B
South St. Islw 71 16 75 A
South St. Rain 52 50 83 D
South St. Rom 42 51 88 C
South St. W1 6 28 80 C
South Tenter St. EC4 8 33 80 B
South Terr. N22 24 29 90 D
South Terr. Surb 101 18 67 C
South Terr. SW7 9 27 78 A
South Vale. Har 44 15 85 A
Southvale Rd. SE3 77 39 76 C
South Vale. SE19 97 33 70 A
Southview Ave. NW10 45 21 85 D
South View. Brom 99 41 69 C
South View Cl. Bex 79 48 74 D
South View Cres. Ilf 40 43 88 D
Southview Dri. E18 27 40 89 B
Southview Gdns. Wall 111 29 63 C
Southview Rd. Brom 88 38 71 B
South View Rd. N8 24 30 89 A
South View Rd. Pnr 19 10 91 B
South Villas. NW1 47 29 84 B
Southville Cl. Eps 109 20 62 B
Southville Cl. Felt 81 09 73 C
Southville Cres. Felt 81 09 73 C
Southville Rd. Felt 81 09 73 C
Southville Rd. Surb 101 16 66 B
Southville. SW8 74 29 76 B
Southwark Bridge. EC4 8 32 80 A
Southwark Bridge Rd. SE1 8 32 79 A
Southwark Park Rd. SE16 63 34 78 A
Southwark Pl. Brom 99 42 68 B
Southwark St. SE1 8 32 80 C
Southwater Cl. E14 57 36 81 D
Southway. Brom 107 40 66 A
Southway. Cars 110 26 62 D
Southway Cl. W12 61 22 79 B
South Way. Croy 106 36 65 C
South Way. Har 20 13 89 C
South Way. N11 24 29 91 A
Southway. N20 15 25 93 A
South Way. N9 18 35 93 A
Southway. NW11 35 25 88 B
Southway. SW20 95 23 68 D
Southway. Wall 111 29 64 A
South Way. Wem 45 19 85 D
Southwell Ave. Nthlt 43 13 84 A
Southwell Gdns. SW7 62 26 78 A
Southwell Grove Rd. E11 39 39 86 A
Southwell Rd. Har 33 17 88 D
Southwell Rd. SE5 75 32 75 A
Southwell Rd. Th Hth 105 31 67 C
South Western Rd. Twick 71 16 74 D
South West India Dock Entrance. E14 64 38 79 A
Southwest Rd. E11 38 38 87 D
South Wharf Rd. W2 1 26 81 D
Southwick Mews. W2 1 26 81 D
Southwick Pl. W2 1 27 81 C
Southwick St. W2 1 27 81 C
South Wlk. W.Wick 107 39 65 C
Southwold Dri. Bark 51 46 85 C
Southwold Rd. Bex 79 49 74 D
Southwold Rd. E5 38 35 86 A
Southwood Ave. King 94 20 69 A
Southwood Ave. N6 36 28 87 B
Southwood Cl. Brom 99 42 68 D
Southwood Cl. Wor Pk 103 23 66 D
Southwood Dri. Surb 102 20 66 C
Southwood Gdns. Esh 101 16 65 C
Southwood Gdns. Ilf 28 43 89 D
Southwood La. N6 36 28 87 A
Southwood Lawn Rd. N6 36 28 87 B
Southwood Park. N6 36 28 87 A
Southwood Rd. SE9 90 43 72 B
South Worple Ave. SW14 72 21 75 A
South Worple Way. SW14 72 20 75 B
South Yd. EC2 4 32 81 B
Sovereign Cl. Ruis 31 09 87 C
Sovereign Cl. W5 54 17 81 A
Sowerby Cl. SE9 77 42 74 B
Space Waye. Felt 69 10 74 A
Spa Cl. SE25 97 33 69 A
Spafield St. EC1 3 31 82 C
Spa Hill. SE19 97 32 69 B
Spalding Rd. NW4 35 23 87 A
Spalding Rd. SW17 86 28 71 D
Spanby Rd. E3 57 37 82 C
Spaniards Cl. NW11 35 26 87 D
Spaniards End. NW3 35 26 87 D
Spaniard's Rd. NW3 35 26 86 A
Spanish Pl. W1 2 28 81 C
Spanish Rd. SW18 73 26 74 A
Spa Rd. SE16 8 33 79 D
Spa Rd. SE16 8 33 79 D
Sparkbridge Rd. Har 21 15 89 C
Sparks Cl. Hamp 92 12 70 A
Sparrow Dri. Orp 108 44 66 D
Sparrow Farm Dri. Felt 82 11 73 B
Sparrow Farm Rd. Eps 109 22 64 B
Sparrow Green. Dag 41 49 86 D
Sparrows La. SE9 90 44 73 C
Sparsholt Rd. Bark 51 45 83 A
Sparsholt Rd. N19 36 30 87 D
Sparta St. SE10 76 38 76 A
Spearman St. SE18 66 43 77 A
Spear Mews. SW5 62 25 78 A
Spears Rd. N19 36 30 87 C
Speart La. Houn 59 12 77 C
Spedan Cl. NW3 35 26 86 C
Speedwell St. SE8 64 37 77 C
Speedy Pl. WC1 3 30 82 A
Speer Rd. Surb 101 15 67 D
Speirs Cl. N.Mal 102 21 67 D
Spekehill SE9 89 42 72 D
Speke Rd. Th Hth 97 32 69 D
Speldhurst Cl. Brom 107 39 67 B
Speldhurst Rd. E9 49 35 84 D
Speldhurst Rd. W4 61 20 79 D
Spellbrook Wlk (off Basire St). N1 48 32 83 A
Spelman St. E1 57 34 81 A
Spelthorne Gr. Sun 91 09 70 D
Spelthorne La. Ashf 91 08 70 C
Spencer Ave. N13 24 30 91 B
Spencer Cl. NW10 54 18 82 B
Spencer Cl. Orp 108 45 65 B
Spencer Dri. N2 35 26 88 C
Spencer Gdns. SW14 72 20 74 A
Spencer Hill Rd. SW19 95 24 70 C
Spencer Hill. SW19 95 24 70 B
Spencer Mews. W6 62 24 77 A
Spencer Park. SW18 73 26 74 B
Spencer Pas. E2 48 34 83 D
Spencer Pl. Croy 105 32 66 B
Spencer Rd. Brom 99 39 70 D
Spencer Rd. E17 26 38 90 C
Spencer Rd. E6 50 41 83 B
Spencer Rd. E Mol 92 14 68 C
Spencer Rd. Har 21 15 90 C
Spencer Rd. Ilf 40 45 87 D
Spencer Rd. Islw 70 14 76 A
Spencer Rd. Mit 104 28 66 A
Spencer Rd. Mit 96 28 68 A
Spencer Rd. N11 16 28 92 B
Spencer Rd. N17 25 34 90 A
Spencer Rd. N8 36 30 88 B
Spencer Rd. Rain 52 50 83 D
Spencer Rd. S Croy 112 33 64 C
Spencer Rd. SW18 73 26 74 B
Spencer Rd. SW20 94 22 69 B
Spencer Rd. Twick 83 15 72 A
Spencer Rd. W3 55 20 80 C
Spencer Rd. W4 61 20 77 C
Spencer Rd. Wem 33 17 86 A
Spencer Rise. NW5 36 28 86 D
Spencer St. EC1 3 31 82 B
Spencer St. Sthl 59 11 79 B
Spencer Wlk. SW15 73 23 75 D
Spenser Gr. N16 48 33 85 A
Spenser Rd. SE24 75 31 74 B
Spenser St. SW1 6 29 79 C
Spensley Wlk. N16 37 32 86 D
Speranza St. SE18 66 45 78 D
Sperling Rd. N17 25 33 90 D
Spert St. E14 57 36 80 A
Speyside. N14 12 29 95 C
Spey St. E14 58 38 81 A
Spey Way. Rom 30 51 91 C
Spezia Rd. NW10 45 22 83 C
Spicer Cl. SE5 75 31 76 D
Spices Yd. Croy 112 32 64 A
Spielman Rd. Dart 80 54 75 D
Spigurnell Rd. N17 25 32 90 B
Spikes Bridge Rd. Sthl 53 12 80 A
Spilsby Cl. NW9 22 21 90 C
Spilsby Rd. Rom 30 54 91 C
Spindlewood Gdns. Croy 112 33 64 A
Spinel Cl. SE18 66 45 78 D
Spingfield Mount. NW9 34 21 88 A
Spinnells Rd. Har 32 12 87 D
Spinney Cl. N.Mal 102 21 67 A
Spinney Dri. Felt 81 08 73 A
Spinney Gdns. Dag 52 48 85 C
Spinney Oak. Brom 99 42 69 C
Spinneys The. Brom 99 42 69 D
Spinney The. Barn 11 25 97 D
Spinney The. N21 17 31 94 A
Spinney The. Sun 91 10 69 A
Spinney The. Sutt 110 23 64 A
Spinney The. SW16 86 29 72 D
Spinney The. Wem 33 16 86 C
Spital Sq. E1 4 33 81 A
Spital St. Dart 80 53 74 D
Spital St. E1 57 34 82 C
Spital Yd. E1 4 33 81 A
Spitfire Way. Houn 59 11 78 C
Spode Wlk. NW6 46 25 85 D
Spondon Rd. N15 25 34 89 C
Spooner's Mews. W3 55 20 80 D
Spooner Wlk. Wall 111 29 64 D
Sportsbank St. SE6 88 38 73 A
Spottons Gr. N17 25 32 90 C
Spratt Hall Rd. E11 39 40 88 C
Spray St. SE18 66 43 78 B
Spreighton Rd. E Mol 92 13 68 D
Sprimont Pl. SW3 9 27 78 D
Springall St. SE15 63 34 77 D
Springbank. N21 12 30 95 D
Springbank Rd. SE13 77 39 74 C
Springbank Wlk. N7 47 29 84 D
Springbourne Ct. Beck 98 38 69 A
Spring Bridge Rd.W5 54 17 80 B
Springclose La. Sutt 110 24 63 A
Spring Cottages. Surb 101 17 67 B
Springcroft Ave. N2 24 27 89 D
Spring Ct. Eps 109 21 62 B
Springdale Rd. N16 48 32 85 B
Spring Dri. Pnr 31 10 88 C
Springfield Ave. Hamp 92 13 70 B
Springfield Ave. N10 24 29 89 A
Springfield Ave. SW20 95 24 68 B
Springfield Cl. N12 15 25 92 D
Springfield Ct. King 93 18 68 A
Springfield Dri. Ilf 40 44 88 C
Springfield. E5 37 34 87 D
Springfield Gdns. Brom 99 42 68 D
Springfield Gdns. E5 37 34 87 D
Springfield Gdns. NW9 34 20 88 B
Springfield Gdns. Ruis 31 10 86 D
Springfield Gdns. Wdf Gn 27 41 91 C
Springfield Gdns. W Wick 106 37 65 B
Springfield Gr. SE7 65 41 77 A
Springfield Gr. Sun 91 10 69 A
Springfield La. NW6 46 25 83 B
Springfield Rd. Bexh 79 49 75 D
Springfield Rd. Brom 99 42 68 D
Springfield Rd. E15 58 39 82 A
Springfield Rd. E17 38 36 88 D
Springfield Rd. E6 50 42 84 D
Springfield Rd. Eps 110 23 62 C
Springfield Rd. Har 33 15 88 C
Springfield Rd. Hay 53 11 80 C
Springfield Rd. King 93 18 68 A
Springfield Rd. N11 16 29 92 C
Springfield Rd. N15 25 34 89 C
Springfield Rd. NW8 46 26 83 A
Springfield Rd. SE26 87 34 71 D
Springfield Rd. SW19 85 25 71 C
Springfield Rd. Tedd 83 16 71 C
Springfield Rd. Th Hth 97 32 69 A
Springfield Rd. Twick 82 13 73 C
Springfield Rd. W7 54 15 80 C
Springfield Rd. Il 111 28 64 D
Springfield Rd. Well 78 46 75 B
Springfield Rise. SE26 87 34 72 D
Springfield Wlk (off Andover Rd). Orp 108 44 66 D
Springfield Wlk. NW6 46 25 83 B
Spring Gdns. E Mol 92 14 68 C
Spring Gdns. N5 48 32 85 C
Spring Gdns. Rom 41 50 88 C
Spring Gdns. SW1 6 29 80 D
Spring Gdns. Wall 111 29 64 C
Spring Gdns. Wdf Gn 27 41 91 C
Spring Gr. Hamp 92 13 69 B
Spring Grove Cres. Houn 70 14 76 A
Spring Grove Rd. Houn 70 14 76 A
Spring Grove Rd. Islw 70 14 76 B
Spring Grove Rd. Rich 71 18 74 B
Spring Gr. W4 61 19 77 A
Springhead Rd. Eri 68 51 77 B
Springhill Cl. SE5 75 32 75 B
Spring Hill. E5 37 34 87 A
Spring Hill. SE26 88 35 71 A
Spring La. Croy 105 34 67 D
Spring La. E5 37 34 87 D
Spring La. SE25 105 34 67 D
Spring Mews. W1 1 27 81 B
Spring Park Ave. Croy 106 35 65 B
Springpark Dri. Beck 98 38 68 A
Springpark Dri. N4 37 32 87 C
Spring Park Rd. Croy 106 35 65 B
Spring Pas. SW15 73 23 75 B
Spring Path. NW3 46 26 85 D
Spring Pl. NW5 47 28 85 D
Springpond Rd. Dag 52 48 85 C
Spring Rd. Felt 81 09 72 D
Springrice Rd. SE13 76 38 74 D
Spring St. Eps 109 21 62 B
Spring St. W2 1 26 81 D
Spring Val. Bexh 79 49 75 D
Springvale Ave. Brent 60 18 78 C
Spring Vale. Dart 80 53 74 D
Spring Vale Terr. W14 62 23 79 D
Spring Villa Rd. Edg 22 19 91 C
Springwater Cl. SE18 78 43 76 A
Springway. Har 32 14 87 B
Springwell Ave. NW10 45 22 83 A
Springwell Cl. SW16 87 31 71 A
Springwell Rd. Houn 70 11 76 B
Springwell Rd. SW16 87 31 71 A
Spring Wlk. E1 57 34 81 A
Springwood Way. Rom 42 52 88 A
Sprowston Mews. E7 50 40 85 C
Sprowston Rd. E7 50 40 85 C
Sprucedale Gdns. Wall 111 30 62 A
Spruce Hills Rd. E17 26 38 90 C
Sprules Rd. SE4 76 36 76 C
Spurfield. E Mol 92 13 68 B
Spurgeon Ave. SE19 97 32 69 B
Spurgeon Rd. SE19 97 32 70 D
Spurgeon St. SE1 8 32 79 D
Spurling Rd. Dag 52 48 84 B
Spurling Rd. SE22 75 33 75 D
Spur Rd. Bark 51 44 83 C
Spur Rd. Felt 69 10 75 D
Spur Rd. Islw 60 16 77 D
Spur Rd. N15 25 32 89 D
Spur Rd. Orp 108 46 65 A
Spurstowe Rd. E8 48 34 84 B
Spurstowe Terr. E8 48 34 85 D
Square The. Cars 111 28 64 C
Square The. Ilf 40 43 87 A
Square The. Rich 71 17 74 B
Square The. W6 62 23 78 C
Squarey St. SW17 85 26 72 C
Squire's Bridge Rd. Shep 91 07 68 A
Squires La. N3 23 26 90 A
Squire's Mount. NW3 35 26 86 D
Squire's Rd. Shep 91 07 68 C
Squires Wood Dri. Chis 99 42 70 D
Squirrel Cl. Houn 70 11 75 A
Squirrels Cl. N12 15 26 92 A
Squirrels Green. Wor Pk 102 22 65 A
Squirrel's Heath Ave. Rom 30 52 89 B
Squirrels Heath La. Horn 30 53 89 D
Squirrels Heath La. Rom 30 53 89 C
Squirrels Heath Rd. Rom 30 54 90 D
Squirrels The. Pnr 20 12 89 B
Squirrel's The. SE13 76 38 75 B
Squirries St. E2 57 34 82 A
Stable Cl. Nthlt 43 13 83 C
Stables End. Orp 108 44 65 C
Stables Way. SE11 63 31 78 C
Stable Way. W10 56 23 81 D
Stable Way. W12 56 23 81 C
Stable Wlk. N2 23 26 90 B
Stable Yd Rd. SW1 6 29 79 A
Stacey Ave. N18 18 35 92 A
Stacey Cl. E10 38 38 88 B
Stacey St. WC2 2 29 81 D
Stackhouse St. SW1 5 27 79 D
Stacy Path. SE5 63 33 77 C
Staddon Ct. Beck 98 36 68 C
Stadium Rd. Dart 80 51 74 B
Stadium Rd. SE18 65 42 77 C
Stadium St. SW10 62 26 77 C
Stadium Way. Wem 45 19 85 A
Staffa Rd. E10 38 36 87 C
Stafford Ave. Horn 30 53 89 B
Stafford Cl. N14 12 29 95 A
Stafford Cl. NW6 56 25 82 A
Stafford Cl. Sutt 110 24 63 A
Stafford Cripps House. SW6 62 24 77 B
Stafford Gdns. Croy 111 30 64 D
Stafford Pl. Rich 83 18 73 B
Stafford Pl. SW1 6 29 79 C
Stafford Rd. Croy 111 30 64 D
Stafford Rd. E3 49 36 83 D
Stafford Rd. E7 50 41 84 B
Stafford Rd. Har 20 14 91 C
Stafford Rd. N Mal 94 20 68 A
Stafford Rd. NW6 56 25 82 A
Stafford Rd. Sid 90 45 71 A
Stafford Rd. Wall 111 29 63 B
Staffordshire St. SE15 75 34 76 A
Stafford St. W1 6 29 80 C
Stafford Terr. W8 62 25 79 A
Stafford Wlk. Rich 71 18 76 A
Staff St. EC1 4 32 82 B
Stag Cl. Edg 22 19 90 D
Staggart Green. Chig 28 46 91 A
Stag La. Edg 22 19 90 D
Stag La. NW9 22 20 89 A
Stag La. SW15 84 21 72 B
Stag Pl. SW1 6 29 79 C
Stag Ride. SW19 84 22 72 C
Stainbank Rd. Mit 96 28 68 B
Stainby Rd. N15 25 33 89 D
Stainer St. SE1 8 32 80 D
Staines Ave. Sutt 103 24 65 A
Staines Rd. Felt 81 09 73 A
Staines Rd. Houn 70 12 75 C
Staines Rd. Ilf 51 44 85 B
Staines Rd. Twick 82 14 72 C
Staines Road E. Sun 92 11 69 D
Staines Road W. Ashf 91 08 70 C
Staines Road W. Sun 91 09 70 D
Stainford Cl. Ashf 81 08 71 D
Stainforth Rd. E17 26 37 89 C
Stainforth Rd. Ilf 40 44 88 D
Staining La. EC2 4 32 81 C
Stainmore Cl. Chis 100 44 69 B
Stainsbury St. E2 49 35 83 C
Stainsby Pl. E14 57 37 81 C
Stainsby Rd. E14 57 37 81 C
Stainton Rd. Enf 14 35 97 A
Stainton Rd. SE6 88 38 73 B
Stainton Rd. SE6 76 38 74 D
Stalbridge St. NW1 1 27 81 A
Stalham St. SE16 63 34 79 D
Stambourne Way. SE19 97 33 70 D
Stambourne Way. W Wick 106 38 65 C
Stamford Brook Ave. W6 61 21 78 B
Stamford Brook Gdns. W6 61 21 79 D
Stamford Brook Rd. W6 61 21 79 D
Stamford Cl. Har 21 15 91 C
Stamford Cl. N15 25 34 89 C
Stamford Cl. NW3 35 26 86 C
Stamford Cl. Sthl 53 13 80 A
Stamford Ct. W6 61 21 78 B
Stamford Dri. Brom 99 39 68 D
Stamford Gdns. Dag 52 47 84 C
Stamford Grove E. N16 37 34 87 C
Stamford Grove W. N16 37 34 87 C
Stamford Hill. N16 37 33 87 D
Stamford Rd. Dag 52 47 84 C
Stamford Rd. E6 50 42 83 A
Stamford Rd. N15 37 34 88 A
Stamford Rd. N1 48 33 84 A
Stamford St. SE1 7 31 80 C
Stamp Pl. E2 48 33 83 D
Stanard Cl. N16 37 33 87 A
Stanborough Cl. Hamp 92 12 70 B
Stanborough Pas. E8 48 33 84 B
Stanborough Rd. Islw 70 14 75 B
Stanbridge Rd. SW15 73 23 75 A
Stanbrook Ct. W1 6 29 80 C
Stanbrook Rd. SE2 66 46 79 B
Stanbury Ct. NW3 47 27 84 B
Stanbury Rd. SE15 75 34 76 D
Stanbury Rd. SE15 76 35 76 C
Stancroft. NW9 34 21 88 A
Standale Gr. Ruis 31 08 88 A
Standard Pl. EC2 4 33 82 A
Standard Rd. Belv 67 49 78 C
Standard Rd. Bexh 79 48 75 C
Standard Rd. Houn 70 12 75 A
Standard Rd. NW10 55 20 82 D
Standen Ave. Horn 42 54 86 C
Standfield Gdns. Dag 52 49 84 A
Standfield Rd. Dag 52 49 85 C
Standish Rd. W6 61 22 78 A
Stane Cl. SW19 95 25 70 D
Stane Way. Eps 109 22 62 C
Stane Way. SE18 65 42 77 C
Stanfield Rd. E3 49 36 83 C
Stanford Cl. Hamp 92 12 70 B
Stanford Cl. Rom 41 49 88 D
Stanford Cl. Ruis 31 08 88 C
Stanford Cl. Wdf Gn 27 42 91 A

Stanford Pl. SE17 63 33 78 A
Stanford Rd. N11 16 27 92 D
Stanford Rd. SW16 96 30 69 C
Stanford Rd. W8 62 25 79 D
Stanford Way. SW16 96 29 69 D
Stanger Rd. SE25 97 34 68 C
Stanham Pl. Dart 80 52 75 C
Stanham Rd. Dart 80 53 74 A
Stanhope Ave. Brom 107 40 66 C
Stanhope Ave. Har 20 14 90 B
Stanhope Ave. N3 23 24 89 B
Stanhope Gate. W1 6 28 80 C
Stanhope Gdns. Dag 41 48 86 D
Stanhope Gdns. Ilf 39 42 87 D
Stanhope Gdns. N4 37 32 88 C
Stanhope Gdns. N6 36 29 88 C
Stanhope Gdns. SW7 62 26 78 A
Stanhope Gr. Beck 98 36 68 D
Stanhope Mews E. SW7 62 26 78 A
Stanhope Mews S. SW7 62 26 78 A
Stanhope Mews W. SW7 62 26 78 A
Stanhope Park Rd. Grnf 53 14 82 C
Stanhope Pl. W2 5 27 80 B
Stanhope Rd. Barn 11 23 95 D
Stanhope Rd. Bexh 79 48 76 C
Stanhope Rd. Cars 111 28 63 C
Stanhope Rd. Croy 105 33 65 C
Stanhope Rd. Dag 41 48 86 D
Stanhope Rd. E17 38 37 88 B
Stanhope Rd. Grnf 53 14 81 A
Stanhope Rd. N12 15 26 92 C
Stanhope Rd. N6 36 29 87 A
Stanhope Rd. Sid 90 46 71 A
Stanhope Row. W1 6 28 80 D
Stanhope St. NW1 2 29 82 A
Stanhope Terr. W2 5 26 80 B
Stanier Cl. SW5 62 24 78 D
Stanlake Mews. W12 56 23 80 C
Stanlake Rd. W12 56 23 80 C
Stanlake Villas. W12 56 23 80 C
Stanley Ave. Bark 51 45 83 D
Stanley Ave. Beck 98 38 68 A
Stanley Ave. Dag 41 48 87 B
Stanley Ave. Grnf 43 14 83 A
Stanley Ave. N.Mal 102 22 67 A
Stanley Ave. Rom 30 52 89 C
Stanley Ave. Wem 44 18 84 C
Stanley Cl. Horn 42 53 86 A
Stanley Cl. Rom 30 52 89 C
Stanley Cl. SW8 10 30 77 B
Stanley Cl. Wem 44 18 84 C
Stanley Cres. W11 56 24 80 B
Stanleycroft Cl. Islw 71 15 76 A
Stanley Ct. Sutt 110 25 63 D
Stanley Ct. W5 54 17 81 A
Stanley Gardens Rd. Tedd 83 15 71 C
Stanley Gdns. Mit 96 28 70 A
Stanley Gdns. NW2 46 23 85 C
Stanley Gdns. W11 56 24 80 B
Stanley Gdns. W3 61 21 79 A
Stanley Gdns. Wall 111 29 63 A
Stanley Gr. Croy 105 31 67 C
Stanley Gr. SW8 74 28 76 C
Stanley Park Dri. Wem 44 18 83 B
Stanley Park Rd. Cars 111 27 63 D
Stanley Park Rd. Wall 111 28 63 B
Stanley Park Rd. Wall 111 28 63 B
Stanley Pas. NW1 47 30 83 C
Stanley Rd. Brom 99 41 68 C
Stanley Rd. Cars 111 28 63 C
Stanley Rd. Croy 105 31 67 C
Stanley Rd. E10 38 37 88 D
Stanley Rd. E12 50 42 85 C
Stanley Rd. E15 49 38 83 B
Stanley Rd. E18 27 39 90 B
Stanley Rd. E4 18 38 94 D
Stanley Rd. Enf 13 33 96 A
Stanley Rd. Har 32 14 86 A
Stanley Rd. Horn 42 53 86 B
Stanley Rd. Houn 70 14 75 C
Stanley Rd. Ilf 40 44 86 B
Stanley Rd. Mit 96 28 70 C
Stanley Rd. Mord 95 25 68 C
Stanley Rd. N10 24 28 91 D
Stanley Rd. N11 16 29 92 D
Stanley Rd. N15 25 31 89 D
Stanley Rd. N2 23 26 89 B
Stanley Rd. N9 17 33 93 B
Stanley Rd. Nthwd 19 10 90 A
Stanley Rd. NW9 34 22 87 A
Stanley Rd. Orp 108 45 66 D
Stanley Rd. Sid 90 46 72 C
Stanley Rd. Sthl 53 12 80 A
Stanley Rd. Sutt 110 25 63 D
Stanley Rd. SW14 72 19 75 D
Stanley Rd. SW19 95 25 70 A
Stanley Rd. Tedd 83 15 71 C
Stanley Rd. Twick 82 14 72 D
Stanley Rd. W3 61 20 79 C
Stanley Rd. Wem 44 18 84 B
Stanley Sq. Cars 111 27 62 B
Stanley St. SE8 64 36 77 D
Stanley Terr. N19 36 30 86 A
Stanley Way. Orp 108 46 67 B
Stanmer St. SW11 74 27 76 C
Stanmore Gdns. Rich 71 18 75 B
Stanmore Gdns. Sutt 103 26 65 C
Stanmore Pl. NW1 47 28 83 B
Stanmore Rd. Belv 67 50 78 A
Stanmore Rd. E11 39 39 87 D
Stanmore Rd. N15 25 31 89 D
Stanmore Rd. Rich 71 18 75 B
Stanmore St. N1 47 30 83 B
Stanmore Terr. Beck 98 37 69 C
Stannard Rd. E8 48 34 84 A
Stannary Pl. SE11 63 31 78 C
Stannary St. SE11 63 31 78 C
Stansden Rd. SW18 85 25 73 A
Stansfeld Hse. SE1 63 33 78 B
Stansfeld Rd. E16 58 41 81 B
Stansfield Rd. Houn 69 10 76 D
Stansfield Rd. SW9 74 30 75 B
Stansgate Rd. Dag 41 49 86 C
Stanstead Cl. Brom 107 39 67 D
Stanstead Gr. SE6 88 36 73 D
Stanstead Manor. Sutt 110 25 63 A
Stanstead Rd. E11 39 40 88 B
Stanstead Rd. SE23 88 36 73 C
Stanstead Rd. SE6 88 36 73 D
Stanswood Gdns. SE5 63 33 77 C
Stanthorpe Cl. SW16 86 30 71 C
Stanthorpe Rd. SW16 86 30 71 A
Stanton Ave. Tedd 93 15 70 A
Stanton Ave. Tedd 83 15 71 C
Stanton Cl. Eps 109 19 64 D
Stanton Cl. Wor Pk 103 23 66 D
Stanton Rd. Croy 105 32 66 A
Stanton Rd. SW20 95 23 69 B
Stanton St. SE15 75 34 76 A
Stanton. SW13 72 21 76 D
Stanton Way. SE26 88 36 71 B
Stanway Gdns. Edg 22 20 91 A
Stanway Gdns. W3 55 19 80 C
Stanway St. N1 48 33 83 C
Stanwell Rd. Felt 81 07 73 B
Stanwick Rd. W14 62 24 78 B
Stapenhill Rd. Wem 33 16 86 D
Staplefield Cl. Pnr 20 12 91 C
Staplefield Cl. SW2 86 30 73 C
Stapleford Ave. Ilf 40 45 88 A
Stapleford Cl. King 94 19 68 A
Stapleford Cl. SW19 85 24 73 A
Stapleford Gdns. Rom 29 49 91 A
Stapleford Rd. Wem 44 17 84 D
Staplehurst Rd. Cars 111 27 63 C
Staplehurst Rd. SE13 77 39 74 A
Staple Inn Bldgs. WC2 3 31 81 A
Staples Cl. SE16 57 36 80 C
Staple St. SE1 8 32 79 B
Stapleton Gdns. Croy 112 31 64 C
Stapleton Hall Rd. N4 36 30 87 B
Stapleton Rd. Bexh 67 48 77 D
Stapleton Rd. Orp 108 45 65 D
Stapleton Rd. SW17 86 28 72 C
Stapley Rd. Belv 67 49 78 C
Stapylton Rd. Barn 11 24 96 A
Star Alley. EC3 8 33 80 A
Starboard Way. E14 64 37 79 C
Starch House La. Ilf 28 44 90 D
Starcross St. NW1 2 29 82 A
Starfield Rd. W12 61 22 79 A
Star & Garter Hill. Rich 83 18 73 A
Star Hill. Dart 80 51 74 A
Starkleigh Way. SE16 63 34 78 C
Star La. E16 58 39 82 D
Starling Cl. Pnr 20 11 89 A
Star Rd. Islw 70 14 76 D
Star Rd. W14 62 24 78 D
Star St. W2 1 27 81 C
Starts Cl. Orp 108 43 65 C
Starts Hill Rd. Orp 108 43 65 D
Star Yd. WC2 3 31 81 C
Statham Gr. N16 37 32 86 D
Statham Gr. N18 17 33 92 C
Station App. Barn 11 26 96 C
Station App. Beck 98 37 69 A
Station App. Bexh 79 48 76 C
Station App. Bexh 79 50 76 C
Station App. Brom 107 40 66 C
Station App. Chis 99 42 70 A
Station App. Chis 100 43 69 C
Station App. Dart 80 54 74 C
Station App. E11 39 40 88 A
Station App. Eps 109 22 64 C
Station App. Esh 101 15 65 D
Station App. Hamp 92 13 69 A
Station App. King 94 19 69 A
Station App. N11 16 28 92 D
Station App. Nthwd 19 09 91 C
Station App. NW10 55 21 82 B
Station App. Orp 108 45 65 B
Station App. Orp 100 46 68 D
Station App. Pnr 20 12 89 C
Station App. Rich 72 19 76 A
Station Approach Rd. W4 61 20 77 C
Station App. Ruis 31 09 87 C
Station App. Ruis 43 11 85 C
Station App. S Croy 112 32 62 B
Station App. S Croy 112 32 62 B
Station App. SE26 88 36 71 D
Station App. SE3 77 40 75 B
Station App. SE9 89 42 73 D
Station App. SE9 77 42 74 A
Station App. Sun 91 10 69 A
Station App. Sutt 110 24 63 C
Station App. SW16 86 30 71 C
Station App. SW6 73 24 75 A
Station App. Well 78 46 76 C
Station App. Wem 44 16 84 B
Station App. Wor Pk 102 22 66 C
Station Ave. Eps 109 21 62 A
Station Ave. N Mal 94 21 68 A
Station Ave. Rich 72 19 76 A
Station Ave. SW9 75 31 75 B
Station Cl. Hamp 92 13 69 B
Station Cl. N12 15 25 92 B
Station Cl. N3 23 25 90 A
Station Cres. N15 25 32 89 D
Station Cres. SE3 65 40 78 C
Station Cres. Wem 44 16 84 B
Stationers Hall Ct. EC4 3 31 81 D
Station Estate. Beck 98 35 68 D
Station Estate Rd. Felt 81 10 73 D
Station Garage Mews. SW16 96 29 70 B
Station Gdns. W4 61 20 77 C
Station Gr. Wem 44 18 84 A
Station Hill. Brom 107 40 65 A
Station La. Horn 42 54 86 A
Station Par. Bark 51 44 84 C
Station Par. Barn 12 28 96 C
Station Par. N14 16 29 94 D
Station Par. NW2 46 23 84 A
Station Par. Rich 72 19 76 A
Station Pas. E18 27 40 90 D
Station Pas. SE15 76 35 76 A
Station Path. SW6 73 24 75 B
Station Pl. N4 37 31 86 A
Station Rd. Barn 11 25 95 B
Station Rd. Belv 67 49 79 C
Station Rd. Bexh 79 48 75 A
Station Rd. Brom 99 39 69 C
Station Rd. Brom 99 40 69 A
Station Rd. Cars 111 27 64 B
Station Rd. Croy 105 32 66 C
Station Rd. Dag 41 47 87 B
Station Rd. Dart 80 51 74 D
Station Rd. E10 38 38 86 C
Station Rd. E12 50 42 85 A
Station Rd. E17 38 36 88 A
Station Rd. E4 18 38 94 B
Station Rd. E7 50 40 85 A
Station Rd. Edg 22 19 91 A
Station Rd. Hamp 92 13 69 B
Station Rd. Har 32 13 88 B
Station Rd. Har 33 15 88 B
Station Rd. Houn 70 13 75 D
Station Rd. Ilf 40 43 86 D
Station Rd. King 93 17 69 B
Station Rd. King 94 19 69 A
Station Rd. N11 16 27 92 D
Station Rd. N17 25 34 89 A
Station Rd. N21 17 31 94 D
Station Rd. N22 24 30 90 D
Station Rd. N22 24 30 91 C
Station Rd. N3 23 25 90 C
Station Rd. N. Belv 67 49 79 D
Station Rd. N.Mal 102 22 67 B
Station Rd. NW10 45 21 83 D
Station Rd. NW4 34 22 88 C
Station Rd. NW7 22 21 91 A
Station Rd. Orp 108 45 65 B
Station Rd. Rom 41 47 87 B
Station Rd. Rom 30 52 89 D
Station Rd. Rom 30 54 90 B
Station Rd. SE20 98 35 70 A
Station Rd. SE25 97 33 68 D
Station Rd. Sid 90 46 72 C
Station Rd. Sun 91 10 70 C
Station Rd. Surb 101 15 66 B
Station Rd. Sutt 110 25 62 C
Station Rd. SW13 72 22 76 C
Station Rd. SW19 95 26 69 B
Station Rd. Tedd 83 15 71 D
Station Rd. Tedd 93 16 70 A
Station Rd. Twick 83 15 73 D
Station Rd. W5 54 18 81 D
Station Rd. W7 54 15 80 C
Station Rd. W Wick 106 38 66 C
Station Rise. SE27 87 31 72 B
Station Sq. Orp 108 44 67 A
Station Sq. Orp 100 46 68 D
Station St. E15 49 38 84 D
Station Terr. NW10 46 23 83 D
Station Terr. SE5 75 32 76 A
Station View. Grnf 43 14 83 B
Station Way. SE15 75 34 76 C
Station Way. Sutt 110 24 63 C
Station Yd. Twick 83 16 73 A
Stauford St. SW1 10 29 78 B
Staunton Rd. King 93 18 70 D
Staunton St. SE8 64 36 77 B
Staveley Cl. E9 49 35 85 C
Staveley Cl. N7 47 30 85 A
Staveley Cl. SE15 76 35 76 A
Staveley Ct. E11 39 40 88 A
Staveley Gdns. W4 72 20 76 B
Staveley Gdns. W4 61 20 77 D
Staveley Rd. Ashf 91 08 70 B
Staveley Rd. W4 61 20 77 D
Staverton Rd. Horn 42 53 88 D
Staverton Rd. NW2 46 23 84 C
Stavordale Rd. Cars 103 26 66 A
Stavordale Rd. N5 48 31 85 B
Stayner's Rd. E1 57 35 82 D
Stayton Rd. Sutt 103 25 65 C
Stead St. SE17 63 32 78 B
Steam Farm La. Felt 69 09 75 D
Stean St. E8 48 33 83 B
Stebbing Way. Bark 51 46 83 C
Stebondale St. E14 64 38 78 A
Stedham Pl. WC1 3 30 81 C
Stedman Cl. Uxb 31 07 86 C
Steedman St. SE17 63 32 78 A
Steeds Rd. N10 24 27 90 D
Steele Rd. E11 50 39 84 A
Steele Rd. Islw 71 16 75 C
Steele Rd. N17 25 33 89 B
Steele Rd. NW10 45 20 83 C
Steele Rd. W4 61 20 79 C
Steele's Mews N. NW3 47 27 84 B
Steele's Mews S. NW3 47 27 84 B
Steele's Rd. NW3 47 27 84 B
Steel's La. E1 57 35 81 C
Steen Way. SE22 75 33 74 A
Steep Hill. SW16 86 29 72 D
Steeple Cl. SW19 85 24 71 C
Steeple Cl. SW6 73 24 76 C
Steeplestone Cl. N18 17 32 92 C
Steeple Wlk (off Maldon Cl). N1 48 32 83 A
Steerforth St. SW18 85 26 72 A
Steers Mead. Mit 96 27 69 B
Stella Rd. SW17 96 27 70 B
Stelling Rd. Eri 67 50 77 D
Stellman Cl. E5 37 34 86 C
Stembridge Rd. SE20 97 34 69 D
Stephen Cl. E8 48 34 83 A
Stephen Cl. Orp 108 45 65 D
Stephendale Rd. SW6 73 26 76 C
Stephen Mews. W1 2 29 81 B
Stephen Rd. Bexh 79 50 75 A
Stephenson Rd. Houn 82 13 73 A
Stephenson Rd. W7 54 15 81 D
Stephenson St. E16 58 39 81 A
Stephenson St. NW10 55 21 82 B
Stephenson Way. NW1 2 29 82 C
Stephen's Rd. E15 50 39 83 C
Stephen St. W1 2 29 81 B
Stepney Cswy. E1 57 35 81 D
Stepney Green. E1 57 35 81 B
Stepney High St. E1 57 35 81 B
Stepney Way. E1 57 35 81 A
Sterling Rd. Enf 13 32 97 B
Sterling St. SW7 5 27 79 C
Sterling Way. N18 17 33 92 C
Sterndale Rd. W14 62 23 79 D
Sterne St. W12 62 23 79 B
Sternhall La. SE15 75 34 75 A
Sternhold Ave. SW2 86 29 72 B
Sterry Cres. Dag 52 49 85 C
Sterry Dri. E Mol 101 15 67 C
Sterry Dri. Eps 109 21 64 A
Sterry Gdns. Dag 52 49 84 A
Sterry Rd. Bark 51 45 83 B
Sterry Rd. Dag 52 49 85 C
Sterry St. SE1 8 32 79 B
Steucers La. SE23 88 36 73 C
Stevedale Rd. Well 79 47 76 C
Stevenage Rd. E6 51 43 84 A
Stevenage Rd. SW6 73 23 76 B
Stevens Ave. E9 49 35 84 A
Stevens Cl. Beck 98 37 70 A
Stevens Cl. Hamp 92 12 70 B
Stevens Cl. Pnr 32 11 88 A
Stevenson Cl. Eri 68 52 77 D
Stevens Rd. Dag 41 47 86 C
Stevens St. SE1 8 33 79 C
Steventon Rd. W12 55 21 80 B
Stewards Holte Wlk. N11 16 28 92 B
Steward St. E1 4 33 81 A
Stewards Wlk. Rom 42 51 88 A
Stewart Ave. Shep 91 07 68 C
Stewart Cl. Hamp 92 12 70 A
Stewart Cl. NW9 34 20 88 C
Stewart Rd. E15 49 38 85 B
Stewartsby Cl. N18 17 32 93 C
Stewart's Gr. SW3 9 27 78 C
Stewart's Rd. SW8 74 29 76 A
Stewart St. E14 64 38 79 A
Stew La. EC4 8 32 80 A
Steyne Rd. W3 55 19 80 D
Steyning Gr. SE9 89 42 71 B
Steynings Way. N12 15 25 92 C
Steyning Way. Houn 70 11 75 C
Stickland Rd. Belv 67 49 78 A
Stickleton Cl. Grnf 53 13 82 B
Stilecroft Gdns. Wem 33 16 86 D
Stile Hall Gdns. W4 61 19 78 C
Stile Path. Sun 91 10 68 A
Stiles Cl. Brom 107 42 67 D
Stillingfleet Rd. SW13 61 22 77 A
Stillington St. SW1 10 29 78 A
Stillness Rd. SE23 76 36 74 D
Stilton Cres. NW10 45 20 84 C
Stipularis Dri. Hay 53 11 82 D
Stirling Rd. E13 50 40 83 D
Stirling Rd. E17 26 36 89 A
Stirling Rd. Har 21 15 89 B
Stirling Rd. N17 25 34 90 A
Stirling Rd. N22 25 31 90 B
Stirling Rd. SW9 74 30 76 C
Stirling Rd. Twick 82 13 73 B
Stirling Rd. W3 61 19 79 D
Stirling Road Path. E17 26 36 89 A
Stiven Cres. Har 32 12 86 D
Stockbury Rd. Croy 106 35 67 C
Stockdale Rd. Dag 41 48 86 B
Stockdove Way. Grnf 54 15 82 B
Stockfield Rd. SW16 86 30 72 D
Stockholm Rd. SE16 64 35 78 C
Stockhurst Cl. SW6 73 23 76 B
Stockingswater La. Enf 14 36 96 B
Stockland Rd. Rom 41 50 88 D
Stock Orchard Cres. N7 47 30 85 D
Stock Orchard St. N7 47 30 85 D
Stockport Rd. SW16 96 29 69 B
Stocksfield Rd. E17 26 38 89 A
Stocks Pl. E14 57 36 80 B
Stock St. E13 50 40 83 C
Stockton Gdns. N17 25 32 91 C
Stockton Rd. N17 25 32 91 C
Stockton Rd. N18 25 34 91 B
Stockwell Ave. SW9 74 30 75 B
Stockwell Ave. SW9 75 31 75 A
Stockwell Gdns. SW9 74 30 76 B
Stockwell Green. SW9 74 30 76 D
Stockwell La. SW9 74 30 76 D
Stockwell Mews. SW9 74 30 76 D
Stockwell Park Cres. SW9 74 30 76 D
Stockwell Park Rd. SW9 74 30 76 D
Stockwell Park Rd. SW9 75 31 76 C
Stockwell Park Wlk. SW9 75 31 75 A
Stockwell Rd. SW9 74 30 75 B
Stockwell St. SE10 64 38 77 A
Stockwell Terr. SW9 74 30 76 B
Stodart Rd. SE20 98 35 69 A
Stofield Gdns. SE9 89 41 72 D
Stoford Cl. SW19 85 24 73 A
Stoke Ave. Ilf 28 46 91 A
Stokenchurch St. SW6 73 25 76 B
Stoke Newington Church St. N16 37 33 86 C
Stoke Newington Common. N16 37 33 86 B
Stoke Newington Rd. N16 48 33 85 B
Stoke Pl. NW10 55 21 82 B
Stoke Rd. King 94 20 70 C
Stokesley St. W12 55 21 81 D
Stokes Rd. Croy 106 35 67 D
Stonard Rd. Dag 51 46 85 B
Stonard Rd. N13 17 31 93 C
Stondon Park. SE23 76 36 74 C
Stondon Wlk. E6 50 41 83 D
Stone Bldgs. WC2 3 30 81 B
Stonebridge Common. E8 48 33 84 D
Stonebridge Park. NW10 45 20 84 D
Stonebridge Rd. N15 37 33 88 B
Stonebridge Way. Wem 45 19 84 B
Stone Cl. Dag 41 48 86 B
Stonecot Cl. Sutt 103 24 66 C
Stonecot Hill. Sutt 103 24 66 A
Stonecroft Rd. Eri 67 50 77 C
Stonecroft Way. Croy 104 30 66 A
Stonecutter St. EC4 3 31 81 D
Stonefield Cl. Bexh 79 49 75 A
Stonefield Cl. Ruis 43 12 85 C
Stonefield St. N1 48 31 83 A
Stonefield Way. Ruis 43 12 85 C
Stonefield Way. SE7 65 41 77 D
Stonehall Ave. Ilf 39 42 88 C
Stoneham Rd. N11 16 29 92 C
Stonehill Cl. SW14 72 20 74 B
Stonehill Rd. SW14 72 20 74 B
Stonehill Rd. W4 61 19 78 C
Stonehills Ct. SE21 87 33 72 C
Stonehorse Rd. Enf 14 35 95 A
Stonehouse Ct. EC2 4 33 81 C
Stoneleigh Ave. Enf 13 34 97 B
Stoneleigh Ave. Wor Pk 102 22 65 C
Stoneleigh Cres. Eps 109 22 64 A
Stoneleigh Ct. Ilf 27 42 89 A
Stoneleigh Par. Eps 109 21 63 B
Stoneleigh Park Ave. Croy 106 35 67 D
Stoneleigh Park Rd. Eps 109 22 64 D
Stoneleigh Pl. W11 56 23 80 B
Stoneleigh Rd. Cars 104 27 66 A
Stoneleigh Rd. Ilf 27 42 89 B
Stoneleigh Rd. N17 25 33 89 B
Stoneleigh St. W11 56 23 80 B
Stoneleigh Terr. N6 36 28 86 B
Stonell's Rd. SW11 74 27 74 D
Stonenest St. N4 36 30 87 D
Stone Park Ave. Beck 98 37 68 D
Stone Pl. Wor Pk 102 22 65 A
Stone Rd. Brom 107 39 67 B
Stones End St. SE1 8 32 79 A
Stone St. Croy 112 31 64 C
Stone Strs. E1 57 35 80 B
Stonewood Rd. Eri 68 51 78 C
Stoney Alley. SE18 78 43 76 C
Stoneyard La. E14 57 37 80 B
Stoneycroft Cl. SE12 89 39 73 B
Stoneycroft Rd. Wdf Gn 27 42 91 A
Stoneydown Ave. E17 26 36 89 C
Stoneydown House. E17 26 36 89 C
Stoney La. EC3 4 33 81 D
Stoney La. SE19 97 33 70 B
Stoney St. SE1 8 32 80 D
Stonhouse St. SW4 74 29 75 B
Stonor Rd. W14 62 24 78 B
Stopford Rd. E13 50 40 83 A
Stopford Rd. SE17 63 31 78 D
Store Rd. E16 66 43 79 A
Store St. E15 49 38 85 D
Store St. WC1 2 29 81 B
Storey Rd. E17 26 36 89 D
Storey Rd. N6 36 27 88 D
Storey's Gate. SW1 6 29 79 B
Storey St. E16 66 43 79 A
Stories Rd. SE5 75 33 75 A
Stork Rd. E7 50 40 84 A
Storksmead Rd. Edg 22 21 91 C
Stork's Rd. SE16 63 34 79 C
Stormont Rd. N6 36 27 87 B
Stormont Rd. SW11 74 28 75 C
Storrington Rd. Croy 105 33 66 D
Story St. N1 47 30 84 D
Stothard Pl. E1 4 33 81 A
Stothard St. E1 57 35 82 C
Stoughton Ave. Sutt 110 24 64 C
Stoughton Cl. SW15 84 22 73 C
Stour Ave. Sthl 59 13 79 C
Stourcliffe St. W1 1 27 81 D
Stourhead Cl. SW19 85 23 73 B
Stourhead Gdns. SW20 94 22 68 A
Stour Rd. Dag 41 49 86 A
Stour Rd. Dart 80 52 75 A
Stour Rd. E3 49 37 84 C
Stourton Ave. Felt 82 12 71 B
Stowage. SE8 64 37 77 A
Stow Cres. E17 26 36 91 C

Stowe Cres. Ruis 31 08 88 C
Stowe Gdns. N9 17 33 94 D
Stowe Pl. N15 25 33 89 A
Stowe Rd. W12 61 22 79 B
Stox Mead. Har 20 14 90 B
Stracey Rd. E7 50 40 85 A
Stracey Rd. NW10 45 20 83 B
Strachan Pl. SW19 95 23 70 A
Stradbroke Dri. Chig 27 43 91 B
Stradbroke Gr. Ilf 27 42 90 D
Stradbroke Rd. N5 48 32 85 A
Stradella Rd. SE24 75 32 74 C
Strafford Ave. Ilf 28 43 90 C
Strafford Rd. Barn 11 24 96 A
Strafford Rd. Houn 70 12 75 B
Strafford Rd. Twick 83 16 73 A
Strafford Rd. W3 61 20 79 A
Strafford St. E14 64 37 79 A
Strahan Rd. E3 57 36 82 A
Straight Rd. Rom 30 53 91 C
Straightsmouth. SE10 64 38 77 C
Straight The. Sthl 59 12 79 A
Straker's Rd. SE15 75 34 75 D
Straker's Rd. SE22 75 34 74 B
Strandfield Cl. SE18 66 45 78 C
Strand La. WC2 7 30 80 B
Strand-on-the-Green. W4 61 19 77 A
Strand-on-the-Green. W4 61 19 77 B
Strand Pl. N18 17 33 92 A
Strand. WC2 7 30 80 B
Strangways Terr. W14 62 24 79 D
Stranraer Way. N1 47 30 84 D
Stratford Ave. W8 62 25 79 D
Stratford Cl. Bark 51 46 84 C
Stratford Cl. Dag 52 50 84 C
Stratford Ct. N Mal 94 20 68 D
Stratford Gr. SW15 73 23 75 D
Stratford Pl. W1 2 28 81 D
Stratford Rd. E13 50 40 83 A
Stratford Rd. Hay 53 11 82 C
Stratford Rd. Sthl 59 12 78 A
Stratford Rd. Th Hth 97 31 68 B
Stratford Rd. W8 62 25 79 C
Stratford Villas. NW1 47 29 84 D
Strathan Cl. SW18 73 24 74 D
Strathaven Rd. SE12 77 40 74 D
Strathblaine Rd. SW11 73 26 75 D
Strathblaine Rd. SW11 74 27 75 C
Strathbrook Rd. SW16 96 30 70 D
Strathcona Rd. Wem 33 17 86 B
Strathdale. SW16 86 30 71 D
Strathdon Dri. SW17 85 26 72 D
Strathearn Ave. Twick 82 14 73 C
Strathearn Pl. W2 5 27 80 A
Strathearn Rd. Sutt 110 25 64 C
Strathearn Rd. SW19 85 25 71 A
Strathede Rd. SE3 65 40 77 C
Strathfield Gdns. Bark 51 44 84 B
Strathleven Rd. SW2 74 30 74 A
Strathmore Gdns. Edg 22 19 90 D
Strathmore Gdns. Horn 42 51 87 D
Strathmore Gdns. N3 23 25 90 B
Strathmore Gdns. W8 56 25 80 C
Strathmore Rd. Croy 105 32 66 B
Strathmore Rd. SW19 85 25 72 C
Strathmore Rd. Tedd 83 15 71 A
Strathnairn St. SE1 63 34 78 A
Strathray Gdns. NW3 47 27 84 A
Strath Terr. SW11 74 27 75 C
Strathville Rd. SW18 85 25 73 D
Strathyre Ave. SW16 97 31 68 A
Stratton Ave. Wall 111 29 62 B
Stratton Cl. Bexh 79 48 75 A
Stratton Cl. Edg 21 18 91 B
Stratton Cl. Houn 70 13 76 A
Stratton Cl. SW19 95 25 69 C
Strattondale St. E14 64 38 79 C
Stratton Dri. Bark 51 45 84 B
Stratton Gdns. Sthl 53 13 81 C
Stratton Rd. Bexh 79 48 75 A
Stratton Rd. Sun 91 09 69 D
Stratton Rd. SW19 95 25 69 C
Stratton St. W1 6 28 80 D
Strauss Rd. W4 61 20 79 B
Strawberry Hill Cl. Twick 83 15 72 D
Strawberry Hill Rd. Twick 83 15 72 D
Strawberry La. Cars 104 28 65 C
Strawberry Vale. N2 23 26 90 B
Strawberry Vale. Twick 83 16 72 C
Streamdale. SE2 66 46 77 B
Streamside Cl. Brom 99 40 68 C
Stream Way. Belv 67 49 77 A
Streatfield Rd. E6 50 42 83 B
Streatfield Rd. Har 21 17 89 B
Streatham Common N. SW16 86 30 71 D
Streatham Common S. SW16 96 30 70 B
Streatham Ct. SW16 86 30 72 C
Streatham High Rd. SW16 96 30 70 C
Streatham High Rd. SW16 86 30 71 A
Streatham Hill SW2 86 30 73 C
Streatham Pl. SW2 86 30 73 A
Streatham Rd. Mit 96 28 69 A
Streatham Rd. SW16 96 28 70 D
Streatham St. WC1 3 30 81 C
Streatham Vale. SW16 96 29 70 C
Streathbourne Rd. SW17 86 28 72 C
Streatley Pl. NW3 46 26 85 A
Streatley Rd. NW6 46 24 84 D
Streimer Rd. E15 49 38 83 C
Strelley Way. W3 55 21 80 A
Stretton Rd. Croy 105 33 66 A
Stretton Rd. Rich 83 17 72 A
Strickland Ave. (off Joyce Green La). Dart 80 54 75 B
Strickland Ave. (off Sharp Way). Dart 80 54 75 B
Strickland Row. SW18 85 26 73 B
Strickland St. SE8 76 37 76 A
Strode Rd. E13 50 39 83 D
Strode Cl. N10 24 28 91 C
Strode Rd. E7 50 40 85 A
Strode Rd. N17 25 33 90 C
Strode Rd. NW10 45 22 84 A
Strode Rd. SW6 62 24 77 C
Strone Rd. E12 50 41 84 B
Strone Rd. E7 50 41 84 A
Strongbow Cres. SE9 77 42 74 B
Strongbow Rd. SE9 77 42 74 B
Strongbridge Cl. Har 32 13 87 C
Stronsa Rd. W12 61 21 79 B
Strood Ave. Rom 41 50 87 D
Stroud Cres. SW15 84 22 72 C
Stroudes Cl. Wor Pk 102 21 66 B
Stroud Field. Nthlt 43 12 84 A
Stroud Gate. Har 43 13 85 B
Stroud Green Gdns. Croy 106 35 66 A
Stroud Green Rd. N4 36 30 87 D
Stroud Green Rd. N4 37 31 87 C
Stroud Green Way. Croy 106 35 67 C
Stroudley Wlk. E3 57 37 82 B
Stroud Rd. SE25 105 34 67 C
Stroud Rd. SW19 85 25 72 C
Stroud Way. Ashf 91 07 70 B
Stroughton Cl. SE11 70 30 78 B
Strout's Pl. E2 4 33 82 B
Strutton Ground. SW1 6 29 79 D
Strype St. E1 4 33 81 B
Stuart Ave. Brom 107 40 66 C
Stuart Ave. Har 32 12 86 D
Stuart Ave. NW9 34 22 87 A
Stuart Ave. W5 60 18 79 B
Stuart Cres. Croy 106 36 65 D
Stuart Cres. N22 24 30 90 B
Stuart Gr. Tedd 83 15 71 C
Stuart Mantle Way. Eri 68 51 77 C
Stuart Pl. Mit 96 27 69 B
Stuart Rd. Bark 51 45 84 D
Stuart Rd. Barn 16 27 94 B
Stuart Rd. Har 21 15 89 B
Stuart Rd. NW6 56 25 82 B
Stuart Rd. Rich 83 16 72 D
Stuart Rd. SE15 76 35 75 C
Stuart Rd. SW19 85 25 72 C
Stuart Rd. Th Hth 97 32 68 C
Stuart Rd. W3 55 20 80 C
Stuart Rd. Well 78 46 76 B
Stuat Evans Cl. Well 79 47 75 A
Stubbs Way. SW19 95 26 69 B
Stucley Pl. NW1 47 28 84 D
Stucley Rd. Houn 59 14 77 C
Studdridge St. SW6 73 25 76 C
Studd St. N1 48 31 83 B
Studholme Ct. NW3 46 25 85 A
Studholme St. SE15 63 34 77 D
Studio Pl. SW1 5 27 79 B
Studios Rd. Shep 91 07 68 A
Studland Cl. Sid 90 45 72 D
Studland Rd. King 93 18 70 A
Studland Rd. SE26 88 35 71 D
Studland Rd. W7 54 15 81 C
Studland St. W6 61 22 78 B
Studley Ave. E4 26 38 91 D
Studley Cl. E5 49 36 85 C
Studley Ct. Sid 90 46 71 D
Studley Dri. Ilf 39 41 88 D
Studley Grange Rd. W7 60 15 79 B
Studley Rd. Dag 52 47 84 D
Studley Rd. E7 50 40 84 B
Studley Rd. SW4 74 30 76 C
Stukeley Rd. E7 50 40 84 D
Stukeley St. WC2 3 30 81 C
Stumps Hill La. Beck 98 37 70 A
Sturdy Rd. SE15 75 34 76 D
Sturge Ave. E17 26 37 90 D
Sturgeon Rd. SE17 63 32 78 C
Sturges Field. Chis 100 44 70 B
Sturgess Ave. NW4 34 22 87 B
Sturge St. SE1 8 32 79 A
Sturmer Way. N7 47 30 85 D
Sturrock Cl. N15 25 32 89 D
Sturry St. E14 57 37 81 D
Sturt St. N1 48 32 83 C
Stutfield St. E1 57 34 81 C
Styles Gdns. SW9 75 31 75 B
Styles Way. Beck 98 38 68 C
Sudbourne Rd. SW2 74 30 74 B
Sudbrooke Rd. SW12 74 28 74 C
Sudbrook Gdns. Rich 83 18 72 C
Sudbrook La. Rich 83 18 72 A
Sudbury Ave. Wem 44 17 85 B
Sudbury Court Dri. Har 33 16 86 C
Sudbury Court Rd. Har 33 16 86 C
Sudbury Cres. Brom 99 40 70 A
Sudbury Cres. Brom 89 40 71 C
Sudbury Cres. Wem 44 16 85 D
Sudbury Croft. Wem 44 15 85 B
Sudbury Gdns. Croy 112 33 64 A
Sudbury Heights Ave. Grnf 44 16 85 C
Sudbury Hill Cl. Wem 33 15 86 D
Sudbury Hill. Har 33 15 86 C
Sudbury Rd. Bark 51 45 85 D
Sudeley St. N1 48 31 83 D
Sudlow Rd. SW18 73 25 74 A
Sudrey St. SE1 8 32 79 A
Suez Ave. Grnf 44 15 83 D
Suez Rd. Enf 14 36 96 C
Suffield Rd. E4 18 37 92 B
Suffield Rd. N15 37 33 88 B
Suffield Rd. SE20 98 35 69 C
Suffolk Ct. Ilf 40 45 88 C
Suffolk La. EC4 8 32 80 B
Suffolk Park Rd. E17 26 36 89 C
Suffolk Pl. SW1 6 29 80 D
Suffolk Rd. Bark 51 45 84 C
Suffolk Rd. Dag 52 50 85 C
Suffolk Rd. Dart 80 54 74 C
Suffolk Rd. E13 58 39 82 B
Suffolk Rd. Enf 13 34 95 B
Suffolk Rd. Har 32 13 88 A
Suffolk Rd. Ilf 40 45 88 C
Suffolk Rd. N15 37 32 88 B
Suffolk Rd. NW10 45 21 84 C
Suffolk Rd. SE25 97 33 68 D
Suffolk Rd. SW13 61 22 77 C
Suffolk Rd. Wor Pk 102 21 65 B
Suffolk St. E7 50 40 85 A
Suffolk St. SW1 6 29 80 D
Sugar Bakers Ct. EC3 4 33 81 C
Sugar House La. E15 49 38 83 C
Sugar Loaf Ct. EC4 8 32 80 A
Sugar Loaf Wlk. E2 57 35 82 A
Sugden Rd. Surb 101 16 66 D
Sugden Rd. SW11 74 28 75 C
Sugden Way. Bark 51 45 83 D
Sulgrave Gdns. W12 62 23 79 A
Sulgrave Rd. W6 62 23 79 C
Sulina Rd. SW2 86 30 73 A
Sulivan Ct. SW6 73 25 76 C
Sulivan Rd. SW6 73 25 75 A
Sullivan Ave. E16 58 41 81 B
Sullivan Cl. E Mol 92 13 68 B
Sullivan Cl. SW11 74 27 75 A
Sullivan Rd. SE11 63 31 78 A
Sultan Rd. E11 27 40 89 D
Sultan St. Beck 98 35 69 D
Sultan St. SE5 63 32 77 C
Sumatra Rd. NW6 46 25 84 A
Sumburgh Rd. SW12 74 28 74 C
Summer Ave. E Mol 101 15 67 A
Summercourt Rd. E1 57 35 81 C
Summerfield Ave. NW6 46 24 83 C
Summerfield La. Surb 101 17 65 B
Summerfield Rd. W5 54 16 82 D
Summerfield St. SE12 89 39 73 B
Summer Gdns. E Mol 101 15 67 A
Summer Hill. Chis 100 43 69 C
Summerhill Cl. Orp 108 45 65 C
Summerhill Gr. Enf 13 33 95 C
Summerhill Rd. Dart 80 53 74 D
Summerhill Rd. N15 25 32 89 D
Summerhouse Ave. Houn 70 12 76 A
Summerhouse Rd. N16 37 33 86 A
Summerland Gdns. N10 24 28 89 B
Summerlands Ave. W3 55 20 80 A
Summerlee Ave. N2 24 27 89 D
Summerlee Gdns. N2 24 27 89 D
Summerley St. SW18 85 25 72 B
Summerley St. SW18 85 25 72 B
Summer Rd. E Mol 101 15 67 A
Summer Rd. Surb 101 15 67 B
Summersby Rd. N6 36 28 88 D
Summers Cl. NW9 34 19 87 D
Summers Cl. Sutt 110 25 63 C
Summers La. N12 24 27 91 A
Summers Row. N12 24 27 91 A
Summers St. EC1 3 31 82 C
Summerstown. SW17 85 26 71 A
Summer Trees. Sun 91 10 69 B
Summerville Gdns. Sutt 110 24 63 B
Summerwood Rd. Islw 71 15 74 D
Summit Ave. NW9 34 20 88 B
Summit Cl. Edg 22 19 91 C
Summit Cl. N14 16 29 93 A
Summit Cl. NW9 22 20 89 D
Summit Ct. NW2 46 24 85 C
Summit Ct. NW2 46 24 85 C
Summit Dri. Wdf Gn 27 41 90 D
Summit Estate. N16 37 34 87 A
Summit Rd. E17 26 37 89 D
Summit Rd. Nthlt 43 13 84 C
Summit Way. N14 16 28 93 B
Summit Way. SE19 97 33 70 C
Sumner Ave. SE15 75 33 76 B
Sumner Bldgs. SE1 8 32 80 C
Sumner Gdns. Croy 105 31 66 C
Sumner Place Mews. SW7 62 26 78 B
Sumner Pl. SW7 62 26 78 B
Sumner Rd. Croy 105 34 66 D
Sumner Rd. Har 32 14 87 A
Sumner Rd. SE15 63 33 77 D
Sumner Rd. SE15 75 34 76 A
Sumner Road S. Croy 105 31 66 C
Sumner St. SE1 6 32 80 C
Sumpter Cl. NW3 46 26 84 A
Sun Alley. Rich 71 18 75 C
Sunbeam Rd. NW10 55 20 82 D
Sunbury Ave. SW14 72 20 75 D
Sunbury Court Rd. Sun 92 11 69 C
Sunbury Cres. Felt 81 09 71 B
Sunbury Cross Centre. Sun 91 09 70 D
Sunbury La. SW11 73 26 76 B
Sunbury Rd. Felt 81 09 71 B
Sunbury Rd. Sutt 103 24 65 C
Sunbury St. SE18 65 42 79 D
Sunbury Way. Felt 82 11 71 C
Suncroft Pl. SE26 88 35 72 C
Sun Ct. EC3 4 32 81 D
Sun Ct. Eri 80 51 76 D
Sunderland Ct. SE22 87 34 73 A
Sunderland Rd. SE23 88 35 72 B
Sunderland Rd. W5 60 17 79 D
Sunderland Terr. W2 56 25 81 D
Sunderland Way. E12 39 41 86 B
Sundew Ave. W12 55 22 80 A
Sundial Ave. SE25 97 33 68 B
Sundorne Rd. SE7 65 41 78 C
Sundown Rd. Ashf 80 08 71 C
Sundra Wlk. E1 57 35 82 D
Sundridge Ave. Brom 99 41 69 B
Sundridge Ave. Chis 99 42 70 C
Sundridge Ave. Well 78 44 75 B
Sundridge Pl. Croy 105 34 66 C
Sundridge Rd. Croy 105 34 66 C
Sunfields Pl. SE3 65 40 77 D
Sunflower Way. Rom 30 53 90 B
Sunkist Way. Wall 111 30 62 A
Sunland Ave. Bexh 79 48 75 C
Sun La. SE3 65 40 77 D
Sunleigh Rd. Wem 44 18 83 A
Sunley Gdns. Grnf 44 16 83 A
Sunmead Rd. Sun 91 10 68 A
Sunna Gdns. Sun 91 10 69 D
Sunningdale Ave. Bark 51 44 84 D
Sunningdale Ave. Felt 82 12 72 A
Sunningdale Ave. Ruis 32 11 87 C
Sunningdale Ave. W3 55 21 80 A
Sunningdale Cl. Stan 21 16 91 C
*Sunningdale Gdns. NW9 34 20 88 A
Sunningdale Gdns. W8 62 25 79 C
Sunningdale. N14 16 29 92 D
Sunningdale Rd. Brom 99 42 68 C
Sunningdale Rd. Sutt 110 24 64 B
Sunningdale. Sthl 53 14 81 C
Sunningfields Cres. NW4 22 22 90 D
Sunningfields Rd. NW4 22 22 89 B
Sunninghill Gdns. 28 46 89 C
Sunninghill Rd. SE13 76 37 76 D
Sunny Bank. SE25 97 34 68 A
Sunny Cres. NW10 45 20 84 C
Sunnycroft Rd. Houn 70 13 76 D
Sunnycroft Rd. SE25 97 34 68 A
Sunnycroft Rd. Sthl 53 13 81 A
Sunnydale Gdns. NW7 22 20 91 B
Sunnydale. Orp 108 43 65 A
Sunnydale Rd. SE12 77 40 74 B
Sunnydene Ave. E4 18 38 92 D
Sunnydene Ave. Ruis 31 10 87 C
Sunnydene Cl. Rom 30 54 91 D
Sunnydene Gdns. Wem 44 17 84 A
Sunnydene St. SE26 88 36 71 A
Sunnyfield Rd. Chis 100 46 68 A
Sunny Gardens Rd. NW4 23 23 89 A
Sunny Hill Ct. NW4 22 22 90 D
Sunny Hill. NW4 22 22 89 B
Sunnyhill Rd. SW16 86 30 71 A
Sunnyhurst Cl. Sutt 103 25 65 C
Sunnymead Ave. Mit 96 29 68 B
Sunnymead Rd. NW9 34 20 87 B
Sunnymead Rd. SW15 72 22 74 B
Sunnymede Ave. Eps 109 21 63 C
Sunnymede Dri. Ilf 28 43 89 D
Sunny Nook Gdns. S Croy 112 32 63 B
Sunny Pl. NW4 23 23 89 C
Sunnyside Dri. E4 18 38 94 A
Sunnyside. NW2 35 24 86 D
Sunnyside Pas. SW19 95 24 70 A
Sunnyside Pl. SW19 95 24 70 A
Sunnyside Rd. E10 38 37 87 C
Sunnyside Rd. Ilf 40 44 86 D
Sunnyside Rd. N19 36 29 87 B
Sunnyside Rd. Tedd 82 14 71 B
Sunnyside Rd. W5 54 17 80 D
Sunnyside Road E. N9 17 34 93 C
Sunnyside Road N. N9 17 34 93 C
Sunnyside Road S. N9 17 34 93 C
Sunnyside. SW19 95 24 70 A
Sunny View. NW9 34 20 88 B
Sunny Way. N12 24 27 91 C
*Sun Pas. SE16 63 34 79 C
Sunray Ave. Brom 107 42 67 D
Sunray Ave. SE24 75 32 75 D
Sunray Ave. SE5 75 32 75 D
Sunray Ave. Surb 102 19 65 B
Sun Rd. W14 62 24 78 D
Sunrise Ave. Horn 42 53 86 C
Sunrise Cl. Felt 82 12 72 D
Sunrise Lodge. Horn 42 53 86 C
Sunset Ave. E4 18 37 94 D
Sunset Gdns. SE25 97 33 69 D
Sunset Rd. SE5 75 32 75 C
Sunset View. Barn 11 24 97 C
Sunshine Way. Mit 96 27 69 D
Sun St. EC2 4 33 81 A
Sun St Pas. EC2 4 33 81 A
Sunwell Cl. SE15 75 34 76 D
Surbiton Cres. King 93 18 68 C
Surbiton Ct. Surb 101 17 67 D
Surbiton Hall Cl. King 93 18 68 C
Surbiton Hill Park. Surb 102 19 67 A
Surbiton Hill Rd. Surb 101 18 67 A
Surbiton Rd. King 93 18 68 C
Surgeon St. SE18 66 43 79 C
Surrendale Pl. W9 56 25 82 C
Surrey Canal Rd. SE14 64 35 77 B
Surrey Cres. W4 61 19 78 C
Surrey Gr. SE17 63 33 78 C
Surrey Gr. Sutt 103 26 65 D
Surrey Lane Estate. SW11 74 27 76 A
Surrey La. SW11 74 27 76 A
Surrey Mews. SE27 87 33 71 A
Surrey Rd. Bark 51 45 84 C
Surrey Rd. Dag 52 49 85 C
Surrey Rd. Har 32 14 88 A
Surrey Rd. SE15 76 35 74 B
Surrey Rd. W Wick 106 37 66 D
Surrey Row. SE1 7 31 79 B
Surrey Sq. SE17 63 33 78 C
Surrey St. Croy 105 32 65 C
Surrey St. E13 58 40 82 B
Surrey St. WC2 7 30 80 B
Surrey Terr. SE17 63 33 78 A
Surridge Gdns. SE19 97 32 70 B
Surr St. N7 47 30 85 C
Surry Mount. SE23 87 34 73 D
Susan Cl. Rom 29 50 89 A
Susannah St. E14 58 38 81 C
Susan Rd. SE3 77 40 76 D
Susan Wood. Chis 100 43 69 A
Sussex Ave. Islw 71 15 75 A
Sussex Ave. Rom 30 54 91 D
Sussex Cl. Ilf 39 42 88 B
Sussex Cl. N19 36 30 86 A
Sussex Cl. N Mal 94 21 68 C
Sussex Cl. Twick 71 16 74 D
Sussex Cres. Nthlt 43 13 84 A
Sussex Gdns. N4 37 32 88 A
Sussex Gdns. N6 36 27 88 B
Sussex Gdns. W2 1 26 81 D
Sussex Mews E. W2 1 26 81 D
Sussex Mews W. W2 5 26 80 B
Sussex Pl. EC3 4 33 81 C
Sussex Pl. N Mal 94 21 68 C
Sussex Pl. NW1 1 27 82 D
Sussex Pl. W2 1 26 81 D
Sussex Rd. Cars 111 27 63 B
Sussex Rd. E6 51 43 83 A
Sussex Rd. Eri 67 49 77 D
Sussex Rd. Har 32 14 88 A
Sussex Rd. Mit 104 30 67 A
Sussex Rd. N Mal 94 21 68 C
Sussex Rd. S Croy 112 32 63 B
Sussex Rd. Sid 90 46 71 D
Sussex Rd. Sthl 59 11 79 D
Sussex Rd. W Wick 106 37 66 D
Sussex Ring. N12 15 25 92 C
Sussex Sq. W2 5 26 80 B
Sussex St. E13 58 40 82 B
Sussex St. SW1 9 28 78 D
Sussex Way. Barn 12 28 95 B
Sussex Way. N19 36 30 86 A
Sussex Wlk. SW9 75 31 75 D
Sutcliffe Cl. NW11 35 25 88 B
Sutcliffe Rd. SE18 66 45 77 A
Sutcliffe Rd. Well 79 47 76 C
Sutherland Ave. Orp 108 45 67 B
Sutherland Ave. Sun 91 09 69 D
Sutherland Ave. W13 54 16 81 D
Sutherland Ave. W9 56 25 82 D
Sutherland Ave. W9 1 26 82 A
Sutherland Ave. Well 78 45 75 C
Sutherland Cl. Barn 11 24 96 C
Sutherland Ct. NW9 34 19 88 B
Sutherland Dri. SW19 95 26 69 B
Sutherland Gdns. Sun 91 09 69 D
Sutherland Gdns. SW14 72 21 75 A
Sutherland Gdns. Wor Pk 102 22 66 D
Sutherland Gr. SW18 85 24 73 B
Sutherland Gr. Tedd 83 15 71 D
Sutherland Pl. W2 56 25 81 C
Sutherland Rd. Belv 67 49 79 C
Sutherland Rd. Croy 105 31 66 A
Sutherland Rd. E17 26 35 89 B
Sutherland Rd. E3 49 36 83 D
Sutherland Rd. End 14 35 95 B
Sutherland Rd. N17 25 34 90 A
Sutherland Rd. N9 17 34 94 D
Sutherland Rd. Sthl 53 12 81 D
Sutherland Rd. W13 54 16 81 C
Sutherland Rd. W4 61 21 77 A
Sutherland Row. SW1 9 28 78 D
Sutherland Sq. SE17 63 32 78 C
Sutherland St. SW1 9 28 78 D
Sutherland Wlk. SE17 63 32 78 C
Sutlej Rd. SE7 65 41 77 C
Sutterton St. N7 47 30 84 B
Sutton Arc. Sutt 110 25 64 D
Sutton Cl. Beck 98 37 69 B
Sutton Cl. Pnr 31 10 88 A
Sutton Common Rd. Sutt 103 25 66 C
Sutton Court Rd. E13 58 41 82 A
Sutton Court Rd. Sutt 110 26 63 A
Sutton Court Rd. W4 61 20 77 A
Sutton Court Roundabout. W4 61 20 77 A
Sutton Cres. Barn 11 23 95 B
Sutton Ct. SE19 97 33 70 D
Sutton Ct. Sutt 110 26 63 A
Sutton Ct. W4 61 20 77 A
Sutton Dene. Houn 70 13 76 B
Sutton Dwellings. N1 48 31 84 D
Sutton Dwellings. SW3 9 27 78 C
Sutton Estate The. W10 56 23 81 A
Sutton Gdns. Bark 51 45 83 C
Sutton Gdns. Croy 105 33 67 B
Sutton Green. Bark 51 45 83 A
Sutton Gr. Sutt 110 26 64 D
Sutton Hall Rd. Houn 59 13 77 C
Sutton La. Houn 70 12 76 D
Sutton Lane S. W4 61 20 77 A
Sutton La. W4 61 20 78 C
Sutton Park Rd. Sutt 110 25 63 B
Sutton Pl. E9 49 35 85 C
Sutton Rd. Bark 51 45 83 A
Sutton Rd. E13 58 39 82 D
Sutton Rd. E17 26 35 90 A
Sutton Rd. Houn 70 13 76 A
Sutton Rd. N10 24 28 90 A
Sutton Row. W1 2 29 81 D
Suttons Ave. Horn 42 53 86 D
Suttons Gdns. Horn 42 53 86 D
Suttons La. Horn 42 53 86 D

Sutton Sq. Houn ...70  12 76 B
Sutton St. E1 ...57  35 81 C
Sutton Way. Houn ...70  12 76 B
Sutton Way. W10 ...56  23 82 C
Swaby Rd. SW18 ...85  26 72 A
Swaffham Way. N22 ...25  31 91 D
Swaffield Rd. SW18 ...85  26 73 A
Swain Rd. Th Hth ...105  32 67 A
Swain's La. N6 ...36  28 86 B
Swainson Rd. W3 ...61  21 79 B
Swains Rd. SW17 ...96  27 70 D
Swaisland Rd. Dart ...80  52 74 D
Swaislands Dri. Dart ...80  51 74 B
Swakeleys Rd. Uxb ...31  07 86 D
Swale Rd. Dart ...80  52 75 C
Swallands Rd. SE6 ...88  37 72 C
Swallow Cl. SE14 ...76  35 76 A
Swallow Dri. Nthlt ...43  13 83 C
Swallowfield Rd. SE7 ...65  40 78 D
Swallow Pas Pl. W1 ...2  28 81 D
Swallow St. W1 ...6  29 80 A
Swanage Rd. E4 ...26  38 91 C
Swanage Rd. SW18 ...73  26 74 C
Swanage Waye. Hay ...53  11 81 C
Swanbridge Rd. Bexh ...79  49 76 B
Swan Cl. Felt ...82  12 71 A
Swan Cl. Orp ...100  46 68 A
Swan Cl. SW3 ...9  27 78 C
Swanfield St. E2 ...4  33 82 B
Swan La. EC4 ...3  32 80 B
Swan La. N20 ...15  26 93 C
Swanley Rd. Well ...79  47 76 A
Swan Mead. SE1 ...8  33 79 C
Swan Mews. SW9 ...74  30 76 D
Swan Pas. E1 ...57  34 80 A
Swan Pl. SW13 ...72  21 76 D
Swan Rd. Felt ...82  12 71 A
Swan Rd. SE16 ...64  35 79 A
Swan Rd. SE18 ...65  41 79 D
Swan Rd. Stal ...53  13 81 D
Swanscombe Rd. W11 ...56  23 80 D
Swanscombe Rd. W4 ...61  21 78 C
Swansea Rd. Enf ...14  35 96 C
Swan St. Islw ...71  16 75 B
Swan St. SE1 ...8  32 79 A
Swanton Gdns. SW19 ...85  23 73 D
Swanton Rd. Eri ...67  49 77 D
Swan Way. Enf ...14  35 97 D
Swanwick Cl. SW15 ...84  21 73 B
Swan Wlk. Rom ...42  51 88 A
Swan Wlk. SW3 ...9  27 77 B
Swan Yd. N1 ...48  31 84 B
Sward Rd. Orp ...108  46 67 C
Swaton Rd. E3 ...57  37 82 C
Swaylands Rd. Belv ...67  49 77 A
Swedenborg Gdns. E1 ...57  34 80 B
Sweeney Cres. SE1 ...8  33 79 B
Sweet Briar Green. N9 ...17  33 93 D
Sweet Briar Gro. N9 ...17  33 93 D
Sweet Briar Wlk. N18 ...17  33 92 B
Sweetmans Ave. Pnr ...20  11 89 B
Sweets Way. N20 ...15  26 93 B
Swetenham Wlk. SE18 ...66  44 78 C
Swete St. E13 ...50  40 83 C
Sweyn Pl. SE3 ...77  40 76 C
Swift Cl. Har ...32  13 86 B
Swift Rd. Felt ...82  12 71 A
Swift Rd. Sthl ...59  13 79 C
Swiftsden Way. Brom ...99  39 70 A
Swift St. SW6 ...73  24 76 A
Swift St. SW6 ...73  24 76 B
Swinbrook Rd. W10 ...56  24 81 A
Swinburne Cres. Croy ...106  35 67 C
Swinburne Rd. SW15 ...72  22 75 C
Swinderby Rd. Wem ...44  18 84 A
Swindon Cl. Ilf ...40  45 87 C
Swindon St. W12 ...56  23 80 C
Swinfield Cl. Felt ...82  12 71 A
Swinford Gdns. SW9 ...75  31 75 B
Swingate La. SE18 ...66  45 77 C
Swinnerton St. E9 ...49  36 85 C
Swinton Cl. Wem ...34  19 87 D
Swinton Pl. WC1 ...3  30 82 B
Swinton St. WC1 ...3  30 82 B
Swithland Gdns. SE9 ...90  43 71 A
Swyncombe Ave. W5 ...60  16 78 B
Sybourn St. E17 ...38  36 87 B
Sycamore Ave. Sid ...78  45 74 D
Sycamore Ave. W5 ...60  17 79 D
Sycamore Cl. Cars ...111  27 64 B
Sycamore Cl. E16 ...58  39 82 C
Sycamore Cl. Nthlt ...43  12 83 A
Sycamore Gdns. Mit ...95  26 69 D
Sycamore Gdns. W6 ...61  22 79 D
Sycamore Gr. N Mal ...94  21 68 A

Sycamore Gr. NW9 ...34  20 87 A
Sycamore Gr. SW19 ...95  23 70 A
Sycamore St. EC1 ...4  32 82 C
Sycamore Way. Th Hth ...105  31 67 A
Sycamore Wlk. Ilf ...28  44 89 C
Sycamore Wlk. W10 ...56  24 82 C
Sydenham Ave. SE26 ...87  34 71 D
Sydenham Hill. SE26 ...87  34 72 C
Sydenham Park Rd. SE26 ...88  35 72 C
Sydenham Pl. SE27 ...87  31 72 D
Sydenham Rd. Croy ...105  32 66 B
Sydenham Rd. SE26 ...88  35 71 D
Sydenham Rise. SE23 ...87  34 72 B
Sydenham Station App. SE26 ...88  35 71 A
Sydmons Ct. SE23 ...87  35 73 A
Sydner Mews. N16 ...48  33 85 B
Sydner Rd. N16 ...48  33 85 B
Sydney Cl. SW3 ...9  26 78 B
Sydney Cres. Ashf ...91  07 70 B
Sydney Elson Rd. E6 ...51  43 83 C
Sydney Gr. NW4 ...35  23 88 A
Sydney Mews. SW3 ...9  26 78 B
Sydney Pl. SW7 ...9  27 78 A
Sydney Rd. Bexh ...79  47 75 D
Sydney Rd. E11 ...39  40 88 D
Sydney Rd. Enf ...13  32 96 D
Sydney Rd. Felt ...81  10 73 C
Sydney Rd. Ilf ...28  44 90 C
Sydney Rd. N10 ...24  28 91 D
Sydney Rd. N8 ...24  31 89 C
Sydney Rd. Rich ...71  18 75 C
Sydney Rd. SE2 ...67  47 79 D
Sydney Rd. Sid ...90  45 71 A
Sydney Rd. Sutt ...110  25 64 A
Sydney Rd. SW20 ...95  23 69 D
Sydney Rd. Tedd ...83  15 71 D
Sydney Rd. W13 ...60  16 79 A
Sydney St. SW3 ...9  27 78 C
Sylvan Ave. Horn ...42  54 88 D
Sylvan Ave. N22 ...25  31 91 C
Sylvan Ave. N3 ...23  25 90 C
Sylvan Ave. NW7 ...22  21 91 A
Sylvan Ave. Rom ...41  48 88 D
Sylvan Cl. S Croy ...112  34 62 D
Sylvan Gdns. Surb ...101  17 66 B
Sylvan Gr. SE15 ...63  34 77 B
Sylvan Hill. SE19 ...97  33 69 A
Sylvan Rd. E11 ...39  40 88 A
Sylvan Rd. E17 ...38  37 88 A
Sylvan Rd. E7 ...50  40 84 B
Sylvan Rd. Ilf ...40  44 86 A
Sylvan Rd. SE19 ...97  33 69 B
Sylvan Way. Dag ...41  46 85 B
Sylverdale Rd. Croy ...105  31 65 D
Sylvester Ave. Chis ...99  42 70 B
Sylvester Path. E8 ...49  34 84 B
Sylvester Rd. E17 ...38  36 87 B
Sylvester Rd. E8 ...49  34 84 B
Sylvester Rd. N2 ...23  26 90 D
Sylvester Rd. Wem ...44  17 85 C
Sylvia Ave. Pnr ...20  12 91 B
Sylvia Gdns. Wem ...45  19 84 D
Symes Mews. NW1 ...47  29 83 C
Symons St. SW3 ...9  27 78 B
Syon La. Islw ...60  15 77 D
Syon Park Gdns. Islw ...60  15 77 D
Tabard St. SE1 ...8  32 79 D
Taber Gr. SW19 ...95  24 70 D
*Tabernacle Ave. E13 ...58  40 82 C
Tabernacle St. EC2 ...4  32 82 D
Tableer Ave. SW4 ...74  29 74 B
Tabley Rd. N7 ...47  30 85 A
Tabor Ct. Sutt ...110  24 63 A
Tabor Gdns. Sutt ...110  24 63 A
Tabor Rd. W6 ...61  22 79 D
Tachbrook Mews. SW1 ...10  29 78 A
Tachbrook Rd. Felt ...81  09 73 B
Tachbrook Rd. Sthl ...59  11 78 B
Tachbrook St. SW1 ...10  29 78 A
Tadema Rd. SW10 ...62  26 78 A
Tadmor Cl. Sun ...91  09 68 D
Tadmor St. W12 ...56  23 80 D
Tadworth Ave. N. Mal ...102  21 67 B
Tadworth Rd. NW2 ...34  22 86 A
Taffey's How. Mit ...96  27 68 A
Taft Way. E3 ...57  37 82 B
Tailworth St. E1 ...57  34 81 A
Tait Rd. Croy ...105  33 66 B
Takeley Cl. Rom ...29  50 90 D
Talacre Rd. NW5 ...47  28 84 A
Talbot Ave. N2 ...23  26 89 D
Talbot Cl. N15 ...25  33 89 D
Talbot Cres. NW4 ...34  22 88 A

Talbot Ct. EC3 ...8  32 80 B
Talbot Gdns. Ilf ...40  46 86 A
Talbot Pl. SE3 ...77  39 76 C
Talbot Rd. Brom ...99  40 68 B
Talbot Rd. Cars ...111  28 64 C
Talbot Rd. Dag ...41  48 84 D
Talbot Rd. E6 ...51  43 83 C
Talbot Rd. E7 ...50  40 85 A
Talbot Rd. Har ...21  15 90 D
Talbot Rd. Islw ...71  16 75 C
Talbot Rd. N15 ...25  33 89 D
Talbot Rd. N22 ...24  29 90 A
Talbot Rd. N6 ...36  28 88 C
Talbot Rd. Sthl ...59  12 78 A
Talbot Rd. Th Hth ...105  32 68 D
Talbot Rd. Twick ...83  15 73 D
Talbot Rd. W11 ...56  24 81 D
Talbot Rd. W13 ...54  16 80 A
Talbot Rd. W2 ...56  25 81 C
Talbot Rd. Wem ...44  17 84 B
Talbot Sq. W2 ...2  26 81 D
Talbot Wlk (off Heron Cl). NW10 ...45  21 84 A
Talbot Wlk. W11 ...56  24 81 C
Talbot Yd. SE1 ...8  32 80 D
Talcott Path. SW2 ...87  31 73 C
Talfourd Pl. SE15 ...75  33 76 B
Talfourd Rd. SE15 ...75  33 76 B
Talgarth Rd. W14 ...62  24 78 C
Talgarth Rd. W6 ...62  23 78 D
Talisman Sq. SE26 ...87  34 71 A
Talisman Way. Wem ...33  18 86 D
Tallack Cl. Har ...21  15 91 C
Tallack Rd. E10 ...38  36 87 D
Tall Elms Cl. Brom ...107  39 67 B
Tall Elms Cl. Brom ...99  39 68 D
Tallis Gr. SE7 ...65  40 77 B
Tallis St. EC4 ...7  31 80 A
Tallis Way. Stan ...21  18 90 C
Talma Gdns. Twick ...83  15 73 A
Talmage Cl. SE23 ...88  35 73 A
Talman Gr. Stan ...21  17 91 B
Talma Rd. SW2 ...75  31 75 C
Talwin St. E3 ...57  37 82 B
Tamarisk Sq. W12 ...55  21 80 B
Tamar Sq. Wdf Gn ...27  40 91 B
Tamar St. SE7 ...65  42 79 C
Tamar Way. N17 ...25  34 89 A
Tamian Way. Houn ...70  11 75 C
Tamworth Ave. Wdf Gn ...27  39 91 A
Tamworth La. Mit. ...96  28 68 B
Tamworth Park. Mit ...96  28 68 B
Tamworth Pl. Croy ...105  32 65 A
Tamworth Rd. Croy ...105  32 65 A
Tamworth St. SW6 ...62  25 77 A
Tancred Rd. N4 ...37  31 88 D
Tandridge Dri. Orp ...108  44 66 D
Tandridge Pl. Orp ...108  44 66 D
Tanfield Ave. NW2 ...34  21 86 D
Tanfield Rd. Croy ...112  32 64 A
Tangent Rd. Rom ...30  53 90 B
Tanglewood Cl. Croy ...106  35 65 C
Tangley Gr. SW15 ...84  21 73 B
Tangley Park Rd. Hamp ...92  12 70 B
Tangley Park Rd. Hamp ...92  12 71 D
Tangmere Gdns. Nthlt ...43  11 83 D
Tangmere Way. NW9 ...22  21 90 C
Tanhurst Wlk. Belv ...67  47 79 D
Tankerton Rd. Surb ...101  18 65 B
Tankerton St. WC1 ...3  30 82 A
Tankerville Rd. SW16 ...96  29 70 D
Tank Hill Rd. Grays ...68  54 78 D
Tankridge Rd. NW2 ...34  22 86 B
Tanners End La. N18 ...17  33 92 C
Tanner's Hill. SE8 ...76  37 76 A
Tanners La. Ilf ...40  44 89 A
Tanner St. Bark ...51  44 84 A
Tanner St. SE1 ...8  33 79 B
Tannery Cl. Dag ...41  49 86 D
Tannington Terr. N4 ...37  31 86 C
Tannsfeld Rd. SE26 ...88  35 71 D
Tansley Cl. N7 ...47  29 85 D
Tanswell St. SE1 ...7  31 79 A
Tansy Cl. Rom ...30  54 91 A
Tantallon Rd. SW12 ...86  28 73 C
Tant Ave. E16 ...58  39 81 D
Tantony Gr. Rom ...29  47 89 B
Tanworth Gdns. Pnr ...11  90 C
Tanza Rd. NW3 ...47  27 85 A
Tapestry Cl. Sutt ...110  25 63 D
Taplow Rd. N13 ...25  32 83 C
Tappesfield Rd. SE15 ...76  35 75 A
Tapping Cl. King ...94  19 70 C
Tapp St. E1 ...57  34 82 D
Tapster St. Barn ...11  24 96 B

Taransay Wlk. N1 ...48  32 84 B
Tarbert Rd. SE22 ...75  33 74 A
Tarbert Wlk. E1 ...57  35 80 A
Target Cl. Felt ...69  09 74 C
Tariff Rd. N17 ...25  34 91 A
Tarleton Gdns. SE23 ...87  34 73 D
Tarling Cl. Sid ...90  46 72 D
Tarling Rd. E16 ...58  39 81 D
Tarling Rd. N2 ...23  26 90 C
Tarling St. E1 ...57  35 81 C
Tarnbank. Enf ...12  30 95 A
Tarn St. SE1 ...8  32 79 C
Tarnwood Park. SE9 ...89  42 73 D
Tarragon Cl. SW16 ...86  29 72 D
Tarver Rd. SE17 ...63  31 78 D
Tarves Way. SE10 ...64  37 77 D
Tash Pl. N11 ...16  29 92 A
Tasker Rd. NW3 ...47  27 85 D
Tasman Rd. SW9 ...74  30 75 A
Tasman Wlk. E16 ...58  41 81 D
Tasso Rd. W6 ...62  24 77 A
Tatam Rd. NW10 ...45  20 84 D
Tate Rd. Sutt ...110  25 64 C
Tatnell Rd. SE23 ...88  36 74 C
Tattersall Cl. SE9 ...77  42 74 A
Tatton Cres. N16 ...33  33 87 B
Tatum St. SE17 ...63  33 78 A
Taunton Ave. Houn ...70  14 76 C
Taunton Ave. SW20 ...94  22 69 D
Taunton Cl. Bexh ...79  50 76 D
Taunton Cl. Sutt ...103  25 66 C
Taunton Dri. Enf ...12  31 96 A
Taunton Pl. NW1 ...1  27 82 D
Taunton Rd. Grnf ...43  13 83 B
Taunton Rd. SE12 ...78  39 74 B
Taunton Way. Stan ...21  18 90 C
Taverners Cl. W11 ...56  24 80 C
Taverner Sq. N5 ...48  32 85 A
Tavern La. SW9 ...74  31 76 C
Tavistock Ave. E17 ...26  36 89 A
Tavistock Ave. Grnf ...44  16 83 C
Tavistock Cl (off Crossway). N16 ...48  33 85 C
Tavistock Cl. Rom ...30  53 90 B
Tavistock Cres. Mit ...96  30 68 C
Tavistock Cres. W11 ...56  24 81 B
Tavistock Gdns. Ilf ...51  45 85 A
Tavistock Gr. Croy ...105  32 66 B
Tavistock Mews. W11 ...56  24 81 D
Tavistock Pl. N14 ...16  28 94 B
Tavistock Pl. WC1 ...3  30 82 C
Tavistock Rd. Brom ...99  40 68 C
Tavistock Rd. Cars ...103  26 66 D
Tavistock Rd. Croy ...105  32 66 D
Tavistock Rd. E15 ...50  39 84 B
Tavistock Rd. E18 ...40  40 89 A
Tavistock Rd. E7 ...39  39 85 B
Tavistock Rd. Edg ...22  19 90 A
Tavistock Rd. N4 ...37  32 88 D
Tavistock Rd. NW10 ...56  21 83 D
Tavistock Rd. W11 ...56  24 81 B
Tavistock Rd. Well ...79  47 76 A
Tavistock Sq. WC1 ...3  29 82 D
Tavistock St. WC2 ...7  30 80 A
Tavistock Terr. N19 ...36  29 86 D
Tavistock Wlk. Cars ...103  26 66 D
Taviton St. WC1 ...3  29 82 D
Tavy Bridge. SE2 ...67  47 79 A
Tavy Cl. SE11 ...11  31 78 C
Tawkesbury Gdns. NW9 ...22  19 89 B
Tawny Way. SE16 ...64  35 78 B
Tayben Ave. Twick ...71  15 74 C
Taybridge Rd. SW11 ...74  28 75 A
Tayburn Cl. E14 ...58  38 81 C
Taylor Ave. Rich ...61  19 79 D
Taylor Cl. Hamp ...92  14 71 C
Taylor Cl. N17 ...25  34 91 C
Taylor Cl. Rom ...29  49 91 C
Taylor Cl. Mit ...96  27 70 D
Taylor Rd. Mit ...86  28 72 B
Taylor Rd. Wall ...111  24 64 B
Taylor's Bldgs. SE18 ...66  43 78 B
Taylor's Cl. Sid ...90  45 72 D
Taylor's Green. W3 ...55  21 81 C
Taylor's La. Barn ...11  24 97 B
Taylor's La. NW10 ...45  21 84 C
Taylor's La. SE26 ...88  34 71 B
Taylor St. SE18 ...66  43 78 B
Taymount Rise. SE23 ...88  35 72 A
Tayport Cl. N1 ...48  30 84 C
Tay Way. Rom ...30  51 90 B
Taywood Rd. Nthlt ...53  12 82 B

Teak Cl. SE16 ...57  36 80 C
Teal Ct. Wall ...111  29 64 C
Teale St. E2 ...48  34 83 C
Tealing Dri. Eps ...109  20 64 B
Teasel Way. E15 ...58  39 82 A
Teather St. SE5 ...63  33 77 C
Tebworth Rd. N17 ...25  33 91 D
Teddington Cl. Eps ...109  20 62 D
Teddington Park Rd. Tedd ...83  15 71 B
Teddington Park. Tedd ...83  15 71 D
Tedworth Gdns. SW3 ...9  27 78 D
Tedworth Sq. SW3 ...9  27 78 D
Tees Ave. Grnf ...44  15 83 D
Teesdale Ave. Islw ...71  16 76 A
Teesdale Cl. E2 ...48  34 83 D
Teesdale Gdns. Islw ...71  16 76 A
Teesdale Gdns. SE25 ...97  33 69 C
Teesdale Rd. E11 ...39  39 87 B
Teesdale St. E2 ...48  34 83 D
Teesdale Yd. E2 ...48  34 83 D
Teeswater Ct. Belv ...67  47 79 D
Tee The. W3 ...55  21 81 C
Teevan Cl. Croy ...105  34 66 A
Teevan Rd. Croy ...105  34 66 A
Teignmouth Cl. Edg ...21  18 90 D
Teignmouth Gdns. Grnf ...54  16 82 A
Teignmouth Rd. NW2 ...46  23 84 B
Teignmouth Rd. Well ...79  47 76 C
Telcote Way. Ruis ...32  11 87 A
Telegraph Hill. NW3 ...35  25 86 D
Telegraph Mews. Ilf ...40  46 87 C
Telegraph Pl. SW15 ...85  23 73 A
Telegraph St. EC2 ...4  32 81 D
Telegraph Track. Cars ...111  28 62 C
Telemann Sq. SE3 ...77  40 75 B
Telephone Pl. W14 ...62  24 77 B
Telferscot Rd. SW12 ...86  29 73 D
Telford Ave. SW2 ...86  30 73 C
Telford Cl. SE19 ...97  33 70 B
Telford Cl. W3 ...55  21 81 A
Telford Dri. Houn ...82  13 73 A
Telford Rd. N11 ...16  29 92 C
Telford Rd. NW9 ...34  22 88 C
Telford Rd. SE9 ...90  44 72 B
Telford Rd. Sthl ...53  13 81 D
Telford Rd. W10 ...56  24 81 A
Telford Way. W3 ...55  21 83 D
Telham Rd. E6 ...51  43 83 C
Tell Gr. SE22 ...75  33 75 D
Tellson Ave. SE18 ...77  41 76 B
Telscombe Cl. Orp ...108  45 65 A
Temeraire St. SE16 ...64  35 79 A
Tempelhof Ave. NW4 ...35  23 87 A
Temperley Rd. SW12 ...86  28 73 A
Templar Pl. Hamp ...92  13 72 C
Templars Ave. NW11 ...35  24 88 D
Templars Cres. N3 ...23  25 90 C
Templars Dri. Har ...20  14 91 B
Templar St. SW9 ...75  31 78 C
Temple Ave. Croy ...106  36 65 D
Temple Ave. Dag ...41  49 87 C
Temple Ave. EC4 ...7  31 80 A
Temple Ave. N20 ...15  26 94 B
Temple Cl. N3 ...23  25 90 D
Templecombe Rd. E9 ...49  35 83 A
Templecombe Way. Mord ...103  24 67 A
Templecroft. Ashf ...91  08 70 B
Temple Fortune Hill. NW11 ...35  25 88 A
Temple Fortune La. NW11 ...35  25 88 C
Temple Gdns. Dag ...41  47 86 D
Temple Gdns. NW11 ...35  24 88 D
Temple Gro. Enf ...13  31 96 B
Temple Gro. NW11 ...35  25 88 C
Temple Hill. Dart ...80  54 74 B
Temple Hill Sq. Dart ...80  54 74 B
Temple La. EC4 ...3  31 80 A
Templeman Rd. W7 ...54  15 81 B
Temple Mead Cl. Stan ...21  16 91 B
Templemead Cl. W3 ...55  21 81 C
Temple Mills La. E15 ...49  38 85 A
Temple Mills Rd. E15 ...49  38 85 A
Temple Pl. WC2 ...7  31 80 B
Temple Rd. Croy ...112  32 64 B
Temple Rd. E6 ...50  42 83 A
Temple Rd. Houn ...70  14 75 C
Temple Rd. N8 ...24  30 89 D
Temple Rd. NW2 ...46  23 85 A
Temple Rd. Rich ...71  18 76 D
Temple Rd. W4 ...61  20 79 C
Temple Rd. W5 ...60  17 78 A
Temple Sheen Rd. SW14 ...72  20 75 C
Temple Sheen. SW14 ...72  20 74 A
Temple St. E2 ...48  34 83 D

Templeton Cl (off Crossway). N16 ...48  33 85 C
Templeton Cl. SE19 ...97  32 69 B
Templeton Pl. SW5 ...62  25 78 A
Templeton Rd. N15 ...37  32 88 D
Temple Way. Sutt ...103  26 65 D
Templewood Ave. NW3 ...35  25 86 D
Templewood Gdns. NW3 ...35  25 86 D
Templewood. W13 ...54  16 81 B
Temple Yd. E2 ...48  34 83 B
Tempsford Cl. Har ...33  15 88 D
Temsford Cl. Har ...20  14 90 C
Tenbury Cl. E7 ...50  41 85 D
Tenbury Ct. SW2 ...86  30 73 C
Tenby Ave. Har ...21  16 90 D
Tenby Cl. N15 ...25  33 89 D
Tenby Cl. Rom ...41  48 88 C
Tenby Ct. E17 ...38  36 88 A
Tenby Gdns. Nthlt ...43  13 84 A
Tenby Rd. E17 ...38  35 88 A
Tenby Rd. Edg ...21  18 90 D
Tenby Rd. Enf ...14  35 96 C
Tenby Rd. Rom ...41  48 88 C
Tenby Rd. Well ...79  47 76 B
Tench St. E1 ...57  34 80 D
Tenda Rd. SE16 ...63  34 78 B
Tendring Way. Rom ...41  47 88 A
Tenham Ave. SW2 ...86  29 72 B
Tenison Ct. W1 ...2  29 80 A
Tenison Way. SE1 ...7  31 80 C
Tenniel Cl. W2 ...56  25 80 B
Tennis Court La. E Mol ...93  15 68 B
Tennison Ave. SE25 ...105  33 67 B
Tennis St. SE1 ...8  32 79 B
Tenniswood Rd. Enf ...13  33 97 A
Tennyson Ave. E11 ...39  40 87 A
Tennyson Ave. E12 ...50  42 84 C
Tennyson Ave. N. Mal ...102  22 67 B
Tennyson Ave. NW9 ...22  20 89 A
Tennyson Ave. Twick ...83  15 72 B
Tennyson Cl. Felt ...69  10 74 C
Tennyson Cl. Well ...78  45 76 B
Tennyson Rd. E10 ...38  37 86 B
Tennyson Rd. E15 ...50  39 84 C
Tennyson Rd. E17 ...38  36 88 D
Tennyson Rd. Houn ...70  14 76 C
Tennyson Rd. NW6 ...46  24 83 B
Tennyson Rd. Rom ...30  53 91 C
Tennyson Rd. SE20 ...98  35 70 D
Tennyson Rd. SW19 ...85  27 72 A
Tennyson Rd. W7 ...54  15 80 B
Tennyson St. SW8 ...74  28 76 D
Tennyson Way. Horn ...51  51 86 B
Tensing Rd. Sthl ...59  13 79 C
Tentelow La. Sthl ...59  13 79 D
Tenterden Cl. NW4 ...23  23 89 B
Tenterden Dri. NW4 ...23  23 89 B
Tenterden Gdns. Croy ...105  34 66 A
Tenterden Gdns. NW4 ...23  23 89 B
Tenterden Rd. Croy ...105  34 66 A
Tenterden Rd. Dag ...41  48 86 B
Tenterden Rd. N17 ...25  33 91 C
Tenterden St. W1 ...2  28 81 B
Tenter Ground. E1 ...4  33 81 B
Tent St. E1 ...57  34 82 D
Terborch Way. SE22 ...75  33 74 A
Teresa Wlk. N10 ...36  28 88 B
Terling Cl. E11 ...39  39 86 D
Terling Rd. Dag ...41  49 86 A
Terling Wlk. N1 ...48  32 83 A
Terminus Pl. SW1 ...6  28 79 D
Terrace Ave. W10 ...56  23 82 A
Terrace Gdns. SW13 ...72  21 76 D
Terrace La. Rich ...71  18 74 C
Terrace Rd. E13 ...50  40 83 A
Terrace Rd. E9 ...49  35 84 D
Terrace The. E12 ...39  42 86 A
Terrace. The. EC4 ...3  31 81 C
Terrace. The. Wem ...46  25 83 A
Terrace The. SW13 ...72  21 76 C
Terrace Wlk. Dag ...52  48 85 C
Terrapin Rd. SW17 ...86  28 72 D
Terretts Pl. N1 ...48  31 83 B
Terrick Rd. N22 ...24  30 90 A
Terrick St. W12 ...55  22 81 D
Terrilands. Pnr ...20  12 89 B
Terront Rd. N15 ...25  32 89 C
Testerton Wlk. W11 ...56  23 80 B
Testwood Rd. W7 ...54  15 80 A
Tetbury Pl. N1 ...48  31 83 B
Tetcott Rd. SW10 ...62  26 77 C
Tetherdown. N10 ...24  28 89 A
Tetterby Way. SE16 ...63  34 78 D
Tetty Way. Brom ...99  40 69 C

Teversham La. SW8 74 30 76 A
Teviot Cl. Well 78 46 76 B
Teviot St. E14 58 38 81 A
Tewkesbury Ave. Pnr 32 12 88 A
Tewkesbury Ave. SE23 87 34 73 B
*Tewkesbury Cl. N15 37 32 88 D
Tewkesbury Rd. Cars 103 26 66 D
Tewkesbury Rd. N15 37 32 88 D
Tewkesbury Rd. W13 54 16 80 A
Tewkesbury Terr. N11 24 29 91 B
Tewson Rd. SE18 66 45 78 C
Teynham Ave. Enf 13 32 95 D
Teynham Green. Brom 107 40 67 A
Teynton Terr. N17 25 32 90 C
Thackeray Ave. N17 25 34 90 C
Thackeray Cl. Har 32 13 87 C
Thackeray Cl. SW19 95 23 70 D
Thackeray Ct. W5 54 18 81 D
Thackeray Gdns. Rom 40 46 87 B
Thackeray Rd. SW8 74 28 76 D
Thackeray St. W8 62 25 79 D
Thakeham Cl. SE26 87 34 71 D
Thakeray Rd. E6 50 41 83 D
Thalias Cl. SE10 64 38 77 B
Thames Ave. Dag 52 50 83 C
Thames Ave. Grnf 44 15 83 D
Thames Bank. SW14 72 20 76 C
Thames Cl. Hamp 92 13 69 D
Thames Dri. Ruis 31 08 88 C
Thames Eyot. Twick 83 16 73 C
Thamesgate Cl. Rich 83 16 71 B
Thameshill Ave. Rom 29 50 90 C
Thameside. Tedd 93 17 70 D
Thames Meadow. E Mol 92 13 68 A
Thames Pl. E14 57 36 80 B
Thamespoint. Tedd 93 17 70 D
Thames Rd. Dart 80 52 75 A
Thames Rd. E16 58 41 80 D
Thames Rd. W4 61 19 77 B
Thames Side. King 93 17 69 B
Thames Side. Surb 101 16 67 D
Thames St. Hamp 92 13 69 D
Thames St. King 93 17 69 C
Thames St. SE10 64 38 77 A
Thames St. Sun 92 11 68 A
Thamesvale Cl. Houn 70 13 76 C
Thames Village. W4 72 20 76 A
Thanescroft Gdns. Croy 105 33 65 C
Thanet Ct. W3 55 19 81 C
Thanet Dri. Brom 107 41 65 D
Thanet Pl. Croy 112 32 64 A
Thanet Rd. Eri 68 51 77 C
Thanet St. WC1 3 30 82 A
Thane Villas. N7 36 30 86 D
Thanington Ct. SE9 78 45 74 C
Tharp Rd. Wall 111 29 64 D
Thatcham Gdns. N20 15 26 94 A
Thatchers Way. Islw 70 14 74 B
Thathes Gr. Rom 29 48 89 C
Thavie's Inn. EC4 3 31 81 C
Thaxted Pl. SW20 95 23 70 D
Thaxted Rd. SE9 90 44 72 A
Thaxton Rd. W14 62 24 77 B
Thayers Farm Rd. Beck 98 36 69 A
Thayer St. W1 2 28 81 C
Theatre St. SW11 74 27 75 B
Theberton St. N1 48 31 83 B
The Cedars. E9 49 35 84 D
The Chevenings. Sid 90 46 72 D
The Curve. W12 55 22 80 A
Theed St. SE1 7 31 80 C
The Hatch. Enf 14 35 97 B
The Link. W3 55 19 81 D
Thelma Gdns. SE3 77 42 76 A
Thelma Gr. Tedd 93 16 70 A
Theobald Cres. Har 20 14 90 A
Theobald Rd. Croy 105 31 65 B
Theobald Rd. E17 38 37 87 A
Theobald's Ave. N12 15 26 92 A
Theobald's Rd. WC1 3 30 81 B
Theobald St. SE1 8 32 79 D
Theodore Rd. SE13 76 38 74 D
Therapia La. Croy 104 29 66 B
Therapia Rd. SE22 76 35 74 C
Theresa Rd. W6 61 22 78 A
Theresa's Wlk. S Croy 112 32 63 B
Thermopylae Gate. E14 64 37 78 B
Theseus Wlk. N1 48 31 83 D
Thesiger Rd. SE20 98 35 70 D
The Sir Oswald Stoll Foundation. SW6 62 25 77 D
The Sunny Rd. Enf 14 35 97 B
Thetford Cl. N22 25 31 91 B
Thetford Gdns. Dag 52 47 83 B
Thetford Rd. Dag 52 47 84 D
Thetford Rd. N.Mal 102 21 67 A
Theydon Gr. Wdf Gn 27 41 91 A
Theydon Rd. E5 38 35 86 A
Theydon St. E17 38 36 87 B
Thicket Cres. Sutt 110 26 64 A
Thicket Gr. Dag 52 47 84 A
Thicket Gr. SE20 97 34 70 C
Thicket Rd. SE20 97 34 70 D
Thicket Rd. Sutt 110 26 64 A
Third Ave. Dag 52 49 83 D
Third Ave. E12 50 42 85 B
Third Ave. E13 58 40 82 A
Third Ave. E17 38 37 88 A
Third Ave. Enf 13 33 95 B
Third Ave. Rom 41 47 88 A
Third Ave. W10 56 24 82 A
Third Ave. W3 55 21 80 D
Third Ave. Wem 33 17 86 B
Third Cl. E Mol 92 14 68 C
Third Cross Rd. Twick 82 14 72 B
Third Way. Wem 45 19 85 B
Thirleby Rd. Edg 22 20 90 B
Thirleby Rd. SW1 6 29 79 C
Thirlmere Ave. Grnf 54 17 82 A
Thirlmere Gdns. Nthwd 19 08 91 A
Thirlmere Gdns. Wem 33 17 87 D
Thirlmere Rd. Bexh 79 50 76 A
Thirlmere Rd. N10 24 28 90 B
Thirlmere Rd. SW16 86 29 71 B
Thirlmere Rise. Brom 99 39 70 B
Thirsk Cl. Nthlt 43 13 84 A
Thirsk Rd. Mit 96 28 70 C
Thirsk Rd. SE25 97 32 68 D
Thirsk Rd. SW11 74 28 75 A
Thirza Rd. Dart 80 54 74 D
Thistlebrook. SE2 67 47 79 C
Thistlecroft Gdns. Stan 21 17 90 D
Thistledene Ave. Har 32 12 86 C
Thistledene. E Mol 101 15 67 C
Thistle Gr. SW10 62 26 78 C
Thistle Gr. SW10 62 26 78 C
Thistlemead. Chis 100 43 69 D
Thistlewaite Rd. E5 37 34 86 D
Thistlewood Cl. N7 36 30 86 B
Thistleworth Cl. Islw 59 14 77 D
Thomas A' Beckett Cl. Wem 44 15 85 B
Thomas Baines Rd. SW11 73 26 75 B
Thomas Doyle St. SE1 7 31 79 D
Thomas La. SE6 88 37 73 A
Thomas More St. E1 57 34 80 C
Thomas More Way. N2 23 26 89 A
Thomas Rd. E14 57 37 81 A
Thomas St. SE18 66 43 78 B
Thompson Ave. Rich 72 19 75 A
Thompson Rd. Dag 41 48 86 D
Thompson Rd. SE22 75 33 74 D
Thompson's Ave. SE5 63 32 77 C
Thomson Cres. Croy 105 31 66 C
Thomson Rd. Har 21 15 89 A
Thorburn Way. SW19 95 26 69 B
Thoresby St. N1 4 32 82 A
Thorkhill Gdns. Surb 101 16 66 C
Thorkhill Rd. Surb 101 16 66 B
Thornaby Gdns. N18 17 34 92 C
Thornburn Sq. SE1 63 34 78 A
Thornbury Ave. Islw 59 14 77 D
Thornbury Cl (off Boleyn Rd). N16 48 33 85 C
Thornbury Rd. Islw 70 14 76 B
Thornbury Rd. SW2 74 30 74 C
Thornby Rd. E5 38 35 86 C
Thorn Cl. Brom 108 43 67 C
Thorncliffe Rd. Sthl 59 12 78 D
Thorncliffe Rd. SW4 74 30 74 C
Thorn Cl. Nthlt 53 12 82 B
Thorncombe Rd. SE22 75 33 74 A
Thorncroft. Horn 42 52 88 D
Thorncroft Rd. Sutt 110 25 64 D
Thorncroft St. SW8 10 30 77 C
Thorndean St. SW18 85 26 72 A
Thorndene Ave. N11 16 28 94 C
Thorndike Ave. Nthlt 43 11 83 B
Thorndike Cl. SW10 62 26 77 C
Thorndike St. SW1 10 29 78 B
Thorndon Cl. Orp 100 45 69 D
Thorndon Gdns. Eps 109 21 64 A
Thorndon Rd. Orp 100 45 69 D
Thorndyke Ct. Pnr 20 12 91 D
Thorne Cl. Ashf 91 08 70 C
Thorne Cl. E11 50 39 85 A
Thorne Cl. E16 58 40 81 C
Thorne Cl. Eri 67 49 77 B
Thorne Cl. N Mal 94 20 68 C
Thorneloe Gdns. Croy 112 31 64 D
Thorne Pas. SW13 72 21 76 C
Thorne Rd. N Mal 94 20 68 C
Thorne Rd. SW8 10 30 77 C
Thorne's Cl. Beck 98 38 68 A
Thorne St. E16 58 39 81 D
Thorne St. SW13 72 21 75 A
Thornet Wood Rd. Brom 100 43 68 A
Thorney Hedge Rd. W4 61 19 78 B
Thorney St. SW1 10 30 78 A
Thornfield Ave. NW7 23 24 90 A
Thornfield Rd. W12 61 22 79 B
Thornford Rd. SE13 76 38 74 A
Thorngate Rd. W9 56 25 82 C
Thorngrove Rd. E13 50 40 83 B
Thornham Gr. E15 49 38 85 D
Thornham St. SE10 64 37 77 B
Thornhaugh Mews. WC1 2 29 82 D
Thornhaugh St. WC1 2 29 82 D
Thornhill Ave. SE18 66 45 77 C
Thornhill Ave. Surb 101 18 65 A
Thornhill Cres. N1 47 30 84 D
Thornhill Gdns. Bark 51 45 84 C
Thornhill Gdns. E10 38 37 86 B
Thornhill Gr. N1 48 31 84 C
Thornhill Rd. Croy 105 32 66 A
Thornhill Rd. E10 38 37 86 B
Thornhill Rd. N1 48 31 84 C
Thornhill Rd. Surb 101 18 65 B
Thornhill Rd. Uxb 31 07 86 C
Thornhill Sq. N1 47 30 84 D
Thornlaw Rd. SE27 87 31 71 B
Thornley Cl. N17 25 34 91 C
Thornley Dri. Har 32 13 86 B
Thornley Pl. E10 65 39 78 C
Thornsbeach Rd. SE6 88 38 72 A
Thornsett Pl. SE20 97 34 69 D
Thornsett Rd. SE20 97 34 69 D
Thornsett Rd. SW18 85 25 73 D
Thornton Ave. Croy 104 30 67 D
Thornton Ave. SW2 86 29 73 D
Thornton Ave. W4 61 21 78 A
Thornton Dene. Beck 98 37 69 C
Thornton Gdns. SW12 86 29 73 D
Thornton Gr. Pnr 20 13 91 A
Thornton Hill. SW19 95 24 70 C
Thornton Pl. W1 1 27 81 B
Thornton Rd. Barn 11 24 96 A
Thornton Rd. Belv 67 49 78 B
Thornton Rd. Brom 89 40 71 C
Thornton Rd. Cars 103 26 66 D
Thornton Rd. Croy 104 30 67 D
Thornton Rd. E11 38 38 86 B
Thornton Rd. Ilf 51 43 85 B
Thornton Rd. SW12 86 29 73 D
Thornton Rd. SW14 72 20 75 B
Thornton Rd. SW19 95 23 70 B
Thornton Rd. Th Hth 105 31 67 A
Thornton Road E. SW19 95 23 70 B
Thornton Row. Th Hth 105 31 67 A
Thorntons Farm Ave. Rom 41 50 86 B
Thornton St. SW9 75 31 76 C
Thornton Way. NW11 35 25 88 B
Thorntree Rd. SE7 65 41 78 D
Thornville St. SE8 76 37 76 A
Thornwood Cl. E18 27 40 90 D
Thornwood Rd. SE13 77 39 74 A
Thorogood Gdns. E15 50 39 85 C
Thorold Rd. Ilf 40 44 87 C
Thorold Rd. N22 24 30 91 C
Thorpebank Rd. W12 55 22 80 C
Thorpe Cl. Horn 42 53 87 B
Thorpe Cl. Orp 108 45 65 A
Thorpe Cl. SE26 88 35 71 B
Thorpe Cl. W10 56 24 81 C
Thorpe Cres. E17 26 36 90 B
Thorpedale Gdns. Ilf 28 43 89 D
Thorpedale Rd. N4 36 30 87 D
Thorpe Hall Rd. E17 26 38 90 A
Thorpe Rd. Bark 51 44 84 D
Thorpe Rd. E17 26 38 90 C
Thorpe Rd. E6 50 42 83 B
Thorpe Rd. E7 50 39 85 B
Thorpe Rd. King 93 18 70 C
Thorpe Rd. N15 37 33 88 C
Thorpewood Ave. SE26 87 34 72 B
Thorpewood Ave. SE26 88 35 72 A
Thorsden Way. SE19 87 33 71 C
Thorverton Rd. NW2 35 24 86 C
Thoydon Rd. E3 49 36 83 C
Thrale Rd. SW16 86 29 71 C
Thrale St. SE1 8 32 80 C
Thrawl St. E1 4 33 81 B
Threadneedle St. EC2 4 32 81 D
Three Colt Cnr. E2 57 34 82 C
Three Colts La. E2 57 34 82 D
Three Colt St. E14 57 36 80 B
Three Corners. Bexh 79 50 76 C
Three Kings Rd. Mit 96 28 68 A
Three Kings Yd. W1 6 28 80 B
Three Mill La. E3 58 38 82 A
Three Nun Ct. EC2 4 32 81 C
Three Oak La. SE1 8 33 79 B
Threshers Pl. W11 56 24 80 A
Thriffwood. SE23 88 35 72 D
Throckmorten Rd. E16 58 40 81 D
Throgmorton Ave. EC2 4 32 81 D
Throgmorton St. EC2 4 32 81 D
Throwley Cl. SE2 67 47 79 C
Throwley Rd. Sutt 110 25 64 D
Throwley Way. Sutt 110 25 64 D
Thrupp Cl. Mit 96 28 69 D
Thrush St. SE17 63 32 78 C
Thruxton Way. (OFF Garnies Cl). SE15 63 33 77 D
Thurbarn Rd. SE6 88 37 71 D
Thurland Rd. SE16 63 34 79 C
Thurlby Cl. Har 33 16 88 C
Thurlby Cl. Wdf Gn 27 42 91 B
Thurlby Rd. SE27 87 31 71 B
Thurlby Rd. Wem 44 17 84 B
Thurleigh Ave. SW12 74 28 74 C
Thurleigh Ct. SW12 74 28 74 C
Thurleigh Rd. SW12 74 28 74 C
Thurleston Ave. Mord 103 24 67 A
Thurlestone Ave. Ilf 51 45 85 B
Thurlestone Ave. N12 24 27 91 B
Thurlestone Rd. SE27 87 31 71 A
Thurloe Cl. SW7 9 27 78 A
Thurloe Gdns. Rom 42 51 88 D
Thurloe Place Mews. SW7 62 26 78 B
Thurloe Pl. SW7 62 26 78 B
Thurloe Pl. SW7 5 27 79 C
Thurloe Sq. SW7 9 27 78 A
Thurloe St. SW7 62 26 78 B
Thuow Gdns. Ilf 28 44 91 B
Thurlow Gdns. Wem 44 17 85 D
Thurlow Hill. SE21 87 32 72 A
Thurlow Park Rd. SE21 87 32 72 A
Thurlow Rd. NW3 46 26 85 D
Thurlow Rd. W7 60 16 79 A
Thurlow St. SE17 63 33 78 C
Thurlow Terr. NW5 47 28 85 C
Thurlow Wlk. SE17 63 33 78 C
Thurlston Rd. Ruis 31 10 86 C
Thurnby Ct. Twick 83 15 72 C
Thursley Gdns. SW19 85 23 72 B
Thursley Rd. SE9 89 42 72 D
Thurso St. SW17 85 26 71 B
Thurstan Rd. SW20 94 22 70 D
Thurston Rd. SE13 76 37 75 B
Thurston Rd. Sthl 53 13 81 C
Thurtle Rd. E2 48 33 83 D
Thwaite Cl. Eri 67 50 77 A
Thyra Gr. N12 23 25 91 B
Tibbatt's Rd. E3 57 37 82 D
Tibbenham Wlk. E13 50 39 83 D
Tibberton Sq. N1 48 32 84 C
Tibbets Cl. SW19 85 23 73 D
Tibbet's Cnr. SW15 85 23 73 B
Tibbet's Ride. SW15 85 23 73 B
Ticehurst Rd. SE23 88 36 72 A
Tichmarsh. Eps 109 20 62 C
Tickford Cl. SE2 67 47 79 A
Tidal Basin Rd. E16 58 39 80 B
Tidenham Gdns. Croy 105 33 65 C
Tideswell Rd. Croy 106 37 65 C
Tideswell Rd. SW15 73 23 74 A
Tideway Cl. Rich 83 17 71 A
Tidey St. E3 57 37 81 A
Tidford Rd. Well 78 45 76 D
Tidworth Rd. E3 57 37 82 C
Tiepigs La. Brom 107 39 66 D
Tiepigs La. W.Wick 107 39 65 B
Tierney Rd. SW2 86 30 73 C
Tiger La. Brom 99 40 68 D
Tiger Way. E5 48 34 85 B
Tilbrook Rd. SE3 77 41 75 B
Tilbury Cl. Orp 100 46 69 D
Tilbury Rd. E10 38 38 87 A
Tilbury Rd. E6 50 42 83 D
Tildesley Rd. SW15 73 23 74 C
Tile Farm Rd. Orp 108 44 65 D
Tilehurst Rd. Sutt 110 24 64 C
Tilehurst Rd. SW18 85 26 73 D
Tile Kiln La. N13 17 32 92 C
Tile Kiln La. N6 36 29 87 C
Tile Kilns La. Uxb 31 07 87 B
Tileyard Rd. N7 47 30 84 C
Tile Yd. E14 57 36 81 D
Tilford Gdns. SW19 85 23 73 D
Tiller Rd. E14 64 37 79 C
Tillett Cl. NW10 45 20 84 A
Tillet Way. E2 57 34 82 A
Tillingbourne Gdns. N3 23 24 89 B
Tillingbourne Green. Orp 100 46 68 C
Tillingbourne Way. N3 23 24 89 D
Tillingham Way. N12 15 25 92 A
Tilling Rd. NW2 34 22 87 D
Tilling Rd. NW2 35 23 87 A
Tillman St. E1 57 34 81 D
Tilloch St. N1 47 30 84 D
Tillotson Rd. Har 20 13 91 C
Tillotson Rd. Ilf 40 43 87 A
Tillotson Rd. N9 17 33 93 B
Tillotson St. E1 57 35 81 B
Tilney Ct. EC1 4 32 82 C
Tilney Gdns. N1 48 32 84 B
Tilney Rd. Dag 52 48 84 B
Tilney Rd. Sthl 59 11 78 A
Tilney St. W1 6 28 80 C
Tilson Gdns. SW2 86 30 73 A
Tilson Rd. N17 25 34 90 A
Tilton St. SW6 62 24 77 A
Tiltwood The. W3 55 20 80 A
Tilt Yard App. SE9 77 42 74 D
Timber Cl. Chis 100 43 69 C
Timbercroft. Eps 109 21 64 A
Timbercroft La. SE18 66 45 77 C
Timberland Rd. E1 57 34 81 D
Timberling Gdns. S Croy 112 32 62 D
Timber Mill Way. SW4 74 29 75 B
Timberslip Dri. Wall 111 29 62 B
Timber St. EC1 4 32 82 C
Timberwharf Rd. N16 37 34 88 C
Timothy Rd. E3 57 36 81 B
Timsbury Wlk. SW15 84 22 73 C
Tindall Cl. Rom 30 54 90 D
Tindal St. SW9 75 31 76 B
Tinderbox Alley. SW14 72 20 75 B
Tinsley Rd. E1 57 35 81 A
Tintagel Cres. SE22 75 33 75 D
Tintagel Gdns. SE22 75 33 75 D
Tintern Ave. NW9 22 19 89 B
Tintern Cl. SW15 73 24 74 A
Tintern Cl. SW19 95 26 70 A
Tintern Gdns. N14 16 29 94 A
Tintern Rd. Cars 103 26 66 D
Tintern Rd. N22 25 32 90 A
Tintern St. SW4 74 30 75 C
Tintern Way. Har 32 13 87 D
Tinto Rd. E16 58 40 82 C
Tinworth St. SE11 10 30 78 D
Tippetts Cl. Enf 13 32 97 A
Tipthorpe Rd. SW11 74 28 75 A
Tipton Dri. Croy 112 33 64 A
Tiptree Cres. Ilf 28 43 89 A
Tiptree Dri. Enf 13 32 96 D
Tirlemont Rd. S Croy 112 32 63 C
Tirrell Rd. Croy 105 32 67 C
Tisbury Ct. W1 6 29 80 B
Tisbury Rd. SW16 96 30 69 C
Tisdall Pl. SE17 63 32 78 B
Titchborne Row. W2 1 27 81 C
Titchfield Rd. Cars 103 26 66 D
Titchfield Rd. NW8 47 27 83 B
Titchfield Wlk. Cars 103 26 66 B
Titchwell Rd. SW18 85 26 73 D
Tite St. SW3 9 27 77 B
Tithe Barn Cl. King 93 18 69 B
Tithe Cl. NW7 22 22 90 A
Tithe Farm Ave. Har 32 13 86 C
Tithe Farm Cl. Har 32 13 86 C
Tithe Wlk. NW7 22 22 90 A
Titley Cl. E4 18 37 92 C
Titmus St. W12 61 22 79 B
Tivendale. N8 24 30 89 A
Tiverton Ave. Ilf 28 43 89 A
Tiverton Dri. SE9 90 44 73 C
Tiverton Rd. Edg 21 18 90 C
Tiverton Rd. Houn 70 14 76 C
Tiverton Rd. N15 237 32 88 D
Tiverton Rd. N18 17 33 92 C
Tiverton Rd. NW10 46 23 83 B
Tiverton Rd. Ruis 31 10 86 C
Tiverton Rd. Wem 44 18 83 C
Tiverton St. SE1 8 32 79 C
Tivoli Gdns. SE18 65 42 78 A
Tivoli Rd. Houn 70 12 75 C
Tivoli Rd. N8 36 29 88 B
Tivoli Rd. SE27 87 32 71 C
Tobago St. E14 64 37 79 A
Tobin Cl. NW3 47 27 84 C
Toby La. E2 57 36 82 C
Todds Wlk. N7 36 30 86 B
Tokenhouse Yd. EC2 4 32 81 D
Token Yd. SW15 73 24 75 C
Tokyngton Ave. Wem 45 19 84 A
Toland Sq. SW15 72 22 74 A
Tolbut Ct. Rom 42 51 88 D
Tolcarne Dri. Pnr 19 10 89 B
Toley Ave. Wem 33 18 87 A
Tollesbury Gdns. Ilf 28 44 89 B
Tollet St. E1 57 35 82 D
Tollgate Dri. SE21 87 33 72 A
Tollgate Rd. E16 58 41 81 B
Tollhouse Way. N19 36 29 86 A
Tollington Park. N4 36 30 86 B
Tollington Pl. N4 36 30 86 B
Tollington Rd. N7 47 30 85 B
Tollington Way. N7 36 30 86 A
Tolmers Sq. NW1 2 29 82 C
Tolsford Rd. E5 48 34 85 D
Tolson Rd. Islw 71 16 75 A
Tolverne Rd. SW20 95 23 69 A
Tolworth Cl. Surb 102 19 66 D
Tolworth Gdns. Rom 41 47 88 B
Tolworth Park Rd. Surb 101 18 65 B
Tolworth Rd. Surb 101 18 65 A
Tolworth Rise N. Surb 102 20 66 C
Tolworth Rise S. Surb 102 20 66 C
Tolworth Underpass. Surb 102 19 65 B
Tomahawk Gdns (off Javelin Way). Nthlt 53 11 82 B
Tom Coombs Cl. SE9 77 42 75 C
Tom Cribb Rd. SE28 66 44 79 D
Tomlin's Gr. E3 57 37 82 A
Tomlinson Cl. E2 4 33 82 B
Tomlins Orchard. Bark 51 44 83 A
Tomlins Terr. E14 57 36 81 B
Tomlins Wlk. N7 36 30 86 B
Tom Mann Cl. Bark 51 45 83 A
Tompion St. EC1 3 31 82 B
Tomswood Ct. Ilf 28 44 90 A
Tomswood Hill Ilf 28 44 91 C
Tomswood Rd. Chig 28 43 91 A
Tonbridge Cres. Har 21 18 89 C
Tonbridge Rd. E Mol 92 12 68 D
Tonbridge Rd. Rom 30 53 91 D
Tonbridge St. WC1 3 30 82 A
Tonfield Rd. Sutt 103 24 66 D
Tonge Cl. Beck 106 37 67 A
Tonsley Hill. SW18 73 25 74 B
Tonsley Pl. SW18 73 25 74 B
Tonsley Rd. SW18 73 25 74 B
Tonsley St. SW18 73 25 74 B
Tonstall Rd. Eps 109 20 62 D
Tonstall Rd. Mit 96 28 69 C
Tooke Cl. Pnr 20 12 90 A
Tooley St. SE1 8 33 80 C
Toorack Rd. Har 20 14 90 D
Tooting Bec Gdns. SW16 86 29 71 B
Tooting Bec Rd. SW12 86 28 72 C
Tooting Bec Rd. SW16 86 29 71 A
Tooting Bwy. SW17 86 27 71 C
Tooting Gr. SW17 86 27 71 C
Tooting High St. SW17 96 27 70 A
Tooting High St. SW17 86 27 71 C
Tootswood Rd. Brom 99 39 68 C
Topaz St. SE11 10 30 78 B
Topham Sq. N17 25 32 90 C
Topham St. EC1 3 31 82 C
Top House Rise. E4 18 38 94 A
Topiary Sq. Rich 71 18 75 B
Topley St. SE9 77 41 75 D
Top Park. Beck 107 39 67 A
Topp Wlk. NW2 35 23 86 A
Topsfield Rd. N8 36 30 88 A
Topsham Rd. SW17 86 28 71 A
Torbay Rd. Har 32 12 86 A
Torbay Rd. NW6 46 24 84 D
Torbay St. NW1 47 28 84 D
Torbridge Cl. Edg 21 18 91 C
Torcross Dri. SE23 88 35 72 A
Torcross Rd. Ruis 32 11 86 C
Tor Gdns. W8 62 25 79 A
Tormead Cl. Sutt 110 25 63 A
Tormount Rd. SE18 66 45 78 C
Toronto Ave. E12 50 42 85 B
Toronto Rd. E11 49 38 85 B
Toronto Rd. Ilf 40 44 87 C
Torquay Gdns. Ilf 27 41 89 D
Torquay St. W2 56 25 81 B
Torrance Cl. Horn 42 53 87 B
Tor Rd. Well 79 47 76 A
Torrens Rd. E15 50 39 84 B
Torrens Rd. SW2 74 30 74 B
Torrens Sq. E15 50 39 84 B
Torrens St. N1 48 31 83 D
Torre Wlk. Cars 104 27 66 C
Torriano Ave. NW5 47 29 85 D
Torriano Cottages. NW5 47 29 85 D

Torridge Gdns. SE15 76 35 75 C
Torridge Rd. Th Hth 105 31 67 B
Torridon Rd. SE13 89 39 73 A
Torridon Rd. SE6 88 38 73 D
Torrington Ave. N12 15 26 92 D
Torrington Ct. SE26 87 34 71 C
Torrington Dri. Har 32 13 86 D
Torrington Gdns. Grnf 44 17 84 C
Torrington Gdns. N11 24 29 91 A
Torrington Gr. N12 16 27 92 C
Torrington Park N12 15 26 92 B
Torrington Pl. WC1 2 29 82 D
Torrington Rd. Dag 41 48 87 D
Torrington Rd. E18 27 40 89 A
Torrington Rd. Grnf 44 17 83 A
Torrington Rd. Ruis 31 10 86 C
Torrington Sq. WC1 2 29 82 D
Torrington Way. Mord 103 25 67 C
Torr Rd. SE20 98 35 70 D
Torver Rd. Har 21 15 89 C
Torver Way. Orp 108 44 65 B
Torwood Rd. SW15 72 22 74 A
Tothill St. SW1 6 29 79 B
Totnes Rd. Well 67 47 77 C
Totnes Wlk. N2 23 26 89 D
Tottenhall Rd. N13 17 31 92 D
Tottenham Ct Rd. W1 2 29 81 B
Tottenham Green East South Side. N15 25 33 89 D
Tottenham Green E. N15 25 33 89 D
Tottenham La. N8 36 30 88 A
Tottenham La. N8 24 30 89 D
Tottenham Mews. W1 2 29 81 A
Tottenham Rd. N1 48 33 84 A
Tottenham St. W1 2 29 81 A
Totterdown St. SW17 86 27 71 D
Totteridge Common. N20 15 23 94 D
Totteridge La. N20 15 25 94 D
Totteridge Village. N20 15 24 94 D
Totternhoe Cl. Har 33 17 88 A
Totton Rd. Th Hth 97 31 68 A
Totty St. E3 49 36 83 C
Toulmin St. SE1 8 32 79 A
Toulon St. SE5 63 32 77 C
Tournay Rd. SW6 62 24 77 D
*Toussaint Wlk. SE16 63 34 79 C
Tovil Cl. SE20 97 34 69 D
Towcester Rd. E3 58 38 82 C
Tower Bridge App. E1 8 33 80 B
Tower Bridge. E1 8 33 80 D
Tower Bridge Rd. SE1 8 33 79 A
Tower Cl. Ilf 28 43 91 B
Tower Cl. Orp 108 45 65 D
Tower Cl. SE20 97 34 70 D
Tower Ct. N16 37 33 87 B
Tower Ct. WC2 3 30 81 C
Tower Gardens Rd. N17 25 32 90 B
Tower Hamlets Rd. E17 26 37 89 A
Tower Hamlets Rd. E7 50 39 85 D
Tower Hill. EC3 8 33 80 B
Tower Mews. E17 26 37 89 C
Tower Rd. Belv 67 50 78 A
Tower Rd. Bexh 79 49 75 C
Tower Rd. Dart 80 53 74 D
Tower Rd. NW10 45 22 84 C
Tower Rd. Orp 108 45 65 D
Tower Rd. Twick 83 15 72 D
Tower Rise. Rich 71 18 75 A
Tower Royal. EC4 8 32 80 A
Towers Pl. Rich 71 18 74 A
Towers Rd. Pnr 20 12 90 A
Towers Rd. Sthl 53 13 82 C
Tower St. WC2 3 30 81 C
Tower Terr. N22 24 30 90 D
Tower View. Croy 106 36 66 A
Towfield Rd. Felt 82 12 72 B
Towncourt Cres. Orp 100 44 68 D
Town Court La. Orp 108 44 66 B
Towncourt Path. N4 37 32 87 C
Towney Mead Ct. Nthlt 43 12 83 D
Towney Mead Ct. Nthlt 43 12 83 D
Towney Mead. Nthlt 43 12 83 D
Towney Mead. Nthlt 43 12 83 D
Town Hall App. N16 48 33 85 A
Town Hall App. N16 48 33 85 A
Town Hall Ave. W4 61 20 78 D
Town Hall Rd. SW11 74 27 75 B
Townholm Cres. W7 60 15 79 D
Townley Ct. E15 50 39 84 B
Townley Rd. Bexh 79 48 74 B
Townley Rd. SE22 75 33 74 A
Townley St. SE17 63 32 78 D
Town Meadow Rd. Brent 60 17 77 D
Townmead Rd. Rich 72 19 76 D
Townmead Rd. SW6 73 26 76 C
Townmead. SW6 73 25 75 B
Town Quay. Bark 51 43 83 B
Town Rd. N9 17 34 93 B
Townsend Ave. N14 16 29 92 B
Townsend La. NW9 34 20 87 B
Townsend Rd. N15 37 33 88 B
Townsend Rd. Sthl 53 12 80 C
Townsend St. SE17 63 33 78 A
Townsend's Yd. N6 36 28 87 D
Townsend Way. Nthwd 19 09 91 D
Townshend Estate. NW8 47 27 83 C
Townshend Rd. Chis 90 43 71 D
Townshend Rd. NW8 47 27 83 A
Townshend Rd. Rich 71 18 75 D
Townshend Terr. Rich 71 18 75 D
Town Sq. Eri 68 51 77 A
Town The. Enf 13 32 96 B
Town Tree Rd. Ashf 81 07 71 C
Towton Rd. SE27 87 32 72 A
Toynbee Rd. SW20 95 24 69 A
Toynbee St. E1 4 33 81 B
Toyne Way. N6 36 27 88 D
Tracey Ave. NW2 46 23 85 C
Tracy Ct. Stan 21 17 91 C
Tradescant Rd. SW8 10 30 77 C
Trading Estate Rd. NW1 55 20 82 C
Trafalar Ct. E6 51 43 83 A
Trafalgar Ave. N17 25 33 91 A
Trafalgar Ave. SE15 63 33 77 B
Trafalgar Ave. Wor Pk 103 23 66 D
Trafalgar Gdns. E1 57 35 81 B
Trafalgar Gr. SE10 64 38 77 B
Trafalgar Pl. N18 17 34 92 C
Trafalgar Rd. SW19 95 26 70 C
Trafalgar Rd. Twick 82 14 72 B
Trafalgar Sq. SW1 7 29 80 D
Trafalgar Sq. WC2 7 30 80 C
Trafalgar St. SE17 63 32 78 D
Trafford Cl. E15 49 37 85 D
Trafford Rd. Th Hth 104 30 67 B
Traherne Lodge. Tedd 83 15 71 D
Tramway Ave. E15 49 38 84 D
Tramway Ave. N9 18 35 94 A
Tramway Path. Mit 96 27 68 C
Tramway Path. Mit 104 28 67 C
Tranmere Rd. N9 17 33 94 B
Tranmere Rd. SW18 85 26 72 A
Tranmere Rd. Twick 82 13 73 B
Tranquil Pas. SE3 77 39 76 D
Tranquil Rise. Eri 68 51 78 C
Tranquil Vale. SE3 77 39 76 C
Transept St. NW1 1 27 81 A
Transmere Cl. Orp 108 44 67 C
Transmere Rd. Orp 108 44 67 C
Transport Ave. Brent 60 16 77 B
Tranton Rd. SE16 63 34 79 C
Traps La. N Mal 94 21 69 A
Travellers Way. Houn 70 11 76 C
Travers Rd. N7 37 31 86 C
Treadgold St. W11 56 23 80 B
Treadway St. E2 48 34 83 D
Treaty Rd. Houn 70 13 75 B
Treaty St. N1 47 30 83 B
Trebeck St. W1 6 28 80 D
Trebovir Rd. SW5 62 25 78 A
Treby St. E3 57 36 82 D
Trecastle Way. N7 47 29 85 B
Tredegar Rd. E3 49 36 83 D
Tredegar Rd. N11 24 29 91 D
Tredegar Sq. E3 57 36 82 B
Tredegar Terr. E3 57 36 82 B
Trederwen Rd. E8 48 34 83 A
Tredown Rd. SE26 88 35 71 C
Tredwell Cl. Brom 99 42 68 C
Tree Cl. Rich 83 17 73 D
Treen Ave. SW13 72 21 75 B
Tree Rd. E16 58 41 81 C
Treetops Cl. SE2 67 48 78 C
Treewall Gdns. Brom 89 40 71 B
Trefgarne Rd. Dag 41 49 86 A
Trefoil Rd. SW18 73 26 74 A
Tregaron Ave. N8 36 30 88 C
Tregaron Gdns. N Mal 94 21 68 C
Tregarvon Rd. SW11 74 28 75 C
Tregenna Ave. Har 43 13 85 A
Tregenna Cl. N14 12 29 95 A
Trego Rd. E9 49 37 84 C
Tregothnan Rd. SW9 75 30 75 A
Tregunter Rd. SW10 62 26 78 C
Trehearn Rd. Ilf 28 44 91 D
Treherne Ct. SW9 75 31 76 B
Trehern Rd. SW14 72 20 75 B
Trehurst St. E5 49 36 85 C
Trelawney Estate. E9 49 35 84 A
Trelawney Rd. Ilf 28 44 91 D
Trelawn Rd. E11 38 38 86 C
Trelawn Rd. SW2 75 31 74 A
Trellis Sq. E3 57 36 82 B
Treloar Gdns. SE19 97 32 70 B
Tremadoc Rd. SW4 74 29 75 D
Tremaine Cl. SE4 76 37 76 C
Tremaine Rd. SE20 97 34 69 D
Tremlett Gr. N19 36 29 86 C
Tremlett Mews. N19 36 29 86 C
Trenance Gdns. Ilf 40 46 86 C
Trenchard Cl. Stan 21 16 91 A
Trenchard Ct. Mord 103 25 67 C
Trenchard St. SE10 64 38 78 C
Trenchold St. SW8 10 30 77 A
Trenholme Cl. SE20 97 34 70 D
Trenholme Rd. SE20 97 34 70 D
Trenholme Terr. SE20 97 34 70 D
Trenmar Gdns. NW10 55 22 82 B
Trent Ave. W5 60 17 79 C
Trent Gdns. N14 12 28 95 D
Trentham Dri. Orp 108 46 67 A
Trentham St. SW18 85 25 73 C
Trent Rd. SW2 74 30 74 B
Trent Way. Wor Pk 103 23 65 C
Trentwood Side. Enf 12 30 96 B
Treport St. SW18 85 25 73 B
Tresco Cl. Brom 99 39 70 A
Trescoe Gdns. Har 32 12 87 A
Tresco Gdns. Ilf 40 46 86 A
Tresco Rd. SE15 75 34 75 D
Tresham Cres. NW8 1 27 82 C
Tresham Rd. Bark 51 45 84 D
Tresham Wlk. E9 49 35 85 C
Tressillian Cres. SE4 76 37 75 A
Tressillian Rd. SE4 76 37 75 A
Trestis Cl. Hay 53 11 81 B
Treswell Rd. Dag 52 48 83 B
Trevanion Rd. W14 62 24 78 C
Treve Ave. Har 32 14 87 B
Trevelyan Ave. E12 50 42 85 B
Trevelyan Cl. Dart 80 54 75 D
Trevelyan Cres. Har 33 17 87 B
Trevelyan Gdns. NW10 46 23 83 A
Trevelyan Rd. E15 50 39 85 B
Trevelyan Rd. SW17 96 27 70 B
Treveris St. SE1 7 31 80 D
Treverton St. W10 56 23 82 D
Treville St. SW15 84 22 73 B
Treviso Rd. SE23 88 35 72 B
Trevithick Dri. Dart 80 54 75 D
Trevithick St. SE8 64 37 77 A
Trevone Gdns. Pnr 32 12 88 C
Trevor Cl. Barn 11 26 95 D
Trevor Cl. Brom 107 40 66 A
Trevor Cl. Islw 71 15 74 B
Trevor Cl. Nthlt 43 11 83 C
Trevor Cl. Stan 21 15 91 D
Trevor Gdns. Edg 22 20 90 B
Trevor Gdns. Nthlt 43 11 83 C
Trevor Pl. SW7 5 27 79 A
Trevor Rd. Edg 22 20 90 B
Trevor Rd. SW19 95 24 70 C
Trevor Rd. Wdf Gn 27 40 91 C
Trevor Sq. SW7 5 27 79 A
Trevor St. SW7 5 27 79 A
Trevose Rd. E17 26 38 90 B
Trewince Rd. SW20 95 23 69 A
Trewint St. SW18 85 26 72 A
Trewsbury Rd. SE26 88 35 71 D
Triandra Way. Hay 53 11 81 B
Triangle Ct. E16 58 41 81 A
Triangle Pl. SW4 74 29 75 D
Triangle Rd. E8 48 34 83 B
Triangle The. E8 48 34 83 B
Triangle The. King 94 20 69 C
Trident Gdns (off Jetstar Way). Nthlt 53 11 82 B
Trident St. SE16 64 35 78 B
Trident Way. Sthl 59 11 79 C
Trigon Rd. SW8 10 30 77 D
Trilby Rd. SE23 88 35 72 B
Trimmer Wlk (off Netley Rd). Brent 60 18 77 A
Trinder Gdns. N19 36 30 87 C
Trinder Rd. Barn 11 23 95 A
Trinder Rd. N19 36 30 87 C
Tring Ave. Sthl 53 12 81 D
Tring Ave. W5 54 18 80 D
Tring Ave. Wem 45 19 84 A
Tring Cl. Ilf 40 44 88 B
Tring Ct. Twick 83 16 71 A
Trinidad Gdns. Dag 52 50 84 D
Trinidad St. E14 57 36 80 B
Trinity Ave. Enf 13 33 95 D
Trinity Ave. N2 23 26 89 B
Trinity Church Rd. SW13 61 22 77 B
Trinity Church Sq. SE1 8 32 79 C
Trinity Cl. Brom 107 42 66 C
Trinity Cl. E11 39 39 86 A
Trinity Cl. Houn 70 12 75 C
Trinity Cl. Nthwd 19 09 91 A
Trinity Cl. NW3 46 26 85 B
Trinity Cl. S Croy 112 33 62 B
Trinity Cl. SE13 76 38 75 D
Trinity Cres. SW17 86 28 72 A
Trinity Estate. SE8 64 36 78 D
Trinity Gdns. E16 58 39 81 B
Trinity Gdns. SW9 74 30 75 D
Trinity Green. E1 57 35 81 A
Trinity Gr. SE10 76 38 76 A
Trinity Pl. EC3 8 33 80 B
Trinity Rd. Ilf 28 44 89 A
Trinity Rd. N22 24 30 90 B
Trinity Rd. N22 24 30 91 C
Trinity Rd. N2 23 26 89 B
Trinity Rd. Rich 71 18 75 B
Trinity Rd. Sthl 53 12 80 C
Trinity Rd. SW17 86 27 72 B
Trinity Rd. SW18 73 26 74 B
Trinity Rd. SW19 95 25 70 A
Trinity Rise. SW2 87 31 73 B
Trinity Sq. EC3 8 33 80 B
Trinity St. E16 58 39 81 B
Trinity St. Enf 13 32 97 C
Trinity St. SE1 8 32 79 A
Trinity St. SE1 8 32 79 D
Trinity Way. W13 55 21 80 B
Trio Pl. SE1 8 32 79 A
Tristan Sq. SE3 77 39 75 A
Tristram Cl. E17 26 38 89 B
Tristram Rd. Brom 89 39 71 B
Triton Sq. NW1 2 29 82 C
Tritton Ave. Croy 111 30 64 A
Tritton Rd. SE21 87 32 72 D
Triumph Cl. Hay 69 08 76 A
Trojan Way. Croy 105 31 65 C
Troon St. E1 57 36 81 C
Trosley Rd. Belv 67 49 77 A
Trossachs Rd. SE22 75 33 74 A
Trothy Rd. SE1 63 34 78 A
Trott Rd. N10 24 28 91 C
Trott St. SW11 74 27 76 A
Troughton Rd. SE7 65 40 78 D
Troutbeck Rd. SE14 76 36 76 A
Trouville Rd. SW4 74 29 74 C
Trowbridge Rd. E9 49 36 84 B
Trowbridge Rd. Rom 30 53 91 B
Trowlock Ave. Tedd 93 17 70 A
Trowlock Way. Tedd 93 17 70 B
Troy Rd. SE19 97 32 70 B
Troy St. SE18 66 43 78 B
Troy Town. SE15 75 34 75 A
Trulock Rd. N17 25 34 91 C
Truman's Rd. N16 48 33 85 D
Trumpers Way. W7 60 15 79 D
Trumpington Rd. E7 50 39 85 B
Trump St. EC2 4 32 81 C
Trundle St. SE1 8 32 79 A
Trundley's Rd. SE8 64 35 78 D
Trundley's Terr. SE8 64 35 78 B
Truro Gdns. Ilf 39 42 87 A
Truro Rd. E17 26 36 89 D
Truro Rd. N22 24 30 91 D
Truro St. NW5 47 28 84 A
Truro Wlk. Rom 30 53 91 A
Truslove Rd. SE27 87 31 71 D
Trussley Rd. W6 62 23 79 C
Trustons Gdns. Horn 42 52 87 A
Trust Wlk. SE21 87 31 73 D
Tryfan Cl. Ilf 39 41 88 B
Tryon St. SW3 9 27 78 D
Tuam Rd. SE18 66 44 77 B
Tubbenden Cl. Orp 108 45 65 C
Tubbenden La. Orp 108 45 65 C
Tubbs Rd. NW10 45 21 83 D
Tuck's Ct. EC4 3 31 81 C
Tudor Ave. Hamp 92 13 70 C
Tudor Ave. Rom 30 52 89 A
Tudor Ave. Wor Pk 109 22 64 B
Tudor Cl. Chis 99 42 69 B
Tudor Cl. Dart 80 52 74 D
Tudor Cl. NW3 47 27 85 C
Tudor Cl. NW7 22 22 91 A
Tudor Cl. NW9 34 20 86 A
Tudor Cl. Pnr 31 10 88 A
Tudor Cl. Sutt 110 23 64 D
Tudor Cl. Sutt 110 24 63 A
Tudor Cl. SW2 74 30 74 D
Tudor Cl. Wall 111 29 63 C
Tudor Court N. Wem 45 19 85 C
Tudor Court S. Wem 45 19 85 C
Tudor Cres. Enf 13 32 97 A
Tudor Cres. Ilf 28 44 91 A
Tudor Ct. E17 38 36 87 B
Tudor Ct. Felt 82 11 71 A
Tudor Ct. N1 48 33 84 A
Tudor Ct. Tedd 93 15 70 B
Tudor Dri. King 83 18 71 C
Tudor Dri. Mord 103 24 66 A
Tudor Dri. Rom 30 52 89 C
Tudor Gdns. NW9 34 20 86 A
Tudor Gdns. Rom 30 52 89 D
Tudor Gdns. SW13 72 21 75 A
Tudor Gdns. Twick 83 15 73 D
Tudor Gdns. W3 55 19 81 C
Tudor Gdns. W Wick 106 38 65 C
Tudor Gr. E9 49 35 84 C
Tudor Pl. Mit 96 27 70 C
Tudor Rd. Ashf 91 08 70 B
Tudor Rd. Bark 51 45 83 B
Tudor Rd. Barn 11 25 96 B
Tudor Rd. Beck 98 38 68 A
Tudor Rd. E4 26 37 91 B
Tudor Rd. E6 50 41 83 A
Tudor Rd. E9 49 35 83 A
Tudor Rd. Hamp 92 13 70 C
Tudor Rd. Har 20 14 90 D
Tudor Rd. Houn 70 14 75 D
Tudor Rd. King 94 19 70 C
Tudor Rd. N9 18 35 94 A
Tudor Rd. Pnr 20 11 90 C
Tudor Rd. SE19 97 33 70 D
Tudor Rd. SE25 105 34 67 B
Tudor Rd. Sthl 53 12 80 A
Tudor St. EC4 7 31 80 A
Tudor Way. N14 16 29 94 D
Tudor Way. Orp 108 44 67 B
Tudor Way. W3 61 19 79 A
Tudway Rd. SE3 77 41 75 C
Tufnail Rd. Dart 80 54 74 D
Tufnell Park Rd. N19 47 29 85 A
Tufnell Park Rd. N7 47 29 85 B
Tufton Gdns. E Mol 92 13 69 D
Tufton Rd. E4 18 37 92 A
Tufton St. SW1 7 30 79 C
Tugela Rd. Croy 105 32 67 D
Tugela St. SE6 88 36 72 B
Tuilerie St. E2 48 34 83 C
Tulip Cl. Rom 30 53 91 B
Tuliptree Ave. Rich 60 18 77 C
Tulse Cl. Beck 98 38 68 A
Tulse Hill. SW2 87 31 73 C
Tulsemere Rd. SE27 87 32 72 A
Tuncombe Rd. N18 17 33 92 A
Tunley Rd. NW10 45 20 83 A
Tunley Rd. SW17 86 28 72 A
Tunmarsh La. E13 58 41 82 A
Tunnel Ave. SE10 65 39 79 C
Tunnel Gdns. N11 24 29 91 C
Tunnel Rd. SE16 64 35 79 A
Tunstall Ave. Ilf 28 46 91 A
Tunstall Rd. Croy 105 33 66 C
Tunstall Rd. SW9 74 30 75 D
Tunstall Wlk (off Ealing Rd). Brent 60 18 77 A
Tunworth Cl. NW9 34 20 88 C
Tunworth Cres. SW15 72 21 74 D
Turenne Cl. SW18 73 26 75 C
Turin Rd. N9 18 35 94 A
Turin St. E2 57 34 82 A
Turkey Oak Cl. SE19 97 33 70 C
Turks Row. SW3 9 27 78 D
Turle Rd. N4 36 30 86 B
Turley Cl. E15 50 39 83 A
Turnagain La. EC4 3 31 81 D
Turnage Rd. Dag 41 48 87 C
Turnant Rd. N17 25 32 90 A
Turnberry Way. Orp 108 44 66 D
Turnchapel Mews. SW4 74 28 75 B
Turner Ave. Mit 96 27 69 B
Turner Ave. N15 25 33 89 C
Turner Ave. Twick 82 14 72 C
Turner Cl. NW11 35 25 88 D
Turner Dri. NW11 35 25 88 D
Turner Rd. E17 26 38 89 A
Turner Rd. Edg 21 18 90 D
Turner Rd. N.Mal 102 20 66 B
Turner's Rd. E3 57 36 81 B
Turner St. E16 58 39 81 D
Turner St. E1 57 34 81 B
Turner's Wood. NW11 35 26 87 C
Turneville Rd. W14 62 24 77 B
Turney Rd. SE21 87 32 73 B
Turney Rd. SE21 75 33 74 C
Turnham Green Terr. W4 61 21 78 A
Turnham Rd. SE4 76 36 74 A
Turnmill St. EC1 3 31 81 B
Turnpike Cl. SE8 64 36 77 D
Turnpike Ct. Bexh 79 47 75 D
Turnpike La. N8 25 31 89 A
Turnpike Link. Croy 105 33 65 A
Turnpin La. SE10 64 38 77 A
Turpentine La. SW1 9 28 78 D
Turpin Ave. Rom 29 49 91 B
Turpington Cl. Brom 107 42 66 A
Turpington La. Brom 107 42 67 C
Turpin Rd. Felt 69 09 74 D
Turpin's La. Wdf 28 43 91 A
Turpin Way. N19 36 29 86 B
Turpin Way. Wall 111 28 63 D
Turquand St. SE17 63 32 78 A
Turret Gr. SW4 74 29 75 A
Turtle Rd. SW16 96 30 69 C
Turton Rd. Wem 44 18 85 C
Turville St. E2 4 33 82 D
Tuscan Rd. SE18 66 44 78 D
Tuskar St. E10 65 39 78 C
T Watson Cott Homes. Barn 11 24 95 A
Tweedale Gr. Ruis 31 08 86 C
Tweeddale Rd. Cars 103 26 66 B
Tweed Glen. Rom 29 50 91 D
Tweed Glen. Rom 29 50 91 D
Tweed Green. Rom 29 50 91 D
Tweed Green. Rom 29 50 91 D
Tweedmouth Rd. E13 50 40 83 D
Tweed Way. Rom 29 50 91 D
Tweedy Rd. Brom 99 40 69 A
Tweezer's Alley. WC2 7 31 80 A
Twelvetrees Cres. E3 58 38 82 C
Twickenham Cl. Croy 104 30 65 D
Twickenham Gdns. Grnf 44 16 85 C
Twickenham Gdns. Har 21 15 91 C
Twickenham Rd. E11 38 38 86 B
Twickenham Rd. Felt 82 13 72 C
Twickenham Rd. Islw 71 16 75 C
Twickenham Rd. Rich 83 16 71 A
Twickenham Rd. Rich 71 17 75 D
Twigg Cl. Eri 68 51 77 C
Twilley St. SW18 85 25 73 A
Twine Ct. E1 57 35 80 A
Twineham Green. N12 15 25 92 A
Twining Ave. Twick 82 14 72 D
Twinn Rd. NW7 23 24 91 A
Twisden Rd. NW5 47 28 85 B
Twybridge Way. NW10 45 20 84 C
Twyford Ave. N2 24 27 89 B
Twyford Ave. W3 55 19 80 A
Twyford Cres. W3 55 19 80 C
Twyford Pl. WC2 3 30 81 D
Twyford Rd. Cars 103 26 66 D
Twyford Rd. Har 32 13 87 B
Twyford Rd. Ilf 51 44 85 C
Twyford St. N1 47 30 83 B
Tyas Rd. E16 58 39 82 D
Tybenham Rd. SW19 95 25 68 A
Tyberry Rd. Enf 14 35 96 A
Tyburn La. Har 33 15 87 B
Tyburn Way. W1 5 27 80 B
Tyers Gate. SE1 8 33 79 A
Tyers St. SE11 10 30 78 D
Tyers Terr. SE11 10 30 78 D
Tyeshurst Cl. SE2 67 48 78 C
Tylecroft Rd. SW16 96 30 69 C
Tyle Green. Horn 30 54 89 D
Tylehurst Gdns. Ilf 51 44 85 C
Tyler Gr. Dart 80 54 75 D
Tylers Gate. Har 33 18 88 C
Tylers Path. Cars 111 27 64 B
Tyler St. E10 65 39 78 C
Tylia Rd. E5 48 34 85 B
Tylney Ave. SE19 87 33 71 D
Tylney Rd. Brom 99 41 69 D
Tylney Rd. E7 50 41 85 A
Tynan Cl. Felt 81 10 73 C
Tyndale La. N1 48 31 84 D
Tyndale Terr. N1 48 31 84 D
Tyndall Rd. E10 38 38 86 A
Tyndall Rd. Well 78 45 75 B
Tynedale Mansions. N1 48 31 84 D
Tyneham Cl. SW11 74 28 75 A
Tyneham Rd. SW11 74 28 75 A
Tynemouth Rd. Mit 96 28 70 C
Tynemouth Rd. N15 25 33 89 D
Tynemouth St. SW6 73 26 76 C
Tyne St. E1 4 33 81 D
Tynwald Ho. SE26 87 34 72 D
Tyrawley Rd. SW6 73 25 76 B
Tyrell Cl. Har 44 15 85 A
Tyrell Ct. Cars 111 27 64 B
Tyrone Rd. E6 50 42 83 D

Tyron Way. Sid 90 45 71 D
Tyrrell Ave. Well 78 46 74 B
Tyrrell Rd. SE22 75 34 75 C
Tyrrel Way. NW9 34 22 87 A
Tyrwhitt Rd. SE4 76 37 75 A
Tysoe St. EC1 3 31 82 A
Tyson Rd. SE23 88 35 73 A
Tyssen Pas. E8 48 33 84 B
Tyssen Rd. N16 37 33 86 D
Tyssen St. E8 48 33 84 B
Tyssen St. N1 48 33 83 C
Tytherton Rd. N19 36 29 86 D

Uamvar St. E14 57 37 81 B
Uckfield Gr. Mit 96 28 69 A
Udall Gdns. Rom 29 49 91 A
Udall St. SW1 10 29 78 A
Udney Park Rd. Tedd 93 16 70 A
Uffington Rd. NW10 45 22 83 B
Uffington Rd. SE27 87 31 71 A
Ufford Cl. Har 20 13 91 C
Ufford Rd. Har 20 13 91 C
Ufford St. SE1 7 31 79 B
Ufton Gr. N1 48 33 84 C
Ufton Rd. N1 48 33 84 C
Ullathorne Rd. SW16 86 29 71 A
Ulleswater Rd. N14 16 30 93 D
Ullin St. E14 58 38 81 A
Ullswater Cl. Brom 99 39 70 C
Ullswater Cl. SW15 84 20 71 B
Ullswater Cres. SW15 84 20 71 B
Ullswater Rd. SE27 87 31 72 B
Ullswater Rd. SW13 61 22 77 C
Ulster Gdns. N13 17 32 92 A
Ulster Pl. NW1 2 28 82 D
Ulundi Rd. SE3 65 39 77 A
Ulva Rd. SW15 73 23 75 D
Ulverscroft Rd. SE22 75 34 74 A
Ulverstone Rd. SE27 87 31 72 B
Ulverston Rd. E17 26 38 90 D
Ulysses Rd. NW6 46 24 85 C
Umberston St. E1 57 34 81 D
Umbria St. SW15 72 22 74 C
Umfreville Rd. N4 37 31 88 D
Underbridge Way. Enf 14 36 96 A
Undercliff Rd. SE13 76 37 75 B
Underhill. Barn 11 25 95 A
Underhill Pas. NW1 47 28 83 B
Underhill Rd. SE22 75 34 74 C
Underhill St. NW1 47 28 83 B
Underne Ave. N14 16 28 93 B
Undershaft. EC3 4 33 81 C
Undershaw Rd. Brom 89 39 72 D
Underwood Rd. E1 57 34 82 C
Underwood Rd. E4 18 37 92 D
Underwood Row. N1 4 32 82 A
Underwood St. N1 4 32 82 A
Underwood The. SE9 89 42 72 B
Undine St. SW17 86 27 71 D
Uneeda Dri. Grnf 43 14 83 B
Unicorn Pas. SE1 8 33 80 C
Union Ct. EC2 4 33 81 C
Union Dri. E2 57 36 82 C
Union Gr. SW8 74 29 76 D
Union Mews. SW4 74 30 76 C
Union Rd. Brom 107 41 67 B
Union Rd. Croy 105 32 66 A
Union Rd. N11 24 29 91 B
Union Rd. Nthlt 43 13 83 C
Union Rd. SW8 74 29 76 D
Union Rd. Wem 44 18 84 A
Union St. Barn 11 24 96 A
Union St. E15 49 38 83 B
Union St. King 93 17 69 D
Union St. N1 48 32 83 A
Union St. SE1 8 32 80 C
Union Wlk. E2 4 33 82 C
Unity Way. SE18 65 41 79 D
University Cl. NW9 22 21 91 D
University Pl. Eri 67 50 77 C
University Rd. SW19 95 26 70 B
University St. WC1 2 29 82 C
Unwin Ave. Felt 69 08 74 B
Unwin Cl. SE15 63 34 77 A
Unwin Rd. Islw 71 15 75 A
Unwin Rd. SW7 5 26 79 D
Upbrook Mews. W2 1 26 81 C
Upcerne Rd. SW10 62 26 77 C
Updale Rd. Sid 90 45 71 B
Upfield. Croy 105 34 65 B
Upfield Rd. W7 54 15 81 B
Upgrove Manor Way. SE24 87 31 73 A
Uphall Rd. Ilf 51 43 85 D
Upham Park Rd. W4 61 21 78 A
Uphill Dri. NW9 34 20 88 A
Upland Court Rd. Rom 30 54 90 D
Upland Rd. Bexh 79 48 75 B
Upland Rd. E13 58 40 82 C
Upland Rd. S Croy 112 32 64 D
Upland Rd. SE22 75 34 74 B
Upland Rd. Sutt 110 26 63 D
Uplands Ave. E17 26 35 90 D
Uplands. Beck 98 37 69 C
Uplands Cl. SW14 72 19 74 B
Uplands Park Rd. Enf 13 31 97 C
Uplands Rd. Barn 16 28 94 C
Uplands Rd. N8 37 31 88 C
Uplands Rd. Orp 108 46 66 D
Uplands Rd. Rom 29 47 89 B
Uplands Rd. Wdf Gn 27 42 91 C
Uplands The. Ruis 31 10 87 A
Uplands Way. N21 13 31 95 A
Upminster Rd. Horn 42 54 86 B
Upney La. Bark 51 45 84 B
Upnor Way. SE17 63 33 78 C
Uppark Dri. Ilf 40 44 88 C
Upper Abbey Rd. Belv 67 49 78 A
Upper Addison Gdns. W14 62 24 79 A
Upper Bardsey Wlk. N1 48 32 84 A
Upper Belgrave St. SW1 6 28 79 C
Upper Berenger Wlk. SW10 62 26 77 D
Upper Berkeley St. W1 1 27 81 D
Upper Beulah Hill. SE19 97 33 69 A
Upper Blantyre Wlk. SW10 62 26 77 D
Upper Brentwood Rd. Rom 30 53 89 A
Upper Brighton Rd. Surb 101 18 66 A
Upper Brockley Rd. SE4 76 36 76 D
Upper Brockley Rd. SE4 76 36 76 D
Upper Brook St. W1 6 28 80 A
Upper Butts. Brent 60 17 77 A
Upper Caldy Wlk. N1 48 32 84 A
Upper Camelford Wlk. W11 56 24 81 C
Upper Cavendish Ave. N3 23 25 89 A
Upper Cheyne Row. SW3 9 27 77 A
Upper Clapton Rd. E5 37 34 86 B
Upper Clarendon Wlk. W11 56 24 81 C
Upper Dartrey Wlk. SW10 62 26 77 D
Upper Dengie Wlk (off Maldon Cl). N1 48 32 83 A
Upper Elmers End Rd. Beck 106 36 67 B
Upper Farm Rd. E Mol 92 12 68 D
Upper Green E. Mit 96 27 68 B
Upper Green W. Mit 96 27 69 D
Upper Grenfell Wlk. W11 56 23 80 B
Upper Grosvenor St. W1 6 28 80 A
Upper Grotto Rd. Twick 83 15 72 B
Upper Ground. SE1 7 31 80 C
Upper Grove Rd. Belv 67 48 77 B
Upper Gr. SE25 97 33 68 D
Upper Gulland Wlk. N1 48 32 84 B
Upper Halliford Rd. Shep 91 09 68 A
Upper Ham Rd. Rich 83 17 71 B
Upper Handa Wlk. N1 48 32 84 A
Upper Harley St. NW1 2 28 82 C
Upper Hawkwell Wlk (off Maldon Cl). N1 48 32 83 A
Upper Holly Hill Rd. Belv 67 49 78 D
Upper James St. W1 6 29 80 A
Upper John St. W1 6 29 80 A
Upper Lismore Wlk. N1 48 32 84 A
Upper Mall. W6 61 22 78 C
Upper Marsh. SE1 7 30 79 B
Upper Montague St. W1 1 27 81 B
Upper Mulgrave Rd. Sutt 110 24 63 C
Upper North St. E14 57 37 81 C
Upper Park Rd. Belv 67 49 78 B
Upper Park Rd. Brom 99 41 69 A
Upper Park Rd. King 94 19 70 A
Upper Park Rd. N11 16 29 92 C
Upper Park Rd. NW3 47 27 85 D
Upper Phillimore Gdns. W8 62 25 79 A
Upper Rainham Rd. Horn 42 51 86 B
Upper Ramsey Wlk. N1 48 32 84 B
Upper Rawreth Wlk (off Basire St). N1 48 32 83 A
Upper Rd. E13 58 40 82 A
Upper Rd. N2 24 27 90 A
Upper Rd. Wall 111 29 64 D
Upper Richmond Rd. SW15 73 23 75 D
Upper Richmond Rd W. Rich 72 19 75 D
Upper Richmond Rd W. SW14 72 20 75 D
Upper Richmond Rd W. SW15 72 21 75 D
Upper Selsdon Rd. S Croy 112 34 62 A
Upper Sheppey Wlk. N1 48 32 84 A
Upper Sheridan Rd. Belv 67 49 78 A
Upper Shirley Rd. Croy 106 35 65 D
Upper Sq. Islw 71 16 75 A
Upper Staithe. W4 72 20 76 A
Upper St Martin's La. WC2 7 30 80 A
Upper St. N1 48 31 83 B
Upper Sunbury Rd. Hamp 92 13 69 A
Upper Sutton La. Houn 70 13 76 A
Upper Tachbrook St. SW1 10 29 78 A
Upper Talbot Wlk. W11 56 24 81 C
Upper Teddington Rd. King 93 17 69 A
Upper Teddington Rd. Tedd 93 17 70 C
Upper Terr. NW3 35 26 86 C
Upper Thames St. EC4 8 32 80 A
Upper Tollington Park. N4 37 31 87 C
Upperton Rd. Sid 90 45 71 D
Upperton Road E. E13 58 41 82 A
Upperton Road W. E13 58 41 82 A
Upper Tooting Park. SW17 86 28 72 A
Upper Tooting Rd. SW17 86 27 72 D
Upper Town Rd. Grnf 53 13 82 D
Upper Tulse Hill. SW2 86 30 73 B
Upper Vernon Rd. Sutt 110 26 64 D
Upper Walthamstow Rd. E17 26 38 89 B
Upper Whistler Wlk. SW10 62 26 77 D
Upper Wickham La. Well 78 46 76 D
Upper Wimpole St. W1 2 28 81 A
Upper Woburn Pl. WC1 2 29 82 B
Uppingham Ave. Stan 21 17 90 C
Upsdell Ave. N13 25 31 91 A
Upstall St. SE5 75 31 76 B
Upton Ave. E7 50 40 84 C
Upton Cl. Bex 79 48 74 D
Upton Cross. E13 50 40 83 A
Upton Dene. Sutt 110 25 63 D
Upton Gdns. Har 33 17 88 C
Upton La. E7 50 40 84 D
Upton Park Rd. E7 50 40 84 D
Upton Rd. Bex 79 48 74 D
Upton Rd. Bexh 79 48 74 A
Upton Rd. Houn 70 13 75 A
Upton Rd. N18 17 34 92 D
Upton Rd S. Bex 79 48 74 D
Upton Rd. SE18 66 44 77 A
Upton Rd. Th Hth 97 32 69 D
Upway. N12 24 27 91 A
Upwood Rd. SE12 77 40 74 C
Upwood Rd. SW16 96 30 69 A
Urban Ave. Horn 42 53 86 C
Urlwin St. SE5 63 32 77 A
Urlwin Wlk. SW9 75 31 76 A
Urmston Dri. SW19 85 24 73 C
Urquhart Ct. Beck 98 36 70 D
Ursula St. SW11 74 27 76 A
Urswick Gdns. Dag 52 48 84 C
Urswick Rd. Dag 52 48 84 C
Urswick Rd. E5 49 35 85 C
Usher Rd. E3 49 36 83 B
Usher Rd. E3 49 36 83 D
Usk Rd. SW11 73 26 75 C
Usk St. E16 58 39 80 B
Usk St. E2 57 35 82 B
Uvedale Rd. Dag 41 49 86 C
Uvedale Rd. Enf 13 32 95 B
Uverdale Rd. SW10 62 26 77 C
Uxbridge Rd. Hamp 82 13 71 B
Uxbridge Rd. Har 20 14 91 D
Uxbridge Rd. King 101 17 67 B
Uxbridge Rd. Pnr 20 12 91 D
Uxbridge Rd. Stan 21 15 91 B
Uxbridge Rd. Sthl 53 13 80 C
Uxbridge Rd. Twick 82 11 72 B
Uxbridge Rd. W12 55 22 80 D
Uxbridge Rd. W13 54 16 80 D
Uxbridge Rd. W3 55 20 80 D
Uxbridge Rd. W5 54 18 80 A
Uxbridge Rd. W7 54 15 80 D
Uxbridge St. W8 56 25 80 C
Uxendon Cres. Wem 33 18 87 C
Uxendon Hill. Wem 33 18 87 B

Valan Leas. Brom 99 39 68 A
Vale Cl. Twick 83 16 72 C
Vale Cl. W9 1 26 82 A
Vale Cottages. Brom 99 40 68 A
Vale Cres. SW15 84 21 71 A
Vale Croft Pnr 32 12 88 A
Vale Ct. Wem 33 17 86 C
Vale Dri. Barn 11 25 95 A
Vale End. SE22 75 33 75 D
Vale Estate The. W3 55 21 80 C
Vale Gr. N4 37 32 87 A
Vale Gr. W3 55 20 80 D
Vale La. W3 55 19 81 A
Vale Lodge. SE23 88 35 72 A
Valence Ave. Dag 41 47 86 B
Valence Circ. Dag 41 48 86 C
Valence Rd. Eri 67 50 77 D
Valence Wood Rd. Dag 41 48 86 C
Valentia Pl. SW9 75 31 75 C
Valentine Ct. SE23 88 35 72 B
Valentine Pl. SE1 7 31 79 B
Valentine Rd. E9 49 35 84 B
Valentine Rd. Har 32 14 86 C
Valentine Row. SE1 7 31 79 B
Valentines Rd. Ilf 40 43 87 D
Valentines Way. Rom 42 51 86 A
Vale of Health. NW3 35 26 86 D
Vale Rd. Brom 100 43 69 C
Vale Rd. E7 50 40 84 B
Vale Rd. Mit 96 29 68 D
Vale Rd. N4 37 32 88 C
Vale Rd N. Surb 101 18 65 A
Vale Rd S. Surb 101 18 65 A
Vale Rd. Sutt 110 25 64 B
Vale Rd. Wor Pk 102 21 65 D
Valerian Way. E15 58 39 82 A
Valerie Ct. Sutt 110 25 63 D
Vale Rise. NW11 35 24 87 D
Vale Row. N5 37 31 86 D
Vale Royal. N7 47 30 84 C
Valeswood Rd. Brom 89 39 71 D
Vale Terr. N4 37 32 87 A
Vale The. Croy 106 35 65 B
Vale The. Felt 69 10 74 D
Vale The. Houn 59 12 77 A
Vale The. N10 24 28 90 A
Vale The. N14 16 29 94 A
Vale The. NW11 35 24 86 A
Vale The. Ruis 43 11 85 A
Vale The. Sun 91 10 70 A
Vale The. SW3 62 26 77 B
Vale The. W3 55 21 80 C
Vale The. Wdf Gn 27 40 91 C
Valetta Gr. E13 50 40 83 C
Valetta Rd. W3 61 21 79 B
Valette St. E9 49 35 84 A
Valiant Cl. Nthlt 53 11 82 B
Valiant Cl. Rom 29 49 90 D
Vallance Rd. E1 57 34 82 C
Vallance Rd. E2 57 34 82 C
Vallance Rd. N22 24 29 90 C
Vallentin Rd. E17 26 38 89 C
Valley Ave. N12 15 26 92 B
Valley Cl. Dart 80 51 74 D
Valley Cl. Pnr 19 10 90 D
Valley Dri. NW9 34 19 88 B
Valleyfield Rd. SW16 86 30 71 D
Valley Fields Cres. Enf 13 31 97 C
Valley Gdns. SW19 95 26 70 D
Valley Gdns. Wem 44 18 84 D
Valley Gr. SE7 65 41 78 C
Valley Mews. Twick 83 16 72 A
Valley Rd. Belv 67 50 78 A
Valley Rd. Brom 99 39 69 C
Valley Rd. Dart 80 51 74 D
Valley Rd. Eri 67 50 78 B
Valley Rd. Orp 100 46 70 D
Valley Rd. SW16 86 30 71 B
Valley Side. E4 18 37 94 C
Valley View. Barn 11 24 95 C
Valley Wlk. Croy 106 35 65 A
Valliere Rd. NW10 55 22 82 A
Valliers Wood Rd. Sid 90 45 73 C
Vallis Way. W13 54 16 81 A
Valmar Rd. SE5 75 32 76 A
Valnay St. SW17 86 27 71 D
Valognes Ave. E17 26 36 90 A
Valonia Gdns. SW18 73 24 74 D
Vambery Rd. SE18 66 44 77 A
Vanbrough Cres. Nthlt 43 11 83 A
Vanbrugh Fields. SE3 65 39 77 D
Vanbrugh Hill. E10 65 39 78 D
Vanbrugh Hill. SE3 65 39 77 B
Vanbrugh Park Rd. SE3 65 39 77 D
Vanbrugh Park Rd W. SE3 65 39 77 D
Vanbrugh Park. SE3 65 39 77 D
Vanbrugh Rd. W4 61 20 79 D
Vanbrugh Terr. SE3 77 39 76 B
Vanburgh Cl. Orp 108 45 66 C
Vancouver Rd. Edg 22 19 90 B
Vancouver Rd. Rich 83 17 71 A
Vancouver Rd. SE23 88 36 72 A
Vanderbilt Rd. SW18 85 26 73 C
Vandome Cl. E16 58 40 81 D
Vandon Pas. SW1 6 29 79 C
Vandon St. SW1 6 29 79 C
Van Dyck Ave. N.Mal 102 20 66 B
Vandyke Cl. SW15 73 23 74 D
Vandyke Cross. SE9 77 42 74 A
Vandy St. EC2 4 33 82 C
Vane Cl. Har 33 18 88 D
Vane Cl. NW3 46 26 85 B
Vanessa Cl. Belv 67 49 78 C
Vane St. SW1 10 29 78 A
Vanguard Cl. Croy 105 31 66 D
Vanguard Cl. Rom 29 49 90 D
Vanguard St. SE8 76 37 76 A
Vanguard Way. Wall 111 30 63 C
Vanoc Gdns. Brom 89 40 71 A
Vansittart Rd. E7 50 40 85 A
Vansittart St. SE14 64 36 77 C
Vanston Pl. SW6 62 25 77 C
Vant Rd. SW17 86 27 71 D
Varcoe Rd. SE16 64 35 78 C
Vardens Rd. SW11 73 26 75 D
Varden St. E1 57 34 81 D
Varley Rd. E16 58 40 81 D
Varna Rd. Hamp 92 13 69 B
Varna Rd. SW6 62 24 77 D
Varndell St. NW1 2 29 82 A
Vartry Rd. N15 37 33 88 C
Vassall Rd. SW9 63 31 77 C
Vauban St. SE16 8 33 79 D
Vaughan Ave. NW4 34 22 88 A
Vaughan Ave. W6 61 21 78 B
Vaughan Cl. Hamp 92 12 70 A
Vaughan Gdns. Ilf 39 42 87 B
Vaughan Rd. E15 50 39 84 B
Vaughan Rd. Har 32 14 88 D
Vaughan Rd. SE5 75 32 75 A
Vaughan Rd. Surb 101 16 66 B
Vaughan Rd. Well 78 45 76 D
Vaughan Williams Cl. SE8 64 37 77 C
Vauxhall Bridge Rd. SW1 10 29 78 A
Vauxhall Bridge. SE1 10 30 78 C
Vauxhall Cross. SE1 10 30 78 C
Vauxhall Gdns. S Croy 112 32 63 A
Vauxhall Gr. SW8 10 30 77 B
Vauxhall St. SE11 10 30 78 D
Vauxhall Wlk. SE11 10 30 78 D
Vawdrey Cl. E1 57 35 82 C
Vectis Gdns. SW17 96 28 70 B
Vectis Rd. SW17 96 28 70 B
Veda Rd. SE13 76 37 75 C
Veldt Way. SE22 75 33 74 A
Venables St. NW8 1 26 81 B
Vencourt Pl. W6 61 22 78 A
Venetian Rd. SE5 75 32 76 C
Venetia Rd. N4 37 31 88 D
Venetia Rd. W5 60 17 79 B
Venner Rd. SE26 88 35 71 C
Venners Cl. Bexh 80 51 76 C
Venn St. SW4 74 29 75 C
Ventnor Ave. Stan 21 16 90 B
Ventnor Dri. N20 15 25 93 D
Ventnor Gdns. Bark 51 45 84 A
Ventnor Rd. SE14 64 35 77 D
Ventnor Rd. Sutt 110 25 63 D
Venue St. E14 58 38 81 A
Venus Rd. SE18 65 42 79 D
Vera Ave. N21 13 31 95 A
Vera Rd. SW6 73 24 76 A
Verbena Gdns. W6 61 22 78 C
Verdant La. SE6 89 39 73 C
Verdayne Ave. Croy 106 35 65 B
Verdun Rd. SE18 66 46 77 A
Verdun Rd. SW13 61 22 77 C
Vereker Dri. Sun 91 10 69 C
Vereker Rd. W14 62 24 78 C
Vere St. W1 2 28 81 D
Vermont Rd. SE19 97 33 70 A
Vermont Rd. Sutt 103 25 65 D
Vermont Rd. SW18 73 25 74 D
Verney Gdns. Dag 52 48 85 A
Verney Rd. Dag 52 48 85 A
Verney Rd. SE16 63 34 78 D
Verney St. NW10 34 20 86 D
Verney Way. SE16 63 34 78 D
Vernham Rd. SE18 66 44 77 A
Vernon Ave. E12 50 42 85 B
Vernon Ave. SW20 95 23 69 D
Vernon Ave. Wdf Gn 27 40 91 D
Vernon Cl. Eps 109 20 63 A
Vernon Cl. Orp 100 46 68 B
Vernon Cres. Barn 12 28 95 C
Vernon Ct. Stan 21 16 90 B
Vernon Dri. Stan 21 16 90 A
Vernon Pl. WC1 3 30 81 A
Vernon Rd. E11 39 39 87 C
Vernon Rd. E15 50 39 84 C
Vernon Rd. E17 38 36 88 B
Vernon Rd. E3 49 36 83 D
Vernon Rd. Felt 81 09 72 B
Vernon Rd. Ilf 40 45 87 D
Vernon Rd. N8 25 31 89 A
Vernon Rd. Sutt 110 26 64 C
Vernon Rd. SW14 72 20 75 B
Vernon Rise. Grnf 43 14 85 D
Vernon Rise. WC1 3 30 82 B
Vernon Sq. WC1 3 30 82 B
Vernon St. W14 62 24 78 A
Vernon Yd. W11 56 24 80 B
Veroan Rd. Bexh 79 48 76 C
Verona Dri. Surb 101 18 65 A
Verona Rd. E7 50 40 84 C
Veronica Cl. Rom 30 53 91 C
Veronica Rd. SW17 86 28 72 B
Veronique Gdns. Ilf 40 44 88 A
Verran Rd. SW12 86 28 73 B
Versailles Rd. SE20 97 34 70 C
Verulam Ave. E17 38 36 87 B
Verulam Rd. Sthl 53 13 82 C
Verulam St. WC1 3 31 81 A
Verwood Rd. Har 20 14 90 C
Vesey Path. E14 57 37 81 D
Vespan Rd. W12 61 22 79 A
Vesta Rd. SE4 76 36 76 C
Vestris Rd. SE23 88 35 72 B
Vestry Mews. SE5 75 33 76 A
Vestry Rd. E17 26 37 89 D
Vestry Rd. SE5 75 33 76 A
Vestry St. N1 4 32 82 B
Vevey St. SE6 88 36 72 B
Veysey Gdns. Dag 41 49 86 C
Viaduct Pl. E2 57 34 82 D
Viaduct Rd. N2 24 27 90 C
Viaduct St. E2 57 34 82 B
Viaduct The. Wem 44 18 83 A
Viaduct Yd. EC1 3 31 81 A
Vian St. SE13 76 37 75 B
Vibart Gdns. SW2 86 30 73 B
Vibart Wlk. N1 47 30 83 A
Vicarage Ave. SE3 65 40 77 C
Vicarage Cl. Eri 67 50 77 A
Vicarage Cl. Nthlt 43 12 84 D
Vicarage Cl. Ruis 31 08 87 B
Vicarage Cres. SW11 73 26 76 B
Vicarage Ct. Felt 81 08 73 A
Vicarage Dri. Bark 51 44 84 C
Vicarage Dri. SW14 72 20 74 B
Vicarage Farm Rd. Houn 70 12 76 A
Vicarage Gate. W8 62 25 79 B
Vicarage Gate. W8 56 25 80 D
Vicarage Gdns. Mit 96 27 68 A
Vicarage Gdns. W8 56 25 80 C
Vicarage Gr. SE5 75 32 76 B
Vicarage La. E15 50 39 84 D
Vicarage La. Eps 109 22 62 A
Vicarage La. Ilf 40 44 87 D
Vicarage Park. SE18 66 44 78 C
Vicarage Path. N8 36 30 87 A
Vicarage Rd. Croy 105 31 65 C
Vicarage Rd. Dag 52 49 84 D
Vicarage Rd. E10 38 37 87 D
Vicarage Rd. E15 50 39 84 D
Vicarage Rd. Horn 42 52 87 C
Vicarage Rd. King 93 17 69 A
Vicarage Rd. N17 25 34 90 A
Vicarage Rd. NW4 34 22 88 C
Vicarage Rd. SE18 66 44 78 C
Vicarage Rd. Sun 91 10 70 A
Vicarage Rd. Sutt 103 25 65 D
Vicarage Rd. SW14 72 20 74 B
Vicarage Rd. Tedd 83 16 71 C
Vicarage Rd. Twick 70 14 74 C
Vicarage Rd. Twick 83 15 72 A
Vicarage Rd. Wdf Gn 27 42 91 C
Vicarage Way. Har 32 13 87 A
Vicarage Way. NW10 34 20 86 D
Vicarage Wlk. SW6 73 26 76 B
Vicar's Cl. E15 50 40 83 A
Vicar's Cl. E9 49 35 83 A
Vicar's Cl. Enf 13 33 97 C
Vicars Hill. SE13 76 37 75 D
Vicar's Moor La. N21 17 31 94 B
Vicars Oak Rd. SE19 97 33 70 A
Vicar's Rd. NW5 47 28 85 C
Vicar's Wlk. Dag 40 46 86 D
Viceroy Cl. N2 24 27 89 C
Viceroy Rd. SW8 74 30 76 A
Vickers Rd. Eri 67 50 78 D
Victor App. Horn 42 53 87 D
Victor Cl. Horn 42 53 87 D
Victor Gdns. Horn 42 53 87 D
Victor Gr. Wem 44 18 84 C
Victoria Arc. SW1 6 28 79 D
Victoria Ave. Barn 11 26 96 D
Victoria Ave. E6 50 41 83 B
Victoria Ave. EC2 4 33 81 A
Victoria Ave. E Mol 92 13 68 B
Victoria Ave. Houn 70 13 74 A
Victoria Ave. N3 23 24 90 B
Victoria Ave. Rom 29 49 91 B
Victoria Ave. S Croy 112 32 62 C
Victoria Ave. Surb 101 17 67 D

Victoria Ave. Wall 104 28 65 C
Victoria Ave. Wem 45 19 84 B
Victoria Cl. E Mol 92 13 68 A
Victoria Cl. Har 33 15 88 D
Victoria Cottages. Rich 72 19 76 A
Victoria Cres. N15 37 33 88 A
Victoria Cres. SE19 97 33 70 A
Victoria Cres. SW19 95 24 70 D
Victoria Ct. W3 61 19 79 A
Victoria Ct. Wem 45 19 84 A
Victoria Dock Rd. E16 58 40 80 A
Victoria Dri. SW19 85 23 73 D
Victoria Emb. EC4 7 31 80 A
Victoria Emb. SW1 7 30 79 A
Victoria Emb. WC2 7 30 80 B
Victoria Gdns. Houn 70 12 76 A
Victoria Gdns. W11 56 25 80 C
Victoria Gr Mews. W2 56 25 80 B
Victoria Gr. N12 15 26 92 D
Victoria Gr. W8 5 26 79 C
Victoria La. Barn 11 24 96 D
Victoria Mews. NW6 46 25 83 A
Victoria Mews. SW4 74 28 75 D
Victorian Gr. N16 37 33 86 C
Victorian Rd. N16 37 33 86 D
Victoria Park Rd. E9 49 36 84 C
Victoria Park Sq. E2 57 35 82 A
Victoria Pl. Rich 71 17 74 B
Victoria Rd. Bark 51 43 84 B
Victoria Rd. Barn 11 26 96 D
Victoria Rd. Bexh 79 49 75 C
Victoria Rd. Brom 107 41 67 B
Victoria Rd. Chis 90 43 71 C
Victoria Rd. Dag 52 50 85 C
Victoria Rd. Dart 80 54 74 A
Victoria Rd. E11 50 39 85 A
Victoria Rd. E13 50 40 83 C
Victoria Rd. E17 26 38 90 C
Victoria Rd. E18 27 40 89 B
Victoria Rd. Eri 68 51 77 A
Victoria Rd. Felt 81 10 73 D
Victoria Rd. King 93 18 69 D
Victoria Rd. Mit 96 27 70 D
Victoria Rd. N15 25 34 89 C
Victoria Rd. N18 17 33 92 B
Victoria Rd. N22 24 29 90 B
Victoria Rd. N4 36 30 87 B
Victoria Rd. N4 37 31 87 C
Victoria Rd. N9 17 33 93 D
Victoria Rd. NW10 55 21 82 C
Victoria Rd. NW4 23 23 89 D
Victoria Rd. Rom 42 51 88 B
Victoria Rd. Ruis 31 10 86 A
Victoria Rd. Ruis 43 11 85 D
Victoria Rd. Sid 90 46 72 C
Victoria Rd. Sthl 59 12 79 D
Victoria Rd. Surb 101 17 67 D
Victoria Rd. Sutt 110 26 64 D
Victoria Rd. SW14 72 20 75 B
Victoria Rd. Tedd 93 16 70 A
Victoria Rd. Twick 83 16 73 B
Victoria Rd. W3 55 20 81 C
Victoria Rd. W5 54 16 81 B
Victoria Rd. W8 5 26 79 C
Victoria Rise. SW4 74 28 75 B
Victoria Scott Ct. Dart 80 51 75 A
Victoria Sq. SW1 6 28 79 D
Victoria St. Belv 67 48 78 D
Victoria St. E15 50 39 84 C
Victoria St. SW1 6 29 79 C
Victoria Terr. Har 33 15 87 C
Victoria Terr. N4 37 31 87 C
Victoria Vils. N9 17 32 92 D
Victoria Villas. Rich 71 18 75 D
Victoria Way. SE7 65 40 78 D
Victor Rd. Har 20 14 89 A
Victor Rd. NW10 55 22 82 B
Victor Rd. SE20 98 35 70 D
Victor Rd. Tedd 83 15 71 A
Victors Dri. Hamp 92 12 70 A
Victor Wlk. Horn 42 53 87 D
Victory Ave. Mord 103 26 67 A
Victory Pl. SE17 63 32 78 B
Victory Pl. SE19 97 33 70 A
Victory Rd. SW19 95 26 70 C
Victory Sq. SE5 63 32 77 D
Victory Way. Rom 29 49 90 B
Victory Wlk. SE8 76 37 76 A
View Cl. Har 20 14 89 D
View Cl. N6 36 27 87 B
Viewfield Rd. SW18 73 24 74 D
Viewland Rd. SE18 66 45 78 D
View Rd. N6 36 27 88 D
View The. SE2 67 48 78 C
Viga Rd. N21 13 31 95 C
Vigilant Cl. SE26 87 34 71 A
Vignoles Rd. Rom 41 49 87 A
Vigo St. W1 6 29 80 A
Viking Rd. Sthl 53 12 80 A
Villacourt Rd. SE18 66 46 77 A
Village Cl. E4 18 38 92 C
Village Green Rd. Dart 80 52 75 C
Village Home The. Ilf 28 44 89 A
Village Rd. Enf 13 33 95 C
Village Rd. N3 23 24 90 C
Village Row. Sutt 110 25 63 C
Village The. SE7 65 41 77 B
Village Way. Ashf 81 07 71 A
Village Way. Beck 98 37 68 A
Village Way E. Har 32 13 87 A
Village Way. NW10 45 20 85 B
Village Way. Pnr 32 12 87 B
Village Way. SE21 75 32 74 D
Villa Rd. SW9 75 31 75 A
Villas Rd. SE18 66 44 78 A
Villa St. SE17 63 32 78 D
Villa St. SE17 63 32 78 D
Villa Wlk. SE17 63 32 78 D
Villers Cl. E10 38 37 86 A
Villiers Ave. Surb 101 18 67 B
Villiers Ave. Twick 82 12 73 D
Villiers Cl. King 93 18 68 D
Villier's Path. Surb 101 18 67 A
Villiers Rd. Beck 98 35 69 D
Villiers Rd. Islw 71 15 76 C
Villiers Rd. King 93 18 68 B
Villiers Rd. NW2 45 22 84 A
Villiers Rd. Sthl 53 12 80 D
Villiers St. WC2 7 30 80 C
Vincam Cl. Twick 82 13 73 A
Vincent Ave. Surb 102 19 65 B
Vincent Cl. Barn 11 25 96 B
Vincent Cl. Brom 99 40 68 D
Vincent Cl. Ilf 28 44 91 A
Vincent Cl. Sid 90 45 73 C
Vincent Dri. Shep 91 09 68 A
Vincent Gdns. NW2 34 21 86 D
Vincent Rd. Croy 105 33 66 A
Vincent Rd. Dag 52 48 84 C
Vincent Rd. E4 26 38 91 B
Vincent Rd. Houn 70 11 75 B
Vincent Rd. Islw 70 14 76 B
Vincent Rd. King 94 19 68 A
Vincent Rd. N15 25 32 89 C
Vincent Rd. N22 25 31 90 C
Vincent Rd. SE18 66 43 78 B
Vincent Rd. W3 61 20 79 C
Vincent Rd. Wem 44 18 84 D
Vincent Row. Hamp 82 14 71 C
Vincent Sq. N22 25 31 90 C
Vincent Sq. SW1 10 29 78 B
Vincent St. E16 58 39 81 B
Vincent St. SW1 10 29 78 B
Vincent Terr. N1 48 31 83 D
Vince St. EC1 4 32 82 B
Vine Cl. Surb 101 18 67 D
Vine Cl. Sutt 103 26 65 C
Vine Ct. E1 57 34 81 A
Vine Ct. Har 33 18 88 C
Vinegar Yd. SE1 8 33 79 A
Vine Gdns. Ilf 51 44 85 C
Vine Hill. EC1 3 31 82 C
Vine La. SE1 8 33 80 C
Vine Pl. Houn 70 13 75 D
Vine Rd. E15 50 39 84 D
Vine Rd. E Mol 92 14 68 C
Vine Rd. SW13 72 21 75 B
Vineries Cl. Dag 52 48 84 B
Vineries The. Enf 13 33 96 A
Vineries The. N14 12 29 95 C
Vinery Villas. NW8 1 27 82 A
Vines Ave. N3 3 25 90 B
Vine St. EC3 8 33 80 B
Vine St. EC3 4 33 81 D
Vine St. Rom 29 50 89 C
Vine St. W1 6 29 80 A
Vineyard Ave. NW7 23 24 91 C
Vineyard Cl. SE6 88 37 73 C
Vineyard Hill Rd. SW19 85 25 71 A
Vineyard Pas. Rich 71 18 74 A
Vineyard Path. SW14 72 20 75 B
Vineyard Rd. Felt 81 10 72 C
Vineyard Row. King 93 17 69 A
Vineyard The. Rich 71 18 74 A
Vineyard Wlk. EC1 3 31 82 C
Vine Yd. SE1 8 32 79 A
Viney Rd. SE13 76 37 75 B
Vining St. SW9 75 31 75 C
Vinlake Ave. Uxb 31 07 86 C
Vinson Cl. Orp 108 46 66 C
Vintners Pl. EC4 8 32 80 A
Viola Ave. Felt 70 11 74 C
Viola Ave. SE2 66 46 78 D
Viola Sq. W12 55 21 80 B
Violet Gdns. Croy 112 31 64 D
Violet Hill. NW8 46 26 83 C
Violet La. Croy 112 31 64 D
Violet Rd. E14 57 37 81 B
Violet Rd. E17 38 37 88 C
Violet Rd. E18 27 40 90 D
Violet Rd. E3 57 37 82 D
Violet St. E2 57 34 82 D
Virgil Pl. W1 1 27 81 B
Virgil St. SE1 7 30 79 D
Virginia Gdns. Ilf 28 44 90 D
Virginia Rd. E2 4 33 82 B
Virginia Rd. Th Hth 97 31 69 B
Virginia St. E1 57 34 80 A
Virginia Wlk. SW2 74 30 74 D
Viscount Gr. Nthlt 53 11 82 B
Viscount St. EC1 4 32 81 A
Viscount Way. Houn 69 09 75 C
Vista Ave. Enf 14 35 97 D
Vista Dri. Ilf 39 41 88 B
Vista The. SE9 89 41 73 B
Vista Way. Har 33 18 88 C
Vivian Ave. NW4 34 22 88 B
Vivian Ave. Wem 45 19 84 B
Vivian Gdns. Wem 45 19 85 C
Vivian Rd. E3 49 36 83 C
Vivian Sq. SE15 75 34 75 B
Vivian Way. N2 35 26 88 B
Vivian Way. N2 24 27 89 C
Vivienne Cl. Twick 71 17 74 D
Voce Rd. SE18 66 44 77 D
Voewood Cl. N.Mal 102 21 67 D
Voltaire Rd. SW4 74 29 75 B
Voluntary Pl. E11 39 40 88 C
Vorley Rd. N19 36 29 86 A
Voss Ct. SW16 96 30 70 A
Voss St. E2 57 34 82 A
Vrow Wlk. E Mol 93 15 68 B
Vulcan Cl. Wall 111 30 63 D
Vulcan Gate. Enf 13 31 97 C
Vulcan Rd. SE4 76 36 76 D
Vulcan Terr. SE4 76 36 76 D
Vulcan Way. N7 47 30 84 B
Vyner Rd. W3 55 20 80 B
Vyner St. E2 48 34 83 B
Vyne The. Bexh 79 49 75 B
Vyse Cl. Barn 11 23 96 C

Wadding St. SE17 63 32 78 B
Waddington Rd. E15 49 38 84 B
Waddington St. E15 49 38 84 B
Waddington Way. SE19 97 32 69 A
Waddon Cl. Croy 105 31 65 C
Waddon Court Rd. Croy 105 31 65 C
Waddon Marsh Way. Croy 104 30 66 D
Waddon New Rd. Croy 105 31 65 B
Waddon Park Ave. Croy 105 31 65 C
Waddon Rd. Croy 105 31 65 D
Waddon Way. Croy 112 31 63 B
Wade Rd. E16 58 41 81 C
Wade's Gr. N21 17 31 94 C
Wade's Hill. N21 17 31 94 A
Wade's La. Tedd 83 16 71 C
Wadeson St. E2 48 34 83 D
Wade's Pl. E14 57 37 80 B
Wadesville Ave. 41 48 87 B
Wadeville Cl. Belv 67 49 78 C
Wadham Ave. E17 26 37 91 D
Wadham Gdns. Grnf 43 14 84 B
Wadham Gdns. NW3 47 27 84 C
Wadham Rd. E17 26 38 90 A
Wadham Rd. SW15 73 24 75 C
Wadhurst Cl. SE20 97 34 69 D
Wadhurst Rd. W4 61 20 79 D
Wadley Rd. E11 39 39 87 A
Wadsworth Cl. Enf 14 35 95 B
Wadsworth Cl. Grnf 44 17 83 C
Wadsworth Rd. Grnf 44 17 83 C
Wager St. E3 57 36 82 D
Waggon La. N18 25 34 91 A
Waghorn Rd. Har 21 17 89 B
Waghorn St. SE15 75 34 75 A
Wagner St. SE15 64 35 77 C
Waid Cl. Dart 80 54 74 D
Waights Ct. King 93 18 69 A
Wainfleet Ave. Rom 29 50 90 C
Wainford Cl. SW19 85 23 73 D
Waite Davies Rd. SE12 89 39 73 D
Waite St. SE15 63 33 77 B
Waithman St. EC4 3 31 81 D
Wakefield Gdns. Ilf 39 42 88 C
Wakefield Gdns. SE19 97 33 70 C
Wakefield Rd. N15 37 33 88 B
Wakefield Rd. N11 16 29 92 D
Wakefield Rd. Rich 71 17 74 B
Wakefield St. E6 50 41 83 B
Wakefield St. E6 50 42 83 A
Wakefield St. N18 17 34 92 C
Wakefield St. WC1 3 30 82 A
Wakehams Hill. Pnr 20 12 89 B
Wakeham St. N1 48 32 84 B
Wakehurst Rd. SW11 74 27 74 B
Wakeling Rd. W7 54 15 81 B
Wakeling St. E14 57 36 81 C
Wakelin Rd. E15 50 39 83 C
Wakeman Rd. NW10 56 23 82 B
Wakemans Hill Ave. NW9 34 20 88 B
Wakerfield Cl. Horn 42 54 88 B
Wakering Rd. Bark 51 44 84 C
Wakley St. EC1 3 31 82 B
Walberswick St. SW8 10 30 77 C
Walbrook. EC4 4 32 81 D
Walburgh St. E1 57 34 81 D
Walcorde Ave. SE17 63 32 78 A
Walcot Rd. Enf 14 36 97 D
Walcot Sq. SE11 63 31 78 A
Waldeck Gr. SE27 87 31 72 D
Waldeck Rd. Dart 80 54 74 D
Waldeck Rd. N15 25 31 89 D
Waldeck Rd. SW14 72 20 75 A
Waldeck Rd. W13 54 16 81 D
Waldeck Rd. W4 61 19 77 A
Waldegrave Ave. Tedd 83 15 71 D
Waldegrave Gdns. Twick 83 15 72 D
Waldegrave Park. Twick 83 15 71 B
Waldegrave Rd. Brom 99 42 68 D
Waldegrave Rd. Dag 41 47 86 A
Waldegrave Rd. N8 25 31 89 A
Waldegrave Rd. SE19 97 33 70 D
Waldegrave Rd. Tedd 83 15 71 D
Waldegrave Rd. Twick 83 15 72 D
Waldegrave Rd. W5 54 18 80 B
Waldegrove. Croy 105 33 65 D
Waldemar Ave. SW6 73 24 76 C
Waldemar Ave. W13 54 17 80 C
Waldemar Rd. SW19 85 25 71 C
Walden Ave. N13 17 32 92 A
Walden Ave. Rain 52 50 83 D
Walden Ave. SE9 89 42 71 B
Walden Cl. Belv 67 48 78 D
Walden Gdns. Th Hth 96 30 68 D
Walden Rd. Chis 99 42 70 B
Walden Rd. Horn 42 53 88 D
Walden Rd. N17 25 32 90 B
Waldenshaw Rd. SE23 88 35 73 C
Walden St. E1 57 34 81 D
Walden Way. Horn 42 53 88 D
Walden Way. Ilf 28 45 91 C
Walden Way. NW7 23 23 91 B
Waldo Pl. Mit 96 27 70 C
Waldo Rd. Brom 99 41 68 B
Waldo Rd. NW10 55 22 82 B
Waldorf Cl. S Croy 112 31 62 B
Waldram Cres. SE23 88 35 73 C
Waldram Park Rd. SE23 88 35 73 D
Waldram Pl. SE23 88 35 73 C
Waldron Gdns. Brom 98 38 68 C
Waldronhyrst. S Croy 112 31 64 B
Waldron Mews. SW3 62 26 77 B
Waldron Rd. Har 33 15 87 C
Waldron Rd. SW18 85 26 72 A
Waldrons Path. S Croy 112 32 64 A
Waldrons. S Croy 112 32 64 A
Waldrons The. Croy 112 32 64 A
Waldron's Yd. Har 32 14 86 B
Waleran Cl. Stan 21 15 91 B
Walerand Rd. SE13 76 38 76 C
Wales Ave. Cars 111 27 64 C
Wales Farm Rd. W3 55 20 81 B
Waleton Acres. Wall 111 29 63 B
Waley St. E1 57 35 81 B
Walfield Ave. N20 15 25 94 B
Walford Rd. N16 48 33 85 A
Walfrey Gdns. Dag 52 48 84 C
Walham Green Arc. SW6 62 25 77 C
Walham Gr. SW6 62 25 77 C
Walham Rise. SW19 95 24 70 A
Walham Yd. SW6 62 25 77 C
Walkden Rd. Chis 90 43 71 C
Walker Cl. Dart 80 51 75 B
Walker Cl. Hamp 92 12 70 B
Walker Cl. SE18 66 44 78 A
Walkerscroft Mead. SE21 87 32 73 D
Walker's Ct. W1 6 29 80 B
Walkford Way. SE15 64 33 77 D
Walkley Rd. Dart 80 52 74 B
Walk Pl. E2 57 36 82 C
Walks The. N2 23 26 89 B
Walk The. Horn 42 54 86 B
Walk The. Sun 91 09 70 D
Wallace Cl. Shep 91 08 68 D
Wallace Cres. Cars 111 27 64 D
Wallace Rd. N1 48 32 84 A
Wallasey Cres. Uxb 31 07 86 C
Wallbutton Rd. SE4 76 36 76 C
Wallcote Ave. NW2 35 23 87 D
Wall End Rd. E6 51 43 83 A
Wallenger Ave. Rom 30 52 89 B
Waller Dri. Nthwd 19 10 90 A
Waller Rd. SE14 76 35 76 D
Wallers Cl. Wdf Gn 27 42 91 B
Wallflower St. W12 55 21 80 B
Wallgrave Rd. SW5 62 25 78 B
Wallhouse Rd. Eri 68 53 77 C
Wallingford Ave. W10 56 23 81 D
Wallington Cl. Ruis 31 08 88 C
Wallington Rd. Ilf 40 45 87 B
Wallington Sq. Wall 111 29 63 A
Wallis Alley. SE1 8 32 79 A
Wallis Cl. SW11 73 26 75 B
Wallis Rd. E9 49 37 84 A
Wallis Rd. Sthl 53 13 81 D
Wallorton Gdns. SW14 72 20 75 D
Wall St. N1 48 32 84 B
Wallwood Rd. E11 38 38 87 B
Wallwood St. E14 57 36 81 B
Walmar Cl. Barn 11 26 97 B
Walmer Cl. Rom 29 49 90 D
Walmer Gdns. W13 60 16 79 A
Walmer Pl. W1 1 27 81 B
Walmer Rd. W10 56 23 81 C
Walmer Rd. W11 56 24 80 A
Walmer St. W1 1 27 81 B
Walmer Terr. SE18 66 44 78 B
Walmgate Rd. Grnf 44 16 83 B
Walmington Fold. N12 15 25 92 C
Walm La. NW2 46 23 84 B
Walney Wlk. N1 48 32 84 A
Walnut Cl. Cars 111 27 64 D
Walnut Cl. Ilf 28 44 89 C
Walnut Gr. Enf 13 32 95 B
Walnut Mews. Sutt 110 26 63 C
Walnuts Rd. Orp 108 46 66 D
Walnut Tree Ave. Mit 96 27 68 A
Walnut Tree Cl. Chis 100 44 69 A
Walnut Tree Cl. SW13 61 21 77 D
Walnut Tree Cotts. SW19 85 24 71 C
Walnut Tree Rd. Brent 60 18 77 A
Walnut Tree Rd. Dag 41 47 86 D
Walnut Tree Rd. E10 65 39 78 C
Walnut Tree Rd. Eri 68 51 78 C
Walnut Tree Rd. Houn 59 12 77 B
Walnut Tree Rd. Shep 91 08 69 C
Walnut Tree Wlk. SE11 63 31 78 A
Walnut Way. Ruis 43 11 84 A
Walpole Ave. Rich 71 18 76 D
Walpole Cl. Pnr 20 13 91 A
Walpole Cl. W13 60 17 79 A
Walpole Cres. Tedd 83 15 71 D
Walpole Gdns. Twick 83 15 72 C
Walpole Gdns. W4 61 20 78 B
Walpole Pl. Tedd 83 15 71 D
Walpole Rd. Brom 107 41 67 B
Walpole Rd. Croy 105 32 65 B
Walpole Rd. E17 26 36 89 C
Walpole Rd. E18 27 39 90 B
Walpole Rd. E6 50 41 84 C
Walpole Rd. N17 25 32 90 C
Walpole Rd. Surb 101 18 67 C
Walpole Rd. SW19 95 26 70 B
Walpole Rd. Tedd 83 15 71 D
Walpole Rd. Twick 83 15 72 A
Walpole St. SW3 9 27 78 D
Walrond Ave. Wem 44 18 85 C
Walsham Cl. N16 37 34 87 C
Walsham Rd. Felt 81 10 73 B
Walsham Rd. SE14 76 35 76 D
Walsingham Gdns. Eps 109 21 64 D
Walsingham Park. Chis 100 44 69 D
Walsingham Rd. E5 37 34 86 D
Walsingham Rd. Enf 13 32 95 B
Walsingham Rd. Mit 104 27 67 B
Walsingham Rd. Orp 100 46 69 B
Walsingham Rd. W13 54 16 80 C
Walters Rd. Enf 14 35 96 C
Walter's Rd. SE25 97 33 68 C
Walter St. E2 57 35 82 B
Walter St. King 93 18 69 A
Walters Yd. Brom 99 40 69 C
Walter Terr. E1 57 35 81 D
Walterton Rd. W9 56 25 82 C
Walter Wlk. Edg 22 20 91 A
Waltham Ave. NW9 34 19 88 C
Waltham Cl. Dart 80 52 74 C
Waltham Dri. Edg 22 19 90 C
Waltham Green Ct. SW6 62 25 77 D
Waltham Park. E17 26 37 90 A
Waltham Park Way. E17 26 37 91 C
Waltham Rd. Cars 104 27 66 C
Waltham Rd. Sthl 59 12 79 C
Waltham Rd. Wdf Gn 27 42 91 A
Walthamstow Ave. E4 26 37 91 C
Waltham Way. E4 18 36 93 B
Waltheof Ave. N17 25 32 90 B
Waltheof Gdns. N17 25 32 90 B
Walton Ave. Har 43 12 85 B
Walton Ave. N Mal 94 21 68 D
Walton Ave. Sutt 103 24 65 D
Walton Cl. E5 38 35 86 D
Walton Cl. Har 20 14 89 D
Walton Cl. NW2 34 22 86 B
Walton Cl. SW8 10 30 77 C
Walton Dri. Har 20 14 89 D
Walton Gdns. Felt 81 09 71 B
Walton Gdns. W3 55 19 81 B
Walton Gdns. Wem 33 18 86 A
Walton Pl. SW3 5 27 79 D
Walton Rd. E12 51 43 85 A
Walton Rd. E13 50 41 83 C
Walton Rd. E Mol 92 13 68 D
Walton Rd. Har 20 14 89 D
Walton Rd. N15 25 33 89 D
Walton Rd. Rom 29 48 91 D
Walton Rd. Sid 90 46 72 D
Walton St. Enf 13 32 97 B
Walton St. SW3 5 27 79 C
Walton Way. W3 55 19 81 B
Walworth Pl. SE17 63 32 78 C
Walworth Rd. SE17 63 32 78 C
Walwyn Ave. Brom 99 41 68 D
Wanborough Dri. SW15 84 22 73 D
Wandle Bank. Croy 104 30 65 C
Wandle Bank. SW19 95 26 70 D
Wandle Court Gdns. Croy 104 30 65 C
Wandle Ct. Eps 109 20 64 A
Wandle Rd. Croy 104 30 65 C
Wandle Rd. Croy 105 32 65 C
Wandle Rd. Mord 103 26 67 B
Wandle Rd. SW17 86 27 72 A
Wandle Rd. Wall 104 28 65 B
Wandle Side. Croy 104 30 65 D
Wandle Side. Wall 104 28 65 D
Wandle Way. Mit 104 27 67 B
Wandon Rd. SW6 62 25 77 D
Wandsworth Bridge Rd. SW6 73 25 76 D
Wandsworth Common West Side. SW18 73 26 74 B
Wandsworth High St. SW18 73 25 74 B
Wandsworth Plain. SW18 73 25 74 B
Wandsworth Rd. SW8 74 29 76 D
Wandsworth Rd. SW8 10 30 77 C
Wangey Rd. Rom 41 47 87 B
Wanless Rd. SE24 75 32 75 A
Wanley Rd. SE5 75 32 75 D
Wanlip Rd. E13 58 40 82 D
Wannock Gdns. Ilf 28 43 91 D
Wansbeck Rd. E9 49 36 84 D
Wansdown Pl. SW6 62 25 77 D
Wansey St. SE17 63 32 78 A
Wansford Rd. Wdf Gn 27 41 90 A
Wanstead Cl. Brom 99 41 69 C
Wanstead Gdns. Ilf 39 41 88 D
Wanstead La. Ilf 39 42 88 C
Wanstead Park Ave. E12 39 41 86 B
Wanstead Park Rd. Ilf 39 42 87 D
Wanstead Pl. E11 39 40 88 A
Wanstead Rd. Brom 99 41 69 C
Wantage Rd. SE12 77 39 74 B
Wantz Rd. Dag 52 49 85 B
Wapping Dock St. E1 57 34 80 D
Wapping High St. E1 57 34 80 D
Wapping La. E1 57 34 80 D
Wapping Wall. E1 57 35 80 C
Warbank La. King 94 21 70 D
Warbeck Rd. W12 61 22 79 B
Warberry Rd. N22 24 30 90 D
Warboys App. King 94 19 70 B
Warboys Cres. E4 18 38 92 C
Warboys Rd. King 94 19 70 B
Warboys Rd. King 84 20 71 C
Warburton Cl. Har 20 14 91 B
Warburton Rd. E8 48 34 83 B
Warburton Rd. Twick 82 13 73 D
Warburton St. E8 48 34 83 B
Warburton Terr. E17 26 37 90 D
Wardale Cl. SE16 64 35 78 A

Ward Cl. Eri 67 50 77 B
Wardell Cl. NW9 22 21 91 C
Warden Ave. Har 32 12 87 D
Warden Rd. NW5 47 28 84 A
Wardens Gr. SE1 8 32 80 C
Wardle St. E9 49 35 85 D
Wardley St. SW18 85 25 73 A
Wardo Ave. SW6 73 24 76 A
Wardour Mews. W1 2 29 81 C
Wardour St. W1 2 29 81 D
Ward Rd. E15 49 38 83 B
Ward Rd. N19 36 29 86 C
Wardrobe Pl. EC4 3 31 81 D
Wardrobe Terr. EC4 7 31 80 B
Wardrobe The. Rich 71 17 74 B
Wards Rd. Ilf 40 44 87 B
Wards Road E. Ilf 40 45 87 A
Wareham Cl. Houn 70 13 75 D
Waremead Rd. Ilf 40 43 88 B
Warfield Rd. Felt 81 09 73 A
Warfield Rd. Hamp 92 13 69 B
Warfield Rd. NW10 56 23 82 B
Wargrave Ave. N15 37 33 88 D
Wargrave Rd. Har 32 14 86 C
Warham Rd. Har 21 15 90 D
Warham Rd. N4 37 31 88 B
Warham Rd. S Croy 112 32 64 C
Warham St. SE5 63 31 77 D
Waring St. SE27 87 32 71 A
Warkworth Gdns. Islw 60 16 77 C
Warkworth Rd. N17 25 32 91 D
Warland Rd. SE18 66 44 77 D
Warley Ave. Dag 41 48 87 B
Warley Rd. Ilf 28 43 90 A
Warley Rd. N9 18 35 93 A
Warley Rd. Wdf Gn 27 40 91 D
Warley St. E2 57 35 82 B
Warlingham Rd. Th Hth 97 31 68 D
Warlock Rd. W9 56 24 82 D
Warlock Rd. W9 56 25 82 C
Warlters Cl. N7 47 30 85 A
Warlters Rd. N7 47 30 85 A
Waltersville Mansions. N19 36 30 87 A
Warltersville Rd. N19 36 30 87 A
Warming Cl. E5 38 35 86 D
Warmington Rd. SE24 75 32 74 C
*Warmington St. E13 58 40 82 C
Warminster Gdns. SE25 97 34 69 C
Warminster Rd. SE25 97 34 69 C
Warminster Sq. SE25 97 34 69 C
Warminster Way. Mit 96 28 69 D
Warndon St. SE16 64 35 78 B
Warneford Rd. Har 21 18 89 A
Warneford St. E9 48 34 83 B
Warner Ave. Sutt 103 24 65 A
Warner Cl. E15 50 39 85 C
Warner Cl. NW9 34 22 87 A
Warner Pl. E2 57 34 82 A
Warner Rd. Brom 99 39 70 D
Warner Rd. E17 26 36 89 C
Warner Rd. N8 24 29 89 D
Warner Rd. SE5 75 32 76 A
Warner St. EC1 3 31 82 C
Warner Yd. EC1 3 31 82 C
Warnham Ct. Rd. Cars 111 27 63 D
Warnham Rd. N12 16 27 92 C
Warple Rd. SW18 73 25 75 D
Warple Way. W3 61 21 79 A
Warren Ave. Brom 99 39 70 C
Warren Ave. E10 38 38 86 D
Warren Ave. Rich 72 19 75 D
Warren Ave. Sutt 110 24 62 D
Warren Cl. Bexh 79 49 74 A
Warren Cl. N9 18 35 94 B
Warren Cl. SE21 87 32 73 A
Warren Cl. Wem 33 17 86 B
Warren Cres. N9 17 33 94 B
Warren Ct. Beck 98 37 70 C
Warren Ct. N1 48 31 83 C
Warren Cutting. King 94 20 70 D
Warrender Rd. N19 47 29 85 A
Warrender Way. Ruis 31 10 87 A
Warren Dri. Grnf 53 14 82 C
Warren Dri. Horn 42 52 86 D
Warren Dri. Ruis 32 11 87 B
Warren Drive N. Surb 102 19 66 D
Warren Drive S. Surb 102 20 66 C
Warren Drive The. E11 39 41 87 A
Warren Footpath. Twick 83 17 73 B
Warren Footpath. Twick 71 17 74 D
Warren Gdns. E15 49 38 85 D
Warren La. SE18 66 43 79 D
Warren Mews. W1 2 29 82 C
Warren Park. King 94 20 70 A
Warren Park Rd. Sutt 111 27 63 A
Warren Rd. Ashf 91 09 70 C
Warren Rd. Bexh 79 49 74 A
Warren Rd. Brom 107 39 65 B
Warren Rd. Brom 107 40 65 A
Warren Rd. Croy 105 33 66 D
Warren Rd. E10 38 38 86 C
Warren Rd. E11 39 41 87 A
Warren Rd. E4 18 38 93 A
Warren Rd. Ilf 40 44 88 B
Warren Rd. King 94 20 70 A
Warren Rd. NW2 34 21 86 B
Warren Rd. SW19 96 27 70 A
Warren Rd. Twick 70 14 74 D
Warren Rise. N Mal 94 20 69 B
Warren St. W1 2 29 82 C
Warren Terr. Rom 29 47 89 D
Warren The. Cars 111 27 62 A
Warren The. E12 50 42 85 A
Warren The. Houn 59 12 77 D
Warren The. Wor Pk 102 20 65 D
Warren Way. NW7 23 24 91 A
Warren Wlk. SE7 65 41 77 A
Warren Wood Cl. Brom 107 40 65 A
Warriner Ave. Horn 42 53 86 B
Warriner Gdns. SW11 74 28 76 A
Warrington Cres. W9 1 26 82 C
Warrington Gdns. Horn 42 53 88 B
Warrington Gdns. W9 1 26 82 C
Warrington Pl. E14 58 38 80 C
Warrington Rd. Croy 105 31 65 D
Warrington Rd. Dag 41 48 86 A
Warrington Rd. Har 33 15 88 A
Warrington Rd. Rich 71 17 74 B
Warrington Sq. Dag 41 47 86 B
Warrior Sq. E12 51 43 85 A
Warspite Rd. SE18 65 42 79 C
Warton Rd. E15 49 38 83 A
Warwick Ave. Har 43 12 85 B
Warwick Ave. W9 56 25 82 D
Warwick Ave. W9 1 26 82 C
Warwick Cl. Barn 11 26 95 B
Warwick Cl. Hamp 92 14 70 C
Warwick Cl. Orp 108 46 65 C
Warwick Cres. W2 1 27 81 A
Warwick Ct. SE15 75 34 76 C
Warwick Ct. WC1 3 30 81 B
Warwick Dene. W5 54 18 80 C
Warwick Dri. SW15 72 22 75 B
Warwick Gdns. Ilf 40 43 87 D
Warwick Gdns. N4 37 32 88 C
Warwick Gdns. Rom 30 53 89 A
Warwick Gdns. Surb 101 15 67 B
Warwick Gdns. W14 62 24 78 B
Warwick Gr. E5 37 34 87 D
Warwick Gr. Surb 101 18 66 B
Warwick House St. SW1 6 29 80 D
Warwick La. EC4 3 31 81 D
Warwick Pl N. SW1 10 29 78 A
Warwick Pl. W5 60 17 79 B
Warwick Pl. W9 1 26 81 A
Warwick Rd. Barn 11 25 96 D
Warwick Rd. E11 39 40 88 B
Warwick Rd. E12 50 42 85 C
Warwick Rd. E15 50 39 84 B
Warwick Rd. E17 26 36 90 D
Warwick Rd. E4 18 37 92 C
Warwick Rd. Houn 69 10 75 B
Warwick Rd. King 93 17 69 A
Warwick Rd. N11 24 29 91 B
Warwick Rd. N18 17 33 92 B
Warwick Rd. N Mal 94 20 68 A
Warwick Rd. SE20 97 34 68 B
Warwick Rd. Sid 90 46 71 D
Warwick Rd. Sthl 59 12 79 D
Warwick Rd. Surb 101 15 67 B
Warwick Rd. Sutt 110 26 64 C
Warwick Rd. SW5 62 25 78 C
Warwick Rd. Th Hth 97 31 68 A
Warwick Rd. Twick 83 15 73 C
Warwick Rd. W14 62 24 78 B
Warwick Rd. W5 54 18 80 C
Warwick Rd. Well 79 47 75 A
Warwick Row. SW1 6 28 79 D
Warwickshire Path. SE8 62 36 77 D
Warwickshire Rd. N16 48 33 85 A
Warwick Sq. EC4 3 31 81 D
Warwick Sq Mews. SW1 10 29 78 A
Warwick Sq. SW1 10 29 78 A
Warwick St. W1 6 29 80 A
Warwick Terr. SE18 66 44 77 B
Warwick Way. SW1 10 29 78 A
Warwick Yd. EC1 4 32 82 C
Washington Ave. E12 50 42 85 B
Washington Rd. E18 27 39 90 D
Washington Rd. E6 50 41 84 C
Washington Rd. King 94 19 69 C
Washington Rd. SW13 61 22 77 C
Washington Rd. Wor Pk 102 22 66 D
Wastdale Mews. SE23 88 35 73 D
Wastdale Rd. SE23 88 35 73 D
Watchfield Ct. W4 61 20 78 C
Watcombe Cottages. Rich 61 19 77 A
Watcombe Pl. SE25 97 34 68 D
Watcombe Rd. SE25 105 34 67 B
Waterbank Rd. SE6 88 38 71 A
Waterbeach Dri. NW9 22 21 90 C
Waterbeach Rd. Dag 52 47 84 A
Waterbrook La. NW4 35 23 88 A
Waterdale Rd. SE2 66 46 77 A
Waterden Rd. E15 49 37 84 A
Waterer Rise. Wall 111 29 63 B
Waterfall Cl. N14 16 29 93 C
Waterfall Rd. N11 16 29 92 A
Waterfall Rd. N14 16 29 93 C
Waterfall Rd. SW19 96 27 70 A
Waterford Rd. SW6 62 25 77 D
Watergate. EC4 7 31 80 B
Watergate St. SE8 64 37 77 A
Watergate Wlk. WC2 7 30 80 C
Water Gdns. The W2 1 27 81 C
Waterhead Cl. Eri 68 51 77 C
Waterhouse Cl. E16 58 41 81 B
Waterhouse Cl. NW3 46 26 85 D
Waterhouse Cl. W6 62 23 78 B
Water La. E15 50 39 84 A
Water La. Ilf 40 45 86 D
Water La. King 93 17 69 B
Water La. Rich 71 17 74 B
Water La. Twick 83 16 73 C
Waterloo Bridge. WC2 7 30 80 B
Waterloo Cl. E9 49 35 85 C
Waterloo Gdns. E2 49 35 83 C
Waterloo Gdns. Rom 41 50 88 D
Waterloo Pas. NW6 46 24 84 D
Waterloo Pl. Rich 71 18 75 C
Waterloo Pl. Rich 61 19 77 A
Waterloo Pl. SW1 6 29 80 D
Waterloo Rd. E10 38 37 87 A
Waterloo Rd. E6 50 41 84 C
Waterloo Rd. E7 50 39 85 D
Waterloo Rd. Ilf 28 44 90 C
Waterloo Rd. NW2 34 22 86 A
Waterloo Rd. Rom 42 51 88 C
Waterloo Rd. SE1 7 31 79 A
Waterloo Rd. SE1 7 31 80 C
Waterloo Rd. Sutt 110 26 64 D
Waterloo Terr. N1 48 31 84 D
Waterlow Ct. NW11 35 25 87 B
Waterlow Rd. N19 36 29 87 C
Waterman St. SW15 73 23 75 B
Watermans Wlk. SE16 57 36 80 C
Watermead. Felt 81 09 73 C
Watermead La. Cars 104 27 66 B
Watermead Rd. SE6 88 38 71 A
Watermen's Sq. SE20 98 35 70 C
Watermill Cl. Rich 83 17 72 C
Watermill La. N18 17 33 92 C
Water Mill Way. Felt 82 13 72 A
Water Rd. Wem 44 18 83 B
Watersedge. Eps 109 20 64 A
Watersfield Way. Edg 21 17 91 D
Waters Gdns. Dag 52 49 85 C
Watersid Beck 98 36 69 B
*Waterside Cl. SE16 63 34 79 A
Waterside. Dart 80 51 74 A
Waterside Pl. NW1 47 28 83 A
Waterside Rd. Sthl 59 13 79 C
Waterson St. E2 4 33 82 B
Watersplash Rd. Shep 91 07 68 C
Waters Rd. King 94 19 69 D
Waters Rd. SE6 89 39 72 C
Waters Sq. King 94 19 68 B
Water St. WC2 7 31 80 A
Water Tower Hill. Croy 112 33 64 A
Waterworks La. E5 38 35 86 B
Waterworks Rd. SW2 74 30 74 D
Waterworks Yd. Croy 105 32 65 C
Watery La. Nthlt 43 11 83 C
Watery La. Sid 100 46 70 B
Watery La. SW20 95 24 69 D
Wates Way. Mit 104 27 67 D
Wateville Rd. N17 25 32 90 A
Watford Cl. SW11 74 27 76 A
Watford Rd. E16 58 40 81 A
Watford Rd. Har 33 16 87 C
Watford Rd. Nthwd 19 09 91 B
Watford Rd. Wem 44 16 85 B
Watford Way. NW4 22 22 89 A
Watford Way. NW7 22 21 91 D
Watkin Rd. Wem 34 19 86 D
Watkinson Rd. N7 47 30 84 B
Watling Ave. Edg 22 20 90 B
Watling Ct. EC4 4 32 81 C
Watling Gdns. NW2 46 24 84 B
Watling St. Bexh 79 50 75 C
Watling St. EC4 4 32 81 C
Watlington Gr. SE26 88 36 71 C
Watney Market. E1 57 34 81 D
Watney Rd. SW14 72 20 75 A
Watneys Rd. Mit 104 29 67 B
Watney St. E1 57 34 81 D
Watson Ave. E6 51 43 84 C
Watson Ave. Sutt 103 24 65 A
Watson Cl. N16 48 32 85 D
Watson Cl. SW19 96 27 70 C
Watson's Mews. W1 1 27 81 A
Watsons Rd. N22 24 30 90 D
Watson's St. SE8 64 37 77 C
Watson St. E13 50 40 83 D
Watsons Yd. NW2 34 21 86 B
Wattcsfield Rd. E5 38 35 86 C
Watts Bridge Rd. Eri 68 51 77 B
Watts Gr. E3 57 37 81 B
Watt's La. Chis 100 44 69 A
Watt's La. Tedd 83 16 71 C
Watts Rd. Surb 101 16 66 A
Watts St. E1 57 34 80 D
Wat Tyler Rd. SE3 76 38 76 D
Wauthier Cl. N13 17 31 92 D
Wavell Dri. Sid 78 45 74 C
Wavel Mews. NW6 46 26 84 A
Wavendon Ave. W4 61 20 78 D
Waveney Ave. SE15 75 34 75 D
Waverley Ave. E4 18 36 92 B
Waverley Ave. Surb 102 20 67 C
Waverley Ave. Sutt 103 26 65 A
Waverley Ave. Twick 82 13 73 C
Waverley Ave. Wem 44 18 85 D
Waverley Cl. Brom 107 41 67 B
Waverley Cl. E18 27 41 90 C
Waverley Cres. Rom 30 53 91 C
Waverley Cres. SE18 66 44 78 D
Waverley Gdns. Bark 51 45 83 C
Waverley Gdns. Ilf 28 44 90 C
Waverley Gdns. Nthwd 19 10 90 A
Waverley Gr. N3 23 24 89 A
Waverley Pl. N4 37 31 87 D
Waverley Pl. NW8 46 26 83 D
Waverley Rd. E17 26 38 89 A
Waverley Rd. E18 27 41 90 A
Waverley Rd. Enf 13 31 96 B
Waverley Rd. Eps 109 22 64 D
Waverley Rd. Har 32 12 87 C
Waverley Rd. N17 25 34 91 D
Waverley Rd. N8 36 30 87 A
Waverley Rd. SE18 66 44 78 D
Waverley Rd. SE25 97 34 68 B
Waverley Rd. Sthl 53 13 80 A
Waverley Way. Cars 111 27 63 A
Waverton Rd. SW18 85 26 73 A
Waverton St. W1 6 28 80 D
Wavertree Rd. E18 27 40 90 C
Wavertree Rd. SW2 86 30 73 D
Waxham. NW5 47 27 85 D
Waxlow Cres. Sthl 53 13 81 C
Waxlow Rd. NW10 45 20 83 D
Waxwell Cl. Pnr 20 11 90 D
Waxwell La. Pnr 20 11 90 D
Wayborne Gr. Ruis 31 08 88 C
Waye Ave. Houn 69 10 76 A
Wayfarer Rd. Nthlt 53 12 82 A
Wayford St. SW11 74 27 76 C
Wayland Ave. E8 48 34 85 C
Wayland Cl. E8 48 34 85 C
Waylett Pl. SE27 87 31 72 D
Waylett Pl. Wem 44 17 85 B
Wayne Cl. Orp 108 45 65 D
Waynflete Ave. Croy 105 31 65 D
Waynflete Sq. W10 56 23 80 B
Waynflete Sq. W10 56 23 81 D
Waynflete St. SW18 85 26 72 A
Wayside Ave. Horn 42 53 86 B
Wayside Cl. N14 12 29 95 C
Wayside Cl. Rom 30 51 89 B
Wayside Ct. Twick 71 17 74 C
Wayside Ct. Wem 34 19 86 C
Wayside Gdns. Dag 52 49 85 C
Wayside Gr. SE9 89 42 71 B
Wayside. NW11 35 24 87 C
Wayside. SW14 72 20 74 A
Weald Cl. Brom 107 42 65 A
Weald La. Har 20 14 90 D
Weald Rise. Har 21 15 90 B
Weald Sq. E5 37 34 86 B
Wealdstone Rd. Sutt 103 24 65 B
Weald The. Chis 99 42 70 B
Weald Way. Rom 41 49 88 D
Wealdwood Gdns. Pnr 20 13 91 B
Weale Rd. E4 18 38 93 D
Weardale Gdns. Enf 13 32 97 B
Weardale Rd. SE13 76 38 75 D
Wear Pl. E2 57 34 82 B
Wearside Rd. SE13 76 37 75 D
Weatherley Cl. E3 57 36 81 B
Weavers House. E11 39 40 88 C
Weaver's La. SE1 8 33 80 C
Weaver St. E1 57 34 82 C
Weaver Wlk SE27 87 31 71 A
Webber Cl. Eri 68 52 77 D
Webber Row. SE1 7 31 79 A
Webber St. SE1 7 31 79 B
Webb Estate. E5 37 34 87 C
*Webb Gdns. E13 58 40 82 C
Webb Rd. SE3 65 39 77 B
Webb's Rd. SW11 74 27 74 B
Webb St. SE1 8 33 79 C
Weber Row. SE1 7 31 79 C
Webster Gdns. W5 54 17 80 D
Webster Rd. E11 38 38 86 C
Webster Rd. SE16 63 34 79 C
Wedderburn Rd. Bark 51 45 83 A
Wedderburn Rd. NW3 46 26 85 D
Wedgewood Wlk. NW6 46 25 85 D
Wedgwood Cl. Nthwd 19 08 91 A
Wedgwood Way. SE19 97 32 70 A
Wedlake Cl. Horn 42 54 87 C
Wedlake St. W10 56 24 82 C
Wedmore Ave. Ilf 28 43 90 A
Wedmore Gdns. N19 36 29 86 B
Wedmore Mews. N19 36 29 86 D
Wedmore Rd. Grnf 53 14 82 B
Wedmore St. N19 36 29 86 D
Wednesbury Gdns. Rom 30 54 91 D
Wednesbury Green. Rom 30 54 91 D
Wednesbury Rd. Rom 30 54 91 D
Weech Rd. NW6 46 25 85 A
Weedington Rd. NW5 47 28 85 C
Weekley Sq. SW11 73 26 75 B
Weigall Rd. SE12 77 40 75 C
Weighhouse St. W1 2 28 81 C
Weighton Rd. Har 20 14 90 B
Weighton Rd. SE20 97 34 69 D
Weihurst Gdns. Sutt 110 26 64 D
Weimar St. SW15 73 24 75 A
Weirdale Ave. N20 16 27 93 B
Weir Hall Ave. N18 25 32 91 B
Weir Hall Gdns. N18 17 32 92 D
Weir Hall Rd. N17 25 32 91 D
Weir Hall Rd. N18 25 32 91 B
Weir Rd. SW12 86 29 73 A
Weir Rd. SW19 85 25 72 D
Weir's Pas. NW1 2 29 82 B
Weiss Rd. SW15 73 23 75 B
Welbeck Ave. Brom 89 40 71 B
Welbeck Ave. Sid 90 46 73 C
Welbeck Cl. Eps 109 22 63 C
Welbeck Cl. N12 15 26 92 D
Welbeck Cl. N.Mal 102 21 67 B
Welbeck Rd. Barn 12 27 95 C
Welbeck Rd. Cars 104 27 66 C
Welbeck Rd. E6 58 41 82 B
Welbeck Rd. Har 32 13 87 D
Welbeck Rd. Sutt 103 26 65 B
Welbeck St. W1 2 28 81 D
Welbeck Way. W1 2 28 81 D
Welbeck Wlk. Cars 104 27 66 C
Welby St. SE5 75 31 76 B
Welch Pl. Pnr 20 11 90 A
Weld Pl. N11 16 28 92 B
Welfare Rd. E15 50 39 84 C
Welford Cl. E5 38 35 86 D
Welham Rd. SW16 96 28 70 B
Welhouse Rd. Cars 104 27 65 A
Wellacre Rd. Har 33 16 88 D
Wellan Cl. Well 78 46 74 B
Wellands Cl. Brom 99 42 69 D
Welland St. SE10 64 38 77 A
Well App. Barn 11 23 95 A
Wellbrook Rd. Orp 108 43 65 D
Wellclose Sq. E1 57 34 80 A
Wellclose St. E1 57 34 80 A
Well Cl. Ruis 32 12 86 C
Wellcome Ave. Dart 80 54 75 C
Well Cottage Cl. E11 39 41 87 A
Well Ct. EC4 4 32 81 C
Well Ct. EC4 4 32 81 C
Welldon Cres. Har 33 15 88 C
Wellers Ct. NW1 47 30 83 C
Weller St. SE1 8 32 79 A
Wellesley Ave. W6 61 22 79 D
Wellesley Court Rd. Croy 105 32 65 B
Wellesley Cres. Twick 83 15 72 C
Wellesley Ct. Sutt 103 24 66 C
Wellesley Ct. Twick 83 15 72 C
Wellesley Gr. Croy 105 32 65 B
Wellesley Pl. NW5 47 28 85 C
Wellesley Rd. Croy 105 32 66 C
Wellesley Rd. E11 39 40 88 A
Wellesley Rd. E17 38 37 88 C
Wellesley Rd. Har 33 15 88 A
Wellesley Rd. Ilf 40 44 87 C
Wellesley Rd. N22 25 31 90 C
Wellesley Rd. NW5 47 28 85 C
Wellesley Rd. Sutt 110 26 63 A
Wellesley Rd. Twick 83 15 72 C
Wellesley Rd. W4 61 19 78 D
Wellesley St. E1 57 35 81 B
Wellesley Terr. N1 4 32 82 A
Wellfield Ave. N10 24 28 89 B
Wellfield Rd. SW16 86 30 71 B
Wellfield Wlk. SW16 86 30 71 D
Wellfield Wlk. SW16 87 31 71 A
Wellford Pl. SW19 85 24 71 A
Wellgarth. Grnf 44 16 84 B
Wellgarth Rd. NW11 35 25 87 D
Well Hall Par. SE9 77 42 75 D
Well Hall Rd. SE9 77 42 75 C
Wellhouse La. Barn 11 23 96 D
Wellhouse Rd. Beck 98 37 68 C
Welling High St. Well 78 46 75 B
Wellington Ave. E4 18 37 93 B
Wellington Ave. Houn 70 13 74 A
Wellington Ave. N15 37 34 88 C
Wellington Ave. N9 17 34 93 B
Wellington Ave. Pnr 20 12 90 B
Wellington Ave. Pnr 20 12 90 B
Wellington Ave. Sid 78 46 74 C
Wellington Ave. Wor Pk 103 23 65 C
Wellington Bldgs. SW1 9 28 78 C
Wellington Cl. Dag 52 50 84 C
Wellington Cl. SE14 76 35 76 B
Wellington Cl. W11 56 25 81 C
Wellington Cres. N Mal 94 20 68 A
Wellington Dri. Dag 52 50 84 C
Wellington Gdns. Hamp 82 14 71 B
Wellington Gdns. SE7 65 41 78 C
Wellington Gr. SE10 64 38 77 D
Wellington Pas. E11 39 40 88 A
Wellington Pl. NW8 1 26 82 B
Wellington Rd. Belv 67 48 78 D
Wellington Rd. Bex 79 47 74 B
Wellington Rd. Brom 99 41 68 C
Wellington Rd. Croy 105 31 66 B
Wellington Rd. Dart 80 53 74 C
Wellington Rd. E10 38 36 87 C
Wellington Rd. E11 239 40 88 A
Wellington Rd. E17 26 36 89 C
Wellington Rd. E6 50 42 83 D
Wellington Rd. E7 50 39 85 D
Wellington Rd. Enf 17 33 94 A
Wellington Rd. Enf 13 33 95 C
Wellington Rd. Felt 69 09 74 A
Wellington Rd. Hamp 82 14 71 B
Wellington Rd. Har 21 15 89 A
Wellington Rd N. Houn 70 12 75 B
Wellington Rd. NW10 56 23 82 B
Wellington Rd. NW8 1 27 82 A
Wellington Rd. Orp 108 46 67 D
Wellington Rd. Pnr 20 12 90 B
Wellington Rd S. Houn 70 12 74 B
Wellington Rd. SW19 85 25 72 A
Wellington Rd. W5 60 17 79 C
Wellington Row. E2 4 33 82 B
Wellington Row. E2 57 34 82 A
Wellington Sq. SW3 9 27 78 D
Wellington St. Bark 51 44 83 A
Wellington St. SE18 66 43 78 A
Wellington St. WC2 7 30 80 B
Wellington Terr. Har 32 14 87 D
Wellington Way. E3 57 37 82 A
Wellington Yd. Rich 71 17 74 B
Welling Way. SE9 78 44 75 B
Welling Way. Well 78 45 75 A
Well La. SW14 72 20 74 A
Wellmeadow Rd. SE13 77 39 74 C
Wellmeadow Rd. SE6 89 39 73 C
Wellmeadow Rd. W7 60 16 78 A
Wellow Wlk. Cars 103 26 66 D
Well Pas. NW3 35 26 86 D
Well Rd. Barn 11 23 95 A
Well Rd. NW3 35 26 86 D
Wells Cl. Nthlt 53 11 82 A
Wells Dri. NW9 34 20 87 D
Wells Gdns. Dag 52 49 85 D
Wells Gdns. Ilf 39 42 87 A

Wells House Rd. NW10 55 21 81 A
Wellside Cl. Barn 11 23 96 C
Wellside Gdns. SW14 72 20 74 A
Wells Mews. W1 2 29 81 C
Wellsmoor Gdns. Brom 100 43 68 A
Wells Park Rd. SE26 87 34 71 B
Wellsprings Cres. Wem 34 19 86 D
Wells Rd. Brom 99 42 69 D
Wells Rd. W12 62 23 79 A
Wells Rise. NW8 47 27 83 B
Wells Sq. WC1 3 30 82 D
Wells St. W1 2 29 81 C
Well St. E15 50 39 84 A
Well St. E9 49 35 84 C
Wellstead Ave. N9 18 35 94 B
Wellstead Rd. E6 51 43 83 C
Wells Terr. N4 37 31 86 A
Wells Way. SE5 63 33 77 A
Wells Way. SW7 5 26 79 D
Wells Yd. N7 48 31 85 C
Well Wlk. NW3 35 26 86 D
Wellwood Rd. Ilf 40 46 87 A
Welsby Ct. W5 54 17 81 A
Welsford St. SE1 63 34 78 A
Welsh Cl. E13 58 40 82 A
Welshpool St. E8 48 34 83 A
Weltje Rd. W6 61 22 78 A
Welton Rd. SE18 66 45 77 C
Welwyn Ave. Felt 69 09 74 D
Welwyn St. E2 57 35 82 B
Wembley Hill Rd. Wem 44 18 85 B
Wembley Park Dri. Wem 33 18 86 D
Wembley Rd. Hamp 92 13 69 A
Wembley Way. Wem 45 19 84 B
Wemborough Rd. Stan 21 17 91 C
Wembury Rd. N6 36 28 87 B
Wemyss Rd. SE3 77 39 76 D
Wendela Ct. Har 33 15 86 A
Wendell Rd. W12 61 21 79 B
Wendling. NW5 47 27 85 D
Wendling Rd. Sutt 103 26 65 B
Wendon St. E3 49 36 83 B
Wendover Dri. N.Mal 102 21 67 D
Wendover Rd. Brom 99 40 68 B
Wendover Rd. NW10 45 21 83 D
Wendover Rd. SE9 77 41 75 B
Wendover Way. Orp 108 46 67 C
Wendover Way. Well 78 46 75 C
Wendy Cl. Enf 13 33 95 D
Wendy Way. Wem 44 18 83 A
Wenlock Ct. N1 48 32 83 D
Wenlock Rd. Edg 22 19 91 B
Wenlock Rd. N1 48 32 83 C
Wenlock St. N1 48 32 83 D
Wennington Rd. E3 49 35 83 D
Wensley Ave. Wdf Gn 27 40 91 C
Wensleydale Ave. Ilf 27 42 90 C
Wensleydale Gdns. Hamp 92 13 70 D
Wensleydale Rd. Hamp 92 13 70 D
Wensley Rd. N18 25 34 91 B
Wentland Cl. SE6 88 38 72 B
Wentland Rd. SE6 88 38 72 B
Wentworth Ave. N3 23 25 91 D
Wentworth Cl. Ashf 81 07 71 B
Wentworth Cl. Mord 103 25 66 A
Wentworth Cl. N3 23 25 91 D
Wentworth Cl. Surb 101 17 65 B
Wentworth Cres. SE15 63 34 77 C
Wentworth Dri. Dart 80 52 74 C
Wentworth Dri. Pnr 31 10 88 A
Wentworth Dwellings. E1 4 33 81 D
Wentworth Gdns. N13 13 31 95 D
Wentworth Hill. Wem 33 18 87 D
Wentworth Mews. E3 57 36 82 B
Wentworth Mews. E3 57 36 82 C
Wentworth Park. N3 23 25 91 D
Wentworth Rd. Barn 11 23 96 B
Wentworth Rd. Croy 105 31 66 A
Wentworth Rd. E12 50 41 85 B
Wentworth Rd. NW11 35 24 87 B
Wentworth Rd. Sthl 59 11 78 B
Wentworth St. E1 4 33 81 B
Wentworth Way. Pnr 20 11 89 D
Wenvoe Ave. Bexh 79 49 76 D
Wernbrook St. SE18 66 44 77 A
Werndee Rd. SE25 97 34 68 C
Werneth Hall Rd. Ilf 28 43 89 A
Wern St. WC1 3 30 82 D
Werrington St. NW1 47 29 83 D
Werter Rd. SW15 73 24 75 C
Wesleyan Pl. NW5 47 28 85 B
Wesley Ave. Houn 70 12 76 D
Wesley Ave. NW10 55 20 82 B
Wesley Cl. Har 32 14 86 A
Wesley Cl. N7 36 30 86 B
Wesley Cl. SE17 63 31 78 B
Wesley Rd. E10 38 38 87 A
Wesley Rd. N2 24 27 90 A
Wesley Rd. NW10 45 20 83 A
Wesley Sq. W11 56 24 81 C
Wesley St. W1 2 28 81 A
Wessex Ave. SW19 95 25 68 A
Wessex Cl. Ilf 40 45 88 C
Wessex Cl. King 94 19 69 B
Wessex Ct. SW15 73 23 74 B
Wessex Dri. Eri 80 51 76 C
Wessex Dri. Pnr 20 12 91 C
Wessex Gdns. NW11 35 24 87 C
Wessex La. Grnf 43 14 83 D
Wessex St. E2 57 35 82 A
Wessex Way. NW11 35 24 87 C
Westacott Cl. N19 36 29 87 D
West App. Orp 108 44 67 A
West Arbour St. E1 57 35 81 D
West Ave. E17 38 37 88 B
West Ave. N2 23 25 89 B
West Ave. N3 23 25 91 A
West Avenue Rd. E17 26 37 89 C
West Ave. NW4 35 23 88 B
West Ave. Pnr 32 12 87 B
West Ave. Sthl 53 12 80 B
West Ave. Wall 111 30 64 C
West Bank. Enf 13 32 97 C
West Bank. N16 37 33 87 A
Westbank Rd. Hamp 92 14 70 A
West Barnes La. N.Mal 102 22 67 B
West Barnes La. N Mal 94 22 68 B
West Barnes La. SW20 94 22 69 D
Westbeech Rd. N22 25 31 89 A
Westbere Rd. NW2 46 24 85 C
Westbourne Ave. Sutt 103 24 65 A
Westbourne Ave. W3 55 20 81 D
Westbourne Cl. Hay 53 11 82 C
Westbourne Cres. W2 5 26 80 B
Westbourne Dri. SE23 88 35 72 B
Westbourne Gdns. W2 56 25 81 D
Westbourne Gr. Bexh 79 49 75 D
Westbourne Gr Mews. W11 56 25 81 C
Westbourne Gr Terr. W2 56 25 81 D
Westbourne Gr. W11 56 25 81 C
Westbourne Gr. W2 56 25 81 D
Westbourne Park Pas. W2 56 25 81 A
Westbourne Park Rd. W2 56 25 81 A
Westbourne Park Villas. W2 56 25 81 B
Westbourne Pl. N9 17 34 93 D
Westbourne Rd. Bexh 67 48 77 C
Westbourne Rd. Croy 105 33 67 D
Westbourne Rd. Felt 81 09 72 D
Westbourne Rd. N7 47 30 84 B
Westbourne Rd. N7 48 31 84 A
Westbourne Rd. SE26 98 35 70 B
Westbourne St. W2 5 26 80 B
Westbourne Terr Mews W2 1 26 81 C
Westbourne Terr Rd. W2 1 27 81 A
Westbourne Terr. W2 1 26 81 C
Westbridge Rd. SW11 74 27 76 A
Westbrook Ave. Hamp 92 12 70 D
Westbrook Cl. Barn 11 26 96 B
Westbrook Cres. Barn 11 26 96 B
Westbrook Cres. Well 79 47 75 A
Westbrooke Rd. SE9 90 44 72 B
Westbrooke Rd. Well 79 47 75 A
Westbrook Rd. Houn 59 12 77 D
Westbrook Rd. SE3 77 40 76 B
Westbrook Rd. Th Hth 97 32 69 D
Westbrook Sq. Barn 11 26 96 B
Westbury Ave. N22 25 31 90 D
Westbury Ave. Sthl 53 13 82 C
Westbury Ave. Wem 44 18 84 C
Westbury Cl. Ruis 31 10 87 A
Westbury Gr. N12 23 25 91 A
Westbury Lodge Cl. Pnr 20 11 89 B
Westbury Pl. Brent 60 17 77 B
Westbury Rd. Bark 51 44 83 B
Westbury Rd. Beck 98 36 68 A
Westbury Rd. Brom 99 41 69 B
Westbury Rd. Croy 105 32 67 D
Westbury Rd. E17 26 37 89 C
Westbury Rd. E7 50 40 84 B
Westbury Rd. Felt 82 11 72 B
Westbury Rd. Ilf 40 43 86 A
Westbury Rd. N11 24 30 91 A
Westbury Rd. N12 15 25 92 D
Westbury Rd. N13 24 30 91 A
Westbury Rd. N.Mal 102 20 67 B
Westbury Rd. SE20 98 35 69 B
Westbury Rd. W5 54 18 81 C
Westbury Rd. Wem 44 18 84 C
Westbury Terr. E7 50 40 84 B
West Carriage Dri. W2 5 27 80 C
West Central St. WC1 3 30 81 C
West Centre Ave. W10 56 23 82 A
West Chantry. Har 20 13 90 B
Westchester Dri. NW4 23 23 89 B
West Cl. Barn 12 28 96 C
West Cl. Grnf 43 14 83 C
West Cl. Hamp 92 12 70 A
West Cl. N9 17 33 93 D
West Cl. Wem 33 18 87 D
Westcombe Ave. Croy 104 30 66 B
Westcombe Dri. Barn 11 25 95 A
Westcombe Hill. SE10 65 40 78 C
Westcombe Hill. SE3 65 40 77 A
Westcombe Park Rd. SE3 65 39 77 D
West Common Rd. Brom 107 40 65 D
Westcoombe Ave SW20 94 21 69 B
Westcote Rd. SW16 96 29 70 A
Westcote Rd. SW16 86 29 71 C
Westcote Rise. Ruis 31 08 87 A
Westcott Cl. N15 37 33 88 D
Westcott Cres. W7 54 15 81 A
Westcott Rd. SE17 63 31 77 B
Westcott Way. Sutt 110 23 62 C
Westcroft Cl. NW2 46 24 85 A
Westcroft Ct. NW9 34 19 88 B
Westcroft Estate. NW2 46 24 85 A
Westcroft Gdns. Mord 95 24 68 D
Westcroft Rd. Cars 111 28 64 A
Westcroft Rd. Wall 111 28 64 B
Westcroft Sq. 6 61 22 78 A
Westcroft Way. NW2 46 24 85 A
West Cromwell Rd. SW5 62 25 78 A
West Cromwell Rd. W14 62 24 78 D
West Cross Route. W10 56 23 80 B
West Cross Route. W11 56 23 80 D
West Cross Way. Brent 60 16 77 B
West Ct. Islw 59 14 77 C
West Ct. Wem 33 17 86 A
Westdale Pas. SE18 66 43 77 B
Westdale Rd. SE18 66 43 77 B
Westdean Ave. SE12 89 41 73 C
Westdean Cl. SW18 73 25 74 D
Westdown Rd. E15 49 38 85 A
Westdown Rd. SE6 88 37 73 A
West Dri. Cars 110 26 62 D
West Dri. Har 20 14 91 B
West Dri. Sutt 110 24 62 A
West Dri. SW16 86 29 71 A
West Drive Gdns. Har 20 14 91 B
West Eaton Pl Mews. SW1 9 28 78 A
West Eaton Pl. SW1 9 28 78 A
West Ella Rd. NW10 45 21 84 C
West End Ave. E10 38 38 88 B
West End Ave. Pnr 20 11 89 D
West End Ct. Pnr 20 11 89 D
West End Gdns. Nthlt 53 11 82 A
West End La. Barn 11 23 96 D
West End La. NW6 46 25 84 B
West End La. Pnr 20 11 89 D
West End Rd. Nthlt 43 11 84 C
West End Rd. Ruis 31 09 86 B
West End Rd. Sthl 53 12 80 C
Westerdale Rd. SE10 65 40 78 C
Westerfield Rd. N15 37 33 88 B
Westergate Rd. SE2 67 48 77 A
Westerham Ave. N9 17 33 93 C
Westerham Dri. Sid 79 47 74 C
Westerham Rd. Brom 107 42 65 C
Westerham Rd. E10 38 37 87 B
Westerley Cres. SE26 88 36 71 D
Western Ave. Dag 52 50 84 B
Western Ave. Grnf 44 15 83 C
Western Ave. Grnf 54 16 82 B
Western Ave. Nthlt 43 12 83 B
Western Ave. NW11 35 23 88 D
Western Ave. Rom 30 53 90 C
Western Ave. W3 55 20 82 C
Western Ave. W5 54 18 82 A
Western Ct. N3 23 25 91 A
Western Gdns. W5 55 19 80 A
Western La. SW12 86 28 73 A
Western Mews. W9 56 24 82 D
Western Par. Barn 11 25 95 B
Western Rd. E13 50 41 83 C
Western Rd. E17 38 38 88 A
Western Rd. Mit 96 27 69 C
Western Rd. N22 24 30 90 D
Western Rd. N2 24 27 89 D
Western Rd. NW10 55 20 82 C
Western Rd. Rom 42 51 88 B
Western Rd. Sthl 59 11 79 D
Western Rd. Sutt 110 25 64 C
Western Rd. SW19 95 26 69 B
Western Rd. SW9 75 31 75 A
Western Rd. W5 54 17 80 B
Westernville Gdns. Ilf 40 44 87 A
Western Way. Barn 11 25 95 D
Western Way. SE28 66 45 79 A
Westferry Rd. E14 64 37 79 A
Westfield Cl. Enf 14 36 96 A
Westfield Cl. Sutt 110 24 64 B
Westfield Dri. Har 21 17 89 D
Westfield Gdns. Har 21 17 89 D
Westfield La. Har 21 17 89 D
Westfield Park. Pnr 20 12 91 D
Westfield Rd. Beck 98 36 69 D
Westfield Rd. Bexh 79 50 75 A
Westfield Rd. Croy 105 31 65 B
Westfield Rd. Dag 52 48 85 B
Westfield Rd. Mit 96 27 69 D
Westfield Rd. Surb 101 17 67 B
Westfield Rd. Sutt 110 24 64 B
Westfield Rd. W13 54 16 80 C
Westfields Ave. SW13 72 21 75 A
Westfields Rd. W3 55 19 81 B
Westfields. SW13 72 21 75 B
Westfield St. SE18 65 41 79 D
Westfield Way. Ruis 31 09 86 D
Westgate Mews. W10 56 24 82 C
Westgate Rd. Beck 98 38 69 A
Westgate Rd. Dart 80 53 74 D
Westgate Rd. SE25 97 34 68 D
Westgate St. E8 48 34 83 B
Westgate Terr. SW10 62 25 77 B
West Gate. W5 54 18 82 A
West Gdns. E1 57 34 80 B
West Gdns. Eps 109 21 62 C
West Gdns. SW17 96 27 70 A
West Gdns. SW17 96 27 70 A
Westglade Ct. Har 33 17 88 B
West Green Rd. N 25 32 89 D
Westgrove La. SE10 76 38 76 A
West Gr. SE10 76 38 76 A
West Gr. Wdf Gn 27 41 91 A
West Halkin St. SW1 6 28 79 C
West Hallowes. SE9 89 42 73 C
West Hall Rd. Rich 72 19 76 B
Westhall Rd. SE5 63 31 77 D
West Ham La. E15 50 39 84 C
West Hampstead Mews. NW6 46 25 84 B
West Harding St. EC4 3 31 81 C
West Hatch Manor. Ruis 31 09 87 D
Westhay Gdns. SW14 72 19 74 B
West Heath Ave. NW11 35 25 87 C
West Heath Cl. Dart 80 51 74 D
West Heath Cl. NW3 35 25 86 C
West Heath Dri. NW11 35 25 87 C
West Heath Gdns. NW3 35 25 86 C
West Heath Rd. Dart 80 51 74 D
West Heath Rd. NW3 35 25 86 D
West Heath Rd. SE2 67 47 77 B
West Hendon Bwy. NW9 34 22 87 A
West Hill Ct. N6 36 28 86 C
West Hill. Dart 80 53 74 D
West Hill Dri. Dart 80 53 74 C
West Hill. Har 33 15 86 A
Westhill Park. N6 36 27 86 B
West Hill Rd. SW18 73 24 74 D
West Hill Rise. Dart 80 53 74 D
West Hill. S Croy 112 33 62 A
West Hill. SW15 85 23 73 B
West Hill. SW15 73 24 74 C
West Hill Way. N20 15 25 94 D
West Hill. Wem 33 18 87 D
West Holme. Eri 79 50 76 A
Westholme Gdns. Ruis 31 10 87 C
Westholme. Orp 108 45 66 B
Westholm. NW11 23 25 89 D
Westhorne Ave. SE12 77 40 74 D
Westhorne Ave. SE9 77 41 74 B
Westhorpe Gdns. NW4 23 23 89 B
Westhorpe Rd. SW15 73 23 75 A
West House Cl. SW19 85 24 73 C
Westhurst Dri. Chis 90 43 71 D
West India Dock Rd. E14 57 37 80 A
Westlake Cl. N13 17 31 93 C
Westlake. SE16 64 35 78 A
Westland Ave. Horn 42 54 87 C
Westland Dri. Brom 107 39 65 B
Westland Pl. N1 4 32 82 B
Westlands Terr. SW12 74 29 74 C
West La. SE16 63 34 79 B
Westlea Rd. W7 60 16 79 C
Westleigh Ave. SW15 73 23 74 A
Westleigh Dri. Brom 99 42 69 A
Westleigh Gdns. Edg 22 19 90 A
West Lodge Ave. W3 55 19 80 C
West Mall. W8 56 25 80 C
West Mead. Eps 109 21 63 A
Westmead Rd. Sutt 110 26 64 B
West Mead. Ruis 43 11 85 A
Westmead. SW15 72 22 74 D
Westmede. Chig 28 44 91 A
West Mews. SW1 10 29 78 A
Westminster Ave. Th Hth 97 31 69 D
Westminster Bridge Rd. SE1 7 31 79 C
Westminster Bridge. SW1 7 30 79 A
Westminster Cl. Ilf 28 44 90 C
Westminster Dri. N13 16 30 92 C
Westminster Gdns. Bark 51 45 83 C
Westminster Gdns. Ilf 28 44 90 D
Westminster Rd. N9 17 34 94 D
Westminster Rd. Sutt 103 26 65 B
Westminster Rd. W7 54 15 80 C
Westmoat Cl. Beck 98 38 70 C
Westmont Rd. Esh 101 15 65 A
Westmoor Gdns. nf 14 35 97 D
Westmoor Rd. Enf 14 35 97 D
Westmoor St. SE7 65 41 79 D
Westmoreland Ave. Horn 30 53 89 C
Westmoreland Ave. Well 78 45 75 C
Westmoreland Bldgs. EC1 4 32 81 A
Westmoreland Dri. Sutt 110 25 62 B
Westmoreland Pl. Brom 99 40 68 A
Westmoreland Pl. SW1 9 28 78 D
Westmoreland Pl. W5 54 17 81 B
Westmoreland Rd. Brom 99 39 68 D
Westmoreland Rd. NW9 21 18 89 B
Westmoreland Rd. SE17 63 32 77 B
Westmoreland Rd. SW13 72 22 76 A
Westmoreland St. W1 2 28 81 A
Westmoreland Wlk. SE17 63 33 78 C
Westmorland Cl. E12 39 41 86 B
Westmorland Cl. Eps 109 21 62 A
Westmorland Cl. Twick 71 16 74 D
Westmorland. Mit 104 30 67 A
Westmorland Rd. E17 38 37 88 C
Westmorland Rd. Har 32 13 88 B
Westmount Rd. SE9 78 43 75 C
West Oak. Beck 98 38 69 B
Westoe Rd. N9 17 34 93 B
Weston Ave. E Mol 92 12 68 D
Weston Ave. Surb 101 15 66 A
Weston Dri. Stan 21 16 90 B
Weston Gdns. Islw 71 15 76 A
Weston Gr. Brom 99 39 69 B
Weston Green. Dag 52 48 85 B
Weston Green Rd. Esh 101 15 66 C
Weston Green Rd. Surb 101 15 66 A
Weston Green. Surb 101 15 66 C
Weston Park Cl. Surb 101 15 66 C
Weston Park. N8 36 30 88 C
Weston Park. Surb 101 15 66 C
Weston Pk. King 93 18 69 C
Weston Rd. Brom 99 39 70 D
Weston Rd. Dag 52 48 85 A
Weston Rd. Enf 13 32 97 D
Weston Rd. Surb 101 15 66 C
Weston Rd. W4 61 20 79 C
Weston Rise. WC1 3 30 82 B
Weston St. SE1 8 32 79 B
Weston St. SE1 8 33 80 C
Weston Wlk. E9 49 35 84 C
Westover Cl. Sutt 110 25 62 B
Westover Rd. SW18 73 26 74 C
Westow Hill. SE19 97 33 70 B
Westow St. SE19 97 33 70 A
West Park Ave. Rich 72 19 76 B
West Park Cl. Rom 41 47 88 B
West Park Rd. Rich 72 19 76 A
West Park. SE9 89 42 73 C
West Pier. E1 57 34 80 D
West Pl. SW19 85 23 71 C
Westpole Ave. Barn 12 28 96 D
Westport Rd. E13 58 40 82 D
Westport St. E1 57 35 81 D
West Poultry Ave. EC1 3 31 81 B
West Quarters. W12 55 22 81 C
West Ramp. Houn 69 07 76 A
West Rd. Barn 16 28 94 C
West Rd. E15 50 39 83 B
West Rd. Felt 81 08 73 B
West Rd. King 94 20 69 A
West Rd. N17 25 34 91 B
West Rd. N2 23 26 90 D
West Rd. Rom 41 47 88 D
West Rd. Rom 41 50 87 B
West Rd. SW3 9 27 77 B
West Rd. SW4 74 29 74 B
West Rd. W5 54 18 81 A
West Ridge Gdns. Grnf 43 14 83 C
Westrow Dri. Bark 51 46 84 A
Westrow Gdns. Ilf 40 45 86 D
West Row. W10 56 24 82 C
West Sheen Vale. Rich 71 18 75 D
West Side Common. SW19 95 23 70 A
Westside. NW4 22 22 90 D
West Smithfield. EC1 3 31 81 B
West Sq. SE11 7 31 79 D
West St. Bexh 79 48 75 B
West St. Brom 99 40 69 C
West St. Cars 111 27 64 B
West St. Croy 112 32 64 A
West St. E11 39 39 86 C
West St. E17 38 37 88 B
West St. E2 48 34 83 D
West St. Eps 109 21 62 D
West St. Eri 68 51 78 C
West St. Har 33 15 87 C
West St La. Cars 111 27 64 B
West Street Pl. Croy 112 32 64 A
West St. Sutt 110 25 64 D
West St. WC2 2 29 81 D
West Temple Sheen. SW14 72 19 74 B
West Tenter St. E1 4 33 81 D
West Towers. Pnr 32 11 88 D
Westview Cl. NW10 45 21 85 D
Westview Cres. N9 17 33 94 A
Westview Dri. Wdf Gn 27 41 90 D
West View. Felt 81 08 73 A
West View. NW4 22 22 89 D
West View. NW4 35 23 88 A
West View. NW4 23 23 89 C
West View Rd. Dart 80 54 74 D
Westville Rd. Surb 101 16 66 A
Westville Rd. W12 61 22 79 A
Westward Rd. E4 18 36 92 D
Westward Way. Har 33 18 88 C
West Warwick Pl. SW1 10 29 78 A
West Way. Cars 110 26 62 D
Westway Cl. SW20 94 22 68 B
West Way. Croy 106 36 65 C
West Way. Edg 22 20 91 A
West Way Gdns. Croy 106 35 65 B
West Way. Houn 70 12 76 B
West Way. N18 17 32 92 B
West Way. NW10 34 20 86 D
West Way. Orp 108 44 67 B
West Way. Pnr 20 11 89 D
West Way. Ruis 31 09 87 D
Westways. Eps 109 21 64 B
Westway. SW20 95 23 68 C
Westway. W10 56 24 81 C
Westway. W12 55 22 80 A
Westway. W2 7 26 81 A
Westway. W9 56 25 81 A
West Way. W Wick 106 38 67 D
Westwell Rd. SW16 96 30 70 A
Westwell Road App. SW16 96 30 70 A
Westwick Gdns. Houn 69 10 76 D
Westwick Gdns. W14 62 23 79 B
West Wlk. Barn 16 28 94 C
West Wlk. NW9 22 21 90 A
West Wlk. W5 54 18 81 A
Westwood Ave. Har 43 13 85 B
Westwood Ave. SE19 97 32 69 A
Westwood Cl. Ruis 31 08 88 C
Westwood Gdns. SW13 72 21 75 B
Westwood Hill. SE26 87 34 71 C
Westwood La. Sid 78 46 74 A
Westwood La. Well 78 45 75 D
Westwood Park. SE23 87 34 73 B
Westwood Rd. E16 58 40 80 D
Westwood Rd. Ilf 40 46 87 A
Westwood Rd. SW13 72 21 75 B
Wetheral Dri. Stan 21 17 90 A
Wetherby Cl. Nthlt 43 13 84 B
Wetherby Gdns. SW5 62 26 78 A
Wetherby Mews. SW5 62 25 78 D
Wetherby Pl. SW7 62 26 78 A
Wetherby Rd. Enf 13 32 97 A
Wetherden St. E17 38 36 87 B
Wetherell Rd. E9 49 35 83 B
Wetherill Rd. N10 24 28 90 A
Wettern Cl. S Croy 112 33 62 C
Wexford Rd. SW12 86 27 73 B
Weybourne St. SW18 85 26 72 A
Weybridge Point. SW11 74 27 76 D
Weybridge Rd. Th Hth 97 31 68 C
Wey Ct. Eps 109 20 64 A
Weydown Cl. SW19 85 24 73 C
Weyhill Rd. E1 57 34 81 C
Weylond Rd. Dag 41 48 86 D
Weyman Rd. SE3 77 41 76 A
Weymarks The. N17 25 32 91 B
Weymouth Ave. W5 60 17 79 C
Weymouth Ct. Sutt 110 25 63 C
Weymouth Mews. W1 2 28 81 B
Weymouth St. W1 2 28 81 B
Weymouth Terr. E2 48 33 83 D

Weymouth Wlk. Stan 21 16 91 A
Whadcoat St. N4 37 31 86 A
Whalebone Ave. Rom 41 48 88 D
Whalebone Gr. Rom 41 48 88 D
Whalebone La. E15 50 39 84 C
Whalebone Lane N. Rom 29 48 90 A
Whalebone Lane S. Dag 41 48 87 D
Whalebone Lane S. Rom 41 48 87 B
Wharfdale Rd. NW1 47 30 83 C
Wharfedale Gdns. Th Hth 96 30 68 B
Wharfedale St. SW10 62 25 78 D
Wharf La. Twick 83 16 73 C
Wharf Pl. E2 48 34 83 B
Wharf Rd. E15 49 38 83 B
Wharf Rd. Enf 14 36 95 C
Wharf Rd. N1 48 32 83 C
Wharf Rd. NW1 47 30 83 B
Wharfside Rd. E16 58 39 81 A
Wharf St. E16 58 39 81 A
Wharncliffe Dri. Sthl 53 14 80 D
Wharncliffe Gdns. SE25 97 33 69 C
Wharncliffe Rd. SE25 97 33 69 C
Wharton Cl. NW10 45 21 84 A
Wharton Rd. Brom 99 40 69 B
Wharton St. WC1 3 30 82 B
Whateley Rd. SE20 98 35 70 D
Whateley Rd. SE22 75 33 74 B
Whatley Ave. SW20 95 24 68 A
Whatman Rd. SE23 88 35 73 B
Wheatfields. Enf 14 36 97 C
Wheathill Rd. SE20 97 34 68 B
Wheatlands. Houn 59 13 77 A
Wheatlands Rd. SW17 86 28 72 C
Wheatley Gdns. N9 17 33 93 A
Wheatley Rd. Islw 71 15 75 B
Wheatley St. W1 2 28 81 A
Wheatley Terrace Rd. Eri 68 51 77 B
Wheatsheaf La. SW6 62 23 77 C
Wheatsheaf La. SW8 10 30 77 C
Wheatsheaf Rd. Rom 42 51 88 D
Wheatsheaf Terr. SW6 62 24 77 D
Wheelers Cross. Bark 51 44 83 D
Wheelers Dri. Ruis 31 08 88 C
Wheeler's St. Sutt 103 25 65 C
Wheel Farm Dri. Dag 41 50 86 C
Wheelwright St. N7 47 30 84 D
Whelan Way. Wall 104 29 65 D
Wheler St. E1 4 33 82 D
Whellock Rd. W4 61 21 79 C
Whetstone Cl. N20 15 26 93 B
Whetstone Park. WC2 3 30 81 D
Whetstone Rd. SE3 77 41 76 D
Whewell Rd. N19 36 30 86 A
Whichcote St. SE1 7 31 80 C
Whidborne St. WC1 3 30 82 A
Whinchat Rd. SE28 66 44 79 D
Whinfell Cl. SW16 86 29 71 D
Whinyates Rd. SE9 77 42 75 A
Whippendell Cl. Orp 100 46 69 B
Whippendell Way. Orp 100 46 69 D
Whipps Cross. E17 38 38 88 B
Whipps Cross Rd. E11 39 39 88 D
Whiskin St. EC1 3 31 82 B
Whistler Gdns. Edg 22 19 90 C
Whistler St. N5 48 31 85 D
Whistler Wlk. SW10 62 26 77 C
Whiston Rd. E2 48 33 83 B
Whitbread Rd. SE4 76 36 75 D
Whitburn Rd. SE13 76 38 75 C
Whitby Ave. NW10 55 19 82 B
Whitby Gdns. NW9 22 19 89 A
Whitby Gdns. Sutt 103 26 65 B
Whitby Rd. Har 32 14 86 C
Whitby Rd. Ruis 32 11 86 A
Whitby Rd. Sutt 103 26 65 B
Whitby St. E1 4 33 82 D
Whitcher Cl. SE14 64 36 77 A
Whitchurch Ave. Edg 21 18 91 D
Whitchurch Cl. Edg 21 18 91 B
Whitchurch Gdns. Edg 21 18 91 B
Whitchurch La. Edg 21 18 91 D
Whitchurch La. Edg 22 19 91 C
Whitchurch Rd. W11 56 23 80 B
Whitcomb Ct. SW1 6 29 80 B
Whitcomb St. WC2 6 29 80 B
White Acre. NW9 22 21 90 C
Whitear Wlk. E15 49 38 84 B
Whitebarn La. Dag 52 49 83 A
Whitebeam Ave. Brom 108 43 67 C
White Bear Pl. NW3 46 26 85 B
White Bear Yd. EC1 3 31 82 C
White Bridge Cl. Felt 69 09 74 D
White Butts Rd. Ruis 32 11 86 D
Whitechapel High St. E1 4 33 81 D
Whitechapel Rd. E1 57 34 81 A
White Church La. E1 57 34 81 C
*White Church Pas. E1 57 34 81 C
White City Cl. W12 56 23 80 A
White City Estate. W12 55 22 80 B
White City Rd. W12 56 23 80 A
*White Conduit St. N1 48 31 83 C
Whitecote Rd. Sthl 53 14 81 C
Whitecroft Cl. Beck 98 38 68 D
Whitecroft Way. Beck 98 38 68 D
Whitecross Pl. EC2 4 32 81 B
Whitecross St. EC1 4 32 81 A
Whitecross St. EC1 4 32 82 C
Whitecross St. EC2 4 32 81 A
Whitefield Ave. NW2 35 23 87 B
Whitefield Cl. SW18 73 24 74 C
Whitefoot La. Brom 88 38 72 D
Whitefoot La. SE6 89 39 72 C
Whitefoot Terr. Brom 89 39 72 D
Whitefriars Ave. Har 21 15 90 C
Whitefriars Dri. Har 21 15 90 C
Whitefriars St. EC4 3 31 81 C
White Gate Gdns. Har 21 15 91 D
White Gdns. Dag 52 49 84 A
Whitegift Centre. Croy 105 32 65 A
Whitehall Ct. SW1 7 30 80 C
Whitehall Gdns. E4 18 38 94 D
Whitehall Gdns. SW1 7 30 80 C
Whitehall Gdns. W3 55 19 80 C
Whitehall Gdns. W4 61 19 77 B
Whitehall La. Eri 80 51 76 D
Whitehall La. Eri 80 52 76 B
Whitehall Park. N19 36 29 87 C
Whitehall Park Rd. W4 61 19 77 B
Whitehall Pl. E7 50 40 85 C
Whitehall Pl. SW1 7 30 80 C
Whitehall Pl. Wall 111 28 64 B
Whitehall Rd. Brom 99 42 68 C
Whitehall Rd. Har 33 15 87 A
Whitehall Rd. Th Hth 105 31 67 A
Whitehall Rd. W7 60 16 79 A
Whitehall St. N17 25 33 91 C
Whitehall. SW1 7 30 80 C
White Hart Ct. EC2 4 33 81 A
White Hart La. N17 25 32 91 D
White Hart La. N22 25 31 91 C
White Hart La. NW10 45 21 84 B
White Hart La. Rom 29 49 90 C
White Hart La. SW13 72 21 75 A
White Hart Rd. Orp 108 46 66 A
White Hart Rd. SE18 66 45 78 A
White Hart Slip. Brom 99 40 69 C
White Hart St. SE11 63 31 78 C
White Hart Yd. SE1 8 32 80 D
Whitehaven Cl. Brom 99 40 68 C
Whitehaven St. NW8 1 27 82 C
Whitehead Cl. SW18 85 26 73 A
Whitehead's Gr. SW3 9 27 78 A
Whiteheath Ave. Ruis 31 08 87 A
Whitehill Rd. Dart 80 52 74 A
White Hill. Rick 19 07 91 A
White Hill. S Croy 112 32 62 D
Whitehorn Gdns. Croy 105 34 65 B
Whitehorn Gdns. Enf 13 32 95 B
White Horse Alley. EC1 3 31 81 B
White Horse Hill. Chis 90 43 71 C
White Horse La. E1 57 35 81 B
Whitehorse La. SE25 97 33 68 A
Whitehorse Rd. Croy 105 32 67 D
White Horse Rd. E1 57 36 81 C
Whitehorse Rd. Th Hth 97 32 68 D
White Horse St. W1 6 28 80 D
White Horse Yd. EC2 4 32 81 D
White House Ct. N14 16 29 93 B
Whitehouse Estate. E10 38 38 88 C
White House La. Enf 13 32 97 A
Whitehouse Way. N14 16 28 93 D
White Kennett St. E1 4 33 81 C
Whitelands Way. Rom 30 53 90 B
White Ledges. W13 54 17 81 C
Whitelegg Rd. E13 50 39 83 D
Whiteley Rd. SE19 87 32 71 D
Whiteleys Way. Felt 82 13 72 C
White Lion Hill. EC4 7 31 80 B
White Lion St. N1 48 31 83 C
White Lion Yd. W1 6 28 80 B
White Lodge Cl. N2 35 26 88 D
White Lodge. SE19 97 31 70 D
White Lodge. Sutt 110 26 63 C
Whitemore Cl. N11 16 28 92 D
White Oak Dri. Beck 98 38 69 C
Whiteoaks La. Grnf 53 14 82 B
White Orchards. N20 15 24 94 D
White Post La. E9 49 37 84 C
White Post St. SE15 64 35 77 C
White Rd. E15 50 39 84 C
Whites Ave. Ilf 40 45 88 C
White's Grounds. SE1 8 33 79 A
White's Meadow. Brom 100 43 68 C
White's Row. E1 4 33 81 B
White's Sq. SW4 74 29 75 D
Whitestile Rd. Brent 60 17 78 D
Whitestone La. NW3 35 26 86 C
Whitestone Walk. NW3 35 26 86 C
White St. Sthl 59 11 79 B
Whitethorn. Horn 42 53 88 C
Whitethorn Pas. E3 57 37 81 A
Whitethorn St. E3 57 37 81 A
Whitewebbs Way. Orp 100 45 69 B
Whitfield Pl. W1 2 29 82 C
Whitfield Rd. Bexh 67 48 77 D
Whitfield Rd. E6 50 41 84 C
Whitfield Rd. SE3 76 38 76 B
Whitfield St. W1 2 29 81 A
Whitford Gdns. Mit 96 27 68 B
Whitgift Ave. S Croy 112 32 64 C
Whitgift St. Croy 105 32 65 C
Whitgift St. SE11 10 30 78 B
Whithers Pl. EC1 4 32 82 C
Whiting Ave. Bark 51 43 84 D
Whitings Rd. Barn 11 23 95 A
Whiting St. SE1 7 31 79 A
Whitington Ave. EC3 4 33 81 C
Whitland Rd. Cars 103 26 66 D
Whitley Rd. N17 25 33 90 C
Whitlock Dri. SW19 85 24 73 C
Whitman Rd. E3 57 36 82 C
Whitmead Cl. S Croy 112 33 63 A
Whitmore Gdns. NW10 46 23 83 C
Whitmore Rd. Beck 98 36 68 B
Whitmore Rd. Har 32 14 87 A
Whitmore Rd. N1 48 33 83 A
Whitnell Way. SW15 73 23 74 A
Whitnell Way. SW15 73 23 74 B
Whitney Ave. Ilf 27 41 89 D
Whitney Rd. E10 38 37 87 B
Whitstable Cl. Beck 98 36 69 B
Whitstable Cl. Ruis 31 09 86 A
Whittaker Ave. Rich 71 17 74 B
Whittaker Rd. E6 50 41 84 D
Whittaker Rd. Sutt 103 24 65 D
Whittaker St. SW1 9 28 78 A
Whitta Rd. E12 50 41 85 B
Whittell Gdns. SE26 88 35 72 C
Whittingstall Rd. SW6 73 24 76 B
Whittington Ct. N2 36 27 88 B
Whittington Rd. N22 24 30 91 A
Whittington Way. Pnr 32 12 88 A
Whittlebury Cl. Cars 111 27 63 D
Whittle Cl. Sthl 53 13 81 D
Whittle Rd. Houn 59 11 77 C
Whittlesea Cl. Har 20 14 91 C
Whittlesea Path. Har 20 14 90 A
Whittlesea Rd. Har 20 14 90 A
Whittlesey St. SE1 7 31 80 C
Whitton Avenue E. Grnf 44 16 85 C
Whitton Avenue W. Grnf 43 14 85 D
Whitton Avenue W. Nthlt 43 14 85 C
Whitton Cl. Grnf 44 16 84 B
Whitton Dene. Houn 70 14 74 A
Whitton Dene. Islw 70 14 74 B
Whitton Dri. Grnf 44 16 84 A
Whitton Manor Rd. Islw 70 14 74 C
Whitton Rd. Houn 70 13 74 B
Whitton Rd. Twick 83 15 73 B
Whitton Rd. Twick 71 15 74 C
Whitton Waye. Houn 70 13 74 C
Whitton Wlk. E3 57 37 82 A
Whitwell Rd. E13 58 40 82 A
Whitworth Rd. SE18 66 43 77 C
Whitworth Rd. SE25 97 33 68 D
Whitworth St. E10 65 39 78 C
Whorlton Rd. SE15 75 34 75 B
Whymark Ave. N22 25 31 89 B
Whytecroft. Houn 59 11 77 D
Whyteville Rd. E7 50 40 84 B
Wickersley Rd. SW11 74 28 75 A
Wickersley Rd. SW11 74 28 76 C
Wickers Oake. SE19 87 33 71 B
Wicker St. E1 57 34 81 D
Wickford St. E1 57 35 82 C
Wickford Way. E17 26 35 89 D
Wickham Ave. Croy 106 36 66 C
Wickham Ave. Sutt 110 23 64 C
Wickham Ch. W.Wick 107 39 66 A
Wickham Cl. Enf 14 35 96 A
Wickham Cl. N.Mal 102 21 67 B
Wickham Cres. W Wick 106 38 65 A
Wickham Ct Rd. W Wick 106 38 65 A
Wickham Gdns. SE4 76 36 75 B
Wickham La. SE2 66 46 77 A
Wickham Mews. SE4 76 36 76 D
Wickham Rd. Beck 98 37 68 B
Wickham Rd. Croy 106 36 65 A
Wickham Rd. E4 26 38 91 C
Wickham Rd. Har 20 14 90 D
Wickham Rd. SE4 76 35 75 B
Wickham St. SE11 10 30 78 D
Wickham St. Well 78 45 76 C
Wickham St. Well 78 46 76 C
Wickham Way. Beck 106 38 67 A
Wick La. E3 49 37 83 A
Wickliffe Ave. N3 23 24 90 C
Wickliffe Gdns. Wem 34 19 86 B
Wicklow St. WC1 3 30 82 B
Wick Rd. E9 49 35 84 B
Wick Rd. Tedd 93 17 70 C
Wicks Cl. SE9 89 41 71 B
Wick Sq. E9 49 36 84 B
Wickwood St. SE5 75 31 76 D
Widdenham Rd. N7 47 30 85 B
Widdicombe Ave. Har 32 12 86 A
Widdin St. E15 50 39 84 C
Widecombe Cl. Rom 30 53 90 B
Widecombe Gdns. Ilf 27 42 89 C
Widecombe Rd. SE9 89 42 72 C
Widecombe Way. N2 23 26 89 D
Widegate St. E1 4 33 81 A
Widenham Cl. Pnr 32 11 88 A
Wide Way. Mit 96 29 68 B
Widley Rd. W9 56 25 82 C
Widmore Lodge Rd. Brom 99 41 69 D
Widmore Rd. Brom 99 41 69 C
Wieland Rd. Nthwd 19 10 91 C
Wigeon Path. SE28 66 44 79 D
Wiggins Mead. NW9 22 21 91 D
Wigginton Ave. Wem 45 19 84 B
Wightman Rd. N4 37 31 88 C
Wightman Rd. N8 25 31 89 C
Wigley Rd. Felt 82 11 73 D
Wigmore Pl. W1 2 28 81 D
Wigmore Rd. Cars 104 27 66 C
Wigmore St. W1 2 28 81 C
Wigmore Wlk. Cars 103 26 65 B
Wigram Rd. E11 39 41 88 C
Wigram Sq. E17 26 38 89 A
Wigston Rd. E13 58 40 82 D
Wigton Gdns. Stan 21 18 90 A
*Wigton Pl. SE11 63 31 78 C
Wigton Rd. E17 26 36 90 B
Wilberforce Rd. N4 37 31 86 B
Wilberforce Rd. NW9 34 22 88 C
Wilberforce Way. SW19 95 23 70 B
Wilbraham Pl. SW1 9 28 78 A
Wilbury Ave. Sutt 110 24 62 D
Wilbury Way. N13 17 32 92 D
Wilby Mews. W11 56 24 80 D
Wilcox Pl. SW1 6 29 79 C
Wilcox Rd. Sutt 110 25 64 B
Wilcox Rd. SW8 10 30 77 C
Wilcox Rd. Tedd 82 14 71 B
Wildcroft Gdns. Edg 21 17 91 B
Wildcroft Manor. SW15 85 23 73 A
Wildcroft Rd. SW15 85 23 73 A
Wild Ct. WC2 3 30 81 D
Wilde Cl. E8 48 34 83 A
Wilde Pl. N13 25 31 91 B
Wilderness Rd. Chis 100 43 70 D
Wilderness The. Hamp 82 13 71 B
Wilderton Rd. N16 37 33 87 A
Wildfell Rd. SE6 88 37 73 B
Wild Goose Dri. SE14 76 35 76 A
Wild Hatch. NW11 35 25 88 C
Wild Oaks Cl. Nthwd 19 09 91 B
Wild's Rents. SE1 8 33 79 C
Wild St. WC2 3 30 81 D
Wildwood Cl. SE12 89 39 73 B
Wildwood Gr. NW3 35 26 87 C
Wildwood. Nthwd 19 08 91 B
Wildwood Rd. NW11 35 26 87 A
Wildwood Rise. NW11 35 26 87 C
*Wilford Cl. Enf 13 32 96 B
Wilford Cl. Nthwd 19 08 91 D
Wilford Rd. Croy 105 32 66 A
Wilfred St. SW1 6 29 79 C
Wilfrid Gdns. W3 55 20 81 A
Wilkes St. E1 4 33 81 B
Wilkes St. E1 4 33 82 D
Wilkinson Cl. Dart 80 54 75 D
Wilkinson Rd. E16 58 41 81 C
Wilkinson St. SW8 10 30 77 D
Wilkinson Way. W4 61 20 79 B
Wilkin St. NW5 47 28 84 B
Wilkin Street Mews. NW5 47 28 84 B
Wilks Pl. N1 48 33 83 C
Willan Rd. N17 25 33 90 C
Willan Wall. E16 58 39 80 B
Willard St. SW8 74 28 75 B
Willcocks Cl. Chess 101 18 65 C
Willcott Rd. W3 55 19 80 D
Will Crooks Gdns. SE9 77 41 75 D
Willenhall Ave. Barn 11 26 95 C
Willenhall Rd. SE18 66 43 78 D
Willersley Ave. Orp 108 44 65 D
Willersley Ave. Sid 90 45 73 B
Willersley Cl. Sid 90 45 73 D
Willesden La. NW2 46 23 84 A
Willesden La. NW6 46 24 84 C
Willes Rd. NW5 47 28 84 B
Willett Cl. Nthlt 53 11 82 A
Willett Cl. Orp 108 45 67 C
Willett Pl. Th Hth 105 31 67 A
Willett Rd. Th Hth 105 31 67 A
Willett Way. Orp 108 45 67 A
Willet Way. SE16 63 34 78 D
William Barefoot Dr. SE9 90 43 72 C
William Bonney Estate. SW4 74 29 75 D
William Booth Rd. SE20 97 34 69 A
William Cl. Rom 29 50 90 B
William Dromey Ct. NW6 46 24 84 D
*William Ellis Way. SE16 63 34 79 C
William Guy Gdns. E3 57 37 82 B
William IV St. WC2 7 30 80 A
William Margrie Cl. SE15 75 34 76 C
William Mews. SW1 5 27 79 B
William Morley Cl. E6 50 41 83 B
William Morris Cl. E17 26 36 89 B
William Rd. NW1 2 29 82 A
William Rd. Sutt 110 26 64 C
William Rd. SW19 95 24 70 C
Williams Ave. E17 26 36 90 B
William's Bldgs. E2 57 35 82 C
Williams Gr. N22 25 31 90 A
Williams La. Mord 103 26 67 A
Williams La. SW14 72 20 76 C
Williamson Cl. E10 65 39 78 D
Williamson St. N7 47 30 85 A
Williamson Way. NW7 23 24 91 A
Williams Rd. Sthl 59 12 78 A
William's Rd. W13 54 16 80 C
William St. Bark 51 44 84 C
William St. Cars 104 27 65 D
William St. E10 38 37 88 D
Williams Terr. Croy 112 31 63 A
William St. N17 25 33 91 C
William St SW1 5 27 79 B
Willifield Way. NW11 35 25 88 A
Willingale Cl. Wdf Gn 27 41 91 A
Willingdon Rd. N22 25 31 90 D
Willingham Terr. NW5 47 29 85 C
Willingham Way. King 94 19 68 A
Willington Rd. SW9 74 30 75 A
Willis Ave. Sutt 111 27 63 A
Willis Rd. Croy 105 32 66 A
Willis Rd. E15 50 39 83 D
Willis Rd. Eri 67 50 78 B
Willis St. E14 57 37 81 D
Willmore End. SW19 95 25 69 D
Willoughby Ave. Croy 111 30 64 B
Willoughby Gr. N17 25 34 91 D
Willoughby La. N17 25 34 91 D
Willoughby Park Rd. N17 25 34 91 D
Willoughby Rd. King 93 18 69 B
Willoughby Rd. N8 25 31 89 C
Willoughby Rd. NW3 46 26 85 B
Willoughby Rd. Twick 71 17 74 B
Willoughby St. WC1 3 30 81 A
Willow Ave. Sid 78 46 74 C
Willow Ave. SW13 72 21 76 D
Willow Bank. Rich 83 16 72 D
Willow Bank. SW6 73 24 75 A
Willow Bridge Rd. N1 48 32 84 A
Willowbrook Rd. SE15 63 33 77 D
Willowbrook Rd. Sthl 59 13 79 C
Willow Cl. Bex 79 48 74 D
Willow Cl. Brent 60 17 77 A
Willow Cl. Brom 107 42 67 B
Willow Cl. Horn 42 52 86 D
Willow Cl. Orp 108 46 66 B
Willowcourt Ave. Har 33 16 88 B
Willow Ct. Wall 111 28 63 D
Willowdene Cl. Twick 82 14 73 A
Willow Dene. Pnr 20 11 90 D
Willow Dri. Barn 11 24 96 C
Willow End. N20 15 25 93 A
Willow End. Surb 101 18 66 C
Willow Gdns. Houn 70 13 76 A
Willow Gdns. Ruis 31 09 86 B
Willow Gr. Chis 100 43 70 B
Willow Gr. E13 50 40 83 C
Willow Green. NW9 22 21 90 A
Willow Gr. Ruis 31 09 87 D
Willowhayne Gdns. Wor Pk 110 23 64 A
Willowherb Wlk. Rom 30 53 91 C
Willow La. Mit 104 27 67 D
Willowmead Cl. W5 54 17 81 B
Willow Mount. Croy 105 33 65 C
Willow Pl. SW1 10 29 78 A
Willow Rd. E12 39 42 86 D
Willow Rd. Enf 13 33 97 C
Willow Rd. Eri 80 52 76 A
Willow Rd. N Mal 94 20 68 C
Willow Rd. NW3 46 26 85 B
Willow Rd. Rom 41 48 88 C
Willow Rd. W5 60 18 79 A
Willows Ave. Mord 103 25 67 B
Willows Cl. Pnr 20 11 90 C
Willow St. E4 18 38 94 B
Willow St. EC2 4 33 82 C
Willow St. Rom 29 50 89 C
Willow Tree Cl. Hay 53 11 82 C
Willow Tree Cl. SW18 85 25 73 D
Willowtree Cl. Uxb 31 08 86 C
Willow Tree La. Hay 53 11 82 D
Willow Vale. Chis 100 43 70 B
Willow Vale. W12 55 22 80 C
Willow View. SW19 95 26 69 B
Willow Way. Eps 109 20 63 B
Willow Way. N3 23 25 91 D
Willow Way. SE26 88 35 72 C
Willow Way. Sun 91 10 68 C
Willow Way. Twick 82 13 72 B
Willow Way. Wem 33 16 86 C
Willow Wlk. Dart 80 53 75 C
Willow Wlk. E17 38 36 88 B
Willow Wlk. Ilf 40 43 86 B
Willow Wlk. N15 25 31 89 D
Willow Wlk. N21 12 30 95 D
Willow Wlk. N2 23 26 90 D
Willow Wlk. Orp 8 43 65 D
Willow Wlk. SE1 63 33 78 B
Willow Wlk. Sutt 103 24 65 D
Willow Wood Cres. SE25 105 33 67 C
Willrose Cres. SE2 66 46 78 D
Wills Cres. Houn 70 13 74 D
Willshaw St. SE14 76 36 76 D
Wilman Gr. E8 48 34 84 C
Wilmar Gdns. W Wick 106 37 66 D
Wilmer Cl. King 83 18 71 D
Wilmer Cres. King 83 18 71 D
Wilmer Gdns (off Hoxton St). N1 48 33 83 A
Wilmer Gdns (off Kingsland Rd). E8 48 33 83 A
Wilmer Lea Cl. E15 49 38 84 D
Wilmer Pl. N16 37 33 86 B
Wilmer Way. N14 16 29 92 B
Wilmington Ave. W4 61 20 77 D
Wilmington Gdns. Bark 51 45 84 C
Wilmington Sq. WC1 3 31 82 A
Wilmington St. WC1 3 31 82 A
Wilmot Cl. N2 23 26 90 C
Wilmot Cl. SE15 63 34 77 C
Wilmot Pl. NW1 47 29 84 C
Wilmot Pl. W7 54 15 80 C
Wilmot Rd. Cars 111 27 64 D
Wilmot Rd. Dart 80 52 74 B
Wilmot Rd. E10 38 37 86 B
Wilmot Rd. N17 25 32 89 B
Wilmot St. E2 57 34 82 B
Wilmount St. SE18 66 43 78 B
Wilna Rd. SW18 85 26 73 A
Wilsham St. W11 56 24 80 C
Wilsmere Dri. Har 21 15 91 D
Wilsmere Dri. Nthlt 43 12 85 C
Wilson Ave. Mit 96 27 69 A
Wilson Gdns. Har 32 14 87 A
Wilson Gr. SE16 63 34 79 B
Wilson Rd. E6 58 41 82 B
Wilson Rd. Har 32 14 87 A
Wilson Rd. Ilf 39 42 87 B
Wilson Rd. SE5 75 33 76 A
Wilson's Ave. N17 25 33 90 D
Wilson's Pl. E14 57 36 81 D
Wilson Sq. EC2 4 32 81 B
Wilson's Rd. W6 62 23 78 D
Wilson St. E17 38 38 88 A
Wilson St. N21 17 31 94 A
Wilthorne Gdns. Dag 52 49 84 D
Wilton Ave. W4 61 21 78 C
Wilton Cres. SW19 95 24 69 B
Wilton Cres. SW1 6 28 79 A
Wilton Dr. Rom 29 50 91 D
Wilton Estate. E8 48 34 84 A
Wilton Gdns. E Mol 92 13 68 A
Wilton Gr. N.Mal 102 21 67 D

| | | |
|---|---|---|
| Wilton Mews. SW1 | 6 | 28 79 D |
| Wilton Pl. Har | 33 | 15 88 D |
| Wilton Pl. SW1 | 6 | 28 79 A |
| Wilton Rd. Barn | 12 | 27 96 D |
| Wilton Rd. Houn | 70 | 11 75 B |
| Wilton Rd. N10 | 24 | 28 90 C |
| Wilton Rd. SE2 | 67 | 47 78 A |
| Wilton Rd. SW19 | 96 | 27 70 C |
| Wilton Rd. SW1 | 10 | 29 78 A |
| Wilton Row. SW1 | 6 | 28 79 A |
| Wilton Row. SW1 | 6 | 28 79 A |
| Wilton Sq. N1 | 48 | 32 83 B |
| Wilton St. SW1 | 6 | 28 79 D |
| Wilton Terr. SW1 | 6 | 28 79 C |
| Wilton Villas. N1 | 48 | 32 83 B |
| Wilton Way. E8 | 48 | 34 84 B |
| Wiltshire Ave. Horn | 30 | 54 89 D |
| Wiltshire Cl. SW3 | 9 | 27 78 B |
| Wiltshire Gdns. Twick | 82 | 14 73 C |
| Wiltshire La. Pnr | 19 | 09 89 B |
| Wiltshire Rd. Orp | 108 | 46 66 A |
| Wiltshire Rd. SW9 | 75 | 31 75 A |
| Wiltshire Rd. Th Hth | 97 | 31 68 A |
| Wiltshire Row. N1 | 48 | 32 83 B |
| Wilverley Cres. N.Mal | 102 | 21 67 C |
| Wimbart Rd. SW2 | 86 | 30 73 B |
| Wimbledon Bridge. SW19 | 95 | 24 70 B |
| Wimbledon Hill Rd. SW19 | 95 | 24 70 A |
| Wimbledon Park Rd. SW18 | 85 | 24 73 B |
| Wimbledon Park Side. SW19 | 85 | 23 73 D |
| Wimbledon Rd. SW17 | 85 | 26 71 A |
| Wimbolt St. E2 | 57 | 34 82 A |
| Wimborne Ave. Hay | 53 | 11 81 C |
| Wimborne Ave. Orp | 100 | 45 68 B |
| Wimborne Ave. Sthl | 59 | 13 78 A |
| Wimborne Cl. SE12 | 77 | 39 74 B |
| Wimborne Cl. Wor Pk | 103 | 23 66 C |
| Wimborne Dri. NW9 | 22 | 19 89 A |
| Wimborne Dri. Pnr | 32 | 12 87 A |
| Wimborne Gdns. W13 | 54 | 16 81 B |
| Wimborne Rd. N17 | 25 | 33 90 C |
| Wimborne Rd. N9 | 17 | 34 93 A |
| Wimborne Way. Beck | 98 | 36 68 C |
| Wimbourne St. N1 | 48 | 32 83 D |
| Wimpole Cl. King | 94 | 19 69 C |
| Wimpole Mews. W1 | 2 | 28 81 B |
| Wimpole St. W1 | 2 | 28 81 B |
| Winans Wlk. SW9 | 75 | 31 76 C |
| Wincanton Cres. Nthlt | 43 | 13 85 D |
| Wincanton Gdns. Ilf | 28 | 43 90 D |
| Wincanton Rd. SW18 | 85 | 24 73 B |
| Winchcombe Rd. Cars | 104 | 27 66 C |
| Winchcomb Gdns. SE9 | 77 | 41 75 B |
| Winchelsea Ave. Bexh | 67 | 48 77 D |
| Winchelsea Cl. SW15 | 73 | 23 74 B |
| Winchelsea Rd. E7 | 50 | 40 85 A |
| Winchelsea Rd. N17 | 25 | 33 89 A |
| Winchelsea Rd. NW10 | 45 | 20 83 B |
| Winchelsey Rise. S Croy | 112 | 33 63 B |
| Winchendon Rd. SW6 | 73 | 24 76 B |
| Winchendon Rd. Tedd | 82 | 14 71 B |
| Winchester Ave. Houn | 59 | 12 77 B |
| Winchester Ave. NW6 | 46 | 24 83 A |
| Winchester Ave. NW9 | 22 | 19 89 A |
| Winchester Cl. Brom | 99 | 39 68 B |
| Winchester Cl. Enf | 13 | 33 95 A |
| Winchester Cl. King | 94 | 19 70 D |
| Winchester Cl. SE17 | 63 | 31 78 B |
| Winchester Dri. Pnr | 32 | 11 88 B |
| Winchester Mews. NW3 | 46 | 26 84 D |
| Winchester Mews. W1 | 2 | 28 81 A |
| Winchester Park. Brom | 99 | 39 68 B |
| Winchester Pl. E8 | 48 | 33 85 D |
| Winchester Pl. N6 | 36 | 28 87 D |
| Winchester Rd. Bexh | 79 | 47 76 D |
| Winchester Rd. Brom | 99 | 39 68 B |
| Winchester Rd. E4 | 26 | 38 91 C |
| Winchester Rd. Felt | 82 | 12 72 D |
| Winchester Rd. Har | 21 | 18 89 C |
| Winchester Rd. Ilf | 40 | 44 86 D |
| Winchester Rd. N6 | 36 | 28 87 B |
| Winchester Rd. N9 | 17 | 34 94 C |
| Winchester Rd. Nthwd | 19 | 10 89 A |
| Winchester Rd. NW3 | 46 | 26 84 D |
| Winchester Rd. Twick | 71 | 16 74 D |
| Winchester Sq. SE1 | 8 | 32 80 D |
| Winchester St. SW1 | 9 | 28 78 D |
| Winchester St. W3 | 61 | 20 79 A |
| Winchester Wlk. SE1 | 8 | 32 80 D |
| Winchet Wlk. Croy | 106 | 35 67 C |
| Winchfield Cl. Har | 33 | 17 88 C |
| Winchfield Rd. SE26 | 88 | 36 71 C |
| Winchilsea Cres. E Mol | 92 | 14 69 C |
| Winchmore Hill Rd. N14 | 16 | 30 94 A |
| Winchmore Hill Rd. N21 | 16 | 30 94 B |
| Winckley Cl. Har | 33 | 18 88 B |
| Wincott St. SE11 | 63 | 31 78 A |
| Wincrofts Dri. SE9 | 78 | 44 75 D |
| Windborough Rd. Cars | 111 | 28 63 C |
| Windermere Ave. Har | 33 | 17 87 A |
| Windermere Ave. N3 | 23 | 25 89 A |
| Windermere Ave. NW6 | 46 | 24 83 A |
| Windermere Ave. Ruis | 32 | 11 87 D |
| Windermere Ave. SW19 | 95 | 25 68 B |
| Windermere Ave. Wem | 33 | 17 87 C |
| Windermere Cl. Orp | 108 | 43 65 D |
| Windermere Ct. SW13 | 61 | 21 77 B |
| Windermere Gdns. Ilf | 39 | 42 88 A |
| Windermere Gr. Wem | 33 | 17 87 C |
| Windermere House. E3 | 57 | 36 82 D |
| Windermere Rd. Bexh | 79 | 50 76 C |
| Windermere Rd. Croy | 105 | 33 66 D |
| Windermere Rd. N10 | 24 | 28 90 B |
| Windermere Rd. N19 | 36 | 29 86 A |
| Windermere Rd. Sthl | 53 | 13 81 A |
| Windermere Rd. SW15 | 84 | 21 71 C |
| Windermere Rd. SW16 | 96 | 29 69 D |
| Windermere Rd. W5 | 60 | 17 79 C |
| Windermere Rd. W.Wick | 107 | 39 65 A |
| Winders Rd. SW11 | 74 | 27 76 C |
| Windfield Cl. SE26 | 88 | 35 71 B |
| Windham Rd. Rich | 71 | 18 75 B |
| Winding Way. Dag | 41 | 47 86 C |
| Windlass Pl. SE8 | 64 | 36 78 A |
| Windlesham Gr. SW19 | 85 | 23 73 D |
| Windley Cl. SE23 | 88 | 35 72 A |
| Windmill Alley. W4 | 61 | 21 78 A |
| Windmill Cl. SE1 | 63 | 34 78 A |
| Windmill Cl. Sun | 91 | 09 70 C |
| Windmill Cl. Surb | 101 | 17 66 A |
| Windmill Ct. NW2 | 46 | 24 84 A |
| Windmill Dri. SW4 | 74 | 28 74 B |
| Windmill Gdns. Enf | 13 | 31 96 A |
| Windmill Gr. Croy | 105 | 32 66 A |
| Windmill Gr. Croy | 105 | 32 67 C |
| Windmill Hill. Enf | 13 | 31 96 B |
| Windmill Hill. NW3 | 35 | 26 86 C |
| Windmill Hill Ruis | 31 | 09 87 B |
| Windmill La. E15 | 49 | 38 84 B |
| Windmill La. Grnf | 53 | 14 81 A |
| Windmill La. Islw | 60 | 15 78 C |
| Windmill La. Sthl | 59 | 14 79 D |
| Windmill La. Surb | 101 | 16 66 B |
| Windmill Pas. W4 | 61 | 21 78 A |
| Windmill Rd. Brent | 60 | 17 77 B |
| Windmill Rd. Croy | 105 | 32 66 A |
| Windmill Rd. Hamp | 82 | 14 71 C |
| Windmill Rd. Mit | 96 | 29 68 C |
| Windmill Rd. N18 | 17 | 33 92 A |
| Windmill Rd. Sun | 91 | 09 69 A |
| Windmill Rd. SW18 | 73 | 26 74 D |
| Windmill Rd. SW19 | 84 | 22 71 B |
| Windmill Rd. W4 | 61 | 21 78 A |
| Windmill Rd. W5 | 60 | 17 78 C |
| Windmill Road W. Sun | 91 | 09 69 A |
| Windmill Row. SE11 | 63 | 31 78 C |
| Windmill St. W1 | 2 | 29 81 B |
| Windmill St. W1 | 2 | 29 81 B |
| Windmill Way. Ruis | 31 | 09 87 D |
| Windmill Wlk. SE1 | 7 | 31 79 A |
| Windmill Wlk. SE1 | 7 | 31 80 C |
| Windover Ave. NW9 | 22 | 20 89 D |
| Windrush Cl. SW11 | 73 | 26 75 D |
| Windrush Cl. W4 | 61 | 20 77 C |
| Windrush La. SE23 | 88 | 35 72 D |
| Windsor Ave. E17 | 26 | 36 90 C |
| Windsor Ave. E Mol | 92 | 13 68 A |
| Windsor Ave. N Mal | 102 | 20 67 A |
| Windsor Ave. Sutt | 103 | 24 65 C |
| Windsor Ave. SW19 | 95 | 26 69 A |
| Windsor Cl. Brent | 60 | 16 77 B |
| Windsor Cl. Har | 32 | 13 86 C |
| Windsor Cl. N3 | 23 | 24 90 C |
| Windsor Cl. Nthwd | 19 | 10 90 C |
| Windsor Cl. SE27 | 87 | 32 71 A |
| Windsor Cres. Har | 32 | 13 86 C |
| Windsor Cres. Wem | 34 | 19 86 D |
| Windsor Ct. N14 | 16 | 29 94 A |
| Windsor Ct. NW11 | 35 | 24 88 C |
| Windsor Ct. Sun | 91 | 10 70 C |
| Windsor Dri. Barn | 12 | 27 95 D |
| Windsor Dri. Dart | 80 | 52 74 C |
| Windsor Gdns. W9 | 56 | 25 82 C |
| Windsor Gr. SE27 | 87 | 32 71 A |
| Windsor Pl. SW1 | 10 | 29 78 A |
| Windsor Rd. Barn | 11 | 24 95 C |
| Windsor Rd. Bexh | 79 | 48 75 C |
| Windsor Rd. Dag | 41 | 48 86 C |
| Windsor Rd. E10 | 38 | 37 86 B |
| Windsor Rd. E11 | 39 | 40 86 A |
| Windsor Rd. E4 | 18 | 37 92 B |
| Windsor Rd. E7 | 50 | 41 85 C |
| Windsor Rd. Har | 20 | 14 90 B |
| Windsor Rd. Horn | 42 | 53 87 A |
| Windsor Rd. Houn | 70 | 11 76 C |
| Windsor Rd. Ilf | 51 | 44 85 A |
| Windsor Rd. Ilf | 40 | 44 86 D |
| Windsor Rd. King | 93 | 18 70 C |
| Windsor Rd. N13 | 17 | 31 93 C |
| Windsor Rd. N17 | 25 | 34 90 C |
| Windsor Rd. N3 | 23 | 24 90 C |
| Windsor Rd. N7 | 36 | 30 86 C |
| Windsor Rd. NW2 | 45 | 22 84 B |
| Windsor Rd. Rich | 71 | 18 76 D |
| Windsor Rd. Sid | 100 | 46 70 B |
| Windsor Rd. Sthl | 59 | 12 79 D |
| Windsor Rd. Sun | 91 | 10 70 A |
| Windsor Rd. Tedd | 82 | 14 71 D |
| Windsor Rd. Th Hth | 97 | 31 69 D |
| Windsor Rd. W5 | 54 | 18 80 A |
| Windsor Rd. Wor Pk | 102 | 22 65 A |
| Windsor St. N1 | 48 | 31 83 B |
| Windsor Terr. N1 | 4 | 32 82 A |
| Windsor Wlk. SE5 | 75 | 32 76 D |
| Windspoint Dri. SE15 | 63 | 34 77 B |
| Windus Rd. N16 | 37 | 33 87 D |
| Windus Wlk. N16 | 37 | 33 87 D |
| Windy Ridge. Brom | 99 | 42 69 A |
| Windy Ridge Cl. SW19 | 85 | 23 71 D |
| Wine Cl. E1 | 57 | 35 80 A |
| Wine Office Ct. EC4 | 3 | 31 81 C |
| Winforton St. SE10 | 76 | 38 76 A |
| Winfrith Rd. SW18 | 85 | 26 73 C |
| Wingate Cres. Croy | 104 | 30 67 C |
| Wingate Rd. Ilf | 51 | 43 85 D |
| Wingate Rd. W6 | 61 | 22 79 D |
| Wingfield Mews. SE15 | 75 | 34 75 A |
| Wingfield Rd. E15 | 50 | 39 85 C |
| Wingfield Rd. E17 | 38 | 37 88 B |
| Wingfield Rd. King | 94 | 19 70 A |
| Wingfield St. SE15 | 75 | 34 75 A |
| Wingford Rd. SW2 | 74 | 30 74 C |
| Wingletye La. Horn | 42 | 54 87 D |
| Wingletye La. Horn | 30 | 54 89 D |
| Wingmore Rd. SE24 | 75 | 32 75 A |
| Wingrave Rd. W6 | 62 | 23 77 A |
| *Wingrave. SE17 | 63 | 32 78 B |
| Wingrove Rd. SE6 | 89 | 39 72 A |
| Winifred Pl. N12 | 15 | 26 92 C |
| Winifred Rd. Dag | 41 | 48 87 C |
| Winifred Rd. Dart | 80 | 52 74 B |
| Winifred Rd. Eri | 68 | 51 78 C |
| Winifred Rd. Hamp | 82 | 13 71 A |
| Winifred Rd. SW19 | 95 | 25 69 A |
| Winifred Terr. E13 | 50 | 40 83 C |
| Winifred Terr. N9 | 17 | 33 94 B |
| Winkfield Rd. E13 | 50 | 40 83 D |
| Winkfield Rd. N22 | 25 | 31 90 A |
| Winkley Ct. Har | 32 | 13 86 C |
| Winkley St. E2 | 48 | 34 83 D |
| Winlaton Rd. Brom | 88 | 38 71 B |
| Winmill Rd. Dag | 41 | 48 86 D |
| Winn Common Rd. SE18 | 66 | 45 78 D |
| Winnett St. W1 | 6 | 29 80 B |
| Winnington Cl. N2 | 35 | 26 88 D |
| Winnington Rd. N2 | 35 | 26 88 D |
| Winn Rd. SE12 | 89 | 40 73 D |
| Winns Ave. E17 | 26 | 36 89 B |
| Winns Mews. N15 | 25 | 33 89 C |
| Winns Terr. E17 | 26 | 37 89 A |
| Winsbeach. E17 | 26 | 38 90 D |
| Winscombe Cres. W5 | 54 | 17 82 D |
| Winscombe St. N19 | 36 | 28 86 B |
| Winsford Rd. SE6 | 88 | 36 72 D |
| Winsford Terr. N18 | 17 | 32 92 D |
| Winsham Gr. SW11 | 74 | 28 74 A |
| Winslade Rd. SW2 | 74 | 30 74 A |
| Winslade Way. SE6 | 88 | 37 73 B |
| Winsland Mews. W2 | 1 | 26 81 D |
| Winsland St. W2 | 1 | 26 81 D |
| Winsley St. W1 | 2 | 29 81 C |
| Winslow Cl. Pnr | 31 | 10 88 D |
| Winslow Rd. W6 | 62 | 23 77 A |
| Winslow Way. Felt | 82 | 12 72 C |
| Winstanley Rd. SW11 | 73 | 26 75 B |
| Winstead Gdns. Dag | 52 | 50 85 C |
| Winston Ave. NW9 | 34 | 21 87 A |
| Winston Cl. Har | 21 | 15 91 B |
| Winston Cl. Rom | 29 | 49 89 D |
| Winston Ct. Har | 20 | 13 91 C |
| Winston Rd. N16 | 48 | 32 85 B |
| Winston Wlk. W4 | 61 | 20 78 B |
| Winter Ave. E6 | 50 | 42 83 A |
| Winterborne Ave. Orp | 108 | 44 65 D |
| Winterbourne Rd. Dag | 41 | 47 86 A |
| Winterbourne Rd. SE6 | 88 | 36 73 D |
| Winterbourne Rd. Th Hth | 97 | 31 68 B |
| Winter Box Wlk. Rich | 71 | 18 74 B |
| Winterbrook Rd. SE24 | 75 | 32 74 C |
| Winterfold Cl. SW19 | 85 | 24 72 A |
| Winters Rd. Surb | 101 | 16 66 B |
| Winterstoke Rd. SE6 | 88 | 36 73 D |
| Winterton Pl. SW10 | 62 | 26 77 A |
| Winterwell Rd. SW2 | 74 | 30 74 A |
| Winthorpe Rd. SW15 | 73 | 24 75 C |
| Winthrop St. E1 | 57 | 34 81 B |
| Winthrop Wlk. Wem | 33 | 18 86 C |
| Winton Ave. N11 | 24 | 29 91 C |
| Winton Cl. N9 | 18 | 35 94 B |
| Winton Gdns. Edg | 21 | 18 91 D |
| Winton Way. SW16 | 87 | 31 71 C |
| Wirral Ho. SE26 | 87 | 34 72 C |
| Wisbeach Rd. Croy | 105 | 32 67 B |
| Wisborough Rd. S Croy | 112 | 33 62 B |
| Wisdons Cl. Dag | 41 | 49 87 D |
| Wise La. NW7 | 22 | 22 91 A |
| Wiseman Rd. E10 | 38 | 37 86 A |
| Wise Rd. E15 | 49 | 38 83 B |
| Wiseton Rd. SW17 | 86 | 27 73 D |
| Wishart Rd. SE3 | 77 | 41 76 D |
| Wisley Rd. Orp | 100 | 46 70 D |
| Wisley Rd. SW11 | 74 | 28 74 A |
| Wistaria Cl. Orp | 108 | 43 65 B |
| Wisteria Rd. SE13 | 76 | 38 75 D |
| Witan St. E2 | 57 | 34 82 B |
| Witcher Pl. NW1 | 47 | 29 84 A |
| Witham Rd. Dag | 52 | 49 85 C |
| Witham Rd. Islw | 70 | 14 76 B |
| Witham Rd. Rom | 42 | 52 88 B |
| Witham Rd. SE20 | 98 | 35 68 A |
| Witham Rd. W13 | 54 | 16 80 C |
| Witherby Cl. Croy | 112 | 33 64 A |
| Witherfield Way. SE16 | 63 | 34 78 D |
| Witherings The. Horn | 42 | 54 88 B |
| Witherington Rd. N5 | 48 | 31 85 C |
| Withers Mead. NW9 | 22 | 21 90 B |
| Witherston Way. SE9 | 90 | 43 72 A |
| Withington Rd. N2 | 24 | 27 90 A |
| Withycombe Rd. SW19 | 85 | 23 73 B |
| Withy La. Ruis | 31 | 08 88 A |
| Withy Mead. E4 | 18 | 38 93 D |
| Witley Gdns. Sthl | 59 | 12 78 B |
| Witley Rd. N19 | 36 | 29 86 A |
| Witney Cl. Pnr | 20 | 12 91 B |
| Witney Path. SE23 | 88 | 35 72 D |
| Wittenham Way. E4 | 18 | 38 93 D |
| Wittersham Rd. Brom | 89 | 39 71 D |
| Wivenhoe Cl. SE15 | 75 | 34 75 B |
| Wivenhoe Ct. Houn | 70 | 12 75 D |
| Wivenhoe Rd. Bark | 51 | 46 83 D |
| Wiverton Rd. SE26 | 88 | 35 71 C |
| Wix Rd. Dag | 52 | 47 83 B |
| Wix's La. SW4 | 74 | 28 75 D |
| Woburn Cl. SW19 | 95 | 26 70 A |
| Woburn Ct. Croy | 105 | 32 66 C |
| Woburn Mews. WC1 | 2 | 29 82 D |
| Woburn Pl. WC1 | 3 | 30 82 C |
| Woburn Rd. Cars | 104 | 27 66 C |
| Woburn Rd. Croy | 105 | 32 66 C |
| Woburn Sq. WC1 | 2 | 29 82 D |
| Woburn Wlk. WC1 | 2 | 29 82 B |
| Woffington Cl. King | 93 | 17 69 A |
| Woking Cl. SW15 | 72 | 21 75 D |
| Woldham Rd. Brom | 99 | 41 68 C |
| Wolfe Cl. Brom | 107 | 40 67 C |
| Wolfe Cres. SE7 | 65 | 41 78 D |
| Wolferton Rd. E12 | 50 | 42 85 B |
| Wolfington Rd. SE27 | 87 | 31 71 B |
| Wolfram Cl. SE13 | 77 | 39 74 A |
| Wolftencroft Cl. SW11 | 74 | 27 75 A |
| Wolseley Ave. SW19 | 85 | 25 72 A |
| Wolseley Gdns. W4 | 61 | 19 77 B |
| Wolseley Rd. Cars | 104 | 28 66 A |
| Wolseley Rd. E7 | 50 | 40 84 D |
| Wolseley Rd. Har | 21 | 15 89 A |
| Wolseley Rd. N22 | 24 | 30 90 B |
| Wolseley Rd. N8 | 36 | 29 88 B |
| Wolseley Rd. Rom | 41 | 50 87 B |
| Wolseley Rd. W4 | 61 | 20 78 A |
| Wolseley St. SE1 | 63 | 34 79 A |
| Wolsey Ave. E17 | 26 | 36 89 B |
| Wolsey Ave. Surb | 101 | 15 67 B |
| Wolsey Cl. Houn | 70 | 14 75 C |
| Wolsey Cl. King | 94 | 19 69 B |
| Wolsey Cl. Sthl | 59 | 14 79 C |
| Wolsey Cl. Wor Pk | 109 | 22 64 A |
| Wolsey Cres. Mord | 103 | 24 66 B |
| Wolsey Dr. King | 93 | 18 70 A |
| Wolsey Gdns. Ilf | 28 | 44 91 A |
| Wolsey Gr. Edg | 22 | 20 91 D |
| Wolsey Mews. NW5 | 47 | 29 84 A |
| Wolsey Rd. Ashf | 91 | 09 70 B |
| Wolsey Rd. E Mol | 92 | 14 68 D |
| Wolsey Rd. Enf | 13 | 34 97 D |
| Wolsey Rd. Hamp | 82 | 14 71 C |
| Wolsey Rd. N1 | 48 | 33 85 C |
| Wolsey St. E1 | 57 | 35 81 A |
| Wolsey Way. Chess | 109 | 19 64 C |
| Wolsley Cl. Dart | 80 | 51 74 A |
| Wolstonbury. N12 | 15 | 25 92 C |
| Wolvercote Rd. SE2 | 67 | 47 79 B |
| Wolverley St. E2 | 57 | 34 82 B |
| Wolverton Ave. King | 94 | 19 69 A |
| Wolverton Gdns. W5 | 54 | 18 80 B |
| Wolverton Gdns. W6 | 62 | 23 78 B |
| Wolverton Rd. Stan | 21 | 17 91 C |
| Wolverton. SE17 | 63 | 33 78 C |
| Wolverton Way. N14 | 12 | 29 95 A |
| Wolves La. N13 | 25 | 31 91 A |
| Wolves La. N22 | 25 | 31 91 C |
| Womersley Rd. N8 | 36 | 30 88 D |
| Wonersh Way. Sutt | 110 | 23 62 B |
| Wonford Cl. King | 94 | 21 69 A |
| Wontner Rd. SW17 | 84 | 22 72 B |
| Woodall Rd. Enf | 14 | 35 95 D |
| Woodbank Rd. Brom | 89 | 39 72 D |
| Woodbastwick Rd. SE26 | 88 | 36 71 C |
| Woodberry Ave. Har | 20 | 14 89 C |
| Woodberry Ave. N21 | 17 | 31 93 B |
| Woodberry Cl. Sun | 91 | 10 70 A |
| Woodberry Cres. N10 | 24 | 28 89 B |
| Woodberry Down. N4 | 37 | 32 87 A |
| Woodberry Gdns. N12 | 23 | 26 91 A |
| Woodberry Gr. N12 | 23 | 26 91 A |
| Woodberry Gr. N4 | 37 | 32 87 A |
| Woodberry Way. E4 | 18 | 38 94 A |
| Woodberry Way. N12 | 23 | 26 91 A |
| Woodbine Cl. Twick | 82 | 14 72 B |
| Woodbine Gr. SE20 | 97 | 34 70 D |
| Woodbine La. Wor Pk | 103 | 23 65 C |
| Woodbine Pl. E11 | 39 | 40 88 D |
| Woodbine Rd. Sid | 90 | 45 73 C |
| Woodbines Ave. King | 93 | 17 68 B |
| Woodbine Terr. E9 | 49 | 35 84 A |
| Woodborough Rd. SW15 | 72 | 22 75 D |
| Woodbourne Ave. SW16 | 86 | 29 72 D |
| Woodbourne Gdns. Wall | 111 | 28 63 D |
| Woodbridge Cl. N7 | 36 | 30 86 B |
| Woodbridge Cl. NW2 | 34 | 22 86 C |
| Woodbridge Ct. Wdf Gn | 27 | 42 91 C |
| Woodbridge Rd. Bark | 51 | 45 85 D |
| Woodbridge St. EC1 | 3 | 31 82 D |
| Woodbrook Rd. SE2 | 66 | 46 77 A |
| Woodburn Cl. NW4 | 35 | 23 88 B |
| Woodbury Cl. Croy | 105 | 33 65 B |
| Woodbury Cl. E11 | 27 | 40 89 D |
| Woodbury Dri. Sutt | 110 | 26 62 C |
| Woodbury Ho. SE26 | 87 | 34 72 D |
| Woodbury Park Rd. W13 | 54 | 16 82 D |
| Woodbury Rd. E17 | 26 | 37 89 D |
| Woodbury St. SW17 | 86 | 27 71 C |
| Woodchester Sq. W2 | 56 | 25 81 B |
| Woodchurch Cl. Sid | 90 | 45 72 C |
| Woodchurch Dri. Brom | 99 | 41 70 D |
| Woodchurch Rd. NW6 | 46 | 26 84 A |
| Wood Cl. E2 | 57 | 34 82 C |
| Wood Cl. Har | 32 | 14 87 B |
| Wood Cl. NW9 | 34 | 20 87 B |
| Woodclyffe Dri. Chis | 100 | 43 69 C |
| Woodcock Dell Ave. Har | 33 | 17 87 B |
| Woodcock Hill. Har | 33 | 17 87 A |
| Woodcombe Cres. SE23 | 88 | 35 73 C |
| Woodcote Ave. Horn | 42 | 52 86 C |
| Woodcote Ave. NW7 | 23 | 23 91 A |
| Woodcote Ave. Th Hth | 97 | 31 68 D |
| Woodcote Ave. Wall | 111 | 28 62 B |
| Woodcote Cl. Enf | 14 | 35 95 C |
| Woodcote Cl. King | 83 | 18 71 D |
| Woodcote Dri. Orp | 108 | 44 66 D |
| Woodcote Dri. Pur | 111 | 29 62 D |
| Woodcote Green. Wall | 111 | 29 62 A |
| Woodcote Mews. Wall | 111 | 28 63 B |
| Woodcote Pl. SE27 | 87 | 31 71 C |
| Woodcote Rd. E11 | 39 | 40 87 A |
| Woodcote Rd. Wall | 111 | 29 63 C |
| Woodcroft Ave. NW7 | 22 | 21 91 A |
| Woodcroft Ave. Stan | 21 | 16 90 A |
| Woodcroft Grnf | 44 | 16 84 A |
| Woodcroft. N21 | 17 | 31 94 C |
| Woodcroft Rd. Th Hth | 105 | 31 67 D |
| Woodcroft. SE9 | 89 | 42 72 D |
| Wood Dri. Chis | 99 | 42 70 A |
| Wood End Ave. Har | 43 | 14 85 A |
| Wood End Cl. Nthlt | 43 | 14 85 D |
| Woodend Gdns. Enf | 12 | 30 96 C |
| Wood End Gdns. Nthlt | 43 | 14 85 D |
| Wood End La. Nthlt | 43 | 14 85 C |
| Woodend Rd. E17 | 26 | 38 90 C |
| Wood End Rd. Har | 44 | 15 85 A |
| Woodend. SE19 | 97 | 32 70 A |
| Woodend. Sutt | 103 | 26 65 A |
| Wood End The. Wall | 111 | 28 62 B |
| Wood End Way. Nthlt | 43 | 14 85 C |
| Wooder Gdns. E7 | 50 | 40 85 A |
| Woodfall Ave. Barn | 11 | 24 95 B |
| Woodfall Rd. N4 | 37 | 31 86 A |
| Woodfall St. SW3 | 9 | 27 78 D |
| Woodfarrs. SE5 | 75 | 32 75 D |
| Woodfield Ave. Cars | 111 | 28 63 A |
| Woodfield Ave. NW9 | 22 | 21 89 C |
| Woodfield Ave. SW16 | 86 | 29 72 D |
| Woodfield Ave. W5 | 54 | 17 82 C |
| Woodfield Ave. Wem | 33 | 17 86 C |
| Woodfield Cl. SE19 | 97 | 32 70 C |
| Woodfield Cres. W5 | 54 | 17 82 D |
| Woodfield Dri. Barn | 16 | 28 94 C |
| Woodfield Dri. Rom | 30 | 52 89 C |
| Woodfield Gdns. N.Mal | 102 | 21 67 B |
| Woodfield Gr. SW16 | 86 | 29 72 D |
| Woodfield La. SW16 | 86 | 29 72 D |
| Woodfield Pl. W9 | 56 | 24 82 D |
| Woodfield Rd. Houn | 69 | 10 76 D |
| Woodfield Rd. Surb | 101 | 15 65 B |
| Woodfield Rd. W5 | 54 | 17 82 C |
| Woodfield Rd. W9 | 56 | 25 81 A |
| Woodfield Way. Horn | 42 | 53 87 D |
| Woodfield Way. N11 | 24 | 29 91 D |
| Woodfines The. Horn | 42 | 53 88 D |
| Woodford Ave. Ilf | 27 | 42 89 D |
| Woodford Bridge Rd. Ilf | 27 | 42 89 C |
| Woodford Cres. Pnr | 19 | 10 90 D |
| Woodford New Rd. E17 | 27 | 39 89 A |
| Woodford New Rd. E18 | 27 | 39 90 A |
| Woodford New Rd. Wdf Gn | 27 | 39 91 D |
| Woodford Pl. Wem | 33 | 18 87 C |
| Woodford Rd. E18 | 27 | 40 89 A |
| Woodford Rd. E7 | 50 | 40 85 B |
| Woodgate Cres. Nthwd | 19 | 10 91 A |
| Woodger Rd. W12 | 62 | 23 79 A |
| Woodgrange Ave. Enf | 13 | 34 95 C |
| Woodgrange Ave. Har | 33 | 17 88 B |
| Woodgrange Ave. N12 | 23 | 26 91 B |
| Woodgrange Ave. W5 | 55 | 19 80 C |
| Woodgrange Cl. Har | 33 | 17 88 B |
| Woodgrange Gdns. Enf | 13 | 34 95 C |
| Woodgrange Rd. E7 | 50 | 40 85 C |
| Woodhall Ave. Pnr | 20 | 12 90 A |
| Woodhall Ave. SE21 | 87 | 33 72 D |
| Woodhall Cres. Horn | 42 | 54 87 D |
| Woodhall Dri. Pnr | 20 | 12 90 A |
| Woodhall Dri. SE21 | 87 | 33 72 D |
| Woodhall Gate. Pnr | 20 | 11 90 B |
| Woodham Ct. E18 | 27 | 39 89 D |
| Woodham Rd. SE6 | 88 | 38 72 C |
| Woodhaven Gdns. Ilf | 28 | 44 89 C |
| Woodhayes. Chis | 100 | 43 70 B |
| Woodhead Dri. Orp | 108 | 45 65 A |
| Woodheyes Rd. NW10 | 45 | 21 85 C |
| Woodhill Cres. Har | 33 | 17 88 D |
| Woodhill. SE18 | 65 | 42 78 A |
| Woodhouse Ave. Grnf | 44 | 15 83 D |
| Woodhouse Cl. Grnf | 44 | 15 83 D |
| Woodhouse Gr. E12 | 50 | 42 84 A |
| Woodhouse Rd. E11 | 39 | 39 86 D |
| Woodhouse Rd. N12 | 24 | 27 91 A |
| Woodhurst Ave. Orp | 108 | 44 67 C |
| Woodhurst Rd. SE2 | 66 | 46 78 A |
| Woodhurst Rd. W3 | 55 | 20 80 A |
| Woodington Cl. SE9 | 78 | 43 74 C |
| Woodison St. E3 | 57 | 36 82 C |
| Woodknoll Dri. Chis | 99 | 42 69 B |
| Wood La. Dag | 41 | 49 86 D |
| Wood La. Islw | 60 | 15 77 D |
| Wood La. N6 | 36 | 28 88 D |
| Woodland App. Grnf | 44 | 16 84 A |
| Woodland Cl. Eps | 109 | 21 63 A |
| Woodland Cl. NW9 | 34 | 20 88 C |
| Woodland Cl. SE19 | 97 | 33 70 A |
| Woodland Cl. Uxb | 31 | 07 86 B |
| Woodland Cres. SE10 | 65 | 39 77 A |
| Woodland Gdns. Islw | 71 | 15 75 A |
| Woodland Gdns. N10 | 36 | 28 88 B |
| Woodland Hill. SE19 | 97 | 33 70 A |
| Woodland Rd. E4 | 18 | 38 94 C |
| Woodland Rd. N11 | 16 | 28 92 D |
| Woodland Rd. SE19 | 97 | 33 70 B |
| Woodland Rd. Th Hth | 97 | 31 68 C |
| Woodland Rise. N10 | 24 | 28 89 D |
| Woodlands Ave. E11 | 39 | 40 87 D |
| Woodlands Ave. Horn | 42 | 54 88 A |

Woodlands Ave. N3 23 26 90 A
Woodlands Ave. N Mal 94 20 69 B
Woodlands Ave. Rom 41 48 87 A
Woodlands Ave. Ruis 32 11 87 B
Woodlands Ave. Sid 90 45 73 C
Woodlands Ave. W3 55 19 80 D
Woodlands Ave. Wor Pk 102 22 65 A
Woodlands. Bexh 79 49 74 B
Woodlands Cl. Brom 99 42 69 D
Woodlands Cl. NW11 35 24 88 A
Woodlands Dri. Stan 21 15 91 B
Woodlands Dri. Sun 92 11 69 C
Woodlands Gr. E10 65 39 78 C
Woodlands Gr. Islw 71 15 76 C
Woodlands. Har 20 13 89 C
Woodlands. N12 23 26 91 A
Woodlands. NW11 35 24 88 A
Woodlands Par. Ashf 91 08 70 A
Woodlands Park Rd. N15 37 32 88 A
Woodlands Park Rd. SE10 65 39 77 A
Woodlands Rd. Bexh 79 48 75 A
Woodlands Rd. Brom 99 42 69 D
Woodlands Rd. E11 39 39 86 A
Woodlands Rd. E17 26 38 89 A
Woodlands Rd. Enf 13 32 97 B
Woodlands Rd. Har 33 15 88 B
Woodlands Rd. Ilf 51 44 85 A
Woodlands Rd. Ilf 40 44 86 C
Woodlands Rd. Islw 70 14 75 B
Woodlands Rd. Islw 71 15 75 A
Woodlands Rd. Islw 71 15 76 D
Woodlands Rd. N9 18 35 94 C
Woodlands Rd. Rom 30 51 89 B
Woodlands Rd. Sthl 53 11 80 D
Woodlands Rd. Surb 101 17 66 B
Woodlands Rd. SW13 72 21 75 B
Woodlands Rise. Grnf 44 16 84 A
Woodlands. SE19 97 32 70 C
Woodlands St. SE13 88 38 73 B
Woodlands. SW20 95 23 68 D
Woodland St (off Dalston La). E8 48 33 84 B
Woodland St (off Forest Rd). E8 48 33 84 B
Woodlands The. Islw 71 15 76 D
Woodlands The. N14 16 28 94 D
Woodlands The. SE13 88 38 73 B
Woodlands The. Wall 111 28 62 B
Woodlands Way. SW15 73 24 74 B
Woodland Terr. SE7 65 42 78 A
Woodland Way. Croy 106 36 66 C
Woodland Way. Mit 96 28 70 C
Woodland Way. Mord 95 24 68 D
Woodland Way. N21 17 31 93 A
Woodland Way. NW7 22 21 91 B
Woodland Way. Orp 108 44 67 A
Woodland Way. SE2 67 47 78 B
Woodland Way. Surb 102 19 65 B
Woodland Way. W Wick 106 38 65 C
Woodland Wlk. Brom 89 39 71 A
Woodland Wlk. E10 65 39 78 C
Wood La. NW9 34 20 87 B
Wood La. Ruis 31 09 86 A
Wood La. W12 56 23 80 A
Woodlawn Cres. Twick 82 13 72 B
Woodlawn Dri. Felt 82 11 72 B
Woodlawn Rd. SW6 73 23 76 B
Woodlawn Rd. SW6 62 23 77 D
Woodlea Dri. Brom 107 39 67 A
Woodlea Gr. Nthwd 19 08 91 A
Woodlea Rd. N16 37 33 86 C
Woodleigh Ave. N12 24 27 91 A
Woodleigh Gdns. SW16 86 30 72 C
Woodley Cl. SW17 96 27 70 D
Wood Lodge Gdns. Brom 99 42 70 C
Wood Lodge La. W Wick 106 38 65 C
Woodlodge. SW19 85 24 71 D
Woodman Mews. W10 55 22 81 B
Woodman Path. Ilf 28 45 91 A
Woodmansterne La. Wall 111 28 62 D
Woodmansterne Rd. Cars 111 27 62 C
Woodmansterne Rd. SW16 96 29 69 B
Woodmere Ave. Croy 106 35 66 B
Woodmere Cl. Croy 106 35 66 B
Woodmere Gdns. Croy 106 35 66 B
Woodmere. SE9 89 42 73 B
Woodmere Way. Beck 106 38 67 B
Woodneigh St. SW6 73 25 76 A
Woodnook Rd. SW16 86 28 71 D
Woodpecker Cl. N9 13 34 95 D
Woodpecker Rd. SE14 64 36 77 A
Woodquest Ave. SE24 75 32 74 A
Wood Rd. Shep 91 07 68 C
Wood Ride. Barn 11 26 97 B
Wood Ride. Orp 100 45 68 C
Woodridge Way. Nthwd 19 09 91 A
Woodridings Ave. Pnr 20 12 90 B
Woodridings Cl. Pnr 20 12 91 D
Woodriffe Rd. E11 38 38 87 B
Wood Rise. Pnr 31 10 88 A
Woodrow Cl. Grnf 44 16 84 D
Woodrow Ct. N17 25 34 91 D
Woodrow. SE18 65 42 78 B
Woodrush Way. Rom 29 47 89 D
Wood's Bldgs. E1 57 34 81 B
Woodseer St. E1 4 33 81 B
Woodseer St. E1 57 34 81 A
Woodsford Sq. W14 62 24 79 A
Woodshire Rd. Dag 41 49 86 D
Woodside Ave. Chis 90 44 71 C
Woodside Ave. Esh 101 15 66 A
Woodside Ave. N10 24 28 89 C
Woodside Ave. N12 15 26 92 A
Woodside Ave. N6 36 27 88 B
Woodside Ave. SE25 105 34 67 B
Woodside Ave. Wem 44 18 83 A
Woodside Cl. Bexh 79 50 75 D
Woodside Cl. Surb 102 20 66 A
Woodside Cl. Wem 44 18 83 A
Woodside Court Rd. Croy 105 34 66 A
Woodside Cres. Sid 90 45 72 C
Woodside Ct. N12 15 25 92 B
Woodside Ct. W5 54 18 80 C
Woodside End. Wem 44 18 83 A
Woodside Gdns. E4 26 37 91 B
Woodside Gdns. N17 25 33 90 D
Woodside Grange Rd. N12 15 25 92 B
Woodside Green. SE25 105 34 67 C
Woodside Gr. N12 15 26 93 C
Woodside La. Bex 79 47 74 D
Woodside La. N12 15 26 93 C
Woodside. NW11 35 25 88 A
Woodside Park Ave. E17 26 38 89 D
Woodside Park Rd. N12 15 26 92 A
Woodside Park. SE25 105 34 67 D
Woodside Pl. Wem 44 18 83 A
Woodside Rd. Bexh 79 50 75 D
Woodside Rd. Brom 107 42 67 A
Woodside Rd. E13 58 41 82 C
Woodside Rd. King 93 18 70 C
Woodside Rd. N22 25 31 91 C
Woodside Rd. N Mal 94 21 69 C
Woodside Rd. Nthwd 19 09 91 D
Woodside Rd. SE25 105 34 67 D
Woodside Rd. Sid 90 45 72 C
Woodside Rd. Sutt 103 26 65 C
Woodside. SW19 85 24 71 D
Woodside Way. Croy 106 35 67 C
Woodside Way. SW16 96 29 69 A
Woods Mews. W1 6 28 80 A
Woodsome Rd. NW5 36 28 86 D
Wood's Pl. SE1 8 33 79 C
Woodspring Rd. SW19 85 24 72 A
Wood's Rd. SE15 75 34 76 B
Wood St. Barn 11 23 96 D
Wood St. Cars 104 28 66 A
Wood St. E16 58 40 80 B
Wood St. E17 26 38 89 C
Woodstead Gr. Edg 21 18 91 A
Wood St. EC2 4 32 81 C
Wood St. King 93 17 69 D
Woodstock Ave. Islw 71 16 74 A
Woodstock Ave. NW11 35 24 87 A
Woodstock Ave. Sthl 53 12 82 B
Woodstock Ave. Sutt 103 24 66 B
Woodstock Ave. W13 60 16 79 C
Woodstock Cl. Stan 21 18 90 C
Woodstock Cres. N9 13 34 95 D
Woodstock Ct. SE12 77 40 74 C
Woodstock Gdns. Beck 98 37 69 B
Woodstock Gdns. Ilf 40 46 86 A
Woodstock Gr. W12 62 23 79 B
Woodstock La N. Surb 101 17 65 A
Woodstock La S. Chess 101 17 65 C
Woodstock Mews. W1 2 28 81 A
Woodstock Rd. Cars 111 28 64 C
Woodstock Rd. Croy 105 32 65 D
Woodstock Rd. E17 26 38 90 D
Woodstock Rd. E7 50 41 84 C
Woodstock Rd. N4 37 31 87 C
Woodstock Rd. NW11 35 24 87 D
Woodstock Rd. W4 61 21 79 C
Woodstock Rd. Wem 44 18 84 D
Woodstock Rise. Sutt 103 24 66 B
Woodstock St. E16 58 39 81 D
Woodstock St. W1 2 28 81 D
Woodstock Terr. E14 57 37 80 B
Woodstock Way. Mit 96 28 69 D
Woodstone Ave. Eps 109 22 64 C
Wood St. W4 61 21 78 C
Woodsyre. SE26 87 33 71 B
Woodthorpe Rd. SW15 72 22 75 D
Woodvale Ave. SE25 97 33 69 D
Wood Vale. N10 36 29 88 A
Wood Vale. SE23 87 34 73 B
Woodvale Wlk. SE27 87 32 71 C
Woodview Ave. E4 18 38 92 A
Woodville Cl. Rich 83 16 71 A
Woodville Cl. SE12 77 40 74 A
Woodville Gdns. Ilf 28 43 89 D
Woodville Gdns. NW11 35 23 87 B
Woodville Gdns. Ruis 31 08 87 A
Woodville Gdns. W5 54 18 81 C
Woodville Rd. Barn 11 25 96 B
Woodville Rd. E11 39 39 87 D
Woodville Rd. E17 26 36 89 D
Woodville Rd. E18 27 40 90 D
Woodville Rd. Mord 95 25 68 C
Woodville Rd. N16 48 33 85 C
Woodville Rd. NW11 35 24 87 A
Woodville Rd. NW6 46 24 83 D
Woodville Rd. Rich 83 17 72 C
Woodville Rd. Th Hth 97 32 68 B
Woodville Rd. W5 54 17 81 D
Woodville St. SE18 65 42 78 A
Woodward Ave. NW4 34 22 88 A
Woodwarde Rd. SE22 75 33 74 D
Woodward Gdns. Dag 52 47 84 C
Woodward Rd. Dag 52 47 84 C
Woodway Cres. Har 33 16 88 C
Wood Way. Orp 108 43 65 A
Woodwell St. SW18 73 26 74 A
Wood Wharf SE10 64 37 77 B
Woodyard Cl. NW5 47 28 85 C
Woodyard La. SE21 87 33 73 A
Woodyates Rd. SE12 89 40 73 B
Woodyates Rd. SE12 77 40 74 C
Woolacombe Rd. SE3 77 41 76 C
Wooler St. SE17 63 32 78 D
Woollaston Rd. N4 37 31 88 D
Woolmead Ave. NW9 34 22 87 A
Woolmer Gdns. N18 17 34 92 C
Woolmer Rd. N18 17 34 92 C
Woolmore St. E14 58 38 80 A
Wool Rd. SW20 94 22 70 B
Woolstaplers Way. SE16 63 34 79 C
Woolston Cl. E17 26 35 90 D
Woolstone Rd. SE23 88 36 72 A
Woolwich Church St. SE18 65 42 79 D
Woolwich Common. SE18 66 43 77 A
Woolwich High St. SE18 66 43 79 C
Woolwich Manorway. E16 66 43 79 B
Woolwich New Rd. SE18 66 43 78 B
Woolwich Rd. Belv 67 48 78 D
Woolwich Rd. Bexh 79 49 75 A
Woolwich Rd. E10 65 39 78 D
Woolwich Rd. E7 65 41 78 A
Woolwich Rd. SE2 67 48 77 A
Wooster Gdns. E14 58 38 81 D
Wootton Cl. Horn 42 53 88 B
Wootton Gr. N3 23 25 90 A
Wootton St. SE1 7 31 80 C
Worbeck Rd. SE20 98 35 69 C
Worcester Ave. N17 25 34 91 C
Worcester Cl. Croy 106 37 65 A
Worcester Cl. Mit 96 28 69 C
Worcester Gdns. Grnf 43 14 84 B
Worcester Gdns. Ilf 39 42 87 A
Worcester Gdns. Wor Pk 102 21 65 C
Worcester Mews. NW3 46 25 84 B
Worcester Park Rd. Wor Pk 102 20 65 D
Worcester Pl. EC4 8 32 80 A
Worcester Rd. E12 50 42 85 B
Worcester Rd. E17 26 35 90 D
Worcester Rd. Sutt 110 25 63 D
Worcester Rd. SW19 85 24 71 D
Wordsworth Ave. E12 50 42 84 C
Wordsworth Ave. E18 27 39 90 D
Wordsworth Ave. Grnf 53 14 82 B
Wordsworth Cl. Rom 30 53 90 A
Wordsworth Dri. Sutt 110 23 64 A
Wordsworth Par. N15 25 31 89 D
Wordsworth Rd. Hamp 82 12 71 B
Wordsworth Rd. N16 48 33 85 A
Wordsworth Rd. SE20 98 35 70 D
Wordsworth Rd. Wall 111 29 63 A
Wordsworth Rd. Well 78 45 76 A
Wordsworth Wlk. NW11 23 25 89 C
Worfield St. SW11 74 27 76 A
Worfield St. SW11 9 27 77 C
Worgan St. SE11 10 30 78 D
Worland Rd. E15 50 39 84 C
World's End La. N21 12 30 96 D
World's End Pas. SW10 62 26 77 D
World's End Pl. SW10 62 26 77 C
Worlidge St. W6 62 23 78 C
Worlingham Rd. SE22 75 33 75 D
Wormholt Rd. W12 55 22 80 C
Wormwood St. EC3 4 33 81 C
Wornington Rd. W10 56 24 81 A
Woronzow Rd. NW8 47 27 83 A
Worple Ave. Islw 71 16 74 A
Worple Ave. SW19 95 23 70 D
Worple Cl. Har 32 12 87 D
Worple Rd. Islw 71 16 75 C
Worple Rd. SW19 95 24 70 B
Worple Rd. SW20 95 23 69 B
Worple Road Mews. SW19 95 24 70 B
Worple St. SW14 72 20 75 B
Worple Way. Har 32 12 87 D
Worple Way. Rich 71 18 75 D
Worship St. EC2 4 33 82 C
Worslade Rd. SW17 85 26 71 B
Worsley Bridge Rd. Beck 88 37 71 C
Worsley Rd. E11 50 39 85 A
Worsopp Dri. SW4 74 29 74 A
Worthfield Cl. Eps 109 20 63 D
Worth Gr. SE17 63 32 78 D
Worthing Cl. E15 50 39 83 A
Worthing Rd. Houn 59 12 77 B
Worthington Rd. Surb 101 18 66 D
Wortley Rd. Croy 105 31 66 A
Wortley Rd. E6 50 41 84 D
Worton Gdns. Islw 70 14 76 D
Worton Rd. Islw 70 14 75 D
Worton Rd. Islw 71 15 75 A
Worton Way. Houn 70 14 76 D
Worton Way. Islw 70 14 76 D
Wotton Rd. NW2 35 23 86 C
Wotton Rd. SE8 64 36 77 B
Wotton Way. Sutt 110 23 62 C
Wouldham Rd. E16 58 39 81 D
Wragby Rd. E11 39 39 86 C
Wrampling Pl. N9 17 34 94 C
Wrangthorn Wlk. Croy 112 31 64 A
Wray Ave. Ilf 28 43 89 A
Wray Cl. Horn 42 53 87 A
Wray Cres. N4 36 30 86 B
Wrayfield Rd. Sutt 110 23 64 B
Wray Rd. Sutt 110 24 62 B
Wrekin Rd. SE18 66 44 77 C
Wren Ave. NW2 46 23 85 A
Wren Ave. Sthl 59 12 78 B
Wren Gdns. Dag 52 47 85 D
Wren Gdns. Horn 42 51 87 D
Wren Path. SE28 66 44 79 D
Wren Rd. Dag 52 47 85 D
Wren Rd. SE5 75 32 76 B
Wren's Ave. Ashf 81 08 71 A
Wren's Park House. E5 37 34 86 B
Wren St. WC1 3 30 82 D
Wrentham Ave. NW10 46 23 83 D
Wrenthorpe Rd. Brom 89 39 71 A
Wrenwood Way. Pnr 19 10 89 D
Wrexham Rd. E3 49 37 83 C
Wricklemarsh Rd. SE3 77 41 76 A
Wrigglesworth St. SE14 64 35 77 D
Wright Cl. SE13 76 38 75 D
Wright Rd. Houn 59 11 77 C
Wright Rd. N1 48 33 84 A
Wright's Green. SW4 74 29 75 D
Wright's La. W8 62 25 79 D
Wrights Pl. NW10 45 20 84 A
Wright's Rd. E3 49 36 83 D
Wrights Rd. SE25 97 33 68 A
Wright's Row. Wall 111 28 64 B
Wrights Wlk. SW14 72 20 75 B
Wrigley Cl. E4 18 38 92 D
Wrotham Rd. Barn 11 24 97 C
Wrotham Rd. NW1 47 29 84 C
Wrotham Rd. W13 54 17 80 C
Wrotham Rd. Well 79 47 76 A
Wrottesley Rd. NW10 45 22 83 C
Wrottesley Rd. SE18 66 44 77 A
Wroughton Rd. SW11 74 27 74 D
Wroughton Terr. NW4 22 22 89 D
Wroxall Rd. Dag 52 47 85 C
Wroxham Gdns. N11 24 29 91 D
Wroxton Rd. SE15 76 35 76 C
Wrythe Green Rd. Cars 104 27 65 D
Wrythe La. Cars 103 26 66 D
Wulfstan St. W12 55 21 81 D
Wyatt Ct. Wem 44 18 83 A
Wyatt Park Rd. SW2 86 30 72 B
Wyatt Rd. Dart 80 51 75 B
Wyatt Rd. E7 50 40 84 A
Wyatt Rd. N5 37 32 86 C
Wyatt's La. E17 26 38 89 A
Wybert St. NW1 2 29 82 C
Wyborne House. NW10 45 20 84 C
Wyborne Way. NW10 45 20 84 C
Wyburn Ave. Barn 11 24 96 B
Wycham Ave. Sid 90 45 73 C
Wyche Gr. S Croy 112 32 63 D
Wych End. Beck 98 36 70 D
Wycherley Cres. Barn 11 25 95 D
Wychwood Ave. Edg 21 17 91 B
Wychwood Ave. Th Hth 97 32 68 A
Wychwood Cl. Edg 21 17 91 B
Wychwood End. N6 36 29 87 A
Wychwood Gdns. Ilf 27 42 89 D
Wychwood Way. Nthwd 19 09 91 D
Wychwood Way. SE19 97 33 70 A
Wycliffe Cl. Well 78 45 76 B
Wycliffe Rd. SW11 74 28 75 A
Wycliffe Rd. SW11 74 28 76 C
Wycliffe Rd. SW19 95 25 70 B
Wyclif St. EC1 3 31 82 B
Wycombe Gdns. NW11 35 25 86 A
Wycombe Rd. Ilf 39 42 88 B
Wycombe Rd. N17 25 34 90 A
Wycombe Rd. Wem 45 19 83 A
Wydehurst Rd. Croy 105 34 66 A
Wydell Cl. Mord 103 23 67 D
Wydeville Manor Rd. SE12 89 40 71 B
Wye Cl. Ashf 81 07 71 B
Wye Cl. Orp 108 45 66 B
Wye Cl. Ruis 31 08 88 C
Wye St. SW11 73 26 75 B
Wyevale Cl. Pnr 19 10 89 A
Wyfields. Ilf 28 43 90 B
Wyfold Rd. SW6 62 24 77 C
Wyhill Wlk. Dag 52 50 84 A
Wyke Gdns. W7 60 16 79 C
Wykeham Ave. Dag 52 47 84 A
Wykeham Ave. Horn 42 53 88 D
Wykeham Green. Dag 52 47 84 A
Wykeham Hill. Wem 33 18 87 D
Wykeham Rd. Har 21 16 89 D
Wykeham Rd. NW4 35 23 88 A
Wykeham Rise. N20 15 24 94 C
Wyke Rd. E3 49 37 84 C
Wyke Rd. SW20 95 23 69 C
Wylchin Cl. Pnr 19 09 89 B
Wyldes Cl. NW11 35 26 87 A
Wyldfield Gdns. N9 17 33 93 B
Wyld Way. Wem 45 19 84 D
Wyleu St. SE23 88 35 73 D
Wylie Rd. Sthl 59 13 79 C
Wyllen Cl. E1 57 35 82 A
Wymering Rd. W9 56 25 82 A
Wymond St. SW15 73 23 75 A
Wynard Terr. SE11 10 30 78 D
Wynash Gdns. Cars 111 27 64 C
Wynaud Ct. N22 24 30 91 B
Wynchgate. Har 21 15 91 C
Wynchgate. N14 16 30 94 C
Wynchgate. N21 16 30 94 A
Wyncroft Cl. Brom 99 42 68 B
Wyndale Ave. NW9 34 19 88 C
Wyndcliff Rd. SE7 65 40 77 B
Wyndcroft Cl. Enf 13 31 96 B
Wyndham Cl. Orp 108 44 66 C
Wyndham Cl. Sutt 110 25 63 C
Wyndham Cres. Houn 70 13 74 C
Wyndham Cres. N19 36 29 86 C
Wyndham Mews. W1 1 27 81 B
Wyndham Pl. W1 1 27 81 B
Wyndham Rd. Barn 16 29 94 D
Wyndham Rd. E6 50 41 84 D
Wyndham Rd. King 93 18 70 D
Wyndham Rd. SE5 63 32 77 C
Wyndham Rd. W13 60 16 79 D
Wyndham St. W1 1 27 81 B
Wyndham Yd. W1 1 27 81 B
Wyneham Rd. SE24 75 32 74 B
Wynell Rd. SE23 88 35 72 D
Wynford Gr. Orp 100 46 68 B
Wynford Rd. N1 47 30 83 D
Wynford Way. SE9 89 42 72 B
Wynlie Gdns. Pnr 19 10 90 D
Wynndale Rd. E18 27 40 90 B
Wynne Rd. SW9 75 31 76 C
Wynn's Ave. Sid 78 46 74 A
Wynnstay Gdns. W8 62 25 79 C
Wynter St. SW11 73 26 75 C
Wynton Gdns. SE25 105 33 67 B
Wynton Gdns. SE25 97 33 68 D
Wynton Pl. W3 55 19 81 D
Wynyard Terr. SE11 10 30 78 D
Wynyatt St. EC1 3 31 82 B
Wyresdale Cres. Grnf 54 15 82 B
Wyteleaf Cl. Ruis 31 08 88 C
Wythburn Pl. W1 1 27 81 D
Wythenshawe Rd. Dag 41 49 86 C
Wythens Wlk. SE9 78 43 74 D
Wythes Cl. Brom 99 42 69 D
Wythfield Rd. SE9 77 42 74 D
Wyvenhoe Rd. Har 43 14 85 A
Wyvern Cl. Orp 108 46 65 D
Wyvern Estate The. N Mal 94 22 68 C
Wyvern Rd. Pur 112 31 62 D
Wyvil Rd. SW8 10 30 77 B
Wyvis St. E14 57 37 81 B

Yabsley St. E14 58 38 80 C
Yalding Rd. SE16 63 34 79 C
Yarborough Rd. SW19 95 26 69 B
Yardbridge Cl. Sutt 110 25 62 D
Yardley Cl. E4 14 37 95 B
Yardley Ct. Sutt 110 23 64 A
Yardley La. E4 14 37 95 B
Yardley St. WC1 3 31 82 A
Yarmouth Cres. N17 37 34 88 B
Yarmouth Pl. W1 6 28 80 D
Yarnton Way. Belv 67 48 79 D
Yarnton Way. SE2 67 47 79 B
Yateley St. SE18 65 41 79 D
Yeading Ave. Har 32 12 87 C
Yeading Fork. Hay 53 11 82 C
Yeading La. Hay 53 11 81 A
Yeading La. Nthlt 53 11 82 A
Yeate St. N1 48 32 84 D
Yeatman Rd. N6 36 27 88 D
Yeldham Rd. W6 62 23 78 D
Yelverton Cl. Rom 30 53 90 B
Yelverton Lodge. Twick 83 17 73 A
Yelverton Rd. SW11 73 26 76 D
Yenston Cl. Mord 103 25 67 C
Yeoman Cl. SE27 87 31 72 D
Yeoman Rd. Nthlt 43 12 84 C
Yeomans Acre. Ruis 31 10 88 C
Yeoman's Row. SW3 5 27 79 C
Yeoman St. SE8 64 36 78 A
Yeomans Way. Enf 14 35 97 C
Yeoman's Yd. E1 8 33 80 B
Yeomen Way. Ilf 28 44 91 A
Yeo St. E3 57 37 81 B
Yeovil Cl. Orp 108 45 65 A
Yerbury Rd. N19 36 29 86 D
Yester Dri. Chis 99 42 70 C
Yester Park. Chis 99 42 70 B
Yester Rd. Chis 99 42 70 D
Yevele Way. Horn 42 54 87 A
Yewdale Cl. Brom 99 39 70 A
Yewfield Rd. NW10 45 21 84 B
Yew Gr. NW2 46 23 85 B
Yew Tree Cl. N21 17 31 94 A
Yew Tree Cl. Well 78 46 76 A
Yew Tree Cl. Wor Pk 102 21 66 C
Yew Tree Gdns. Rom 41 48 88 A
Yew Tree Gdns. Rom 41 50 88 B
Yewtree Rd. Beck 98 36 68 B
Yew Tree Rd. W12 55 21 80 B
Yew Tree Wlk. Houn 70 12 74 B
Yew Tree Wlk. Pur 112 32 62 C
Yew Wlk. Har 33 15 87 C
Yoakley Rd. N16 37 33 86 A
Yoke Cl. N7 47 30 84 A
Yolande Gdns. SE9 77 42 74 A
Yonge Park. N4 37 31 86 C
York Ave. SE17 63 32 78 C
York Ave. Sid 90 45 72 B
York Ave. Stan 21 16 90 D
York Ave. SW14 72 20 74 A
York Ave. W7 54 15 80 C
York Bldgs. WC2 7 30 80 A
York Bridge. NW1 2 28 82 C
York Cl. Mord 95 25 68 D
York Cl. W7 54 15 80 C
York Gate. N14 16 29 94 A
York Gate. NW1 2 28 82 C
York Gr. SE15 76 35 76 A
York Hill. SE27 87 31 72 D
York House Pl. W8 62 25 79 B
Yorkland Ave. Well 78 45 75 D
York Mews. Ilf 40 43 86 C
York Mews. NW5 47 28 85 D
York Par. Brent 60 17 78 D
York Pl. Ilf 40 43 86 B
York Pl. SW11 73 26 75 B
York Pl. WC2 7 30 80 A
York Rd. Barn 11 26 95 B
York Rd. Brent 60 17 78 D
York Rd. Croy 105 31 66 A
York Rd. E10 38 38 86 C
York Rd. E17 38 35 88 B
York Rd. E4 18 37 92 C
York Rd. E7 50 40 84 A
York Rd. Houn 70 13 75 B
York Rd. Ilf 40 43 86 A

**Yorkland Ave. Well**

| | | | |
|---|---|---|---|
| Yorkland Ave. Well | 78 | 45 75 | D |
| York Rd. King | 93 | 18 70 | D |
| York Rd. N11 | 24 | 29 91 | B |
| York Rd. N18 | 17 | 34 92 | D |
| York Rd. N21 | 17 | 32 94 | B |
| York Rd. Nthwd | 19 | 10 90 | C |
| York Rd. Rich | 71 | 18 74 | B |
| York Rd. SE1 | 7 | 30 79 | B |
| York Rd. Sutt | 110 | 25 63 | C |
| York Rd. SW11 | 73 | 26 75 | B |
| York Rd. SW18 | 73 | 26 75 | C |
| York Rd. SW19 | 95 | 26 70 | A |
| York Rd. Tedd | 83 | 15 71 | A |
| York Rd. W3 | 55 | 20 81 | D |
| York Rd. W5 | 60 | 17 79 | C |
| York Rise. NW5 | 36 | 28 86 | D |
| Yorkshire Cl. N16 | 37 | 33 86 | D |
| Yorkshire Gdns. N18 | 17 | 34 92 | D |
| Yorkshire Grey Yd. WC1 | 3 | 30 81 | B |
| Yorkshire Rd. E14 | 57 | 36 81 | C |
| Yorkshire Rd. Mit | 96 | 30 68 | C |
| York Sq. E14 | 57 | 36 81 | C |
| York St. Bark | 51 | 44 83 | A |
| York St. Mit | 104 | 28 66 | A |
| York St. Twick | 83 | 16 73 | C |
| York St. W1 | 1 | 27 81 | B |
| York Terr. Eri | 79 | 50 76 | A |
| York Terr E. NW1 | 2 | 28 82 | C |
| York Terr W. NW1 | 2 | 28 82 | C |
| Yorkton St. E2 | 48 | 34 83 | C |
| York Way Ct. N1 | 47 | 30 83 | A |
| York Way. Felt | 82 | 12 72 | D |
| York Way. N1 | 47 | 30 83 | A |
| York Way. N7 | 47 | 30 84 | A |
| York Way. N20 | 16 | 27 93 | D |
| Youngmans Cl. Enf | 13 | 32 97 | A |
| Young Rd. E16 | 58 | 41 81 | C |
| Young's Bldgs. EC1 | 4 | 32 82 | C |
| Youngs Rd. Ilf | 40 | 44 88 | D |
| Young St. W8 | 62 | 25 79 | B |
| Yoxley App. Ilf | 40 | 44 88 | C |
| Yoxley Dri. Ilf | 40 | 44 88 | C |
| Yukon Rd. SW12 | 86 | 28 73 | B |
| Yuletide Cl. NW10 | 45 | 21 84 | C |
| Zampa Rd. SE16 | 64 | 35 78 | C |
| *Zander Ct. E2 | 57 | 34 82 | A |
| Zangwill Rd. SE3 | 77 | 41 76 | B |
| Zealand Rd. E3 | 49 | 36 83 | C |
| Zelah Rd. Orp | 108 | 46 66 | B |
| Zennor Rd. SW12 | 86 | 29 73 | C |
| Zenoria St. SE22 | 75 | 33 75 | D |
| Zermatt Rd. Th Hth | 97 | 32 68 | C |
| Zetland St. E14 | 58 | 38 81 | A |
| Zion Pl. Th Hth | 97 | 32 68 | D |
| Zoar St. SE1 | 8 | 32 80 | C |
| Zoffany St. N19 | 36 | 29 86 | B |